SEVENTH EDITION

ADVANCED ACCOUNTING

Floyd A. Beams
John A. Brozovsky
Craig D. Shoulders
Virginia Polytechnic Institute and State University

PRENTICE HALL, Upper Saddle River, New Jersey 07458

Executive Editor: *Annie Todd*
Editorial Assistant: *Fran Toepfer*
Editor-in-Chief: *P. J. Boardman*
Executive Marketing Manager: *Beth Toland*
Production Editor: *Marc Oliver*
Manufacturing Buyer: *Lisa DiMaulo*
Senior Manufacturing Supervisor: *Paul Smolenski*
Senior Manufacturing/Prepress Manager: *Vincent Scelta*
Design Manager: *Patricia Smythe*
Art Manager: *Jayne Conte*
Cover Art: *Bruce Kenselaar*
Cover Design: *Kiwi Design*
Composition: *UG*

Beams, Floyd A.
 Advanced accounting / Floyd A. Beams, John A. Brozovsky, Craig
 D. Shoulders.—7th ed.
 p. cm.
 Includes bibliographical references and index.
 ISBN 0-13-597873-4
 1. Accounting. I. Brozovsky, John A. II. Shoulders, Craig D. III.
Title.
 HF5635 .B41517 1999
 657′.046—dc21
                                                             98-32388
                                                               CIP

Prentice-Hall International (UK) Limited, London
Prentice-Hall of Australia Pty. Limited, Sydney
Prentice-Hall Canada, Inc., Toronto
Prentice-Hall Hispanoamericana, S.A., Mexico
Prentice-Hall of India Private Limited, New Delhi
Prentice-Hall of Japan, Inc., Tokyo
Pearson Education Asia Pte. Ltd., Singapore
Editora Prentice-Hall do Brasil, Ltda., Rio de Janeiro

Printed in the United States of America

10 9 8 7 6 5 4 3 2

Contents

Preface

This seventh edition of *Advanced Accounting* contains 21 chapters plus two appendices and is designed for financial accounting courses above the intermediate level. The seventh edition has been updated to reflect recent business developments and changes in accounting standards and regulatory requirements. The chapter content is revised for better and more efficient coverage.

An important feature of this book is its student orientation, and special effort was expended to maintain that emphasis in this seventh edition. The student-oriented features include the shading of working paper entries, presenting working papers on single upright pages, and integrating excerpts from business publications and corporate annual reports in the text. A student orientation is also reflected in the assignment material, which is designed to provide variety and maintain student interest. The text includes many exhibits that summarize complex material and both clarify and reinforce the underlying concepts. All exhibits should be read and reviewed in conjunction with the text. The assignment material, including items from past CPA Examinations, is closely aligned with chapter coverage. In addition, the names of parent and subsidiary companies begin with P and S for convenient identification and reference.

NEW TO THIS EDITION

The most important changes in this seventh edition of *Advanced Accounting* include:

- Chapter 10 has been updated to include changes in the handling of earnings per share introduced in *Statement No. 128*. The tax section was also modified to incorporate the deductibility of goodwill in "taxable" business combinations.
- Chapter 13 has been updated to incorporate the new hedging rules introduced in *Statement No. 133*, "Accounting for Derivative Instruments and Hedging Activities."
- Chapter 15 has been updated for the modification of segment reporting according to *Statement No. 131*.
- Chapters 19 through 21 have been totally reorganized and updated. The addition of a government and not-for-profit expert in Dr. Craig Shoulders has provided a very significant improvement in the handling of the not-for-profit area of accounting.

ORGANIZATION

The first 11 chapters cover business combinations, the equity and cost methods of accounting for investments in common stock, and consolidated financial statements. This emphasis reflects the importance of business combinations and consolidations in advanced accounting courses, as well as in financial accounting and reporting practices.

Accounting standards for business combinations under the purchase and pooling of interests methods are introduced in Chapter 1, along with applicable accounting and reporting standards. Chapter 1 also provides relevant background material relating to the form and economic impact of business combinations. The Financial Accounting Standards Board (FASB) has indicated that it plans to move toward aligning the standards of U.S. generally accepted accounting principles with those of other nations, particularly those of our NAFTA trading partners. For example, the standard-setting boards of the United States and Canada held joint meetings in their deliberations on revised segment reporting principles (*Statement No. 131*), and the FASB's stated objectives for the earnings-per-share standard (*Statement No. 128*) include making EPS computations similar to those of other countries. In light of this trend, it is likely that the long-awaited standards for consolidation principles will also reflect some movement toward international standards. Differences in international accounting related to business combinations are introduced in Chapter 1.

The equity method of accounting as a one-line consolidation is discussed in Chapter 2 and integrated throughout subsequent chapters on consolidations. This parallel one-line consolidation/consolidation coverage permits alternate computations for such key concepts as consolidated net income and consolidated retained earnings and helps the instructor explain the objectives of consolidation procedures. It also permits students to check their logic by alternative approaches to key computations.

The one-line consolidation is established as the standard for a parent company in accounting for its subsidiaries, but the coverage does not ignore situations in which the parent company uses the cost method or an incomplete equity method to account for its subsidiaries and other investees. These methods are illustrated in the text and included in assignment material so that students are prepared for consolidation assignments regardless of the method used by the parent company in accounting for its subsidiary investments.

Accounting and reporting matters related to pooled subsidiaries are integrated into Chapters 3 through 11. Consolidated financial statements and push-down accounting are introduced in Chapter 3. Chapter 3 also includes an illustration of two methods considered by the FASB for allocating the purchase price to (1) the *total* fair values of the subsidiary's identifiable net assets and *purchased* goodwill and (2) the *total* fair values of the subsidiaries identifiable net assets and *implied* goodwill.

Chapter 4 introduces the student to consolidation working paper techniques and procedures. The three-section, financial statement working paper approach is presented as basic, but the trial balance approach is also illustrated and included in the problem material. Consolidation working papers for a parent company that uses the equity method as a one-line consolidation are presented first to set the standard. Subsequently, working papers are illustrated under an incomplete (or simple) equity method and the cost method, both for the year of acquisition and the following year.

Consolidation under the cost and incomplete equity methods is illustrated using both the traditional approach (alternate working paper entries) and the conversion-to-equity approach (adjusted to the equity method through a schedule and a working paper entry).

Intercompany transactions involving inventories, plant assets, and bonds are covered in Chapters 5, 6, and 7. Chapter 8 covers ownership changes in subsidiaries.

Chapter 9 covers complex affiliation structures, and Chapter 10 covers subsidiaries with preferred stock, consolidated earnings per share, and income taxation for consolidated entities.

Chapter 11 covers consolidation theories, leveraged buyouts, push-down accounting, and corporate joint ventures. An appendix to the chapter discusses current cost implications for consolidations. Chapters 9, 10, and 11 cover specialized topics, so their coverage is not essential background for assignment of subsequent chapters.

Chapter 12 covers accounting and reporting practices for branch operations, including the use of perpetual inventory practices in the combining working papers. The use of perpetual inventory procedures makes the combining working paper entries for branches compatible with those for consolidations.

Foreign currency issues continue to be important to American business enterprises. The survival of many American businesses depends on access to foreign markets, suppliers, and capital. Chapter 13 covers foreign currency transactions, including imports and exports and forward or similar contracts to hedge against exchange losses. It has been updated for *FASB Statement 133*. Chapter 14 covers translation and remeasurement of foreign-entity financial statements, one-line consolidations of equity investees, consolidation of foreign subsidiaries for external reporting purposes, and combining foreign branch operations.

Chapter 15 examines disclosures for industry segments and interim financial reporting and has been updated for *FASB Statement 131*. Chapter 16 covers organization, operations, and dissolution of partnership entities, and Chapter 17 extends partnership coverage to liquidations.

Chapter 18 covers corporate liquidations, reorganizations, and debt restructurings for financially distressed companies.

Chapters 19 and 20 provide an introduction to governmental accounting, and the final chapter (Chapter 21) introduces accounting for voluntary health and welfare organizations, hospitals, and colleges and universities. These chapters have been totally reorganized and updated to provide the best available assistance for the student to gain a basic grasp of not-for-profit accounting.

Appendix A provides an overview of SEC accounting requirements, and Appendix B provides a review of fiduciary accounting for estates and trusts.

SUPPLEMENTARY MATERIALS

The supplementary materials for the seventh edition of *Advanced Accounting* include three manuals:

- The solutions manual
- A resource manual that contains (a) comprehensive outlines of all chapters; (b) class illustrations; (c) descriptions of all exercises and problems, including estimated times for completion; (d) alternative lesson plans covering different chapters; and (e) a checklist for students of key figures in the problems
- A test bank manual

The following additional material is available to adopters:

- Transparencies for solutions to exercises and problems
- A diskette containing test material (This is the same as the material contained in the manual.)
- Excel spreadsheet templates for consolidation and other working paper problems
- Partially completed working papers for consolidation and other working paper problems in the textbook (These working papers are hard copy of the Excel templates included on the diskettes.)

ACKNOWLEDGMENTS

Many people have made valuable contributions to the seventh edition of *Advanced Accounting* and we are happy to recognize their contributions. We are indebted to the many users of prior editions for their helpful comments and constructive criticism. We also acknowledge the help and encouragement that we received from our students at Virginia Tech who, often unknowingly, participated in class-testing of various sections of the manuscript.

I also want to thank Wayne E. Leininger, Larry Killough, and Richard E. Sorensen of the Pamplin College of Business at Virginia Tech for the understanding and support that made seven editions of *Advanced Accounting* possible.

Our gratitude goes to the reviewers who helped us shape this edition: Charles Fazzi, Robert Morris College; Saleha B. Khumawala, University of Houston; Donald E. Keller, University of California-Chico; and Frederic M. Stiner, University of Delaware.

We would like to thank the Prentice Hall book team for their hard work and dedication: Annie Todd, Fran Toepfer, Marc Oliver, Lisa DiMaulo, Beth Toland, and Bob Prokop.

FLOYD A. BEAMS
JOHN A. BROZOVSKY
CRAIG D. SHOULDERS

1

Business Combinations

In general terms, **business combinations** unite previously separate business entities. Although the overriding objective of business combinations must be profitability, the immediate concern of many combinations is to gain operating efficiencies through horizontal or vertical integration of operations or to diversify business risks through conglomerate operations.

Horizontal integration is the combination of firms in the same business lines and markets. The 1997 business combination between Atmos Energy Corporation and United Cities Gas Company, both natural gas utilities, is an example of horizontal integration. The combined company serves more than one million customers in 12 states and expects cost savings from the combined operations of $375 million over the next 10 years.

Vertical integration is the combination of firms with operations in different, but successive, stages of production and/or distribution. Tultex Corporation, already a vertically-integrated company that spins yarn, knits, dyes, cuts, and sews activewear and sports apparel, acquired California Shirt Sales and T-Shirt City in 1997. Both companies are apparel distributors and will provide Tultex with distribution outlets for its manufactured goods.

Conglomeration is the combination of firms with unrelated and diverse products and/or service functions. Firms may diversify to reduce the risk associated with a particular line of business, or to even out cyclical earnings, such as a utility's acquisition of a manufacturing company. Several utilities combined with telephone companies after the 1996 Telecommunications Act allowed utilities to enter the telephone business. For example, in November 1997, Texas Utilities Company acquired Lufkin-Conroe Communications Company, a local-exchange telephone company, to diversify into a communication business.

Reasons for Business Combinations

If expansion is a proper goal of business enterprise, why does a business expand through combination rather than by building new facilities? Among the many possible reasons for electing business combination as the vehicle for expansion are:

> **Cost Advantage.** It is frequently less expensive for a firm to obtain needed facilities through combination than through development. This is particularly true in periods of inflation.

Lower Risk. The purchase of established product lines and markets is usually less risky than developing new products and markets. Business combination is especially less risky when the objective is diversification. For companies in industries already plagued with excess manufacturing capacity, business combinations may be the only way to grow.

Fewer Operating Delays. Plant facilities acquired through a business combination are operative and already meet environmental and other governmental regulations. The time to market is critical, especially in the technology industry. Firms constructing new facilities can expect numerous delays in construction, as well as in getting the necessary governmental approval to commence operations. Environmental impact studies alone can take months or even years to complete.

Avoidance of Takeovers. Many companies combine to avoid being acquired themselves. Smaller companies tend to be more vulnerable to corporate takeovers, so many of them adopt aggressive buyer strategies as the best defense against takeover attempts by other companies.

Acquisition of Intangible Assets. Business combinations bring together both intangible and tangible resources. Thus, the acquisition of patents, mineral rights, research, customer databases, or management expertise may be a primary motivating factor in a particular business combination.

Other Reasons. Firms may choose a business combination over other forms of expansion for business tax advantages (for example, tax-loss carryforwards), for personal income and estate-tax advantages, and for personal reasons. One of several motivating factors in the 1998 business combination of Wheeling-Pittsburgh Steel, a subsidiary of WHX, with Handy & Harman was Handy & Harman's overfunded pension plan, which virtually eliminated Wheeling-Pittsburgh Steel's unfunded pension liability. The egos of company management and takeover specialists may play an important role in some business combinations.

Antitrust Considerations

Federal antitrust laws prohibit business combinations that restrain trade or impair competition. The U.S. Department of Justice and the Federal Trade Commission (FTC) have primary responsibility for enforcing federal antitrust laws. For example, in 1997 the FTC blocked Staples's proposed $4.3 billion acquisition of Office Depot, arguing in federal court that the takeover would be anticompetitive. Business combinations in particular industries are subject to review by additional federal agencies. For example, the Federal Reserve Board reviews bank mergers, the Department of Transportation scrutinizes mergers of companies under its jurisdiction, the Department of Energy has jurisdiction over some electric utility mergers, and the Federal Communications Commission (FCC) rules on the transfer of communication licenses. After the Justice Department cleared a $23 billion merger between Bell Atlantic Corporation and Nynex Corporation, the merger was delayed by the FCC because of its concern that consumers would be deprived of competition. The FCC later approved the merger. Such disputes are settled in federal courts.

In addition to federal antitrust laws, most states have some type of statutory takeover regulations. Some states aim at preventing or delaying hostile takeovers of the business enterprises incorporated in their states. On the other hand, some states have passed antitrust exemption laws to protect hospitals from antitrust laws when they pursue cooperative projects.

Interpretations of antitrust laws vary from one administration to another, from department to department, and from state to state. Even the same department under the same administration can change its mind. A completed business combination can be reexamined by the FTC at any time. Deregulation in the banking, telecommunication, and utility industries permits business combinations that once would have been forbidden. In 1997, the Justice Department and the FTC jointly issued new guidelines for evaluating proposed business combinations that allow companies to argue that cost savings or better products could offset potential anticompetitive effects of a merger.

THE FORM OF BUSINESS COMBINATIONS

Business combination is a general term that encompasses all forms of combining previously separate business entities. Such combinations are **acquisitions** when one corporation acquires the productive assets of another business entity and integrates those assets into its own operations. Business combinations are also acquisitions when one corporation obtains operating control over the productive facilities of another entity by acquiring a majority of its outstanding voting stock. The acquired company need not be dissolved; that is, the acquired company does not have to go out of existence.

The terms **merger** and **consolidation** are often used as synonyms for acquisitions. However, in accounting there is a difference. A merger entails the dissolution of all but one of the business entities involved. A consolidation entails the dissolution of all the business entities involved and the formation of a new corporation.

A *merger* occurs when one corporation takes over all the operations of another business entity and that entity is dissolved. For example, Company A purchases the assets of Company B directly from Company B for cash, other assets, or Company A securities (stocks, bonds, or notes). This business combination is an acquisition, but it is not a merger unless Company B goes out of existence. Alternatively, Company A may purchase the stock of Company B directly from Company B's stockholders for cash, other assets, or Company A securities. This acquisition will give Company A operating control over Company B's assets. It will not give Company A legal ownership of the assets unless it acquires all of Company B stock and elects to dissolve Company B (again, a merger).

A *consolidation* occurs when a new corporation is formed to take over the assets and operations of two or more separate business entities, and those previously separate entities are dissolved. For example, Company D, a newly formed corporation, may acquire the net assets of Companies E and F by issuing stock directly to Companies E and F. In this case, Companies E and F may continue to hold Company D stock for the benefit of their stockholders (an acquisition), or they may distribute the Company D stock to their stockholders and go out of existence (a consolidation). In either case, Company D acquires ownership of the assets of Companies E and F. Alternatively, Company D could issue its stock directly to the stockholders of Companies E and F in exchange for a majority of their shares. In this case, Company D controls the assets of Company E and Company F, but it does not obtain legal title unless Companies E and F are dissolved. Company D must acquire all the stock of Companies E and F and dissolve those companies if their business combination is to be a consolidation. If Companies E and F are not dissolved, Company D will operate as a holding company, and Companies E and F will be its subsidiaries.

Future references in this chapter will use the term merger in the technical sense of a business combination in which all but one of the combining companies go out of existence. Similarly, the term consolidation will be used in its technical sense to refer to a business combination in which all the combining companies are dissolved and a new corporation is formed to take over their net assets. Consolidation is also used in accounting to refer to the accounting process of combining parent and subsidiary financial statements, such as in the expressions "principles of consolidation," "consolidation procedures," and "consolidated financial statements." In future chapters, the meanings of the terms will depend on the context in which they are found.

THE ACCOUNTING CONCEPT OF A BUSINESS COMBINATION

The accounting concept of a business combination is given in *Accounting Principles Board (APB) Opinion No. 16*, "Business Combinations," which became effective on November 1, 1970. According to the APB:

> A business combination occurs when a corporation and one or more incorporated or unincorporated businesses are brought together into one accounting entity. The single entity carries on the activities of the previously separate, independent enterprises.[1]

Note that the accounting concept of a business combination emphasizes the single entity and the independence of the combining companies before their union. Although one or more of the combining companies may lose its separate legal identity, dissolution of the legal entities is not necessary within the accounting concept.

Previously separate businesses are brought together into one entity when their business resources and operations come under the control of a single management

---

[1]*APB Opinion No. 16*, paragraph 1.

team. Such control within one business entity is established in business combinations in which:

1 One or more corporations become subsidiaries,
2 One company transfers its net assets to another, or
3 Each company transfers its net assets to a newly formed corporation.[2]

A corporation becomes a **subsidiary** when another corporation acquires a majority (more than 50%) of its outstanding voting stock.[3] Thus, one corporation need not acquire all the stock of another corporation to consummate a business combination. In business combinations in which less than 100% of the voting stock of other combining companies is acquired, the combining companies necessarily retain their separate legal identities and separate accounting records even though they have become one entity for primary reporting purposes.

Business combinations in which one company transfers its net assets to another can be consummated in a variety of ways, but the acquiring company must acquire substantially all the net assets in any case. Alternatively, each combining company can transfer its net assets to a newly formed corporation. Since the newly formed corporation has no net assets of its own, it issues its stock to the other combining companies or to their stockholders or owners.

A Brief Background on Accounting for Business Combinations

Accounting for business combinations is one of the most important and interesting topics of accounting theory and practice. At the same time, accounting for business combinations is one of the most complex and controversial areas of accounting thought. Business combinations are important and interesting because they involve financial transactions of enormous magnitudes, business empires, success stories and personal fortunes, executive genius, and management fiascos. By their nature, they necessarily involve the takeover of entire companies. Business combinations are complex because each one is unique and must be evaluated in terms of its economic substance, irrespective of its legal form.

Much of the controversy concerning accounting requirements for business combinations involves the pooling of interests method, which became generally accepted in 1950 when the Committee on Accounting Procedure issued *Accounting Research Bulletin (ARB) No. 40*. Although there are conceptual difficulties with the pooling method, the underlying problem that arose with *ARB No. 40* was the introduction of alternative methods of accounting for business combinations (pooling versus purchase). Numerous financial interests are involved in a business combination, and alternate accounting procedures may not be neutral with respect to different interests. That is, the individual financial interests and the final plan of combination may be affected by the method of accounting.

Current accounting requirements for business combinations are found in *APB Opinion No. 16*, which continues to recognize both the pooling and the purchase methods of accounting for business combinations, but not as alternative methods of accounting for the same business combination. Even so, two very different methods of accounting for business combinations continue to be generally accepted. Currently, the Financial Accounting Standards Board (FASB) has a number of projects related to business combinations and consolidations on its agenda, including the possible elimination of the pooling of interest method of accounting for business combinations.

Methods of Accounting for Business Combinations

There are two generally accepted methods of accounting for business combinations: **the pooling of interests method** and the **purchase method**. However, the two methods "are not alternatives in accounting for the same business combination."[4] A business combination that meets the criteria of *APB Opinion No. 16* for a pooling of interests must be accounted for under the pooling method. All other business combinations

---

[2]Ibid., paragraph 5.

[3]The Financial Accounting Standards Board favors a consolidation policy based on control of another enterprise, rather than majority ownership.

[4]Ibid., paragraph 43.

must be accounted for under the purchase method. The two methods are based on different assumptions about the nature of a business combination.

Pooling of Interests Method   An underlying assumption of the pooling of interests method is that the ownership interests of the combining companies are united and continue relatively unchanged in the new accounting entity. Because none of the combining companies is considered to have acquired the other combining companies, there is no purchase, no purchase price, and, accordingly, no new basis of accountability. Under the pooling method, the assets and liabilities of the combining companies are carried forward to the combined entity at book value. Therefore, any goodwill on the books of the other combining companies will be included as an asset on the books of the surviving (pooled) entity. Retained earnings of the combining companies are also carried forward to the pooled entity (subject to certain limitations to be explained later). Income of the pooled entity includes the incomes of the combining companies for the entire year, regardless of the date on which the business combination is consummated.

Separate companies in a business combination may have used different accounting methods for recording assets and liabilities. In a pooling of interests combination, the amounts recorded by the separate companies under different accounting methods "may be adjusted to the same basis of accounting if the change would otherwise have been appropriate for the separate company. A change in accounting method to conform the individual methods should be applied retroactively, and the financial statements presented for prior periods should be restated."[5] For example, if one company in a pooling of interests business combination prices its inventories at last-in, first-out (LIFO) cost and the other company at first-in, first-out (FIFO) cost, the historical cost data may be adjusted to either LIFO or FIFO to conform accounting methods.

Purchase Method   The purchase method is based on the assumption that a business combination is a transaction in which one entity acquires the net assets of the other combining companies. Under the purchase method, the acquiring corporation records the assets received and liabilities assumed at their fair values. The cost of the acquired company is determined in the same manner as for other transactions. This cost is allocated to identifiable assets and liabilities acquired according to their fair values at the date of combination. Any excess of cost over the fair value of net assets acquired is allocated to goodwill and amortized over a maximum period of 40 years. Retained earnings of the acquiring corporation under the purchase method might be decreased as a result of the business combination, but it could never be increased. The income of the acquiring company includes its own income for the period, plus the income of the acquired companies that is earned after the date of the business combination.

The use of different accounting methods (for example, LIFO versus FIFO) by the separate companies in a purchase business combination is not a relevant factor in recording a combination accounted for as a purchase, because all assets and liabilities of the acquired company are recorded at their fair values.

Although these descriptions of the pooling and purchase methods are short, they introduce the two methods and indicate the significant differences in accounting that can result from using one method rather than the other. The two methods are covered in more detail in subsequent sections of this chapter.

Conditions for Pooling

The pooling of interests concept is based on the assumption that it is possible to unite ownership interests through the exchange of equity securities without an acquisition of one combining company by another.[6] Accordingly, application of the concept is limited to those business combinations in which the combining entities exchange equity securities and the operations and ownership interests continue in a new accounting entity. In *APB Opinion No. 16*, the APB sought to prevent pooling of interests accounting for business combinations that were incompatible with the pooling concept. It did this by specifying (in paragraphs 45 through 48 of *Opinion No. 16*) 12 condi-

---

[5]Ibid., paragraph 52.

[6]The underlying assumptions of pooling have been challenged by many writers in accounting. For example, see *Accounting Research Study No. 5*, "A Critical Study of Accounting for Business Combinations," by Arthur R. Wyatt (New York: American Institute of Certified Public Accountants, 1963). FASB considered eliminating pooling of interest in 1997.

tions that must be met for the pooling of interests method to be used. These conditions are summarized under the headings used by the APB.

Attributes of Combining Companies   Two of the conditions for a pooling of interests are classified as attributes of the combining companies. The first condition is that each of the combining companies is autonomous and has not been a subsidiary or division of another corporation within two years before the plan of combination is initiated. The date of initiation is whichever is earlier: the public announcement of the ratio of exchange of stock or the notification of the stockholders of the exchange ratio. The *exchange ratio* is the ratio of the number of shares of the issuing company's stock to be exchanged for each share of the other combining company's stock on the date of consummation of the pooling. The second condition is that each of the combining companies be *independent* of the others. This is interpreted to mean that the other combining companies together own no more than 10% of the voting stock of any combining company.

Manner of Combining Interests   Seven conditions for pooling are classified under this heading. First, the combination must be effected in a *single transaction* or be completed in accordance with a specific plan within one year after the plan is initiated. Failure to meet the one-year requirement will not prevent the pooling treatment if consummation is delayed by lawsuits, regulatory agencies, or other factors beyond the control of management. Second, one corporation (the issuing corporation) *must offer and issue only common stock* in exchange for substantially all (90% or more) of the outstanding voting stock of another company (a combining company) on the date the plan is consummated. The number of shares assumed to be exchanged excludes shares of the combining company held by the issuing company when the plan is initiated, shares acquired by the issuing company before the plan is consummated, and shares outstanding after the plan is consummated. If the combining company holds shares in the issuing company, these shares must be converted into an equivalent number of shares of the combining company and also deducted from outstanding shares to determine the number of shares assumed to be exchanged. The reason for this adjustment is that part of the shares issued by the issuing company are used to reacquire its own shares. Such shares are not issued to acquire stock of the other combining company.[7]

The third condition for pooling is that *none of the combining companies changes the equity interest* of the voting common stock in contemplation of effecting the combination within two years before initiation of the plan of combination or between the dates of initiation and consummation. A fourth condition is that each of the combining companies *reacquires shares of voting common stock only for purposes other than business combination,* and that no company reacquires more than a normal number of shares between the dates the plan is initiated and consummated. This restriction on treasury stock transactions generally does not apply to shares purchased for stock option or compensation plans.

The fifth condition requires that the proportionate interest of each individual common stockholder in each of the combining companies remains the same as a result of the exchange of stock to effect the combination. For example, if Stockholder A held 100 shares in the other combining company and Stockholder B held 200 shares, then Stockholder B's interest in the pooled entity must be twice that of A's for the combination to be a pooling of interests.

Condition 6 specifies that the voting rights in the combined corporation be immediately exercisable by the stockholders. The final condition requires resolution of the combination on the date of consummation, with no provisions pending that relate to the issue of securities or other considerations.

Absence of Planned Transactions   The last group of conditions for a pooling of interests focuses on planned transactions of the combined entity. First, the combined corporation must *not* retire or reacquire stock issued to effect the combination. Second, the combined corporation must *not* enter into financial arrangements (such as loan guarantees) for the benefit of former stockholders of a combining company.

---

[7]Paragraph 99 of *Opinion No. 16* provided certain exceptions to the test of minority stock held prior to combination and the 90 percent "substantially all" test. These exceptions, commonly referred to as the *grandfather clause,* were intended to provide a five-year period of transition to the rules of *Opinion No. 16.* Although the grandfather clause initially was scheduled to expire on October 31, 1975, it was extended indefinitely by *FASB Statement No. 10.*

Exhibit 1–1   Twelve Conditions for Pooling (APB Opinion No. 16)

Finally, the combined corporation must *not* plan to dispose of a significant part of the assets of the combining companies within two years after the combination. Plans to dispose of assets that represent duplicate facilities are permissible.

    If all 12 of these conditions are met, the business combination is accounted for as a pooling of interests; otherwise, the purchase method must be used. Exhibit 1–1 reviews the 12 conditions for a pooling of interests.

Computations for the "Substantially All" Test

Although most of the conditions for pooling are easily understood, the second condition (the "substantially all" test) under the "Manner of Combining Interests" heading requires illustration. Assume that Pat Corporation and Sam Corporation enter into a plan of business combination on May 1, 20X1, in which Pat will acquire Sam's outstanding stock by issuing one share of Pat stock for each two shares of Sam. The agreed-upon exchange ratio is 0.5 to 1. When the plan of combination is initiated, Sam Corporation has 10,000 shares of voting common stock outstanding, of which 200 shares are already owned by Pat. After the plan of combination is initiated, Pat purchases for cash an additional 200 shares of Sam stock directly from Sam's stockholders, and Sam purchases for cash 200 shares of Pat stock from Pat's stockholders. The business combination is consummated on July 1, 20X1, with Pat issuing 4,500 shares of its own stock for 9,000 shares of Sam. Sam's former stockholders continue to hold 600 shares of Sam stock.

    To meet the "substantially all" test, Pat Corporation must issue its own stock for 90% or more of Sam's stock. Although it appears that the 90% pooling test is met, the computation shown in Exhibit 1–2 indicates otherwise. The Sam shares held by Pat

Shares Assumed to Be Exchanged	
Sam's outstanding shares on July 1, 20X1	10,000
Deduct:	
Combining company shares held by issuing company:	
Sam shares held by Pat on May 1, 20X1	−200
Sam shares acquired by Pat during May 20X1	−200
Equivalent number of issuing company shares held by combining company:	
Equivalent number of Sam shares represented by	
Sam's 200 shares of Pat (200/0.5 exchange ratio)	−400
Sam shares outstanding after consummation	−600
Sam shares assumed to be exchanged in the combination	8,600
Shares Required to Be Exchanged	
10,000 outstanding shares of Sam on July 1, 20X1 × 90%	9,000
90% Test	
The 8,600 shares assumed exchanged is less than the required 9,000. Thus, the business combination is not a pooling of interests.	

Exhibit 1–2   "Substantially All" Test for a Pooling of Interests

and the Pat shares held by Sam disqualify the business combination for the pooling treatment, even though Pat issued its own stock for 90% of Sam's outstanding shares on the date of consummation of the plan.

NOTE TO THE STUDENT

The exhibits in this book are an integral part of the learning experience, and they should be studied in conjunction with the related text. In other words, the exhibits should be reviewed as they are introduced in the text. Exhibits contain information and explanations that are essential for understanding the material, and this information is often not provided elsewhere.

APPLICATION OF THE POOLING OF INTERESTS METHOD

A business combination that meets the conditions for a pooling of interests must be accounted for as a pooling. The accounting, however, is affected by the form of the business combination. In the case of a merger or a consolidation, there is only one surviving entity for which accounting records must be maintained and for which financial reports must be issued. Similarly, when one entity in a business combination receives the net assets of other combining companies, that receiving entity is the relevant entity for accounting and reporting purposes. By contrast, business combinations in which the combining entities continue to operate in a parent company–subsidiary relationship involve more complex accounting problems because the accounting records are maintained by the separate legal entities (parent company and subsidiaries), but the reporting for the combined entity requires the issuance of consolidated financial statements.

Combining Stockholders' Equities in a Pooling

In a pooling of interests, the recorded assets and liabilities of the separate companies become the assets and liabilities of the surviving (combined) corporation. Because total assets and liabilities equal the sum of the combining entities, so must the total equities. The capital stock of the surviving corporation must equal the par or stated value of outstanding shares (after the issuance of the new shares). Ordinarily, the retained earnings of the surviving corporation will be equal to the total retained earnings of the combining companies, but this is not possible when the par or stated value of outstanding shares of the surviving entity exceeds the paid-in capital of the combining companies. If total paid-in capital of the combining companies exceeds the par or stated value of outstanding shares of the surviving entity, the amount of the excess becomes the additional paid-in capital of the surviving entity, and the total retained earnings of the combining companies becomes the retained earnings of the surviving entity. Alternatively, if the par or stated value of outstanding shares of the surviving entity exceeds the total paid-in capital of the combining companies, the combined retained earnings balance is reduced by the excess, and the surviving entity has no additional paid-in capital.

These relationships can be shown through a series of illustrations. Assume that immediately before their pooling of interests business combination, the stockholders' equity accounts for Jake Corporation and Kate Corporation are as follows:

	Jake Corporation	Kate Corporation	Total
Capital stock, $10 par	$100,000	$ 50,000	$ 150,000
Additional paid-in capital	10,000	20,000	30,000
Total paid-in capital	110,000	70,000	180,000
Retained earnings	50,000	30,000	80,000
Net assets and equity	$160,000	$100,000	$260,000

In cases 1, 2, and 3 that follow, the pooling is in the form of a *merger*, in which Jake Corporation is the issuing corporation and the surviving entity. In cases 4, 5, and 6, the pooling is in the form of a *consolidation*, and Pete Corporation is formed to take over the net assets of Jake and Kate. Jake and Kate disappear.

Case 1: Merger; Paid-in Capital Exceeds Stock Issued   Jake, the surviving corporation, issues 5,000 shares of its stock for the net assets of Kate. In this case, the $180,000 total paid-in capital of the combining companies exceeds the $150,000 capital stock of Jake, the surviving entity, by $30,000. As a result of the merger, Jake has capital stock of $150,000, additional paid-in capital of $30,000, and retained earnings of $80,000, for a total equity of $260,000. The entry on Jake's books to record the pooling is:

Net assets	$100,000	
Capital stock, $10 par		$50,000
Additional paid-in capital		20,000
Retained earnings		30,000

    To record issuance of 5,000 shares in a pooling of
      interests with Kate Corporation.

The summary designation *net assets* is used only to simplify this illustration. If separate accounting records are to be maintained for Kate, the debit in this entry would be to *investment in Kate*. If separate accounting records are not maintained for Kate, the individual asset and liability accounts are debited or credited, rather than the summary designation net assets.

Kate records its dissolution by closing out its ledger as follows:

Capital stock, $10 par	$ 50,000	
Additional paid-in capital	20,000	
Retained earnings	30,000	
Net assets		$100,000

    To record merger with Jake Corporation and final dissolution.

Case 2: Merger; Paid-in Capital Exceeds Stock Issued   Jake, the surviving corporation, issues 7,000 shares of its stock for the net assets of Kate. In this case, the $180,000 total paid-in capital of the combining companies exceeds the $170,000 capital stock of Jake by $10,000. As a result, Jake has capital stock of $170,000, additional paid-in capital of $10,000, and retained earnings of $80,000, for a total equity of $260,000. Observe that the net assets of the surviving entity still are equal to the total recorded assets of the combining companies. Jake records the pooling as follows:

Net assets	$100,000	
Capital stock, $10 par		$ 70,000
Retained earnings		30,000

    To record issuance of 7,000 shares in a pooling with
      Kate Corporation.

Case 3: Merger; Stock Issued Exceeds Paid-in Capital   Jake, the surviving entity, issues 9,000 shares of its stock for the net assets of Kate. In this case, the $190,000 capital stock of Jake exceeds the $180,000 total paid-in capital of the combining companies by $10,000. The result is that Jake will have capital stock of $190,000, no additional paid-in capital, and retained earnings of $70,000. Notice that the maximum retained earnings that can be combined ($80,000) has been reduced by the $10,000 excess of capital stock over paid-in capital. The entry on Jake's books is:

Net assets	$100,000	
Additional paid-in capital	10,000	
Capital stock, $10 par		$ 90,000
Retained earnings		20,000

    To record issuance of 9,000 shares in a pooling with
      Kate Corporation.

The previous cases illustrated accounting procedures for a merger accounted for as a pooling of interests. Accounting procedures for consolidation of Jake and Kate are illustrated by assuming that Pete Corporation is formed to take over the net assets of Jake and Kate Corporations.

Case 4: Consolidation; Paid-in Capital Exceeds Stock Issued   Pete Corporation issues 15,000 shares of $10 par capital stock, 10,000 to Jake and 5,000 to Kate, for their net assets. In this case, the stockholders' equity of Pete, the surviving entity, is the same as for Jake Corporation in Case 1. Pete, however, opens its books with the following entry:

Net assets	$260,000	
Capital stock, $10 par		$150,000
Additional paid-in capital		30,000
Retained earnings		80,000

    To record issuance of 10,000 shares to Jake and 5,000
    shares to Kate in a business combination accounted
    for as a pooling of interests.

The $180,000 combined paid-in capital of Jake and Kate exceeds the $150,000 capital stock of Pete, the surviving entity, so the $30,000 excess is the additional paid-in capital of the pooled entity. Also, the $80,000 maximum retained earnings is pooled.

Case 5: Consolidation; Paid-in Capital Exceeds Stock Issued   Pete Corporation issues 17,000 shares of $10 par capital stock, 11,000 to Jake and 6,000 to Kate, for their net assets. The stockholders' equity of Pete in this case is the same as Jake's stockholders' equity in Case 2. Pete records the consolidation as follows:

Net assets	$260,000	
Capital stock, $10 par		$170,000
Additional paid-in capital		10,000
Retained earnings		80,000

    To record issuance of 11,000 shares to Jake and 6,000
    shares to Kate in a business combination accounted
    for as a pooling of interests.

The $180,000 total paid-in capital of the combining entities exceeds the $170,000 capital stock of Pete, therefore, the $10,000 excess is the additional paid-in capital of the pooled entity, and the $80,000 maximum retained earnings is pooled.

Case 6:Consolidation; Stock Issued Exceeds Paid-in Capital   Pete Corporation issues 19,000 shares of $10 par capital stock, 12,000 to Jake and 7,000 to Kate, for their net assets. Pete's stockholders' equity in this case is the same as Jake's stockholders' equity in Case 3. The entry on Pete's books to record the pooling is as follows:

Net assets	$260,000	
Capital stock, $10 par		$190,000
Retained earnings		70,000

    To record issuance of 12,000 shares to Jake and 7,000
    shares to Kate in a business combination accounted
    for as a pooling of interests.

The $190,000 capital stock of Pete, the surviving entity, exceeds the $180,000 total paid-in capital of Jake and Kate, so the maximum pooled retained earnings is reduced by the $10,000 excess to $70,000, and the pooled entity has no additional paid-in capital.

Summary Balance Sheets   A summary balance sheet for the surviving entity in each of the six pooling of interests business combinations is shown in Exhibit 1–3.

Treasury Stock in a Pooling   Under the provisions of *APB Opinion No. 16*, a corporation that distributes treasury stock in a pooling of interests should first account for those shares as retired so that their issuance will be recorded in the same manner as previously unissued stock.[8]

Stock of One Combining Company Held by Another Combining Company   Accounting for the stock of one combining company held by another combining company depends on whether the stock is stock of the surviving entity. An investment in the common stock of the surviving entity is returned to the surviving company in the combination and should be treated as treasury stock of the combined entity. Alternatively, an investment in another combining company by the surviving entity should be treated as stock retired as part of the combination.[9]

---

[8]*APB Opinion No. 16*, paragraph 54.
[9]Ibid., paragraph 55.

	Merger Jake's Books			Consolidation Pete's Books		
	Case 1	Case 2	Case 3	Case 4	Case 5	Case 6
Net assets	$260,000	$260,000	$260,000	$260,000	$260,000	$260,000
Capital stock, $10 par	$150,000	$170,000	$190,000	$150,000	$170,000	$190,000
Additional paid-in capital	30,000	10,000	—	30,000	10,000	—
Retained earnings	80,000	80,000	70,000	80,000	80,000	70,000
Stockholders' equity	$260,000	$260,000	$260,000	$260,000	$260,000	$260,000

Exhibit 1–3   *Summary Balance Sheets for the Six Pooling of Interests Cases*

This requirement is illustrated by assuming that Kam Corporation owns 200 shares of Lax Corporation common stock at the consummation of the Kam and Lax merger. Kam carries its investment in Lax account at its $3,000 cost. Summary data for Kam and Lax are as follows:

	Kam	Lax
Investment in Lax	$ 3,000	—
Other assets	197,000	$300,000
Total	$200,000	$300,000
Capital stock, $10 par	$100,000	$200,000
Additional paid-in capital	50,000	30,000
Retained earnings	50,000	70,000
Total	$200,000	$300,000

If Kam is the surviving entity and issues 19,800 shares to Lax (a 1:1 exchange ratio), the pooling of interests merger is recorded on Kam's books as:

Net assets	$300,000	
Capital stock, $10 par		$198,000
Additional paid-in capital		29,000
Retained earnings		70,000
Investment in Lax		3,000
To record merger with Lax Corporation.		

If Lax is the surviving entity and issues 10,000 shares of its own stock for 10,000 shares of Kam (a 1:1 exchange ratio), the pooling of interests merger is recorded on the books of Lax as:

Net assets	$197,000	
Treasury stock	3,000	
Capital stock, $10 par		$100,000
Additional paid-in capital		50,000
Retained earnings		50,000
To record merger with Kam Corporation.		

In each of these examples, the net assets of the surviving entity are $3,000 less than the recorded assets of the combining companies. The related effect on the combined stockholders' equity is to reduce paid-in capital when the investment is in the combining company and to record treasury stock when the investment is in stock of the surviving entity.

Reporting Combined Operations in a Pooling of Interests

When a business combination is treated as a pooling of interests, the financial statements of the surviving (combined) entity are prepared as though the companies had been combined as of the beginning of the year. This means that the results of operations of a pooled company are the same regardless of whether the business combination is consummated at the beginning of the period, at midyear, or at year-end. The revenue and expenses of the combined entity before combination during an accounting period should be recorded in the records of the surviving entity when the business combination is consummated.

The accounting entries to record a midyear pooling are illustrated in cases 1 and 2 that follow for the July 1, 20X5 pooling of interests of Tom and Mini corporations. Trial balances for the two companies at June 30, 20X5 are as follows:

	Tom Corporation	Mini Corporation
Other assets	$750,000	$290,000
Expenses	150,000	60,000
Total debits	$900,000	$350,000
Capital stock, $10 par	$500,000	$200,000
Retained earnings	200,000	50,000
Revenues	200,000	100,000
Total credits	$900,000	$350,000

Case 1: Merger   Tom Corporation, the surviving entity, issues 22,000 shares of $10 par common stock for the net assets of Mini Corporation on July 1, 20X5. The entry on Tom's books to record the merger is:

July 1, 20X5

Other assets	$ 290,000	
Expenses	60,000	
Capital stock, $10 par		$220,000
Retained earnings		30,000
Revenues		100,000

To record issuance of 22,000 shares in a pooling merger with Mini Corporation.

Immediately after this entry has been recorded, Tom Corporation's trial balance will include the following:

	Debits	Credits
Other assets	$1,040,000	
Expenses	210,000	
Capital stock		$ 720,000
Retained earnings		230,000
Revenues		300,000
	$1,250,000	$1,250,000

Note that the $250,000 maximum amount of retained earnings that could have been pooled has been reduced by $20,000, the excess of the $720,000 capital stock of the surviving corporation over the $700,000 paid-in capital of the combining corporations.

Case 2: Consolidation   Wall Corporation is formed to consolidate the operations of Tom and Mini corporations. On July 1, 20X5 Wall issues 72,000 shares of $10 par common stock for the net assets of Tom and Mini, 50,000 shares to Tom and 22,000 shares to Mini. The entry on the books of Wall Corporation to record the pooling of interests is:

July 1, 20X5

Other assets	$1,040,000	
Expenses	210,000	
Capital stock, $10 par		$720,000
Retained earnings		230,000
Revenues		300,000

To record issuance of 72,000 shares in the Tom and Mini pooling of interests.

The par value of outstanding stock of Wall Corporation is the same as in Case 1 in which Tom was the surviving entity, therefore, the trial balance of Wall Corporation immediately after the combination will be the same as for Tom Corporation in Case 1.

Expenses Related to Pooling Combinations

The costs incurred to effect a business combination and to integrate the operations of the combining companies in a pooling are expenses of the combined corporation. This treatment is required by *APB Opinion No. 16* and is consistent with the pooling concept of combining operations and shareholders' interests without an acquisition and without raising new capital. For example, costs of registering and issuing securities, providing stockholders with information, paying accountants' and consultants' fees, and paying finder's fees to those who discovered the "combinable" situation are recorded as expenses of the combined entity in the period in which they are incurred. If Tom or Mini corporation in the preceding cases had incurred accountants' fees, consultants' fees, costs of security registration, and other costs of combining, the combined net assets of the surviving entity would have been less and combined expenses would have been greater. However, the capital stock and pooled retained earnings recorded at July 1, 20X5 would have been the same.

As discussed previously, financial statements of a pooled entity for the year of combination should be presented as if the combination had been consummated at the beginning of the period. In addition, if comparative financial statements for prior years are presented, they must be restated on a combined basis with disclosure of the fact that the statements of previously separate companies have been combined.[10]

ACCOUNTING FOR BUSINESS COMBINATIONS UNDER THE PURCHASE METHOD

All business combinations that do not meet the conditions for pooling must be recorded under the purchase method. In general, the **purchase method** follows the same accounting principles for recording a business combination as are followed in accounting for assets and liabilities under generally accepted accounting principles. The cost to the purchasing entity of acquiring another company in a purchase business combination is measured by the amount of cash disbursed or the fair value of other assets distributed or securities issued. The cost of the acquired company also includes the direct costs of combination (such as accounting, legal, consulting, and finder's fees), other than those for the registration or issuance of equity securities. Registration and issuance costs of equity securities issued in a purchase combination are charged against the fair value of securities issued, usually as a reduction of additional paid-in capital. Indirect costs such as management salaries, depreciation, and rent are expenses under both the pooling and purchase methods. Costs incurred to close duplicate facilities are indirect costs and should be expensed.[11]

To illustrate, assume that Poppy Corporation issues 100,000 shares of $10 par common stock for the net assets of Sunny Corporation in a purchase business combination on July 1, 20X5. The market price of Poppy common stock on this date is $16 per share. Additional direct costs of the business combination consist of SEC fees of $5,000, accountants' fees in connection with the SEC registration statement of $10,000, costs of printing and issuing the common stock certificates of $25,000, and finder's and consultants' fees of $80,000.

The issuance of the 100,000 shares is recorded on Poppy's books as:

Investment in Sunny	$1,600,000	
Common stock, $10 par		$1,000,000
Additional paid-in capital		600,000

To record issuance of 100,000 shares of $10 par common stock with a par value of $16 per share in a purchase business combination with Sunny Corporation.

---

[10]*APB Opinion No. 20*, "Accounting Changes," paragraph 34. Restatement of all prior-period financial statements presented is required for a change in the reporting entity if the results are material.

[11]*FASB Technical Bulletin No. 85-5.*

Additional direct costs of the business combination are recorded as:

Investment in Sunny	$80,000	
Additional paid-in capital	40,000	
Cash (or other net assets)		$120,000

To record additional direct costs of combining with Sunny
Corporation: $80,000 for finder's and consultants' fees and
$40,000 for registering and issuing equity securities.

Registration and issuance costs of $40,000 are treated as a reduction of the fair value of the stock issued and are charged to additional paid-in capital. Other direct costs of the business combination ($80,000) are added to the cost of acquiring Sunny Corporation. The total cost to Poppy of acquiring Sunny is $1,680,000, the amount entered in the investment in Sunny account. It is desirable to accumulate the total cost incurred in purchasing another company in a single investment account, regardless of whether the other combining company is dissolved or the combining companies continue to operate in a parent-subsidiary relationship. If Sunny Corporation is dissolved, its identifiable net assets are recorded on Poppy's books at their fair values, and any excess of investment cost over fair value is recorded as goodwill. In this case, the balance recorded in the investment in Sunny account is allocated by means of an entry on Poppy's books. Such an entry might appear as follows:

Receivables	$XXX	
Inventories	XXX	
Plant assets	XXX	
Goodwill	XXX	
Accounts payable		$ XXX
Notes payable		XXX
Investment in Sunny		1,680,000

To record allocation of the $1,680,000 cost of acquiring
Sunny Corporation to identifiable net assets according
to their fair values, and to goodwill.

If Poppy and Sunny corporations were to operate as parent company and subsidiary, the entry to allocate the investment in Sunny balance would not be recorded by Poppy. Instead, Poppy would account for its investment in Sunny by means of the investment in Sunny account, and the allocation of the investment cost to identifiable net assets acquired would be made in the consolidation process. Because of the additional complications of accounting for parent-subsidiary operations, the remainder of this chapter is limited to business combinations in which a single acquiring entity receives the net assets of the other combining companies. Subsequent chapters cover parent-subsidiary operations and the preparation of consolidated financial statements.

Cost Allocation in a Purchase Business Combination

The first step in allocating the cost of an acquired company is to determine the fair values of all identifiable tangible and intangible assets acquired and liabilities assumed. This can be a monumental task, but much of the work is done before and during the negotiating process of the proposed merger. Companies generally retain outside appraisers to determine fair market values. Guidelines for assigning amounts to specific categories of assets received and liabilities assumed in the purchase are provided in *APB Opinion No. 16*, paragraph 88. In general the guidelines are as follows:

- Marketable securities—net realizable value
- Merchandise inventories and finished goods—net realizable value less a reasonable profit[12]
- Work-in-process inventories—net realizable value less a reasonable profit
- Raw materials—current replacement costs
- Receivables—present values determined at current interest rates less an allowance for uncollectibility

---

[12]Net realizable value of assets is the estimated selling price in the ordinary course of business less reasonably predictable costs of completion and disposal. ARB 43, Chapter 4, "Inventory Pricing," paragraph 8.

- Plant and equipment—current replacement costs for similar capacity if the assets are to be used, and net realizable value for assets to be sold
- Other assets, including land, natural resources, and nonmarketable securities—appraisal values
- Identifiable intangible assets—appraisal values
- Liabilities—present value determined at appropriate current interest rates

Fair values for all identifiable assets and liabilities are determined regardless of whether they are recorded on the books of the acquired company. For example, an acquired company may have expensed the costs of developing patents, blueprints, formulas, and the like under the provisions of *FASB Statement No. 2*, "Accounting for Research and Development Costs." However, fair values should be assigned to such identifiable intangible assets of an acquired company in a business combination accounted for as a purchase.[13] Similarly, *FASB Statement No. 87*, "Employers' Accounting for Pensions," requires that when the acquired company is an employer with a defined benefit pension plan, the assignment of the purchase price at the date of combination should include either a liability (the amount of projected benefit obligation in excess of plan assets) or an asset (the amount of plan assets in excess of the projected benefit obligation).

No value is assigned to goodwill on the books of an acquired subsidiary under *APB Opinion No. 16* because such goodwill is an unidentifiable asset, and because the goodwill resulting from the business combination is valued directly as the excess of cost over fair value of identifiable assets acquired.

FASB Statement No. 38, "Accounting for Preacquisition Contingencies of Purchased Enterprises," identifies the time needed to quantify the assets acquired and liabilities assumed in a purchase business combination as an allocation period. If the fair value of a preacquisition contingency, other than the tax benefit of a loss carryforward, can be determined in the allocation period, it is included in allocating the purchase price. Even if the fair value is not determinable during the allocation period, amounts that can be reasonably estimated for contingencies that are considered probable are included in the allocation. After the allocation period (usually no more than one year after consummation), any adjustment from a preacquisition contingency is included in net income of the period.

Contingent Consideration in a Purchase Business Combination Some purchase business combinations provide for additional payments to the previous stockholders of the acquired company, contingent on future events or transactions. Guidance in accounting for contingent consideration in a purchase business combination is provided in *APB Opinion No. 16*. (Recall that contingent consideration is prohibited under pooling of interests combinations.) The contingent consideration may involve the distribution of cash or other assets or the issuance of debt or equity securities. Contingent consideration that is determinable at the date of acquisition is recorded as part of the cost of combination. Contingent consideration that is not determinable at the date of acquisition is recognized when the contingency is resolved and the consideration is issued or becomes issuable.

When the contingency involves future earnings levels, the fair market value of the consideration distributed or issued is recognized as an additional cost (usually goodwill) of the acquired company. The additional cost should be amortized over the remaining life of the asset.

If the contingency is based on security prices, the recorded cost of the acquired company should not change. Instead, when the contingency is resolved, the additional consideration that is distributed is recorded at its fair market value. Securities issued and recorded at the date of acquisition should be written down proportionately. When capital stock is issued, the write-down would usually be to other paid-in capital. A write-down of debt securities would result in recording a discount on debt. Such a discount would be amortized from the date of settlement of the contingency.

Cost and Fair Value Compared After fair values have been assigned to all identifiable assets acquired and liabilities assumed, the investment cost is compared with the total fair value of identifiable assets less liabilities. If the investment cost exceeds net

---

[13]*FASB Interpretation No. 4*, "Applicability of *FASB Statement No. 2* to Business Combinations Accounted for by the Purchase Method," February 1975, paragraph 4.

fair value, it is allocated first to identifiable net assets according to their fair values, and the excess is allocated to goodwill. Amounts assigned to goodwill and to identifiable intangible assets should be amortized over the period to be benefitted, but not in excess of the maximum period of 40 years (see *APB Opinion No. 17*, "Intangible Assets"). Straight-line amortization is required "unless a company demonstrates that another systematic method is more appropriate."

In some business combinations, the total fair value of identifiable assets acquired over liabilities assumed may exceed the cost of the acquired company. Accounting procedures to dispose of the excess fair value in this situation are explained in paragraph 91 of *APB Opinion No. 16*:

> An excess over cost should be allocated to reduce proportionately the values assigned to noncurrent assets (except long-term investments in marketable securities) in determining their fair values. If the allocation reduces the noncurrent assets to zero value, the remainder of the excess over cost should be classified as a deferred credit and should be amortized systematically to income over the period estimated to be benefitted but not in excess of forty years.

Illustration of a Purchase Combination

Pitt Corporation acquires the net assets of Seed Company in a purchase combination consummated on December 27, 20X5. The assets and liabilities of Seed Company on this date, at their book values and at fair values, are as follows:

	Book Value	Fair Value
Assets		
Cash	$ 50,000	$ 50,000
Net receivables	150,000	140,000
Inventories	200,000	250,000
Land	50,000	100,000
Buildings—net	300,000	500,000
Equipment—net	250,000	350,000
Patents	—	50,000
Total assets	$1,000,000	$1,440,000
Liabilities		
Accounts payable	$ 60,000	$ 60,000
Notes payable	150,000	135,000
Other liabilities	40,000	45,000
Total liabilities	$ 250,000	$ 240,000
Net assets	$ 750,000	$1,200,000

Case 1: Goodwill Pitt Corporation pays $400,000 cash and issues 50,000 shares of Pitt Corporation $10 par common stock with a market value of $20 per share for the net assets of Seed Company. The entries to record the business combination on the books of Pitt Corporation on December 27, 20X5 are as follows:

Investment in Seed Company	$1,400,000	
Cash		$400,000
Common stock, $10 par		500,000
Additional paid-in capital		500,000
To record issuance of 50,000 shares of $10 par common plus $400,000 cash in a purchase business combination with Seed Company.		
Cash	$ 50,000	
Net receivables	140,000	
Inventories	250,000	
Land	100,000	
Buildings	500,000	
Equipment	350,000	
Patents	50,000	
Goodwill	200,000	
Accounts payable		$ 60,000
Notes payable		135,000

Other liabilities		45,000
Investment in Seed Company		1,400,000

> To assign the cost of Seed Company to identifiable
> assets acquired and liabilities assumed on the basis
> of their fair values and to goodwill.

The amounts assigned to the assets and liabilities are based on fair values, except for goodwill. Goodwill is determined by subtracting the $1,200,000 fair value of identifiable net assets acquired from the $1,400,000 purchase price for Seed Company's net assets.

Case 2: Negative Goodwill   Pitt Corporation issues 40,000 shares of its $10 par common stock with a market value of $20 per share, and it also gives a 10%, five-year note payable for $200,000 for the net assets of Seed Company. Journal entries on Pitt's books to record the Pitt/Seed business combination as a purchase on December 27, 20X5 are as follows:

Investment in Seed Company	$1,000,000	
Common stock, $10 par		$ 400,000
Additional paid-in capital		400,000
10% Note payable		200,000

> To record issuance of 40,000 shares of $10 par
> common stock plus a $200,000, 10% note in a
> purchase business combination with Seed Company.

Cash	$ 50,000	
Net receivables	140,000	
Inventories	250,000	
Land	80,000	
Buildings	400,000	
Equipment	280,000	
Patents	40,000	
Accounts payable		$ 60,000
Notes payable		135,000
Other liabilities		45,000
Investment in Seed Company		1,000,000

> To assign the cost of Seed Company to current assets and
> liabilities on the basis of their fair value and to noncurrent
> assets on the basis of fair value less a proportionate share
> of the excess of the fair value over investment cost.

The amounts assigned to the individual asset and liability accounts in the above entry are determined in accordance with the provisions of *APB Opinion No. 16* for purchase business combinations. The $1,200,000 fair value of the identifiable net assets acquired exceeds the $1,000,000 purchase price by $200,000, so the amounts otherwise assignable to noncurrent assets are reduced by 20 percent ($200,000 excess/$1,000,000 fair value of noncurrent assets). The reduction in specific noncurrent assets is as follows:

	Fair Value of Noncurrent Assets	Less 20% Reduction for the Excess of Fair Value over Cost*	Amounts Assignable to Noncurrent Assets
Land	$ 100,000	$ 20,000	$ 80,000
Buildings	500,000	100,000	400,000
Equipment	350,000	70,000	280,000
Patents	50,000	10,000	40,000
Total	$1,000,000	$200,000	$800,000

*Alternatively, the reduction in individual noncurrent assets for the excess of fair value over cost could be computed as:

Land	$100,000/$1,000,000 × $200,000 =	$ 20,000
Buildings	$500,000/$1,000,000 × $200,000 =	100,000
Equipment	$350,000/$1,000,000 × $200,000 =	70,000
Patents	$50,000/$1,000,000 × $200,000 =	10,000
		$200,000

In some instances, the excess fair value over cost may be so large that a balance remains after noncurrent assets have been reduced to zero. The remaining excess in this case should be reported as a deferred credit with a descriptive title other than negative goodwill.

When the fair value of net assets acquired in a purchase business combination exceeds investment cost, the excess is commonly referred to as **negative goodwill**. The designation negative goodwill is a misnomer because a firm either has goodwill (excess earning power) or does not have goodwill, but it cannot have minus goodwill. Even so, the designation is widely used by accountants to describe the excess of fair value acquired over cost in a business combination.

The Goodwill Controversy

Goodwill is defined as the excess of the investment cost over the fair value of assets received. Theoretically, it is a measure of the present value of the combined company's projected future excess earnings over the normal earnings of a similar business. This measurement requires considerable speculation. Therefore, the amount that is generally capitalized as goodwill is the portion of the purchase price left over after all other identifiable tangible and intangible assets and liabilities are valued. Errors in the valuation of other assets will impact on the amount capitalized as goodwill.

Goodwill is amortized over its useful life, but not longer than 40 years. In view of the obsolescence factor in modern technology, many accountants believe that a 40-year amortization period for intangible assets acquired in a business combination is much too long. For example, the competitive advantage of high tech assets is generally assumed to be less than five years. The Securities and Exchange Commission (SEC) encourages acquirers to select realistic useful lives, rather than 40 years.

Once goodwill is on the books of a company, it can become a nuisance and a serious drag on earnings. The SEC generally has not permitted a large write-off unless the company has operating losses or projects operating losses, and the goodwill asset has become impaired by a significant event or downward change in the company's business environment. The accounting rules are not clear on the issue of when goodwill has become impaired, and the SEC's position continues to evolve on a case-by-case basis.

Some accountants argue that goodwill should be written off immediately because goodwill has no value separate from the firm. Others prefer capitalization and no write-off. They argue that goodwill does not necessarily decrease in value and should be viewed as a permanent investment. Still others agree that goodwill should be amortized, but that the amortization period should be no longer than five to 20 years.

In addition to the accounting problems—difficulties in establishing a useful life, depression of earnings through amortization for years, and uncertainty in determining when the goodwill asset is impaired—there are also income tax controversies relating to goodwill. In some cases, goodwill amortization is deductible for tax purposes over a 15-year period. The tax consequences of goodwill are discussed in Chapter 10.

International Accounting for Goodwill   U.S. companies have long complained that the accounting rule for goodwill puts them at a disadvantage in competing against foreign companies for merger partners. In some countries, for example, the immediate write-off of goodwill to stockholders' equity is permitted. Even though the balance sheet of the combined company may show minus net worth, the company can begin showing income from the merged operations immediately. Companies in most industrial countries capitalize and amortize goodwill acquired in business combinations. The amortization periods vary. The maximum amortization period in Australia and Sweden is 20 years, and, in Japan, it is five years. In some countries, goodwill amortization is deductible for tax purposes, which makes short amortization periods popular.

The North American Free Trade Agreement (NAFTA) increased trade and investments between Canada, Mexico, and the United States and also increased the need for the harmonization of accounting standards. The standard-setting bodies of the three trading partners are looking at ways to narrow the differences in accounting standards. Canadian companies amortize goodwill over the period benefitted, not to exceed 40 years; Mexican companies amortize intangibles over the period benefitted, not to exceed 20 years. Negative goodwill from business combinations of Mexican companies is reported as a component of stockholders' equity and is not amortized.

The International Accounting Standards Committee (IASC) is a private-sector organization formed in 1973 to develop international accounting standards and promote harmonization of accounting standards worldwide. *International Accounting Standard No. 22* mandates the capitalization of goodwill with a maximum five-year amortization period. If it can be justified, the amortization period can be extended to 20 years. Although more than 95 accounting organizations from all over the world are members, the IASC does not have the authority to require compliance with its standards.

POOLING AND PURCHASE METHODS COMPARED

An indication of the relative importance of the purchase and pooling methods of accounting for business combinations is found in the 1997 edition of *Accounting Trends & Techniques*, page 52. Data on business combinations from the American Institute of Certified Public Accountants (AICPA) annual survey of six hundred stockholders' reports are as follows:

	1996	1995	1994	1993
Pooling of interest	32	32	19	21
Purchase method	256	244	215	200
Total business combinations in survey	288	276	234	221

Poolings of interests accounted for twelve percent or less of the business combinations in the AICPA survey in each of the four years. The issuance of *APB Opinion No. 16* in 1970 restricted the application of the pooling method. The percentage of combinations accounted for as poolings has decreased in most years since then. The conditions for a pooling are difficult to interpret when applied to complex capital structures. Numerous interpretations and informal rulings by the SEC have made it ever more difficult to structure a business combination as a pooling. Even so, poolings account for some of the largest business combinations.

     In spite of the underlying assumption that there is no acquisition in a pooling of interests, statements such as this one describing a proposed business combination between Suiza Foods Corporation and Morningstar Group are common: "The purchase will be accounted for as a pooling of interests transaction to avoid hefty charges against earnings for goodwill."[14] Richard Dieter writes: "In almost all business combinations that are accounted for as poolings of interests, an economic event has taken place whereby one entity has acquired another. To not account for these very significant transactions at their economic value further erodes the credibility of the continuing financial statements."[15]

IASC Proposal for Poolings   The IASC has proposed an international accounting standard for poolings of interests that would permit only combinations between companies of approximately equal fair value to be accounted for by the pooling method. This would rule out many U.S. business combinations that are currently accounted for as poolings.

Comparative Illustration of the Pooling and Purchase Methods

Comparative trial balances for Black Corporation and White Corporation at December 30, 20X6, just before the Black and White merger, together with the fair value of White's identifiable assets and liabilities, are shown in Exhibit 1–4.

     The Black and White merger was consummated on December 31, 20X6, with Black Corporation, the surviving entity, issuing 50,000 shares of $10 par common stock with a total market value of $885,000 for the net assets of White Corporation. The cost of registering and issuing the common stock was $20,000, and other direct costs of the business combination amounted to $40,000. These costs were paid by Black Corporation on December 31, 20X6.

Journal Entries   Journal entries to record the Black and White merger as a pooling of interests are compared with entries necessary to record the merger as a purchase in Exhibit 1–5. The first set of entries compares the differences in recording the stock

---

[14] *The Wall Street Journal*, September 30, 1997, A4.

[15] Richard Dieter, "Is Now the Time to Revisit Accounting for Business Combinations?" *The CPA Journal*, LIX, 7 (July 1989), p. 48.

COMPARATIVE TRIAL BALANCES
DECEMBER 30, 20X6

	Black Corporation per Books	White Corporation per Books	White Corporation Fair Values
Cash	$ 475,000	$ 125,000	$125,000
Receivables—net	600,000	300,000	300,000
Inventories	800,000	200,000	250,000
Plant and equipment—net	1,200,000	350,000	450,000
Cost of goods sold	1,000,000	325,000	
Other expenses	325,000	100,000	
Total debits	$4,400,000	$1,400,000	
Accounts payable	$ 300,000	$ 180,000	$180,000
Other liabilities	200,000	120,000	120,000
Capital stock, $10 par	1,500,000	500,000	
Additional paid-in capital	200,000	40,000	
Retained earnings	650,000	110,000	
Sales	1,550,000	450,000	
Total credits	$4,400,000	$1,400,000	

Exhibit 1–4   *Premerger Book Value and Fair Value Information*

issued by Black Corporation in the merger. Under the pooling method, the investment in White is recorded at $650,000, the book value of White's net assets on January 1, 20X6 (capital stock plus additional paid-in capital plus retained earnings). Under the purchase method, the investment in White is recorded at the $885,000 market value of the shares issued by Black Corporation on December 31, 20X6, the date on which the business combination was consummated. The retained earnings of Black and White are combined in the entry to record the stock issuance under the pooling of interests method, but there is no change in Black Corporation's retained earnings when the combination is recorded as a purchase.

	Pooling of Interests		Purchase	
Issuance of Securities				
Investment in White	$650,000		$885,000	
Capital stock, $10 par		$500,000		$500,000
Additional paid-in capital		40,000		385,000
Retained earnings		110,000		—
Direct Costs of Combination				
Expenses	$ 60,000		$ —	
Investment in White	—		40,000	
Additional paid-in capital	—		20,000	
Cash		$ 60,000		$ 60,000
Allocation of Investment				
Cash	$125,000		$125,000	
Receivables—net	300,000		300,000	
Inventories	200,000		250,000	
Plant and equipment—net	350,000		450,000	
Goodwill	—		100,000	
Cost of goods sold	325,000		—	
Other expense	100,000		—	
Accounts payable		$180,000		$180,000
Other liabilities		120,000		120,000
Sales		450,000		—
Investment in White		650,000		925,000

Exhibit 1–5   *Differences in Recording the Black and White Merger under the Pooling of Interests and Purchase Methods*

Journal entries to record additional costs of the business combination under the pooling and purchase methods are shown in a second section of Exhibit 1–5. All additional costs of combination are expenses when the combination is recorded as a pooling of interests. Under the purchase method, security registration and issuance costs ($20,000) are charged against additional paid-in capital, and the other direct costs of combination ($40,000) are added to the cost of acquiring White Corporation.

A third set of comparative journal entries in Exhibit 1–5 shows assignment of the investment in White balance to specific assets and liabilities, and in the case of a pooling of interests, to sales and expenses. Assets and liabilities are recorded at their fair market values when the purchase method is applied and at their book values under the pooling method. The excess of investment cost ($925,000) over the fair value of identifiable net assets ($825,000) is recorded as goodwill under the purchase method. In subsequent years the $100,000 allocated to goodwill will be amortized over the period to be benefitted, but not more than the maximum period of 40 years. This amortization will increase expenses and decrease income under the purchase method in future years. The excess of fair value over historical cost to White, which was allocated to inventories ($50,000) and to plant and equipment ($100,000) under purchase accounting, also will increase future expenses and decrease future income as compared with the pooling method. Thus, income of Black Corporation in subsequent years will be lower if the Black and White merger is recorded as a purchase rather than a pooling of interests.

Financial Statements　The combined financial statements for Black Corporation for 20X6 are compared in Exhibit 1–6 for the purchase and pooling methods. The differences in the comparative income statements result from the combining of sales

---

BLACK CORPORATION
COMPARATIVE FINANCIAL STATEMENTS
FOR THE YEAR ENDED DECEMBER 31, 20X6

	Pooling of Interests Method	Purchase Method
Income Statement		
Sales	$ 2,000,000	$ 1,550,000
Cost of sales	(1,325,000)	(1,000,000)
Other expenses	(485,000)	(325,000)
Net income	$　190,000	$　225,000
Retained Earnings Statement		
Retained earnings January 1, 20X6 (as reported)	$　650,000	$　650,000
Increase from pooling	110,000	
Retained earnings January 1, 20X6 (as restated)	760,000	
Net income	190,000	225,000
Retained earnings December 31, 20X6	$　950,000	$　875,000
Balance Sheet		
Assets		
Cash	$　540,000	$　540,000
Receivables—net	900,000	900,000
Inventories	1,000,000	1,050,000
Plant and equipment—net	1,550,000	1,650,000
Goodwill	—	100,000
Total assets	$ 3,990,000	$ 4,240,000
Liabilities and stockholders' equity		
Accounts payable	$　480,000	$　480,000
Other liabilities	320,000	320,000
Capital stock, $10 par	2,000,000	2,000,000
Additional paid-in capital	240,000	565,000
Retained earnings	950,000	875,000
Total liabilities and stockholders' equity	$ 3,990,000	$ 4,240,000

Exhibit 1–6　*Comparative Financial Statements for the Black and White Merger in the Year of Business Combination*

and expenses under the pooling method but not under purchase accounting. An additional difference is reflected in charging additional costs of combination to expense under the pooling method.

Total assets of Black Corporation at December 31, 20X6, are $4,240,000 under the purchase method and $3,990,000 under the pooling method. This $250,000 balance-sheet difference is the result of allocating the excess of cost over book value acquired to inventories, plant and equipment, and goodwill under the purchase method.

The comparative balance sheets in Exhibit 1–6 show additional paid-in capital of $240,000 and $565,000 under the pooling and purchase methods, respectively. Additional paid-in capital under the pooling method is equal to the excess of paid-in capital of the combining companies ($2,240,000) over the capital stock of the combined entity ($2,000,000). The $565,000 additional paid-in capital under purchase accounting is equal to the $200,000 beginning balance, plus $385,000 from the issuance of the 50,000 shares in excess of par value, less the $20,000 cost of registering and issuing the securities in the business combination.

The pooled retained earnings of Black Corporation exceed the retained earnings of Black under the purchase method by $75,000. This difference stems from combining retained earnings under the pooling method, as well as from the income differences discussed earlier. Note that significant differences in accounting for the retained earnings of a combined entity are possible under generally accepted accounting principles (GAAP). Accordingly, users of financial statements of combined entities should be careful not to interpret the reported retained earnings balances as amounts legally available for dividends. Such interpretations are questionable when the reports are for separate legal entities, and they are even more suspect when two or more entities are combined into one accounting entity.

DISCLOSURE REQUIREMENTS FOR A POOLING

The combined corporation must disclose that the business combination was accounted for as a pooling of interests. In addition, financial statement notes for the period of pooling should include the names of the combined companies, a description of the shares issued, the details of the results of operations of the separate companies before pooling, the nature of any asset adjustments to adopt the same accounting practices, the details of the effect on retained earnings of changing the fiscal period of a combining company, and a reconciliation of the issuing company's revenue and earnings with combined amounts after the pooling. When a new corporation is formed in a pooling, this last disclosure requirement can be met by disclosing the earnings of the separate companies that comprise the combined earnings for the period.[16]

DISCLOSURE REQUIREMENTS FOR A PURCHASE

Notes to the financial statements of the acquiring corporation must disclose that the business combination was accounted for by the purchase method. The notes also should provide the name and a brief description of the acquired company; the period for which results of operations of the acquired company are included in the income statement; the cost of the acquired company and, if applicable, the number and valuation of shares of stock issued or issuable, and a description of any contingent payments. A description of the plan for amortization of acquired goodwill should also be included. Information relating to several minor acquisitions may be combined for disclosure purposes.

For material acquisitions, the financial statement notes for the period of combination should include supplemental information on a pro forma basis as follows: (1) the results of operations for the current period as though the companies had combined at the beginning of the period and (2) the results of operations for the immediately preceding period as though the companies had combined at the beginning of that period, if comparative financial statements are presented.[17] Disclosures of these pro forma results are not required for nonpublic enterprises.[18]

---

[16]*APB Opinion No. 16*, paragraph 64.

[17]Ibid., paragraphs 95 and 96.

[18]*FASB Statement No. 79*, "Elimination of Certain Disclosures for Business Combinations by Nonpublic Enterprises," 1984, paragraph 4.

SUMMARY

A business combination occurs when two or more separate businesses are brought together into one accounting entity. There are two generally accepted methods of accounting for business combinations—purchase and pooling of interests—but these methods are not alternatives in accounting for the same business combination. All combinations that do not meet the conditions for the pooling of interests method must be accounted for as purchases. A pooling of interests involves an exchange of voting common shares, the combining of stockholders' equities, and the recording of assets and liabilities of the combining companies at their book values. Purchase accounting requires the recording of assets acquired and liabilities assumed at their fair values at the time of combination. The illustrations in this chapter are for business combinations for which there is only one surviving entity. Later chapters cover accounting and reporting for parent-subsidiary operations in which more than one of the combining companies continue to exist as separate legal entities.

SELECTED READINGS

Accounting Interpretations Nos. 1–39 of APB Opinion No. 16. New York: American Institute of Certified Public Accountants, 1970–73.

Accounting Principles Board Opinion No. 16. "Business Combinations." New York: American Institute of Certified Public Accountants, 1970.

Accounting Principles Board Opinion No. 17. "Intangible Assets." New York: American Institute of Certified Public Accountants, 1970.

BEIER, RAYMOND J. "Do Acquirers Have Carte Blanche to Get Rid of Goodwill?" *Mergers & Acquisitions* (November/December 1993), pp. 6–8.

BERESFORD, DENNIS R., and BRUCE J. ROSEN. "Accounting for Preacquisition Contingencies." *The CPA Journal* (March 1982), pp. 39–42.

CATLETT, GEORGE R., and NORMAN O. OLSON. "Accounting for Goodwill." *Accounting Research Study No. 10.* New York: American Institute of Certified Public Accountants, 1968.

DAVIS, MICHAEL. "Goodwill Accounting: Time for an Overhaul." *Journal of Accountancy* (June 1992), pp. 75–83.

DEMOVILLE, WIG, and GEORGE A. PETRIE, "Accounting for a Bargain Purchase in a Business Combination," *Accounting Horizons* (September 1989), pp. 38–43.

DIETER, RICHARD. "Is Now the Time to Revisit Accounting for Business Combinations?" *The CPA Journal* (July 1989), pp. 44–48.

DUVALL, LINDA, ROSS JENNINGS, JOHN ROBINSON, and ROBERT B. THOMPSON II. "Can Investors Unravel the Effects of Goodwill Accounting?" *Accounting Horizons* (June 1992), pp. 1–14.

GRINYER, J. R., A. RUSSELL, and M. WALKER. "The Rationale for Accounting for Goodwill." *The British Accounting Review* (September 1990), pp. 223–235.

JOHNSON, JEANNIE D., and MICHAEL G. TEARNEY. "Goodwill—An Eternal Controversy." *The CPA Journal* (April 1993), pp. 58–62.

MORTENSEN, ROGER. "Accounting for Business Combinations in the Global Economy: Purchase, Pooling, or ___" *Journal of Accounting Education* Vol. 12, No. 1 (1994), pp. 81–87.

NURNBERG, HUGO, and JAN SWEENEY. "The Effect of Fair Values and Historical Costs on Accounting for Business Combinations." *Issues in Accounting Education* (Fall 1989), pp. 375–395.

Statement of Financial Accounting Standards No. 38. "Accounting for Preacquisition Contingencies of Purchased Enterprises—an Amendment of *APB Opinion No. 16.*" Stamford, CT: Financial Accounting Standards Board, 1980.

Statement of Financial Accounting Standards No. 87. "Employers' Accounting for Pensions." Stamford, CT: Financial Accounting Standards Board, 1985.

WYATT, ARTHUR R. "A Critical Study of Accounting for Business Combinations." *Accounting Research Study No. 5.* New York: American Institute of Certified Public Accountants, 1963.

ASSIGNMENT MATERIAL

QUESTIONS

1 Describe the accounting concept of a business combination.
2 Is dissolution of all but one of the separate legal entities necessary in order to have a business combination? Explain.
3 What is the distinction between a business combination, a merger, and a consolidation?
4 Explain the basic differences between the purchase and pooling of interests methods of accounting for business combinations.

5 Identify the twelve conditions that must be met for a business combination to be accounted for as a pooling of interests.

6 Ordinarily, the retained earnings of the surviving corporation in a pooling of interests will be equal to the combined retained earnings of the combining companies. Under what conditions would the combined retained earnings be less than or greater than the total retained earnings of the combining companies?

7 The term *instant earnings* has been cited as an undesirable feature of the pooling of interests method. In what sense does pooling of interests accounting give rise to the so-called instant earnings? Explain.

8 Compare the costs of effecting a business combination under the purchase and pooling of interests methods.

9 When does goodwill result from a business combination? How does goodwill affect reported net income after a business combination?

10 What is negative goodwill? Describe the accounting procedures necessary to record and account for negative goodwill.

11 Why are purchase and pooling of interests business combinations accounted for differently?

12 Explain how the direct and indirect costs of combination are recorded for purchase business combinations and for poolings of interests.

EXERCISES

E 1-1 1 A business combination in which a new corporation is formed to take over the assets and operations of two or more separate business entities, and those previously separate entities are dissolved, is a:
   a Consolidation
   b Merger
   c Pooling of interests
   d Purchase

2 Which one of the following items is a requirement for a pooling of interests?
   a Fair value accounting
   b Amortization of goodwill
   c Exchange of common shares
   d Dissolution of all but one of the combining entities

3 In a purchase business combination, the direct costs of registering and issuing equity securities are:
   a Added to the parent/investor company's investment account
   b Charged against other paid-in capital of the combined entity
   c Deducted from income in the period of combination
   d None of the above

4 Which of the following accounts would be adjusted to its fair market value in a merger accounted for under the purchase method, regardless of the price paid?
   a Inventories
   b Goodwill
   c Patents
   d Equipment

5 A pooling of interests was consummated with the stockholders of the other combining corporation exchanging two of their shares for each share of stock of the issuing company. The exchange ratio in this pooling is:
   a 2
   b 0.5
   c 3
   d 1.5

6 The issuing company in a pooling of interests may issue treasury shares for the stock of the other combining corporation if the treasury stock is:
   a Acquired for cash to affect the business combination
   b Accounted for on a cost basis
   c Reissued at its current market value
   d First retired and then reissued

7 Corporation A and Corporation B combine in 20X2 in a pooling of interests business combination. Which of the following dates is the date of initiation of the plan for this business combination?
   a A consulting firm arranges a meeting between the officers and directors of the two companies on January 5, 20X2.
   b A public announcement is made on March 1, 20X2, that the exchange ratio will be 1.2 to 1.
   c Stockholders are notified that the officers of the two companies have agreed upon the 1.2 to 1 exchange ratio on March 15, 20X2.

    d Stockholders of the two companies vote to accept the terms of the proposed business combination on May 15, 20X2.

  8 Which one of the following criteria is *not* a condition for a pooling of interests?

    a Each of the combining firms must be autonomous.

    b The combination must be completed in a single transaction or in accordance with a specific plan that is completed within one year of its initiation.

    c Each combining corporation other than the issuing corporation must be dissolved as of the date on which the combination is consummated.

    d The proportionate interest of each individual common stockholder in each of the combining companies remains the same as a result of stock exchanged to effect the combination.

  9 An excess of the fair value of net assets acquired in a purchase business combination over the price paid is:

    a Reported as a deferred credit and amortized over a maximum period of 40 years

    b Applied to a reduction of noncash assets before a deferred credit may be reported

    c Applied to reduce noncurrent assets other than marketable securities to zero before a deferred credit may be reported

    d Applied to reduce goodwill to zero before a deferred credit may be reported

10 When retained earnings of a combining company in a pooling are adjusted to conform accounting principles with those of the pooled entity, the accounting change

    a Disqualifies the combination for pooling of interests treatment

    b Is recorded as an initial entry in the pooled firm's records

    c Is unacceptable if the effect is to increase retained earnings

    d Is acceptable if the change would have been appropriate for the separate company

E 1-2   **1** The criteria for a pooling of interests are *not* met if:

    a The combined entity plans to sell duplicate facilities

    b The issuing company pays cash for 1% of the shares of the other combining company between the initiation and consummation dates

    c The voting rights relating to the shares issued to effect the pooling will not be effective until a year after consummation of the plan

    d The business combination takes more than six months from the date of initiation to complete

  2 The exchange ratio in a pooling of interests is the:

    a Ratio of the market value per share of the issuing company's stock to the market value per share of the combining company's stock

    b Ratio of the total market value of stock issued to the total market value of stock received

    c Ratio of the number of shares of the issuing company's stock to be exchanged for each share of the other combining company's stock on the date of consummation

    d Ratio of the number of shares of the acquired company's stock to be exchanged for each share of the issuing company's stock

  3 The expensing of indirect costs of a business combination is required for:

    a Purchase but not pooling combinations

    b Pooling but not purchase combinations

    c Both purchase and pooling combinations

    d Neither purchase nor pooling combinations

  4 The maximum retained earnings that can be combined in a pooling of interests is reduced by the excess of:

    a Paid-in capital of the combining entities over the capital stock of the pooled entity

    b Additional paid-in capital of the combining entities over capital stock of the pooled entity

    c Capital stock of the pooled entity over total paid-in capital of the combining entities

    d Capital stock of the pooled entity over additional paid-in capital of the combining entities

  5 In a pooling of interests business combination, stock of the other combining company held by the issuing corporation is treated as:

    a An investment to be accounted for under the equity method

    b Stock retired in the pooling

    c Treasury stock of the pooled entity

    d None of the above

  6 The capital stock of the surviving entity in a 100% pooling of interests is equal to:

    a Capital stock of the issuing company plus the capital stock issued for shares of the other combining companies

    b Combined capital stock of the combining entities

    c Capital stock of the pooled entity over the paid-in capital of the other combining entities

    d None of the above

  7 Immediately before the business combination of Posey and Sharrel corporations in which Sharrel Corporation was dissolved, Posey held 500 shares of Sharrel common stock, and

Sharrel held 200 shares of Posey common stock. Posey issued 4,750 of its shares for the remaining 9,500 outstanding shares of Sharrel when the business combination was consummated. Which statement regarding this pooling of interests is correct?

   a The 500 shares of Sharrel stock held by Posey will be treated as shares retired in the pooling of interests.

   b The 200 shares of Posey stock held by Sharrel will be treated as treasury shares of the pooled entity.

   c The exchange ratio in this pooling is 0.5 to 1.

   d All of the above statements are correct.

8 Cork Corporation acquires Dart Corporation in a business combination accounted for as a purchase. Which of the following would be excluded from the process of assigning fair values for purposes of recording the purchase?

   a Patents developed by Dart because the costs were expensed under the provisions of *FASB Statement No. 2*, "Accounting for Research and Development Costs"

   b Dart's mortgage payable because it is fully secured by land that has a market value far in excess of the mortgage

   c An asset or liability amount for over- or underfunding of Dart's defined benefit pension plan

   d None of the above would be excluded

E 1-3 Pappy Corporation exchanged 11,000 of its common shares for 33,000 common shares of Snippy Corporation in consummation of a business combination on July 1, 20X6. Just before consummation, Pappy held 2,000 shares of Snippy common stock and Snippy held 1,000 shares of Pappy common stock. After the business combination, 2,000 shares of Snippy stock remained outstanding.

Required

   1 What was the exchange ratio in the business combination?

   2 How many shares of Snippy common stock were outstanding before consummation of the business combination?

   3 How many shares will be assumed to be exchanged under the "substantially all" test for a pooling?

   4 Is the "substantially all" test for a pooling of interests met in the Pappy-Snippy business combination?

E 1-4 Baloney Corporation and Nayle Company enter into a plan of business combination in which Baloney will issue one share of common stock for every three shares of Nayle common stock. On the date of initiation of the business combination, Baloney held 500 shares of Nayle's common stock, and Nayle held 100 shares of Baloney common stock. Between the date of initiation and the date of consummation, Baloney purchased an additional 400 shares of Nayle common in the stock market. Nayle had 50,000 shares of common stock outstanding throughout the period. On the date of consummation, Baloney issued 16,000 shares of common stock for 48,000 shares of Nayle's common stock. Nayle's old stockholders still hold 1,100 shares of Nayle common.

Required: How many shares of Nayle stock are assumed to be exchanged in the combination under the "substantially all" test for a pooling of interests?

E 1-5 **[AICPA adopted]**

   1 Dan Corporation offered to exchange two shares of Dan common stock for each share of Boone Company common stock. On the initiation date, Dan held 3,000 shares of Boone common and Boone held 500 shares of Dan common. In later cash transactions, Dan purchased 2,000 shares of Boone common and Boone purchased 2,500 shares of Dan common. At all times, the number of common shares outstanding was 1,000,000 for Dan and 100,000 for Boone. After consummation, Dan held 100,000 Boone common shares. The number of shares considered exchanged in determining whether this combination should be accounted for by the pooling of interests method is:

   a 190,000

   b 95,000

   c 93,500

   d 89,000

   2 Fast Corporation paid $50,000 cash for the net assets of Agge Company, which consisted of the following:

	Book Value	Fair Value
Current assets	$10,000	$14,000
Plant and equipment	40,000	55,000
Liabilities assumed	(10,000)	(9,000)
	$40,000	$60,000

The plant and equipment acquired in this business combination should be recorded at:
- **a** $55,000
- **b** $50,000
- **c** $45,833
- **d** $45,000

3 The business combination of Jax Company—the issuing company—and the Bell Corporation was consummated on March 14, 20X3. At the initiation date, Jax held 1,000 shares of Bell. If the combination is accounted for as a pooling of interests, the 1,000 shares of Bell held by Jax will be accounted for as:
- **a** Retired stock
- **b** 1,000 shares of treasury stock
- **c** (1,000/the exchange rate) shares of treasury stock
- **d** (1,000 × the exchange rate) shares of treasury stock

4 On April 1, 20X9 the Jack Company paid $800,000 for all the issued and outstanding common stock of Ann Corporation in a transaction properly accounted for as a purchase. The recorded assets and liabilities of Ann Corporation on April 1, 20X9 follow:

Cash	$ 80,000
Inventory	240,000
Property and equipment (net of accumulated depreciation of $320,000)	480,000
Liabilities	(180,000)

On April 1, 20X9 it was determined that the inventory of Ann had a fair value of $190,000, and the property and equipment (net) had a fair value of $560,000. What is the amount of goodwill resulting from the business combination?
- **a** $0
- **b** $50,000
- **c** $150,000
- **d** $180,000

E 1-6 Carrier Corporation issued 100,000 shares of $20 par common stock for all the outstanding stock of Homer Corporation in a business combination consummated on July 1, 20X5. Carrier Corporation common stock was selling at $30 per share at the time the business combination was consummated. Out-of-pocket costs of the business combination were as follows:

Finder's fee	$50,000
Accountants' fee (advisory)	10,000
Legal fees (advisory)	20,000
Printing costs	5,000
SEC registration costs and fees	12,000
Total	$97,000

1 If the business combination is treated as a pooling of interests, the acquisition cost of the combination will be:
- **a** $3,097,000
- **b** $2,097,000
- **c** $2,080,000
- **d** None of the above

2 If the combination is treated as a purchase, the acquisition cost of the combination will be:
- **a** $3,097,000
- **b** $3,080,000
- **c** $3,017,000
- **d** None of the above

E 1-7 Franklin and Harlow corporations were combined on April 1, 20X3 in a pooling of interests business combination, and Harlow was dissolved. For the year 20X3, the companies had the following earnings records:

Franklin Corporation (January 1–April 1)	$ 40,000
Franklin Corporation (April 1–December 31)	660,000
Harlow Corporation (January 1–April 1)	200,000

1 Franklin, the surviving corporation, will report income for 20X3 of:
- **a** $660,000
- **b** $700,000
- **c** $860,000
- **d** $900,000

2 Franklin's financial statement notes for 20X3 should include:
  a A description of all classes of preferred and common stock exchanged in the consummation of the pooling
  b A reconciliation of Franklin's revenue and earnings with combined amounts after the pooling of interests
  c A description of any contingent payments that may result in 20X4 from the pooling of interests
  d The cost of acquiring Harlow

E 1-8 Patter Corporation issues 500,000 shares of its own $10 par common stock for all the outstanding stock of Simpson Corporation in a merger consummated on July 1, 20X7. On this date, Patter stock is quoted at $20 per share. Summary balance sheet data for the two companies at July 1, 20X7, just before combination, are as follows:

	Patter	Simpson
Current assets	$18,000,000	$1,500,000
Plant assets	22,000,000	6,500,000
Total assets	$40,000,000	$8,000,000
Liabilities	$12,000,000	$2,000,000
Common stock, $10 par	20,000,000	3,000,000
Additional paid-in-capital	3,000,000	1,000,000
Retained earnings	5,000,000	2,000,000
Total equities	$40,000,000	$8,000,000

1 If the business combination is treated as a pooling of interests, the pooled retained earnings immediately after the combination will be:
  a $5,000,000   **c** $7,000,000
  b $6,000,000   **d** $8,000,000
2 If the business combination is treated as a pooling of interests, the additional paid-in capital immediately after the combination will be:
  a $5,000,000   **c** $3,000,000
  b $4,000,000   **d** $2,000,000
3 If the business combination is treated as a purchase and Simpson's identifiable net assets have a fair value of $9,000,000, Patter's balance sheet immediately after the combination will show goodwill of:
  a $1,000,000   **c** $3,000,000
  b $2,000,000   **d** $4,000,000

E 1-9 The stockholders' equities of Pillow Corporation and Sleep-bank Corporation at January 1, 20X7, were as follows:

	Pillow	Sleep-bank
Capital stock, $10 par	$1,500,000	$ 800,000
Other paid-in capital	200,000	400,000
Retained earnings	600,000	300,000
Stockholders' equity	$2,300,000	$1,500,000

On January 2, 20X7 Pillow issued 150,000 of its shares with a market value of $20 per share for all of Sleep-bank's shares, and Sleep-bank was dissolved. On the same day, Pillow paid $5,000 to register and issue the shares and $10,000 for other direct costs of combination.

Required
  1 Prepare the stockholders' equity section of Pillow Corporation's balance sheet immediately after the business combination on January 3, 20X7 assuming that the business combination is a pooling of interests.
  2 Prepare the stockholders' equity section of Pillow Corporation's balance sheet immediately after the business combination on January 3, 20X7 assuming that the business combination is *not* a pooling of interests.

E 1-10 IceAge Company issued 120,000 shares of $10 par common stock with a fair value of $2,550,000 for all the voting common stock of Jester Company. In addition, IceAge incurred the following additional costs:

Legal fees to arrange the business combination	$25,000
Cost of SEC registration including accounting and legal fees	12,000

Cost of printing and issuing new stock certificates		3,000
Indirect costs of combining, including allocated overhead and executive salaries		20,000

Immediately before the business combination in which Jester Company was dissolved, Jester's assets and equities were as follows:

	Book Value	Fair Value
Current assets	$1,000,000	$1,100,000
Plant assets	1,500,000	2,200,000
Liabilities	300,000	300,000
Common stock	2,000,000	
Retained earnings	200,000	

Required
1 Assume that the business combination is a pooling of interests. Prepare all journal entries on IceAge's books to record the business combination.
2 Assume that IceAge's acquisition is a purchase business combination. Prepare all journal entries on IceAge's books to record the business combination.

E 1-11 On January 1, 20X2 Placate Corporation held 2,000 shares of Service Corporation common stock acquired at $15 per share several years earlier. On this date, Placate issued 1.5 of its $10 par shares for each of the other 98,000 outstanding shares of Service in a pooling of interests in which Service Corporation was dissolved. Service Corporation's after-closing trial balance on December 31, 20X1, consisted of the following:

Current assets	$ 800,000	
Plant and equipment—net	1,500,000	
Liabilities		$ 200,000
Capital stock, $5 par		500,000
Additional paid-in capital		1,000,000
Retained earnings		600,000
	$2,300,000	$2,300,000

Required: Prepare a journal entry (or entries) on Placate's books to account for the pooling of interests. (Hint: Do not forget to consider the 2,000 shares of Service held by Placate on January 1, 20X2.)

E 1-12 Blair Corporation, the surviving company in a pooling of interests, exchanges 20,000 of its treasury shares for 10,000 shares of Tuby Corporation's common stock on July 1. At the time of the exchange, Tuby holds 1,000 shares of Blair stock acquired several years ago at $10 per share. The equity accounts of Blair and Tuby immediately before the pooling are as follows:

	Blair	Tuby
Capital stock, $10 par	$700,000	$100,000
Additional paid-in capital	40,000	74,000
Retained earnings	200,000	45,000
	940,000	219,000
Treasury stock, 20,000 shares	180,000	
Total stockholders' equity	$760,000	$219,000

Required: Prepare the stockholders' equity section of Blair's balance sheet immediately after the business combination.

E 1-13 Tansy Corporation issues its own common stock for all the outstanding shares of Vatters Corporation in a pooling of interests business combination on January 1, 20X2. The balance sheets of the two companies at December 31, 20X1, were as follows:

	Tansy	Vatters
Current assets	$15,000,000	$ 4,000,000
Plant assets—net	40,000,000	6,000,000
Total assets	$55,000,000	$10,000,000
Liabilities	$10,000,000	$ 3,000,000

(Continued)

	Tansy	Vatters
Common stock, $10 par	30,000,000	4,000,000
Additional paid-in capital	3,000,000	2,000,000
Retained earnings	12,000,000	1,000,000
Total equities	$55,000,000	$10,000,000

Required: Prepare balance sheets for Tansy Corporation on January 1, 20X2, immediately after the pooling of interest in which Vatters is dissolved under the following assumptions:
1 Tansy issues 800,000 of its common shares for all of Vatters's outstanding shares.
2 Tansy issues 1,000,000 of its common shares for all of Vatters's outstanding shares.

E 1-14 On January 1, 20X2, Danders Corporation pays $200,000 cash and also issues 18,000 shares of $10 par common stock with a market value of $330,000 for all the outstanding common shares of Harrison Corporation. In addition, Danders pays $30,000 for registering and issuing the 18,000 shares and $70,000 for the other direct costs of the business combination in which Harrison Corporation is dissolved. Summary balance sheet information for the companies immediately before the merger is as follows:

	Danders Book Value	Harrison Book Value	Harrison Fair Value
Cash	$350,000	$ 40,000	$ 40,000
Inventories	120,000	80,000	100,000
Other current assets	30,000	20,000	20,000
Plant assets—net	260,000	180,000	280,000
Total assets	$760,000	$320,000	$440,000
Current liabilities	$160,000	$ 30,000	$ 30,000
Other liabilities	80,000	50,000	40,000
Common stock, $10 par	420,000	200,000	
Retained earnings	100,000	40,000	
Total liabilities and owners equity	$760,000	$320,000	

Required: Prepare all journal entries on Danders Corporation's books to account for the business combination.

PROBLEMS

P 1-1 Gladfresh and Farmstone Corporations enter into a business combination accounted for as a pooling of interests in which Farmstone is dissolved. Net assets and stockholders' equities of the two companies immediately before the pooling follow:

	Gladfresh	Farmstone
Net assets	$1,000,000	$800,000
Capital stock, $10 par	$ 400,000	$200,000
Additional paid-in capital	200,000	300,000
Total paid-in capital	600,000	500,000
Retained earnings	400,000	300,000
Total stockholders' equity	$1,000,000	$800,000

Required
1 Prepare the journal entry on Gladfresh Corporation's books to record the pooling with Farmstone if Gladfresh issues 35,000, $10 par common shares in exchange for all Farmstone common shares.
2 Prepare the journal entry on Gladfresh Corporation's books to record the pooling with Farmstone if Gladfresh issues 77,000, $10 par common shares in exchange for all Farmstone common shares.

P 1-2 Quatro Corporation initiated a plan to pool its interests with Tertio Corporation on January 1, 20X1. On this date:
1 Quatro held 40,000 of Tertio's 750,000 shares of authorized and issued common stock, acquired by Quatro at a cost of $600,000.`
2 Tertio held 5,000 shares of Quatro's $10 par common stock acquired at $60 per share.

3 Tertio held 50,000 shares of its own common stock (treasury shares) reacquired at $30 per share.

On October 1, 20X1, Quatro issued 330,000 of its $10 par shares for 660,000 shares of Tertio. The stockholders' equity of Tertio on October 1, just before the exchange of shares in which Tertio was dissolved, consisted of the following:

Capital stock, $10 par	$7,500,000
Retained earnings	3,500,000
Less: Treasury shares	(1,500,000)
Total stockholders' equity	$9,500,000

The direct costs of the business combination consisted of $20,000 to register and issue the common stock and $380,000 in other costs of combination. These costs were paid in cash by Quatro.

Required

1 How many of Tertio's shares are required to be exchanged to meet the "substantially all" test for a pooling of interests?

2 How many of Tertio's shares will be assumed to be exchanged to determine if the "substantially all" test is met?

3 Prepare the journal entries on Quatro's books in summary form to record the business combination as a pooling. (Hint: Use an "other net assets" account to record Tertio's net assets other than its investment in Quatro, and make a separate entry to account for Pond's investment in Tertio and Tertio's investment in Quatro.)

P 1-3 Summary information is given for David Company and Carol Company at July 1, 20X7. The quoted market price of David common stock on July 1, 20X7 is $40 per share.

	David Company per Books	Carol Company per Books	Carol Company Fair Values
Current assets	$24,000,000	$ 8,000,000	$ 9,000,000
Plant assets	26,000,000	22,000,000	26,000,000
Total assets	$50,000,000	$30,000,000	$35,000,000
Liabilities	$15,000,000	$ 5,000,000	$ 5,000,000
Common stock, $10 par	20,000,000	10,000,000	
Additional paid-in capital	1,000,000	1,000,000	
Retained earnings	14,000,000	14,000,000	
Total equities	$50,000,000	$30,000,000	

Required

1 Assume that David Company issues 1,000,000 shares of its own stock for all the outstanding stock of Carol Company on July 1, 20X7, in a purchase business combination in which Carol Company is dissolved.

   a Calculate the goodwill from the business combination.

   b Prepare a journal entry to record the combination.

   c Determine total paid-in capital of David Company immediately after the business combination.

2 Assume that David Company issues 500,000 shares of its own stock for all the outstanding stock of Carol Company on July 1, 20X7, in a purchase business combination in which Carol Company is dissolved.

   a Determine the excess or deficiency of investment cost over the fair value of net assets acquired.

   b Prepare a journal entry to record the combination.

   c Determine the additional paid-in capital and retained earnings of David Company immediately after the business combination.

P 1-4 Comparative balance sheets for Pine and Sain Corporations at December 31, 20X1, are as follows:

	Pine	Sain
Current assets	$130,000	$ 60,000
Land	50,000	100,000
Buildings—net	300,000	100,000
Equipment—net	220,000	240,000
Total assets	$700,000	$500,000

(Continued)

	Pine	Sain
Current liabilities	$ 50,000	$ 60,000
Capital stock, $10 par	500,000	200,000
Additional paid-in capital	50,000	140,000
Retained earnings	100,000	100,000
Total equities	$700,000	$500,000

On January 2, 20X2, Pine issues 30,000 shares of its stock with a market value of $20 per share for all the outstanding shares of Sain Corporation in a purchase business combination. Sain is dissolved. The recorded book values reflect fair values, except for the buildings of Pine, which have a net realizable value of $400,000, and the current assets of Sain, which have a net realizable value of $100,000.

Pine pays the following expenses in connection with the business combination:

Costs of registering and issuing securities	$15,000
Other direct costs of combination	25,000

Required: Prepare the balance sheet of Pine Corporation immediately after the purchase business combination.

P 1-5   On January 2, 20X2, Pelican Corporation enters into a business combination with Seabird Corporation in which Seabird is dissolved. Pelican pays $825,000 for Seabird, the consideration consisting of 33,000 shares of Pelican $10 par common stock with a market value of $25 per share. In addition, Pelican pays the following expenses in cash at the time of the merger:

Finders' fee	$ 35,000
Accounting and legal fees	65,000
Registration and issuance costs of securities	40,000
	$140,000

Balance sheet and fair value information for the two companies on December 31, 20X1, immediately before the merger, is as follows:

	Pelican Book Value	Seabird Book Value	Seabird Fair Value
Cash	$ 150,000	$ 30,000	$ 30,000
Accounts receivable—net	230,000	50,000	40,000
Inventories	520,000	80,000	120,000
Land	400,000	100,000	150,000
Buildings—net	1,000,000	200,000	300,000
Equipment—net	500,000	300,000	250,000
Total assets	$2,800,000	$760,000	$890,000
Accounts payable	$ 300,000	$ 40,000	$ 40,000
Note payable	600,000	200,000	180,000
Capital stock, $10 par	800,000	300,000	
Other paid-in capital	600,000	50,000	
Retained earnings	500,000	170,000	
Total liabilities and owners equity	$2,800,000	$760,000	

Required: Prepare a balance sheet for Pelican Corporation as of January 2, 20X2, immediately after the merger, assuming the merger is treated as a purchase.

P 1-6   On January 2, 20X7, Persis Corporation issues its own $10 par common stock for all the outstanding stock of Sineco Corporation in a purchase business combination. Sineco is dissolved. In addition, Persis pays $20,000 for registering and issuing securities and $30,000 for other costs of combination. The market price of Persis's stock on January 2, 20X7, is $30 per share.

Relevant balance sheet information for Persis and Sineco corporations on January 1, 20X7, just before the business combination, is as follows:

	Persis Historical Cost	Sineco Historical Cost	Sineco Fair Value
Cash	$ 120,000	$ 10,000	$ 10,000
Inventories	50,000	30,000	60,000
Other current assets	100,000	90,000	100,000
Land	80,000	20,000	100,000
Plant and equipment—net	650,000	200,000	350,000
Total assets	$1,000,000	$350,000	$620,000
Liabilities	$ 200,000	$ 50,000	$ 50,000
Capital stock, $10 par	500,000	100,000	
Additional paid-in capital	200,000	50,000	
Retained earnings	100,000	150,000	
Total liabilities and owners equity	$1,000,000	$350,000	

Required

1 Assume that Persis issues 25,000 shares of its stock for all of Sineco's outstanding shares.
   a Prepare journal entries to record the business combination of Persis and Sineco.
   b Prepare a balance sheet for Persis Corporation immediately after the business combination.

2 Assume that Persis issues 15,000 shares of its stock for all of Sineco's outstanding shares.
   a Prepare journal entries to record the business combination of Persis and Sineco.
   b Prepare a balance sheet for Persis Corporation immediately after the business combination.

P 1-7 On January 2, 20X4 Dual and Cowhill corporations merge their operations through a business combination accounted for as a pooling of interests. The $300,000 direct costs of combination are paid in cash by the surviving entity on January 2, 20X4. At December 31, 20X3 Cowhill held 25,000 shares of Dual stock acquired at $20 per share. Summary balance sheet information for Dual and Cowhill corporations at December 31, 20X3 is as follows:

	Dual Corporation	Cowhill Corporation
Current assets	$ 6,500,000	$ 4,500,000
Plant and equipment—net	10,000,000	10,000,000
Investment in Dual		500,000
Total assets	$16,500,000	$15,000,000
Liabilities	$ 1,500,000	$ 3,000,000
Common stock, $10 par	10,000,000	8,000,000
Additional paid-in capital	2,000,000	3,000,000
Retained earnings	3,000,000	1,000,000
Total equities	$16,500,000	$15,000,000

Required

1 Assume that the surviving corporation is Dual Corporation and that Dual issues 1,000,000 shares of its own stock for all the outstanding shares of Cowhill Corporation.
   a Prepare journal entries on the books of Dual Corporation to record the business combination.
   b Prepare a balance sheet for Dual Corporation on January 2, 20X4 immediately after the business combination.

2 Assume that the surviving corporation is Cowhill Corporation and that Cowhill issues 1,200,000 shares of its own stock for all the outstanding shares of Dual Corporation.
   a Prepare journal entries on the books of Cowhill Corporation to record the business combination.
   b Prepare a balance sheet for Cowhill Corporation on January 2, 20X4 immediately after the business combination.

P 1-8 Patio Corporation was formed on January 2, 20X3 to consolidate the operations of EPA Corporation and Century Corporation. Summary balance sheets for the two companies at December 31, 20X2 are as follows:

	EPA Corporation	Century Corporation
Assets		
Cash	$ 3,000,000	$ 1,000,000
Receivables—net	3,500,000	1,500,000
Inventories	6,000,000	7,000,000
Land	1,000,000	2,000,000
Buildings—net	7,500,000	3,000,000
Equipment—net	3,000,000	5,500,000
Total assets	$24,000,000	$20,000,000
Liabilities and Stockholders' Equity		
Accounts payable	$ 2,700,000	$ 2,300,000
Bonds payable	3,000,000	—
Capital stock	10,000,000	6,000,000
Additional paid-in capital	4,300,000	2,700,000
Retained earnings	4,000,000	9,000,000
Total liabilities and stockholders' equity	$24,000,000	$20,000,000

Additional Information

1 The stockholders of the combining corporations agree to the following plan of combination:
   a Stockholders of EPA Corporation are to receive 1,300,000 common shares of $10 par stock of Patio Corporation for their 5,000,000 shares of $2 par capital stock.
   b Stockholders of Century Corporation are to receive 1,200,000 common shares of Patio Corporation for their 1,000,000 shares of $6 stated value capital stock.
   c Both EPA Corporation and Century Corporation are to be dissolved.
2 The business combination is treated as a pooling of interests with January 2, 20X3 as the date of initiation and consummation of the plan.
3 The inventories of Patio are to be maintained on a FIFO basis. Accordingly, Century's December 31, 20X2 LIFO inventory is adjusted to its $8,000,000 FIFO cost.
4 Cost of registering and issuing securities in the combination amount to $60,000, and other direct costs of combination total $140,000. These costs are paid by Patio on January 2, 20X3 from cash obtained from the other combining companies.

Required

1 Prepare journal entries on the books of Patio Corporation to:
   a Record the issuance of 1,300,000 shares to the stockholders of EPA Corporation
   b Record the issuance of 1,200,000 shares to the stockholders of Century Corporation
   c Record payment of the costs of business combination
2 Prepare a balance sheet for Patio Corporation at January 2, 20X3, immediately after the business combination has been consummated.

P 1-9 The balance sheets of Phule Corporation and Sen Corporation at December 31, 20X2 are summarized together with fair value information as follows:

	Phule Corporation		Sen Corporation	
	Book Value	Fair Value	Book Value	Fair Value
Assets				
Cash	$115,000	$115,000	$ 10,000	$ 10,000
Receivables—net	40,000	40,000	20,000	20,000
Inventories	120,000	150,000	50,000	30,000
Land	45,000	100,000	30,000	100,000
Buildings—net	200,000	300,000	100,000	150,000
Equipment—net	180,000	245,000	90,000	150,000
Total assets	$700,000	$950,000	$300,000	$460,000
Equities				
Accounts payable	$ 90,000	$ 90,000	$ 30,000	$ 30,000
Other liabilities	100,000	90,000	60,000	70,000
Capital stock, $10 par	300,000		100,000	

(Continued)

Other paid-in capital	100,000		80,000
Retained earnings	110,000		30,000
Total equities	$700,000		$300,000

On January 1, 20X3 Phule Corporation acquired all of Sen Corporation's outstanding stock for $300,000. Phule paid $100,000 cash and issued a five-year, 12% note for the balance. Sen Corporation was dissolved.

Required
1 Prepare a schedule to show how the investment cost is allocated to identifiable assets and liabilities.
2 Prepare a balance sheet for Phule Corporation on January 1, 20X3 immediately after the business combination.

P 1-10 On January 1, 20X7 Ainsley Corporation issues 500,000 shares of its capital stock for all of Biker Corporation's outstanding shares and Biker is dissolved. The fair value of Ainsley's common stock on this date is $25 per share. The book values and fair values of Ainsley and Biker at December 31, 20X6 are as follows:

	Ainsley Corporation		Biker Corporation	
	Book Value	Fair Value	Book Value	Fair Value
Assets				
Cash	$ 3,000,000	$ 3,000,000	$ 1,000,000	$ 1,000,000
Receivables—net	5,500,000	5,500,000	2,000,000	2,000,000
Inventories (LIFO)	6,000,000	7,000,000	3,500,000	4,000,000
Other current assets	1,500,000	1,500,000	500,000	600,000
Plant assets—net	16,000,000	19,000,000	5,000,000	7,400,000
Total assets	$32,000,000	$36,000,000	$12,000,000	$15,000,000
Equities				
Accounts payable	$ 5,000,000	$ 5,000,000	$ 1,800,000	$ 1,800,000
Other liabilities	3,800,000	4,000,000	3,200,000	3,000,000
Capital stock, $10 par	15,000,000		3,000,000	
Other paid-in capital	3,000,000		1,200,000	
Retained earnings	5,200,000		2,800,000	
Total equities	$32,000,000		$12,000,000	

Required: Prepare comparative balance sheets for Ainsley Corporation immediately after the business combination, assuming that (a) the combination is a pooling of interests and (b) the combination is a purchase.

P 1-11 Celistia Corporation paid $2,500,000 for Dawn Corporation's voting common stock on January 2, 20X7, and Dawn was dissolved. The purchase price consisted of 100,000 shares of Celistia's common stock with a market value of $2,000,000, plus $500,000 cash. In addition, Celistia paid $50,000 for registering and issuing the 100,000 shares of common stock and $100,000 for other costs of combination. Balance sheet information for the companies immediately before the business combination is summarized as follows:

	Celistia Book Value	Dawn Book Value	Dawn Fair Value
Cash	$ 3,000,000	$ 240,000	$ 240,000
Accounts receivable—net	1,300,000	360,000	360,000
Notes receivable—net	1,500,000	300,000	300,000
Inventories	2,500,000	420,000	500,000
Other current assets	700,000	180,000	200,000
Land	2,000,000	100,000	200,000
Buildings—net	9,000,000	600,000	1,200,000
Equipment—net	10,000,000	800,000	600,000
Total assets	$30,000,000	$3,000,000	$3,600,000
Accounts payable	$ 1,000,000	$ 300,000	$ 300,000
Mortgage payable—10%	5,000,000	700,000	600,000
Capital stock, $10 par	10,000,000	1,000,000	
Other paid-in capital	8,000,000	600,000	
Retained earnings	6,000,000	400,000	
Total equities	$30,000,000	$3,000,000	

1 Prepare journal entries for Celistia Corporation to record its acquisition of Dawn Corporation, including all allocations to individual asset and liability accounts.
2 Prepare a balance sheet for Celistia Corporation on January 2, 20X7, immediately after the acquisition and dissolution of Dawn.

2

Stock Investments— Investor Accounting and Reporting

Chapter 1 illustrated business combinations in which one surviving entity received the net assets of the other combining companies. The net assets and operations of all combining companies were integrated into those of a single legal and accounting entity with one record-keeping system. When an investment account was used to record a business combination in Chapter 1, its balance was eliminated immediately through allocation to individual asset and liability accounts.

Chapter 2 looks at equity investments in which the investment accounts are maintained on a continuous basis. It includes accounting for investments under the fair value/cost (fair value for marketable securities and cost for nonmarketable securities) method, in which the investor company does not have the ability to influence the activities of the investee, as well as accounting under the equity method, in which the investor company can exercise significant influence over the investee's operations. The chapter also includes accounting under the equity method, in which the investor is able to control the operations of the investee through stock ownership. This latter situation involves ownership of more than 50% of the voting stock of the investee company and is the result of a business combination in which "one or more companies become subsidiaries."[1]

This chapter covers parent company accounting for its subsidiaries under the purchase method, but it does *not* cover poolings of interests or consolidated financial statements. Consolidated financial statements for parent and subsidiary companies appear in Chapter 3 and subsequent chapters.

ACCOUNTING FOR STOCK INVESTMENTS

Generally accepted accounting principles (GAAP) for recording common stock acquisitions require that the investment be recorded at its cost. The basic guidelines for measuring the cost of common stock acquired in a purchase business combination also apply to common stock investments of less than 50% of the voting stock of another corporation. Investment cost includes cash disbursed; the fair value of other assets given or securities issued; and additional direct costs of obtaining the investment, other than the costs of registering and issuing equity securities, which are charged to additional paid-in capital.

---

[1]*APB Opinion No. 16*, "Business Combinations," paragraph 5.

One of the two basic methods of accounting for noncurrent, common stock investments generally applies—the **fair value method** or the **equity method**. If the fair value method is used, the investment should be accounted for according to the provisions of *FASB Statement No. 115*, "Accounting for Certain Investments in Debt and Equity Securities." If the equity method of accounting applies, the investment is accounted for under the provisions of *APB Opinion No. 18*, "The Equity Method of Accounting for Investments in Common Stock," as amended by *FASB Statement No. 94*, "Consolidation of All Majority-owned Subsidiaries."

Concepts Underlying Fair Value/Cost and Equity Methods

Under the **fair value/cost method** (also referred to as the cost method), investments in common stock are recorded at cost, and dividends from subsequent earnings are reported as dividend income. There is an exception. Dividends received in excess of the investor's share of earnings after the stock is acquired are considered returns of capital (or liquidating dividends) and are recorded as reductions in the investment account.[2] Equity securities that have a readily determinable fair value are classified as either trading securities (securities bought and held principally for the purpose of resale in the near term) or available-for-sale securities (investments not classified as trading securities) under the provisions of *FASB Statement No. 115*, "Accounting for Certain Investments in Debt and Equity Securities." Both classifications are carried at their fair values and report realized gains, losses, and dividends as earnings. However, unrealized gains and losses from the trading-securities classification are included in earnings. Unrealized gains and losses from the available-for-sale securities classification are reported at a net amount as a separate line item under other comprehensive income. *FASB Statement 130* allows other comprehensive income to be reported either on the income statement, as a separate statement of comprehensive income, or in a statement of changes in equity. These amounts would accumulate in the equity section of the balance sheet in the account titled *accumulated other comprehensive income*. *FASB Statement No. 115* does not apply to investments in equity securities accounted for under the equity method or to investments in consolidated subsidiaries.

The **equity method** of accounting is essentially accrual accounting for equity investments that enable the investor firm to exercise significant influence over the investee firm. Under the equity method, the investments are recorded at cost and are adjusted for earnings, losses, and dividends. The investor company reports its share of the investee's earnings as investment income and its share of the investee's losses as investment loss. The investment account is increased for investment income and decreased for investment losses. Dividends received from investees are disinvestments under the equity method, and they are recorded as decreases in the investment account. Thus, investment income under the equity method reflects the investor's share of the net income of the investee, and the investment account reflects the investor's share of the investee's net assets.

An investment in voting stock that gives the investor the ability to exercise significant influence over the financial and operating policies of the investee should be accounted for by the equity method of accounting. This is explained in paragraph 17 of *APB Opinion No. 18*:

> The Board concludes that the equity method of accounting for an investment in common stock should . . . be followed by an investor whose investment in voting stock gives it the ability to exercise significant influence over operating and financial policies of an investee even though the investor holds 50% or less of the voting stock.

The ability to exert significant influence is based on a 20% ownership test as provided by the APB:

> An investment (direct or indirect) of 20% or more of the voting stock of an investee should lead to a presumption that in the absence of evidence to the contrary an investor has the ability to exercise significant influence over an investee. Conversely, an investment of less than 20% of the voting stock of an investee should lead to a presumption

---

[2]*APB Opinion No. 18*, "The Equity Method of Accounting for Investments in Common Stock," paragraph 6a.

that an investor does not have the ability to exercise significant influence unless such ability can be demonstrated.[3]

An investor may be able to exert significant influence over its investee with an investment interest of less than 20%, according to *Opinion No. 18*. The following statement note from the *Ameritech 1994 Annual Report* (page 41) is an example of the exception:

On December 22, 1993, the company made an investment of $437.5 million for a 15% share in the Hungarian telephone company MATAV. The company's investment is being accounted for using the equity method, since the company exercises significant operating influence. Goodwill of approximately $210 million is being amortized by the straight-line method over a period of 40 years.

The equity method should not be applied if the investor's ability to exert significant influence is temporary or if the investees are foreign companies operating under severe exchange restrictions or controls.[4] Another statement note (partial) from the *Ameritech 1994 Annual Report* (page 40) contained the following disclosure:

On September 12, 1990, Ameritech and Bell Atlantic Corporation purchased all of the shares of Telecom Corporation of New Zealand Limited (New Zealand Telecom), the state-owned telephone company in New Zealand, for approximately $2.5 billion.

After stock sales required by the New Zealand government in the purchase agreement, which were completed in September 1993, the company's share of ownership is 24.8%. Stock sales of New Zealand Telecom in 1993 resulted in an after-tax gain of $61.7 million.

The company's long-term investment in New Zealand Telecom is accounted for under the equity method. Goodwill of approximately $290 million associated with this investment is being amortized by the straight-line method over a period of 40 years. The portion of the company's investment that was required to be sold was accounted for under the cost method.

FASB Interpretation No. 35 cites (1) opposition by the investee that challenges the investor's influence, (2) surrender of significant stockholder rights by agreement between investor and investee, (3) concentration of majority ownership, (4) inadequate or untimely information to apply the equity method, and (5) failure to obtain representation on the investee's board of directors as indicators of an investor's inability to exercise significant influence.[5] Application of the equity method should be discontinued when the investor's share of losses reduces the carrying amount of the investment to zero.

The Equity Method and FASB Statement No. 94   A parent company may use the equity method to account for its subsidiary investments, even though the financial statements of the subsidiaries are subsequently included in the consolidated financial statements for the parent company and its subsidiaries. In other words, the parent company maintains the "investment in subsidiary account" by taking up its share of the subsidiary's income and reducing the investment account for its share of subsidiary dividends declared. Under the equity method, the parent company's income and consolidated net income are equal. They reflect the income of the parent company and its subsidiaries as a single economic entity.

Before the issuance of *Statement No. 94* in 1987, parent companies were able to determine their own consolidation policies, and they had broad discretion in deciding whether to consolidate particular subsidiaries. Unconsolidated subsidiaries (in other words, subsidiaries whose assets and liabilities were not consolidated with those of the parent company) were accounted for by the equity method and *reported* in the parent's financial statements as equity investments. However, the provisions of *Statement No. 94* require that all majority-owned subsidiaries be consolidated, except where control is likely to be temporary or where control does not lie with the majority interests. Examples of control of a subsidiary not resting with the parent include a subsidiary in legal reorganization or in bankruptcy, or a subsidiary operating under severe foreign exchange restrictions or other governmentally imposed uncertainties. An investment in an unconsolidated subsidiary is reported in the parent's financial

---

[3]Ibid., paragraph 17.

[4]Ibid., footnotes 4 and 7.

[5]*FASB Interpretation No. 35*, 1981, paragraph 3.

statements by either the cost or equity method, according to the significant influence provisions of *APB Opinion No. 18*. Chapter 3 discusses situations in which certain subsidiaries should not be consolidated.

Accounting Procedures Under the Fair Value/Cost and Equity Methods

Assume that Pilzner Company acquires 2,000 of the 10,000 outstanding shares of Sud Corporation at $50 per share on July 1, equal to the book value and fair value of Sud's net assets. Sud Corporation's net income for the entire year is $50,000, and dividends of $20,000 are paid on November 1. If there is evidence of an inability to exercise significant influence, Pilzner should apply the fair value/cost method, revaluing the investment account to fair market value at the end of the accounting period. Otherwise, the equity method is required. Accounting by Pilzner Company under the two methods is as follows:

Entry on July 1 to Record the Investment:

Cost Method			*Equity Method*		
Investment in Sud	$100,000		Investment in Sud	$100,000	
Cash		$100,000	Cash		$100,000

Entry on November 1 to Record Dividends:

Cost Method			*Equity Method*		
Cash	$ 4,000		Cash	$ 4,000	
Dividend income		$ 4,000	Investment in Sud		$ 4,000

Entry on December 31 to Recognize Earnings:

Cost Method		*Equity Method*		
None (Assume that the stock is either nonmarketable or has a market price = $50 per share so that no revaluing is needed.)		Investment in Sud	$ 5,000	
		Income from Sud		$ 5,000
		($50,000 × 1/2 year × 20%)		

Under the fair value/cost method, Pilzner recognizes income of $4,000 and reports its investment in Sud at its $100,000 cost. Under the equity method, Pilzner recognizes $5,000 in income and reports the investment in Sud at $101,000 (equal to $100,000 cost plus $5,000 income less $4,000 dividends received).

The entries to illustrate the fair value/cost method reflect the usual situation in which the investor records dividend income equal to dividends actually received. An exception to this usual fair value/cost method situation arises when dividends are received in excess of the investor's share of earnings after the investment is acquired. From the investor's point of view, dividends in excess of the investor's share of earnings since acquisition of the investment are a return of capital or liquidating dividends. For example, if Sud's net income for the year had been $30,000, Pilzner's share would have been $3,000 ($30,000 × 1/2 year × 20%). The $4,000 dividend received exceeds the $3,000 equity in Sud's income, so the $1,000 excess would be considered a return of capital and credited to the investment in Sud account. Assuming that Pilzner records the $4,000 cash received on November 1 as dividend income, a year-end entry to adjust dividend income and the investment account would be needed. Such an entry would be recorded as follows:

Dividend income	$ 1,000	
Investment in Sud		$ 1,000
To adjust dividend income and investment accounts for dividends received in excess of earnings.		

This entry reduces dividend income to Pilzner's $3,000 share of income earned after July 1 and reduces the investment in Sud to $99,000, the new fair value/cost basis for the investment. If, after the liquidating dividend, the stock had a value of $120,000, then another entry would be required to increase the investment to its fair value.

Allowance to adjust available-for-sale securities to market value	$21,000	
Other comprehensive income		$21,000

Economic Consequences of Using the Fair Value/Cost and Equity Methods

The different methods of accounting (fair value/cost and equity) result in different investment amounts in the balance sheet of the investor corporation and different income amounts in the income statement. When the investor can significantly influence or control the operations of the investee, including dividend declarations, the fair value/cost method is unacceptable. By influencing or controlling investee dividend decisions, the investor corporation is able to manipulate its own investment income. The possibility of income manipulation does not exist when the financial statements of a parent company/investor are consolidated with the statements of a subsidiary/investee because the consolidated statements are the same, regardless of which method of accounting is used.

Although the equity method is not a substitute for consolidation, the income reported by a parent company/investor in its separate income statement under the equity method of accounting is generally the same as the income reported in consolidated financial statements for a parent company and its subsidiary.

EQUITY METHOD OF ACCOUNTING—A ONE-LINE CONSOLIDATION

The equity method of accounting is often called a **one-line consolidation**. This is because the investment is reported in a single amount on one line of the investor company's balance sheet, and investment income is reported in a single amount on one line of the investor's income statement (except when the investee has extraordinary or other "below-the-line" items that require separate disclosure). "One-line consolidation" also means that a parent company/investor's income and stockholders' equity are the same when a subsidiary company/investee is accounted for under a complete and correct application of the equity method as when the financial statements of parent company and subsidiary are consolidated. Consolidated financial statements show the same income and the same net assets but include the details of revenues and expenses and assets and liabilities.

The equity method involves many complexities; in fact, it involves the same computational complexities encountered in preparing consolidated financial statements. For this reason, the equity method is the standard of parent company accounting for its subsidiaries, and the one-line consolidation is integrated throughout the consolidation chapters of this book. This parallel one-line consolidation/consolidation coverage permits students and practitioners alike to check their work through alternative computations of such key financial statement items as consolidated net income and consolidated retained earnings.

Basic accounting procedures for applying the equity method are the same whether the investor has the ability to exercise significant influence over the investee (20% or 50% ownership) or the ability to control the investee (more than 50% ownership). This is important because investments of more than 50% are business combinations and are subject to the provisions of *APB Opinion No. 16.* Thus, the accounting principles that apply to purchase business combinations also apply to accounting for investments of 20% to 100% under the equity method. The difference between the way *Opinion No. 16* provisions are applied in this chapter and the way they are applied in Chapter 1 arises because:

1 Both the investor and investee companies continue to exist as separate legal entities with their own accounting systems.
2 The equity method applies to only one of those entities—the investor company.
3 The investor's equity interest may range from 20% to 100%.

Equity Investments at Acquisition

Equity investments in voting common stock of other entities are subject to the provisions of *APB Opinion No. 16,* so the investment cost is measured by the cash disbursed or the fair value of other assets distributed or securities issued. Similarly, direct costs of registering and issuing equity securities are charged against additional paid-in capital, and other direct costs of acquisition are added to the acquisition cost. The total investment cost is entered in an investment account under the one-line consolidation concept.

Assume that Payne Company purchases 30% of Sloan Company's outstanding voting common stock on January 1, 20X2 from existing stockholders for $2,000,000 cash plus 200,000 shares of Payne Company $10 par common stock with a market value of $15 per share. Additional cash costs of the equity interest consist of $50,000 for registration of the shares and $100,000 for consulting and advisory fees. These events would be recorded by Payne Company with the following journal entries:

January 1, 20X2

Investment in Sloan	$5,000,000	
Common stock		$2,000,000
Additional paid-in capital		1,000,000
Cash		2,000,000

    To record acquisition of a 30% equity investment in
       Sloan Company.

January 1, 20X2

Investment in Sloan	$ 100,000	
Additional paid-in capital	50,000	
Cash		$ 150,000

    To record additional direct costs of purchasing a 30%
       equity interest in Sloan.

Under a one-line consolidation, these entries can be made without knowledge of book value or fair value of Sloan Company's assets and liabilities.

Assignment of Excess Cost Over Underlying Equity

Information regarding the individual assets and liabilities of Sloan Company at the time of the purchase is important because subsequent accounting under the equity method entails accounting for any differences between the investment cost and the underlying equity in the net assets of the investee.

Assume that the following book value and fair value information for Sloan Company at December 31, 20X1 is available:

	Book Value	Fair Value
Cash	$ 1,500,000	$ 1,500,000
Receivables—net	2,200,000	2,200,000
Inventories	3,000,000	4,000,000
Other current assets	3,300,000	3,100,000
Equipment—net	5,000,000	8,000,000
Total assets	$15,000,000	$18,800,000
Accounts payable	$ 1,000,000	$ 1,000,000
Note payable, due January 1, 20X7	2,000,000	1,800,000
Common stock	10,000,000	
Retained earnings	2,000,000	
Total liabilities and stockholders'		
equity	$15,000,000	

The underlying equity in the net assets of Sloan Company is $3,600,000 (30% of the $12,000,000 book value of Sloan Company's net assets), and the difference between the investment cost and the underlying equity is $1,500,000. This difference must be assigned to the identifiable assets and liabilities based on their fair values, and any remaining difference is allocated to goodwill. Exhibit 2–1 illustrates the assignment to identifiable net assets and goodwill.

The asset and liability information given in Exhibit 2–1 is not recorded separately on the books of Payne Company. Instead, the $1,500,000 excess cost over underlying equity is included in Payne's investment in Sloan account. Under the equity method of accounting, this difference is eliminated by periodic charges

PAYNE COMPANY AND ITS 30%-OWNED EQUITY INVESTEE,
SLOAN COMPANY

Investment in Sloan					$5,100,000
Book value of the interest acquired					
(30% × $12,000,000 equity of Sloan)					(3,600,000)
Total excess of cost over book value acquired					$1,500,000

Assignment to Identifiable Net Assets and Goodwill

	Fair Value	−	Book Value ×	% Interest Acquired =	Amount Assigned
Inventories	$4,000,000		$3,000,000	30%	$ 300,000
Other current assets	3,100,000		3,300,000	30	(60,000)
Equipment	8,000,000		5,000,000	30	900,000
Note payable	1,800,000		2,000,000	30	60,000
Total assigned to identifiable net assets					1,200,000
Remainder assigned to goodwill					300,000
Total excess of cost over book value acquired					$1,500,000

Exhibit 2–1   *Schedule for Allocating the Excess of Investment Cost Over the Book Value
of the Interest Acquired*

(debits) and credits to income from the investment and by equal credits or charges to the investment account. Thus, the original difference between investment cost and book value acquired will disappear over the remaining lives of identifiable assets and liabilities or over a maximum period of 40 years (the maximum life that could be assigned to goodwill). The one exception is amounts assigned to land, which are not amortized.

The $300,000 assigned to goodwill in Exhibit 2–1 was determined as a remainder of the total excess over amounts assigned to identifiable assets and liabilities. However, the amount could have been computed directly as the excess of investment cost of $5,100,000 over the $4,800,000 fair value of Sloan's net assets acquired (30% × $16,000,000). If the difference between cost and underlying book value cannot be related to identifiable assets and liabilities, it is considered goodwill (or negative goodwill).

Accounting for Excess of Investment Cost Over Book Value Acquired

Assume that Sloan Company pays dividends of $1,000,000 on July 1, 20X2 and reports net income of $3,000,000 for the year. The excess cost over book value acquired is amortized as follows:

	20X2 Amortization Rates
Excess Allocated to:	
Inventories—sold in 20X2	100%
Other current assets—disposed of in 20X2	100%
Equipment—depreciated over 20 years	5%
Note payable—due in 5 years	20%
Goodwill—40-year maximum	2.5%

Payne Company makes the following entries under a one-line consolidation to record its dividends and income from Sloan:

July 1, 20X2		
Cash	$300,000	
Investment in Sloan		$300,000
To record dividends received from Sloan		
($1,000,000 × 30%).		

December 31, 20X2
Investment in Sloan	$900,000	
Income from Sloan		$900,000

    To record equity in income of Sloan
        ($3,000,000 × 30%).

December 31, 20X2
Income from Sloan	$300,000	
Investment in Sloan		$300,000

    To record write-off of excess allocated to inventory
        items that were sold in 20X2.

December 31, 20X2
Investment in Sloan	$ 60,000	
Income from Sloan		$ 60,000

    To record income credit for overvalued other current
        assets disposed of in 20X2.

December 31, 20X2
Income from Sloan	$ 45,000	
Investment in Sloan		$ 45,000

    To record depreciation on excess allocated to
        undervalued equipment with a 20-year remaining
        use life ($900,000 ÷ 20 years).

December 31, 20X2
Income from Sloan	$ 12,000	
Investment in Sloan		$ 12,000

    To amortize the excess allocated to the overvalued
        note payable over the remaining life of the note
        ($60,000 ÷ 5 years).

December 31, 20X2
Income from Sloan	$ 7,500	
Investment in Sloan		$ 7,500

    To amortize the excess allocated to goodwill
        ($300,000 ÷ 40 years).

    The last six journal entries all involve the income and investment accounts, so Payne could record its income from Sloan for 20X2 in a single entry at December 31, 20X2, as follows:

Investment in Sloan	$595,500	
Income from Sloan		$595,500

    To record equity income from 30% investment
        in Sloan as follows:

Equity in Sloan's reported income ($3,000,000 × 30%)	$900,000
Amortization of excess cost over book value:	
Inventories sold in 20X2 ($300,000 × 100%)	(300,000)
Other current assets sold in 20X2 ($60,000 × 100%)	60,000
Equipment ($900,000 × 5% depreciation rate)	(45,000)
Note payable ($60,000 × 20% amortization rate)	(12,000)
Goodwill ($300,000 × 2.5% amortization rate)	(7,500)
Total investment income from Sloan	$595,500

    Payne Company reports its investment in Sloan at December 31, 20X2 on one line of its balance sheet at $5,395,500 ($5,100,000 cost + $595,500 income − $300,000 dividends), and its income from Sloan for 20X2 at $595,500 on one line of its income statement. Sloan's net assets (stockholders' equity) increased by $2,000,000 during 20X2 to $14,000,000, and Payne's share of this underlying equity is 30%, or $4,200,000. The $1,195,500 difference between the investment balance and the underlying equity at December 31, 20X2 represents the unamortized excess of investment cost over book value acquired. This amount can be confirmed by subtracting the $304,500 net amortization for 20X2 from the original excess of $1,500,000.

When the full $1,500,000 excess has been amortized, the investment balance will be equal to its underlying book value—30% of the common stockholders' equity of Sloan. A summary of these observations follows:

	Stockholders' Equity of Sloan A	Underlying Equity (30% of Sloan's Equity) B	Investment in Sloan Account Balance C	Unamortized Cost/Book Value Differential C − B
January 1, 20X2	$12,000,000	$3,600,000	$5,100,000	$1,500,000
Dividends, July 20X2	(1,000,000)	(300,000)	(300,000)	
Income, 20X2	3,000,000	900,000	900,000	
Amortization, 20X2			(304,500)	(304,500)
December 31, 20X2	$14,000,000	$4,200,000	$5,395,500	$1,195,500

Excess of Book Value Acquired Over Investment Cost

The book value of the interest acquired in an investee corporation may be greater than the investment cost. This situation indicates that the identifiable net assets of the investee corporation are overvalued or that the interest was acquired at a bargain price. If the total excess relates to overvalued assets (in other words, investment cost is equal to fair value), the excess is assigned to reduce the specific assets that are overvalued. However, if identifiable net assets are recorded at their fair values, the excess of fair value (and book value) of the interest acquired over investment cost is negative goodwill. Negative goodwill is assigned to reduce noncurrent assets other than marketable securities, as explained in Chapter 1.

Amounts assigned to reduce specific assets are amortized over the assets' remaining useful lives. The income effect of such amortization under a one-line consolidation is the reverse of the goodwill situation that reduces income and investment account balances. That is, both the investment and investment income accounts of the investor corporation are increased when an excess of book value over cost is amortized.

To illustrate, assume that Post Corporation purchases 50% of the outstanding voting common stock of Taylor Corporation on January 1, 20X6 for $40,000. A summary of the changes in Taylor's stockholders' equity during 20X6 appears as follows:

Stockholders' equity January 1, 20X6	$100,000
Add: Income for 20X6	20,000
Deduct: Dividends paid July 1	(5,000)
Stockholders' equity December 31, 20X6	$115,000

The $10,000 excess of book value acquired over investment cost ($100,000 × 50% − $40,000) was due to inventory items and equipment that were overvalued on Taylor's books. Taylor's January 1, 20X6 inventory was overvalued by $2,000 and was sold in December 20X6. The remaining $18,000 overvaluation related to equipment with a 10-year remaining useful life from January 1, 20X6. No goodwill or negative goodwill results because the $40,000 cost is equal to fair value acquired (50% × $80,000).

The assignment of the difference between book value acquired and investment cost is as follows:

Cost of the investment in Taylor	$ 40,000
Less: Underlying book value of Post's 50% interest in Taylor ($100,000 stockholders' equity × 50%)	(50,000)
Excess book value over cost	$(10,000)
Excess assigned to:	
Inventories ($2,000 overvaluation × 50% owned)	$ (1,000)
Equipment ($18,000 overvaluation × 50% owned)	(9,000)
Excess book value over cost	$(10,000)

Journal entries to account for Post Corporation's investment in Taylor Corporation during 20X6 are as follows:

January 1, 20X6

Investment in Taylor	$40,000	
Cash		$40,000

To record purchase of 50% of Taylor's outstanding
  voting stock.

July 1, 20X6

Cash	$ 2,500	
Investment in Taylor		$ 2,500

To record dividends received ($5,000 × 50%).

December 31, 20X6

Investment in Taylor	$10,000	
Income from Taylor		$10,000

To recognize equity in the income of Taylor
  ($20,000 × 50%).

December 31, 20X6

Investment in Taylor	$ 1,900	
Income from Taylor		$ 1,900

To amortize excess of book value over investment
  cost assigned to:

Inventory ($1,000 × 100%)	$ 1,000
Equipment ($9,000 × 10%)	900
Total	$ 1,900

Because assets were purchased at less than book value, Post reports investment income from Taylor for 20X6 of $11,900 ($10,000 + $1,900), and an investment in Taylor balance at December 31, 20X6 of $49,400 ($40,000 + $11,900 − $2,500). Amortization of the excess of book value over investment cost increases Post's investment in Taylor balance by $1,900 during 20X6.

Negative Goodwill

Assume that Post Corporation also acquires a 25% interest in Saxon Corporation for $110,000 on January 1, 20X6, at which time Saxon's net assets consist of the following:

	Book Value	Fair Value	Excess Fair Value
Inventories	$240,000	$260,000	$20,000
Other current assets	100,000	100,000	
Equipment—net	50,000	50,000	
Buildings—net	140,000	200,000	60,000
	530,000	610,000	
Less: Liabilities	130,000	130,000	
Net assets	$400,000	$480,000	$80,000

Saxon's net income and dividends for 20X6 are $60,000 and $40,000, respectively. The undervalued inventory items were sold during 20X6 and the buildings and equipment each had four-year remaining useful lives when Post acquired its 25% interest. Exhibit 2–2 illustrates the assignment of the excess cost over book value.

In reviewing Exhibit 2–2, notice that the excess cost over book value is first assigned to fair values of identifiable net assets, after which the negative goodwill is reassigned to reduce noncurrent assets other than marketable securities.

```
POST CORPORATION AND ITS 25%-OWNED EQUITY INVESTEE,
SAXON CORPORATION
_____

Investment cost                                              $110,000
Book value acquired ($400,000 × 25%)                         (100,000)
    Excess cost over book value acquired                     $ 10,000

                              Assignment    Reassignment
                                  to        of Negative       Final
                              Fair Value      Goodwill      Assignment

Inventory ($20,000 × 25%)       $ 5,000                       $ 5,000
Equipment—net                      —        $(2,000)*          (2,000)
Buildings—net ($60,000 × 25%)   15,000        (8,000)*          7,000
Negative goodwill              (10,000)        10,000
    Excess cost over book
    value acquired             $10,000           0            $10,000

*Based on fair values:  $50,000/$250,000 to equipment
                        $200,000/$250,000 to buildings
```

Exhibit 2–2   *Schedule for Allocating Negative Goodwill*

Journal entries for Post Corporation to account for its investment in Saxon Corporation during 20X6 follow:

```
January 1, 20X6
Investment in Saxon                          $110,000
    Cash                                                  $110,000
  To record purchase of a 25% interest in Saxon's
  voting stock.


20X6
Cash                                         $ 10,000
    Investment in Saxon                                   $ 10,000
  To record dividends received ($40,000 × 25%).


December 31, 20X6
Investment in Saxon                          $  8,750
    Income from Saxon                                     $  8,750
  To recognize investment income from Saxon computed
  as follows:
    25% of Saxon's $60,000 net income                     $ 15,000
    Excess allocated to inventories                         (5,000)
    Excess allocated to equipment ($2,000 ÷ 4 years)           500
    Excess allocated to buildings ($7,000 ÷ 4 years)        (1,750)
                                                          $  8,750
```

Post Corporation's investment in Saxon balance at December 31, 20X6 is $108,750, and the underlying book value of the investment is $105,000 ($420,000 × 25%). The $3,750 difference consists of the $5,250 unamortized excess assigned to buildings less the $1,500 unamortized negative goodwill assigned to equipment.

INTERIM ACQUISITIONS OF AN INVESTMENT INTEREST

The detail of accounting for equity investments is increased when acquisitions are made within an accounting period (interim acquisitions). Additional computations are needed in determining the underlying equity at the time of acquisition and the investment income for the year. Stockholders' equity of the investee company is computed by adding income earned since the last statement date to the beginning stockholders' equity and subtracting dividends declared to the date of purchase. In accounting for interim acquisitions, it is assumed that income of the investee is earned proportionately throughout the year, unless there is evidence to the contrary.

Assume that Petron Corporation acquires 40% of the voting common stock of Fairview Company for $80,000 on October 1, 20X8. Fairview's net assets (owners' equity) at January 1, 20X8 are $150,000, and it reports net income of $25,000 for 20X8 and declares $15,000 dividends on July 1. The book values of Fairview's assets and liabilities are equal to fair values on October 1, 20X8 except for a building worth $60,000 and recorded at $40,000. The building has a 20-year remaining useful life from October 1, and any goodwill is to be amortized over five years. Generally accepted accounting principles require application of the equity method and assignment of any difference between investment cost and book value acquired first to identifiable assets and liabilities and then to goodwill.

The excess of Petron's investment cost over the book value of its 40% interest in Fairview is computed and assigned to identifiable assets and goodwill, as shown in Exhibit 2–3.

Journal entries on Petron's books to account for the 40% equity interest in Fairview for 20X8 are as follows:

October 1, 20X8

Investment in Fairview	$80,000	
Cash		$80,000

To record acquisition of 40% of Fairview's voting stock.

December 31, 20X8

Investment in Fairview	$ 2,500	
Income from Fairview		$ 2,500

To record equity in Fairview's income (40% × $25,000 × 1/4 year).

December 31, 20X8

Income for Fairview	$ 100	
Investment in Fairview		$ 100

To record amortization of excess of cost over book value allocated to the undervalued building ($8,000 ÷ 20 years) × 1/4 year.

Income from Fairview	$ 525	
Investment in Fairview		$ 525

To record amortization of the excess of cost over book value allocated to goodwill ($10,500 ÷ 5 years) × 1/4 year.

At December 31, 20X8, after the entries are posted, Petron's investment in Fairview account will have a balance of $81,875 ($80,000 cost + $1,875 income). This investment account balance is $17,875 more than the $64,000 underlying book value of Petron's interest in Fairview on that date (40% × $160,000). The $17,875 consists of the original excess cost over book value acquired of $18,500 less the $625 amortized in 20X8.

PETRON CORPORATION AND ITS 40%-OWNED EQUITY INVESTEE, FAIRVIEW CORPORATION

Investment cost		$80,000
Less: Share of Fairview equity on October 1		
Beginning equity	$150,000	
Add: Income to October 1	18,750	
Less: Dividends	(15,000)	
	153,750	
Times: Interest purchased	40%	(61,500)
Excess cost over book value		$18,500
Excess assigned to:		
Buildings [($60,000 − $40,000) × 40%]		$ 8,000
Goodwill (remainder)		10,500
Excess cost over book value		$18,500

Exhibit 2–3   *Schedule for Allocating the Excess of Investment Cost Over Book Value Acquired*

INVESTMENT IN A STEP-BY-STEP ACQUISITION

An investor may acquire an ability to exercise significant influence over the operating and financial policies of an investee corporation in a series of stock acquisitions, rather than in a single purchase. For example, an investor may acquire a 10% interest in an investee and later acquire another 10% interest. The original 10% interest should be accounted for by the fair value/cost method until a 20% interest is attained. When the interest owned reaches 20%, however, the equity method is adopted and the investment and retained earnings accounts are adjusted retroactively.

Assume that Hop Corporation acquires a 10% interest in Skip Corporation for $750,000 on January 2, 20X2 and another 10% interest for $850,000 on January 2, 20X3. The stockholders' equity of Skip Corporation on the dates of these acquisitions is as follows:

	January 2, 20X2	January 2, 20X3
Capital stock	$5,000,000	$5,000,000
Retained earnings	2,000,000	2,500,000
Total stockholders' equity	$7,000,000	$7,500,000

Hop Corporation is not able to relate the excess of investment cost over book value acquired to identifiable net assets. Accordingly, the excess of cost over book value from each of the acquisitions is goodwill with a 10-year amortization period.

On January 2, 20X3 when the second 10% is acquired, Hop Corporation adopts the equity method of accounting for its 20% interest. This involves converting the carrying value of the original 10% interest from its $750,000 cost to its correct carrying value on an equity basis. The entry to adjust the investment account of Hop Corporation is:

January 2, 20X3

Investment in Skip	$45,000	
Retained earnings		$45,000

    To adjust the investment in Skip account from a cost to an equity basis as follows: Share of Skip's retained earnings increase during 20X2 of $50,000 [$500,000 × 10% interest held during the year] less $5,000 goodwill amortization for 20X2 [($750,000 cost − 700,000 book value acquired) ÷ 10 years] equals the retroactive adjustment from accounting change of $45,000.

Skip's $500,000 retained earnings increase for 20X2 represents its income less dividends for 20X2. Hop reports its share of dividends received from Skip as income under the cost method, therefore, Hop's income for 20X2 under the equity method is greater by 10% of Skip's retained earnings increase for 20X2 and less by the $5,000 goodwill amortization that is not charged to income under the fair value/cost method.

Changes in the cost, equity, and consolidation methods of accounting for subsidiaries and investments are changes in the reporting entity that require restatement of prior-period financial statements if the effect is material.[6]

SALE OF AN EQUITY INTEREST

When an investor sells a portion of an equity investment that reduces its interest in the investee below 20% or less than a level necessary to exercise significant influence, the equity method of accounting is no longer appropriate for the remaining interest. The investment is accounted for under the cost method from this time forward, and the investment account balance after the sale becomes the new cost basis. No other adjustments are required, and the investor accounts for the investment under the fair value/cost method in the usual manner. Gain or loss from the equity interest sold is

---

[6]See *APB Opinion No. 20*, "Accounting Changes," paragraph 34.

the difference between the selling price and the book value of the equity interest immediately before the sale.

To illustrate, Leighton Industries acquires 320,000 shares (a 40% interest) in Sergio Corporation on January 1, 20X1 for $580,000. Sergio's stockholders' equity is $1,200,000, and the book values of its assets and liabilities equal their fair values. The $100,000 goodwill is amortized over 10 years at a rate of $10,000 a year. Leighton accounts for its investment in Sergio under the equity method during the years 20X1 through 20X3, and at December 31, 20X3 the balance of the investment account is $670,000, equal to 40% of Sergio's $1,500,000 stockholders' equity plus $70,000 unamortized goodwill.

On January 1, 20X4 Leighton sells 80% of its holdings in Sergio (256,000 shares) for $600,000, reducing its interest in Sergio to 8% (40% × 20%). The book value of the interest sold is $536,000, or 80% of the $670,000 balance of the investment in Sergio account. Leighton recognizes a gain on the sale of its interest in Sergio of $64,000 ($600,000 selling price less $536,000 book value of the interest sold). The balance of the investment in Sergio account after the sale is $134,000 ($670,000 less $536,000 interest sold). Leighton determines that it can no longer exercise significant influence over Sergio, and accordingly, it switches to the fair value/cost method and accounts for its investment under the provisions of *FASB Statement No. 115*, with the $134,000 balance becoming the new cost basis of the investment.

STOCK PURCHASES DIRECTLY FROM THE INVESTEE

Previous illustrations have assumed that the investor corporation purchased its shares from existing stockholders of the investee corporation. In that situation, the interest acquired was equal to the shares acquired divided by the investee's outstanding shares. If shares are purchased directly from the issuing corporation, however, the investor's interest is determined by the shares acquired divided by the shares outstanding after the new shares are issued by the investee.

Assume that Karl Corporation purchases 20,000 shares of previously unissued common stock directly from Master Corporation for $450,000 on January 1, 20X8. Master's stockholders' equity at December 31, 20X7 consists of $200,000 of $10 par common stock and $150,000 retained earnings.

Karl's interest in Master Corporation is 50%, computed as follows:

A	Shares purchased by Karl		20,000 shares
B	Shares outstanding after new shares are issued:		
	Outstanding December 31, 20X7	20,000	
	Issued to Karl	20,000	40,000 shares
	Karl's interest in Master: A/B = 50%		

The book value of the interest acquired by Karl is $400,000, determined by multiplying the 50% interest acquired by Master's $800,000 stockholders' equity immediately after the issuance of the additional 20,000 shares. Computations are as follows:

Master's stockholders' equity before issuance ($200,000 capital stock + $150,000 retained earnings)	$350,000
Sale of 20,000 shares to Karl	450,000
Master's stockholders' equity after issuance	800,000
Karl's percentage ownership	50%
Book value acquired by Karl	$400,000

INVESTEE CORPORATION WITH PREFERRED STOCK

The equity method applies to investments in common stock, and some adjustments in applying the equity method are necessary when an investee has preferred as well as common stock outstanding. These adjustments require:

1 Allocation of the investee corporation's stockholders' equity into preferred and common equity components upon acquisition in order to determine the book value of the common stock investment

2 Allocation of the investee's net income into preferred and common income components to determine the investor's share of the investee's income to common stockholders

Assume that Tech Corporation's stockholders' equity is $6,000,000 at the beginning of 20X3 and $6,500,000 at the end of 20X3. Its net income and dividends for 20X3 are $700,000 and $200,000, respectively.

	January 1, 20X3	December 31, 20X3
10% cumulative preferred stock, $100 par	$ 1,000,000	$ 1,000,000
Common stock, $10 par	3,000,000	3,000,000
Other paid-in capital	500,000	500,000
Retained earnings	1,500,000	2,000,000
	$6,000,000	$6,500,000

If Mornet Corporation pays $2,500,000 on January 2, 20X3 for 40% of Tech's outstanding common stock, the investment is evaluated as follows:

Cost of 40% common interest in Tech		$2,500,000
Book value (and fair value) acquired:		
Stockholders' equity of Tech	$6,000,000	
Less: Preferred stockholders' equity	1,000,000	
Common stockholders' equity	5,000,000	
Percent acquired	40%	2,000,000
Goodwill		$ 500,000

The equity of preferred stockholders is equal to the par value of outstanding preferred stock, increased by the greater of any call or liquidating premium and by preferred dividends in arrears.

Mornet's income from Tech for 20X3 from its 40% interest is computed:

Tech's net income for 20X3	$700,000
Less: Preferred income ($1,000,000 × 10%)	100,000
Income to common	$600,000
Share of Tech's common income ($600,000 × 40%)	$240,000
Less: Goodwill amortization ($500,000 ÷ 40 years)	(12,500)
Income from Tech for 20X3	$227,500

APB Opinion No. 18, paragraph 9k, provides that when an investee company has cumulative preferred stock outstanding, an investor in common stock computes its share of earnings or losses after deducting preferred dividends, whether or not preferred dividends are declared. Additional coverage of accounting matters related to investees with preferred stock outstanding is provided in Chapter 10.

EXTRAORDINARY ITEMS, CUMULATIVE-EFFECT-TYPE ADJUSTMENTS, AND OTHER CONSIDERATIONS

In accounting for a stock investment under the equity method, the investor corporation reports its share of the ordinary income of an investee on one line of its income statement. However, the one-line consolidation does not apply to the reporting of investment income when the investee corporation's income consists of extraordinary items or cumulative-effect-type adjustments. In this case, the investment income must be separated into its ordinary, extraordinary, and cumulative-effect components and reported accordingly.

Assume that Carl Corporation owns 40% of the outstanding stock of Homer Corporation and that Homer's income for 20X5 consists of the following:

Income from continuing operations before extraordinary item	$500,000
Extraordinary item—casualty loss (less applicable income taxes of $25,000)	(50,000)
Net income	$450,000

Carl records its investment income from Homer as follows:

Investment in Homer	$180,000	
Casualty loss—Investee	20,000	
Income from Homer		$200,000

To record investment income from Homer.

The $200,000 income from Homer is reported as investment income by Carl, and the $20,000 casualty loss is reported along with any extraordinary items that Carl may have had during the year. If Homer had a cumulative-effect-type adjustment, it would be recorded in similar fashion and reported along with Carl's cumulative-effect-type adjustments, if any. A gain or loss on an investee's disposal of a segment of a business would be treated similarly.

Other Requirements of the Equity Method

In reporting its share of earnings and losses of an investee under the equity method, an investor corporation must eliminate the effect of profits and losses on transactions between the investor and investee corporations until they are realized. This involves adjusting the investment and investment income accounts in a manner similar to that illustrated previously for identifiable net assets and goodwill. Transactions of an investee that change the investor's share of the net assets of the investee corporation also involve adjustments under the equity method of accounting. These and other complexities of the equity method are covered in subsequent chapters, along with related consolidation procedures. Chapter 10 covers preferred stock, earnings per share, and income tax considerations.

DISCLOSURES FOR EQUITY INVESTEES

The extent to which separate disclosure should be provided for equity investments depends on the significance (materiality) of such investments to the financial position and results of operations of the investor company. If equity investments are significant, the investor should disclose the following information, parenthetically or in financial statement notes or schedules:

1 The name of each investee and percentage of ownership in common stock
2 The accounting policies of the investor with respect to investments in common stock
3 The difference, if any, between the amount at which an investment is carried and the amount of underlying equity in net assets, including the accounting treatment of the difference.

Additional disclosures for material equity investments include the aggregate value of each identified investment for which quoted market prices are available and summarized information regarding the assets, liabilities, and results of operations of the investees. Firms that made these disclosures for nonconsolidated subsidiaries under *APB Opinion No. 18* are required to continue the disclosures under *FASB Statement No. 94*, even though the subsidiaries now are consolidated.

An excerpt from the Whirlpool Corporation 1997 Annual Report is presented in Exhibit 2–4 to illustrate the disclosure requirements. Financial information is summarized for all significant equity investees as a group. Whirlpool's share of underlying net assets of these investees is listed as "investment in affiliated companies" in the balance sheet, and its share of the investees' net income is included in the income statement as "equity in affiliated companies." The operating activities section of Whirlpool's consolidated statement of cash flows shows "equity in net losses (earnings) of affiliated companies, including dividends received" as an adjustment to net income.

WHIRLPOOL CORPORATION 1997 ANNUAL REPORT
NOTES TO CONSOLIDATED FINANCIAL STATEMENTS
NOTE 5, AFFILIATED COMPANIES

The Company has a 49% direct voting interest in a Mexican company (Vitromatic, S.A. de C.V.) and direct voting interests ranging from 10% to 40% in several other international companies principally engaged in the manufacture and sale of major home appliances or related component parts. Prior to consolidation of the company's Brazilian subsidiary for the last two months of 1997 (Refer to Note 1), results were reflected as equity earnings of affiliated companies. The company's share of Brazilian results for 1997 was $78 million excluding restructuring and operating charges and $64 million including restructuring and operating charges.

Equity in the net earnings (losses) of affiliated companies, net of related taxes, is as follows:

(millions of dollars)	1997	1996	1995
Brazilian affiliates	$ 60	$ 92	$ 70
Mexican affiliate	5	(3)	—
Other	2	4	2
Total equity earnings (losses)	$ 67	$ 93	$ 72

Combined condensed financial information for all affiliated operating companies (excluding Brazil in 1997) follows:

December 31 (millions of dollars)	1997	1996
Current assets	$ 275	$1,365
Other assets	372	1,090
	$ 647	$2,455
Current liabilities	$ 303	$ 795
Other liabilities	160	380
Stockholders' equity	184	1,280
	$ 647	$2,455

Year ended December 31 (millions of dollars)	1997	1996	1995
Net sales	$ 937	$3,112	$2,772
Cost of products sold	$ 596	$2,323	$2,122
Net earnings	$ 17	$ 265	$ 192
Dividends and fees paid to Whirlpool by affiliates	$ 5	$ 20	$ 20

Exhibit 2–4   *Financial Statement Disclosures for Equity Investments*

Related Party Transactions

FASB Statement No. 57, "Related Party Disclosures," explains that there is no presumption of arm's-length bargaining between related parties. The statement identifies material transactions between affiliated companies as related party transactions requiring financial statement disclosure. The required disclosures include:

1 The nature of the relationship
2 A description of the transaction
3 The dollar amounts of the transaction and any change from the previous period in the method used to establish the terms of the transaction for each income statement presented
4 Amounts due to or due from related parties at the balance sheet date for each balance sheet presented

Related party disclosures for affiliated companies are illustrated in Exhibit 2–5 for Chevron Corporation. Chevron's 1997 Annual Report identifies the Caltex Group of Companies as Chevron's largest equity affiliate.

CHEVRON CORPORATION 1997 ANNUAL REPORT.
NOTE 12. INVESTMENTS AND ADVANCES [PARTIAL]
(in millions of dollars)

The company's transactions with affiliated companies are summarized in the following table. These are primarily for the purchase of Indonesian crude oil from CPI, the sale of crude oil and products to CPC's refining and marketing companies, the sale of natural gas to NGC, and the purchase of natural gas and natural gas liquids from NGC.

"Accounts and notes receivable" in the consolidated balance sheet include $145 and $258 at December 31, 1997 and 1996, respectively, of amounts due from affiliated companies. "Accounts payable" include $57 and $39 at December 31, 1997 and 1996, respectively, of amounts due to affiliated companies.

	Year Ended December 31		
	1997	1996	1995
Sales to Caltex Group	$1,335	$1,708	$1,330
Sales to NGC	1,822	676	—
Sales to other affiliates	8	18	10
Total sales to affiliate	$3,165	$2,402	$1,340
Purchases from Caltex Group	$ 932	$1,022	$ 934
Purchases from NGC	854	269	—
Purchases from other affiliates	16	41	40
Total purchases from affiliates	$1,802	$1,332	$ 974

Exhibit 2–5   *Related Party Disclosures for Affiliates*

SUMMARY

A flow chart summary of accounting procedures for business investments is presented in Exhibit 2–6. Investments in the voting common stock of an investee corporation are accounted for under the fair value/cost method if the investment does not give the investor an ability to exercise significant influence over the investee. Otherwise, the equity method (a one-line consolidation) should normally be used. In the absence of evidence to the contrary, a 20% ownership test is used to determine if the investor has the ability to exercise significant influence over the investee.

The equity method is referred to as a one-line consolidation because its application produces the same net income and stockholders' equity for the investor as would result from consolidation of the financial statements of the investor and investee corporations. Under the one-line consolidation, the investment is reflected in a single amount on one line of the investor's balance sheet, and the investor's income from the investee is reported on one line of the investor's income statement, except when the investee's income includes extraordinary or cumulative-effect-type items.

As indicated in the flow chart in Exhibit 2–6, the equity method is equally applicable to investments accounted for under the pooling and purchase methods, even though the initial recording of a stock investment under the two methods is different. The flow chart also indicates that consolidated statements are generally required for investments in excess of 50% of the voting stock of the investee and that the one-line consolidation (equity method) is used in reporting investments of 20% to 50% in the investor's financial statements and in consolidated financial statements.

NOTE TO THE STUDENT

In solving problems in the areas of business combinations, equity investments, and consolidations, it is frequently necessary to make assumptions about the nature of the difference between investment cost and book value of the net assets acquired, the amortization period for goodwill, the timing of income earned within an accounting

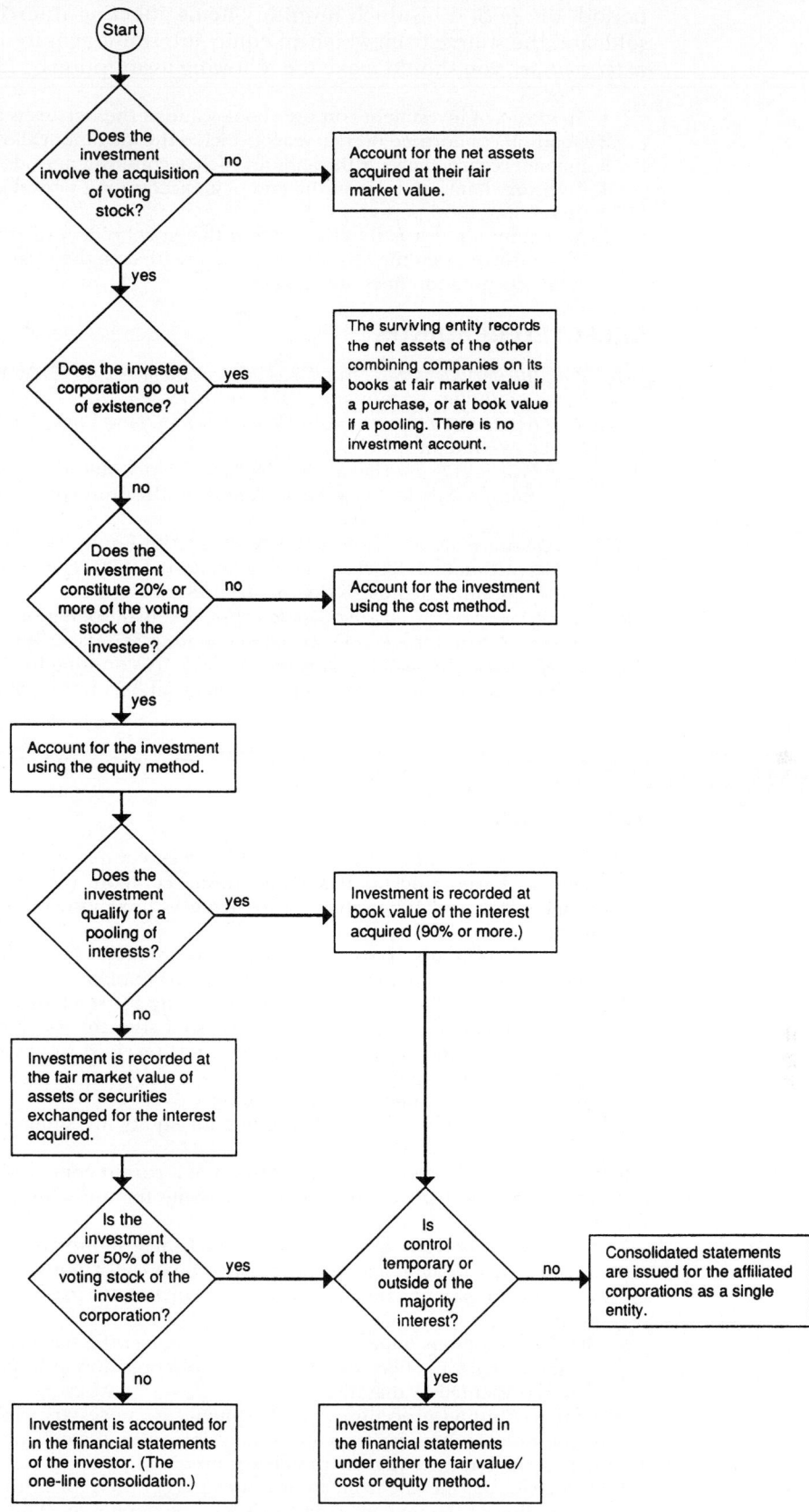

Exhibit 2–6   *Accounting for Equity Investments Generally*

period, the period in which inventory items affecting intercompany investments are sold, and the source from which an equity interest is acquired. *In the absence of evidence to the contrary*, you should make the following assumptions:

1 An excess of investment cost over book value of the net assets acquired is goodwill.
2 Goodwill is amortized over 40 years (which is the maximum allowable amortization period).
3 Income is earned evenly throughout each accounting period.
4 Inventory items on hand at the end of an accounting period are sold in the immediately succeeding fiscal period.
5 An equity interest is purchased from the stockholders of the investee company rather than directly from the investee corporation (that is, the total outstanding stock of the investee corporation does not change).

SELECTED READINGS

Accounting Interpretations Nos. 1 and 2 of APB Opinion No. 17. New York: American Institute of Certified Public Accountants, 1971 and 1973.
Accounting Interpretation No. 1 of APB Opinion No. 18. New York: American Institute of Certified Public Accountants, 1971.
Accounting Principles Board Opinion No. 18. "The Equity Method of Accounting for Investments in Common Stock." New York: American Institute of Certified Public Accountants, 1971.
FASB Interpretation No. 35. "Criteria for Applying the Equity Method of Accounting for Investments in Common Stock." An interpretation of *APB Opinion No. 18.* Stamford, CT: Financial Accounting Standards Board, May 1981.
Statement of Financial Accounting Standards No. 94. "Consolidation of All Majority-owned Subsidiaries." Stamford, CT: Financial Accounting Standards Board, 1986.
Statement of Financial Accounting Standards No. 115. "Accounting for Certain Investments in Debt and Equity Securities." Norwalk, CT: Financial Accounting Standards Board, 1993.

ASSIGNMENT MATERIAL

QUESTIONS

1 How are the accounts of investor and investee companies affected when the investor acquires stock from stockholders of the investee company (for example, a New York Stock Exchange purchase)? When the investor acquires previously unissued stock directly from the investee?
2 Would goodwill arising from an equity investment of more than 20% be recorded separately on the books of the investor corporation? Explain.
3 Under the fair value/cost method of accounting for stock investments, an investor records dividends received from earnings accumulated after the investment is acquired as dividend income. How does an investor treat dividends received from earnings accumulated before an investment is acquired?
4 Describe the equity method of accounting.
5 Why is the equity method of accounting for equity investments frequently referred to as a one-line consolidation?
6 Is there a difference between the amount of a parent company's net income under the equity method and the consolidated net income for the same parent company and its subsidiaries?
7 What is the difference in reporting income from a subsidiary in the parent company's separate income statement and in consolidated financial statements?
8 How does a parent company/investor record amortization of goodwill on its separate books?
9 Cite the conditions under which you would expect the balance of an equity investment account on a balance sheet date subsequent to acquisition to be equal to the underlying book value represented by that investment.
10 What accounting procedures or adjustments are necessary when an investor uses the cost method of accounting for an investment in common stock, and later increases the investment such that the equity method is required?
11 Ordinarily, the income from an investment accounted for by the equity method is reported on one line of the investor company's income statement. When would more than one line of the income statement of the investor be required to report such income?
12 Describe the accounting adjustments needed when a 25% equity interest in an investee company is decreased to a 15% equity interest.

13 Does cumulative preferred stock in the capital structure of an investee affect the way that an investor company accounts for its 30% common stock interest? Explain.

EXERCISES

E 2-1
1 Indicators of an investor company's inability to exercise significant influence over an investee are provided in *FASB Interpretation No. 35*. Which of the following is *not* included among those indicators?
   a Surrender of significant stockholder rights by agreement
   b Concentration of majority ownership
   c Failure to obtain representation on the investee's board
   d Inability to control the investee's operating policies
2 A 20% common stock interest in an investee company:
   a Must be accounted for under the equity method
   b Is accounted for by the cost method because over 20% is required for the application of the equity method
   c Is presumptive evidence of an ability to exercise significant influence over the investee
   d Enables the investor to apply either the cost or the equity method
3 The cost of a 25% interest in the voting stock of an investee that is recorded in the investment account includes:
   a Cash disbursed, the book value of other assets given or securities issued, and additional direct and indirect costs of obtaining the investment, other than the cost of registering and issuing equity securities
   b Cash disbursed, the book value of other assets given or securities issued, additional direct costs of obtaining the investment and registering and issuing equity securities
   c Cash disbursed, the fair value of other assets given or securities issued, and additional direct costs of obtaining the investment, other than the cost of registering and issuing equity securities
   d Cash disbursed, the fair value of other assets given or securities issued, and additional direct costs of obtaining the investment and registering and issuing equity securities
4 The underlying equity of an investment at acquisition:
   a Is recorded in the investment account under the equity method
   b Minus the cost of the investment is assigned to goodwill or negative goodwill
   c Is equal to the fair value of the investee's net assets times the percent acquired
   d Is equal to the book value of the investee's net assets times the percent acquired
5 Jarret Corporation is a 25%-owned equity investee of Marco Corporation. During 20X1 Marco receives $12,000 in dividends from Jarret. How does the $12,000 dividend affect Marco's financial position and results of operations?
   a Increases assets
   b Decreases investment
   c Increases income
   d Decreases income

E 2-2 **[AICPA adapted]**
1 Investor Company owns 40% of Alimand Corporation. During the calendar year 20X5, Alimand had net earnings of $100,000 and paid dividends of $10,000. Investor mistakenly recorded these transactions using the cost method rather than the equity method of accounting. What effect would this have on the investment account, net earnings, and retained earnings, respectively?
   a Understate, overstate, overstate
   b Overstate, understate, understate
   c Overstate, overstate, overstate
   d Understate, understate, understate
2 The corporation exercises control over an affiliate in which it holds a 40% common stock interest. If its affiliate completed a fiscal year profitably but paid *no* dividends, how would this affect the investor corporation?
   a Result in an increased current ratio
   b Result in increased earnings per share
   c Increase several turnover ratios
   d Decrease book value per share
3 An investor uses the cost method to account for an investment in common stock. A portion of the dividends received this year were in excess of the investor's share of investee's earnings after the date of the investment. The amount of dividend revenue that should be reported in the investor's income statement for this year would be:
   a Zero
   b The total amount of dividends received this year

c The portion of the dividends received this year that were in excess of the investor's share of investee's earnings after the date of investment

d The portion of the dividends received this year that were *not* in excess of the investor's share of investee's earnings after the date of investment

4 On January 1, 20X8 Grade Company paid $300,000 for 20,000 shares of Medium Company's common stock, which represents a 15% investment in Medium. Grade does not have the ability to exercise significant influence over Medium. Medium declared and paid a dividend of $1 per share to its stockholders during 20X8. Medium reported net income of $260,000 for the year ended December 31, 20X8. The balance in Grade's balance sheet account "Investment in Medium Company" at December 31, 20X8 should be

    a $280,000   **c** $319,000

    b $300,000   **d** $339,000

5 On January 2, 20X1 Troquel Corporation bought 15% of Zafacon Corporation's capital stock for $30,000. Troquel accounts for this investment by the cost method. Zafacon's net income for the years ended December 31, 20X1 and December 31, 20X2 were $10,000 and $50,000, respectively. During 20X2 Zafacon declared a dividend of $70,000. No dividends were declared in 20X1. How much should Troquel show on its 20X2 income statement as income from this investment?

    a $1,575   **c** $9,000

    b $7,500   **d** $10,500

6 Pare purchased 10% of Tot Company's 100,000 outstanding shares of common stock on January 2, 20X2 for $50,000. On December 31, 20X2 Pare purchased an additional 20,000 shares of Tot for $150,000. There was no goodwill as a result of either acquisition, and Tot had not issued any additional stock during 20X2. Tot reported earnings of $300,000 for 20X2. What amount should Pare report in its December 31, 20X2 balance sheet as investment in Tot?

    a $170,000   **c** $230,000

    b $200,000   **d** $290,000

7 On January 1, 20X2 Point purchased 10% of Iona Company's common stock. Point purchased additional shares, bringing its ownership up to 40% of Iona's common stock outstanding, on August 1, 20X2. During October 20X2, Iona declared and paid a cash dividend on all of its outstanding common stock. How much income from the Iona investment should Point's 20X2 income statement report?

    a 10% of Iona's income for January 1 to July 31, 20X2 plus 40% of Iona's income for August 1 to December 31, 20X2

    b 40% of Iona's income for August 1 to December 31, 20X2, only

    c 40% of Iona's 20X2 income

    d Amount equal to dividends received from Iona

8 On January 2, 20X3 Kean Company purchased a 30% interest in Pod Company for $250,000. On this date, Pod's stockholders' equity was $500,000. The carrying amounts of Pod's identifiable net assets approximated their fair values, except for land, whose fair value exceeded its carrying amount by $200,000. Pod reported net income of $100,000 for 20X3 and paid no dividends. Kean accounts for this investment using the equity method and amortizes goodwill over 10 years. In its December 31, 20X3, balance sheet, what amount should Kean report as investment in subsidiary?

    a $210,000   **c** $270,000

    b $220,000   **d** $276,000

E 2-3   Trevor Corporation's stockholders' equity at December 31, 20X1 consisted of the following:

Capital stock, $10 par, 60,000 shares issued and outstanding	$ 600,000
Additional paid-in capital	150,000
Retained earnings	250,000
Total stockholders' equity	$1,000,000

On January 1, 20X2 Bowman Corporation purchased 20,000 previously unissued shares of Trevor stock directly from Trevor for $500,000.

Required

    1 Calculate Bowman Corporation's percentage ownership in Trevor.

    2 Determine the goodwill from Bowman's investment in Trevor.

E 2–4   Carson Corporation pays $600,000 for a 30% interest in Medley Corporation on July 1, 20X2 when the book value of Medley's net assets equals fair value. Carson amortizes any goodwill from this investment over 20 years. Information relating to Medley follows:

Capital stock, $1 par	$ 600,000	$ 600,000
Retained earnings	400,000	500,000
Total stockholders' equity	$1,000,000	$1,100,000
Medley's net income earned evenly throughout 20X2		$200,000
Medley's dividends for 20X2 (paid $50,000 on March 1 and $50,000 on September 1)		$100,000

Required: Calculate Carson's income from Medley for 20X2.

E 2-5   Dokey Company acquired a 30% interest in Oakey on January 1, 20X1 for $2,000,000 cash. Dokey assigned the $500,000 cost over book value of the interest acquired to the following assets:

Inventories	$100,000 (sold in 20X1)
Building	$200,000 (4-year remaining life at January 1, 20X1)
Goodwill	$200,000 (40-year amortization period)

During 20X1 Oakey reported net income of $800,000 and paid $200,000 dividends.

Required
1 Determine Dokey's income from Oakey for 20X1.
2 Determine the December 31, 20X1 balance of the investment in Oakey account.

E 2-6   Martin Corporation purchased a 40% interest in Neighbors Corporation for $500,000 on January 1, 20X1 at book value, when Neighbors' assets and liabilities were recorded at their fair values. During 20X1, Neighbors reported net income of $300,000 as follows:

Income from continuing operations	$350,000
Less: Loss from discontinued operations	50,000
Net income	$300,000

Required: Prepare the journal entry on Martin Corporation's books to recognize income from the investment in Neighbors for 20X1.

E 2-7   1 On January 3, 20X7 Harrison Company purchases a 15% interest in Bennett Corporation's common stock for $50,000 cash. Harrison accounts for the investment using the cost method. Bennett's net income for 20X7 is $20,000, but it declares no dividends. In 20X8, Bennett's net income is $80,000, and it declares dividends of $120,000. What is the correct balance of Harrison's investment in Bennett account at December 31, 20X8?
   a $47,000   c $62,000
   b $50,000   d $65,000
2 Screwsbury Corporation's stockholders' equity at December 31, 20X7 follows:

Capital stock, $100 par	$3,000,000
Additional paid-in capital	500,000
Retained earnings	500,000
Total stockholders' equity	$4,000,000

On January 3, 20X8 Screwsbury sells 10,000 shares of previously unissued $100 par common stock to Pannell Corporation for $1,400,000. On this date the recorded book values of Screwsbury's assets and liabilities equal their fair values. Goodwill from Pannell's investment in Screwsbury at the date of purchase is:
   a 0   c $300,000
   b $50,000   d $400,000
3 On January 1, 20X2 Leighton Company paid $300,000 for a 20% interest in Monroe Corporation's voting common stock, at which time Monroe's stockholders' equity consisted of $600,000 capital stock and $400,000 retained earnings. Leighton was not able to exercise any influence over the operations of Monroe and accounted for its investment in Monroe using the cost method. During 20X2, Monroe had net income of $200,000 and paid dividends of $150,000. The balance of Leighton's investment in Monroe account at December 31, 20X2 is:
   a $330,000   c $307,500
   b $310,000   d $300,000

4 Jollytime Corporation owns a 40% interest in Krazy Products acquired several years ago at book value. Krazy Products' income statement for 20X2 contains the following information:

Income before extraordinary item	$200,000
Extraordinary loss	50,000
Net income	$150,000

Jollytime should report income from Krazy Products in its income from continuing operations for 20X2 at:

a $20,000		**c** $80,000	
b $60,000		**d** $100,000	

E 2-8 Raython Corporation owns a 40% interest in the outstanding common stock of Treaton Corporation, having acquired its interest for $2,400,000 on **January 1, 20X2** when Treaton's stockholders' equity was $4,000,000. The cost/book value differential was allocated to inventories that were undervalued by $100,000 and sold in 20X2, to equipment with a four-year remaining life that was undervalued by $200,000, and the remainder to goodwill with a 10-year amortization period.

The balance of Treaton's stockholders' equity at **December 31, 20X6** is $5,500,000, and all changes therein are the result of income earned and dividends paid.

Required: Determine the balance of Raython's investment in Treaton account at December 31, 20X6.

E 2-9 Runner Company had net income of $400,000 and paid dividends of $200,000 during 20X7. Runner's stockholders' equity on December 31, 20X6 and December 31, 20X7 is summarized as follows:

	December 31, 20X6	December 31, 20X7
10% cumulative preferred stock, $100 par	$ 300,000	$ 300,000
Common stock, $1 par	1,000,000	1,000,000
Additional paid-in capital	2,200,000	2,200,000
Retained earnings	500,000	700,000
Stockholders' equity	$4,000,000	$4,200,000

On January 2, 20X7 Nickie Corporation purchased 300,000 common shares of Runner at $4 per share and also paid $50,000 direct costs of acquiring the investment.

Required: Determine (1) Nickie's income from Runner for 20X7 and (2) the balance of the investment in Runner account at December 31, 20X7.

E 2-10 Arbor Corporation acquired 25% of Tree Corporation's outstanding common stock on October 1, 20X2 for $600,000. A summary of Tree's adjusted trial balances on this date and at December 31, 20X2 follows:

	December 31, 20X2	October 1, 20X2
Debits		
Current assets	$ 500,000	$ 250,000
Plant assets—net	1,500,000	1,550,000
Expenses (including cost of goods sold)	800,000	600,000
Dividends (paid in July)	200,000	200,000
	$3,000,000	$2,600,000
Credits		
Current liabilities	$ 300,000	$ 200,000
Capital stock (no change during 20X2)	1,000,000	1,000,000
Retained earnings January 1, 20X2	500,000	500,000
Sales	1,200,000	900,000
	$3,000,000	$2,600,000

Arbor uses the equity method of accounting. No information is available concerning the fair values of Tree's assets and liabilities.

1 Determine Arbor's investment income from Tree Corporation for the year ended December 31, 20X2.
2 Compute the correct balance of Arbor's investment in Tree account at December 31, 20X2.

E 2-11 Summary balance sheet and income information for Twizzle Company for two years is as follows:

	January 1, 20X7	December 31, 20X7	December 31, 20X8
Current assets	$100,000	$120,000	$150,000
Plant assets	400,000	480,000	500,000
	$500,000	$600,000	$650,000
Liabilities	$ 80,000	$100,000	$100,000
Capital stock	300,000	300,000	300,000
Retained earnings	120,000	200,000	250,000
	$500,000	$600,000	$650,000

	20X7	20X8
Net income	$200,000	$100,000
Dividends	120,000	50,000

On January 2, 20X7 Ratterman Corporation purchases 10% of Twizzle Company for $50,000 cash, and it accounts for its investment in Twizzle using the fair value method. On December 31, 20X7 the fair value of all of Twizzle's stock is $1,000,000. On January 2, 20X8 Ratterman purchases an additional 10% interest in Twizzle stock for $100,000 and adopts the equity method to account for the investment. The fair values of Twizzle's assets and liabilities were equal to their book values as of the time of both stock purchases.

Required
1 Prepare a journal entry to adjust the investment in Twizzle account to an equity basis on January 2, 20X8.
2 Determine Ratterman's income from Twizzle for 20X8.

E 2-12 The stockholders' equity of Tall Corporation at December 31, 20X1 was $380,000, consisting of the following:

Capital stock, $10 par (24,000 shares outstanding)	$240,000
Additional paid-in capital	60,000
Retained earnings	80,000
Total stockholders' equity	$380,000

On January 1, 20X2, Tall Corporation, which was in a tight working capital position, sold 12,000 shares of previously unissued stock to River Corporation for $250,000. All of Tall's identifiable assets and liabilities were recorded at their fair values on this date except for a building with a 10-year remaining useful life that was undervalued by $60,000. During 20X2, Tall Corporation reported net income of $120,000 and paid dividends of $90,000.

Required: Prepare all journal entries necessary for River Corporation to account for its investment in Tall for 20X2.

E 2-13 BIP Corporation paid $195,000 for a 30% interest in Crown Corporation on December 31, 20X3, when Crown's equity consisted of $500,000 capital stock and $200,000 retained earnings. The price paid by BIP reflected the fact that Crown's inventory (on a FIFO basis) was overvalued by $50,000. The overvalued inventory items were sold in 20X4.

During 20X4 Crown paid dividends of $100,000 and reported income as follows:

Income before extraordinary items	$170,000
Extraordinary loss (net of tax effect)	20,000
Net income	$150,000

Required
1 Prepare all journal entries necessary to account for BIP's investment in Crown for 20X4.
2 Determine the correct balance of BIP's investment in Crown account at December 31, 20X4.

3 Assume that BIP's net income for 20X4 consists of $1,000,000 sales, $700,000 expenses, and its investment income from Crown. Prepare an income statement for BIP Corporation for 20X4.

E 2-14 Valley Corporation paid $290,000 for 40% of the outstanding common stock of Water Corporation on January 2, 20X3. During 20X3, Water paid dividends of $48,000 and reported net income of $108,000. A summary of Water's stockholders' equity at December 31, 20X2 and 20X3 follows:

December 31,	20X2	20X3
8% cumulative preferred stock, $100 par	$100,000	$100,000
Common stock, $10 par	300,000	300,000
Premium on preferred stock	10,000	10,000
Other paid-in capital	90,000	90,000
Retained earnings	100,000	160,000
Total stockholders' equity	$600,000	$660,000

Required: Calculate Valley Corporation's income from Water for 20X3 and its investment in Water account balance at December 31, 20X3.

PROBLEMS

P 2-1 Ritter Corporation paid $343,000 for a 30% interest in Telly Corporation's outstanding voting stock on April 1, 20X5. At December 31, 20X4, Telly had net assets of $1,000,000 and only common stock outstanding. During 20X5, Telly declared and paid dividends of $20,000 each quarter on March 15, June 15, September 15, and December 15 ($80,000 in total). Telly's 20X5 income was reported as follows:

Income before extraordinary item	$120,000
Extraordinary gain, December 20X5	40,000
Net income	$160,000

Required: Determine the following:
1 Goodwill from the investment in Telly
2 Income from Telly for 20X5
3 Investment in Telly account balance at December 31, 20X5
4 Ritter's equity in Telly's net assets at December 31, 20X5
5 Unamortized goodwill at December 31, 20X5
6 The amount of extraordinary gain that Ritter will show on its 20X5 income statement

P 2-2 Putter Company paid $110,000 for an 80% interest in Siegel Company on July 1, 20X8 when Siegel Company had total equity of $110,000. Siegel Company reported earnings of $10,000 for 20X8 and declared dividends of $8,000 on November 1, 20X8.

Required: Give the entries to record these facts on the books of Putter Company:
1 Assuming that Putter Company uses the cost method of accounting for its subsidiaries.
2 Assuming that Putter Company uses the equity method of accounting for its subsidiaries. (Any difference between investment cost and book value acquired is to be amortized over a 10-year period.)

P 2-3 Vatter Company acquired a 30% interest in the voting stock of Zelda Company for $331,000 on January 1, 20X2, when Zelda's stockholders' equity consisted of capital stock of $600,000 and retained earnings of $400,000. At the time of Vatter's investment, Zelda's assets and liabilities were recorded at their fair values, except for inventories that were undervalued by $30,000 and a building with a 10-year remaining useful life that was overvalued by $60,000. Any goodwill from the investment is amortized over 40 years. Zelda has income for 20X2 of $100,000 and pays dividends of $50,000.

Required
1 Compute Vatter's income from Zelda for 20X2.
2 What is the balance of Vatter's investment in Zelda account at December 31, 20X2?
3 What is Vatter's share of Zelda's recorded net assets at December 31, 20X2?

P 2-4 Diller Corporation paid $380,000 for 40% of Dormer Corporation's outstanding voting common stock on July 1, 20X7. Dormer's stockholders' equity on January 1, 20X7 was $500,000, consisting of $300,000 capital stock and $200,000 retained earnings.

During 20X7, Dormer had net income of $100,000, and on November 1, 20X7 Dormer declared dividends of $50,000.

Dormer's assets and liabilities were stated at their fair values on July 1, 20X7 except for land that was undervalued by $30,000 and equipment with a five-year remaining useful life that was undervalued by $50,000.

Required: Prepare all the journal entries (other than closing entries) on the books of Diller Corporation during 20X7 to account for the investment in Dormer.

P 2-5 Earth-Q Corporation paid $1,680,000 for a 30% interest in Tremor Corporation's outstanding voting stock on January 1, 20X4. The book values and fair values of Tremor's assets and liabilities on January 1, along with amortization data, are as follows:

	Book Value	Fair Value
Cash	$ 400,000	$ 400,000
Accounts receivable—net	700,000	700,000
Inventories (sold in 20X4)	1,000,000	1,200,000
Other current assets	200,000	200,000
Land	900,000	1,700,000
Buildings—net (10-year remaining life)	1,500,000	2,000,000
Equipment—net (7-year remaining life)	1,200,000	500,000
Total assets	$5,900,000	$6,700,000
Accounts payable	$ 800,000	$ 800,000
Other current liabilities	200,000	200,000
Bonds payable (due January 1, 20X9)	1,000,000	1,100,000
Capital stock, $10 par	3,000,000	
Retained earnings	900,000	
Total equities	$5,900,000	

Tremor Corporation reported net income of $1,200,000 for 20X4 and paid dividends of $600,000. Any goodwill from the investment is amortized over 20 years.

Required
  1 Prepare a schedule to allocate the investment cost/book value differentials relating to Earth-Q's investment in Tremor.
  2 Calculate Earth-Q's income from Tremor for 20X4.
  3 Determine the balance of Earth-Q's investment in Tremor account at December 31, 20X4.

P 2-6 Pauly Corporation purchased for cash 6,000 shares of voting common stock of Stapleton Corporation at $16 per share on July 1, 20X7. On this date, Stapleton's equity consisted of $100,000 of $10 par capital stock, $20,000 retained earnings from prior periods, and $10,000 current earnings (for one-half of 20X7).

Stapleton's income for 20X7 was $20,000, and it paid dividends of $12,000 on November 1, 20X7.

All of Stapleton's assets and liabilities were stated at their fair values at July 1, 20X7, and any differences between investment cost and book value acquired should be amortized over a 10-year period.

Required: Compute the correct amounts for each of the following items using the equity method of accounting for Pauly's investment:
  1 Pauly Corporation's income from its investment in Stapleton for the year ended December 31, 20X7
  2 The balance of Pauly's investment in Stapleton account at December 31, 20X7
  3 Pauly's unamortized goodwill from its investment in Stapleton at December 31, 20X9
(Note: Assumptions on page 56 are needed for this problem.)

P 2-7 Dill Corporation acquired 30% of the voting stock of Larkspur Company at book value on July 1, 20X1. During 20X3, Larkspur paid dividends of $80,000 and reported income of $250,000 as follows:

Income before extraordinary item	$150,000
Extraordinary gain (tax credit from operating loss carryforward)	100,000
Net income	$250,000

Required: Show how Dill's income from Larkspur should be reported for 20X3 by means of a partial income statement for Dill Corporation.

P 2-8 Hazel Corporation purchased a 10% interest in Brady Company on January 1, 20X1, for $20,000 and an additional 20% interest for $50,000 on July 1, 20X3. The fair value of Hazel's

10% interest in Brady was worth $22,000 on December 31, 20X1, $25,000 on December 31, 20X2, and $21,000 on December 31, 20X3. The Brady stock was consistently classified as an available-for-sale security. Brady had total stockholders' equity of $150,000 when the 10% interest was acquired and $235,000 when the 20% interest was acquired. Any difference between investment cost and book value acquired is to be amortized over a 10-year period. Brady reported net income and paid dividends for the years 20X1 through 20X4 as follows:

	20X1	20X2	20X3	20X4
Net income for the year	$50,000	$60,000	$70,000	$90,000
Dividends paid in November	30,000	30,000	30,000	40,000

Hazel accounts for its investment in Brady in accordance with generally accepted accounting principles.

Required
  1 Determine Hazel's investment income from Brady for 20X3.
  2 Determine Hazel's prior-period adjustment for 20X3 relating to this investment and prepare any necessary journal entries to update the investment account at the point of the purchase of additional shares.
  3 Calculate the balance of Hazel's investment in Brady account at December 31, 20X4, for its 30% interest.
  4 On January 1, 20X5 Brady increases its outstanding shares from 10,000 to 12,000 by selling 2,000 shares to Hazel for $70,000. What adjustment should Hazel make in its investment in Brady account on this date?

P 2-9 Sigma Corporation became a subsidiary of Provo Corporation on July 1, 20X4, when Provo paid $1,980,000 cash for 90% of Sigma's outstanding common stock. The price paid by Provo reflected the fact that Sigma's inventories were undervalued by $50,000 and its plant assets were overvalued by $500,000. Sigma sold the undervalued inventory items during 20X4 but continues to hold the overvalued plant assets that had a remaining useful life of nine years from July 1, 20X4.

During the years 20X4 through 20X6, Sigma's paid-in capital consisted of $1,500,000 capital stock and $500,000 additional paid-in capital. Sigma's retained earnings statements for 20X4, 20X5, and 20X6 were as follows:

	Year Ended December 31, 20X4	Year Ended December 31, 20X5	Year Ended December 31, 20X6
Retained earnings January 1	$525,000	$600,000	$700,000
Add: Net income	250,000	300,000	200,000
Deduct: Dividends (declared in December)	(175,000)	(200,000)	(150,000)
Retained earnings December 31	$600,000	$700,000	$750,000

Provo uses the equity method in accounting for its investment in Sigma.

Required
  1 Compute Provo Corporation's income from its investment in Sigma for 20X4.
  2 Determine the balance of Provo Corporation's investment in Sigma account at December 31, 20X5.
  3 Prepare the journal entries necessary for Provo to account for its investment in Sigma for 20X6.

P 2-10 Creape Corporation exchanged 40,000 previously unissued no par common shares for a 40% interest in Tantani Corporation on January 1, 20X8. The assets and liabilities of Tantani on that date were as follows:

	Book Value	Fair Value
Cash	$ 100,000	$ 100,000
Accounts receivable-net	200,000	200,000
Inventories	500,000	600,000
Land	100,000	300,000
Buildings-net	600,000	400,000
Equipment-net	400,000	500,000
Total assets	$1,900,000	$2,100,000

(Continued)

	Book Value	Fair Value
Liabilities	$ 900,000	$ 900,000
Capital stock	700,000	
Retained earnings	300,000	
Total equities	$1,900,000	

The direct cost of issuing the shares of stock was $10,000, and other direct costs of combination were $40,000.

Required
1 Assume that the January 1, 20X8 market price for Creape's shares is $12 per share. Prepare a schedule to allocate the investment cost/book value differentials.
2 Assume that the January 1, 20X8 market price for Creape's shares is $7 per share. Prepare a schedule to allocate the investment cost/book value differentials.

P 2-11 Prudy Corporation made three investments in Spandix during 20X5 and 20X6 as follows:

Date Acquired	Shares Acquired	Cost
July 1, 20X5	3,000	$ 48,750
January 1, 20X6	6,000	99,000
October 1, 20X6	9,000	162,000

Spandix Corporation's stockholders' equity on January 1, 20X5 consisted of 20,000 shares of $10 par common stock and retained earnings of $100,000. Prudy's initial intention was to buy a controlling interest in Spandix, so it never considered its investment in Spandix as a trading security. Spandix stock had a market value of $16.50 on December 31, 20X5 and $19.00 on December 31, 20X6.

Spandix had net income of $40,000 and $60,000 in 20X5 and 20X6 respectively, and paid dividends of $15,000 on May 1 and November 1 of 20X5 and 20X6 ($60,000 total for the two years).

Prudy Corporation accounts for its investment in Spandix using the equity method of accounting. It amortizes differences between investment cost and book value acquired over a 10-year period from the date of acquisition.

Required: Compute the following amounts:
1 Prudy's income from its investment in Spandix for 20X5
2 The balance of Prudy's investment in Spandix account at December 31, 20X5
3 Prudy's income from its investments in Spandix for 20X6
4 The balance of Prudy's investment in Spandix account at December 31, 20X6

P 2-12 Pilot Corporation purchased 40% of the voting stock of Sassy Corporation on July 1, 20X5 for $300,000. On that date Sassy's stockholders' equity consisted of capital stock of $500,000, retained earnings of $150,000, and current earnings (just half of 20X5) of $50,000. Income is earned proportionately throughout each year.

The investment in Sassy account of Pilot Corporation and the retained earnings account of Sassy Corporation for 20X5 through 20X8 are summarized as follows:

RETAINED EARNINGS (SASSY)

Dividends November 1, 20X5	$40,000	Balance January 1, 20X5	$150,000
Dividends November 1, 20X6	40,000	Earnings 20X5	100,000
Dividends November 1, 20X7	50,000	Earnings 20X6	80,000
Dividends November 1, 20X8	50,000	Earnings 20X7	130,000
		Earnings 20X8	120,000

INVESTMENT IN SASSY (PILOT)

Investment July 1, 20X5 40%	$300,000	Dividends 20X5	$16,000
Income 20X5	40,000	Dividends 20X6	16,000
Income 20X6	32,000	Dividends 20X7	20,000
Income 20X7	52,000	Dividends 20X8	20,000
Income 20X8	48,000		

Required
1 Determine the correct amount of the investment in Sassy that should appear in Pilot's December 31, 20X8 balance sheet. Assume a 10-year period for any difference between investment cost and book value acquired.

2 Prepare any journal entry (entries) on Pilot's books to bring the investment in Sassy account up to date on December 31, 20X8, assuming that the books have not been closed at year-end 20X8.

P 2-13 Publican Corporation acquired a 70% interest in Samaritan Corporation on April 1, 20X3, when it purchased 14,000 of Samaritan's 20,000 outstanding shares in the open market at $13 per share. Additional costs of acquiring the shares consisted of $5,000 brokerage fees and $5,000 legal and consulting fees. Samaritan Corporation's balance sheets on January 1 and April 1, 20X3 are summarized as follows:

	January 1, 20X3 (per books)	April 1, 20X3 (per books)	April 1, 20X3 (fair values)
Cash	$ 40,000	$ 45,000	$ 45,000
Inventories	35,000	60,000	50,000
Other current assets	25,000	20,000	20,000
Land	30,000	30,000	50,000
Equipment—net	100,000	95,000	135,000
Total assets	$230,000	$250,000	$300,000
Accounts payable	$ 45,000	$ 40,000	$ 40,000
Other liabilities	15,000	20,000	20,000
Capital stock, $5 par	100,000	100,000	
Retained earnings January 1	70,000	70,000	
Current earnings		20,000	
Total liabilities and equity	$230,000	$250,000	

Additional Information

1 The overvalued inventory items were sold in September 20X3.

2 The undervalued items of equipment had a remaining useful life of four years on April 1, 20X3.

3 Samaritan's net income for 20X3 was $80,000 ($60,000 from April to December 31, 20X3).

4 On December 1, 20X3, Samaritan declared dividends of $2 per share, payable on January 10, 20X4.

5 Any unidentified assets of Samaritan are to be amortized over a period of 10 years.

Required

1 Prepare a schedule showing how the difference between Publican's investment cost and book value acquired should be allocated to identifiable and/or unidentifiable assets.

2 Calculate Publican's investment income from Samaritan for 20X3.

3 Determine the correct balance of Publican's Investment in Samaritan account at December 31, 20X3.

P 2-14 Use the information in Problem 2-13, except change the per share market price to $7 per share.

Required

1 Prepare a schedule showing how the difference between Publican's investment cost and book value acquired should be allocated to identifiable and/or unidentifiable assets.

2 Calculate Publican's investment income from Samaritan for 20X3.

3 Determine the correct balance of Publican's Investment in Samaritan account at December 31, 20X3.

3

An Introduction to Consolidated Financial Statements

This chapter contains background material necessary for understanding consolidated financial statements and also provides an overview of the procedures involved in the consolidation process. The purchase method of accounting for business combinations is applied in the first part of the chapter, and pooled subsidiaries are covered at the end of the chapter. The parent company/investor is assumed to use the equity method of accounting for subsidiary investments. Further discussions of business combinations in this book assume purchase accounting unless the pooling of interests method is specifically identified.

Required consolidated financial statements include a consolidated balance sheet, a consolidated income statement, a consolidated retained earnings statement, and a consolidated statement of cash flows. The consolidated balance sheet and consolidated income and retained earnings statements that are introduced in this chapter are prepared from the separate financial statements of the parent company and its subsidiaries. The consolidated statement of cash flows, however, is prepared from consolidated income statements and consolidated balance sheets. The consolidated statement of cash flows is introduced in an appendix to Chapter 4.

BUSINESS COMBINATIONS CONSUMMATED THROUGH STOCK ACQUISITIONS

The accounting concept of a business combination, as described in *APB Opinion No. 16,* clearly includes those combinations in which one or more companies become subsidiaries of a common parent corporation. A corporation becomes a subsidiary when another corporation acquires a controlling interest in its outstanding voting stock. Ordinarily, one corporation gains control of another corporation directly by acquiring a majority (more than 50%) of its voting stock. A corporation may also gain control of another corporation through indirect stock ownership. Indirect stock-ownership situations are covered in Chapter 9 of this book.[1] Until Chapter 9, assume that direct ownership of a majority of the voting stock of another corporation is required for control and in order to have a parent-subsidiary relationship.

A business combination is consummated when one corporation acquires more than 50% of the voting stock of another corporation, but once a parent-subsidiary re-

---

[1]See *ARB No. 51*, "Consolidated Financial Statements," paragraph 2.

lationship is established, the purchase of additional subsidiary shares is not a business combination. In other words, separate entities can combine only once. Increasing a controlling interest is simply an additional investment. The acquisition of additional shares of a subsidiary is accounted for by the purchase method, as explained in paragraph 43 of *APB Opinion No. 16*:

> The acquisition after the effective date of this Opinion of some or all of the stock held by minority stockholders of a subsidiary—whether acquired by the parent, the subsidiary itself, or another affiliate—should be accounted for by the purchase method rather than by the pooling of interests method.

The Reporting Entity

A business combination brings two previously separate corporations under the control of a single management team (the officers and directors of the parent company). Although both corporations continue to exist as separate legal entities, the purchase creates a new reporting entity that encompasses all operations controlled by the management of the parent company.

When an investment in voting stock creates a parent-subsidiary relationship, the purchasing entity (parent company) and the entity acquired (subsidiary) continue to function as separate entities and to maintain their accounting records on a separate legal basis. Separate parent company and subsidiary financial statements are converted into consolidated financial statements that reflect the financial position and the results of operations of the combined entity. The new reporting entity is responsible for reporting to the stockholders and creditors of the parent company and to other interested parties.

The Parent-Subsidiary Relationship

A corporation that owns more than 50% of the voting stock of another corporation is able to control that corporation through its stock ownership, and a **parent-subsidiary relationship** exists between the two corporations. When parent-subsidiary relationships exist, the companies are affiliated. Often the term **affiliate** is used to mean subsidiary, and the two terms are used interchangeably in this book and throughout much of the literature of accounting. The FASB Exposure Draft, "Consolidated Financial Statements: Policy and Procedures," defined affiliate as: "an entity that, directly or indirectly through one or more intermediaries, controls, is controlled by, or is under common control with another entity. A parent and its subsidiary(ies) are affiliates and subsidiaries of a common parent are affiliates." In many annual reports, however, the term *affiliate* is used to include all investments accounted for by the equity method. The following excerpt from the Sun Company 1997 Annual Report (page 37) is an example of this latter usage of the term *affiliate*: "Affiliated companies over which the company has the ability to exercise significant influence but that are not controlled (generally 20 to 50% owned) are accounted for by the equity method."

Other companies have adopted the term *associated* to refer to equity investments of 20% to 50% of the voting interests in other companies. The Kimberly-Clark Corporation 1997 Annual Report (page 31) explains that "Investments in significant nonconsolidated companies which are at least 20 percent owned are stated at cost plus equity in undistributed net income. These latter companies are referred to as equity companies."

An affiliation structure with two subsidiaries is illustrated in Exhibit 3–1, which shows Percy Company owning 90% of the voting stock of San Del Corporation and 80% of the voting stock of Saltz Corporation. Percy Company owns 90% of the voting stock of San Del, and stockholders outside the affiliation structure own the other 10%. These outside stockholders are the minority stockholders, and their interest is referred to as a **minority interest**. Outside stockholders have a 20% minority interest in Saltz Corporation.

Percy Company and each of its subsidiaries are separate legal entities for which separate accounting records are maintained. In its separate records Percy Company uses the equity method described in Chapter 2 to account for its investments in San Del and Saltz corporations. For reporting purposes, however, the equity method of reporting usually does not result in the most meaningful financial statements. This is

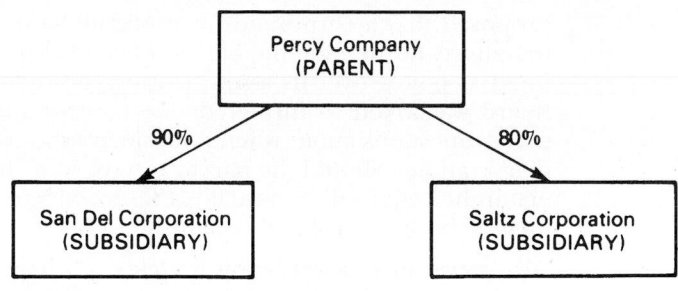

Exhibit 3–1 *Affiliation Structure*

because the parent, through its stock ownership, is able to elect subsidiary directors and control subsidiary decisions, including dividend declarations. Although affiliated companies are separate legal entities, there is really only one economic entity because all resources are under control of a single management—the directors and officers of the parent company.

The opening paragraph of *ARB No. 51*, "Consolidated Financial Statements," states that:

> The purpose of consolidated statements is to present, primarily for the benefit of stockholders and creditors of the parent company, the results of operations and the financial position of a parent company and its subsidiaries essentially as if the group were a single company with one or more branches or divisions.

Thus, consolidated statements are intended primarily for the parent company's investors, rather than for the minority stockholders and subsidiary creditors. (The subsidiary, as a separate legal entity, continues to report the results of its own operations to the minority shareholders.)

Consolidation Policy

Consolidated financial statements provide much information that is not included in the separate statements of the parent corporation, and they are usually required for fair presentation of the financial position and results of operations for a group of affiliated companies. The usual condition for consolidation is ownership of more than 50% of the voting stock of another company. Under the provisions of *FASB Statement No. 94*, "Consolidation of All Majority-owned Subsidiaries," a subsidiary can be excluded from consolidation in only two situations: (1) where control is likely to be temporary or (2) where control does not rest with the majority owner. Control does not rest with the majority owner if the subsidiary is in legal reorganization, or in bankruptcy, or operating under severe foreign exchange restrictions, controls, or other governmentally imposed uncertainties.

History *ARB No. 51*, issued in 1959, allowed parent company management broad discretion in determining consolidation policy as long as the objective was to provide the most meaningful financial presentation in the circumstances. Many firms adopted a policy of excluding from consolidation those subsidiaries whose operations differed greatly from those of the parent company. Manufacturing and merchandising companies routinely excluded their finance, insurance, and real estate subsidiaries. These "nonhomogeneous" subsidiaries were included in the financial statements as unconsolidated subsidiaries and accounted for by the equity method. As explained in Chapter 2, accounting by the equity method provides the same net income as consolidating the accounts of the parent and subsidiary corporations. However, the assets, liabilities, revenues, and expenses of the unconsolidated subsidiary are not included in the financial statements under the equity method. It was concern over the possible omission of significant amounts of debt from the balance sheet that prompted the issuance of *FASB Statement No. 94* in 1987.

The FASB is considering a consolidation policy based on control, rather than majority ownership. The FASB issued *Preliminary Views on Major Issues Related to Consolidation Policy* in 1994 and an exposure draft, "Consolidated Financial Statements: Policy and Procedures," in 1995. Both the *Preliminary Views* and the exposure draft proposed that a corporation consolidate all entities that it controls unless control is temporary at the time the business becomes a subsidiary. Control of an entity was defined as power over its assets. During the redeliberations of the exposure draft, the Board was asked to further define control and clarify the presumption of control. Other questions about when a subsidiary should be consolidated arose during the redeliberations: Should the parent receive some level of benefits? Should a level of ownership be required? Eventually, the Board agreed that a consolidation policy should include both control and benefits.[2]

Disclosure of Consolidation Policies   A description of significant accounting policies is required for financial reporting under *APB Opinion No. 22*, "Disclosure of Accounting Policies," and traditionally, consolidation policy disclosures were among the most frequent of all policy disclosures. *FASB Statement No. 94* eliminates acceptable alternative consolidation policies, so consolidation policy disclosures under *APB Opinion No. 22* are only needed to report exceptions (temporary control or inability to control) to the *Statement 94* requirement for consolidation of all majority-owned subsidiaries. Even so, the disclosure of consolidation policies in annual reports is not likely to decline significantly because the SEC requires publicly held companies to report their consolidation policies under Regulation S-X, Rule 3A-03. Consolidation policy is usually presented under a heading such as "principles of consolidation" or "basis of consolidation." The WHX Corporation 1997 Annual Report (page 27) contains a typical consolidation policy note:

> The consolidated financial statements include the accounts of all subsidiary companies. All significant intercompany accounts and transactions are eliminated in consolidation. The Company uses the equity method of accounting for investments in unconsolidated companies owned 20% or more.

Parent and Subsidiary with Different Fiscal Periods

When the fiscal periods of the parent company and its subsidiaries are different, consolidated statements are prepared for and as of the end of the parent's fiscal period. If the difference in fiscal periods is not in excess of three months, it usually is acceptable to use the subsidiary's statements for its fiscal year for consolidation purposes, with disclosure of "the effect of intervening events which materially affect the financial position or results of operations."[3] Otherwise, the statements of the subsidiary should be adjusted so that they correspond as closely as possible to the fiscal period of the parent company. The 1997 H.J. Heinz Company Annual Report (page 39) includes the following explanation of its fiscal year: "H.J. Heinz Company (the 'company') operates on a 52- or 53-week fiscal year ending the Wednesday nearest April 30. However, certain foreign subsidiaries have earlier closing dates to facilitate timely reporting."

CONSOLIDATED BALANCE SHEET AT DATE OF ACQUISITION

A consolidated entity is a fictitious (conceptual) reporting entity. It is based on the assumption that the separate legal and accounting entities of a parent and its subsidiaries can be combined into a single meaningful set of financial statements for external reporting purposes. It is important to note that the consolidated entity is a fictitious reporting entity that does not have transactions and does not maintain a ledger of accounts.

Parent Acquires 100 Percent of Subsidiary at Book Value

Exhibit 3–2 shows the basic differences between separate company and consolidated balance sheets. Penn Corporation acquires 100% of Skelly Corporation at its book value and fair value of $40,000 in a purchase business combination on January 1, 20X1. The balance sheets shown in Exhibit 3–2 are prepared immediately after the investment. Penn's "investment in Skelly" appears in the separate balance sheet of Penn, but not in the consolidated balance sheet for Penn and Subsidiary. When the

---

[2]Financial Accounting Series, *Status Report 295*, November 26, 1997.

[3]*ARB No. 51*, paragraph 5.

| | Separate Balance Sheets | | Consolidated Balance Sheet |
	Penn	Skelly	Penn and Subsidiary
Assets			
Current assets			
Cash	$ 20,000	$10,000	$ 30,000
Other current assets	45,000	15,000	60,000
Total current assets	65,000	25,000	90,000
Plant assets	75,000	45,000	120,000
Less: Accumulated depreciation	(15,000)	(5,000)	(20,000)
Total plant assets	60,000	40,000	100,000
Investment in Skelly—100%	40,000	—	—
Total assets	$165,000	$65,000	$190,000
Liabilities and Stockholders' Equity			
Current liabilities			
Accounts payable	$ 20,000	$15,000	$ 35,000
Other current liabilities	25,000	10,000	35,000
Total current liabilities	45,000	25,000	70,000
Stockholders' equity			
Capital stock	100,000	30,000	100,000
Retained earnings	20,000	10,000	20,000
Total stockholders' equity	120,000	40,000	120,000
Total liabilities and			
stockholders' equity	$165,000	$65,000	$190,000

Exhibit 3–2   *100 Percent Ownership Acquired at Book Value*

balance sheets are consolidated, the investment in Skelly account (Penn's books) and the stockholders' equity accounts (Skelly's books) are eliminated because they are reciprocal—both representing the net assets of Skelly Corporation at January 1, 20X1. The nonreciprocal accounts of Penn and Skelly are combined and included in the consolidated balance sheet of Penn Corporation and Subsidiary. Note that the consolidated balance sheet is not merely a summation of account balances of the affiliated corporations. Reciprocal accounts are eliminated in the process of consolidation, and only nonreciprocal accounts are combined. The capital stock that appears in a consolidated balance sheet is the capital stock of the parent company, and the consolidated retained earnings is the retained earnings of the parent company.

Parent Acquires 100 Percent of Subsidiary—with Goodwill

The consolidated balance sheet presented in Exhibit 3–2 was prepared for a parent company that purchased all the stock of Skelly Corporation at book value. If, instead, Penn purchases all of Skelly's stock for $50,000, there will be a $10,000 excess of investment cost over book value acquired ($50,000 investment cost less $40,000 stockholders' equity of Skelly). The $10,000 appears in the consolidated balance sheet at acquisition as an asset of $10,000. In the absence of evidence that identifiable net assets are undervalued, this asset is assumed to be goodwill. Procedures for preparing a consolidated balance sheet are illustrated in Exhibit 3–3 for Penn Corporation, assuming that Penn pays $50,000 for the outstanding stock of Skelly.

Only one working paper entry is needed to consolidate the balance sheets of Penn and Skelly at acquisition. The entry is reproduced in general journal form for convenient reference:

a	Capital stock	$30,000	
	Retained earnings	10,000	
	Goodwill	10,000	
	Investment in Skelly		$50,000

To eliminate reciprocal investment and equity accounts and to assign the excess of investment cost over book value acquired to goodwill.

PENN CORPORATION AND SUBSIDIARY
CONSOLIDATED BALANCE SHEET WORKING PAPERS
JANUARY 1, 20X1

	Penn	100% Skelly	Adjustments and Eliminations		Consolidated Balance Sheet
			Debits	Credits	
Assets Cash	$ 10,000	$ 10,000			$ 20,000
Other current assets	45,000	15,000			60,000
Plant assets	75,000	45,000			120,000
Accumulated depreciation	(15,000)	(5,000)			(20,000)
Investment in Skelly	50,000			a 50,000	
Goodwill			a 10,000		10,000
Total assets	$165,000	$ 65,000			$190,000
Liabilities and Equity Accounts payable	$ 20,000	$ 15,000			$ 35,000
Other current liabilities	25,000	10,000			35,000
Capital stock—Penn	100,000				100,000
Retained earnings—Penn	20,000				20,000
Capital stock—Skelly		30,000	a 30,000		
Retained earnings—Skelly		10,000	a 10,000		
Total liabilities and stockholders' equity	$165,000	$ 65,000			$190,000

a To eliminate reciprocal investment and equity accounts and to assign the excess of investment cost over book value acquired to goodwill.

Exhibit 3–3   *100 Percent Ownership, Cost $10,000 Greater than Book Value*

Entries such as those shown in Exhibit 3–3 are only working paper adjustments and eliminations and *are not recorded in the accounts of the parent or subsidiary corporations.* The entries will never be journalized or posted. Their only purpose is to facilitate completion of the working papers to consolidate a parent and subsidiary at and for the period ended on a particular date. In this book, working paper entries are shaded to avoid confusing them with actual journal entries that are recorded in the accounts of the parent and subsidiary companies.

In future periods the difference between the investment account balance and the subsidiary equity will decline as goodwill is amortized. If goodwill is amortized over a 10-year period, the difference between the balance in the investment in Skelly account and total stockholders' equity of Skelly at December 31, 20X1 will be $9,000; at December 31, 20X5, $5,000; and so on.

Parent Acquires 90 Percent of Subsidiary—with Goodwill

Assume that instead of acquiring all of Skelly's outstanding stock, Penn acquires 90% of Skelly's stock for $50,000. In this case, the excess of investment cost over book value acquired is $14,000 ($50,000 cost less $36,000 book value acquired), and there is a minority interest in Skelly of $4,000 ($40,000 equity × 10% minority interest). The working papers in Exhibit 3–4 illustrate procedures for preparing the consolidated balance sheet for Penn and Skelly under the 90% ownership assumption.

PENN CORPORATION AND SUBSIDIARY
CONSOLIDATED BALANCE SHEET WORKING PAPERS
JANUARY 1, 20X1

	Penn	90% Skelly	Adjustments and Eliminations Debits	Credits	Consolidated Balance Sheet
Assets					
Cash	$ 10,000	$ 10,000			$ 20,000
Other current assets	45,000	15,000			60,000
Plant assets	75,000	45,000			120,000
Accumulated depreciation	(15,000)	(5,000)			(20,000)
Investment in Skelly	50,000			a 50,000	
Goodwill			a 14,000		14,000
Total assets	$165,000	$ 65,000			$194,000
Liabilities and Equity					
Accounts payable	$ 20,000	$ 15,000			$ 35,000
Other current liabilities	25,000	10,000			35,000
Capital stock—Penn	100,000				100,000
Retained earnings—Penn	20,000				20,000
Capital stock—Skelly		30,000	a 30,000		
Retained earnings—Skelly		10,000	a 10,000		
	$165,000	$ 65,000			
Minority interest				a 4,000	4,000
Total liabilities and stockholders' equity					$194,000

a To eliminate reciprocal investment and equity balances, assign the $14,000 excess of investment cost ($50,000) over book value acquired ($36,000) to goodwill, and recognize a $4,000 minority interest in the net assets of Skelly ($40,000 equity × 10% minority interest).

Exhibit 3–4 *90 Percent Ownership, Cost $14,000 Greater than Book Value*

The working paper entry to consolidate the balance sheets of Penn and Skelly and recognize the minority interest in Skelly at the date of acquisition is:

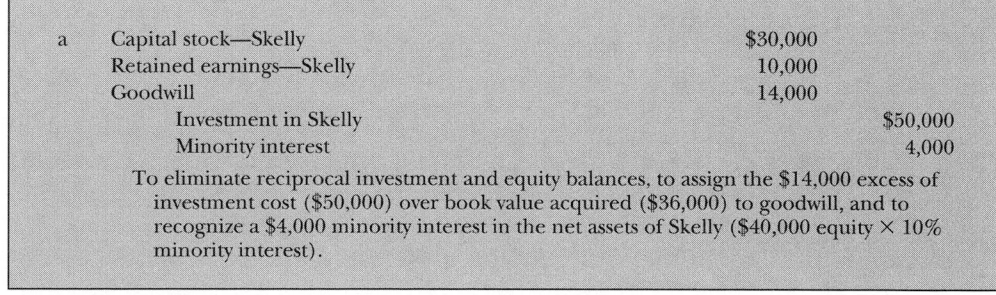

a	Capital stock—Skelly	$30,000	
	Retained earnings—Skelly	10,000	
	Goodwill	14,000	
	Investment in Skelly		$50,000
	Minority interest		4,000

To eliminate reciprocal investment and equity balances, to assign the $14,000 excess of investment cost ($50,000) over book value acquired ($36,000) to goodwill, and to recognize a $4,000 minority interest in the net assets of Skelly ($40,000 equity × 10% minority interest).

Minority Interest

All the assets and liabilities of the subsidiary are included in the consolidated balance sheet, and a separate deduction is made for the minority interest's share of subsidiary net assets.

Working papers provide the basis of preparing formal financial statements, and the question arises as to how the $4,000 minority interest that appears in Exhibit 3–4 would be reported in a formal balance sheet. Although practice varies with respect to classification, the minority interest in subsidiaries is generally shown in a single amount in the liability section of the consolidated balance sheet, frequently under the heading of noncurrent liabilities.[4] Conceptually, the classification of minority stockholder interests as liabilities is inconsistent because the interests of minority stockholders represent equity investments in the consolidated net assets by stockholders outside the affiliation structure. The alternatives are to include the minority interest in consolidated stockholders' equity or in a separate minority interest section. When classified as stockholders' equity, the minority interest should be separated from the equity of majority stockholders, that is, stockholders of the parent company. (See Chapter 11 for more discussion on the presentation of minority interests.)

The FASB, as part of its consolidations project, made the following *tentative decisions* in its discussions on the presentation of a noncontrolling interest:

- A noncontrolling interest in a subsidiary should be displayed and labeled in the consolidated balance sheet as a separate component of equity.
- Income attributable to the noncontrolling interest is not an expense or a loss but a deduction from consolidated net income to compute income attributable to the controlling interest.
- Both components of consolidated net income (net income attributable to noncontrolling interest and net income attributable to controlling interest) should be disclosed on the face of the consolidated income statement.

CONSOLIDATED BALANCE SHEETS AFTER ACQUISITION

The account balances of both parent and subsidiary corporations change to reflect their separate operations after the parent-subsidiary relationship is established. Subsequently, additional adjustments are necessary to eliminate other reciprocal balances. If a consolidated balance sheet is prepared between the time a subsidiary declares and the time it pays dividends, the parent's books will show a dividend receivable account that is the reciprocal of a dividends payable account on the books of the subsidiary. Such balances do not represent amounts receivable or payable outside the affiliated grouping; therefore, they must be reciprocals that are eliminated in preparing consolidated statements. Other intercompany receivables and payables, such as accounts receivable and accounts payable, are reciprocal items that are eliminated in preparing consolidated statements.

The balance sheets of Penn and Skelly corporations at December 31, 20X1, one year after affiliation, contain the following:

	Penn	Skelly
Cash	$ 22,400	$15,000
Dividends receivable	9,000	—
Other current assets	41,000	28,000
Plant assets	75,000	45,000
Accumulated depreciation	(20,000)	(8,000)
Investment in Skelly (90%)	57,600	—
Total assets	$185,000	$80,000
Accounts payable	$ 30,000	$15,000
Dividends payable	—	10,000
Other current liabilities	20,000	5,000
Capital stock	100,000	30,000
Retained earnings	35,000	20,000
Total equities	$185,000	$80,000

Assumptions

1 Penn acquired a 90% interest in Skelly for $50,000 on January 1, 20X1 when Skelly's stockholders' equity was $40,000 (see Exhibit 3–4).

---

[4] *Accounting Trends & Techniques–1997* shows that 147 of the 600 reporting corporations reported minority interest in the "Other Noncurrent Liabilities" section of the balance sheet (p. 243).

2 The accounts payable of Skelly include $5,000 owed to Penn.
3 Goodwill is amortized over a 10-year period.
4 During 20X1 Skelly had income of $20,000 and declared $10,000 dividends.

Consolidated balance sheet working papers reflecting the above information are shown in Exhibit 3–5. The balance in the investment in Skelly account at December 31, 20X1 is determined using the equity method of accounting. Calculations of the December 31, 20X1 investment account balance are as follows:

Original investment January 1, 20X1	$50,000
Add: 90% of Skelly's $20,000 net income for 20X1	18,000
Deduct: 90% of Skelly's $10,000 dividends for 20X1	(9,000)
Deduct: Goodwill amortization ($14,000 ÷ 10 years)	(1,400)
Investment account balance December 31, 20X1	$57,600

PENN CORPORATION AND SUBSIDIARY
CONSOLIDATED BALANCE SHEET WORKING PAPERS
DECEMBER 31, 20X1

	Penn	90% Skelly	Adjustments and Eliminations Debits	Credits	Consolidated Balance Sheet
Assets					
Cash	$ 22,400	$ 15,000			$ 37,400
Dividends receivable	9,000			b 9,000	
Other current assets	41,000	28,000		c 5,000	64,000
Plant assets	75,000	45,000			120,000
Accumulated depreciation	(20,000)	(8,000)			(28,000)
Investment in Skelly	57,600			a 57,600	
Goodwill			a 12,600		12,600
Total assets	$185,000	$ 80,000			$206,000
Liabilities and Equity					
Accounts payable	$ 30,000	$ 15,000	c 5,000		$ 40,000
Dividends payable		10,000	b 9,000		1,000
Other current liabilities	20,000	5,000			25,000
Capital stock—Penn	100,000				100,000
Retained earnings—Penn	35,000				35,000
Capital stock—Skelly		30,000	a 30,000		
Retained earnings—Skelly		20,000	a 20,000		
	$185,000	$ 80,000			
Minority interest				a 5,000	5,000
Total liabilities and stockholders' equity					$206,000

a To eliminate reciprocal investment and equity balances, record unamortized goodwill ($14,000 less $1,400 amortization), and enter the minority interest ($50,000 × 10%).

b To eliminate reciprocal dividends receivable and payable amounts (90% of $10,000 dividends payable of Skelly).

c To eliminate intercompany accounts receivable and accounts payable.

Exhibit 3–5 *90 Percent Ownership, Consolidation One Year After Acquisition*

Even though the amounts involved are different, the *process* of consolidating balance sheets after acquisition is basically the same as at acquisition. In all cases, the amount of the subsidiary investment account is eliminated and the equity accounts of the subsidiary are eliminated. The excess of the investment account balance over the book value of the interest owned (goodwill in this illustration) is entered in the working papers during the process of eliminating reciprocal investment and equity balances. Goodwill does not appear on the books of the parent and is added to the asset listing when the working papers are prepared. The minority interest is equal to the percentage of minority ownership times the equity of the subsidiary at the balance sheet date. Consolidated retained earnings is equal to the parent company's retained earnings.

The working paper entries necessary to consolidate the balance sheets of Penn and Skelly are reproduced in general journal form for convenient reference:

a	Capital stock—Skelly	$30,000	
	Retained earnings—Skelly	20,000	
	Goodwill	12,600	
	Investment in Skelly		$57,600
	Minority interest		5,000
	To eliminate reciprocal investment and equity balances, record unamortized goodwill ($14,000 less $1,400 amortization for 20X1), and enter the minority interest ($50,000 × 10%).		
b	Dividends payable	$ 9,000	
	Dividends receivable		$ 9,000
	To eliminate reciprocal dividends receivable and payable amounts (90% of $10,000 dividends payable of Skelly).		
c	Accounts payable	$ 5,000	
	Accounts receivable		$ 5,000
	To eliminate intercompany accounts receivable and accounts payable.		

ALLOCATION OF EXCESS TO IDENTIFIABLE NET ASSETS AND GOODWILL

The excess of investment cost over the book value acquired in the Penn-Skelly illustration was assigned to goodwill. An underlying assumption of that assignment of the excess is that the book values and fair values of identifiable assets and liabilities are equal. When the evidence indicates that fair values exceed book values or book values exceed fair values, however, the excess must be allocated accordingly.

Effect of Allocation on Consolidated Balance Sheet at Acquisition

In acquisitions involving parent-subsidiary relationships, the cost/book value differentials are not recorded on the books of the parent companies or subsidiaries. Therefore, the amounts that appear in a consolidated balance sheet of a parent company and its subsidiary are entered through working paper procedures that adjust the subsidiary book values to reflect the cost-book value differentials. The amount of adjustment to individual asset and liability accounts is determined by means of the approach illustrated in Chapter 2 for one-line consolidations.

On December 31, 20X1 Pilot purchases 90% of Sand Corporation's outstanding voting common stock directly from Sand Corporation's stockholders for $5,000,000 cash plus 100,000 shares of Pilot Corporation $10 par common stock with a market value of $5,000,000. Additional costs of combination consist of $100,000 for registering and issuing the common stock and $200,000 for other costs of combination. These additional costs are paid in cash by Pilot. Pilot and Sand must continue to operate as parent company and subsidiary because 10% of Sand's shares are outstanding and held by minority stockholders.

Comparative book value and fair value information for Pilot and Sand immediately before their combination on December 31, 20X1 appear in Exhibit 3–6. Pilot records the business combination on its books with the following journal entries:

	Pilot Corporation		Sand Corporation	
	Per Books	Fair Values	Per Books	Fair Values
Assets				
Cash	$ 6,600,000	$ 6,600,000	$ 200,000	$ 200,000
Receivables—net	700,000	700,000	300,000	300,000
Inventories	900,000	1,200,000	500,000	600,000
Other current assets	600,000	800,000	400,000	400,000
Land	1,200,000	11,200,000	600,000	800,000
Buildings—net	8,000,000	15,000,000	4,000,000	5,000,000
Equipment—net	7,000,000	9,000,000	2,000,000	1,700,000
Total assets	$25,000,000	$44,500,000	$8,000,000	$9,000,000
Liabilities and Equity				
Accounts payable	$ 2,000,000	$ 2,000,000	$ 700,000	$ 700,000
Notes payable	3,700,000	3,500,000	1,400,000	1,300,000
Common stock, $10 par	10,000,000		4,000,000	
Additional paid-in capital	5,000,000		1,000,000	
Retained earnings	4,300,000		900,000	
Total liabilities and stockholders' equity	$25,000,000		$8,000,000	

Exhibit 3–6   *Preacquisition Book and Fair Value Balance Sheets*

Investment in Sand	$10,000,000	
Common stock		$1,000,000
Additional paid-in capital		4,000,000
Cash		5,000,000

To record acquisition of 90% of Sand Corporation's
outstanding stock for $5,000,000 in cash and 100,000
shares of Pilot common stock with a value of $5,000,000.

Investment in Sand	$ 200,000	
Additional paid-in capital	100,000	
Cash		$ 300,000

To record additional costs of combining with Sand.

These are the only entries necessary on Pilot's books to record the business combination of Pilot and Sand. No entries are recorded by Sand because Pilot acquired its 90% interest directly from Sand's stockholders. The balance sheet information given in Exhibit 3–6 is not used in recording the business combination on Pilot's books, but it is used in preparing the consolidated balance sheet for the combined entity immediately after combination.

Allocating the Cost/Book Value Differential   The adjustments necessary to combine the balance sheets of parent and subsidiary corporations are determined by *assigning* the difference between investment cost and the book value acquired to identifiable assets and liabilities and then to goodwill for any remainder. The schedule in Exhibit 3–7 illustrates the adjustment necessary to consolidate the balance sheets of Pilot and Sand at December 31, 20X1.

Although the book values of assets and liabilities are not used in determining fair values for individual assets and liabilities (these are usually determined by management), book values are used in the mechanical process of combining the balance sheets of parent and subsidiary.

The underlying book value of the 90% interest acquired in Sand Corporation is $5,310,000 (as shown in Exhibit 3–7), and the excess of investment cost over book value acquired is $4,890,000. This excess is allocated first to the identifiable assets acquired and liabilities assumed, and the remainder is assigned to goodwill. The amounts assigned to identifiable assets and liabilities are for 90% of the fair value and book value difference because the price paid by Pilot Corporation is for 90% of the identifiable assets less liabilities of Sand Corporation. The other 10% in Sand's identifiable net assets relates to the interests of minority stockholders that are not adjusted

PILOT CORPORATION AND ITS 90%-OWNED SUBSIDIARY,
SAND CORPORATION

Investment in Sand—cost	$10,200,000
Book value of interest acquired	
90% × $5,900,000 equity of Sand	(5,310,000)
Total excess of cost over book value acquired	$ 4,890,000

Allocation of Identifiable Assets and Liabilities

	Fair Value	−	Book Value	×	Interest Acquired	=	Excess Allocated
Inventories	$ 600,000		$ 500,000		90%		$ 90,000
Land	800,000		600,000		90		180,000
Buildings	5,000,000		4,000,000		90		900,000
Equipment	1,700,000		2,000,000		90		(270,000)
Notes payable	1,300,000		1,400,000		90		90,000
Total allocated to identifiable net assets							990,000
Remainder allocated to goodwill							3,900,000
Total excess of cost over book value acquired							$4,890,000

Exhibit 3–7 *Schedule for Allocating the Excess of Investment Cost over the Book Value of the Interest Acquired*

to their fair values on the basis of the price paid by Pilot for its 90% interest.[5] The cost/book value differences are determined by and allocated to the interest acquired by the parent/investor.

Working Paper Procedures to Enter Allocations in Consolidated Balance Sheet
The allocation of the excess cost over book value as determined in Exhibit 3–7 is incorporated into a consolidated balance sheet through working paper procedures. These procedures are illustrated in Exhibit 3–8 for Pilot and Sand as of the date of their affiliation.

The consolidated balance sheet working papers show two working paper entries for the consolidation. Entry a is reproduced in general journal form as follows:

a	Unamortized excess	$4,890,000	
	Common stock, $10 par—Sand	4,000,000	
	Additional paid-in capital—Sand	1,000,000	
	Retained earnings—Sand	900,000	
	Investment in Sand		$10,200,000
	Minority interest—10%		590,000

This working paper entry eliminates reciprocal investment in Sand and stockholders' equity amounts of Sand, establishes the minority interest in Sand, and enters the total unamortized excess from Exhibit 3–7.

A second working paper entry allocates the unamortized excess to individual assets and liabilities and to goodwill.

b	Inventories	$ 90,000	
	Land	180,000	
	Buildings—net	900,000	
	Goodwill	3,900,000	
	Notes payable	90,000	
	Equipment—net		$ 270,000
	Unamortized excess		4,890,000

---

[5]Revaluation of all assets and liabilities of a subsidiary on the basis of the price paid by the parent for its majority interest is supported by the entity theory of consolidations. Entity theory is covered in Chapter 11.

PILOT CORPORATION AND SUBSIDIARY
CONSOLIDATED BALANCE SHEET WORKING PAPERS
AFTER COMBINATION ON DECEMBER 31, 20X1

	Pilot	90% Sand	Adjustments and Eliminations		Consolidated Balance Sheet
			Debits	Credits	
Assets					
Cash	$ 1,300,000	$ 200,000			$ 1,500,000
Receivables—net	700,000	300,000			1,000,000
Inventories	900,000	500,000	b 90,000		1,490,000
Other current assets	600,000	400,000			1,000,000
Land	1,200,000	600,000	b 180,000		1,980,000
Buildings—net	8,000,000	4,000,000	b 900,000		12,900,000
Equipment—net	7,000,000	2,000,000		b 270,000	8,730,000
Investment in Sand	10,200,000			a 10,200,000	
Goodwill			b 3,900,000		3,900,000
Unamortized excess			a 4,890,000	b 4,890,000	
Total assets	$29,900,000	$8,000,000			$32,500,000
Liabilities and Equity					
Accounts payable	$ 2,000,000	$ 700,000			$ 2,700,000
Notes payable	3,700,000	1,400,000	b 90,000		5,010,000
Common stock— Pilot	11,000,000				11,000,000
Other paid-in capital—Pilot	8,900,000				8,900,000
Retained earnings— Pilot	4,300,000				4,300,000
Common stock— Sand		4,000,000	a 4,000,000		
Other paid-in capital—Sand		1,000,000	a 1,000,000		
Retained earnings— Sand		900,000	a 900,000		
	$29,900,000	$8,000,000			
Minority interest				a 590,000	590,000
Total liabilities and stockholders' equity					$32,500,000

a To eliminate reciprocal subsidiary investment and equity balances, establish minority interest, and enter the unamortized excess.
b To allocate the unamortized excess to identifiable assets, liabilities, and goodwill.

Exhibit 3–8 *90 Percent Ownership, Excess Allocated to Identifiable Net Assets and Goodwill*

The unamortized excess account is used to simplify working paper entries when the investment cost/book value differential is allocated to numerous asset and liability items. But it is not needed when the total excess is allocated to goodwill, as in Exhibits 3–4 and 3–5. Working paper entries a and b enter equal debits and credits to the unamortized excess, so the account has no final effect on the consolidated balance sheet.

Debit and credit working paper amounts are combined with the line items shown in the separate statements of Pilot and Sand to produce the amounts shown in the consolidated balance sheet column. Sand is a partially owned subsidiary, so its assets and liabilities are not included in the consolidated balance sheet at either their fair values or their book values. Instead, the consolidated assets and liabilities include Pilot's assets and liabilities at book value, plus Sand's assets and liabilities at book value, plus or minus unamortized cost/book value differentials from Pilot's investment in Sand.

Effect of Amortization on Consolidated Balance Sheet After Acquisition

The effect of amortizing the $4,890,000 excess on the December 31, 20X2 consolidated balance sheet is based on the following assumptions about the operations of Pilot and Sand during 20X2, and about the relevant amortization periods of the assets and liabilities to which the excess was allocated in Exhibit 3–7. These assumptions are:

Income for 20X2
Sand's net income	$ 800,000
Pilot's income excluding income from Sand	2,523,500

Dividends Paid in 20X2
Sand	$ 300,000
Pilot	1,500,000

Amortization of Excess
Undervalued inventories—sold in 20X2
Undervalued land—still held by Sand; no amortization
Undervalued buildings—useful life 45 years from January 1, 20X2
Overvalued equipment—useful life 5 years from January 1, 20X2
Overvalued notes payable—retired in 20X2
Goodwill—to be amortized over 40 years

At December 31, 20X2 Pilot's investment in Sand account has a balance of $10,406,500, consisting of the original $10,200,000 cost, increased by $476,500 investment income from Sand, and decreased by $270,000 dividends received from Sand. Pilot's income from Sand for 20X2 is calculated under a one-line consolidation as follows:

Equity in Sand's net income ($800,000 × 90%)		$720,000
Add: Amortization of overvalued equipment		
($270,000 ÷ 5 years)		54,000
Deduct: Amortization of excess allocated to:		
Inventories (sold in 20X2)	$ 90,000	
Land	—	
Buildings ($900,000 ÷ 45 years)	20,000	
Notes payable (retired in 20X2)	90,000	
Goodwill ($3,900,000 ÷ 40 years)	97,500	(297,500)
Income from Sand 20X2		$476,500

Pilot's net income for 20X2 is $3,000,000, consisting of income from its own operations of $2,523,500 plus $476,500 income from Sand. Sand's stockholders' equity increased $500,000 during 20X2, from $5,900,000 to $6,400,000. Pilot's retained earnings increased $1,500,000, from $4,300,000 at December 31, 20X1 to $5,800,000 at December 31, 20X2. This information is reflected in consolidated balance sheet working papers for Pilot and Subsidiary at December 31, 20X2 in Exhibit 3–9.

PILOT CORPORATION AND SUBSIDIARY
CONSOLIDATED BALANCE SHEET WORKING PAPERS
ON DECEMBER 31, 20X2

	Pilot	90% Sand	Adjustments and Eliminations Debits	Credits	Consolidated Balance Sheet
Assets					
Cash	$ 253,500	$ 100,000			$ 353,500
Receivables—net	540,000	200,000			740,000
Inventories	1,300,000	600,000			1,900,000
Other current assets	800,000	500,000			1,300,000
Land	1,200,000	600,000	b 180,000		1,980,000
Buildings—net	9,500,000	3,800,000	b 880,000		14,180,000
Equipment—net	8,000,000	1,800,000		b 216,000	9,584,000
Investment in Sand	10,406,500			a 10,406,500	
Goodwill			b 3,802,500		3,802,500
Unamortized excess			a 4,646,500	b 4,646,500	
Total assets	$32,000,000	$7,600,000			$33,840,000
Liabilities and Equity Accounts payable	$ 2,300,000	$1,200,000			$ 3,500,000
Notes payable	4,000,000				4,000,000
Common stock— Pilot	11,000,000				11,000,000
Other paid-in capital—Pilot	8,900,000				8,900,000
Retained earnings— Pilot	5,800,000				5,800,000
Common stock— Sand		4,000,000	a 4,000,000		
Other paid-in capital—Sand		1,000,000	a 1,000,000		
Retained earnings— Sand		1,400,000	a 1,400,000		
	$32,000,000	$7,600,000			
Minority interest				a 640,000	640,000
Total liabilities and stockholders' equity					$33,840,000

a To eliminate reciprocal subsidiary investment and equity balances, establish minority interest, and enter the unamortized excess.
b To allocate the unamortized excess to identifiable assets and goodwill.

Exhibit 3–9   *90 Percent Ownership, Unamortized Excess One Year After Acquisition*

Working papers entries are reproduced as follows:

a	Common stock—Sand	$4,000,000	
	Other paid-in capital—Sand	1,000,000	
	Retained earnings—Sand	1,400,000	
	Unamortized excess	4,646,500	
	Investment in Sand		$10,406,500
	Minority interest		640,000
	To eliminate reciprocal subsidiary investment and equity accounts, establish minority interest, and enter the unamortized excess.		
b	Land	$ 180,000	
	Buildings—net	880,000	
	Goodwill	3,802,500	
	Equipment—net		$ 216,000
	Unamortized excess		4,646,500
	To allocate the unamortized excess to identifiable assets and goodwill.		

The differences in the adjustments and eliminations in Exhibits 3–8 and 3–9 result from changes that occurred between December 31, 20X1 when the investment was acquired, and December 31, 20X2 after the investment had been held for one year. The following schedule provides the basis for the working paper entries that appear in Exhibit 3–9.

	Unamortized Excess December 31, 20X1	Amortization 20X2	Unamortized Excess December 31, 20X2
Inventories	$ 90,000	$ 90,000	$ —
Land	180,000	—	180,000
Buildings—net	900,000	20,000	880,000
Equipment—net	(270,000)*	(54,000)*	(216,000)*
Notes payable	90,000	90,000	—
Goodwill	3,900,000	97,500	3,802,500
	$4,890,000	$243,500	$4,646,500

*Excess book value over fair value.

The consolidated balance sheet working paper adjustments in Exhibit 3–9 show elimination of reciprocal stockholders' equity and investment in Sand balances. This elimination, entry a, involves debits to Sand's stockholders' equity accounts of $6,400,000, a credit to the minority interest in Sand of $640,000, and a credit to the investment in Sand account of $10,406,500. The difference between these debits and credits totals $4,646,500, representing the unamortized excess of investment over book value acquired on December 31, 20X2, and is entered in the working papers as unamortized excess.

The undervalued inventory items and the overvalued notes payable on Sand's books at December 31, 20X1, were fully amortized in 20X2 (the inventory was sold and the notes payable were retired), therefore, these items do not require balance sheet adjustments at December 31, 20X2. The remaining items—land, $180,000; buildings, $880,000; equipment, $216,000 (overvaluation); and goodwill, $3,802,500—account for the $4,646,500 unamortized excess and are entered in the consolidated balance sheet working papers through working paper entry b, which allocates the unamortized excess as of the balance sheet date. Technically, the working paper entries shown in Exhibit 3–9 are combination adjustment and elimination entries, because the investment in Sand and stockholders' equity accounts of Sand are eliminated, the minority interest is reclassified into a single amount representing 10% of Sand's stockholders' equity, and the asset accounts are adjusted.

CONSOLIDATED INCOME STATEMENT

Comparative separate-company and consolidated income and retained earnings statements for Pilot Corporation and Subsidiary are shown in Exhibit 3–10. These statements reflect the previous assumptions and amounts that were used in preparing the consolidated balance sheet working papers for Pilot and Sand. Detailed revenue and expense items have been added to illustrate the consolidated income statement, but all assumptions and amounts are completely compatible with those already introduced. Adjustment and elimination entries have not been included in the illustration. These entries are covered extensively in Chapter 4.

The difference between a consolidated income statement and an unconsolidated income statement of the parent company lies in the detail presented rather than the net income amount. This can be seen in Exhibit 3–10 by comparing the separate income statement of Pilot with the consolidated income statement of Pilot and Subsidiary.

Pilot's separate income statement shows the revenues and expenses from Pilot's own operations plus its investment income from Sand.[6] By contrast, the consolidated income statement column shows the revenues and expenses of both Sand and Pilot but does not show the investment income from Sand. The $476,500 investment income is excluded because the consolidated income statement includes the detailed revenues ($2,200,000), expenses ($1,400,000), net amortization of the excess ($243,500), and the minority interest deduction ($80,000) that account for the investment income. The net amortization is reflected in the consolidated income statement by increasing cost of goods sold for the $90,000 undervalued inventories that were

---

PILOT AND SAND CORPORATIONS
SEPARATE COMPANY AND CONSOLIDATED STATEMENTS
OF INCOME AND RETAINED EARNINGS
FOR THE YEAR ENDED DECEMBER 31, 20X2

| | Separate Company | | |
	Pilot	Sand	Consolidated
Sales	$ 9,523,500	$2,200,000	$11,723,500
Investment income from Sand	476,500		
Total revenue	10,000,000	2,200,000	11,723,500
Less: Operating expenses			
Cost of sales	4,000,000	700,000	4,790,000
Depreciation expense—buildings	200,000	80,000	300,000
Depreciation expense—equipment	700,000	360,000	1,006,000
Goodwill amortization	—	—	97,500
Other expenses	1,800,000	120,000	1,920,000
Total operating expense	6,700,000	1,260,000	8,113,500
Operating income	3,300,000	940,000	3,610,000
Nonoperating item:			
Interest expense	300,000	140,000	530,000
Net income	**$ 3,000,000**	**$ 800,000**	
Total consolidated income			3,080,000
Less: Minority interest income			80,000
Consolidated net income			**$ 3,000,000**
Retained earnings December 31, 20X1	4,300,000	900,000	4,300,000
	7,300,000	1,700,000	7,300,000
Deduct: Dividends	1,500,000	300,000	1,500,000
Retained earnings December 31, 20X2			
	$ 5,800,000	$1,400,000	$ 5,800,000

Exhibit 3–10   Separate Company and Consolidated Income and Retained Earnings Statements

---

[6]A parent company's income from subsidiary investments is referred to as income from subsidiary, equity in subsidiary earnings, investment income from subsidiary, or by other descriptive captions.

sold in 20X2, increasing depreciation expense on buildings for the $20,000 amortization on the excess allocated to buildings, decreasing depreciation on equipment for the $54,000 amortization of the excess allocated to overvalued equipment, increasing interest expense for the $90,000 allocated to overvalued notes payable that were retired in 20X2, and adding a new expense category to reflect the $97,500 goodwill amortization.

Consolidated income statements, like consolidated balance sheets, are more than summations of the income accounts of affiliated companies. A summation of all income statement items for Pilot and Sand would result in a combined income figure of $3,800,000, whereas consolidated net income is only $3,000,000. The $800,000 difference between these two amounts lies in the investment income of $476,500, the $243,500 net amortization, and the $80,000 income allocated to minority stockholders.

Note that consolidated net income represents income to the stockholders of the parent corporation. Income of minority stockholders is a deduction in the determination of consolidated net income.

If the parent company sells merchandise to its subsidiary, or vice versa, there will be intercompany purchases and sales on the separate books of the parent and its subsidiary. Intercompany purchases and sales balances are reciprocals that must be eliminated in preparing consolidated income statements because they do not represent purchases and sales to parties outside the consolidated entity. Adjustments for intercompany sales and purchases reduce revenue (sales) and expenses (cost of goods sold) by the same amount and therefore have no effect on consolidated net income. Reciprocal rent income and expense amounts are likewise eliminated without affecting consolidated net income.

Numerous other adjustments and eliminations arise in the preparation of consolidated income statements, where the objective is to show the income for a parent company and its subsidiaries *as if* there were only one legal and accounting entity. Discussion of these additional complications is postponed until Chapter 4 and later chapters.

Observe that Pilot's separate retained earnings are identical to consolidated retained earnings. As expected, the $5,800,000 ending consolidated retained earnings in Exhibit 3–10 is the same amount that appears in the consolidated balance sheet for Pilot and Subsidiary at December 31, 20X2 (see Exhibit 3–9).

PUSH-DOWN ACCOUNTING

In the pilot and Sand illustration, the investment was recorded on the books of Pilot at cost, and allocation of the purchase price to identifiable assets and liabilities and goodwill was accomplished through working paper adjusting entries. In some instances, the allocation of the purchase price may be recorded in the subsidiary accounts, in other words, pushed down to the subsidiary records. Push-down accounting affects the books of the subsidiary and separate subsidiary financial statements. It does not alter consolidated financial statements, and in fact, simplifies the consolidation process.

The SEC requires push-down accounting for SEC filings when a subsidiary is substantially wholly owned with no publicly held debt or preferred stock outstanding.

Pack Corporation gives 5,000 shares of Pack $10 par common stock and $100,000 cash for all the capital stock of Simm Company, a closely held company, on January 3, 20X7. At this time, Pack's stock is quoted on a national exchange at $55 a share. Simm's balance sheet and fair value information on January 3 is summarized as follows:

	Book Value	Fair Value
Cash	$ 30,000	$ 30,000
Accounts receivable—net	90,000	90,000
Inventories	130,000	150,000
Land	30,000	70,000
Buildings—net	150,000	130,000
Equipment—net	80,000	120,000
	$510,000	$590,000

(Continued)

	Book Value	Fair Value
Current liabilities	$100,000	$100,000
Long-term debt	150,000	150,000
Capital stock, $10 par	150,000	
Retained earnings	110,000	
	$510,000	

Under push-down accounting, Pack records its investment in Simm in the usual manner:

Investment in Simm	$375,000	
Cash		$100,000
Capital stock, $10 par		50,000
Paid-in capital		225,000

To record acquisition of Simm Company.

An entry must also be made on Simm's books on January 3 to record the new asset bases, including goodwill, in its accounts. Because Simm is considered similar to a new entity, it also has to reclassify retained earnings. Simm makes the following entry to record the push-down values:

Inventories	$ 20,000	
Land	40,000	
Equipment—net	40,000	
Goodwill	35,000	
Retained earnings	110,000	
Building—net		$ 20,000
Push-down capital		225,000

A separate balance sheet prepared for Simm Company immediately after the business combination on January 3 includes the following accounts and amounts:

Cash	$ 30,000
Accounts receivable—net	90,000
Inventories	150,000
Land	70,000
Buildings—net	130,000
Equipment—net	120,000
Goodwill	35,000
	$625,000
Current liabilities	$100,000
Long-term debt	150,000
Capital stock, $10 par	150,000
Push-down capital	225,000
	$625,000

In consolidating the balance sheets of Pack and Simm at January 3, 20X7 after the push-down entries are made on Simm's books, the investment in Simm account on Pack's books is eliminated against Simm's capital stock and push-down capital, and the other accounts are combined.

The arguments for and against push-down accounting and an illustration of push-down accounting with minority interest are considered in more detail in Chapter 11.

ALLOCATION OF THE PURCHASE PRICE TO TOTAL FAIR VALUES OF THE SUBSIDIARY

The FASB Exposure Draft, "Consolidated Financial Statements: Policy and Procedures," proposed recognizing a subsidiary's identifiable assets and liabilities other than goodwill at their fair values at the time of the business combination, if the parent company acquired control of the subsidiary in a single-step purchase. Only the goodwill actually purchased by the parent company would be recognized. In its redeliberations of consolidation policy and procedures, however, the Board changed its mind about goodwill in favor of recognizing goodwill attributable to both the controlling and noncontrolling interests in the consolidated balance sheet at the time of acquisition. To illustrate the two methods contemplated by the Board, assume that Pet Corporation acquires a 60% interest in Sun Corporation for $210,000 when the book values and fair values of Sun's assets and liabilities are as follows:

	Book Value	Fair Value
Assets		
Cash	$ 10,000	$ 10,000
Receivables	60,000	60,000
Inventories	120,000	150,000
Plant assets-net	280,000	300,000
	$470,000	$520,000
Equities		
Payables	$230,000	$230,000
Capital stock	200,000	
Retained earnings	40,000	
	$470,000	

A fair value of Sun Corporation is determined by dividing the purchase price by the interest acquired, in this case, 60%. Thus, the full value of the company according to the FASB must be $350,000 ($210,000 ÷ 60%). The fair value of the identifiable net assets is $290,000 and implied goodwill is $60,000. Under the method first favored by the FASB however, only the $36,000 goodwill actually purchased ($60,000 × 60%) is recognized.

Under the method later favored by the FASB, the full $60,000 implied goodwill is recognized. The amounts to be included in a consolidated balance sheet prepared immediately after the business combination under both methods are compared to the amounts included under current generally accepted accounting principles:

	Fair Value with Purchased Goodwill	Fair Value with Implied Goodwill	Current GAAP
Cash	$ 10,000	$ 10,000	$ 10,000
Receivables	60,000	60,000	60,000
Inventories	150,000	150,000	138,000
Plant assets—net	300,000	300,000	292,000
Goodwill	36,000	60,000	36,000
Total assets	556,000	580,000	536,000
Payables	230,000	230,000	230,000
Net assets	$326,000	$350,000	$306,000

Goodwill under the first method is the same as goodwill computed under current GAAP [$210,000 cost − ($290,000 fair value × 60% acquired) = $36,000]; however, net assets included in a consolidated balance sheet are $20,000 less under GAAP.

POOLED SUBSIDIARIES

The pooling of interests method of accounting for business combinations was covered in Chapter 1, where the conditions for poolings of interests were discussed in some detail. It was assumed in that chapter that the combining corporations, other than the one issuing the stock, were dissolved. However, neither merger nor consolidation is necessary in a pooling. This point was clearly established by the APB in paragraph 49 of *Opinion No. 16*:

> Dissolution of a combining company is not a condition for applying the pooling of interests method of accounting for a business combination. One or more combining companies may be subsidiaries of the issuing corporation after the combination is consummated if the other conditions are met.

If the other combining entities are not dissolved in a pooling of interests, the issuing corporation records the stock acquired as an investment at the subsidiary book value for the pooled net assets. In this case, a parent-subsidiary relationship is established between the issuing corporation (parent) and the other combining corporations (subsidiaries), and consolidated financial statements are needed to combine the operations of the separate entities for external reporting.

The discussion in this chapter assumes that the combining corporations are not dissolved and that parent-subsidiary accounting and reporting procedures are appropriate. Except for initial differences in recording the investment in pooled companies and combining stockholders' equities in the year of combination, the parent company accounts for its investments in pooled corporations under the usual equity method. The investment account is increased for investment income and decreased for subsidiary dividends and losses.

Accounting for Subsidiary Investments in Poolings of Interests

The parent company (issuer) records its investments in pooled companies at the book value of the net assets acquired in the other combining companies. In recording its investment in a pooled company, the parent company also combines its retained earnings with the retained earnings of the other combining company and adjusts its additional paid-in capital to reflect the paid-in capital of the pooled corporation. To illustrate the initial recording, assume that Pink Corporation issues its own capital stock for all the outstanding voting stock of Silver Corporation on January 1, 20X1. Immediately before the pooling, the stockholders' equity accounts for the combining corporations are as follows:

	Pink Corporation	Silver Corporation
Capital stock, $10 par	$1,500,000	$ 500,000
Additional paid-in capital	100,000	200,000
Retained earnings	400,000	300,000
Total stockholders' equity	$2,000,000	$1,000,000

If Pink Corporation issues 50,000 shares of its own stock for the outstanding stock of Silver, the investment is recorded:

Investment in Silver	$1,000,000	
Capital stock—Pink		$500,000
Additional paid-in capital		200,000
Retained earnings		300,000

The par value of stock issued by Pink is equal to the outstanding stock of Silver, so all of Silver's retained earnings and additional paid-in capital is recorded on Pink Corporation's books.

This entry assumes that the parent will record the additional paid-in capital and retained earnings from the pooling in its existing equity accounts. This assumption is consistent with the pooling concept that a single entity emerges from the combining of previously separate companies, but the separate companies do continue to exist as separate legal entities when the combining companies are not dissolved. Retained earnings and other capital accounts are affected by legal considerations, so it may be desirable to maintain separate accounts for equity changes that result from a pooling without dissolution. If such separation is deemed necessary, it can be achieved by designating the accounts "Additional Paid-in Capital from Pooling" and "Retained Earnings from Pooling." This type of account separation is not reflected in the entries illustrated in this chapter.

The issuance of 90,000 shares of Pink Corporation in the pooling would be recorded:

Investment in Silver	$1,000,000	
Additional paid-in capital	100,000	
Capital stock		$900,000
Retained earnings		200,000

In this case, the par value of capital stock issued by Pink ($900,000) exceeds the paid-in capital of Silver ($700,000) plus the additional paid-in capital of Pink ($100,000). Accordingly, the retained earnings that would otherwise be combined has to be reduced by the $100,000 difference.

If Pink Corporation issues 40,000 shares for all of Silver Corporation's stock, its investment is recorded:

Investment in Silver	$1,000,000	
Capital stock		$400,000
Additional paid-in capital		300,000
Retained earnings		300,000

This entry combines the maximum retained earnings of Silver and credits Pink's additional paid-in capital for $300,000. This credit to additional paid-in capital consists of the additional paid-in capital of Silver ($200,000), plus the excess of capital stock of Silver ($500,000) over the par value of shares issued by Pink ($400,000).

In each of the three situations, the stockholders' equity of Pink Corporation is increased by $1,000,000, such that Pink's stockholders' equity reflects the $3,000,000 stockholders' equity of the pooled entity. In consolidating the balance sheets of Pink Corporation and Silver Corporation on the date of the pooling, the reciprocal investment in Silver and stockholders' equity of Silver amounts are eliminated, and the consolidated balance sheet shows the stockholders' equity accounts of Pink Corporation. The consolidation working paper entries are the same in all three situations:

Capital stock—Silver	$ 500,000	
Additional paid-in capital—Silver	200,000	
Retained earnings—Silver	300,000	
Investment in Silver		$1,000,000

Note that the investment account is equal to the equity of Silver so there is no excess of investment balance over underlying equity of Silver.

After the pooling, Pink Corporation increases its investment in Silver account for 100% of Silver's income and decreases it for 100% of Silver's dividends, thereby maintaining the reciprocal relationship between the investment in Silver account and the total stockholders' equity of Silver. By using the equity method of accounting, Pink's net income is equal to consolidated net income, and Pink's retained earnings is equal to consolidated retained earnings.

Pooling of Interests with Minority Interest

The parent company in a pooling combination must acquire at least 90% of the outstanding shares of each combining subsidiary. Shares not acquired by the parent are accounted for as a minority interest. The minority interest can be no greater than 10% of the outstanding subsidiary shares before the pooling because additional holdings by minority interests would violate the 90% "substantially all" test for poolings. If the "substantially all" test is met, could a minority stockholder exchange some, but not all, of his or her shares for shares in the issuing corporation? The APB responded to this question by stating that under the pooling method "each common stockholder of the combining company must either agree to exchange all of his shares for shares of the issuing corporation or refuse to exchange any of his shares."[7]

If Pink Corporation in the previous illustration had issued 50,000 shares of its own stock for 90% of the outstanding voting stock of Silver, the investment would have been recorded as follows:

Investment in Silver	$900,000	
Capital stock		$500,000
Additional paid-in capital		130,000
Retained earnings		270,000

---

[7]AICPA Accounting Interpretations of APB Opinion No. 16, Interpretation No. 25, November 1971.

This entry on Pink's books records the investment in Silver at 90% of the book value of Silver's net assets and combines $270,000 of Silver's retained earnings with Pink's retained earnings. Only 90% of Silver's stock was acquired, so a maximum of 90% of Silver's retained earnings can be combined. The $130,000 credit to additional paid-in capital is the excess of 90% of the paid-in capital of Silver over the par value of capital stock issued by Pink [($700,000 × 90%) − $500,000 = $130,000].

Total paid-in capital of the combining entities less the minority stockholders' share can also be compared with the parent's outstanding capital stock after the pooling. If total paid-in capital is greater, the excess is the parent's additional paid-in capital after the pooling. If capital stock is greater, additional paid-in capital of the parent will be zero, and the excess is the amount by which maximum pooled retained earnings must be reduced. To illustrate, Pink's $1,600,000 paid-in capital plus 90% of Silver's $700,000 paid-in capital exceeds Pink's $2,000,000 capital stock after the pooling by $230,000. This represents Pink's $100,000 additional paid-in capital before the pooling plus the $130,000 added here.

Issuance of 40,000 shares of Pink stock for the 90% interest would have been recorded as follows:

Investment in Silver	$900,000	
Capital stock		$400,000
Additional paid-in capital		230,000
Retained earnings		270,000

The effects of the 10% minority interest in Silver under the various assumptions discussed above are illustrated in Exhibit 3–11. The stockholders' equity of Pink is $2,900,000 immediately after the pooling, regardless of the number of shares issued. This $2,900,000 represents Pink's $2,000,000 stockholders' equity before the pooling, plus the $900,000 book value recorded in the investment in Silver account.

The $3,000,000 stockholders' equity shown in the consolidated or pooled balance sheet consists of Pink Corporation's stockholders' equity immediately after the pooling, plus $100,000 minority interest (10% of Silver's $1,000,000 stockholders'

Stockholders' Equity	Pink	Silver	Consolidated (Pooled) Balance Sheet
A. Issuance of 50,000 Shares for a 90% Interest			
Capital stock, $10 par	$2,000,000	$ 500,000	$2,000,000
Additional paid-in capital	230,000	200,000	230,000
Retained earnings	670,000	300,000	670,000
Minority interest			100,000
Stockholders' equity	$2,900,000	$1,000,000	$3,000,000
B. Issuance of 90,000 Shares for a 90% Interest			
Capital stock, $10 par	$2,400,000	$ 500,000	$2,400,000
Additional paid-in capital	—	200,000	—
Retained earnings	500,000	300,000	500,000
Minority interest			100,000
Stockholders' equity	$2,900,000	$1,000,000	$3,000,000
C. Issuance of 40,000 Shares for a 90% Interest			
Capital stock, $10 par	$1,900,000	$ 500,000	$1,900,000
Additional paid-in capital	330,000	200,000	330,000
Retained earnings	670,000	300,000	670,000
Minority interest			100,000
Stockholders' equity	$2,900,000	$1,000,000	$3,000,000

Exhibit 3–11 *Comparison of Stockholders' Equity Pooling Under Different Assumptions*

equity). In consolidation working papers, the following entry would be required to eliminate the reciprocal investment and equity amounts in all three situations:

Capital stock—Silver	$500,000	
Additional paid-in capital—Silver	200,000	
Retained earnings—Silver	300,000	
Investment in Silver		$900,000
Minority interest		100,000

This entry eliminates the equity accounts of Silver and the investment in Silver, and it establishes the 10% minority interest. Net assets in a pooling are accounted for on the basis of book value, so there is no excess of investment account balance over book value acquired to allocate to identifiable assets or goodwill.

Acquisition of Minority Shares

APB Opinion No. 16 specifically precludes firms from using the pooling method for acquisition of shares held by minority stockholders. If Pink Corporation acquires the remainder of Silver Corporation's outstanding shares after consummation of the business combination, the acquisition is not accounted for as a pooling of interests, even if the transaction is consummated through an exchange of shares. Although not a business combination, the acquisition of the additional shares is accounted for under the purchase method, and the transaction is recorded on a fair value basis. The result is a revaluation of 10% of the net assets of Silver Corporation.

SUMMARY

Consolidated financial statements are usually required for the fair presentation of financial position and the results of operations of a parent company and its subsidiaries. Consolidated financial statements are not merely summations of parent company and subsidiary financial statement items. Reciprocal amounts are eliminated, and only nonreciprocal amounts are combined and included in consolidated statements. The investment in subsidiary and the subsidiary stockholders' equity accounts are eliminated in the preparation of consolidated financial statements because they are reciprocal, both representing the net assets of the subsidiary. Sales, borrowing, and leasing transactions between parent and subsidiaries also give rise to reciprocal amounts that must be eliminated in the consolidating process.

The stockholders' equity amounts that appear in the consolidated balance sheet are those of the parent company, except for the equity of minority stockholders, which may be reported as a separate item within or outside of consolidated stockholders' equity. Consolidated net income is a measurement of income to the stockholders of the parent company. Any income accruing to the benefit of minority stockholders is a deduction in determination of consolidated net income. Parent company net income and retained earnings are equal to consolidated net income and consolidated retained earnings, respectively.

The pooling of interests method of accounting involves combination through the exchange of shares. If only the issuing corporation survives, the accounting is done as explained in Chapter 1. If the combining corporations continue to exist as separate legal entities, the companies are accounted for according to parent-subsidiary procedures with the following amendments:

1 The parent company/issuer records the subsidiary investment at its book value. Stock issued is credited for the par value of shares issued, retained earnings are combined to the extent possible, and additional paid-in capital is increased or decreased as necessary to account for differences between the par value of stock issued and paid-in capital of the other combining company.
2 Maximum retained earnings that can be combined with the parent's retained earnings is equal to the parent's ownership percentage times the subsidiary's retained earnings.
3 Earnings of combining companies are pooled for the entire year in which the business combination is consummated.

The equity method is used in accounting for investments in pooled subsidiaries. If it is correctly applied, the parent company's investment account will be equal to the underlying subsidiary equity; parent company income will be equal to consolidated (pooled) income; and parent company equity account balances will equal the consolidated (pooled) equity balances. These equalities are established in the year in which the pooling takes place. In subsequent years, the parent company accounts for its investments in pooled subsidiaries in the same manner as for purchased subsidiaries, and the consolidation procedures are the same as those for purchased subsidiaries.

SELECTED READINGS

Accounting Principles Board Opinion No. 16. "Business Combinations." New York: American Institute of Certified Public Accountants, 1970.

American Accounting Association's Financial Accounting Standards Committee. "Comment Letter to the FASB Discussion Memorandum 'New Basis of Accounting.'" *Accounting Horizons* (March 1994), pp. 119–121.

American Accounting Association's Financial Accounting Standards Committee. "Response to the FASB Discussion Memorandum 'Consolidation Policy and Procedures.'" *Accounting Horizons* (June 1994) pp. 120–125.

American Accounting Association's Financial Accounting Standards Committee. "Response to FASB Special Report, 'Issues Associated with the FASB Project on Business Combinations'" *Accounting Horizons* (March 1998), pp. 87–89.

Bossio, Ronald J. and Gisele Dion. "Revisiting Consolidated Financial Statements." *The CPA Journal* (February 1995), pp. 46–49.

Committee on Accounting Procedure. *Accounting Research Bulletin No. 51.* "Consolidated Financial Statements." New York: American Institute of Certified Public Accountants, 1959.

DeMoville, Wig, and A. George Petrie. "Accounting for a Bargain Purchase in a Business Combination." *Accounting Horizons* (September 1989), pp. 38–43.

Financial Accounting Standards Board. *An Analysis of Issues Related to Consolidation Policy and Procedures.* Discussion Memorandum. Norwalk, CT: Financial Accounting Standards Board, 1991.

Financial Accounting Standards Board. *Preliminary Views on Major Issues Related to Consolidation Policy.* Financial Accounting Series. Norwalk, CT: Financial Accounting Standards Board, 1994.

Johnson, L. Todd, and Kimberley R. Petrone. "Is Goodwill an Asset" *Accounting Horizons* (September 1998), pp. 293–303.

Pacter, Paul. "Revising GAAP for Consolidations: Join the Debate." *The CPA Journal* (July 1992), pp. 38–47.

Statement of Financial Accounting Standards No. 94. "Consolidation of All Majority-owned Subsidiaries." Stamford, CT: Financial Accounting Standards Board, 1987.

ASSIGNMENT MATERIAL

QUESTIONS

1 When does a corporation become a subsidiary of another corporation?

2 In allocating the excess of investment cost over book value acquired of a subsidiary, are the amounts allocated to identifiable assets and liabilities (land and notes payable, for example) recorded separately in the accounts of the parent company? Explain.

3 If the fair value of a subsidiary corporation's land was $100,000 and its book value $90,000 when the parent company acquired its 100% interest for cash, at what amount would the land be included in the consolidated balance sheet of the two corporations immediately after the acquisition? Would your answer be different if the parent company had acquired an 80% interest?

4 Define or explain the terms *parent company, subsidiary company, affiliated companies,* and *associated companies.*

5 What is a minority interest?

6 Describe the circumstances under which the accounts of a subsidiary would not be included in the consolidated financial statements.

7 Who are the primary users for which consolidated financial statements are intended?

8 What amount of capital stock is reported in a consolidated balance sheet?

9 In what general ledger would you expect to find the account "goodwill from consolidation"?

10 How should the parent company's investment in subsidiary account be classified in a consolidated balance sheet? In the parent company's separate balance sheet?

11 Name some reciprocal accounts that might be found in the separate records of a parent company and its subsidiaries.

12 Why are reciprocal amounts eliminated in the preparation of consolidated financial statements?

13 How does the stockholders' equity of the parent company that uses the equity method of accounting differ from the consolidated stockholders' equity of the parent company and its subsidiaries?

14 Is there a difference in the amounts reported in the statement of retained earnings of a parent that uses the equity method of accounting and the amounts that appear in the consolidated retained earnings statement?

15 Is minority interest income an expense? Explain.

16 Describe how the total minority interest at the end of an accounting period is determined.

17 What special procedures are required to consolidate the statements of a parent company that reports on a calendar year basis and a subsidiary whose fiscal year ends on October 31?

18 When are parent-subsidiary accounting procedures applicable to a pooling business combination?

19 How does a parent company account for its investments in pooled subsidiaries?

20 Under what conditions does a parent company pool (or combine) all the retained earnings of its 100% owned subsidiaries?

21 Assume that a parent company makes the following journal entry to record its investment in a subsidiary under the pooling method:

Investment in Schwan	$1,300,000	
Capital stock, $10 par		$1,000,000
Additional paid-in capital		120,000
Retained earnings		180,000

Explain the components of the above entry in terms of what you would expect each of the amounts to represent.

22 Assume that the following entry is made by a parent company in recording its investment in a pooled subsidiary:

Investment in Starling	$1,250,000	
Additional paid-in capital	150,000	
Capital stock, $10 par		$1,000,000
Retained earnings		400,000

Did the parent company pool maximum retained earnings? Explain. Will the pooled additional paid-in capital be more or less than the parent company's additional paid-in capital before the pooling? Explain.

23 A parent company acquires 92% of the voting stock of a subsidiary in a pooling of interests that was consummated in 20X4 and an additional 4% of the subsidiary stock in 20X5. How should the acquisition of the additional 4% be accounted for by the parent company?

24 Does the acquisition of shares held by minority stockholders constitute a business combination?

(*Note:* Don't forget the assumptions on page 56 when working exercises and problems in this chapter.)

EXERCISES

E 3-1

1 A 75% owned subsidiary should not be consolidated under the provisions of *FASB Statement No. 94*, "Consolidation of All Majority-owned Subsidiaries," when:
  a Its operations are dissimilar from those of the parent company
  b Control of the subsidiary does not lie with the parent company
  c There is a dominant minority interest in the subsidiary
  d Management feels that consolidation would not provide the most meaningful financial statements

2 Under the provisions of *FASB Statement No. 94*, an 80%-owned subsidiary that cannot be consolidated must be accounted for:
  a Under the equity method
  b Under the cost method
  c Under the equity method if the parent can exercise significant influence over the subsidiary
  d At market value if the subsidiary is in bankruptcy

3 Consolidated statements for Porter Corporation and its 60%-owned investee, Spinelli Company, will not be prepared under the provisions of *FASB Statement No. 94* if:
  a The fiscal periods of Porter and Spinelli are more than three months apart
  b Porter is a major manufacturing company and Spinelli is an insurance company
  c Spinelli is a foreign company
  d Porter will spinoff all Spinelli shares to Porter stockholders within the next year

4 Armor Industries owns 7,000,000 shares of Babbitt Corporation's outstanding common stock (a 70% interest). The remaining 3,000,000 outstanding common shares of Babbitt are held by Ottman Insurance Company. On Armor Industries' consolidated financial statements, Ottman Insurance Company is considered:

a An investee

b An associated company

c An affiliated company

d A minority interest

5 Pella Corporation owns a 60% interest in Sanico Company and an 80% interest in Talbert Company. Pella consolidates its investment in Sanico, but Talbert, which is currently under protection of the bankruptcy court, is not consolidated, and Pella accounts for this investment by the equity method. Which statement is correct?

a Consolidated retained earnings will not reflect the earnings of Talbert.

b Consolidated net income will be the same as if both subsidiaries were consolidated.

c The individual assets and liabilities of Sanico and Talbert are reflected in Pella's consolidated statements.

d Minority income will be reported the same as if both subsidiaries were consolidated.

6 On January 1, 20X4, Paxton Company purchased 75% of the outstanding shares of Salem Company at a cost exceeding the book value and fair value of Salem's net assets. Using the following notations, describe the amount at which the plant assets will appear in a consolidated balance sheet of Paxton Company and Subsidiary prepared immediately after the acquisition:

P_{bv} = book value of Paxton's plant assets

P_{fv} = fair value of Paxton's plant assets

S_{bv} = book value of Salem's plant assets

S_{fv} = fair value of Salem's plant assets

a. $P_{bv} + S_{bv} \pm 0.75(S_{fv} - S_{bv})$

b. $P_{bv} + 0.75(S_{bv}) \pm 0.75(S_{fv} - S_{bv})$

c. $P_{bv} + 0.75(S_{fv})$

d. $P_{fv} + S_{bv} \pm 0.75(S_{fv} - S_{bv})$

E 3-2 **1** Under *FASB Statement No. 94*, "Consolidation of All Majority-owned Subsidiaries," a parent company should exclude a subsidiary from consolidation if:

a It measures income from the subsidiary under the equity method

b The subsidiary is in a regulated industry

c The subsidiary is a foreign entity whose books are recorded in a foreign currency

d The parent expects to sell the subsidiary investment within a year

2 The FASB's primary motivation for issuing *FASB Statement No. 94*, "Consolidation of All Majority-owned Subsidiaries," was to:

a Ensure disclosure of all loss contingencies

b Prevent the use of off-balance sheet financing

c Improve comparability of the statements of cash flows

d Establish criteria for exclusion of finance and insurance subsidiaries from consolidation

3 Parent company and consolidated financial statement amounts would not be the same for:

a Capital stock

b Retained earnings

c Investments in unconsolidated subsidiaries

d Investments in consolidated subsidiaries

4 Minority interest, as it appears in a consolidated balance sheet, refers to:

a Owners of less than 50% of the parent company's stock

b Parent's interest in subsidiary companies

c Interest expense on subsidiary's bonds payable

d Equity in the subsidiary's net assets held by stockholders other than the parent

5 Pat Corporation acquired an 80% interest in Sal Corporation on January 1, 20X4 and issued consolidated financial statements at and for the year ended December 31, 20X4. Pat and Sal had issued separate company financial statements in 20X3.

a The change in reporting entity is reported by restating the financial statements of all prior periods presented as consolidated statements.

b The cumulative effect of the change in reporting entity is shown in a separate category of the income statement net of tax.

c The income effect of the error is charged or credited directly to beginning retained earnings.

d The income effect of the accounting change is spread over the current and future periods.

6 The minority interest income that appears in the consolidated income statement is computed as follows:

a Consolidated net income is multiplied by the minority interest percentage

b The subsidiary's income less amortization of cost/book value differentials is multiplied by the minority interest percentage

    c Subsidiary net income is subtracted from consolidated net income

    d Subsidiary income determined for consolidated statement purposes is multiplied by the minority interest percentage

7 The retained earnings that appears on the consolidated balance sheet of a parent company and its 60%-owned subsidiary is:

    a The parent company's retained earnings plus 100% of the subsidiary's retained earnings

    b The parent company's retained earnings plus 60% of the subsidiary's retained earnings

    c The parent company's retained earnings

    d Pooled retained earnings

8 A corporation is contemplating acquiring 90% of another corporation, by either (a) issuing common stock in exchange for 90% of the outstanding stock of the combining corporation in a pooling of interests or (b) paying cash for 90% of the outstanding stock in a purchase business combination. Which of the following items would be reported in the consolidated financial statements at the same amount, regardless of the accounting method used?

    a Minority interest   **c** Retained earnings

    b Goodwill   **d** Capital stock

E 3-3 **[AICPA adapted]**

Use the following information in answering questions 1 and 2:

    Apex Company acquired 70% of the outstanding stock of Nadir Corporation. The separate balance sheet of Apex immediately after the acquisition and the consolidated balance sheet are as follows:

	Apex	Consolidated
Current assets	$106,000	$146,000
Investment in Nadir—cost	100,000	—
Goodwill	—	8,100
Fixed assets—net	270,000	370,000
	$476,000	$524,100
Current liabilities	$ 15,000	$ 28,000
Capital stock	350,000	350,000
Minority interest	—	35,100
Retained earnings	111,000	111,000
	$476,000	$524,100

    Of the excess payment for the investment in Nadir, $10,000 was ascribed to undervaluation of its fixed assets. The balance of the excess payment was ascribed to goodwill. Current assets of Nadir included a $2,000 receivable from Apex, which arose before they became related on an ownership basis.

    The following two items relate to Nadir's separate balance sheet prepared at the time Apex acquired its 70% interest in Nadir.

1 What was the total of the current assets on Nadir's separate balance sheet immediately before Apex acquired its 70% interest?

    a $38,000   **c** $42,000

    b $40,000   **d** $104,000

2 What was the total stockholders' equity on Nadir's separate balance sheet at the time Apex acquired its 70% interest?

    a $64,900   **c** $100,000

    b $70,000   **d** $117,000

3 Cobb Company's current receivables from affiliated companies at December 31, 20X5 are (1) a $75,000 cash advance to Hill Corporation (Cobb owns 30% of the voting stock of Hill and accounts for the investment by the equity method), (2) a receivable of $260,000 from Vick Corporation for administrative and selling services (Vick is 100%-owned by Cobb and is included in Cobb's consolidated financial statements), and (3) a receivable of $200,000 from Ward Corporation for merchandise sales on credit (Ward is a 90%-owned, unconsolidated subsidiary of Cobb accounted for by the equity method). In the current assets section of its December 31, 20X5 consolidated balance sheet, Cobb should report accounts receivable from investees in the amount of:

    a $180,000   **c** $275,000

    b $255,000   **d** $535,000

Use the following information in answering questions 4 and 5:

    On January 1, 20X3 Owen Corp. purchased all of Sharp Corp.'s common stock for $1,200,000. On that date, the fair values of Sharp's assets and liabilities equaled their carrying amounts of $1,320,000 and $320,000, respectively. Owen's policy is to amortize intangibles over 10 years. During 20X3, Sharp paid cash dividends of $20,000.

Selected information from the separate balance sheets and income statements of Owen and Sharp as of December 31, 20X3 and for the year then ended follows:

	Owen	Sharp
Balance sheet accounts		
Investment in subsidiary	$1,300,000	—
Retained earnings	1,240,000	$ 560,000
Total stockholders' equity	2,620,000	1,120,000
Income statement accounts		
Operating income	$ 420,000	$ 200,000
Equity in earnings of Sharp	120,000	—
Net income	400,000	140,000

4 In Owen's 20X3 consolidated income statement, what amount should be reported for amortization of goodwill?
  a $0   **c** $18,000
  b $12,000   **d** $20,000

5 In Owen's December 31, 20X3 consolidated balance sheet, what amount should be reported as total retained earnings?
  a $1,240,000   **c** $1,380,000
  b $1,360,000   **d** $1,800,000

6 Wright Corp. has several subsidiaries that are included in its consolidated financial statements. In its December 31, 20X2 trial balance, Wright had the following intercompany balances before eliminations:

	Debit	Credit
Current receivable due from Main Co.	$ 32,000	
Noncurrent receivable from Main	114,000	
Cash advance to Corn Corp.	6,000	
Cash advance from King Co.		$ 15,000
Intercompany payable to King		101,000

In its December 31, 20X2 consolidated balance sheet, what amount should Wright report as intercompany receivables?
  a $152,000   **c** $36,000
  b $146,000   **d** $0

E 3-4 Pina Corporation paid $900,000 for a 90% interest in Santa Maria Corporation on January 1, 20X1 at a price $30,000 in excess of underlying book value. The excess *was allocated* $12,000 to undervalued equipment with a three-year remaining useful life and $18,000 to goodwill with a 10-year write-off period. The income statements of Pina and Santa Maria for 20X1 are summarized as follows:

	Pina	Santa Maria
Sales	$2,000,000	$800,000
Income from Santa Maria	90,000	
Cost of sales	(1,000,000)	(400,000)
Depreciation expense	(200,000)	(120,000)
Other expenses	(400,000)	(180,000)
Net income	$ 490,000	$100,000

Required
  1 Calculate the unamortized goodwill that should appear in the consolidated balance sheet of Pina and Subsidiary at December 31, 20X1.
  2 Calculate consolidated net income for 20X1.

E 3-5 On December 31, 20X2, the separate company financial statements for Panderman Corporation and its 70%-owned subsidiary, Sadisman Corporation, had the following account balances related to dividends:

	Panderman	Sadisman
Dividends for 20X2	$600,000	$400,000
Dividends payable at December 31, 20X2	300,000	100,000

1 At what amount will dividends be shown in the consolidated retained earnings statement?
2 At what amount should dividends payable be shown in the consolidated balance sheet?

E 3-6 On January 1, 20X2 Pascal Corporation issues 50,000 previously unissued shares of $10 par common stock for 90% of Sunset Corporation's outstanding common shares in a business combination accounted for as a pooling of interests. Balance sheet information for Pascal and Sunset at December 31, 20X1 follows:

	Pascal Book Value	Sunset Book Value	Sunset Fair Value
Current assets	$ 4,000,000	$ 800,000	$ 900,000
Plant assets—net	6,000,000	1,400,000	1,500,000
	$10,000,000	$2,200,000	$2,400,000
Liabilities	$ 4,000,000	$ 800,000	$ 800,000
Capital stock, $10 par	3,000,000	800,000	
Additional paid-in capital	2,000,000	400,000	
Retained earnings	1,000,000	200,000	
	$10,000,000	$2,200,000	

Required

1 Prepare the journal entry on Pascal's books to account for the business combination.
2 Prepare a consolidated balance sheet for Pascal and Subsidiary on January 1, 20X2, immediately after the business combination.

E 3-7 Book values and fair values of Slider Corporation's assets and liabilities on December 31, 20X5 are as follows:

	Book Value	Fair Value
Cash	$ 70,000	$ 70,000
Accounts receivable—net	80,000	80,000
Inventories	80,000	100,000
Land	150,000	200,000
Buildings-net	350,000	500,000
Equipment-net	220,000	300,000
	$950,000	$1,250,000
Accounts payable	$100,000	$ 100,000
Note payable	140,000	150,000
Capital stock	500,000	
Retained earnings	210,000	
	$950,000	

On January 1, 20X6 Portal Corporation acquires all of Slider's capital stock for $1,250,000 cash. The acquisition is recorded using push-down accounting.

Required

1 Prepare the January 1 journal entry on Slider's books to record push-down values.
2 Prepare a balance sheet for Slider Corporation immediately after the business combination on January 1 under push-down accounting.

E 3-8 Summary income statement information for Pasture Corporation and its 70%-owned subsidiary, Situation Specialists Corporation, for the year 20X2 is as follows:

	Pasture	Situation Specialists
Sales	$1,000,000	$400,000
Income from Situation Specialist	49,000	—
Cost of sales	(600,000)	(200,000)
Depreciation expense	(50,000)	(40,000)
Other expenses	(199,000)	(90,000)
Net income	$ 200,000	$ 70,000

Required

    1 Assume that Pasture acquired its 70% interest in Situation Specialists at book value on January 1, 20X1 when Situation Specialist's assets and liabilities were equal to their recorded book values. There were no intercompany transactions during 20X1 and 20X2. Prepare a consolidated income statement for Pasture Corporation and Subsidiary for 20X2.

    2 Assume that Pasture acquired its 70% interest in Situation Specialist on January 1, 20X1 at a price $20,000 in excess of book value and that $10,000 *was allocated* to a reduction of overvalued equipment with a five-year remaining useful life and $30,000 to goodwill with a 10-year amortization period. There were no intercompany transactions during 20X1 and 20X2. Prepare a consolidated income statement for Pasture Corporation and Subsidiary for 20X2.

E 3-9   Poball Corporation acquired an 80% interest in Softcan Corporation on January 2, 20X2 for $700,000. On this date the capital stock and retained earnings of the two companies were as follows:

	Poball	Softcan
Capital stock	$1,800,000	$500,000
Retained earnings	800,000	100,000

The assets and liabilities of Softcan were stated at their fair values when Poball acquired its 80% interest. Poball uses the equity method to account for its investment in Softcan.

    Net income and dividends for 20X2 for the affiliated companies were:

	Poball	Softcan
Net income	$300,000	$90,000
Dividends declared	180,000	50,000
Dividends payable December 31, 20X2	90,000	25,000

Required: Calculate the amounts at which the following items should appear in the consolidated balance sheet on December 31, 20X2:

    1 Capital stock

    2 Goodwill

    3 Consolidated retained earnings

    4 Minority interest

    5 Dividends payable

E 3-10   Paskey and Salam corporations' balance sheets at December 31, 20X7 are summarized as follows:

	Paskey	Salam
Cash	$255,000	$ 60,000
Other assets	200,000	175,000
Total assets	$455,000	$235,000
Liabilities	$ 70,000	$ 35,000
Capital stock, par $10	300,000	175,000
Additional paid-in capital	50,000	15,000
Retained earnings	35,000	10,000
Total equities	$455,000	$235,000

    Paskey acquired 80% of the voting stock of Salam on January 2, 20X8 at $15 per share. The fair values of Salam's net assets were equal to their book values on January 2, 20X8.

    During 20X8 Paskey reported earnings of $55,000, including income from Salam of $16,000, and paid dividends of $25,000. Salam's earnings for 20X8 were $20,000 and its dividends were $15,000.

Required: Prepare the stockholders' equity section of the December 31, 20X8 consolidated balance sheet for Paskey Corporation and Subsidiary.

E 3-11   Comparative income statements of Peekos Corporation and Slogger Corporation for the year ended December 31, **20X4** are as follows:

	Peekos	Slogger
Sales	$1,600,000	$500,000
Income from Slogger	126,500	—
Total revenue	1,726,500	500,000
Less: Cost of goods sold	900,000	200,000
Operating expenses	400,000	150,000
Total expenses	1,300,000	350,000
Net income	$ 426,500	$150,000

Additional Information

1 Slogger is a 90%-owned subsidiary of Peekos, acquired by Peekos for $820,000 on January 1, **20X2**, when Slogger's stockholders' equity was $700,000.

2 The excess of the cost of Peekos's investment in Slogger over book value acquired *was allocated* $30,000 to inventories that were sold in **20X2**, $20,000 to equipment with a four-year remaining useful life, and the remainder to goodwill.

Required: Prepare a consolidated income statement for Peekos Corporation and Subsidiary for the year ended December 31, **20X4**.

E 3-12 Pholmes Corporation and Shurlock Corporation consummated a pooling of interests business combination on January 1, 20X8, with both companies continuing their operations in a parent-subsidiary relationship. Stockholders' equities of the two companies immediately before the pooling consisted of the following:

	Pholmes	Shurlock
Common stock, $10 par	$ 500,000	$300,000
Additional paid-in capital	500,000	50,000
Retained earnings	200,000	150,000
Total stockholders' equity	$1,200,000	$500,000

Required: Prepare partial balance sheets showing consolidated stockholders' equity for Pholmes Corporation and Subsidiary on January 1, 20X8, immediately after the pooling, under each of the following assumptions:

1 Pholmes Corporation issues 25,000 shares of previously unissued common stock with a market value of $25 per share for all of the outstanding stock of Shurlock Corporation.

2 Pholmes Corporation issues 35,000 shares of previously unissued common stock with a market value of $25 per share for 90% of the outstanding stock of Shurlock Corporation.

PROBLEMS

P 3-1 On December 31, 20X2 Pennyvale Corporation purchased 80% of the stock of Sutherland Sales Company at book value. The data reported on their separate balance sheets immediately after the acquisition follow. At December 31, 20X2 Pennyvale Corporation owes Sutherland Sales $5,000 on accounts payable.

	Pennyvale Corporation	Sutherland Sales
Assets		
Cash	$ 32,000	$ 18,000
Accounts receivable	45,000	34,000
Inventories	143,000	56,000
Investment in Sutherland	200,000	
Equipment—net	380,000	175,000
	$800,000	$283,000
Liabilities and Stockholders' Equity		
Accounts payable	$ 40,000	$ 33,000
Common stock, $10 par	460,000	150,000
Retained earnings	300,000	100,000
	$800,000	$283,000

Required

1 Prepare a consolidated balance sheet for Pennyvale Corporation and Subsidiary at December 31, 20X2.

2 Compute consolidated net income for 20X3 assuming that Pennyvale Corporation reported separate income of $170,000 and Sutherland Sales Company reported net income of $90,000. (Separate income does *not* include income from the investment in Sutherland Sales.)

P 3-2 Parlor Corporation acquired 70% of the outstanding common stock of Setting Corporation on January 1, 20X3 for $178,000 cash. Immediately after this acquisition the balance sheet information for the two companies was as follows:

	Parlor Book Value	Setting Book Value	Setting Fair Value
Assets			
Cash	$ 32,000	$ 20,000	$ 20,000
Receivables—net	80,000	30,000	30,000
Inventories	70,000	30,000	50,000
Land	100,000	50,000	60,000
Buildings—net	110,000	70,000	90,000
Equipment—net	80,000	40,000	30,000
Investment in Setting	178,000	—	—
Total assets	$650,000	$240,000	$280,000
Liabilities and Stockholders' Equity			
Accounts payable	$ 90,000	$ 80,000	$ 80,000
Other liabilities	10,000	50,000	40,000
Capital stock, $10 par	500,000	100,000	
Retained earnings	50,000	10,000	
Total equities	$650,000	$240,000	

Required

1 Prepare a schedule to allocate the difference between the cost of the investment in Setting and the book value of the interest acquired by Parlor to identifiable and unidentifiable net assets.

2 Prepare a consolidated balance sheet for Parlor Corporation and Subsidiary at January 1, 20X3.

P 3-3 PJ Corporation pays $2,700,000 for an 80% interest in Softback Books Corporation on January 1, 20X2, at which time the book value and fair value of Softback Books' net assets are as follows:

	Book Value	Fair Value
Current assets	$1,000,000	$1,500,000
Equipment—net	2,000,000	3,000,000
Other plant assets—net	1,000,000	1,000,000
Liabilities	(1,500,000)	(1,500,000)
Net assets	$2,500,000	$4,000,000

Required: Prepare a schedule to allocate the cost/book value differentials to Softback Books' net assets.

P 3-4 Pharm Corporation purchased a block of Specht Company common stock for $260,000 cash on January 1, 20X8. Separate company and consolidated balance sheets prepared immediately after the acquisition are summarized as follows:

PHARM CORPORATION AND SUBSIDIARY
CONSOLIDATED BALANCE SHEET AT JANUARY 1, 20X8

	Pharm	Specht	Consolidated
Assets			
Current assets	$ 190,000	$100,000	$ 290,000
Investment in Specht	260,000	—	—
Plant assets—net	550,000	200,000	758,000
Goodwill	—	—	44,000
Total assets	$1,000,000	$300,000	$1,092,000

(Continued)

PHARM CORPORATION AND SUBSIDIARY
CONSOLIDATED BALANCE SHEET AT JANUARY 1, 20X8

	Pharm	Specht	Consolidated
Equities			
Liabilities	$ 400,000	$ 40,000	$ 440,000
Capital stock, $10 par	500,000	200,000	500,000
Retained earnings	100,000	60,000	100,000
Minority interest	—	—	52,000
Total equities	$1,000,000	$300,000	$1,092,000

Required: Reconstruct the schedule to allocate the cost/book value differential from Pharm's investment in Specht.

P 3-5 Adjusted trial balances for Palmer and Sorrel Corporations at December 31, 20X2 are as follows:

	Palmer	Sorrel
Debits		
Current assets	$ 240,000	$100,000
Plant assets—net	500,000	300,000
Investment in Sorrel	410,000	—
Cost of sales	300,000	300,000
Other expenses	100,000	50,000
Dividends	50,000	—
	$1,600,000	$750,000
Credits		
Liabilities	$ 450,000	$210,000
Capital stock	300,000	50,000
Retained earnings	340,000	90,000
Sales	500,000	400,000
Income from Sorrel	10,000	—
	$1,600,000	$750,000

Palmer purchased all the stock of Sorrel for $400,000 cash on January 1, 20X2 when Sorrel's stockholders' equity consisted of $50,000 capital stock and $90,000 retained earnings. Sorrel's assets and liabilities were fairly valued except for inventory items that were undervalued by $20,000 and sold in 20X2, and plant assets that were undervalued by $40,000 and had a remaining useful life of four years from the date of business combination. Palmer uses a 20-year amortization period for goodwill.

Required: Prepare a consolidated balance sheet for Palmer Corporation and Subsidiary at December 31, 20X2.

P 3-6 Perry Corporation paid $400,000 cash for 90% of Sim Corporation's common stock on January 1, 20X6 when Sim had $300,000 capital stock and $100,000 retained earnings. The book values of Sim's assets and liabilities were equal to fair values. During 20X6 Sim reported net income of $20,000 and declared $10,000 dividends on December 31. Balance sheets for Perry and Sim at December 31, 20X6 are as follows:

	Perry	Sim
Assets		
Cash	$ 42,000	$ 20,000
Receivables—net	50,000	130,000
Inventories	400,000	50,000
Land	150,000	200,000
Equipment—net	600,000	100,000
Investment in Sim	408,000	—
	$1,650,000	$500,000
Equities		
Accounts payable	$ 410,000	$ 80,000
Dividends payable	60,000	10,000
Capital stock	1,000,000	300,000
Retained earnings	180,000	110,000
	$1,650,000	$500,000

Required: Prepare consolidated balance sheet working papers for Perry Corporation and Subsidiary for 20X6.

P 3-7 Portly Corporation acquired 80% of the outstanding stock of Slender Corporation for $280,000 cash on January 3, 20X5, on which date Slender's stockholders' equity consisted of capital stock of $200,000 and retained earnings of $50,000.

There were no changes in the outstanding stock of either corporation during 20X5 and 20X6. At December 31, 20X6 the adjusted trial balances of Portly and Slender are as follows:

	Portly	Slender
Debits		
Current assets	$ 204,000	$ 75,000
Plant assets—net	400,000	300,000
Investment in Slender—80%	336,000	—
Cost of goods sold	250,000	120,000
Other expenses	50,000	30,000
Dividends	60,000	25,000
	$1,300,000	$550,000
Credits		
Current liabilities	$ 162,000	$ 50,000
Capital stock	500,000	200,000
Retained earnings	200,000	100,000
Sales	400,000	200,000
Income from Slender	38,000	—
	$1,300,000	$550,000

Additional Information

1 All of Slender's assets and liabilities were recorded at their fair values on January 3, 20X5.
2 The current liabilities of Slender at December 31, 20X6 include dividends payable of $10,000.

Required: Determine the amounts that should appear in the consolidated statements of Portly Corporation and Subsidiary at December 31, 20X6 for each of the following:

1 Minority interest income
2 Current assets
3 Income from Slender
4 Capital stock
5 Investment in Slender
6 Excess of investment cost over book value acquired
7 Consolidated net income
8 Consolidated retained earnings, December 31, 20X5
9 Consolidated retained earnings, December 31, 20X6
10 Minority interest, December 31, 20X6

P 3-8 **[AICPA adapted]**

On January 1, 20X6 Todd Corporation made the following investments:

1 Acquired for cash, 80% of the outstanding common stock of Meadow Corporation at $70 per share. The stockholders' equity of Meadow on January 1, 20X6 consisted of the following:

Common stock, par value $50	$50,000
Retained earnings	20,000

2 Acquired for cash, 70% of the outstanding common stock of Van Corporation at $40 per share. The stockholders' equity of Van on January 1, 20X6 consisted of the following:

Common stock, par value $20	$60,000
Capital in excess of par value	20,000
Retained earnings	40,000

After these investments were made, Todd was able to exercise significant influence over the operations of both companies.

An analysis of the retained earnings of each company for 20X6 is as follows:

	Todd	Meadow	Van
Balance January 1, 20X6	$240,000	$20,000	$40,000
Net income (loss)	104,600	36,000	(12,000)
Cash dividends paid	(40,000)	(16,000)	(9,000)
Balance December 31, 20X6	$304,600	$40,000	$19,000

Required

1 What entries should have been made on the books of Todd during 20X6 to record the following?
   a Investments in subsidiaries
   b Subsidiary dividends received
   c Parent's share of subsidiary income or loss
2 Compute the amount of minority interest in each subsidiary's stockholders' equity at December 31, 20X6.
3 What amount should be reported as consolidated retained earnings of Todd Corporation and subsidiaries as of December 31, 20X6?
4 Compute the correct balances of Todd's investment in Meadow and investment in Van accounts at December 31, 20X6.

P 3-9 Pansy Corporation purchased 90% of Snowdrop Corporation's outstanding stock for $3,000,000 cash on January 1, 20X2 when Snowdrop's stockholders' equity consisted of $2,000,000 capital stock and $700,000 retained earnings. The $570,000 excess *was allocated* $350,000 to undervalued equipment with a seven-year remaining useful life, and $220,000 to goodwill that is amortized over 10 years. Snowdrop's net income and dividends for 20X2 were $500,000 and $200,000, respectively. Comparative balance sheet data for Pansy and Snowdrop corporations at December 31, 20X2 are as follows:

	Pansy	Snowdrop
Cash	$ 300,000	$ 200,000
Receivables—net	600,000	400,000
Dividends receivable	90,000	—
Inventory	700,000	600,000
Land	600,000	700,000
Buildings—net	2,000,000	1,000,000
Equipment—net	1,500,000	800,000
Investment in Snowdrop	3,198,000	—
	$8,988,000	$3,700,000
Accounts payable	$ 300,000	$ 600,000
Dividends payable	500,000	100,000
Capital stock	7,000,000	2,000,000
Retained earnings	1,188,000	1,000,000
	$8,988,000	$3,700,000

Required: Prepare consolidated balance sheet working papers for Pansy Corporation and Subsidiary on December 31, 20X2.

P 3-10 The consolidated balance sheet of Pandora Corporation and its 80% subsidiary, Snaplock Corporation, contains the following items on December 31, 20X6:

Cash	$ 20,000
Inventories	180,000
Other current assets	70,000
Plant assets—net	270,000
Goodwill from consolidation	60,000
	$600,000
Liabilities	$120,000
Capital stock	400,000
Retained earnings	30,000
Minority interests	50,000
	$600,000

Pandora Corporation uses the equity method of accounting for its investment in Snaplock. Snaplock Corporation stock was acquired by Pandora on January 1, 20X2 when Snaplock's capital stock was $200,000 and its retained earnings was $20,000. The fair values of Snaplock's net assets were equal to their book values on January 1, 20X2, and there have been no changes in outstanding stock of either Pandora or Snaplock since January 1, 20X2.

Goodwill is being amortized over a 20-year period.

Required: Determine the following:

1 The purchase price of Pandora's investment in Snaplock stock on January 1, 20X2.
2 The total of Snaplock's stockholders' equity on December 31, 20X6.
3 The balance of Pandora's investment in Snaplock account at December 31, 20X6.
4 The balances of Pandora's retained earnings and capital stock accounts on December 31, 20X6.

P 3-11 Pope Corporation acquired a 70% interest in Stubb Corporation on January 1, 20X3 for $670,000, when Stubb's stockholders' equity consisted of $500,000 capital stock and $300,000 retained earnings. On this date, the book value of Stubb's assets and liabilities was equal to the fair value, except for inventories that were undervalued by $20,000 and sold in 20X3, and plant assets that were undervalued by $80,000 and had a remaining useful life of eight years from January 1. Any goodwill is amortized over 20 years. Stubb's net income and dividends for 20X3 were $70,000 and $10,000, respectively.

Separate company balance sheet information for Pope and Stubb corporations at December 31, 20X3 follows:

	Pope	Stubb
Cash	$ 60,000	$ 20,000
Accounts receivable—customers	440,000	200,000
Accounts receivable from Pope	—	10,000
Dividends receivable	7,000	—
Inventories	500,000	320,000
Land	100,000	150,000
Plant assets—net	700,000	350,000
Investment in Stubb	689,000	—
	$2,496,000	$1,050,000
Accounts payable—suppliers	$ 300,000	$ 80,000
Account payable to Stubb	10,000	—
Dividends payable	40,000	10,000
Long-term debt	600,000	100,000
Capital stock	1,000,000	500,000
Retained earnings	546,000	360,000
	$2,496,000	$1,050,000

Required: Prepare consolidated balance sheet working papers for Pope Corporation and Subsidiary at December 31, 20X3.

P 3-12 A summary of changes in Pendleton Corporation's investment in Shasti account from January 1, 20X4 to December 31, 20X6 follows:

INVESTMENT IN SHASTI (80%)

January 1, 20X4 Cost	$760,000		
Income—20X4	60,000	Dividends —20X4	$ 32,000
—20X5	76,000	—20X5	40,000
—20X6	92,000	—20X6	48,000
		to balance	868,000√
	$988,000		$988,000
December 31, 20X6			
Balance forward	$868,000		

Additional Information

1 Pendleton acquired its 80% interest in Shasti Corporation when Shasti had capital stock of $600,000 and retained earnings of $300,000.
2 Dividends declared by Shasti Corporation in each of the years 20X4, 20X5, and 20X6 were equal to 50% of Shasti Corporation's reported net income.
3 Shasti Corporation's assets and liabilities were stated at their fair values on January 1, 20X4.

Required: Compute the following amounts:

1 Shasti Corporation's dividends declared in 20X5
2 Shasti Corporation's net income for 20X5
3 Unamortized goodwill at December 31, 20X5
4 Minority interest income for 20X6

5 Minority interest at December 31, 20X6

6 Consolidated net income for 20X6, assuming that Pendleton's separate income for 20X6 is $280,000

P 3-13 Separate balance sheets for Peyton Corporation and Sidney Corporation at December 31, 20X7 are as follows:

	Peyton	Sidney
Assets		
Cash	$ 50,000	$ 20,000
Other current assets	150,000	80,000
Land	300,000	50,000
Buildings	600,000	200,000
Less: Accumulated depreciation	(200,000)	(50,000)
	$900,000	$300,000
Liabilities and Stockholders' Equity		
Current liabilities	$100,000	$ 50,000
Common stock, $10 par	600,000	100,000
Additional paid-in capital	60,000	75,000
Retained earnings	140,000	75,000
	$900,000	$300,000

Peyton issued 10,000 shares of its own common stock with a market value of $300,000 on January 2, 20X8 in exchange for 80% of Sidney's outstanding stock. All of Sidney's assets and liabilities were recorded at their fair values, except for buildings that had a fair value of $170,000 and a remaining useful life of five years.

Required

1 At what amount would each of the following items appear in Peyton's consolidated balance sheet prepared on January 2, 20X8, immediately after the business combination?

  a Total current assets

  b Total plant and equipment (land and buildings less accumulated depreciation)

  c Common stock

  d Additional paid-in capital

  e Retained earnings

2 Assume that Sidney has net income of $40,000 and pays dividends of $20,000 during 20X8, and that Peyton has income from its own operations (does not include investment income) of $90,000 during 20X8 and pays dividends of $50,000. Determine the correct amounts for each of the following:

  a Peyton's income from Sidney for 20X8

  b Peyton's investment in Sidney account at December 31, 20X8

  c Consolidated net income for 20X8

  d Consolidated retained earnings at December 31, 20X8

  e Minority interest at December 31, 20X8

P 3-14 Portland Corporation purchased 80% of the voting common stock of Sidney Corporation for $2,760,000 cash on January 2, 20X3. On this date, before combination, the book value and fair value of Portland and Sidney were as follows:

	Portland Corporation		Sidney Corporation	
	Book Value	Fair Value	Book Value	Fair Value
Cash	$ 3,000,000	$ 3,000,000	$ 60,000	$ 60,000
Receivables—net	800,000	800,000	200,000	200,000
Inventories	1,100,000	1,200,000	400,000	500,000
Other current assets	900,000	900,000	150,000	200,000
Land	3,100,000	4,000,000	500,000	600,000
Buildings—net	6,000,000	8,000,000	1,000,000	1,800,000
Equipment—net	3,500,000	4,500,000	800,000	600,000
	$18,400,000	$22,400,000	$3,110,000	$3,960,000
Accounts payable	$ 400,000	$ 400,000	$ 200,000	$ 200,000
Other liabilities	1,500,000	1,600,000	610,000	560,000
Capital stock, $10 par	15,000,000		2,000,000	
Retained earnings	1,500,000		300,000	
	$18,400,000		$3,110,000	

Required

    1 Prepare a schedule showing how the excess of Portland's investment cost over book value acquired should be allocated.

    2 Prepare a consolidated balance sheet.

P 3-15 Use the information in Problem 3–14, except change the amount of cash that Portland Corporation paid for the 80% interest in Sidney Corporation to $1,660,000. [*Hint:* Portland's $3,000,000 cash less $1,660,000 paid for the 80% interest in Sidney equals $1,340,000. Portland's cash of $1,340,000 plus Sidney's cash of $60,000 equals $1,400,000 consolidated cash, rather than the $300,000 consolidated cash ($240,000 + $60,000) in Problem 3–14.]

Required

    1 Prepare a schedule to allocate the cost/book value differential.

    2 Prepare a consolidated balance sheet immediately after the business combination.

P 3-16 Penguin Corporation and Salty Corporation consummate a business combination on December 31, 20X8, with Penguin exchanging its previously unissued $10 par common shares for common stock held by Salty's stockholders. The combination meets all the requirements for a pooling of interests, and the companies expect to continue their own operations in a parent company-subsidiary relationship. Summary balance sheet data for the two companies at December 31, 20X8 are as follows:

	Penguin	Salty
Assets		
Current assets	$ 8,000,000	$4,000,000
Plant assets	12,000,000	3,000,000
Total assets	$20,000,000	$7,000,000
Liabilities and Stockholders' Equity		
Current liabilities	$ 1,000,000	$2,000,000
Long-term liabilities	3,000,000	—
Common stock, $10 par	10,000,000	3,000,000
Additional paid-in capital	1,000,000	1,500,000
Retained earnings	5,000,000	500,000
Total equities	$20,000,000	$7,000,000

Required: Prepare a partial balance sheet showing consolidated stockholders' equity for Penguin Corporation and Subsidiary at December 31, 20X8 immediately after the pooling of interests under each of the following assumptions:

    1 Penguin issues 300,000 shares of its common stock for all the outstanding shares of Salty Corporation.

    2 Penguin issues 500,000 shares of its common stock for all the outstanding shares of Salty Corporation.

    3 Penguin issues 300,000 shares of its common stock for 90% of the outstanding shares of Salty Corporation.

    4 Penguin issues 500,000 shares of its common stock for 90% of the outstanding shares of Salty Corporation.

4

Consolidation Techniques and Procedures

This chapter examines procedures for consolidating the financial statements of parent and subsidiary companies. Some differences in the consolidation process result from different methods of parent company accounting for its subsidiary investments. Consolidation working papers for a parent company/investor that uses the equity method of accounting are illustrated first to set the standard for good consolidation procedures. Next, the illustrations are repeated for an incomplete equity method and the cost method of parent company accounting. Subsequently, the chapter examines additional complexities that arise from errors and omissions in the separate company records and detailed allocations of cost/book value differentials. The final section of the chapter illustrates the trial balance working paper format, which is an alternative to the financial statement format used in other sections of the chapter.

Chapter 3 presented the balance sheet working papers used to organize the information needed for consolidated balance sheets. By contrast, this chapter presents working papers that develop the information needed for consolidated balance sheets and income and retained earnings statements. A consolidated statement of cash flows is illustrated in the appendix to this chapter.

CONSOLIDATION UNDER THE EQUITY METHOD

Basic procedures used to consolidate the financial statements of affiliated companies are explained in conjunction with the following example of a parent company that uses the equity method of accounting for its subsidiary. Subsequently, the example is changed to illustrate differences in consolidation procedures that arise when the parent company accounts for its subsidiary under an incomplete equity method and the cost method.

Equity Method—Year of Acquisition

Prep Corporation pays $87,000 for 80% of the outstanding voting stock of Snap Corporation on January 1, 20X5 when Snap Corporation's stockholders' equity consists of $60,000 capital stock and $30,000 retained earnings. The $15,000 excess of investment cost over book value acquired [$87,000 − ($90,000 × 80%)] is allocated to goodwill with a 10-year amortization period, and Snap's net income and dividends are as follows:

	20X5	20X6
Net income	$25,000	$30,000
Dividends	15,000	15,000

Financial statements for Prep and Snap corporations for 20X5 are presented in the first two working paper columns of Exhibit 4–1. Prep's $18,500 income from Snap for 20X5 consists of 80% of Snap's $25,000 net income for 20X5 less $1,500 goodwill amortization. Its $93,500 investment in Snap account at December 31, 20X5 consists of $87,000 investment cost plus $18,500 income from Snap, less $12,000 dividends received from Snap during 20X5.

Numerous consolidation approaches and any number of different adjustment and elimination combinations will result in correct amounts for the consolidated financial statements. The adjustment and elimination entries that appear in the working papers *do not affect the general ledger accounts of either the parent or its subsidiaries.* Adjusting or eliminating accounts or balances simply means that the amounts listed in the separate company columns of the working papers are either (1) adjusted before inclusion in the consolidated statement column or (2) eliminated and do not appear in the consolidated statement column. A single working paper entry often adjusts some items and eliminates others. It is the objective of the working paper entry, not its classification as adjusting or eliminating, that is important in developing working paper skills and in understanding the consolidation process.

The checkmarks beside the net income and ending retained earnings amounts in the separate statement columns of Exhibit 4–1 are intended as reminders that these items are not subject to adjustment or elimination. This is because consolidated net income consists of consolidated revenues less consolidated expenses, and if adjustments are needed, they should relate to individual revenue and expense items rather than net income. Similarly, the retained earnings amount that appears in the consolidated balance sheet consists of beginning consolidated retained earnings plus consolidated net income less parent company dividends. If errors or omissions have occurred such that parent company retained earnings and consolidated retained earnings are not equal, the amount of the parent company's beginning retained earnings is corrected through working paper entries to adjust it to beginning consolidated retained earnings. Parent company net income and retained earnings amounts under the equity method are equal to consolidated net income and retained earnings, so retained earnings adjustments are needed only when the parent company fails to apply the equity method as a one-line consolidation. Because Prep Corporation (Exhibit 4–1) has applied the equity method correctly, its net income of $68,500 is equal to consolidated net income, and both its beginning and ending retained earnings amounts are equal to the $5,000 and $43,500 consolidated retained earnings amounts, respectively.

The first entry in the Exhibit 4–1 working paper is journalized as:

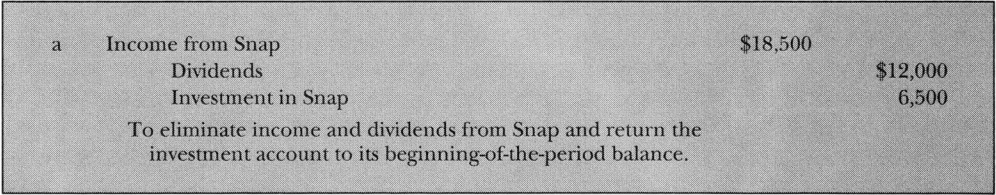

a	Income from Snap	$18,500	
	Dividends		$12,000
	Investment in Snap		6,500

To eliminate income and dividends from Snap and return the investment account to its beginning-of-the-period balance.

Recall that working paper entries are shaded to avoid confusion with journal entries that are recorded by parent companies and subsidiaries. Investment income is eliminated because the consolidated income statement shows the details of revenue and expense rather than the one-line consolidation reflected in the income from Snap account. Dividends received from the subsidiary are eliminated because they are mere transfers within the consolidated entity for which the statements are being prepared. The difference between income from subsidiary recognized on the books of

PREP CORPORATION AND SUBSIDIARY
CONSOLIDATION WORKING PAPERS
FOR THE YEAR ENDED DECEMBER 31, 20X5

	Prep	80% Snap	Adjustments and Eliminations	Minority Interest	Consolidated Statements
Income Statement Revenue	$250,000	$ 65,000			$315,000
Income from Snap	18,500		a 18,500		
Expenses	(200,000)	(40,000)	c 1,500		(241,500)
Minority interest income ($25,000 × 20%)				$ 5,000	(5,000)
Net income	$ 68,500	$ 25,000			$ 68,500
Retained Earnings Retained earnings—Prep	$ 5,000				$ 5,000
Retained earnings—Snap		$ 30,000	b 30,000		
Add: Net income	68,500√	25,000√			68,500
Deduct: Dividends	(30,000)	(15,000)	a 12,000	(3,000)	(30,000)
Retained earnings December 31, 20X5	$ 43,500	$ 40,000			$ 43,500
Balance Sheet Cash	$ 40,000	$ 10,000			$ 50,000
Other current assets	90,000	50,000			140,000
Investment in Snap	93,500		a 6,500 b 87,000		
Plant and equipment	300,000	100,000			400,000
Accumulated depreciation	(50,000)	(30,000)			(80,000)
Goodwill			b 15,000 c 1,500		13,500
	$473,500	$130,000			$523,500
Liabilities	$ 80,000	$ 30,000			$110,000
Capital stock	350,000	60,000	b 60,000		350,000
Retained earnings	43,500√	40,000√			43,500
	$473,500	$130,000			
Minority interest January 1, 20X5 ($90,000 × 20%)			b 18,000	18,000	
Minority interest December 31, 20X5				$20,000	20,000
					$523,500

Exhibit 4–1 *Equity Method—Working Papers for Year of Acquisition*

the parent company and the dividends received represents the change in the investment account for the period. The $6,500 credit to the investment in Snap account reduces that account to its $87,000 beginning-of-the-period balance and thereby establishes reciprocity between the investment in Snap and Snap's stockholders' equity at January 1, 20X5.

Working paper entry b from Exhibit 4–1 is journalized as follows:

b	Retained earnings—Snap (beginning)	$30,000	
	Capital stock—Snap	60,000	
	Goodwill	15,000	
	Investment in Snap		$87,000
	Minority interest		18,000

To eliminate reciprocal equity and investment balances, establish beginning minority interest, and enter unamortized goodwill.

This entry eliminates reciprocal investment and equity balances, enters the unamortized excess of investment cost over book value acquired as of the beginning of the year, and constructs beginning minority interest ($90,000 × 20%) as a separate item. Observe that entry b eliminates reciprocal investment and equity balances as of the beginning of the period and enters minority interest as of the same date. Therefore, the goodwill (cost/book value differential) portion of the entry is also a beginning-of-the-period unamortized amount.

Many accountants prefer to eliminate only the parent's percentage of the capital stock and retained earnings of the subsidiary and to transfer the amount not eliminated directly to the minority interest column. Although the difference is solely a matter of preference, the approach used here emphasizes that all the individual stockholders' equity accounts of a subsidiary are eliminated in the process of consolidation.

Entry c in the working papers of Exhibit 4–1 enters the current year's goodwill amortization as an expense of the consolidated entity and reduces unamortized goodwill from its $15,000 unamortized balance at January 1 to its $13,500 unamortized balance at December 31, 20X5.

c	Expenses	$ 1,500	
	Goodwill		$ 1,500

To enter current amortization of goodwill.

This working paper entry to adjust consolidated expenses is needed even though Prep Corporation amortized goodwill on its separate books under the equity method. Prep's amortization of the goodwill is reflected in its income from Snap account, and working paper entry a eliminated that account for consolidation purposes in order to disaggregate the revenue and expense components in reporting consolidated income.

Sequence of Working Paper Entries

The sequence of the working paper entries in Exhibit 4–1 is both logical and necessary. Entry a adjusts the investment in Snap for changes during 20X5, and entry b eliminates the investment in Snap after adjustment to its beginning-of-the-period balance in entry a. Entry b also enters unamortized goodwill in the working papers as of the beginning of the period. Subsequently, entry c amortizes the goodwill for the current period and reduces the asset goodwill to its unamortized amount at the balance sheet date. As additional complexities of consolidation are encountered, the sequence of working paper adjustments and eliminations is expanded to the following:

1 Adjustments for errors and omissions in the separate parent company and subsidiary statements
2 Adjustments to eliminate intercompany profits and losses
3 Adjustments to eliminate income and dividends from subsidiary and adjust the investment in subsidiary to its beginning-of-the-period balance
4 Eliminations of reciprocal investment in subsidiary and subsidiary equity balances
5 Allocation and amortization of cost/book value differentials (from step 4)
6 Elimination of other reciprocal balances (intercompany receivables and payables, revenues and expenses, and so on)

Although other sequences of working paper entries may be adequate in a given consolidation, the above sequence will always work. It is recommended that you learn it and apply it throughout your study of consolidation.

After all adjustments and eliminations are entered in the working papers, the minority interest in subsidiary net income is computed and entered as an addition in the minority interest column (deduction for loss) and a deduction in the consolidated income statement (addition for loss). The $3,000 dividends of Snap that are not eliminated reflect dividends paid to minority stockholders and are carried to the minority interest column as a deduction. The minority interest reflected in the consolidated balance sheet is computed in the working papers as beginning minority interest plus minority interest income less minority interest dividends. In case the ownership in a subsidiary increases during a period, the minority interest computation will reflect the minority interest at the balance sheet date, with minority interest income and dividends also reflecting the ending minority interest percentages.

Some accountants prefer to use a working paper entry for inserting the minority interest income and dividend items into the consolidation worksheet. For example, these items for the Prep-Snap consolidation could have been incorporated with the following working paper entry:

Minority interest income	$5,000	
Dividends		$3,000
Minority interest		2,000

This approach explains all minority interest components through consolidation working paper entries, but it tends to increase the size of the spreadsheet. Note that the investment in subsidiary balances are always eliminated when a subsidiary is consolidated. Although the investment in subsidiary account may be adjusted to establish reciprocity, it never appears in a consolidated balance sheet when the subsidiary accounts are consolidated. Likewise, investment income from subsidiaries that are consolidated is always eliminated. Consolidated net income is computed by deducting consolidated expenses and minority interest income from consolidated revenues. It is *not* determined by adjusting the separate net incomes of parent and subsidiary. Note the arrows from the consolidated income statement to the consolidated retained earnings statement and from the consolidated retained earnings statement to the consolidated balance sheet in Exhibit 4–1. These arrows simply indicate that consolidated net income is determined from consolidated revenue and expense and carried to the consolidated retained earnings statement, and the consolidated retained earnings is carried to the consolidated balance sheet.

Consolidated retained earnings at the end of the period is computed in the working papers as the sum of beginning consolidated retained earnings and consolidated net income less parent company dividends. If a complete equity method of accounting has been used, beginning consolidated retained earnings will equal beginning parent company retained earnings. In the absence of a correct equity method of accounting, the beginning retained earnings of the parent must be adjusted in years after the year of acquisition to convert it to beginning consolidated retained earnings. Capital stock and other paid-in capital accounts appearing in a consolidated balance sheet are those of the parent company.

Equity Method—Year Subsequent to Acquisition

Prep Corporation maintains its 80% ownership interest in Snap throughout 20X6, recording income from Snap of $22,500 for the year (80% of Snap's $30,000 net income less $1,500 goodwill amortization). At December 31, 20X6, Prep's investment in Snap account has a balance of $104,000, determined as follows:

Investment cost January 1, 20X5	$ 87,000
Income from Snap—20X5	18,500
Dividends from Snap—20X5	−12,000
Investment in Snap December 31, 20X5	93,500
Income from Snap—20X6	22,500
Dividends from Snap—20X6	−12,000
Investment in Snap December 31, 20X6	$104,000

The only intercompany transaction between Prep and Snap during 20X6 was a $10,000 noninterest-bearing loan to Snap during the third quarter of the year.

Consolidation working papers for Prep Corporation and Subsidiary for the year 20X6 are presented in Exhibit 4–2.

There were no errors or omissions or intercompany profits relating to the consolidation, so the first working paper entry is to eliminate income and dividends from Snap as follows:

a	Income from Snap	$22,500	
	Dividends		$12,000
	Investment in Snap		10,500
	To eliminate income and dividends from Snap and return the investment account to its beginning-of-the-period balance.		

This entry adjusts the investment in Snap account to its $93,500 December 31, 20X5 balance and establishes reciprocity with Snap's stockholders' equity at December 31, 20X5.

Entry b eliminates investment in Snap and stockholders' equity of Snap as follows:

b	Retained earnings—Snap	$40,000	
	Capital stock—Snap	60,000	
	Goodwill	13,500	
	Investment in Snap		$93,500
	Minority interest		20,000
	To eliminate reciprocal investment and equity balances, establish beginning minority interest, and enter unamortized goodwill.		

Entry b eliminates the investment in Snap and stockholders' equity of Snap amounts at December 31, 20X5 and enters the minority interest at December 31, 20X5, therefore the $13,500 investment cost/book value difference reflects unamortized goodwill at December 31, 20X5. Thus, entry c amortizes this amount to the $12,000 balance at December 31, 20X6.

c	Expenses	$ 1,500	
	Goodwill		$ 1,500
	To enter current goodwill amortization.		

The final working paper entry eliminates intercompany notes payable and notes receivable balances because the amounts are not assets and liabilities of the consolidated entity.

d	Note payable—Prep	$10,000	
	Note receivable—Snap		$10,000
	To eliminate reciprocal receivable and payable balances.		

The intercompany loan was noninterest bearing, so the note receivable and the note payable are the only reciprocal balances created by the intercompany transaction. Additional eliminations for reciprocal interest income and interest expense and interest receivable and interest payable balances would have been needed if the intercompany loan had been interest bearing.

Compare the consolidation working papers of Exhibit 4–2 with those of Exhibit 4–1. Notice that the December 31, 20X5 minority interest from Exhibit 4–1 is the beginning minority interest in Exhibit 4–2. Also note that the unamortized goodwill in the consolidated balance sheet of Exhibit 4–1 is the beginning-of-the-period unamortized goodwill in Exhibit 4–2.

PREP CORPORATION AND SUBSIDIARY
CONSOLIDATION WORKING PAPERS
FOR THE YEAR ENDED DECEMBER 31, 20X6

	Prep	80% Snap	Adjustments and Eliminations	Minority Interest	Consolidated Statements
Income Statement Revenue	$300,000	$ 75,000			$375,000
Income from Snap	22,500		a 22,500		
Expenses	(244,000)	(45,000)	c 1,500		(290,500)
Minority interest income ($30,000 × 20%)				$ 6,000	(6,000)
Net income	$ 78,500	$ 30,000			$ 78,500
Retained Earnings Retained earnings—Prep	$ 43,500				$ 43,500
Retained earnings—Snap		$ 40,000	b 40,000		
Net income	78,500√	30,000√			78,500
Dividends	(45,000)	(15,000)	a 12,000	(3,000)	(45,000)
Retained earnings December 31, 20X6	$ 77,000	$ 55,000			$ 77,000
Balance Sheet Cash	$ 46,000	$ 20,000			$ 66,000
Note receivable—Snap	10,000		d 10,000		
Other current assets	97,000	70,000			167,000
Investment in Snap	104,000		a 10,500 b 93,500		
Plant and equipment	300,000	100,000			400,000
Accumulated depreciation	(60,000)	(40,000)			(100,000)
Goodwill			b 13,500 c 1,500		12,000
	$497,000	$150,000			$545,000
Note payable—Prep		$ 10,000	d 10,000		
Liabilities	$ 70,000	25,000			$ 95,000
Capital stock	350,000	60,000	b 60,000		350,000
Retained earnings	77,000√	55,000√			77,000
	$497,000	$150,000			
Minority interest January 1, 20X6 ($100,000 × 20%)			b 20,000	20,000	
Minority interest December 31, 20X6				$23,000	23,000
					$545,000

Exhibit 4–2   *Equity Method—Working Papers for Year Subsequent to Acquisition*

CONSOLIDATION UNDER AN INCOMPLETE EQUITY METHOD

When the equity method is correctly applied, the parent company's net income is equal to consolidated net income, and the parent company's retained earnings is equal to consolidated retained earnings. This equality of parent company and consolidated income and retained earnings amounts does not always exist. It is absent when the equity method is applied incorrectly, or when the cost method of accounting for subsidiary investments is used. For example, a parent company, in applying the equity method of accounting, may not amortize the difference between investment cost and book value acquired on its separate books, or it may not eliminate intercompany profits or losses. Such omissions result in an incomplete application of the equity method of accounting.[1] Other errors in applying the equity method of accounting result in similar misstatements of parent company income and retained earnings.

The problem of a misapplication of the equity method of accounting or use of the cost method in accounting for subsidiary investments may not be as serious as it first appears because the accountant must prepare correct consolidated financial statements, regardless of how the parent company accounts for its subsidiary investment. There is no violation of generally accepted accounting principles as long as the consolidated financial statements prepared for issuance to stockholders are correct and the parent/investor company issues no other audited financial statements. The continued use of either the cost method or an incomplete application of the equity method of accounting by many firms is based on the assumed issuance of consolidated financial statements as the only statements prepared for stockholders of the primary reporting entity. When bankers require audited, parent company financial statements to support lines of credit and long-term loans, the statements should reflect the equity method as a one-line consolidation.

Incomplete Equity Method—Year of Acquisition

To illustrate consolidation procedures under an incomplete equity method, assume the same information from the Prep-Snap illustration, except that Prep has not amortized goodwill on its separate books. Prep's income statement for 20X5 would show income from Snap of $20,000 and net income of $70,000, rather than $18,500 and $68,500 shown under the equity method in Exhibit 4–1. This same $1,500 difference is reflected in Prep's investment in Snap account ($95,000 rather than $93,500) and Prep's retained earnings ($45,000 instead of $43,500) at December 31, 20X5.

One of the first things that the accountant does in consolidating the financial statements of affiliated companies is determine how the parent company has accounted for its subsidiary investment(s). A simple check of the relationship between the parent company's equity in the subsidiary's net income and the income recognized by the subsidiary will usually reveal the parent company's method of accounting. The fact that Prep's $20,000 income from Snap is equal to 80% of Snap's $25,000 net income for 20X5 provides evidence of an incomplete equity method. Further evidence lies in the fact that Prep's investment in Snap account of $95,000 at December 31, 20X5 is $15,000 greater than the underlying equity ($100,000 × 80%) on that date, indicating that no goodwill amortization has occurred.

Conversion to Equity Method Approach   One approach to preparing consolidation working papers when the parent company has not accounted for its subsidiary by the equity method is to convert the parent company's accounts to the equity method as the first working paper entry. The remaining working paper entries would be the same as if the equity method had been used. If Prep uses an incomplete equity method, the first entry in the working papers is a conversion to the equity method:

Income from Snap	$1,500	
Investment in Snap		$1,500
To correct for the omission of goodwill amortization on Prep's books.		

---

[1]Incomplete applications of the equity method are frequently encountered in textbook problems and illustrations and on CPA examinations.

This entry converts the parent company's accounts to the equity method, after which the other working paper entries for 20X5 would be the same as those illustrated in Exhibit 4–1 under the equity method. The working paper entry illustrated above could also be recorded on Prep's separate records to adjust to the equity method as a one-line consolidation. If Prep's books have been closed for 20X5, the correcting entry on Prep's books would be a debit to retained earnings and a credit to investment in Snap for $1,500.

Traditional Approach   Consolidation working papers may be prepared without an initial conversion to the equity method. Exhibit 4–3 shows consolidation working papers for Prep Corporation and Subsidiary for 20X5 under an incomplete equity method and no conversion to the equity method.

The consolidation working paper entries for 20X5 from Exhibit 4–3 are reproduced in journal form as follows:

a	Income from Snap	$20,000	
	Dividends		$12,000
	Investment in Snap		8,000
	To establish reciprocity as of the beginning of the period.		
b	Retained earnings—Snap	$30,000	
	Capital stock—Snap	60,000	
	Goodwill	15,000	
	Investment in Snap		$87,000
	Minority interest		18,000
	To eliminate reciprocal equity and investment amounts, establish minority interest at the beginning of the period, and set up the original goodwill at acquisition.		
c	Expenses	$ 1,500	
	Goodwill		$ 1,500
	To adjust expenses to reflect current goodwill amortization.		

Compare the working paper entries in Exhibit 4–3 with those in Exhibit 4–1 under the equity method. Notice that the entries and amounts are the same except for entry a, where the $20,000 debit to income from Snap does not include goodwill amortization, and the $8,000 credit to investment in Snap simply reflects the investment increase for 20X5 as reported on Prep's books. Even so, the objective of that entry is the same as the comparable working paper entry in Exhibit 4–1—to eliminate investment income and dividends received, and to adjust the investment account to its beginning-of-the-period balance.

Prep's failure to amortize goodwill in accounting for its investment in Snap has a minimal effect on the consolidation working papers for 20X5 because Prep's January 1, 20X5 investment in Snap ($87,000) and retained earnings ($5,000) are not affected by the omission. The omission does, of course, create an inequality between Prep's net income ($70,000) and consolidated net income ($68,500), and between Prep's retained earnings ($45,000) and consolidated retained earnings ($43,500) at December 31, 20X5. Consolidated financial statements are unaffected by the parent company's method of accounting for its investment, so the consolidated financial statements for an incomplete equity method (Exhibit 4–3) are identical with those prepared under a correct equity method (Exhibit 4–1).

Incomplete Equity Method—Year Subsequent to Acquisition

Application of the incomplete equity method has a greater effect on consolidation working paper procedures in years subsequent to the year of acquisition because the omissions affect beginning investment and retained earnings amounts on the parent company's books. Prep's investment in Snap account at December 31, 20X6 is $107,000, compared with $104,000 in Exhibit 4–2 under the equity method. This $3,000 difference reflects the omission of goodwill amortization for both 20X5 and 20X6. The omissions affect Prep's beginning retained earnings in 20X6 by $1,500 ($45,000 rather than $43,500), and ending retained earnings in 20X6 by $3,000 ($80,000 instead of $77,000).

PREP CORPORATION AND SUBSIDIARY
CONSOLIDATION WORKING PAPERS
FOR THE YEAR ENDED DECEMBER 31, 20X5

	Prep	80% Snap	Adjustments and Eliminations	Minority Interest	Consolidated Statements
Income Statement					
Revenue	$250,000	$ 65,000			$315,000
Income from Snap	20,000		a 20,000		
Expenses	(200,000)	(40,000)	c 1,500		(241,500)
Minority interest income ($25,000 × 20%)				$ 5,000	(5,000)
Net income	$ 70,000	$ 25,000			$ 68,500
Retained Earnings					
Retained earnings—Prep	$ 5,000				$ 5,000
Retained earnings—Snap		$ 30,000	b 30,000		
Add: Net income	70,000√	25,000√			68,500
Deduct: Dividends	(30,000)	(15,000)	a 12,000	(3,000)	(30,000)
Retained earnings December 31, 20X5	$ 45,000	40,000			$ 43,500
Balance Sheet					
Cash	$ 40,000	$ 10,000			$ 50,000
Other current assets	90,000	50,000			140,000
Investment in Snap	95,000		a 8,000 b 87,000		
Plant and equipment	300,000	100,000			400,000
Accumulated depreciation	(50,000)	(30,000)			(80,000)
Goodwill			b 15,000 c 1,500	1,500	13,500
	$475,000	$130,000			$523,500
Liabilities	$ 80,000	$ 30,000			$110,000
Capital stock	350,000	60,000	b 60,000		350,000
Retained earnings	45,000√	40,000√			43,500
	$475,000	$130,000			
Minority interest January 1, 20X5 ($90,000 × 20%)			b 18,000	18,000	
Minority interest December 31, 20X5				$20,000	20,000
					$523,500

Exhibit 4–3   *Incomplete Equity Method—Working Papers for Year of Acquisition*

Conversion to the Equity Method Approach   Consolidation working papers for 20X6 can be prepared by converting the parent company's accounts to the equity method as the first entry in the consolidation process. A first working paper entry corrects for the omissions on Prep's books as follows:

a	Income from Snap	$ 1,500	
	Retained earnings—Prep	1,500	
	Investment in Snap		$ 3,000
	To correct income from Snap for the omission of the current year's goodwill amortization and correct Prep's beginning retained earnings for prior years' goodwill amortization.		

After this conversion to equity working paper entry, the other entries would be the same as those illustrated in Exhibit 4–2. Assuming that Prep's books have been closed at December 31, 20X6, Prep could convert to the equity method as of January 1, 20X7, with a $3,000 correcting entry to debit retained earnings and credit the investment in Snap account.

Traditional Approach   Exhibit 4–4 shows the consolidation working papers for Prep and Snap that are prepared without an initial conversion to the equity method. Although the consolidated financial statements presented in Exhibit 4–4 are identical with those shown in Exhibit 4–2 under the equity method, a working paper change is necessary.

The working paper entries for 20X6 in journal form are as follows:

a	Income from Snap	$24,000	
	Dividends		$12,000
	Investment in Snap		12,000
	To establish reciprocity as of the beginning of the period.		
b	Retained earnings—Snap	$40,000	
	Capital stock—Snap	60,000	
	Goodwill	15,000	
	Investment in Snap		$95,000
	Minority interest		20,000
	To eliminate reciprocal equity and investment amounts, establish minority interest at the beginning of the period, and set up the original goodwill at acquisition.		
c	Expenses	$ 1,500	
	Retained earnings—Prep	1,500	
	Goodwill		$ 3,000
	To adjust expenses to reflect current goodwill amortization and to charge Prep's retained earnings for goodwill amortization omitted in 20X5.		
d	Note payable—Prep	$10,000	
	Note receivable—Snap		$10,000
	To eliminate reciprocal note payable and receivable amounts.		

Entry a eliminates the income from Snap (as recognized on Prep's books) and the dividends received from Snap and adjusts the investment in Snap to its beginning-of-the-year amount on Prep's books. Entry b eliminates Snap's beginning-of-the-period equity balances and the investment in Snap at the beginning of the year and enters minority interest at its beginning-of-the-year amount. Because the goodwill (cost/book value differential) was not amortized by Prep, the debit to goodwill reflects the original goodwill, a difference that will remain as long as Prep uses the incomplete equity method. The fact that goodwill is amortized for consolidation purposes does not affect this generalization because working paper entries are not recorded on parent company books.

Entry c for 20X6 includes an additional $1,500 adjustment for 20X5 amortization that was not recorded by Prep. The $1,500 debit in 20X6 to Prep's retained earnings converts Prep's beginning retained earnings to beginning consolidated retained earnings. That is, it reduces Prep's December 31, 20X5 retained earnings of $45,000

PREP CORPORATION AND SUBSIDIARY
CONSOLIDATION WORKING PAPERS
FOR THE YEAR ENDED DECEMBER 31, 20X6

	Prep	80% Snap	Adjustments and Eliminations	Minority Interest	Consolidated Statements
Income Statement					
Revenue	$300,000	$ 75,000			$375,000
Income from Snap	24,000		a 24,000		
Expenses	(244,000)	(45,000)	c 1,500		(290,500)
Minority interest income ($30,000 × 20%)				$ 6,000	(6,000)
Net income	$ 80,000	$ 30,000			$ 78,500
Retained Earnings					
Retained earnings—Prep	$ 45,000		c 1,500		$ 43,500
Retained earnings—Snap		$ 40,000	b 40,000		
Net income	80,000√	30,000√			78,500
Dividends	(45,000)	(15,000)	a 12,000	(3,000)	(45,000)
Retained earnings December 31, 20X6	$ 80,000	$ 55,000			$ 77,000
Balance Sheet					
Cash	$ 46,000	$ 20,000			$ 66,000
Note receivable—Snap	10,000		d 10,000		
Other current assets	97,000	70,000			167,000
Investment in Snap	107,000		a 12,000 b 95,000		
Plant and equipment	300,000	100,000			400,000
Accumulated depreciation	(60,000)	(40,000)			(100,000)
Goodwill			b 15,000 c 3,000		12,000
	$500,000	$150,000			$545,000
Note payable—Prep		$ 10,000	d 10,000		
Liabilities	$ 70,000	25,000			$ 95,000
Capital stock	350,000	60,000	b 60,000		350,000
Retained earnings	80,000√	55,000√			77,000
	$500,000	$150,000			
Minority interest January 1, 20X6 ($100,000 × 20%)			b 20,000	20,000	
Minority interest December 31, 20X6				$23,000	23,000
					$545,000

Exhibit 4–4 Incomplete Equity Method—Working Papers for Year Subsequent to Acquisition

to consolidated retained earnings of $43,500, as shown in the consolidated balance sheet at December 31, 20X5. The $3,000 credit to goodwill in working paper entry c reflects two years' amortization and reduces goodwill to its $12,000 unamortized balance at December 31, 20X6. The last working paper entry to eliminate reciprocal notes payable and receivable balances is not affected by the method of parent company accounting for its subsidiaries.

CONSOLIDATION UNDER THE COST METHOD

The cost method of accounting for subsidiary investments emphasizes the concept of legal entity, as opposed to the equity method, which emphasizes the economic entity under control of a single management team. Under the cost method, income is recognized only when dividends are declared by the subsidiary. The investment account remains unchanged except when dividends reduce subsidiary retained earnings below retained earnings at the date of acquisition of the investment, or when significant and permanent subsidiary losses impair subsidiary capital. Dividend income rather than investment income appears on the parent company's income statement when the cost method is used.

Differences from applying the cost, incomplete equity, and equity methods are reflected in the parent company's investment in subsidiary (assets) and retained earnings (equities) balances. No other balance sheet accounts are affected.

Consolidation under the cost method can be accomplished in either of two ways. One approach for consolidating a subsidiary accounted for by the cost method is to use the conversion to equity method. The first consolidation working paper entry converts the statements to equity, after which the remaining working paper entries are the same as under the equity method. The other approach uses a set of traditional working paper entries to consolidate a parent company and its subsidiary accounted for by the cost method. The traditional approach begins with an entry to adjust the investment in subsidiary account for the parent company's share of subsidiary retained earnings increases since acquisition, and to credit parent company retained earnings for the same amount to convert beginning parent company retained earnings to beginning consolidated retained earnings. This adjustment is not needed for consolidations in the period of acquisition because the parent's beginning investment and retained earnings balances will not have been affected. A second entry eliminates reciprocal dividend income and dividends paid amounts, and a third entry eliminates reciprocal investment and equity balances and enters beginning-of-the-period goodwill and minority interest. The traditional method is easier to use for consolidations in the year of acquisition, but it gets complicated in years after acquisition, especially if there are intercompany transactions between the two affiliates. Both the conversion to equity approach and the traditional approach are illustrated for the Prep and Snap consolidation.

Cost Method—Conversion to Equity Approach

Year of Acquisition   Consolidation under the cost method can be accomplished by converting to the equity method in the first entry in the working papers. The remaining working paper entries are then the same as under the equity method. The cost-to-equity conversion in the year of acquisition is simplified by the fact that the investment is recorded at its cost. The entry on Prep's separate books in 20X5 to record dividend income of $12,000 fails to recognize its equity in Snap's undistributed income [80% × ($25,000 income − $15,000 dividends)] or to provide for the $1,500 goodwill amortization. Thus, Prep's dividend income from Snap of $12,000 and net income of $62,000 under the cost method are each understated by Prep's $6,500 equity in Snap's undistributed income less amortization for 20X5. The conversion to equity approach in the year of acquisition is illustrated in Exhibit 4–5.

Conversion to the equity method requires the following working paper entry:

a	Dividend income	$12,000	
	Investment in Snap	6,500	
	Income from Snap		$18,500
	To correct income and investment account for the cost method.		

PREP CORPORATION AND SUBSIDIARY
CONSOLIDATION WORKING PAPERS
FOR THE YEAR ENDED DECEMBER 31, 20X5

	Prep	80% Snap	Adjustments and Eliminations		Minority Interest	Consolidated Statements
Income Statement						
Revenue	$250,000	$ 65,000				$315,000
Dividend income	12,000		a 12,000			
Income from Snap			b 18,500	a 18,500		
Expenses	(200,000)	(40,000)	d 1,500			(241,500)
Minority interest income ($25,000 × 20%)					$ 5,000	(5,000)
Net income	$ 62,000	$ 25,000				$ 68,500
Retained Earnings						
Retained earnings—Prep	$ 5,000					$ 5,000
Retained earnings—Snap		$ 30,000	c 30,000			
Add: Net income	62,000√	25,000√				68,500
Deduct: Dividends	(30,000)	(15,000)		b 12,000	(3,000)	(30,000)
Retained earnings December 31, 20X5	$ 37,000	$ 40,000				$ 43,500
Balance Sheet						
Cash	$ 40,000	$ 10,000				$ 50,000
Other current assets	90,000	50,000				140,000
Investment in Snap	87,000		a 6,500	b 6,500 c 87,000		
Plant and equipment	300,000	100,000				400,000
Accumulated depreciation	(50,000)	(30,000)				(80,000)
Goodwill			c 15,000	d 1,500		13,500
	$467,000	$130,000				$523,500
Liabilities	$ 80,000	$ 30,000				$110,000
Capital stock	350,000	60,000	c 60,000			350,000
Retained earnings	37,000√	40,000√				43,500
	$467,000	$130,000				
Minority interest January 1, 20X5 ($90,000 × 20%)				c 18,000	18,000	
Minority interest December 31, 20X5					$20,000	20,000
						$523,500

Exhibit 4–5 *Cost Method—Year of Acquisition (Conversion to Equity)*

This entry enters income from Snap for 20X5 under the equity method, eliminates dividend income (distributed income from Snap), and adjusts the investment in Snap account for Prep's equity in undistributed income ($10,000 × 80%) less $1,500 goodwill amortization. If Prep chooses to adopt the equity method, this entry can be recorded in Prep's separate records to make the conversion.

The other working paper entries for 20X5 from Exhibit 4–5 are journalized as follows:

b	Income from Snap	$18,500	
	Dividends		$12,000
	Investment in Snap		6,500
	To eliminate income and dividends of Snap and return the investment account to its beginning-of-the-period balance.		
c	Retained earnings—Snap	$30,000	
	Capital stock—Snap	60,000	
	Goodwill	15,000	
	Investment in Snap		$87,000
	Minority interest		18,000
	To enter reciprocal investment and equity balances, establish beginning minority interest, and enter unamortized goodwill.		
d	Expenses	$ 1,500	
	Goodwill		$ 1,500
	To enter current goodwill amortization.		

A comparison of these last three working paper entries with those in Exhibit 4–1 shows that they are identical. Obviously, when the cost method is used, parent company net income and ending retained earnings ($62,000 and $37,000, respectively) are not equal to their consolidated financial statement counterparts because the parent has not taken up its share of the subsidiary's undistributed earnings, and it has not amortized the cost/book value differentials from the investment.

Year Subsequent to Acquisition   The cost-to-equity conversion in the consolidation working papers is more complex in periods after the year in which the subsidiary investment is acquired. This is because the parent's prior-year income was misstated by use of the cost method, which failed to recognize the parent's equity in any undistributed income of the subsidiary or to provide for amortization of cost/book value differentials. The balance sheet effect of the cost method is to misstate the investment in subsidiary and retained earnings balances at year-end by equal amounts. Thus, the cost-to-equity conversion in years after acquisition requires adjustments for prior-year effects to the investment in subsidiary and the parent's beginning retained earnings accounts. It also requires adjustment for those effects occurring in the year of consolidation (current period) to the investment in subsidiary and the income from subsidiary accounts. Exhibit 4–6 illustrates the cost-to-equity conversion approach for years subsequent to the year of acquisition.

The cost-to-equity conversion in the working papers for the Prep/Snap example for 20X6 is analyzed in terms of the components needed for conversion. Amounts that decrease the accounts are in parentheses.

	Prep's Retained Earnings 12/31/X5	Investment in Snap	Income from Snap	Dividend Income
Prior-Year Effect				
80% of Snap's $10,000 undistributed income for 20X5 (see note)	$ 8,000	$ 8,000		
Goodwill amortization—20X5	(1,500)	(1,500)		

(Continued)

	Prep's Retained Earnings 12/31/X5	Investment in Snap	Income from Snap	Dividend Income
Current-Year Effect				
Reclassify dividend income as investment decrease ($15,000 dividend × 80%)		(12,000)		$(12,000)
Equity in 20X6 income of Snap ($30,000 × 80%)		24,000	$24,000	
Goodwill amortization— 20X6		(1,500)	(1,500)	
20X6 working paper adjustments	$ 6,500	$ 17,000	$22,500	$(12,000)

Note: A corporation's undistributed earnings are reflected in its retained earnings balances. Therefore, the changes in a subsidiary's retained earnings from the date of its acquisition to a subsequent evaluation date are ordinarily the changes in a subsidiary's undistributed earnings for cost-to-equity conversions. In this example, the computation is 80% × ($40,000 retained earnings at December 31, 20X5 less $30,000 retained earnings at January 1, 20X5).

This analysis provides the basis for working paper entry a in the consolidation working papers of Prep Corporation and Subsidiary for 20X6 (see Exhibit 4–6).

a	Dividend income	$12,000	
	Investment in Snap	17,000	
	Income from Snap		$22,500
	Retained earnings—Prep		6,500
	To correct income and investment amounts to the equity basis.		

The other working paper entries for 20X6 are the same as those illustrated for the equity method in Exhibit 4–2. If the corporation chooses to convert from the cost to the equity method of parent company accounting, it can record entry a on its separate books before closing in 20X6. Alternatively, the entry to convert to the equity method after the books are closed at December 31, 20X6 would be a debit to the investment in Snap account and a credit to retained earnings for $17,000.

Cost Method—Traditional Approach

Year of Acquisition Consolidation procedures for the cost method using the *traditional approach* are illustrated in Exhibits 4–7 and 4–8 for Prep Corporation and its 80%-owned subsidiary, Snap Corporation. On the cost basis, Prep's investment in Snap remains at $87,000 throughout 20X5 and 20X6, and the only entries made by Prep are to record receipt of 80% of the dividends declared by Snap. The entry in 20X5 and again in 20X6 is:

Cash	$12,000	
Dividend income		$12,000
To record receipt of 80% of $15,000 dividends paid by Snap.		

The consolidated financial statements that appear in the working papers in Exhibit 4–7 are exactly the same as those shown in Exhibits 4–1 and 4–3, but the working paper entries are slightly different.

Entry a is journalized as follows:

a	Dividend income	$12,000	
	Dividends		$12,000
	To eliminate reciprocal dividend income and dividends paid to Prep.		

PREP CORPORATION AND SUBSIDIARY
CONSOLIDATION WORKING PAPERS
FOR THE YEAR ENDED DECEMBER 31, 20X6

	Prep	80% Snap	Adjustments and Eliminations		Minority Interest	Consolidated Statements
Income Statement Revenue	$300,000	$ 75,000				$375,000
Dividend income	12,000		a 12,000			
Income from Snap			b 22,500	a 22,500		
Expenses	(244,000)	(45,000)	d 1,500			(290,500)
Minority interest income ($30,000 × 20%)					$ 6,000	(6,000)
Net income	$ 68,000	$ 30,000				$ 78,500
Retained Earnings Retained earnings—Prep	$ 37,000			a 6,500		$ 43,500
Retained earnings—Snap		$ 40,000	c 40,000			
Net income	68,000√	30,000√				78,500
Dividends	(45,000)	(15,000)		b 12,000	(3,000)	(45,000)
Retained earnings December 31, 20X6	$ 60,000	$ 55,000				$ 77,000
Balance Sheet Cash	$ 46,000	$ 20,000				$ 66,000
Note receivable—Snap	10,000			e 10,000		
Other current assets	97,000	70,000				167,000
Investment in Snap	87,000		a 17,000	b 10,500 c 93,500		
Plant and equipment	300,000	100,000				400,000
Accumulated depreciation	(60,000)	(40,000)				(100,000)
Goodwill			c 13,500	d 1,500		12,000
	$480,000	$150,000				$545,000
Note payable—Prep		$ 10,000	e 10,000			
Liabilities	$ 70,000	25,000				$ 95,000
Capital stock	350,000	60,000	c 60,000			350,000
Retained earnings	60,000√	55,000√				77,000
	$480,000	$150,000				
Minority interest January 1, 20X6 ($100,000 × 20%)				c 20,000	20,000	
Minority interest December 31, 20X6					$23,000	23,000
						$545,000

Exhibit 4–6   *Cost Method—Year Subsequent to Acquisition (Conversion to Equity)*

PREP CORPORATION AND SUBSIDIARY
CONSOLIDATION WORKING PAPERS
FOR THE YEAR ENDED DECEMBER 31, 20X5

	Prep	80% Snap	Adjustments and Eliminations	Minority Interest	Consolidated Statements
Income Statement					
Revenue	$250,000	$ 65,000			$315,000
Dividend income	12,000		a 12,000		
Expenses	(200,000)	(40,000)	c 1,500		(241,500)
Minority interest income ($25,000 × 20%)				$ 5,000	(5,000)
Net income	$ 62,000	$ 25,000			$ 68,500
Retained Earnings					
Retained earnings—Prep	$ 5,000				$ 5,000
Retained earnings—Snap		$ 30,000	b 30,000		
Add: Net income	62,000√	25,000√			68,500
Deduct: Dividends	(30,000)	(15,000)	a 12,000	(3,000)	(30,000)
Retained earnings December 31, 20X5	$ 37,000	$ 40,000			$ 43,500
Balance Sheet					
Cash	$ 40,000	$ 10,000			$ 50,000
Other current assets	90,000	50,000			140,000
Investment in Snap	87,000		b 87,000		
Plant and equipment	300,000	100,000			400,000
Accumulated depreciation	(50,000)	(30,000)			(80,000)
Goodwill			b 15,000 c 1,500		13,500
	$467,000	$130,000			$523,500
Liabilities	$ 80,000	$ 30,000			$110,000
Capital stock	350,000	60,000	b 60,000		350,000
Retained earnings	37,000√	40,000√			43,500
	$467,000	$130,000			
Minority interest January 1, 20X5 ($90,000 × 20%)			b 18,000	18,000	
Minority interest December 31, 20X5				$20,000	20,000
					$523,500

Exhibit 4–7   *Cost Method—Year of Acquisition (Traditional Approach)*

**PREP CORPORATION AND SUBSIDIARY
CONSOLIDATION WORKING PAPERS
FOR THE YEAR ENDED DECEMBER 31, 20X6**

	Prep	80% Snap	Adjustments and Eliminations		Minority Interest	Consolidated Statements
Income Statement						
Revenue	$300,000	$ 75,000				$375,000
Dividend income	12,000		b 12,000			
Expenses	(244,000)	(45,000)	d 1,500			(290,500)
Minority interest income ($30,000 × 20%)					$ 6,000	(6,000)
Net income	$ 68,000	$ 30,000				$ 78,500
Retained Earnings						
Retained earnings—Prep	$ 37,000		d 1,500	a 8,000		$ 43,500
Retained earnings—Snap		$ 40,000	c 40,000			
Net income	68,000√	30,000√				78,500
Dividends	(45,000)	(15,000)		b 12,000	(3,000)	(45,000)
Retained earnings December 31, 20X6	$ 60,000	$ 55,000				$ 77,000
Balance Sheet						
Cash	$ 46,000	$ 20,000				$ 66,000
Note receivable—Snap	10,000			e 10,000		
Other current assets	97,000	70,000				167,000
Investment in Snap	87,000		a 8,000	c 95,000		
Plant and equipment	300,000	100,000				400,000
Accumulated depreciation	(60,000)	(40,000)				(100,000)
Goodwill			c 15,000	d 3,000		12,000
	$480,000	$150,000				$545,000
Note payable—Prep		$ 10,000	e 10,000			
Liabilities	$ 70,000	25,000				$ 95,000
Capital stock	350,000	60,000	c 60,000			350,000
Retained earnings	60,000√	55,000√				77,000
	$480,000	$150,000				
Minority interest January 1, 20X6 ($100,000 × 20%)				c 20,000	20,000	
Minority interest December 31, 20X6					$23,000	23,000
						$545,000

Exhibit 4–8 Cost Method—Working Papers for Year Subsequent to Acquisition (Traditional Approach)

This working paper entry eliminates reciprocal dividend income and dividends paid amounts. The $3,000 subsidiary dividends not eliminated relate to the 20% minority interest and are deducted in the minority interest column. Entry b is reconstructed as follows:

b	Retained earnings—Snap (beginning)	$30,000	
	Capital stock—Snap	60,000	
	Goodwill	15,000	
	Investment in Snap		$87,000
	Minority interest		18,000
	To eliminate reciprocal investment and equity amounts and establish beginning minority interest and goodwill amounts.		

Reciprocity between the investment in Snap account on Prep's books and the capital stock and beginning retained earnings accounts on Snap's books exists because these items are stated at their January 1, 20X5, amounts. Entry b simply eliminates reciprocal investment and equity amounts and enters beginning-of-the-period goodwill and minority interest.

Entry c for current amortization of goodwill is exactly the same as that for Exhibits 4–1 and 4–3.

c	Expenses	$ 1,500	
	Goodwill		$ 1,500
	To enter current goodwill amortization.		

Year Subsequent to Acquisition   More significant differences in traditional working paper procedures under the cost and equity methods of accounting for subsidiary investments occur in periods subsequent to the year in which the investment is acquired. These differences are illustrated in Exhibit 4–8 by extending the Prep/Snap illustration to the year 20X6.

Again, the consolidated statements that appear in Exhibit 4–8 are exactly the same as those in Exhibits 4–2 and 4–4, but the working paper entries are different. Entry a in Exhibit 4–8 establishes reciprocity between the investment in Snap at January 1, 20X6, and the subsidiary equity amounts at the same date.

a	Investment in Snap	$ 8,000	
	Retained earnings—Prep (beginning)		$ 8,000
	To establish reciprocity between the investment account and Snap's equity accounts.		

The $8,000 amount is Prep's share of the increase in Snap's retained earnings (undistributed income) from the January 1, 20X5 date of acquisition to the January 1, 20X6 beginning of the 20X6 period of consolidation. Alternatively, the $8,000 amount is 80% of Snap's $25,000 income for 20X5, less 80% of Snap's $15,000 dividends declared in 20X5 ($20,000 − $12,000). Observe that working paper entry a adjusts for the omission of undistributed income under the cost method, but that it does not adjust for amortization of cost/book value differentials that are also omitted under the cost method. These latter items are adjusted in working paper entries c and d.

Entry b eliminates reciprocal dividend income and dividends paid amounts as follows:

b	Dividend income	$12,000	
	Dividends		$12,000
	To eliminate dividend income and dividends paid to Prep.		

Entry c in the working papers is journalized as follows:

c	Retained earnings—Snap (beginning)	$40,000	
	Capital stock—Snap	60,000	
	Goodwill	15,000	
	Investment in Snap		$95,000
	Minority interest		20,000
	To eliminate reciprocal investment and equity accounts, establish beginning minority interest, and enter original goodwill.		

This entry eliminates the reciprocal investment in Snap account, as adjusted in entry a, against Snap's capital stock and retained earnings balances at January 1, 20X6. It also enters the original $15,000 goodwill and the beginning-of-the-period minority interest.

Entry d adjusts expenses for the current amortization of goodwill, adjusts Prep's beginning retained earnings for the 20X5 goodwill amortization that was not recorded by Prep, and reduces the goodwill to $12,000, its correct unamortized balance at December 31, 20X6.

d	Retained earnings—Prep (beginning)	$ 1,500	
	Expenses	1,500	
	Goodwill		$ 3,000
	To enter current goodwill amortization and correct Prep's beginning retained earnings for prior years' amortization.		

Entry e eliminates reciprocal note payable and note receivable accounts.

c	Note payable—Prep	$10,000	
	Note receivable—Snap		$10,000
	To eliminate reciprocal note payable and note receivable amounts.		

LOCATING ERRORS

The last part of consolidation working papers to be completed is the consolidated balance sheet section. Most errors made in consolidating the financial statements will show up when the consolidated balance sheet does not balance. If the consolidated balance sheet fails to balance after totals have been recomputed, individual items should be checked to ensure that all items have been included. Omissions involving the minority interest income in the consolidated income statement and minority interest equity in the consolidated balance sheet occur frequently because these items do not appear on the separate company statements. The equality of debits and credits in the working paper entries is checked by totaling the adjustment and elimination columns. Although proper coding of each working paper entry minimizes this type of error, many accountants prefer to total the adjustment and elimination columns as a regular working paper procedure.

EXCESS ALLOCATED TO IDENTIFIABLE NET ASSETS

Consolidation working paper procedures for allocating an excess of investment cost over underlying book value to specific assets and liabilities are similar to those illustrated for goodwill. The working paper entries are more complex, however, because more accounts are affected and additional allocation, amortization, and depreciation schemes are required. These additional working paper complexities are illustrated here for Pate Corporation and its 90%-owned subsidiary, Solo Corporation.

Pate acquired its equity interest in Solo on December 31, 20X5 for $365,000 cash, when Solo's stockholders' equity consisted of $200,000 capital stock and $50,000 retained earnings. On the date that Solo became a subsidiary of Pate, the following assets of Solo had book values different from their fair values:

	Fair Value	Book Value	Undervaluation (Overvaluation)
Inventories	$ 60,000	$ 50,000	$ 10,000
Land	60,000	30,000	30,000
Buildings	180,000	100,000	80,000
Equipment	70,000	90,000	(20,000)
	$370,000	$270,000	$100,000

Based on this information, Pate allocated the $140,000 excess cost over book value acquired [$365,000 cost − (90% × $250,000 equity of Solo)] to identifiable assets and goodwill, as shown in the following schedule:

	Undervaluation (Overvaluation)	Interest Acquired	Excess Allocation	Amortization Period
Inventories	$10,000 ×	90% =	$ 9,000	Sold in 20X6
Land	30,000	90	27,000	None
Buildings—net	80,000	90	72,000	36 years
Equipment—net	(20,000)	90	(18,000)	9 years
Goodwill—remainder			50,000	10 years
			$140,000	

The schedule also shows the amortization periods assigned to the undervalued and overvalued assets and goodwill.

Consolidation at Acquisition

Consolidated balance sheet working papers for Pate Corporation and Subsidiary immediately after the business combination on December 31, 20X5 are shown in Exhibit 4–9. The excess cost over book value allocation is reasonably complex, so an unamortized excess account is used in the working papers. The first working paper entry eliminates reciprocal investment in Solo and stockholders' equity accounts of Solo, enters the 10% minority interest in Solo, and debits the unamortized excess account for the $140,000 excess cost over book value acquired. A second working paper entry allocates the excess to identifiable net assets and goodwill. The amounts allocated in the second working paper entry are the original allocations because the accounts of Pate and Solo are being consolidated immediately after the business combination.

Consolidation After Acquisition

Solo reports $60,000 net income for 20X6 and declares dividends of $10,000 on June 1 and December 1 ($20,000 total for 20X6). The June 1 dividend is paid on July 1, but the December 1 dividend remains unpaid at December 31, 20X6. During 20X6, Solo sells the undervalued inventory items, but the undervalued land and buildings and overvalued equipment are still in use by Solo at December 31, 20X6. On the date of business combination, the buildings had a remaining useful life of 36 years, and the equipment, nine years. Goodwill is being amortized over 10 years.

During 20X6 Solo borrows $20,000 from Pate on a noninterest-bearing note. Solo repays the note on December 30, but the repayment check to Pate was in transit and was not reflected in Pate's separate balance sheet at December 31, 20X6.

Pate made the following journal entries in 20X6 to account for its investment in Solo.

	Pate	90% Solo	Adjustments and Eliminations		Consolidated Balance Sheet
Assets					
Cash	$ 20,000	$ 5,000			$ 25,000
Receivables—net	90,000	25,000			115,000
Inventories	80,000	50,000	b 9,000		139,000
Land	60,000	30,000	b 27,000		117,000
Buildings—net	200,000	100,000	b 72,000		372,000
Equipment—net	135,000	90,000		b 18,000	207,000
Investment in Solo	365,000			a 365,000	
Goodwill			b 50,000		50,000
Unamortized excess			a 140,000	b 140,000	
Totals	$950,000	$300,000			$1,025,000
Liabilities and Equity					
Accounts payable	$130,000	$ 50,000			$ 180,000
Capital stock—Pate	700,000				700,000
Retained earnings—Pate	120,000				120,000
Capital stock—Solo		200,000	a 200,000		
Retained earnings—Solo		50,000	a 50,000		
Minority interest				a 25,000	25,000
Totals	$950,000	$300,000			$1,025,000

Exhibit 4–9 *Consolidation at Acquisition*

July 1, 20X6

Cash	$ 9,000	
Investment in Solo		$9,000

To record dividends from Solo ($10,000 × 90%).

December 31, 20X6

Investment in Solo	$40,000	
Income from Solo		$40,000

To record investment income from Solo determined as follows:

Share of Solo's net income ($60,000 × 90%)	$54,000
Amortization of excess allocated to:	
Inventories ($9,000 × 100% recognized)	−9,000
Buildings ($72,000 ÷ 36 years)	−2,000
Equipment ($18,000 ÷ 9 years)	+2,000
Goodwill ($50,000 ÷ 10 years)	−5,000
Income from Solo for 20X6	$40,000

These entries show that Pate has used a one-line consolidation in accounting for its $40,000 income from Solo for 20X6, but it has failed to recognize Solo's December 1 dividend declaration. Accordingly, Pate's investment in Solo at December 31, 20X6, is overstated by $9,000 (90% of Solo's $10,000 December 1 dividend declaration). Consolidation working papers for Pate and Subsidiary for 20X6 in Exhibit 4–10 show Pate's investment in Solo at $396,000 ($365,000 cost plus $40,000 income less $9,000

PATE CORPORATION AND SUBSIDIARY
CONSOLIDATION WORKING PAPERS
FOR THE YEAR ENDED DECEMBER 31, 20X6

	Pate	90% Solo	Adjustments and Eliminations		Minority Interest	Consolidated Statements
Income Statement						
Sales	$900,000	$300,000				$1,200,000
Income from Solo	40,000		c 40,000			
Cost of goods sold	(600,000)	(150,000)	e 9,000			(759,000)
Operating expenses	(190,000)	(90,000)	f 2,000 h 5,000	g 2,000		(285,000)
Minority interest income ($60,000 × 10%)					$ 6,000	(6,000)
Net income	$150,000	$ 60,000				$ 150,000
Retained Earnings						
Retained earnings—Pate	$120,000					$ 120,000
Retained earnings—Solo		$ 50,000	d 50,000			
Net income	150,000√	60,000√				150,000
Dividends	(100,000)	(20,000)		c 18,000	(2,000)	(100,000)
Retained earnings December 31, 20X6	$170,000	$ 90,000				$ 170,000
Balance Sheet						
Cash	$ 8,000	$ 15,000	b 20,000			$ 43,000
Accounts receivable—net	76,000	25,000				101,000
Note receivable—Solo	20,000			b 20,000		
Inventories	90,000	60,000				150,000
Land	60,000	30,000	e 27,000			117,000
Buildings—net	190,000	110,000	e 72,000	f 2,000		370,000
Equipment—net	150,000	120,000	g 2,000	e 18,000		254,000
Investment in Solo	396,000			a 9,000 c 22,000 d 365,000		
Dividends receivable			a 9,000	i 9,000		
Goodwill			e 50,000	h 5,000		45,000
Unamortized excess			d 140,000	e 140,000		
	$990,000	$360,000				$1,080,000
Accounts payable	$120,000	$ 60,000				$ 180,000
Dividends payable		10,000	i 9,000			1,000
Capital stock	700,000	200,000	d 200,000			700,000
Retained earnings	170,000√	90,000√				170,000
	$990,000	$360,000				
Minority interest January 1, 20X6				d 25,000	25,000	
Minority interest December 31, 20X6					$29,000	29,000
						$1,080,000

Exhibit 4–10   *Consolidation After Acquisition*

dividends received), whereas the correct amount is $387,000. The overstatement is corrected in working paper entry a of Exhibit 4–10:

a	Dividends receivable	$ 9,000	
	Investment in Solo		$ 9,000
	To correct investment balance for unrecorded dividends receivable.		

This entry is different from previous working paper entries because it represents a real adjustment that should be recorded on Pate's books.

Working paper entry b adjusts for the $20,000 cash in transit from Solo to Pate at December 31, 20X6:

b	Cash	$ 20,000	
	Note receivable—Solo		$ 20,000
	To enter receipt of intercompany note receivable.		

This working paper entry is also a real adjustment and one that should be recorded by Pate on its separate books. If entries a and b are not recorded as correcting entries on the separate books of Pate, however, they will be recorded in the normal course of events in 20X7 when Pate receives the $9,000 dividend and the $20,000 note repayment checks from Solo. Year-end transactions between affiliated companies always need to be examined to make sure that they are reflected in the records of both parent and subsidiary companies.

Entry c eliminates the income from Solo and 90% of Solo's dividends, and it adjusts the investment in Solo account to its $365,000 beginning-of-the-period balance. Entry d eliminates the reciprocal investment in Solo account and the stockholders' equity accounts of Solo, records the 10% minority interest at the beginning of the period, and enters the $140,000 excess.

c	Income from Solo	$ 40,000	
	Dividends		$ 18,000
	Investment in Solo		22,000
	To eliminate income and dividends of Solo and return investment account to beginning-of-the-period balance.		
d	Retained earnings—Solo	$ 50,000	
	Capital stock—Solo	200,000	
	Unamortized excess	140,000	
	Investment in Solo		$365,000
	Minority interest—January 1		25,000
	To eliminate reciprocal investment and equity amounts, establish beginning minority interest, and enter unamortized excess.		

The unamortized excess entered in working paper entry d is allocated to identifiable assets and goodwill as of December 31, 20X5 in entry e and amortized in entries f, g, and h. A schedule to support these allocations and amortizations should be completed for convenience in preparing the working paper entries and to provide documentation for subsequent consolidations.

	Unamortized Excess December 31, 20X5	Amortization 20X6	Unamortized Excess December 31, 20X6
Inventories	$ 9,000	$ 9,000	$ —
Land	27,000	—	27,000
Buildings—net	72,000	2,000	70,000
Equipment—net	(18,000)	(2,000)	(16,000)
Goodwill	50,000	5,000	45,000
	$140,000	$14,000	$126,000

With the exception of the $9,000 excess allocated to cost of goods sold, the allocation in working paper entry e of Exhibit 4–10 is the same as the allocation in working paper entry b in the consolidated balance sheet working papers of Exhibit 4–9.

The $9,000 excess assigned to inventories is allocated to cost of goods sold because the related undervalued inventories from December 31, 20X5 were sold in 20X6, thus increasing cost of goods sold in the 20X6 consolidated income statement. Working paper entry e is journalized as follows:

e	Cost of goods sold	$ 9,000	
	Land	27,000	
	Buildings—net	72,000	
	Goodwill	50,000	
	Equipment—net		$ 18,000
	Unamortized excess		140,000
	To allocate unamortized excess to identifiable assets and goodwill.		

Working paper entries f, g, and h are necessary to increase operating expenses for depreciation on the $72,000 excess allocated to undervalued buildings, to decrease operating expenses for excessive depreciation on the $18,000 assigned to overvalued equipment, and to increase operating expenses for amortization of the $50,000 originally assigned to goodwill, respectively. Entry h for amortizing goodwill has been illustrated previously and requires no further explanation. Entry f for recording depreciation on the excess allocated to buildings is procedurally the same as the adjustment for goodwill, except that buildings—net of depreciation is credited. The credit is to accumulated depreciation or to buildings—net when the buildings are shown on a net-of-depreciation basis. The $2,000 debit to equipment—net and credit to operating expenses in working paper entry g corrects for excessive depreciation on the overvalued equipment. Procedurally, this adjustment is the exact opposite of entry f, which corrects for underdepreciation on the buildings:

f	Operating expenses	$ 2,000	
	Buildings—net		$ 2,000
	To enter current depreciation on excess allocated to buildings.		
g	Equipment—net	$ 2,000	
	Operating expenses		$ 2,000
	To adjust current depreciation for excess allocated to reduce equipment.		
h	Operating expenses	$ 5,000	
	Goodwill		$ 5,000
	To enter current amortization of goodwill.		

Working paper entry i eliminates reciprocal dividends payable and dividends receivable amounts:

i	Dividends payable	$ 9,000	
	Dividends receivable		$ 9,000
	To eliminate reciprocal receivables and payables.		

The $1,000 dividends payable of Solo that is not eliminated relates to the minority interest. It is included among consolidated liabilities because it represents an amount payable outside the consolidated entity.

TRIAL BALANCE WORKING PAPER FORMAT

The trial balance approach to consolidation working papers brings together the adjusted trial balances for affiliated companies. Both the financial statement approach and the trial balance approach generate the same information, so the selection is based on user preference. If completed financial statements are available, the financial statement approach is easier to use because it provides measurements of parent and subsidiary income, retained earnings, assets, and equities that are needed in the consolidating process. If the accountant is given adjusted trial balances to consolidate, the trial balance approach may be more convenient.

Working paper entries illustrated in this chapter are designed for convenient switching between the financial statement and trial balance approaches for consolidation working papers. Recall that only account balances are adjusted or eliminated. Net income is not an account balance, so it is not subject to adjustment. All nominal accounts are assumed to be open and to permit adjustment. The only retained earnings amount that appears in an adjusted trial balance is the beginning retained earnings amount. Therefore, by working with beginning retained earnings amounts and by adjusting only actual accounts, the adjustments and eliminations are exactly the same whether the trial balance approach or the financial statement approach is used.

Consolidation Example—Trial Balance Format and Equity Method

Consolidation working papers using the trial balance format are illustrated in Exhibit 4–11 for Pibb Corporation and its 90%-owned subsidiary, Shad Corporation. Pibb acquired its interest in Shad on January 1, 20X1, at a price $14,000 in excess of underlying book value, and assigned the excess to goodwill with a 10-year amortization period.

A summary of changes in Pibb's investment in Shad account from the date of acquisition to December 31, 20X2, the report date, is as follows:

Investment cost January 1, 20X1	$50,000
Add: Income—20X1 (90% of Shad's $10,000 net income less $1,400 amortization of goodwill)	7,600
Investment balance December 31, 20X1	57,600
Add: Income—20X2 (90% of Shad's $20,000 net income less $1,400 amortization of goodwill)	16,600
Deduct: Dividends received from Shad (90% × $10,000)	−9,000
Investment balance December 31, 20X2	$65,200

The working papers presented in Exhibit 4–11 reflect the additional assumptions that Pibb sold merchandise to Shad during 20X2 for $14,000, and that, as of December 31, 20X2, Shad owed Pibb $5,000 from the sale. The merchandise was sold by Shad to its customers, so all profit from the sale was realized by the consolidated entity during 20X2.

Separate adjusted trial balances are presented in the first two columns of Exhibit 4–11. As shown in the exhibit, debit-balance accounts are presented first and totaled, and credit-balance accounts are presented and totaled below the debit-balance accounts.

The working paper entries to prepare consolidated financial statements using the trial balance format are the same as those for the financial statement approach. However, the accounts in a trial balance are classified according to their debit and credit balances, so the locations of the accounts vary from those found in the financial statement format. Also, only beginning-of-the-period retained earnings amounts are found in a trial balance, and, accordingly, the checkmarks used in the financial statement format for net income and ending retained earnings amounts are not needed.

Working paper entries to consolidate the trial balances of Pibb and Subsidiary at December 31, 20X2 are as follows:

a	Sales	$14,000	
	Cost of goods sold		$14,000
	To eliminate reciprocal sales and cost of sales from intercompany purchases.		
b	Income from Shad	$16,600	
	Dividends		$ 9,000
	Investment in Shad		7,600
	To eliminate income and dividends from Shad and adjust the investment account to its beginning-of-the-year amount.		
c	Common stock—Shad	$30,000	
	Retained earnings—Shad	20,000	
	Goodwill	12,600	
	Investment in Shad		$57,600
	Minority interest (10%)		5,000

PIBB CORPORATION AND SUBSIDIARY CONSOLIDATION WORKING PAPERS FOR THE YEAR ENDED DECEMBER 31, 20X2

	Pibb	90% Shad	Adjustments and Eliminations	Income Statement	Retained Earnings	Minority Interest	Balance Sheet
Debits							
Cash	$ 6,800	$ 20,000					$ 26,800
Accounts receivable	30,000	15,000	e 5,000				40,000
Inventories	50,000	25,000					75,000
Plant and equipment	75,000	45,000					120,000
Investment in Shad	65,200		b 7,600 c 57,600				
Cost of goods sold	80,000	30,000	a 14,000	$(96,000)			
Operating expenses	19,600	20,000	d 1,400	(41,000)			
Dividends	15,000	10,000	b 9,000		$(15,000)	$(1,000)	
Goodwill			c 12,600 d 1,400				11,200
	$341,600	$165,000					$273,000
Credits							
Accumulated depreciation	$ 25,000	$ 11,000					$ 36,000
Accounts payable	45,000	34,000	e 5,000				74,000
Common stock	100,000	30,000	c 30,000				100,000
Retained earnings	35,000	20,000	c 20,000		35,000		
Sales	120,000	70,000	a 14,000	176,000			
Income from Shad	16,600		b 16,600				
	$341,600	$165,000					
Minority interest January 1, 20X2			c 5,000			5,000	
Minority interest income ($20,000 × 10%)				(2,000)		2,000	
Consolidated net income				$ 37,000	37,000		
Consolidated retained earnings December 31, 20X2					$ 57,000		57,000
Minority interest December 31, 20X2						$6,000	6,000
							$273,000

Exhibit 4–11 *Trial Balance Approach for Working Papers*

After all adjustments and eliminations are entered in the working papers, items not eliminated are carried to the Income Statement, Retained Earnings Statement, Minority Interest, or Balance Sheet columns. Next, minority interest income is computed independently. It is included in the Income Statement column as a deduction and in the Minority Interest column as an addition. An inconvenience of the trial balance approach can be seen at this point because Shad's $20,000 net income has to be computed from the revenue and expense data before it can be multiplied by the minority interest percentage. Subsidiary net income is shown directly when the financial statement approach is used.

The Consolidated Income Statement column is totaled and carried to the Consolidated Retained Earnings Statement column. The Consolidated Retained Earnings Statement column is totaled and carried to the Consolidated Balance Sheet column, and the Minority Interest column is totaled and carried to the Consolidated Balance Sheet column. Finally, Consolidated Balance Sheet debits and credits are totaled, and the working papers are completed. Consolidated financial statements can be prepared directly from the Consolidated Income Statement, Consolidated Retained Earnings Statement, and Consolidated Balance Sheet columns.

SUMMARY

The objective of preparing working papers is to produce meaningful financial reports for a consolidated business entity. Working papers are merely tools for organizing and manipulating data. All the computations for consolidated financial statements can be determined independent of consolidation working papers if the objective is clearly understood.

The method of accounting for a subsidiary investment must be known before parent and subsidiary financial statements can be consolidated. Several approaches can be used to determine the method used by the parent company in accounting for its subsidiaries. For example, a dividend income account, rather than an income from subsidiary account, on the parent company's books suggests that the cost method is being used. Also, an investment in subsidiary account balance equal to the original cost of the interest acquired provides evidence of the cost method. Alternatively, an income from subsidiary account equal to the parent company's share of subsidiary net income, or an investment in subsidiary account equal to underlying book value plus original cost/book value differentials, provides evidence that the parent company is using an incomplete equity method.

Once the method of accounting is known, appropriate adjustments are made in the working papers to produce correct consolidated financial statements. Generally, the worksheet variations resulting from different methods of accounting for the same subsidiary investment are not great.

APPENDIX: CONSOLIDATED STATEMENT OF CASH FLOWS

The consolidated statement of cash flows (SCF) is prepared from consolidated income statements and consolidated balance sheets, rather than from the separate parent company and subsidiary statements. With minor exceptions, the preparation of a consolidated SCF involves the same analysis and procedures that are used in preparing the SCF for separate entities.

Consolidated balance sheets at December 31, 20X5 and 20X6 and the 20X6 consolidated income statement for Polski Corporation and its 80%-owned subsidiary, Seed Corporation, are presented in Exhibit 4–12. Consolidated balance sheets at the beginning and end of the year are used to calculate the year's changes, which must be explained in the SCF. Other information pertinent to the preparation of Polski's consolidated SCF is as follows:

1 During 20X6, Seed sold land that cost $20,000 to outside entities for $10,000 cash.
2 Polski issued a $300,000, two-year note on January 8, 20X6, for new equipment.
3 Goodwill amortization from the Polski-Seed business combination is $10,000 per year.
4 Polski received $10,000 dividends from its investments in equity investees.
5 Changes in plant assets not explained above are due to provisions for depreciation.

POLSKI CORPORATION AND SUBSIDIARY
COMPARATIVE BALANCE SHEETS
AT DECEMBER 31

	20X6	20X5	Year's Change Increase (Decrease)
Cash	$ 255,000	$ 180,000	$ 75,000
Accounts receivable—net	375,000	270,000	105,000
Inventories	250,000	205,000	45,000
Equity investments	100,000	95,000	5,000
Land	80,000	100,000	(20,000)
Buildings—net	200,000	220,000	(20,000)
Equipment—net	800,000	600,000	200,000
Goodwill	90,000	100,000	(10,000)
	$2,150,000	$1,770,000	$380,000
Accounts payable	$ 250,000	$ 270,000	$(20,000)
Dividends payable	20,000	20,000	—
Note payable due 20X8	300,000	—	300,000
Common stock	500,000	500,000	—
Other paid-in capital	300,000	300,000	—
Retained earnings	670,000	600,000	70,000
Minority interest—20%	110,000	80,000	30,000
	$2,150,000	$1,770,000	$380,000

CONSOLIDATED INCOME STATEMENT
FOR THE YEAR ENDED DECEMBER 31, 20X6

Sales		$750,000
Income from equity investees		15,000
Total revenue		765,000
Less expenses:		
Cost of goods sold	$ 300,000	
Depreciation expense	120,000	
Goodwill amortization	10,000	
Wages and salaries	54,000	
Other operating expenses	47,000	
Interest expense	24,000	
Loss on sale of land	10,000	(565,000)
Total consolidated income		200,000
Less: Minority interest income		(50,000)
Consolidated net income		150,000
Consolidated retained earnings January 1, 20X6		600,000
Less: Cash dividends paid		(80,000)
Consolidated retained earnings December 31, 20X6		$670,000

Exhibit 4–12   *Consolidated Balance Sheets and Income Statement for Polski and Subsidiary*

The SCF is prepared using a single concept—cash and cash equivalents. Two presentations for reporting net cash flows from operations are permitted. The indirect method begins with consolidated net income and includes adjustments for items not providing or using cash to arrive at net cash flows from operations. Under the direct method, cash received from customers and investment income are offset against cash paid to suppliers, employees, governmental units, and so on in arriving at net cash flows from operations. Although the Financial Accounting Standards Board has expressed a preference for the direct method of reporting net cash flows from operations,[2] the 1997 issue of *Accounting Trends & Techniques* reported that 11 of 600 surveyed companies presenting a statement of cash flows used the direct method, and 589 used the indirect method.

[2]*FASB Statement No. 95*, "Statement of Cash Flows," paragraph 119.

Consolidated Statement of Cash Flows—Indirect Method

A consolidated SCF is presented in Exhibit 4–13 for Polski Corporation and Subsidiary under the indirect method. This statement is based on the consolidated balance sheet changes and the 20X6 consolidated income statement that appears in Exhibit 4–12 for Polski Corporation and Subsidiary. A statement of cash flows worksheet that organizes the information for statement preparation is presented in Exhibit 4–14 using the schedule approach. The consolidated SCF is prepared directly from the "cash flow from operations," "cash flow—investing activities," and "cash flow—financing activities" columns of the worksheet in Exhibit 4–14.

Minority interest income is an increase in the cash flow from operating activities because minority interest income increases consolidated assets and liabilities in exactly the same manner as consolidated net income. Similarly, minority interest dividends are deducted along with majority interest dividends in reporting the cash flows from financing activities.

Income and Dividends from Investees Under the Indirect and Direct Methods

Income from equity investees is an item that requires special attention in the consolidated SCF when the indirect method is used. Income from equity investees increases income without increasing cash because the increase is reflected in the investment account. Conversely, dividends received from equity investees increase cash but do not affect income because the decrease is reflected in the investment account. The net amount of these items (the change in the investment account) is deducted from (or added to) net income in the "cash flows from operating activities" section of the SCF. An excess of dividends received over equity income would be added. When the direct method of reporting cash flows from operating activities is used, dividends received

---

POLSKI CORPORATION AND SUBSIDIARY
CONSOLIDATED STATEMENT OF CASH FLOWS
FOR THE YEAR ENDED DECEMBER 31, 20X6

Cash Flows from Operating Activities		
Consolidated net income		$ 150,000
Adjustments to reconcile net income to cash		
provided by operating activities:		
Minority interest income	$ 50,000	
Undistributed income—equity investees	(5,000)	
Loss on sale of land	10,000	
Depreciation on equipment	100,000	
Depreciation on buildings	20,000	
Amortization of goodwill	10,000	
Increase in accounts receivable	(105,000)	
Increase in inventories	(45,000)	
Decrease in accounts payable	(20,000)	15,000
Net cash flows from operating activities		165,000
Cash Flows from Investing Activities		
Proceeds from sale of land	$ 10,000	
Net cash flows from investing activities		10,000
Cash Flows from Financing Activities		
Payment of cash dividends—majority	$(80,000)	
Payment of cash dividends—minority	(20,000)	
Net cash flows from financing activities		(100,000)
Increase in cash for 20X6		75,000
Cash on January 1, 20X6		180,000
Cash on December 31, 20X6		$ 255,000
Listing of Noncash Investing and Financing Activities		
Equipment purchased for $300,000 by issuing a two-year note payable		

Exhibit 4–13 *Consolidated Statement of Cash Flows—Indirect Method*

POLSKI CORPORATION AND SUBSIDIARY
WORKING PAPERS FOR THE STATEMENT OF CASH FLOWS (INDIRECT METHOD)
FOR THE YEAR ENDED DECEMBER 31, 20X6

	Year's Change	Reconciling Items		Cash Flow—from Operations	Cash Flow—Investing Activities	Cash Flow—Financing Activities
		Debit	Credit			
Asset Changes						
Cash	75,000					
Accounts receivable—net	105,000		k 105,000			
Inventories	45,000		l 45,000			
Equity investments	5,000		e 5,000			
Land	(20,000)	f 20,000				
Buildings—net	(20,000)	i 20,000				
Equipment—net	200,000	h 100,000	g 300,000			
Goodwill	(10,000)	j 10,000				
Total asset changes	380,000					
Equity Changes						
Accounts payable	(20,000)		m 20,000			
Dividends payable	0					
Note payable due 20X8*	300,000	g 300,000				
Common stock	0					
Other paid-in capital	0					
Retained earnings	70,000	a 150,000	b 80,000			
Minority interest	30,000	c 50,000	d 20,000			
Total equity changes	380,000					
Consolidated net income			a 150,000	150,000		
Minority interest income			c 50,000	50,000		
Income–equity investees		e 5,000		(5,000)		
Loss on sale of land			f 10,000	10,000		
Depreciation on equipment			h 100,000	100,000		
Depreciation on buildings			i 20,000	20,000		
Amortization of goodwill			j 10,000	10,000		
Increase in receivables		k 105,000		(105,000)		
Increase in inventories		l 45,000		(45,000)		
Decrease in accounts payable		m 20,000		(20,000)		
Proceeds from sale of land			f 10,000		10,000	
Payment of dividends—majority		b 80,000				(80,000)
Payment of dividends—minority		d 20,000				(20,000)
		925,000	925,000	165,000	10,000	(100,000)

Cash flows from operations $165,000
Cash flows from investing activities   10,000
Cash flows from financing activities   (100,000)
Increase in cash for 20X6 = cash change above $ 75,000

*Noncash investing and financing transaction: equipment purchased for $300,000 by issuing a 2-year note payable.

Exhibit 4–14   Worksheet for Consolidated SCF—Indirect Method

from equity investees are reported directly as cash flows from operating activities without the complications involved with the indirect method.

Consolidated Statement of Cash Flows—Direct Method

A consolidated SCF for Polski Corporation and Subsidiary under the direct method is presented in Exhibit 4–15. This statement is identical to the one presented in Exhibit 4–13, except for cash flows from operating activities. Under the direct method, the consolidated income statement items that involve cash flows are converted from the accrual to the cash basis, and those items that do not involve cash are explained in notes or schedules supporting the cash flow statement. Exhibit 4–16 shows a worksheet that organizes information for a consolidated statement of cash flows under the direct method. The SCF is prepared directly from the last three columns of the worksheet.

POLSKI CORPORATION AND SUBSIDIARY
CONSOLIDATED STATEMENT OF CASH FLOWS
FOR THE YEAR ENDED DECEMBER 31, 20X6

Cash Flows from Operating Activities

Cash received from customers		$645,000
Dividends received from equity investees		10,000
Less: Cash paid to suppliers	$365,000	
Cash paid to employees	54,000	
Paid for other operating items	47,000	
Cash paid for interest expense	24,000	(490,000)
Net cash flows from operating activities		165,000

Cash Flows from Investing Activities

Proceeds from sale of land	$ 10,000	
Net cash flows from investing activities		10,000

Cash Flows from Financing Activities

Payment of cash dividends—majority interests	$(80,000)	
Payment of cash dividends—minority interests	(20,000)	
Net cash flows from financing activities		(100,000)
Increase in cash for 20X6		75,000
Cash on January 1, 20X6		180,000
Cash on December 31, 20X6		$255,000

Listing of Noncash Investment and Financing Activities
Equipment was purchased for $300,000 through
the issuance of a 2-year note payable

Reconciliation of Consolidated Net Income to Operating Cash Flows
Cash Flows from Operating Activities

Consolidated net income		$150,000
Adjustments to reconcile net income to cash provided by operating activities:		
Minority interest income	$ 50,000	
Undistributed income-equity investees	(5,000)	
Loss on sale of land	10,000	
Depreciation on equipment	100,000	
Depreciation on buildings	20,000	
Amortization of goodwill	10,000	
Increase in accounts receivable	(105,000)	
Increase in inventories	(45,000)	
Decrease in accounts payable	(20,000)	15,000
Net cash flows from operating activities		$165,000

Exhibit 4–15   *Consolidated Statement of Cash Flows—Direct Method*

In comparing the cash flow statements in Exhibits 4–13 and 4–15, observe that the cash flows from investing and financing activities are identical. The significant differences lie in the presentation of cash flows from operating activities and the additional schedule to reconcile consolidated net income to operating cash flows under the direct method. Although the presentation in Exhibit 4–15 under the direct method may be less familiar, it is somewhat easier to interpret.

SELECTED READING

Statement of Financial Accounting Standards No. 95. "Statement of Cash Flows." Stamford, CT: Financial Accounting Standards Board, 1987.

ASSIGNMENT MATERIAL

QUESTIONS

1 How are consolidated financial statements affected by the manner in which the parent company accounts for its subsidiary investments?

2 Is it ever acceptable for a parent company to use the cost method of accounting for its investments in subsidiary corporations? Explain.

	Year's Change	Reconciling Items		Cash Flow from Operations	Cash Flow—Investing Activities	Cash Flow—Financing Activities
		Debit	Credit			
Asset Changes						
Cash	75,000					
Accounts receivable—net	105,000		a 105,000			
Inventories	45,000		c 45,000			
Equity investments	5,000		b 5,000			
Land	(20,000)	h 20,000				
Buildings—net	(20,000)	f 20,000				
Equipment—net	200,000	e 100,000	d 300,000			
Goodwill	(10,000)	g 10,000				
Total asset changes	380,000					
Equity Changes						
Accounts payable	(20,000)		c 20,000			
Dividends payable	0					
Note payable due 20X8**	300,000	d 300,000				
Common stock	0					
Other paid-in capital	0					
Retained earnings*	70,000					
Minority interest	30,000	i 50,000	j 20,000			
Total equity changes	380,000					
*Retained earnings changes**						
Sales	750,000	a 105,000		645,000		
Income—equity investees	15,000	b 5,000		10,000		
Cost of goods sold	(300,000)	c 65,000		(365,000)		
Depreciation on equipment	(100,000)		e 100,000			
Depreciation on buildings	(20,000)		f 20,000			
Goodwill amortization	(10,000)		g 10,000			
Wage and salaries	(54,000)			(54,000)		
Other operating expenses	(47,000)			(47,000)		
Interest expense	(24,000)			(24,000)		
Loss on sale of land	(10,000)		h 10,000			
Minority interest income	(50,000)		i 50,000			
Dividends paid by Polski	(80,000)		k 80,000			
Change in retained earnings	70,000					
Payment of dividends—majority		k 80,000				(80,000)
Payment of dividends—minority		j 20,000				(20,000)
Proceeds from the land sale			h 10,000		10,000	
		775,000	775,000	165,000	10,000	(100,000)

*Retained earnings changes replace the retained earnings account for reconciling purposes.

**Noncash investing and financing transaction: equipment purchased for $300,000 by issuing a 2-year note payable.

Exhibit 4–16   Worksheet for Consolidated SCF—Direct Method

3 If a parent company in accounting for its subsidiary investment amortizes goodwill on its separate books, why is it necessary to include an adjustment for goodwill amortization in the consolidation working papers?

4 How is minority interest income entered in consolidation working papers? Is there an alternative method?

5 How are the working paper procedures for the investment in subsidiary, income from subsidiary, and subsidiary's stockholders' equity accounts alike?

6 If a parent company uses the equity method but does not amortize the difference between investment cost and book value acquired on its separate books, its net income and retained earnings will not equal consolidated net income and consolidated retained earnings. How does this affect consolidation working paper procedures?

7 Are working paper adjustments and eliminations entered on the parent company books? The subsidiary books? Explain.

8 The financial-statement and trial-balance working paper approaches illustrated in the chapter generate comparable information, so why learn both approaches?

9 Can the method used by a parent company in accounting for its subsidiary investments be determined by examining the separate financial statements of the parent and subsidiary companies?

10 How is reciprocity established between a parent company's investment account and the equity accounts of its subsidiary when the cost method is used?

11 In what way do the adjustment and elimination entries for consolidation working papers differ for the financial statement and trial balance approaches?

12 When is it necessary to adjust the parent company's retained earnings account in the preparation of consolidation working papers? In answering this question, explain the relationship between parent company retained earnings and consolidated retained earnings.

13 What approach would you use to check the accuracy of the consolidated retained earnings and minority interest amounts that appear in the balance sheet section of completed consolidation working papers?

14 *Appendix:* Explain why minority interest income is added to consolidated net income in determining cash flows from operating activities.

15 *Appendix:* Consolidated net income is a measurement of income to the stockholders of the parent company, but does a change in cash as reflected in a statement of cash flows also relate to the stockholders of the parent company?

(*Note:* Don't forget the assumptions on page 56 when working exercises and problems in this chapter.)

EXERCISES

E 4-1   1 Working paper entries normally:
   a Are posted to the general ledger accounts of one or more of the affiliated companies
   b Are posted to the general ledger accounts only when the financial statement approach is used
   c Are posted to the general ledger accounts only when the trial balance approach is used
   d Do not affect the general ledger accounts of any of the affiliated companies

2 Working paper techniques assume nominal accounts are:
   a Open when the financial statement approach is used
   b Open when the trial balance approach is used
   c Open in all cases
   d Closed

3 Most errors made in consolidating financial statements will appear when:
   a The consolidated balance sheet does not balance
   b Consolidated net income does not equal parent company net income
   c The retained earnings amount on the balance sheet does not equal the amount on the retained earnings statement
   d Adjustment and elimination column totals do not equal

4 Net income on consolidation working papers is:
   a Adjusted when the parent company uses the cost method
   b Adjusted when the parent company uses the equity method
   c Adjusted in all cases
   d Not an account balance and not subject to adjustment

5 On consolidation working papers, individual stockholders' equity accounts of a subsidiary are:
   a Added to parent company stockholders' equity accounts
   b Eliminated
   c Eliminated only to the extent of minority interest
   d Eliminated to the extent of the parent company's interest

6 On consolidation working papers, investment income from a subsidiary is:
   a Added to the investment account
   b Added to the parent company's beginning retained earnings
   c Allocated between majority and minority stockholders
   d Eliminated

7 On consolidation working papers, the investment in consolidated subsidiary account balances are:
   a Allocated between majority and minority interests
   b Always eliminated
   c Carried forward to the consolidated balance sheet
   d Eliminated when the financial statement approach is used

8 On consolidation working papers, consolidated net income is determined by:
   a Adding net income of the parent and subsidiary companies
   b Deducting consolidated expenses and minority interest income from consolidated revenues

c Making adjustments to the parent company's income

d Subtracting minority interest income from parent company net income

9 On consolidation working papers, consolidated end-of-the-period retained earnings is determined by:

    a Adding beginning consolidated retained earnings and consolidated net income and subtracting parent company dividends

    b Adding end-of-the-period retained earnings of the affiliated companies

    c Adjusting beginning parent-company retained earnings for subsidiary profits and dividends

    d Adjusting the parent company's retained earnings account balance

10 Under the trial balance approach to consolidation working papers, which of the following is used?

    a Unadjusted trial balances

    b Adjusted trial balances

    c Postclosing trial balances

    d Either a or b, depending on the circumstances

E 4-2   Ponder Corporation purchased 80% of the outstanding voting common stock of Sally Forth Corporation on January 2, 20X5 for $300,000 cash. Sally Forth's balance sheets on this date and on December 31, 20X5 are as follows:

SALLY FORTH CORPORATION BALANCE SHEETS

	January 2, 20X5	December 31, 20X5
Inventory	$ 50,000	$ 20,000
Other current assets	50,000	80,000
Plant assets—net	200,000	220,000
Total assets	$300,000	$320,000
Liabilities	$ 50,000	$ 60,000
Capital stock	150,000	150,000
Retained earnings	100,000	110,000
Total equities	$300,000	$320,000

Additional Information

    1 Ponder uses the equity method of accounting for its investment in Sally Forth.

    2 Sally Forth's 20X5 net income and dividends were $70,000 and $60,000, respectively.

    3 Sally Forth's inventory, which was sold in 20X5, was undervalued by $12,500 at January 2, 20X5.

Required

    1 What is Ponder's income from Sally Forth for 20X5?

    2 What is the minority interest income for 20X5?

    3 What is the total minority interest at December 31, 20X5?

    4 What will be the balance of Ponder's investment in Sally Forth account at December 31, 20X5 if investment income from Sally Forth is $50,000? *Ignore* your answer to 1.

    5 What is consolidated net income for Ponder Corporation and Subsidiary if Ponder's net income for 20X5 is $180,200? (Assume income from subsidiary is $50,000.)

E 4-3   **1** Peggy Corporation owns a 70% interest in Sandy Corporation, acquired several years ago at book value. On December 31, 20X4, Sandy mailed a check for $10,000 to Peggy in part payment of a $20,000 account with Peggy. Peggy had not received the check when its books were closed on December 31. Peggy Corporation had accounts receivable of $150,000 (including the $20,000 from Sandy), and Sandy had accounts receivable at $220,000 at year-end. In the consolidated balance sheet of Peggy Corporation and Subsidiary at December 31, 20X4, accounts receivable will be shown in the amount of:

    a $370,000   **c** $350,000

    b $360,000   **d** $304,000

Use the following information in answering questions 2 and 3.

    Primrose Corporation purchased a 70% interest in Starman Corporation on January 1, 20X1 for $15,000,000, when Starman's stockholders' equity consisted of $3,000,000 common stock, $10,000,000 additional paid-in capital, and $2,000,000 retained earnings. Income and dividend information for Starman for 20X1, 20X2, and 20X3 is as follows:

	20X1	20X2	20X3
Net income (or loss)	$1,000,000	$200,000	$(500,000)
Dividends	400,000	100,000	—

2 Primrose reported separate income of $12,000,000 for 20X3. Consolidated net income for 20X3 is:

  a $11,387,500   **c** $11,537,500
  b $11,500,000   **d** $11,650,000

3 Primrose's investment in Starman balance at December 31, 20X3, under the equity method is:

  a $14,800,000   **c** $14,960,000
  b $14,802,500   **d** $15,137,500

E 4-4 Peacourt Corporation acquired 80% of Schooner Corporation's outstanding voting common stock on January 1, 20X3 for $28,000,000, when Schooner's stockholders' equity consisted of $20,000,000 common stock and $10,000,000 retained earnings. Peacourt accounts for its investment in Schooner under the cost method, but for purposes of preparing consolidated financial statements, any goodwill on the investment is amortized over a 10-year period.

Schooner reported income and dividends for the years 20X3, 20X4, and 20X5 as follows:

	20X3	20X4	20X5
Net income	$1,000,000	$ 500,000	$1,500,000
Dividends	600,000	600,000	600,000

Required: Prepare the journal entry on January 1, 20X6 for Peacourt to convert its investment in Schooner to the equity method.

E 4-5 Pinto Corporation purchases a 75% interest in Saab Corporation for $2,000,000 cash on July 1, 20X8, when Saab Corporation has capital stock of $1,200,000, retained earnings of $400,000, and current earnings of $400,000. The $500,000 excess of investment cost over book value acquired is allocated $100,000 to undervalued inventory items (sold in 20X8) and $400,000 to goodwill with a 10-year write-off period.

Saab's total earnings for 20X8 are $800,000, and it pays dividends of $300,000 on December 1, 20X8. Pinto's income for 20X8 is $720,000, including investment income from Saab of $300,000. At December 31, 20X8 Pinto's investment in Saab account has a balance of $2,075,000.

Required: Compute the following amounts:

  1 Minority interest income for 20X8
  2 Minority interest on December 31, 20X8
  3 Consolidated net income for 20X8
  4 The correct balance of Pinto's investment in Saab account at December 31, 20X8
  5 Goodwill at December 31, 20X8 to be included in the consolidated balance sheet

E 4-6 Abbreviated trial balances of Pardee and Sayers corporations at December 31, 20X5 follow:

	Pardee	Sayers
Current assets	$ 240,000	$ 130,000
Land	300,000	50,000
Plant and equipment—net	1,000,000	450,000
Investment in Sayers—90%	410,000	
Cost of sales	1,000,000	300,000
Other expenses	250,000	120,000
Dividends	100,000	50,000
	$3,300,000	$1,100,000
Current liabilities	$ 255,000	$ 100,000
Common stock	1,000,000	300,000
Retained earnings	500,000	200,000
Sales	1,500,000	500,000
Dividend income	45,000	
	$3,300,000	$1,100,000

Pardee acquired a 90% interest in Sayers for $410,000 cash on January 1, 20X1, when Sayers' stockholders' equity consisted of $300,000 capital stock and $100,000 retained earnings. Any difference between investment cost and book value acquired related to equipment with a 10-year life from January 1, 20X1. (*Hint:* Pardee uses the cost method.)

  1 The amount of adjustment needed to convert the investment in Sayers account to an equity basis as of January 1, 20X5, is computed:

  a 100%($200,000 − $100,000) − $5,000
  b 90%($200,000 − $100,000) − $20,000

  c 100%($200,000 − $100,000) + $20,000
  d 90%($200,000 − $100,000) + $5,000
 2 Consolidated net income for 20X5 is:
  a $322,000   **c** $330,000
  b $317,000   **d** $362,000
 3 Minority interest in Sayers at December 31, 20X5, is:
  a $50,000   **c** $53,000
  b $58,000   **d** $68,000
 4 Dividends to the minority stockholders for 20X5 are:
  a $50,000   **c** $10,000
  b $20,000   **d** $5,000

E 4-7 S'Brain Corporation's outstanding capital stock (and paid-in capital) has been $200,000 since the company was organized in 20X4. S'Brain's retained earnings account since 20X4 is summarized as follows:

RETAINED EARNINGS

Dividends December 1, 20X4	$20,000	Net income 20X4	$50,000
Dividends December 1, 20X5	20,000	Net income 20X5	70,000
Dividends December 1, 20X6	30,000	Net income 20X6	10,000
Dividends December 1, 20X7	40,000	Net income 20X7	60,000

  Pinky Corporation purchased 75% of S'Brain's outstanding stock on January 1, 20X6, for $300,000. During 20X7 Pinky's income, excluding its investment income from S'Brain, was $90,000.

Required
 1 Prepare the journal entries, other than closing entries, on Pinky's books to account for its investment in S'Brain during 20X7 under the *cost method.*
 2 Determine the balance of Pinky's investment in S'Brain account at December 31, 20X7 under the *cost method.*
 3 Prepare the journal entries, other than closing entries, on Pinky's books to account for its investment in S'Brain for 20X7 under the *equity method.*
 4 Determine the balance of Pinky's investment in S'Brain account at December 31, 20X7 under the *equity method.*
 5 Compute consolidated net income for Pinky Corporation and Subsidiary for 20X7.

E 4-8 **[AICPA adapted]**
The following balance sheets as of the current date are for Parent Company and Subsidiary:

	Parent	Consolidated
Assets		
Current assets	$218,000	$363,000
Plant assets	93,000	154,000
Investment in subsidiary	145,000	—
	$456,000	$517,000
Equities		
Current liabilities	$ 83,000	$150,000
Minority interest	—	29,200
Capital stock	320,000	320,000
Retained earnings	53,000	17,800
	$456,000	$517,000

  Parent Company uses the cost (legal-basis) method of accounting for its investment in 80% of the capital stock of Subsidiary.
  A $7,000 excess of book value acquired over investment cost was allocated to reduce an overvaluation of Subsidiary's land account and is included in the above plant assets valuation.
 1 The stockholders' equity of Subsidiary at the time Parent purchased its interest was:
  a $190,000   **c** $159,000
  b $172,500   **d** $152,000
 2 The balance in the capital stock account of Subsidiary at the time Parent purchased its interest was:
  a $150,000   **c** $100,000
  b $125,000   **d** Indeterminable

3 The current stockholders' equity of Subsidiary is:
 a $173,000   c $152,000
 b $159,000   d $146,000
4 The current balance in the retained earnings account of Subsidiary is:
 a $152,000   c $146,000
 b $150,000   d Indeterminable
5 The current working capital of Subsidiary is:
 a $145,000   c $78,000
 b $125,000   d $67,000

E 4-9 Photronic Industries acquires an 80% interest in Silicon Corporation for $160,000 cash, its book value on January 1, 20X5. Silicon's capital stock and retained earnings on this date totaled $200,000.

Photronic reported net income for 20X5 at $120,000 and paid dividends during 20X5 of $60,000. Silicon's net income and dividends for 20X5 were $60,000 and $25,000, respectively.

Required
1 Assume that Photronic uses the cost method of accounting for its investment in Silicon.
 a At what amount should the investment in Silicon appear on Photronic's books at December 31, 20X5?
 b Compute consolidated net income for 20X5.
2 Assume that Photronic uses the equity method of accounting for its investment in Silicon.
 a At what amount should the investment in Silicon appear on Photronic's books at December 31, 20X5?
 b Compute consolidated net income for 20X5.
 c Compute minority interest at December 31, 20X5.

E 4-10 The stockholder's equity accounts of Penair Corporation and Stine Corporation at December 31, 20X5 were as follows:

	Penair Corporation	Stine Corporation
Capital stock	$1,200,000	$500,000
Retained earnings	500,000	100,000
Total	$1,700,000	$600,000

On January 1, 20X6, Penair Corporation acquired an 80% interest in Stine Corporation for $580,000. The excess of cost over book value acquired was due to Stine Corporation's equipment being undervalued by $50,000 and the remainder due to goodwill. The undervalued equipment had a five-year remaining useful life when Penair acquired its interest. Goodwill is being amortized over a 10-year period.

The income and dividends of Penair and Stine for 20X6 and 20X7 are as follows:

	Penair		Stine	
	20X6	20X7	20X6	20X7
Net income	$340,000	$350,000	$120,000	$150,000
Dividends	240,000	250,000	80,000	90,000

Required
1 Assume that Penair Corporation uses the equity method of accounting for its investment in Stine.
 a Determine consolidated net income for Penair Corporation and Subsidiary for 20X6.
 b Compute the balance of Penair's investment in Stine account at December 31, 20X6.
 c Compute minority interest income for 20X6.
 d Compute minority interest at December 31, 20X7.
2 Compute consolidated net income for Penair Corporation and Subsidiary for 20X6 assuming that Penair uses the equity method of accounting except that it does not amortize the difference between cost and book value acquired on its separate books. (*Hint:* Determine separate income of Penair Corporation as a first step in your computation.)

E 4-11 **Appendix**
1 In preparing a statement of cash flows, the cost of acquiring a subsidiary is reported:
 a As an operating activity under the direct method
 b As an operating activity under the indirect method
 c As an investing activity
 d As a financing activity

2 In computing cash flows from operating activities under the direct method, the following item is an addition:

a Cash dividends from equity investees

b Collection of principal on a loan made to a subsidiary

c Minority interest dividends

d Minority interest income

3 In computing cash flows from operating activities under the indirect method, the following item is an addition to consolidated net income:

a Minority interest dividends

b Minority interest income

c Income from equity investees in excess of dividends received

d Amortization of negative goodwill

4 In computing cash flows from operating activities under the direct method, the following item is an addition:

a Sales

b Minority interest income

c Cash received from customers

d Depreciation expense

5 Dividends paid as presented in a consolidated cash flow statement are:

a Parent company dividends

b Subsidiary dividends

c Parent and subsidiary dividends

d Parent and minority interest dividends

E 4-12   Appendix

Information needed to prepare the "cash flow from operating activities" section of Party Corporation's consolidated statement of cash flows for 20X2, is included in the following list:

Amortization of goodwill	$ 8,000
Consolidated net income	75,000
Decrease in accounts payable	10,000
Depreciation expense	60,000
Increase in accounts receivable	52,500
Increase in inventories	22,500
Loss on sale of land	50,000
Minority interest income	25,000
Minority interest dividends	12,000
Undistributed income of equity investees	2,500

Required: Prepare the "cash flows from operating activities" section of Party's consolidated statement of cash flows under the indirect method.

E 4-13   Appendix

The information needed to prepare the "cash flow from operating activities" section of Prolax Corporation's consolidated statement of cash flows for 20X2, is included in the following list:

Cash received from customers	$322,500
Cash paid to suppliers	182,500
Cash paid to employees	27,000
Cash paid for other operating items	23,500
Cash paid for interest expense	12,000
Cash proceeds from sale of land	60,000
Minority interest dividends	10,000
Dividends received from equity investees	7,000

Required: Prepare the "cash flows from operating activities" section of Prolax's consolidated statement of cash flows under the direct method.

PROBLEMS

P 4-1 Pearl Corporation purchased 75% of the outstanding voting stock of Seine Corporation for $2,500,000 on January 1, 20X2. Seine's stockholders' equity on this date consisted of the following:

Capital stock, $10 par	$1,000,000
Additional paid-in capital	600,000
Retained earnings December 31, 20X1	800,000
Total stockholders' equity	$2,400,000

The excess of investment cost over book value of the net assets acquired was allocated 10% to undervalued inventory (sold in 20X2), 40% to plant assets with a remaining useful life of eight years, and 50% to unidentifiable intangible assets with a 10-year write-off period.

Comparative trial balances of Pearl Corporation and Seine Corporation at December 31, 20X6 are as follows:

	Pearl	Seine
Other assets—net	$3,850,000	$2,600,000
Investment in Seine—75%	2,080,000	—
Expenses (including cost of sales)	3,180,000	600,000
Dividends	500,000	200,000
	$9,610,000	$3,400,000
Capital stock, $10 par	$3,000,000	$1,000,000
Additional paid-in capital	850,000	600,000
Retained earnings	1,530,000	800,000
Sales	4,000,000	1,000,000
Income from Seine	230,000	—
	$9,610,000	$3,400,000

Required: Determine the amounts that would appear in the consolidated financial statements of Pearl Corporation and Subsidiary for each of the following items:
1 Goodwill at December 31, 20X6
2 Minority interest income for 20X6
3 Consolidated retained earnings at December 31, 20X5
4 Consolidated retained earnings at December 31, 20X6
5 Consolidated net income for 20X6
6 Minority interest at December 31, 20X5
7 Minority interest at December 31, 20X6
8 Dividends payable at December 31, 20X6

P 4-2   Pane Company paid $88,000 for an 80% interest in Sizzle Company on January 5, 20X1, when Sizzle's capital stock was $60,000 and its retained earnings $40,000. Trial balances for the companies at December 31, 20X1 are as follows:

	Pane	Sizzle
Cash	$ 2,500	$ 15,000
Accounts receivable	15,000	25,000
Other assets	120,000	100,000
Investment in Sizzle	88,000	—
Cost of goods sold	50,000	30,000
Operating expenses	25,000	40,000
Dividends	20,000	10,000
	$320,500	$220,000
Liabilities	$ 80,000	$ 30,000
Capital stock	100,000	60,000
Paid-in excess	10,000	—
Retained earnings	22,500	40,000
Sales	100,000	90,000
Dividend income	8,000	—
	$320,500	$220,000

The only entries that Pane Company made in regard to the investment in Sizzle Company are as follows:

January 5, 20X1

| Investment in Sizzle | $88,000 | |
| Cash | | $88,000 |

November 15, 20X1

| Cash | $8,000 | |
| Dividend income | | $8,000 |

Goodwill is to be amortized over a 10-year period. Assets and liabilities of Sizzle are stated at their fair values.

Required

1 Prepare a balance sheet for Pane Company at December 31, 20X1.
2 Prepare a consolidated income statement for Pane Company and Subsidiary for 20X1.
3 Prepare a consolidated balance sheet for Pane Company and Subsidiary at December 31, 20X1.

P 4-3 Palm Corporation acquired 70% of the outstanding voting stock of Sail Corporation for $45,500 cash on January 1, 20X8 when Sail's stockholders' equity was $65,000. All the assets and liabilities of Sail were stated at their fair values when Palm acquired its 70% interest.

Financial statements of the two corporations at and for the year ended December 31, 20X8 are summarized as follows:

	Palm	Sail
Combined Income and Retained Earnings Statements for the Year Ended December 31, 20X8		
Sales	$310,000	$100,000
Income from Sail	10,500	—
Cost of goods sold	(200,000)	(65,000)
Operating expenses	(77,000)	(20,000)
Net income	43,500	15,000
Add: Retained earnings January 1, 20X8	65,000	11,000
Deduct: Dividends	(30,000)	(10,000)
Retained earnings December 31, 20X8	$ 78,500	$ 16,000
Balance Sheet at December 31, 20X8		
Cash	$ 45,500	$ 15,000
Receivables—net	60,000	30,000
Inventories	24,000	20,000
Plant and equipment—net	120,000	35,000
Investment in Sail	49,000	—
Total assets	$298,500	$100,000
Accounts payable	$ 30,000	$ 18,000
Other liabilities	20,000	12,000
Capital stock, $10 par	150,000	50,000
Other paid-in capital	20,000	4,000
Retained earnings	78,500	16,000
Total equities	$298,500	$100,000

Required

1 Prepare consolidation working papers for Palm Corporation and Subsidiary for 20X8.
2 Prepare a consolidated income statement and a consolidated balance sheet for Palm Corporation and Subsidiary.

P 4-4 Pan Corporation acquired a controlling interest in Saf Corporation on January 1, 20X2. Financial statements of Pan and Saf corporations for the year 20X2 are as follows:

	Pan	Saf
Combined Income and Retained Earnings Statements for the Year Ended December 31, 20X2		
Sales	$400,000	$100,000
Income from Saf	17,000	—
Cost of sales	(250,000)	(50,000)
Other expenses	(97,000)	(26,000)
Net income	70,000	24,000
Add: Retained earnings January 1, 20X2	180,000	34,000
Deduct: Dividends	(50,000)	(16,000)
Retained earnings December 31, 20X2	$200,000	$ 42,000
Balance Sheet at December 31, 20X2		
Cash	$ 61,000	$ 15,000
Accounts receivable—net	80,000	20,000
Dividends receivable from Saf	6,000	—
Inventories	95,000	10,000
Note receivable from Pan	—	5,000

(Continued)

	Pan	Saf
Land	65,000	30,000
Buildings—net	170,000	80,000
Equipment—net	130,000	50,000
Investment in Saf	183,000	—
Total assets	$790,000	$210,000
Accounts payable	$ 85,000	$ 10,000
Note payable to Saf	5,000	—
Dividends payable	—	8,000
Capital stock, $10 par	500,000	150,000
Retained earnings	200,000	42,000
Total equities	$790,000	$210,000

Required: Prepare consolidation working papers for Pan Corporation and Subsidiary for the year ended December 31, 20X2. Only the information provided in the financial statements is available, and accordingly, your solution will require some standard assumptions. (*Hint:* Determine Pan's interest in Saf as a first step.)

P 4-5 Pari Corporation acquired a 70% interest in Soul Corporation's outstanding voting common stock on January 1, 20X1 for $500,000 cash. The stockholders' equity of Soul on this date consisted of $500,000 capital stock and $100,000 retained earnings. The difference between the price paid by Pari and the underlying equity acquired in Soul was *allocated* $5,000 to Soul's undervalued inventory, $14,000 to undervalued buildings, $21,000 to undervalued equipment, and $40,000 to goodwill.

The undervalued inventory items were sold during 20X1, and the undervalued buildings and equipment had remaining useful lives of seven years and three years, respectively. Depreciation is straight line.

At December 31, 20X1 Soul's accounts payable include $10,000 owed to Pari. This $10,000 account payable is due on January 15, 20X2. Pari sold equipment with a book value of $15,000 for $25,000 on June 1, 20X1. This is not an intercompany sale transaction. Separate financial statements for Pari and Soul for 20X1 are summarized as follows:

	Pari	Soul
Combined Income and Retained Earnings Statements for the Year Ended December 31, 20X1		
Sales	$ 800,000	$700,000
Income from Soul	55,000	—
Gain on equipment	10,000	—
Cost of sales	(300,000)	(400,000)
Depreciation expense	(155,000)	(60,000)
Other expenses	(160,000)	(140,000)
Net income	250,000	100,000
Add: Retained earnings January 1, 20X1	300,000	100,000
Deduct: Dividends	(200,000)	(50,000)
Retained earnings December 31, 20X1	$ 350,000	$150,000
Balance Sheet at December 31, 20X1		
Cash	$ 86,000	$ 60,000
Accounts receivable—net	100,000	70,000
Dividends receivable	14,000	—
Inventories	150,000	100,000
Other current assets	70,000	30,000
Land	50,000	100,000
Buildings—net	140,000	160,000
Equipment—net	570,000	330,000
Investment in Soul	520,000	—
Total assets	$1,700,000	$850,000
Accounts payable	$ 200,000	$ 85,000
Dividends payable	100,000	20,000
Other liabilities	50,000	95,000
Capital stock, $10 par	1,000,000	500,000
Retained earnings	350,000	150,000
Total equities	$1,700,000	$850,000

Required: Prepare consolidation working papers for Pari Corporation and Subsidiary for the year ended December 31, 20X1. Use an unamortized excess account.

P 4-6   Separate company financial statements for Pen Corporation and its subsidiary, Syn Company, at and for the year ended December 31, 20X3 are summarized as follows:

	Pen	Syn
Combined Income and Retained Earnings Statements		
for the Year Ended December 31, 20X3		
Sales	$400,000	$100,000
Income from Syn	20,600	—
Cost of sales	(250,000)	(50,000)
Expenses	(100,600)	(26,000)
Net income	70,000	24,000
Add: Retained earnings January 1, 20X3	180,000	34,000
Deduct: Dividends	(50,000)	(16,000)
Retained earnings December 31, 20X3	$200,000	$ 42,000
Balance Sheet at December 31, 20X3		
Cash	$ 18,000	$ 15,000
Accounts receivable—net	80,000	20,000
Dividends receivable from Syn	7,200	—
Note receivable from Pen	—	5,000
Inventory	95,000	10,000
Investment in Syn	224,800	—
Land	65,000	30,000
Buildings—net	170,000	80,000
Equipment—net	130,000	50,000
Total assets	$790,000	$210,000
Accounts payable	$ 85,000	$ 10,000
Note payable to Syn	5,000	—
Dividends payable	—	8,000
Capital stock, $10 par	500,000	150,000
Retained earnings	200,000	42,000
Total equities	$790,000	$210,000

Additional Information
1 Pen Corporation acquired 13,500 shares of Syn Company stock for $15 per share on January 1, 20X2, when Syn's stockholders' equity consisted of $150,000 capital stock and $15,000 retained earnings.
2 Syn Company's land was undervalued when Pen acquired its interest, and accordingly, $14,000 of the cost/book value differential was allocated to land. Any remaining differential is goodwill.
3 Syn Company owes Pen $5,000 on account, and Pen owes Syn $5,000 on a note payable.

Required: Prepare consolidation working papers for Pen Corporation and Subsidiary for the year ended December 31, 20X3.

P 4-7   Prim Corporation acquired a 100% interest in Stan Corporation in a pooling of interests on January 1, 20X6 when Stan's equity consisted of $1,000,000 capital stock and $200,000 retained earnings. Prim exchanged 100,000 of its shares with a market value of $1,350,000 for all Stan's outstanding shares.

Additional Information
1 Prim uses the equity method of accounting for Stan.
2 Stan's inventories were undervalued by $2,000 and its equipment by $10,000 on January 1, 20X6. The inventory items were sold in 20X6, and the equipment had a 10-year remaining useful life at the time.
3 Stan mailed a $10,000 check to Prim on December 31, 20X8 in settlement of an account receivable. Prim did not record the collection until 20X9. Accordingly, its December 31, 20X8 receivables are overstated.
4 In accounting for its investment in Stan for 20X8, Prim failed to record its share of Stan's dividends declared but not paid in 20X8.
5 Separate company financial statements for Prim Corporation and Stan Corporation at and for the year ended December 31, 20X8 are summarized as follows:

	Prim	Stan
Combined Income and Retained Earnings Statements		
for the Year Ended December 31, 20X8		
Sales	$1,900,000	$1,000,000
Income from Stan	200,000	—
Cost of sales	(800,000)	(400,000)
Depreciation expense	(200,000)	(100,000)
Interest expense	(200,000)	—
Operating expense	(400,000)	(300,000)
Net income	500,000	200,000
Add: Retained earnings January 1, 20X8	1,300,000	400,000
Deduct: Dividends	(400,000)	(150,000)
Retained earnings December 31, 20X8	$1,400,000	$ 450,000
Balance Sheet at December 31, 20X8		
Cash	$ 150,000	$ 60,000
Receivables—net	350,000	140,000
Inventories	1,000,000	150,000
Land	600,000	100,000
Buildings—net	1,500,000	500,000
Equipment—net	1,900,000	800,000
Investment in Stan	1,500,000	—
Total assets	$7,000,000	$1,750,000
Accounts payable	$ 400,000	$ 250,000
Dividends payable	100,000	50,000
Bond interest payable	100,000	—
10% bonds payable	2,000,000	—
Common stock, $10 par	2,500,000	1,000,000
Other paid-in capital	500,000	—
Retained earnings	1,400,000	450,000
Total equities	$7,000,000	$1,750,000

Required: Prepare working papers to consolidate the financial statements of Prim Corporation and Subsidiary at and for the year ended December 31, 20X8.

P 4-8 Plastik Corporation acquired 80% of Seldane Corporation's common stock on January 1, 20X2 for $210,000 cash. The stockholders' equity of Seldane at this time consisted of $150,000 capital stock and $50,000 retained earnings. The difference between the price paid by Plastik and the underlying equity acquired in Seldane was due to a $12,500 undervaluation of Seldane's inventory, a $25,000 undervaluation of Seldane's equipment, and goodwill.

The undervalued inventory items were sold by Seldane during 20X2, and the undervalued equipment had a remaining useful life of five years. Any goodwill is amortized over 20 years. Straight-line depreciation is used.

Seldane owed Plastik $4,000 on accounts payable at December 31, 20X2.

The separate financial statements of Plastik and Seldane corporations at and for the year ended December 31, 20X2 are as follows:

	Plastik	Seldane
Combined Income and Retained Earnings Statements		
for the Year Ended December 31, 20X2		
Sales	$200,000	$110,000
Income from Seldane	17,000	—
Cost of sales	(80,000)	(40,000)
Depreciation expense	(40,000)	(20,000)
Other expenses	(25,500)	(10,000)
Net income	71,500	40,000
Add: Retained earnings January 1, 20X2	75,000	50,000
Deduct: Dividends	(40,000)	(20,000)
Retained earnings December 31, 20X2	$106,500	$ 70,000
Balance Sheet at December 31, 20X2		
Cash	$ 29,500	$ 30,000
Trade receivables—net	28,000	40,000
Dividends receivable	8,000	—

(Continued)

	Plastik	Seldane
Inventories	40,000	30,000
Land	15,000	30,000
Buildings—net	65,000	70,000
Equipment—net	200,000	100,000
Investment in Seldane	211,000	—
Total assets	$596,500	$300,000
Accounts payable	$ 40,000	$ 50,000
Dividends payable	100,000	10,000
Other liabilities	50,000	20,000
Capital stock, $10 par	300,000	150,000
Retained earnings	106,500	70,000
Total equities	$596,500	$300,000

Required: Prepare consolidation working papers for Plastik Corporation and Subsidiary at and for the year ended December 31, 20X2.

P 4-9 Pill Corporation paid $170,000 for an 80% interest in Stud Corporation on December 31, 20X1, when Stud's stockholders' equity consisted of $100,000 capital stock and $50,000 retained earnings. A summary of the changes in Pill's investment in Stud account from December 31, 20X1 to December 31, 20X5 follows:

Investment cost December 31, 20X1		$170,000
Increases		
80% of Stud's income 20X2 through 20X5		112,000
		282,000
Decreases		
80% of Stud's dividends 20X2 through 20X5	$56,000	
Amortization of excess cost over book value:		
Allocated to inventories, $7,000 (sold in 20X2)	7,000	
Allocated to plant assets, $18,000 (depreciated		
over a nine-year period) 20X2 through 20X5	8,000	
Allocated to goodwill, $25,000 (amortized over		
a five-year period) 20X2 through 20X5	20,000	91,000
Investment balance December 31, 20X5		$191,000

Financial statements for Pill and Stud at and for the year ended December 31, 20X5 are summarized as follows:

	Pill	Stud
Combined Income and Retained Earnings Statements		
for the Year Ended December 31, 20X5		
Sales	$300,000	$200,000
Income from Stud	25,000	—
Cost of sales	(180,000)	(140,000)
Other expenses	(50,000)	(20,000)
Net income	95,000	40,000
Add: Retained earnings January 1, 20X5	255,000	100,000
Deduct: Dividends	(50,000)	(20,000)
Retained earnings December 31, 20X5	$300,000	$120,000
Balance Sheet at December 31, 20X5		
Cash	$ 41,000	$ 35,000
Trade receivables—net	60,000	55,000
Dividends receivable	8,000	—
Advance to Stud	25,000	—
Inventories	125,000	35,000
Plant assets—net	300,000	175,000
Investment in Stud	191,000	—
Total assets	$750,000	$300,000

(Continued)

	Pill	Stud
Accounts payable	$ 50,000	$ 45,000
Dividends payable	—	10,000
Advance from Pill	—	25,000
Capital stock	400,000	100,000
Retained earnings	300,000	120,000
Total equities	$750,000	$300,000

Additional Information

    1 The accounts payable of Stud at December 31, 20X5 include $5,000 owed to Pill.

    2 Pill advanced $25,000 to Stud during 20X3. This advance is still outstanding.

    3 Half of Stud's 20X5 dividends will be paid in January 20X6.

Required: Prepare working papers to consolidate the balance sheets only of Pill and Stud corporations at December 31, 20X5.

P 4-10 Pat Corporation acquired an 80% interest in Sci Corporation for $240,000 on January 1, 20X5, when Sci's stockholders' equity consisted of $200,000 capital stock and $25,000 retained earnings. The excess cost over book value acquired was allocated to plant assets that were undervalued by $50,000 and to goodwill. The undervalued plant assets had a four-year useful life and goodwill is amortized over 10 years.

Additional Information

    1 Pat's accounts receivable includes $5,000 owed to Sci.

    2 Sci mailed its check for $20,000 to Pat on December 30, 20X6 in settlement of the advance.

    3 A $10,000 dividend was declared by Sci on December 30, 20X6, but not recorded by Pat.

    4 Financial statements for Pat and Sci corporations for 20X6 follow:

	Pat	Sci
Statements of Income and Retained Earnings		
for the Year Ended December 31, 20X6		
Sales	$900,000	$300,000
Income from Sci	36,000	—
Cost of sales	(600,000)	(150,000)
Operating expenses	(190,000)	(90,000)
Net income	146,000	60,000
Add: Retained earnings January 1	120,000	50,000
Less: Dividends	(100,000)	(20,000)
Retained earnings December 31	$166,000	$ 90,000
Balance Sheet at December 31, 20X6		
Cash	$ 6,000	$ 15,000
Accounts receivable—net	26,000	20,000
Inventories	82,000	60,000
Advance to Sci	20,000	—
Other current assets	80,000	5,000
Land	160,000	30,000
Plant assets—net	340,000	230,000
Investment in Sci	276,000	—
Total assets	$990,000	$360,000
Accounts payable	$ 24,000	$ 15,000
Dividends payable	—	10,000
Other liabilities	100,000	45,000
Capital stock	700,000	200,000
Retained earnings	166,000	90,000
Total liabilities and stockholders' equity	$990,000	$360,000

Required: Prepare consolidation working papers for Pat Corporation and Subsidiary for 20X6.

P 4-11 Separate company and consolidated financial statements are presented for Powderhouse Corporation and its subsidiary, Starmark Corporation, at and for the year ended December 31, 20X9.

	Powerhouse	Starmark	Consolidated
Income Statement			
Sales	$1,000,000	$400,000	$1,400,000
Income from Starmark	80,000	—	—
Cost of goods sold	(500,000)	(150,000)	(650,000)
Operating expenses	(385,000)	(150,000)	(545,000)
Minority interest income	—	—	(10,000)
Net income	$ 195,000	$100,000	$ 195,000
Retained Earnings Statement			
Retained earnings January 1, 20X9	$ 350,000	$150,000	$ 350,000
Add: Net income	195,000	100,000	195,000
Deduct: Dividends	(100,000)	(50,000)	(100,000)
Retained earnings December 31, 20X9	$ 445,000	$200,000	$ 445,000
Balance Sheet			
Cash	$ 118,000	$ 25,000	$ 143,000
Accounts receivable—net	155,000	50,000	200,000
Dividends receivable	27,000	—	—
Inventories	250,000	175,000	425,000
Plant assets—net	500,000	300,000	815,000
Investment in Starmark	445,000	—	—
Goodwill	—	—	25,000
Total assets	$1,495,000	$550,000	$1,608,000
Accounts payable	$ 150,000	$ 70,000	$ 215,000
Dividends payable	50,000	30,000	53,000
Capital stock, $10 par	700,000	100,000	700,000
Additional paid-in capital	150,000	150,000	150,000
Retained earnings	445,000	200,000	445,000
Minority interest	—	—	45,000
Total equities	$1,495,000	$550,000	$1,608,000

Required: Reproduce in general journal form the working paper adjustments and eliminations that were made to consolidate the financial statements of Powderhouse and its subsidiary, Starmark, at December 31, 20X9. Include a working paper entry for minority interest income, dividends, and equity. Goodwill had a remaining useful life of six years at January 1, 20X9.

P 4-12 Comparative adjusted trial balances for Ply Corporation and Ski Corporation at December 31, 20X5, 20X6, and 20X7 are given here. Ply Corporation acquired an 80% interest in Ski Corporation on January 1, 20X6, for $80,000 cash. Except for inventory items that were undervalued by $1,000 and equipment that was undervalued by $4,000, all of Ski's identifiable assets and liabilities were stated at their fair values on December 31, 20X5.

Ski Corporation sold the undervalued inventory items during 20X6 but continues to own the equipment, which had a four-year remaining useful life as of December 31, 20X5.

	December 31, 20X5		December 31, 20X6		December 31, 20X7	
	Ply	Ski	Ply	Ski	Ply	Ski
Cash	$100,000	$ 30,000	$ 24,700	$ 15,000	$ 26,700	$ 20,000
Trade receivables—net	30,000	15,000	25,000	20,000	45,000	30,000
Dividends receivable	—	—	4,000	—	4,000	—
Inventories	50,000	20,000	40,000	30,000	40,000	30,000
Plant and equipment—net	90,000	60,000	100,000	55,000	95,000	60,000
Investment in Ski	—	—	86,300	—	94,300	—
Cost of sales	100,000	40,000	105,000	35,000	110,000	35,000
Operating expenses	20,000	30,000	35,000	30,000	30,000	35,000
Dividends	10,000	5,000	10,000	5,000	15,000	10,000
	$400,000	$200,000	$430,000	$190,000	$460,000	$220,000
Accounts payable	$ 30,000	$ 35,000	$ 20,700	$ 15,000	$ 17,700	$ 25,000
Dividends payable	10,000	—	9,000	5,000	6,000	5,000
Capital stock	100,000	40,000	100,000	40,000	100,000	40,000
Other paid-in capital	60,000	20,000	60,000	20,000	60,000	20,000
Retained earnings	50,000	25,000	70,000	30,000	90,300	40,000
Sales	150,000	80,000	160,000	80,000	170,000	90,000
Income from Ski	—	—	10,300	—	16,000	—
	$400,000	$200,000	$430,000	$190,000	$460,000	$220,000

Required: Prepare consolidation working papers for Ply Corporation and Subsidiary for 20X6 and 20X7 using the financial statement approach. (*Hint:* Ply Corporation's accountant applied the equity method correctly for 20X6 but misapplied the equity method for 20X7.)

P 4-13 Separate company financial statements for Phil Corporation and its 70%-owned subsidiary, Simm Corporation, at December 31, 20X8 are summarized as follows:

	Phil	Simm
Combined Income and Retained Earnings Statements for the Year Ended December 31, 20X8		
Sales	$500,000	$100,000
Income from Simm	21,000	—
Cost of sales	(240,000)	(40,000)
Expenses	(174,000)	(30,000)
Net income	107,000	30,000
Add: Retained earnings January 1, 20X8	110,000	40,000
Deduct: Dividends	(70,000)	(20,000)
Retained earnings December 31, 20X8	$147,000	$ 50,000
Balance Sheet at December 31, 20X8		
Cash	$ 56,000	$ 30,000
Accounts receivable	40,000	20,000
Inventories	60,000	15,000
Plant assets—net	220,000	105,000
Investment in Simm	121,000	—
Total assets	$497,000	$170,000
Accounts payable	$ 50,000	$ 40,000
Capital stock	300,000	80,000
Retained earnings	147,000	50,000
Total equities	$497,000	$170,000

Phil acquired its interest in Simm on January 1, 20X6 for $100,000, when Simm's outstanding capital stock was $80,000 and its retained earnings, $20,000. Of the excess of cost over book value, $10,000 was allocated to inventories that were sold in 20X6 and the remainder to goodwill with a 10-year amortization period.

Required: Prepare consolidation working papers for Phil Corporation and Subsidiary for the year ended December 31, 20X8.

P 4-14 Puff Corporation acquired a 60% interest in Scot Corporation for $200,000 on January 1, 20X5, when the stockholders' equity of Scot consisted of $200,000 capital stock and $25,000 retained earnings. The excess cost over book value acquired was allocated to machinery that was undervalued by $50,000 and to goodwill. The undervalued machinery is being depreciated over four years and goodwill is being amortized over 10 years.

Financial statements for Puff and Scot Corporations for 20X6 are summarized as follows:

	Puff	Scot
Combined Income and Retained Earnings Statements for the Year Ended December 31, 20X6		
Net sales	$900,000	$300,000
Dividends from Scot	6,000	—
Cost of goods sold	(600,000)	(150,000)
Operating expenses	(190,000)	(90,000)
Net income	116,000	60,000
Add: Retained earnings January 1, 20X6	112,000	50,000
Less: Dividends	(100,000)	(20,000)
Retained earnings December 31, 20X6	$128,000	$ 90,000
Balance Sheet at December 31, 20X6		
Cash	$ 26,000	$ 15,000
Accounts receivable—net	26,000	20,000
Inventories	82,000	60,000
Other current assets	80,000	5,000
Land	160,000	30,000

(Continued)

	Puff	Scot
Plant and equipment—net	340,000	230,000
Investment in Scot	200,000	—
Total assets	$914,000	$360,000
Accounts payable	$ 24,000	$ 15,000
Dividends payable	—	10,000
Other liabilities	62,000	45,000
Capital stock	700,000	200,000
Retained earnings	128,000	90,000
Total equities	$914,000	$360,000

Additional Information

1 A $10,000 dividend was declared by Scot on December 30, 20X6, but not recorded by Puff.
2 Puff's accounts receivable includes $5,000 due from Scot.

Required: Prepare consolidation working papers for Puff Corporation and Subsidiary for the year ended December 31, 20X6.

P 4-15 Pappa Bee Industries acquired its interest in Sue Bee Company for cash on July 1, 20X1, when Sue Bee had capital stock of $50,000 and retained earnings of $21,000. Of the excess of investment cost over book value acquired, $15,000 was allocated to plant and equipment with a five-year remaining useful life and the remainder to goodwill with a 10-year life as of the date of combination. No changes in the outstanding common stock of either company have occurred since July 1, 20X1.

Pappa Bee loaned Sue Bee $100,000 at 8 percent interest on June 30, 20X4, with interest payable semiannually. All interest in the financial statements relate to this loan.

The separate company financial statements for Pappa Bee Industries and its subsidiary Sue Bee Company at June 30, 20X5 are summarized as follows:

	Pappa Bee	Sue Bee
Combined Income and Retained Earnings Statements for the Year Ended June 30, 20X5		
Sales	$500,000	$250,000
Dividend income	57,000	—
Interest income	8,000	—
Cost of sales	(300,000)	(120,000)
Interest expense	—	(8,000)
Other expenses	(150,000)	(60,000)
Net income	115,000	62,000
Add: Beginning retained earnings	148,000	81,000
Deduct: Dividends	(50,000)	(60,000)
Retained earnings June 30, 20X5	$213,000	$ 83,000
Balance Sheet at June 30, 20X5		
Cash	$ 69,300	$ 22,000
Accounts receivable—net	60,000	30,000
Interest receivable	4,000	—
Dividends receivable	14,250	—
Other current assets	100,000	75,000
Plant and equipment	300,000	200,000
Less: Accumulated depreciation	(72,000)	(50,000)
Investment in Sue Bee	102,450	—
Note receivable—8%	100,000	—
Total assets	$678,000	$277,000
Accounts payable	$ 40,000	$ 25,000
Dividends payable	25,000	15,000
Interest payable	—	4,000
Note payable—8%	—	100,000
Capital stock	400,000	50,000
Retained earnings	213,000	83,000
Total equities	$678,000	$277,000

Required

1 Prepare a conversion to equity schedule for Pappa Bee's investment in Sue Bee Company.
2 Prepare consolidation working papers for Pappa Bee Industries and Subsidiary for the year ended June 30, 20X5.

P 4-16 Peter Pepper Company paid $100,000 for a 90% interest in Simple Pear on January 5, 20X2, when Simple Pear's capital stock was $60,000 and its retained earnings $20,000. Trial balances for the companies at December 31, 20X5 are as follows:

	Peter Pepper	Simple Pear
Cash	$ 11,000	$ 15,000
Accounts receivable	15,000	25,000
Plant assets	220,000	180,000
Investment in Simple Pear	138,000	—
Cost of goods sold	50,000	30,000
Operating expenses	25,000	40,000
Dividends	20,000	10,000
	$479,000	$300,000
Accumulated depreciation	$ 90,000	$ 50,000
Liabilities	80,000	30,000
Capital stock	100,000	60,000
Paid-in excess	20,000	—
Retained earnings	73,000	70,000
Sales	100,000	90,000
Income from Simple Pear	16,000	—
	$479,000	$300,000

The excess of investment cost over book value acquired was allocated $8,000 to undervalued inventory items that were sold in 20X2 and the remainder to goodwill having a remaining useful life of 10 years from January 1, 20X2.

Required
1. Summarize the changes in Peter Pepper Company's investment in Simple Pear account from January 5, 20X2 through December 31, 20X5.
2. Prepare consolidation working papers for Peter Pepper Company and Subsidiary for the year 20X5 using the trial balance approach for your working papers.

P 4-17 Peggy Corporation owns 90% of the voting stock of Super Corporation and 25% of the voting stock of Ellen Corporation.

The 90% interest in Super was acquired for $20,000 cash on January 1, 20X5, when Super's stockholders' equity was $20,000 ($18,000 capital stock and $2,000 retained earnings).

Peggy's 25% interest in Ellen was purchased for $7,000 cash on July 1, 20X5, when Ellen's stockholders' equity was $24,000 ($15,000 capital stock, $6,000 retained earnings, and $3,000 current earnings—first half of 20X5).

The difference between investment cost and book value acquired is considered goodwill and is being amortized over 10 years.

Adjusted trial balances of the three associated companies at December 31, 20X5 are presented as follows:

	Peggy	Super	Ellen
Cash	$ 16,950	$ 4,000	$ 1,000
Other current assets	40,000	11,000	10,000
Plant assets—net	120,000	14,000	20,000
Investment in Super—90%	21,600	—	—
Investment in Ellen—25%	6,450	—	—
Cost of sales	60,000	16,000	15,000
Other expenses	25,000	7,000	9,000
Dividends (paid in November)	10,000	3,000	5,000
Total debits	$300,000	$55,000	$60,000
Current liabilities	$ 25,000	$ 7,000	$ 9,000
Capital stock	150,000	18,000	15,000
Retained earnings	20,000	2,000	6,000
Sales	100,000	28,000	30,000
Income from Super	4,300	—	—
Income from Ellen	700	—	—
Total credits	$300,000	$55,000	$60,000

Required
1. Reconstruct the journal entries that were made by Peggy Corporation during 20X5 to account for its investments in Super and Ellen corporations.

2 Prepare an income statement, a retained earnings statement, and a balance sheet for Peggy Corporation for December 31, 20X5.

3 Prepare consolidation working papers (trial balance format) for Peggy and Subsidiary for 20X5.

4 Prepare consolidated financial statements other than the cash flows statement for Peggy Corporation and Subsidiary for the year ended December 31, 20X5.

P 4-18 Appendix

The accountant for Pillory Corporation collected the following information that he thought might be useful in the preparation of the company's consolidated statement of cash flows:

Cash paid for purchase of equipment	$ 270,000
Cash paid for other expenses	450,000
Cash paid to suppliers	630,000
Cash received from customers	1,600,000
Cash received from sale of land	500,000
Cash received from treasury stock sold	400,000
Dividends from equity investees	40,000
Dividends paid to minority stockholders	20,000
Dividends paid to Pillory's stockholders	50,000
Gain on sale of land	200,000
Income from equity investees	80,000
Interest received from short-term loan	5,000
Minority interest income	45,000

Required: Prepare the "cash flows from operating activities" section of the consolidated statement of cash flows for Pillory Corporation and Subsidiaries using the *direct method* of presentation.

P 4-19 Appendix

Comparative consolidated financial statements for Pesek Corporation and its 90%-owned subsidiary, Snider Corporation, at and for the years ended December 31, 20X8 and 20X7 are as follows:

PESEK CORPORATION AND SUBSIDIARY COMPARATIVE CONSOLIDATED FINANCIAL STATEMENTS

	Year 20X8	Year 20X7	20X8–20X7
Income and Retained Earnings Statements for the Year			*Change*
Sales	$ 675,000	$ 600,000	$ 75,000
Cost of sales	(350,000)	(324,500)	(25,500)
Depreciation expense	(51,000)	(51,000)	0
Other operating expenses	(139,000)	(120,500)	(18,500)
Minority interest income	(5,000)	(4,000)	(1,000)
Consolidated net income	130,000	100,000	30,000
Add: Beginning retained earnings	190,000	130,000	60,000
Less: Dividends	(40,000)	(40,000)	0
Ending retained earnings	$ 280,000	$ 190,000	$ 90,000
Balance Sheets at December 31			
Assets			
Cash	$ 55,500	$ 65,000	$ (9,500)
Accounts receivable—net	85,000	80,000	5,000
Inventories	140,000	120,000	20,000
Other current assets	100,000	81,000	19,000
Plant and equipment—net	674,000	600,000	74,000
Goodwill	19,000	19,500	(500)
Total assets	$1,073,500	$ 965,500	$108,000
Equities			
Accounts payable	$ 85,000	$ 63,000	$ 22,000
Dividends payable	21,000	17,000	4,000
Long-term liabilities	35,000	46,000	(11,000)
Capital stock	500,000	500,000	0
Other paid-in capital	120,000	120,000	0
Retained earnings	280,000	190,000	90,000
Minority interest—10%	32,500	29,500	3,000
Total equities	$1,073,500	$ 965,500	$108,000

Required: Prepare a consolidated statement of cash flows for Pesek Corporation and Subsidiary for the year ended December 31, 20X8, using either the indirect method or the direct method. All changes in plant assets are due to asset acquisitions and depreciation. Snider's net income and dividends for 20X8 are $50,000 and $20,000, respectively.

P 4-20   Appendix [AICPA adapted]

The consolidated working paper balances of Bush, Inc. and its subsidiary, Dorr Corporation, as of December 31, 20X6 and 20X5 are as follows:

	20X6	20X5	Net Change Increase (Decrease)
Assets			
Cash	$ 313,000	$ 195,000	$118,000
Marketable equity securities at cost (MES)	175,000	175,000	—
Allowance to reduce MES to market	(13,000)	(24,000)	11,000
Accounts receivable—net	418,000	440,000	(22,000)
Inventories	595,000	525,000	70,000
Land	385,000	170,000	215,000
Plant and equipment	755,000	690,000	65,000
Accumulated depreciation	(199,000)	(145,000)	(54,000)
Goodwill—net	57,000	60,000	(3,000)
Total assets	$2,486,000	$2,086,000	$400,000
Liabilities and Stockholders' Equity			
Note payable, current portion	$ 150,000	$ 150,000	$ —
Accounts and accrued payables	595,000	474,000	121,000
Note payable, long-term portion	300,000	450,000	(150,000)
Deferred income taxes	44,000	32,000	12,000
Minority interest in Dorr	179,000	161,000	18,000
Common stock—$10 par	580,000	480,000	100,000
Additional paid-in capital	303,000	180,000	123,000
Retained earnings	335,000	195,000	140,000
Treasury stock at cost	—	(36,000)	36,000
Total equities	$2,486,000	$2,086,000	$400,000

Additional Information

   1 On January 20, 20X6 Bush issued 10,000 shares of its common stock for land having a fair value of $215,000.
   2 On February 5, 20X6 Bush reissued all of its treasury stock for $44,000.
   3 On May 15, 20X6 Bush paid a cash dividend of $58,000 on its common stock.
   4 On August 8, 20X6 equipment was purchased for $127,000.
   5 On September 30, 20X6 equipment was sold for $40,000. The equipment cost $62,000 and had a carrying amount of $34,000 on the date of sale.
   6 On December 15, 20X6 Dorr Corporation paid a cash dividend of $50,000 on its common stock.
   7 Deferred income taxes represent timing differences relating to the use of accelerated depreciation methods for income tax reporting and the straight-line method for financial reporting.
   8 Consolidated net income for 20X6 was $198,000. Dorr's net income was $110,000.
   9 Bush owns 70% of its subsidiary, Dorr Corporation. There was no change in the ownership interest in Dorr during 20X5 and 20X6. There were no intercompany transactions other than the dividend paid to Bush by its subsidiary.

Required: Prepare a consolidated statement of cash flows for Bush and Subsidiary for the year ended December 31, 20X6. Use the *indirect method.*

P 4-21   Appendix

Comparative consolidated financial statements for Pilgrim Corporation and its 80%-owned subsidiary at and for the year ended December 31, 20X7 and 20X6 are summarized as follows:

PILGRAM CORPORATION AND SUBSIDIARY
COMPARATIVE CONSOLIDATED FINANCIAL STATEMENTS
AT AND FOR THE YEAR ENDED DECEMBER 31

	Year 20X7	Year 20X6	Year's Change 20X7–20X6
Income and Retained Earnings			
Sales	$2,600,000	$2,400,000	$200,000
Income—equity investees	60,000	50,000	10,000
Cost of sales	(1,450,000)	(1,408,000)	(42,000)
Depreciation expense	(200,000)	(150,000)	(50,000)
Other operating expenses	(470,000)	(462,000)	(8,000)
Minority interest income	(40,000)	(30,000)	(10,000)
Net income	500,000	400,000	100,000
Retained earnings, January 1	1,000,000	700,000	300,000
Dividends	(150,000)	(100,000)	(50,000)
Retained earnings, December 31	$1,350,000	$1,000,000	$350,000
Balance Sheet			
Cash	$ 430,000	$ 360,000	$ 70,000
Accounts receivable—net	750,000	540,000	210,000
Inventories	700,000	700,000	0
Plant and equipment—net	1,800,000	1,500,000	300,000
Equity investments	430,000	400,000	30,000
Goodwill	190,000	200,000	(10,000)
Total assets	$4,300,000	$3,700,000	$600,000
Accounts payable	$ 492,000	$ 475,000	$ 17,000
Dividends payable	38,000	25,000	13,000
Long-term note payable	600,000	400,000	200,000
Capital stock	1,000,000	1,000,000	0
Other paid-in capital	600,000	600,000	0
Retained earnings	1,350,000	1,000,000	350,000
Minority interest—20%	220,000	200,000	20,000
Total equities	$4,300,000	$3,700,000	$600,000

Required: Prepare a consolidated statement of cash flows for Pilgrim Corporation and Subsidiary for the year ended December 31, 20X7. Assume that all changes in plant assets are due to asset acquisitions and depreciation. Income and dividends from 20%- to 50%-owned investees for 20X7 were $60,000 and $30,000, respectively. Pilgram's only subsidiary reported $200,000 net income for 20X7 and declared $100,000 dividends during the year. Goodwill amortization for 20X7 is $10,000.

5

Intercompany Profit Transactions— Inventories

Consolidated statements are prepared to show the financial position and the results of operations of two or more affiliated companies as if they were one business enterprise. Therefore, the effects of transactions between the affiliated companies (referred to as intercompany transactions) must be eliminated from consolidated financial statements. Intercompany transactions may result in reciprocal account balances on the books of the affiliated companies. For example, intercompany sales transactions produce reciprocal sales and purchases (or cost of goods sold) balances, as well as reciprocal balances for accounts receivable and accounts payable. Intercompany loan transactions produce reciprocal notes receivable and notes payable balances, as well as reciprocal interest income and interest expense balances. These intercompany transactions are intracompany transactions from the viewpoint of the consolidated entity; therefore, their effects must be eliminated in the consolidation process.

In addition to reciprocal account balances, gains and losses from intercompany transactions must be eliminated until realized through use or through sale outside of the consolidated entity. As stated in *Accounting Research Bulletin (ARB) No. 51*, consolidated statements "should not include gain or loss on transactions among the companies in the group. Accordingly, any intercompany profit or loss on assets remaining within the group shall be eliminated; the concept usually applied for this purpose is gross profit or loss."[1]

ARB No. 51 also notes in paragraph 14 that the amount of intercompany profit that should be eliminated is not affected by the existence of a minority interest and should be eliminated in its entirety. The reason for eliminating intercompany profits and losses is that the management of the parent company is able to control all intercompany transactions, including authorization and pricing, without arm's-length bargaining between the affiliated companies. In eliminating the effect of intercompany profits and losses from consolidated statements, however, the issue is not whether the intercompany transactions were or were not at arm's length. *The objective is to show the income and financial position of the consolidated entity as they would have appeared if the intercompany transactions had never taken place*, irrespective of the amounts involved in such transactions. The same reasoning applies to the measurement of the investment account and investment income under a one-line consolidation. In the case of a one-line consolidation, however, evidence that intercompany transactions were not at arm's length

---

[1]*ARB No. 51*, "Consolidated Financial Statements," paragraph 6.

may necessitate additional adjustments for fair presentation of the parent company's income and financial position in separate parent company financial statements. These additional adjustments are covered in *Accounting Interpretation No. 1 of APB Opinion No. 18*, "The Equity Method of Accounting for Investments in Common Stock."

Most intercompany transactions involving gains and losses can be grouped as inventory items, plant assets, and bonds. Consolidation procedures involving inventory items are discussed in this chapter, and those involving plant assets and bonds are covered in subsequent chapters. Although the discussion and illustrations in this chapter relate to intercompany profit situations, the examples also provide a basis for analyzing and accounting for intercompany losses. Tax considerations are covered in Chapter 10.

INTERCOMPANY INVENTORY TRANSACTIONS

Revenue is recognized (recorded as revenue) when it is realized, that is, when it is earned. For revenue to be earned from the viewpoint of the consolidated entity, there must be a sale to outside entities. Revenue on sales between affiliated companies cannot be recognized until merchandise is sold outside of the consolidated entity. No consolidated income results from transfers between affiliated companies. The sale of inventory items by one company to an affiliated company produces reciprocal sales and purchases accounts when the purchasing entity has a periodic inventory system and reciprocal sales and cost of goods sold accounts when the purchasing entity uses a perpetual inventory system. These reciprocal sales and cost of goods sold (or purchases) amounts must be eliminated in preparing a consolidated income statement, in order to report sales and cost of goods sold for the consolidated entity; eliminating equal sales and cost of goods sold has no effect on consolidated net income.

Elimination of Intercompany Purchases and Sales

Intercompany sales and purchases of affiliated companies are eliminated in the consolidation process in order to report consolidated sales and purchases (or cost of goods sold) at amounts purchased from and sold to outside entities. When a periodic inventory system is used, the working paper entry to eliminate intercompany sales and purchases is simply a debit to sales and a credit to purchases. The working paper elimination under a perpetual inventory system, used throughout this book, is a debit to sales and a credit to cost of goods sold. The reason is that in a perpetual inventory system, intercompany purchases are included in the separate cost of goods sold account of the purchasing affiliate. These observations are illustrated for Pint Corporation and its subsidiary, Shep Corporation.

Pint Corporation formed a subsidiary, Shep Corporation, in 20X1 to retail a special line of Pint's merchandise. All Shep's purchases are made from Pint Corporation at 20% above Pint's cost. During 20X1 Pint sold merchandise that cost $20,000 to Shep for $24,000, and Shep sold all the merchandise to its customers for $30,000. Journal entries relating to the merchandise are recorded on the separate books of Pint and Shep as follows:

PINT'S BOOKS

Inventory	$20,000	
Accounts payable		$20,000
To record purchases on account from other entities.		
Accounts receivable—Shep	$24,000	
Sales		$24,000
To record intercompany sales to Shep.		
Cost of sales	$20,000	
Inventory		$20,000
To record cost of sales to Shep.		

SHEP'S BOOKS

Inventory	$24,000	
Accounts payable—Pint		$24,000
To record intercompany purchases from Pint.		
Accounts receivable	$30,000	
Sales		$30,000
To record sales to customers outside the consolidated entity.		

Cost of sales			$24,000	
Inventory				$24,000
To record cost of sales to customers.				

At year-end 20X1, Pint's sales include $24,000 sold to Shep, and its cost of sales includes the $20,000 cost of merchandise transferred to Shep. Shep's sales consist of $30,000 in merchandise sold to other entities, and its cost of sales consists of the $24,000 transfer price from Pint. Pint and Shep are considered one entity for reporting purposes, so their combined sales and cost of sales are overstated by $24,000. That overstatement is eliminated in the consolidation working papers, where measurements for consolidated sales and cost of sales are finalized. The working paper elimination is as follows:

	Pint	100% Shep	Adjustments and Eliminations	Consolidated
Sales	$24,000	$30,000	a 24,000	$30,000
Cost of sales	20,000	24,000	a 24,000	20,000
Gross profit	$ 4,000	$ 6,000		$10,000

The working paper elimination has no effect on consolidated net income because equal sales and cost of sales amounts are eliminated, and combined gross profit is equal to consolidated gross profit. However, the elimination is necessary to reflect merchandising activity accurately for the consolidated entity that purchased merchandise for $20,000 (Pint) and sold it for $30,000 (Shep). The fact that Pint's separate records include $4,000 gross profit on the merchandise and Shep's records show $6,000 is irrelevant in reporting the consolidated results of operations. In addition to eliminating the intercompany profit items, it is necessary to eliminate intercompany receivables and payables in the consolidation process.

Elimination of Unrealized Profit in Ending Inventory

The consolidated entity realizes and recognizes the full amount of intercompany profit on sales between affiliated companies in the period in which the merchandise is resold to outside entities. Until the merchandise is resold, however, any profit or loss on intercompany sales is unrealized, and its effect must be eliminated in the consolidation process. Any unrealized profit or loss on intercompany sales is reflected in the *ending inventory of the purchasing affiliate* because that inventory reflects the intercompany transfer price rather than cost to the consolidated entity. The elimination is a debit to cost of goods sold and a credit to the ending inventory for the amount of unrealized profit. The credit reduces the inventory to its cost basis to the consolidated entity; and the debit, when considered in conjunction with the elimination of intercompany purchases, reduces cost of goods sold to its cost basis. These relationships are illustrated by continuing the Pint and Shep example for 20X2.

During 20X2 Pint sold merchandise that cost $30,000 to Shep for $36,000, and Shep sold all but $6,000 of this merchandise to its customers for $37,500. Journal entries relating to the merchandise transferred intercompany during 20X2 are as follows:

PINT'S BOOKS

Inventory	$30,000	
Accounts payable		$30,000
To record purchase on account from other entities.		
Accounts receivable—Shep	$36,000	
Sales		$36,000
To record intercompany sales to Shep.		
Cost of sales	$30,000	
Inventory		$30,000
To record cost of sales to Shep.		

Inventory	$36,000	
Accounts payable—Pint		$36,000

To record intercompany purchases from Pint.

Accounts receivable	$37,500	
Sales		$37,500

To record sales to customers outside the consolidated entity.

Cost of sales	$30,000	
Inventory		$30,000

To record cost of sales to outside entities.

Pint's sales for 20X2 include $36,000 sold to Shep, and its cost of sales reflects the $30,000 cost of merchandise transferred to Shep. Shep's $37,500 sales for 20X2 consist of merchandise acquired from Pint, and its $30,000 cost of sales is equal to 5/6, or $30,000/$36,000, of the $36,000 transfer price of merchandise acquired from Pint. The remaining merchandise acquired from Pint in 20X2 stays in Shep's December 31, 20X2 inventory at the $6,000 transfer price, which includes $1,000 unrealized profit.

Working Paper Entries   From the viewpoint of the consolidated entity, merchandise that cost $30,000 was transferred intracompany.

- $25,000 (or 5/6) of this merchandise was then sold to outside entities for $37,500
- $5,000 (or 1/6) remains in inventory at year-end
- The consolidated entity has realized a gross profit of $12,500

These consolidated results are accomplished through working paper entries that eliminate the effects of the intercompany transactions from sales, cost of sales, and inventory. Although a single working paper entry can be made to reduce combined sales by $36,000, combined cost of sales by $35,000, and inventory by $1,000, two working paper entries are ordinarily used in order to separate the elimination of intercompany sales and purchases from the elimination (deferral) of unrealized profit.

The working paper eliminations are as follows:

	Pint	Shep	Adjustments and Eliminations		Consolidated
Income Statement Sales	$36,000	$37,500	a 36,000		$37,500
Cost of sales	30,000	30,000	b 1,000	a 36,000	25,000
Gross profit	$ 6,000	$ 7,500			$12,500
Balance Sheet Inventory		$ 6,000		b 1,000	$ 5,000

The first working paper entry eliminates intercompany sales and purchases and is journalized as follows:

a	Sales	$36,000	
	Cost of sales		$36,000
	To eliminate intercompany sales and purchases.		

This entry is procedurally the same as the one made in 20X1 to eliminate intercompany purchases and sales.

A second entry defers the $1,000 intercompany profit that remains unrealized ($13,500 combined gross profit − $12,500 consolidated gross profit) and reduces the ending inventory from $6,000 to its $5,000 cost to the consolidated entity.

b	Cost of sales	$1,000	
	Inventory		$1,000

To eliminate intercompany profit from cost of sales and inventory.

The debit to cost of sales reduces profit by increasing consolidated cost of sales, and the credit reduces the valuation of inventory for consolidated statement purposes from the intercompany transfer price to cost. From the viewpoint of the consolidated entity, Shep's ending inventory is overstated by the $1,000 unrealized profit. An overstated ending inventory understates cost of sales and overstates gross profit, so the error is corrected with working paper entry b, which increases (debits) cost of sales and decreases (credits) the overstated ending inventory. This elimination entry reduces consolidated gross profit by $1,000 (income effect) and consolidated ending inventory by $1,000 (balance sheet effect).

These two working paper entries should be learned at this time because they are always the same, regardless of additional complexities that have yet to be introduced.

Equity Method On December 31, 20X2, Pint computes its investment income in the usual manner, except that the $1,000 intercompany profit must be deferred. In Pint's one-line consolidation entry, income from Shep will be reduced by the $1,000 unrealized profit in the ending inventory, and accordingly, the investment in Shep account will also be reduced $1,000.

Recognition of Unrealized Profit in Beginning Inventory

Unrealized profit in an ending inventory is realized for consolidated statement purposes when the merchandise is sold outside the consolidated entity. Ordinarily, realization occurs in the immediately succeeding fiscal period, so the recognition is simply deferred for consolidated statement purposes until the following year. Recognition of the previously unrealized profit requires a working paper credit to cost of goods sold because the amount of the beginning inventory is reflected in cost of goods sold when the perpetual system is used. The direction of the sale, minority ownership percentage, and parent company method of accounting for the subsidiary may complicate the related working paper debits. These complications do not affect consolidated gross profit, however, and the previous example is extended to reflect 20X3 operations for Pint and Shep.

During 20X3 Pint Corporation sold merchandise that cost $40,000 to Shep for $48,000, and Shep sold 75% of the merchandise for $45,000. Shep also sold the items in the beginning inventory with a transfer price of $6,000 to its customers for $7,500. Journal entries relating to the merchandise transferred intercompany are as follows:

PINT'S BOOKS

Inventory	$40,000	
Accounts payable		$40,000
To record purchase on account from other entities.		
Accounts receivable—Shep	$48,000	
Sales		$48,000
To record intercompany sales to Shep.		
Cost of sales	$40,000	
Inventory		$40,000
To record cost of sales to Shep.		

SHEP'S BOOKS

Inventory	$48,000	
Accounts payable—Pint		$48,000
To record intercompany purchases from Pint.		
Accounts receivable	$52,500	
Sales		$52,500
To record sales of $45,000 and $7,500 to outside entities.		

Cost of sales			$42,000	
Inventory				$42,000

To record cost of sales ($48,000 transfer price × 75% sold) and $6,000 from beginning inventory.

Shep sold 75% of the merchandise purchased from Pint, so its ending inventory in 20X3 is $12,000 ($48,000 × 25%), and that inventory includes $2,000 unrealized profit [$12,000 − ($12,000/1.2 transfer price)].

Working Paper Entries   From the viewpoint of the consolidated entity, merchandise that cost $40,000 was transferred intercompany:

- $30,000 of this merchandise, plus $5,000 beginning inventory, was sold for $52,500
- $10,000 remained in inventory at year-end 20X3
- The consolidated entity realized a gross profit of $17,500

These consolidated results are reflected in the consolidation working papers that eliminate the effects of intercompany transactions from sales, cost of sales, and inventory. Three working paper entries are used to eliminate intercompany purchases and sales, recognize previously deferred profit from beginning inventory, and defer unrealized profit in the ending inventory, as follows:

	Pint	Shep	Adjustments and Eliminations		Consolidated
Income Statement					
Sales	$48,000	$52,500	a 48,000		$52,500
Cost of sales	40,000	42,000	c 2,000	a 48,000 b 1,000	35,000
Gross profit	$ 8,000	$10,500			$17,500
Balance Sheet					
Inventory		$12,000		c 2,000	$10,000
Investment in Shep	XXX		b 1,000		

The working paper entries to eliminate the effects of intercompany transactions between Pint and Shep for 20X3 are journalized as follows:

a	Sales		$48,000	
	Cost of sales			$48,000
	To eliminate intercompany purchases and sales.			
b	Investment in Shep		$ 1,000	
	Cost of sales			$ 1,000
	To recognize previously deferred profit from beginning inventory.			
c	Cost of sales		$ 2,000	
	Inventory			$ 2,000
	To defer unrealized profit in ending inventory.			

Working paper entries a and c are procedurally the same as the entries for 20X2. Their purpose is to eliminate intercompany purchases and sales and defer unrealized profit in the ending inventory. From the consolidated viewpoint, the $1,000 overstated beginning inventory overstates cost of sales in 20X3. Entry b recognizes previously deferred profit from 20X2 by reducing consolidated cost of sales, and thereby increasing consolidated gross profit. The related debit to the investment in Shep account adjusts for the one-line consolidation entry that reduced the investment in Shep account in 20X2 to defer unrealized profit in the ending inventory of that year. Although the credit side of this working paper entry is always the same, additional complexities sometimes arise with the debit side of the entry.

The Pint–Shep example illustrates the effects of intercompany inventory transactions on consolidated sales, cost of sales, and gross profit, and these effects are always the same. But the example did not cover the effects of intercompany inventory transactions on minority interest computations or on parent company accounting under the equity method. These ramifications are discussed and illustrated next.

DOWNSTREAM AND UPSTREAM SALES

A sale by a parent company to a subsidiary is designated as a **downstream sale**, and a sale by a subsidiary to its parent is designated as an **upstream sale**. The upstream and downstream designations relate to the usual diagram of affiliation structures that places the parent company at the top. Thus, sales from top to bottom are downstream, and sales from bottom to top are upstream.

Reciprocal sales and cost of goods sold (or purchases) amounts are eliminated in consolidated financial statements regardless of whether the sales are upstream or downstream. Likewise, any unrealized gross profit in inventories is eliminated in its entirety for both downstream and upstream sales. However, the effect of unrealized profits on separate parent company statements (as investor) and on consolidated financial statements (which show income to the majority stockholders) is determined by both the direction of the intercompany sales activity and the percentage ownership of subsidiary companies, except for 100%-owned subsidiaries, which have no minority ownership.

In the case of downstream sales, the parent company's separate income includes the full amount of any unrealized profit (included in its sales and cost of sales accounts), and the subsidiary's income is not affected. When sales are upstream, the subsidiary company's net income includes the full amount of any unrealized profit (included in its sales and cost of sales accounts), and the parent company's separate income is not affected. The full amount of intercompany sales and cost of sales is eliminated in the consolidation process, regardless of whether the sales are downstream or upstream. However, the minority interest income *may be affected* if the subsidiary's net income includes unrealized profit (the upstream situation). It *is not affected* if the parent company's separate income includes unrealized profit (the downstream situation) because the minority shareholders have an interest only in the income of the subsidiary. When subsidiary net income is overstated (from the viewpoint of the consolidated entity) because it includes unrealized profit, the income allocated to minority interests should be based on the *realized income of the subsidiary*. A subsidiary's realized income is its reported net income adjusted for intercompany profits from upstream sales.

Minority interest income *may be affected* by unrealized profit from upstream sales because accounting standards are not definitive with respect to the computation. *ARB No. 51*, paragraph 14, provides that "the elimination of intercompany profit or loss may be allocated proportionately between majority and minority interests," but does not require such allocation. The alternative to allocation is to eliminate intercompany profits and losses from upstream sales in the same manner as for downstream sales, charging (crediting) the full amount of unrealized gain (loss) to the parent's income.

The approach that allocates unrealized profits and losses from upstream sales proportionately between minority and majority interests is conceptually superior because it applies the viewpoint of the consolidated entity consistently to both majority and minority interests. That is, both consolidated net income and minority interest income are computed on the basis of income that is realized from the viewpoint of the consolidated entity. In addition, material amounts of unrealized profits and losses from upstream sales may be allocated between majority and minority interests in accounting practice. *Accordingly, unrealized profits and losses from upstream sales are allocated proportionately between consolidated net income (majority interests) and minority interest income (minority interests) throughout this book.* Consistent treatment between consolidation procedures and the equity method of accounting (the one-line consolidation) is accomplished by using the same allocation approach in accounting for the parent company/investor's interest under the equity method.

Downstream and Upstream Effects on Income Computations

Assume that the separate incomes of a parent company and its 80%-owned subsidiary for 20X5 are as follows:

	Parent	Subsidiary
Sales	$600,000	$300,000
Cost of sales	300,000	180,000
Gross profit	300,000	120,000
Expenses	100,000	70,000
Parent's separate income	$200,000	
Subsidiary's net income		$ 50,000

Intercompany sales during the year are $100,000, and the December 31, 20X5 inventory includes $20,000 unrealized profit.

Minority Interest Income Computation If the intercompany sales are downstream, the $20,000 unrealized profit is reflected in the parent company's sales and cost of sales accounts, and the subsidiary's $50,000 net income is equal to its realized income. In this case the minority interest income computation is unaffected by the intercompany transactions and is computed:

$$\$50,000 \text{ net income of subsidiary} \times 20\% = \underline{\$10,000}$$

If the intercompany sales are upstream, the $20,000 unrealized profit is reflected in the subsidiary's sales and cost of sales accounts and the subsidiary's realized income is $30,000. In this case the minority interest income computation is:

$$(\$50,000 \text{ net income of subsidiary} - \$20,000 \text{ unrealized}) \times 20\% = \underline{\$6,000}$$

Consolidated Net Income Computation Comparative consolidated income statements for the parent and its 80%-owned subsidiary under the two assumptions are shown in Exhibit 5–1. In examining the exhibit, note that the only difference in the computation of consolidated net income under the two assumptions lies in the computation of minority interest income. This is because the eliminations for intercompany purchases and sales and intercompany inventory profits are the same, regardless of whether the sales are downstream or upstream. Parent company net income under the equity method is equal to consolidated net income, so the approach used in computing income from subsidiary must be consistent with the approach used in determining consolidated net income. For downstream sales, the full amount of unrealized

---

PARENT CORPORATION AND SUBSIDIARY
CONSOLIDATED INCOME STATEMENTS
FOR THE YEAR ENDED DECEMBER 31, 20X5

	Downstream Sales	Upstream Sales
Sales ($900,000 − $100,000)	$800,000	$800,000
Cost of sales ($480,000 + $20,000 − $100,000)	400,000	400,000
Gross profit	400,000	400,000
Expenses ($100,000 + $70,000)	170,000	170,000
Total realized income	230,000	230,000
Less: Minority interest income	10,000	6,000
Consolidated net income	$220,000	$224,000

Exhibit 5–1 *Consolidated Income Effect of Downstream and Upstream Sales*

profit is charged against income from subsidiary, but for upstream sales, only the parent's proportionate share is charged against its investment income from subsidiary. Computations are as follows:

	Downstream	Upstream
Parent's separate income	$200,000	$200,000
Add: Income from subsidiary		
Downstream		
Equity in subsidiary's reported income less unrealized profit [($50,000 × 80%) − $20,000]	20,000	
Upstream		
Equity in subsidiary realized income [($50,000 − $20,000) × 80%]		24,000
Parent (and consolidated) net income	$220,000	$224,000

UNREALIZED PROFITS FROM DOWNSTREAM SALES

Sales by a parent company to its subsidiaries increase parent company sales, cost of goods sold, and gross profit but do not affect the income of subsidiaries until the merchandise is resold to outside parties. The full amount of gross profit on merchandise sold downstream and remaining in subsidiary inventories increases parent company income, so the full amount must be eliminated from the parent company income statement under the equity method of accounting. Consistent with the one-line consolidation concept, this is done by reducing investment income and the investment account. In consolidated financial statements, unrealized gross profit is eliminated by increasing consolidated cost of goods sold and reducing merchandise inventory to a cost basis to the consolidated entity. The overstatement of the ending inventory from the consolidated viewpoint understates consolidated cost of goods sold.

Deferral of Intercompany Profit in Period of Intercompany Sale

The following example illustrates the deferral of unrealized profits on downstream sales. Porter Corporation owns 90% of the voting stock of Sorter Corporation. Separate income statements of Porter and Sorter for 20X7, before consideration of unrealized profits, are as follows:

	Porter	Sorter
Sales	$100,000	$50,000
Cost of goods sold	60,000	35,000
Gross profit	40,000	15,000
Expenses	15,000	5,000
Operating income	25,000	10,000
Income from Sorter	9,000	—
Net income	$ 34,000	$10,000

Porter's sales include $15,000 to Sorter at a profit of $6,250, and Sorter's December 31, 20X7 inventory includes 40% of the merchandise from the intercompany transaction. The $2,500 unrealized profit in Sorter's inventory ($6,000 transfer price less $3,500 cost) is reflected in Porter's operating income. On its separate books, Porter takes up its share of Sorter's income and defers recognition of the unrealized profit with the following entries:

Investment in Sorter	$9,000	
Income from Sorter		$9,000
To record share of Sorter's income.		
Income from Sorter	$2,500	
Investment in Sorter		$2,500
To eliminate unrealized profit on sales to Sorter.		

The second entry on Porter's books reduces Porter's income from Sorter from $9,000 to $6,500. In consolidated financial statements, reciprocal sales and cost of goods sold, as well as all unrealized profit, must be eliminated. These working paper adjustments are shown in the partial working papers in Exhibit 5–2.

The full amount of intercompany sales is deducted from sales and cost of goods sold in entry a. Working paper entry b then corrects cost of goods sold for the unrealized profit at year-end and reduces the inventory to its cost basis to the consolidated entity. Note that working paper entries a and b are equivalent to a single debit to sales for $15,000, a credit to cost of goods sold for $12,500, and a credit to inventory for $2,500.

In examining Exhibit 5–2, observe that Porter's net income on an equity basis is equal to consolidated net income. This equality would not have occurred without the one-line consolidation adjustment that reduced Porter's income from $34,000 to $31,500. The $1,000 minority interest income shown in Exhibit 5–2 is not affected by the unrealized profit on Porter's sales because minority stockholders share only in subsidiary profit and Sorter's reported income for 20X7 (equal to its realized income) is unaffected by the unrealized profit in its inventory. (Sorter's goods available for sale and its ending inventory are overstated by the amount of unrealized profit, but its cost of goods sold is not affected by the unrealized profit in its ending inventory.)

Recognition of Intercompany Profit upon Sale to Outside Entities

Now assume that the merchandise acquired from Porter during 20X7 is sold by Sorter during 20X8, and there are no intercompany transactions between Porter and Sorter during 20X8. Separate income statements for 20X8 before consideration of the $2,500 unrealized profit in Sorter's beginning inventory are as follows:

	Porter	Sorter
Sales	$120,000	$60,000
Cost of goods sold	80,000	40,000
Gross profit	40,000	20,000
Expenses	20,000	5,000
Operating income	20,000	15,000
Income from Sorter	13,500	—
Net income	$ 33,500	$15,000

Porter's operating income for 20X8 is unaffected by the unrealized profit in Sorter's December 31, 20X7 inventory. But Sorter's 20X8 profit is affected because the $2,500 overstatement of Sorter's beginning inventory overstates cost of goods sold from a consolidated viewpoint. From Porter's viewpoint, the unrealized profit from 20X7 is realized in 20X8, and its investment income is recorded and adjusted as follows:

Investment in Sorter	$13,500	
Income from Sorter		$13,500
To record investment income from Sorter.		
Investment in Sorter	$ 2,500	
Income from Sorter		$ 2,500
To record realization of profit from 20X7 intercompany sales to Sorter.		

The effect of this entry is to increase Porter's investment from $13,500 to $16,000 and Porter's net income from $33,500 to $36,000. These adjusted amounts are reflected in the partial working papers for Porter and Sorter for the year 20X8 as shown in Exhibit 5–3.

In examining the partial working papers in Exhibit 5–3, note that entry a debits the investment in Sorter account and credits cost of goods sold for $2,500. The beginning inventory of Sorter has already been closed to cost of goods sold under a perpetual inventory system, so the inventory cannot be adjusted. The adjustment to the investment account is necessary to increase the investment account at the beginning of the year to reflect realization during 20X8 of the unrealized profit that was deferred

PORTER AND SUBSIDIARY, SORTER
PARTIAL WORKING PAPERS
FOR THE YEAR ENDED DECEMBER 31, 20X7

	Porter	90% Sorter	Adjustments and Eliminations		Consolidated
Income Statement Sales	$100,000	$50,000	a 15,000		$135,000
Income from Sorter	6,500		c 6,500		
Cost of goods sold	(60,000)	(35,000)	b 2,500	a 15,000	(82,500)
Expenses	(15,000)	(5,000)			(20,000)
Minority interest income ($10,000 × 10%)					(1,000)
Net income	$ 31,500	$10,000			$ 31,500
Balance Sheet Inventory		$ 7,500		b 2,500	$ 5,000
Investment in Sorter	XXX			c 6,500	

a Eliminates reciprocal sales and cost of goods sold.
b Adjusts cost of goods sold and ending inventory to a cost basis to the consolidated entity.
c Eliminates investment income and adjusts the investment in Sorter account to the January 1, 20X7 balance.

Exhibit 5–2   *Inventory Profit on Downstream Sales in Year of Intercompany Sales*

at the end of 20X7. *This adjustment reestablishes reciprocity between the investment balance at January 1, 20X8, and the subsidiary equity account at the same date. It is important to record this adjustment before eliminating reciprocal investment and equity balances.* The computation of minority interest income in Exhibit 5–3 is not affected because the sales are downstream.

PORTER AND SUBSIDIARY, SORTER
PARTIAL WORKING PAPERS
FOR THE YEAR ENDED DECEMBER 31, 20X8

	Porter	90% Sorter	Adjustments and Eliminations		Consolidated
Income Statement Sales	$120,000	$60,000			$180,000
Income from Sorter	16,000		b 16,000		
Cost of goods sold	(80,000)	(40,000)		a 2,500	(117,500)
Expenses	(20,000)	(5,000)			(25,000)
Minority interest income ($15,000 × 10%)					(1,500)
Net income	$ 36,000	$15,000			$ 36,000
Balance Sheet Investment in Sorter	XXX		a 2,500	b 16,000	

a Adjusts cost of goods sold to a cost basis and adjusts the investment account balance to reestablish reciprocity with the beginning subsidiary equity accounts.
b Eliminates investment income and adjusts the investment account to its January 1, 20X8 balance.

Exhibit 5–3   *Inventory Profit on Downstream Sales in Year After Intercompany Sales*

Unrealized inventory profits in consolidated financial statements are self-correcting over any two accounting periods and are subject to the same type of analysis as inventory errors. Total consolidated net income for Porter and Sorter for 20X7 and 20X8 is unaffected by the $2,500 deferral in 20X7 and recognition in 20X8. The significance of the adjustments lies in the accurate statement of the income of the consolidated entity for each period.

UNREALIZED PROFITS FROM UPSTREAM SALES

Sales by a subsidiary to its parent company increase the sales, cost of goods sold, and gross profit of the subsidiary, but they do not affect the operating income of the parent until the merchandise is resold by the parent to other entities. The parent's net income is affected, however, because the parent recognizes its share of the subsidiary's income on an equity basis. If the selling subsidiary is a 100%-owned affiliate, the parent defers 100% of any unrealized profit in the year of intercompany sale. If the subsidiary is a partially owned affiliate, the parent company defers only its proportionate share of the unrealized subsidiary profit.

Deferral of Intercompany Profit in Period of Intercompany Sale

Assume that Salt Corporation (subsidiary) sells merchandise that it purchased for $7,500 to Park Corporation (parent) for $20,000 during 20X7 and that Park Corporation sold 60% of the merchandise to outsiders during the year for $15,000. At year-end the unrealized inventory profit is $5,000 (cost $3,000, but included in Park's inventory at $8,000). If Salt reports net income of $50,000 for 20X7, Park's proportionate share is recognized as shown in Exhibit 5–4. The exhibit compares parent company accounting for a one-line consolidation of a 100%-owned subsidiary and a 75%-owned subsidiary.

As the illustration shows, if Park records 100% of Salt's income under the equity method, it must eliminate 100% of any unrealized profit included in that income. However, if Park records only 75% of Salt's income under the equity method, it must eliminate only 75% of any unrealized profit included in Salt's income. In both cases, all the unrealized profit recorded by Park is eliminated from Park's income and investment accounts.

The elimination of unrealized inventory profits from upstream sales in consolidated financial statements results in the elimination of 100% of all unrealized inven-

---

Part A
If Salt is a 100%-Owned Subsidiary

Investment in Salt	$50,000	
Income from Salt		$50,000
To record 100% of Salt's reported income as income from subsidiary.		
Income from Salt	$ 5,000	
Investment in Salt		$ 5,000
To defer 100% of the unrealized inventory profits reported by Salt until realized.		

A single entry for $45,000 [($50,000 − $5,000) × 100%] is equally acceptable.

Part B
If Salt is a 75%-Owned Subsidiary

Investment in Salt	$37,500	
Income from Salt		$37,500
To record 75% of Salt's reported income as income from subsidiary.		
Income from Salt	$ 3,750	
Investment in Salt		$ 3,750
To defer 75% of the unrealized inventory profits reported by Salt until realized.		

A single entry for $33,750 [($50,000 − $5,000) × 75%] is equally acceptable.

Exhibit 5–4   *Entries for a One-Line Consolidation on the Books of Park*

	Park	75% Salt	Adjustments and Eliminations	Consolidated
PARK AND SUBSIDIARY, SALT (75% OWNED)				
PARTIAL CONSOLIDATION WORKING PAPERS				
FOR THE YEAR ENDED DECEMBER 31, 20X7				
Income Statement				
Sales	$250,000	$150,000	a 20,000	$380,000
Income from Salt	33,750		c 33,750	
Cost of goods sold	(100,000)	(80,000)	b 5,000 a 20,000	(165,000)
Expenses	(50,000)	(20,000)		(70,000)
Minority interest income ($50,000 − $5,000) × 25%				(11,250)
Net income	$133,750	$ 50,000		$133,750
Balance Sheet				
Inventory	$ 10,000		b 5,000	$ 5,000
Investment in Salt	XXX		c 33,750	

a To eliminate reciprocal intercompany sales and cost of goods sold amounts.

b To adjust cost of goods sold and inventory to a cost basis.

c To eliminate investment income and to adjust the investment in Salt account to its beginning-of-the-period balance.

Exhibit 5–5   *Inventory Profit on Upstream Sales in Year of Intercompany Sales*

tory profits from consolidated sales and cost of goods sold accounts. However, because consolidated net income is a measurement of income to the stockholders of the parent company, minority interest income is reduced for its proportionate share of any unrealized profit of the subsidiary. This involves deducting the minority interest's share of unrealized profits from the minority interest's share of the subsidiary's reported net income. Thus, the effect on consolidated net income of unrealized profits from upstream sales is the same as the effect on parent company income under the equity method of accounting.

Partial consolidation working papers for Park Corporation and its 75%-owned subsidiary Salt Corporation are illustrated in Exhibit 5–5. Although the amounts for sales, cost of goods sold, and expenses are presented without explanation, the data provided are consistent with previous assumptions for Park and Salt corporations.

The $33,750 income from Salt that appears in Park's separate income statement in Exhibit 5–5 is explained in Part B of Exhibit 5–4. Minority interest income is computed by subtracting unrealized profit from Salt's reported income and multiplying by the minority interest percentage. Failure to adjust the minority interest income for unrealized profit will result in a lack of equality between parent company net income on an equity basis and consolidated net income. This potential problem is, of course, absent in the case of a 100%-owned subsidiary because there is no minority interest.

Recognition of Intercompany Profit upon Sale to Outside Entities

The effect of unrealized profits in a beginning inventory on parent company and consolidated net incomes is just the opposite of the effect of unrealized profits in an ending inventory. That is, the relationship between unrealized profits in ending inventories (year of intercompany sale) and consolidated net income is direct, whereas the

	Park	75% Salt	Adjustments and Eliminations	Consolidated
PARK AND SUBSIDIARY, SALT (75% OWNED) **PARTIAL CONSOLIDATION WORKING PAPERS** **FOR THE YEAR ENDED DECEMBER 31, 20X8**				
Income Statement Sales	$275,000	$160,000		$435,000
Income from Salt	48,750		b 48,750	
Cost of goods sold	(120,000)	(85,000)	a 5,000	(200,000)
Expenses	(60,000)	(15,000)		(75,000)
Minority interest income ($60,000 + $5,000) × 25%				(16,250)
Net income	$143,750	$ 60,000		$143,750
Balance Sheet Investment in Salt	XXX		a 3,750 b 48,750	
Minority interest: January 1, 20X8			a 1,250	

a To reduce cost of goods sold to a cost basis to the consolidated entity and adjust the investment in Salt account to establish reciprocity between it and subsidiary equity at January 1, 20X8, and to eliminate intercompany profit from beginning minority interest.
b To eliminate investment income and adjust the investment in Salt account to its January 1, 20X8, balance.

Exhibit 5–6 *Inventory Profit on Upstream Sales in Year After Intercompany Sales*

relationship between unrealized profit in beginning inventories (year of sale to outside entities) and consolidated net income is inverse. This is illustrated by continuing the Park and Salt example to show realization during 20X8 of the $5,000 unrealized profit in the December 31, 20X7 inventories. Assume that there are no intercompany transactions between Park and Salt during 20X8, that Salt is a 75%-owned subsidiary of Park, and that Salt reports income of $60,000 for 20X8. Park records its share of Salt's income under the equity method as follows:

Investment in Salt	$45,000	
Income from Salt		$45,000
To record 75% of Salt's reported income as income from subsidiary.		
Investment in Salt	$ 3,750	
Income from Salt		$ 3,750
To record realization during 20X8 of 75% of the $5,000 unrealized inventory profits of Salt from 20X7.		

Consolidation procedures for unrealized profits in beginning inventories from upstream sales are illustrated for Park and Subsidiary in Exhibit 5–6. Several of the items in Exhibit 5–6 differ from those for upstream sales with unrealized profit in the ending inventory (Exhibit 5–5). In particular, cost of goods sold is overstated (because of the overstated beginning inventory) and requires a worksheet adjustment to reduce it to a cost basis. This is shown in working paper entry a, which also adjusts the investment account and beginning minority interest. *The allocation between the investment balance (75%) and the minority interest (25%) is required for unrealized profits in beginning inventories from upstream sales to correct for prior-year effects on the investment account and the minority interest.*

CONSOLIDATION EXAMPLE—INTERCOMPANY PROFITS FROM DOWNSTREAM SALES

Seay Corporation is a 90%-owned subsidiary of Peak Corporation, acquired for $94,500 cash on July 1, 20X1, when Seay's net assets consisted of $100,000 capital stock and $5,000 retained earnings. The cost of Peak's 90% interest in Seay was equal to book value and fair value of the interest acquired ($105,000 × 90%), and accordingly, no allocation to identifiable and unidentifiable assets was necessary.

Peak sells inventory items to Seay on a regular basis, and the intercompany transaction data for 20X5 are as follows:

Sales to Seay in 20X5 (cost $15,000), selling price	$20,000
Unrealized profit in Seay's inventory at December 31, 20X4	2,000
Unrealized profit in Seay's inventory at December 31, 20X5	2,500
Seay's accounts payable to Peak December 31, 20X5	10,000

Equity Method

At December 31, 20X4 Peak's investment in Seay account had a balance of $128,500. This balance consisted of Peak's 90% equity in Seay's $145,000 net assets on that date less $2,000 unrealized profit in Seay's December 31, 20X4 inventory.

During 20X5 Peak made the following entries on its books for its investment in Seay under the equity method:

Cash	$ 9,000	
Investment in Seay		$ 9,000
To record dividends from Seay ($10,000 × 90%).		
Investment in Seay	$26,500	
Income from Seay		$26,500
To record income from Seay for 20X5 computed as follows:		
Equity in Seay's net income ($30,000 × 90%)		$27,000
Add: 20X4 inventory profit recognized in 20X5		2,000
Less: 20X5 inventory profit deferred at year-end		−2,500
		$26,500

The intercompany sales that led to the unrealized inventory profits were downstream, so the full amount of profit deferred in 20X4 is recognized in 20X5, and the full amount of the unrealized inventory profit originating in 20X5 is deferred at December 31, 20X5. Peak's investment in Seay account increased from $128,500 at January 1, 20X5 to $146,000 at December 31, 20X5, the entire change consisting of $26,500 income less $9,000 dividends for the year. These amounts are shown in the separate company columns of the consolidation working papers for Peak Corporation and Subsidiary for the year ended December 31, 20X5, that appear in Exhibit 5–7.

The working paper entries in Exhibit 5–7 are presented in journal form as follows:

a	Sales	$ 20,000	
	Cost of goods sold		$ 20,000
	To eliminate intercompany sales and related cost of goods sold amounts.		
b	Investment in Seay	$ 2,000	
	Cost of goods sold		$ 2,000
	To adjust cost of goods sold and the beginning investment balance for unrealized profits in the beginning inventory.		
c	Cost of goods sold	$ 2,500	
	Inventory		$ 2,500
	To eliminate unrealized profit in the ending inventory and to increase cost of goods sold to a cost basis to the consolidated entity.		

d	Income from Seay	$ 26,500	
	Dividends		$ 9,000
	Investment in Seay		17,500

To eliminate the investment income and 90% of the
dividends of Seay and to reduce the investment account
to its beginning-of-the-period balance, plus the $2,000
from entry b.

e	Capital stock—Seay	$100,000	
	Retained earnings—Seay	45,000	
	Investment in Seay		$130,500
	Minority interest		14,500

To eliminate reciprocal investment and equity balances
and record beginning minority interest.

f	Accounts payable	$ 10,000	
	Accounts receivable		$ 10,000

To eliminate reciprocal payables and receivables from
intercompany sales.

In examining the working papers of Peak Corporation and Subsidiary in Exhibit 5–7, note that Peak's net income ($126,500) is equal to consolidated net income, and Peak's retained earnings amount ($270,500) is equal to consolidated retained earnings. These equalities are expected from a correct application of the equity method of accounting. The sales that gave rise to the intercompany profits in Seay's inventories were downstream, so neither beginning minority interest ($14,500) nor minority interest income ($3,000) was affected by the intercompany transactions.

Incomplete Equity Method

Assume that Peak failed to consider its intercompany transactions in accounting for its investment in Seay during 20X4 and 20X5. In that case, both Peak's investment in Seay and its retained earnings account balances at December 31, 20X4 would be $2,000 greater than under the equity method. This $2,000 overstatement is the result of failing to reduce investment and investment income amounts for the $2,000 unrealized profit in 20X4. The amount of overstatement of Peak's investment in Seay and retained earnings balances would increase by $500 to $2,500 at December 31, 20X5 because the $2,000 unrealized profits deferred in 20X4 would not be recognized in Peak's 20X5 income and the $2,500 unrealized profit at year-end 20X5 would not be excluded from Peak's income. These observations can be summarized as follows:

	Incomplete Equity Method	− Overstated + Understated	= Equity Method
Investment balance at December 31, 20X4	$130,500	−$2,000	$128,500
Income from Seay in 20X5	27,000	+2,000 } −2,500	26,500
Dividends received in 20X5	(9,000)		(9,000)
Investment balance at December 31, 20X5	$148,500	−$2,500	$146,000

The errors of omitting the intercompany inventory profits affect the investment in Seay and retained earnings accounts of Peak by the same amount.

PEAK CORPORATION AND SUBSIDIARY
CONSOLIDATION WORKING PAPERS
FOR THE YEAR ENDED DECEMBER 31, 20X5

	Peak	90% Seay	Adjustments and Eliminations		Minority Interest	Consolidated Statements
Income Statement Net sales	$1,000,000	$300,000	a 20,000			$1,280,000
Income from Seay	26,500		d 26,500			
Cost of goods sold	(550,000)	(200,000)	c 2,500	a 20,000 b 2,000		(730,500)
Other expenses	(350,000)	(70,000)				(420,000)
Minority interest income ($30,000 × 10%)					$ 3,000	(3,000)
Net income	$ 126,500	$ 30,000				$ 126,500
Retained Earnings Retained earnings—Peak	$ 194,000					$ 194,000
Retained earnings—Seay		$ 45,000	e 45,000			
Net income	126,500√	30,000√				126,500
Dividends	(50,000)	(10,000)		d 9,000	(1,000)	(50,000)
Retained earnings December 31, 20X5	$ 270,500	$ 65,000				$ 270,500
Balance Sheet Cash	$ 30,000	$ 5,000				$ 35,000
Accounts receivable	70,000	20,000		f 10,000		80,000
Inventories	90,000	45,000		c 2,500		132,500
Other current assets	64,000	10,000				74,000
Plant and equipment	800,000	120,000				920,000
Investment in Seay	146,000		b 2,000	d 17,500 e 130,500		
	$1,200,000	$200,000				$1,241,500
Accounts payable	$ 80,000	$ 15,000	f 10,000			$ 85,000
Other liabilities	49,500	20,000				69,500
Capital stock	800,000	100,000	e 100,000			800,000
Retained earnings	270,500√	65,000√				270,500
	$1,200,000	$200,000				
Minority interest January 1, 20X5				e 14,500	14,500	
Minority interest December 31, 20X5					$16,500	16,500
						$1,241,500

Exhibit 5–7 *Intercompany Profits on Downstream Sales—Equity Method*

Conversion to Equity Method Approach   The working papers for Peak and Seay for 20X5 can be converted to the equity method with the following working paper entry to correct for the omissions on Peak's books:

a	Income from Seay	$ 500	
	Retained earnings—Peak (beginning)	2,000	
	Investment in Seay		$ 2,500

After this working paper correction is entered, the other working paper entries would be the same as those illustrated in the consolidation working papers of Exhibit 5–7. This entry could also be recorded on the separate books of Peak before closing in 20X5 to correct for all prior errors resulting from the misapplication of the equity method.

Traditional Working Paper Solution for Incomplete Equity Method   The initial approach to consolidating Peak and Seay financial statements under an incomplete equity method was to convert the income from subsidiary, investment in subsidiary, and retained earnings balances to a complete equity basis. Alternatively, the consolidation working paper entries can be adjusted to accommodate an incomplete equity method without conversion to the equity basis. This alternative working paper approach is illustrated in Exhibit 5–8.

Only entries b and d are different from those appearing in Exhibit 5–7 under the equity method. These two working paper entries are reproduced for convenient reference:

b	Retained earnings—Peak January 1	$ 2,000	
	Cost of goods sold		$ 2,000
	To adjust cost of goods sold and Peak's beginning-of-the-period retained earnings for unrealized profits in the beginning inventory.		
d	Income from Seay	$27,000	
	Dividends		$ 9,000
	Investment in Seay		18,000
	To eliminate investment income (as recorded by Peak) and 90% of Seay's dividends and to reduce the investment account to its beginning-of-the-period balance.		

Beginning parent company retained earnings is overstated because Peak failed to eliminate the $2,000 unrealized profits in 20X4. The amount of the overstatement is the difference between the transfer price and historical cost of the merchandise sold downstream. Entry b decreases Peak's beginning retained earnings and cost of goods sold for realized profits in the beginning inventory. Entry d eliminates the investment income recognized on Peak's books and dividends received from Seay. The investment account is also adjusted to its beginning-of-the-period balance in entry d.

Cost Method

If Peak had accounted for its investment in Seay using the cost method, the investment account and the December 31, 20X5 retained earnings would be understated by equal amounts in the parent's separate balance sheet. Also, instead of income from Seay, the income statement for 20X5 would show dividend income of $9,000. The investment in Seay account would be $94,500—the original amount paid by Peak for its investment.

Conversion to Equity Method Approach   The cost-to-equity conversion schedule in Exhibit 5–9 is based on the same data as under the equity method for Peak and Seay, except that Peak maintains its investment in Seay account using the cost method. The objective of the schedule is to provide information necessary to adjust the working paper accounts to what they would have been had the equity method been used.

PEAK CORPORATION AND SUBSIDIARY
CONSOLIDATION WORKING PAPERS
FOR THE YEAR ENDED DECEMBER 31, 20X5

	Peak	90% Seay	Adjustments and Eliminations		Minority Interest	Consolidated Statements
Income Statement Net sales	$1,000,000	$300,000	a 20,000			$1,280,000
Income from Seay	27,000		d 27,000			
Cost of goods sold	(550,000)	(200,000)	c 2,500	a 20,000 b 2,000		(730,500)
Other expenses	(350,000)	(70,000)				(420,000)
Minority interest income ($30,000 × 10%)					$ 3,000	(3,000)
Net income	$ 127,000	$ 30,000				$ 126,500
Retained Earnings Retained earnings—Peak	$ 196,000		b 2,000			$ 194,000
Retained earnings—Seay		$ 45,000	e 45,000			
Net income	127,000√	30,000√				126,500
Dividends	(50,000)	(10,000)		d 9,000	(1,000)	(50,000)
Retained earnings December 31, 20X5	$ 273,000	$ 65,000				$ 270,500
Balance Sheet Cash	$ 30,000	$ 5,000				$ 35,000
Accounts receivable	70,000	20,000		f 10,000		80,000
Inventories	90,000	45,000		c 2,500		132,500
Other current assets	64,000	10,000				74,000
Plant and equipment	800,000	120,000				920,000
Investment in Seay	148,500			d 18,000 e 130,500		
	$1,202,500	$200,000				$1,241,500
Accounts payable	$ 80,000	$ 15,000	f 10,000			$ 85,000
Other liabilities	49,500	20,000				69,500
Capital stock	800,000	100,000	e 100,000			800,000
Retained earnings	273,000√	65,000√				270,500
	$1,202,500	$200,000				
Minority interest January 1, 20X5				e 14,500	14,500	
Minority interest December 31, 20X5					$16,500	16,500
						$1,241,500

Exhibit 5–8   *Incomplete Equity Method*

	Retained Earnings 12/31/X4	Investment in Seay	Income from Seay	Dividend Income
Prior Year's Effect				
90% of Seay's increase in undistributed earnings from July 1, 20X1, to December 31, 20X4 ($45,000 − $5,000) × 90%	$36,000	$36,000		
Unrealized profit in Seay's inventory at December 31, 20X4	(2,000)	(2,000)		
Current Year's Effect				
Reclassify dividend income as investment decrease ($10,000 × 90%)		(9,000)		$(9,000)
Equity in Seay's income for 20X5 ($30,000 × 90%)		27,000	$27,000	
Unrealized profit in Seay's December 31, 20X4 inventory		2,000	2,000	
Unrealized profit in Seay's December 31, 20X5 inventory		(2,500)	(2,500)	
20X5 working paper adjustments to convert from cost to equity	$34,000	$51,500	$26,500	$(9,000)

Exhibit 5–9   *Peak and Subsidiary Cost-Equity Conversion Schedule*

The following consolidation working paper entry is prepared from the schedule:

a	Dividend income	$ 9,000	
	Investment in Seay	51,500	
	Retained earnings—Peak		$ 34,000
	Income from Seay		26,500

To eliminate dividend income, enter income from Seay, adjust the investment in Seay account to an equity basis, and convert Peak's retained earnings to beginning consolidated retained earnings.

After this working paper adjustment is entered, the other working paper entries are exactly the same as those in Exhibit 5–7 under the equity method. This entry may also be recorded on the parent company books before closing in 20X5 to convert the parent company records to an equity basis.

Traditional Working Paper Solution for Cost Method   When Peak accounts for its investment in Seay by the cost method, the financial statements of Peak and Seay can be consolidated without converting to the equity method. Exhibit 5–10 illustrates consolidation working papers when the parent company accounts for its investment under the cost method without a working paper entry for conversion to the equity method.

Working paper entries from Exhibit 5–10 are reproduced for convenient reference:

a	Sales	$ 20,000	
	Cost of goods sold		$ 20,000
	To eliminate intercompany sales and related cost of goods sold.		
b	Retained earnings—Peak January 1	$ 2,000	
	Cost of goods sold		$ 2,000
	To adjust cost of goods sold and Peak's beginning-of-the-period retained earnings for unrealized profits in the beginning inventory.		

PEAK CORPORATION AND SUBSIDIARY
CONSOLIDATION WORKING PAPERS
FOR THE YEAR ENDED DECEMBER 31, 20X5

	Peak	90% Seay	Adjustments and Eliminations		Minority Interest	Consolidated Statements
Income Statement Net sales	$1,000,000	$300,000	a 20,000			$1,280,000
Dividend income	9,000		d 9,000			
Cost of goods sold	(550,000)	(200,000)	c 2,500	a 20,000 b 2,000		(730,500)
Other expenses	(350,000)	(70,000)				(420,000)
Minority interest income ($30,000 × 10%)					$ 3,000	(3,000)
Net income	$ 109,000	$ 30,000				$ 126,500
Retained Earnings Retained earnings—Peak	$ 160,000		b 2,000	e 36,000		$ 194,000
Retained earnings—Seay		$ 45,000	f 45,000			
Net income	109,000√	30,000√				126,500
Dividends	(50,000)	(10,000)		d 9,000	(1,000)	(50,000)
Retained earnings December 31, 20X5	$ 219,000	$ 65,000				$ 270,500
Balance Sheet Cash	$ 30,000	$ 5,000				$ 35,000
Accounts receivable	70,000	20,000		g 10,000		80,000
Inventories	90,000	45,000		c 2,500		132,500
Other current assets	64,000	10,000				74,000
Plant and equipment	800,000	120,000				920,000
Investment in Seay	94,500		e 36,000	f 130,500		
	$1,148,500	$200,000				$1,241,500
Accounts payable	$ 80,000	$ 15,000	g 10,000			$ 85,000
Other liabilities	49,500	20,000				69,500
Capital stock	800,000	100,000	f 100,000			800,000
Retained earnings	219,000√	65,000√				270,500
	$1,148,500	$200,000				
Minority interest January 1, 20X5				f 14,500	14,500	
Minority interest December 31, 20X5					$16,500	16,500
						$1,241,500

Exhibit 5–10 *Intercompany Profits and Downstream Sales—Cost Method*

c	Cost of goods sold	$ 2,500	
	Inventories		$ 2,500
	To eliminate unrealized profits in ending inventory.		
d	Dividend income	$ 9,000	
	Dividends		$ 9,000
	To eliminate dividend income and 90% of Seay's dividends.		
e	Investment in Seay	$ 36,000	
	Retained earnings—Peak January 1		$ 36,000
	To increase Peak's beginning retained earnings for its share of Seay's retained earnings increase between the date of acquisition and the beginning of the period.		
f	Capital stock—Seay	$100,000	
	Retained earnings—Seay	45,000	
	Investment in Seay		$130,500
	Minority interest January 1		14,500
	To eliminate reciprocal investment and equity balances.		
g	Accounts payable	$ 10,000	
	Accounts receivable		$ 10,000
	To eliminate reciprocal receivables and payables.		

Entries a, b, and c are the same as those in Exhibit 5–8 under the incomplete equity method. Under the cost method, the balance of Peak's investment in Seay account remains at the $94,500 original cost. Peak recognizes dividend income but does not record its share of Seay's income or eliminate intercompany profits.

Entry d eliminates dividend income and 90% of Seay's dividends. Entry e establishes reciprocity between the investment in Seay account balance and Seay's equity balances at the beginning of the period ($145,000 × 90%). Entries f and g are the same as under the equity method.

CONSOLIDATION EXAMPLE—INTERCOMPANY PROFITS FROM UPSTREAM SALES

Smith Corporation is an 80%-owned subsidiary of Poch Corporation, acquired for $480,000 on January 2, 20X6 when Smith's stockholders' equity consisted of $500,000 capital stock and $100,000 retained earnings. The investment cost was equal to the book value and fair value of Smith's net assets acquired, so no cost/book value differential resulted from the business combination.

Smith Corporation sells inventory items to Poch Corporation on a regular basis. The intercompany transaction data for 20X7 are as follows:

Sales to Poch in 20X7	$300,000
Unrealized profit in Poch's inventory, December 31, 20X6	40,000
Unrealized profit in Poch's inventory, December 31, 20X7	30,000
Intercompany accounts receivable and payable at December 31, 20X7	50,000

Equity Method

At December 31, 20X6, Poch's investment in Smith had an account balance of $568,000, consisting of $600,000 underlying equity in Smith's net assets ($750,000 × 80%) less 80% of the $40,000 unrealized profit in Poch's December 31, 20X6 inventory from upstream sales.

During 20X7 Poch made the following entries to account for its investment in Smith under the equity method:

Cash	$40,000	
Investment in Smith		$40,000
To record dividends from Smith ($50,000 × 80%).		

Investment in Smith	$88,000	
Income from Smith		$88,000

To record income from Smith for 20X7 computed as follows:

Equity in Smith's net income ($100,000 × 80%)	$80,000
Add: 80% of $40,000 unrealized profit deferred in 20X6	32,000
Less: 80% of $30,000 unrealized profit at December 31, 20X7	−24,000
	$88,000

The intercompany sales that led to the unrealized inventory profits in 20X6 and 20X7 were upstream, and, accordingly, only 80% of the $40,000 unrealized profit from 20X6 is recognized by Poch in 20X7. Similarly, only 80% of the $30,000 unrealized profit from 20X7 sales is deferred by Poch at December 31, 20X7. Poch's investment in Smith account was increased by the $88,000 income from Smith during 20X7 and decreased by $40,000 dividends received from Smith. Thus, the $568,000 investment in Smith account at December 31, 20X6 increased to $616,000 at December 31, 20X7. These amounts, combined with other compatible information to provide complete separate company financial statements, are shown in the separate company columns of the consolidation working papers for Poch Corporation and Subsidiary in Exhibit 5–11.

The working paper entries in Exhibit 5–11 are presented below in journal form for convenient reference.

a	Sales	$300,000	
	Cost of goods sold		$300,000
	To eliminate reciprocal sales and cost of goods sold amounts.		
b	Investment in Smith	$ 32,000	
	Minority interest	8,000	
	Cost of goods sold		$ 40,000
	To adjust cost of goods sold for unrealized profit in beginning inventory and to allocate the unrealized profit 80% to the parent's investment account and 20% to minority interest.		
c	Cost of goods sold	$ 30,000	
	Inventory		$ 30,000
	To eliminate unrealized profit from ending inventory and cost of goods sold.		
d	Income from Smith	$ 88,000	
	Dividends		$ 40,000
	Investment in Smith		48,000
	To eliminate investment income and 80% of the dividends by Smith and to reduce the investment account to its beginning balance.		
e	Retained earnings—Smith	$250,000	
	Capital stock—Smith	500,000	
	Investment in Smith		$600,000
	Minority interest		150,000
	To eliminate reciprocal investment and equity balances and to enter beginning minority interest.		
f	Accounts payable	$ 50,000	
	Accounts receivable		$ 50,000
	To eliminate reciprocal accounts receivable and payable.		

The consolidation working paper entries, as presented in Exhibit 5–11, are similar to those in the Peak/Seay illustration. Only entry b, which allocates the unrealized profit in Poch's beginning inventory between investment in Smith (80%) and minority interest (20%), is significantly different. Allocation is necessary because the unreal-

POCH CORPORATION AND SUBSIDIARY
CONSOLIDATION WORKING PAPERS
FOR THE YEAR ENDED DECEMBER 31, 20X7

	Poch	80% Smith	Adjustments and Eliminations		Minority Interest	Consolidated Statements
Income Statement Sales	$3,000,000	$1,500,000	a 300,000			$4,200,000
Income from Smith	88,000		d 88,000			
Cost of goods sold	(2,000,000)	(1,000,000)	c 30,000	a 300,000 b 40,000		(2,690,000)
Other expenses	(588,000)	(400,000)				(988,000)
Minority interest income[†]					$ 22,000	(22,000)
Net income	$ 500,000	$ 100,000				$ 500,000
Retained Earnings Retained earnings—Poch	$1,000,000					$1,000,000
Retained earnings—Smith		$ 250,000	e 250,000			
Net income	500,000√	100,000√				500,000
Dividends	(400,000)	(50,000)		d 40,000	(10,000)	(400,000)
Retained earnings December 31, 20X7	$1,100,000	$ 300,000				$1,100,000
Balance Sheet Cash	$ 200,000	$ 50,000				$ 250,000
Accounts receivable	700,000	100,000		f 50,000		750,000
Inventories	1,100,000	200,000		c 30,000		1,270,000
Other current assets	384,000	150,000				534,000
Plant and equipment—net	2,000,000	500,000				2,500,000
Investment in Smith	616,000		b 32,000	d 48,000 e 600,000		
	$5,000,000	$1,000,000				$5,304,000
Accounts payable	$ 500,000	$ 150,000	f 50,000			$ 600,000
Other liabilities	400,000	50,000				450,000
Capital stock	3,000,000	500,000	e 500,000			3,000,000
Retained earnings	1,100,000√	300,000√				1,100,000
	$5,000,000	$1,000,000				
Minority interest January 1, 20X7			b 8,000	e 150,000	142,000	
Minority interest December 31, 20X7					$154,000	154,000
						$5,304,000

† Minority interest income ($100,000 + $40,000 – $30,000) × 20% = $22,000.

Exhibit 5–11 *Intercompany Profits on Upstream Sales—Equity Method*

ized profit arises from an upstream sale and was included in Smith's reported income for 20X6. Poch's share of the $40,000 unrealized profit is only 80%. The other 20% relates to minority interests, and, accordingly, the $8,000 charge is necessary to reduce beginning minority interest from $150,000 (20% of Smith's reported equity of $750,000) to $142,000—20% of Smith's realized equity of $710,000 ($750,000 − $40,000) at December 31, 20X6.

Minority Interest   In computing minority interest income for 20X7, it is necessary to adjust Smith's reported net income for unrealized profits before multiplying by the minority interest percentage. The computation is:

Reported net income of Smith	$100,000
Add: Inventory profits from 20X6 realized in 20X7	+ 40,000
Deduct: Unrealized profits at December 31, 20X7	−30,000
Smith's realized income for 20X7	110,000
Minority interest percentage	20%
Minority interest income	$ 22,000

The $154,000 minority interest at December 31, 20X7 is determined in the working papers by adding minority interest income of $22,000 to beginning minority interest of $142,000 and subtracting minority interest dividends. An alternative computation that may be used as a check is to deduct unrealized profit in the December 31, 20X7 inventory from Smith's equity at December 31, 20X7, and multiply the resulting realized equity of Smith by the 20% minority interest [($800,000 − $30,000) × 20% = $154,000]. The advantage of this approach is that only unrealized profits at the balance sheet date need to be considered in the computation.

Incomplete Equity Method

Now assume that Poch Corporation has failed to consider its intercompany transactions in accounting for its investment in Smith for 20X6 and 20X7. In that case, both Poch's investment in Smith and its retained earnings account balances at December 31, 20X6 would be $32,000 greater than under the equity method. This $32,000 overstatement is the result of Poch's failure to reduce investment and investment income accounts for 80% of the $40,000 unrealized inventory profit in 20X6. By December 31, 20X7, the overstatement would decrease to $24,000 because the $32,000 deferred from 20X6 would not be recognized in Poch's income for 20X7, and the $24,000 unrealized profit for 20X7 (80% of $30,000 unrealized profit at December 31, 20X7) would not be excluded from Poch's 20X7 income. These observations can be summarized by comparison with the equity method example already illustrated:

	Incomplete Equity Method	− + Overstated Understated	= Equity Method (see Exhibit 5–11)
Investment balance at December 31, 20X6	$600,000	−$32,000	$568,000
Income from Smith in 20X7	80,000	+ 32,000 − 24,000 }	88,000
Dividends received in 20X7	(40,000)		(40,000)
Investment balance at December 31, 20X7	$640,000	−$24,000	$616,000

Conversion to Equity Method Approach   The errors from omitting the intercompany profits in 20X6 and 20X7 affect the investment in Smith and retained earnings accounts of Poch by equal amounts.

A working paper entry to correct for the omissions on Poch's books in the 20X7 consolidation working papers of Poch and Subsidiary is as follows:

a	Retained earnings—Poch	$32,000	
	Income from Smith		$ 8,000
	Investment in Smith		24,000

This working paper entry converts the separate accounts of Poch from the incomplete equity to the equity method for working paper utilization. After the conversion is entered in the working papers, the other working paper entries will be the same as those illustrated in the consolidation working papers of Exhibit 5–11. The conversion entry could also be recorded in Poch's separate records before closing in 20X7 to correct for the 20X6 and 20X7 errors of omission.

Traditional Working Paper Solution for Incomplete Equity Method The traditional approach to consolidating the financial statements of Poch and Smith under an incomplete equity method is illustrated in Exhibit 5–12. Beginning parent company retained earnings is overstated by Poch's share of the unrealized profits in Poch's December 31, 20X6 inventory of goods acquired from Smith. Entry b eliminates the $40,000 cost-of-goods-sold effect of the intercompany profits in Poch's beginning inventory, and allocates it 80% to Poch's beginning-of-the-period retained earnings and 20% to beginning-of-the-period minority interest. Entry d eliminates income from Smith (as recorded by Poch) and 80% of Smith's dividends, and reduces the investment account to its beginning-of-the-period balance. Other entries in Exhibit 5–12 are the same as those under the equity method.

Cost Method

If Poch Corporation had used the cost method of accounting for its investment in Smith for 20X6 and 20X7, its investment in Smith account would remain at $480,000, the original cost of the investment. Assume the same facts for Poch and Smith as shown in Exhibit 5–11 under the equity method, except that Poch's investment in Smith is accounted for by the cost method.

Conversion to Equity Method Approach Data for the working paper entry to convert Poch's cost-based accounting records to the equity basis are provided in the cost-equity conversion schedule that appears in Exhibit 5–13. The information in the cost-equity conversion schedule is used in constructing a consolidation working paper entry for Poch and Smith as follows:

a	Dividend income	$ 40,000	
	Investment in Smith	136,000	
	Income from Smith		$88,000
	Retained earnings—Poch		88,000
	To eliminate dividend income, enter income from Smith, adjust the investment in Smith account to an equity basis, and convert Poch's beginning retained earnings into beginning consolidated retained earnings.		

This entry should be entered as the first working paper adjustment, after which other working paper entries are the same as those prepared when the equity method is used. The cost-equity conversion entry may be recorded on the parent company books before closing in 20X7 to convert the parent company records to an equity basis.

Traditional Working Paper Solution for the Cost Method Exhibit 5–14 illustrates working paper procedures to consolidate the financial statements of Poch and Smith without converting to the equity method. Entries a, b, and c under the cost method are identical to those under an *incomplete equity method.* Entry d eliminates dividend income and 80% of Smith's dividends. Entry e takes up Poch's share of Smith's retained earnings increase between the date of acquisition of the investment and the begin-

POCH CORPORATION AND SUBSIDIARY
CONSOLIDATION WORKING PAPERS
FOR THE YEAR ENDED DECEMBER 31, 20X7

	Poch	80% Smith	Adjustments and Eliminations		Minority Interest	Consolidated Statements
Income Statement						
Sales	$3,000,000	$1,500,000	a 300,000			$4,200,000
Income from Smith	80,000		d 80,000			
Cost of goods sold	(2,000,000)	(1,000,000)	c 30,000	a 300,000		
				b 40,000		(2,690,000)
Other expenses	(588,000)	(400,000)				(988,000)
Minority interest income†					$ 22,000	(22,000)
Net income	$ 492,000	$ 100,000				$ 500,000
Retained Earnings						
Retained earnings—Poch	$1,032,000		b 32,000			$1,000,000
Retained earnings—Smith		$ 250,000	e 250,000			
Net income	492,000√	100,000√				500,000
Dividends	(400,000)	(50,000)		d 40,000	(10,000)	(400,000)
Retained earnings December 31, 20X7	$1,124,000	$ 300,000				$1,100,000
Balance Sheet						
Cash	$ 200,000	$ 50,000				$ 250,000
Accounts receivable	700,000	100,000		f 50,000		750,000
Inventories	1,100,000	200,000		c 30,000		1,270,000
Other current assets	384,000	150,000				534,000
Plant and equipment—net	2,000,000	500,000				2,500,000
Investment in Smith	640,000			d 40,000		
				e 600,000		
	$5,024,000	$1,000,000				$5,304,000
Accounts payable	$ 500,000	$ 150,000	f 50,000			$ 600,000
Other liabilities	400,000	50,000				450,000
Capital stock	3,000,000	500,000	e 500,000			3,000,000
Retained earnings	1,124,000√	300,000√				1,100,000
	$5,024,000	$1,000,000				
Minority interest January 1, 20X7			b 8,000	e 150,000	142,000	
Minority interest December 31, 20X7					$154,000	154,000
						$5,304,000

†Minority interest income ($100,000 + $40,000 − $30,000) × 20% = $22,000.

Exhibit 5–12   Incomplete Equity Method

	Poch's Retained Earnings 12/31/X6	Investment in Smith	Income from Smith	Dividend Income
Prior Years' Effect				
80% of increase in Smith's undistributed earnings from January 2, 20X6 to December 31, 20X6 ($250,000 − $100,000) × 80%	$120,000	$120,000		
80% of unrealized profit in Poch's December 31, 20X6, inventory ($40,000 × 80%)	(32,000)	(32,000)		
Current Years' Effect				
Reclassify dividend income as investment decrease ($50,000 dividends × 80%)		(40,000)		$(40,000)
Equity in Smith's 20X7 income ($100,000 × 80%)		80,000	$ 80,000	
80% of unrealized profit in Poch's December 31, 20X6 inventory		32,000	32,000	
80% of unrealized profit in Poch's December 31, 20X7 inventory ($30,000 × 80%)		(24,000)	(24,000)	
20X7 working paper adjustments to convert from cost to equity	$ 88,000	$136,000	$ 88,000	$(40,000)

Exhibit 5–13 *Poch and Subsidiary Cost-Equity Conversion Schedule*

ning of 20X7, thereby establishing reciprocity between the investment account at the beginning of the period and 80% of Smith's $750,000 equity at the same date. Entries d and e are reproduced for convenient reference:

d	Dividend income	$ 40,000	
	Dividends		$ 40,000
	To eliminate dividend income and 80% of Smith's dividends.		

e	Investment in Smith	$120,000	
	Retained earnings—Poch January 1		$120,000
	To establish reciprocity between parent's beginning-of-the-period retained earnings and the investment account at the same date.		

Entry f eliminates reciprocal investment and equity balances and enters beginning minority interest the same as under the *equity method.* Entry g eliminates reciprocal accounts receivable and payable.

SUMMARY

Intercompany sales and purchases of inventory items result in reciprocal sales and cost of goods sold amounts that do not reflect merchandising activity of the consolidated entity. Such intercompany transactions also give rise to unrealized intercompany profits that are required to be deferred until they are realized by subsequent sales outside of the consolidated entity. Except for affiliation structures with only 100%-owned subsidiaries, the direction of intercompany sales is important. The full amount of the unrealized intercompany profit from downstream sales is charged against parent company and consolidated net income. In the case of upstream sales, however, unrealized profits are charged to consolidated net income and minority interest income on the basis of majority and minority ownership. Intercompany profits

POCH CORPORATION AND SUBSIDIARY
CONSOLIDATION WORKING PAPERS
FOR THE YEAR ENDED DECEMBER 31, 20X7

	Poch	80% Smith	Adjustments and Eliminations		Minority Interest	Consolidated Statements
Income Statement						
Sales	$3,000,000	$1,500,000	a 300,000			$4,200,000
Dividend income	40,000		d 40,000			
Cost of goods sold	(2,000,000)	(1,000,000)	c 30,000	a 300,000 b 40,000		(2,690,000)
Other expenses	(588,000)	(400,000)				(988,000)
Minority interest income†					$ 22,000	(22,000)
Net income	$ 452,000	$ 100,000				$ 500,000
Retained Earnings						
Retained earnings—Poch	$ 912,000		b 32,000	e 120,000		$1,000,000
Retained earnings—Smith		$ 250,000	f 250,000			
Net income	452,000√	100,000√				500,000
Dividends	(400,000)	(50,000)		d 40,000	(10,000)	(400,000)
Retained earnings December 31, 20X7	$ 964,000	$ 300,000				$1,100,000
Balance Sheet						
Cash	$ 200,000	$ 50,000				$ 250,000
Accounts receivable	700,000	100,000		g 50,000		750,000
Inventories	1,100,000	200,000		c 30,000		1,270,000
Other current assets	384,000	150,000				534,000
Plant and equipment—net	2,000,000	500,000				2,500,000
Investment in Smith	480,000		e 120,000	f 600,000		
	$4,864,000	$1,000,000				$5,304,000
Accounts payable	$ 500,000	$ 150,000	g 50,000			$ 600,000
Other liabilities	400,000	50,000				450,000
Capital stock	3,000,000	500,000	f 500,000			3,000,000
Retained earnings	964,000√	300,000√				1,100,000
	$4,864,000	$1,000,000				
Minority interest January 1, 20X7			b 8,000	f 150,000	142,000	
Minority interest December 31, 20X7					$154,000	154,000
						$5,304,000

† Minority interest income ($100,000 + $40,000 – $30,000) × 20% = $22,000.

Exhibit 5–14   Intercompany Profits on Upstream Sales—Cost Method

Assumptions:
1 Parent company's income, excluding income from subsidiary, is $100,000.
2 90%-owned subsidiary reports net income of $50,000.
3 Unrealized profit in beginning inventory is $5,000.
4 Unrealized profit in ending inventory is $10,000.

	Downstream Assume that P Sells to S	Upstream Assume that S Sells to P
P's Net Income—Equity Method		
P's separate income	$100,000	$100,000
P's share of S's reported net income:		
($50,000 × 90%)	45,000	45,000
Add: Unrealized profit in beginning inventory:		
($5,000 × 100%)	5,000	
($5,000 × 90%)		4,500
Deduct: Unrealized profit in ending inventory:		
($10,000 × 100%)	(10,000)	
($10,000 × 90%)		(9,000)
P's net income	$140,000	$140,500
Consolidated Net Income		
P's separate income plus S's net income	$150,000	$150,000
Adjustments for unrealized profits:		
Beginning inventory ($5,000 × 100%)	5,000	5,000
Ending inventory ($10,000 × 100%)	(10,000)	(10,000)
Total realized income	145,000	145,000
Less: Minority interest income:		
($50,000 × 10%)	(5,000)	
($50,000 + $5,000 − $10,000) × 10%		(4,500)
Consolidated net income	$140,000	$140,500

Exhibit 5–15 *Summary Illustration—Unrealized Inventory Profits*

that are deferred in one period are subsequently recognized in the period in which the related inventory items are sold to nonaffiliated entities. A summary illustration of the effect of intercompany profit eliminations on parent company and consolidated net income is presented in Exhibit 5–15.

Under the assumption that P sells to S, P's net income and consolidated net income are exactly the same as if the sales involving the unrealized profits had never taken place. In that case, P's separate income would have been $95,000 ($100,000 + $5,000 − $10,000), and P's income from S would have been $45,000 ($50,000 × 90%), for a total of $140,000. Under the assumption that S sells to P, P's net income and consolidated net income are exactly the same as if the intercompany sales involving unrealized profits had never taken place. In that case, P's separate income would have been $100,000 (as given), and S's net income would have been $45,000 ($50,000 + $5,000 − $10,000). P's $100,000 separate income plus P's income from S of $40,500 ($45,000 × 90%) is equal to P's net income and consolidated net income.

SELECTED READINGS

Accounting Interpretation No. 1 of APB Opinion No. 18. New York: American Institute of Certified Public Accountants, 1971.

Accounting Principles Board Opinion No. 18. "The Equity Method of Accounting for Investments in Common Stock." New York: American Institute of Certified Public Accountants, 1971.

Accounting Research Bulletin No. 51. "Consolidated Financial Statements." New York: American Institute of Certified Public Accountants, 1959.

Financial Accounting Standards Board. Discussion Memorandum. *An Analysis of Issues Related to Consolidation Policy and Procedures.* Financial Accounting Series. Norwalk, CT: Financial Accounting Standards Board, 1991.

ASSIGNMENT MATERIAL

QUESTIONS

1 The effect of unrealized profits and losses on sales between affiliated companies is eliminated in preparing consolidated financial statements. When are profits and losses on such sales realized for consolidated statement purposes?

2 In eliminating unrealized profit on intercompany sales of inventory items, should gross profit or net profit be eliminated?

3 Is the amount of intercompany profit to be eliminated from consolidated financial statements affected by the existence of a minority interest? Explain.

4 What effect does the elimination of intercompany sales and purchases (or cost of goods sold) have on consolidated net income?

5 What effect does the elimination of intercompany accounts receivable and accounts payable have on consolidated working capital?

6 Explain the designations *upstream sales* and *downstream sales*. Of what significance are these designations in computing parent company and consolidated net income?

7 Would failure to eliminate unrealized profit in inventories at December 31, 20X6 have any effect on consolidated net income in 20X7? 20X8?

8 Under what circumstances is minority interest income affected by intercompany sales activity?

9 How does a parent company adjust its investment income for unrealized profit on sales it makes to its subsidiaries (a) in the year of the sale and (b) in the year in which the subsidiaries sell the related merchandise to outsiders?

10 How is the combined cost of goods sold affected by unrealized profit in (a) the beginning inventory of the subsidiary and (b) the ending inventory of the subsidiary?

11 Is the effect of unrealized profit on consolidated cost of goods sold influenced by (a) the existence of a minority interest and (b) the direction of intercompany sales?

12 Unrealized profit in the ending inventory is eliminated in consolidation working papers by increasing cost of sales and decreasing the inventory account. How is unrealized profit in the beginning inventory reflected in the consolidation working papers?

13 Describe the computation of minority interest income in a year in which there is unrealized inventory profit from upstream sales in both the beginning and ending inventories of the parent company.

14 Consolidation working paper procedures are usually based on the assumption that any unrealized profit in the beginning inventory of one year is realized through sales in the following year. If the related merchandise is not sold in the succeeding period, would the assumption result in an incorrect measurement of consolidated net income?

   (*Note:* Don't forget the assumptions on page 56 when working exercises and problems in this chapter.)

EXERCISES

E 5-1

1 Intercompany profit elimination entries in consolidation working papers are prepared in order to:
   a Nullify the effect of intercompany transactions on consolidated statements
   b Defer intercompany profit until realized
   c Allocate unrealized profits between majority and minority interests
   d Reduce consolidated income

2 The direction of intercompany sales (upstream or downstream) does not affect consolidation working paper procedures when the intercompany sales between affiliated companies are made:
   a At fair value   c At book value
   b Above market value   d To a 100%-owned subsidiary

3 Peterson Corporation sells inventory items for $100,000 to Steven Corporation, its 80%-owned subsidiary. The consolidated working paper entry to eliminate the effect of this intercompany sale will include a debit to sales for:
   a $100,000
   b $80,000
   c The amount remaining in Steven's ending inventory
   d 80% of the amount remaining in Steven's ending inventory

4 Sarah Corporation, a 90%-owned subsidiary of Painter Corporation, buys half of its raw materials from Painter. The transfer price is exactly the same price as Sarah pays to buy identical raw materials from outside suppliers and the same price as Painter sells the materials to unrelated customers. In preparing consolidated statements for Painter Corporation and Subsidiary:
   a The intercompany transactions can be ignored because the transfer price represents arm's-length bargaining

    b Any unrealized profit from intercompany sales remaining in Painter's ending inventory must be offset against the unrealized profit in Painter's beginning inventory

    c Any unrealized profit on the intercompany transactions in Sarah's ending inventory is eliminated in its entirety

    d Only 90% of any unrealized profit on the intercompany transactions in Sarah's ending inventory is eliminated

5 Pritchard Corporation sells an inventory item to its subsidiary, Shinault Company, to be used as a plant asset by Shinault. The working paper entry to eliminate intercompany profits in the year of sale will **not** include:

    a A debit to sales   **c** A credit to inventories

    b A credit to cost of sales   **d** A credit to plant assets

6 Smeltzer Corporation regularly sells inventory items to its parent, Pullano Corporation. In preparing the consolidated income statement, which of the following items would *not* be affected by the direction (upstream or downstream) of these intercompany sales?

    a Consolidated gross profit   **c** Consolidated net income

    b Minority interest income   **d** Consolidated retained earnings

7 Pentacost Corporation regularly sells inventory items to its subsidiary, Schumaker Corporation. If unrealized profits in Schumaker's 20X2 year-end inventory exceed the unrealized profits in its 20X3 year-end inventory:

    a Combined cost of sales will be greater than consolidated cost of sales in 20X3

    b Combined cost of sales will be less than consolidated cost of sales in 20X3

    c Combined gross profit will be greater than consolidated gross profit in 20X3

    d Combined sales will be less than consolidated sales in 20X3

8 Spartacus Corporation is a 90%-owned subsidiary of Plymouth Corporation, acquired on January 1, 20X7 at a price equal to book value and fair value. Plymouth accounts for its investment in Spartacus using the equity method of accounting. The only intercompany transactions between the two affiliates in 20X7 and 20X8 are as follows:

    20X7   Plymouth sold inventory items that cost $200,000 to Spartacus for $250,000. One-fourth of this merchandise remains unsold at December 31, 20X7.

    20X8   Plymouth sold inventory items that cost $300,000 to Spartacus for $375,000. One-third of this merchandise remains unsold at December 31, 20X8.

At December 31, 20X8 Plymouth's investment in Spartacus account:

    a Will equal its underlying equity in Spartacus

    b Will be $12,500 greater than its underlying equity in Spartacus

    c Will be $25,000 less than its underlying equity in Spartacus

    d Will be $12,500 less than its underlying equity in Spartacus

E 5-2   **[AICPA adapted]**

1 Perez, Inc., owns 80% of Senior, Inc. During 20X2, Perez sold goods with a 40% gross profit to Senior. Senior sold all of these goods in 20X2. For 20X2 consolidated financial statements, how should the summation of Perez and Senior income statement items be adjusted?

    a Sales and cost of goods sold should be reduced by the intercompany sales.

    b Sales and cost of goods sold should be reduced by 80% of the intercompany sales.

    c Net income should be reduced by 80% of the gross profit on intercompany sales.

    d No adjustment is necessary.

2 Clark Company had the following transactions with affiliated parties during 20X2:

    • Sales of $60,000 to Dean, with $20,000 gross profit. Dean had $15,000 of this inventory on hand at year-end. Clark owns a 15% interest in Dean and does not exert significant influence.

    • Purchases of raw materials totaling $240,000 from Kent Corporation, a wholly owned subsidiary. Kent's gross profit on the sale was $48,000. Clark had $60,000 of this inventory remaining on December 31, 20X2.

Before eliminating entries, Clark had consolidated current assets of $320,000. What amount should Clark report in its December 31, 20X2, consolidated balance sheet for current assets?

    a $320,000   **c** $308,000

    b $317,000   **d** $303,000

3 Parker Corporation owns 80% of Smith's Inc. common stock. During 20X1, Parker sold Smith $250,000 of inventory on the same terms as sales made to third parties. Smith sold all of the inventory purchased from Parker in 20X1. The following information pertains to Smith's and Parker's sales for 20X1:

	Parker	Smith
Sales	$1,000,000	$700,000
Cost of sales	400,000	350,000
	$ 600,000	$350,000

What amount should Parker report as cost of sales in its 20X1 consolidated income statement?

    a $750,000   **c** $500,000

    b $680,000   **d** $430,000

E 5-3

1 The separate incomes of Philly Corporation and Silvio Corporation, a 100%-owned subsidiary of Philly, for 20X3 are $1,000,000 and $500,000, respectively. Philly sells all of its output to Silvio at 150% of Philly's cost of production. During 20X2 and 20X3 Philly's sales to Silvio were $4,500,000 and $3,500,000, respectively. Silvio's inventory at December 31, 20X2 included $1,500,000 of the merchandise acquired from Philly, and its December 31, 20X3 inventory included $1,200,000 of such merchandise.

A consolidated income statement for Philly Corporation and Subsidiary for 20X3 should show consolidated net income of:

a $1,100,000   **c** $1,500,000
b $1,400,000   **d** $1,600,000

Use the following information in answering questions 2 and 3:

Pansy Corporation owns 75% of the voting common stock of Saturn Corporation, acquired at book value during 20X5. Selected information from the accounts of Pansy and Saturn for 20X7 are as follows:

	Pansy	Saturn
Sales	$900,000	$500,000
Cost of sales	490,000	190,000

During 20X7 Pansy sold merchandise to Saturn for $50,000, at a gross profit to Pansy of $20,000. Half of this merchandise remained in Saturn's inventory at December 31, 20X7. Saturn's December 31, 20X6 inventory included unrealized profit of $4,000 on goods acquired from Pansy.

2 In a consolidated income statement for Pansy Corporation and Subsidiary for the year 20X7, consolidated sales should be:

a $1,450,000   **c** $1,362,500
b $1,400,000   **d** $1,350,000

3 In a consolidated income statement for Pansy Corporation and Subsidiary for the year 20X7, consolidated cost of sales should be:

a $686,000   **c** $636,000
b $680,000   **d** $624,000

E 5-4 Pride Corporation owns an 80% interest in Sedita Corporation, and at December 31, 20X1, Pride's investment in Sedita on an equity basis was equal to 80% of Sedita's stockholders' equity. During 20X2, Sedita sells merchandise to Pride for $100,000, at a gross profit to Sedita of $20,000. At December 31, 20X2 half of this merchandise is included in Pride's inventory. Separate incomes for Pride and Sedita for 20X2 are summarized as follows:

	Pride	Sedita
Sales	$500,000	$300,000
Cost of sales	(250,000)	(200,000)
Gross profit	250,000	100,000
Operating expenses	(125,000)	(40,000)
Separate incomes	$125,000	$ 60,000

1 Pride's income from Sedita for 20X2 is:

a $48,000   **c** $38,000
b $40,000   **d** $28,000

2 Consolidated cost of sales for 20X2 is:

a $460,000   **c** $440,000
b $450,000   **d** $360,000

3 Minority interest income for 20X2 is:

a $12,000   **c** $4,000
b $10,000   **d** $2,000

E 5-5 Parcon Corporation owns an 80% interest in Shelly Corporation acquired several years ago. Shelly regularly sells merchandise to its parent at 125% of Shelly's cost. Gross profit data of Parcon and Shelly for the year 20X6 are as follows:

	Parcon	Shelly
Sales	$1,000,000	$800,000
Cost of goods sold	800,000	640,000
Gross profit	$ 200,000	$160,000

During 20X6 Parcon purchased inventory items from Shelly at a transfer price of $400,000. Parcon's December 31, 20X5 and 20X6 inventories included goods acquired from Shelly of $100,000 and $125,000, respectively.

1 Consolidated sales of Parcon Corporation and Subsidiary for 20X6 were:
    a $1,800,000   **c** $1,400,000
    b $1,425,000   **d** $1,240,000

2 The unrealized profits in the year-end 20X5 and 20X6 inventories were:
    a $100,000 and $125,000, respectively
    b $80,000 and $100,000, respectively
    c $20,000 and $25,000, respectively
    d $16,000 and $20,000, respectively

3 Consolidated cost of goods sold of Parcon Corporation and Subsidiary for 20X6 was:
    a $1,024,000   **c** $1,052,800
    b $1,045,000   **d** $1,056,000

E 5-6   **1** Patti Corporation owns 70% of Susan Company's common stock, acquired January 1, 20X4. Goodwill from the investment is being amortized at a rate of $20,000 per year. Susan regularly sells merchandise to Patti at 150% of Susan's cost. Patti's December 31, 20X4 and 20X5 inventories include goods purchased intercompany of $112,500 and $33,000, respectively. The separate incomes (do not include investment income) of Patti and Susan for 20X5 are summarized as follows:

	Patti	Susan
Sales	$1,200,000	$ 800,000
Cost of sales	(600,000)	(500,000)
Other expenses	(400,000)	(100,000)
Separate incomes	$ 200,000	$ 200,000

Total consolidated income should be allocated to consolidated net income and minority interest income in the amounts of:
    a $338,550 and $67,950, respectively
    b $358,550 and $60,000, respectively
    c $346,500 and $60,000, respectively
    d $346,500 and $67,950, respectively

2 Packman acquired a 60% interest in Slocum on January 1, 20X3 for $360,000, when Slocum's net assets had a book value and fair value of $600,000. During 20X3 Packman sold inventory items that cost $600,000 to Slocum for $800,000, and Slocum's inventory at December 31, 20X3 included one-fourth of this merchandise. Packman reported separate income from its own operations (excludes investment income) of $300,000, and Slocum reported a net loss of $150,000 for 20X3. Consolidated net income for Packman Corporation and Subsidiary for 20X3 is:
    a $260,000   **c** $160,000
    b $180,000   **d** $100,000

3 Santini Corporation, a 75%-owned subsidiary of Parnell Corporation, sells inventory items to its parent at 125% of cost. Inventories of the two affiliated companies for 20X9 are as follows:

	Parnell	Santini
Beginning inventory	$400,000	$250,000
Ending inventory	500,000	200,000

Parnell's beginning and ending inventories include merchandise acquired from Santini of $150,000 and $200,000, respectively. If Santini reports net income of $300,000 for 20X9, Parnell's income from Santini will be:
    a $255,000   **c** $215,000
    b $217,500   **d** $195,000

E 5-7   Pansy Corporation owns an 80% interest in the common stock of Sheridan Corporation, acquired several years ago at book value. Pansy regularly sells merchandise to Sheridan. Information relevant to the intercompany sales and profits of Pansy and Sheridan for 20X4, 20X5, and 20X6 is as follows:

	20X4	20X5	20X6
Sales to Sheridan	$100,000	$120,000	$200,000
Unrealized profit in Sheridan's inventory at December 31	30,000	40,000	20,000
Sheridan's separate income	500,000	550,000	475,000
Pansy's separate income (does not include investment income)	300,000	400,000	350,000

Required: Prepare a schedule showing consolidated net income for each of the three years.

E 5-8 The separate incomes (which do not include investment income) of Pycus Corporation and Sylvia Corporation, its 80%-owned subsidiary, for 20X6 were determined as follows:

	Pycus	Sylvia
Sales	$400,000	$100,000
Less: Cost of sales	200,000	60,000
Gross profit	200,000	40,000
Other expenses	100,000	30,000
Separate incomes	$100,000	$ 10,000

During 20X6 Pycus sold merchandise that cost $20,000 to Sylvia for $40,000, and at December 31, 20X6 half of these inventory items remained unsold by Sylvia.

Required: Prepare a consolidated income statement for Pycus Corporation and Subsidiary for the year ended December 31, 20X6.

E 5-9 Income statement information for the year 20X3 for Purgatory Corporation and its 60%-owned subsidiary, Seven Corporation, is as follows:

	Purgatory	Seven
Sales	$900,000	$350,000
Cost of sales	400,000	250,000
Gross profit	500,000	100,000
Operating expenses	250,000	50,000
Seven's net income		$ 50,000
Purgatory's separate income	$250,000	

Intercompany sales for 20X3 are upstream (from Seven to Purgatory) and total $100,000. Purgatory's December 31, 20X2 and December 31, 20X3 inventories contain unrealized profits of $5,000 and $10,000, respectively.

Required
1 Compute minority interest income for 20X3.
2 Compute consolidated sales, cost of sales, and total consolidated income for 20X3.

E 5-10 Papillion Corporation purchased an 80% interest in Saiki Corporation for $600,000 on January 1, 20X7 at which time Saiki's stockholders' equity consisted of $500,000 common stock and $200,000 retained earnings. The excess cost over book value was assigned to goodwill with a 10-year amortization period. Comparative income statements for the two corporations for 20X8 are as follows:

	Papillion	Saiki
Sales	$1,000,000	$500,000
Income from Saiki	112,000	
Cost of sales	(400,000)	(250,000)
Depreciation expense	(130,000)	(40,000)
Other expenses	(90,000)	(60,000)
Net income	$ 492,000	$150,000

Dividends of Papillion and Saiki for all of 20X8 were $300,000 and $100,000, respectively. During 20X7 Saiki sold inventory items to Papillion for $80,000. This merchandise cost Saiki $50,000 and one-third of it remained in Papillion's December 31, 20X7 inventory. During 20X8 Saiki's sales to Papillion amounted to $90,000. This merchandise cost Saiki $60,000 and one-half of it remained in Papillion's December 31, 20X8 inventory.

Required: Prepare a consolidated income statement for Papillion Corporation and Subsidiary for the year ended December 31, 20X8.

E 5-11 Spud Corporation is a 90%-owned subsidiary of Pear Corporation, acquired by Pear at book value, which was also equal to its fair value on January 1, 20X2. Pear uses the equity method of accounting for its investment in Spud, but it does not make adjustments for intercompany profit transactions [an incomplete equity method]. Separate income statements for Pear and Spud for 20X2 and 20X3 are as follows:

	Pear 20X2	Pear 20X3	Spud 20X2	Spud 20X3
Sales	$1,000,000	$1,200,000	$500,000	$700,000
Income from Spud	90,000	135,000		
Cost of sales	(600,000)	(720,000)	(300,000)	(350,000)
Other expenses	(200,000)	(250,000)	(100,000)	(200,000)
Net income	$ 290,000	$ 365,000	$100,000	$150,000

Intercompany sales from Spud to Pear were $80,000 during 20X2 and $120,000 during 20X3. Unrealized profits included in ending inventories from these intercompany sales amounted to $8,000 at December 31, 20X2 and $24,000 at December 31, 20X3.

1 Consolidated cost of sales for 20X3 should be:
   a $950,000   **c** $934,000
   b $966,000   **d** $926,000

2 Minority interest income for 20X3 should be:
   a $16,600   **c** $13,400
   b $15,000   **d** $12,600

3 Consolidated net income for 20X3 should be:
   a $381,000   **c** $365,000
   b $379,400   **d** $350,600

E 5-12 On January 1, 20X1 Pres Corporation acquired 60% of the voting common shares of Suey Corporation at an excess of cost over book value of $1,000,000. This excess was attributed to plant assets with a remaining useful life of five years. For the year ended December 31, 20X8 Suey prepared *condensed* financial statements as follows:

Condensed Balance Sheet at December 31, 20X8

Current assets (except inventory)	$ 600,000
Inventories	300,000
Plant assets—net	5,000,000
Total assets	$5,900,000
Liabilities	$ 400,000
Capital stock	3,400,000
Retained earnings	2,100,000
Total equities	$5,900,000

Condensed Statement of Income and Retained Earnings

Sales	$1,000,000
Cost of sales	(500,000)
Other expenses	(300,000)
Net income	200,000
Add: Retained earnings January 1, 20X8	2,000,000
Less: Dividends	(100,000)
Retained earnings December 31, 20X8	$2,100,000

Suey regularly sells inventory items to Pres at a price of 120% of cost. In 20X7 and 20X8 sales from Suey to Pres are:

	20X7	20X8
Sales at selling price	$840,000	$960,000
Inventory unsold by Pres on December 31	120,000	360,000

1 Under the equity method, Pres reports investment income from Suey for 20X8 of:
   a $120,000   **c** $80,000
   b $96,000   **d** $104,000 loss

2 Minority interest on December 31, 20X8 is:
   a $2,200,000   **c** $2,176,000
   b $2,184,000   **d** $2,140,000

3 On the books of Pres Corporation, the investment account is properly reflected on December 31, 20X8 at:
   a $3,240,000   **c** $3,276,000
   b $3,264,000   **d** Not enough information is given.

[AICPA adapted]

Selected information from the separate and consolidated balance sheets and income statements of Pard, Inc. and its subsidiary, Spin Company, as of December 31, 20X6 and for the year then ended is as follows:

	Pard	Spin	Consolidated
Balance sheet accounts			
Accounts receivable	$ 26,000	$ 19,000	$ 39,000
Inventory	30,000	25,000	52,000
Investment in Spin	67,000	—	—
Goodwill	—	—	30,000
Minority interest	—	—	10,000
Stockholders' equity	154,000	50,000	154,000
Income statement accounts			
Revenues	$200,000	$140,000	$308,000
Cost of goods sold	150,000	110,000	231,000
Gross profit	50,000	30,000	77,000
Equity in earnings of Spin	11,000	—	—
Amortization of goodwill	—	—	2,000
Net income	36,000	20,000	40,000

During 20X6, Pard sold goods to Spin at the same markup on cost that Pard uses for all sales. At December 31, 20X6 Spin had not paid for all of these goods and still held 37.5% of them in inventory.

Pard acquired its interest in Spin on January 2, 20X3. Pard's policy is to amortize goodwill by the straight-line method.

1 What was the amount of intercompany sales from Pard to Spin during 20X6?
   a $3,000   **c** $29,000
   b $6,000   **d** $32,000
2 At December 31, 20X6, what was the amount of Spin's payable to Pard for intercompany sales?
   a $3,000   **c** $29,000
   b $6,000   **d** $32,000
3 In Pard's consolidated balance sheet, what was the carrying amount of the inventory that Spin purchased from Pard?
   a $3,000   **c** $9,000
   b $6,000   **d** $12,000
4 What is the percent of minority interest ownership in Spin?
   a 10 percent   **c** 25 percent
   b 20 percent   **d** 45 percent
5 Over how many years has Pard chosen to amortize goodwill?
   a 15   **c** 23
   b 19   **d** 40

E 5-14 Pepper Corporation recorded $65,000 investment income from Sneeze Corporation, its 80%-owned subsidiary, for the year 20X7, and $70,000 for the year 20X8. This investment income represented 80% of Sneeze's reported income of $81,250 and $87,500 in 20X7 and 20X8, respectively. Pepper's net income (including investment income) for 20X7 was $240,000, and for 20X8 it was $160,000.

During 20X7 Pepper sold merchandise to Sneeze for $180,000. This merchandise cost Pepper $130,000, and 40% of it was inventoried by Sneeze at December 31, 20X7.

Pepper sold merchandise that cost $150,000 to Sneeze for $210,000 during 20X8. The December 31, 20X8 inventory of Sneeze included $63,000 of this merchandise.

Required
   1 Compute the following:
      a Pepper's income from Sneeze on a correct equity basis for 20X7 and 20X8
      b Consolidated net income for 20X7 and 20X8
   2 Prepare journal entries to correct Pepper's books at December 31, 20X8, assuming that closing entries at December 31, 20X8 have not been made.

E 5-15 Speck Corporation is an 80%-owned subsidiary of Pearl Corporation, acquired at book value on January 1, 20X2 when Speck's assets and liabilities were equal to their fair values. During 20X2 Speck sold $12,000 merchandise to Pearl at a 25% gross profit (cost to Speck was $9,000). At December 31, 20X2 Pearl included 40% of this merchandise in its inventory at its purchase price from Speck.

Income statements for Pearl and Speck Corporations for 20X2 follow:

	Pearl	Speck
Sales	$300,000	$100,000
Income from Speck	12,000	—
Cost of sales	(200,000)	(75,000)
Other expenses	(50,000)	(10,000)
Net income	$ 62,000	$ 15,000

Required: Prepare a consolidated income statement for Pearl Corporation and Subsidiary for the year 20X2.

E 5-16 The consolidated income statement of Pullen and Swain for 20X2 was as follows:

Sales	$1,380,000
Cost of sales	(920,000)
Operating expenses	(160,000)
Income to 20% minority interest in Swain	(40,000)
Consolidated net income	$ 260,000

After the consolidated income statement was prepared, it was discovered that intercompany sales transactions had not been considered and that unrealized profits had not been eliminated. Information concerning these items follows:

	Cost	Selling Price	Unsold at Year-End
20X1 Sales—Pullen to Swain	$160,000	$180,000	25%
20X2 Sales—Swain to Pullen	90,000	120,000	40

Required: Prepare a corrected consolidated income statement for Pullen and Swain for the year ended December 31, 20X2.

PROBLEMS

P 5-1 Pargo Corporation acquired all the voting common stock of Silor Corporation several years ago in a pooling of interests business combination. A summary of the separate income amounts of Pargo and Silor before consideration of any intercompany transactions for the year 20X2 is as follows:

	Pargo	Silor
Sales	$1,000,000	$600,000
Cost of sales	600,000	300,000
Gross profit	400,000	300,000
Operating expenses	200,000	200,000
Operating income	$ 200,000	$100,000

During 20X2 Pargo sold merchandise that cost $140,000 to Silor for $200,000. Two-fifths of this merchandise remains in Silor's inventory at December 31, 20X2. This is the first year in which any intercompany transaction has occurred, and there were no other intercompany transactions during the year.

Required
1 Calculate consolidated cost of sales for 20X2.
2 Prepare the consolidated income statement for Pargo Corporation and Subsidiary for the year 20X2.

P 5-2 Proctor Corporation acquired its 90% interest in Samel Corporation at its book value of $360,000 on January 1, 20X7 when Samel had capital stock of $300,000 and retained earnings of $100,000.

The December 31, 20X7 and 20X8 inventories of Proctor included merchandise acquired from Samel of $30,000 and $40,000, respectively. Samel realizes a gross profit of 40% on all merchandise sold. During 20X7 and 20X8, sales by Samel to Proctor were $60,000 and $80,000, respectively.

Summary adjusted trial balances for Proctor and Samel at December 31, 20X8, follow:

	Proctor	Samel
Cash	$ 100,000	$ 20,000
Receivables—net	200,000	50,000
Inventories	240,000	100,000
Plant assets—net	250,000	480,000
Investment in Samel—90%	435,600	—
Cost of sales	800,000	390,000
Other expenses	340,000	160,000
Dividends	100,000	50,000
	$2,465,600	$1,250,000
Accounts payable	$ 150,000	$ 90,000
Other liabilities	60,000	60,000
Capital stock, $10 par	500,000	300,000
Retained earnings	369,200	150,000
Sales	1,300,000	650,000
Income from Samel	86,400	—
	$2,465,600	$1,250,000

Required: Prepare a combined consolidated income and retained earnings statement for Proctor Corporation and Subsidiary for the year ended December 31, 20X8.

P 5-3 Sadly is a 75%-owned subsidiary of Proud Corporation, acquired by Proud at book value (also fair value) on January 2, 20X4. Comparative income statements for Proud and Sadly for 20X6 are as follows:

	Proud	Sadly
Net sales	$500,000	$200,000
Cost of goods sold	300,000	120,000
Gross profit	200,000	80,000
Operating expenses	60,000	30,000
Operating income	140,000	50,000
Income from Sadly	37,500	—
Net income	$177,500	$ 50,000

Additional Information
1 Sadly made sales to Proud of $60,000 in 20X5 and $100,000 in 20X6.
2 Proud's inventories at December 31, 20X5 and December 31, 20X6 included merchandise on which Sadly reported profit of $15,000 and $24,000 during 20X5 and 20X6, respectively.
3 Proud has not eliminated the effect of intercompany profits in accounting for its investment in Sadly.

Required
1 Prepare any entries necessary to adjust Proud's investment in Sadly account at December 31, 20X6 and income from Sadly for 20X6.
2 Determine the following:
   a Consolidated cost of goods sold for 20X6
   b Minority interest income for 20X6
   c Consolidated net income for 20X6

P 5-4 Plum Corporation paid $2,900,000 for all the outstanding voting common stock of Star Corporation on January 2, 20X1 when Star's stockholders' equity consisted of $1,500,000 common stock and $1,000,000 retained earnings. The excess cost over book value acquired was allocated to goodwill with a 10-year amortization period.

Financial information relating to Star's income, dividends, and retained earnings for 20X7 and 20X8 is summarized as follows:

	20X7	20X8
Net income as reported	$ 400,000	$ 700,000
Dividends	200,000	300,000
Retained earnings, December 31	1,500,000	1,900,000

During 20X8 Plum sold inventory items to Star for $120,000, and $20,000 intercompany profit from the sales was unrealized at December 31. Star's December 31, 20X7 inventory included $30,000 unrealized profit on merchandise acquired from Plum.

Plum uses the cost method of accounting for its investment in Star, and accordingly, Plum's investment in Star account balance has remained at $2,900,000 since acquisition.

Plum's retained earnings balances at year-end 20X7 and 20X8 are $4,700,000 and $5,300,000, respectively.

Required
1 Determine the correct balance of Plum's investment in Star account at December 31, **20X7** under the equity method.
2 Determine Plum's income from Star under the equity method for 20X8.
3 Prepare a schedule to convert from the cost to the equity method in the consolidation working papers for 20X8.
4 Prepare a consolidation working paper entry for 20X8 to convert Plum's accounts to an equity basis for consolidation purposes. The entry should be based on the schedule prepared in 3.

P 5-5 Comparative income statements for Probe Corporation and its 70%-owned subsidiary, Seek Corporation, for 20X3 are summarized as follows:

	Probe	Seek
Sales	$1,000,000	$600,000
Cost of sales	480,000	310,000
Gross profit	520,000	290,000
Operating expenses	300,000	180,000
Separate income	220,000	110,000
Income from Seek	77,000	—
Net income	$ 297,000	$110,000

Additional Information
1 Probe acquired its interest in Seek on January 1, 20X2 at a price $360,000 in excess of the fair value of the interest acquired. A fair value/book value differential of $100,000 (based on the interest acquired) has been assigned to equipment with a 10-year life.
2 Probe sells inventory items to Seek on a regular basis, with intercompany sales data as follows:

	20X2	20X3
Probes's sales to Seek	$300,000	$420,000
Probes's cost of sales to Seek	200,000	280,000
Percent unsold at December 31	40%	25%

Required
1 Prepare a corrected income statement for Probe Corporation for 20X3 with Seek Corporation being treated as an equity investee.
2 Prepare a consolidated income statement for Probe Corporation and Subsidiary for 20X3.

P 5-6 Putt Corporation acquired a 90% interest in Slam Corporation at book value on January 1, 20X5. Intercompany purchases and sales and inventory data for 20X5, 20X6, and 20X7 are as follows:

	Sales by Slam to Putt	Intercompany Profit in Putt's Inventory at December 31
20X5	$200,000	$15,000
20X6	150,000	12,000
20X7	300,000	24,000

Selected data from the financial statements of Putt and Slam at and for the year ended December 31, 20X7 are as follows:

	Putt	Slam
Income Statement		
Sales	$900,000	$600,000
Cost of sales	625,000	300,000
Expenses	225,000	150,000
Income from Slam	124,200	—

(Continued)

	Putt	Slam
Balance Sheet		
Inventory	$150,000	$ 80,000
Retained earnings December 31, 20X7	425,000	220,000
Capital stock	500,000	300,000

Required: Prepare well-organized schedules showing computations for each of the following:
1 Consolidated cost of sales for 20X7
2 Minority interest income for 20X7
3 Consolidated net income for 20X7
4 Minority interest at December 31, 20X7

P 5-7 Potter Company owns controlling interests in Scan and Tray corporations, having acquired an 80% interest in Scan in 20X1, and a 90% interest in Tray on January 1, 20X2. Potter's investments in Scan and Tray were at book value equal to fair value.

Inventories of the affiliated companies at December 31, 20X2 and December 31, 20X3 were as follows:

	December 31, 20X2	December 31, 20X3
Potter inventories	$60,000	$54,000
Scan inventories	38,750	31,250
Tray inventories	24,000	36,000

Potter sells to Scan at a 25% markup based on cost, and Tray sells to Potter at a 20% markup based on cost. Potter's beginning and ending inventories for 20X3 consisted of 40% and 50%, respectively, of goods acquired from Tray. All of Scan's inventories consisted of merchandise acquired from Potter.

Required
1 Calculate the inventory that should appear in the December 31, 20X2 consolidated balance sheet.
2 Calculate the inventory that should appear in the December 31, 20X3 consolidated balance sheet.

P 5-8 Comparative income statements of Stuff Corporation for the calendar years 20X7, 20X8, and 20X9 are as follows:

	20X7	20X8	20X9
Sales	$4,000,000	$4,250,000	$4,750,000
Cost of sales	2,100,000	2,200,000	2,500,000
Gross profit	1,900,000	2,050,000	2,250,000
Operating expenses	1,500,000	1,600,000	1,900,000
Net income	$ 400,000	$ 450,000	$ 350,000

Additional Information
1 Stuff was a 75%-owned subsidiary of Plier Corporation throughout the 20X7–20X9 period. Plier's separate income (excludes income from Stuff) was $1,800,000, $1,700,000, and $2,000,000 in 20X7, 20X8, and 20X9, respectively. Plier acquired its interest in Stuff at its underlying book value, which was equal to fair value on July 1, 20X6.
2 Plier sold inventory items to Stuff during 20X7 at a gross profit to Plier of $200,000. Half the merchandise remained in Stuff's inventory at December 31, 20X7. Total sales by Plier to Stuff in 20X7 were $500,000. The remaining merchandise was sold by Stuff in 20X8.
3 Plier's inventory at December 31, 20X8 included items acquired from Stuff on which Stuff made a profit of $100,000. Total sales by Stuff to Plier during 20X8 were $400,000.
4 There were no unrealized profits in the December 31, 20X9 inventories of either Stuff or Plier.
5 Plier uses the equity method of accounting for its investment in Stuff.

Required
1 Prepare a schedule showing Plier's income from Stuff for each of the years 20X7, 20X8, and 20X9.
2 Compute Plier's net income for each of the years 20X7, 20X8, and 20X9.
3 Prepare a schedule of consolidated net income for Plier Corporation and Subsidiary for each of the years 20X7, 20X8, and 20X9, beginning with the separate incomes of the two affiliated corporations and including minority interest computations.

P 5-9   Comparative separate company and consolidated balance sheets for Pharm Corporation and its 80%-owned subsidiary, Silky Corporation, at year end 20X2 are as follows:

	Pharm	Silky	Consolidated
Assets			
Cash	$ 180,000	$ 40,000	$ 220,000
Inventories	200,000	160,000	360,000
Other current assets	70,000	150,000	170,000
Plant assets—net	500,000	350,000	850,000
Investment in Silky	630,000	—	—
Goodwill	—	—	150,000
	$1,580,000	$700,000	$1,750,000
Equities			
Accounts payable	$ 80,000	$ 50,000	$ 120,000
Dividends payable	100,000	50,000	110,000
Capital stock, $10 par	1,000,000	500,000	1,000,000
Retained earnings	400,000	100,000	400,000
Minority interest	—	—	120,000
	$1,580,000	$700,000	$1,750,000

Investigation reveals that the consolidated balance sheet is in error because Pharm Corporation has not amortized goodwill and it has not eliminated unrealized inventory profits. The investment in Silky was acquired on January 1, 20X1 at a price $150,000 in excess of the book value and fair value. The original plan was to amortize goodwill over 20 years. Unrealized profits in Silky's December 31, 20X1 and 20X2 inventories of merchandise acquired from Pharm were $30,000 and $50,000, respectively. Intercompany receivables of $10,000 are included in other current assets.

Required: Prepare consolidated balance sheet working papers on December 31, 20X2 for Pharm Corporation and Subsidiary.

P 5-10   Pane Corporation acquired 100% of Seal Corporation's outstanding voting common stock on January 1, 20X1 for $660,000 cash. Seal's stockholders' equity on this date consisted of $300,000 capital stock and $300,000 retained earnings. The difference between the price paid by Pane and the underlying equity acquired in Seal *was allocated* $30,000 to Seal's undervalued inventory and the remainder to goodwill with a five-year write-off period. The undervalued inventory items were sold by Seal during 20X1.

Pane made sales of $100,000 to Seal at a gross profit of $40,000 during 20X1, and during 20X2, Pane made sales of $120,000 to Seal at a gross profit of $48,000. One-half the 20X1 sales were inventoried by Seal at year-end 20X1, and one-fourth the 20X2 sales were inventoried by Seal at year-end 20X2. Seal owed Pane $17,000 on account at December 31, 20X2.

The separate financial statements of Pane and Seal corporations at and for the year ended December 31, 20X2 are summarized as follows:

	Pane	Seal
Combined Income and Retained Earnings Statements for the Year Ended December 31, 20X2		
Sales	$ 800,000	$400,000
Income from Seal	102,000	—
Cost of sales	(400,000)	(200,000)
Depreciation expense	(110,000)	(40,000)
Other expenses	(192,000)	(60,000)
Net income	200,000	100,000
Beginning retained earnings	600,000	380,000
Less: Dividends	(100,000)	(50,000)
Retained earnings December 31, 20X2	$ 700,000	$430,000
Balance Sheet at December 31, 20X2		
Cash	$ 54,000	$ 37,000
Receivables–net	90,000	60,000
Inventories	100,000	80,000
Other assets	70,000	90,000
Land	50,000	50,000

(Continued)

	Pane	Seal
Buildings–net	200,000	150,000
Equipment–net	500,000	400,000
Investment in Seal	736,000	—
Total assets	$1,800,000	$867,000
Accounts payable	$ 160,000	$ 47,000
Other liabilities	340,000	90,000
Common stock, $10 par	600,000	300,000
Retained earnings	700,000	430,000
Total equities	$1,800,000	$867,000

Required: Prepare working papers to consolidate the financial statements of Pane Corporation and Subsidiary at and for the year ended December 31, 20X2.

P 5-11 Patty Corporation acquired a 75% interest in Sue Corporation for $300,000 on January 1, 20X7 when Sue's equity consisted of $150,000 capital stock and $50,000 retained earnings. The fair values of Sue's assets and liabilities were equal to their book values on this date, and any goodwill is to be amortized over a 15-year period. Patty uses the equity method of accounting for Sue.

During 20X7 Patty sold inventory items to Sue for $80,000, and at December 31, 20X7 Sue's inventory included items on which there were $10,000 unrealized profits. During 20X8 Patty sold inventory items to Sue for $130,000, and at December 31, 20X8 Sue's inventory included items on which there were $20,000 unrealized profits.

On December 31, 20X8 Sue owed Patty $15,000 on account for merchandise purchases.

The financial statements of Patty and Sue corporations at and for the year ended December 31, 20X8 are summarized as follows:

	Patty	Sue
Combined Income and Retained Earnings Statements for the Year Ended December 31, 20X8		
Sales	$ 600,000	$400,000
Income from Sue	92,500	
Cost of sales	(270,000)	(210,000)
Operating expenses	(145,000)	(40,000)
Net income	227,500	150,000
Beginning retained earnings	172,500	90,000
Deduct: Dividends	(150,000)	(50,000)
Retained earnings December 31, 20X8	$ 300,000	$190,000
Balance Sheet at December 31, 20X8		
Cash	$ 85,000	$ 30,000
Accounts receivable	165,000	100,000
Dividends receivable	15,000	—
Inventories	60,000	80,000
Land	80,000	50,000
Buildings–net	230,000	100,000
Equipment–net	200,000	140,000
Investment in Sue	365,000	—
Total assets	$1,200,000	$500,000
Accounts payable	$ 225,000	$100,000
Dividends payable	70,000	20,000
Other liabilities	155,000	40,000
Common stock, $10 par	450,000	150,000
Retained earnings	300,000	190,000
Total equities	$1,200,000	$500,000

Required: Prepare consolidation working papers for Patty Corporation and Subsidiary for the year ended December 31, 20X8.

P 5-12 Poly Corporation purchased a 90% interest in Susan Corporation on December 31, 20X4 for $275,000 cash, when Susan had capital stock of $200,000 and retained earnings of $50,000. All Susan's assets and liabilities were recorded at their fair values when Poly acquired its interest. The excess of cost over book value is being amortized over a 10-year period.

The Poly/Susan affiliation is a vertically integrated merchandising operation, with Susan selling all of its output to Poly Corporation at 140% of its cost. Poly sells the merchandise acquired from Susan at 150% of its purchase price from Susan. All of Poly's December 31, 20X6 and December 31, 20X7 inventories of $28,000 and $42,000, respectively, were acquired from Susan. Susan's December 31, 20X6 and December 31, 20X7 inventories were $80,000 each.

Poly's accounts payable at December 31, 20X7 includes $10,000 owed to Susan from 20X7 purchases.

Comparative financial statements for Poly Corporation and Susan Corporation at and for the year ended December 31, 20X7 are as follows:

	Poly	Susan
Combined Income and Retained Earnings Statement for the Year Ended December 31, 20X7		
Sales	$819,000	$560,000
Income from Susan	81,400	—
Cost of sales	(546,000)	(400,000)
Other expenses	(154,400)	(60,000)
Net income	200,000	100,000
Add: Beginning retained earnings	120,000	70,000
Deduct: Dividends	(100,000)	(50,000)
Retained earnings December 31, 20X7	$220,000	$120,000
Balance Sheet at December 31, 20X7		
Cash	$ 75,800	$ 50,000
Inventory	42,000	80,000
Other current assets	60,000	20,000
Plant assets–net	300,000	300,000
Investment in Susan	312,200	—
Total assets	$790,000	$450,000
Current liabilities	$170,000	$130,000
Capital stock	400,000	200,000
Retained earnings	220,000	120,000
Total equities	$790,000	$450,000

Required: Prepare consolidation working papers for Poly Corporation and Subsidiary for the year ended December 31, 20X7.

P 5-13 Sert is a 90%-owned subsidiary of Phil Corporation, acquired by Phil in 20X1 at a price $5,000 in excess of fair value. The excess was amortized over a five-year period beginning with 20X1. Comparative financial statements for Phil and Sert for the year ended December 31, 20X8 are presented as follows:

	Phil	Sert
Combined Income and Retained Earnings Statement for the Year Ended December 31, 20X8		
Sales	$500,000	$100,000
Income from Sert	27,000	—
Cost of sales	(240,000)	(40,000)
Expenses	(174,000)	(30,000)
Net income	113,000	30,000
Add: Beginning retained earnings	110,000	40,000
Deduct: Dividends	(70,000)	(20,000)
Retained earnings December 31, 20X8	$153,000	$ 50,000
Balance Sheet at December 31, 20X8		
Cash	$ 63,000	$ 30,000
Accounts receivable	40,000	20,000
Inventories	60,000	15,000
Plant assets–net	220,000	105,000
Investment in Sert	117,000	—
Total assets	$500,000	$170,000
Accounts payable	$ 47,000	$ 40,000
Capital stock	300,000	80,000
Retained earnings	153,000	50,000
Total equities	$500,000	$170,000

During 20X8 Phil sold merchandise to Sert for $10,000. This merchandise cost Phil $6,000 and was not paid for or resold by Sert until 20X9. Phil's inventory at December 31, 20X7 included merchandise acquired from Sert on which Sert reported a profit during 20X7 of $5,000.

Required

    1 Prepare correcting entries for Phil's investment in Sert.
    2 Prepare consolidation working papers for 20X8 after adjusting the separate statements of Phil for prior errors and omissions.

P 5-14 Panda and Soapy corporations were combined in a pooling of interests that was consummated on January 1, 20X7. Panda issued 35,000 of its previously unissued common shares for all of Soapy's outstanding shares, and Soapy became a 100%-owned subsidiary of Panda. Adjusted trial balances for the two companies at December 31, 20X6 immediately before the pooling and at December 31, 20X7, one year after the pooling, are as follows:

PANDA CORPORATION AND SOAPY CORPORATION
ADJUSTED TRIAL BALANCES

| | December 31, 20X6 | | December 31, 20X7 | |
	Panda	Soapy	Panda	Soapy
Cash	$ 180,000	$ 40,000	$ 155,000	$ 120,000
Accounts receivable	200,000	100,000	220,000	130,000
Dividends receivable			20,000	
Inventories	120,000	70,000	205,000	80,000
Land	100,000	50,000	100,000	50,000
Building–net	500,000	150,000	700,000	140,000
Equipment–net	400,000	160,000	470,000	200,000
Investment in Soapy			530,000	
Cost of sales	550,000	200,000	600,000	240,000
Other expenses	250,000	150,000	300,000	160,000
Dividends	100,000	80,000	100,000	80,000
Total debits	$2,400,000	$1,000,000	$3,400,000	$1,200,000
Accounts payable	$ 225,000	$ 40,000	$ 300,000	$ 50,000
Dividends payable	25,000	20,000	25,000	20,000
Other liabilities	150,000	40,000	165,000	60,000
Capital stock, $10 par	500,000	200,000	850,000	200,000
Other paid-in capital	200,000	80,000	130,000	80,000
Retained earnings	300,000	120,000	590,000	190,000
Sales	1,000,000	500,000	1,200,000	600,000
Income from Soapy			140,000	
Total credits	$2,400,000	$1,000,000	$3,400,000	$1,200,000

During 20X7 Soapy sold inventory items to Panda for $150,000, at a markup of 150% of cost to Soapy. Panda inventoried all of this merchandise on December 31, 20X7.

Required: Prepare a consolidated income statement, a consolidated retained earnings statement, and a consolidated balance sheet for Panda Corporation and Subsidiary at and for the year ended December 31, 20X7.

6

Intercompany Profit Transactions—Plant Assets

Transactions between affiliated companies involving the sale and purchase of plant assets create unrealized profits and losses to the consolidated entity. Such profits and losses are eliminated (deferred) in reporting the results of operations and the financial position of the consolidated entity. They are also eliminated in reporting the financial position and results of operations of a parent company under the equity method of accounting. The adjustments to eliminate the effects of intercompany profits on plant assets are similar to, but not identical with, those for unrealized inventory profits. Unrealized inventory profits are self-correcting over any two accounting periods, but unrealized profits or losses on plant assets affect the financial statements until the related assets are sold outside the consolidated entity or are exhausted through use by the purchasing affiliate. This chapter covers concepts and procedures involved in eliminating the effect of unrealized profits on plant assets in one-line consolidations under the equity method of accounting and in consolidated statements.[1]

INTERCOMPANY PROFITS ON NONDEPRECIABLE PLANT ASSETS

The transfer of nondepreciable plant assets between affiliated companies at a price other than book value gives rise to unrealized profit or loss to the consolidated entity. An intercompany gain or loss appears in the income statement of the selling affiliate in the year of sale. However, such gain or loss is unrealized, and its effects must be eliminated from investment income in a one-line consolidation by the parent company. Its effects must also be eliminated in preparing consolidated financial statements.

The direction of intercompany sales of plant assets, like intercompany sales of inventory items, is important in evaluating the effect of unrealized profit on parent company and consolidated financial statements. Any gain or loss on sales downstream from

---

[1]Most public utilities are subject to rate-of-return regulations. *FASB Statement No. 71*, "Accounting for the Effects of Certain Types of Regulations," states that "if rates are based on allowable costs that include reasonable intercompany profits, the company should not eliminate those intercompany profits in its financial statements." Thus, the *1993 Ameritech Annual Report* (page 29) includes the following note: "The original cost of telecommunications plant acquired from Ameritech Services, Inc., a wholly-owned centralized procurement and support subsidiary of the Ameritech Bell Companies, includes a return on investment to Ameritech Services, Inc. which is not eliminated in consolidation." As more and more industries are being deregulated these *FASB Statement No. 71* modifications will become less common.

parent to subsidiary is initially included in parent company income and must be eliminated. The amount of elimination is 100%, regardless of the minority interest percentage. Any profit or loss from upstream sales from subsidiary to parent is initially included in subsidiary accounts. The parent company recognizes only its share of the subsidiary's income, so only the parent's proportionate share of unrealized profits should be eliminated. The effect on consolidated net income is the same as for the parent.

This section of the chapter discusses and illustrates accounting practices for intercompany sales of land. Both downstream and upstream sales are covered.

Downstream Sale of Land

Stan Corporation is a 90%-owned subsidiary of Park Corporation, acquired for $270,000 on January 1, 20X5. Investment cost was equal to book value and fair value of the interest acquired. Stan's net income for 20X5 was $70,000, and Park's income, excluding its income from Stan, was $90,000. Park's income includes a $10,000 unrealized gain on land that cost $40,000 and was sold to Stan for $50,000. Accordingly, Park makes the following entries in accounting for its investment in Stan at December 31, 20X5:

Investment in Stan	$63,000	
Income from Stan		$63,000
To record 90% of Stan's $70,000 reported income.		
Income from Stan	$10,000	
Investment in Stan		$10,000
To eliminate unrealized profit on land sold to Stan.		

Consolidation working papers for Park and Subsidiary for 20X5 are presented in Exhibit 6–1. Separate summary financial statements for Park and Stan appear in the first two columns of the working papers.

Gain on the sale of land should not appear in the consolidated income statement, and the land should be included in the consolidated balance sheet at its cost of $40,000. Entry a eliminates the gain on sale of land and reduces the land account to $40,000—its cost to the consolidated entity. This is the only entry that is significantly different from adjustments and eliminations illustrated in previous chapters.

a	Gain on sale of land	$10,000	
	Land		$10,000
	To eliminate gain on intercompany sale of land and reduce land to its cost basis.		

The overvalued land will continue to appear in the separate balance sheet of Stan in subsequent years until it is sold outside of the consolidated entity, but the gain on land does not appear in the separate income statements of Park in subsequent years. Therefore, entry a as shown in Exhibit 6–1 is applicable only in the year of the intercompany sale.

Years Subsequent to Intercompany Sale The working paper adjustment to reduce land to its cost to the consolidated entity in years subsequent to the year of the intercompany sale is as follows for downstream sales:

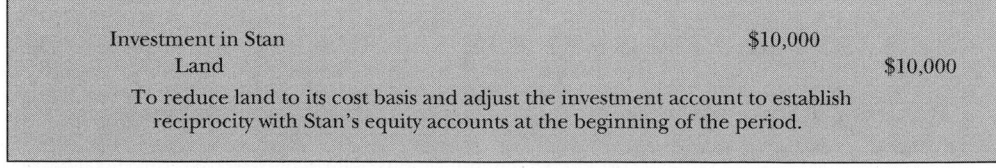

Investment in Stan	$10,000	
Land		$10,000
To reduce land to its cost basis and adjust the investment account to establish reciprocity with Stan's equity accounts at the beginning of the period.		

The debit to the investment account adjusts its balance to establish reciprocity with the subsidiary equity accounts at the beginning of each subsequent period in

PARK CORPORATION AND SUBSIDIARY CONSOLIDATION
WORKING PAPERS FOR THE YEAR ENDED DECEMBER 31, 20X5

	Park	90% Stan	Adjustments and Eliminations		Minority Interest	Consolidated Statements
Income Statement						
Sales	$380,000	$220,000				$600,000
Income from Stan	53,000		b	53,000		
Gain on sale of land	10,000		a	10,000		
Expenses (including cost of goods sold)	(300,000)	(150,000)				(450,000)
Minority interest income ($70,000 × 10%)					$ 7,000	(7,000)
Net income	$143,000	$ 70,000				$143,000
Retained Earnings						
Retained earnings—Park	$207,000					$207,000
Retained earnings—Stan		$100,000	c 100,000			
Add: Net income	143,000√	70,000√				143,000
Retained earnings December 31, 20X5	$350,000	$170,000				$350,000
Balance Sheet						
Other assets	$477,000	$350,000				$827,000
Land		50,000	a	10,000		40,000
Investment in Stan	323,000		b c	53,000 270,000		
	$800,000	$400,000				$867,000
Liabilities	$ 50,000	$ 30,000				$ 80,000
Capital stock	400,000	200,000	c 200,000			400,000
Retained earnings	350,000√	170,000√				350,000
	$800,000	$400,000				
Minority interest January 1, 20X5			c	30,000	30,000	
Minority interest December 31, 20X5					$37,000	37,000
						$867,000

a Eliminates gain on sale of land and reduces land to a cost basis.
b Eliminates investment income and reduces the investment account to its January 1, 20X5 balance.
c Eliminates reciprocal equity and investment amounts and establishes beginning minority interest.

Exhibit 6–1   *Intercompany Profit from Downstream Sale of Land*

which the land is held. For example, the investment account balance at December 31, 20X5 is $323,000. This is $10,000 less than Park's underlying equity in Stan of $333,000 on that date ($370,000 × 90%). The difference arises from the entry on the parent company books to reduce investment income and the investment account for the intercompany profit in the year of sale.

Sale in Subsequent Year to Outside Entity

Assume that Stan uses the land for three years and sells it for $65,000 in 20X9. In the year of sale, Stan will report a $15,000 gain ($65,000 proceeds less $50,000 cost), but the gain to the consolidated entity is $25,000 ($65,000 proceeds less $40,000 cost to Park).

Park recognizes its gain on the land in 20X9 under the equity method of accounting by adjusting its investment income in that year. The entry on Park's books is:

Investment in Stan	$10,000	
Income from Stan		$10,000
To recognize previously deferred profit on sale of land to Stan.		

This entry on Park's separate books reestablishes equality between the investment account and 90% of the equity of Stan on the same date.

The following working paper entry is required to adjust the $15,000 gain to Stan to the $25,000 consolidated gain on the land:

Investment in Stan	$10,000	
Gain on land		$10,000
To adjust gain on land to the $25,000 gain to the consolidated entity.		

This entry in the year of sale is almost the same as the working paper entry in each of the years 20X6, 20X7, and 20X8 to eliminate the unrealized profit from the land account. The difference is that the credit is to gain because the land no longer appears on the separate books of Park or Stan.

Upstream Sale of Land

To illustrate the accounting for upstream sales of nondepreciable plant assets, assume that Park purchases the land referred to in the previous section during 20X5 from its 90%-owned affiliate, Stan. As before, Stan's net income for 20X5 is $70,000 and Park's income, excluding its income from Stan, is $90,000. However, the $10,000 unrealized profit on the intercompany sale of land is now reflected in the income of Stan, rather than Park. In accounting for its investment in Stan at year-end 20X5, Park makes the following entries:

Investment in Stan	$63,000	
Income from Stan		$63,000
To record 90% of Stan's reported net income.		

Income from Stan	$ 9,000	
Investment in Stan		$ 9,000
To eliminate 90% of the $10,000 unrealized profit on land purchased from Stan.		

The combined effect of these entries is to record Park's investment income for 20X5 in the amount of $54,000 ($63,000 − $9,000). Note that the $54,000 investment income consists of 90% of Stan's $60,000 realized income for 20X5 ($70,000 reported income less $10,000 unrealized gain on land). Park's net income for 20X5 is $144,000 ($90,000 separate income plus $54,000 investment income), as compared with $143,000 in the case of the downstream sale. The difference lies in the $1,000 unrealized gain attributed to minority interest and charged against minority interest income.

Consolidation working papers for Park Corporation and Subsidiary for 20X5 are presented in Exhibit 6–2. The working papers are based on the same information as the working papers in Exhibit 6–1 except for minor changes necessary to switch to the upstream sale situation.

The adjustments reflected in the consolidation working papers in Exhibit 6–2 are the same as those in Exhibit 6–1 except for the amount of entry b, which is $54,000 rather than $53,000. Entry a eliminates the full amount of the gain on the sale of land and reduces the land to its cost basis to the consolidated entity whether the intercompany sale is upstream or downstream.

PARK CORPORATION AND SUBSIDIARY CONSOLIDATION
WORKING PAPERS FOR THE YEAR ENDED DECEMBER 31, 20X5

	Park	90% Stan	Adjustments and Eliminations	Minority Interest	Consolidated Statements
Income Statement Sales	$390,000	$210,000			$600,000
Income from Stan	54,000		b 54,000		
Gain on sale of land		10,000	a 10,000		
Expenses (including cost of goods sold)	(300,000)	(150,000)			(450,000)
Minority interest income ($70,000 – $10,000) × 10%				$ 6,000	(6,000)
Net income	$144,000	$ 70,000			$144,000
Retained Earnings Retained earnings—Park	$207,000				$207,000
Retained earnings—Stan		$100,000	c 100,000		
Add: Net income	144,000√	70,000√			144,000
Retained earnings December 31, 20X5	$351,000	$170,000			$351,000
Balance Sheet Other assets	$427,000	$400,000			$827,000
Land	50,000		a 10,000		40,000
Investment in Stan	324,000		b 54,000 c 270,000		
	$801,000	$400,000			$867,000
Liabilities	$ 50,000	$ 30,000			$ 80,000
Capital stock	400,000	200,000	c 200,000		400,000
Retained earnings	351,000√	170,000√			351,000
	$801,000	$400,000			
Minority interest January 1, 20X5			c 30,000	30,000	
Minority interest December 31, 20X5				$36,000	36,000
					$867,000

a Eliminates gain on sale of land and reduces land to a cost basis.
b Eliminates investment income and reduces the investment account to its January 1, 20X5 balance.
c Eliminates reciprocal equity and investment amounts and establishes beginning minority interest.

Exhibit 6–2   *Intercompany Profit from Upstream Sale of Land*

Minority Interest Income   Minority interest income is $7,000 in Exhibit 6–1 but only $6,000 in Exhibit 6–2. Minority interest is charged with its share of the unrealized gain on Stan's sale of land to Park. This is done in the consolidation working papers by converting Stan's reported net income into realized income and multiplying by the minority interest percentage. Thus, the $6,000 minority interest income is 10% of Stan's $60,000 realized income.

Year Subsequent to Intercompany Sale   While Park continues to hold the land in subsequent years, the consolidation working papers will require an adjusting entry to reduce the land account to its cost basis to the consolidated entity. The working paper entry to eliminate unrealized profit from the land account is:

Investment in Stan	$9,000	
Minority interest	1,000	
Land		$10,000

To reduce land to its cost basis and adjust the investment account and beginning minority interest to establish reciprocity with Stan's equity accounts at the beginning of the period.

Minority interest is entered in the working papers at the minority interest share of *reported* subsidiary equity when reciprocal investment and subsidiary equity accounts are eliminated, so the foregoing adjustment is needed to reduce minority interest to its *realized* amount each time consolidation working papers are prepared. In other words, this adjustment is necessary to make the beginning minority interest in 20X6 equal to ending minority interest in 20X5, and so on.

Sale in Subsequent Year to Outside Entity

Assume that Park uses the land for three years and sells it for $65,000 in 20X9. In the year of sale, Park will report a $15,000 gain ($65,000 proceeds less $50,000 cost), but the gain to the consolidated entity is $25,000, allocated $24,000 [$15,000 + ($10,000 × 0.9)] to majority stockholders (consolidated net income) and $1,000 to minority stockholders.

Park adjusts its investment income from Stan in 20X9 with the following entry:

Investment in Stan	$9,000	
Income from Stan		$ 9,000

To recognize previously deferred intercompany profit on land.

The $15,000 gain on the sale of land plus the $9,000 increase in investment income on Park's books equals the $24,000 effect on consolidated net income in 20X9.

In the consolidation working papers, the adjustment of the $15,000 gain of Park to the $25,000 consolidated gain requires the following working paper entry:

Investment in Stan	$9,000	
Minority interest	1,000	
Gain on land		$10,000

To adjust gain on land to the $25,000 gain to the consolidated entity.

The $10,000 gain is allocated between the investment in Stan (90%) and minority interest (10%).

INTERCOMPANY PROFITS ON DEPRECIABLE PLANT ASSETS

Intercompany sales of plant assets subject to depreciation, depletion, or amortization result in unrealized gains and losses that are reflected in the accounts of the selling affiliate. The effects of these gains and losses are eliminated from parent company and consolidated financial statements until they are realized by the consolidated entity *through sale to other entities or through use within the consolidated entity.* The adjustments to eliminate the effect of unrealized gains and losses on parent company and consolidated financial statements are more complex than in the case of nondepreciable assets. This additional complexity stems from the depreciation (or depletion or amortization) process that affects parent company and consolidated income in each year in which the related assets are held by affiliated companies.

The discussion of intercompany sales of plant assets in this section is limited to depreciable assets, but the analysis and procedures illustrated apply equally to assets subject to depletion or amortization. Intercompany gains and losses from downstream sales of depreciable plant assets are considered initially, and the upstream sale situation is covered next.

Downstream Sales of Depreciable Plant Assets

The initial effect of unrealized gains and losses from downstream sales of depreciable assets is the same as for nondepreciable assets. Gains or losses appear in the parent company accounts in the year of sale and must be eliminated by the parent company in determining its investment income under the equity method of accounting. Similarly, such gain or loss is eliminated from consolidated statements by removing the gain or loss and reducing the plant assets to their depreciated cost to the consolidated entity.

Downstream Sale at the End of a Year   Assume that Perry Corporation sells machinery to its 80%-owned subsidiary, Soper Corporation, on December 31, 20X2. The machinery has an undepreciated cost of $50,000 on this date (cost $90,000 and accumulated depreciation $40,000), and it is sold to Soper for $80,000. Journal entries to record the sale and purchase on Perry's and Soper's books are as follows:

PERRY'S BOOKS

Cash	$80,000	
Accumulated depreciation	40,000	
Machinery		$90,000
Gain on sale of machinery		30,000

SOPER'S BOOKS

Machinery	$80,000	
Cash		$80,000

The gain on Perry's books is unrealized at December 31, 20X2, and, accordingly, Perry adjusts its investment income for 20X2 under the equity method of accounting for the full amount of the unrealized gain:

Income from Soper	$30,000	
Investment in Soper		$30,000

The gain on machinery should not appear in the consolidated income statement for 20X2, and the machinery should be included in the consolidated balance sheet at $50,000, its depreciated cost to the consolidated entity. This effect is accomplished by a consolidation working paper adjustment as follows:

Gain on sale of machinery	$30,000	
Machinery		$30,000

Alternatively, the working paper entry could be recorded by debiting gain on sale of machinery for $30,000, debiting machinery for $10,000, and crediting accumulated depreciation—machinery for $40,000. Conceptually, this entry is superior because it results in reporting plant assets and accumulated depreciation at the amounts that would have been shown if the intercompany sale had not taken place. From a practical viewpoint, however, the additional detail is usually not justified by cost/benefit considerations, because the same net asset amounts are obtained without the additional recordkeeping costs. The examples in this book reflect the more practical approach.

No adjustment of the minority interest is necessary, because Soper's income is unaffected by the intercompany sale. Note that the analysis up to this point is equivalent to the one for the intercompany sale of land discussed earlier in this chapter.

Downstream Sale at the Beginning of a Year   If the sale from Perry to Soper had occurred on January 1, 20X2, the machinery would have been depreciated by Soper during 20X2, and any depreciation on the unrealized gain would be considered a piecemeal recognition of the gain during 20X2. Assume that on January 1, 20X2, the date of the intercompany sale, the machinery has a five-year remaining useful life and no expected residual value at December 31, 20X6. Straight-line depreciation is used. The journal entries to record the sale and purchase are the same as for the December 31 sale, however, Soper also records depreciation expense of $16,000 for 20X2 ($80,000 ÷ 5 years). Of this $16,000 depreciation, $10,000 is based on cost to the consolidated entity ($50,000 cost ÷ 5 years), and $6,000 is based on the $30,000 unrealized gain ($30,000 ÷ 5 years). The $6,000 is considered a piecemeal recognition of one-fifth of the $30,000 unrealized gain on the intercompany transaction. Conceptually, this is equivalent to the sale to other entities of one-fifth of the services remaining in the machinery.[2]

In eliminating the effect of the intercompany sale from its investment in Soper account for 20X2, Perry Corporation makes the following entries:

Income from Soper	$30,000	
Investment in Soper		$30,000
Investment in Soper	$ 6,000	
Income from Soper		$ 6,000

Thus, elimination of the effect of the intercompany sale reduces Perry's investment income in 20X2 by $24,000 ($30,000 unrealized gain less $6,000 realized through depreciation). Although Soper's income is decreased by the $6,000 excess depreciation during 20X2, the $6,000 is considered realized through use, and, accordingly, no adjustment of the minority interest income is necessary.

Effect of Downstream Sale on Consolidation Working Papers   The effect of the January 1 intercompany sale of machinery on the consolidated financial statements is illustrated in partial consolidation working papers as follows:

	Perry	80% Soper	Adjustments and Eliminations		Consolidated Statements
Income Statement					
Gain on sale of machinery	$30,000		a 30,000		
Depreciation expense		$16,000		b 6,000	$10,000
Balance Sheet					
Machinery		$80,000		a 30,000	$50,000
Accumulated depreciation		16,000	b 6,000		10,000

The first consolidation working paper entry eliminates the $30,000 unrealized gain on machinery and reduces machinery to its cost basis to the consolidated entity at the time of intercompany sale. Depreciation expense and accumulated depreciation are reduced in the second entry in order to adjust these items to the depreciated cost basis to the consolidated entity at December 31, 20X2. Minority interest computations are not affected by the working paper adjustments because the sale was downstream.

In each of the years 20X3 through 20X6, Perry Corporation adjusts its investment income for the piecemeal recognition of the previously unrecognized gain on the machinery with the following entry:

---

[2]It is assumed that the machine services have entered the cost of goods delivered to customers during the current period. If, instead, they are included in inventory, realization has not yet occurred and appropriate adjustments should be made. This additional refinement is not justified when the amounts involved are immaterial.

20X3, 20X4, 20X5, and 20X6		
Investment in Soper	$ 6,000	
Income from Soper		$ 6,000

Accordingly, by December 31, 20X6, the end of the useful life of the machinery, Perry will have recognized the full $30,000 gain as investment income. Its investment account balance will reflect the elimination and piecemeal recognition of the unrealized gain as follows:

Year	Elimination of Gain on Machinery	Piecemeal Recognition of Gain Through Depreciation	Effect on Investment Balance at December 31
20X2	$−30,000	$+6,000	$−24,000
20X3		+6,000	−18,000
20X4		+6,000	−12,000
20X5		+6,000	− 6,000
20X6		+6,000	0

In consolidation working papers, it is necessary to establish reciprocity between the investment and subsidiary equity accounts at the beginning of the period before eliminating reciprocal balances. Thus, the effect of the unrealized gain on the December 31, 20X2 investment account is eliminated in 20X3 consolidation working papers with the working paper entry:

Investment in Soper	$24,000	
Accumulated depreciation	6,000	
Machinery		$30,000

This entry for 20X3 is included in the partial consolidation working papers shown in Exhibit 6–3 for Perry and Soper. The exhibit shows consolidation eliminations for each subsequent year (after 20X2) in which the unrealized gain on machinery would require working paper adjustment.

The partial working papers in Exhibit 6–3 show two working paper adjustments for each of the years 20X3 through 20X6. Two entries for each year are used in order to isolate the effect on beginning-of-the-period balances and current-year changes. Current-year changes only affect depreciation expense and accumulated depreciation in equal amounts, so the entries can be combined and frequently are combined in subsequent illustrations and in problem solutions.

Upstream Sales of Depreciable Plant Assets

Upstream sales of depreciable assets from subsidiary to parent company result in unrealized gains or losses in the subsidiary accounts in the year of sale (unless the assets are sold at their book values). In computing its investment income in the year of sale, the parent company adjusts its share of the reported income of the subsidiary for (1) its share of any unrealized gain on the sale and (2) its share of any piecemeal recognition of such unrealized gain through the depreciation process.

Effect of Upstream Sale on the Affiliated Companies' Separate Books   The effect of a gain on an upstream sale is illustrated by the following example. Pruitt Corporation purchases a truck from its 80%-owned subsidiary, Scott Corporation, on January 1, 20X4. Other information is as follows:

Scott's reported net income for 20X4	$50,000
Use life of the truck at January 1, 20X4	3 years
Depreciation method	straight line
Trade-in value of the truck at December 31, 20X6	$ 3,000
Cost of truck to Scott	$14,000
Accumulated depreciation on truck at December 31, 20X3	$ 5,000

PERRY CORPORATION AND SUBSIDIARY PARTIAL CONSOLIDATION WORKING PAPERS FOR THE YEARS 20X3, 20X4, 20X5, AND 20X6

	Perry	80% Soper	Adjustments and Eliminations		Consolidated Statements
20X3					
Income Statement					
Depreciation expense		$16,000		b 6,000	$10,000
Balance Sheet—December 31					
Machinery		80,000		a 30,000	50,000
Accumulated depreciation		32,000	a 6,000 b 6,000		20,000
Investment in Soper	XXX*		a 24,000		
20X4					
Income Statement					
Depreciation expense		$16,000		b 6,000	$10,000
Balance Sheet—December 31					
Machinery		80,000		a 30,000	50,000
Accumulated depreciation		48,000	a 12,000 b 6,000		30,000
Investment in Soper	XXX*		a 18,000		
20X5					
Income Statement					
Depreciation expense		$16,000		b 6,000	$10,000
Balance Sheet—December 31					
Machinery		80,000		a 30,000	50,000
Accumulated depreciation		64,000	a 18,000 b 6,000		40,000
Investment in Soper	XXX*		a 12,000		
20X6					
Income Statement					
Depreciation expense		$16,000		b 6,000	$10,000
Balance Sheet—December 31					
Machinery		80,000		a 30,000	50,000
Accumulated depreciation		80,000	a 24,000 b 6,000		50,000
Investment in Soper	XXX*		a 6,000		

*Whatever the balance of the investment account, it will be less than the underlying book value of the investment at the beginning of the year by the amount of the unrealized profit.

a Eliminates unrealized profit from machinery and accumulated depreciation as of the beginning of the year and adjusts the investment in Soper account to establish reciprocity with Soper's equity accounts at the beginning of the period.

b Eliminates the current year's effect of unrealized profit from depreciation expense and accumulated depreciation.

Exhibit 6–3 *Downstream Sale of Depreciable Asset—Years Subsequent to Sale*

If Scott sells the truck to Pruitt for $12,000 cash, Scott and Pruitt make the following journal entries on their separate books for 20X4:

SCOTT'S BOOKS

January 1, 20X4 (sale of truck)

Cash	$12,000	
Accumulated depreciation	5,000	
Trucks		$14,000
Gain on sale of truck		3,000
To record sale of truck.		

PRUITT'S BOOKS

January 1, 20X4 (purchase of truck)

Trucks	$12,000	
Cash		$12,000
To record purchase of truck.		

December 31, 20X4 (depreciation expense)

Depreciation expense	$ 3,000	
Accumulated depreciation		$ 3,000
To record depreciation for one year [($12,000 cost − $3,000 scrap) ÷ 3 years]		

December 31, 20X4 (investment income)

Investment in Scott	$38,400	
Income from Scott		$38,400
To record investment income for 20X4 computed as follows:		
Share of Scott's reported net income ($50,000 × 80%)		$40,000
Less: Unrealized gain on truck ($3,000 × 80%)		−2,400
Add: Piecemeal recognition of gain		
[($3,000 gain ÷ 3 years) × 80%]		+800
Investment income for 20X4		$38,400

The deferral of the intercompany gain on the truck decreases Pruitt's investment income for 20X4 by $1,600 (from $40,000 to $38,400). This is 80% of the unrealized gain at December 31, 20X4 ($3,000 unrealized gain from sale − $1,000 piecemeal recognition through depreciation × 80%). Pruitt will recognize the remaining $1,600 during 20X5 and 20X6 at the rate of $800 per year.

Effect of Upstream Sale on Consolidation Working Papers   To illustrate the working paper procedures for Pruitt and Scott, the following investment and equity balances—and changes in them—are included as additional assumptions.

	Investment in Scott 80%	80% of the Equity of Scott	100% of the Equity of Scott
December 31, 20X3	$400,000	$400,000	$500,000
Income—20X4	+38,400	+40,000	+50,000
December 31, 20X4	438,400	440,000	550,000
Income—20X5	+40,800	+40,000	+50,000
December 31, 20X5	479,200	480,000	600,000
Income—20X6	+40,800	+40,000	+50,000
December 31, 20X6	$520,000	$520,000	$650,000

Pruitt's investment in Scott account at December 31, 20X4 is $1,600 below its underlying book value ($438,400 compared with $440,000), and at December 31, 20X5 it is $800 below its underlying book value ($479,200 compared with $480,000).

By December 31, 20X6 the $3,000 gain on the truck has been realized through depreciation. Pruitt's share of that gain ($2,400) has been recognized at the rate of $800 per year in 20X4, 20X5, and 20X6. Thus, reciprocity between Pruitt's investment account and its underlying book value is reestablished at the end of 20X6.

Partial consolidation working paper for 20X4, the year of sale, appear next, followed by the working paper entries in journal form.

20X4: YEAR OF SALE

	Pruitt	80% Scott	Adjustments and Eliminations		Minority Interest	Consolidated Statements
Income Statement Income from Scott	$ 38,400		c 38,400			
Gain on sale of truck		$ 3,000	b 3,000			
Depreciation expense	3,000			a 1,000		$ 2,000
Minority interest income					$ 9,600	9,600
Balance Sheet Trucks	$ 12,000			b 3,000		$ 9,000
Accumulated depreciation	3,000		a 1,000			2,000
Investment in Scott	438,400			c 38,400 d 400,000		
Equity of Scott—January 1		$500,000	d 500,000			
Minority interest—January 1				d 100,000	100,000	
Minority interest—December 31					$109,600	109,600

a	Accumulated depreciation		$ 1,000	
	Depreciation expense			$ 1,000
	To eliminate the current year's effect of unrealized gain from depreciation accounts.			
b	Gain on sale of truck		$ 3,000	
	Trucks			$ 3,000
	To eliminate unrealized gain and to reduce trucks to a cost basis.			
c	Income from Scott		$ 38,400	
	Investment in Scott			$ 38,400
	To eliminate investment income and to adjust the investment account to its beginning-of-the-period balance.			
d	Equity of Scott January 1, 20X4		$500,000	
	Investment in Scott			$400,000
	Minority interest January 1, 20X4			100,000
	To eliminate reciprocal investment and equity accounts and to establish beginning minority interest.			

Note that minority interest income of $9,600 for 20X4 is computed as 20% of Scott's realized income of $48,000 [($50,000 − $3,000 + $1,000) × 20%].

Partial consolidation working papers and the working paper entries in journal form for 20X5, the first subsequent year after the upstream sale, are as follows:

	Pruitt	80% Scott	Adjustments and Eliminations				Minority Interest	Consolidated Statements
Income Statement Income from Scott	$ 40,800		c	40,800				
Depreciation expense	3,000				a	1,000		$ 2,000
Minority interest income							$ 10,200	10,200
Balance Sheet Trucks	$ 12,000				b	3,000		$ 9,000
Accumulated depreciation	6,000		a b	1,000 1,000				4,000
Investment in Scott	479,200		b	1,600	c d	40,800 440,000		
Equity of Scott— January 1		$550,000	d	550,000				
Minority interest— January 1			b	400	d	110,000	109,600	
Minority interest— December 31							$119,800	119,800

a	Accumulated depreciation		$ 1,000	
	Depreciation expense			$ 1,000
	To eliminate the effect of the 20X4 unrealized gain from current depreciation accounts.			
b	Accumulated depreciation		$ 1,000	
	Investment in Scott		1,600	
	Minority interest January 1, 20X5		400	
	Trucks			$ 3,000
	To eliminate the effect of 20X4 unrealized gain from accumulated depreciation and truck accounts and to charge the unrealized gain of $2,000 at January 1 to the investment account (80%) and minority interest (20%).			
c	Income from Scott		$ 40,800	
	Investment in Scott			$ 40,800
	To eliminate investment income and to adjust the investment account to its beginning-of-the-period balance.			
d	Equity of Scott January 1, 20X5		$550,000	
	Investment in Scott			$440,000
	Minority interest January 1, 20X5			110,000
	To eliminate reciprocal investment and equity accounts and to establish beginning minority interest.			

Minority interest income of $10,200 for 20X5 consists of 20% of Scott's reported net income of $50,000 plus 20% of the $1,000 gain realized through depreciation in 20X5. In 20X6 the computation of minority interest income is the same as in 20X5.

To explain further, minority interest income in 20X4 (the year of sale) is decreased by $400, the minority interest's share of the $2,000 gain not realized through depreciation in 20X4. The beginning equity of Scott is not affected by the intercompany sale in 20X4, so beginning minority interest is unaffected and does not require adjustment. Depreciation expense for each of the years 20X4, 20X5, and 20X6 of

$3,000 is reduced to $2,000 by a working paper adjustment of $1,000. The $2,000 depreciation expense that appears in the consolidated income statement is simply one-third of the book value less residual value of the truck at the time of intercompany sale [($9,000 − $3,000) ÷ 3 years].

Effect of Upstream Sale on Subsequent Years   In 20X5, the first subsequent year after the intercompany sale, both the beginning investment account and the beginning minority interest are affected by the unrealized gain. Working paper entry b allocates the $2,000 unrealized gain 80% to the investment in Scott account and 20% to beginning minority interest. The debit to the investment in Scott account adjusts for the $1,600 difference between the investment account and 80% of Scott's equity at December 31, 20X4. The $400 debit to minority interest is necessary to adjust beginning minority interest in 20X5 to $109,600, equal to the ending minority interest in 20X4.

In the partial consolidation working papers for 20X6, the second subsequent year after the upstream sale, the amounts allocated are $800 to the investment account and $200 to minority interest because only $1,000 of the initial $3,000 unrealized gain is unrealized at January 1, 20X6. No further adjustments are necessary in 20X7 because the full amount of the unrealized gain has been realized through depreciation. Observe that the truck account less accumulated depreciation at December 31, 20X6 is equal to the $3,000 residual value of the truck on that date (trucks, $9,000, less accumulated depreciation, $6,000).

20X6: SECOND SUBSEQUENT YEAR

	Pruitt	80% Scott	Adjustments and Eliminations		Minority Interest	Consolidated Statements
Income Statement						
Income from Scott	$ 40,800		c 40,800			
Depreciation expense	3,000			a 1,000		$ 2,000
Minority interest income					$ 10,200	10,200
Balance Sheet						
Trucks	$ 12,000			b 3,000		$ 9,000
Accumulated depreciation	9,000		a 1,000			
			b 2,000			6,000
Investment in Scott	520,000		b 800	c 40,800		
				d 480,000		
Equity of Scott—January 1		$600,000	d 600,000			
Minority interest—January 1			b 200	d 120,000	119,800	
Minority interest— December 31					$130,000	130,000

a	Accumulated depreciation		$1,000	
	Depreciation expense			1,000
	To eliminate the effect of the 20X4 unrealized gain from current depreciation accounts.			
b	Accumulated depreciation		$2,000	
	Investment in Scott		800	
	Minority interest January 1, 20X5		200	
	Trucks			$ 3,000
	To eliminate the effect of 20X4 unrealized gain from accumulated depreciation and truck accounts and to charge the unrealized gain of $1,000 at January 1 to the investment account (80%) and minority interest (20%).			

c	Income from Scott	$ 40,800	
	Investment in Scott		$ 40,800
	To eliminate investment income and to adjust the investment account to its beginning-of-the-period balance.		
d	Equity of Scott January 1, 20X5	$600,000	
	Investment in Scott		$480,000
	Minority interest January 1, 20X5		120,000
	To eliminate reciprocal investment and equity accounts and to establish beginning minority interest.		

PLANT ASSETS SOLD AT OTHER THAN FAIR VALUE

An intercompany sale of plant assets at a loss requires special evaluation to make sure that the loss is not one that the selling affiliate should have recognized on its separate books prior to the intercompany sale (or in the absence of an intercompany sale). For example, if a parent company sells a machine with a book value of $30,000 to its 90%-owned subsidiary for $20,000 on January 1, 20X4, a question should arise as to the fair value of the asset at the time of sale. If the fair value is in fact $20,000, then the parent company should have written the asset down to its $20,000 fair value before the sale and recognized the actual loss on its separate company books. If the fair value is $30,000, then the propriety of the parent company's action is suspect because the majority stockholders lose and the minority stockholders gain on the exchange. Parent company officers and directors may be charged with improper stewardship.

Similar suspicions arise if a subsidiary sells an asset to the parent at less than its fair value, because the transaction would have to have been approved by parent company officials who also serve as directors of the subsidiary.

Intercompany sales at prices above fair value also create inequities. The Federal Trade Commission charged Nynex Corporation with overcharging its own telephone subsidiaries for equipment, supplies, and services. The telephone companies were fined $1.4 million for passing the costs of the overpayments along to their customers.[3]

Consolidation with Loss on Intercompany Sale

Consolidation procedures to recognize intercompany losses are essentially the same as those to eliminate unrealized gains. Assume that the machine referred to above had a remaining useful life of five years when it was sold to the 90%-owned subsidiary for $20,000. The parent company has a $10,000 unrealized loss that is recognized on a piecemeal basis over five years. If the subsidiary's net income for 20X4 is $200,000 and there are no other intercompany transactions, the parent records its income from subsidiary as follows:

Investment in Subsidiary	$188,000	
Income from Subsidiary		$188,000
To record income for 20X4 determined as follows:		
Equity in subsidiary's income ($200,000 × 90%)		$180,000
Add: Unrealized loss on machine		10,000
Less: Piecemeal recognition of loss		
($10,000 ÷ 5 years)		(2,000)
		$188,000

Consolidation working paper entries relating to the intercompany loss for 20X4 would be as follows:

Machinery	$10,000	
Loss on sale of machinery		$10,000
To eliminate unrealized intercompany loss on downstream sale.		
Depreciation expense	$ 2,000	
Accumulated depreciation		$ 2,000
To increase depreciation expense to reflect depreciation on a cost basis.		

---

[3] *The Wall Street Journal*, February 21, 1990, p. B8.

In the years 20X5 through 20X8, the parent company's income from subsidiary will be reduced by $2,000 each year under the equity method of accounting. Consolidated net income is also reduced by $2,000 each year through working paper entries to eliminate the effect of the intercompany loss. The elimination reduces consolidated income by increasing depreciation expense to a cost basis for consolidated statement purposes. In 20X5 the working paper entry would be:

Machinery	$10,000	
Depreciation expense	2,000	
Accumulated depreciation		$4,000
Investment in Subsidiary		8,000
To eliminate the effects of intercompany sale at a loss.		

An upstream sale of plant assets at a loss would be accounted for in similar fashion, except that the intercompany loss and its piecemeal recognition would be allocated proportionately to majority stockholders (investment income and consolidated net income) and minority interests.

CONSOLIDATION EXAMPLE—UPSTREAM AND DOWNSTREAM SALES OF PLANT ASSETS

Plank Corporation acquired a 90% interest in Sharp Corporation at its underlying book value of $450,000 on January 3, 20X5. Since Plank Corporation acquired its interest in Sharp, the two corporations have participated in the following transactions involving plant assets:

1 On July 1, 20X5 Plank sold land to Sharp at a gain of $5,000. Sharp resold the land to outside entities during 20X7 at a loss to Sharp of $1,000.
2 On January 2, 20X6 Sharp sold equipment with a five-year remaining useful life to Plank at a gain of $20,000. This equipment was still in use by Plank at December 31, 20X7.
3 On January 5, 20X7 Plank sold a building to Sharp at a gain of $32,000. The remaining useful life of the building on this date was eight years, and Sharp still owned the building at December 31, 20X7.

Comparative financial statements for Plank and Sharp corporations for 20X7 are shown in the separate company columns of the consolidation working papers in Exhibit 6–4.

Equity Method

An examination of the consolidation working papers in Exhibit 6–4 shows that Plank Corporation uses the equity method of accounting. This is shown by the fact that Plank's net income of $300,000 is equal to consolidated net income, as well as by the equality of Plank's retained earnings and consolidated retained earnings. A reconciliation of Plank's investment in Sharp account at December 31, 20X6 and December 31, 20X7 follows:

Underlying equity in Sharp December 31, 20X6	
($600,000 equity of Sharp × 90%)	$540 000
Less: Unrealized profit on land	(5,000)
Less: 90% of unrealized profit on equipment ($16,000 × 90%)	(14,400)
Investment in Sharp December 31, 20X6	520,600
Add: Income from Sharp 20X7 (90% of Sharp's $80,000 net income + $5,000 gain on land + $3,600 piecemeal recognition of gain on equipment − $28,000 unrealized profit on building)	52,600
Less: Dividends received 20X7	(27,000)
Investment in Sharp December 31, 20X7	$546,200

Plank Corporation sold land to Sharp in 20X5 at a gain of $5,000. This gain was realized in 20X7 when Sharp sold the land to another entity. However, Sharp sold the

PLANK CORPORATION AND SUBSIDIARY CONSOLIDATION
WORKING PAPERS—FOR THE YEAR ENDED DECEMBER 31, 20X7

	Plank	90% Sharp	Adjustments and Eliminations		Minority Interest	Consolidated Statements
Income Statement Sales	$2,000,000	$700,000				$2,700,000
Gain on building	32,000		c 32,000			
Loss (or gain) on land		(1,000)		a 5,000		4,000
Income from Sharp	52,600		d 52,600			
Cost of goods sold	(1,000,000)	(320,000)				(1,320,000)
Depreciation expense	(108,000)	(50,000)	b 4,000 c 4,000			(150,000)
Other expenses	(676,600)	(249,000)				(925,600)
Minority interest income					$ 8,400	(8,400)
Net income	$ 300,000	$ 80,000				$ 300,000
Retained Earnings Retained earnings—Plank	$ 400,000					$ 400,000
Retained earnings—Sharp		$200,000	e 200,000			
Net income	300,000√	80,000√				300,000
Dividends	(200,000)	(30,000)		d 27,000	(3,000)	(200,000)
Retained earnings December 31, 20X7	$ 500,000	$250,000				$ 500,000
Balance Sheet Cash	$ 131,800	$ 32,000				$ 163,800
Other current assets	200,000	150,000				350,000
Land	160,000	40,000				200,000
Buildings	500,000	232,000		c 32,000		700,000
Accumulated depreciation—buildings	(200,000)	(54,000)	c 4,000			(250,000)
Equipment	620,000	400,000		b 20,000		1,000,000
Accumulated depreciation—equipment	(258,000)	(100,000)	b 8,000			(350,000)
Investment in Sharp	546,200		a 5,000 b 14,400	d 25,600 e 540,000		
	$1,700,000	$700,000				$1,813,800
Current liabilities	$ 200,000	$ 50,000				$ 250,000
Capital stock	1,000,000	400,000	e 400,000			1,000,000
Retained earnings	500,000√	250,000√				500,000
	$1,700,000	$700,000				
Minority interest January 1, 20X7			b 1,600	e 60,000	58,400	
Minority interest December 31, 20X7					$63,800	63,800
						$1,813,800

Exhibit 6–4   *Intercompany Sales of Plant Assets—Equity Method*

land at a $1,000 loss based on the transfer price, and the net result is a $4,000 gain for the consolidated entity during 20X7. Working paper entry a converts the $1,000 loss included in Sharp's separate income to a $4,000 consolidated gain.

a	Investment in Sharp	$ 5,000	
	Gain on land		$ 5,000
	To recognize previously deferred gain on land.		

Entry b relates to the $20,000 intercompany profit on Sharp's sale of equipment to Plank at the beginning of 20X6. The working paper adjustment is:

b	Investment in Sharp	$ 14,400	
	Minority interest January 1	1,600	
	Accumulated depreciation—equipment	8,000	
	Depreciation expense		$ 4,000
	Equipment		20,000
	To eliminate unrealized profit on upstream sale of equipment.		

Depreciation on the unrealized gain is $4,000 per year ($20,000 ÷ 5 years), and the portion unrealized at the beginning of 20X7 was $16,000, the original gain less piecemeal recognition of $4,000 through depreciation in 20X6. The sale was upstream, so the $16,000 unrealized profit is allocated 90% and 10% to investment in Sharp ($14,400) and beginning minority interest ($1,600), respectively. The $14,400 is debited to the investment in Sharp account because Plank used the equity method of accounting.

Working paper entry c eliminates intercompany profit on the buildings that Plank sold to Sharp in 20X7 at a gain of $32,000:

c	Gain on buildings	$ 32,000	
	Accumulated depreciation—buildings	4,000	
	Buildings		$ 32,000
	Depreciation expense		4,000
	To eliminate unrealized gain on the downstream sale of buildings.		

The transaction occurred at the beginning of the current year, so prior-period balances were not affected by the sale. The $32,000 gain is eliminated in the adjustment, and buildings are reduced to reflect their cost to the consolidated entity. Depreciation expense and accumulated depreciation amounts relating to the unrealized gain are also eliminated.

Entry d in the consolidation working papers eliminates income from Sharp and 90% of Sharp's dividends, and it credits the investment in Sharp for the $25,600 difference in order to establish reciprocity between investment and equity accounts at the beginning of the year. Entry e eliminates reciprocal investment and equity accounts and establishes the minority interest at the beginning of the year.

d	Income from Sharp	$ 52,600	
	Dividends		$ 27,000
	Investment in Sharp		25,600
	To eliminate income and dividends from subsidiary.		
e	Retained earnings—Sharp	$200,000	
	Capital stock—Sharp	400,000	
	Investment in Sharp		$540,000
	Minority interest—beginning		60,000
	To eliminate reciprocal investment and equity balances.		

The $8,400 deduction for minority interest income in the consolidated income statement of Exhibit 6–4 is equal to 10% of Sharp's reported income for 20X7 plus the piecemeal recognition of the gain in 20X7 from Sharp's sale of equipment to Plank [($80,000 + $4,000) × 10%]. At December 31, 20X7 the minority interest's share of the unrealized gain on the equipment is $1,200. This $1,200 is reflected in the $63,800 minority interest that is shown in the consolidated balance sheet. If the effect of the unrealized gain applicable to minority interest had not been eliminated, minority interest in the consolidated balance sheet would be $65,000, 10% of Sharp's reported equity at December 31, 20X7.

Incomplete Equity Method

If Plank Corporation had used an incomplete equity method and failed to consider intercompany transactions in accounting for its investment in Sharp, its separate financial statements would show overstated amounts for beginning and ending retained earnings, investment income, net income, and the investment in Sharp.

Conversion to Equity Method Approach   Computations to support the working paper entry to convert Plank's separate accounts to the equity method are shown in the following incomplete equity-to-equity conversion schedule:

	Plank's Beginning Retained Earnings	Investment in Sharp	Income from Sharp
Prior Year's Effect			
Sale of land to Sharp in 20X5	$ −5,000	$ −5,000	
Purchase of equipment from Sharp on January 1, 20X6 ($20,000 gain × 90%)	−18,000	−18,000	
Piecemeal recognition through 20X6 depreciation of equipment [($20,000 gain ÷ 5 years) × 90%]	+3,600	+3,600	
Current Year's Effect			
Sharp's sale of land to outside entity		+5,000	$ +5,000
Sale of building to Sharp on January 5, 20X7		−32,000	−32,000
Piecemeal recognition of gain on equipment—20X7		+3,600	+3,600
Piecemeal recognition of gain on building through depreciation ($32,000 gain ÷ 8 years)		+4,000	+4,000
Working paper adjustment to convert to the equity method	$−19,400	$−38,800	$−19,400

The working paper entry prepared from the schedule is:

Retained earnings—Plank January 1	$19,400	
Income from Sharp	19,400	
Investment in Sharp		$38,800

The equality of these numbers is coincidental, because the retained earnings adjustment consists of overstatements from prior sales of land and equipment, and the income adjustment consists of recognition of previously deferred gain on land, piecemeal recognition of the gain on equipment, and the gain on buildings less related piecemeal recognition.

After entering the conversion to equity entry in the consolidation working papers, all other working paper entries should be the same as those in Exhibit 6–4 under the equity method.

Traditional Working Paper Solution for Incomplete Equity Method   Exhibit 6–5 illustrates working paper procedures to consolidate the financial statements of Plank and Sharp when Plank uses an incomplete equity method of accounting and consolidates without converting to the equity method.

PLANK CORPORATION AND SUBSIDIARY CONSOLIDATION
WORKING PAPERS—FOR THE YEAR ENDED DECEMBER 31, 20X7

	Plank	90% Sharp	Adjustments and Eliminations		Minority Interest	Consolidated Statements
Income Statement Sales	$2,000,000	$700,000				$2,700,000
Gain on building	32,000		c 32,000			
Loss (or gain) on land		(1,000)		a 5,000		4,000
Income from Sharp	72,000		d 72,000			
Cost of goods sold	(1,000,000)	(320,000)				(1,320,000)
Depreciation expense	(108,000)	(50,000)	b 4,000	c 4,000		(150,000)
Other expenses	(676,600)	(249,000)				(925,600)
Minority interest income					$ 8,400	(8,400)
Net income	$ 319,400	$ 80,000				$ 300,000
Retained Earnings Retained earnings—Plank	$ 419,400		a 5,000 b 14,400			$ 400,000
Retained earnings—Sharp		$200,000	e 200,000			
Net income	319,400√	80,000√				300,000
Dividends	(200,000)	(30,000)		d 27,000	(3,000)	(200,000)
Retained earnings December 31, 20X7	$ 538,800	$250,000				$ 500,000
Balance Sheet Cash	$ 131,800	$ 32,000				$ 163,800
Other current assets	200,000	150,000				350,000
Land	160,000	40,000				200,000
Buildings	500,000	232,000		c 32,000		700,000
Accumulated depreciation—buildings	(200,000)	(54,000)	c 4,000			(250,000)
Equipment	620,000	400,000		b 20,000		1,000,000
Accumulated depreciation—equipment	(258,000)	(100,000)	b 8,000			(350,000)
Investment in Sharp	585,000		d 45,000	e 540,000		
	$1,738,800	$700,000				$1,813,800
Current liabilities	$ 200,000	$ 50,000				$ 250,000
Capital stock	1,000,000	400,000	e 400,000			1,000,000
Retained earnings	538,800√	250,000√				500,000
	$1,738,800	$700,000				
Minority interest January 1, 20X7			b 1,600	e 60,000	58,400	
Minority interest December 31, 20X7					$63,800	63,800
						$1,813,800

Exhibit 6–5 *Incomplete Equity Method—Traditional Approach*

Notice that the entries are similar to those in Exhibit 6–4, except that the debit amounts in entries a and b are to the parent's beginning retained earnings instead of the investment account. This is because the parent did not eliminate intercompany unrealized profits in prior years through a one-line consolidation of its investment in Sharp. The working paper entries from Exhibit 6–5 are reproduced for convenient reference as follows:

a	Retained earnings—Plank January 1	$ 5,000	
	Gain on land		$ 5,000
	To recognize previously deferred gain on land.		
b	Retained earnings—Plank January 1	$ 14,400	
	Accumulated depreciation—equipment	8,000	
	Minority interest January 1	1,600	
	Equipment		$ 20,000
	Depreciation expense		4,000
	To eliminate unrealized profit on upstream sale of equipment.		
c	Gain on building	$ 32,000	
	Accumulated depreciation	4,000	
	Buildings		$ 32,000
	Depreciation expense		4,000
	To eliminate unrealized gain on downstream sale of building.		
d	Income from Sharp	$ 72,000	
	Dividends		$ 27,000
	Investment in Sharp		45,000
	To eliminate investment income (as recorded by Plank) and dividends, and return investment account to its beginning-of-the-period balance under an incomplete equity method.		
e	Retained earnings—Sharp	$200,000	
	Capital stock—Sharp	400,000	
	Investment in Sharp		$540,000
	Minority interest		60,000
	To eliminate reciprocal equity and investment balances and enter beginning minority interest.		

Cost Method

Now assume that Plank has used the cost method in accounting for its investment in Sharp. Under the cost method, Plank's investment in Sharp account remains at the $450,000 original investment. Net income and retained earnings are understated by Plank's share of Sharp's undistributed income plus or minus any unrealized intercompany profits.

Conversion to Equity Method Approach The working paper entry to convert Plank's cost-based accounting records from the cost to the equity method in journal form is:

Investment in Sharp	$ 96,200	
Dividend income	27,000	
Income from Sharp		$ 52,600
Retained earnings—Plank January 1		70,600
To adjust Plank's account balances to an equity basis as a first step in consolidating its subsidiary.		

Data to support the working paper entry are provided in the following cost-equity conversion schedule:

	Plank's Beginning Retained Earnings	Investment in Sharp	Income from Sharp	Dividend Income
Prior Year's Effect				
90% of Sharp's increase in undistributed income for 20X5 and 20X6 [($600,000 − $500,000) × 90%]	$+90,000	$+90,000		
Gain on sale of land to Sharp	−5,000	−5,000		
Gain on purchase of equipment from Sharp	−18,000	−18,000		
Piecemeal recognition of gain on equipment through depreciation ($4,000 × 90%)	+3,600	+3,600		
Current Year's Effect				
Reclassify dividend income as decrease in investment		−27,000		$−27,000
Share of Sharp's reported income ($80,000 × 90%)		+72,000	$+72,000	
Sharp's sale of land to outside entity		+5,000	+5,000	
Gain from sale of building to Sharp		−32,000	−32,000	
20X7 piecemeal recognition of gain on equipment ($4,000 × 90%)		+3,600	+3,600	
20X7 piecemeal recognition of gain on building ($32,000 ÷ 8 years)		+4,000	+4,000	
Working paper entry to convert cost to equity method	$+70,600	$+96,200	$+52,600	$−27,000

As in the case of the conversion from incomplete equity to the equity method, after this first correcting entry is made in the working papers to convert Plank's accounting for its investment in Sharp to the equity method, the rest of the working paper entries are the same as those in Exhibit 6–4.

Traditional Working Paper Solution for Cost Method   Exhibit 6–6 illustrates working paper procedures to consolidate the financial statements of Plank and Sharp when Plank uses the cost method to account for its investment in Sharp and consolidates without converting to the equity method.

Working paper entries a, b, and c under the cost method are identical to those under an incomplete equity method. Entry d eliminates dividend income against dividends. Entry e takes up Plank's share of the increase in Sharp's retained earnings from the date of acquisition to the beginning of 20X7. In other words, entry e establishes reciprocity between the investment and equity balances to the beginning of the year. Entry f then eliminates the reciprocal investment and equity balances and enters beginning-of-the-period minority interest. These last three working paper entries are journalized as follows:

d	Dividend income—Sharp	$27,000	
	Dividends		$27,000
	To eliminate dividend income.		
e	Investment in Sharp	$90,000	
	Retained earnings—Plank January 1		$90,000
	To increase parent's beginning retained earnings for its share of Sharp's retained earnings increase between date of acquisition and beginning of the period.		

PLANK CORPORATION AND SUBSIDIARY CONSOLIDATION
WORKING PAPERS—FOR THE YEAR ENDED DECEMBER 31, 20X7

	Plank	90% Sharp	Adjustments and Eliminations	Minority Interest	Consolidated Statements
Income Statement Sales	$2,000,000	$700,000			$2,700,000
Gain on building	32,000		c 32,000		
Loss (or gain) on land		(1,000)	a 5,000		4,000
Dividends from Sharp	27,000		d 27,000		
Cost of goods sold	(1,000,000)	(320,000)			(1,320,000)
Depreciation expense	(108,000)	(50,000)	b 4,000 c 4,000		(150,000)
Other expenses	(676,600)	(249,000)			(925,600)
Minority interest income				$ 8,400	(8,400)
Net income	$ 274,400	$ 80,000			$ 300,000
Retained Earnings Retained earnings—Plank	$ 329,400		a 5,000 b 14,400 e 90,000		$ 400,000
Retained earnings—Sharp		$200,000	f 200,000		
Net income	274,400√	80,000√			300,000
Dividends	(200,000)	(30,000)	d 27,000	(3,000)	(200,000)
Retained earnings December 31, 20X7	$ 403,800	$250,000			$ 500,000
Balance Sheet Cash	$ 131,800	$ 32,000			$ 163,800
Other current assets	200,000	150,000			350,000
Land	160,000	40,000			200,000
Buildings	500,000	232,000	c 32,000		700,000
Accumulated depreciation—buildings	(200,000)	(54,000)	c 4,000		(250,000)
Equipment	620,000	400,000	b 20,000		1,000,000
Accumulated depreciation—equipment	(258,000)	(100,000)	b 8,000		(350,000)
Investment in Sharp	450,000		e 90,000 f 540,000		
	$1,603,800	$700,000			$1,813,800
Current liabilities	$ 200,000	$ 50,000			$ 250,000
Capital stock	1,000,000	400,000	f 400,000		1,000,000
Retained earnings	403,800√	250,000√			500,000
	$1,603,800	$700,000			
Minority interest January 1, 20X7			b 1,600 f 60,000	58,400	
Minority interest December 31, 20X7				$63,800	63,800
					$1,813,800

Exhibit 6–6   *Cost Method—Traditional Approach*

f	Retained earnings—Sharp	$200,000	
	Capital stock—Sharp	400,000	
	Investment in Sharp		$540,000
	Minority interest		60,000

To eliminate reciprocal investment and equity balances
and enter beginning minority interest.

Comparison of Results Under the Three Methods

Regardless of the method (equity, incomplete equity, or cost) used by the parent in accounting for its subsidiary, or the approach used in the working papers to consolidate the financial statements of the parent and subsidiary, the final consolidated financial statements will always be the same. A summary of the differences in the financial statement items of Plank under the equity, incomplete equity, and cost methods is as follows:

	Equity Method	Incomplete Equity Method	Cost Method
Income Statement			
Income from Sharp	$ 52,600	$ 72,000	—
Dividend income from Sharp	—	—	$ 27,000
Net income	300,000	319,400	274,400
Retained Earnings Statement			
Retained earnings January 1, 20X7	400,000	419,400	329,400
Net income	300,000	319,400	274,400
Dividends (no difference)	(200,000)	(200,000)	(200,000)
Retained earnings December 31, 20X7	500,000	538,800	403,800
Balance Sheet			
Investment in Sharp	546,200	585,000	450,000
Retained earnings December 31, 20X7	500,000	538,800	403,800

INVENTORY ITEMS PURCHASED FOR USE AS OPERATING ASSETS

Intercompany asset transactions do not always fall neatly into the categories of inventory items or plant assets. For example, inventory items may be sold for use in the operations of an affiliated company. In this case, any gross profit on the sale will be realized for consolidated statement purposes as the property is depreciated by the purchasing affiliate.

Assume that Premier Electronics Company sells a computer that it manufactures at a cost of $150,000 to Service Valley Corporation, its 100%-owned subsidiary, for $200,000. The computer has a five-year expected useful life, and straight-line depreciation is used. Premier's separate income statement includes $200,000 intercompany sales, but Service Valley's cost of sales does *not* include intercompany purchases, because the purchase price is reflected in its plant assets, and the $50,000 gross profit is reflected in its equipment account. Working paper entries to consolidate the financial statements of Premier and Service Valley in the year of sale are:

Sales	$200,000	
Cost of sales		$150,000
Equipment		50,000

To eliminate intercompany sales and to reduce cost of sales
and equipment for the cost and gross profit, respectively.

Accumulated depreciation	$ 10,000	
Depreciation expense		$ 10,000

To eliminate depreciation on the gross profit from the sale ($50,000 ÷ 5 years).

228 CHAPTER SIX

Recognition of the remaining $40,000 unrealized profit will occur as Service Valley depreciates the computer over its remaining four-year useful life. Assuming that Premier adjusts its investment in Service Valley account for the unrealized profit on the sale under the equity method, the working paper entry for the second year will be:

Investment in Service Valley	$40,000	
Accumulated depreciation—equipment	20,000	
Equipment		$50,000
Depreciation expense		10,000

To reduce equipment to its cost basis to the consolidated entity, to eliminate the effects of the intercompany sale from depreciation expense and accumulated depreciation, and to establish reciprocity between beginning-of-the-period equity and investment amounts.

Working paper entries for the remaining three years of the computer's useful life will include the same debit and credit items, but the accumulated depreciation debit will increase by $10,000 in each subsequent year to a maximum of $50,000, and the debits to investment in Service Valley will decrease by $10,000 in each subsequent year as the gross profit is realized. The credit amounts are the same in each year.

SUMMARY

The effects of intercompany gains and losses on plant assets must be eliminated from consolidated financial statements until the gains and losses are realized by the consolidated entity through use or through sale of the assets. Realization through use results from the depreciation recorded by the purchasing affiliate. Although all unrealized profit must be eliminated from the consolidated statements, consolidated net income is adjusted for all unrealized gains and losses in the case of downstream sales. For upstream sales, however, the total amount of unrealized gains and losses is allocated between consolidated net income and minority interest income. One-line consolidation procedures for parent company financial statements must be compatible with consolidation procedures in order to maintain the equality of parent company income under the equity method and consolidated net income. A summary illustration comparing the effect of intercompany sales of plant assets on parent company and consolidation income statements is presented in Exhibit 6–7.

ASSIGNMENT MATERIAL

QUESTIONS

1 What is the objective of eliminating the effects of intercompany sales of plant assets in the preparation of consolidated financial statements?

2 In accounting for unrealized profits and losses from intercompany sales of plant assets, does it make any difference if the parent company is the purchaser or the seller? Would your answer be different if the subsidiary were 100% owned?

3 When are unrealized gains and losses from intercompany sales of land realized from the viewpoint of the selling affiliate?

4 How is the computation of minority interest income affected by downstream sales of land? By upstream sales of land?

5 Consolidation working paper entries are made to eliminate 100% of the unrealized profit from the land account in downstream sales of land. Is 100% also eliminated for upstream sales of land?

6 How are unrealized gains and losses from intercompany transactions involving depreciable assets eventually realized?

7 Describe the computation of minority interest income in the year of an upstream sale of depreciable plant assets.

8 How does a parent company eliminate the effects of unrealized gains on intercompany sales of plant assets under the equity method?

9 What is the effect of intercompany sales of plant assets on parent company and consolidated net income in years subsequent to the year of sale?

10 Explain the sequence of working paper adjustments and eliminations when unrealized gains and losses on plant assets are involved. Is your answer affected by the method used by the

Assumptions

1 Parent Company's income, excluding income from Subsidiary, is $100,000.
2 90%-owned Subsidiary reported net income of $50,000.
3 An intercompany sale of land resulted in a gain of $5,000.
4 The land is still held within the consolidated entity.

	Downstream	Upstream
	Assume that P sells to S	Assume that S sells to P
P's Net Income—Equity Method		
P's separate income	$100,000	$100,000
P's share of S's reported net income	45,000	45,000
Deduct: Unrealized gain from land		
($5,000 × 100%)	(5,000)	
($5,000 × 90%)		(4,500)
P's net income	$140,000	$140,500
Consolidated Net Income		
P's separate income plus S's net income	$150,000	$150,000
Less: Unrealized gain on land	(5,000)	(5,000)
Total realized income	145,000	145,000
Less: Minority interest income		
($50,000 × 10%)	(5,000)	
($50,000 − $5,000) × 10%		(4,500)
Consolidated net income	$140,000	$140,500

Note that P's net income and consolidated net income are the same as if the intercompany transaction had never taken place. In the downstream example, P's separate income would have been $95,000 ($100,000 − $5,000 gain) without the intercompany transaction, and S's reported income would have remained at $50,000. P's separate income of $95,000, plus P's $45,000 income from S ($50,000 × 90%), equals $140,000.

In the upstream example, P's separate income would have been unchanged at $100,000 in the absence of the intercompany transaction, but S's reported income would have been only $45,000 ($50,000 − $5,000 gain). P's separate income of $100,000, plus P's $40,500 income from S ($45,000 × 90%), equals $140,500. Although helpful in understanding the nature of accounting procedures, these assumptions concerning what the incomes would have been without the intercompany transactions lack economic realism because they ignore the productive use of the land.

Exhibit 6–7 *Summary Illustration—Unrealized Profit from Plant Assets*

parent company in accounting for its subsidiary investment? Is your answer affected by whether the intercompany transaction occurred in the current year or in prior years?

(*Note:* Don't forget the assumptions on page 56 when working exercises and problems in this chapter.)

EXERCISES

E 6-1 Use the following information in answering questions 1 and 2:

Parent Company sells land with a book value of $5,000 to Subsidiary Company for $6,000 in 20X1. Subsidiary Company holds the land during 20X2. Subsidiary Company sells the land for $8,000 to an outside entity in 20X3.

1 In 20X1 the unrealized gain:
   a To be eliminated is affected by the minority interest percentage
   b Is initially included in the subsidiary's accounts and must be eliminated from Parent Company's income from Subsidiary Company under the equity method
   c Is eliminated from consolidated net income by a working paper entry that includes a credit to the land account for $1,000
   d Is eliminated from consolidated net income by a working paper entry that includes a credit to the land account for $6,000
2 Which of the following statements is true?
   a Under the equity method, Parent Company's investment in Subsidiary account will be $1,000 less than its underlying equity in Subsidiary throughout 20X2.
   b No working paper adjustments for the land are required to 20X2 if Parent Company has applied the equity method correctly.
   c A working paper entry debiting gain on sale of land and crediting land will be required each year until the land is sold outside the consolidated entity.

d In 20X3, the year of Subsidiary's sale to an outside entity, the working paper adjustment for the land will include a debit to gain on sale of land for $2,000.

Use the following information in answering questions 3 and 4:

Perry Corporation sold machinery to its 80%-owned subsidiary, Samuel Corporation, for $100,000 on December 31, 20X1. The cost of the machinery to Perry was $80,000, the book value at the time of sale was $60,000, and the machinery had a remaining useful life of five years.

3 How will the intercompany sale affect Perry's income from Samuel and Perry's net income for 20X1?

	Perry's Income from Samuel	Perry's Net Income
a	No effect	No effect
b	Increased	No effect
c	Decreased	No effect
d	No effect	Decreased

4 How will the consolidated assets and consolidated net income for 20X1 be affected by the intercompany sale?

	Consolidated Net Assets	Consolidated Net Income
a	No effect	Decreased
b	Decreased	Decreased
c	Increased	No effect
d	No effect	No effect

E 6-2 Samit Corporation is a 90%-owned subsidiary of Parsen Corporation, acquired by Parsen in 20X2. During 20X5 Parsen sells land to Samit for $50,000 for which it paid $25,000. Samit owns this land at December 31, 20X5.

Required

1 How and in what amount will the sale of land affect Parsen's income from Samit and net income for the year 20X5 and the balance of Parsen's investment in Samit account on December 31, 20X5?

2 How will the consolidated financial statements of Parsen Corporation and Subsidiary for 20X5 be affected by the intercompany sale of land?

3 If Samit still owns the land at December 31, 20X6, how will Parsen's income from Samit and net income for 20X6 be affected and what will be the effect on Parsen's investment in Samit account on December 31, 20X6?

4 If Samit sells the land during 20X7 for $50,000, how will Parsen's income from Samit and total consolidated income for 20X7 be affected?

E 6-3 Silverman Corporation is a 90%-owned subsidiary of Pruitt Corporation, acquired several years ago at book value equal to fair value. For the years 20X1 and 20X2, Pruitt and Silverman report the following:

	20X1	20X2
Pruitt's separate income	$300,000	$400,000
Silverman's net income	80,000	60,000

The only intercompany transaction between Pruitt and Silverman during 20X1 and 20X2 was the January 1, 20X1 sale of land. The land had a book value of $20,000 and was sold intercompany for $30,000, its appraised value at the time of sale.

1 Assume that the land was sold by Pruitt to Silverman and that Silverman still owns the land at December 31, 20X2.

   a Calculate consolidated net income for 20X1 and 20X2.

   b Calculate minority interest income for 20X1 and 20X2.

2 Assume that the land was sold by Silverman to Pruitt and Pruitt still holds the land at December 31, 20X2.

   a Calculate consolidated net income for 20X1 and 20X2.

   b Calculate minority interest income for 20X1 and 20X2.

E 6-4 Income information for 20X2 taken from the separate company financial statements of Park Corporation and its 75%-owned subsidiary, Skyline Corporation, is presented as follows:

	Park	Skyline
Sales	$1,000,000	$460,000
Gain on sale of building	20,000	—
Income from Skyline	75,000	—
Cost of goods sold	(500,000)	(260,000)
Depreciation expense	(100,000)	(60,000)
Other expenses	(200,000)	(40,000)
Net income	$ 295,000	$100,000

Park's gain on sale of building relates to a building with a book value of $40,000 and a 10-year remaining useful life that was sold to Skyline for $60,000 on January 1, 20X2.

Required

1 At what amount will the gain on sale of building appear on the consolidated income statement of Park and Subsidiary for the year 20X2?
2 Calculate consolidated depreciation expense for 20X2.
3 Calculate consolidated net income for Park and Subsidiary for 20X2.
4 What entry should be made on Park's books on December 31, 20X2 (after the books are closed) to correct the accounts to an equity basis?

E 6-5   Salmark is a 90%-owned subsidiary of Pigwich Corporation, acquired at book value several years ago. Comparative separate company income statements for these affiliated corporations for 20X6 are as follows:

	Pigwich Corporation	Salmark Corporation
Sales	$1,500,000	$700,000
Income from Salmark	108,000	—
Gain on building	30,000	—
Income credits	1,638,000	700,000
Cost of sales	1,000,000	400,000
Operating expenses	300,000	150,000
Income debits	1,300,000	550,000
Net income	$ 338,000	$150,000

On January 5, 20X6 Pigwich sold a building with a 10-year remaining useful life to Salmark at a gain of $30,000. Salmark paid dividends of $100,000 during 20X6.

Required

1 Reconstruct the journal entries made by Pigwich during 20X6 to account for its investment in Salmark. Explanations of the journal entries are required.
2 Prepare a consolidated income statement for Pigwich Corporation and Subsidiary for 20X6.

E 6-6   **[AICPA adapted]**

1 On January 1, 20X5 the Jonas Company sold equipment to its wholly owned subsidiary, Neptune Company, for $1,800,000. The equipment cost Jonas $2,000,000; accumulated depreciation at the time of sale was $500,000. Jonas was depreciating the equipment on the straight-line method over twenty years with no salvage value, a procedure that Neptune continued. On the consolidated balance sheet at December 31, 20X5 the cost and accumulated depreciation, respectively, should be:
  a $1,500,000 and $600,000   c $1,800,000 and $500,000
  b $1,800,000 and $100,000   d $2,000,000 and $600,000
2 In the preparation of consolidated financial statements, intercompany items for which eliminations will not be made are:
  a Purchases and sales where the parent employs the equity method
  b Receivables and payables where the parent employs the cost method
  c Dividends received and paid where the parent employs the equity method
  d Dividends receivable and payable where the parent employs the equity method
3 Dunn Corporation owns 100% of Grey Corporation's common stock. On January 2, 20X6, Dunn sold to Grey for $40,000 machinery with a carrying amount of $30,000. Grey is depreciating the acquired machinery over a five-year life by the straight-line method. The net adjustments to compute 20X6 and 20X7 consolidated income before income tax would be an increase (decrease) of:

	20X6	20X7
a	$ (8,000)	$2,000
b	$ (8,000)	$0
c	$(10,000)	$2,000
d	$(10,000)	$0

4 Port Company owns 100% of Salem Company. On January 1, 20X2, Port sold Salem delivery equipment at a gain. Port had owned the equipment for two years and used a five-year straight-line depreciation rate with no residual value. Salem is using a three-year straight-line depreciation rate with no residual value for the equipment. In the consolidated income statement, Salem's recorded depreciation expense on the equipment for 20X2 will be decreased by:

a 20% of the gain on sale
b 33.33% of the gain on sale
c 50% of the gain on sale
d 100% of the gain on sale

E 6-7   1 Schoenfeld Corporation is an 80%-owned subsidiary of Poindexter Corporation. In 20X1 Schoenfeld sold land that cost $15,000 to Poindexter for $25,000. Poindexter held the land for eight years before reselling it in 20X9 to Elroy Company, an unrelated entity, for $55,000. The consolidated income statement for Poindexter and its subsidiary, Schoenfeld, will show a gain on the sale of land of:

a $40,000   c $30,000
b $32,000   d $24,000

2 On January 3, 20X8 Pella Corporation sells equipment with a book value of $90,000 to its 100%-owned subsidiary, Satterman Corporation, for $120,000. The equipment has a remaining useful life of three years with no salvage at the time of transfer. Satterman uses the straight-line method of depreciation. As a result of this intercompany transaction, Pella's investment in Satterman account balance at December 31, 20X8 will be:

a $20,000 greater than its underlying equity interest
b $20,000 less than its underlying equity interest
c $30,000 less than its underlying equity interest
d $10,000 greater than its underlying equity interest

3 Pentex Corporation sells equipment with a book value of $80,000 to Shirley Company, its 75%-owned subsidiary, for $100,000 on January 1, 20X8. Shirley determines that the remaining useful life of the equipment is four years and that straight-line depreciation is appropriate. The December 31, 20X8 *separate* company financial statements of Pentex and Shirley show equipment—net of $500,000 and $300,000, respectively. Consolidated equipment—net will be:

a $800,000   c $780,000
b $785,000   d $650,000

4 Parolari Corporation sold equipment with a remaining three-year useful life and a book value of $14,500 to its 80%-owned subsidiary, Sarafin Corporation, for $16,000 on January 2, 20X4. A consolidated working paper entry on December 31, 20X4 to eliminate the unrealized profits from the intercompany sale of equipment will include:

a A debit to gain on sale of equipment for $1,000
b A debit to gain on sale of equipment for $1,500
c A credit to depreciation expense for $1,500
d A debit to machinery for $1,500

5 A subsidiary sells equipment with a four-year remaining useful life to its parent at a $12,000 gain on January 1, 20X2. The effect of this intercompany transaction on the parent company's investment income from its subsidiary for 20X2 will be:

a An increase of $12,000 if the subsidiary is 100% owned
b An increase of $9,000 if the subsidiary is 100% owned
c A decrease of $9,000 if the subsidiary is 100% owned
d A decrease of $3,600 if the subsidiary is 60% owned

6 On January 1, 20X8 Sartin Corporation, a 60%-owned subsidiary of Pollyparts Company, sells a building with a book value of $300,000 to its parent for $350,000. At the time of sale, the building has an estimated remaining life of 10 years with no salvage value. Pollyparts uses straight-line depreciation. If Sartin reports net income of $1,000,000 for 20X8, minority interest income will be:

a $450,000   c $382,000
b $400,000   d $355,000

E 6-8   A summary of the separate income of Pod Corporation and the net income of its 75%-owned subsidiary, Seiver Corporation, for 20X6 is as follows:

	Pod	Seiver
Sales	$500,000	$300,000
Gain on sale of machinery	10,000	
Cost of goods sold	(200,000)	(130,000)
Depreciation expense	(50,000)	(30,000)
Other expenses	(80,000)	(40,000)
Separate incomes (excludes investment income)	$180,000	$100,000

Seiver Corporation sold machinery with a book value of $40,000 to Pod Corporation for $65,000 on January 2, 20X4. At the time of the intercompany sale, the machinery had a remaining useful life of five years. Pod uses straight-line depreciation. Pod used the machinery until December 28, 20X6, at which time it was sold to another entity for $36,000.

Required: Prepare a consolidated income statement for Pod Corporation and Subsidiary for 20X6.

E 6-9 Pepper Corporation owns 40% of the outstanding voting stock of Salt Corporation, acquired for $100,000 on July 1, 20X4 when Salt's common stockholders' equity was $200,000. The excess of investment cost over book value acquired was due to valuable patents owned by Salt and expected to give Salt a competitive advantage until July 1, 20X9.

Salt's net income for 20X4 was $40,000 (for the entire year), and for 20X5 Salt's net income was $60,000. Pepper's December 31, 20X4 and 20X5 inventories included unrealized profit on goods acquired from Salt in the amounts of $4,000 and $6,000, respectively. At December 31, 20X4 Pepper sold land to Salt at a gain of $2,000. This land is still owned by Salt at December 31, 20X5.

Required

1 Compute Pepper's investment income from Salt for 20X4 on the basis of a one-line consolidation.
2 Compute Pepper's investment income from Salt for 20X5 on the basis of a one-line consolidation.

E 6-10 Plain Corporation has an 80% interest in Simple Corporation, its only subsidiary. The 80% interest was acquired on July 1, 20X3 for $400,000, at which time Simple's equity consisted of $300,000 capital stock and $100,000 retained earnings. The excess of cost over book value was allocated to buildings with a 20-year remaining useful life.

On December 31, 20X5 Simple sold equipment with a remaining useful life of four years to Plain at a gain of $20,000. Plain Corporation had separate income for 20X5 of $500,000 and for 20X6 of $600,000.

Income and retained earnings data for Simple Corporation for 20X5 and 20X6 are as follows:

	20X5	20X6
Retained earnings January 1	$150,000	$200,000
Add: Net income	100,000	110,000
Deduct: Dividends	−50,000	−60,000
Retained earnings December 31	$200,000	$250,000

Required

1 Compute Plain Corporation's income from Simple, net income, and consolidated net income for each of the years 20X5 and 20X6.
2 Compute the correct balances of Plain Corporation's investment in Simple at December 31, 20X5 and 20X6, assuming no changes in Simple's outstanding stock since Plain acquired its interest.

E 6-11 Ped Industries manufactures heavy equipment used in construction and excavation. On January 3, 20X5 Ped sold a piece of equipment from its inventory that cost $180,000 to its 60%-owned subsidiary, Spano Corporation, at Ped's standard price of twice its cost. Spano is depreciating the equipment over six years using straight-line depreciation and no salvage value.

Required

1 Determine the net amount at which this equipment will be included in the consolidated balance sheets for Ped Industries and Subsidiary at December 31, 20X5 and 20X6.
2 Ped accounts for its investment in Spano as a one-line consolidation. Prepare the consolidation working paper entries related to this intercompany sale that are necessary to consolidate the financial statements of Ped and Spano at December 31, 20X5 and 20X6.

E 6-12 Income data from the records of Pasco Corporation and Slocum Corporation, Pasco's 80%-owned susidiary, for the years 20X1 through 20X4 follow:

	20X1	20X2	20X3	20X4
Pasco's separate income	$200,000	$150,000	$40,000	$120,000
Slocum's net income	60,000	70,000	80,000	90,000

Pasco acquired its interest in Slocum on January 1, 20X1 at a price of $40,000 *less* than book value. The $40,000 was assigned to a reduction of plant assets with a remaining useful life of 10 years.

On July 1, 20X1, Slocum sold land that cost $25,000 to Pasco for $30,000. This land was resold by Pasco for $35,000 in 20X4.

Pasco sold machinery to Slocum for $100,000 on January 2, 20X2. This machinery had a book value of $75,000 at the time of sale and is being depreciated by Slocum at the rate of $20,000 per year.

Pasco's December 31, 20X3 inventory included $8,000 unrealized profit on merchandise acquired from Slocum during 20X3. This merchandise was sold by Pasco during 20X4.

Required: Prepare a schedule to calculate the consolidated net income of Pasco Corporation and Subsidiary for each of the years 20X1, 20X2, 20X3, and 20X4.

PROBLEMS

P 6-1 The separate income statements of Pearl Corporation and its 90%-owned subsidiary, Sear Corporation, for 20X3 are summarized as follows:

	Pearl	Sear
Sales	$1,000,000	$600,000
Income from Sear	90,000	—
Gain on equipment	40,000	—
Cost of sales	(600,000)	(400,000)
Other expenses	(200,000)	(100,000)
Net income	$ 330,000	$100,000

Investigation reveals that the effects of certain intercompany transactions are not included in Pearl's income from Sear. Information about those intercompany transactions follows:

1 Inventories—Sales of inventory items from Pearl to Sear are summarized as follows:

	20X2	20X3
Intercompany sales	$100,000	$150,000
Cost of intercompany sales	60,000	90,000
Percentage unsold at year-end	50%	40%

2 Plant Assets—Pearl sold equipment with a book value of $60,000 to Sear for $100,000 on January 1, 20X3. Sear is depreciating the equipment on a straight-line basis (no scrap) over a four-year period.

Required

1 Determine the correct amount of Pearl's income from Sear for 20X3.
2 Prepare a consolidated income statement for Pearl Corporation and Subsidiary for 20X3.

P 6-2 Comparative balance sheets for Pony Corporation and its 90%-owned subsidiary, Sox Corporation, on December 31, 20X8, are as follows:

	Pony Corporation	Sox Corporation
Assets		
Cash	$ 3,200,000	$ 1,200,000
Receivables—net	4,760,000	2,000,000
Inventories	4,040,000	1,800,000
Land	4,700,000	1,000,000
Building—net	8,000,000	4,000,000
Equipment—net	14,000,000	6,000,000
Investment in Sox	11,300,000	—
Total assets	$50,000,000	$16,000,000

(Continued)

	Pony Corporation	Sox Corporation
Liabilities and Stockholders' Equity		
Accounts payable	$ 4,000,000	$ 2,000,000
Other liabilities	8,000,000	2,000,000
Common stock	30,000,000	10,000,000
Retained earnings	8,000,000	2,000,000
Total equities	$50,000,000	$16,000,000

Pony acquired its 90% interest in Sox for cash on December 31, 20X5 at a price $500,000 in excess of underlying book value. The excess was due to goodwill having a 10-year amortization period.

Sox Corporation's inventories at December 31, 20X8 included merchandise acquired from Pony at a price $50,000 in excess of its cost to Pony. Unrealized profit in Sox's December 31, 20X7 inventories acquired from Pony were $40,000.

During 20X8 Sox sold land to Pony at a gain of $200,000. Pony's land account at December 31, 20X8 includes the full $700,000 paid for the land. Pony uses the equity method of accounting for its investment in Sox but has applied the equity method without amortizing goodwill or adjusting for unrealized profits (an incomplete equity method).

Required: Prepare a consolidated balance sheet for Pony Corporation and Subsidiary at December 31, 20X8.

P 6-3 Prime Corporation owns 80% of the outstanding voting stock of Select Corporation, having acquired its interest at book value when Select Corporation was incorporated on January 2, 20X5. Comparative income statements for Prime and Select for 20X5 and 20X6 are as follows:

	20X5		20X6	
	Prime	Select	Prime	Select
Sales	$500,000	$200,000	$600,000	$250,000
Gain on machinery	10,000	—	—	—
Gain on land	—	—	—	5,000
Dividend income	40,000	—	40,000	—
Total revenue	550,000	200,000	640,000	255,000
Inventory January 1	80,000	40,000	70,000	50,000
Purchases	300,000	100,000	400,000	120,000
Goods available for sale	380,000	140,000	470,000	170,000
Inventory December 31	70,000	50,000	90,000	60,000
Cost of goods sold	310,000	90,000	380,000	110,000
Gross profit	240,000	110,000	260,000	145,000
Operating expenses	80,000	60,000	100,000	80,000
Net income	$160,000	$ 50,000	$160,000	$ 65,000

Additional Information

1 Prime Corporation uses the cost method of accounting for its investment in Select.
2 The $10,000 gain relates to machinery sold to Select at the beginning of 20X5. Select still held the machinery on December 31, 20X6 and is depreciating it at the rate of 20% per year. The $5,000 relates to land sold to Prime at the beginning of 20X6.
3 Intercompany sales and inventory data for 20X5 and 20X6 are as follows:

	20X5	20X6
Sales by Prime to Select	$40,000	—
Sales by Select to Prime	—	$50,000
Unrealized profit in Select's December 31 inventory	$ 8,000	—
Unrealized profit in Prime's December 31 inventory	—	$10,000

Required: Prepare comparative 20X5 and 20X6 consolidated income statements for Prime Corporation and Subsidiary. You may use a single line for cost of sales in your comparative income statements.

P 6-4 Parch Corporation acquired a 90% interest in Sarg Corporation's outstanding voting common stock on January 1, 20X1 for $630,000 cash. The stockholder's equity of Sarg on this date consisted of $500,000 capital stock and $200,000 retained earnings.

The separate financial statements of Parch and Sarg corporations at and for the year ended December 31, 20X1 are summarized as follows:

	Parch	Sarg
Combined Income and Retained Earnings Statement		
for the Year Ended December 31, 20X1		
Sales	$ 700,000	$ 500,000
Income from Sarg	70,000	—
Gain on land	—	10,000
Gain on equipment	20,000	—
Cost of sales	(300,000)	(300,000)
Depreciation expense	(90,000)	(35,000)
Other expenses	(200,000)	(65,000)
Net income	200,000	110,000
Beginning retained earnings	600,000	200,000
Dividends	(100,000)	(50,000)
Retained earnings December 31, 20X1	$ 700,000	$ 260,000
Balance Sheet at December 31, 20X1		
Cash	$ 35,000	$ 30,000
Accounts receivable—net	90,000	110,000
Inventories	100,000	80,000
Other current items	70,000	40,000
Land	50,000	70,000
Buildings—net	200,000	150,000
Equipment—net	500,000	400,000
Investment in Sarg	655,000	—
	$1,700,000	$ 880,000
Accounts payable	$ 160,000	$ 50,000
Other liabilities	340,000	70,000
Capital stock, $10 par	500,000	500,000
Retained earnings	700,000	260,000
	$1,700,000	$ 880,000

During 20X1 Parch made sales of $50,000 to Sarg at a gross profit of $15,000. One-third of these sales were inventoried by Sarg at year-end. Sarg owed Parch $10,000 on open account at December 31, 20X1.

Sarg sold land that cost $20,000 to Parch for $30,000 on July 1, 20X1. Parch still owns the land. On January 1, 20X1 Parch sold equipment with a book value of $20,000 and a remaining useful life of four years to Sarg for $40,000. Sarg uses straight-line depreciation and assumes no salvage value on this equipment.

Required: Prepare consolidation working papers for Parch Corporation and Subsidiary for the year ended December 31, 20X1.

P 6-5   Sim Corporation, a 90%-owned subsidiary of Pal Corporation, was acquired on January 1, 20X7 at a price $40,000 in excess of underlying book value. The excess was allocated $20,000 to buildings with a five-year remaining useful life and $20,000 to goodwill with a 10-year amortization period. Separate company financial statements for Pal and Sim for 20X8 are as follows:

	Pal	Sim
Combined Income and Retained Earnings Statement		
for the Year Ended December 31, 20X8		
Sales	$300,000	$100,000
Income from Sim	25,000	—
Gain on sale of equipment	9,000	—
Cost of sales	(140,000)	(50,000)
Operating expenses	(60,000)	(10,000)
Net income	134,000	40,000
Add: Beginning retained earnings	146,000	70,000
Less: Dividends	(60,000)	(20,000)
Retained earnings, December 31, 20X8	$220,000	$ 90,000

(Continued)

	Pal	Sim
Balance Sheet at December 31, 20X8		
Cash	$100,000	$ 17,000
Accounts receivable	90,000	50,000
Dividends receivable	9,000	—
Inventories	20,000	8,000
Land	40,000	15,000
Buildings—net	135,000	50,000
Equipment—net	165,000	60,000
Investment in Sim	141,000	—
Total assets	$700,000	$200,000
Accounts payable	$ 98,000	$ 30,000
Dividends payable	15,000	10,000
Other liabilities	67,000	20,000
Capital stock	300,000	50,000
Retained earnings	220,000	90,000
Total equities	$700,000	$200,000

Additional Information

1 Pal sold inventory items to Sim during 20X7 and 20X8 as follows:

	20X7	20X8
Sales	$30,000	$20,000
Cost of sales to Pal	15,000	10,000
Unrealized profit at December 31	5,000	4,000

2 Pal sold land that cost $7,000 to Sim for $10,000 during 20X7. The land is still owned by Sim.

3 In January 20X8 Pal sold equipment with a book value of $21,000 to Sim for $30,000. The equipment is being depreciated by Sim over a three-year period using the straight-line method.

4 On December 30, 20X8 Sim remitted $2,000 to Pal for merchandise purchases. The remittance was not recorded by Pal until January 5, 20X9 and it is not reflected in Pal's financial statements at December 31, 20X8.

Required: Prepare consolidation working papers for Pal Corporation and Subsidiary for the year ended December 31, 20X8.

P 6-6 Pall Corporation acquired a 90% interest in Stor Corporation on January 1, 20X3 for $236,000, at which time Stor's capital stock and retained earnings were $150,000 and $90,000, respectively. The $20,000 cost/book value differential is goodwill with a 10-year amortization period. Financial statements for Pall and Stor for 20X4 are as follows:

	Pall	Stor
Combined Income and Retained Earnings Statement for the Year Ended December 31, 20X4		
Sales	$ 450,000	$190,000
Income from Stor	38,000	—
Gain on land	5,000	—
Cost of sales	(200,000)	(100,000)
Operating expenses	(113,000)	(40,000)
Net income	180,000	50,000
Add: Retained earnings January 1	200,000	120,000
Less: Dividends	(150,000)	(20,000)
Retained earnings, December 31, 20X4	$ 230,000	$150,000
Balance Sheet at December 31, 20X4		
Cash	$ 167,000	$ 14,000
Accounts receivable	180,000	100,000
Dividends receivable	18,000	—
Inventories	60,000	36,000
Land	100,000	30,000
Buildings—net	280,000	80,000
Machinery—net	330,000	140,000
Investment in Stor	265,000	—
	$1,400,000	$400,000

(Continued)

	Pall	Stor
Accounts payable	$ 200,000	$ 50,000
Dividends payable	30,000	20,000
Other liabilities	140,000	30,000
Capital stock	800,000	150,000
Retained earnings	230,000	150,000
	$1,400,000	$400,000

Additional Information

1 Pall sold inventory items to Stor for $60,000 during 20X3 and $72,000 during 20X4. Stor's inventories at December 31, 20X3 and 20X4 included unrealized profits of $10,000 and $12,000, respectively.

2 On July 1, 20X3 Pall Corporation sold machinery with a book value of $28,000 to Stor for $35,000. The machinery had a useful life of 3.5 years at the time of intercompany sale and straight-line depreciation is used.

3 During 20X4, Pall sold land with a book value of $15,000 to Stor for $20,000.

4 Pall's accounts receivable on December 31, 20X4 includes $10,000 due from Stor Corporation.

5 Pall uses the equity method of accounting for its 90% interest in Stor.

Required: Prepare consolidation working papers for Pall Corporation and Subsidiary for the year ended December 31, 20X4.

P 6-7 Financial statements for Pill Corporation and Sank Corporation for 20X6 are summarized as follows:

	Pill	Sank
Combined Income and Retained Earnings Statement for the Year Ended December 31, 20X6		
Sales	$210,000	$130,000
Income from Sank	31,900	—
Gain on sale of land	—	10,000
Depreciation expense	(40,000)	(30,000)
Other expenses	(110,000)	(60,000)
Net income	91,900	50,000
Add: Beginning retained earnings	140,400	50,000
Deduct: Dividends	(30,000)	—
Retained earnings December 31, 20X6	$202,300	$100,000
Balance Sheet at December 31, 20X6		
Current assets	$200,000	$170,000
Plant assets	550,000	350,000
Accumulated depreciation	(120,000)	(70,000)
Investment in Sank	322,300	—
Total assets	$952,300	$450,000
Current liabilities	$150,000	$ 50,000
Capital stock	600,000	300,000
Retained earnings	202,300	100,000
Total equities	$952,300	$450,000

Additional Information

1 Pill acquired an 80% interest in Sank on January 2, 20X4 for $290,000, when Sank's stockholders' equity consisted of $300,000 capital stock and no retained earnings. The excess of investment cost over book value of the net assets acquired related 50% to undervalued inventories (subsequently sold in 20X4) and 50% to goodwill with a 10-year amortization period.

2 Sank sold equipment to Pill for $25,000 on January 1, 20X5, at which time the equipment had a book value of $10,000 and a five-year remaining useful life. (Included in plant assets in the financial statements.)

3 During 20X6 Sank sold land to Pill at a profit of $10,000. (Included in plant assets in the financial statements.)

4 Pill uses the equity method in accounting for its investment in Sank.

Required: Prepare consolidation working papers for Pill Corporation and Subsidiary for the year ended December 31, 20X6.

P 6-8   Port Corporation acquired all the outstanding stock of Skip Corporation on April 1, 20X1 for $15,000,000, when Skip's stockholders' equity consisted of $5,000,000 capital stock and $2,000,000 retained earnings. The purchase price reflected a $500,000 undervaluation of Skip's inventory on this date (sold in 20X1) and a $3,500,000 undervaluation of Skip's buildings (remaining useful life seven years from April 1, 20X1). Goodwill from the acquisition is being amortized over 40 years.

During 20X2, Skip sold land that cost $1,000,000 to Port for $1,500,000. Port resold the land for $2,200,000 during 20X5.

Port sells inventory items to Skip on a regular basis. Information relevant to such sales is as follows:

	Sales to Skip	Cost to Port	Percentage Unsold by Skip at Year-End	Percentage Unpaid by Skip at Year-End
20X1	$ 500,000	$300,000	0%	0%
20X2	1,000,000	600,000	30	50
20X3	1,200,000	720,000	18	30
20X4	1,000,000	600,000	25	20
20X5	1,500,000	900,000	20	20

Skip sold equipment with a book value of $800,000 to Port on January 3, 20X5 for $1,600,000. This equipment had a remaining useful life of four years at the time of sale.

Port uses the equity method of accounting for its investment in Skip. The financial statements for Port and Skip corporations are summarized as follows:

	Port	Skip
Combined Income and Retained Earnings Statement for the Year Ended December 31, 20X5		
Sales	$26,000,000	$11,000,000
Gain on land	700,000	—
Gain on equipment	—	800,000
Income from Skip	1,280,000	—
Cost of sales	(15,000,000)	(5,000,000)
Depreciation expense	(3,700,000)	(2,000,000)
Other expenses	(4,280,000)	(2,800,000)
Net income	5,000,000	2,000,000
Add: Beginning retained earnings	12,000,000	4,000,000
Deduct: Dividends	(3,000,000)	(1,000,000)
Retained earnings December 31, 20X5	$14,000,000	$ 5,000,000
Balance Sheet at December 31, 20X5		
Cash	$ 1,170,000	$ 500,000
Accounts receivable—net	2,000,000	1,500,000
Inventories	5,000,000	2,000,000
Land	4,000,000	1,000,000
Buildings—net	15,000,000	4,000,000
Equipment—net	10,000,000	4,000,000
Investment in Skip	13,930,000	—
Total assets	$51,100,000	$13,000,000
Accounts payable	$ 4,100,000	$ 1,000,000
Other liabilities	7,000,000	2,000,000
Capital stock	26,000,000	5,000,000
Retained earnings	14,000,000	5,000,000
Total equities	$51,100,000	$13,000,000

Required: Prepare consolidation working papers for Port Corporation and Subsidiary for the year ended December 31, 20X5.

P 6-9   Pic Corporation acquired an 80% interest in Sic Company on January 1, 20X5, for $136,000. Sic's capital stock and retained earnings on that date were $100,000 and $70,000, respectively.

At the beginning of 20X5, Sic sold a machine to Pic for $10,000. The machine had cost Sic $7,000, had depreciated $2,000 while being used by Sic, and had a remaining useful life of five years from the date of sale.

Trial balances of the two companies on December 31, 20X5 and 20X6 are as follows:

	20X5		20X6	
	Pic	Sic	Pic	Sic
Debits:				
Cash and equivalents	$ 50,000	$ 30,000	$ 63,000	$ 30,000
Other current assets	130,000	70,000	140,000	80,000
Plant and equipment	400,000	200,000	440,000	245,000
Investment in Sic	160,000	—	192,000	—
Cost of sales	250,000	130,000	260,000	140,000
Depreciation expense	50,000	25,000	50,000	25,000
Other expenses	60,000	20,000	55,000	30,000
	$1,100,000	$475,000	$1,200,000	$550,000
Credits:				
Accumulated depreciation	$ 150,000	$ 50,000	$ 200,000	$ 75,000
Liabilities	100,000	50,000	48,000	40,000
Capital stock	300,000	100,000	300,000	100,000
Retained earnings	126,000	70,000	190,000	100,000
Sales	400,000	200,000	430,000	235,000
Gain on plant asset	—	5,000	—	—
Income from Sic	24,000	—	32,000	—
	$1,100,000	$475,000	$1,200,000	$550,000

Required: Prepare consolidation working papers for Pic Corporation and Subsidiary for the year ended December 31, 20X5 and the year ended December 31, 20X6.

P 6-10 Park Corporation acquired an 80% interest in Spin Corporation on January 1, 20X6 for $108,000 cash, when Spin's capital stock was $100,000 and retained earnings, $10,000. The difference between investment cost and book value acquired is being amortized over a 10-year period.

Separate company financial statements for Park and Spin corporations on December 31, 20X9 are summarized as follows:

	Park	Spin
Combined Income and Retained Earnings Statement for the Year Ended December 31, 20X9		
Sales	$650,000	$120,000
Income from Spin	42,000	—
Cost of sales	(390,000)	(40,000)
Other expenses	(170,000)	(30,000)
Net income	132,000	50,000
Add: Beginning retained earnings	95,600	20,000
Deduct: Dividends	(70,000)	(20,000)
Retained earnings December 31, 20X9	$157,600	$ 50,000
Balance Sheet at December 31, 20X9		
Cash	$ 58,000	$ 20,000
Accounts receivable	40,000	20,000
Inventories	60,000	35,000
Plant assets	290,000	205,000
Accumulated depreciation	(70,000)	(100,000)
Investment in Spin	121,600	—
Total assets	$499,600	$180,000
Accounts payable	$ 42,000	$ 30,000
Capital stock	300,000	100,000
Retained earnings	157,600	50,000
Total equities	$499,600	$180,000

Additional Information
1 Spin's sales include intercompany sales of $8,000, and Park's December 31, 20X9 inventory includes $1,000 profit on goods acquired from Spin. Park's December 31, 20X8 inventory contained $2,000 profit on goods acquired from Spin.
2 Park owes Spin $4,000 on account.

3 On January 1, 20X8 Spin sold plant assets to Park for $60,000. These assets had a book value of $40,000 on that date and are being depreciated by Park over a five-year period.

4 Park uses the equity method to account for its investment in Spin.

Required: Prepare consolidation working papers for Park Corporation and Subsidiary for the year 20X9.

P 6-11 Pike Corporation issued 10,000 of its own $10 par shares for 90% of Shad Corporation's outstanding common shares on January 1, 20X7 in a pooling of interests business combination. Shad's stockholders' equity consisted of $100,000 capital stock, $50,000 other paid-in capital, and $50,000 retained earnings at the time of the pooling. Pike recorded the pooling as follows:

Investment in Shad (90%)	$180,000	
Capital stock, $10 par		$100,000
Other paid-in capital		35,000
Retained earnings		45,000

Separate company financial statements for Pike and Shad on December 31, 20X8 are summarized as follows:

	Pike	Shad
Income Statement for 20X8		
Sales	$ 600,000	$200,000
Income from Shad	63,500	—
Gain on equipment	18,000	—
Cost of sales	(270,000)	(100,000)
Operating expenses	(121,500)	(20,000)
Net income	$ 290,000	$ 80,000
Retained Earnings for 20X8		
Retained earnings December 31, 20X7	$ 70,000	$ 90,000
Add: Net income	290,000	80,000
Deduct: Dividends	(150,000)	(40,000)
Retained earnings December 31, 20X8	$ 210,000	$130,000
Balance Sheet at December 31, 20X8		
Cash	$ 166,500	$ 23,000
Accounts receivable	180,000	100,000
Dividends receivable	18,000	—
Inventories	60,000	27,000
Land	100,000	30,000
Buildings—net	280,000	100,000
Equipment—net	330,000	120,000
Investment in Shad	215,500	—
Total assets	$1,350,000	$400,000
Accounts payable	$ 225,000	$ 60,000
Dividends payable	30,000	20,000
Other liabilities	150,000	40,000
Capital stock, $10 par	600,000	100,000
Other paid-in capital	135,000	50,000
Retained earnings	210,000	130,000
Total equities	$1,350,000	$400,000

During 20X7 and 20X8, the intercompany transactions between these affiliated companies were as follows:

Inventory Items: During 20X7 Pike sold inventory items that cost $30,000 to Shad for $50,000. Half of these items were inventoried by Shad at December 31, 20X7. During 20X8, Pike sold inventory items that cost $20,000 to Shad for $40,000, and 40% of these items were inventoried by Shad at December 31, 20X8. Also, Shad owed Pike $5,000 at December 31, 20X8.

Plant Assets: On January 12, 20X7 Shad sold land with a book value of $10,000 to Pike for $15,000 and a building with a book value of $50,000 to Pike for $70,000. The building is being depreciated over a four-year period. On January 1, 20X8 Shad purchased equipment with a six-year remaining useful life from Pike at a gain to Pike of $18,000.

Required: Prepare consolidation working papers for Pike Corporation and Subsidiary at and for the year ended December 31, 20X8.

Cain Corporation acquired all the outstanding $10 par value voting common stock of Frey Corporation on January 1, 20X9, in exchange for 25,000 shares of its $10 par value voting common stock. On December 31, 20X8, Cain's common stock had a closing market price of $30 per share on a national stock exchange. The acquisition was appropriately accounted for as a purchase. Both companies continued to operate as separate business entities, maintaining separate accounting records with years ending December 31.

On December 31, 20X9, the companies had condensed financial statements as follows:

	Cain	Frey
Income Statement for the Year Ended December 31, 20X9		
Net sales	$3,800,000	$1,500,000
Dividends from Frey	40,000	—
Gain on sale of warehouse	30,000	—
Cost of goods sold	(2,360,000)	(870,000)
Operating expenses (including depreciation)	(1,100,000)	(440,000)
Net income	$ 410,000	$ 190,000
Retained Earnings Statement for the Year Ended December 31, 20X9		
Retained earnings—beginning	$ 440,000	$ 156,000
Add: Net income	410,000	190,000
Less: Dividends paid	—	(40,000)
Retained earnings December 31, 20X9	$ 850,000	$ 306,000
Balance Sheet at December 31, 20X9		
Assets		
Cash	$ 570,000	$ 150,000
Accounts receivable—net	860,000	350,000
Inventories	1,060,000	410,000
Land, plant and equipment	1,320,000	680,000
Accumulated depreciation	(370,000)	(210,000)
Investment in Frey (at cost)	750,000	—
Total assets	$4,190,000	$1,380,000
Liabilities and Stockholders' Equity		
Accounts payable and accrued expenses	$1,340,000	$ 594,000
Common stock, $10 par	1,700,000	400,000
Additional paid-in capital	300,000	80,000
Retained earnings	850,000	306,000
Total equities	$4,190,000	$1,380,000

Additional Information

1 There were no changes in the common stock and additional paid-in capital accounts during 20X9 except the one necessitated by Cain's acquisition of Frey.

2 At the acquisition date, the fair value of Frey's machinery exceeded its book value by $54,000. The excess cost will be amortized over the estimated average remaining life of six years. The fair values of all of Frey's other assets and liabilities were equal to their book values. Any goodwill resulting from the acquisition will be amortized over a 20-year period.

3 On July 1, 20X9 Cain sold a warehouse facility to Frey for $129,000 cash. At the time of the sale, Cain's book values were $33,000 for the land and $66,000 for the undepreciated cost of the building. Based on a real estate appraisal, Frey allocated $43,000 of the purchase price to land and $86,000 to building. Frey is depreciating the building over its estimated five-year remaining useful life by the straight-line method with no salvage value.

4 During 20X9, Cain purchased merchandise from Frey at an aggregate invoice price of $180,000, which included a 100% markup on Frey's cost. At December 31, 20X9, Cain owed Frey $86,000 on these purchases, and $36,000 of this merchandise remained in Cain's inventory.

Required: Prepare working papers to consolidate the financial statements of Cain and Frey for the year 20X9. (*Note:* Conversion to equity is an inefficient approach to the solution for this problem because the consolidation is in the year of acquisition.)

P 6-13 Separate company and consolidated financial statements for Pape Corporation and its only subsidiary, Sach Corporation, for 20X2 are summarized here. Pape acquired its interest in Sach on January 1, 20X1 at a price in excess of book value.

PAPE CORPORATION AND SUBSIDIARY
SEPARATE COMPANY AND CONSOLIDATED FINANCIAL STATEMENTS
AT AND FOR THE YEAR ENDED DECEMBER 31, 20X2

	Pape	Sach	Consolidated
Income Statement			
Sales	$ 500,000	$300,000	$ 716,000
Income from Sach	17,000	—	—
Gain on equipment	20,000	—	—
Cost of sales	(200,000)	(150,000)	(275,000)
Depreciation expense	(60,000)	(40,000)	(95,000)
Other expenses	(77,000)	(60,000)	(141,000)
Minority interest income	—	—	(5,000)
Net income	$ 200,000	$ 50,000	$ 200,000
Retained Earnings			
Retained earnings	$ 250,000	$120,000	$ 250,000
Net income	200,000	50,000	200,000
Dividends	(100,000)	(30,000)	(100,000)
Retained earnings	$ 350,000	$140,000	$ 350,000
Balance Sheet			
Cash	$ 17,500	$ 35,000	$ 52,500
Accounts receivable—net	50,000	30,000	70,000
Dividends receivable	13,500	—	—
Inventories	90,000	60,000	136,000
Other current assets	70,000	40,000	110,000
Land	50,000	20,000	70,000
Buildings—net	100,000	50,000	150,000
Equipment—net	300,000	265,000	550,000
Investment in Sach	309,000	—	—
Goodwill	—	—	32,000
Total assets	$1,000,000	$500,000	$1,170,500
Accounts payable	$ 60,000	$ 50,000	$ 100,000
Dividends payable	—	15,000	1,500
Other liabilities	90,000	95,000	185,000
Capital stock, $10 par	500,000	200,000	500,000
Retained earnings	350,000	140,000	350,000
Minority interest December 31, 20X2	—	—	34,000
Total equities	$1,000,000	$500,000	$1,170,500

Required: Answer the following questions about the financial statements of Pape and Sach.

1 What is Pape Corporation's percentage interest in Sach Corporation? Provide a computation to explain your answer.

2 Does Pape use a one-line consolidation in accounting for its investment in Sach? Explain your answer.

3 Were there intercompany sales between Pape and Sach in 20X2? If so, show computations.

4 Are there unrealized inventory profits on December 31, 20X2? If so, show computations.

5 Provide computations to explain the difference between the combined separate-company cost of sales and consolidated cost of sales.

6 Explain the difference between combined separate-company and the consolidated "equipment—net" line item by reconstructing the working paper entry(s) that was (were) apparently made.

7 Are there intercompany receivables and payables? If so, identify them and state their amounts.

8 Beginning with the minority interest at January 1, 20X2, provide calculations of the $34,000 minority interest at December 31, 20X2.

9 What was the amount of unamortized goodwill at December 31, 20X1? Show computations.

10 Provide computations to explain the $309,000 investment in Sach account balance on December 31, 20X2.

7

Intercompany Profit Transactions—Bonds

Companies frequently hold the debt instruments of affiliated companies. Such intercompany borrowing and lending activity is justified on the basis of convenience, efficiency, and flexibility. Even though each affiliate is a separate legal entity, the management of the parent company is in a position to negotiate all loans between affiliated companies, and a decision to borrow from or loan directly to affiliated companies is really only a decision to transfer funds among affiliates. Direct loans among affiliates produce reciprocal receivable and payable accounts for both principal and interest, as well as reciprocal income and expense accounts. These reciprocal accounts are eliminated in the preparation of consolidated financial statements because the intercompany receivables and payables do not reflect assets or obligations of the consolidated entity.

Special problems of accounting for intercompany bonds and notes arise when one company purchases the debt instruments of an affiliate from outside entities. Such purchases constitute a retirement of debt from the viewpoint of the consolidated entity, even though the debt remains outstanding from the viewpoint of the debtor corporation as a separate legal entity. That is, the issuing affiliate (debtor corporation) accounts for its debt obligations as if they were held by unaffiliated entities, and the purchasing affiliate accounts for its investment in the affiliate's obligations as if they were the obligations of unaffiliated entities. Consolidated statements, however, are prepared to show the financial position and results of operations that would have resulted if the issuing corporation had purchased and retired its own debt.

INTERCOMPANY BOND TRANSACTIONS

At the time a company issues bonds, its bond liability will reflect the current market rate of interest. However, subsequent changes in the market rate of interest will create a disparity between the book value and the market value of that liability. If the market rate of interest increases, the market value of the liability will be less than book value and the issuing company will have *realized* a gain as a result. The gain is *not recognized* on the issuing company's books under generally accepted accounting principles. Similarly, a decline in the market rate of interest gives rise to a *realized* loss that is *not recognized*. These realized but unrecognized gains and losses are required to be disclosed in the financial statements or footnotes in accordance with *FASB Statement No. 107*, "Disclosure about Fair Value of Financial Instruments."

Realized but unrecognized gains or losses on outstanding bonds can be recognized by retiring the outstanding bonds. The parent company, which controls all debt retirement and other decisions for the consolidated entity, has the following options:

1 The *issuing company* (parent or subsidiary) can use its available resources to purchase and *retire its own bonds.*
2 The *issuing company* (parent or subsidiary) can borrow money from unaffiliated entities at the market rate of interest and use the proceeds to *retire its own bonds.* (This option constitutes refunding.)
3 The *issuing company* can borrow money from an affiliated company and use the proceeds to *retire its own bonds.*
4 An *affiliated company* (parent or subsidiary) can purchase the bonds of the issuing company, in which case the bonds are *constructively retired.*

The first three options result in an **actual retirement** of the bonds. The previously unrecognized gain or loss in these three situations is recognized by the issuing company and is appropriately included in measuring consolidated net income. The fourth option results in a **constructive retirement**. This means that the bonds are retired for consolidated statement purposes because the bond investment and the bonds payable items of the parent and the subsidiary are reciprocals that must be eliminated in the consolidation process. The difference between the book value of the bond liability and the purchase price of the bond investment is a gain or loss for consolidated statement purposes. It is also a gain or loss for parent company accounting under the equity method (one-line consolidation). The gain or loss is not recognized on the books of the issuing company, whose bonds are held as an investment by the purchasing affiliate.

Although the constructive retirement is different in form, the substance of the debt extinguishment is the same as for the other three options from the viewpoint of the consolidated entity. Also, the effect of a constructive retirement on consolidated statements is the same as for an actual retirement. The gain or loss is a gain or loss of the issuing company that has been realized by changes in the market rate of interest after the bonds were issued, and it is recognized for consolidated statement purposes when the bonds are repurchased and held within the consolidated entity.

CONSTRUCTIVE GAINS AND LOSSES ON INTERCOMPANY BONDS

If the price paid by one affiliate to acquire the debt of another is greater than the book value of the liability (par value plus unamortized premium or less unamortized discount and issuance costs), a constructive loss on the retirement of debt occurs. Alternatively, if the price paid is less than the book value of the debt, a constructive gain results. The gain or loss is referred to as *constructive* because it is a gain or loss that is realized and recognized from the viewpoint of the consolidated entity, but it is not recorded on the separate books of the affiliated companies at the time of purchase.

Constructive gains and losses on bonds are (1) realized gains and losses from the consolidated viewpoint (2) that arise when a company purchases the bonds of an affiliate (3) from other entities (4) at a price other than the book value of the bonds. No gains or losses result from the purchase of an affiliate's bonds at book value or from direct lending and borrowing between affiliated companies.

Some accounting theorists argue that constructive gains and losses on intercompany bond transactions should be allocated between the purchasing and issuing affiliates according to the par value of the bonds. For example, if Parent Company pays $99,000 for $100,000 par of Subsidiary Company's outstanding bonds with $2,000 unamortized premium, the $3,000 constructive gain ($102,000 less $99,000) is allocated $1,000 to Parent and $2,000 to Subsidiary. The alternative to this **par value theory** is the **agency theory**, under which the affiliate that purchases the intercompany bonds acts as agent for the issuing company, under directions from Parent Company management. Under agency theory, the $3,000 constructive gain is assigned to Subsidiary Company (the issuing company), and the consolidated statement effect is the same as if Subsidiary Company had purchased its own bonds for $99,000. Although not supported by a separate theory, constructive gains and losses are sometimes assigned 100% to the parent company on the basis of expediency. That is, the accounting is less complicated.

Changes in market interest rates generate gains and losses for the issuing company, so accounting procedures should assign such gains and losses to the issuing affiliate, irrespective of the form of the transaction (direct retirement by the issuing company or purchase by an affiliate). Failure to assign the full amount of a constructive gain or loss to the issuing affiliate results in recognizing form over substance in debt retirement transactions. The substance of a transaction should be considered over its form (incidentally, this is what consolidation is all about), therefore, the agency theory is conceptually superior, and, accordingly, constructive gains and losses are assigned to the issuing affiliate in this book.

Most corporate long-term debt is in the form of outstanding bonds, so the analysis in this chapter relates to bonds even though it also applies to other types of debt instruments. Straight-line rather than effective interest amortization of premiums and discounts is used in the illustrations throughout the chapter. This is done to make the illustrations easier to follow and help students learn the concepts involved without the added complexity of effective interest computations. It should be understood that the *effective interest method is generally superior* to the straight-line method.[1] This discussion of intercompany bond transactions among affiliated companies also applies to companies associated through ownership of 20% or more of the voting stock of another company and accounted for under the equity method.

The first illustration in this section assumes that the subsidiary purchases parent company bonds (in other words, the parent company is the issuing affiliate) and the constructive gain or loss is assigned to the parent company. In the second illustration, the parent company purchases bonds issued by the subsidiary, and the constructive gain or loss is assigned to the subsidiary.

Acquisition of Parent Company Bonds

Assume that Sugar Corporation is an 80%-owned affiliate of Peach Corporation and that Peach Corporation sells $1,000,000 par of 10%, 10-year mortgage bonds at par value to the public on January 2, 20X6. One year later, on December 31, 20X6, Sugar purchases $100,000 of these outstanding bonds for $104,500 through the bond market. The purchase by Sugar results in the constructive retirement of $100,000 of Peach bonds and a constructive loss of $4,500 ($104,500 paid to retire bonds with a book value of $100,000).

Peach adjusts its investment income and investment accounts at December 31, 20X6 to record the constructive loss under the equity method of accounting. The entry on Peach's books is:

Income from Sugar	$4,500	
Investment in Sugar		$4,500
To adjust income from Sugar for the constructive loss on bonds.		

Without this entry, the income of Peach on an equity basis would not equal consolidated net income.

The $4,500 constructive loss is charged against Peach's share of Sugar's reported income because Peach is the issuing company for the bonds. Under the agency theory, the full amount of any constructive gain or loss on bonds is assigned to the issuing affiliate. The parent company is the issuing affiliate, so the analysis is similar to one for a downstream sale, and the full amount is charged to Peach and to consolidated net income.

The $4,500 constructive loss appears in the consolidated income statement of Peach Corporation and Subsidiary for 20X6, and the 10% mortgage bond issue is reported at $900,000 in the consolidated balance sheet at December 31, 20X6. This is accomplished through the following working paper adjustment:

Loss on constructive retirement of bonds	$ 4,500	
10% mortgage bonds payable	100,000	
Investment in bonds		$104,500
To enter loss and eliminate reciprocal bond investment and liability amounts.		

---

[1] *APB Opinion No. 21*, "Interest on Receivables and Payables," which generally requires the effective interest method of amortization, does not apply to "transactions between parent and subsidiary companies and between subsidiaries of a common parent." Paragraph 3f.

Gains and losses on the early extinguishment of debt, if material, are classified as extraordinary items under *FASB Statement No. 4,* "Reporting Gains and Losses from Extinguishment of Debt."

Acquisition of Subsidiary Bonds

Assume that Sugar sold $1,000,000 par of 10%, 10-year mortgage bonds to the public on January 2, 20X6 and that Peach acquires $100,000 par of these bonds for $104,500 on December 31, 20X6 in the bond market. The purchase by Peach results in a constructive retirement of $100,000 par of Sugar bonds and a constructive loss of $4,500 to the consolidated entity. Only 80% of the constructive loss is charged to majority stockholders because the purchase of subsidiary bonds is equivalent to an upstream sale, where the intercompany transactions affect minority interest income.

In accounting for its investment in Sugar under the equity method, Peach recognizes 80% of the constructive loss with the following entry:

Income from Sugar	$3,600	
Investment in Sugar		$3,600

The consolidation working paper adjustment in the year of the intercompany bond purchase is the same as that illustrated for the intercompany purchase of Peach bonds. However, the $3,600 decrease in consolidated net income (to equate it with the one-line consolidation effect) consists of the $4,500 constructive loss less the $900 minority interest share of the loss, which reduces minority interest income and thereby increases consolidated net income.

To summarize, when the parent company is the issuing affiliate, no allocation of gains and losses from intercompany bond transactions is necessary. When the subsidiary is the issuing affiliate, intercompany gains and losses on bonds must be allocated between consolidated net income and minority interest income in the consolidated income statement. In a one-line consolidation, the parent company recognizes only its proportionate share of the constructive gain or loss on bonds issued by a subsidiary.

PARENT COMPANY BONDS PURCHASED BY SUBSIDIARY

A constructive retirement of parent company bonds occurs when the outstanding bonds of the parent are purchased by an affiliated company. The purchasing subsidiary records the amount paid as an investment in bonds. This is the only entry made by either the purchasing or the issuing affiliate at the time of intercompany purchase. Thus, any gain or loss that results from the constructive retirement is *not* recorded in the separate accounts of the affiliated companies, but rather is reflected in the difference between the bond liability and bond investment accounts on the books of the parent and subsidiary companies.

To illustrate, assume that Sue is a 70%-owned subsidiary of Pam, acquired at its $56,000 book value on December 31, 20X2, when Sue had capital stock of $50,000 and retained earnings of $30,000. Pam has $100,000 par of 10% bonds outstanding with a $1,000 unamortized premium on January 1, 20X4, at which time Sue Company purchases $10,000 par of these bonds for $9,500 from an investment broker. This purchase results in a constructive retirement of 10% of Pam's bonds and a $600 constructive gain, computed as follows:

Book value of bonds purchased [10% × ($100,000 par + $1,000 premium)]	$10,100
Purchase price	9,500
Constructive gain on bond retirement	$ 600

The only entry Sue makes at the time the Pam bonds are purchased is:

Investment in Pam bonds	$9,500	
Cash		$9,500
To record acquisition of Pam bonds at 95.		

Equity Method

If consolidated financial statements are prepared immediately after the constructive retirement, the working paper entry to eliminate the intercompany bond investment and liability balances will include the $600 gain as follows:

January 1, 20X4		
10% bonds payable	$10,000	
Premium on bonds	100	
Investment in Pam bonds		$9,500
Gain on retirement of bonds		600

As a result of this working paper entry, the consolidated income statement reflects the gain, the investment in Pam bonds is eliminated, and the consolidated balance sheet shows the bond liability to holders outside the consolidated entity at $90,900 ($90,000 par plus $900 unamortized premium).

During 20X4, Pam will amortize the bond premium on its separate books and Sue will amortize the discount on its bond investment. Assuming that interest is paid on January 1 and July 1, that the bonds mature on January 1, 20X9 (five years after purchase), and that straight-line amortization is used, Pam will amortize 20% of the bond premium and Sue will amortize 20% of the discount as follows:

PAM'S BOOKS

July 1		
Interest expense	$5,000	
Cash		$5,000
($100,000 par × 10% × 1/2 year)		

December 31		
Interest expense	$5,000	
Interest payable		$5,000
($100,000 par × 10% × 1/2 year)		

December 31		
Premium on bonds	$ 200	
Interest expense		$ 200
($1,000 premium ÷ 5 years)		

SUE'S BOOKS

July 1		
Cash	$ 500	
Interest income		$ 500
($10,000 par × 10% × 1/2 year)		

December 31		
Interest receivable	$ 500	
Interest income		$ 500
($10,000 par × 10% × 1/2 year)		

December 31		
Investment in Pam bonds	$ 100	
Interest income		$ 100
($500 discount ÷ 5 years)		

At December 31, 20X4, after the foregoing entries are posted, the ledgers of Pam and Sue show the following balances:

Pam's Books

10% bonds payable	$100,000
Premium on bonds	800
Interest expense	9,800

Sue's Books

Investment in Pam bonds	$ 9,600
Interest income	1,100

The difference between the bond investment ($9,600) and 10% of Pam's bond liability ($10,080) is now $480 rather than $600. The reason is that there has been a piecemeal realization and recognition of the constructive gain on the separate books of Pam and Sue. This piecemeal recognition occurred during 20X4 as Pam amortized $20 premium and Sue amortized $100 discount on bonds that were constructively retired on January 1, 20X4. This difference is reflected in interest expense and interest income accounts relating to the constructively retired bonds. That is, interest income of $1,100 less 10% of $9,800 interest expense equals $120, or 20% of the original constructive gain. The working paper entries to eliminate reciprocal bond accounts at December 31, 20X4 are:

10% bonds payable	$10,000	
Premium on bonds	80	
Investment in Pam bonds		$9,600
Gain on retirement of bonds		480
Interest income	$ 1,100	
Interest expense		$ 980
Gain on retirement of bonds		120
Interest payable	$ 500	
Interest receivable		$ 500

Because 20X4 is the year in which the bonds are constructively retired, the combined gain that is entered by these working paper entries is $600, the original gain. If the working paper entries were combined, the gain would appear as a single amount. Note that the amount of piecemeal recognition of a constructive gain or loss is always the difference between the intercompany interest expense and interest income amounts that are eliminated. The fact that the piecemeal recognition was 20% of the $600 gain is the result of straight-line amortization, a relationship that would not hold under the effective interest method.

Separate company financial statements for Pam and Sue are included in the first two columns of the consolidation working papers in Exhibit 7–1. Except for the investment in Sue and the income from Sue accounts, the amounts shown reflect all previous assumptions and computations.

Pam's investment income of $2,020 is computed:

70% of Sue's reported income of $2,200	$1,540
Add: Constructive gain on bonds	600
	2,140
Less: Piecemeal recognition of constructive gain	
($600 ÷ 5 years)	120
Income from Sue	$2,020

Separate entries on the books of Pam to record the investment income from Sue under a one-line consolidation are:

Investment in Sue	$1,540	
Income from Sue		$1,540

To record investment income from Sue ($2,200 × 70%).

Investment in Sue	$ 600	
Income from Sue		$ 600

To adjust income from Sue for 100% of the $600 constructive gain on bonds.

Income from Sue	$ 120	
Investment in Sue		$ 120

To adjust income from Sue for the piecemeal recognition of the constructive gain on bonds that occurred during 20X4. (Either $600 gain ÷ 5 years or $1,100 interest income − $980 interest expense.)

PAM CORPORATION AND SUBSIDIARY
CONSOLIDATION WORKING PAPERS
FOR THE YEAR ENDED DECEMBER 31, 20X4

	Pam	70% Sue	Adjustments and Eliminations		Minority Interest	Consolidated Statements
Income Statement						
Sales	$ 40,000	$ 20,000				$ 60,000
Income from Sue	2,020		c	2,020		
Gain on retirement of bonds			a	480		600
			b	120		
Interest income		1,100	b	1,100		
Expenses including cost of sales	(19,100)	(18,900)				(38,000)
Interest expense	(9,800)		b	980		(8,820)
Minority interest income ($2,200 × 30%)					$ 660	(660)
Net income	$ 13,120	$ 2,200				$ 13,120
Retained Earnings						
Retained earnings—Pam	$ 49,000					$ 49,000
Retained earnings—Sue		$ 40,000	d 40,000			
Add: Net income	13,120√	2,200√				13,120
Retained earnings December 31, 20X4	$ 62,120	$ 42,200				$ 62,120
Balance Sheet						
Other assets	$398,800	$191,000				$589,800
Interest receivable		500	e	500		
Investment in Sue	65,020		c	2,020		
			d	63,000		
Investment in Pam bonds		9,600	a	9,600		
	$463,820	$201,100				$589,800
Other liabilities	$ 95,900	$108,900				$204,800
Interest payable	5,000		e	500		4,500
10% bonds payable	100,000		a 10,000			90,000
Premium on bonds	800		a	80		720
Common stock	200,000	50,000	d 50,000			200,000
Retained earnings	62,120√	42,200√				62,120
	$463,820	$201,100				
Minority interest January 1, 20X4			d 27,000		27,000	
Minority interest December 31, 20X4					$27,660	27,660
						$589,800

Exhibit 7–1 Parent Company Bonds Held by Subsidiary

The $600 constructive gain is added to Pam's share of the reported income of Sue because it is realized from the consolidated viewpoint. This constructive gain is recognized on the separate books of the affiliated companies as they continue to account for the $10,000 par of bonds deemed to be constructively retired on January 1, 20X4.

Pam's investment income for 20X4 is increased by $480 from the constructive retirement of the bonds ($600 constructive gain less $120 piecemeal recognition of the gain). In the years 20X5, 20X6, 20X7, and 20X8, Pam's investment income will be reduced $120 each year as the constructive gain is recognized on the separate books of Pam and Sue. In other words, in addition to recording its share of the reported income of Sue in each of these four years, Pam makes the following entry to adjust its income from Sue for the piecemeal recognition of the constructive gain:

Income from Sue	$120	
Investment in Sue		$120

At January 1, 20X9, the maturity date of the bonds, the full amount of the constructive gain will have been recognized, and Pam's investment in Sue account will be equal to 70% of the equity of Sue.

The working paper entries to consolidate the financial statements of Pam Corporation and Subsidiary for 20X4 (see Exhibit 7–1) are reproduced in general journal form:

a	10% bonds payable	$10,000		
	Premium on bonds	80		
	Gain on retirement of bonds		$ 480	
	Investment in Pam bonds		9,600	
	To enter gain and eliminate reciprocal bond investment and bond liability amounts.			
b	Interest income	$ 1,100		
	Interest expense		$ 980	
	Gain on retirement of bonds		120	
	To eliminate reciprocal interest income and interest expense amounts.			
c	Income from Sue	$ 2,020		
	Investment in Sue		$ 2,020	
	To establish reciprocity.			
d	Retained earnings—Sue	$40,000		
	Common stock—Sue	50,000		
	Investment in Sue		$63,000	
	Minority interest January 1, 20X4		27,000	
	To eliminate reciprocal investment and equity accounts and set up beginning minority interest.			
e	Interest payable	$ 500		
	Interest receivable		$ 500	
	To eliminate reciprocal interest payable and interest receivable amounts.			

The first working paper entry eliminates 10% of Pam's bond liability and Sue's bond investment and also enters $480 of the gain on retirement of bonds. This $480 is that part of the $600 constructive gain that has not been recognized on the separate books of Pam and Sue as of December 31, 20X4.

Reciprocal interest expense and interest income are eliminated in entry b. The difference between the interest expense and interest income amounts represents that part of the constructive gain that was recognized on the separate books of Pam and Sue through amortization in 20X4. This amount is $120 and, when credited to the gain on retirement of bonds, brings the gain up to the original $600. As mentioned earlier, if entries a and b had been combined, the constructive gain would have been entered in the working papers as one amount.

Working paper entry c eliminates investment income and adjusts the investment in Sue account to its beginning-of-the-period balance. Entry d eliminates Pam's investment in Sue, and the equity accounts of Sue, and establishes the beginning-of-the-period minority interest.

Entry e of the consolidation working papers eliminates reciprocal interest payable and interest receivable amounts on the intercompany bonds. This results in showing interest payable in the consolidated balance sheet at $4,500, the nominal interest payable for one-half year on the $90,000 par of bonds held outside of the consolidated entity. Note that minority interest computations in Exhibit 7–1 are not affected by the intercompany bond holdings. This is because Pam issued the bonds, and the full amount of the constructive gain is assigned to the issuing company.

Incomplete Equity and Cost Methods

If an incomplete equity method of accounting or the cost method had been used by Pam in accounting for its investment in Sue, Pam's separate financial statements would show balances that differ from those illustrated under the equity method as follows:

	Equity Method	Incomplete Equity Method	Cost Method
Income Statement			
Income from Sue	$ 2,020	$ 1,540	—
Pam's net income	13,120	12,640	$11,100
Retained Earnings			
Retained earnings January 1, 20X4	49,000	49,000	42,000
Net income	13,120	12,640	11,100
Retained earnings December 31, 20X4	62,120	61,640	53,100
Balance Sheet			
Investment in Sue	65,020	64,540	56,000
Retained earnings December 31, 20X4	62,120	61,640	53,100

Assuming that Pam has used an incomplete equity method of accounting for its investment in Sue and has not adjusted for the constructive gain, the following working paper entry would adjust Pam's accounts to the equity method:

Incomplete Equity Method		
Investment in Sue	$ 480	
Income from Sue		$ 480

The conversion entry that would be required if the cost method had been used would be as follows:

Cost Method		
Investment in Sue	$9,020	
Retained earnings January 1, 20X4		$7,000
Income from Sue		2,020

After the conversion entry (incomplete equity to equity or cost to equity) is entered in the working papers, all other working paper entries to consolidate the financial statements of Pam and Sue for 20X4 are the same as those illustrated in Exhibit 7–1 under the equity method.

Effect on Consolidated Statements in Subsequent Years

In subsequent years until the intercompany bonds are retired, Pam and Sue will continue to account for the bonds on their separate books—reporting interest expense (Pam) of $980 and interest income (Sue) of $1,100. The $120 difference is recognized

PAM'S BOOKS

	December 31,			
	20X5	20X6	20X7	20X8
Interest expense	$ 9,800	$ 9,800	$ 9,800	$ 9,800
Interest payable	5,000	5,000	5,000	5,000
Bonds payable	100,000	100,000	100,000	100,000
Premium on bonds	600	400	200	—

SUE'S BOOKS

	December 31,			
	20X5	20X6	20X7	20X8
Interest income	$1,100	$1,100	$1,100	$ 1,100
Interest receivable	500	500	500	500
Investment in Pam bonds	9,700	9,800	9,900	10,000

Exhibit 7–2   *Year-End Account Balances Relating to Intercompany Bonds*

on Pam's separate books as an adjustment of investment income. In consolidated financial statements for 20X5 through 20X8, all balances related to the intercompany bonds are eliminated. The year-end balances related to the intercompany bonds on the separate books of Pam and Sue are shown in Exhibit 7–2.

A single adjusting and eliminating entry in the consolidation working papers for 20X5 could be used for items relating to the intercompany bonds:

Interest income	$ 1,100	
Interest payable	500	
10% bonds payable	10,000	
Premium on bonds	60	
Interest expense		$ 980
Interest receivable		500
Investment in Pam bonds		9,700
Investment in Sue		480

This entry eliminates reciprocal interest income and interest expense amounts, reciprocal interest receivable and payable amounts, and reciprocal bond investment and bond liability amounts. The remaining difference of $480 is credited to the investment in Sue account to establish reciprocity between Pam's investment in Sue and the equity accounts of Sue at the beginning of 20X5. This is necessary because Pam increased its investment account in 20X4 when it adjusted its investment income account for the constructive gain. In other words, Pam's investment in Sue account exceeded its underlying book value in Sue by $480 at December 31, 20X4. The 20X5 working paper entry to adjust the investment in Sue account establishes reciprocity with the equity accounts of Sue and is entered in the consolidation working papers before reciprocal investment and equity amounts are eliminated.

Similar working paper adjustments are necessary in 20X6, 20X7, and 20X8. For example, the consolidation working paper credit to the investment in Sue account will be $360 in 20X6, $240 in 20X7, and $120 in 20X8.

SUBSIDIARY BONDS PURCHASED BY PARENT

The illustration in this section is similar to that for Pam and Sue, except that the subsidiary is the issuing affiliate and the constructive retirement of bonds results in a loss to the consolidated entity.

Pro Corporation owns a 90% interest in the voting common stock of Sky Corporation, having purchased its interest in Sky at its book value of $92,250 a number of years ago when Sky's capital stock was $100,000 and its retained earnings were $2,500. At December 31, 20X3, Sky had $100,000 par of 10% bonds outstanding with unamortized discount of $3,000. These bonds have interest payment dates of January 1 and July 1 and mature in five years, on January 1, 20X9.

On January 2, 20X4, Pro Corporation purchases 50% of Sky's outstanding bonds for $51,500 cash. This transaction results in a loss of $3,000 from the viewpoint of the consolidated entity because a liability of $48,500 (50% of $97,000 book value of the bonds) is constructively retired at a cost of $51,500. The loss is assigned to Sky Corporation under the theory that the management of the parent company acts as agent for Sky, the issuing company, in all intercompany bond transactions.

During 20X4, Sky records interest expense on the bonds of $10,600 [($100,000 par × 10%) + $600 discount amortization]. Of this interest expense, $5,300 relates to the intercompany bonds. Pro records interest income from its investment in bonds during 20X4 of $4,700 [($50,000 par × 10%) − $300 premium amortization]. The $600 difference between the interest expense and the interest income on the intercompany bonds reflects recognition of one-fifth of the constructive loss during 20X4. At December 31, 20X4, $2,400 of the constructive loss has not been recognized on the books of Pro and Sky through premium amortization (Pro's books) and discount amortization (Sky's books).

Equity Method

Sky reports net income of $7,500 for 20X4, and Pro computes its $4,590 income from Sky as follows:

90% of Sky's $7,500 reported income	$6,750
Deduct: $3,000 constructive loss × 90%	(2,700)
Add: $600 recognition of constructive loss × 90%	540
Investment income from Sky	$4,590

The journal entries that Pro makes to account for its investment in Sky during 20X4 are:

December 31, 20X4

Investment in Sky	$6,750	
Income from Sky		$6,750

    To record 90% of Sky's reported income for 20X4.

December 31, 20X4

Income from Sky	$2,700	
Investment in Sky		$2,700

    To adjust investment income from Sky for 90% of the loss on the constructive retirement of Sky's bonds. (This entry could be made on January 1, 20X4.)

December 31, 20X4

Investment in Sky	$ 540	
Income from Sky		$ 540

    To adjust investment income from Sky for 90% of the $600 piecemeal recognition of the constructive loss on Sky bonds during 20X4.

In future years until the bonds mature, Pro's income from Sky should be computed by adding $540 annually to its share of the reported income of Sky.

Pro Corporation's investment in Sky account at December 31, 20X4 has a balance of $105,840. This balance is equal to the underlying book value of Pro's investment in Sky at January 1, 20X4 plus $4,590 investment income from Sky for 20X4:

Investment in Sky January 1, 20X4 ($112,500 × 90%)	$101,250
Add: Income from Sky	4,590
Investment in Sky December 31, 20X4	$105,840

PRO CORPORATION AND SUBSIDIARY
CONSOLIDATION WORKING PAPERS
FOR THE YEAR ENDED DECEMBER 31, 20X4

	Pro	90% Sky	Adjustments and Eliminations		Minority Interest	Consolidated Statements
Income Statement						
Sales	$257,500	$142,500				$400,000
Income from Sky	4,590		c	4,590		
Interest income	4,700		b	4,700		
Expenses including cost of sales	(216,790)	(124,400)				(341,190)
Interest expense		(10,600)		b 5,300		(5,300)
Loss on retirement of bonds			a	2,400		(3,000)
			b	600		
Minority interest income					$ 510	(510)
Net income	$ 50,000	$ 7,500				$ 50,000
Retained Earnings						
Retained earnings—Pro	$130,000					$130,000
Retained earnings—Sky		$ 12,500	d	12,500		
Add: Net income	50,000√	7,500√				50,000
Retained earnings December 31, 20X4	$180,000	$ 20,000				$180,000
Balance Sheet						
Other assets	$340,460	$250,000				$590,460
Interest receivable	2,500			e 2,500		
Investment in Sky	105,840			c 4,590		
				d 101,250		
Investment in Sky bonds	51,200			a 51,200		
	$500,000	$250,000				$590,460
Other liabilities	$120,000	$ 27,400				$147,400
Interest payable		5,000	e	2,500		2,500
10% bonds payable		100,000	a	50,000		50,000
Discount on bonds		(2,400)		a 1,200		(1,200)
Capital stock	200,000	100,000	d 100,000			200,000
Retained earnings	180,000√	20,000√				180,000
	$500,000	$250,000				
Minority interest January 1, 20X4				d 11,250	11,250	
Minority interest December 31, 20X4					$11,760	11,760
						$590,460

Exhibit 7–3   *Subsidiary Bonds Held by Parent*

Consolidated financial statement working papers for Pro Corporation and Subsidiary are presented in Exhibit 7–3. The constructive loss of $3,000 on the intercompany bonds appears in the consolidated income statement for 20X4. Because $50,000 par of Sky bonds have been constructively retired, the consolidated balance sheet shows bonds payable of $50,000 and discount on bonds of $1,200 related to the bonds held outside of the consolidated entity.

Effect of Constructive Loss on Minority Interest Income and Consolidated Net Income
The minority interest income for 20X4 is $510 [($7,500 − $3,000 + $600) × 10%]. The constructive loss is assigned to Sky, so the minority interest is charged for 10% of the $3,000 constructive loss and credited for 10% of the $600 piecemeal recognition of the constructive loss during 20X4. Accordingly, minority interest income for 20X4 is 10% of Sky's $5,100 realized income, and *not* 10% of Sky's $7,500 reported net income.

The effect of the constructive loss is to reduce consolidated net income for 20X4 by $2,160. This reduction is reflected in the consolidated income statement through the inclusion of the $3,000 loss on the constructive retirement of the bonds, through the elimination of interest income of $4,700 and interest expense of $5,300, and through the reduction of minority interest income by $240 (from $750 based on reported net income of Sky to $510 minority interest income for the year). The effect can be analyzed as follows:

Consolidated Net Income—20X4

Decreased by:	
Constructive loss	$3,000
Elimination of interest income	4,700
Total decreases	$7,700
Increased by:	
Elimination of interest expense	$5,300
Reduction of minority interest income ($750 − $510)	240
Total increases	$5,540
Effect on consolidated net income for 20X4	$2,160

Observe that the reduction of minority interest income is similar to the reduction of expenses. A decrease in minority interest income increases consolidated net income and vice versa.

Consolidation Working Paper Entries   The entries shown in the consolidation working papers of Exhibit 7–3 are similar to those in the Pam/Sue illustration in Exhibit 7–1 except for amounts and the shift to a constructive loss situation. As in the previous illustration, working papers entries a and b are separated for illustrative purposes, but they could have been combined into a single entry as follows:

Loss on retirement of bonds	$ 3,000	
Interest income	4,700	
10% bonds payable	50,000	
Discount on bonds		$ 1,200
Investment in Sky bonds		51,200
Interest expense		5,300

Incomplete Equity and Cost Methods

If Pro had used an incomplete equity method or the cost method in accounting for its investment in Sky, its separate financial statements for 20X4 would contain amounts that differ from those under the equity method as follows:

	Equity Method	Incomplete Equity Method	Cost Method
Income Statement			
Income from Sky	$ 4,590	$ 6,750	—
Pro's net income	50,000	52,160	$ 45,410
			(Continued)

	Equity Method	Incomplete Equity Method	Cost Method
Retained Earnings			
Retained earnings January 1	130,000	130,000	121,000
Net income	50,000	52,160	45,410
Retained earnings December 31	180,000	182,160	166,410
Balance Sheet			
Investment in Sky	105,840	108,000	92,250
Retained earnings December 31	180,000	182,160	166,410

An entry in the consolidation working papers to convert from an incomplete equity to the equity method of accounting for 20X4 would be as follows:

Income from Sky	$ 2,160	
Investment in Sky		$ 2,160

The only difference between the incomplete and complete equity methods lies in the constructive gain, so the conversion entry only affects the year 20X4. The amount is 90% of the $3,000 constructive loss less 90% of the $600 piecemeal recognition of the loss.

If the cost method had been used by Pro, the cost-to-equity working paper conversion for the 20X4 consolidation would be:

Investment in Sky	$13,590	
Income from Sky		$ 4,590
Retained earnings January 1		9,000

When the conversion entry under the incomplete equity method or the cost method is entered in the working papers, the adjusted amounts of Pro will reflect the equity method of accounting as a one-line consolidation. Subsequently, the remaining working paper entries to consolidate the statements of Pro and Sky will be the same as those illustrated in Exhibit 7–3 under the equity method.

Effect on Consolidated Statements in Subsequent Years

The loss on the retirement of bonds only appears in the consolidated income statement in the year in which the bonds are constructively retired. In subsequent years, the portion of the constructive loss that has not been recognized through premium and discount amortization on the separate books of Pro and Sky will be allocated between the investment account (the majority interest) and minority interest. For example, the combined working paper entry to eliminate the bond investment and bonds payable and the interest income and interest expense amounts in 20X5 would be as follows:

Investment in Sky	$ 2,160	
Minority interest—beginning	240	
Interest income	4,700	
10% bonds payable	50,000	
Discount on bonds		$ 900
Investment in Sky bonds		50,900
Interest expense		5,300

The allocation of the unrecognized loss between the investment in Sky ($2,160) and minority interest ($240) in the entry is dictated by the assignment of the constructive loss to Sky. The loss is a subsidiary loss, so minority interest must share in the loss.

In computing minority interest for 20X5, 10% of the $600 constructive loss recognized in 20X5 is added to the minority interest share of income reported by Sky. This adjustment of minority interest income is required each year through 20X8. By December 31, 20X8, the bond investment will have been reduced to $50,000 through premium amortization, and the intercompany bond liability will have been increased to $50,000 through discount amortization.

The effect of the intercompany bond holdings on consolidated net income for 20X5 through 20X8 is to increase consolidated net income by $540 each year. Under the equity method of accounting, Pro's income from Sky and net income will also be increased by $540 in each of the years. Computations showing the effect on consolidated net income for the years 20X5 through 20X8 follow:

Consolidated Net Income—20X5 Through 20X8

Increased by:
Elimination of interest expense $5,300

Decreased by:
Elimination of interest income $4,700
Increase in minority interest income
    ($600 piecemeal recognition × 10%)   60
        Total decreases $4,760
Annual effect on consolidated net income $ 540

Exhibit 7–4 summarizes the intercompany bond account balances that appear on the separate books of Pro and Sky at year-end 20X5 through 20X8. The exhibit

SUMMARY OF INTERCOMPANY BOND ACCOUNT BALANCES ON SEPARATE BOOKS

December 31,	20X5	20X6	20X7	20X8
Pro's Books				
Investment in Sky bonds	$ 50,900	$ 50,600	$ 50,300	$ 50,000
Interest income	4,700	4,700	4,700	4,700
Interest receivable	2,500	2,500	2,500	2,500
Sky's Books				
10% bonds payable	$100,000	$100,000	$100,000	$100,000
Discount on bonds	1,800	1,200	600	—
Interest expense	10,600	10,600	10,600	10,600
Interest payable	5,000	5,000	5,000	5,000

SUMMARY OF CONSOLIDATION WORKING PAPER ADJUSTMENTS

December 31,	20X5	20X6	20X7	20X8
Debits				
Investment in Sky (90%)*	$ 2,160	$ 1,620	$ 1,080	$ 540
Minority interest (10%)*	240	180	120	60
Interest income	4,700	4,700	4,700	4,700
10% bonds payable†	50,000	50,000	50,000	50,000
Interest payable	2,500	2,500	2,500	2,500
Credits				
Discounts on bonds†	$ 900	$ 600	$ 300	$ —
Investment in Sky bonds	50,900	50,600	50,300	50,000
Interest expense†	5,300	5,300	5,300	5,300
Interest receivable	2,500	2,500	2,500	2,500

*The unrecognized portion of the constructive loss at the beginning of the year is charged 90% to the investment in Sky account and 10% to minority interest.

†Elimination of 50% of Sky's bonds, 50% of the unamortized discount on the bonds, and 50% of the current interest expense on the bonds.

Exhibit 7–4 *Subsidiary Bonds Held by Parent—Years Subsequent to Year of Intercompany Purchase*

PIMA CORPORATION AND SUBSIDIARY
CONSOLIDATION WORKING PAPERS
FOR THE YEAR ENDED DECEMBER 31, 20X5

	Pima	80% Sioux	Adjustments and Eliminations		Minority Interest	Consolidated Statements
Income Statement						
Sales	$200,000	$ 99,150				$299,150
Income from Sioux	23,900		b 23,900			
Interest income		850	a 850			
Interest expense	(1,000)			a 750		(250)
Other expenses	(142,900)	(70,000)				(212,900)
Minority interest income					$ 6,000	(6,000)
Net income	$ 80,000	$ 30,000				$ 80,000
Retained Earnings						
Retained earnings—Pima	$100,000					$100,000
Retained earnings—Sioux		$ 55,000	c 55,000			
Net income	80,000√	30,000√				80,000
Dividends	(60,000)	(20,000)		b 16,000	(4,000)	(60,000)
Retained earnings December 31, 20X5	$120,000	$ 65,000				$120,000
Balance Sheet						
Investment in Sioux	$132,400		a 500 b 7,900 c 124,000			
Bond investment—Pima		$ 7,100	a 7,100			
Other assets	367,600	172,900				$540,500
	$500,000	$180,000				$540,500
10% bonds payable	$ 10,000		a 7,500			$ 2,500
Other liabilities	170,000	$ 15,000				185,000
Capital stock	200,000	100,000	c 100,000			200,000
Retained earnings	120,000√	65,000√				120,000
	$500,000	$180,000				
Minority interest January 1, 20X5				c 31,000	31,000	
Minority interest December 31, 20X5					$33,000	33,000
						$540,500

Exhibit 7–5 *Intercompany Bonds After Acquisition—Equity Method*

also summarizes the consolidation working paper adjustments that are required to consolidate the financial statements of Pro and Sky for years subsequent to the year of intercompany purchase of Sky bonds. Because the investment in Sky account is involved, the working paper entries shown in Exhibit 7–4 are made before reciprocal investment and subsidiary equity amounts are eliminated.

The working paper entries shown in Exhibit 7–4 eliminate those amounts that would have been eliminated from the separate statements of Pro and Sky if the bonds had in fact been retired in 20X4. The objective is to produce the consolidated financial statements as they would have appeared if Sky had purchased and retired its own bonds.

CONSOLIDATION IN YEARS AFTER INTERCOMPANY BOND PURCHASE UNDER DIFFERENT ASSUMPTIONS

This section illustrates consolidation procedures in years after an intercompany bond purchase under several different parent company accounting assumptions. The first consolidation working paper (Exhibit 7–5) shows consolidation when the parent has accounted for its subsidiary by the equity method. The next two working paper exhibits show consolidation procedures when an incomplete equity method and a cost method of accounting are used and a conversion to equity is the first step in the working papers. This is followed with the same example using the traditional approach to consolidation working papers under an incomplete equity and a cost method of accounting.

Pima Corporation acquired an 80% interest in Sioux Corporation on January 1, 20X4 at its book value of $120,000, when the stockholders' equity of Sioux consisted of $100,000 common stock and $50,000 retained earnings. The only intercompany transactions between the two companies occurred on December 31, 20X4, when Sioux purchased 75% of Pima's $10,000 par, 10% outstanding bonds for $7,000. These bonds were issued at par and mature in five years on December 31, 20X9. During 20X4, Sioux reported net income of $25,000 and paid $20,000 dividends. Comparisons of Pima's income from Sioux for 20X4 and its investment in Sioux at December 31, 20X4 under the equity, incomplete equity, and cost methods of accounting are as follows:

	Equity Method	Incomplete Equity Method	Cost Method
Income (dividends) from Sioux	$ 20,500	$ 20,000	$ 16,000
Investment in Sioux 80%	124,500	124,000	120,000

The $500 differences in Pima's income and investment in Sioux amounts under the equity and incomplete equity methods are due to the $500 constructive gain on the intercompany purchase of bonds [($10,000 × 75%) − $7,000]. Pima's bonds were constructively retired, so no part of the gain is allocated to minority interests. Pima's dividend income under the cost method differs from income from Sioux under the incomplete equity method by $4,000, or 80% of Sioux's $5,000 undistributed income from 20X4. Under the cost method, Pima's investment in Sioux remains at its $120,000 cost on January 1, 20X4.

During 20X5, Sioux reported $30,000 net income and paid $20,000 dividends, and the only intercompany transactions between Pima and Sioux relate to the $750 interest ($10,000 par × 10% interest × 75% owned) that Pima paid to Sioux and the $16,000 dividends that Sioux paid to Pima. Pima's total interest expense for 20X5 is $1,000, and Sioux's interest income is $850, consisting of $750 nominal interest plus $100 discount amortization. The changes in Pima's investment in Sioux from acquisition to December 31, 20X5 are compared under the equity, incomplete equity, and cost methods of parent company accounting as follows:

	Equity Method	Incomplete Equity Method	Cost Method
Investment balance January 1, 20X4	$120,000	$120,000	$120,000
Income from Sioux—20X4	20,500	20,000	—
Dividends received	(16,000)	(16,000)	—
Investment balance December 31, 20X4	124,500	124,000	120,000
Income from Sioux—20X5:			
Equity in Sioux's income	24,000	24,000	—
Piecemeal recognition of gain on bonds	(100)	—	—
Dividends	(16,000)	(16,000)	—
Investment balance December 31, 20X5	$132,400	$132,000	$120,000

This information is reflected in comparative consolidation working papers for Pima and Sioux for 20X5 in Exhibit 7–5 for the equity method, Exhibit 7–6 for the incomplete equity method, and Exhibit 7–7 for the cost method. Under the equity method of consolidation illustrated in Exhibit 7–5, Pima's net income of $80,000 is equal to consolidated net income, and its beginning and ending retained earnings are equal to the respective consolidated retained earnings amounts. The first working paper entry in Exhibit 7–5 eliminates intercompany interest income and interest expense amounts, and intercompany bond investment and bond liability amounts, and credits the investment in Sioux for the $500 constructive gain that had not been recognized on the separate books of Pima and Sioux at the beginning of the period.

a	Interest income	$ 850	
	10% bonds payable	7,500	
	Interest expense		$ 750
	Bond investment—Pima		7,100
	Investment in Sioux 80%		500

The second working paper entry in Exhibit 7–5 eliminates the income from Sioux and 80% of dividends paid by Sioux and returns the investment in Sioux to its beginning-of-the-period amount:

b	Income from Sioux	$ 23,900	
	Dividends		$ 16,000
	Investment in Sioux 80%		7,900

The last working paper entry eliminates reciprocal investment and equity amounts and enters beginning minority interest.

c	Common stock—Sioux	$100,000	
	Retained earnings—Sioux	55,000	
	Investment in Sioux 80%		$124,000
	Minority interest		31,000

Conversion to Equity Approach   These three working paper entries are also used in consolidating the financial statements of Pima and Sioux under an incomplete equity method (Exhibit 7–6) and the cost method (Exhibit 7–7) after an initial conversion to equity entry is entered in the working papers. The working paper entry in Exhibit 7–6 to convert from an incomplete equity to the equity method is as follows:

a	Income from Sioux	$ 100	
	Investment in Sioux 80%	400	
	Retained earnings—Pima		$ 500

PIMA CORPORATION AND SUBSIDIARY
CONSOLIDATION WORKING PAPERS
FOR THE YEAR ENDED DECEMBER 31, 20X5

	Pima	80% Sioux	Adjustments and Eliminations		Minority Interest	Consolidated Statements
Income Statement						
Sales	$200,000	$ 99,150				$299,150
Income from Sioux	24,000		a	100		
			c	23,900		
Interest income		850	b	850		
Interest expense	(1,000)			b 750		(250)
Other expenses	(142,900)	(70,000)				(212,900)
Minority interest income					$ 6,000	(6,000)
Net income	$ 80,100	$ 30,000				$ 80,000
Retained Earnings						
Retained earnings—Pima	$ 99,500			a 500		$100,000
Retained earnings—Sioux		$ 55,000	d 55,000			
Net income	80,100√	30,000√				80,000
Dividends	(60,000)	(20,000)		c 16,000	(4,000)	(60,000)
Retained earnings December 31, 20X5	$119,600	$ 65,000				$120,000
Balance Sheet						
Investment in Sioux	$132,000			b 500		
			a 400	c 7,900		
				d 124,000		
Bond investment—Pima		$ 7,100		b 7,100		
Other assets	367,600	172,900				$540,500
	$499,600	$180,000				$540,500
10% bonds payable	$ 10,000		b	7,500		$ 2,500
Other liabilities	170,000	$ 15,000				185,000
Capital stock	200,000	100,000	d 100,000			200,000
Retained earnings	119,600√	65,000√				120,000
	$499,600	$180,000				
Minority interest January 1, 20X5				d 31,000	31,000	
Minority interest December 31, 20X5					$33,000	33,000
						$540,500

Exhibit 7–6 *Intercompany Bonds After Acquisition—Incomplete Equity Method*

PIMA CORPORATION AND SUBSIDIARY
CONSOLIDATION WORKING PAPERS
FOR THE YEAR ENDED DECEMBER 31, 20X5

	Pima	80% Sioux	Adjustments and Eliminations		Minority Interest	Consolidated Statements
Income Statement						
Sales	$200,000	$ 99,150				$299,150
Dividend income	16,000		a 16,000			
Income from Sioux			c 23,900	a 23,900		
Interest income		850	b 850			
Interest expense	(1,000)			b 750		(250)
Other expenses	(142,900)	(70,000)				(212,900)
Minority interest income					$ 6,000	(6,000)
Net income	$ 72,100	$ 30,000				$ 80,000
Retained Earnings						
Retained earnings—Pima	$ 95,500			a 4,500		$100,000
Retained earnings—Sioux		$ 55,000	d 55,000			
Net income	72,100√	30,000√				80,000
Dividends	(60,000)	(20,000)		c 16,000	(4,000)	(60,000)
Retained earnings December 31, 20X5	$107,600	$ 65,000				$120,000
Balance Sheet						
Investment in Sioux	$120,000		a 12,400	b 500 c 7,900 d 124,000		
Bond investment—Pima		$ 7,100		b 7,100		
Other assets	367,600	172,900				$540,500
	$487,600	$180,000				$540,500
10% bonds payable	$ 10,000		b 7,500			$ 2,500
Other liabilities	170,000	$ 15,000				185,000
Capital stock	200,000	100,000	d 100,000			200,000
Retained earnings	107,600√	65,000√				120,000
	$487,600	$180,000				
Minority interest January 1, 20X5				d 31,000	31,000	
Minority interest December 31, 20X5					$33,000	33,000
						$540,500

Exhibit 7–7 *Intercompany Bonds After Acquisition—Cost Method*

This working paper entry corrects Pima's beginning retained earnings for the $500 constructive gain that was not recorded under an incomplete equity method, and it adjusts income from Sioux for the $100 piecemeal recognition of the constructive gain that was not charged to investment income under the incomplete equity method. The $400 debit to investment in Sioux corrects that account for the constructive gain for 20X4, less piecemeal recognition for 20X5, neither of which was recorded under the incomplete equity method. The other working paper entries in Exhibit 7–6 are the same as those illustrated for the equity method.

The consolidation illustrated in Exhibit 7–7 assumes that Pima uses the cost method in accounting for its investment in Sioux and that the balance of its investment in Sioux account is equal to the $120,000 cost at January 1, 20X4. Entry a in the working papers of Exhibit 7–7 converts the accounts of Pima to an equity basis for working paper purposes.

a	Dividend income	$16,000	
	Investment in Sioux 80%	12,400	
	Income from Sioux		$23,900
	Retained earnings—Pima (beginning)		4,500

A cost-equity conversion schedule is probably the best explanation of this working paper entry. After the conversion entry is entered in the working papers of Exhibit 7–7, the other working paper entries are the same as if the equity method had been used. Pima could also convert its separate accounts to the equity method by entering an equivalent entry before closing its books for 20X5. The conversion schedule is as follows:

	Pima's Beginning Retained Earnings	Investment in Sioux	Income from Sioux	Dividend Income
Prior Year's Effect				
80% of $5,000 undistributed income from 20X4	$4,000	$ 4,000		
Constructive gain for 20X4	500	500		
Current Year's Effect				
Reclassify dividend income as investment decrease		(16,000)		$(16,000)
80% share of Sioux's $30,000 net income		24,000	$24,000	
Piecemeal recognition of gain ($500 ÷ 5 years, or $850 interest income − $750 interest expense)		(100)	(100)	
Conversion entry amounts	$4,500	$12,400	$23,900	$(16,000)

Traditional Approach The financial statements of Pima and Sioux can be consolidated without an initial conversion to equity. Procedures under the traditional approach are shown in the next two exhibits. Working papers for an incomplete equity method under the traditional approach are presented in Exhibit 7–8.

If Pima has accounted for its investment in Sioux using an incomplete equity method as shown in Exhibit 7–8, the financial statements can be consolidated using the following set of working paper entries:

a	10% bonds payable	$ 7,500	
	Bond investment—Pima		$ 7,100
	Retained earnings—Pima January 1		400
	To eliminate intercompany bond investment and bond liability amounts and correct Pima's beginning-of-the-period retained earnings for the constructive gain.		

PIMA CORPORATION AND SUBSIDIARY
CONSOLIDATION WORKING PAPERS–NO CONVERSION TO EQUITY
FOR THE YEAR ENDED DECEMBER 31, 20X5

	Pima	80% Sioux	Adjustments and Eliminations		Minority Interest	Consolidated Statements
Income Statement						
Sales	$200,000	$ 99,150				$299,150
Income from Sioux	24,000		c 24,000			
Interest income		850	b 850			
Interest expense	(1,000)			b 750		(250)
Other expenses	(142,900)	(70,000)				(212,900)
Minority interest income					$ 6,000	(6,000)
Net income	$ 80,100	$ 30,000				$ 80,000
Retained Earnings						
Retained earnings—Pima	$ 99,500			a 400		
				b 100		$100,000
Retained earnings—Sioux		$ 55,000	d 55,000			
Net income	80,100√	30,000√				80,000
Dividends	(60,000)	(20,000)		c 16,000	(4,000)	(60,000)
Retained earnings December 31, 20X5	$119,600	$ 65,000				$120,000
Balance Sheet						
Investment in Sioux	$132,000			c 8,000		
				d 124,000		
Bond investment—Pima		$ 7,100		a 7,100		
Other assets	367,600	172,900				$540,500
	$499,600	$180,000				$540,500
10% bonds payable	$ 10,000		a 7,500			$ 2,500
Other liabilities	170,000	$ 15,000				185,000
Capital stock	200,000	100,000	d 100,000			200,000
Retained earnings	119,600√	65,000√				120,000
	$499,600	$180,000				
Minority interest January 1, 20X5				d 31,000	31,000	
Minority interest December 31, 20X5					$33,000	33,000
						$540,500

Exhibit 7–8 *Intercompany Bonds After Acquisition—Incomplete Equity Method (Traditional Approach)*

b	Interest income	$ 850		
	Interest expense		$ 750	
	Retained earnings		100	

To eliminate intercompany interest income and
expense and adjust for piecemeal recognition of
the constructive gain.

c	Income from Sioux	$ 24,000		
	Dividends		$ 16,000	
	Investment in Sioux		8,000	

To eliminate investment income (as recorded by Pima),
80% of Sioux's dividends, and return the investment
account to its beginning-of-the-period balance.

d	Retained earnings—Sioux	$ 55,000		
	Capital Stock—Sioux	100,000		
	Investment in Sioux		$124,000	
	Minority interest January 1		31,000	

To eliminate reciprocal investment and equity amounts
and enter beginning-of-the-period minority interest.

Now assume that Pima has used the cost method in accounting for its investment in Sioux, and that it consolidates the financial statements under the traditional approach without a conversion to equity. Working papers are presented in Exhibit 7–9.

The working paper entries from Exhibit 7–9 are reproduced for convenient reference as follows:

a	Investment in Sioux	$ 4,000		
	Retained earnings—Pima January 1		$ 4,000	

To take up 80% of Sioux's increase in stockholders'
equity between the date of acquisition and
the beginning of the current period.

b	10% bonds payable	$ 7,500		
	Bond investment—Pima		$ 7,100	
	Retained earnings—Pima January 1		400	

To eliminate intercompany bond investment and
bond liability amounts and increase Pima's
beginning-of-the-period retained earnings for
the constructive gain on the bonds.

c	Interest income	$ 850		
	Interest expense		$ 750	
	Retained earnings—Pima January 1		100	

To eliminate intercompany interest income and
expense and adjust for piecemeal recognition of
the constructive gain.

d	Dividend income	$ 16,000		
	Dividends		$ 16,000	

To eliminate dividend income and 80% of Sioux's
dividends.

e	Retained earnings—Sioux	$ 55,000		
	Capital stock—Sioux	100,000		
	Investment in Sioux		$124,000	
	Minority interest January 1		31,000	

To eliminate reciprocal investment and equity amounts
and enter beginning-of-the-period minority interest.

PIMA CORPORATION AND SUBSIDIARY CONSOLIDATION WORKING PAPERS—NO CONVERSION TO EQUITY FOR THE YEAR ENDED DECEMBER 31, 20X5

	Pima	80% Sioux	Adjustments and Eliminations		Minority Interest	Consolidated Statements
Income Statement Sales	$200,000	$ 99,150				$299,150
Dividend income	16,000		d 16,000			
Interest income		850	c 850			
Interest expense	(1,000)			c 750		(250)
Other expenses	(142,900)	(70,000)				(212,900)
Minority interest income					$ 6,000	(6,000)
Net income	$ 72,100	$ 30,000				$ 80,000
Retained Earnings Retained earnings—Pima	$ 95,500			a 4,000 b 400 c 100		$100,000
Retained earnings—Sioux		$ 55,000	e 55,000			
Net income	72,100√	30,000√				80,000
Dividends	(60,000)	(20,000)		d 16,000	(4,000)	(60,000)
Retained earnings December 31, 20X5	$107,600	$ 65,000				$120,000
Balance Sheet Investment in Sioux	$120,000		a 4,000	e 124,000		
Bond investment—Pima		$ 7,100		b 7,100		
Other assets	367,600	172,900				$540,500
	$487,600	$180,000				$540,500
10% bonds payable	$ 10,000		b 7,500			$ 2,500
Other liabilities	170,000	$ 15,000				185,000
Capital stock	200,000	100,000	e 100,000			200,000
Retained earnings	107,600√	65,000√				120,000
	$487,600	$180,000				
Minority interest January 1, 20X5				e 31,000	31,000	
Minority interest December 31, 20X5					$33,000	33,000
						$540,500

Exhibit 7–9   Intercompany Bonds After Acquisition—Cost Method (Traditional Approach)

SUMMARY

Transactions in which one corporation acquires the outstanding bonds of an affiliated company result in constructive gains and losses except when the bonds are purchased at their book value. Constructive gains and losses are realized from the viewpoint of the consolidated entity when the bonds are purchased by an affiliate, and they should be reflected in the income of the parent company and consolidated net income in the year of purchase. Gains and losses on parent company bonds are similar to unrealized gains and losses on downstream sales and do not require allocation between minority and majority interests. However, constructive gains and losses on bonds in which a subsidiary is the issuing entity should be allocated between minority interest and consolidated net income. Constructive gains or losses on intercompany bonds are recognized on the books of the purchasing and issuing corporations as they amortize differences between the book value and par value of bonds.

A summary illustration comparing the effect of constructive gains and losses from intercompany bond transactions on parent company and consolidated net incomes is presented in Exhibit 7–10.

Assumptions

1 Parent Company's income, excluding income from Subsidiary, was $100,000 for 20X6.
2 90% owned Subsidiary reported net income of $50,000 for 20X6.
3 $100,000 of 10% bonds payable are outstanding with $6,000 unamortized premium as of January 1, 20X6.
4 $50,000 par of the bonds were purchased for $51,500 on January 2, 20X6.
5 The bonds mature on January 1, 20X9.

	S Acquires P's Bonds (similar to downstream)	P Acquires S's Bonds (similar to upstream)
P's Net Income—Equity Method		
P's separate income	$100,000	$100,000
P's share of S's reported net income	45,000	45,000
Add: Constructive gain on bonds		
($53,000 − $51,500) × 100%	1,500	
($53,000 − $51,500) × 90%		1,350
Deduct: Piecemeal recognition of constructive gain		
($1,500 gain ÷ 3 years) × 100%	(500)	
($1,500 gain ÷ 3 years) × 90%		(450)
P's net income	$146,000	$145,900
Consolidated Net Income		
P's separate income plus S's net income	$150,000	$150,000
Add: Constructive gain on bonds	1,500	1,500
Eliminate: Interest expense (increase)	4,000	4,000
Interest income (decrease)	(4,500)	(4,500)
Total realized income	151,000	151,000
Less: Minority interest income		
($50,000 × 10%)	(5,000)	
($50,000 + $1,500 − $500) × 10%		(5,100)
Consolidated net income	$146,000	$145,900

P's net income and consolidated net income of $146,000 when S acquires P's bonds are the same as if the bonds had actually been retired by P at the end of 20X6. In that case, P's separate income would have been $101,000 ($100,000 plus $1,000 constructive gain), and S's net income would have been unchanged. P's $101,000 plus P's $45,000 share of S's reported net income equals $146,000. An assumption of retirement at year-end is necessary because the interest expense of P and the interest income of S are both realized and recognized during 20X6. The amount of the gain is $1,000 ($1,500 less $500 realized and recognized during the current year).

P's net income and consolidated net income of $145,900 when P acquires S's bonds are the same as if the bonds had actually been retired by S at the end of 20X6. In that case, P's separate income would have been unchanged at $100,000, and S's reported net income would have been $51,000 ($50,000 plus $1,000 constructive gain). P's $100,000 separate income plus P's $45,900 share of S's reported income ($51,000 × 90%) equals $145,900. Again, the assumption of retirement at year-end is necessary because the interest income of P and the interest expense of S are realized and recognized during the current year.

Exhibit 7–10   *Summary Illustration—Constructive Gains and Losses on Intercompany Bonds*

ASSIGNMENT MATERIAL

QUESTIONS

1 What reciprocal accounts arise when one company borrows from an affiliated company?

2 Do direct lending and borrowing transactions between affiliated companies give rise to unrealized gains or losses? To unrecognized gains or losses?

3 What are constructive gains and losses? Describe a transaction involving a constructive gain.

4 A company has a $1,000,000 bond issue outstanding with unamortized premium of $10,000 and unamortized issuance cost of $5,300. What is the book value of its liability? If an affiliated company purchases half the bonds in the market at 98, what is the gain or loss? Is the gain or loss actual or constructive?

5 Compare a constructive gain on intercompany bonds with an unrealized gain on the intercompany sale of land.

6 Describe the process by which constructive gains on intercompany bonds are realized and recognized on the books of the separate affiliated companies. Does recognition of a constructive gain in consolidated financial statements precede or succeed recognition on the books of the affiliated companies?

7 If a subsidiary purchases parent company bonds at a price in excess of their recorded book value, is the gain or loss attributed to the parent company or the subsidiary? Explain.

8 The following information related to intercompany bond holdings was taken from the adjusted trial balances of a parent company and its 90%-owned subsidiary four years before the bond issue matured:

	Parent	Subsidiary
Investment in S bonds, $50,000 par	$49,000	
Interest receivable	2,500	
Interest expense		$ 9,000
10% bonds payable, $100,000 par		100,000
Bond premium		4,000
Interest income	5,250	
Interest payable		5,000

Construct the consolidation working paper entries necessary to eliminate reciprocal balances (a) assuming that the parent acquired its intercompany bond investment at the beginning of the current year, and (b) assuming that the parent company acquired its intercompany bond investment two years prior to the date of the adjusted trial balance.

9 Prepare a journal entry (or entries) to account for the parent company investment income for the current year if the reported income of its 80%-owned subsidiary is $50,000 and the consolidated entity has a $4,000 constructive gain from the subsidiary's acquisition of parent company bonds.

10 Calculate the parent company's income from its 75%-owned subsidiary if the reported net income of the subsidiary for the period is $100,000 and the consolidated entity has a constructive loss of $8,000 from the parent's acquisition of subsidiary bonds.

11 If a parent company reports interest expense of $4,300 with respect to bonds held intercompany and the subsidiary reports interest income of $4,500 for the same bonds, (a) was there a constructive gain or loss on the bonds? (b) is the gain or loss attributed to the parent company or the subsidiary? and (c) what does the $200 difference between interest income and interest expense represent?

12 How are intercompany receivables and payables of equity investees reported in parent company and consolidated financial statements?

EXERCISES

E 7-1   1 Which of the following is not a characteristic of a constructive retirement of bonds from an intercompany bond transaction?

a Bonds are retired for consolidated statement purposes only

b The reciprocal intercompany bond investment and bond liability amounts are eliminated in the consolidation process

c Any gain or loss from the intercompany bond transaction is recognized on the books of the issuing affiliate

d For consolidated statement purposes, the gain or loss on the constructive retirement of bonds is the difference between the book value of the bond liability and the purchase price of the bond investment

2 When bonds are purchased in the market by an affiliate, the book value of the intercompany bond liability is:

    a The par value of the bonds less unamortized issuance costs and less unamortized discount or plus unamortized premium

    b The par value of the bonds less issuance costs, less unamortized discount or plus unamortized premiums, and less the costs incurred to purchase the bond investment

    c The par value of the bonds

    d The par value of the bonds less the discount or plus the premium at the time of issuance

3 Constructive gains and losses:

    a Arise when one company purchases the bonds of an affiliate or lends money directly to the affiliate to repurchase its own bonds

    b Are realized gains and losses from the viewpoint of the issuing affiliate

    c Are always assigned to the parent company because its management makes the decisions for intercompany transactions

    d Are realized and recognized from the viewpoint of the consolidated entity

4 Straight-line interest amortization of bond premium and discounts is used as an expedient in this book. However, the effective interest rate method is generally required under GAAP. When using the effective interest rate method:

    a The amount of the piecemeal recognition of a constructive gain or loss is the difference between the intercompany interest expense and interest income that is eliminated

    b The piecemeal recognition of a constructive gain or loss is recorded in the separate accounts of the affiliated companies

    c No piecemeal recognition of the constructive gain or loss is required for consolidated statement purposes

    d The issuing and the purchasing affiliates do not amortize the discounts and premiums on their separate books because the bonds are retired

E 7-2 Showalter Corporation is a 70%-owned subsidiary of Pavone Corporation. On January 1, 20X3, Showalter purchased $600,000 par of Pavone's $900,000 outstanding bonds for $602,000 in the bond market. Pavone's bonds have an 8% interest rate, pay interest on January 1 and July 1, and mature on January 1, 20X7. There was $48,000 unamortized premium on the bond issue on January 1, 20X3. Assume straight-line amortization.

1 The constructive gain or loss that should appear in the consolidated income statement of Pavone Corporation and Subsidiary for 20X3 is:

    a $30,000 gain   **c** $2,000 loss

    b $46,000 gain   **d** $30,000 loss

2 Interest expense that should appear in the 20X3 consolidated income statement for Pavone's bond issue is:

    a $28,000   **c** $20,800

    b $24,000   **d** $20,000

E 7-3 Palmer Corporation's long-term debt on January 1, 20X5 consists of $400,000 par value of 10% bonds payable due on January 1, 20X9, with unamortized discount of $8,000. On January 2, 20X5, Scott Corporation, Palmer's 90%-owned subsidiary, purchased $80,000 par of Palmer's 10% bonds for $76,000. Interest payment dates are January 1 and July 1, and straight-line amortization is used.

1 On the consolidated income statement of Palmer Corporation and Subsidiary for 20X5, a gain or loss should be reported in the amount of:

    a $5,600   **c** $2,400

    b $4,000   **d** $2,000

2 Bonds payable of Palmer less unamortized discount appears in the consolidated balance sheet at December 31, 20X5 in the amount of:

    a $392,000   **c** $320,000

    b $394,000   **d** $315,200

3 The amount of the constructive gain or loss that is unrecognized on the separate books of Palmer and Scott at December 31, 20X5 is:

    a $2,400   **c** $1,800

    b $2,200   **d** 0

4 Interest expense on Palmer bonds appears in the consolidated income statement for 20X5 at:

    a $42,000   **c** $33,600

    b $40,000   **d** $32,000

5 Consolidated net income for 20X6 will be affected by the intercompany bond transactions as follows:

    a Increased by 100% of the constructive gain from 20X5

    b Decreased by 25% of the constructive gain from 20X5

    c Increased by 25% of the constructive loss from 20X5

    d Decreased by (25% × 90%) of the constructive loss from 20X5

E 7-4 Paul Corporation acquired an 80% interest in Sally Corporation on January 1, 20X1 for $400,000 in excess of book value and fair value. Paul amortizes goodwill over 10 years.

On January 1, 20X4, Paul had $1,000,000 par, 8% bonds outstanding with $40,000 unamortized discount. On this date, Sally purchased $400,000 par of Paul's bonds at par. The bonds mature on January 1, 20X8 and pay interest on January 1 and July 1.

Paul's separate income, not including investment income, for 20X4 is $800,000 and Sally's reported net income is $500,000.

Required: Determine the following:
1 Consolidated net income for Paul Corporation and Subsidiary for 20X4
2 Minority interest income for 20X4

E 7-5 Comparative income statements for Prim Corporation and its 100%-owned subsidiary, Saddie Corporation, for the year ended December 31, 20X9 are summarized as follows:

	Prim	Saddie
Sales	$1,000,000	$500,000
Income from Saddie	226,000	—
Bond interest income (includes discount amortization)	—	22,000
Cost of sales	(670,000)	(200,000)
Operating expenses	(150,000)	(100,000)
Bond interest expense	(50,000)	—
Net income	$ 356,000	$222,000

Prim purchased its interest in Saddie at book value on January 1, 20X1. On January 1, 20X2, Prim sold $500,000 par of 10%, 10-year bonds to the public at par value, and on January 1, 20X9, Saddie purchased $200,000 par of the bonds at 97. Both companies use straight-line amortization. There are no other intercompany transactions between the affiliated companies.

Required: Prepare a consolidated income statement for Prim Corporation and Subsidiary for the year ended December 31, 20X9.

E 7-6 On January 1, 20X1, Pike Corporation sold $200,000 par value of 8% bonds in the bond market for $208,000. The bonds have interest payment dates of January 1 and July 1 and mature in 10 years from date of issue.

Sack Corporation, Pike's 100% pooled subsidiary, purchased $100,000 par of Pike's 8% bonds in the bond market for $95,000 on January 1, 20X6. Both entities use straight-line amortization for bond investments and liabilities.

Comparative balance sheets for Pike and Sack corporations at December 31, 20X6 are summarized as follows:

	Pike	Sack
Assets		
Cash	$ 83,000	$ 25,000
Bond interest receivable	—	4,000
Other receivables	60,000	25,000
Inventories	120,000	70,000
Plant assets—net	250,000	180,000
Investment in Sack stock	385,600	—
Investment in Pike bonds	—	96,000
Total assets	$898,600	$400,000
Equities		
Accounts payable	$ 28,000	$ 20,000
Bond interest payable	8,000	—
8% bonds payable	200,000	—
Premium on bonds payable	3,200	—
Common stock $10 par	400,000	300,000
Retained earnings	259,400	80,000
Total equities	$898,600	$400,000

Required: Prepare a consolidated balance sheet for Pike Corporation and Subsidiary at December 31, 20X6.

E 7-7 Platt Corporation owns a 70% interest in Smedley Corporation acquired several years ago at book value equal to fair value. On January 1, 20X2, Smedley had outstanding $1,000,000 of 9% bonds with a book value of $990,000. On this date, Platt purchased $500,000 of Smedley's 9% bonds for $503,000. The bonds are due on January 1, 20X6 and pay interest on January 1 and July 1.

Required
1 Determine the gain or loss on the constructive retirement of Smedley bonds.
2 Smedley reports net income of $14,000 for 20X2. Determine Platt's income from Smedley.

E 7-8 Comparative balance sheets of Pitt Corporation and Slick Corporation at December 31, 20X4 follow:

	Pitt	Slick
Assets		
Accounts receivable—net	$ 1,024,300	$ 300,000
Interest receivable	10,000	—
Inventories	3,000,000	500,000
Other current assets	98,500	200,000
Plant assets—net	3,840,000	2,500,000
Investment in Slick stock	1,830,800	—
Investment in Slick bonds	196,400	—
Total assets	$10,000,000	$3,500,000
Liabilities and Stockholders' Equity		
Accounts payable	$ 400,000	$ 139,000
Interest payable	—	50,000
10% bonds payable	—	1,000,000
Premium on bonds payable	—	36,000
Capital stock	8,000,000	2,000,000
Retained earnings	1,600,000	275,000
Total equities	$10,000,000	$3,500,000

Pitt acquired 80% of Slick's capital stock for $1,660,000 on January 1, 20X2, when Slick's capital stock was $2,000,000 and its retained earnings was $75,000.

On January 1, 20X4, Pitt acquired $200,000 par of Slick 10% bonds in the bond market for $195,500, on which date the unamortized premium for bonds payable on Slick's books was $45,000. The bonds pay interest on January 1 and July 1 and mature on January 1, 20X9. (Assume straight-line amortization.)

1 The gain or loss on the constructive retirement of $200,000 of Slick bonds on January 1, 20X4 is reported in the 20X4 consolidated income statement in the amount of:
   a $13,500   c $10,500
   b $11,500   d $7,000
2 The portion of the constructive gain or loss on Slick bonds that remains unrecognized on the separate books of Pitt and Slick at December 31, 20X4 is:
   a $12,000   c $10,500
   b $10,800   d $9,200
3 Consolidated bonds payable at December 31, 20X4 should be reported at:
   a $1,036,000   c $828,800
   b $1,000,000   d $800,000

E 7-9 The consolidated balance sheet of Partie Corporation and Saydo Corporation (its 80%-owned subsidiary) at December 31, 20X1 includes the following items related to an 8%, $1,000,000 outstanding bond issue:

Current Liabilities	
Bond interest payable (6 months' interest due January 1, 20X2)	$ 40,000
Long-Term Liabilities	
8% bonds payable (maturity date January 1, 20X7)	$1,000,000
Less: Unamortized discount	30,000
Total long-term liabilities	$ 970,000

Partie Corporation is the issuing corporation and straight-line amortization is applicable. Saydo purchases $600,000 par of the outstanding bonds of Partie on July 1, 20X2 for $574,800.

Required
1 Calculate the following:
   a The gain or loss on constructive retirement of the bonds
   b The consolidated bond interest expense for 20X2
   c The consolidated bond liability at December 31, 20X2

2 How would the amounts determined in 1 be different if Partie had purchased Saydo's bonds?

E 7-10 The balance sheets of Picker Company and Skidden Corporation, an 80%-owned subsidiary of Picker, at December 31, 20X3 are as follows:

	Picker	Skidden
Assets		
Cash	$ 2,440,000	$2,500,000
Accounts receivable—net	3,000,000	300,000
Other current assets	8,000,000	1,200,000
Plant assets—net	15,000,000	5,500,000
Investment in Skidden	6,560,000	—
Total assets	$35,000,000	$9,500,000
Liabilities and Stockholders' Equity		
Accounts payable	$ 750,000	$ 230,000
Interest payable	250,000	50,000
10% bonds payable (due January 1, 20X9)	5,000,000	1,000,000
Discount on bonds payable	(100,000)	—
Premium on bonds payable	—	20,000
Capital stock	25,000,000	7,000,000
Retained earnings	4,100,000	1,200,000
Total liabilities and stockholders' equity	$35,000,000	$9,500,000

Required

1. Assume that Skidden purchases $2,000,000 par of Picker's bonds for $1,900,000 on January 2, 20X4 and that semiannual interest is paid on July 1 and January 1. Determine the amounts at which the following items should appear in the consolidated financial statements of Picker and Skidden at and for the year ended December 31, 20X4.
   a. Gain or loss on bond retirement
   b. Interest payable
   c. Bonds payable at par value
   d. Investment in Picker bonds
2. Disregard 1 above and assume that Picker purchases $1,000,000 par of Skidden's bonds for $1,030,000 on January 2, 20X4, and that semiannual interest on the bonds is paid on July 1 and January 1. Determine the amounts at which the following items will appear in the consolidated financial statements of Picker and Skidden at and for the year ended December 31, 20X4.
   a. Gain or loss on bond retirement
   b. Interest expense (assume straight-line amortization)
   c. Interest receivable
   d. Bonds payable at book value

E 7-11 Perdue Corporation has $2,000,000 of 12% bonds outstanding on December 31, 20X2 with unamortized premium of $60,000. These bonds pay interest semiannually on July 1 and January 1 and mature on January 1, 20X8.

On January 1, 20X3, Shelly Corporation, an 80%-owned subsidiary of Perdue, purchases $500,000 par of Perdue's outstanding bonds in the market for $490,000.

Additional Information

1. Perdue and Shelly use the straight-line method of amortization.
2. The financial statements are consolidated.
3. Perdue's bonds are the only outstanding bonds of the affiliated companies.
4. Shelly's net income for 20X3 is $200,000 and for 20X4, $300,000.

Required

1. Compute the constructive gain or loss that will appear in the consolidated income statement for 20X3.
2. Prepare a consolidation entry (entries) for 20X3 to eliminate the effect of the intercompany bondholdings.
3. Compute the amounts that will appear in the consolidated income statement for 20X4 for the following:
   a. Constructive gain or loss
   b. Minority interest income
   c. Bond interest expense
   d. Bond interest income

4 Compute the amounts that will appear in the consolidated balance sheet at December 31, 20X4 for the following:
   a Investment in Perdue bonds
   b Book value of bonds payable
   c Bond interest receivable
   d Bond interest payable

E 7-12 Comparative income statements for Parrish Corporation and its 80%-owned subsidiary, Sandwood Corporation, for the year ended December 31, 20X3 are summarized as follows:

	Parrish	Sandwood
Sales	$1,200,000	$600,000
Income from Sandwood	260,800	—
Bond interest income (includes discount amortization)	91,000	—
Cost of sales	(750,000)	(200,000)
Operating expenses	(200,000)	(200,000)
Bond interest expense	—	(60,000)
Net income	$ 601,800	$140,000

Parrish purchased its 80% interest in Sandwood at book value on January 1, 20X2, when Sandwood's assets and liabilities were equal to their fair values.

On January 1, 20X3, Parrish paid $783,000 to purchase all of Sandwood's $1,000,000, 6% outstanding bonds. The bonds were issued at par on January 1, 20X1, pay interest semiannually on June 30 and December 31, and mature on December 31, 20X9.

Required: Prepare a consolidated income statement for Parrish Corporation and Subsidiary for the year ended December 31, 20X3.

E 7-13 Public Corporation, which owns an 80% interest in Spede Corporation, purchases $100,000 of Spede Corporation 8% bonds at 106 on July 1, 20X6. The bonds pay interest on January 1 and July 1 and mature on July 1, 20X9. Public uses the equity method of accounting for its investment in Spede. Selected data from the December 31, 20X6 trial balances of the two companies are as follows:

	Public	Spede
Interest receivable	$ 4,000	$ —
Investment in Spede 8% bonds	105,000	—
Bond discount	—	15,000
Interest payable	—	40,000
8% bonds payable	—	1,000,000
Interest income	3,000	—
Interest expense	—	86,000
Gain or loss on intercompany bonds		

Required
   1 Determine the amounts for each of the foregoing items that will appear in the consolidated financial statements on or for the year ended December 31, 20X6.
   2 Prepare in general journal form the working paper adjustments and eliminations related to the foregoing bonds that are required to consolidate the financial statements of Public and Spede corporations for the year ended December 31, 20X6.
   3 Prepare in general journal form the working paper adjustments and eliminations related to the bonds that are required to consolidate the financial statements of Public and Spede corporations for the year ended December 31, 20X7.

E 7-14 Pappy Corporation acquired an 80% interest in Sonny Corporation at book value equal to fair value on January 1, 20X7, at which time Sonny's capital stock and retained earnings were $100,000 and $40,000, respectively. On January 1, 20X8, Sonny purchased $50,000 par of Pappy's 8%, $100,000 par bonds for $48,800 three years before maturity. Interest payment dates are January 1 and July 1. During 20X8, Sonny reports interest income of $4,400 in connection with the bonds and Pappy reports interest expense of $8,000.

Additional Information
   1 Pappy's separate income for 20X8 is $200,000.
   2 Sonny's net income for 20X8 is $50,000.
   3 Pappy accounts for its investment by the equity method.
   4 Straight-line amortization is applicable.

Required

    1 Determine the gain or loss on the bonds.
    2 Prepare the journal entries for Sonny to account for its bond investment during 20X8.
    3 Prepare the journal entries for Pappy to account for its bonds payable during 20X8.
    4 Prepare the journal entry for Pappy to account for its 80% investment in Sonny for 20X8.
    5 Calculate minority interest income and consolidated net income for 20X8.

PROBLEMS

P 7-1   Partial adjusted trial balances for Pongo Corporation and its 90%-owned subsidiary, Song Corporation, for the year ended December 31, 20X6 are as follows:

	Pongo Corporation Debit (Credit)	Song Corporation Debit (Credit)
Interest receivable	$ —	$ 1,000
Investment in Pongo bonds	—	52,700
Interest payable	(2,000)	—
8% bonds payable, due April 1, 20X9	(100,000)	—
Discount on bonds payable	1,800	—
Interest income	—	(2,100)
Interest expense	8,800	—

Song Corporation acquired $50,000 par of Pongo bonds on April 1, 20X6 for $53,600. The bonds pay interest on April 1 and October 1 and mature on April 1, 20X9.

Required

    1 Compute the gain or loss on the bonds that will appear in the 20X6 consolidated income statement.
    2 Determine the amounts of interest income and interest expense that will appear in the 20X6 consolidated income statement.
    3 Determine the amounts of interest receivable and interest payable that will appear in the December 31, 20X6 consolidated balance sheet.
    4 Prepare in general journal form the consolidation working paper entries needed to eliminate the effect of the intercompany bonds for 20X6.

P 7-2   Intercompany transactions between Pewter Corporation and Steel Corporation, its 80%-owned subsidiary, from January 20X1, when Pewter acquired its controlling interest, to December 31, 20X4 are summarized as follows:

    20X1   Pewter sold inventory items that cost $60,000 to Steel for $80,000. Steel sold $60,000 of these inventory items in 20X1 and $20,000 of them in 20X2.

    20X2   Pewter sold inventory items that cost $30,000 to Steel for $40,000. All of these items were sold by Steel during 20X3.

    20X3   Steel sold land with a book value of $40,000 to Pewter at its fair market value of $55,000. This land is to be used as a future plant site by Pewter.

    20X3   Pewter sold equipment with a four-year remaining useful life to Steel on January 1 for $80,000. This equipment had a book value of $50,000 at the time of sale and was still in use by Steel at December 31, 20X4.

    20X4   Steel purchased $100,000 par of Pewter's 10% bonds in the bond market for $106,000 on January 1, 20X4. These bonds had a book value of $98,000 when acquired by Steel and mature on January 1, 20X8.

The separate income of Pewter (does not include income from Steel) and the reported net income of Steel for the years 20X1 through 20X4 were:

	20X1	20X2	20X3	20X4
Separate income of Pewter	$500,000	$375,000	$460,000	$510,000
Net income of Steel	100,000	120,000	110,000	120,000

Required: Compute Pewter's net income (and consolidated net income) for each of the years 20X1 through 20X4. A schedule with columns for 20X1, 20X2, 20X3, and 20X4 is suggested as the most efficient approach for solution of this problem. (Use straight-line depreciation and amortization and take a full year's depreciation on the equipment sold to Steel in 20X3.)

P 7-3 Comparative balance sheets for Phil Corporation and Sam Corporation at December 31, 20X4 are summarized as follows:

	Phil	Sam
Assets		
Cash	$ 25,000	$19,400
Accounts receivable	32,200	25,000
Inventories	30,000	16,000
Plant and equipment	50,000	30,000
Accumulated depreciation	(10,000)	(4,000)
Bond discount	—	3,600
Investment in Sam stock (90%)	46,000	—
Investment in Sam bonds	20,800	—
	$194,000	$90,000
Liabilities and Equity		
Accounts payable	$ 25,500	$10,000
Bonds payable (10%)	—	40,000
Common stock	100,000	30,000
Retained earnings	68,500	10,000
	$194,000	$90,000

Additional Information
1 Phil acquired its 90% interest in Sam Corporation on January 1, 20X1.
2 Phil uses the equity method of accounting but does not adjust for the excess of cost over book value acquired or for intercompany profits.
3 The difference between Phil's investment in Sam stock account and the underlying book value of Phil's equity interest relates to undervalued plant and equipment that had an expected useful life of 10 years on January 1, 20X1.
4 Sam's December 31, 20X4 inventory includes $2,000 profit on goods acquired from Phil.
5 Phil acquired $20,000 par of Sam bonds on January 1, 20X4. The bonds mature on December 31, 20X8, and the premium is amortized by the straight-line method.

Required: Prepare a consolidated balance sheet for Phil Corporation and Subsidiary at December 31, 20X4.

P 7-4 Pile Corporation acquired 100% of Scud Corporation's outstanding common stock at its underlying book value on January 1, 20X4, when Scud's equity consisted of $100,000 capital stock, $35,000 other paid-in capital, and $35,000 retained earnings. Scud's assets and liabilities were recorded at their fair values on this date.

Pile uses the equity method in accounting for Scud but has made no adjustment relative to the intercompany bond holdings of Pile and Scud. Scud's investment in Pile's bonds consists of $50,000 par value of Pile's 10% bonds that were purchased by Scud for $48,000 on January 2, 20X4. These bonds mature on January 1, 20X8 and have semiannual interest payment dates of July 1 and January 1. The combined income and retained earnings statements and balance sheets of Pile and Scud at and for the year ended December 31, 20X4 are summarized as follows:

	Pile	Scud
Combined Income and Retained Earnings Statements for the Year Ended December 31, 20X4		
Sales	$150,000	$ 55,000
Income from Scud	25,000	—
Interest income	—	5,500
Cost of sales	(73,000)	(20,000)
Depreciation expense	(28,000)	(9,000)
Interest expense	(9,000)	—
Other expenses	(30,000)	(6,500)
Net income	35,000	25,000
Add: Beginning retained earnings	65,000	35,000
Less: Dividends	(10,000)	(20,000)
Retained earnings December 31, 20X4	$ 90,000	$ 40,000
Balance Sheet at December 31, 20X4		
Cash	$ 15,000	$ 9,000
Accounts receivable	20,000	10,000
Interest receivable	—	2,500

(Continued)

	Pile	Scud
Inventories	60,000	10,000
Land	70,000	20,000
Plant and equipment—net	140,000	100,000
Investment in Scud stock	175,000	—
Investment in Pile bonds	—	48,500
Total assets	$480,000	$200,000
Accounts payable	$ 42,000	$ 25,000
Interest payable	5,000	—
10% bonds payable	100,000	—
Premium on bonds payable	3,000	—
Capital stock, $10 par	200,000	100,000
Other paid-in capital	40,000	35,000
Retained earnings	90,000	40,000
Total equities	$480,000	$200,000

Required: Prepare consolidation working papers for Pile Corporation and Subsidiary for the year 20X4.

P 7-5 Paul Corporation acquired an 80% interest in Silas Corporation on January 1, 20X1 for $46,000, when Silas had capital stock of $26,000 and retained earnings of $6,500. The excess of investment cost over book value acquired was due to a $15,000 understatement of plant and equipment with a remaining useful life of 15 years, and to goodwill, which is being amortized over a 10-year period.

Paul Corporation holds $25,000 par of Silas Corporation bonds acquired on January 1, 20X4 for $24,000. The bonds mature on January 1, 20X9.

Silas Corporation sells merchandise to Paul Corporation at a markup of 20% based on cost. Intercompany sales during 20X4 totaled $8,000. Paul's December 31, 20X4 inventory includes $4,500 of merchandise acquired from Silas, and the beginning inventory includes $2,250 of such merchandise. Accounts payable of Paul Corporation includes $1,500 owed to Silas on intercompany sales.

Separate company financial statements for Paul Corporation and its 80%-owned subsidiary, Silas Corporation, for the year ended December 31, 20X4 are summarized as follows:

	Paul	Silas
Combined Income and Retained Earnings Statement for the Year Ended December 31, 20X4		
Sales	$ 56,600	$ 20,000
Income from Silas	3,200	—
Interest income	2,700	—
Cost of goods sold	(28,000)	(7,000)
Operating expenses	(12,000)	(4,200)
Interest expense	—	(4,800)
Net income	22,500	4,000
Add: Beginning retained earnings	42,000	14,000
Deduct: Dividends	(15,000)	(2,000)
Retained earnings December 31, 20X4	$ 49,500	$ 16,000
Balance Sheet at December 31, 20X4		
Cash	$ 15,000	$ 31,000
Accounts receivable	12,200	25,000
Inventories	30,000	8,000
Plant and equipment	50,000	40,000
Less: Accumulated depreciation	(10,000)	(4,000)
Investment in Silas stock	53,600	—
Investment in Silas bonds	24,200	—
Total assets	$175,000	$100,000
Accounts payable	$ 25,500	$ 7,200
Bonds payable, 10%	—	50,000
Premium on bonds	—	800
Common stock	100,000	26,000
Retained earnings	49,500	16,000
Total equities	$175,000	$100,000

Required: Prepare consolidated financial statement working papers for Paul Corporation and Subsidiary for the year ended December 31, 20X4.

P 7-6 Plum Corporation purchased 90% of Star Corporation's outstanding voting common stock at its book value for $207,000 cash on January 1, 20X2, when Star's stockholders' equity consisted of $200,000 capital stock and $30,000 retained earnings. Financial statements for Plum and Star for the year 20X3 are as follows:

	Plum	Star
Combined Income and Retained Earnings Statement for the Year Ended December 31, 20X3		
Sales	$380,000	$210,000
Income from Star	36,000	—
Interest income	—	12,000
Gain on equipment	30,000	—
Cost of sales	(180,000)	(140,000)
Depreciation expense	(58,000)	(22,000)
Operating expenses	(78,000)	(20,000)
Interest expense	(20,000)	—
Net income	110,000	40,000
Add: Retained earnings January 1, 20X3	125,000	50,000
Less: Dividends	(60,000)	(30,000)
Retained earnings December 31, 20X3	$175,000	$ 60,000
Balance Sheet at December 31, 20X3		
Cash	$ 49,000	$ 19,000
Accounts receivable	110,000	60,000
Interest receivable	—	5,000
Inventories	90,000	30,000
Land	20,000	10,000
Buildings—net	70,000	30,000
Equipment—net	227,000	150,000
Investment in Star stock	234,000	—
Investment in Plum bonds	—	96,000
Total assets	$800,000	$400,000
Accounts payable	$115,000	$140,000
Interest payable	10,000	—
10% bonds payable	200,000	—
Capital stock, $1 par	300,000	200,000
Retained earnings	175,000	60,000
Total equities	$800,000	$400,000

Additional Information

1 Star Corporation sold inventory items to Plum for $60,000 during 20X2, and one-half of this merchandise was inventoried by Plum at year-end. Star's sales to Plum Corporation during 20X3 were $90,000, and two-thirds of this merchandise was included in Plum's year-end 20X3 inventory. Star's sales to Plum are at 150% of Star's cost.

2 Star's accounts receivable at December 31, 20X3 included $30,000 due from Plum Corporation.

3 Plum Corporation sold equipment with a book value of $50,000 and a five-year remaining useful life to Star for $80,000 on July 1, 20X3. This equipment remains in use by Star Corporation. Straight-line depreciation to the nearest month is applicable.

4 On January 1, 20X3, Star Corporation paid $94,000 for $100,000 par of Plum Corporation's five-year, 10% bonds. These bonds have interest payment dates of July 1 and January 1 and mature January 1, 20X6.

5 Plum Corporation applies the equity method of accounting without considering intercompany transactions.

Required: Prepare working papers to consolidate the financial statements of Plum Corporation and Subsidiary at and for the year ended December 31, 20X3.

P 7-7 Peter Corporation acquired an 80% interest in Cher Corporation on January 1, 20X4 for $320,000, at which time Cher had capital stock of $200,000 outstanding and retained earnings of $100,000. The price paid by Peter reflected a $100,000 undervaluation of Cher's plant and equipment. This equipment had a remaining useful life of eight years when Peter acquired its interest.

Separate company and consolidated financial statements for Peter Corporation and its subsidiary, Cher Corporation, for the year ended December 31, 20X6 are as follows:

	Peter	Cher	Consolidated
Combined Income and Retained Earnings Statement for the Year Ended December 31, 20X6			
Sales	$ 180,000	$100,000	$230,000
Income from Cher	20,000	—	—
Interest income	—	8,000	—
Cost of goods sold	(110,000)	(60,000)	(110,000)
Operating expenses	(30,000)	(18,000)	(58,000)
Interest expense	(18,000)	—	(9,000)
Loss	—	—	(3,000)
Minority interest income	—	—	(8,000)
Net income	42,000	30,000	42,000
Add: Beginning retained earnings	294,000	135,000	294,000
Deduct: Dividends	(20,000)	(15,000)	(20,000)
Ending retained earnings	$ 316,000	$150,000	$316,000
Balance Sheet at December 31, 20X6			
Cash	$ 60,000	$ 26,000	$ 86,000
Accounts receivable	120,000	60,000	165,000
Inventories	100,000	50,000	140,000
Plant and equipment	500,000	200,000	780,000
Accumulated depreciation	(100,000)	(50,000)	(180,000)
Investment in Cher stock	320,000		
Investment in Peter bonds	—	104,000	—
Total assets	$1,000,000	$390,000	$991,000
Accounts payable	$ 80,000	$ 40,000	$105,000
10% bonds payable	200,000	—	100,000
Premium on bonds	4,000	—	2,000
Common stock	400,000	200,000	400,000
Retained earnings	316,000	150,000	316,000
Minority interest	—	—	68,000
Total equities	$1,000,000	$390,000	$991,000

Cher sells merchandise to Peter but never purchases from Peter. On January 1, 20X6, Cher purchased $100,000 par of 10% Peter Corporation bonds for $106,000. These bonds mature on December 31, 20X8, and Cher expects to hold the bonds until maturity. Both Cher and Peter use straight-line amortization.

Required: Show computations for each of the following items:
1 The $3,000 loss in the consolidated income statement
2 The $230,000 consolidated sales
3 Consolidated cost of goods sold of $110,000
4 Intercompany profit in beginning inventories
5 Intercompany profit in ending inventories
6 Consolidated accounts receivable of $165,000
7 Minority interest income of $8,000
8 Minority interest at December 31, 20X6
9 Investment in Cher stock at December 31, 20X5
10 Investment income account of $20,000 (Peter's books)

P 7-8   [AICPA adapted]
Selected amounts from the separate unconsolidated financial statements of Poe Corp. and its 90%-owned subsidiary, Shaw Co., at December 31, 20X2 are as follows.

	Poe	Shaw
Selected Income Statement Amounts		
Sales	$710,000	$530,000
Cost of goods sold	490,000	370,000
Gain on sale of equipment	—	21,000
Earnings from investment in subsidiary	61,000	—
Interest expense	—	16,000
Depreciation	25,000	20,000

(Continued)

	Poe	Shaw
Selected Balance Sheet Amounts		
Cash	$ 50,000	$ 15,000
Inventories	229,000	150,000
Equipment	440,000	360,000
Accumulated depreciation	(200,000)	(120,000)
Investment in Shaw	189,000	—
Investment in bonds	100,000	—
Discount on bonds	(9,000)	—
Bonds payable	—	(200,000)
Common stock	(100,000)	(10,000)
Additional paid-in capital	(250,000)	(40,000)
Retained earnings	(402,000)	(140,000)
Selected Statement of Retained Earnings Amounts		
Beginning balance December 31, 20X1	$272,000	$100,000
Net income	210,000	70,000
Dividends paid	80,000	30,000

Additional Information

1 On January 2, 20X2, Poe purchased 90% of Shaw Co.'s 100,000 outstanding common stock for cash of $155,000. On that date, Shaw's stockholders' equity equaled $150,000 and the fair values of Shaw's assets and liabilities equaled their carrying amounts. Poe has accounted for the acquisition as a purchase. Poe's policy is to amortize intangibles over 10 years.

2 On September 4, 20X2, Shaw paid cash dividends of $30,000.

3 On December 31, 20X2, Poe recorded its equity in Shaw's earnings.

4 On January 3, 20X2, Shaw sold equipment with an original cost of $30,000 and a carrying value of $15,000 to Poe for $36,000. The equipment had a remaining life of three years and was depreciated using the straight-line method by both companies.

5 During 20X2, Shaw sold merchandise to Poe for $60,000, which included a profit of $20,000. At December 31, 20X2, half of this merchandise remained in Poe's inventory.

6 On December 31, 20X2, Poe paid $91,000 to purchase half of the outstanding bonds issued by Shaw. The bonds mature on December 31, 20X8 and were originally issued at par. These bonds pay interest annually on December 31 of each year, and the interest was paid to the prior investor immediately before Poe's purchase of the bonds.

Required: Determine the amounts at which the following items will appear in the consolidated financial statements of Poe Corporation and Subsidiary for the year ended December 31, 20X2:

1 Cash
2 Equipment less accumulated depreciation
3 Investment in Shaw
4 Bonds payable
5 Common stock
6 Beginning retained earnings
7 Dividends paid
8 Gain on retirement of bonds
9 Cost of goods sold
10 Interest expense
11 Depreciation expense

P 7-9 Financial statements for Paar Corporation and its 75%-owned subsidiary, Sahl Corporation, for 20X4 are summarized as follows.

	Paar	Sahl
Combined Income and Retained Earnings Statement for the Year Ended December 31, 20X4		
Sales	$630,000	$500,000
Gain on plant	30,000	—
Income from Sahl	52,000	—
Cost of goods sold	(350,000)	(300,000)
Depreciation expense	(76,000)	(40,000)
Interest expense	(20,000)	—
Other expenses	(46,000)	(60,000)
Net income	220,000	100,000

(Continued)

	Paar	Sahl
Add: Beginning retained earnings	150,000	100,000
Deduct: Dividends	(160,000)	(80,000)
Retained earnings December 31, 20X4	$210,000	$120,000

Balance Sheet at December 31, 20X4

	Paar	Sahl
Cash	$ 27,000	$ 81,000
Bond interest receivable	—	5,000
Other receivables—net	40,000	30,000
Inventories	80,000	50,000
Land	90,000	70,000
Buildings—net	150,000	180,000
Equipment—net	140,000	90,000
Investment in Sahl	343,000	—
Investment in Paar bonds	—	94,000
Total assets	$870,000	$600,000
Accounts payable	$ 50,000	$ 80,000
Bond interest payable	10,000	—
10% bonds payable	200,000	—
Common stock	400,000	400,000
Retained earnings	210,000	120,000
Total equities	$870,000	$600,000

Paar Corporation acquired its interest in Sahl at book value during 20X1, when the fair values of Sahl's assets and liabilities were equal to their recorded book values.

Additional Information

1 Paar uses the equity method in accounting for its investment in Sahl.
2 Intercompany sales of merchandise between the two affiliated companies totaled $50,000 during 20X4. All intercompany balances have been paid except for $10,000 in transit from Sahl to Paar at December 31, 20X4.
3 Unrealized profits in Sahl's inventories of merchandise acquired from Paar were $12,000 at December 31, 20X3 and $15,000 at December 31, 20X4.
4 Sahl sold equipment with a six-year remaining useful life to Paar on January 2, 20X2 at a gain of $24,000. The equipment is still in use by Paar.
5 Paar sold a plant to Sahl on July 1, 20X4. The land was sold at a gain of $10,000 and the building, which had a remaining useful life of 10 years, at a gain of $20,000.
6 Sahl purchased $100,000 par of Paar 10% bonds in the open market for $94,000 plus $5,000 accrued interest on December 31, 20X4. Interest is paid semiannually on January 1 and July 1, and the bonds mature on January 1, 20X9.

Required: Prepare consolidation working papers for Paar Corporation and Subsidiary for the year ended December 31, 20X4.

P 7-10 Puter Corporation acquired a 90% interest in Surry Corporation in 20X4 in a pooling of interests business combination. The pooling was correctly recorded by Puter on the date of consummation. Financial statements for Puter and Surry corporations at and for the year ended December 31, 20X7 are summarized as follows.

	Puter	Surry
Combined Income and Retained Earnings Statements		
for the Year Ended December 31, 20X7		
Sales	$300,000	$100,000
Income from Surry	50,300	—
Interest income	—	4,000
Cost of sales	(140,000)	(45,000)
Depreciation expense	(15,000)	(5,000)
Operating expense	(20,000)	(4,000)
Interest expense	(10,000)	—
Net income	165,300	50,000
Add: Beginning retained earnings	114,600	35,000
Deduct: Dividends	(60,000)	(20,000)
Retained earnings December 31, 20X7	$219,900	$ 65,000

(Continued)

	Puter	Surry
Balance Sheet at December 31, 20X7		
Cash	$ 90,000	$ 17,000
Accounts receivable—net	110,000	35,000
Interest receivable	—	2,500
Inventories	50,000	30,000
Land	70,000	15,000
Buildings—net	140,000	50,000
Equipment—net	160,000	90,000
Investment in Surry	174,900	—
Investment in Puter bonds	—	45,500
Total assets	$794,900	$285,000
Accounts payable	$120,000	$ 85,000
Interest payable	5,000	—
10% bonds payable	100,000	—
Capital stock, $10 par	300,000	100,000
Additional paid-in capital	50,000	35,000
Retained earnings	219,900	65,000
Total equities	$794,900	$285,000

Additional Information

1 Surry purchased inventory items from Puter during 20X6 and 20X7 as follows:

	Sales	Cost of Sales	Gross Profit	Unsold December 31
20X6	$30,000	$20,000	$10,000	$15,000
20X7	40,000	25,000	15,000	16,000

2 Puter paid Surry $20,000 on January 5, 20X6 for equipment that had a book value of $12,000 on Surry's books and a four-year remaining useful life. Straight-line depreciation is used.

3 Surry paid $44,000 for $50,000 par of Puter's 10% bonds on July 1, 20X7. Puter issued the bonds at par in 20X1 and the bonds mature on July 1, 20X9. Interest payment dates are January 1 and July 1. Straight-line amortization is used.

4 Puter uses the equity method to account for its interest in Surry.

Required: Prepare consolidation working papers for Puter Corporation and Subsidiary at and for the year ended December 31, 20X7.

P 7-11 [AICPA adapted]

Madison, Inc., acquired all the outstanding $10 par voting common stock of Adams Corporation on December 31, 20X9, in exchange for 90,000 shares of its $10 par voting common stock in a business combination that meets all the conditions for a pooling of interests. On the acquisition date, Madison's common stock had a closing market price of $26 per share on a national stock exchange. Both corporations continued to operate as separate businesses maintaining separate accounting records with years ending December 31.

Additional Information

1 Madison recorded its investment in Adams at the underlying equity in the net assets of Adams of $2,205,000.

2 On December 31, 20X9, Adams's assets and liabilities had fair values equal to the book balances with the exception of land, which had a fair value of $400,000.

3 Madison's accounting policy is to amortize excess cost over fair market value of net assets acquired over a 40-year period.

4 On December 15, 20X9, Adams paid a cash dividend of $3 per share on its common stock.

5 Adams's long-term debt consisted of 9%, 10-year bonds, issued at face value on June 30, 20X5 and due in 10 years. Interest is paid semiannually on June 30 and December 31. Madison had purchased Adams's bonds at face value of $250,000. There was no change in Madison's ownership of Adams's bonds through December 31, 20X9.

6 During the three-month period ended December 31, 20X9, Madison purchased merchandise from Adams at an aggregate invoice price of $600,000. Madison had not paid for the merchandise as of December 31, 20X9. The amount of profit realized by Adams on these transactions was $120,000. At December 31, 20X9, one-half of the merchandise remained in Madison's inventory. There were no intercompany merchandise transactions before October 1, 20X9.

7 The 20X9 net income amounts per books of Madison and Adams were $2,100,000 and $1,125,000, respectively.

8 The balances in retained earnings on December 31, 20X8 were $1,600,000 and $275,000 for Madison and Adams, respectively.

On December 31, 20X9, after nominal accounts were closed and immediately after acquisition, the condensed balance sheets for both corporations were as follows:

	Madison	Adams
Assets		
Cash	$ 750,000	$ 300,000
Accounts receivable—net	1,950,000	750,000
Inventories	2,100,000	950,000
Land	500,000	200,000
Depreciable assets—net	4,160,000	1,800,000
Investment in Adams Corporation	2,205,000	—
Long-term investments and other assets	785,000	350,000
Total assets	$12,450,000	$4,350,000
Liabilities and Stockholders' Equity		
Accounts payable and other current liabilities	$ 1,750,000	$ 945,000
Long-term debt	1,500,000	1,200,000
Common stock, $10 par	3,000,000	900,000
Additional paid-in capital	1,370,000	175,000
Retained earnings	4,830,000	1,130,000
Total liabilities and equity	$12,450,000	$4,350,000

Required

1 Prepare consolidated balance sheet working papers for Madison and its subsidiary, Adams Corporation, as of December 31, 20X9.

2 Prepare a consolidated statement of retained earnings for the year ended December 31, 20X9.

8

Consolidations— Changes in Ownership Interests

This chapter considers several separate topics related to changes in parent company/investor ownership interests. These topics include parent/investor accounting and consolidation procedures for interim acquisitions of stock, midyear poolings, piecemeal acquisitions of a controlling interest, sales of ownership interests, and changes in ownership interests through investee stock issuances and treasury stock transactions.

ACQUISITIONS DURING AN ACCOUNTING PERIOD

Previous chapters in this book have illustrated consolidations for subsidiary acquisitions at the beginning of an accounting period. When a subsidiary is acquired during an accounting period, some consolidation adjustments have to be made in order to account for the income of the subsidiary that was earned prior to its acquisition and included in the purchase price. Such income is referred to as *preacquisition earnings* to distinguish it from income of the consolidated entity. Similarly, *preacquisition dividends* are dividends paid on stock before its acquisition during an accounting period that require consolidation adjustments in the period of acquisition.

Preacquisition Earnings

Conceptually, *preacquisition earnings* (also referred to as *purchased income*) can be eliminated from consolidated income by either of two methods. It can be eliminated by excluding the sales and expenses of the subsidiary prior to acquisition from consolidated sales and expenses. Or it can be eliminated by including the sales and expenses of the subsidiary in the consolidated income statement for the full year and deducting preacquisition income as a separate item.

Assume, for example, that Patter Corporation purchases a 90% interest in Sissy Company on April 1, 20X6 for $213,750. Sissy's income, dividends, and stockholders' equity for 20X6 are summarized as follows:

	January 1 to April 1	April 1 to December 31	January 1 to December 31
Income			
Sales	$ 25,000	$ 75,000	$100,000
Cost of sales and expenses	12,500	37,500	50,000
Net income	$ 12,500	$ 37,500	$ 50,000
Dividends	$ 10,000	$ 15,000	$ 25,000

	January 1	April 1	December 31
Stockholder's Equity			
Capital stock	$200,000	$200,000	$200,000
Retained earnings	35,000	37,500	60,000
Stockholders' equity	$235,000	$237,500	$260,000

Sissy's income from January 1 to April 1, 20X6 is $12,500 ($25,000 sales − $12,500 expenses), and Sissy's equity at April 1 is $237,500. Therefore, the book value acquired by Patter ($237,500 × 90% interest) is equal to the $213,750 purchase price of Sissy stock.

In recording income from its investment in Sissy at year-end, Patter makes the following entry:

Investment in Sissy	$33,750	
Income from Sissy		$33,750

To record income from the last three quarters
of 20X6 ($37,500 × 90%).

The effect of recording investment income on an equity basis is to increase Patter's income by $33,750, so the effect on consolidated net income must also be $33,750. Conceptually, the consolidated income statement is affected as follows:

Sales (last three quarters of 20X6)	$ 75,000
Expenses (last three quarters of 20X6)	(37,500)
Minority interest income (last three quarters of 20X6)	(3,750)
Effect on consolidated net income	$ 33,750

This solution poses two practical problems. First, the income of the 10% minority interest for 20X6 is $5,000 for the full year, even though it is only $3,750 for the last nine months. Second, by consolidating sales and expenses for only nine months of the year, the consolidated income statement does not provide a basis for projecting future annual sales and expenses for the consolidated entity. In considering these problems, the Committee on Accounting Procedure of the AICPA in *ARB No. 51* (paragraph 11) expressed the opinion that the most meaningful consolidated income statement presentation results from including the sales and expenses in the consolidated income statement for the full year and deducting preacquisition income as a separate item. The committee recommended consolidating subsidiary accounts in the following manner:

Sales (full year)	$100,000
Expenses (full year)	(50,000)
Preacquisition income	(11,250)
Minority interest income	(5,000)
Effect on consolidated net income	$ 33,750

Preacquisition Dividends

Dividends paid on stock prior to its acquisition during an accounting period (preacquisition dividends) are eliminated in the consolidation process because they are not a part of the equity acquired. Sissy paid $25,000 dividends during 20X6, but $10,000 of this amount was paid before the acquisition by Patter. Accordingly, Patter makes the following entry in accounting for dividends actually received.

Cash	$13,500	
Investment in Sissy		$13,500
To record dividends received ($15,000 × 90%).		

The preacquisition dividends relating to the 90% interest acquired by Patter are eliminated in the consolidation process along with the preacquisition earnings. These eliminations are included in the working paper entry that eliminates reciprocal investment in subsidiary and subsidiary equity balances in order to compensate for the fact that subsidiary equity balances are eliminated as of the beginning of the period and the investment balance is eliminated as of the date of acquisition within the period. The allocations of income and dividends for Sissy can be summarized as follows:

	Majority Interest (Patter and Consolidated)	Minority Interest (10%)	Preacquisition Eliminations	Total
Sissy's net income	$33,750	$5,000	$11,250	$50,000
Sissy's dividends	13,500	2,500	9,000	25,000

Consolidation

Consolidation procedures for midyear acquisitions are illustrated in Exhibit 8–1 for Patter and Subsidiary. The $234,000 investment in Sissy balance in Patter's balance sheet consists of the $213,750 cost plus $33,750 income less $13,500 dividends received. Although other amounts in the separate statements of Patter and Sissy are introduced for the first time in the consolidation working papers, they are entirely compatible with the previous assumptions and data for Patter and Sissy corporations.

Working paper entry a eliminates the income from Sissy and dividends received from Sissy, and returns the investment in Sissy account to its $213,750 balance at acquisition on April 1, 20X6.

a	Income from Sissy	$ 33,750	
	Dividends—Sissy		$ 13,500
	Investment in Sissy		20,250
	To eliminate investment income and the dividends received from Sissy and adjust the investment in Sissy to its cost on April 1, 20X6.		

This entry does not reflect new procedures, but care must be exercised to eliminate only dividends actually received (90% × $15,000), rather than the ownership percentage times dividends paid by the subsidiary for the year.

The second working paper entry in Exhibit 8–1 does reflect new working paper procedures because it contains items for preacquisition earnings and dividends. It is journalized as follows:

b	Preacquisition income	$ 11,250	
	Capital stock—Sissy	200,000	
	Retained earnings—Sissy	35,000	
	Dividends—Sissy		$ 9,000
	Investment in Sissy		213,750
	Minority interest—beginning		23,500
	To eliminate reciprocal investment and equity balances, to record preacquisition income and beginning minority interest, and to eliminate preacquisition dividends.		

In examining this entry, note that preacquisition income less preacquisition dividends of $2,250 is equal to the $213,750 investment cost on April 1, 20X6 less 90% of Sissy's equity on January 1, 20X6. Also note that beginning minority interest is 10% of Sissy's January 1, 20X6 equity. In case of *increases* in ownership interests during a period, minority interest is computed for the minority shares outstanding at year-end.

PATTER CORPORATION AND SUBSIDIARY
CONSOLIDATION WORKING PAPERS
FOR THE YEAR ENDED DECEMBER 31, 20X6

	Patter	90% Sissy	Adjustments and Eliminations		Minority Interest	Consolidated Statements
Income Statement Sales	$300,000	$100,000				$400,000
Income from Sissy	33,750		a 33,750			
Expenses including cost of goods sold	(200,000)	(50,000)				(250,000)
Minority interest income ($50,000 × 10%)					$ 5,000	(5,000)
Preacquisition income			b 11,250			(11,250)
Net income	$133,750	$ 50,000				$133,750
Retained Earnings Retained earnings—Patter	$266,250					$266,250
Retained earnings—Sissy		$ 35,000	b 35,000			
Net income	133,750√	50,000√				133,750
Dividends	(100,000)	(25,000)	a 13,500 b 9,000		(2,500)	(100,000)
Retained earnings December 31, 20X6	$300,000	$ 60,000				$300,000
Balance sheet Other assets	$566,000	$260,000				$826,000
Investment in Sissy	234,000		a 20,250 b 213,750			
	$800,000	$260,000				$826,000
Capital stock	$500,000	$200,000	b 200,000			$500,000
Retained earnings	300,000√	60,000√				300,000
	$800,000	$260,000				
Minority interest January 1, 20X6			b 23,500		23,500	
Minority interest December 31, 20X6					$26,000	26,000
						$826,000

Exhibit 8–1 *Preacquisition Income and Dividends in Consolidation Working Papers*

Preacquisition income is introduced in the working papers through a working paper entry. Subsequently, it is carried to the consolidated income statement as a deduction in measuring consolidated net income. The classification of preacquisition income in a consolidated income statement parallels the classification of minority interest income. Consolidation working papers in subsequent accounting periods are *not affected* by midyear acquisitions.

Sissy's 10% ending minority interest is held outside of the consolidated entity for the entire year, so the minority interest computation is simply 10% of Sissy's equity at the beginning of the year plus 10% of Sissy's net income for the year less 10% of the dividends declared by Sissy during the year.

POOLING OF INTERESTS DURING AN ACCOUNTING PERIOD

When a pooling of interests takes place during an accounting period, the income of the combining companies is consolidated for the entire year irrespective of the date of combination. In addition, prior-period financial statements are restated to show the effect of the pooling for all prior periods reported. The requirement to pool the income of combining companies for the entire year of combination has important implications for recording investments in pooled companies within an accounting period and in accounting for such investments under the equity method of accounting. Income and retained earnings of the parent under the equity method of accounting should be equal to consolidated or pooled income and retained earnings. Therefore, the investment in a pooled company is recorded at the book value of the interest acquired at the beginning of the period of pooling, adjusted downward for dividends paid prior to combination, but not adjusted upward for preacquisition earnings.

Accounting Procedures for Midyear Poolings

Assume that Pete Corporation issues 10,000 shares of its own $10 par common stock for all the outstanding voting stock of Skag Corporation at July 1, 20X5 in a pooling of interests. Summary financial information for Skag Corporation at June 30 and at December 31, 20X5 is as follows:

	Six Months Ended June 30, 20X5	Year Ended December 31, 20X5
Net assets	$160,000	$170,000
Capital stock, $10 par	$100,000	$100,000
Retained earnings December 31, 20X4	50,000	50,000
Income	20,000	40,000
Dividends	(10,000)	(20,000)
Stockholders' equity	$160,000	$170,000

Pete Corporation records its investment in Skag on June 30, 20X5 as follows:

Investment in Skag	$160,000	
Capital stock, $10 par		$100,000
Retained earnings		40,000
Income from Skag		20,000

The $40,000 credit to retained earnings is equal to the December 31, 20X4 retained earnings less $10,000 dividends paid prior to the pooling. The entry for the pooling treatment provides for including a full year's earnings in investment income.

During the six months of 20X5, Pete records the receipt of $10,000 dividends from Skag, and at December 31, 20X5 it records income from Skag of $20,000. Pete's journal entries are:

Cash	$10,000	
Investment in Skag		$10,000
To record dividends received ($10,000 × 100%).		
Investment in Skag	$20,000	
Income from Skag		$20,000
To record investment income ($20,000 × 100%) for the second six months.		

The investment in Skag account at December 31, 20X5 is $170,000 ($160,000 + $20,000 − $10,000), equal to Skag's recorded net assets on that date.

Consolidation working papers for Pete and Skag for 20X5 are presented in Exhibit 8–2.

Only three working paper entries are needed to consolidate the financial statements of the pooled companies. Entry a eliminates investment income and subsidiary

PETE CORPORATION AND SUBSIDIARY
CONSOLIDATION WORKING PAPERS
FOR THE YEAR ENDED DECEMBER 31, 20X5

	Pete	100% Skag	Adjustments and Eliminations		Consolidated Statements
Income Statement Income from Skag	$ 40,000		a 40,000		
Revenue less expenses	100,000	$ 40,000			$140,000
Net income	$140,000	$ 40,000			$140,000
Retained Earnings Retained earnings—Pete	$240,000				$240,000
Retained earnings—Skag		$ 50,000	b 10,000 c 40,000		
Net income	140,000√	40,000√			140,000
Dividends	(50,000)	(20,000)		a 10,000 b 10,000	(50,000)
Retained earnings December 31, 20X5	$330,000	$ 70,000			$330,000
Balance Sheet Investment in Skag	$170,000			a 30,000 c 140,000	
Other net assets	760,000	$170,000			$930,000
	$930,000	$170,000			$930,000
Capital stock	$600,000	$100,000	c 100,000		$600,000
Retained earnings	330,000√	70,000√			330,000
	$930,000	$170,000			$930,000

Exhibit 8–2 *Consolidation Working Papers for Pooling of Interests*

dividends and credits the investment account for the difference. Entry b eliminates preacquisition dividends, and entry c eliminates reciprocal investment and equity balances. The working paper entries are reproduced for convenient reference.

a	Income from Skag		$ 40,000	
		Dividends		$ 10,000
		Investment in Skag		30,000
	To eliminate income from Skag and dividends and credit investment account for the difference.			
b	Retained earnings—Skag		$ 10,000	
		Dividends		$ 10,000
	To eliminate preacquisition dividends.			
c	Retained earnings—Skag		$ 40,000	
	Capital stock—Skag		100,000	
		Investment in Skag		$140,000
	To eliminate reciprocal investment and equity balances.			

The consolidated net income of $140,000 shown in Exhibit 8–2 is equal to the net income of Pete. Consolidated retained earnings of $330,000 at December 31, 20X5 is also equal to Pete's retained earnings. Two items in the consolidation working papers are unusual and require some comment. Skag's dividends for the entire year ($20,000) are eliminated because there is no minority interest, and because the dividends to be reflected in the consolidated retained earnings statement are those paid by Pete, the parent company. Also, Pete's beginning retained earnings and beginning consolidated retained earnings of $240,000 are $10,000 less than the $250,000 combined retained earnings of the pooled companies at January 1, 20X5.[1] The difference is the result of eliminating the $10,000 dividends paid by Skag before consummation of the pooling. Although other approaches for correcting the inconsistencies of the pooling requirements are available, the one illustrated was selected because it maintains a correct correspondence between the investment and underlying equity accounts, between parent company income and consolidated income, and between parent company and consolidated retained earnings.

Reporting Pooled Retained Earnings

The reporting of consolidated retained earnings for 20X5 does not parallel the one-line consolidation entries presented above because reconciliation with Pete Corporation's $200,000 retained earnings at December 31, 20X4 is required. Therefore, consolidated retained earnings in the period of pooling would be presented as follows:

PETE CORPORATION AND SUBSIDIARY
CONSOLIDATED (POOLED) RETAINED EARNINGS
FOR THE YEAR ENDED DECEMBER 31, 20X5

Retained earnings December 31, 20X4 as previously reported		$200,000
Pooling Adjustment		
Retained earnings of Skag, December 31, 20X4		50,000
Retained earnings (pooled), December 31, 20X4		250,000
Net income (pooled income)—20X5		140,000
Dividends—20X5		
To Pete shareholders	$50,000	
To Skag shareholders before pooling	10,000	60,000
Retained earnings, December 31, 20X5		$330,000

This presentation enables readers of Pete's financial statements to view the effect of the pooling from the perspective of amounts presented in prior years.

PIECEMEAL ACQUISITIONS

A corporation may acquire an interest in another corporation in a series of separate stock purchases over a period of time. This type of acquisition poses no new problems of analysis if the parent accounts for its investment on an equity basis. However, it does increase the details of computing investment income and consolidated net income. These details are discussed and accounting procedures for them are illustrated in this section.

Poca Corporation acquires a 90% interest in Sark Corporation in a series of separate stock purchases between July 1, 20X3 and October 1, 20X5. Data concerning the acquisitions and interests acquired are as follows:

Year Date	Interest Acquired	Investment Cost	Equity January 1	Income for Year	Equity at Acquisition	Equity December 31
20X3 July 1	20%	$30,000	$100,000	$50,000	$125,000	$150,000
20X4 April 1	40%	$74,000	$150,000	$40,000	$160,000	$190,000
20X5 October 1	30%	$81,000	$190,000	$40,000	$220,000	$230,000

---

[1]Pete's retained earnings at December 31, 20X4 was $200,000. This amount was increased to $240,000 when the pooling was recorded.

The net assets of Sark Corporation are stated at their fair values, and the excess of investment cost over book value acquired in each case is due to goodwill with a 10-year amortization period. Accordingly, the initial goodwill from each of the three acquisitions is computed:

Year	Investment Cost	Book Value and Fair Value Acquired	Goodwill
20X3	$30,000	($125,000 × 20%) = $25,000	$ 5,000
20X4	$74,000	($160,000 × 40%) = $64,000	$10,000
20X5	$81,000	($220,000 × 30%) = $66,000	$15,000

The interests are acquired within each accounting period, so the consolidated income statements show preacquisition income in the years 20X4 and 20X5. Partial-year amortization is necessary for the goodwill arising in each of the three accounting periods.

At December 31, 20X5, Poca's investment in Sark account balance is $233,625, consisting of $185,000 total cost, plus income of $48,625 (Poca's share of Sark's net income less goodwill amortization) during the period 20X3 through 20X5. For purposes of computing gain or loss on subsequent sales, Poca should keep a record for each of the investments. This record could be contained in a schedule such as the following:

		20% Interest	40% Interest	30% Interest	Total
Investment cost		$30,000	$ 74,000	$81,000	$185,000
Investment income	20X3	4,750	—	—	4,750
	20X4	7,500	11,250	—	18,750
	20X5	7,500	15,000	2,625	25,125
		$49,750	$100,250	$83,625	$233,625

When the financial statements of Poca and Sark are consolidated in the years 20X4 and 20X5, preacquisition income will appear in the consolidated income statements. Except for the preacquisition income item, no unusual consolidating procedures result from piecemeal acquisitions. Exhibit 8–3 shows consolidation working papers for Poca Corporation and Subsidiary for 20X5. Additional data, which are compatible with previous information for the Poca/Sark example, are provided for illustrative purposes.

The working paper entries are reproduced for convenient reference:

a	Income from Sark	$ 25,125	
	Investment in Sark		$ 25,125

To eliminate investment income and return investment account to its beginning-of-the-period balance plus the $81,000 new investment.

b	Preacquisition income	$ 9,000	
	Retained earnings—Sark	90,000	
	Capital stock—Sark	100,000	
	Goodwill	28,500	
	Investment in Sark		$208,500
	Minority interest January 1		19,000

To eliminate investment in Sark and Sark's equity balances, and enter preacquisition income, unamortized goodwill, and beginning-of-the-period minority interest balances.

c	Expenses	$ 1,875	
	Goodwill		$ 1,875

To record current year's goodwill amortization.

POCA CORPORATION AND SUBSIDIARY
CONSOLIDATION WORKING PAPERS
FOR THE YEAR ENDED DECEMBER 31, 20X5

	Poca	90% Sark	Adjustments and Eliminations	Minority Interest	Consolidated Statements
Income Statement Sales	$274,875	$150,000			$424,875
Income from Sark	25,125		a 25,125		
Expenses including cost of sales	(220,000)	(110,000)	c 1,875		(331,875)
Preacquisition income			b 9,000		(9,000)
Minority interest income ($40,000 × 10%)				$ 4,000	(4,000)
Net income	$ 80,000	$ 40,000			$ 80,000
Retained Earnings Retained earnings—Poca	$220,000				$220,000
Retained earnings—Sark		$ 90,000	b 90,000		
Net income	80,000√	40,000√			80,000
Retained earnings December 31, 20X5	$300,000	$130,000			$300,000
Balance Sheet Other assets	$466,375	$300,000			$766,375
Investment in Sark	233,625		a 25,125 b 208,500		
Goodwill			b 28,500 c 1,875		26,625
	$700,000	$300,000			$793,000
Liabilities	$100,000	$ 70,000			$170,000
Capital stock	300,000	100,000	b 100,000		300,000
Retained earnings	300,000√	130,000√			300,000
	$700,000	$300,000			
Minority interest January 1, 20X5			b 19,000	19,000	
Minority interest December 31, 20X5				$23,000	23,000
					$793,000

Exhibit 8–3 *Piecemeal Acquisition of a Controlling Interest*

Preacquisition income of $9,000 relates to the 30% interest acquired on October 1, 20X5 ($40,000 Sark's income × 30% interest × $\frac{3}{4}$ year). The income of the minority interest for 20X5 is computed on the basis of the 10% minority ownership at December 31, 20X5. Goodwill of $26,625 as shown in the consolidated balance sheet of Exhibit 8–3 is equal to the initial unamortized goodwill of $30,000 ($5,000 + $10,000 + $15,000) less amortization of $250 in 20X3, $1,250 in 20X4, and $1,875 in 20X5. Except for these three items, the consolidation working paper procedures are equivalent to those used in previous chapters.

SALE OF OWNERSHIP INTERESTS

When a parent company/investor sells an ownership interest, the gain or loss on the sale is computed as the difference between the proceeds from the sale and the book value of the investment interest sold. The book value of the investment should, of course, reflect the equity method of accounting when the investor is able to exercise significant influence over the investee corporation. If a parent company acquires its interest in several different purchases, the shares sold must be identified with particular acquisitions. This is usually done on the basis of specific identification or the first-in, first-out flow assumption.

The following information will be used to illustrate sale of ownership interests, both at the beginning of the period and during the period. Sergio Corporation is a 90%-owned subsidiary of Pablo Corporation. Pablo's investment in Sergio account at January 1, 20X7 has a balance of $288,000, consisting of its underlying equity in Sergio plus $18,000 unamortized goodwill with a remaining amortization period of two years. Sergio's stockholders' equity at January 1, 20X7 consists of $200,000 capital stock and $100,000 retained earnings. During 20X7, Sergio reports income of $36,000, earned proportionately throughout the year, and pays dividends of $20,000 on July 1.

Sale of an Interest at the Beginning of the Period

If Pablo Corporation sells a 10% interest in Sergio (one-ninth of its holdings) on January 1, 20X7 for $40,000, an $8,000 gain on sale will be recorded on Pablo's books and the investment in Sergio account will be reduced $32,000 ($288,000 ÷ 9). The $8,000 gain is a gain for consolidated statement purposes as well as for Pablo as a separate entity. The sale of the 10% interest reduces Pablo's ownership percentage in Sergio to 80% and increases the minority interest to 20%. It also reduces Pablo's goodwill by $\frac{1}{9}$ of the total or $2,000.

During 20X7, Pablo accounts for its 80% interest under the equity method of accounting and records income of $20,800 ($36,000 net income of Sergio × 80% − $8,000 goodwill amortization) and a reduction in its investment account for dividends received. At December 31, 20X7, Pablo's investment in Sergio account has a balance of $260,800, computed as follows:

Investment balance January 1, 20X7	$288,000
Less: Book value of interest sold	32,000
	256,000
Add: Income less dividends ($20,800 − $16,000)	4,800
Investment balance December 31, 20X7	$260,800

The investment balance at year-end consists of Pablo's underlying equity in Sergio of $252,800 ($316,000 × 80%) plus $8,000 unamortized goodwill on the 80% interest still owned. Consolidation working papers for Pablo Corporation and Subsidiary as shown in Exhibit 8–4 illustrate the effect of a decrease in an ownership interest on working paper procedures.

The sale of the interest was at the beginning of the period, so the effect of the sale on consolidation procedures for 20X7 is minimal. The working paper entries from Exhibit 8–4 are in general journal form.

a	Income from Sergio	$ 20,800	
	Dividends—Sergio		$ 16,000
	Investment in Sergio		4,800
	To eliminate income and dividends from Sergio and return the investment account to its beginning-of-the-period balance after the sale of the 10% interest.		

PABLO CORPORATION AND SUBSIDIARY
CONSOLIDATION WORKING PAPERS
FOR THE YEAR ENDED DECEMBER 31, 20X7

	Pablo	80% Sergio	Adjustments and Eliminations		Minority Interest	Consolidated Statements
Income Statement						
Sales	$600,000	$136,000				$736,000
Income from Sergio	20,800		a 20,800			
Gain on sale	8,000					8,000
Cost of sales and expenses	(508,800)	(100,000)	c 8,000			(616,800)
Minority interest income ($36,000 × 20%)					$ 7,200	(7,200)
Net income	$120,000	$ 36,000				$120,000
Retained Earnings						
Retained earnings—Pablo	$210,000					$210,000
Retained earnings—Sergio		$100,000	b 100,000			
Net income	120,000√	36,000√				120,000
Dividends	(80,000)	(20,000)		a 16,000	(4,000)	(80,000)
Retained earnings December 31, 20X7	$250,000	$116,000				$250,000
Balance Sheet						
Other assets	$639,200	$350,000				$989,200
Investment in Sergio†	260,800			a 4,800 b 256,000		
Goodwill			b 16,000	c 8,000		8,000
	$900,000	$350,000				$997,200
Liabilities	$150,000	$ 34,000				$184,000
Capital stock	500,000	200,000	b 200,000			500,000
Retained earnings	250,000√	116,000√				250,000
	$900,000	$350,000				
Minority interest January 1, 20X7				b 60,000	60,000	
Minority interest December 31, 20X7					$63,200	63,200
						$997,200

†The $256,000 elimination in entry b is equal to the $288,000 beginning balance less the $32,000 book value of the 10% investment interest sold.

Exhibit 8–4 Sale of a 10 Percent Interest at the Beginning of the Period

b Capital stock—Sergio	$200,000	
Retained earnings—Sergio	100,000	
Goodwill	16,000	
Investment in Sergio		$256,000
Minority interest (20%)		60,000
To eliminate reciprocal investment and equity balances, and to record unamortized goodwill and beginning minority interest.		
c Amortization of goodwill	$ 8,000	
Goodwill		$ 8,000
To record the current year's amortization.		

Working paper entry a reduces the investment in Sergio to its $256,000 beginning-of-the-period balance after sale of the 10% interest, and entry b enters goodwill and minority interest based on amounts immediately after the 10% interest was sold. The last entry simply reflects current-period goodwill amortization related to the remaining 80% interest. The $8,000 gain on sale is included in Pablo's income statement and is carried directly to the consolidated income statement without adjustment.

Sale of an Interest During an Accounting Period

If Pablo Corporation sells the 10% interest in Sergio Corporation on April 1, 20X7 for $40,000, the sale may be recorded as of April 1, 20X7 or, as an expedient, as of January 1, 20X7. Assuming that the sale is recorded as of January 1, 20X7, Pablo records the $8,000 gain on sale the same as in the beginning-of-the-year sale situation and makes the same one-line consolidation entries as those illustrated in the earlier example. Consistency with the one-line consolidation requires that the consolidated financial statements be prepared using the same beginning-of-the-period sale assumption. That is, minority interest income is computed for a 20% minority interest outstanding throughout 20X7, and beginning and ending minority interest amounts are based on a 20% minority interest. This alternative beginning-of-the-period sale assumption does not affect parent company or consolidated net income because any difference in the gain or loss on sale is exactly offset by differences in computing the income from subsidiary under a one-line consolidation, and in computing amortization and minority interest amounts in the consolidated financial statements.[2]

If the sale is recorded as of April 1, 20X7, the gain on sale will be $7,350, computed as:

Selling price of 10% interest		$40,000
Less: Book value of the interest sold:		
Investment balance January 1	$288,000	
Equity in income		
$36,000 × $\frac{1}{4}$ year × 90%	8,100	
Less: Amortization		
$18,000 ÷ 2 years × $\frac{1}{4}$ year	(2,250)	
	293,850	
Portion of investment sold	× $\frac{1}{9}$	32,650
Gain		$ 7,350

Journal entries on Pablo's books during 20X7 to account for the 10% interest sold and its investment in Sergio are as follows:

[2]If recorded as of the beginning of the period, dividends actually received on the interest sold prior to sale must be considered in calculating the gain or loss on sale, and consolidation procedures must be adjusted accordingly.

April 1, 20X7

Investment in Sergio	$ 5,850	
Income from Sergio		$ 5,850

   To record income for first quarter 20X7 ($8,100 equity
     in income less $2,250 amortization).

Cash	$40,000	
Investment in Sergio		$32,650
Gain on sale of investment		7,350

   To record sale of a 10% interest in Sergio. (See
     earlier computations.)

July 1, 20X7

Cash	$16,000	
Investment in Sergio		$16,000

   To record dividends received ($20,000 × 80%).

December 31, 20X7

Investment in Sergio	$15,600	
Income from Sergio		$15,600

   To record income for last three quarters of 20X7
     computed as follows:

Equity in income $36,000 × $\frac{3}{4}$ year × 80%		$21,600
Goodwill amortization:		
Unamortized January 1	$18,000	
Amortization January 1 to April 1	2,250	
Unamortized April 1 before sale	15,750	
Less: Goodwill on interest		
sold ($15,750 ÷ 9)	1,750	
Unamortized April 1 after sale	14,000	
Amortization April 1 to December 31		
$14,000 ÷ 7/4 years × $\frac{3}{4}$ years		6,000
Income from Sergio		$15,600

The income from Sergio for 20X7 is $21,450, consisting of $5,850 the first quarter and $15,600 the last three quarters of the year. At year-end, the investment in Sergio account has the same $260,800 balance as in the beginning-of-the-period sale illustration, but the balance involves different amounts:

Investment balance January 1	$288,000
Less: Book value of interest sold	32,650
	255,350
Add: Income less dividends	5,450
Investment balance December 31	$260,800

The investment balance at year-end is the same as before because Pablo holds the same ownership interest as under the beginning-of-the-year sale assumption. Further, Pablo has received the same cash inflow from the investment ($40,000 proceeds from the sale and $16,000 dividends), and therefore should report the same income. The income effects under the different assumptions are explained as follows:

	Sale at or Assumed at Beginning of Period	Sale Within the Accounting Period
Gain on sale of investment	$ 8,000	$ 7,350
Income from Sergio	20,800	21,450
Total income effect	$28,800	$28,800

The total income effect on Pablo's net income is the same, so the effect on the consolidated financial statements also must be the same. Consolidation working papers for a sale within an accounting period are illustrated in Exhibit 8–5.

PABLO CORPORATION AND SUBSIDIARY
CONSOLIDATION WORKING PAPERS
FOR THE YEAR ENDED DECEMBER 31, 20X7

	Pablo	80% Sergio	Adjustments and Eliminations		Minority Interest	Consolidated Statements
Income Statement Sales	$600,000	$136,000				$736,000
Income from Sergio	21,450		a 21,450			
Gain on sale	7,350					7,350
Cost of sales and expenses	(508,800)	(100,000)	c 8,250			(617,050)
Minority interest income†					$ 6,300	(6,300)
Net income	$120,000	$ 36,000				$120,000
Retained Earnings Retained earnings—Pablo	$210,000					$210,000
Retained earnings—Sergio		$100,000	b 100,000			
Net income	120,000√	36,000√				120,000
Dividends	(80,000)	(20,000)		a 16,000	(4,000)	(80,000)
Retained earnings December 31, 20X7	$250,000	$116,000				$250,000
Balance Sheet Other assets	$639,200	$350,000				$989,200
Investment in Sergio	260,800			a 5,450 b 255,350		
Goodwill			b 16,250	c 8,250		8,000
	$900,000	$350,000				$997,200
Liabilities	$150,000	$ 34,000				$184,000
Capital stock	500,000	200,000	b 200,000			500,000
Retained earnings	250,000√	116,000√				250,000
	$900,000	$350,000				
Minority interest January 1, 20X7				b 30,000	30,000	
Minority interest April 1, 20X7				b 30,900	30,900	
Minority interest December 31, 20X7					$63,200	63,200
						$997,200

†Minority interest income = ($36,000 × 10% × 1 year) + ($36,000 × 10% × $\frac{3}{4}$ year)

Exhibit 8–5 *Sale of a 10 Percent Interest Within an Accounting Period*

Working paper entries to consolidate the financial statements of Pablo and Sergio are journalized as follows:

a	Income from Sergio	$ 21,450	
	Dividends—Sergio		$ 16,000
	Investment in Sergio		5,450
b	Capital stock—Sergio	$200,000	
	Retained earnings—Sergio	100,000	
	Goodwill	16,250	
	Investment in Sergio		$255,350
	Minority interest January 1		30,000
	Minority interest April 1		30,900
c	Amortization of goodwill	$ 8,250	
	Goodwill		$ 8,250

Minority Interest Computations   The minority interest amounts that are entered in entry b are separated for illustrative purposes but do not have to be separated. One part of the minority interest calculation is based on the 10% minority interest at the beginning of the period ($300,000 equity of Sergio at January 1 × 10%), and the other part reflects the book value of the 10% increase in minority interest from the April 1 sale ($309,000 equity of Sergio on April 1 × 10%). Note that a dual calculation is also needed for minority interest income [($36,000 × 10%) + ($36,000 × 10% × $\frac{3}{4}$ year)] for midyear sale situations. The investment in Sergio was decreased when the interest was sold on April 1, therefore, the $255,350 credit in working paper entry b reflects the $288,000 beginning investment balance less the $32,650 book value of the investment interest sold on April 1.

Except for the items discussed, the working papers in Exhibits 8–4 and 8–5 are comparable, and the resulting consolidated financial statements are equivalent in all material respects. Because of the additional complexity involved when a sale is recorded as of the actual sale date, it is more efficient to use the beginning-of-the-period sale assumption. Use of a beginning-of-the-period assumption is also practical because current earnings information is usually not available during an accounting period.

CHANGES IN OWNERSHIP INTERESTS FROM SUBSIDIARY STOCK TRANSACTIONS

Subsidiary stock issuances provide a means of expanding the operations of a subsidiary through external financing. Both the expansion and the financing decisions are, of course, controlled by the parent company. Parent company management may decide to construct a new plant for the subsidiary and to finance the construction by selling additional subsidiary stock to the parent. Subsidiary operations may also be expanded through the issuance of subsidiary stock to the public. For example, the following note appeared in the *1996 USX Corporation Annual Report* (p. 42):

> In 1996, an aggregate of 6.9 million shares of RMI Titanium Company (RMI) common stock was sold in a public offering at a price of $18.50 per share and total net proceeds of $121 million. Included in the offering were 2.3 million shares sold by USX for net proceeds of $40 million. USX recognized a total pretax gain of $53 million, of which $34 million was attributable to the shares sold by USX and $19 million was attributable to the increase in value of USX's investment as a result of the shares sold by RMI. The income tax effect related to the total gain was $19 million. As a result of this transaction, USX's ownership in RMI decreased from approximately 50% to 27%. USX continues to account for its investment in RMI under the equity method of accounting.

In the case of a partially owned subsidiary, minority stockholders may exercise their preemptive rights to subscribe to additional stock issuances in proportion to their holdings.

Subsidiary operations may be curtailed if the parent company management decides to have the subsidiary reacquire its own shares.

A parent company/investor's ownership in a subsidiary/investee may change as a result of subsidiary sales of additional shares or through subsidiary purchases of its own shares. The effect of such activities on the parent company/investor depends on the price at which additional shares are sold or treasury stock is purchased, and on whether the parent company is directly involved in transactions with the subsidiary. In accounting for an equity investment under a one-line consolidation, *APB Opinion No. 18* stipulates that "a transaction of an investee of a capital nature that affects the investor's share of stockholders' equity of the investee should be accounted for as if the investee were a consolidated subsidiary."[3]

Sale of Additional Shares by a Subsidiary

Assume that Purdy Corporation owns an 80% interest in Stroh Corporation and that Purdy's investment in Stroh is $180,000 on January 1, 20X7, equal to 80% of Stroh's $200,000 stockholders' equity plus $20,000 unamortized goodwill. Stroh's equity on this date consists of:

Capital stock, $10 par	$100,000
Additional paid-in capital	60,000
Retained earnings	40,000
Total stockholders' equity	$200,000

Subsidiary Sells Shares to Parent   If Stroh sells an additional 2,000 shares of stock to Purdy *at book value of $20 per share* on January 2, 20X7, Purdy's investment in Stroh will increase by $40,000 to $220,000, and its interest in Stroh will increase from 80% (8,000 ÷ 10,000 shares) to $83\frac{1}{3}\%$ (10,000 ÷ 12,000 shares). The amount paid for the 2,000 additional shares is equal to book value, so Purdy's investment in Stroh still reflects the $20,000 unamortized goodwill:

	January 1 Before Sale	January 2 After Sale
Stroh's stockholders' equity	$200,000	$240,000
Purdy's interest	80%	$83\frac{1}{3}\%$
Purdy's equity in Stroh	160,000	200,000
Unamortized goodwill	20,000	20,000
Investment in Stroh balance	$180,000	$220,000

If Stroh sells the 2,000 shares to Purdy *at $35 per share*, Purdy's investment in Stroh will increase to $250,000 ($180,000 + $70,000 additional investment), and its ownership interest will increase from 80% to $83\frac{1}{3}\%$. Now Purdy's investment in Stroh reflects a $25,000 excess of investment balance over underlying book value. The additional $5,000 excess is the result of Purdy's $70,000 payment to increase its equity in Stroh by $65,000 and is analyzed as follows:

Price paid by Purdy (2,000 shares × $35)		$ 70,000
Book value acquired:		
Underlying book value after purchase ($200,000 + $70,000) × $83\frac{1}{3}\%$	$225,000	
Underlying book value before purchase ($200,000 × 80%)	160,000	
Book value acquired		65,000
Excess cost over book value acquired		$ 5,000

The $5,000 excess is assigned to identifiable assets or goodwill as appropriate and amortized over the remaining life of undervalued assets, or over a maximum of forty years if assigned to goodwill. Purdy should amortize the $20,000 unamortized goodwill at January 1, 20X1 without changing the initial amortization plan.

Now assume that Stroh sells the 2,000 shares to Purdy at *$15 per share* (or $5 per share below book value). Purdy's ownership interest increases from 80% to $83\frac{1}{3}\%$ as

---

[3]*APB Opinion No. 18*, "The Equity Method of Accounting for Investments in Common Stock," paragraph 19e.

before, and its investment in Stroh increases by $30,000 to $210,000. As a result of paying less than book value for the shares, however, book value acquired exceeds investment cost:

Price paid by Purdy (2,000 shares × $15)		$ 30,000
Book value acquired:		
Underlying book value after purchase		
($200,000 + $30,000) × $83\frac{1}{3}$%	$191,667	
Underlying book value before purchase		
($200,000 × 80%)	160,000	
Book value acquired		31,667
Excess book value acquired over cost		$ 1,667

Conceptually, the $1,667 excess book value acquired over cost should be assigned to reduce overvalued identifiable net assets. The practical solution, however, is to charge the excess book value to any unamortized goodwill from investments in the same company's stock. In this example, reduce unamortized goodwill from $20,000 to $18,333.

Subsidiary Sells Shares to Outside Entities   Assume that Stroh sells the 2,000 additional shares to other entities (minority stockholders). Purdy's ownership interest declines from 80% (8,000 ÷ 10,000 shares) to $66\frac{2}{3}$% (8,000 ÷ 12,000 shares), regardless of the selling price of the shares. But the effect on Purdy's investment in Stroh account depends upon the selling price of the shares. The effect of the sale on Purdy's underlying book value in Stroh under each of three issuance assumptions ($20, $35, and $15 per share) is:

	January 2, 20X1 After Sale		
	Sale at $20	Sale at $35	Sale at $15
Stroh's stockholders' equity	$240,000	$270,000	$230,000
Interest owned	$66\frac{2}{3}$%	$66\frac{2}{3}$%	$66\frac{2}{3}$%
Purdy's equity in Stroh after issuance	160,000	180,000	153,333
Purdy's equity in Stroh before issuance	160,000	160,000	160,000
Increase (decrease) in Purdy's equity in Stroh	0	$ 20,000	$ (6,667)

Sale to outside entities at $20 per share does not affect Purdy's equity in Stroh because the selling price is equal to book value. If the stock is sold at $35 per share (above book value), Purdy's equity in Stroh will increase by $20,000, and if it is sold at $15 per share (below book value), Purdy's equity in Stroh will decrease by $6,667.

Two methods of accounting for the effect of the decreased ownership percentage on the parent company's books are (1) to adjust the additional paid-in capital and the parent's investment account balances for the change in underlying equity and (2) to treat the decrease in ownership as a sale and recognize gain or loss for the difference between book value of the investment interest sold and the parent's share of the proceeds from the subsidiary's stock issuance.

The first approach is supported by *APB Opinion No. 9*, which excludes adjustments from transactions in a company's own stock from the determination of net income "under all circumstances."[4] From the viewpoint of the consolidated entity, the issuance of subsidiary shares to the public is a transaction in a company's own shares. Entries to record the changes in underlying equity on Purdy's books under this first method are:

Sale at $20 Per Share (Book Value)
None

Sale at $35 Per Share (Above Book Value)

Investment in Stroh	$20,000	
Additional paid-in capital		$20,000

---

[4] *APB Opinion No. 9*, "Reporting the Results of Operations," paragraph 28.

Sale at $15 Per Share (Below Book Value)
Additional paid-in capital[5]	$ 6,667	
Investment in Stroh		$ 6,667

Under this method, unamortized cost/book value differentials are not adjusted for the decreased ownership percentage.

Traditionally, the method just illustrated was the only one accepted by the accounting profession and the SEC. In 1980, however, the AICPA released an Issues Paper, "Accounting in Consolidation for Issuances of a Subsidiary's Stock," in which it recommended the recognition of gains or losses on subsidiary stock sales. Then, in 1983, the SEC issued *Staff Accounting Bulletin (SAB) 51*, which allows SEC companies to follow the recommendations of the Issues Paper for previously unissued shares, provided that the subsidiary shares are sold in a public offering and are not part of a broader reorganization that will involve other capital transactions. Subsequently, in 1989, the SEC, in *SAB 84*, affirmed that a parent company can record a gain in the consolidated income statement on its subsidiary's sale of stock to the public if the per share offering price is greater than the carrying value of the subsidiary on the parent company's books. However, *SAB 84* restricts recognition of gain when there are concerns about realization of the gain. *SAB 84* prohibits gain recognition on subsidiary stock sales to the public if the registrant plans to repurchase the shares, if the subsidiary is a newly formed nonoperating entity or a research and development company, or if the subsidiary is a company whose continued existence is in question.

The argument in favor of gain or loss recognition is that there is no substantive difference between subsidiary stock sales that reduce a parent's investment and direct sales of stock by the parent. The FASB has not acted on the matter, so neither the Issues Paper nor *SAB 51* constitutes generally accepted accounting principles at this time. Also, although *SAB 51* is permissive and not mandatory, it may help establish preferability for a firm that changes its accounting policy to recognize gains on subsidiary stock sales.

Under the second method of gain or loss recognition, Purdy is assumed to have sold $16\frac{2}{3}\%$ of its interest in Stroh [$(80\% - 66\frac{2}{3}\%) \div 80\%$] in exchange for $66\frac{2}{3}\%$ of the proceeds from the subsidiary sale of stock. Thus, the entries on Purdy's books under the three selling-price assumptions are:

Sale at $20 Per Share (Book Value)
Loss on sale	$ 3,333	
Investment in Stroh		$ 3,333

Computation: ($40,000 × $66\frac{2}{3}\%$) − ($180,000 × $16\frac{2}{3}\%$)

Sale at $35 Per Share (Above Book Value)
Investment in Stroh	$16,667	
Gain on sale		$16,667

Computation: ($70,000 × $66\frac{2}{3}\%$) − ($180,000 × $16\frac{2}{3}\%$)

Sale at $15 Per Share (Below Book Value)
Loss on sale	$10,000	
Investment in Stroh		$10,000

Computation: ($30,000 × $66\frac{2}{3}\%$) − ($180,000 × $16\frac{2}{3}\%$)

The different gain or loss amounts under this method and the amounts of adjustment to additional paid-in capital under the first method lie solely in the $3,333 unamortized goodwill [$20,000 × ($80\% - 66\frac{2}{3}\%$) ÷ 80%] applicable to the reduction in ownership percentage. Unamortized goodwill related to the interest assumed to be sold is only considered when gain or loss is recognized, and in the absence of unamortized cost/book value differences, the amounts are identical.

Summary of Subsidiary Stock Sales Concepts   Sales of stock by a subsidiary to its parent do not result in gain or loss recognition or adjustments to additional paid-in capital, but they do result in cost/book value differentials equal to the parent company's share of the difference in the subsidiary's stockholders' equity immediately before and immediately after the sale of stock.

---

[5]This debit is to retained earnings when the parent company's additional paid-in capital is insufficient to stand the charge.

Sales of stock by a subsidiary to outside parties are considered capital transactions under generally accepted accounting principles, and they require adjustment of the parent's investment and additional paid-in capital accounts except when the shares are sold at book value. The amount of adjustment is the difference between the underlying book value of the interest held immediately before and after the additional shares are issued to outsiders. The SEC permits recognition of gains or losses on subsidiary stock sales to the public—with certain restrictions. Such gain or loss is determined by comparing the parent's share of proceeds from the stock issue with the book value of the investment interest assumed to be sold. Alternatively, the gain or loss can be determined by adjusting the change in the parent's underlying book value in the subsidiary for any unamortized cost/book value differentials related to the interest assumed to be sold.

If a parent company and outside investors purchase shares of a subsidiary in relation to existing stock ownership (ratably), no adjustments to additional paid-in capital will be necessary, regardless of whether the stock is sold at book value, below book value, or above book value. Similarly, no excess or deficiency of investment cost over book value for the parent company can result from this situation. This is true because the increased investment is necessarily equal to the parent's increase (or decrease) in underlying book value from the ratable purchase of additional shares.

Treasury Stock Transactions by a Subsidiary

The acquisition of treasury stock by a subsidiary decreases subsidiary equity and subsidiary shares outstanding. If the treasury stock is acquired from minority shareholders at book value, no change in the parent's share of subsidiary equity results even though the parent's percentage ownership increases. Purchase of its own shares from minority stockholders at an amount above or below book value decreases or increases the parent's share of subsidiary book value and at the same time increases the parent's ownership percentage. This latter situation requires an entry on the parent company's books to adjust the investment in subsidiary balance, and to charge or credit additional paid-in capital for the difference in the parent's share of subsidiary book value before and after the treasury stock transaction.

Assume that Shelly Company is an 80% subsidiary of Pointer Corporation and that Shelly has 10,000 shares of common stock outstanding at December 31, 20X7. On January 1, 20X8, Shelly purchases 400 shares of its own stock from minority stockholders. The effect of this treasury stock acquisition on Pointer's share of Shelly's book value is summarized in Exhibit 8–6 under three different assumptions regarding the purchase price of the treasury shares.

Pointer's equity in Shelly Company before the purchase of the 400 shares of treasury stock by Shelly was $160,000, and its ownership interest was 80%, as shown in the first column of Exhibit 8–6. The purchase of the 400 treasury shares by Shelly increases Pointer's ownership percentage to $83\frac{1}{3}\%$ (or 8,000 of 9,600 outstanding shares), regardless of the price paid by Shelly to reacquire the shares. If Shelly purchases the 400 shares at their $20 per share book value, Pointer's share of Shelly's equity remains at $160,000, as shown in the second column of Exhibit 8–6, even though its interest increases to $83\frac{1}{3}\%$. In this case, no adjustment is required.

If Shelly purchases the 400 shares of treasury stock at $30 per share, Pointer's equity decreases by $3,333 to $156,667, as shown in column 3 of Exhibit 8–6. The decrease is recorded on Pointer's books with the following entry:

Additional paid-in capital	$3,333	
Investment in Shelly		$3,333
To record an investment decrease from Shelly's purchase		
of treasury stock in excess of book value.		

This entry reduces Pointer's investment in Shelly to its share of the underlying book value in Shelly and also reduces additional paid-in capital. Treasury stock transactions are of a capital nature, so they do not affect gain or loss.

The third situation illustrated in Exhibit 8–6 (column 4) assumes that Shelly purchases 400 shares of treasury stock at $15 per share ($5 per share below book value). As a result of Shelly's acquisition of its own shares, Pointer's share of Shelly's

EQUITY OF SHELLY COMPANY

	Column 1 Before Purchase of Treasury Stock	Column 2 After Purchase of 400 Shares at $20	Column 3 After Purchase of 400 Shares at $30	Column 4 After Purchase of 400 Shares at $15
Capital stock, $10 par	$100,000	$100,000	$100,000	$100,000
Retained earnings	100,000	100,000	100,000	100,000
	200,000	200,000	200,000	200,000
Less: Treasury stock (cost)	—	8,000	12,000	6,000
Total equity	$200,000	$192,000	$188,000	$194,000
Pointer's interest	$\frac{4}{5}$*	$\frac{5}{6}$†	$\frac{5}{6}$†	$\frac{5}{6}$†
Pointer's share of Shelly's book value	$160,000	$160,000	$156,667	$161,667

*8,000 out of 10,000 outstanding shares.
†8,000 out of 9,600 outstanding shares.

Exhibit 8–6 *Purchase of Treasury Stock by Subsidiary*

equity increases from $160,000 to $161,667. This increase of $1,667 requires the following adjustment on Pointer's books:

Investment in Shelly	$1,667	
Additional paid-in capital		$1,667

    To record an investment increase from Shelly's purchase
    of treasury shares below book value.

The parent company adjustments illustrated here for changes resulting from subsidiary treasury stock transactions are supported by current accounting principles that prohibit the recognition of gain or loss from treasury stock transactions, but at the same time require the equity method of accounting with elimination of any differences between the investment and its underlying book value over a maximum period of 40 years. The parent's accounting for subsidiary treasury stock transactions is based on the book value of the net assets. During the time treasury shares are held, the book value of net assets would change due to the subsidiary's operations. If the treasury shares are eventually resold, the parent would account for this change on the basis of the book value of the assets at the time of sale. It should be understood, however, that *frequent and insignificant treasury stock transactions by a subsidiary tend to be offsetting with respect to purchases and sales and do not require the adjustments illustrated.*

STOCK DIVIDENDS AND STOCK SPLITS BY A SUBSIDIARY

Stock dividends and splits by substantially owned subsidiaries are not common unless the minority interest is actively traded in the security markets. This is because the management of the parent company controls such actions and there is ordinarily no advantage to the consolidated entity or the parent company from increasing the number of subsidiary shares outstanding through stock splits or stock dividends. Even if a subsidiary does split its stock or issue a stock dividend, the effect of such actions on consolidation procedures is minimal.

A stock split by a subsidiary increases the number of shares outstanding, but it does not affect either the net assets of the subsidiary or the individual equity accounts. Also, parent company and minority interest ownership percentages are unaffected by subsidiary stock splits and, accordingly, parent company accounting and consolidation procedures are unaffected. These same observations apply to stock dividends by subsidiaries except that the individual subsidiary equity accounts are changed in the case of stock dividends. This change occurs because retained earnings equal to par or stated value or to the market price of the additional shares issued is transferred to paid-in capital.[6] Although the capitalization of retained earnings does not affect parent company accounting for its subsidiaries, it does change the amounts of capital stock, additional paid-in capital, and retained earnings to be eliminated in the consolidation process.

Pictor Corporation owns 80% of the outstanding stock of Sorry Company acquired on January 1, 20X5 for $160,000. Sorry's stockholders' equity on that date was as follows:

Capital stock, $10 par	$100,000
Additional paid-in capital	20,000
Retained earnings	80,000
Total stockholders' equity	$200,000

During 20X5, Sorry had net income of $30,000 and paid cash dividends of $10,000. Pictor increased its investment in Sorry for its investment income of $24,000 ($30,000 × 80%) and decreased it for dividends received of $8,000 ($10,000 × 80%). Thus, Pictor's investment in Sorry account at December 31, 20X5 was $176,000.

On the basis of the information given, the consolidation working papers for Pictor Corporation and Subsidiary for 20X5 would include the following adjustments and eliminations:

Income from Sorry	$ 24,000	
Dividends		$ 8,000
Investment in Sorry		16,000
Capital stock—Sorry	$100,000	
Additional paid-in capital—Sorry	20,000	
Retained earnings—Sorry	80,000	
Investment in Sorry		$160,000
Minority interest—beginning		40,000

If Sorry had also declared and issued a 10% stock dividend on December 31, 20X5, when its stock was selling at $40 per share, the stock dividend would have been recorded by Sorry Corporation as follows:

Stock dividend on common	$40,000	
Capital stock, $10 par		$10,000
Additional paid-in capital		30,000

This stock dividend does not affect Pictor's accounting for its investment in Sorry, but it does affect the consolidation working papers, because Sorry's capital stock has increased to $110,000 ($100,000 + $10,000) and its additional paid-in capital has increased to $50,000 ($20,000 + $30,000). Consolidation working paper adjustment and elimination entries for 20X5 would be as follows:

Income from Sorry	$ 24,000	
Dividends		$ 8,000
Investment in Sorry		16,000
Capital stock—Sorry	$110,000	
Additional paid-in capital—Sorry	50,000	
Retained earnings—Sorry	80,000	
Investment in Sorry		$160,000
Minority interest—beginning		40,000
Stock dividend on common		40,000

---

[6]See *ARB No. 43*, Chapter 7, paragraph 10 through 14, for accounting procedures relating to stock dividends.

The $40,000 stock dividend account is eliminated along with the reciprocal investment and equity balances, because it is really an offset to $10,000 of the capital stock and $30,000 of the additional paid-in capital amounts. In 20X6 and subsequent years, the retained earnings account will reflect the $40,000 decrease from the stock dividend and no further complications will result.

SUMMARY

When a parent company purchases a subsidiary during an accounting period, the preacquisition earnings relating to the interest acquired are deducted in computing consolidated net income. Preacquisition dividends on an interest acquired during an accounting period are also eliminated in the consolidation process. Accounting for a midyear pooling of interests involves consolidating the incomes of the pooled affiliates for the entire year. The investment is recorded at its book value at the beginning of the period, adjusted for dividends paid prior to combination.

The acquisition of a controlling interest in another company through a series of separate stock purchases over a period of time increases the detail involved in accounting for the total investment under the equity method. It also complicates the preparation of consolidated financial statements because the investment cost/book value differential has to be related to each acquisition on the basis of the total interest held.

When a parent company/investor sells an ownership interest in a subsidiary/investee corporation, the gain or loss on sale is equal to the difference between the selling price and the book value of the investment interest sold. However, if the investment is not accounted for on an equity basis, it has to be adjusted to an equity basis before gain or loss on sale is computed. The sale of an interest in a subsidiary during an accounting period increases the minority interest and necessitates some changes in the computation of minority interest income.

The sale of additional shares by a subsidiary changes the parent's percentage ownership in the subsidiary unless the shares are sold to the parent company and minority shareholders in proportion to their holdings. The direct sale of additional shares to the parent company increases the parent's interest and decreases the minority shareholders' interest. The issuance of additional shares to minority stockholders or outside entities by the subsidiary decreases the parent's percentage interest and increases the minority shareholders' interests. Similar changes in majority and minority ownership interests result from a subsidiary's treasury stock transactions. Such changes require special care in accounting for a parent company's investment under the equity method and in preparing consolidated financial statements.

Parent company accounting and consolidation procedures are not affected by subsidiary stock splits. However, subsidiary stock dividends may lead to changes in the consolidation working papers.

SELECTED READINGS

Committee on Accounting Procedure. *Accounting Research Bulletin No. 51*. "Consolidated Financial Statements." New York: American Institute of Certified Public Accountants, 1959.

Financial Accounting Series. *Exposure Draft*. "Consolidated Financial Statements: Policy and Procedures." Norwalk, CT: Financial Accounting Standards Boards, 1995.

AICPA Accounting Standards Executive Committee. *Issues Paper*. "Accounting in Consolidation for Issuance of a Subsidiary Stock." New York: American Institute of Certified Public Accountants, 1980.

AICPA Committee on Accounting Procedure. *Accounting Research Bulletin No. 43*. "Restatement and Revision of Accounting Research Bulletins." New York: American Institute of Certified Public Accountants, 1953.

ASSIGNMENT MATERIAL

QUESTIONS

1 Explain the terms *preacquisition earnings* and *preacquisition dividends*.
2 How are preacquisition earnings accounted for by a parent company under the equity method? How are they accounted for in the consolidated income statement?
3 Assume that an 80% investor of Sub Company acquires an additional 10% interest in Sub halfway through the current fiscal period. Explain the effect of the 10% acquisition by the

parent company on minority interest income for the period and on total minority interest at the end of the current period.

4 Isn't preacquisition income really minority interest income? If so, why separate preacquisition income and minority interest income in the consolidated income statement?

5 What modifications to the usual equity method of accounting are required on a parent company's books in accounting for a midyear pooling of interests? (In other words, how is equality established between parent company and consolidated net income for midyear poolings?)

6 Assume that Pam Corporation purchases plant and equipment from Sam Corporation in January 20X8 and that a pooling business combination between Pam and Sam is consummated in September 20X8. Is the plant asset transaction an intercompany transaction for which gains and losses must be eliminated in the consolidated statements for the year ended December 31, 20X8? Explain.

7 How is the gain or loss determined for the sale of part of an investment interest that is accounted for as a one-line consolidation? Is the amount of gain or loss affected by the accounting method used by the investor?

8 When a parent company sells a part of its interest in a subsidiary during an accounting period, is the income applicable to the interest sold up to the time of sale included in consolidated net income and parent company income under the equity method? Explain.

9 Assume that a subsidiary has 10,000 shares of stock outstanding, of which 8,000 shares are owned by the parent company. What equity method adjustment would be necessary on the parent company books if the subsidiary sells 2,000 additional shares of its own stock to outside interests at book value? At an amount in excess of book value?

10 Assume that a subsidiary has 10,000 shares of stock outstanding, of which 8,000 shares are owned by the parent company. If the parent company purchases an additional 2,000 shares of stock directly from the subsidiary at book value, how should the parent company record its additional investment? Would your answer have been different if the purchase of the 2,000 shares had been made above book value? Explain.

11 How do the treasury stock transactions of a subsidiary affect the parent company's accounting for its investment under the equity method?

12 Can gains or losses to a parent company (investor) result from a subsidiary's (investee's) treasury stock transactions? Explain.

13 Do common stock dividends and stock splits by a subsidiary affect the amounts that appear in the consolidated financial statements? Explain, indicating the items, if any, that would be affected.

(*Note:* Don't forget the assumptions on page 56 when working exercises and problems in this chapter.)

EXERCISES

E 8-1 Pie Corporation increases its ownership interest in its subsidiary, Sweet Corporation, from 70% on January 1, 20X6 to 90% at July 1, 20X6. Sweet's net income for 20X6 is $100,000, and it declares $30,000 dividends on March 1 and $30,000 on September 1.

Required: Show the allocation of Sweet's net income and dividends among majority interests, minority interests, and preacquisition interests.

E 8-2 On January 1, 20X9, Pinnacle Industries purchased a 40% interest in Superstore Corporation for $800,000, when Superstore's stockholders' equity consisted of $1,000,000 capital stock and $1,000,000 retained earnings. On September 1, 20X9, Pinnacle purchased an additional 20% interest in Superstore for $420,000. Both purchases were made at book value equal to fair value.

Superstore had income for 20X9 or $240,000, earned evenly throughout the year, and it paid dividends of $60,000 in April and $60,000 in October.

Required: Compute the following:
 1 Pinnacle's income from Superstore for 20X9
 2 Preacquisition income that will appear on the consolidated income statement of Pinnacle and Subsidiary for 20X9
 3 Minority interest income for 20X9

E 8-3 Peat Corporation owns 100% (300,000 shares) of the outstanding shares of Swamp Corporation's common stock on January 1, 20X1. Its investment in Swamp account on this date is $4,400,000, equal to Swamp's $4,000,000 stockholders' equity plus $400,000 goodwill with a remaining write-off period of 10 years. During 20X1, Swamp reports net income of $600,000 and pays no dividends.

On April 1, 20X1, Peat sells a 15% interest (45,000 shares) in Swamp for $750,000, thereby reducing its holdings to 85%.

Required: Prepare the journal entries needed for Peat to account for its investment in Swamp for 20X1, using a beginning-of-the-period sales assumption.

E 8-4 The balance of Pauley Corporation's investment in Savage Company account at December 31, 20X5 was $436,000, consisting of 80% of Savage's $500,000 stockholders' equity on that date and $36,000 unamortized goodwill with a remaining amortization period of three years.

On May 1, 20X6, Pauley sold a 20% interest in Savage (one-fourth of its holdings) for $130,000. During 20X6, Savage had net income of $150,000, and on July 1, 20X6, Savage declared dividends of $80,000.

Required
  1 Determine the gain or loss on sale of the 20% interest.
  2 Calculate Pauley's income from Savage for 20X6.
  3 Determine the balance of Pauley's investment in Savage account at December 31, 20X6.

E 8-5 Phrog Corporation paid $1,290,000 cash for 70% of the common stock of Stork Corporation on June 1, 20X9. The assets and liabilities of Stork were fairly valued and any cost/book value differential is goodwill with a 10-year amortization period. Data related to the stockholders' equity of Stork are as follows:

Stockholders' Equity December 31, 20X8

Common stock, $10 par	$1,000,000
Retained earnings	480,000
Total stockholders' equity	$1,480,000

Income and dividends—20X9	
Net income (earned evenly throughout the year)	$240,000
Dividends (declared and paid in equal amounts in January, April, July, and October)	120,000

Required
  1 Determine the following
    a Goodwill from the investment in Stork
    b Phrog's income from Stork for 20X9
    c The investment in Stork account balance at December 31, 20X9
  2 Prepare the working paper entries needed to consolidate the financial statements of Phrog and Stork corporations for 20X9.

E 8-6 On October 1, 20X2, Pelvis Corporation issued 30,000 shares of $10 par common stock with a market value of $30 per share for a 90% interest in Solace Corporation in a pooling of interests business combination. Direct costs of the combination, which are paid by Pelvis, total $40,000 for registering and issuing the shares and $35,000 for other items.

On January 1, 20X2, the book value (equal to fair value) of Solace's net assets was $912,500. Solace's net income for 20X2 is $100,000, earned evenly throughout the year, and Solace declares dividends of $25,000 on June 1 and $25,000 on December 1. Pelvis's separate income for 20X2 is $300,000 *excluding* the direct costs of combination.

Required: Determine consolidated net income for Pelvis Corporation and Subsidiary for 20X2.

E 8-7 Preisendorf Corporation issued 150,000 shares of its $10 par common stock for 90% of the outstanding shares of Schenck Corporation on May 1, 20X6 in a pooling of interests business combination. Trial balances of Schenck on May 1 (immediately before the pooling) and on December 31, 20X6 (before closing) are summarized as follows:

	May 1	December 31
Debits		
Current assets	$ 380,000	$ 520,000
Plant assets	1,400,000	1,300,000
Expenses	400,000	1,200,000
Dividends	70,000	210,000
	$2,250,000	$3,230,000
Credits		
Liabilities	$ 250,000	$ 230,000
Common stock, $10 par	1,000,000	1,000,000
Retained earnings	500,000	500,000
Sales	500,000	1,500,000
	$2,250,000	$3,230,000

Required

1 Determine Preisendorf's investment income and dividends from its investment in Schenck for 20X6.

2 Compute the balance of Preisendorf's investment in Schenck account on December 31, 20X6.

E 8-8 The stockholders' equities of Petal Corporation and its 80%-owned subsidiary, Sower Corporation, on December 31, 20X2 are as follows:

	Petal	Sower
Common stock, $10 par	$10,000,000	$6,000,000
Retained earnings	4,000,000	3,000,000
Total stockholders' equity	$14,000,000	$9,000,000

Petal's investment in Sower account balance on December 31, 20X2 is equal to its underlying book value. On January 2, 20X3, Sower issued 60,000 previously unissued common shares directly to Petal at $25 per share.

Required

1 Calculate the balance of Petal's investment in Sower account on January 2, 20X3 after the new investment is recorded.

2 Determine the goodwill, if any, from Petal's purchase of the 60,000 new shares.

E 8-9 The stockholders' equity of Pod Corporation and its 80%-owned subsidiary, Sod Corporation, on December 31, 20X1 appear as follows:

	Pod	Sod
Common stock, $10 par	$5,000,000	$2,200,000
Retained earnings	2,000,000	1,000,000
Total	$7,000,000	$3,200,000

Pod's investment in Sod account on this date is equal to its underlying book value. On January 1, 20X2, Sod issues 30,000 previously unissued common shares for $20 per share.

Required

1 If Pod purchases the 30,000 shares directly from Sod, what is Pod's percentage ownership in Sod after the new shares are acquired?

2 If Sod sells the 30,000 previously unissued common shares to the public, what is Pod's percentage ownership in Sod after the new issuance?

3 If Sod sells the 30,000 shares to the public, prepare the journal entry on Pod's books to account for the effect of the issuance on its investment in Sod account assuming that *no* gain or loss is recognized.

4 If Sod sells the 30,000 shares to the public, prepare the journal entry on Pod's books to account for the effect of the issuance on its investment in Sod account assuming that a gain or loss is recognized.

E 8-10 Padgett Corporation issued 420,000 of its $5 par common shares for 90% of Stockard Corporation's $10 par common shares in a pooling of interests that was consummated on September 1, 20X6. Prior to the pooling, Padgett's stockholders' equity consisted of $10,000,000 common stock, $100,000 other paid-in capital, and $4,000,000 retained earnings. Summary financial information for Stockard at January 1, September 1, and December 31, 20X6 follows:

	Balance January 1	8 Months Ended September 1	Year-End December 31
Net assets	$3,100,000	$3,400,000	$3,550,000
Capital stock, $10 par	$2,000,000	$2,000,000	$2,000,000
Other paid-in capital	200,000	200,000	200,000
Retained earnings	900,000	900,000	900,000
Net income		400,000	650,000
Dividends		(100,000)	(200,000)
Stockholders' equity	$3,100,000	$3,400,000	$3,550,000

Required

1 Prepare the journal entry to record the pooling of interests on September 1, 20X6.

2 Prepare the entry or entries to account for the investment in Stockard during 20X6.

E 8-11   Primetime Corporation owns two-thirds (600,000 shares) of the outstanding $1 par common stock of Satellite Equipment Company on January 1, 20X2. In order to raise cash to finance an expansion program, Satellite issues an additional 100,000 shares of its common stock for $5 per share on January 3, 20X2. Satellite's stockholders' equity before and after the new stock issuance is as follows:

	Before Issuance	After Issuance
Common stock, $1 par	$ 900,000	$1,000,000
Additional paid-in capital	600,000	1,000,000
Retained earnings	600,000	600,000
Total stockholders' equity	$2,100,000	$2,600,000

Required

1 Assume that Primetime purchases all 100,000 shares of common stock directly from Satellite.
   a What is Primetime's percentage ownership interest in Satellite after the purchase?
   b Calculate goodwill from Primetime's acquisition of the 100,000 shares of Satellite.
2 Assume that the 100,000 shares of common stock are sold to Ivanhoe Company, one of Satellite's minority stockholders.
   a What is Primetime's percentage ownership interest in Satellite after the new shares are sold to Ivanhoe?
   b Calculate the change in underlying book value of Primetime's investment in Satellite after the sale to Ivanhoe.
   c Prepare the journal entry on Primetime's books to recognize the increase or decrease in underlying book value computed in b above assuming that gain or loss is *not* recognized.

E 8-12   The stockholder's equity of Sum Corporation at December 31, 20X5, 20X6, and 20X7 is as follows:

	December 31,		
	20X5	20X6	20X7
Capital stock, $10 par	$200,000	$200,000	$200,000
Retained earnings	80,000	160,000	220,000
	$280,000	$360,000	$420,000

Sum reported income of $80,000 in 20X6 and paid no dividends. In 20X7, Sum reported net income of $80,000 and declared dividends of $10,000 on May 1 and $10,000 on November 1. Income was earned evenly in both years.

Plum Corporation acquired 4,000 shares of Sum common stock on April 1, 20X6 for $64,000 cash and another 8,000 shares on July 1, 20X7 for $166,000. Any cost/book value differential is goodwill with a 10-year amortization period.

Required: Determine the following:
1 Plum's income from Sum for 20X6 and 20X7
2 Minority interest at December 31, 20X7
3 Preacquisition income in 20X7
4 Balance of the investment in Sum account at December 31, 20X7

E 8-13   Piccolo Corporation acquired a 90% interest in Sandridge Mines on July 1, 20X4 for $675,000. The stockholders' equity of Sandridge Mines at December 31, 20X3 was as follows:

Capital stock	$500,000
Retained earnings	200,000
Total	$700,000

During 20X4 and 20X5, Sandridge Mines reported income and declared dividends in the following amounts:

	20X4	20X5
Net income	$100,000	$80,000
Dividends (December)	50,000	30,000

On July 1, 20X5, Piccolo Corporation sold a 10% interest (or one-ninth of its investment) in Sandridge Mines for $85,000.

1 Determine Piccolo's investment income for 20X4 and 20X5, and its investment balance on December 31, 20X4 and 20X5.
2 Determine minority interest income for 20X4 and 20X5, and the total of minority interest on December 31, 20X4 and 20X5.

E 8-14 Summarized adjusted trial balances for Polly Corporation and Seay Corporation on August 31, 20X6, just prior to their *pooling of interests* on September 1, 20X6, are as follows:

	Polly	Seay
Assets	$16,000,000	$5,500,000
Expenses	9,000,000	3,000,000
Dividends	2,000,000	500,000
	$27,000,000	$9,000,000
Liabilities	$ 3,000,000	$1,500,000
Common stock, $10 par	8,000,000	2,000,000
Other paid-in capital	1,000,000	500,000
Retained earnings	3,000,000	1,000,000
Sales	12,000,000	4,000,000
	$27,000,000	$9,000,000

Polly's separate income for the year ended December 31, 20X6 was $4,500,000 and its dividends for 20X6 totaled $4,000,000. Seay Corporation's net income for 20X6 was $1,500,000 and its dividends were $1,000,000.

Required

1 Prepare journal entries on Polly's books (a) to record its issuance of 400,000 common shares on September 1, 20X6 for all of the outstanding common stock of Seay, and (b) to account for its investment in Seay for 20X6, assuming that Polly and Seay continue to exist as parent company and subsidiary.
2 Prepare the stockholders' equity section of the consolidated balance sheet of Polly Corporation and Subsidiary on December 31, 20X6.

E 8-15 [AICPA adapted]

On June 30, 20X8, Purl Corporation issued 150,000 shares of its $20 par common stock, for which it received all of Scott Corporation's common stock. The fair value of the common stock issued is equal to the book value of Scott's net assets. Both corporations continued to operate as separate businesses, maintaining accounting records with years ending December 31. Net income from separate company operations and dividends paid were:

	Purl	Scott
Net income		
Six months ended June 30, 20X8	$750,000	$225,000
Six months ended December 31, 20X8	825,000	375,000
Dividends paid		
March 25, 20X8	950,000	—
November 15, 20X8	—	300,000

On December 31, 20X8, Scott held in its inventory merchandise acquired from Purl on December 1, 20X8 for $150,000, which included a $45,000 markup.

1 Assume that the business combination qualifies for treatment as a purchase. In the 20X8 consolidated income statement, net income should be reported at:
  a $1,650,000   **c** $1,950,000
  b $1,905,000   **d** $2,130,000

2 Assume that the business combination qualifies for treatment as a pooling of interests. In the 20X8 consolidated income statement, net income should be reported as:
  a $1,905,000   **c** $2,130,000
  b $1,950,000   **d** $2,175,000

E 8-16 [AICPA adapted]

On June 30, 20X7, Post, Inc. issued 630,000 shares of its $5 par common stock, for which it received 180,000 shares (90%) of Shaw Corporation's $10 par common stock in a business combination appropriately accounted for as a pooling of interests. The stockholders' equities immediately before the combination were:

	Post	Shaw
Common stock	$ 6,500,000	$2,000,000
Additional paid-in capital	4,400,000	1,600,000
Retained earnings	6,100,000	5,400,000
	$17,000,000	$9,000,000

Both corporations continued to operate as separate businesses, maintaining accounting records with years ending December 31. For 20X7, net income and dividends paid from separate company operations were:

	Post	Shaw
Net income		
Six months ended June 30, 20X7	$1,000,000	$300,000
Six months ended December 31, 20X7	1,100,000	500,000
Dividends paid		
April 1, 20X7	1,300,000	—
October 1, 20X7	—	350,000

1 In the June 30, 20X7 consolidated balance sheet, common stock should be reported at:
  a $9,650,000   c $8,500,000
  b $9,450,000   d $8,300,000

2 In the June 30, 20X7 consolidated balance sheet, additional paid-in capital should be reported at:
  a $4,400,000   c $5,840,000
  b $4,490,000   d $6,000,000

3 In the June 30, 20X7 consolidated balance sheet, retained earnings should be reported at:
  a $6,100,000   c $10,960,000
  b $9,660,000   d $11,500,000

4 In the 20X7 consolidated income statement, net income should be reported at:
  a $2,550,000   c $2,820,000
  b $2,600,000   d $2,900,000

5 In the December 31, 20X7 consolidated balance sheet, total minority interest should be reported at:
  a $950,000   c $915,000
  b $945,000   d $900,000

E 8-17 Panda Corporation purchased a 75% interest in Sanyo Corporation in the open market on January 1, 20X3 for $700,000. A summary of Sanyo's stockholders' equity on December 31, 20X2 and 20X3 is as follows:

	December 31	
	20X2	20X3
Capital stock, $10 par	$400,000	$ 400,000
Additional paid-in capital	300,000	300,000
Retained earnings	100,000	300,000
Total stockholders' equity	$800,000	$1,000,000

On January 1, 20X4, Sanyo sold an additional 10,000 shares of its own $10 par stock for $30 per share. Panda amortizes any excess or deficiency of investment cost over book value acquired over a 10-year period.

Required: Compute the following:
  1 The underlying book value of the interest in Sanyo held by Panda on December 31, 20X3
  2 Panda's percentage ownership interest in Sanyo on January 3, 20X4, assuming that Panda purchased the 10,000 additional shares directly from Sanyo
  3 Panda's investment in Sanyo on January 3, 20X4, assuming that Panda purchased the additional shares directly from Sanyo
  4 Panda's percentage ownership interest in Sanyo on January 3, 20X4, assuming that Sanyo sold the 10,000 additional shares to investors outside the consolidated entity
  5 Panda's investment in Sanyo on January 3, 20X4, assuming that Sanyo sold the 10,000 additional shares to investors outside the consolidated entity and no gain or loss is recognized

E 8-18 Puckett Corporation's investment in Saton Company account had a balance of $475,000 at December 31, 20X3. This balance consisted of unamortized goodwill of $35,000 (seven-year remaining amortization period) and 80% of Saton's $550,000 stockholders' equity.

On January 2, 20X4, Saton increased its outstanding shares from 10,000 to 12,000 shares by selling 2,000 additional shares directly to Puckett at $70 per share. Saton's net income for 20X4 is $90,000, and in December 20X4 it pays $60,000 dividends.

Required: Prepare all journal entries other than closing entries to account for Puckett's investment in Saton during 20X4. Any difference between investment cost and book value acquired is assumed to be goodwill with a 10-year amortization period.

E 8-19 Patrick Corporation paid $1,800,000 for 90,000 shares of Striper Corporation's 100,000 outstanding shares on January 1, 20X1, when Striper's stockholders' equity consisted of $1,000,000 of $10 par common stock and $500,000 retained earnings. The excess cost over book value acquired was assigned to goodwill with a 10-year amortization period. On January 2, 20X3, Striper sold an additional 20,000 shares to the public for $600,000 and its stockholders' equity before and after issuance of the additional 20,000 shares was as follows:

	January 1, 20X3 (Before Issuance)	January 2, 20X3 (After Issuance)
$10 par common stock	$1,000,000	$1,200,000
Additional paid-in capital	—	400,000
Retained earnings	800,000	800,000
Total stockholders' equity	$1,800,000	$2,400,000

Required

1 Determine Patrick's investment in Striper account balance on January 1, 20X3.
2 Prepare the entry on Patrick's books to account for its decreased ownership interest if gain or loss is not recognized.
3 Prepare the entry on Patrick's books to account for its decreased ownership interest if gain or loss is recognized.

PROBLEMS

P 8-1 A summary of the changes in the stockholders' equity of Spindle Corporation from January 1, 20X4 to December 31, 20X5 appears as follows:

	Capital Stock $10 Par	Additional Paid-in Capital	Retained Earnings	Total Equity
Balance January 1, 20X4	$500,000	—	$ 50,000	$550,000
Dividends, December 20X4	—	—	(50,000)	(50,000)
Income, 20X4	—	—	100,000	100,000
Balance December 31, 20X4	$500,000	—	$100,000	$600,000
Sale of stock January 1, 20X5	100,000	$ 62,000	—	162,000
Dividends, December 20X5	—	—	(60,000)	(60,000)
Income, 20X5	—	—	150,000	150,000
Balance December 31, 20X5	$600,000	$ 62,000	$190,000	$852,000

Paper Corporation purchases 40,000 shares of Spindle Corporation's outstanding stock on July 1, 20X4 in the open market for $620,000 and an additional 10,000 shares directly from Spindle for $162,000 on January 1, 20X5. Any excess of investment cost over book value acquired is due to goodwill with a 10-year amortization period.

Required

1 Determine the balance of Paper's investment in Spindle account on December 31, 20X4.
2 Compute Paper's investment income from Spindle for 20X5.
3 Determine the balance of Paper's investment in Spindle account on December 31, 20X5.

P 8-2 Prince Corporation purchased 960,000 shares of Smithtown Corporation's common stock (an 80% interest) for $21,200,000 on January 1, 20X6. The $2,000,000 excess of investment cost over book value acquired was allocated to goodwill with a 10-year amortization period.

On January 1, 20X8, Smithtown sold 400,000 previously unissued shares of common stock to the public for $30 per share. Smithtown's stockholders' equity on January 1, 20X6, when Prince acquired its interest, and on January 1, 20X8, immediately before and after the issuance of additional shares, was as follows:

	January 1, 20X6	January 1, 20X8 Before Issuance	January 1, 20X8 After Issuance
Common stock, $10 par	$12,000,000	$12,000,000	$16,000,000
Other paid-in capital	4,000,000	4,000,000	12,000,000
Retained earnings	8,000,000	10,000,000	10,000,000
Total	$24,000,000	$26,000,000	$38,000,000

Required

1 Calculate the balance of Prince's investment in Smithtown account on January 1, 20X8 before the additional stock issuance.

2 Determine Prince's percentage interest in Smithtown on January 1, 20X8 immediately after the additional stock issuance.

3 Prepare a journal entry on Prince's books to adjust for the additional share issuance on January 1, 20X8 if gain or loss is not recognized.

4 Prepare a journal entry on Prince's books to adjust for the additional share issuance on January 1, 20X8 if the issuance is treated as a sale and gain or loss is recognized (as permitted by the SEC).

P 8-3 Patterson Corporation owned a 90% interest in Shawnee Corporation, and during 20X5 the following changes occurred in Shawnee's equity and Patterson's investment in Shawnee:

	Shawnee's Stockholders' Equity	Unamortized Goodwill	Investment in Shawnee (90%)
Balance, January 1, 20X5	$1,000,000	$49,500	$ 949,500
Income—20X5	250,000	(4,500)	220,500
Dividends—20X5	(150,000)	—	(135,000)
Balance, December 31, 20X5	$1,100,000	$45,000	$1,035,000

During 20X6, Shawnee Corporation's net income was $280,000, and it declared $40,000 dividends each quarter of the year.

Patterson reduced its interest in Shawnee to 80% on July 1, 20X6 by selling Shawnee shares for $120,000.

Required

1 Prepare the journal entry on Patterson's books to record the sale of Shawnee shares as of the actual date of sale.

2 Prepare the journal entry on Patterson's books to record the sale of Shawnee shares as of January 1, 20X6.

3 Prepare a schedule to reconcile the answers to (1) and (2).

P 8-4 Panama Corporation owns 300,000 of 360,000 outstanding shares of Shenandoah Corporation, and its $8,700,000 investment in Shenandoah account balance on December 31, 20X4 is equal to the underlying equity interest in Shenandoah. A summary of Shenandoah's stockholders' equity at December 31, 20X4 is as follows:

Common stock, $10 par, 500,000 shares authorized, 400,000 shares issued, of which 40,000 are treasury shares	$ 4,000,000
Additional paid-in capital	2,500,000
Retained earnings	5,500,000
	12,000,000
Less: Treasury shares at cost	1,560,000
Total stockholders' equity	$10,440,000

Because of a cash shortage, Panama has decided to reduce its ownership interest in Shenandoah from a $\frac{5}{6}$ interest to a $\frac{3}{4}$ interest and is considering the following options:

Option 1. Sell 30,000 of the 300,000 shares held in Shenandoah.

Option 2. Instruct Shenandoah to issue 40,000 shares of previously unissued stock.

Option 3. Instruct Shenandoah to reissue the 40,000 shares of treasury stock.

Assume that the shares can be sold at the current market price of $50 per share under each of the three options and that any tax consequences can be ignored. Panama's stockholders' equity at December 31, 20X4 consists of $10,000,000 par value of common stock, $3,000,000 additional paid-in capital, and $7,000,000 retained earnings.

Required: Compare the consolidated stockholders' equity on January 1, 20X5 under each of the three options. (*Hint:* Prepare journal entries on Panama's books as an initial step to your solution.)

P 8-5 Pallo Products Company purchased 9,000 shares of Sala Corporation's $50 par common stock at $90 per share on January 1, 20X5, when Sala had capital stock of $500,000 and retained earnings of $300,000. During 20X5, Sala Corporation had net income of $50,000 but declared no dividends.

On January 1, 20X6, Sala Corporation sold an additional 5,000 shares of stock at $100 per share. Sala's net income for 20X6 was $70,000 and no dividends were declared.

Required: Determine the following:
1 The balance of Pallo Products Company's investment in Salo account on December 31, 20X5. (Use a 10-year amortization period for goodwill.)
2 The goodwill (or negative goodwill) that should appear in the consolidated balance sheet at December 31, 20X6, assuming that Pallo Products Company purchased the 5,000 shares issued on January 1, 20X6.
3 Additional paid-in capital from consolidation at December 31, 20X6, assuming that Sala sold the 5,000 shares issued on January 1, 20X6 to outside entities.
4 Minority interest at December 31, 20X6, assuming that Sala sold the 5,000 shares issued on January 1, 20X6 to outsiders.

P 8-6 Post Corporation purchased a 70% interest in Stake Corporation on January 2, 20X6 for $94,000, when Stake had capital stock of $100,000 and retained earnings of $20,000. On June 30, 20X7, Post purchased an additional 20% interest for $38,000.

Comparative financial statements for Post and Stake corporations at and for the year ended December 31, 20X7 are summarized as follows:

	Post	Stake
Combined Income and Retained Earnings Statement		
for the Year Ended December 31, 20X7		
Sales	$400,000	$200,000
Income from Stake	24,000	—
Cost of sales	(250,000)	(150,000)
Expenses	(50,000)	(20,000)
Net income	124,000	30,000
Add: Beginning retained earnings	200,000	50,000
Less: Dividends, December 1, 20X7	(64,000)	(10,000)
Retained earnings, December 31, 20X7	$260,000	$ 70,000
Balance Sheet at December 31, 20X7		
Other assets	$432,000	$200,000
Investment in Stake	168,000	—
Total assets	$600,000	$200,000
Liabilities	$ 40,000	$ 30,000
Common stock	300,000	100,000
Retained earnings	260,000	70,000
Total equities	$600,000	$200,000

Required
1 Prepare a schedule explaining the $168,000 balance in Post's investment in Stake account at December 31, 20X7.
2 Compute the amount of goodwill that should appear in the December 31, 20X7 consolidated balance sheet. Assume a 10-year amortization period.
3 Prepare a schedule showing computations of the amount of consolidated net income for 20X7.
4 Compute consolidated retained earnings on December 31, 20X7.
5 Compute minority interest on December 31, 20X7.

P 8-7 Comparative separate company and consolidated balance sheets for Percy Corporation and its 70%-owned subsidiary, Sawyer Corporation, at year-end 20X6 were as follows:

	Percy	Sawyer	Consolidated
Cash	$ 100,000	$ 70,000	$ 170,000
Inventories	800,000	100,000	900,000
Other current assets	500,000	130,000	630,000
Plant assets—net	3,500,000	800,000	4,300,000
Investment in Sawyer	600,000	—	—
Goodwill	—	—	40,000
Total assets	$5,500,000	$1,100,000	$6,040,000

(Continued)

	Percy	Sawyer	Consolidated
Current liabilities	$ 500,000	$ 300,000	$ 800,000
Capital stock, $10 par	3,000,000	500,000	3,000,000
Other paid-in capital	1,000,000	100,000	1,000,000
Retained earnings	1,000,000	200,000	1,000,000
Minority interest	—	—	240,000
Total equities	$5,500,000	$1,100,000	$6,040,000

Sawyer's net income for 20X7 was $150,000 and its dividends for the year were $80,000 ($40,000 on March 1 and $40,000 on September 1). On April 1, 20X7, Percy increased its interest in Sawyer to 80% by purchasing 5,000 shares in the market at $19 per share.

Percy's goodwill from its 70% interest is being amortized $8,000 per year, and any goodwill from the 10% interest will be amortized over a 10-year period.

Separate incomes of Percy and Sawyer for the year 20X7 are computed as follows:

	Percy	Sawyer
Sales	$2,000,000	$1,200,000
Cost of sales	(1,200,000)	(700,000)
Gross profit	800,000	500,000
Depreciation expense	(400,000)	(300,000)
Other expenses	(100,000)	(50,000)
Separate incomes	$ 300,000	$ 150,000

Required

1 Prepare a consolidated income statement for Percy Corporation and Subsidiary for the year ended December 31, 20X7.

2 Prepare a schedule to show how Sawyer's net income and dividends for 20X7 are allocated among minority interests, majority interests, and other interests.

P 8-8 Proctor Corporation issues 55,000 of its shares for 90% of Simon Corporation's outstanding common shares in a pooling of interests consummated on April 1, 20X5. Adjusted trial balances for Proctor and Simon on April 1, 20X5, before the pooling, and on December 31, 20X5 are summarized as follows:

	April 1, 20X5		December 31, 20X5	
	Proctor	Simon	Proctor	Simon
Debits				
Cash	$ 100,000	$ 80,000	$ 278,000	$ 70,000
Other assets	2,000,000	550,000	2,400,000	650,000
Investment in Simon	—	—	522,000	—
Dividends	100,000	20,000	400,000	80,000
Expenses	800,000	300,000	2,300,000	1,200,000
	$3,000,000	$950,000	$5,900,000	$2,000,000
Credits				
Liabilities	$ 400,000	$ 50,000	$ 124,000	$ 140,000
Capital stock, $10 par	1,000,000	300,000	1,550,000	300,000
Other paid-in capital	100,000	200,000	—	200,000
Retained earnings	600,000	60,000	636,000	60,000
Sales	900,000	340,000	3,500,000	1,300,000
Income from Simon	—	—	90,000	—
	$3,000,000	$950,000	$5,900,000	$2,000,000

Required: Prepare consolidated balance sheet working papers for Proctor Corporation and Subsidiary as of December 31, 20X5.

P 8-9 Pop Corporation acquired an 80% interest in Sat Corporation on October 1, 20X2 for $82,400, equal to 80% of the underlying equity of Sat on that date plus $16,000 goodwill. Financial statements for Pop and Sat corporations for 20X2 are as follows:

	Pop	Sat
Combined Income and Retained Earnings Statement		
for the Year Ended December 31, 20X2		
Sales	$112,000	$ 50,000
Income from Sat	3,700	
Cost of sales	(60,000)	(20,000)
Operating expenses	(25,100)	(6,000)
Net income	30,600	24,000
Retained earnings January 1	30,000	20,000
Dividends	(20,000)	(10,000)
Retained earnings December 31, 20X2	$ 40,600	$ 34,000
Balance Sheet at December 31, 20X2		
Cash	$ 5,100	$ 7,000
Accounts receivable	10,400	17,000
Note receivable	5,000	10,000
Inventories	30,000	16,000
Plant assets—net	88,000	60,000
Investment in Sat	82,100	—
Total assets	$220,600	$110,000
Accounts payable	$ 15,000	$ 16,000
Notes payable	25,000	10,000
Capital stock	140,000	50,000
Retained earnings	40,600	34,000
Total equities	$220,600	$110,000

Additional Information

1 In November 20X2, Pop sold inventory items to Sat for $12,000 at a gross profit of $3,000. One-third of these items remained in Sat's inventory at December 31, 20X2, and $6,000 remained unpaid.

2 Sat's dividends were declared in equal amounts on March 15 and November 15, and its income was earned in proportionate amounts throughout each quarter of the year.

3 Pop applies the equity method of accounting such that its net income is equal to consolidated net income.

Required: Prepare working papers to consolidate the financial statements of Pop Corporation and Subsidiary for the year ended December 31, 20X2.

P 8-10 Pal Corporation paid $175,000 for a 70% interest in Sid Corporation's outstanding stock on April 1, 20X6. Sid's stockholders' equity on January 1, 20X6 consisted of $200,000 capital stock and $50,000 retained earnings.

Accounts and balances taken from the financial statements for Pal and Sid at and for the year ended December 31, 20X6 are as follows:

	Pal	Sid
Combined Income and Retained Earnings Statement		
for the Year Ended December 31, 20X6		
Sales	$287,100	$150,000
Income from Sid	12,300	—
Gain	12,000	2,000
Interest income	—	5,850
Expenses (includes cost of goods sold)	(200,000)	(117,850)
Interest expense	(11,400)	—
Net income	100,000	40,000
Add: Beginning retained earnings	250,000	50,000
Less: Dividends	(50,000)	(20,000)
Retained earnings December 31, 20X6	$300,000	$ 70,000
Balance Sheet at December 31, 20X6		
Cash	$ 17,000	$ 4,000
Interest receivable	—	6,000
Inventories	140,000	60,000
Other current assets	110,000	20,000
Plant assets—net	502,700	107,300
Investment in Sid common	180,300	—
Investment in Pal bonds	—	102,700
Total assets	$950,000	$300,000

(Continued)

	Pal	Sid
Interest payable	$ 6,000	$ —
Other current liabilities	38,600	30,000
12% bonds payable	100,000	—
Premium on bonds	5,400	—
Common stock	500,000	200,000
Retained earnings	300,000	70,000
Total equities	$950,000	$300,000

Additional Information

1 Sid Corporation paid $102,850 for all of Pal's outstanding bonds on July 1, 20X6. These bonds were issued on January 1, 20X6, bear interest at 12%, have interest payment dates of July 1 and January 1, and mature 10 years from the date of issue. The $6,000 premium on the issue is being amortized under the straight-line method.

2 Other current liabilities of Sid Corporation on December 31, 20X6 include $10,000 dividends declared on December 15 and unpaid at year-end. Sid also declared $10,000 dividends on March 15, 20X6.

3 Pal Corporation sold equipment to Sid on July 1, 20X6 for $30,000. This equipment was purchased by Pal on July 1, 20X3 for $36,000 and is being depreciated over a six-year period under the straight-line method (no scrap).

4 Sid sold land that cost $8,000 to Pal for $10,000 on October 15, 20X6. Pal still owns the land.

5 Pal uses the equity method of accounting for its 70% interest in Sid.

Required: Prepare consolidation working papers for Pal Corporation and Subsidiary for the year ended December 31, 20X6.

P 8-11 Poco Corporation acquired a 70% interest in Sam Corporation on January 1, 20X1 for $450,000 cash. The stockholders' equity of Sam when Poco acquired its 70% interest consisted of $300,000 capital stock and $200,000 retained earnings. On July 1, 20X2, Poco acquired an additional 10% interest in Sam for $77,500 to bring its interest in Sam to 80%. The financial statements of Poco and Sam corporations at and for the year ended December 31, 20X2 are as follows:

	Poco	Sam
Combined Income and Retained Earnings Statement for the Year Ended December 31, 20X2		
Sales	$900,000	$500,000
Income from Sam	32,500	—
Gain on machinery	40,000	—
Cost of sales	(400,000)	(300,000)
Depreciation expense	(90,000)	(60,000)
Other expenses	(160,000)	(40,000)
Net income	322,500	100,000
Add: Beginning retained earnings	150,000	250,000
Less: Dividends	(200,000)	(50,000)
Retained earnings December 31, 20X2	$272,500	$300,000
Balance Sheet at December 31, 20X2		
Cash	$ 20,000	$ 80,000
Accounts receivable	90,000	30,000
Dividends receivable	20,000	—
Inventories	90,000	70,000
Other current items	20,000	80,000
Land	50,000	40,000
Buildings—net	60,000	105,000
Machinery—net	100,000	320,000
Investment in Sam	539,500	—
Total assets	$989,500	$725,000
Accounts payable	$177,000	$ 40,000
Dividends payable	100,000	25,000
Other liabilities	140,000	60,000
Capital stock, $10 par	300,000	300,000
Retained earnings	272,500	300,000
Total equities	$989,500	$725,000

Additional Information

1 The cost/book value differential from Poco's two purchases of interests in Sam was allocated to goodwill with a 20-year write-off period.
2 Poco Corporation sold inventory items to Sam during 20X1 for $60,000, at a gross profit of $10,000. During 20X2, Poco's sales to Sam were $48,000, at a gross profit of $8,000. Half of the 20X1 intercompany sales were inventoried by Sam at year-end 20X1, and three-fourths of the 20X2 sales remained unsold by Sam at year-end 20X2. Sam owes Poco $25,000 from 20X2 purchases.
3 At year-end 20X1, Sam purchased land from Poco for $20,000. The cost of this land to Poco was $12,000.
4 Poco sold machinery with a book value of $40,000 to Sam for $80,000 on July 8, 20X2. The machinery had a five-year useful life at this time. Sam uses straight-line depreciation without considering salvage value on the machinery.
5 Poco uses a one-line consolidation in accounting for Sam. Both Poco and Sam corporations declared their dividends for the year 20X2 in equal amounts in June and December.

Required: Prepare working papers to consolidate the financial statements of Poco Corporation and Subsidiary for the year ended December 31, 20X2.

P 8-12 Pak Corporation acquired an 85% interest in Sly Corporation on August 1, 20X2 for $522,750, equal to 85% of the underlying equity of Sly on that date.

In August 20X2, Sly sold inventory items to Pak for $60,000 at a gross profit of $15,000. One-third of these items remained in Pak's inventory at December 31, 20X2.

On September 30, 20X2, Pak sold an inventory item (equipment) to Sly for $50,000 at a gross profit to Pak of $10,000. When this equipment was placed in service by Sly, it had a five-year remaining useful life and no expected scrap value.

Sly's dividends were declared in equal amounts on June 15 and December 15, and its income was earned in relatively equal amounts throughout each quarter of the year. Pak applies the equity method of accounting, such that its net income is equal to consolidated net income. Financial statements for Pak and Sly are summarized as follows:

	Pak	Sly
Combined Income and Retained Earnings Statement for the Year Ended December 31, 20X2		
Sales	$ 910,000	$400,000
Income from Sly	7,500	—
Cost of sales	(500,000)	(250,000)
Operating expenses	(200,000)	(90,000)
Net income	217,500	60,000
Add: Beginning retained earnings	192,500	100,000
Deduct: Dividends	(100,000)	(40,000)
Retained earnings December 31, 20X2	$ 310,000	$120,000
Balance Sheet at December 31, 20X2		
Cash	$ 33,750	$ 10,000
Dividends receivable	17,000	—
Accounts receivable—net	120,000	70,000
Inventories	300,000	150,000
Plant assets—net	880,000	500,000
Investment in Sly—85%	513,250	—
Total assets	$1,864,000	$730,000
Accounts payable	$ 154,000	$ 90,000
Dividends payable	—	20,000
Capital stock	1,400,000	500,000
Retained earnings	310,000	120,000
Total equities	$1,864,000	$730,000

Required: Prepare consolidation working papers for Pak Corporation and Subsidiary for the year ended December 31, 20X2.

P 8-13 Separate company financial statements for Pin Corporation and its 90%-owned subsidiary, Sit Corporation, for the year ended December 31, 20X8 are summarized as follows:

	Pin	Sit

Combined Income and Retained Earnings Statement for the Year Ended December 31, 20X8

	Pin	Sit
Sales	$1,265,000	$ 600,000
Income from Sit	85,000	—
Cost of goods sold	(800,000)	(300,000)
Depreciation expense	(180,000)	(70,000)
Other expenses	(120,000)	(120,000)
Loss on plant assets	—	(10,000)
Net income	250,000	100,000
Add: Beginning retained earnings	300,000	150,000
Deduct: Dividends	(150,000)	(50,000)
Retained earnings December 31, 20X8	$ 400,000	$ 200,000

Balance Sheet at December 31, 20X8

	Pin	Sit
Cash	$ 220,000	$ 160,000
Receivables	200,000	160,000
Inventory	170,000	140,000
Plant and equipment	1,417,500	720,000
Accumulated depreciation	(272,500)	(180,000)
Investment in Sit	765,000	—
Total assets	$2,500,000	$1,000,000
Current liabilities	$ 300,000	$ 100,000
Other liabilities	300,000	200,000
Capital stock	1,500,000	500,000
Retained earnings	400,000	200,000
Total equities	$2,500,000	$1,000,000

Additional Information

1. Pin acquired an 80% interest in Sit's common stock on January 5, 20X5 for $600,000 and an additional 10% interest on July 1, 20X8 for $82,500. These two acquisitions were made in the open market at regularly quoted exchange prices.
2. Sit's capital stock and retained earnings on January 1, 20X5 were $500,000 and $100,000, respectively.
3. Any difference between investment cost and book value acquired relates to assets not specifically identifiable and is amortized over a 10-year period.
4. Sit paid dividends of $25,000 on April 1 and October 1 of 20X8.
5. Pin sold $50,000 merchandise to Sit during 20X8. The gross profit of $10,000 on this merchandise is included in Sit's December 31, 20X8 inventory. Sit owed Pin $20,000 from intercompany purchases at December 31, 20X8.
6. The amount of intercompany profit in Sit's beginning inventory on goods acquired from Pin amounted to $5,000.
7. Sit sold machinery with a book value of $40,000 to Pin for $30,000 on July 2, 20X8. At the time of sale, the machinery had a remaining useful life of five years and was being depreciated by Pin on a straight-line basis.

Required: Prepare the consolidation working papers for Pin and Subsidiary for the year ended December 31, 20X8.

P 8-14 Financial statements for Poe and Spy corporations for 20X4 are summarized as follows:

	Poe	Spy

Combined Income and Retained Earnings Statement for the Year Ended December 31, 20X4

	Poe	Spy
Sales	$463,750	$130,000
Income from Spy	18,750	—
Gain on Spy stock	17,500	—
Cost of sales	(260,000)	(100,000)
Other expenses	(140,000)	(10,000)
Net income	100,000	20,000
Add: Beginning retained earnings	200,000	30,000
Deduct: Dividends	(50,000)	(10,000)
Retained earnings December 31, 20X4	$250,000	$ 40,000

(Continued)

	Poe	Spy
Balance Sheet at December 31, 20X4		
Cash	$107,500	$ 20,000
Inventories	100,000	50,000
Other current assets	110,000	30,000
Plant assets	300,000	200,000
Investment in Spy	182,500	—
Total assets	$800,000	$300,000
Accounts payable	$150,000	$ 60,000
Capital stock	400,000	200,000
Retained earnings	250,000	40,000
Total equities	$800,000	$300,000

Due to a working capital shortage and other financial problems, Poe sold a 25% interest in Spy, its 100%-owned subsidiary, on October 1, 20X4 for $75,000. Spy was formed by Poe in 20X1 to manufacture miscellaneous furniture for Poe, and all of Spy's sales are made to Poe at 130% of Spy's cost. A summary of Spy's sales to Poe from 20X1 through 20X4 follows:

	Sales for the Year	Spy's Cost of Sales for the Year	Percent Unsold by Poe at December 31	Percent of Sales Unpaid at December 31
20X1	$ 91,000	$ 70,000	10%	20%
20X2	104,000	80,000	5	10
20X3	117,000	90,000	20	15
20X4	130,000	100,000	10	10

Additional Information

1 During 20X4, Spy declared dividends of $5,000 on April 1 and $5,000 on November 1.

2 The $182,500 balance of Poe's investment in Spy account is determined as follows:

Investment cost in 20X1 (when Spy was formed)	$200,000
Add: Income less dividends 20X1 through 20X3	30,000
	230,000
Less: Book value of investment sold ($230,000 × 25%)	(57,500)
	172,500
Add: Income from Spy 20X4	
($15,000 × 100%) + ($5,000 × 75%)	18,750
Less: Dividends from Spy in 20X4	
($5,000 × 100%) + ($5,000 × 75%)	(8,750)
Investment in Spy	$182,500

3 The auditor for Poe has determined that the correct balance of the investment in Spy account at December 31, 20X4 should be $177,750, computed as 75% of Spy's $237,000 *realized* equity. The auditor recommends that the following entry be made to correct the accounts because the books have been closed on December 31, 20X4:

Retained earnings	$4,750	
Investment in Spy		$4,750

The auditor further recommends that Poe adopt and use a correct equity method of accounting for 20X5 and subsequent years.

Required: Prepare consolidation working papers for Poe Corporation and Subsidiary for the year ended December 31, 20X4.

P 8-15   Financial statements for the Psi and Skrye corporations at and for the year ended December 31, 20X6 are summarized as follows:

	Psi	Skrye
Combined Income and Retained Earnings Statement		
for the Year Ended December 31, 20X6		
Sales	$ 613,840	$250,200
Income from Skrye	35,660	—
Interest income	—	4,800
Cost of sales	(400,000)	(170,000)
Operating expenses	(141,400)	(45,000)
Interest expense	(8,600)	—
Net income	99,500	40,000
Add: Beginning retained earnings	200,000	80,000
Deduct: Dividends	(50,000)	(20,000)
Retained earnings, December 31, 20X6	$ 249,500	$100,000
Balance Sheet at December 31, 20X6		
Cash	$ 47,500	$ 8,600
Accounts receivable—net	88,240	67,000
Inventories	120,000	40,000
Investment in Skrye stock	343,760	—
Investment in Psi bonds	—	49,400
Plant assets—net	500,000	200,000
Total assets	$1,099,500	$365,000
Accounts payable	$ 50,000	$ 11,000
Other current liabilities	9,200	4,000
9% bonds payable	100,000	—
Premium on bonds payable	800	—
Capital stock, $10 par	500,000	150,000
Other paid-in capital	190,000	100,000
Retained earnings	249,500	100,000
Total equities	$1,099,500	$365,000

Psi Corporation issued 20,000 shares of its $10 par capital stock for 90% of the outstanding voting stock of Skrye Company in a *pooling of interests* business combination on July 1, 20X5. On January 1, 20X5, Skrye's stockholders' equity consisted of $150,000, $10 par capital stock, other paid-in capital of $100,000, and retained earnings of $60,000. Psi recorded the pooling correctly on July 1. Skrye's net income for 20X5 was $40,000, earned evenly throughout the year, and dividends, paid on December 1, were $20,000.

On July 1, 20X6, Psi acquired an additional 5% interest in Skrye for $29,500 cash. This acquisition is accounted for by the purchase method under the provisions of *APB Opinion No. 16*. Book values of Skrye's net assets were equal to fair values at the times of purchase, and any excess of investment cost over book value acquired is to be amortized over a 10-year period.

Additional Information
20X5
1 Skrye sold merchandise that cost Skrye $20,000 to Psi for $24,000 during 20X5. One-fourth of that merchandise remained in Psi's December 31, 20X5 inventory.
2 On December 31, 20X5, Skrye acquired $50,000 par of Psi's 9% bonds for $49,100 cash. These bonds, which mature on December 31, 20X8 and pay interest on June 30 and December 31, had a book value of $50,600 when acquired by Skrye.
20X6
3 Skrye sold merchandise that cost $40,000 to Psi for $48,000 during 20X6. Psi sold 85% of this merchandise, and at December 31, 20X6, $7,200 of the merchandise remained in Psi's inventory.
4 At December 31, 20X6, Psi owed Skrye $2,040 for merchandise purchased.
5 Skrye's $40,000 net income for 20X6 was earned evenly throughout the year. Its $20,000 dividends were paid on December 1.

Required: Prepare consolidation working papers for Psi Corporation and Subsidiary for the year ended December 31, 20X6.

P 8-16 **[AICPA adapted]**
Presented here are the condensed financial statements (unconsolidated) of Royal Company and its subsidiary, Butler Company, for the year ended December 31, 20X5.

	Royal	Butler
Combined Income and Retained Earnings Statement for the Year Ended December 31, 20X5		
Sales	$4,000,000	$1,700,000
Cost of sales	(2,982,000)	(1,015,000)
Operating expenses	(400,000)	(377,200)
Dividend income	75,000	—
Subsidiary income	232,000	—
Interest expense	—	(7,800)
Net income	925,000	300,000
Add: Retained earnings January 1, 20X5	2,100,000	640,000
Deduct: Dividends	(170,000)	(100,000)
Retained earnings December 31, 20X5	$2,855,000	$ 840,000
Balance Sheet at December 31, 20X5		
Cash	$ 486,000	$ 249,600
Accounts receivable	235,000	185,000
Inventories	475,000	355,000
Machinery and equipment	2,231,000	530,000
Investment in Butler stock	954,000	—
Investment in Butler bonds	58,000	—
Total assets	$4,439,000	$1,319,600
Accounts payable	$ 384,000	$ 62,000
Bonds payable	—	120,000
Unamortized discount on bonds payable	—	(2,400)
Common stock	1,200,000	250,000
Contributed capital	—	50,000
Retained earnings	2,855,000	840,000
Total liabilities and owners' equity	$4,439,000	$1,319,600

Additional Information

1 On January 3, 20X3, Royal acquired from John Roth, the sole stockholder of Butler Company, both a patent valued at $40,000 and 80% of the outstanding stock of Butler for $440,000 cash. The net book value of Butler's stock on the date of acquisition was $500,000, and the book values of the individual assets and liabilities were equal to their fair market values. Royal charged the entire $440,000 to the account "Investment in Butler Company." The patent, for which no amortization has been charged, had a remaining legal life of four years as of January 3, 20X3.

2 On July 1, 20X5, Royal reduced its investment in Butler to 75% of Butler's outstanding common stock, by selling shares for $70,000 to an unaffiliated company at a profit of $16,000. Royal recorded the proceeds as a credit to its investment account.

3 For the six months ended June 30, 20X5, Butler had net income of $140,000. Royal recorded 80% of this amount on its books of account prior to the time of sale.

4 During 20X4, Butler sold merchandise to Royal for $130,000, which was at a markup of 30% over Butler's cost. On January 1, 20X5, $52,000 of this merchandise remained in Royal's inventory. This merchandise was subsequently sold by Royal in February 20X5 at a profit of $8,000.

5 In November 20X5, Royal sold merchandise to Butler for the first time. Royal's cost for this merchandise was $80,000, and the sale was made at 120% of cost. Butler's inventory at December 31, 20X5 contained merchandise that was purchased from Royal at a cost to Butler of $24,000.

6 On December 31, 20X5, there was a $45,000 payment-in-transit from Butler Company to Royal Company. Accounts receivable and accounts payable include intercompany receivables and payables. In December 20X5, Butler declared and paid cash dividends of $100,000 to its stockholders.

7 On December 31, 20X5, Royal purchased 50% of the outstanding bonds issued by Butler for $58,000. The bonds mature on December 31, 20X9 and were originally issued at a discount. On December 31, 20X5, the balance in Butler's account "Unamortized Discount on Bonds Payable" was $2,400. It is the intention of the management of Royal to hold these bonds until their maturity.

Required: Prepare consolidated financial statement working papers for Royal Company and Subsidiary for the year ended December 31, 20X5.

P 8-17 Comparative consolidated financial statements for Poff Corporation and its subsidiary, Sato Corporation, at and for the years ended December 31, 20X4 and 20X3 follow.

POFF CORPORATION AND SUBSIDIARY COMPARATIVE CONSOLIDATED FINANCIAL STATEMENTS AT AND FOR THE YEARS ENDED DECEMBER 31, 20X4 AND 20X3

	Year 20X4	Year 20X3	Year's Change 20X4 – 20X3
Income Statement			
Sales	$3,050,000	$2,850,000	$ 200,000
Gain on 10% interest	5,700		5,700
Cost of sales	(1,750,700)	(1,690,000)	(60,700)
Depreciation expense	(528,000)	(508,000)	(20,000)
Other expenses	(455,000)	(392,000)	(63,000)
Minority income	(22,000)	(10,000)	(12,000)
Net income	$ 300,000	$ 250,000	$ 50,000
Retained Earnings			
Retained earnings—beginning	$1,000,000	$ 950,000	$ 50,000
Net income	300,000	250,000	50,000
Dividends	(200,000)	(200,000)	0
Retained earnings—ending	$1,100,000	$1,000,000	$ 100,000
Balance Sheet			
Cash	$ 46,500	$ 50,500	$ (4,000)
Accounts receivable—net	87,500	90,000	(2,500)
Inventories	377,500	247,500	130,000
Prepaid expenses	68,000	88,000	(20,000)
Equipment	2,970,000	2,880,000	90,000
Accumulated depreciation	(1,542,000)	(1,044,000)	(498,000)
Land and buildings	960,000	960,000	0
Accumulated depreciation	(300,000)	(272,000)	(28,000)
Total assets	$2,667,500	$3,000,000	$ (332,500)
Accounts payable	$ 140,000	$ 343,500	$ (203,500)
Dividends payable	52,500	52,500	0
Long-term notes payable	245,000	545,000	(300,000)
Capital stock, $10 par	1,000,000	1,000,000	0
Retained earnings	1,100,000	1,000,000	100,000
Minority interest	130,000	59,000	71,000
Total equities	$2,667,500	$3,000,000	$ (332,500)

Required: Prepare a consolidated statement of cash flows for Poff Corporation and Subsidiary for the year ended December 31, 20X4. The changes in equipment are due to a $100,000 equipment acquisition, current depreciation, and the sale of one-ninth of the cost/book value differential allocated to equipment ($10,000) and related accumulated depreciation ($2,000). This reduction in the unamortized cost/book value differential results from selling a 10% interest in Sato for $72,700 and thereby reducing its interest from 90% to 80%. Sato's net income and dividends for 20X4 were $110,000 and $50,000, respectively. Use the indirect method.

9

Indirect and Mutual Holdings

The previous chapters of this book presented stock ownership situations in which an investor or parent company directly owned some or all of the voting stock of an investee. The equity method of accounting is appropriate in those situations and equally appropriate when an investor indirectly owns 20% or more of an investee's voting stock. Consolidation is appropriate when one corporation, directly or indirectly, owns a majority of the outstanding voting stock of another corporation.[1]

This chapter discusses parent company accounting and consolidation procedures for indirect ownership situations under the heading of "Indirect Holdings." The chapter also considers additional complexities that arise when affiliated corporations hold the voting stock of each other. Affiliation structures of this type are covered under the heading of "Mutual Holdings." Discussion of **mutual holding** relationships logically follows the coverage of **indirect holdings** because such relationships constitute a special type of indirect holdings—the type in which affiliates indirectly own themselves. Although consolidation procedures for indirectly held and mutually held affiliates are more complex than for directly held affiliates, the basic consolidation objectives remain the same. Most of the problems involve measuring the separate realized income of the separate entities and allocating it between majority and minority interests.

AFFILIATION STRUCTURES

The potential complexity of corporate affiliation structures is limited only by one's imagination. Even so, the general types of affiliation structures are not difficult to identify. The more basic types of affiliation structures are illustrated in Exhibit 9–1.

Although Exhibit 9–1 illustrates affiliation structures for parent and subsidiary corporations, the diagrams are equally applicable to investor and investee corporations associated through the direct or indirect ownership of 20% or more of the voting stock of an investee corporation. **Direct holdings** result from direct investments in the voting stock of one or more investees. Indirect holdings are investments that enable the investor to control or significantly influence the decisions of an investee not directly owned through an investee that is directly owned. Two types of indirect own-

---

[1]*APB Opinion No. 18*, "The Equity Method of Accounting for Investments in Common Stock," paragraphs 3c and 17.

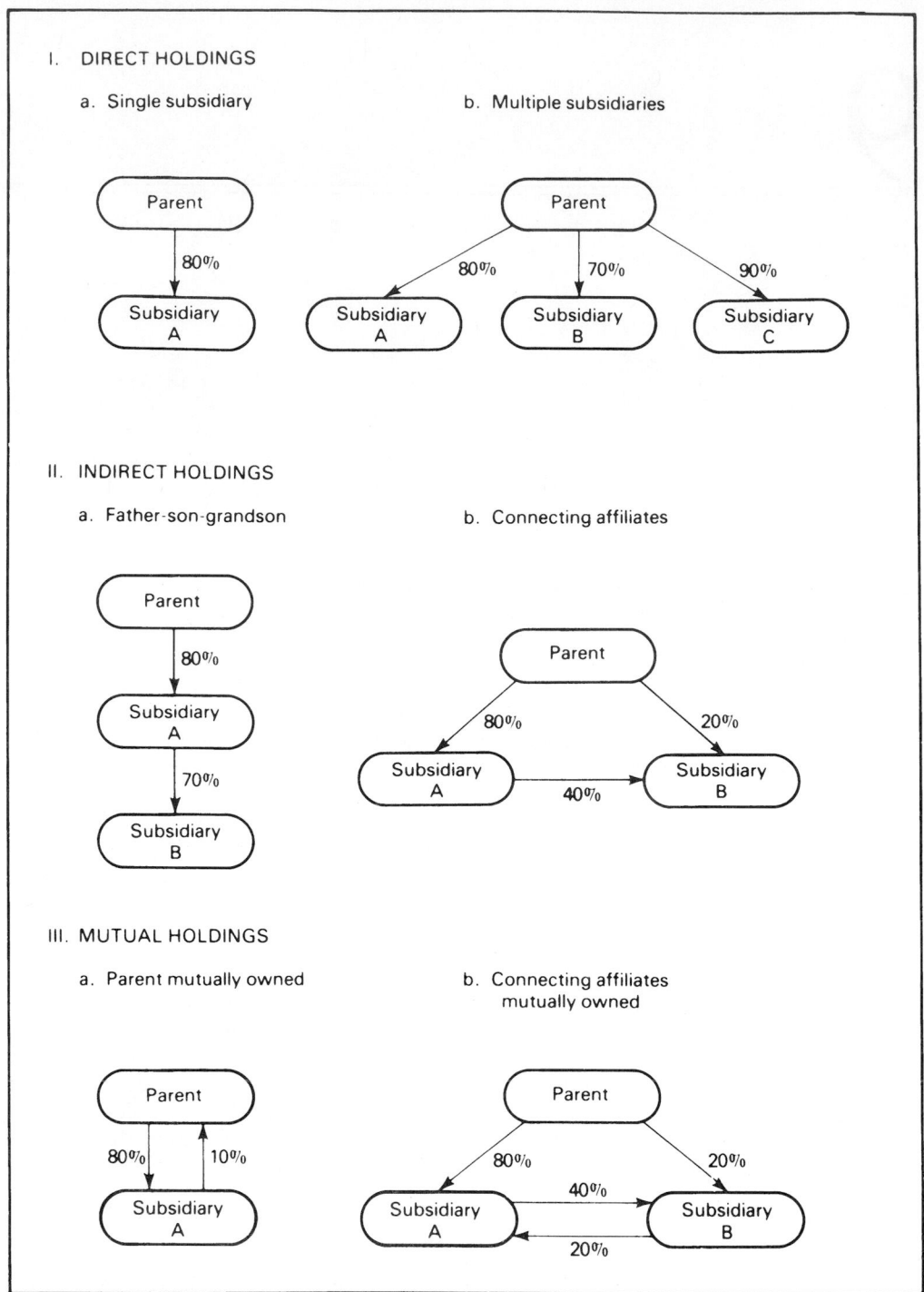

Exhibit 9–1 *Affiliation Structures*

ership structures are illustrated in Exhibit 9–1—the **father-son-grandson relationship** and the **connecting affiliates relationship**.

In the father-son-grandson diagram, the parent directly owns an 80% interest in Subsidiary A and indirectly owns a 56% interest (80% × 70%) in Subsidiary B. Minority shareholders own the other 44% of B—the 30% held directly by minority holders of B stock plus 14% held by the 20% minority holders of A stock (20% × 70%). The parent company indirectly holds 56% of Subsidiary B stock, so consolidation of Subsidiary B is clearly appropriate. It is not the direct and indirect ownership of the parent company, however, that determines whether an affiliate should be consolidated. The decision to consolidate is based on whether a majority of the stock of an affiliate is held within the affiliation structure, thus giving the parent an ability to control the operations of the affiliate.

If Subsidiary A in the father-son-grandson diagram of Exhibit 9–1 had owned 60% of the stock of Subsidiary B, the parent's indirect ownership in Subsidiary B would have been 48% (80% × 60%), and the minority shareholders' interest would have been 52% [40% + (20% × 60%)]. Consolidation of Subsidiary B would still be appropriate, because 60% of B's stock is held within the affiliation structure.

In the illustration of connecting affiliates, the parent holds 20% of Subsidiary B stock directly and 32% (80% × 40%) indirectly for a total direct and indirect ownership of 52%. The other 48% of Subsidiary B is held 40% by B's minority shareholders and 8% (20% × 40%) indirectly by A's minority shareholders.

In the first affiliation diagram for mutual holdings, the parent owns 80% of the stock of Subsidiary A, and Subsidiary A owns 10% of the stock of the parent. Thus, 10% of the parent's stock is held within the affiliation structure and 90% is outstanding. In Diagram b for mutual holdings, the parent is not a party to the mutual holding relationship, but Subsidiary A owns 40% of Subsidiary B, and Subsidiary B owns 20% of Subsidiary A. The complexity involved in this latter case requires the use of simultaneous equations or other appropriate mathematical procedures to allocate incomes and equities among the affiliated corporations.

INDIRECT HOLDINGS—FATHER-SON-GRANDSON STRUCTURE

The major problems encountered in connection with indirect-control situations involve the determination of earnings and equities of the affiliated companies on an equity basis. Once the income and equity accounts of the affiliated companies have been adjusted to an equity basis, the consolidation procedures are the same for indirect as for direct-ownership situations. The mechanics involved in the consolidation process may be cumbersome, however, because of the additional detail required to consolidate the operations of multiple entities.

Assume that Poe Corporation acquires 80% of the stock of Shaw Corporation on January 1, 20X1 and that Shaw acquires 70% of the stock of Turk Corporation on January 1, 20X2. Both Poe's investment in Shaw and Shaw's investment in Turk are made at book value. Trial balances for the three corporations on January 1, 20X2, immediately after Shaw acquires its 70% interest in Turk, are as follows:

	Poe	Shaw	Turk
Other assets	$400,000	$195,000	$190,000
Investment in Shaw (80%)	200,000	—	—
Investment in Turk (70%)	—	105,000	—
	$600,000	$300,000	$190,000
Liabilities	$100,000	$ 50,000	$ 40,000
Capital stock	400,000	200,000	100,000
Retained earnings	100,000	50,000	50,000
	$600,000	$300,000	$190,000

Separate earnings of the three corporations (that is, earnings excluding investment income) and dividends for 20X2 are:

	Poe	Shaw	Turk
Separate earnings	$100,000	$50,000	$40,000
Dividends	60,000	30,000	20,000

Equity Method of Accounting for Father-Son-Grandson Affiliates

In accounting for investment income for 20X2 on an equity basis, Shaw determines its investment income from Turk before Poe determines its investment income from Shaw. Shaw accounts for its investment in Turk for 20X2 with the following entries:

SHAW'S BOOKS

Cash	$14,000	
Investment in Turk		$14,000
To record dividends received from Turk ($20,000 × 70%).		
Investment in Turk	$28,000	
Income from Turk		$28,000
To record income from Turk ($40,000 × 70%).		

Shaw's net income for 20X2 is $78,000 ($50,000 separate income plus $28,000 income from Turk), and its investment in Turk account balance at December 31, 20X2 is $119,000 ($105,000 beginning balance, plus $28,000 income, less $14,000 dividends).

Poe's entries to account for its investment in Shaw for 20X2 are as follows:

POE'S BOOKS

Cash	$24,000	
Investment in Shaw		$24,000
To record dividends received from Shaw ($30,000 × 80%).		
Investment in Shaw	$62,400	
Income from Shaw		$62,400
To record income from Shaw ($78,000 × 80%).		

Poe's net income for 20X2 is 162,400 ($100,000 separate income plus $62,400 income from Shaw), and its investment in Shaw account balance at December 31, 20X2 is $238,400 ($200,000 beginning balance, plus $62,400 income, less $24,000 dividends). Consolidated net income for Poe Corporation and Subsidiaries for 20X2 is $162,400, equal to Poe's net income on an equity basis.

Computational Approaches for Consolidated Net Income

Poe's income and consolidated net income can be determined independently by alternative methods. Computation in terms of the definition of consolidated net income is:

Poe's separate earnings	$100,000
Add: Poe's share of Shaw's separate earnings ($50,000 × 80%)	40,000
Add: Poe's share of Turk's separate earnings ($40,000 × 80% × 70%)	22,400
Poe's net income and consolidated net income	$162,400

Computation of parent and consolidated net income in terms of the consolidated income statement presentation involves the deduction of minority interest income from combined separate earnings:

Combined separate earnings:		
Poe	$100,000	
Shaw	50,000	
Turk	40,000	$190,000
Less: Minority interest incomes:		
Direct minority interest in Turk's income ($40,000 × 30%)	$ 12,000	
Indirect minority interest in Turk's income ($40,000 × 70% × 20%)	5,600	
Direct minority interest in Shaw's income ($50,000 × 20%)	10,000	27,600
Poe's net income and consolidated net income		$162,400

Still another computational approach is to use a schedule such as the following:

	Poe	Shaw	Turk
Separate earnings	$100,000	$ 50,000	$40,000
Allocate Turk's income to Shaw:			
($40,000 × 70%)	—	+28,000	−28,000
Allocate Shaw's income to Poe			
($78,000 × 80%)	+62,400	−62,400	—
Consolidated net income	$162,400		
Minority interest income		$ 15,600	$12,000

Schedules are often helpful in making allocations for complex affiliation structures. This is particularly true when intercompany profits are involved and when the equity method of accounting is not used or is applied incorrectly. The schedule illustrated here shows parent company and consolidated net income, as well as minority interest income. It also shows Shaw's investment income from Turk ($28,000) and Poe's investment income from Shaw ($62,400).

Consolidation Working Papers—Equity Method

Consolidation working papers for Poe Corporation and Subsidiaries for the year 20X2 are illustrated in Exhibit 9–2. The working papers show that no new consolidation procedures have been introduced. Consolidation working paper entries a and b eliminate investment income, dividends, and investment and equity balances for Shaw's investment in Turk. Entries c and d eliminate investment income, dividends, and investment and equity balances for Poe's investment in Shaw. Turk's $45,000 beginning minority interest is simply the 30% direct minority interest percentage times Turk's $150,000 equity at the beginning of 20X2. Minority interest income of Turk is 30% of Turk's $40,000 reported income. Similarly, the $50,000 beginning minority interest in Shaw is 20% of Shaw's $250,000 equity at January 1, 20X2, and the $15,600 minority interest income of Shaw is 20% of Shaw's reported net income. Consolidated net income and consolidated retained earnings of $162,400 and $202,400, respectively, are equal to Poe's net income and retained earnings.

Consolidation Working Papers—Cost Method

Now assume that Poe paid $192,000 for its investment in Shaw on January 1, 20X1, when Shaw's capital stock was $200,000 and retained earnings was $40,000. If Poe and Shaw corporations had used the cost method of accounting, their investment incomes for 20X2 and their investment accounts at December 31, 20X2 would have appeared as follows:

Poe's Books
Investment in Shaw (cost) — $192,000
Dividend income from Shaw — 24,000

Shaw's Books
Investment in Turk (cost) — $105,000
Dividend income from Turk — 14,000

These amounts are shown in the separate company columns of the working papers for Poe and Subsidiaries as illustrated in Exhibit 9–3. Except for the first two working paper entries to convert from the cost to the equity method, the working paper procedures are the same as those shown in Exhibit 9–2.

Turk is lowest in the affiliation structure, so Shaw's investment in Turk should be converted to the equity method first with the following working paper entry:

a	Investment in Turk	$14,000	
	Dividend income from Turk	14,000	
	Income from Turk		$28,000

POE CORPORATION AND SUBSIDIARIES CONSOLIDATION
WORKING PAPERS FOR THE YEAR ENDED DECEMBER 31, 20X2

	Poe	80% Shaw	70% Turk	Adjustments and Eliminations	Minority Interest	Consolidated Statements
Income Statement						
Sales	$200,000	$140,000	$100,000			$440,000
Income from Shaw	62,400			c 62,400		
Income from Turk		28,000		a 28,000		
Expenses including cost of goods sold	(100,000)	(90,000)	(60,000)			(250,000)
Minority income—Shaw					$ 15,600	(15,600)
Minority income—Turk					12,000	(12,000)
Net income	$162,400	$ 78,000	$ 40,000			$162,400
Retained Earnings						
Retained earnings—Poe	$100,000					$100,000
Retained earnings—Shaw		$ 50,000		d 50,000		
Retained earnings—Turk			$ 50,000	b 50,000		
Net income	162,400√	78,000√	40,000√			162,400
Dividends	(60,000)	(30,000)	(20,000)	a 14,000 c 24,000	(12,000)	(60,000)
Retained earnings December 31, 20X2	$202,400	$ 98,000	$ 70,000			$202,400
Balance Sheet						
Other assets	$461,600	$231,000	$200,000			$892,600
Investment in Shaw	238,400			c 38,400 d 200,000		
Investment in Turk		119,000		a 14,000 b 105,000		
	$700,000	$350,000	$200,000			$892,600
Liabilities	$ 97,600	$ 52,000	$ 30,000			$179,600
Capital stock—Poe	400,000					400,000
Capital stock—Shaw		200,000		d 200,000		
Capital stock—Turk			100,000	b 100,000		
Retained earnings	202,400√	98,000√	70,000√			202,400
	$700,000	$350,000	$200,000			
Minority interest in Turk, January 1, 20X2				b 45,000	45,000	
Minority interest in Shaw, January 1, 20X2				d 50,000	50,000	
Minority interest December 31, 20X2					$110,600	110,600
						$892,600

Minority interest income—Shaw, $78,000 × 20% = $15,600.
Minority interest income—Turk, $40,000 × 30% = $12,000.

Exhibit 9–2   *Indirect Holdings—Father-Son-Grandson Type (Equity Method)*

POE CORPORATION AND SUBSIDIARIES CONSOLIDATION
WORKING PAPERS FOR THE YEAR ENDED DECEMBER 31, 20X2

	Poe	80% Shaw	70% Turk	Adjustments and Eliminations		Minority Interests	Consolidated Statements
Income Statement							
Sales	$200,000	$140,000	$100,000				$440,000
Dividends from Shaw	24,000			b 24,000			
Income from Shaw				e 62,400	b 62,400		
Dividends from Turk		14,000		a 14,000			
Income from Turk				c 28,000	a 28,000		
Expenses including cost of goods sold	(100,000)	(90,000)	(60,000)				(250,000)
Minority income—Shaw						$ 15,600	(15,600)
Minority income—Turk						12,000	(12,000)
Net income	$124,000	$ 64,000	$ 40,000				$162,400
Retained Earnings							
Retained earnings—Poe	$ 92,000				b 8,000		$100,000
Retained earnings—Shaw		$ 50,000		f 50,000			
Retained earnings—Turk			$ 50,000	d 50,000			
Net income	124,000√	64,000√	40,000√				162,400
Dividends	(60,000)	(30,000)	(20,000)		c 14,000	(12,000)	(60,000)
					e 24,000		
Retained earnings December 31, 20X2	$156,000	$ 84,000	$ 70,000				$202,400
Balance Sheet							
Other assets	$461,600	$231,000	$200,000				$892,600
Investment in Shaw (cost)	192,000			b 46,400	e 38,400		
					f 200,000		
Investment in Turk (cost)		105,000		a 14,000	c 14,000		
					d 105,000		
	$653,600	$336,000	$200,000				$892,600
Liabilities	$ 97,600	$ 52,000	$ 30,000				$179,600
Capital stock—Poe	400,000						400,000
Capital stock—Shaw		200,000		f 200,000			
Capital stock—Turk			100,000	d 100,000			
Retained earnings	156,000√	84,000√	70,000√				202,400
	$653,600	$336,000	$200,000				
Minority interest in Turk, January 1, 20X2					d 45,000	45,000	
Minority interest in Shaw, January 1, 20X2					f 50,000	50,000	
Minority interest December 31, 20X2						$110,600	110,600
							$892,600

Exhibit 9–3   *Indirect Holdings—Father-Son-Grandson Type (Cost Method)*

Shaw's beginning-of-the-period retained earnings balance was not affected by the cost method, and accordingly, the cost-to-equity conversion merely involves reclassifying the $14,000 dividends as a decrease in the investment in Turk (debit dividend income and credit investment in Turk for $14,000) and taking up 70% of Turk's net income (debit investment in Turk and credit income from Turk for $28,000). After this adjustment, Shaw's realized net income on an equity basis is $78,000.

Poe's 80% investment in Shaw is converted to the equity method in a second working paper entry as follows:

b	Dividend income from Shaw	$24,000	
	Investment in Shaw	46,400	
	Income from Shaw		$62,400
	Retained earnings—Poe		8,000

This cost-to-equity working paper conversion entry involves both prior periods (20X1) and the current period (20X2), so a regular cost-equity conversion schedule is needed.

	Poe's Beginning Retained Earnings	Investment in Shaw	Income from Shaw	Dividend Income
Prior Year's Effect				
80% of Shaw's $10,000 undistributed income from 20X1	$8,000	$ 8,000		
Current Year's Effect				
Reclassify dividend income as decrease in investment		(24,000)		$(24,000)
80% of Shaw's realized income on an equity basis ($78,000 × 80%)		62,400	$62,400	
Working paper adjustments	$8,000	$46,400	$62,400	$(24,000)

After the cost-equity conversion entries are entered in the working papers (entries a and b), the adjusted financial statement items are the same amounts as those shown in Exhibit 9–2 under the equity method. The remaining working paper entries in Exhibit 9–3 (entries c, d, e, and f) are the same as those illustrated in Exhibit 9–2 under the equity method.

INDIRECT HOLDINGS—CONNECTING AFFILIATES STRUCTURE

Pet Corporation owns a 70% interest in Sal Corporation and a 60% interest in Ty Corporation. In addition, Sal Corporation owns a 20% interest in Ty. The affiliation structure of Pet Corporation and Subsidiaries is diagrammed as follows:

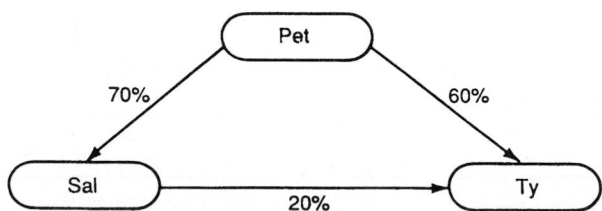

Data relevant to the investments of Pet and Sal are summarized as follows:

	Pet's Investment in Sal (70%) Acquired January 1, 20X5	Pet's Investment in Ty (60%) Acquired January 1, 20X4	Sal's Investment in Ty (20%) Acquired January 1, 20X1
Cost	$178,000	$100,000	$20,000
Less: Book value acquired	(168,000)	(90,000)	(20,000)
Goodwill	$ 10,000	$ 10,000	—
Investment Balance December 31, 20X5			
Cost	$178,000	$100,000	$20,000
Add: Share of investees' pre–20X6 income less dividends	7,000	18,000	16,000
Deduct: Goodwill amortization at 10% per year	(1,000)	(2,000)	—
Balance December 31, 20X5	$184,000	$116,000	$36,000

During 20X6, Pet, Sal, and Ty had earnings from their own operations of $70,000, $35,000, and $20,000 and declared dividends of $40,000, $20,000, and $10,000, respectively. Pet's separate earnings of $70,000 included an unrealized gain of $10,000 from the sale of land to Sal during 20X6. Sal's separate earnings of $35,000 included unrealized profit of $5,000 on inventory items sold to Pet for $15,000 during 20X6 and remaining in Pet's December 31, 20X6 inventory. A schedule for the computation of consolidated net income and minority interest income for the Pet/Sal/Ty affiliation for 20X6 is shown in Exhibit 9–4.

Equity Method of Accounting for Connecting Affiliates

Before allocating the separate earnings of Sal and Ty to Pet, any unrealized profits included in such earnings should be eliminated. Exhibit 9–4 shows the allocation of Ty's income as 20% to Sal and 60% to Pet. This allocation must precede the allocation of Sal's income to Pet because Sal's income includes $4,000 investment income from Ty.

In accounting for its investment in Ty for 20X6, Sal makes the following entries:

Cash	$2,000	
Investment in Ty		$2,000
To record dividends received from Ty ($10,000 × 20%).		
Investment in Ty	$4,000	
Income from Ty		$4,000
To record income from Ty ($20,000 × 20%).		

	Pet	Sal	Ty
Separate earnings	$70,000	$35,000	$20,000
Deduct: Unrealized profit	−10,000	−5,000	—
Separate realized earnings	60,000	30,000	20,000
Allocate Ty's income:			
20% to Sal	—	+4,000	−4,000
60% to Pet	+12,000	—	−12,000
Allocate Sal's income:			
70% to Pet	+23,800	−23,800	—
Deduct goodwill amortization:			
from Pet's 70% investment in Sal	−1,000	—	—
from Pet's 60% investment in Ty	−1,000	—	—
Pet's net income and consolidated net income	$93,800		
Minority interest income		$10,200	$ 4,000

Exhibit 9–4 *Income Allocation Schedule*

Sal's investment in Ty account at December 31, 20X6 has a balance of $38,000, the $36,000 balance at December 31, 20X5, plus $4,000 investment income, less $2,000 dividends. Sal's income from Ty is not reduced for the $5,000 unrealized profit on inventory items sold to Pet because Ty is not involved in the intercompany sale. Sal's $39,000 net income includes $5,000 unrealized profit, which is eliminated when Sal's realized income is allocated to Pet and Sal's minority stockholders.

Pet makes the following entries in accounting for its investments during 20X6:

Investment in Ty

Cash	$ 6,000	
Investment in Ty		$ 6,000
To record dividends received from Ty ($10,000 × 60%).		

Investment in Ty	$11,000	
Income from Ty		$11,000
To record income from Ty computed as follows:		
60% of Ty's $20,000 reported income		$12,000
Less: Goodwill amortization ($10,000 × 10%)		1,000
		$11,000

Investment in Sal

Cash	$14,000	
Investment in Sal		$14,000
To record dividends received from Sal ($20,000 × 70%).		

Investment in Sal	$12,800	
Income from Sal		$12,800
To record income from Sal computed as follows:		
70% of Sal's reported income of $39,000		$27,300
Less: 70% of Sal's unrealized inventory profit of $5,000		−3,500
Less: 100% of unrealized gain on land		−10,000
Less: Goodwill amortization ($10,000 × 10%)		−1,000
		$12,800

Pet's investment accounts at December 31, 20X6 show the following balances:

	Investment in Sal—70%	Investment in Ty—60%
Balance December 31, 20X5	$184,000	$116,000
Add: Investment income	12,800	11,000
Deduct: Dividends	−14,000	−6,000
Balance December 31, 20X6	$182,800	$121,000

Consolidation Working Papers—Equity Method

Consolidated statement working papers for Pet Corporation and Subsidiaries for 20X6 are presented in Exhibit 9–5.

The adjustment and elimination entries are reproduced in journal form for convenient reference.

a	Sales	$15,000	
	Cost of sales		$15,000
	To eliminate reciprocal sales and cost of sales.		
b	Cost of sales	$ 5,000	
	Inventory		$ 5,000
	To eliminate unrealized intercompany profit from inventory at December 31, 20X6.		
c	Gain on land	$10,000	
	Plant assets—net		$10,000
	To eliminate unrealized profit from intercompany sale of land.		

d Income from Ty .... $ 15,000
       Dividends (Ty's) .... $ 8,000
       Investment in Ty (60%) 5,000
       Investment in Ty (20%) 2,000
    To eliminate income from Ty and dividends from Ty and
      to adjust the investment in Ty accounts.

e Retained earnings—Ty, January 1, 20X6 ..... $ 80,000
   Goodwill 8,000
   Capital stock—Ty 100,000
       Investment in Ty (60%) $116,000
       Investment in Ty (20%) 36,000
       Minority interests—Ty 36,000
    To eliminate reciprocal investment and equity amounts of
      Ty and to establish goodwill and minority interest
      at January 1, 20X6.

f Other expenses .... $ 1,000
       Goodwill .... $ 1,000
    To record amortization of goodwill from Pet's investment
      in Ty for 20X6.

g Income from Sal .... $ 12,800
   Investment in Sal 1,200
       Dividends (Sal's) .... $ 14,000
    To eliminate income from Sal and dividends from Sal and
      to adjust the investment in Sal account.

h Retained earnings—Sal, January 1, 20X6 ... $ 50,000
   Goodwill 9,000
   Capital stock—Sal 200,000
       Investment in Sal $184,000
       Minority interest—Sal 75,000
    To eliminate reciprocal investment and equity amounts
      in Sal and to establish goodwill and minority interest
      at January 1, 20X6.

i Other expenses .... $ 1,000
       Goodwill .... $ 1,000
    To record amortization of goodwill from Pet's investment in Sal for 20X6.

A check on the $117,200 minority interest at December 31, 20X6 as shown in Exhibit 9–5 may be helpful at this point. The minority interest can be confirmed as follows:

	Minority Interest in Sal 30%	Minority Interest in Ty 20%	Total Minority Interest
Book value at December 31, 20X6:			
Sal $269,000 × 30%	$ 80,700	—	$ 80,700
Ty $190,000 × 20%	—	$ 38,000	38,000
Less: Unrealized profit of Sal			
$5,000 × 30%	(1,500)	—	(1,500)
Minority interest December 31, 20X6	$ 79,200	$ 38,000	$117,200

Except for the deduction of 30% of the $5,000 unrealized inventory profit on Sal's upstream sale to Pet, the minority interest is stated at its underlying book value at December 31, 20X6.

	Pet	Sal	Ty	Adjustment and Eliminations		Minority Interests	Consolidated Statements
Income Statement Sales	$200,000	$150,000	$100,000	a 15,000			$435,000
Income from Sal	12,800			g 12,800			
Income from Ty	11,000	4,000		d 15,000			
Gain on land	10,000			c 10,000			
Cost of sales	(100,000)	(80,000)	(50,000)	b 5,000	a 15,000		(220,000)
Other expenses	(40,000)	(35,000)	(30,000)	f 1,000 i 1,000			(107,000)
Minority income—Sal ($39,000 − $5,000) × .3						$ 10,200	(10,200)
Minority income—Ty ($20,000 × .2)						4,000	(4,000)
Net income	$ 93,800	$ 39,000	$ 20,000				$ 93,800
Retained Earnings Retained earnings—Pet	$220,000						$220,000
Retained earnings—Sal		$ 50,000		h 50,000			
Retained earnings—Ty			$ 80,000	e 80,000			
Net income	93,800√	39,000√	20,000√				93,800
Dividends	(40,000)	(20,000)	(10,000)		d 8,000 g 14,000	(8,000)	(40,000)
Retained earnings December 31, 20X6	$273,800	$ 69,000	$ 90,000				$273,800
Balance Sheet Other assets	$ 46,200	$ 22,000	$ 85,000				$153,200
Inventories	50,000	40,000	15,000		b 5,000		100,000
Plant assets—net	400,000	200,000	100,000		c 10,000		690,000
Investment in Sal (70%)	182,800			g 1,200	h 184,000		
Investment in Ty (60%)	121,000				d 5,000 e 116,000		
Investment in Ty (20%)		38,000			d 2,000 e 36,000		
Goodwill				e 8,000 h 9,000	f 1,000 i 1,000		15,000
	$800,000	$300,000	$200,000				$958,200
Liabilities	$126,200	$ 31,000	$ 10,000				$167,200
Capital stock—Pet	400,000						400,000
Capital stock—Sal		200,000		h 200,000			
Capital stock—Ty			100,000	e 100,000			
Retained earnings	273,800√	69,000√	90,000√				273,800
	$800,000	$300,000	$200,000				
Minority interest in Ty, January 1, 20X6					e 36,000	36,000	
Minority interest in Sal, January 1, 20X6					h 75,000	75,000	
Minority interest December 31, 20X6						$117,200	117,200
							$958,200

PET CORPORATION AND SUBSIDIARIES CONSOLIDATION WORKING PAPERS FOR THE YEAR ENDED DECEMBER 31, 20X6

Exhibit 9–5 *Connecting Affiliates with Intercompany Profits (Equity Method)*

MUTUAL HOLDINGS—PARENT STOCK HELD BY SUBSIDIARY

When affiliated companies hold ownership interests in each other, a mutual-holding situation exists. Parent company stock held by the subsidiary is not outstanding from the consolidated viewpoint and should not be reported as outstanding stock in a consolidated balance sheet.[2] For example, if Pace Corporation owns a 90% interest in Salt Corporation, and Salt owns a 10% interest in Pace, the 10% interest held by Salt is not outstanding for consolidation purposes and neither is the 90% interest in Salt held by Pace. Consolidation practice requires the exclusion of both the 10% and the 90% interests from consolidated financial statements, and the question is not whether the 10% interest in Pace should be excluded, but rather how should it be eliminated in the consolidation process. The elimination procedures depend on the method used in accounting for the investment.

Two methods of accounting for parent company stock held by a subsidiary are generally acceptable—the treasury stock approach and the conventional approach. The **treasury stock approach** considers parent company stock held by a subsidiary to be treasury stock of the consolidated entity. Accordingly, the investment account on the books of the subsidiary is maintained on a cost basis and is deducted at cost from stockholders' equity in the consolidated balance sheet. The **conventional approach** is to account for the subsidiary investment in parent company stock on an equity basis and to eliminate the subsidiary investment account against the parent company equity accounts in the usual manner. Although both approaches are acceptable, they do not result in equivalent consolidated financial statements. In particular, the consolidated retained earnings and minority interest amounts are usually different under the two methods.

Treasury Stock Approach

Assume that Pace Corporation acquired a 90% interest in Salt Corporation on January 1, 20X5 for $270,000, when Salt's capital stock was $200,000 and its retained earnings, $100,000. In addition, Salt Corporation purchased a 10% interest in Pace Corporation on January 5, 20X5 for $70,000, when Pace's capital stock was $500,000 and its retained earnings, $200,000. Trial balances for Pace and Salt on December 31, 20X5, before either company recorded its investment income, were as follows:

	Pace	Salt
Debits		
Other assets	$480,000	$260,000
Investment in Salt (90%)	270,000	—
Investment in Pace (10%)	—	70,000
Expenses including cost of goods sold	70,000	50,000
	$820,000	$380,000
Credits		
Capital stock, $10 par	$500,000	$200,000
Retained earnings	200,000	100,000
Sales	120,000	80,000
	$820,000	$380,000

Consolidation in Year of Acquisition   If the treasury stock approach is used, Salt Corporation has no investment income for 20X5, and Pace's share of Salt's $30,000 income ($80,000 sales − $50,000 expenses) is $27,000 ($30,000 × 90%). Consolidation working papers for Pace Corporation and Subsidiary for 20X5 are shown in Exhibit 9–6. In examining the working papers, notice that Salt's investment in Pace is reclassified as treasury stock and deducted from stockholders' equity in the consolidated balance sheet.

---

[2]*ARB No. 51*, "Consolidated Financial Statements," paragraph 13.

PACE CORPORATION AND SUBSIDIARY CONSOLIDATION
WORKING PAPERS FOR THE YEAR ENDED DECEMBER 31, 20X5

	Pace	90% Salt	Adjustments and Eliminations	Minority Interests	Consolidated Statements
Income Statement Sales	$120,000	$ 80,000			$200,000
Investment income	27,000		a 27,000		
Expenses including cost of goods sold	(70,000)	(50,000)			(120,000)
Minority interest income				$ 3,000	(3,000)
Net income	$ 77,000	$ 30,000			$ 77,000
Retained Earnings Retained earnings—Pace	$200,000				$200,000
Retained earnings—Salt		$100,000	b 100,000		
Net income	77,000√	30,000√			77,000
Retained earnings December 31, 20X5	$277,000	$130,000			$277,000
Balance Sheet Other assets	$480,000	$260,000			$740,000
Investment in Salt (90%)	297,000		a 27,000 b 270,000		
Investment in Pace (10%)		70,000	c 70,000		
	$777,000	$330,000			$740,000
Capital stock—Pace	$500,000				$500,000
Capital stock—Salt		$200,000	b 200,000		
Retained earnings	277,000√	130,000√			277,000
	$777,000	$330,000			
Treasury stock			c 70,000		(70,000)
Minority interest January 1, 20X5			b 30,000	30,000	
Minority interest December 31, 20X5				$ 33,000	33,000
					$740,000

Exhibit 9–6 *Parent Stock Held by Subsidiary—Treasury Stock Approach (Year of Acquisition)*

Consolidation in Subsequent Years   During 20X6 the separate earnings and dividends of Pace and Salt corporations are as follows:

	Pace	Salt
Separate earnings	$60,000	$40,000
Dividends	30,000	20,000

Under the treasury stock approach, Salt records dividend income of $3,000 from Pace (10% of Pace Corporation's $30,000 dividends) and reports its net income for 20X6 under the cost method in the amount of $43,000.

Pace Corporation accounts for its investment in Salt under the equity method as follows:

Cash	$18,000	
Investment in Salt		$18,000
To record 90% of $20,000 dividends paid by Salt.		
Investment in Salt	$38,700	
Income from Salt		$38,700
To record 90% of Salt's $43,000 income for 20X6.		
Income from Salt	$ 3,000	
Dividends		$ 3,000

    To eliminate intercompany dividends of $3,000 (10% of Pace's
$30,000 dividends paid to Salt) and to adjust investment income
for Pace's dividends that are included in Salt's income.

Thus, Pace records investment income from Salt of $35,700 ($38,700 − $3,000) and an investment account increase of $20,700 during 20X6 ($38,700 − $18,000). The increase of $20,700 in Pace's investment in Salt account is equal to 90% of Salt's $40,000 separate earnings, plus 90% of the $3,000 dividends paid to Salt that accrued to the benefit of Pace, less 90% of Salt's $20,000 dividends. Pace Corporation's investment income from Salt consists of 90% of Salt's $40,000 separate earnings, less $300 (the part of the $3,000 dividends from Pace that accrues to the benefit of Salt Corporation's minority stockholders).

Consolidation working papers for Pace and Subsidiary for 20X6 are shown in Exhibit 9–7. The $317,700 balance in Pace's investment in Salt account is computed as follows:

Investment in Salt (90%) December 31, 20X5	$297,000
Add: 90% of Salt's reported income	38,700
Deduct: 90% of Salt's dividends	(18,000)
Investment in Salt (90%) December 31, 20X6	$317,700

Pace's investment in Salt was acquired at book value, so the investment in Salt account balance can also be computed as 90% of Salt's equity at December 31, 20X6 ($353,000 × 90% = $317,700).

Entry a in the consolidation working papers shown in Exhibit 9–7 is affected by the $3,000 dividend adjustment under the equity method and is reproduced for convenient reference:

a	Income from Salt	$35,700	
	Dividend income	3,000	
	Dividends		$18,000
	Investment in Salt		20,700

This entry is unusual because both Pace Corporation's investment income from Salt and Salt's dividend income from Pace are eliminated in the process of adjusting the investment in Salt account to its $297,000 beginning-of-the-period balance. The other working paper adjustments are similar to those in Exhibit 9–6.

Although Pace Corporation paid dividends of $30,000 during 20X6, only $27,000 was paid to outside stockholders. Thus, Pace's retained earnings statement and the consolidated retained earnings statement show $27,000 dividends rather than $30,000. The consolidated balance sheet shows a $70,000 equity deduction for the cost of Salt's investment in Pace. This amount is the same as was shown in the working papers in Exhibit 9–6.

Conventional Approach

The consolidated balance sheets in Exhibits 9–6 and 9–7 for the treasury stock approach consolidated 100% of Pace Corporation's capital stock and retained earnings and deducted the cost of Salt's 10% investment in Pace from the consolidated stockholders' equity. Under the conventional approach, parent company stock held by a

PACE CORPORATION AND SUBSIDIARY CONSOLIDATION
WORKING PAPERS FOR THE YEAR ENDED DECEMBER 31, 20X6

	Pace	90% Salt	Adjustments and Eliminations	Minority Interests	Consolidated Statements
Income Statement					
Sales	$140,000	$100,000			$240,000
Income from Salt	35,700		a 35,700		
Dividend income		3,000	a 3,000		
Expenses including cost of goods sold	(80,000)	(60,000)			(140,000)
Minority interest income $43,000 × 10%				$ 4,300	(4,300)
Net income	$ 95,700	$ 43,000			$ 95,700
Retained Earnings					
Retained earnings—Pace	$277,000				$277,000
Retained earnings—Salt		$130,000	b 130,000		
Net income	95,700√	43,000√			95,700
Dividends	(27,000)	(20,000)	a 18,000	(2,000)	(27,000)
Retained earnings December 31, 20X6	$345,700	$153,000			$345,700
Balance Sheet					
Other assets	$528,000	$283,000			$811,000
Investment in Salt (90%)	317,700		a 20,700 b 297,000		
Investment in Pace (10%)		70,000	c 70,000		
	$845,700	$353,000			$811,000
Capital stock—Pace	$500,000				$500,000
Capital stock—Salt		$200,000	b 200,000		
Retained earnings	345,700√	153,000√			345,700
	$845,700	$353,000			
Treasury stock			c 70,000		(70,000)
Minority interest January 1, 20X6			b 33,000	33,000	
Minority interest December 31, 20X6				$35,300	35,300
					$811,000

Exhibit 9–7 *Parent Stock Held by Subsidiary—Treasury Stock Approach (Year After Acquisition)*

subsidiary is considered constructively retired, and the capital stock and retained earnings applicable to the interest held by the subsidiary do not appear in the consolidated financial statements.

Salt's acquisition of Pace stock under the conventional procedure is considered a constructive retirement of 10% of Pace's capital stock. A consolidated balance sheet for Pace and Subsidiary at the time of acquisition shows capital stock and retained earnings applicable to the 90% of Pace Corporation's equity held outside of the consolidated entity as follows:

	January 1, 20X5	
	Pace	Consolidated
Capital stock	$500,000	$450,000
Retained earnings	200,000	180,000
Total stockholders' equity	$700,000	$630,000

It is generally agreed that the consolidated balance sheet should show the capital stock and retained earnings applicable to majority stockholders outside the consolidated entity. However, this treatment raises a question concerning the applicability of the equity method of accounting to mutual holdings involving parent company stock. Specifically, is the equity method of accounting applicable to affiliation structures that involve investments in the parent company? If so, the parent company's (investor's) "net income for the period and its stockholders' equity at the end of the period are the same regardless of whether an investment in a subsidiary is accounted for under the equity method or the subsidiary is consolidated."[3]

In spite of some reservations that have been expressed about the applicability of the equity method to mutually held parent company stock, the position taken in this book is that the equity method is applicable and, in fact, required by *APB Opinion No. 18*. Paragraph 19e of that Opinion states that "a transaction of an investee of a capital nature that affects the investor's share of stockholders' equity of the investee should be accounted for as if the investee were a consolidated subsidiary." In accounting for Pace's investment in Salt, this requirement is applied as follows:

January 1, 20X5

Investment in Salt (90%)	$270,000	
Cash		$270,000

   To record acquisition of a 90% interest in Salt
     at book value.

January 5, 20X5

Capital stock, $10 par	$ 50,000	
Retained earnings	20,000	
Investment in Salt		$ 70,000

   To record the constructive retirement of 10% of Pace's outstanding
     stock as a result of Salt's purchase of Pace stock.

These entries reduce parent company capital stock and retained earnings to reflect amounts applicable to majority stockholders outside the consolidated entity. The reduction of the investment in Salt account is based on the theory that parent company stock purchased by a subsidiary is, in effect, returned to the parent company and constructively retired.

By recording the constructive retirement of the parent company stock on parent company books, parent company equity reflects the equity of stockholders outside the consolidated entity. These are the shareholders for which the consolidated statements are intended. In addition, recording the constructive retirement as indicated establishes consistency between capital stock and retained earnings for the parent's outside stockholders (90%) and parent company net income, dividends, and earnings per share, which also relate to the 90% outside stockholders of the parent. Financial statement notes should explain the details of the constructive retirement.

Allocation of Mutual Income   When the conventional method of accounting for mutually held stock is used, the income of the parent on an equity basis cannot be determined until the income of the subsidiary has been determined on an equity basis, and vice versa. This is because the incomes are mutually related. The solution to the problem of determining parent and subsidiary incomes lies in the use of some mathematical

---

[3] *APB Opinion No. 18*, paragraph 19.

procedure, the most common procedure being the use of simultaneous equations and substitution. The allocation of income to the affiliated entities and to outside stockholders is accomplished in two steps. First, the incomes of Pace and Salt are computed on a consolidated basis, which includes the mutual income held by the affiliates. Next, these amounts are multiplied by the percentage ownership held within the affiliated group and the minority interest percentage to determine consolidated net income on an equity basis and minority interest income.

In the first step, the incomes of Pace and Salt on a consolidated basis for 20X5 can be determined mathematically as follows:

P = the income of Pace on a consolidated basis (includes mutual income)

S = the income of Salt on a consolidated basis (includes mutual income)

Then,

$$P = \text{Pace's separate earnings of } \$50,000 + 90\% \; S$$
$$S = \text{Salt's separate earnings of } \$30,000 + 10\% \; P$$

By substitution,

$$P = \$50,000 + .9(\$30,000 + .1P)$$
$$P = \$50,000 + \$27,000 + .09P$$
$$P = \underline{\$84,615}$$
$$S = \$30,000 + (\$84,615 \times .1)$$
$$S = \underline{\$38,462}$$

These solutions are not final solutions because some of the income (mutual income) has been double-counted. The combined separate earnings of Pace and Salt is only $80,000 ($50,000 + $30,000), but P plus S equals $123,077 ($84,615 + $38,462). In the next step, Pace's net income on an equity basis is determined by multiplying the value determined for P in the equation by the 90% interest outstanding, and minority interest income is determined by multiplying the value determined for S by the minority interest percentage. In other words, *Pace's net income on an equity basis is 90% of $84,615, or $76,154, and the minority interest income is 10% of $38,462, or $3,846.* Pace's net income (and consolidated net income) of $76,154, plus minority interest income of $3,846, is equal to the $80,000 separate earnings of Pace and Salt.

Accounting for Mutual Income Under the Equity Method   Pace Corporation records its investment income for 20X5 on an equity basis as follows:

Investment in Salt	$26,154	
Income from Salt		$26,154
To record income from Salt.		

The $26,154 income from Salt is equal to 90% of Salt's $38,462 income on a consolidated basis, less 10% of Pace's $84,615 income on a consolidated basis [($38,462 × 90%) − ($84,615 × 10%)]. This represents Pace's 90% interest in Salt's income less Salt's 10% interest in Pace's income. An alternative calculation that gives the same result is to deduct Pace's separate earnings from its net income ($76,154 − $50,000).

Assume that Salt Corporation accounts for its investment in Pace on a cost basis because its interest in Pace is only 10%. Pace did not declare dividends during 20X5, so Salt would have no investment income for the year, and its investment account would remain at the $70,000 original cost of the 10% interest.

Consolidation Under the Equity Method   Consolidation working papers for Pace Corporation and Subsidiary under the conventional procedure for 20X5 are presented in Exhibit 9–8. The investment in Salt (90%) is shown in the working papers at $226,154 (the $270,000 initial investment, plus $26,154 investment income, less the $70,000 reduction for the constructive retirement of Pace's stock). Entry a in the working papers eliminates the $70,000 investment in Pace (Salt's books) and increases Pace's investment in Salt account to $296,154. This entry reflects the construc-

PACE CORPORATION AND SUBSIDIARY
CONSOLIDATION WORKING PAPERS
FOR THE YEAR ENDED DECEMBER 31, 20X5

	Pace	90% Salt	Adjustments and Eliminations		Minority Interests	Consolidated Statements
Income Statement						
Sales	$120,000	$ 80,000				$200,000
Income from Salt	26,154		b 26,154			
Expenses including cost of sales	(70,000)	(50,000)				(120,000)
Minority interest income (see equation)					$ 3,846	(3,846)
Net income	$ 76,154	$ 30,000				$ 76,154
Retained Earnings						
Retained earnings—Pace	$180,000					$180,000
Retained earnings—Salt		$100,000	c 100,000			
Net income	76,154√	30,000√				76,154
Retained earnings December 31, 20X5	$256,154	$130,000				$256,154
Balance Sheet						
Other assets	$480,000	$260,000				$740,000
Investment in Salt (90%)	226,154		a 70,000	b 26,154 c 270,000		
Investment in Pace (10%)		70,000		a 70,000		
	$706,154	$330,000				$740,000
Capital stock—Pace	$450,000					$450,000
Capital stock—Salt		$200,000	c 200,000			
Retained earnings	256,154√	130,000√				256,154
	$706,154	$330,000				
Minority interest January 1, 20X5			c 30,000		30,000	
Minority interest December 31, 20X5					$33,846	33,846
						$740,000

Exhibit 9–8 Parent Stock Held by Subsidiary—Conventional Approach (Year of Acquisition)

tive retirement of Pace stock that was charged to Pace's investment in Salt account. Entry b eliminates investment income of $26,154 and reduces the investment account to its $270,000 cost at January 5, 20X5. Entry c eliminates the reciprocal investment in Salt and equity of Salt amounts and establishes the minority interest in Salt at $30,000 (10% of $300,000) at the beginning of 20X5.

In examining the working papers in Exhibit 9–8, observe that the net income, capital stock, and retained earnings in the separate statements of Pace Corporation are equal to consolidated net income, capital stock, and retained earnings. This equality would not have existed without the entry to record the constructive retirement of stock on Pace Corporation's books.

Consolidation in Subsequent Years   The separate earnings and dividends of Pace and Salt for 20X6 are as follows:

	Pace	Salt
Separate earnings	$60,000	$40,000
Dividends	30,000	20,000

Application of the conventional method of accounting involves the following mathematical computations for Pace and Salt for 20X6:

P = Pace's income on a consolidated basis (includes mutual income)
S = Salt's income on a consolidated basis (includes mutual income)

Basic equations:

$$P = \$60,000 + .9S$$
$$S = \$40,000 + .1P$$

Substitution:

$$P = \$60,000 + .9(\$40,000 + .1P)$$
$$.91P = \$96,000$$
$$P = \underline{\$105,495}$$
$$S = \$40,000 + .1(\$105,495)$$
$$S = \underline{\$50,549}$$

These computed amounts for P and S include mutual income that then must be eliminated. The amounts are used in determining consolidated net income and minority interest income as follows:

Pace's net income (and consolidated net income)	
$105,495 × 90% outside ownership	$ 94,945
Minority interest income $50,549 × 10%	5,055
Total separate earnings of Pace and Salt	$100,000

If Salt accounts for its investment in Pace under the cost method, it will record dividend income from Pace of $3,000 for 20X6 (10% of Pace's dividends). Alternatively, Salt will record income from Pace of $10,550 ($105,495 × 10%) if it uses the equity method.

Pace accounts for its investment in Salt on an equity basis as follows:

Cash	$18,000	
Investment in Salt		$18,000
To record 90% of Salt's $20,000 dividend for 20X6.		

Investment in Salt	$34,945	
Income from Salt		$34,945

To record investment income computed as follows: $94,945 Pace's net income less $60,000 Pace's separate earnings = $34,945. An alternative computation: 90% of Salt's income on a consolidated basis ($50,549 × 90%), less 10% of Pace's income on a consolidated basis ($105,495 × 10%) = $34,945.

Investment in Salt	$3,000	
Dividends		$3,000

To eliminate parent company dividends paid to Salt and to adjust the investment in Salt account.

Pace's investment in Salt account at December 31, 20X6 will have a balance of $246,099 under the equity method. This balance is computed:

Investment in Salt, December 31, 20X5	$226,154
Add: Investment income	34,945
Add: Dividends paid to Salt	3,000
Deduct: Dividends received from Salt	−18,000
Investment in Salt, December 31, 20X6	$246,099

Consolidation working papers for Pace Corporation and Subsidiary for 20X6 are shown in Exhibit 9–9, which assumes that Salt accounts for its investment in Pace under the cost method. The equity method of accounting has been applied by Pace. Therefore, parent company net income of $94,945 is equal to consolidated net income. Parent company capital stock and retained earnings amounts also are equal to their corresponding consolidated statement amounts. The working paper adjustments in Exhibit 9–9 are procedurally equivalent to those shown earlier in the chapter.

Conversion to Equity Method on Separate Company Books   It is helpful at this point to consider the computations that would be necessary to correct consolidated retained earnings and minority interest if the equity method of accounting had not been used by Pace. First, it would be necessary to determine the separate net asset increases of the mutually held companies. This increase is computed for Pace and Salt from January 1, 20X5 to December 31, 20X6 as follows:

	Pace	Salt	Total
Separate earnings—20X5	$ 50,000	$ 30,000	$ 80,000
Separate earnings—20X6	+60,000	+40,000	+100,000
Less: Dividends declared	−30,000	−20,000	−50,000
Add: Dividends received from affiliates	+18,000	+3,000	+21,000
Increase in net assets	$ 98,000	$ 53,000	$151,000

Once the separate net asset increases are determined, the simultaneous equations used earlier for determining income allocations would be used in allocating the separate net asset increases to consolidated retained earnings and to minority interest. The computations for Pace and Salt would be:

$P =$ increase in net assets of Pace on a consolidated basis since acquisition by Salt

$S =$ increase in net assets of Salt on a consolidated basis since acquisition by Pace

Basic equations:

$$P = \$98,000 + .9S$$
$$S = \$53,000 + .1P$$

By substitution,

$$P = \$98,000 + .9(\$53,000 + .1P)$$
$$P = \$98,000 + \$47,700 + .09P$$
$$.91P = \$145,700$$
$$P = \underline{\$160,110}$$
$$S = \$53,000 + (.1 \times \$160,110)$$
$$S = \underline{\$69,011}$$

These computations (which still include mutual amounts) could be used to allocate the $151,000 net asset increase to consolidated retained earnings and minority interest as follows:

Pace's retained earnings increase (or increase in consolidated retained earnings) = $160,110 × 90%	$144,099
Minority interest's retained earnings increase = $69,011 × 10%	6,901
Total net asset increase	$151,000

PACE CORPORATION AND SUBSIDIARY
CONSOLIDATION WORKING PAPERS
FOR THE YEAR ENDED DECEMBER 31, 20X6

	Pace	90% Salt	Adjustments and Eliminations		Minority Interests	Consolidated Statements
Income Statement Sales	$140,000	$ 100,000				$240,000
Income from Salt	34,945		b 34,945			
Dividend income		3,000	b 3,000			
Expenses including cost of sales	(80,000)	(60,000)				(140,000)
Minority interest income (see equation)					$ 5,055	(5,055)
Net income	$ 94,945	$ 43,000				$ 94,945
Retained Earnings Retained earnings—Pace	$256,154					$256,154
Retained earnings—Salt		$130,000	c 130,000			
Net income	94,945√	43,000√				94,945
Dividends	(27,000)	(20,000)		b 18,000	(2,000)	(27,000)
Retained earnings December 31, 20X6	$324,099	$ 153,000				$324,099
Balance Sheet Other assets	$528,000	$283,000				$811,000
Investment in Salt (90%)	246,099		a 70,000	b 19,945 c 296,154		
Investment in Pace (10%)		70,000		a 70,000		
	$774,099	$ 353,000				$811,000
Capital stock—Pace	$450,000					$450,000
Capital stock—Salt		$ 200,000	c 200,000			
Retained earnings	324,099√	153,000√				324,099
	$774,099	$ 353,000				
Minority interest January 1, 20X6				c 33,846	33,846	
Minority interest December 31, 20X6					$36,901	36,901
						$811,000

Exhibit 9–9   *Parent Stock Held by Subsidiary—Conventional Approach (Year After Acquisition)*

At acquisition, Pace's retained earnings were $200,000, and they were adjusted downward to $180,000 for the constructive retirement of 10% of Pace's stock. Thus, the correct amount of consolidated retained earnings at December 31, 20X6 can be computed independently as $180,000 + $144,099, or $324,099. This computation provides a convenient check on the $324,099 retained earnings shown in the consolidated balance sheet in Exhibit 9–9.

Minority interest in Salt Corporation at January 1, 20X5 was $30,000 ($300,000 equity × 10%). The minority interest at December 31, 20X6 is computed $30,000 + $6,901, or $36,901. This computation confirms the $36,901 minority interest that appears in the consolidation working papers of Exhibit 9–9.

SUBSIDIARY STOCK MUTUALLY HELD

Parent company stock that is held within an affiliation structure is not outstanding and must not be reported as outstanding stock either in the parent company statements under the equity method of accounting or in consolidated financial statements. Two generally accepted approaches for eliminating the effect of mutually held parent company stock—the treasury stock approach and the conventional approach—were explained and illustrated in the previous section of this chapter. In this section, *the mutually held stock involves subsidiaries holding the stock of each other, and the treasury stock approach is not applicable.*

Consider the following diagram of the affiliation structure of Poly, Seth, and Uno. Poly owns an 80% interest in Seth directly. Seth has a 70% interest in Uno, and Uno has a 10% interest in Seth. There is a 10% minority interest in Seth and a 30% minority interest in Uno.

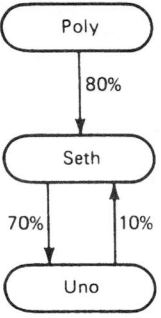

The acquisitions of Poly, Seth, and Uno were as follows:

1 Poly acquired its 80% interest in Seth Corporation on January 2, 20X5 for $260,000, when the stockholders' equity of Seth consisted of capital stock of $200,000 and retained earnings of $100,000 ($20,000 goodwill).
2 Seth acquired its 70% interest in Uno Corporation for $115,000 on January 3, 20X6, when the stockholders' equity of Uno consisted of $100,000 capital stock and $50,000 retained earnings ($10,000 goodwill).
3 Uno acquired its 10% interest in Seth for $40,000 on December 31, 20X6, when the stockholders' equity of Seth consisted of $200,000 capital stock and $200,000 retained earnings (no goodwill).

Accounting Prior to Mutual Holding Relationship

Assume that the recorded net assets from the investments described were equal to their fair values at the time of acquisition and that any excess of investment over net assets acquired was allocated to goodwill with 10-year amortization periods. After-closing trial balances for Poly, Seth, and Uno at December 31, 20X6 are presented as follows:

	Poly	Seth	Uno
Cash	$ 64,000	$ 40,000	$ 20,000
Other current assets	200,000	85,000	80,000
Plant and equipment—net	500,000	240,000	110,000
Investment in Seth (80%)	336,000	—	—
Investment in Uno (70%)	—	135,000	—
Investment in Seth (10%)	—	—	40,000
	$1,100,000	$500,000	$250,000
Liabilities	$ 200,000	$100,000	$ 70,000
Capital stock	500,000	200,000	100,000
Retained earnings	400,000	200,000	80,000
	$1,100,000	$500,000	$250,000

The balance in Poly's investment in Seth account at December 31, 20X6 is $336,000, computed as follows:

Cost	$260,000
Add: 80% of Seth's $40,000 income less dividends—20X5	32,000
80% of Seth's $60,000 income less dividends—20X6	48,000
Deduct: Amortization of excess of cost over book value	
[$260,000 − ($300,000 × 80%)] × 10%: 20X5	−2,000
20X6	−2,000
	$336,000

The balance of Uno's 10% investment in Seth account at December 31, 20X6 is equal to the $40,000 cost of the investment on that date. Assume that this 10% investment in Seth is accounted for on a cost basis, even though the equity method might be used because absolute control lies with the parent company.

Seth's $135,000 investment in Uno at December 31, 20X6 is computed as follows:

Investment in Uno January 3, 20X6—cost	$115,000
Add: 70% of Uno's $30,000 income less dividends—20X6	21,000
Deduct: Amortization of excess of cost over book value	
acquired for 20X6:	
[$115,000 − ($150,000 × 70%)] × 10%	−1,000
	$135,000

Accounting for Mutually Held Subsidiaries

During 20X7, the three affiliated companies had income from their separate operations and dividends as follows:

	Poly	Seth	Uno	Total
Income from separate operations	$112,000	$51,000	$40,000	$203,000
Dividends declared	50,000	30,000	20,000	100,000

The total separate incomes of the three companies are allocated under the conventional approach. An adjustment for goodwill amortization is necessary because goodwill amortization is not considered in determining income from separate operations, but it is required for the determination of investment income on an equity basis.

Income Allocation Computations   Income allocation computations for the affiliated companies are as follows:

P = separate income of Poly + $.8S$ − $2,000 goodwill amortization
S = separate income of Seth + $.7U$ − $1,000 goodwill amortization
U = separate income of Uno + $.1S$ − 0 goodwill amortization
P = $112,000 + $.8S$ − $2,000
S = $51,000 + $.7U$ − $1,000
U = $40,000 + $.1S$

Solve for S (amounts are rounded to nearest $1):

S = $51,000 + .7($40,000 + .1S) − $1,000 = $78,000 + .07S
$.93S$ = $78,000
S = $83,871
U = $40,000 + .1($83,871)
U = $48,387
P = $112,000 + .8($83,871) − $2,000
P = $177,097

Total income for the affiliated group is allocated to:

Consolidated net income (equal to Poly's net income)	$177,097
Minority interest in Seth's income ($83,871 × 10%)	8,387
Minority interest in Uno's income ($48,387 × 30%)	14,516
Total separate income less goodwill amortization	$200,000

Computations of Investment Account Balances A summary of the investment account balances at December 31, 20X7 is as follows:

	Poly (Equity Method)	Seth (Equity Method)	Uno (Cost Method)*
Investment balances December 31, 20X6	$336,000	$135,000	$40,000
Add: Investment income			
Poly ($83,871 × .8) − $2,000	65,097	—	—
Seth ($48,387 × .7) − $1,000	—	32,871	—
Deduct: Dividends received:			
Poly ($30,000 × .8)	(24,000)	—	—
Seth ($20,000 × .7)	—	(14,000)	—
Investment balance December 31, 20X7	$377,097	$153,871	$40,000

*$3,000 dividend income and dividends received amounts for Uno's 10% investment in Seth do not affect the investment account because the cost method is used by Uno.

Consolidation Working Papers—Equity Method The investment incomes and balances as summarized previously are reflected in the consolidation working papers that appear in Exhibit 9–10. Separate company financial statements of Poly, Seth, and Uno are shown in the first three columns of the consolidation working papers. Consolidation working paper entries a, b, and c eliminate investment income (including dividend income of Uno) and intercompany dividend balances, and adjust the investment accounts to their beginning-of-the-period balances. Working paper entry d eliminates reciprocal equity and investment balances for Uno, records the $9,000 beginning-of-the-period unamortized goodwill from Seth's investment in Uno, and establishes the $54,000 beginning minority interest in Uno (computed as $180,000 × 30%). Entry e eliminates reciprocal equity and investment balances for Seth (both Poly's 80% and Uno's 10%), records the $16,000 beginning-of-the-period unamortized goodwill from Poly's investment in Seth, and establishes the $40,000 beginning minority interest in Seth (computed as $400,000 × 10%). Although there are two investment in Seth accounts and two elimination entries could have been made, *it is convenient to prepare one entry for each entity, Seth in this case, rather than for each investment account.* The final working paper entry records amortization of goodwill for the year.

Poly accounts for its investment in Seth as a one-line consolidation, so consolidated net income of $177,097 for 20X7 and consolidated retained earnings of $527,097 at December 31, 20X7 are equal to the corresponding amounts in the separate financial statements of Poly. Minority interest income is determined by equation, as demonstrated earlier.

SUMMARY

One corporation may control another corporation through direct or indirect ownership of its voting stock. Indirect holdings give the investor an ability to control or significantly influence the operations of the investee not directly owned through an investee that is directly owned. The major problem encountered in consolidating the financial statements of companies involved in indirect control situations lies in allocating income and equities among majority and minority stockholders. Several computational approaches are available for such allocations, but the schedule approach is probably the best overall approach because of its simplicity, and because it provides a step-by-step reference of all allocations made.

When affiliated companies hold the stock of each other, the stock is not outstanding from the viewpoint of the consolidated entity. The effect of mutually held

POLY CORPORATION AND SUBSIDIARIES CONSOLIDATION
WORKING PAPERS—FOR THE YEAR ENDED DECEMBER 31, 20X7

	Poly	Seth	Uno	Adjustments and Eliminations	Minority Interests	Consolidated Statements
Income Statement						
Sales	$ 412,000	$161,000	$100,000			$ 673,000
Income from Seth (80%)	65,097			c 65,097		
Income from Uno (70%)		32,871		b 32,871		
Dividend income (10%)			3,000	a 3,000		
Cost of sales	(220,000)	(70,000)	(40,000)			(330,000)
Expenses	(80,000)	(40,000)	(20,000)	f 3,000		(143,000)
Minority income—Seth†					$ 8,387	(8,387)
Minority income—Uno†					14,516	(14,516)
Net income	$ 177,097	$ 83,871	$43,000			$ 177,097
Retained Earnings Retained earnings—Poly	$400,000					$ 400,000
Retained earnings—Seth		$200,000		e 200,000		
Retained earnings—Uno			$ 80,000	d 80,000		
Add: Net income	177,097√	83,871√	43,000√			177,097
Deduct: Dividends	(50,000)	(30,000)	(20,000)	a 3,000 b 14,000 c 24,000	(9,000)	(50,000)
Retained earnings December 31, 20X7	$ 527,097	$253,871	$103,000			$ 527,097
Balance Sheet Cash	$ 60,000	$ 30,000	$ 43,000			$ 133,000
Other current assets	250,000	80,000	70,000			400,000
Plant and equipment—net	550,000	300,000	130,000			980,000
Investment in Seth (80%)	377,097			c 41,097 e 336,000		
Investment in Uno (70%)		153,871		b 18,871 d 135,000		
Investment in Seth (10%)			40,000	e 40,000		
Goodwill—Poly				e 16,000 f 2,000		14,000
Goodwill—Seth				d 9,000 f 1,000		8,000
	$1,237,097	$563,871	$283,000			$1,535,000
Liabilities	$ 210,000	$110,000	$ 80,000			$ 400,000
Capital stock—Poly	500,000					500,000
Capital stock—Seth		200,000		e 200,000		
Capital stock—Uno			100,000	d 100,000		
Retained earnings	527,097√	253,871√	103,000√			527,097
	$1,237,097	$563,871	$283,000			
Minority interest in Uno, January 1, 20X7				d 54,000	54,000	
Minority interest in Seth, January 1, 20X7				e 40,000	40,000	
Minority interest December 31, 20X7					$107,903	107,903
						$1,535,000

†Minority income in Seth is 10% of $83,871 = $8,387; minority income in Uno is 30% of $48,387 = $14,516.

Exhibit 9–10   *Consolidation Involving Mutually Held Subsidiary Stock*

parent company stock is eliminated from consolidated financial statements by either the treasury stock approach or the conventional approach. The treasury stock approach involves deducting the investment in parent company stock on a cost basis from consolidated stockholders' equity. Under the conventional approach, the investment in parent company stock is treated as constructively retired by adjusting the parent's investment in subsidiary and parent's equity accounts to reflect a one-line consolidation. The subsidiary's investment in parent account is then eliminated against the parent's investment in subsidiary account.

Mutual investments by subsidiaries in the stock of each other are accounted for under the conventional method of eliminating reciprocal investment and equity balances. The treasury stock approach is not applicable to such mutually held investments because only parent company stock and retained earnings appear in the consolidated financial statements. Under the conventional method, simultaneous equations are used to allocate income and equities among mutually held companies.

SELECTED READINGS

CHILDS, WILLIAM HERBERT. *Consolidated Financial Statements: Principles and Procedures.* Ithaca, NY: Cornell University Press, 1949 (especially see Chapter 8, "Indirect and Reciprocal Relationships").

Committee on Accounting Procedure. *Accounting Research Bulletin No. 51.* "Consolidated Financial Statements." New York: American Institute of Certified Public Accountants, 1959.

MINCH, ROLAND A. and ENRICO PETRI. "Reporting Income for Reciprocal Parent-Subsidiary Stockholdings." *CPA Journal* (July 1975), pp. 36–40.

MOONITZ, MAURICE, "Mutual Stockholdings in Consolidated Statements." *Journal of Accountancy* (October 1939), pp. 227–35.

PETRI, ENRICO, and ROLAND A. MINCH. "The Treasury Stock Method and Conventional Method in Reciprocal Stockholdings—An Amalgamation." *Accounting Review* (April 1974), pp. 330–341.

WEIL, ROMAN L. "Reciprocal or Mutual Holdings: Allocating Earnings and Selecting the Accounting Method." *Accounting Review* (October 1973), pp. 749–58.

ASSIGNMENT MATERIAL QUESTIONS

QUESTIONS

(Questions 1 through 8 relate to indirect holdings. Questions 9 through 16 relate to mutual holdings.)

1 What is an indirect holding of the stock of an affiliated company?

2 P owns a 60% interest in S, and S owns a 40% interest in T. Should T be consolidated? If not, how should T be included in the consolidated statements of P Company and Subsidiaries?

3 Prepare diagrams of two types of affiliation structures involving indirect ownership. Compute the direct and indirect ownership held by majority and minority stockholders for each of your diagrams.

4 Distinguish between indirect holding affiliation structures and mutual holding affiliation structures.

5 Parent Company owns 70% of the voting stock of Subsidiary A, and Subsidiary A owns 70% of the stock of Subsidiary B. Is the inside ownership of Subsidiary B more than 50%? Should Subsidiary B be included in the consolidated statements of Parent and Subsidiaries? Explain.

6 Pat Corporation owns 80% of the stock of Sam Corporation, and Sam Corporation owns 70% of the stock of Stan Corporation. Separate earnings of Pat, Sam, and Stan are $100,000, $80,000, and $50,000, respectively. Compute consolidated net income and minority interest income under two different approaches.

7 In using the schedule approach for allocating income of subsidiaries to majority and minority stockholders in an indirect holding affiliation structure, why is it necessary to begin with the lowest subsidiary in the affiliation tier?

8 P owns 80% of $S1$, and $S1$ owns 70% of $S2$. Separate incomes of P, $S1$, and $S2$ are $20,000, $10,000, and $5,000, respectively, for 20X1. During 20X1, $S1$ sold land to P at a gain of $1,000. Compute $S1$'s income on an equity basis. Discuss why you did or did not adjust $S1$'s investment in $S2$'s account for the unrealized gain.

9 If a parent company owns 80% of the voting stock of a subsidiary, and the subsidiary in turn owns 20% of the stock of the parent, what kind of affiliation structure is involved? Explain.

10 How is the treasury stock approach applied to the elimination of mutually held stock?

11 Are the treasury stock and conventional approaches equally applicable to all mutual holdings? Explain.

12 Under the treasury stock approach, a mutually held subsidiary accounts for its investment in the parent company on a cost basis. Are dividends received by the subsidiary from the parent company included in investment income of the parent under the equity method of accounting?

13 Describe the concept of a constructive retirement of parent company stock. Should the parent company adjust its equity accounts when its stock is constructively retired?

14 P's separate earnings are $50,000, and S's separate earnings are $20,000. P owns an 80% interest in S, and S owns a 10% interest in P. What is the amount of consolidated net income?

15 How do consolidation procedures for mutual holdings involving the father-son-grandson type of affiliation structure differ from those for mutually held parent company stock?

16 If all companies in an affiliation structure account for their investments on an equity basis, how can minority interests be determined without the use of simultaneous equations?

EXERCISES

(Exercises 9–1 through 9–8 relate to indirect holdings. Exercises 9–9 through 9–14 relate to mutual holdings.)

E 9-1 On January 1, 20X2, Pent Corporation purchased a 60% interest in Sal Corporation at book value (equal to fair value). At the time of Pent's acquisition, Sal owned a 60% interest in Terp Corporation (acquired at book value equal to fair value) and a 15% interest in Wint Company. The four companies had the following separate incomes and dividends for 20X2 (separate income does not include investment income or dividend income):

	Separate Income	Dividends
Pent Corporation	$800,000	$300,000
Sal Corporation	500,000	200,000
Terp Corporation	200,000	100,000
Wint Company	300,000	100,000

Required: Determine consolidated net income and minority interest income for Pent Corporation and Subsidiaries.

E 9-2 Pumba Corporation owns 60% of Simba Corporation and 80% of Timon Corporation. Timon owns 20% of Simba Corporation. Separate income and loss data (not including investment income) for the three affiliates for 20X6 are as follows:

Pumba	$400,000 separate income
Simba	150,000 separate income
Timon	(200,000) separate loss

There are no cost/book value differentials or unrealized profits to consider in measuring 20X6 income.

Required: Calculate consolidated net income for Pumba Corporation and Subsidiaries for 20X6.

E 9-3 The affiliation structure for Place Corporation and its affiliates is as follows:

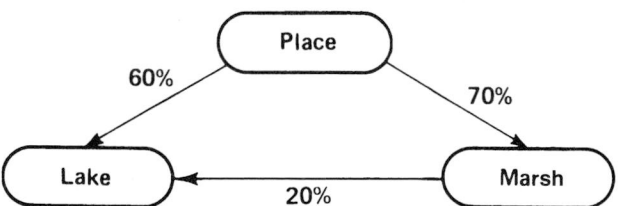

During 20X6 the separate incomes of these affiliated companies were as follows:

Place	$200,000
Lake	80,000
Marsh	70,000

Lake's income includes $20,000 unrealized profit on land sold to Marsh during 20X6.

Required: Prepare a schedule that shows the allocation of income among the affiliated companies and also shows consolidated net income and minority interest income for the year 20X6.

E 9-4 The affiliation structure for Paine Corporation and its subsidiaries is as follows:

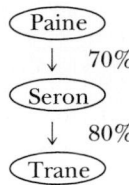

Paine
↓ 70%
Seron
↓ 80%
Trane

Separate incomes of Paine, Seron, and Trane Corporations for 20X1 are $360,000, $160,000, and $100,000, respectively.

1 The equation for determining Paine's income from Seron on a one-line consolidation basis for 20X1 is:
   a $160,000 × 70%
   b ($160,000 × 70%) + ($100,000 × 80%)
   c ($160,000 × 70%) + ($100,000 × 56%)
   d 70% × ($160,000 + $100,000)

2 Minority interest income for Paine Corporation and Subsidiaries for 20X1 is determined as follows:
   a $30% × $160,000
   b (30% × $160,000) + (20% × $100,000)
   c (30% × $160,000) + (24% × $100,000)
   d (30% × $160,000) + (44% × $100,000)

3 Consolidated net income can be determined by the following equation:
   a $620,000 − ($160,000 × 30%)
   b $620,000 − ($160,000 × 30%) − ($100,000 × 20%)
   c $620,000 − ($160,000 × 30%) − ($100,000 × 20%) − ($100,000 × 30% × 90%)
   d $620,000 − ($160,000 × 30%) − ($100,000 × 44%)

E 9-5 Pal Corporation owns 80% each of the voting common stock of Sal and Tall corporations. Sal owns 60% of the voting common stock of Ulti Corporation and 10% of the voting stock of Tall Corporation. Tall owns 70% of the voting stock of Val Corporation and 10% of the voting stock of Ulti.

The affiliated companies had separate incomes during 20X5 as follows:

Pal Corporation	$50,000
Sal Corporation	30,000
Tall Corporation	35,000
Ulti Corporation	(20,000) loss
Val Corporation	40,000

The only intercompany profits included in the separate incomes of the affiliated companies consisted of $5,000 on merchandise that Pal acquired from Tall and which remained in Pal's December 31, 20X5 inventory.

Required
   1 Prepare a diagram of the affiliation structure.
   2 Compute consolidated net income and minority interest income for Pal Corporation and Subsidiaries.

E 9-6 Pete Corporation owns 90% of the stock of Mike Corporation and 70% of the stock of Nina Corporation. Mike owns 70% of the stock of Ople Corporation and 10% of the stock of Nina Corporation. Nina Corporation owns 20% of the stock of Ople Corporation.

Separate incomes for these corporations for the year ended December 31, 20X4 are as follows:

Pete	$65,000
Mike	18,000
Nina	28,000
Ople	9,000

During 20X4, Mike sold land to Nina at a profit of $4,000. Ople sold inventory items to Pete at a profit of $8,000, half of which remains in Pete's inventory. Pete purchased for $15,000 Nina's bonds, which had a book value of $17,000 on December 31, 20X4.

Required: Calculate consolidated net income and minority interest income for 20X4.

E 9-7 The affiliation structure for a group of interrelated companies is diagrammed as follows:

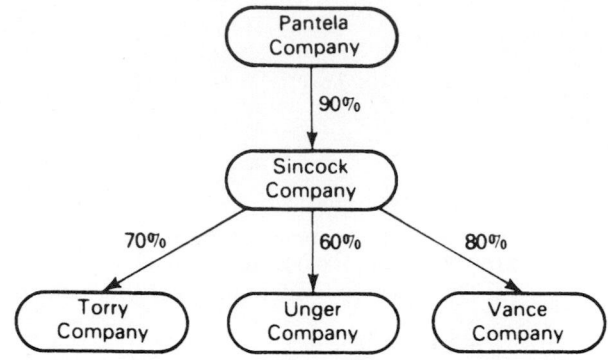

The investments in these companies were acquired at book value in 20X1, and there are no unrealized or constructive profits or losses.

Separate incomes and dividends for the companies for 20X4 are:

	Separate Income (Loss)	Dividends
Pantela	$620,000	$200,000
Sincock	175,000	100,000
Torry	200,000	80,000
Unger	(50,000)	none
Vance	120,000	60,000

1 The minority interest in Torry Company's net income for 20X4 is:
   a $60,000   c $126,000
   b $74,000   d $140,000
2 The income of the minority stockholders of Vance Company for 20X4 is:
   a $24,000   c $55,200
   b $48,000   d $72,000
3 The total minority interest income that should be shown in the consolidated income statement of Pantela Company and Subsidiaries for 20X4 is:
   a $122,100   c $102,100
   b $105,100   d $38,100
4 Consolidated net income for Pantela Company and Subsidiaries for 20X4 is:
   a $962,900   c $620,000
   b $940,900   d $342,900
5 Pantela Company's investment in Sincock account should reflect a net increase for the year 20X4 in the amount of:
   a $381,000   c $312,900
   b $342,900   d $252,900

E 9-8 Pasko Corporation owns an 80% interest in Savoy Corporation and a 70% interest in Trent Corporation. Trent owns a 10% interest in Savoy. These investment interests were acquired at book value.

The net incomes of the affiliated companies for 20X1 were as follows:

Pasko	$240,000
Savoy	80,000
Trent	40,000

On December 31, 20X1, Pasko's inventory included $10,000 of unrealized profits on merchandise purchased from Savoy during 20X1, and Savoy's land account reflected $15,000 unrealized profit on land purchased from Trent during 20X1. These unrealized profits have not been eliminated from the net income amounts shown. Except for adjustments related to unrealized profits, the net income amounts were determined on a correct equity basis.

1 The separate incomes of Pasko, Savoy, and Trent for 20X1 were:
   a $240,000, $80,000, and $32,000, respectively
   b $148,000, $80,000, and $32,000, respectively
   c $148,000, $72,000, and $40,000, respectively
   d $240,000, $72,000, and $40,000, respectively

2 The separate realized incomes of Pasko, Savoy, and Trent for 20X1 were:
  a $138,000, $80,000, and $25,000, respectively
  b $138,000, $70,000, and $25,000, respectively
  c $123,000, $80,000, and $17,000, respectively
  d $148,000, $70,000, and $17,000, respectively
3 Consolidated net income for Pasko Corporation and Subsidiaries for 20X1 was:
  a $220,800   **c** $214,400
  b $215,900   **d** $212,400
4 Minority interest income that should be shown in the consolidated income statement for Pasko Corporation and Subsidiaries for 20X1 is:
  a $23,600   **c** $19,100
  b $21,200   **d** $14,200

E 9-9   Pant Corporation owns an 80% interest in Solo Company, acquired at book value, and Solo owns a 30% interest in Pant, acquired at book value. Separate incomes (not including investment income) of the two affiliates for 20X4 are:

Pant	$3,000,000
Solo	$1,500,000

Required: Construct a diagram of the affiliation structure. Compute consolidated net income for Pant Corporation and Subsidiary for the year 20X4 using the conventional (equation) approach.

E 9-10   Intercompany investment percentages and 20X1 separate earnings for three affiliated companies are as follows:

	Percentage Interest in Smedley	Percentage Interest in Tweed	Separate Earnings
Packard Corporation	70%		$200,000
Smedley Corporation		80%	120,000
Tweed Corporation	10%		80,000

Required
  1 Construct a diagram of the affiliation structure.
  2 Compute consolidated net income and minority interest income for Packard Corporation and Subsidiaries for 20X1.

E 9-11   **[AICPA adapted]**
D. Akron, Inc., owns 80% of the capital stock of Benson Company and 70% of the capital stock of Cashin, Inc. Benson Company owns 15% of the capital stock of Cashin, Inc. Cashin, Inc. in turn, owns 25% of the capital stock of Akron, Inc. These ownership interrelationships are illustrated in the following diagram:

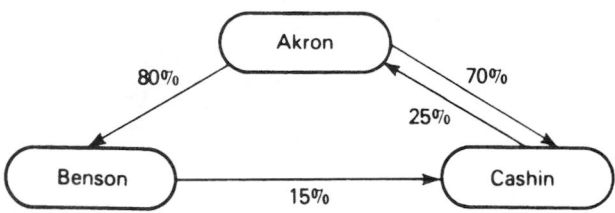

Income before adjusting for interests in intercompany income for each corporation follows:

Akron, Inc.	$190,000
Benson Company	170,000
Cashin, Inc.	230,000

The following notations relate to the questions below:

A = Akron's consolidated income—its separate income plus its share of the consolidated incomes of Benson and Cashin

B = Benson's consolidated income—its separate income plus its share of the consolidated income of Cashin

C = Cashin's consolidated income—its separate income plus its share of the consolidated income of Akron

1 The equation, in a set of simultaneous equations, that computes A is:

   a $A = .75(190,000 + .8B + .7C)$

   b $A = 190,000 + .8B + .7C$

   c $A = .75(190,000) + .8(170,000) + .7(230,000)$

   d $A = .75(190,000) + .8B + .7C$

2 The equation, in a set of simultaneous equations, that computes B is:

   a $B = 170,000 + .15C - .75A$

   b $B = 170,000 + .15C$

   c $B = .2(170,000) + .15(230,000)$

   d $B = .2(170,000) + .15C$

3 Cashin's minority interest in total consolidated income is:

   a $.15(230,000)$

   b $230,000 + .25A$

   c $.15(230,000) + .25A$

   d $.15C$

4 Benson's minority interest in total consolidated income is:

   a $34,316   **c** $45,755

   b $25,500   **d** $30,675

E 9-12   Petty Corporation owns 90% of Soma Corporation's common stock, acquired at book value equal to fair value, and Soma Corporation owns 15% of Petty Corporation, acquired at book value. Separate incomes and dividends of these affiliated companies for 20X3 are as follows:

	Separate Incomes	Dividends
Petty Corporation	$100,000	$50,000
Soma Corporation	60,000	30,000

1 If the treasury stock approach is used, Petty's income and consolidated net income for 20X3 will be computed:

   a $100,000 + (90\% \times \$60,000)$

   b $100,000 + (90\% \times \$67,500)$

   c $100,000 + (90\% \times \$67,500) - (90\% \times \$30,000)$

   d $100,000 + \$60,000 - (10\% \times \$67,500)$

2 If the conventional approach is used, Petty's income on a consolidated basis is denoted $P = \$100,000 + .9S$, and Soma's income on a consolidated basis is denoted $S = \$60,000 + .15P$. Given these equations, consolidated net income is equal to:

   a P **c** $P - .1S$

   b $.85P$ **d** $P + S - .15S$

E 9-13   The affiliation structure of Pusan Corporation and Subsidiaries is diagrammed as follows:

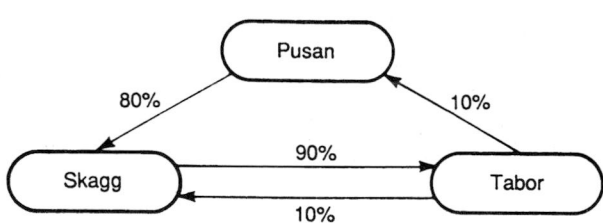

Each of the corporations uses the cost method of accounting for its investments. Separate earnings and dividends paid for 20X6 are as follows:

	Separate Earnings	Dividends
Pusan	$50,000	$20,000
Skagg	42,000	10,000
Tabor	20,000	none

Skagg sells merchandise to Pusan on which there is unrealized profit in Pusan's beginning inventory of $3,000 and in the ending inventory of $5,000.

Required: Compute consolidated net income and minority interest income for Pusan Corporation and Subsidiaries for the year ended December 31, 20X6.

E 9-14   Pumel Corporation acquired a 70% interest in Scat Corporation for $240,000 on January 2, 20X5, when Scat's equity consisted of $200,000 capital stock and $50,000 retained earnings.

The excess is being amortized over a 10-year period, and Pumel accounted for its investment in Scat during 20X5 as follows:

Investment cost January 2, 20X5	$240,000
Income from Scat [($40,000 × 70%) − $6,500]	21,500
Dividends from Scat ($20,000 × 70%)	(14,000)
Investment balance December 31, 20X5	$247,500

On January 3, 20X6, Scat acquired a 10% interest in Pumel at its $60,000 book value. No intercompany profit transactions have occurred between these companies. Their separate incomes and dividends for 20X6 were as follows:

	Pumel	Scat
Separate income 20X6	$120,000	$50,000
Dividends	60,000	30,000

Required

1 Determine the balance of Pumel's investment in Scat account on December 31, 20X6 if the treasury stock approach is used for Scat's investment in Pumel.
2 Compute consolidated net income and minority interest income if the conventional approach is used for Scat's investment in Pumel. Also determine the amount of Pumel's income from Scat and the balance in Pumel's investment in Scat account at December 31, 20X6.

PROBLEMS

(Problems 9–1 through 9–7 relate to indirect holdings. Problems 9–8 through 9–13 relate to mutual holdings.)

P 9-1 The investments of Perez Corporation and its affiliates were as follows throughout 20X3.

	Percentage Owned
Perez Corporation:	
Investment in Alice Company	60%
Investment in Betty Company	80
Investment in Carol Company	70
Alice Company:	
Investment in Donna Company	70
Betty Company:	
Investment in Alice Company	20
Investment in Effie Company	90
Effie Company:	
Investment in Carol Company	10

Perez and all its affiliates account for their investments on a cost basis. All differences between investment costs and book values acquired were fully amortized for consolidated statement purposes in prior years. All prior-year adjustments have been properly made on Perez's books, and the only unrealized profits within the affiliated grouping during 20X3 resulted from the sale of equipment by Alice to Effie at a gain of $15,000, of which $3,000 was depreciated during 20X3.

Net incomes and losses as reported under the cost method, and dividends for Perez and affiliates for 20X3 were as follows:

	Net Income (Loss)	Dividends
Perez Corporation	$110,000	$50,000
Alice Company	20,000	10,000
Betty Company	35,000	20,000
Carol Company	(15,000)	none
Donna Company	(20,000)	5,000
Effie Company	40,000	15,000

Required

1 Diagram the affiliation structure of Perez and affiliates.
2 Prepare a schedule of the allocation of income for Perez and Subsidiaries to consolidated net income and minority interest income.

P 9-2 Palmore Corporation owns an 80% interest in Summit Corporation and a 10% interest in Tonkin Corporation. Summit owns a 70% interest in Tonkin Corporation. The investments were acquired at book value several years ago.

Both Palmore and Summit corporations account for their investments by applying the equity method without eliminating the effects of intercompany profits. During 20X6, Tonkin sold merchandise that cost $30,000 to Palmore for $60,000. Half of this merchandise is included in Palmore's December 31, 20X6 inventory. Also, Palmore sold equipment with a book value of $50,000 and a remaining useful life of three years to Summit for $62,000 on January 2, 20X5. This equipment is expected to be in use by Summit until December 31, 20X7.

Comparative income statements for these affiliated companies for 20X6 follow:

	Palmore	Summit	Tonkin	Total
Comparative Income Statements				
for the Year Ended December 31, 20X6				
Sales	$600,000	$200,000	$180,000	$980,000
Income from Summit	76,000	—	—	76,000
Income from Tonkin	5,000	35,000	—	40,000
Cost of sales	(350,000)	(80,000)	(90,000)	(520,000)
Other expenses	(100,000)	(60,000)	(40,000)	(200,000)
Net income	$231,000	$ 95,000	$ 50,000	$376,000

Required: Prepare a consolidated income statement for Palmore Corporation and Subsidiaries for 20X6.

P 9-3 The affiliation structure for Pida Corporation and its subsidiaries is diagrammed as follows:

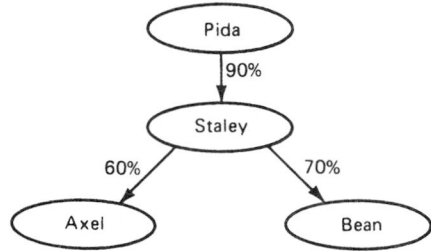

The separate incomes and dividends for the affiliated companies for 20X8 are:

	Pida	Staley	Axel	Bean
Separate income (loss)	$500,000	$300,000	$150,000	$(20,000)
Dividends	200,000	140,000	50,000	none

Additional Information
1 Axel sold land to Staley during 20X8 at a $20,000 gain. The land is still held by Staley.
2 Staley is amortizing the goodwill on its investment in Axel at the rate of $14,000 per year.
3 Pita is amortizing the remaining goodwill in Staley of $360,000 over its remaining nine-year life.

Required: Prepare a schedule to compute consolidated net income and minority interest income for each subsidiary for the year 20X8.

P 9-4 A summary of the assets and equities of Posey Corporation and its 80%-owned subsidiary, Seaton Corporation, at December 31, 20X1 is given as follows:

	Posey	Seaton
Assets	$ 800,000	$350,000
Investment in Seaton (80%)	200,000	—
Total assets	$1,000,000	$350,000
Liabilities	$ 150,000	$100,000
Capital stock	600,000	200,000
Retained earnings	250,000	50,000
Total equities	$1,000,000	$350,000

On January 2, 20X2, Seaton acquired a 70% interest in Thayer Corporation for $150,000. Thayer's net assets of $200,000 were recorded at their fair values on this date. The equity of Thayer on December 31, 20X1 consisted of $150,000 capital stock and $50,000 retained earnings. Data concerning the operations of the three affiliated corporations for 20X2 are as follows:

	Separate Earnings	Dividends	Unrealized Profit Included in Separate Earnings
Posey	$150,000	$50,000	$10,000
Seaton	50,000	30,000	—
Thayer	30,000	10,000	5,000

Posey Corporation's $10,000 unrealized profit resulted from the sale of land to Thayer. Thayer's unrealized profit is from sales of merchandise items to Seaton and included in Seaton's inventory at December 31, 20X2.

Required
1 Prepare all journal entries required on the books of Posey and Seaton to account for their investments for 20X2 on an equity basis. Goodwill is to be amortized over a 10-year period.
2 Compute the net income of Posey, the net income of Seaton, and total minority interest income for 20X2.
3 Prepare a schedule showing the assets and equities of Posey, Seaton, and Thayer on December 31, 20X2, assuming liabilities of $150,000, $100,000, and $50,000 for Posey, Seaton, and Thayer, respectively.

P 9-5 Panda, Ape, Baboon, and Chimp corporations have intercompany stock holdings acquired as follows:
1 January 20X1: Panda acquired 90% of Ape for $380,000, when Ape had capital stock of $300,000 and retained earnings of $100,000.
2 January 20X2: Ape acquired 80% of Baboon for $220,000, when Baboon had capital stock of $100,000 and retained earnings of $75,000.
3 January 20X2: Ape acquired 70% of Chimp for $155,000, when Chimp had capital stock of $100,000 and retained earnings of $50,000.

All the investments are maintained on a cost basis, and the differences between the investment costs and book values acquired are to be amortized over 10-year periods.

During 20X1, Ape had net income of $80,000 and paid dividends of $40,000. During 20X2, Ape had net income of $125,000 ($80,000 separate income, plus $24,000 dividend income from Baboon, and $21,000 dividend income from Chimp) and paid dividends of $60,000. During 20X2, Baboon had net income of $50,000 and paid dividends of $30,000, and Chimp had net income of $30,000 and paid dividends of $30,000.

Required
1 Prepare a schedule to show the correct balances of the investment accounts on an equity basis on December 31, 20X2.
2 Prepare journal entries to convert the investment accounts to an equity basis just before the books of Panda and Ape are closed on December 31, 20X2.

P 9-6 Patter Industries owns a 70% interest in Quiet Company, an 80% interest in Ridder Corporation, and a 90% interest in Stall Company. Quiet Company, in turn, owns a 60% interest in Time Corporation. Ridder Corporation owns a 20% interest in Time and a 10% interest in Stall. All the companies purchased their interests at book value several years ago and maintain their investment accounts on a cost basis.

During 20X7, the affiliated companies reported income and dividends as follows:

	Patter	Quiet	Ridder	Stall	Time
Income	$180,000	$56,000	$66,000	$80,000	$30,000
Dividends	20,000	30,000	30,000	40,000	10,000

At December 31, 20X7, Quiet held inventory items acquired from Patter on which Patter had made a profit of $6,000. Patter held land acquired from Time at a price $3,000 in excess of Time's cost.

Required
1 Construct a diagram of the affiliation structure.
2 Compute realized income for each company.

3 Prepare a table showing separate realized income for each company divided into consolidated net income and minority interest income, and total consolidated net income and total minority interest income for the affiliated group.

P 9-7 Comparative financial statements for Pony Corporation and its subsidiaries, Star and Teel corporations, at and for the year ended December 31, 20X9 are summarized as follows:

	Pony	Star	Teel
Income and Retained Earnings Statement for the Year Ended December 31, 20X9			
Sales	$500,000	$300,000	$100,000
Income from Star	72,000	—	—
Income from Teel	12,500	10,000	—
Cost of sales	(240,000)	(150,000)	(60,000)
Other expenses	(160,000)	(70,000)	(15,000)
Net income	184,500	90,000	25,000
Add: Beginning retained earnings	115,500	160,000	45,000
Deduct: Dividends	(80,000)	(40,000)	(10,000)
Ending retained earnings	$220,000	$210,000	$ 60,000
Balance Sheet at December 31, 20X9			
Cash	$ 67,000	$ 36,000	$ 10,000
Accounts receivable—net	70,000	50,000	20,000
Inventories	110,000	75,000	35,000
Plant and equipment—net	140,000	425,000	115,000
Investment in Star (80%)	508,000	—	—
Investment in Teel (50%)	95,000	—	—
Investment in Teel (40%)	—	74,000	—
Total assets	$990,000	$660,000	$180,000
Accounts payable	$ 70,000	$ 40,000	$ 15,000
Other liabilities	100,000	10,000	5,000
Capital stock	600,000	400,000	100,000
Retained earnings	220,000	210,000	60,000
Total equities	$990,000	$660,000	$180,000

Additional Information

1 Pony acquired its 80% interest in Star Corporation for $420,000 on January 2, 20X7, when Star had capital stock of $400,000 and retained earnings of $100,000. The excess of cost over book value acquired relates to equipment that had a remaining useful life of four years from January 1, 20X7.

2 Pony acquired its 50% interest in Teel Corporation for $75,000 on July 1, 20X7, when Teel's equity consisted of $100,000 capital stock and $20,000 retained earnings. Star acquired its 40% interest in Teel on December 31, 20X8 for $68,000, when Teel's capital stock was $100,000 and its retained earnings, $45,000. The difference between investment costs and book value acquired is considered goodwill.

3 Although Pony and Star use the equity method in accounting for their investments, they do not apply the method to intercompany profits or to differences between investment cost and book value acquired.

4 At December 31, 20X8, the inventory of Star included inventory items acquired from Pony at a profit of $8,000. This merchandise was sold during 20X9.

5 Teel sold merchandise that had cost $30,000 to Star for $50,000 during 20X9. All of this merchandise is held by Star at December 31, 20X9. Star owes Teel $10,000 on this merchandise.

6 Goodwill is to be amortized over a 10-year period.

Required: Prepare consolidation working papers for Pony Corporation and Subsidiaries for the year ended December 31, 20X9.

P 9-8 A schedule of intercompany investment interests and separate earnings for Parish Corporation, Swift Corporation, and Tolbert Corporation is presented as follows:

	Percentage Interest in Swift	Percentage Interest in Tolbert	Separate Earnings Current Year
Parish Corporation	80%	50%	$200,000
Swift Corporation	—	20	100,000
Tolbert Corporation	10	—	50,000

Required

1 Prepare a diagram of the affiliation structure of Parish Corporation and Subsidiaries.

2 Compute consolidated net income and minority interest income assuming no investment differences or unrealized profits.

3 Compute consolidated net income and minority interest income assuming $10,000 unrealized inventory profits on Tolbert's sales to Swift and a $20,000 gain on Parish's sale of land to Swift.

P 9-9 Consider the following intercompany relationships:

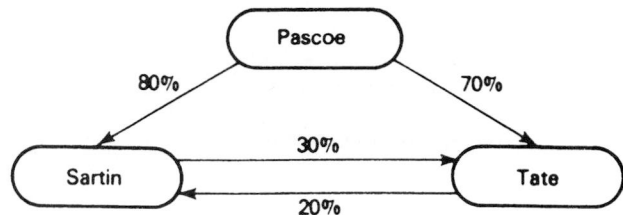

Separate trial balances at December 31, 20X6 are summarized as follows:

	Pascoe	Sartin	Tate
Other assets	$ 500,000	$400,000	$300,000
Investment in Sartin	350,000	—	90,000
Investment in Tate	300,000	100,000	—
	$1,150,000	$500,000	$390,000
Liabilities	$ 200,000	$150,000	$100,000
Capital stock	650,000	200,000	200,000
Retained earnings	300,000	150,000	90,000
	$1,150,000	$500,000	$390,000

All investment accounts are maintained on a cost basis. The investments in Sartin Corporation were made when Sartin had retained earnings of $115,000. The investments in Tate Corporation were made when Tate had retained earnings of $50,000.

Required

1 Prepare a consolidated balance sheet. Sartin and Tate purchases were made five years ago, and all purchase price/book value differentials were assigned to goodwill with a 10-year life.

2 Prepare a proof of consolidated retained earnings.

P 9-10 Punk Corporation paid $135,000 for a 90% interest in the voting common stock of Sub-one Corporation on January 1, 20X1, when Sub-one's equity was $150,000. At that time, Sub-one owned an 80% interest in Sub-two, having acquired its interest at book value of $72,000 several years earlier when Sub-two's equity was $90,000. Sub-two owned a 10% interest in Punk Corporation at the time Sub-one acquired its interest in Sub-two Company.

Data from the financial statements of each of the affiliated companies on December 31, 20X1 are as follows:

	Net Income	Dividends	Subsidiary Investment (at cost)
Punk	$140,000	$70,000	$135,000
Sub-one	60,000	40,000	72,000
Sub-two	25,000	10,000	18,000

At December 31, 20X1, Punk holds inventory items acquired from Sub-one on which there are intercompany profits of $2,000. The investment accounts are maintained on a cost basis.

Required

1 Prepare a diagram of the affiliation structure of Punk Corporation and Subsidiaries. (The structure is referred to as a *circuit affiliation.*)

2 Prepare a schedule to compute separate earnings of each of the affiliated companies.

3 Determine consolidated net income and minority interest income using the treasury stock approach for holdings of parent company stock.

4 Determine consolidated net income and minority interest income using the conventional approach. (Use the same type of equations as for mutual holdings.)

P 9-11 Prill Corporation acquired a 90% interest in Skill Corporation for $355,000 cash on January 2, 20X4, when Skill had capital stock of $200,000 and retained earnings of $150,000. Skill purchased its 10% interest in Prill in 20X5 for $80,000. The excess of Prill's investment cost over book value acquired is due to goodwill, which is being amortized over eight years.

Comparative financial statements for Prill and Skill at and for the year ended December 31, 20X8 are summarized as follows:

	Prill	Skill
Combined Income and Retained Earnings Statement for the Year December 31, 20X8		
Sales	$400,000	$100,000
Investment income	27,000	—
Dividend income	—	10,000
Cost of goods sold	(200,000)	(50,000)
Expenses	(50,000)	(30,000)
Net income	177,000	30,000
Add: Beginning retained earnings	300,000	200,000
Deduct: Dividends	(100,000)	(20,000)
Retained earnings December 31, 20X8	$377,000	$210,000
Balance Sheet at December 31, 20X8		
Other assets	$491,000	$420,000
Investment in Skill (90%)	409,000	—
Investment in Prill (10%)	—	80,000
Total assets	$900,000	$500,000
Liabilities	$123,000	$ 90,000
Capital stock	400,000	200,000
Retained earnings	377,000	210,000
Total equities	$900,000	$500,000

Required: Prepare consolidation working papers for Prill Corporation and Subsidiary using the treasury stock approach for the mutual holding.

P 9-12 Paroll Corporation acquired an 80% interest in Scimp Corporation for $180,000 cash on January 1, 20X1, when Scimp had capital stock of $50,000 and retained earnings of $150,000. The excess of investment cost over book value acquired is due to goodwill, which is being amortized over five years. Scimp purchased its 20% interest in Paroll at book value on January 2, 20X1 for $100,000.

Comparative financial statements for Paroll and Scimp at and for the year ended December 31, 20X2 are summarized as follows:

	Paroll	Scimp
Combined Income and Retained Earnings Statement for the Year December 31, 20X2		
Sales	$140,000	$100,000
Income from Scimp	28,000	—
Dividend income	—	4,000
Gain on sale of land	—	3,000
Expenses	(80,000)	(60,000)
Net income	88,000	47,000
Add: Beginning retained earnings	405,710	180,000
Deduct: Dividends	(16,000)	(20,000)
Retained earnings December 31, 20X2	$477,710	$207,000
Balance Sheet at December 31, 20X2		
Other assets	$448,000	$157,000
Investment in Scimp (80%)	109,710	—
Investment in Paroll (20%)	—	100,000
Total assets	$557,710	$257,000
Capital stock	$ 80,000	$ 50,000
Retained earnings	477,710	207,000
Total equities	$557,710	$257,000

1 Paroll's separate earnings and dividends for 20X2 were $60,000 and $20,000, respectively. Scimp's separate earnings and dividends in 20X2 were $40,000 and $20,000, respectively.
2 Scimp sold land to an outside interest for $7,000 on January 3, 20X2 that it purchased from Paroll on January 3, 20X1 for $4,000. The land had originally cost Paroll $2,000.

Required: Prepare consolidation working paper entries and the consolidated working papers for Paroll Corporation and Subsidiary using the conventional approach for the mutual holding.

P 9-13 Pan Corporation (Panco) purchased an 80% interest in Stoker Corporation (Stoco) for $170,000 on January 1, 20X1, when Stoco's equity was $200,000. The excess of cost over book value is goodwill that is being amortized over a 10-year period.

At December 31, 20X2, the balance of Panco's investment in Stoco account is $208,000, and the stockholders' equity of the two corporations is as follows:

	Panco	Stoco
Capital stock	$600,000	$150,000
Retained earnings	200,000	100,000
Total	$800,000	$250,000

On January 2, 20X3, Stoco acquires a 10% interest in Panco for $80,000. Separate earnings and dividends for 20X3 are:

	Panco	Stoco
Separate earnings	$100,000	$40,000
Dividends	50,000	20,000

Required

1 Compute consolidated net income and minority interest income for 20X3 using the conventional approach.
2 Prepare journal entries to account for Panco's investment in Stoco for 20X3 under the equity method (conventional approach).
3 Prepare journal entries on Stoco's books to account for its investment in Panco under the equity method (conventional approach).
4 Compute Panco's and Stoco's net incomes for 20X3.
5 Determine the balances of Panco's and Stoco's investment accounts on December 31, 20X3.
6 Determine the total stockholders' equity of Panco and Stoco on December 31, 20X3.
7 Compute the minority interest in Stoco on December 31, 20X3.
8 Prepare the adjustment and elimination entries that are needed to consolidate the financial statements of Panco and Stoco for the year ended December 31, 20X3.
9 Prepare the adjustment and elimination entries that are needed to consolidate the balance sheets of Panco and Stoco on December 31, 20X3.

P 9-14 Comparative adjusted trial balances for Pamol Corporation and its 90%-owned subsidiary, Seward Corporation, on December 31, 20X8 follow.

Adjusted Trial Balances at December 31, 20X8	Pamol	Seward
Debits		
Cash	$ 77,000	$ 60,000
Receivables—net	90,000	80,000
Inventory	100,000	70,000
Plant and equipment	800,000	340,000
Investment in Seward (90%)	473,000	—
Investment in Pamol (5%)	—	60,000
Cost of goods sold	400,000	150,000
Depreciation expense	100,000	40,000
Other expenses	50,000	60,000
Loss on sale of land	—	10,000
Dividends	60,000	30,000
Total debits	$2,150,000	$900,000

(Continued)

Adjusted Trial Balances at December 31, 20X8	Pamol	Seward
Credits		
Accumulated depreciation	$ 190,000	$ 90,000
Payables	200,000	50,000
Capital stock, $10 par	800,000	300,000
Retained earnings	215,000	150,000
Sales	700,000	307,000
Investment income	45,000	—
Dividend income	—	3,000
Total credits	$2,150,000	$900,000

Additional Information

1 Pamol acquired its 90% interest in Seward for $365,000 on January 1, 20X4, when Seward had capital stock of $300,000 and retained earnings of $50,000. The excess of cost over book value acquired was allocated to goodwill and is being amortized over a 10-year period.

2 Seward's investment in Pamol was made on January 1, 20X8. The investment is accounted for on a cost basis and the financial statements are consolidated using the treasury stock approach.

3 Pamol's January 1, 20X8 inventory included merchandise acquired from Seward on which Seward had reported a $10,000 gross profit. Seward made sales of $50,000 to Pamol during 20X8, half of which were not paid for at December 31, 20X8. Intercompany profit in Pamol's December 31, 20X8 inventory of merchandise acquired from Seward amounted to $5,000.

4 On July 1, 20X7, Pamol sold equipment to Seward at a profit of $15,000. The equipment had a five-year remaining useful life on that date and is being depreciated on a straight-line basis.

5 On October 1, 20X8, Seward sold land to Pamol at a loss of $10,000.

Required: Prepare consolidation working papers for Pamol Corporation and Subsidiary for the year ended December 31, 20X8. Use the financial statement format and prepare a schedule to convert to the equity method.

10

Subsidiary Preferred Stock, Consolidated Earnings per Share, and Consolidated Income Taxation

This chapter covers three miscellaneous topics relating to consolidation: consolidation of a subsidiary with preferred stock in its capital structure, consolidated earnings per share, and accounting for income taxes of consolidated entities. These topics tend to be detailed and technical, and the illustrations often use simplifying assumptions to minimize details and emphasize significant concepts and relationships. An intermediate accounting background in all three areas is assumed.

SUBSIDIARIES WITH PREFERRED STOCK OUTSTANDING

The existence of preferred stock in the capital structure of a subsidiary corporation complicates the consolidation process, but the basic procedures do not change. Parent company/investor accounting under the equity method is also affected when an investee company has preferred stock outstanding. The complications stem from the need to consider the contractual rights of preferred stockholders in allocating the investee company's equity and income between preferred and common stock components.

Most preferred stock issues are cumulative, nonparticipating, and nonvoting. In addition, preferred stock issues usually have preference rights in liquidation and frequently are callable at prices in excess of the par or liquidating values. Net income of an investee corporation with preferred stock outstanding is allocated first to preferred stockholders based on the preferred stock contract, and the remainder is allocated to common stockholders. Similarly, the stockholders' equity of an investee is allocated first to preferred stockholders based on the preferred stock contract, and the remainder is allocated to common stockholders.

When preferred stock has a call or redemption price, this amount is used in allocating the investee's equity to preferred stockholders. In the absence of a redemption provision, the equity allocated to preferred would be based on par value of the stock plus any liquidation premium. In addition, any dividends in arrears on cumulative preferred stock must be included in the equity allocated to preferred stockholders. For nonparticipating preferred stock, income is assigned to preferred stockholders on the basis of the preference rate or amount. If the preferred stock is cumulative and nonparticipating, the current year's income assigned to the preferred stockholders is the current year's dividend requirement, irrespective of whether the directors declare only current-year dividends, current-year dividends plus prior-year arrearages, or no dividends at all. Income is assigned to noncumulative, nonparticipating preferred stock only if dividends are declared and only in the amount declared.

Subsidiary with Preferred Stock Not Held by Parent

Assume that Poe Corporation purchases 90% of Sol Corporation's outstanding common stock for $395,500 on January 1, 20X2 and that Sol Corporation's stockholders' equity on December 31, 20X1 was as follows:

$10 preferred stock, $100 par, cumulative, nonparticipating, callable at $105 per share	$100,000
Common stock, $10 par	200,000
Other paid-in capital	40,000
Retained earnings	160,000
Total stockholders' equity	$500,000

There were no preferred dividends in arrears as of January 1, 20X2. During 20X2, Sol reported net income of $50,000 and paid dividends of $30,000 ($20,000 on common stock and $10,000 on preferred stock). Sol's assets and liabilities were stated at their fair values when Poe acquired its interest, so any excess of investment cost over book value acquired is goodwill to be amortized over a 10-year period.

In comparing the price paid for the 90% interest in Sol with the book value of the interest acquired, Sol's December 31, 20X1 equity is separated into its preferred and common stock components:

Stockholders' equity of Sol	$500,000
Less: Preferred stockholders' equity (1,000 shares × $105 per share call price)	105,000
Common stockholders' equity	$395,000

The price paid for 90% of the common equity of Sol is compared with the book value (and fair value) acquired to determine goodwill:

Price paid for 90% common stock interest	$395,500
Less: Book value and fair value acquired ($395,000 × 90%)	355,500
Goodwill (10-year amortization period)	$ 40,000

Sol's $50,000 net income for 20X2 is allocated $10,000 to preferred stock (1,000 shares × $10 per share) and $40,000 to common stock. The entries to account for Poe's investment in Sol for 20X2 are:

January 1, 20X2

Investment in Sol common	$395,500	
Cash		$395,500

To record acquisition of 90% of Sol's common stock.

During 20X2

Cash	$ 18,000	
Investment in Sol common		$ 18,000

To reduce investment in Sol for dividends received ($20,000 × 90%).

December 31, 20X2

Investment in Sol common	$ 32,000	
Income from Sol		$ 32,000

To record equity in Sol's income less goodwill amortization [($40,000 × 90%) − $4,000 amortization].

In consolidating the financial statements of Poe and Sol for 20X2 (see Exhibit 10–1), Sol's $520,000 stockholders' equity at December 31, 20X2 is assigned to preferred and common stock components as follows:

POE CORPORATION AND SUBSIDIARY CONSOLIDATION
WORKING PAPERS FOR THE YEAR ENDED DECEMBER 31, 20X2

	Poe	90% Sol	Adjustments and Eliminations	Minority Interest	Consolidated Statements
Income Statement Sales	$ 618,000	$300,000			$ 918,000
Income from Sol (cm)	32,000		b 32,000		
Expenses—including cost of goods sold	(450,000)	(250,000)	d 4,000		(704,000)
Minority interest income (cm) ($40,000 × 10%)				$ 4,000	(4,000)
Minority interest income (pf) ($10,000 × 100%)				10,000	(10,000)
Net income	$ 200,000	$ 50,000			$ 200,000
Retained Earnings Retained earnings—Poe	$ 300,000				$ 300,000
Retained earnings—Sol		$160,000	a 5,000 c 155,000		
Net income	200,000√	50,000√			200,000
Dividends (cm)	(100,000)	(20,000)	b 18,000	(2,000)	(100,000)
Dividends (pf)		(10,000)		(10,000)	
Retained earnings December 31, 20X2	$ 400,000	$180,000			$ 400,000
Balance Sheet Other assets	$1,290,500	$600,000			$1,890,500
Investment in Sol (cm)	409,500		b 14,000 c 395,500		
Goodwill			c 40,000 d 4,000		36,000
	$1,700,000	$600,000			$1,926,500
Liabilities	$ 200,000	$ 80,000			$ 280,000
Preferred stock—Sol		100,000	a 100,000		
Common stock	1,000,000	200,000	c 200,000		1,000,000
Other paid-in capital	100,000	40,000	c 40,000		100,000
Retained earnings	400,000√	180,000√			400,000
	$1,700,000	$600,000			
Minority interest (pf) January 1, 20X2			a 105,000	105,000	
Minority interest (cm) January 1, 20X2			c 39,500	39,500	
Minority interest December 31, 20X2				$146,500	146,500
					$1,926,500

Exhibit 10–1   *Preferred and Common Stock in the Affiliation Structure*

Total stockholders' equity		$520,000
Less: Preferred stockholders' equity (1,000 shares × $105 call price per share)		105,000
Common stockholders' equity		$415,000

Minority Interest in Preferred Stock   The *minority interest* in Sol at December 31, 20X2 consists of 100% of the preferred stockholders' equity and 10% of the common stockholders' equity, or $146,500 [($105,000 × 100%) + ($415,000 × 10%)]. Similarly, *minority interest income* for 20X2 consists of 100% of the income to preferred stockholders and 10% of the income to common stockholders, or $14,000 [($10,000 × 100%) + ($40,000 × 10%)]. This information is reflected in the consolidation working papers for Poe Corporation and Subsidiary in Exhibit 10–1.

Except for working paper entry a, the working paper entries are the same as those encountered in earlier chapters. Entry a is reproduced in journal form as follows:

a	Preferred stock—Sol	$100,000	
	Retained earnings—Sol	5,000	
	Minority interest—preferred		$105,000

Entry a reclassifies the preferred stockholders' equity as a minority interest. The $105,000 preferred equity at the beginning of the period exceeded the $100,000 par value, so the $5,000 excess is debited to Sol's retained earnings. This charge to Sol's retained earnings is made because the preferred stockholders have a maximum claim on Sol's retained earnings for the $5,000 call premium.

The consolidated income statement of Exhibit 10–1 shows separate deductions for minority interest income applicable to preferred ($10,000) and common stock ($4,000). This division is helpful in preparing working papers, but a consolidated income statement prepared from the working papers would ordinarily show minority interest income as one amount. Also, Exhibit 10–1 shows total minority interest in Sol at December 31, 20X2 on one line of the consolidated balance sheet in the single amount of $146,500. Although the consolidation working papers contain the information to separate this amount into preferred and common components, the separation is ordinarily not used for basic financial reporting, because all individual subsidiary equity accounts are typically eliminated in the consolidation process.[1] Consolidated financial statements are intended primarily for the stockholders and creditors of the parent company, and it is not expected that the minority stockholders could benefit significantly from the information contained in them.

Subsidiary Preferred Stock Acquired by Parent

A parent company's purchase of the outstanding preferred stock of a subsidiary results in a retirement of the stock purchased from the viewpoint of the consolidated entity. The stock is retired for consolidated statement purposes because its book value no longer appears as a minority interest in the consolidated balance sheet. However, the retirement is really a constructive retirement because the investment in preferred (parent's books) and the preferred stock equity (subsidiary's books) are reported as outstanding in the separate financial statements of the parent and subsidiary companies.

The constructive retirement of a subsidiary's preferred stock through purchase by the parent company is reported as an actual retirement in the consolidated financial statements. That is, the equity related to the preferred stock held by the parent and the investment in preferred stock are eliminated, and any difference is charged or credited to the additional paid-in capital that would otherwise be reported in the consolidated balance sheet.[2] Parent company stockholders' equity in a one-line consolidation is equal to consolidated stockholders' equity, so comparable accounting requires

---

[1]Minority interest in a subsidiary's preferred stock is sometimes reported as outstanding stock of the consolidated entity with notation of the name of the issuing corporation. This reporting practice is usually confined to regulated companies.

[2]The parent company retained earnings is reduced when additional paid-in capital is insufficient to absorb an excess of purchase price over book.

that the parent company adjust its investment in subsidiary preferred stock to its book value at acquisition and charge or credit its additional paid-in capital for the difference between the price paid for the investment and its underlying book value. The investment in preferred stock is accounted for on the basis of its book value, not on the basis of the cost or equity method.

Constructive Retirement of Subsidiary Preferred Stock   Sol Corporation experiences a net loss of $40,000 in 20X3 and no dividends are paid. Its stockholders' equity decreases from $520,000 at December 31, 20X2 (see Exhibit 10–1) to $480,000 at December 31, 20X3. Poe's 90% investment in Sol decreases from $409,500 at year-end 20X2 to $360,500 at year-end 20X3. The $49,000 decrease in Poe's investment in Sol common account is computed as follows:

Net loss of Sol	$40,000
Add: Income to preferred[3] (1,000 shares × $10)	10,000
Loss to common	50,000
Poe's ownership interest	90%
Decreased equity for Sol's loss	45,000
Add: Goodwill amortization ($40,000 ÷ 10 years)	4,000
Loss from Sol for 20X3	$49,000

The $360,500 investment in Sol common at December 31, 20X3 can be checked as follows:

Stockholders' equity of Sol, December 31, 20X3	$480,000
Less: Preferred stockholders' equity [1,000 shares × ($105 per share call price + $10 per share dividend arrearage)]	115,000
Common stockholders' equity, December 31, 20X3	365,000
Poe's ownership interest	90%
Share of Sol's common stockholders' equity	328,500
Add: Unamortized goodwill ($40,000 − $8,000)	32,000
Investment in Sol common, December 31, 20X3	$360,500

On January 1, 20X4, Poe responded to the depressed price of Sol's preferred stock and purchased 800 shares (an 80% interest) at $100 per share. The $80,000 price paid is less than the $92,000 book value of the stock that is constructively retired ($115,000 × 80%), so Poe records the investment in Sol preferred as follows:

Investment in Sol preferred	$80,000	
Cash		$80,000
To record purchase of 80% of Sol's preferred stock.		

Investment in Sol preferred	$12,000	
Other paid-in capital		$12,000
To adjust other paid-in capital to reflect the constructive retirement.		

Sol reports net income of $20,000 for 20X4, but it again passes dividends for the year. Poe accounts for its investments during 20X4 as follows:

Investment in Sol preferred	$ 8,000	
Income from Sol preferred		$ 8,000
To record 80% of the $10,000 increase in Sol's preferred dividend arrearage.		

Investment in Sol common	$ 5,000	
Income from Sol common		$ 5,000
To record equity in Sol's income to common less goodwill amortization [($20,000 net income − $10,000 preferred income) × 90%] − $4,000 amortization.		

---

[3]A deduction of cumulative preferred dividends in computing income to common stockholders is required by *APB Opinion No. 18*, paragraph 19k, regardless of whether such dividends are declared.

A summary of Sol's preferred and common stockholders' equity and Poe's investment account balances at the end of 20X4 are:

Sol's Stockholders' Equity, December 31, 20X4

Total stockholders' equity ($480,000 on January 1, 20X4 plus $20,000 net income for 20X4)	$500,000
Less: Preferred stockholders' equity [1,000 shares × ($105 call price + $20 dividends in arrears)]	125,000
Common stockholders' equity	$375,000

Poe's Investment Accounts, December 31, 20X4

Investment in Sol preferred ($125,000 preferred equity × 80% owned)	$100,000
Investment in Sol common ($375,000 common equity × 90% owned + $28,000 unamortized goodwill)	$365,500

This information for 20X4 is reflected in consolidation working papers for Poe and Sol corporations in Exhibit 10–2.

The working paper entries for 20X4 are similar to those in Exhibit 10–1 for the year 20X2, except for items related to the investment in Sol's preferred stock. Procedures to eliminate the preferred equity and investment accounts parallel those for common stock. First, Poe's income from Sol preferred is eliminated against the investment in Sol preferred. This working paper entry (entry a) reduces the investment in Sol preferred to its $92,000 adjusted balance at January 1, 20X4. Next, the investment in Sol preferred and the preferred equity of Sol as of January 1, 20X4 are eliminated in working paper entry b. This entry also enters the preferred minority interest as of the beginning of the year. Entries a and b are reproduced in journal form as follows:

a	Income from Sol preferred	$ 8,000	
	Investment in Sol preferred		$ 8,000
b	Preferred stock—Sol	$100,000	
	Retained earnings—Sol	15,000	
	Investment in Sol preferred		$92,000
	Minority interest in Sol preferred		23,000

The remaining entries (c, d, and e) are the same as those for consolidations involving common stock only.

The working papers in Exhibit 10–2 show Poe Corporation's income equal to consolidated net income and its stockholders' equity equal to consolidated stockholders' equity. These equalities result from parent company entries to adjust the preferred stock investment account to its underlying equity at acquisition and to accrue dividend arrearages on cumulative preferred stock.

Preferred Stock Investment Maintained on Cost Basis If the constructive retirement were *not* recorded by Poe at the time of purchase, the investment in Sol preferred would remain at its $80,000 cost throughout 20X4, and no preferred income would be recognized. In this case, the consolidation working paper entry to eliminate the preferred investment and equity amounts would be:

Retained earnings—Sol	$ 15,000	
Preferred stock—Sol	100,000	
Investment in Sol preferred		$80,000
Minority interest in Sol preferred		23,000
Other paid-in capital—Poe		12,000

To eliminate reciprocal preferred equity and investment amounts, establish minority interest at the beginning of the period (20% × $115,000 beginning book value of preferred), and adjust Poe's other paid-in capital account for the difference between the purchase price and underlying book value of the preferred stock.

	Poe	90% Sol	Adjustments and Eliminations	Minority Interest	Consolidated Statements
Income Statement Sales	$ 690,000	$280,000			$ 970,000
Income from Sol (cm)	5,000		c 5,000		
Income from Sol (pf)	8,000		a 8,000		
Expenses—including cost of goods sold	(583,000)	(260,000)	e 4,000		(847,000)
Minority interest income (cm) ($10,000 × 10%)				$ 1,000	(1,000)
Minority interest income (pf) ($10,000 × 20%)				$ 2,000	(2,000)
Net income	$ 120,000	$ 20,000			$120,000
Retained Earnings Retained earnings—Poe	$450,000				$ 450,000
Retained earnings—Sol		$140,000	b 15,000 d 125,000		
Net income	120,000√	20,000√			120,000
Dividends	(70,000)	—			(70,000)
Retained earnings December 31, 20X4	$ 500,000	$160,000			$ 500,000
Balance Sheet Other assets	$1,334,500	$600,000			$1,934,500
Investment in Sol (pf)	100,000		a 8,000 b 92,000		
Investment in Sol (cm)	365,500		c 5,000 d 360,500		
Goodwill (cm)			d 32,000 e 4,000		28,000
	$1,800,000	$600,000			$1,962,500
Liabilities	$ 188,000	$100,000			$ 288,000
Preferred stock—Sol		100,000	b 100,000		
Common stock	1,000,000	200,000	d 200,000		1,000,000
Other paid-in capital	112,000	40,000	d 40,000		112,000
Retained earnings	500,000√	160,000√			500,000
	$1,800,000	$600,000			
Minority interest (pf) January 1, 20X4 ($115,000 × 20%)			b 23,000	23,000	
Minority interest (cm) January 1, 20X4 ($365,000 × 10%)			d 36,500	36,500	
Minority interest Decemer 31, 20X4				$62,500	62,500
					$1,962,500

Exhibit 10–2 *Parent Company Holds Subsidiary's Common and Preferred Stock*

Comparison of Cost Method and Constructive Retirement   The consolidated financial statements will be the same whether the investment in preferred stock remains at its original cost or is adjusted to book value in the parent company's books. However, by adjusting the parent company's additional paid-in capital for the constructive retirement of subsidiary preferred stock, further paid-in capital adjustments in the consolidation process are avoided. Under the cost method, a working paper entry to adjust additional paid-in capital is needed each time parent company and subsidiary statements are consolidated.

PARENT COMPANY AND CONSOLIDATED EARNINGS PER SHARE

A parent company's net income and earnings per share (EPS) under the equity method are equal to consolidated net income and consolidated EPS. However, the computational differences involved in determining parent company and consolidated net income (that is, one-line consolidation versus consolidation) do not extend to EPS calculations. Parent company and consolidated EPS calculations are identical. EPS procedures for equity investors who are able to exercise significant influence over their investees are the same as those for parent company investors. Although parent company and subsidiary relationships are addressed in this section, the discussion and illustrations are equally applicable to investments accounted for under the equity method.[4]

Parent company procedures for computing EPS depend on the subsidiary's capital structure. When the subsidiary (or equity investee) has *no* potentially dilutive securities, the procedures applied in computing consolidated EPS are the same as for separate entities. When the subsidiary does have potentially dilutive securities outstanding, however, the potential dilution has to be considered in computing the parent company's diluted EPS. Basic EPS is computed the same way for a consolidated entity as for separate entities (assuming the equity method is used). The nature of the adjustment to parent company EPS calculations depends on whether the subsidiary's potentially dilutive securities are convertible into subsidiary or parent company common stock. If convertible into subsidiary common stock, the potential dilution is reflected in subsidiary EPS computations, which are then used in determining parent company (and consolidated) EPS. If the dilutive securities of the subsidiary are convertible into parent company stock, they are treated as parent company dilutive securities and are included directly in computing the parent company EPS.[5] In this latter case, subsidiary EPS computations are not needed (or used) in parent company EPS computations.

General formats for EPS calculations involving these situations are summarized in Exhibit 10–3 for diluted EPS. The first column of Exhibit 10–3 shows parent company computations for diluted EPS when the subsidiary has no potentially dilutive securities. In this case, the EPS computations are the same as those for unrelated entities, and no adjustments are necessary for subsidiary income included in parent company income, provided that the equity method has been applied correctly.

Dilutive Securities of Subsidiary Convertible into Subsidiary Shares

The second column of Exhibit 10–3 summarizes parent company EPS computations when subsidiary potentially dilutive securities are convertible into subsidiary common shares. Diluted earnings of the parent company (the numerators of the EPS calculations) are adjusted by excluding the parent's **equity in subsidiary realized income** and replacing that equity with the parent's share of diluted earnings of the subsidiary. Equity in subsidiary realized income is the parent's percentage interest in reported income of the subsidiary adjusted for the effects of intercompany profits from upstream sales and constructive gains or losses of the subsidiary. This adjustment to remove the

---

[4]The provisions of *FASB Statement No. 128*, "Earnings per Share," that apply to subsidiaries also apply to investments accounted for by the equity method. See *APB Opinion No. 18*, "The Equity Method of Accounting for Investments in Common Stock," footnote 8 as amended by FASB Statement No. 128.

[5]*FASB Statement No. 128* paragraphs 62–63.

	Subsidiary Does Not Have Potentially Dilutive Securities Outstanding	Subsidiary Has Potentially Dilutive Securities Convertible into Subsidiary Common Stock	Subsidiary Has Potentially Dilutive Securities Convertible into Parent Company Common Stock
Numerator in Dollars ($)			
Income to parent's common stockholders	$$$	$$$	$$$
Add: Adjustments for parent's dilutive securities	+$	+$	+$
Add: Adjustments for subsidiary's potentially dilutive securities convertible into parent company stock	NA	NA	+$
Replacement calculation (must result in a net decrease)			
Deduct: Parent's equity in subsidiary's realized income	NA	−$	NA
Add: Parent's equity in subsidiary's diluted earnings	NA	+$	NA
Parent's diluted earnings = a	$$$	$$$	$$$
Denominator in Shares (Y)			
Parent's common shares outstanding	YYY	YYY	YYY
Add: Shares represented by parent's potentially dilutive securities	+Y	+Y	+Y
Add: Shares represented by subsidiary's potentially dilutive securities convertible into parent company common shares	NA	NA	+Y
Parent's common shares and common share equivalents = b	YYY	YYY	YYY
Parent Company and Consolidated Diluted EPS	a/b	a/b	a/b

NA—Not applicable.

Exhibit 10–3   *Parent Company and Consolidated Diluted EPS Calculations*

potential dilution from the parent's diluted earnings is based on separate EPS computations for the subsidiary. These computations of subsidiary EPS are made only for the purpose of calculating the parent's EPS, and they are not necessarily the same as those prepared by the subsidiary for its own external reporting.

Note that "parent's equity in subsidiary's realized income" in column 2 of Exhibit 10–3 differs from "parent's income from subsidiary," which includes amortization of goodwill and other valuation differentials and the income effects of all intercompany transactions. The parent company's investment valuation differentials, unrealized profits from downstream sales, and constructive gains and losses assigned to the parent do not affect the equity of the subsidiary's security holders, therefore, these items are not considered in the replacement calculation. In other words, the replacement calculation relates only to the parent's equity in subsidiary realized income.

The subsidiary's diluted EPS are used in determining diluted earnings of the parent company (see column 2 of Exhibit 10–3), so EPS computations for the subsidiary (based on subsidiary realized income) are made as a first step in computing the parent company's EPS. In computing the subsidiary's diluted earnings, unrealized profits of the subsidiary are eliminated and constructive gains and losses of the subsidiary are included. The resulting EPS calculations of the subsidiary are reflected in the parent company EPS calculation, by replacing the "parent's equity in subsidiary's realized income" with the "parent's equity in subsidiary's diluted earnings." The parent company's equity in the subsidiary's diluted earnings is determined by multiplying the subsidiary shares owned by the parent by the subsidiary's diluted EPS. This replacement allocates the subsidiary's realized income for EPS purposes to holders of the subsidiary's common stock and potentially dilutive securities, rather than only to the subsidiary's common stockholders.

Diluted Securities of Subsidiary Convertible into Parent Company Shares

Parent company common shares (the denominators of EPS computations) are identical in columns 1 and 2 of Exhibit 10–3 but are increased in column 3 for subsidiary securities that are convertible into parent company common stock. This adjustment in column 3 is necessary when the subsidiary's potentially dilutive securities are potentially dilutive securities of the parent company, rather than of the subsidiary. When potentially dilutive securities of a subsidiary are convertible into parent common stock, income attributable to these securities under the "if converted" method must be added back in calculating the parent's diluted earnings. Thus, column 3 of Exhibit 10–3 includes the item "adjustment for subsidiary's dilutive securities convertible into parent common stock," which is not applicable when the subsidiary does not have potentially dilutive securities (column 1), or such securities are convertible into subsidiary common stock (column 2).

SUBSIDIARY WITH CONVERTIBLE PREFERRED STOCK

Plant Corporation purchases 90% of Seed Corporation's outstanding voting common stock for $328,000 on January 1, 20X2. On this date, the stockholders' equity of the two corporations consists of the following:

	Plant	Seed
Common stock, $5 par, 200,000 shares issued and outstanding	$1,000,000	
Common stock, $10 par, 20,000 shares outstanding		$200,000
10% cumulative, convertible preferred stock, $100 par, 1,000 shares outstanding		100,000
Retained earnings	500,000	120,000
Total stockholders' equity	$1,500,000	$420,000

During 20X2, Seed reports $50,000 net income and pays $25,000 dividends, $10,000 to preferred and $15,000 to common. Plant's net income for 20X2 is $182,000, determined as follows:

Income from Plant's operations		$150,000
Income from Seed ($50,000 net income − $10,000 preferred income) × 90%	$36,000	
Less: Goodwill amortization [$328,000 cost − ($320,000 common equity × 90%)] ÷ 10 years	(4,000)	32,000
Plant's net income		$182,000

Subsidiary Preferred Convertible into Subsidiary Common

Assume that Seed's preferred stock is convertible into 12,000 shares of Seed's common stock and that neither Plant nor Seed has other potentially dilutive securities outstanding. Seed's diluted EPS is $1.5625 [$50,000 earnings ÷ (20,000 common shares + 12,000 share dilution)], and Plant's diluted EPS is $0.87, computed as follows:

Net income of Plant (equal to income to common)	$182,000
Replacement of Plant's equity in Seed's realized income ($40,000 × 90%)	(36,000)
with Plant's equity in Seed's diluted earnings (18,000 shares of Seed × Seed's $1.5625 diluted EPS)	28,125
Plant's diluted earnings = a	$174,125
Plant's outstanding shares = b	200,000
Plant's diluted EPS = a ÷ b	$ 0.87

The $7,875 potential dilution reflected in Plant's diluted earnings results from replacing Plant's equity in Seed's realized income with Plant's equity in Seed's diluted earnings per share. Note that Plant's equity in Seed's realized income is $36,000, but Plant's income from Seed is $32,000. The $4,000 difference is goodwill amortization that relates to the parent company and is not subject to replacement in EPS computations.

Subsidiary Preferred Convertible into Parent Company Common

Assume that Seed's preferred stock is convertible into 24,000 shares of Plant's common stock and that neither Plant nor Seed has other potentially dilutive securities outstanding. Seed's diluted EPS (not used in Plant's EPS computations) is $2 per share ($40,000 income to common ÷ 20,000 common shares outstanding), because the preferred stock is not a dilutive security of Seed Corporation. Plant's diluted EPS is computed as follows:

Net income of Plant (equal to income to common)	$182,000
Add: Income to preferred stockholders of Seed assumed to be converted	10,000
Plant's diluted earnings = a	$192,000
Plant's outstanding shares	200,000
Add: Seed's preferred shares assumed converted	24,000
Plant's common shares and common stock equivalents = b	224,000
Plant's diluted EPS = a ÷ b	$ 0.86

Preferred income is added to Plant's net income because no income is allocated to the preferred stock assumed to be converted.

SUBSIDIARY WITH OPTIONS AND CONVERTIBLE BONDS

Paddy Corporation has $1,500,000 income from its own operations for 20X3 and $300,000 income from Syd Corporation, its 80%-owned subsidiary. The $300,000 income from Syd consists of 80% of Syd's $450,000 net income for 20X3, less 80% of a $50,000 unrealized gain on land purchased from Syd, less $20,000 amortization of the excess of investment cost over the book value acquired in Syd. Outstanding securities of the two corporations throughout 20X3 are:

Paddy: Common stock, 1,000,000 shares

Syd: Common stock, 400,000 shares
           Options to purchase 60,000 shares of stock at $10 per share (average market price is $15 per share)
           7% convertible bonds, $1,000,000 par outstanding, convertible into 80,000 shares of common stock

Options and Bonds Convertible into Subsidiary Common Stock

Assume that the options and bonds are convertible into Syd's common stock. Computations for Syd's diluted EPS are shown in Exhibit 10–4. Under the treasury stock approach for options and warrants, the effect of options on EPS is dilutive when the

	Syd's Diluted EPS
Syd's income to common stockholders	$450,000
Less: Unrealized profit on sale of land	(50,000)
Add: Net-of-tax interest expense assuming subsidiary bonds converted into subsidiary shares ($1,000,000 × 7% × 66% assumed net-of-tax effect)	46,200
Subsidiary adjusted earnings = a	$446,200
Syd's common shares outstanding	400,000
Incremental shares assuming exercise of options [60,000 shares − ($600,000 proceeds from exercise of options ÷ $15 market price)]	20,000
Additional shares assuming bonds converted into subsidiary shares	80,000
Syd's adjusted shares = b	500,000
Syd's EPS = a ÷ b	$ 0.89

Exhibit 10–4   *Subsidiary's EPS Computations*

average market price of the common shares to which the options apply exceeds the exercise price. If holders of Syd's options had exercised their rights to acquire 60,000 shares of Syd's common stock at $10 per share, Syd would have received $600,000 cash. Under the treasury stock approach, Syd is assumed to use this cash to reacquire 40,000 shares of its own stock ($600,000 ÷ $15 average market price). This assumed exercise and repurchase of treasury shares increases Syd's outstanding common stock for EPS computations by 20,000 shares.

The convertible bonds must also be included in Syd's diluted EPS computations. Under the *if converted* method, $46,200 net-of-tax interest is included in Syd's diluted earnings, and the 80,000 shares issuable upon conversion are included in calculating Syd's diluted common shares.

Syd's $0.89 diluted EPS is used in the EPS computations for Paddy Corporation. Exhibit 10–5 shows computations for Paddy's diluted EPS.

In the computation of Paddy's diluted earnings, Paddy's equity in Syd's realized income ($320,000) was replaced with Paddy's share of Syd's diluted earnings ($284,800). This replacement decreases Paddy's diluted earnings by $35,200. This dilution results from allocating Syd's $400,000 realized income plus $46,200 net-of-tax interest effect from the convertible bonds to holders of Syd's common shares, options, and convertible bonds, rather than just to Syd's common stockholders.

Options and Bonds Convertible into Parent's Common Stock

Computations for Paddy's diluted EPS are presented in Exhibit 10–6 under the assumption that Syd Corporation's options are convertible into 60,000 shares of Paddy Corporation's common stock and that Syd Corporation's bonds are convertible into 80,000 shares of Paddy Corporation's common stock. Under these assumptions, Syd's

	Paddy's Diluted EPS
Paddy's income to common stockholders	$1,800,000
Replacement of Paddy's $320,000 equity in Syd's realized income [($450,000 − $50,000 unrealized profit) × 80%]	(320,000)
with Paddy's $284,800 equity in Syd's diluted EPS (320,000 shares × Syds $0.89 diluted EPS)	284,800
Paddy's adjusted earnings = a	$1,764,800
Paddy's outstanding common shares = b	1,000,000
Paddy's EPS = a ÷ b	$ 1.76

Exhibit 10–5   *Parent's EPS Computations—Dilution Relates to Subsidiary Shares*

	Paddy's Diluted EPS
Paddy's income to common stockholders	$1,800,000
Add: Net-of-tax interest assuming subsidiary bonds converted into parent's common stock ($1,000,000 × 7% × 66% net-of-tax effect)	46,200
Parent's adjusted earnings = a	$1,846,200
Paddy's outstanding shares	1,000,000
Incremental shares assuming options converted into parent's shares [60,000 shares − ($600,000 proceeds from exercise of options ÷ $15 market price)]	20,000
Additional shares assuming subsidiary bonds are converted into parent shares	80,000
Parent's adjusted shares = b	1,100,000
Parent's EPS = a ÷ b	$ 1.68

Exhibit 10–6   *Parent's EPS Computations—Dilution Relates to Parent Shares*

diluted EPS is not needed or used in determining Paddy's EPS because subsidiary EPS computations are only used for replacement computations when subsidiary dilutive securities are convertible into subsidiary shares. The subsidiary dilutive securities are convertible into parent company shares in this example, so only parent company EPS computations are needed.

ACCOUNTING FOR INCOME TAXES OF CONSOLIDATED ENTITIES

This section of the chapter on accounting for income taxes of consolidated entities begins with a discussion of which companies may file consolidated tax returns, the advantages and disadvantages of filing consolidated tax returns, and the status of accounting pronouncements on income taxes. Temporary differences in consolidated and separate tax returns are discussed, and income tax allocation procedures are illustrated for a parent company and subsidiary that file separate tax returns. Next, four cases compare consolidation procedures when a parent company and subsidiary file separate tax returns with those necessary when a consolidated tax return is filed. A final section looks at the tax basis of assets and liabilities acquired in a purchase business combination.

Some consolidated entities prepare consolidated income tax returns and pay taxes on consolidated taxable income. Others prepare income tax returns for each affiliate and pay taxes on the taxable income included in those separate returns. The right of a consolidated entity to file a consolidated income tax return is contingent upon classification as an *affiliated group* under Sections 1501 through 1505 of the Internal Revenue Code. An affiliated group exists when a common parent corporation owns at least 80% of the voting power of all classes of stock and 80% or more of the total value of all outstanding stock of each of the includable corporations. The common parent must meet the 80% requirements directly for at least one includable corporation (USIRC 1504[a]).

A consolidated entity that is an affiliated group may elect to file consolidated income tax returns. All other consolidated entities *must* file separate income tax returns for each affiliated company.

Advantages of Filing Consolidated Tax Returns

The primary advantages of filing a consolidated return are:

1 Losses of one affiliate are offset against income of other members of the affiliated group. However, loss carryforwards at the time of acquisition of an acquired affiliate can be offset only against taxable income of the affiliate.
2 Intercorporate dividends are excluded from taxable income.
3 Intercompany profits are deferred from income until realized (but unrealized losses are also deferred until realized).

Exclusion of intercorporate dividends is not a unique advantage of filing a consolidated tax return because a consolidated entity that is classified as an affiliated group is allowed a 100% exclusion on dividends received from members of the same group, even if it elects not to file consolidated tax returns. In addition, corporate taxpayers can deduct 80% of the dividends received from domestic corporations that are 20%- to 80%-owned and can deduct 70% of the dividends received from domestic corporations that are less than 20%-owned.

Disadvantages of Filing Consolidated Tax Returns

Consolidated entities that file consolidated tax returns lose some of the flexibility of entities that file separate returns. For example, each subsidiary included in a consolidated tax return must use the parent's taxable year. Different years can be used when separate returns are filed. The election to file a consolidated return commits an entity to consolidated returns year after year. It is difficult to get permission to stop filing consolidated returns. Also, deconsolidated corporations cannot rejoin the affiliated group for five years.

FASB Statement No. 109, "Accounting for Income Taxes," is the primary source of GAAP for accounting for income taxes.[6] The objectives of accounting for income taxes under *Statement No. 109* are to recognize the amount of taxes payable or refundable for the current year and to recognize deferred tax liabilities and assets for the future tax consequences of events that have been recognized in the financial statements or tax returns. Events that have future tax consequences are designated *temporary differences* to separate them from events that do not have tax consequences, such as interest on municipal obligations. The tax consequences of temporary differences must be considered in the measurement of income for a period. Some accounting/income tax differences are the same, regardless of whether separate-entity or consolidated income tax returns are filed, whereas others depend on the kind of return filed. For example, unrealized and constructive gains and losses from intercompany transactions are temporary differences when separate returns are filed because the individual entities are taxed on the income included in their separate returns. However, these items are *not* temporary differences when consolidated returns are filed because adjustments to defer intercompany profits until realized are reflected in both the consolidation working papers and the consolidated tax return. Dividends received from members of an affiliated group are excluded from taxation, regardless of whether separate or consolidated returns are filed, but dividends received from affiliates that are not members of an affiliated group are taxed currently, subject to the 80% dividends-received deduction.

Temporary Differences from Undistributed Earnings of Subsidiaries and Equity Investees

Accounting requirements under the equity method of accounting are generally the same for investments of 20% to 50% of the voting stock of an investee as for subsidiary investments. Investors pay income taxes currently on dividends received (distributed income) from equity investees and subsidiaries that are not members of an affiliated group, and investors are required to provide for deferred income taxes on their shares of undistributed income of their investees. That is, a temporary difference results when an investor's equity in its investees' income exceeds dividends received. Under *APB Opinion No. 23*, the parent company/investor could avoid the general presumption that all undistributed earnings will be transferred to the parent company by showing that undistributed earnings of the subsidiary had been invested indefinitely. *Statement 109* amends *APB Opinion No. 23* to remove the exception and require the parent company/investor to treat the undistributed income of their domestic subsidiaries as temporary differences, unless the tax law provides a means by which the investment can be recovered tax-free. (The *Opinion 23* exception is continued for undistributed earnings of foreign subsidiaries and foreign joint ventures and undistributed earnings of domestic subsidiaries that arose before the effective date of *Statement No. 109*.)

In accounting for the *tax effect* of a temporary difference relating to income from equity investees, the one-line consolidation concept is *not* used because investment income is included in the investor's income *before* income taxes—in other words, on a pretax basis. If undistributed earnings of an investee is the only temporary difference, a parent company or equity investor provides for income taxes on its share of undistributed income by debiting income tax expense and crediting deferred income taxes. The temporary difference related to undistributed earnings is, of course, only one of several possible differences that interact to produce the combined tax impact.

Accounting for Distributed and Undistributed Income

Assume that Parson Corporation owns a 30% interest in Seaton Corporation, a domestic corporation. Seaton reports $600,000 net income for the current year and pays dividends of $200,000. An income tax rate of 34% is applicable. (The 34% tax rate is the *only* enacted tax rate applicable throughout this illustration.) Parson's share of Seaton's distributed and undistributed income is analyzed as follows:

---

[6]The one notable exception was *APB Opinion No. 23*, "Accounting for Income Taxes—Special Areas."

Share of distributed earnings (dividends) $200,000 × 30%	$ 60,000	
Share of undistributed earnings (retained earnings increase) $400,000 × 30%	120,000	
Equity in Seaton's earnings $600,000 × 30%	$180,000	

Parson is taxed currently on 20% of the $60,000 dividends received because Seaton is a domestic corporation that qualifies for the 80% dividends-received deduction. The income tax expense equals income tax liability for this part of Parson's income from Seaton. The current tax liability is $4,080 ($60,000 dividends received × 20% taxable × 34% tax rate). No income tax is due currently on Parson's share of Seaton's undistributed earnings, but accounting standards require that income taxes attributable to that temporary difference be recognized as if the earnings had been remitted as dividends during the current period. Assuming that undistributed earnings is the only temporary difference, Parson makes the following entry to provide for income taxes on its share of Seaton's undistributed earnings:

December 31, 20XX

Income tax expense	$8,160	
Deferred income taxes		$8,160

To provide for taxes on undistributed earnings of
Seaton ($120,000 × 20% taxable × 34% rate).

The same procedures for income taxes on undistributed earnings apply to parent company investors, but not to dividends received from members of an affiliated group because 100% of those dividends are excluded from taxable income of the group.

Unrealized Gains and Losses from Intercompany Transactions

Unrealized and constructive gains and losses from intercompany transactions create temporary differences that may affect deferred tax calculations when separate income tax returns are filed. (This is *not* true when consolidated tax returns are filed.) In the case of an unrealized gain, the selling entity includes the gain in its separate tax return and pays the tax due on the transaction. The unrealized gain is eliminated in the consolidation process, so the income taxes related to the gain should be deferred. Similarly, an unrealized loss may reduce deferred tax expense or add to a deferred tax asset.

The tax effects of temporary differences from unrealized gains and losses on intercompany transactions are included in measuring the income tax expense of the selling affiliate. Under this approach, the consolidated income tax expense is equal to the combined income tax expense of the consolidated entities, and intercompany profit items are eliminated on a gross basis. Similarly, this approach permits the parent company/investor to eliminate intercompany profits on a gross, rather than a net-of-tax basis. (When intercompany profits are eliminated on a net-of-tax basis by the parent company/investor, a consolidation working paper entry is needed to convert the combined income tax expense of the affiliated companies into consolidated income tax expense, and to adjust the deferred tax asset or liability amounts to a consolidated basis.)

Assume that Petit Corporation sells merchandise that cost $100,000 to Sellman Corporation, its 75%-owned subsidiary, for $200,000, and that 70% of this merchandise is inventoried by Sellman at year-end. A 34% tax rate is applicable, and Petit pays $34,000 income tax on the transaction during the current year. Sellman is a 75%-owned subsidiary, so separate tax returns are required. (Again, assume that the intercompany transaction is the only temporary difference and that the 34% tax rate is the only enacted rate.) Relevant consolidation and one-line consolidation entries are as follows:

Consolidation Working Paper Entries—Year of Sale

Sales	$200,000	
Cost of sales		$200,000
To eliminate intercompany sales and purchases		

Cost of sales	$70,000	
Inventory		$70,000
To eliminate unrealized profit on intercompany merchandise remaining in inventory ($200,000 − $100,000) × 70%.		

Petit's One-Line Consolidation Entry—Year of Sale

Income from Sellman	$70,000	
Investment in Sellman		$70,000
To eliminate unrealized profit on sales to Sellman ($70,000 unrealized profit × 100%).		

If Sellman sells the merchandise in the next period, the consolidation and one-line consolidation entries in that year will be:

Consolidation Working Paper Entry—Year of Realization

Investment in Sellman	$70,000	
Cost of sales		$70,000
To recognize previously deferred profit on inventory and to adjust Petit's beginning investment in Sellman account to reflect realization.		

Petit's One-Line Consolidation Entry—Year of Realization

Investment in Sellman	$70,000	
Income from Sellman		$70,000
To reinstate previously deferred profit on intercompany sales.		

If the sale had been upstream from Sellman to Petit, the $34,000 tax on the intercompany profit would have been paid by Sellman, but Sellman would show $23,800 ($70,000 × 34%) of that amount as a deferred tax asset, rather than as income tax expense for the year. The consolidation working paper entry to eliminate the intercompany profit in the year of sale would be for $70,000, the same amount as in the downstream example. Minority interest income in the year of sale would be decreased $17,500 (25% × $70,000 unrealized gain), and the amount of the one-line consolidation entry to eliminate the effect of the unrealized profit on Petit's books would be for $52,500 (75% × $70,000), rather than $70,000 as in the downstream example.

SEPARATE COMPANY TAX RETURNS WITH INTERCOMPANY GAIN

This section provides an extended illustration of income tax allocation for a parent company and its subsidiary that file separate income tax returns. Paco Corporation paid $375,000 cash for a 75% interest in Step Corporation on January 1, 20X1, when Step's equity consisted of $300,000 capital stock and $200,000 retained earnings. At the time Paco acquired its interest in Step, Paco had a deferred income tax liability of $10,200, consisting of $30,000 tax/book depreciation differences that reverse in equal ($7,500) amounts over the years 20X2 through 20X5.

On January 8, 20X1, Paco sold equipment to Step at a gain of $20,000. Step is depreciating the equipment on a straight-line basis over five years. Comparative income and retained earnings data for 20X1 are as follows:

	Paco	Step
Sales	$380,000	$300,000
Gain on equipment sale	20,000	—
Income from Step	23,600	—
Cost of sales	(200,000)	(180,000)
Operating expenses	(100,000)	(40,000)
Income tax expense	(31,253)	(27,200)
Net income	92,347	52,800
Add: Beginning retained earnings	357,653	200,000
Deduct: Dividends (December)	(50,000)	(28,000)
Retained earnings December 31, 20X1	$400,000	$224,800

Under *Statement No. 109*, Paco is required to provide for income taxes on its share of Step's $24,800 undistributed earnings ($52,800 net income less $28,000 dividends). The 80% dividends-received deduction is applicable to dividends received from Step. A flat 34% income tax rate is assumed for Paco and Step. Paco's deferred tax computation on the undistributed earnings is therefore $1,265 [($24,800 × 75% owned × 20% taxable) = $3,720 × 34% tax rate].

One-Line Consolidation

Paco makes the following journal entries to account for its investment in Step during 20X1:

January 1, 20X1

Investment in Step	$375,000	
Cash		$375,000

    To record purchase of a 75% interest in Step.

December 20X1

Cash	$ 21,000	
Investment in Step		$ 21,000

    To record dividends received from Step ($28,000 × 75%).

December 31, 20X1

Investment in Step	$ 23,600	
Income from Step		$ 23,600

    To record income from Step computed as follows:

Paco's share of Step's net income ($52,800 × 75%)	$ 39,600
Less: Unrealized profit on sale of equipment	(20,000)
Add: Piecemeal recognition of gain ($20,000 ÷ 5 years)	4,000
Income from Step	$ 23,600

Note that in computing its investment income from Step, Paco takes up its share of Step's income on which taxes have been paid by Step.

At December 31, 20X1, Paco's investment in Step account has a balance of $377,600 ($375,000 beginning balance + $23,600 income from Step − $21,000 dividends), and Paco's share of Step's equity is $393,600 ($524,800 × 75%). The $16,000 difference ($377,600 − $393,600) is the $16,000 unrealized profit from the downstream sale of equipment.

Income Tax Expense Based on Separate Returns

Step's $27,200 income tax expense is simply 34% of Step's $80,000 pretax accounting income, but Paco's income tax expense of $31,253 requires further analysis. In accordance with the provisions of *FASB Statement No. 109*, Paco's income tax expense is calculated as follows:

Tax on Paco's operating income ($380,000 sales − $200,000 cost of sales − $100,000 operating expenses) × 34%	$27,200
Tax on gain from sale of equipment ($20,000 × 34%)	6,800
Tax on dividends received ($21,000 × 20% taxable) × 34%	1,428
Income taxes currently payable	35,428
Less: Decrease in deferred income taxes ($16,000 unrealized gain on equipment at year-end − $3,720 taxable share of Step's undistributed earnings) × 34%	(4,175)
Income tax expense	$31,253

A schedule to support the computation of Paco's income tax expense is provided in Exhibit 10–7. Only one tax rate (34%) is applicable, so the schedule approach is not necessary, but it may be helpful. The calculation for future dividends in the schedule is ($52,800 net income − $28,000 dividends) × 75% owned × 20% taxable portion.

Paco's interest in Step is only 75%, so separate tax returns are required, and income taxes are payable on the $20,000 intercompany gain on the equipment sold to Step. Paco also pays income taxes on dividends received from Step, less an 80%

Temporary Difference	20X1	20X2	20X3	20X4	20X5	Future Years
Depreciation		$7,500	$7,500	$7,500	$7,500	
Gain on equipment	$20,000					
Piecemeal recognition	(4,000)	(4,000)	(4,000)	(4,000)	(4,000)	
Future dividends	(3,720)	—	—	—	—	$3,720
Taxable in future years		3,500	3,500	3,500	3,500	3,720
Enacted tax rate		34%	34%	34%	34%	34%
Deferred tax liability		$1,190	$1,190	$1,190	$1,190	$1,265

Exhibit 10–7 *Schedule of Deferred Income Tax Liability at December 31, 20X1*

dividends received deduction. The multiplication of dividends received and undistributed income by 20% in calculating Paco's income tax expense effectively takes the 80% dividends-received deduction into account without calculating the amount of the deduction and subtracting it from distributed (dividends) or undistributed earnings.

Step's $27,200 income tax expense is equal to the tax liability indicated on its separate return because it has no temporary differences. Paco's income tax expense of $31,253 consists of $35,428 currently payable, less a $4,175 decrease in deferred income taxes for the year. The balance of Paco's deferred income taxes at December 31 is $6,025 ($10,200 beginning balance − $4,175 decrease for the year). Step and Paco record their income tax expenses as follows:

Step's Books—December 31, 20X1

Income tax expense	$27,200	
Income taxes currently payable		$27,200
To accrue income taxes for 20X1.		

Paco's Books—December 31, 20X1

Income tax expense	$31,253	
Deferred income taxes	4,175	
Income taxes currently payable		$35,428
To accrue income taxes for 20X1.		

Consolidation Working Papers

Consolidation working papers for Paco Corporation and Subsidiary are presented in Exhibit 10–8. The working paper entries are the same as those encountered in earlier chapters except for the inclusion of income tax considerations. Observe that Paco's income tax expense plus Step's income tax expense equal the $58,453 consolidated income tax expense.

Paco paid income taxes on the $20,000 gain on the intercompany sale of equipment. This gain is not recognized for consolidated statement purposes so a temporary difference exists for which income tax allocation procedures are required.

Working Paper Entry for 20X2

The working paper entry for 20X2 to eliminate the effect of the unrealized profit from the intercompany sale of equipment is as follows:

Investment in Step	$16,000	
Accumulated depreciation	8,000	
Equipment		$20,000
Depreciation expense		4,000
To eliminate unrealized profit from downstream sale of equipment.		

PACO CORPORATION AND SUBSIDIARY
CONSOLIDATION WORKING PAPERS
FOR THE YEAR ENDED DECEMBER 31, 20X1

	Paco	Step	Adjustments and Eliminations	Minority Interest	Consolidated Statements
Income Statement Sales	$380,000	$300,000			$680,000
Gain on equipment	20,000		a 20,000		
Income from Step	23,600		c 23,600		
Cost of sales	(200,000)	(180,000)			(380,000)
Operating expense	(100,000)	(40,000)	b 4,000		(136,000)
Income tax expense	(31,253)	(27,200)			(58,453)
Minority interest income				$ 13,200	(13,200)
Net income	$ 92,347	$ 52,800			$ 92,347
Retained Earnings Retained earnings—Paco	$357,653				$357,653
Retained earnings—Step		$200,000	d 200,000		
Net income	92,347√	52,800√			92,347
Dividends	(50,000)	(28,000)	c 21,000	(7,000)	(50,000)
Ending retained earnings	$400,000	$224,800			$400,000
Balance Sheet Other assets	$362,400	$432,000			$794,400
Equipment	120,000	200,000	a 20,000		300,000
Accumulated depreciation	(60,000)	(50,000)	b 4,000		(106,000)
Investment in Step	377,600		c 2,600 d 375,000		
	$800,000	$582,000			$988,400
Deferred tax liability	$ 6,025				$ 6,025
Income tax liability	35,428	$ 27,200			62,628
Other liabilities	58,547	30,000			88,547
Capital stock	300,000	300,000	d 300,000		300,000
Retained earnings	400,000√	224,800√			400,000
	$800,000	$582,000			
Beginning minority interest			d 125,000	125,000	
Ending minority interest				$131,200	131,200
					$988,400

Exhibit 10–8   Consolidation Working Papers with Separate Tax Returns

The income tax expense in 20X2 will be equal to the income tax currently payable, adjusted for the change in the deferred tax asset or liability that occurs in 20X2.

EFFECT OF CONSOLIDATED AND SEPARATE COMPANY TAX RETURNS ON CONSOLIDATED PROCEDURES

This section compares consolidation procedures for a parent company and its subsidiary when separate company and consolidated tax returns are filed. Under the provisions of *FASB Statement No. 109*, the income tax expense and the income from subsidiary are the same in both cases. When consolidated tax returns are filed, the tax liability is allocated among the parent company and its subsidiaries.

Allocation of Consolidated Income Tax to Affiliates

A subsidiary that is part of a group filing a consolidated tax return is required to disclose its current and deferred income tax expense amounts and any tax-related balances due to or from affiliates in its separate financial statements. Although no single method of allocating consolidated income tax expense among affiliates is prescribed, the method used must be disclosed.

Four methods currently used in the allocation of consolidated income taxes to affiliates are:[7]

- **Separate return method.** Each subsidiary computes income taxes as if it were filing a separate return.
- **Agreement method.** Tax expense is allocated by agreement between parent and subsidiaries.
- **With-or-without method.** The income tax provision is computed for the group with and without the pretax income of the subsidiary. The subsidiary's income tax expense is the difference.
- **Percentage allocation method.** Consolidated income tax expense is allocated to a subsidiary on the basis of its pretax income as a percentage of consolidated pretax income.

The percentage allocation method is the one used for illustrations in this book.

Background Information for Consolidated and Separate Tax Return Illustrations

The following illustrations for Pool Corporation and its 90%-owned subsidiary, Sal Corporation, compare consolidation procedures used when consolidated tax returns are filed with consolidation procedures necessary when separate-company tax returns are filed. The income tax effects of intercompany profits from both upstream and downstream inventory sales are also illustrated.

On January 1, 20X3, Pool acquired 90% of the outstanding voting stock of Sal for $435,000, when Sal had $300,000 capital stock and $100,000 retained earnings. The $75,000 excess is goodwill with a 15-year amortization period, and it is now deductible for tax purposes. Post August 10, 1993 goodwill from a taxable purchase transaction is tax deductible using a 15-year tax life (Section 197 of the tax code). Additional information follows:

1 A flat 34% enacted income tax rate applies to all years.
2 Pool and Sal are an affiliated group entitled to the 100% dividend exclusion.
3 Sal pays dividends of $20,000 during 20X3.
4 Intercompany sales are $40,000, of which $10,000 represents unrealized profits at year-end 20X3.
5 Pretax operating incomes for the two affiliates are:

---

[7]Terry E. Allison and Paula Bevels Thomas, "Uncharted Territory: Subsidiary Financial Reporting," *Journal of Accountancy* (October 1989), p. 80.

	Pool	Sal
Sales	$900,000	$500,000
Cost of sales	(500,000)	(350,000)
Expenses	(250,000)	(100,000)
Pretax operating income	$150,000	$ 50,000

Cases 1 and 2 illustrate a temporary difference for unrealized profits from downstream sales that originates in the current year and reverses in the succeeding year. Subsequently, Cases 3 and 4 repeat illustrations 1 and 2 using an upstream sale assumption as the only temporary difference.

Case 1: Consolidated Tax Return with Downstream Sales

Assume that a consolidated tax return is filed and that the intercompany sales are downstream. The consolidated income tax return includes the $200,000 combined operating income (Pool's $150,000 operating income plus Sal's $50,000 operating income), less $10,000 unrealized profit and the $5,000 goodwill amortization. The consolidated income tax expense will be $62,900 ($185,000 × 34%). The $62,900 income tax expense is equal to the $62,900 consolidated income tax liability because the unrealized profits are eliminated in the consolidation working papers and in the consolidated income tax return. In addition, no tax is assessed on the $18,000 dividends that Pool receives from Sal.

The $62,900 consolidated income tax liability is allocated to Pool and Sal based on the amounts of their income that are included in the $185,000 consolidated taxable income. The intercompany sales are downstream in this case, so the allocation is:

$$\text{Pool} = \frac{\$150,000 - \$10,000 - \$5,000}{\$185,000} \times \$62,900 = \$45,900$$

$$\text{Sal} = \frac{\$50,000}{\$185,000} \times \$62,900 = \$17,000$$

The income tax expense amounts determined in this allocation are recorded by Pool and Sal as follows:

Pool's Books—December 31, 20X3

Income tax expense	$45,900	
Income taxes currently payable		$45,900
To record share of the consolidated income tax liability.		

Sal's Books—December 31, 20X3

Income tax expense	$17,000	
Income taxes currently payable		$17,000
To record share of the consolidated income tax liability.		

After this tax allocation is entered, Sal's net income will be $33,000 ($50,000 − $17,000 income tax), and Pool's income from Sal is recorded as follows:

December 31, 20X3

Investment in Sal	$14,700	
Income from Sal		$14,700
To record investment income from Sal computed as follows:		
Share of Sal's net income ($33,000 × 90%)		$29,700
Less: Goodwill amortization		(5,000)
Less: Unrealized profit in inventory		(10,000)
Income from Sal		$14,700

The full amount of the unrealized inventory profit is deducted because the sale is downstream and no tax is assessed on unrealized profits when consolidated income tax returns are used. Consolidation working papers for Pool and Subsidiary are presented in Exhibit 10–9.

POOL CORPORATION AND SUBSIDIARY CONSOLIDATION
WORKING PAPERS FOR THE YEAR ENDED DECEMBER 31, 20X3

	Pool	Sal	Adjustments and Eliminations		Minority Interest	Consolidated Statements
Income Statement Sales	$900,000	$500,000	a 40,000			$1,360,000
Income from Sal	14,700		c 14,700			
Cost of goods sold	(500,000)	(350,000)	b 10,000	a 40,000		(820,000)
Expenses (excluding income taxes)	(250,000)	(100,000)	e 5,000			(355,000)
Income tax expense	(45,900)	(17,000)				(62,900)
Minority income					$ 3,300	(3,300)
Net income	$118,800	$ 33,000				$ 118,800
Retained Earnings Retained earnings—Pool	$352,900					$ 352,900
Retained earnings—Sal		$100,000	d 100,000			
Net income	118,800√	33,000√				118,800
Dividends	(80,000)	(20,000)		c 18,000	(2,000)	(80,000)
Retained earnings December 31, 20X3	$391,700	$113,000				$ 391,700
Balance Sheet Inventory	$183,300	$ 80,000		b 10,000		$ 253,300
Other assets	375,000	520,000				895,000
Investment in Sal	431,700		c 3,300	d 435,000		
Goodwill			d 75,000	e 5,000		70,000
	$990,000	$600,000				$1,218,300
Income taxes payable	$ 45,900	$ 17,000				$ 62,900
Other liabilities	152,400	170,000				322,400
Capital stock	400,000	300,000	d 300,000			400,000
Retained earnings	391,700√	113,000√				391,700
	$990,000	$600,000				
Minority interest January 1				d 40,000	40,000	
Minority interest December 31					$41,300	41,300
						$1,218,300

Exhibit 10–9   *Consolidated Tax Return—Unrealized Profit from Downstream Sales*

Related working paper entries are presented in general journal form:

a	Sales	$ 40,000	
	Cost of goods sold		$ 40,000
	To eliminate intercompany sales and purchases.		
b	Cost of goods sold	$ 10,000	
	Inventory		$ 10,000
	To eliminate intercompany profits from downstream sale.		
c	Income from Sal	$ 14,700	
	Investment in Sal	3,300	
	Dividends		$ 18,000
	To eliminate investment income and dividends and adjust the investment in Sal account to its beginning-of-the-period balance.		
d	Capital stock—Sal	$300,000	
	Retained earnings—Sal	100,000	
	Goodwill	75,000	
	Investment in Sal		$435,000
	Minority interest—beginning		40,000
	To eliminate reciprocal beginning-of-the-period investment and equity amounts, establish beginning-of-the-period goodwill and minority interest.		
e	Expenses	$ 5,000	
	Goodwill		$ 5,000
	To enter current amortization of goodwill.		

Case 2: Separate Tax Returns with Downstream Sales

Assume that the intercompany sales are downstream (from Pool to Sal) and that separate income tax returns are filed. Sal has an income tax liability of $17,000 and reports net income of $33,000. Pool records income from Sal of $14,700, computed as follows:

Share of Sal's net income ($33,000 × 90%)	$29,700
Less: Goodwill amortization ($75,000 ÷ 15 years)	(5,000)
Less: Unrealized profit	(10,000)
Income from Sal	$14,700

Pool's income tax currently payable is 34% of its $150,000 operating income, less $5,000 goodwill amortization, or $49,300. Pool's income tax expense is $45,900, computed as follows:

Income tax currently payable	$49,300
Less: Increase in deferred tax asset from temporary difference ($10,000 unrealized profit × 34% tax rate)	(3,400)
Income tax expense	$45,900

These observations are reflected in the consolidation working papers in Exhibit 10–10.

Income taxes currently payable that will appear in the consolidated balance sheet is $66,300 ($49,300 for Pool plus $17,000 for Sal). The difference between the consolidated income tax expense ($62,900) and income taxes currently payable ($66,300) is the $3,400 deferred income tax asset for the $10,000 unrealized profit.

POOL CORPORATION AND SUBSIDIARY CONSOLIDATION
WORKING PAPERS FOR THE YEAR ENDED DECEMBER 31, 20X3

	Pool	Sal	Adjustments and Eliminations		Minority Interest	Consolidated Statements
Income Statement						
Sales	$900,000	$500,000	a 40,000			$1,360,000
Income from Sal	14,700		c 14,700			
Cost of goods sold	(500,000)	(350,000)	b 10,000	a 40,000		(820,000)
Expenses (excluding income taxes)	(250,000)	(100,000)	e 5,000			(355,000)
Income tax expense	(45,900)	(17,000)				(62,900)
Minority income					$ 3,300	(3,300)
Net income	$118,800	$ 33,000				$ 118,800
Retained Earnings						
Retained earnings—Pool	$352,900					$ 352,900
Retained earnings—Sal		$100,000	d 100,000			
Net income	118,800√	33,000√				118,800
Dividends	(80,000)	(20,000)		c 18,000	(2,000)	(80,000)
Retained earnings December 31, 20X3	$391,700	$113,000				$ 391,700
Balance Sheet						
Inventory	$183,300	$ 80,000		b 10,000		$ 253,300
Deferred tax asset	3,400					3,400
Other assets	375,000	520,000				895,000
Investment in Sal	431,700		c 3,300	d 435,000		
Goodwill			d 75,000	e 5,000		70,000
	$993,400	$600,000				$1,221,700
Income taxes payable	$ 49,300	$ 17,000				$ 66,300
Other liabilities	152,400	170,000				322,400
Capital stock	400,000	300,000	d 300,000			400,000
Retained earnings	391,700√	113,000√				391,700
	$993,400	$600,000				
Minority interest January 1				d 40,000	40,000	
Minority interest December 31					$41,300	41,300
						$1,221,700

Exhibit 10–10 Separate Tax Return—Unrealized Profit from Downstream Sales

The $62,900 income tax expense appearing in the consolidated income statement can be computed independently as follows:

Consolidated income before income taxes and minority income ($1,460,000 sales − $920,000 cost of goods sold − $355,000 expenses)	$185,000
Tax rate	34%
Income tax expense	$ 62,900

Compare Exhibits 10–9 and 10–10. Income tax expense and income from subsidiary are the same whether separate tax returns or consolidated tax returns are filed. However, there is a difference in income tax currently payable and in the deferred income tax liability.

When the consolidated tax return is filed, income tax expense is equal to income tax currently payable because no tax is assessed on the unrealized intercompany profit. Consolidated income tax expense is the same whether separate company or consolidated income tax returns are filed. However, with separate tax returns, Pool's income tax expense consists of $49,300 income tax currently payable, less the $3,400 deferred tax asset related to the $10,000 temporary difference.

Case 3: Consolidated Tax Return with Upstream Sales

Now assume that the intercompany sales are upstream (from Sal to Pool). If a consolidated return is filed, the consolidated income tax expenses will be $62,900, the same as in the downstream example, but the allocation to Pool and Sal will be changed because $10,000 of Sal's $50,000 pretax income is not included in consolidated taxable income. The allocation is:

$$\text{Pool} = \frac{\$150,000 - \$5,000}{\$185,000} \times \$62,900 = \$49,300$$

$$\text{Sal} = \frac{\$50,000 - \$10,000}{\$185,000} \times \$62,900 = \$13,600$$

These amounts are recorded in the separate company books as follows:

Pool's Books—December 31, 20X3

Income tax expense	$49,300	
Income taxes currently payable		$49,300
To record share of consolidated income taxes		

Sal's Books—December 31, 20X3

Income tax expense	$13,600	
Income taxes currently payable		$13,600
To record share of consolidated income taxes		

Sal's net income is $36,400 ($50,000 pretax income less $13,600 income tax expense), and Pool's income from Sal is determined as follows:

Share of Sal's net income ($36,400 × 90%)	$32,760
Less: Goodwill amortization ($75,000 ÷ 15 years)	(5,000)
Less: Unrealized profit from upstream sales ($10,000 × 90%)	(9,000)
Income from Sal	$18,760

Consolidation working papers to illustrate the effect of this upstream sales example appear in Exhibit 10–11. Minority interest income of $2,640 is computed as 10% of Sal's realized income of $26,400 ($36,400 net income − $10,000 unrealized profit). The consolidated income tax expense of $62,900 is the same as in the downstream sale example, but consolidated net income is $660 greater because the $10,000

POOL CORPORATION AND SUBSIDIARY CONSOLIDATION
WORKING PAPERS FOR THE YEAR ENDED DECEMBER 31, 20X3

	Pool	Sal	Adjustments and Eliminations		Minority Interest	Consolidated Statements
Income Statement						
Sales	$900,000	$500,000	a 40,000			$1,360,000
Income from Sal	18,760		c 18,760			
Cost of goods sold	(500,000)	(350,000)	b 10,000	a 40,000		(820,000)
Expenses (excluding income taxes)	(250,000)	(100,000)	e 5,000			(355,000)
Income tax expense	(49,300)	(13,600)				(62,900)
Minority income					$ 2,640	(2,640)
Net income	$119,460	$ 36,400				$ 119,460
Retained Earnings						
Retained earnings—Pool	$352,900					$ 352,900
Retained earnings—Sal		$100,000	d 100,000			
Net income	119,460√	36,400√				119,460
Dividends	(80,000)	(20,000)	c 18,000		(2,000)	(80,000)
Retained earnings December 31, 20X3	$392,360	$116,400				$ 392,360
Balance Sheet						
Inventory	$183,300	$ 80,000		b 10,000		$ 253,300
Other assets	375,000	520,000				895,000
Investment in Sal	435,760		c 760 d 435,000			
Goodwill			d 75,000	e 5,000		70,000
	$994,060	$600,000				$1,218,300
Income taxes payable	$ 49,300	$ 13,600				$ 62,900
Other liabilities	152,400	170,000				322,400
Capital stock	400,000	300,000	d 300,000			400,000
Retained earnings	392,360√	116,400√				392,360
	$994,060	$600,000				
Minority interest January 1			d 40,000		40,000	
Minority interest December 31					$40,640	40,640
						$1,218,300

Exhibit 10–11 *Consolidated Tax Return—Unrealized Profit from Upstream Sale*

unrealized gain and the related $3,400 tax allocation effect are attributed to subsidiary operations. Thus, minority interest income is $660 less than in the downstream sale examples and consolidated net income is $660 more ($119,460 instead of $118,800 in Exhibits 10–9 and 10–10). The minority interest income computation in Exhibit 10–11 eliminates 100% of the $10,000 unrealized profit because no tax is paid on unrealized profits when consolidated returns are filed.

Case 4: Separate Tax Returns with Upstream Sales

Assume that the intercompany sales are upstream (from Sal to Pool) and that separate income tax returns are filed. Sal's income tax currently payable, as determined from its separate income tax return is $17,000, because income taxes are assessed on Sal's $50,000 pretax income, which includes the $10,000 unrealized profit. However, Sal's income tax expense is only $13,600, computed as follows:

Income tax currently payable	$17,000
Less: Increase in deferred tax asset from temporary difference ($10,000 unrealized profit × 34% tax rate)	(3,400)
Income tax expense	$13,600

Sal's net income is $36,400, as in Case 3, and Pool records its income from Sal at $18,760, determined as follows:

Pool's share of Sal's net income ($36,400 × 90%)	$32,760
Less: Goodwill amortization ($75,000 ÷ 15 years)	(5,000)
Less: Unrealized profit from upstream sales ($10,000 × 90% owned)	(9,000)
Pool's income from Sal	$18,760

This information is reflected in Exhibit 10–12, which shows working papers when separate returns are filed and unrealized inventory profit results from upstream sales.

In comparing Exhibit 10–11 and 10–12, note that the income tax expense and the income from the subsidiary are the same whether separate or consolidated tax returns are filed. There is, however, a difference in income tax currently payable and in the deferred income tax liability. When separate tax returns are filed, the consolidated income tax expense consists of the following:

	Pool	Sal	Consolidated
Income taxes currently payable	$49,300	$17,000	$66,300
Deferred income tax asset	—	(3,400)	(3,400)
Income tax expense	$49,300	$13,600	$62,900

Thus, the consolidated income statement will show income tax expense of $62,900, and the consolidated balance sheet will show a current liability for income tax currently payable of $66,300 and a current asset for the $3,400 deferred income tax asset.

BUSINESS COMBINATIONS

For income tax purposes, the term "reorganization" refers to certain corporate restructurings or combinations that are tax-free under Internal Revenue Code Section 368. Reorganization transactions include mergers, recapitalizations, and divisions of corporations. Failure to meet any of the required conditions specified in the Code may disqualify a reorganization so that the transaction loses its tax-free status. Although seven types of transactions (Type A through Type G) are described in the Code as reorganizations, only three will be mentioned here.

POOL CORPORATION AND SUBSIDIARY CONSOLIDATION
WORKING PAPERS FOR THE YEAR ENDED DECEMBER 31, 20X3

	Pool	Sal	Adjustments and Eliminations		Minority Interest	Consolidated Statements
Income Statement						
Sales	$900,000	$500,000	a 40,000			$1,360,000
Income from Sal	18,760		c 18,760			
Cost of goods sold	(500,000)	(350,000)	b 10,000	a 40,000		(820,000)
Expenses (excluding income taxes)	(250,000)	(100,000)	e 5,000			(355,000)
Income tax expense	(49,300)	(13,600)				(62,900)
Minority income					$ 2,640	(2,640)
Net income	$119,460	$ 36,400				$ 119,460
Retained Earnings						
Retained earnings—Pool	$352,900					$ 352,900
Retained earnings—Sal		$100,000	d 100,000			
Net income	119,460√	36,400√				119,460
Dividends	(80,000)	(20,000)		c 18,000	(2,000)	(80,000)
Retained earnings December 31, 20X3	$392,360	$116,400				$ 392,360
Balance Sheet						
Inventory	$183,300	$ 80,000		b 10,000		$ 253,300
Deferred tax asset		3,400				3,400
Other assets	375,000	520,000				895,000
Investment in Sal	435,760			c 760		
				d 435,000		
Goodwill			d 75,000	e 5,000		70,000
	$994,060	$603,400				$1,221,700
Income taxes payable	$ 49,300	$ 17,000				$ 66,300
Other liabilities	152,400	170,000				322,400
Capital stock	400,000	300,000	d 300,000			400,000
Retained earnings	392,360√	116,400√				392,360
	$994,060	$603,400				
Minority interest January 1				d 40,000	40,000	
Minority interest December 31					$40,640	40,640
						$1,221,700

Exhibit 10–12   *Separate Tax Returns—Unrealized Profit from Upstream Sale*

- **Merger or Consolidation.** A merger occurs when one corporation acquires another corporation, primarily for the acquiring company's stock (but some other consideration may be given), and the acquired corporation is dissolved. Its assets and liabilities are taken over by the acquiring corporation. A consolidation occurs when two or more companies combine to form a new corporation and the original corporations are dissolved.[8]
- **Acquiring Another Corporation's Stock.** If a corporation exchanges any of its voting stock (*and no other consideration is given*) for stock of another corporation, and it controls the second corporation immediately after the exchange, the transaction is a reorganization. Control means ownership of at least 80% of the voting stock and at least 80% of all other classes of stock.
- **Acquiring Another Corporation's Assets.** If a corporation exchanges any of its voting stock (and generally nothing else) for substantially all of another corporation's property, the transaction is a reorganization. The assumption of liabilities does not disqualify this transaction as a tax-free reorganization.

These summaries are brief and nontechnical. The point is, the qualifications under the tax Code for an exchange of shares to be a tax-free reorganization are *not identical* to the qualifications under accounting principles for a pooling of interests business combination. Purchase business combinations may be either taxable or tax-free, and structuring the transaction to meet the goals of both buyer and seller is an important part of the negotiating process for any business combination.

In a taxable business combination, the assets and liabilities of the acquired corporation are revalued to reflect the fair value acquired. The seller recognizes gain or loss equal to the fair value of the consideration received, less the tax bases of the assets or stock sold. In a tax-free reorganization, the tax bases of the assets and liabilities are carried forward with no revaluation.

The Revenue Recognition Act of 1993 allows a tax deduction for amortization of goodwill and other intangible assets (called Section 197 intangible assets). This deduction is only allowed when taxes have been paid (gain or loss recognized) by the seller on the purchase transaction.[9] All Section 197 intangible assets are amortized for tax purposes over a 15-year period, regardless of their useful lives.

Purchase Business Combinations

FASB Statement No. 109 requires that a deferred tax liability or deferred tax asset be recognized for the difference between the book values (tax bases) and the assigned values of the assets and liabilities (except goodwill, negative goodwill, and leveraged leases) acquired in a purchase business combination.[10] In other words, the assets and liabilities acquired are recorded at their gross fair values, and a deferred tax asset or liability is recorded for the related tax effect in a tax-free reorganization. A difference between book value and tax value only occurs when the assets are not written up to fair value for tax purposes as they are for book purposes. When the assets are written up for tax purposes, the only differences between written-up book value and tax basis should have already been accounted for in the purchased company's separate books as a deferred tax asset or liability (due to an original difference between book and tax value at the point of purchase).

The tax-free business combination of Platt and Shad is used to illustrate the computation of a deferred tax liability for the book value/fair value differentials, and for the determination of goodwill. On January 1, 20X2, Platt Corporation paid $400,000 for 60% of the outstanding voting stock of Shad Corporation, when Shad's stockholders' equity consisted of $300,000 capital stock and $200,000 retained earnings. Book values were equal to fair values of Shad's assets and liabilities except for a building and land. The building had a book value of $80,000, a fair value of $120,000, and a remaining useful life of eight years. The land had a book value of $50,000 and a fair value of $150,000. Any goodwill is to be amortized over 40 years. The tax rate applicable to both companies is 34%, and an 80% dividends deduction applies.

---

[8]The accounting concepts of mergers and consolidations were discussed in Chapter 1.

[9]The company's liabilities may or may not be assumed in the transaction.

[10]Under *APB Opinion No. 11*, the amounts assigned to the assets and liabilities in a purchase business combination were net-of-tax amounts.

The $100,000 excess of cost over book value acquired [$400,000 cost −
($500,000 book value of net assets × 60% interest)] is allocated as follows:

	Book Value	Pretax Fair Value	Difference	Platt's 60% Interest × the Difference
Building	$80,000	$120,000	$ 40,000	$ 24,000
Land	50,000	150,000	100,000	60,000
Revaluation of assets (gross amount)				84,000
Less: Deferred tax on revaluation ($84,000 × 34%)				(28,560)
Net differential from revaluation of assets				55,440
Goodwill				44,560
Excess cost over book value acquired				$100,000

The $24,000 assigned to the building and the $8,160 related deferred tax
($24,000 × 34%) will be written off over the building's remaining eight-year useful
life at the annual amounts of $3,000 and $1,020, respectively. Thus, consolidated net
income will be decreased by $1,980 each year on an after-tax basis. The $60,000
revaluation of the land and the $20,400 deferred tax on the revalued land will re-
main on the books until the land is sold to outside entities. *FASB Statement No. 109*
elected to not assign a deferred tax liability to the goodwill account (when the goodwill is not deductible), due to the difficulty in the simultaneous calculation of the
residual account, goodwill, and a deferred tax assignment to this residual account.
They also decided that not much incremental information would be added by this
calculation.

Equity Method of Accounting for Purchase Business Combinations

During 20X2, Shad has net income of $100,000 and pays dividends of $40,000. Platt
makes the following entries on its separate books to account for its investment in
Shad.

Investment in Shad	$400,000	
Cash		$400,000

To record purchase of a 60% interest in Shad Corporation.

Cash	$ 24,000	
Investment in Shad		$ 24,000

To record receipt of dividends from Shad ($40,000 × 60%).
Note that Platt must also provide for income taxes on its
share of the $60,000 undistributed earnings of Shad
($36,000 × 20% taxable × 34% tax rate = $2,448
deferred taxes).

Investment in Shad	$ 56,906	
Income from Shad		$ 56,906

To record income from Shad and the related amortization
of deferred tax liability on the building computed as follows:

Share of Shad's income ($100,000 × 60%)	$ 60,000
Less: Goodwill amortization ($44,560 ÷ 40 years)	(1,114)
Less: Depreciation on excess allocated to building	(3,000)
Add: Amortization of deferred taxes on building	1,020
Income from Shad	$ 56,906

The stockholders' equity of Shad at December 31, 20X2 consists of $300,000
capital stock and $260,000 retained earnings. The balance of Platt's investment in
Shad account is $432,906. An analysis of the investment account balance shows the
following:

	January 1, 20X2	20X2 Change	December 31, 20X2
Book value of investment	$300,000	$36,000	$336,000
Unamortized excess:			
Building	24,000	(3,000)	21,000
Land	60,000		60,000
Deferred income taxes	(28,560)	1,020	(27,540)
Goodwill	44,560	(1,114)	43,446
Investment balance	$400,000	$32,906	$432,906

Working Paper Entries

When Platt prepares consolidation working papers at December 31, 20X2, the investment in Shad account will have a balance of $432,906 ($400,000 original investment + $56,906 income from Shad − $24,000 dividends). The working paper entries are shown in general journal form as follows.

a	Income from Shad	$ 56,906	
	Dividends		$ 24,000
	Investment in Shad		32,906

To eliminate income and dividends from Shad and adjust the investment in Shad account to its beginning-of-the-period balance.

b	Capital stock—Shad	$300,000	
	Retained earnings—Shad	200,000	
	Building	24,000	
	Land	60,000	
	Goodwill	44,560	
	Investment in Shad		$400,000
	Deferred taxes on revaluation		28,560
	Minority interest—beginning		200,000

To eliminate reciprocal investment and equity balances, establish beginning minority interest, enter beginning-of-the-period cost/book value differentials, and enter deferred taxes on revaluation.

c	Depreciation expense	$ 3,000	
	Accumulated depreciation—building		$ 3,000

To record depreciation on excess allocated to building.

d	Deferred income taxes on revaluation	$ 1,020	
	Income tax expense		$ 1,020

To record amortization of deferred taxes.

e	Goodwill amortization	$ 1,114	
	Goodwill		$ 1,114

To record amortization of goodwill.

FINANCIAL STATEMENT DISCLOSURES FOR INCOME TAXES

Deferred tax assets or liabilities are divided into two categories, a current amount and a noncurrent amount, for balance sheet presentation. Under *FASB Statement No. 109*, deferred tax liabilities and assets are classified as current or noncurrent based on the classification of the related asset or liability for financial reporting. If the deferred item is not related to an asset or liability for financial reporting, its classification depends on the reversal date of the temporary difference. In addition, the significant components of income tax expense or benefit are required to be disclosed in the financial statements or notes to the financial statements.

Disclosures are also required for income tax expense and benefits allocated to continuing operations, discontinued operations, extraordinary items, cumulative-effect-type items, and prior-period adjustments.

SUMMARY

When the capital structure of a subsidiary or equity investee includes outstanding preferred stock, the investee's equity and income are allocated to the preferred stockholders based on the preferred contract, and then to common stockholders. If the subsidiary's preferred stock is not held by the parent company, the preferred income and equity are included in minority interest. From the viewpoint of the consolidated entity, any of the subsidiary's preferred stock held by the parent is considered retired for consolidated statement purposes.

Consolidated and parent company earnings-per-share computations are identical, and the procedures used in computing parent company earnings per share also apply to investor accounting under the equity method. Parent company (investor) relationships do not affect EPS computations unless the subsidiary (investee) has outstanding potentially dilutive securities. When a subsidiary has potentially dilutive securities outstanding, the computational adjustments for EPS differ according to whether the subsidiary's potentially dilutive securities are convertible into subsidiary common stock or parent company common stock.

A consolidated entity classified as an affiliated group may elect to file consolidated tax returns. All other consolidated entities file separate income tax returns. In determining taxable income, consolidated entities that are members of an affiliated group can exclude all dividends received from group members. Affiliated groups that elect to file consolidated tax returns avoid paying taxes on unrealized profits and can offset losses of one group member against income of other group members.

Investors with equity investees and subsidiaries that are not members of an affiliated group pay income taxes currently on a portion of dividends received and provide for deferred income taxes on their share of undistributed income of their investees.

Unrealized and constructive gains and losses from intercompany transactions create temporary differences that may affect deferred tax calculations when separate company tax returns are filed.

A purchase business combination for accounting purposes may be a taxable combination or tax-free reorganization under the Internal Revenue Code.

In a purchase business combination, the cost/book value differential is allocated to the assets and liabilities acquired at gross fair values, and a deferred tax asset or deferred tax liability is recorded for the related tax effect.

SELECTED READINGS

ALLISON, TERRY E. and PAULA THOMAS. "Uncharted Territory: Subsidiary Financial Reporting." *Journal of Accountancy* (October 1989), pp. 76–84.

Accounting Principles Board Opinion No. 18. "The Equity Method of Accounting for Investments in Common Stock." New York: American Institute of Certified Public Accountants, 1971.

COUGHLAN, JOHN W. "ESOs and EPS" *Accounting Horizons* (March 1997), pp. 25–38.

DILLEY, STEVEN C. and JAMES C. YOUNG. "A Pragmatic Approach to Amortization of Intangibles." *The CPA Journal* (December 1994), pp. 46–55.

ENGLEBRECHT, TED D., GOVIND IYER, and STEVEN C. COLBURN. "Type F Reorganizations and the Impact of the *Jobco Manufacturing Company* Decision." *The CPA Journal* (February 1994), pp. 28–32.

FINANCIAL ACCOUNTING STANDARDS BOARD. EITF Issue No. 93–7. *Uncertainties Related to Income Taxes in a Purchase Business Combination.* Norwalk, CT: Financial Accounting Standards Board, 1993.

FULLER, DAVID N. "Amortizing Intangibles—A Break-Even Analysis." *Journal of Accountancy* (June 1994), pp. 31–34.

GREGORY, GEORGE J. THOMAS R. PETREE, and RANDALL J. VITRAY. "*FASB 109*: Planning for Implementation and Beyond." *Journal of Accountancy* (December 1992), pp. 44–50.

MANDEL, GARY B. "The Ability to Reconsolidate After Disaffiliation." *The CPA Journal* (January 1993), pp. 61–62.

Statement of Financial Accounting Standards No. 109. "Accounting for Income Taxes." Norwalk, CT: Financial Accounting Standards Board, 1992.

Statement of Financial Accounting Standards No. 128. "Earnings Per Share." Norwalk, CT: Financial Accounting Standards Board, 1997.

WILLENS, ROBERT. "Amortization of Intangibles: Is a Mergers and Acquisitions Boom Imminent?" *The CPA Journal* (November 1993), pp. 46–47 and 91–94.

ASSIGNMENT MATERIAL

QUESTIONS

1 Arom Corporation has 100,000 outstanding shares of no par common stock and 5,000 outstanding shares of $100 par, cumulative, 10% preferred stock. Arom Corporation's net income for the current year is $300,000, and its stockholders' equity at the end of the current year is as follows:

10% cumulative preferred stock, $100 par	$ 500,000
Common stock, $10 par	1,000,000
Additional paid-in capital	600,000
Retained earnings	400,000
Total stockholders' equity	$2,500,000

Flora Corporation owns 60% of the outstanding common stock of Arom, acquired at book value several years ago. Compute Flora's investment income for the current year and the balance of its investment in Arom account at the end of the current year.

2 Refer to the information in question 1. Assume that Arom pays two years' preferred dividend requirements during the current year. Would this affect your computation of Flora's investment income for the current year? If so, recompute Flora's investment income.

3 How should preferred stock of a subsidiary be shown in a consolidated balance sheet in each case?
   a If it is held 100% by the parent company
   b If it is held 50% by parent company and 50% by outside interests
   c If it is held 100% by outside interests

4 Describe the computation of minority interest income for an 80%-owned subsidiary with both preferred and common stock outstanding.

5 How does consolidated earnings per share differ from parent company earnings per share?

6 Do investments in nonconsolidated subsidiaries and 20%- to 50%-owned investees affect the nature of the investor company's earnings per share calculations?

7 Under what conditions will the procedures used in computing a parent company's earnings per share be the same as those for a company without equity investments?

8 It may be necessary to compute the earnings per share for subsidiaries and equity investees before parent company (and consolidated) earnings per share can be determined. When are the subsidiary earnings-per-share computations used in calculating parent company earnings per share?

9 Potentially dilutive securities of a subsidiary may be converted into parent company common stock or subsidiary common stock. Describe how these situations affect the parent company's EPS procedures.

10 In computing diluted earnings for a parent company, it may be necessary to replace the parent's equity in subsidiary realized income with the parent company's equity in the subsidiary's diluted earnings. Does this replacement calculation involve the goodwill amortization and unrealized profits that are included in the parent company's income from subsidiary?

11 Are consolidated income tax returns required for all consolidated entities? Discuss.

12 Can a consolidated entity that is classified as an "affiliated group" under the IRS Code elect to file separate tax returns for each affiliate?

13 What are the primary advantages of filing a consolidated tax return?

14 Some or all of the dividends received by a corporation from domestic affiliated companies may be excluded from federal income taxation. When are all of the dividends excluded?

15 Describe the nature of the tax effect of temporary differences that arise from use of the equity method of accounting.

16 Does a parent company/investor provide for income taxes on the undistributed earnings of a subsidiary by adjusting investment and investment income accounts? Explain.

17 When do unrealized and constructive gains and losses create temporary differences for a consolidated entity?

EXERCISES

E 10-1   [AICPA adapted]
   1 [Preferred stock] Moss Corporation owns 20% of Dubro Corporation's preferred stock and 80% of its common stock. Dubro's stock outstanding on December 31, 20X3 is as follows:

10% cumulative preferred stock	$100,000
Common stock	700,000

Dubro reported net income of $60,000 for the year ended December 31, 20X3. What amount should Moss record as equity in earnings of Dubro for the year ended December 31, 20X3?

a $42,000   c $48,400
b $48,000   d $50,000

2 [Tax] Taft Corporation uses the equity method to account for its 25% investment in Flame, Inc. During 20X2, Taft received dividends of $30,000 from Flame and recorded $180,000 as its equity in the earnings of Flame. Additional information follows:

• The dividends received from Flame are eligible for the 80% dividends-received deduction.
• There are no other temporary differences.
• Enacted income tax rates are 30% for 20X2 and thereafter.

In its December 31, 20X2 balance sheet, what amount should Taft report for deferred income tax liability?

a $9,000   c $45,000
b $10,800   d $54,000

3 [Tax] In 20X2, Portal Corporation received $100,000 in dividends from Sal Corporation, its 80%-owned subsidiary. What net amount of dividend income should Portal include in its 20X2 consolidated tax return?

a $100,000   c $70,000
b $80,000   d $0

4 [Tax] Potter Corporation and Sly Corporation file consolidated tax returns. In January 20X3, Potter sold land, with a basis of $60,000 and a fair value of $75,000, to Sly for $100,000. Sly sold the land in December 20X4 for $125,000. In its 20X4 and 20X3 tax returns, what amount of gain should be reported for these transactions in the consolidated return?

	20X4	20X3
a	$25,000	$40,000
b	$50,000	$0
c	$50,000	$25,000
d	$65,000	$0

E 10-2   **[Preferred stock]**

The stockholders' equity of Star Corporation at December 31, 20X1 was as follows:

10% cumulative preferred stock, $100 par, callable at $105, 10,000 shares issued and outstanding, with one year's dividends in arrears	$1,000,000
Common stock, $10 par, 100,000 shares issued and outstanding	1,000,000
Additional paid-in capital	2,000,000
Retained earnings	4,000,000
Total stockholders' equity	$8,000,000

On January 1, 20X2, Portland Corporation purchased 90% of Star Corporation's common stock at $90 per share. Star's assets and liabilities were recorded at their fair values when Portland acquired its 90% interest. Any cost/book value differential is to be amortized over a 10-year period. During 20X2, Star reported net income of $1,200,000 and paid dividends of $600,000.

Required: Calculate the following:
1 The cost/book value differential from Portland's investment in Star
2 Portland's income from Star for 20X2
3 The balance of Portland's investment in Star at December 31, 20X2
4 Total minority interest in Star on December 31, 20X2

E 10-3   **[Preferred Stock]**

The stockholders' equity of Sommerfeld Corporation at December 31, 20X5 was as follows:

12% preferred stock, cumulative, nonparticipating, $100 par, callable at 105	$ 600,000
Common stock, $10 par	1,000,000
Other paid-in capital	140,000
Retained earnings	760,000
Total stockholders' equity	$2,500,000

Parnell Corporation purchased 80% of Sommerfeld's common stock on January 2, 20X6 for $1,536,000. During 20X6, Sommerfeld reported a $100,000 net loss and paid no dividends. During 20X7, Sommerfeld reported $500,000 net income and declared dividends of $344,000.

Required

    1 Compute the cost/book value differential from Parnell's investment in Sommerfeld.

    2 Determine Parnell's income (loss) from Sommerfeld for 20X6.

    3 Determine Parnell's income (loss) from Sommerfeld for 20X7.

    4 Compute the balance of Parnell's investment in Sommerfeld account on December 31, 20X7.

E 10-4 **[Preferred stock]**

Penzance Corporation owns 80% of Sandalwood Corporation's common stock, having acquired the interest at book value on December 31, 20X4. During 20X5, Penzance's separate income is $3,000,000 and Sandalwood's net income is $500,000. Penzance and Sandalwood declare dividends in 20X5 of $1,000,000 and $300,000, respectively.

    The stockholders' equity of Sandalwood at December 31, 20X4 and 20X5 consists of the following:

	December 31, 20X4	December 31, 20X5
12% cumulative preferred stock, $100 par, callable at 105 per share	$1,000,000	$1,000,000
Common stock, $10 par	2,000,000	2,000,000
Other paid-in capital	300,000	300,000
Retained earnings	700,000	900,000
Total stockholders' equity	$4,000,000	$4,200,000

Required

    1 Determine the cost of Penzance's investment in Sandalwood on December 31, 20X4 if Sandalwood has one year's preferred dividends in arrears on that date.

    2 Calculate Penzance's net income (and consolidated net income) and minority interest income for 20X5.

    3 Calculate the underlying book value of Penzance's investment in Sandalwood on December 31, 20X5.

E 10-5 **[Preferred stock]**

The stockholders' equity of Shoshone Corporation on December 31, 20X4 was as follows:

15% preferred stock, $100 par, cumulative, nonparticipating, with one year's dividends in arrears	$1,000,000
Common stock, $10 par	2,000,000
Other paid-in capital	200,000
Retained earnings	300,000
Total stockholders' equity	$3,500,000

    Pimlico Corporation acquired 50% of Shoshone's preferred stock for $600,000 and 80% of its common stock for $2,000,000 on January 1, 20X5. Shoshone reported net income of $400,000 and paid dividends of $300,000 in 20X5.

Required

    1 Prepare the journal entries (two entries) to record Pimlico's 50% investment in Shoshone preferred stock.

    2 Calculate the excess cost/book value differential from Pimlico's 80% investment in Shoshone common.

    3 Compute Pimlico's income from Shoshone—preferred for 20X5.

    4 Compute Pimlico's income from Shoshone—common for 20X5 (assume a 10-year amortization period for the cost/book value differential).

    5 Calculate the minority interest in Shoshone that will appear in the consolidated balance sheet of Pimlico Corporation and Subsidiary on December 31, 20X5.

E 10-6 **[Preferred stock]**

Perry Corporation purchased 60% of Sketch Corporation's outstanding preferred stock for $6,500,000 and 70% of its outstanding common stock for $35,000,000 on January 1, 20X7. Sketch's stockholders' equity on December 31, 20X6 consisted of the following:

10% cumulative, $100 par, preferred stock, callable at $105 (100,000 shares issued and outstanding with one year's dividends in arrears)	$10,000,000
Common stock, $10 par	30,000,000
Other paid-in capital	5,000,000
Retained earnings	15,000,000
Total stockholders' equity	$60,000,000

SUBSIDIARY PREFERRED STOCK, EPS, AND TAXATION   **399**

Required

1 Determine the cost/book value differentials from Perry's investments in Sketch.

2 Without bias on your part, assume that the cost/book value differential applicable to the preferred investment is a negative $400,000. Describe the accounting treatment of the preferred cost/book value differential if the preferred investment is treated as a constructive retirement for consolidation purposes.

E 10-7   [EPS]

1 A parent company and its 100%-owned subsidiary have only common stock outstanding (10,000 shares for the parent and 3,000 shares for the subsidiary), and neither company had issued other potentially dilutive securities. The equation to compute consolidated EPS for the parent company and its subsidiary is:

   a (Net income of parent + net income of subsidiary) ÷ 13,000 shares

   b (Net income of parent + net income of subsidiary) ÷ 10,000 shares

   c Net income of parent ÷ 13,000 shares

   d Net income of parent ÷ 10,000 shares

2 A parent company has a 90% interest in a subsidiary that has no potentially dilutive securities outstanding. In computing consolidated EPS:

   a Subsidiary common shares are added to parent company common shares and common share equivalents

   b Subsidiary EPS and parent company EPS amounts are combined

   c Subsidiary EPS computations are not needed

   d Subsidiary EPS computations are used in computing basic earnings

3 In computing a parent company's diluted EPS, it may be necessary to subtract the parent's equity in subsidiary realized income and replace it with the parent's equity in subsidiary diluted earnings. The subtraction in this replacement computation is affected by:

   a Constructive gain from purchase of parent company bonds

   b Current amortization of goodwill from investment in the subsidiary

   c Unrealized profits from downstream sales

   d Unrealized profits from upstream sales

E 10-8   [EPS]

Palor Corporation's net income for 20X9 is $316,000, including $160,000 income from Solaid Corporation, its 80%-owned subsidiary. The income from Solaid consists of $176,000 equity in income less $16,000 goodwill amortization. Palor has 300,000 shares of $10 par common stock outstanding, and Solaid has 50,000 shares of $10 par common stock outstanding throughout 20X9. In addition, Solaid has 10,000 outstanding warrants to acquire 10,000 shares of Solaid common stock at $10 per share. The average market price of Solaid's common stock was $20 per share during 20X9.

1 For purposes of calculating Palor Corporation's (and consolidated) diluted earnings per share, Solaid's diluted earnings are:

   a $220,000   c $176,000

   b $200,000   d $160,000

2 For purposes of calculating Palor Corporation's (and consolidated) diluted earnings per share, Solaid's outstanding common shares and common share equivalents are:

   a 60,000 shares   c 55,000 shares

   b 56,000 shares   d 50,000 shares

3 For purposes of calculating Palor Corporation's (and consolidated) earnings per share, assume that Solaid's diluted EPS is $4 per share. Palor Corporation's (and consolidated) diluted earnings will be:

   a $316,000   c $156,000

   b $300,000   d $140,000

4 If Solaid's diluted earnings for 20X9 are $4 per share, Palor Corporation's (and consolidated) diluted earnings per share will be:

   a $1.64   c $1.04

   b $1.59   d $1.00

E 10-9   EPS

The following information is available regarding Putman Corporation and its 80%-owned subsidiary, Sheridan Corporation, at and for the year ended December 31, 20X2:

	Putman	Sheridan
Outstanding common stock	8,000 shares	5,000 shares
Warrants to purchase 1,000 shares of Sheridan common stock at $9 per share (average market price is $15)		1,000 warrants

(Continued)

	Putman	Sheridan
Net income	$20,000	$18,000
Income from Sheridan ($14,400 − $2,400 amortization of excess cost over book value acquired)	$12,000	

Required: Determine consolidated earnings per share (both basic and diluted).

E 10-10 [EPS]

The income statements of Prince Corporation and its 80%-owned subsidiary, Stanley Corporation, for 20X6 are as follows:

	Prince	Stanley
Sales	$1,270,000	$740,000
Income from Stanley (see note)	13,920	—
Cost of sales	(700,000)	(470,000)
Expenses	(462,000)	(230,000)
Income before taxes	121,920	40,000
Provision for income taxes	(41,453)	(13,600)
Net income	$ 80,467	$ 26,400

[*Note:* Income from Stanley is computed as ($26,400 reported income × 80%) − $2,000 goodwill amortization − $5,200 unrealized profit in Stanley's inventory.]

Prince had 10,000 shares of common stock and 1,200 shares of $100 par, 10% cumulative preferred stock outstanding throughout 20X6. Stanley had 20,000 shares of common stock and warrants to purchase 5,000 shares of Stanley common stock at $24 outstanding throughout 20X6. The average market price of Stanley common stock was $30 per share.

Required: Compute Prince's (and consolidated) basic and diluted EPS.

E 10-11 [EPS]

Poway Corporation owns an 80% interest in Scony Corporation. Poway does not have common stock equivalents or other potentially dilutive securities outstanding, so it calculated its EPS for 20X7 as follows:

$$\frac{\$1,000,000 \text{ separate income } + \$480,000 \text{ income from Scony}}{1,000,000 \text{ outstanding common shares of Poway}} = \$1.48$$

An examination of Poway's income from Scony shows that it is determined correctly as 80% of Scony's $630,000 net income less $24,000 goodwill amortization. Poway's EPS computation is in error, however, because it fails to consider outstanding warrants of Scony that permit their holders to acquire 10,000 shares of Scony common stock at $24 per share and increase Scony's outstanding common stock to 60,000 shares. The average price of Scony common stock during 20X7 was $40.

Required

1 Compute Scony Corporation's diluted EPS for use in the determination of consolidated EPS.
2 Compute consolidated EPS for 20X7 (both basic and diluted).

E 10-12 [Tax]

1 Income taxes are currently due on intercompany profits when
  a Profits originate from upstream sales
  b Separate company tax returns are filed
  c Consolidated tax returns are filed
  d Affiliates are accounted for as unconsolidated subsidiaries
2 The right of a consolidated entity to file a consolidated income tax return is contingent upon:
  a Ownership by a common parent of all the voting stock of group members
  b Ownership by a common parent of 90% of the voting stock of group members
  c Classification as an affiliated group
  d Direct or indirect ownership of a majority of the outstanding stock of all group members
3 When affiliates are classified as an affiliated group for tax purposes, the group:
  a Excludes unrealized profits from intercompany transactions from taxable income
  b Must file a consolidated income tax return
  c May file separate income tax returns
  d Pays lower income taxes

4 Deferred income taxes are provided for unrealized profits from intercompany transactions when:
  a A consolidated tax return is filed
  b Separate company tax returns are filed
  c The unrealized profits are from upstream sales
  d The consolidated entity is an affiliated group

E 10-13 **[Tax]**

1 When Petty Corporation acquired its 100% interest in Simon Corporation in a tax-free reorganization, Simon's equipment had a fair value of $6,000,000 and a book value and tax basis of $4,000,000. If Petty's effective tax rate is 34%, how much of the purchase price should be allocated to equipment and to deferred income taxes?
  a $4,000,000 and $0, respectively
  b $5,320,000 and $680,000, respectively
  c $6,000,000 and $680,000, respectively
  d $6,000,000 and $2,040,000, respectively

2 Carl Corporation, whose effective income tax rate is 34%, received $200,000 dividends from its 30%-owned domestic equity investee during the current year and recorded $500,000 equity in the investee's income. Carl's income tax expense for the year should include taxes on the investment of:
  a $13,600 **c** $34,000
  b $20,400 **d** $68,000

3 During 20X1, Palmer Corporation reported $60,000 investment income from Springer Corporation, its 30%-owned investee, and received $30,000 dividends from Springer. Palmer's effective income tax rate is 34%, and it is entitled to an 80% dividends-received deduction on dividends received from Springer. On the basis of this information, Palmer should:
  a Report investment income from Springer of $57,960
  b Increase its investment in Springer for 20X1 in the amount of $27,960
  c Credit its deferred income taxes in the net amount of $2,040 for the year 20X1
  d Debit its deferred income taxes in the net amount of $2,040 for the year 20X1

4 Polines Corporation owns 35% of the voting stock of Sissy Corporation, a domestic corporation. During 20X1, Sissy reports net income of $100,000 and pays dividends of $50,000. Polines' effective income tax rate is 34%. What amounts should Polines record as income taxes currently payable and deferred income taxes from its investment in Sissy?
  a $17,000 and $0, respectively
  b $5,950 and $5,950, respectively
  c $3,400 and $3,400, respectively
  d $1,190 and $1,190, respectively

5 Pint Corporation and its 100%-owned domestic subsidiary, Star Corporation, are classified as an affiliated group for tax purposes. During the current year, Star pays $80,000 in cash dividends. Assuming a 34% income tax rate, how much income tax expense on this dividend should be reported in the consolidated income statement of Pint Corporation and Subsidiary?
  a $0 **c** $5,440
  b $27,200 **d** $2,720

E 10-14 **[Tax]**

The pretax accounting incomes of Pruit Corporation and its 100%-owned subsidiary, Solo Company, for 20X1 are as follows:

	Pruit	Solo
Sales	$1,000,000	$500,000
Gain on land	200,000	—
Total revenue	1,200,000	500,000
Cost of sales	500,000	300,000
Gross profit	700,000	200,000
Operating expenses	400,000	100,000
Pretax accounting income	$ 300,000	$100,000

The only intercompany transaction during 20X1 was a gain on land sold to Solo. Assume a 34% flat income tax rate.

Required
  1 What amount should be shown on the consolidated income statement as income tax expense if separate company tax returns are filed?
  2 Compute the consolidated income tax expense if a consolidated tax return is filed.
  3 What would be the income taxes currently payable if separate income tax returns are filed? If a consolidated return is filed?

E 10-15   **[Tax]**

Paxton Corporation and its 70%-owned subsidiary, Sutter Corporation, have pretax operating incomes for 20X8 as follows:

	Paxton	Sutter
Sales	$8,000,000	$4,000,000
Gain on equipment	200,000	—
Cost of sales	(5,000,000)	(2,000,000)
Other expenses	(1,800,000)	(1,200,000)
Pretax income	$1,400,000	$ 800,000

Paxton received $280,000 dividends from Sutter during 20X8. Goodwill from Paxton's investment in Sutter is being amortized at a rate of $50,000 per year (the same time horizon is used for both book and tax purposes, and the goodwill is tax-deductible).

On January 1, 20X8, Paxton sold equipment to Sutter at a $200,000 gain. Sutter is depreciating the equipment at a rate of 20% per year. A flat 34% tax rate is applicable to both companies.

Required: Prepare a consolidated income statement for Paxton Corporation and Subsidiary for 20X8. (Assume no deferred tax balance on January 1, 20X8.)

E 10-16   **[Tax]**

Sullivan Corporation is a 100%-owned subsidiary of Peddicord Corporation. During the current year, Peddicord sold merchandise that cost $50,000 to Sullivan for $100,000. A 34% income tax rate is applicable, and 80% of the merchandise remains unsold by Sullivan at year-end.

Required

1 Prepare comparative one-line consolidation entries relating to the unrealized profit when separate and consolidated income tax returns are filed.
2 Prepare comparative consolidation working paper entries in general journal form relating to the intercompany sales transaction and the related income tax effect when separate and consolidated income tax returns are filed.

E 10-17   **[Tax]**

Sweeney Corporation, an 80%-owned subsidiary of Pioneer Corporation, sold equipment with a book value of $150,000 to Pioneer for $250,000 at December 31, 20X3. Separate income tax returns are filed, and a 34% income tax rate is applicable to both Pioneer and Sweeney.

Required

1 Prepare a one-line consolidation entry for Pioneer to eliminate the effect of the intercompany transaction.
2 Prepare working paper entries in general journal form to eliminate the unrealized profit.
3 Assume that the reported net income of Sweeney is $800,000 and that the sale of equipment is the only intercompany transaction between Pioneer and Sweeney. What is the minority interest's share of total consolidated income?

PROBLEMS

P 10-1   **[Preferred stock]**

Parrella Corporation paid $3,100,000 for 180,000 shares of Stanley Corporation's outstanding voting common stock on January 1, 20X5, when the stockholders' equity of Stanley consisted of:

10% cumulative, preferred stock, $100 par. Liquidation preference is $105 per share, and 10,000 shares are issued and outstanding with one year's dividends in arrears	$1,000,000
Common stock, $10 par, 200,000 shares issued and outstanding	2,000,000
Other paid-in capital	500,000
Retained earnings	650,000
Total stockholders' equity	$4,150,000

During 20X5, Stanley reported net income of $500,000 and declared dividends of $400,000. Any cost/book value differential is goodwill to be amortized over a 40-year period.

Required: Calculate the following:
1 Goodwill from Parrella's investment in Stanley
2 Parrella's income from Stanley for 20X5

3 Minority interest income for 20X5
4 Minority interest in Stanley at December 31, 20X5
5 Parrella's investment in Stanley account balance at December 31, 20X5

P 10-2 **[Preferred stock]**

Pulsen Corporation acquired 80% of Starky Corporation's preferred stock for $175,000 and 90% of Starky's common stock for $650,000 on July 1, 20X7. Starky's stockholders' equity on December 31, 20X7 was as follows:

Stockholders' Equity	
9% preferred stock, cumulative, nonparticipating,	
$100 par, call price $105	$200,000
Common stock, $10 par	500,000
Paid-in capital in excess of par	40,000
Retained earnings	160,000
Total stockholders' equity	$900,000

Starky Corporation had net income of $24,000 in 20X6 and $46,000 in 20X7, but it declared no dividends in either year. Assume that preferred dividends accrue ratably throughout each year and that Starky's net assets were fairly valued on July 1, 20X7.

Required

1 Determine the account balances of Pulsen Corporation's investments in Starky's preferred and common stocks at December 31, 20X7 on the basis of a one-line consolidation. Use a 10-year amortization period for any goodwill.
2 Prepare working paper entries to consolidate the balance sheets of Pulsen and Starky at December 31, 20X7.

P 10-3 **[Preferred stock]**

Financial statements for Pat and Sal corporations for 20X4 are summarized as follows:

	Pat	Sal
Combined Income and Retained Earnings Statements		
for the Year Ended December 31, 20X4		
Sales	$1,233,000	$700,000
Income from Sal	67,000	—
Cost of sales	(610,000)	(400,000)
Other expenses	(390,000)	(210,000)
Net income	300,000	90,000
Add: Retained earnings January 1, 20X4	500,000	200,000
Less: Dividends	(200,000)	(50,000)
Retained earnings December 31, 20X4	$ 600,000	$240,000
Balance Sheet at December 31, 20X4		
Cash	$ 181,000	$ 50,000
Other current assets	200,000	300,000
Plant assets—net	900,000	600,000
Investment in Sal	719,000	—
Total assets	$2,000,000	$950,000
Current liabilities	$200,000	$60,000
$10 preferred stock	—	100,000
Common stock	1,200,000	500,000
Other paid-in capital	—	50,000
Retained earnings	600,000	240,000
Total equities	$2,000,000	$950,000

Pat owns 90,000 shares of Sal's outstanding voting common stock at December 31, 20X4. These shares were acquired in two lots as follows:

	Date	Shares	Purchase Price
Lot 1	January 1, 20X3	70,000	$500,000
Lot 2	April 1, 20X4	20,000	152,000

The stockholders' equity of Sal at year-end 20X2, 20X3, and 20X4 was as follows:

	December 31,		
	20X2	20X3	20X4
$10 preferred stock, $100 par, cumulative with no dividends in arrears	$100,000	$100,000	$100,000
Common stock, $5 par	500,000	500,000	500,000
Other paid-in capital	50,000	50,000	50,000
Retained earnings	150,000	200,000	240,000
Total stockholders' equity	$800,000	$850,000	$890,000

Sal's net income for 20X4 is $90,000, earned proportionately throughout the year, and its quarterly dividends of $12,500 are declared on March 15, June 15, September 15, and December 15. Any goodwill from Pat's stock acquisitions is amortized over 10 years. There are no intercompany receivables or payables at December 31, 20X4, and there have been no intercompany transactions other than dividends.

Required: Prepare consolidation working papers for Pat Corporation and Subsidiary for 20X4.

P 10-4 **[Preferred stock]**

Pari Corporation acquired an 80% interest in Sak Corporation common stock for $240,000 on January 1, 20X5, when Sak's stockholders' equity consisted of $200,000 common stock, $100,000 preferred stock, and $25,000 retained earnings. The excess was allocated to goodwill with a five-year amortization period.

Intercompany sales of inventory items from Pari to Sak were $50,000 in 20X5 and $60,000 in 20X6. The cost of these items to Pari was 60% of the selling price to Sak, and Sak inventoried $30,000 of the intercompany sales items at December 31, 20X5 and $40,000 at December 31, 20X6. Intercompany receivables and payables from these sales were $10,000 at December 31, 20X5 and $5,000 at December 31, 20X6.

Sak sold land that cost $10,000 to Pari for $20,000 during 20X5. During 20X6, Pari resold the land outside the consolidated entity for $30,000.

On July 1, 20X6, Pari purchased all of Sak's bonds payable in the open market for $91,000. These bonds were issued at par, have interest payment dates of June 30 and December 31, and mature on June 30, 20X9.

Sak declared and paid dividends of $10,000 on its cumulative preferred stock and $10,000 on its common stock in each of the years 20X5 and 20X6.

Financial statements for Pari and Sak corporations at and for the year ended December 31, 20X6 are summarized as follows:

	Pari	Sak
Combined Income and Retained Earnings Statement for the Year Ended December 31, 20X6		
Sales	$900,000	$300,000
Gain on land	10,000	—
Interest income	6,500	—
Income from Sak	38,000	—
Cost of sales	(600,000)	(140,000)
Operating expenses	(208,500)	(90,000)
Interest expense	—	(10,000)
Net income	146,000	60,000
Add: Beginning retained earnings	120,000	50,000
Deduct: Dividends	(100,000)	(20,000)
Retained earnings December 31, 20X6	$166,000	$ 90,000
Balance Sheet at December 31, 20X6		
Cash	$ 5,500	$ 15,000
Accounts receivable	26,000	20,000
Inventories	80,000	60,000
Other current assets	100,000	5,000
Land	160,000	30,000
Plant and equipment—net	268,000	420,000
Investment in Sak—bonds	92,500	—
Investment in Sak—stock	258,000	—
Total assets	$990,000	$550,000

(Continued)

	Pari	Sak
Accounts payable	$ 24,000	$ 15,000
10% bonds payable	—	100,000
Other liabilities	100,000	45,000
10% preferred stock	—	100,000
Common stock	700,000	200,000
Retained earnings	166,000	90,000
Total equities	$990,000	$550,000

Required: Prepare consolidation working papers for Pari Corporation and Subsidiary for the year ended December 31, 20X6.

P 10-5 **[EPS]**

Palace Corporation has $108,000 income from its own operations for 20X3 and $42,000 income from Skinner Corporation, its 70%-owned subsidiary. Skinner's net income of $60,000 consists of $66,000 operating income less $6,000 net-of-tax interest on its outstanding 10% convertible debenture bonds. Throughout 20X3, Palace has 100,000 shares of common stock outstanding, and Skinner has 50,000 outstanding common shares.

Required

    1 Compute Palace's diluted earnings per share for 20X3, assuming that Skinner's convertible bonds are convertible into 10,000 shares of Skinner's common stock.

    2 Compute Palace's diluted earnings per share for 20X3, assuming that Skinner's convertible bonds are convertible into 10,000 shares of Palace's common stock.

P 10-6 **[EPS]**

Pensacola Corporation owns an 80% interest in Sheridan Company. Throughout 20X8, Pensacola had 20,000 shares of common stock outstanding. Sheridan had the following securities outstanding:

- 10,000 shares of common stock.
- Options to purchase 2,000 shares of Sheridan common at $15 per share.
- 1,000 shares of 10%, $100 par, convertible, preferred stock that are convertible into 3,000 shares of Sheridan common stock.

Income data for the affiliated companies for 20X8 are as follows:

	Pensacola	Sheridan
Separate incomes	$120,000	$55,000
Income from Sheridan ($45,000 income to common × 80%) − $6,000 goodwill amortization	30,000	
	$150,000	$55,000

Required: Compute basic and diluted earnings per share for Pensacola Corporation and Subsidiary for 20X8, assuming average market prices for Sheridan common stock of $30 per share.

P 10-7 **[EPS]**

Protein Corporation owns 80% of Starch Corporation's outstanding common stock. The 80% interest was acquired in 20X2 at $40,000 in excess of book value due to undervalued equipment with an eight-year remaining useful life. Outstanding securities of the two companies throughout 20X3 and at December 31, 20X3 are:

	Protein	Starch
Common stock, $5 par	20,000 shares	—
Common stock, $10 par	—	6,000 shares
14% cumulative, convertible, preferred stock, $100 par	—	1,000 shares

    Starch Corporation's net income is $50,000 for 20X3, and Protein's net income consists of $70,000 separate income and $23,800 income from Starch.

Required

    1 Compute consolidated basic and diluted earnings per share, assuming that the preferred stock is convertible into 4,000 shares of Starch Corporation's common stock.

    2 Compute consolidated basic and diluted earnings per share, assuming that the preferred stock is convertible into 5,000 shares of Protein's common stock.

P 10-8 **[EPS]**

Premble Company owns 40,000 of 50,000 outstanding shares of Smithfield Company, and during 20X6, it recognizes income from Smithfield as follows:

Share of Smithfield's net income ($500,000 × 80%)	$400,000
Goodwill amortization	(50,000)
Unrealized profit—downstream sales	(40,000)
Unrealized profit—upstream sales ($60,000 × 80%)	(48,000)
Income from Smithfield	$262,000

Premble's net income (and consolidated net income) for 20X6 is $1,262,000, consisting of separate income from Premble of $1,000,000 and $262,000 income from Smithfield. Premble has 100,000 shares of common stock outstanding, but it does not have common stock equivalents or other potentially dilutive securities.

Smithfield has $100,000 par of 10% convertible bonds outstanding that are convertible into 10,000 shares of Smithfield common stock. The net-of-tax interest on the bonds is $6,400, and Smithfield's diluted earnings per share for purposes of computing consolidated earnings per share is determined as follows:

Net income	$500,000
Add: Net-of-tax interest on convertible bonds	6,400
Less: Unrealized profit on upstream sales	(60,000)
a Diluted earnings	$446,400
Common shares outstanding	50,000
Shares issuable upon conversion of bonds	10,000
b Common shares and equivalents	60,000
Diluted earnings per share a ÷ b	$ 7.44

Required: Compute Premble Company's and consolidated diluted earnings per share for 20X6.

P 10-9 **[EPS]**

Pike Corporation's net income for 20X6 consists of the following:

Separate income		$320,000
Income from Sim Corporation:		
80% of Sim's income to common	$160,000	
Less: Goodwill amortization	(4,000)	
Less: Unrealized profits on equipment sold to Sim	(10,000)	
Less: 80% of unrealized profit on land purchased from Sim	(16,000)	130,000
Net income for 20X6		$450,000

Additional Information

1 Pike has 100,000 shares of common stock, and Sim has 50,000 shares of common and 10,000 shares of $10 cumulative, convertible, preferred stock outstanding throughout 20X6. The preferred stock is convertible into 30,000 shares of Sim stock.

2 Sim has warrants outstanding that permit their holders to purchase 10,000 shares of Sim Corporation common stock at $15 per share (average market price $20).

3 Sim's reported net income for 20X6 is $300,000, allocated $100,000 to preferred stockholders and $200,000 to common stockholders.

4 Pike owned 40,000 shares of Sim common stock throughout 20X6.

Required: Compute Pike Corporation's (and consolidated) basic and diluted EPS.

P 10-10 **[Tax]**

Pactor Corporation and its 100%-owned subsidiary, Shram Corporation, are members of an affiliated group with pretax accounting incomes as follows:

	Pactor	Shram
Sales	$1,200,000	$700,000
Gain on sale of land	50,000	
Cost of sales	(600,000)	(300,000)
Operating expenses	(350,000)	(250,000)
Pretax accounting income	$ 300,000	$150,000

The gain reported by Pactor relates to land sold to Shram during the current year. A flat 34% income tax rate is applicable.

Required: Prepare income statements for Pactor Corporation assuming (a) that separate income tax returns are filed and (b) that a consolidated income tax return is filed. (*Note:* Pactor applies the equity method as a one-line consolidation.)

P 10-11 **[Tax]**

Panama Corporation paid $590,000 cash for a 70% interest in Silky Corporation's outstanding common stock on January 2, 20X5, when the equity of Silky consisted of $500,000 common stock and $300,000 retained earnings. The excess cost over book value acquired is goodwill with a 15-year amortization period.

In December 20X5, Silky sold inventory items to Panama at a gross profit of $50,000 (selling price $120,000 and cost $70,000), and all these items were included in Panama's inventory at December 31, 20X5.

Silky paid dividends of $50,000 in 20X5, and an 80% dividends-received deduction is applicable. A flat 34% income tax rate is applicable to both companies.

Separate pretax incomes of Panama and Silky for 20X5 are as follows:

	Panama	Silky
Sales	$4,000,000	$1,000,000
Cost of sales	(2,000,000)	(550,000)
Operating expenses	(1,500,000)	(250,000)
Pretax income	$ 500,000	$ 200,000

Required

1 Determine income tax currently payable and income tax expense for Panama and Silky for 20X5.

2 Calculate Panama's income from Silky for 20X5.

3 Prepare a consolidated income statement for Panama and Silky for 20X5.

P 10-12 **[Tax]**

Taxable incomes for Pulaski Corporation and Stewart Corporation, its 70%-owned subsidiary, for 20X3 are as follows:

	Pulaski	Stewart
Sales	$500,000	$300,000
Dividends received from Stewart	28,000	
Total revenue	528,000	300,000
Cost of expenses	250,000	120,000
Operating expenses	78,000	80,000
Total deductions	328,000	200,000
Taxable income	$200,000	$100,000

Additional Information

1 Pulaski acquired its interest in Stewart at book value on December 31, 20X2.

2 Stewart paid dividends of $40,000 in 20X3.

3 Pulaski sold $90,000 merchandise to Stewart during 20X3, and there was $10,000 unrealized profit from the sales at year-end.

4 A flat 34% income tax rate is applicable.

5 Pulaski is eligible for the 80% dividends-received deduction.

Required: Prepare consolidation income statement working papers for Pulaski Corporation and Subsidiary for 20X3.

P 10-13 **[Tax]**

Pen Corporation acquired a 90% interest in Soo Corporation in a taxable transaction on January 1, 20X5 for $900,000, when Soo had $500,000 capital stock and $400,000 retained earnings. The $90,000 excess cost over book value is goodwill with a 15-year amortization period. Pen and Soo are an affiliated group for tax purposes.

During 20X5, Pen sold land to Soo at a $20,000 profit. Soo still holds the land. Soo paid dividends of $50,000. A flat 34% tax rate applies to Pen and Soo. Income statements for Pen and Soo corporations, and a consolidated income statement for Pen Corporation and Subsidiary are summarized as follows:

	Pen	Soo	Consolidated
Sales	$800,000	$200,000	$1,000,000
Gain on sale of land	20,000	—	—
Income from Soo	30,430	—	—
Cost of sales	(400,000)	(75,000)	(475,000)
Other expenses	(150,000)	(30,000)	(186,000)
Income tax expense	(82,960)	(32,300)	(115,260)
Minority interest income	—	—	(6,270)
Net income	$217,470	$ 62,700	$ 217,470

Required: Reconstruct all the working paper entries needed to consolidate the financial statements of Pen Corporation and Subsidiary for 20X5.

P 10-14   [Tax]

Parson Corporation acquired all the stock of Studio Corporation on January 1, 20X5 for $280,000 cash, when the book values and fair values of Studio's assets and liabilities were as follows:

	Book Values (Tax Bases)	Fair Values
Current assets	$100,000	$100,000
Land	20,000	60,000
Buildings—net	80,000	110,000
Equipment—net	60,000	70,000
Assets	$260,000	$340,000
Liabilities	$ 90,000	$ 90,000
Capital stock	150,000	
Retained earnings	20,000	
Equities	$260,000	

Studio's buildings have a remaining life of 10 years, and the equipment has a useful life of two years from the date of the business combination. Any goodwill is amortized by Parson over 15 years. During 20X5, Studio had income of $50,000 and paid dividends of $20,000. Parson and Studio are subject to a 35% tax rate.

Required

1. Prepare a schedule to allocate the excess cost over book value to Studio's assets, liabilities, deferred taxes, and goodwill at January 1, 20X5, assuming the purchase was a taxable transaction.
2. Prepare a schedule to allocate the excess cost over book value to Studio's assets, liabilities, deferred taxes, and goodwill at January 1, 20X5, assuming the purchase was a tax-free reorganization.
3. Compute Parson's income from Studio for 20X5 under both options.

P 10-15   [Tax]

The pretax operating incomes of Pommer Corporation and Sooner Corporation, its 70%-owned subsidiary, for the year 20X8 are as follows:

	Pommer	Sooner
Sales	$8,000,000	$4,000,000
Gain on equipment	500,000	—
Cost of sales	(5,000,000)	(2,000,000)
Other expenses	(2,100,000)	(1,200,000)
Pretax income (excluding Pommer's income from Sooner)	$1,400,000	$ 800,000

Additional Information

1. Pommer received $280,000 dividends from Sooner during 20X8.
2. Goodwill from Pommer's investment in Sooner is being amortized at $50,000 per year (15-year original life).
3. Pommer sold equipment to Sooner at a gain of $500,000 on January 1, 20X8. Sooner is depreciating the equipment at a rate of 20% per year.

4 A flat 34% tax rate is applicable.

5 Pommer provides for income taxes on undistributed income from Sooner.

Required

1 Determine the separate income tax expenses for Pommer and Sooner.

2 Determine Pommer's income from Sooner on an equity basis.

3 Prepare a consolidated income statement for Pommer Corporation and Subsidiary for the year ended December 31, 20X8.

P 10-16 **[Tax]**

On January 3, 20X7, Phoenix Corporation purchased a 90% interest in Selica Corporation at a price $120,000 in excess of book value and fair value. The excess is goodwill with a 10-year amortization period. During 20X7, Phoenix sold inventory items to Selica for $100,000, and $15,000 profit from the sale remained unrealized at year-end. Selica sold land to Phoenix during the year at a gain of $30,000.

Additional Information

1 The companies are an affiliated group for tax purposes.

2 Selica declared and paid dividends of $100,000 in 20X7.

3 Phoenix and Selica file separate income tax returns and a 34% tax rate is applicable to both companies.

4 Phoenix uses a correct equity method in accounting for its investment in Selica.

5 Pretax accounting incomes, excluding Phoenix's income from Selica, are as follows:

	Phoenix	Selica
Sales	$3,815,000	$2,000,000
Gain on land	—	30,000
Cost of sales	(2,200,000)	(1,200,000)
Other expenses	(1,000,000)	(400,000)
Pretax accounting income	$ 615,000	$ 430,000

Required: Calculate the following:

1 Selica's net income

2 Phoenix's income from Selica

3 Phoenix's net income

P 10-17 **[Tax]**

The 20X3 consolidated income tax return of Peabody Corporation and Subsidiary, Sylvester Company (90%-owned), is summarized as follows:

Sales		$390,000
Cost of sales		180,000
Gross profit		210,000
Operating expenses:		
Depreciation expense	$ 40,000	
Other expenses	20,000	60,000
Consolidated taxable income		150,000
Tax rate		× 34%
Income taxes payable (equal to income tax expense)		$ 51,000

Pretax accounting incomes for Peabody, Sylvester, and Peabody and Sylvester Consolidated are as follows:

	Peabody	Sylvester	Consolidated
Sales	$300,000	$150,000	$390,000
Cost of sales	(150,000)	(70,000)	(180,000)
Goodwill amortization (valuation differential)			(10,000)
Depreciation expense	(25,000)	(15,000)	(40,000)
Other expense	(15,000)	(5,000)	(20,000)
Pretax accounting income	$110,000	$ 60,000	$140,000

The $10,000 differential between consolidated taxable income and consolidated pretax accounting income lies in Peabody's goodwill amortization, which is not deductible for tax purposes because it originated from a tax-free purchase transaction. Peabody sold inventory items to Sylvester for $60,000, and the $20,000 gross profit on the sale remains unrealized at December 31, 20X3.

Required

    1 Show how the $51,000 consolidated income tax expense should be allocated to Peabody and Sylvester.

    2 Compute Peabody's income from Sylvester on the basis of a one-line consolidation.

    3 Prepare an income statement for Peabody Corporation for 20X3.

    4 Prepare a consolidated income statement for Peabody Corporation and Subsidiary for 20X3.

11

Consolidation Theories, Push-Down Accounting, and Corporate Joint Ventures

Previous chapters of this book have described practices used in the preparation of consolidated financial statements and explained the rationale for those practices. The concepts and procedures discussed in earlier chapters reflect the **contemporary theory** of consolidated statements. This contemporary theory has evolved from accounting practice, and it does *not* reflect an interconsistent approach to the preparation of consolidated financial statements. Instead, contemporary theory reflects parts of both parent company theory (proprietary theory) and entity theory.[1]

Parent company theory is based on the assumption that consolidated financial statements are an extension of parent company statements and should be prepared from the viewpoint of parent company stockholders. Under parent company theory, consolidated statements are prepared for the benefit of the stockholders of the parent company, and it is not expected that minority stockholders can benefit significantly from the statements. Consolidated net income under parent company theory is a measurement of income to the parent company stockholders.

Certain problems and inconsistencies in accounting procedures under parent company theory arise in the case of less-than-100%-owned subsidiaries. For example, the minority interest is a liability from the viewpoint of parent company stockholders, and published statements frequently report the minority interest in the liability section of the consolidated balance sheet. Similarly, minority interest income is an expense from the viewpoint of majority stockholders. However, shareholder interests, whether majority or minority, are not liabilities under any of the accepted concepts of a liability, and income to shareholders does not meet the requirements for expense recognition.[2] The problem lies in the majority shareholder viewpoint.

Entity theory represents an alternative view of consolidation. This theory was developed by Professor Maurice Moonitz and published by the American Accounting Association in 1944 under the title *The Entity Theory of Consolidated Statements*. The

---

[1]Parent company theory is sometimes referred to as the conventional theory [for example, see Eldon S. Hendriksen, *Accounting Theory*, 4th ed. (Homewood, IL: Richard D. Irwin, 1982), p. 469]. As viewed here, however, the differences between parent company and contemporary theory are sufficiently important to merit separate identification.

[2]Hendriksen points out that probably the strongest justification for including minority interest with the liabilities or between the liabilities and capital is the fact that "the creditors of the parent have only a secondary claim against the assets of a subsidiary, on the same level as the claim of the minority interest." See *Accounting Theory*, p. 472.

focal point of entity theory is that the consolidated statements reflect the viewpoint of the total business entity, under which all resources controlled by the entity are valued consistently. Under entity theory, the income of minority interests is a distribution of the total income of the consolidated entity, and the interests of minority stockholders are a part of consolidated stockholders' equity. Entity theory requires that the income and equity of a subsidiary be determined for all stockholders, so that the total amounts can be allocated between majority and minority shareholders in a consistent manner. This is accomplished under entity theory by imputing a total value for the subsidiary on the basis of the price paid by the parent company for its majority interest. The excess of total value of the subsidiary over the book value of subsidiary net assets is assigned 100% to identifiable assets and to goodwill. In this manner, subsidiary assets (including goodwill) and liabilities are consolidated at their fair values, which are applicable to both minority and majority interests.

COMPARISON OF CONSOLIDATION THEORIES

The basic differences between parent company theory, entity theory, and contemporary theory are compared in Exhibit 11–1. Parent company theory adopts the viewpoint of parent company stockholders, and entity theory focuses on the total consolidated entity. By contrast, contemporary theory identifies the primary users of consolidated financial statements as the stockholders and creditors of the parent company, but assumes the objective of reporting financial position and results of operations of a single business entity. Thus, the viewpoint of contemporary theory, as reflected in *ARB No. 51*, appears to be a compromise between the parent company and entity theories.

Income Reporting

Consolidated net income is a measurement of income to parent company stockholders under both the parent company and contemporary theories. Entity theory, however, requires a computation of income to all equity holders, which is labeled "total consolidated net income." Total consolidated net income is then assigned to minority and majority stockholders, with appropriate disclosure on the face of the income statement. Consolidated net income under existing practice reflects parent company theory. This is evidenced by the practice of reporting minority interest income as an expense and the equity of minority stockholders as a liability. However, the preferred accounting practices under contemporary theory are to show minority interest income as a separate deduction in the determination of consolidated net income, and to report the equity of minority shareholders as a single amount within the consolidated stockholders' equity classification.

In its deliberations on consolidations, the Financial Accounting Standards Board tentatively decided that a noncontrolling interest in a subsidiary should be labeled and displayed as a separate component of equity in the consolidated balance sheet. Further, income attributable to the noncontrolling interest is not an expense or a loss, but it is a deduction from consolidated net income in computing income attributable to the controlling interest. The consolidated income statement should disclose both the portion of consolidated net income attributable to the controlling interest and the portion attributable to noncontrolling interests.[3]

Asset Valuation

Perhaps the greatest difference between parent company theory and entity theory lies in the valuation of subsidiary net assets. Under parent company theory, subsidiary assets are initially consolidated at their book values, plus the parent company's share of any excess of their fair values over their book values. In other words, subsidiary assets are revalued only to the extent of the net assets (including goodwill) acquired by the parent company. The minority interest in subsidiary net assets is consolidated at book value. Although this approach reflects the cost principle from the viewpoint of the parent company, it leads to inconsistent treatment of majority and minority interests

---

[3]Financial Accounting Standards Board, *Financial Accounting Series No. 145-A*, "Status Report No. 260," January 6, 1995, p. 6.

	Parent Company Theory	Entity Theory	Contemporary Theory
Basic purpose and users of consolidated financial statements:	Consolidated statements are an extension of parent company statements. They are prepared for the benefit and from the viewpoint of the stockholders of the parent company.	Consolidated statements are prepared from the viewpoint of the total consolidated entity and are intended for all parties having an interest in the entity.	Consolidated statements present the financial position and results of operations of a single business enterprise but are prepared primarily for the benefit of the stockholders and creditors of the parent company. (*ARB No. 51*, paras. 2 and 7)
Consolidated net income:	Consolidated net income is income to the stockholders of the parent company.	Total consolidated net income is income to all equity holders of the consolidated entity.	Consolidated net income is income to the stockholders of the parent company.
Minority interest income:	Minority interest income is an expense from the viewpoint of the parent company stockholders. It is measured on the basis of the subsidiary as a separate legal entity.	Minority interest income is an allocation of total consolidated net income to minority stockholders.	Minority interest income is a deduction in determining consolidated net income, but not an expense. Instead, it is an allocation of realized income of the entity between majority and minority interests.
Equity of minority interests:	Equity of minority stockholders is a liability from the viewpoint of the parent company stockholders. Its measurement is based on the subsidiary's legal equity.	Equity of minority stockholders is a part of consolidated stockholders' equity. Its reporting is equivalent to the presentation accorded the equity of majority stockholders.	Equity of minority stockholders is a part of consolidated stockholders' equity. It is presented as a single amount because it is not expected that minority interests will benefit from the disclosure.
Consolidation of subsidiary net assets:	Parent's share of subsidiary net assets is consolidated on the basis of the price paid by the parent for its interest. The minority interest's share is consolidated at book value.	All net assets of a subsidiary are consolidated at their fair values imputed on the basis of the price paid by the parent for its interest. Thus, majority and minority interests in net assets are valued consistently.	Subsidiary net assets are consolidated at book value plus the excess of the parent company's investment cost over the book value of the interest acquired. The excess is required to be amortized over a maximum period of 40 years.
Unrealized gains and losses:	100% elimination from consolidated net income for downstream sales and elimination of the parent company's share for upstream sales.	100% elimination in determining total consolidated net income with allocation between majority and minority interests for upstream sales.	100% elimination from revenue and expense accounts with allocation between majority and minority interests for upstream sales. (*ARB No. 51,* paras. 7 and 13)
Constructive gains and losses on debt retirement:	100% recognition in consolidated net income on retirement of parent company debt, and recognition of the parent company's share for retirement of subsidiary debt.	100% recognition in total consolidated net income with allocation between majority and minority interests for retirement of subsidiary debt.	100% recognition in revenue and expense accounts with allocation between majority and minority interests for retirement of subsidiary debt.

Exhibit 11–1 *Comparison of Consolidation Theories*

in the consolidated financial statements, and to a balance sheet valuation that reflects neither historical cost nor fair value.

Under entity theory, subsidiary assets and liabilities are consolidated at their fair values, and the majority and minority interests in those net assets are accounted for consistently. However, this consistent treatment is obtained through the questionable practice of imputing a total subsidiary valuation on the basis of the price paid by the parent company for its majority interest. Conceptually, this valuation approach has considerable appeal when the parent acquires essentially all of the subsidiary's stock for cash. It has much less appeal when the parent acquires a slim majority of subsidiary outstanding stock for noncash assets or through an exchange of shares. An investor may be willing to pay a premium for the rights to *control* an investee (an investment of more than 50%), but not willing to purchase the remaining stock at the inflated price.

Additional problems with the imputed total valuation of a subsidiary under entity theory develop after the parent company acquires its interest. *Once the parent is able to exercise absolute control over the subsidiary, the shares held by minority stockholders do not represent equity ownership in the usual sense.* Typically, the stock of a subsidiary will be "delisted" after a business combination, leaving the parent company as the only viable purchaser for minority shares. In this case, minority shareholders are at the mercy of the parent company. A minority share does not have the same equity characteristics as a majority share.

Contemporary theory conforms to the practices of parent company theory in the consolidation of subsidiary assets and liabilities. Although a conceptual superiority for entity theory in this area is frequently granted, there are practical disadvantages. The price paid by the parent company for its majority interest is not currently considered a valid basis for valuation of minority interests. Even the current practice of measuring the equity of minority shareholders at book value is criticized because it tends to overstate the value of the minority interest (primarily due to the restricted marketability of minority shares).

Unrealized Gains and Losses

A difference between the parent company and entity theories of consolidation also exists in the treatment of unrealized gains and losses from intercompany transactions (see Exhibit 11–1). Although there is general agreement that 100% of all unrealized gains and losses from downstream sales should be eliminated, gains and losses arising from upstream sales are accorded different treatment under parent company and entity theories. Under parent company theory, unrealized gains and losses from upstream sales are eliminated to the extent of the parent company's ownership percentage in the subsidiary. The portion of unrealized gains and losses not eliminated relates to the minority interest and, from the parent company viewpoint, is considered to be realized by minority shareholders.

All unrealized gains and losses are eliminated in determining total consolidated net income under entity theory. In the case of upstream sales, however, the amounts eliminated are allocated between income to minority and majority stockholders according to their respective ownership percentages.

The elimination of unrealized gains and losses under contemporary theory follows the pattern and consistency of entity theory. All unrealized gains and losses are required to be eliminated under the provisions of *ARB No. 51*, paragraph 13, but "the elimination of the intercompany profit or loss may be allocated proportionately between the majority and minority interests." Presumably, the assignment of the full amount of unrealized gains and losses to majority interests would also be acceptable under *ARB No. 51*. This latter approach was not used in earlier chapters of this book because of its inherent inconsistency for consolidation purposes and because its use seems incompatible with requirements for the equity method of accounting. If unrealized gains and losses from upstream sales are not allocated between majority and minority interests, the parent company's income and equity will not equal consolidated net income and equity unless the same inconsistency is applied under the equity method.

Constructive Gains and Losses

The pattern of accounting for constructive gains and losses from intercompany debt acquisitions under the three theories parallels the pattern of accounting for unrealized gains and losses (see Exhibit 11–1). Gains and losses on the constructive retirement of debt under contemporary theory are accounted for in the same manner as under entity theory.

Many of the requirements of the contemporary theory of consolidation are specified by FASB Accounting Standards. As noted earlier in the chapter, these requirements do not constitute an interconsistent theory of consolidated financial statements; instead, they contain elements of both parent company theory and entity theory. Although the contemporary theory of consolidation lacks internal consistency, the theory does adhere reasonably well to other components of accounting theory, such as the cost principle and the basic elements of financial statements.

The Economic Unit Concept—Purchased Goodwill

Chapter 3 (page 85) introduced an accounting procedure for business combinations in which a subsidiary's identifiable assets and liabilities, other than goodwill, are reported at their fair values. Only the goodwill actually purchased by the parent company is recorded. This method, entitled the "economic unit concept—purchased goodwill," is described in the FASB's Discussion Memorandum, *An Analysis of Issues Related to Consolidation Policy and Procedures.* Supporters for this method argue that it is inappropriate to consolidate the controlling interest's portion of the subsidiary's assets and liabilities at fair value and the noncontrolling interest's portion at book value. Under this method, the subsidiary's identifiable assets and liabilities are consistently valued at their fair value in the consolidation process at the date of the business combination. The desire for consistency does not extend to goodwill, however. Supporters of this approach recognize that the parent company may be willing to pay a substantial premium for control of another company, and the control premium may have little to do with the fair value of the subsidiary. Thus, no implied value of goodwill is computed, and only the goodwill actually paid for is reported in the consolidated statements. (See Chapter 3 for an illustration).

In October 1995, the FASB issued an exposure draft, "Consolidated Financial Statements: Policy and Procedures," that would have required accounting for the acquisition of a subsidiary using the "economic unit concept—purchased goodwill" method. However, the exposure draft was not adopted as a FASB statement. Since then, the Board has *tentatively* decided that purchased goodwill meets the definition of an asset and should be measured as the difference between the fair value of the purchase consideration and the fair value of the net assets acquired. This is consistent with *APB Opinion No. 16* requirements. The Board will also consider a procedure by which goodwill would be reviewed periodically for impairment. If a FASB standard based on entity theory or the economic unit concept—purchased goodwill method is issued, it will become part of the contemporary theory. Contemporary theory continues to evolve with changes in accounting standards.

ILLUSTRATION—CONSOLIDATION UNDER PARENT COMPANY AND ENTITY THEORIES

Differences between the various consolidation theories may be more comprehensible when numerical examples are used. The following section relates to the purchase business combination of Pedrich and Sandy corporations on January 1, 20X2. Assume that Pedrich Corporation acquires a 90% interest in Sandy Corporation for $198,000 cash on January 1, 20X2. Comparative balance sheets of the two companies immediately before the acquisition are as follows:

	Pedrich		Sandy	
	Book Value	Fair Value	Book Value	Fair Value
Cash	$220,000	$220,000	$ 5,000	$ 5,000
Accounts receivable—net	80,000	80,000	30,000	35,000
Inventory	90,000	100,000	40,000	50,000
Other current assets	20,000	20,000	10,000	10,000
Plant assets—net	220,000	300,000	60,000	80,000
Total assets	$630,000	$720,000	$145,000	$180,000
Liabilities	$ 80,000	$ 80,000	$ 25,000	$ 25,000
Capital stock, $10 par	400,000		100,000	
Retained earnings	150,000		20,000	
Total equities	$630,000		$145,000	

The $198,000 purchase price for the 90% interest implies a $220,000 total value for Sandy's Corporation's net assets ($198,000 ÷ 90%). Under entity theory, all subsidiary assets and liabilities are revalued and reflected in the consolidated statements on the basis of the $220,000 implied total valuation. Under parent company theory, the total implied value is not reflected in the consolidated financial statements, therefore, only 90% of the subsidiary's net assets are revalued. Although *the different theories do not affect parent company accounting under the equity method*, they do result in different amounts for consolidated assets, liabilities, and minority interests.

Entity Theory   In the Pedrich-Sandy example, the $100,000 excess of implied value over the $120,000 book value of Sandy's net assets under entity theory is assigned to identifiable net assets and goodwill as follows:

	Fair Value		Book Value		Excess Fair Value
Accounts receivable—net	$35,000	–	$30,000	=	$ 5,000
Inventories	50,000	–	40,000	=	10,000
Plant assets—net	80,000	–	60,000	=	20,000
Goodwill (remainder)	—		—		65,000
Total implied value over book value					$100,000

Parent Company Theory   The amounts assigned to identifiable net assets and goodwill in accordance with parent company theory (and contemporary theory) would be 90% of the foregoing amounts:

Accounts receivable—net	$ 5,000 × 90% = $ 4,500
Inventories	10,000 × 90% = 9,000
Plant assets—net	20,000 × 90% = 18,000
Goodwill	65,000 × 90% = 58,500
Total purchase price over book value acquired	$90,000

Goodwill   Goodwill under the two theories can be determined independently. Under entity theory, the $65,000 goodwill is equal to the total implied value of Sandy's net assets over the fair value of Sandy's net assets ($220,000 − $155,000). Under parent company theory, the $58,500 goodwill is equal to the investment cost less 90% of the fair value of Sandy's identifiable net assets ($198,000 − $139,500). The $10,000 additional amount assigned to identifiable assets and goodwill under entity theory ($100,000 − $90,000) is reflected in the minority interest classification in a consolidated balance sheet.[4]

Consolidation at Acquisition

Consolidated balance sheet working papers for Pedrich Corporation and Subsidiary are compared in Exhibit 11–2 under parent company and entity theories. In examining the working papers, recall that contemporary theory is the same as parent company theory in matters relating to the initial consolidation of subsidiary assets and liabilities.

The comparative working papers in Exhibit 11–2 begin with separate balance sheets of the affiliated companies and use established procedures for consolidating the separate balance sheets. Although the working papers could be modified under parent company theory to reflect the minority interest among the liabilities, this modification does not seem necessary. Such classification differences can be reflected in the consolidated statements without changing working paper procedures. Under parent company theory, 90% of the excess of fair value over book value of identifiable net assets is allocated to identifiable assets and liabilities, and the $58,500 excess of investment cost over fair value acquired is allocated to goodwill. Minority interest of $12,000 for parent company theory is equal to 10% of the $120,000 book value of

---

[4]Under the "economic unit concept—purchased goodwill" approach, Sandy's identifiable assets and liabilities at acquisition would be reported at their fair values (as in entity theory), but only purchased goodwill ($58,500 as in parent company theory) would be reported.

PEDRICH CORPORATION AND SUBSIDIARY
CONSOLIDATED BALANCE SHEET WORKING PAPERS AT JANUARY 1, 20X2

	Pedrich	90% Sandy	Adjustments and Eliminations		Consolidated
Parent Company Theory					
Assets					
Cash	$ 22,000	$ 5,000			$ 27,000
Accounts receivable—net	80,000	30,000	b 4,500		114,500
Inventories	90,000	40,000	b 9,000		139,000
Other current assets	20,000	10,000			30,000
Plant assets—net	220,000	60,000	b 18,000		298,000
Investment in Sandy	198,000			a 198,000	
Goodwill			b 58,500		58,500
Unamortized excess			a 90,000	b 90,000	
Total assets	$630,000	$145,000			$667,000
Liabilities and Equity					
Liabilities	$ 80,000	$ 25,000			$105,000
Capital stock	400,000	100,000	a 100,000		400,000
Retained earnings	150,000	20,000	a 20,000		150,000
Minority interest				a 12,000	12,000
Total equities	$630,000	$145,000			$667,000
Entity Theory					
Assets					
Cash	$ 22,000	$ 5,000			$ 27,000
Accounts receivable—net	80,000	30,000	b 5,000		115,000
Inventories	90,000	40,000	b 10,000		140,000
Other current assets	20,000	10,000			30,000
Plant assets—net	220,000	60,000	b 20,000		300,000
Investment in Sandy	198,000			a 198,000	
Goodwill			b 65,000		65,000
Unamortized excess			a 100,000	b 100,000	
Total assets	$630,000	$145,000			$677,000
Liabilities and Equity					
Liabilities	$ 80,000	$ 25,000			$105,000
Capital stock	400,000	100,000	a 100,000		400,000
Retained earnings	150,000	20,000	a 20,000		150,000
Minority interest				a 22,000	22,000
Total equities	$630,000	$145,000			$677,000

Exhibit 11–2 *Balance Sheet Working Paper Comparisons*

Sandy's net assets at the time of acquisition. Under entity theory, the full excess of fair value over book value is assigned to identifiable net assets, and the excess of implied value over fair value is entered as goodwill. The $22,000 minority interest is 10% of the implied value of Sandy's net assets.

Consolidated assets under parent company theory consist of the book value of combined assets plus 90% of the excess of the fair value of Sandy's assets over their book value. Under entity theory, consolidated assets consist of the book value of Pedrich's assets plus the fair value of Sandy's assets. Although all assets of Sandy are consolidated at their fair values, total consolidated assets do not reflect fair values under either theory because the assets of the parent company are not revalued at the time of a business combination.

Consolidation After Acquisition

Differences between parent company theory and entity theory can be explained further by examining the operations of Pedrich Corporation and Sandy Corporation for 20X2. The following assumptions are made:

1 Sandy's net income and dividends for 20X2 are $35,000 and $10,000, respectively.
2 The excess of fair value over book value of Sandy's accounts receivable and inventories at January 1, 20X2 is realized during 20X2.
3 Sandy's plant assets are being depreciated at a 5% annual rate, and goodwill from consolidation is to be amortized over a 10-year period.

Equity Method   Under these assumptions, Pedrich records $11,250 investment income from Sandy for 20X2, computed under the equity method as follows:

Share of Sandy's net income ($35,000 × 90%)	$31,500
Less: Realization of excess allocated to receivables ($5,000 × 90%)	(4,500)
Realization of excess allocated to inventories ($10,000 × 90%)	(9,000)
Depreciation on excess allocated to plant assets ($20,000 × 90%) ÷ 20 years	(900)
Amortization of goodwill ($65,000 × 90%) ÷ 10 years	(5,850)
Income from Sandy for 20X2	$11,250

Pedrich's investment in Sandy account under the equity method has a balance of $200,250 at December 31, 20X2. This investment balance consists of the $198,000 investment cost, plus $11,250 investment income for 20X2, less $9,000 dividends received from Sandy during 20X2. Accounting under the equity method is not affected by the viewpoint adopted for consolidating the financial statements of affiliated companies, therefore, *the separate statements of Pedrich and Sandy will be the same at December 31, 20X2, regardless of the theory adopted.*

Consolidation Procedures   Consolidated net income under parent company theory is the same as the income allocated to parent company stockholders under entity theory. Therefore, the differences between parent company and entity theories lie solely in the manner of consolidating parent and subsidiary financial statements, and in reporting the financial position and results of operations in the consolidated financial statements. These differences are reflected in consolidation working papers for Pedrich Corporation and Subsidiary under parent company theory in Exhibit 11–3 and under entity theory in Exhibit 11–4. Again, the working paper procedures have not been modified to reflect differences in financial statement classification. Differences in financial statement presentation for Pedrich Corporation and Subsidiary are illustrated in Exhibits 11–5 and 11–6, which show financial statements prepared from the working papers.

In comparing the consolidation working papers under parent company theory in Exhibit 11–3 with those under entity theory in Exhibit 11–4, note that the working paper adjustment and elimination entries have the same debit and credit items, but the amounts are different for all working paper entries other than entry a. Accounting for the subsidiary investment under the equity method is the same for both consolidation

PEDRICH CORPORATION AND SUBSIDIARY
CONSOLIDATION WORKING PAPERS—YEAR ENDED DECEMBER 31, 20X2

	Pedrich	90% Sandy	Adjustments and Eliminations		Minority Interest	Consolidated Statements
Income Statement Sales	$600,000	$200,000				$800,000
Income from Sandy	11,250		a	11,250		
Cost of sales	(300,000)	(120,000)	c	9,000		(429,000)
Operating expenses	(211,250)	(45,000)	c d e	4,500 900 5,850		(267,500)
Minority income†					$ 3,500	(3,500)
Net income	$100,000	$ 35,000				$100,000
Retained Earnings Retained earnings	$150,000	$ 20,000	b	20,000		$150,000
Net income	100,000√	35,000√				100,000
Dividends	(80,000)	(10,000)	a	9,000	(1,000)	(80,000)
Retained earnings December 31, 20X2	$170,000	$ 45,000				$170,000
Balance Sheet Cash	$ 29,750	$ 13,000				$ 42,750
Accounts receivable—net	90,000	32,000				122,000
Inventories	100,000	48,000				148,000
Other current assets	30,000	17,000				47,000
Plant assets—net	200,000	57,000	c 18,000	d 900		274,100
Investment in Sandy	200,250			a 2,250 b 198,000		
Goodwill			c 58,500	e 5,850		52,650
Unamortized excess			b 90,000	c 90,000		
	$650,000	$167,000				$686,500
Liabilities	$ 80,000	$ 22,000				$102,000
Capital stock	400,000	100,000	b 100,000			400,000
Retained earnings	170,000√	45,000√				170,000
	$650,000	$167,000				
Minority interest January 1, 20X2				b 12,000	12,000	
Minority interest December 31, 20X2					$14,500	14,500
						$686,500

† Minority interest income $35,000 × 10% = $3,500.

Exhibit 11–3   *Parent Company Theory*

PEDRICH CORPORATION AND SUBSIDIARY
CONSOLIDATION WORKING PAPERS—YEAR ENDED DECEMBER 31, 20X2

	Pedrich	90% Sandy	Adjustments and Eliminations		Minority Interest	Consolidated Statements
Income Statement Sales	$600,000	$200,000				$800,000
Income from Sandy	11,250		a 11,250			
Cost of sales	(300,000)	(120,000)	c 10,000			(430,000)
Operating expenses	(211,250)	(45,000)	c 5,000 d 1,000 e 6,500			(268,750)
Minority income†					$ 1,250	(1,250)
Net income	$100,000	$ 35,000				$100,000
Retained Earnings Retained earnings	$150,000	$ 20,000	b 20,000			$150,000
Net income	100,000√	35,000√				100,000
Dividends	(80,000)	(10,000)		a 9,000	(1,000)	(80,000)
Retained earnings December 31, 20X2	$170,000	$ 45,000				$170,000
Balance Sheet Cash	$ 29,750	$ 13,000				$ 42,750
Accounts receivable—net	90,000	32,000				122,000
Inventories	100,000	48,000				148,000
Other current assets	30,000	17,000				47,000
Plant assets—net	200,000	57,000	c 20,000	d 1,000		276,000
Investment in Sandy	200,250			a 2,250 b 198,000		
Goodwill			c 65,000	e 6,500		58,500
Unamortized excess			b 100,000	c 100,000		
	$650,000	$167,000				$694,250
Liabilities	$ 80,000	$ 22,000				$102,000
Capital stock	400,000	100,000	b 100,000			400,000
Retained earnings	170,000√	45,000√				170,000
	$650,000	$167,000				
Minority interest January 1, 20X2				b 22,000	22,000	
Minority interest December 31, 20X2					$22,250	22,250
						$694,250

† Minority interest income ($35,000 − $22,500 amortization) × 10% = $1,250

Exhibit 11–4 Entity Theory

PEDRICH CORPORATION AND SUBSIDIARY
CONSOLIDATED INCOME STATEMENTS
FOR THE YEAR ENDED DECEMBER 31, 20X2

Parent Company Theory

Sales		$800,000
Less: Cost of sales	$429,000	
Operating expenses	267,500	
Minority interest income	3,500	
Total expenses		700,000
Consolidated net income		$100,000

Entity Theory

Sales		$800,000
Less: Cost of sales	$430,000	
Operating expenses	268,750	
Total expenses		698,750
Total consolidated net income		$101,250
Distribution: to minority stockholders	$ 1,250	
to majority stockholders	$100,000	

Contemporary Theory

Sales		$800,000
Less: Cost of sales	$429,000	
Operating expenses	267,500	
Total expenses		696,500
Total consolidated income		103,500
Less: Minority interest income		3,500
Consolidated net income		$100,000

Exhibit 11–5   *Consolidated Income Statements Under Alternative Theories*

PEDRICH CORPORATION AND SUBSIDIARY
CONSOLIDATED BALANCE SHEETS
AT DECEMBER 31, 20X2

	Parent Company Theory	Entity Theory	Contemporary Theory
Assets			
Cash	$ 42,750	$ 42,750	$ 42,750
Accounts receivable—net	122,000	122,000	122,000
Inventories	148,000	148,000	148,000
Other current assets	47,000	47,000	47,000
Total current assets	359,750	359,750	359,750
Plant assets—net	274,100	276,000	274,100
Goodwill	52,650	58,500	52,650
Total noncurrent assets	326,750	334,500	326,750
Total assets	$686,500	$694,250	$686,500
Liabilities and Equity			
Liabilities	$102,000	$102,000	$102,000
Minority interest	14,500	—	—
Total liabilities	116,500	102,000	102,000
Capital stock	400,000	400,000	400,000
Retained earnings	170,000	170,000	170,000
Minority interest	—	22,250	14,500
Total stockholders' equity	570,000	592,250	584,500
Total equities	$686,500	$694,250	$686,500

Exhibit 11–6   *Consolidated Balance Sheets Under Alternative Theories*

theories, so the entry to eliminate investment income and intercompany dividends, and to adjust the investment account to its beginning-of-the-period balance (entry a), is exactly the same under parent company theory as under entity theory.

The remaining adjustment and elimination entries in Exhibit 11–3 under parent company theory are the same as under the contemporary theory used in earlier chapters. Entry b eliminates reciprocal subsidiary equity amounts, establishes beginning minority interest at book value ($120,000 × 10%) and enters the unamortized excess. Entry c then allocates the excess of investment cost over book value acquired: $9,000 to cost of sales (for undervalued inventory items realized during 20X2), $4,500 to operating expense (for undervalued receivables realized during 20X2), $18,000 to plant assets (for undervalued plant assets at the beginning of 20X2), and $58,500 to goodwill (for unamortized goodwill at the beginning of 20X2). Entries d and e reflect current depreciation on the excess allocated to plant assets ($18,000 × 5%) and current amortization on the amount allocated to goodwill ($58,500 ÷ 10 years), respectively. Minority interest income of $3,500 is simply 10% of Sandy's $35,000 reported net income.

Entries b, c, d, and e in Exhibit 11–4 under entity theory have the same objective as those for the same items under parent company theory, except for amounts that relate to the minority interest. Beginning minority interest under entity theory is $22,000, equal to 10% of the $220,000 implied total value of Sandy Corporation at January 1, 20X2. Beginning minority interest under entity theory is $10,000 greater than beginning minority interest of $12,000 under parent company theory. The additional $10,000 relates to the allocation of 100% of the excess fair value over book value of Sandy's net assets at acquisition under entity theory. In other words, working paper entry b under entity theory is equivalent to entry b under parent company theory, plus the additional $10,000 unamortized excess applicable to minority interest.

b	Unamortized excess	$100,000	
	Capital stock	100,000	
	Retained earnings January 1, 20X2	20,000	
	Investment in Sandy		$198,000
	Minority interest January 1, 20X2		22,000

To eliminate reciprocal investment and equity balances, establish beginning minority interest, and enter the unamortized excess amount.

Entry c under entity theory is equivalent to entry c under parent company theory, plus the additional excess fair value over book value amounts.

c	Cost of sales	$ 10,000	
	Operating expenses	5,000	
	Plant assets	20,000	
	Goodwill	65,000	
	Unamortized excess		$100,000

To allocate unamortized excess to identifiable assets and goodwill.

Working paper entry d for depreciation on the excess allocated to plant assets is $1,000 under entity theory, compared with $900 under parent company theory. The $100 difference is simply the 5% depreciation rate applied to the additional $2,000 allocated to plant assets under entity theory. Current amortization of goodwill under entity theory (entry e) is $6,500, compared with $5,850 under parent company theory. The $650 difference is equal to one-tenth of the extra $6,500 assigned to goodwill under entity theory.

Minority interest income under entity theory is $1,250, consisting of 10% of Sandy's $35,000 income, less 10% of the $22,500 amortization on the $100,000 implied value/book value differential. Alternatively, minority interest income can be computed as follows:

Share of Sandy's reported income $35,000 × 10%	$3,500
Less: Operating expenses for realization of excess allocated to receivables $5,000 × 10%	(500)
Cost of sales for realization of excess allocated to inventory $10,000 × 10%	(1,000)
Depreciation on excess allocated to plant assets $20,000 ÷ 20 years × 10%	(100)
Amortization of goodwill $65,000 ÷ 10 years × 10%	(650)
Minority interest income	$1,250

Comparison of Consolidated Income Statements   The additional expenses that are deducted in determining total consolidated net income under entity theory can be summarized as follows:

	Parent Company Theory	Entity Theory
Operating expenses (for receivables)	$ 4,500	$ 5,000
Cost of sales (for inventory)	9,000	10,000
Operating expenses (for depreciation)	900	1,000
Operating expenses (for amortization)	5,850	6,500
	$20,250	$22,500

The $2,250 additional expenses ($22,500 − $20,250) under entity theory are exactly offset by the lower minority interest income ($3,500 − $1,250). Thus, income to the parent company stockholders is the same under the two theories, even though there are differences in the amounts reported and in the way the amounts are disclosed in the consolidated income statements. These differences are shown in Exhibit 11–5, which compares consolidated income statements for Pedrich Corporation and Subsidiary under parent company theory, entity theory, and contemporary theory.

Consolidated net income under parent company theory is the same as under contemporary theory, however, contemporary theory does not show minority interest income as an expense. The reporting of income under entity theory shows a final amount for "Total Consolidated Net Income" of $103,500 and distribution of that income to minority and parent company stockholders. Although the amounts shown for Pedrich Corporation and Subsidiary are identical under parent company and contemporary theories, this equivalence would not have existed if there had been unrealized profits from upstream sales or constructive gains or losses from intercompany purchases of subsidiary debt. Consolidation procedures for these items are the same under contemporary theory as under entity theory.

The reporting formats under the three consolidation theories vary somewhat, but it may be helpful to note the following relationships:

1 If a subsidiary investment is made at book value and the book values of individual assets and liabilities are equal to their fair values, the income statement amounts should be the same under entity theory as under contemporary theory.
2 In the absence of intercompany transactions, the income statement amounts should be the same under parent company theory as under contemporary theory.
3 In the absence of minority interests, the income statement amounts should be the same under all three theories.

Comparison of Consolidated Balance Sheets   Comparative balance sheets for Pedrich Corporation and Subsidiary at December 31, 20X2 are illustrated in Exhibit 11–6 under each of the three theories. The amount of total assets is the same under parent company and contemporary theories but is greater under entity theory. The difference in total assets is $7,750 ($694,250 − $686,500), and it consists of the unamortized excess of implied value over book value of Sandy's net assets. This difference relates to goodwill of $5,850 ($58,500 − $52,650) and plant assets of $1,900 ($276,000 − $274,100).

Total liabilities and equity are the same under parent company theory and contemporary theory, but liabilities are $14,500 greater under parent company theory because minority interest is classified as a liability. Stockholders' equity is $14,500 greater under contemporary theory because minority interest is classified as a part of stockholders' equity.

The difference between total liabilities and equity under the entity and contemporary theories lies solely in the $7,750 ($22,250 − $14,500) greater minority interest under entity theory. As in the case of the income generalizations, balance sheet amounts under the parent company and contemporary theories will be the same in the absence of intercompany transactions, and under entity and contemporary theories in the absence of a difference between investment cost and book value acquired. In the absence of minority interests, all balance sheet amounts should be identical under the three theories.

Other Views of Minority Interest   Some accountants believe that minority interest should not appear as a separate line item in consolidated financial statements. One suggestion for eliminating minority interest from consolidated statements is to report total consolidated income as the bottom line in the consolidated income statements, with separate *footnote disclosure* of majority and minority interests in the income. Consistent treatment in the consolidated balance sheet would require total consolidated equity to be reported as a single line item, with separate footnote disclosure of the equity of majority and minority interests.

Another suggestion for excluding reference to minority interest in consolidated financial statements is to consolidate only the majority-owned portion of the revenues, expenses, assets, and liabilities of less-than-100%-owned subsidiaries. Proportional consolidation is discussed in the last section of this chapter under accounting for corporate joint ventures.

PUSH-DOWN ACCOUNTING AND OTHER BASIS CONSIDERATIONS

Under the contemporary, entity, and parent company theories discussed in the first section of this chapter, cost/book value differentials were allocated to the individual identifiable assets and liabilities and goodwill by working paper entries in the process of consolidating the financial statements of the parent and subsidiary. The books of the subsidiary were not affected by the price paid by the parent for its ownership interest.

In certain situations, the SEC requires that the fair values of the acquired subsidiary's assets and liabilities, which represent the parent company's cost basis under the provisions of *APB Opinion No. 16*, be recorded in the separate financial statements of the purchased subsidiary. In other words, the values are "pushed down" to the subsidiary's statements.[5] The SEC requires the use of push-down accounting for SEC filings when a subsidiary is substantially wholly owned (usually 97%) with no substantial publicly held debt or preferred stock outstanding.

The SEC's argument is that when the parent controls the form of ownership of an entity, the basis of accounting for purchased assets and liabilities should be the same, regardless of whether the entity continues to exist or is merged into the parent's operations. However, when a subsidiary has outstanding public debt or preferred stock, or when a significant minority interest exists, the parent company may not be able to control the form of ownership. The SEC encourages push-down accounting in these circumstances, but does not require it.

The AICPA Issues Paper "Push-Down Accounting" (October 30, 1979) describes **push-down accounting** as

> the establishment of a new accounting and reporting basis for an entity in its separate financial statements, based on a purchase transaction in the voting stock of the entity, that results in a substantial change of ownership of the outstanding voting stock of the entity.

---

[5] *SEC Staff Accounting Bulletin*, No. 54, 1983. For further clarification of the SEC's position, see *Staff Accounting Bulletin*, No. 73, 1987.

When push-down accounting is not used in an acquisition, the allocation of the purchase price to identifiable net assets and goodwill is done in the consolidation working papers. The consolidated financial statements reflect the purchase allocation. If the subsidiary records the allocation in its financial statements under push-down accounting, the consolidation process is simplified.

Push-down accounting is controversial only in the separate company statements of the subsidiary that are issued to minority interests, creditors, and other interested parties. Critics of push-down accounting argue that the purchase transaction between the parent company/investor and the subsidiary's old stockholders does not justify a new accounting basis for the subsidiary's assets and liabilities under historical cost principles. The subsidiary is not a party to the transaction—it receives no new funds; it sells no assets. Proponents counter that the price paid by the new owners provides the most relevant basis for measuring the subsidiary's assets, liabilities, and results of operations.

Push-down accounting is not consistently applied among the supporters of the concept, although, in practice, a subsidiary's assets are usually revalued on a proportional basis. What percentage of minority interest constitutes a significant minority interest that would preclude the use of push-down accounting? Should the allocation be done on a proportional basis if less than a 100% change in ownership has occurred?[6] These are questions in need of authoritative answers.

In the illustration that follows, the Pedrich-Sandy example is extended using both a proportional allocation for the purchase of a 90% interest in Sandy (a parent company theory approach) and a 100% allocation, in which the entity's market value as a whole is imputed from the purchase price of the 90% interest (an entity theory approach).

Push-Down Procedures in Year of Acquisition

Recall that Pedrich acquired its 90% interest for $198,000 cash on January 1, 20X2 (see page 416). If push-down accounting is used and only 90% of Sandy's identifiable net assets are revalued (parent company theory), the $90,000 cost/book value differential is allocated as follows:

	Book Value	Push-Down Adjustment	Book Value After Push Down
Cash	$ 5,000	—	$ 5,000
Accounts receivable—net	30,000	$ 4,500	34,500
Inventory	40,000	9,000	49,000
Other current assets	10,000	—	10,000
Plant assets—net	60,000	18,000	78,000
Goodwill	—	58,500	58,500
	$145,000	$ 90,000	$235,000
Liabilities	$ 25,000	—	$ 25,000
Capital stock	100,000	—	100,000
Retained earnings	20,000	$(20,000)	—
Push-down capital	—	110,000	110,000
	$145,000	$ 90,000	$235,000

The push-down adjustment on Sandy's separate books is recorded as follows:

Accounts receivable	$ 4,500	
Inventory	9,000	
Plant assets	18,000	
Goodwill	58,500	
Retained earnings	20,000	
Push-down capital		$110,000

---

[6]Colley and Volkan argue that once an entity controls another entity through stock ownership of more than 50%, the minority stockholders are not owners in the usual sense. There is only one owner, the parent, and the minority holders are "investors." They contend that this argument supports the use of push-down accounting for all majority-owned subsidiaries and, further, that it supports a total revaluation approach (in other words, imputing values for 100% of the subsidiary's net assets). See J. Ron Colley and Ara G. Volkan, "Business Combinations: Goodwill and Push-down Accounting," *The CPA Journal* (August 1988), p. 74.

If a total value of $220,000 is imputed from the purchase price of the 90% interest in Sandy under entity theory ($198,000 cost ÷ 90%), the $100,000 excess is pushed down on Sandy's books as follows:

	Book Value	Push-Down Adjustment	Book Value After Push Down
Cash	$ 5,000	—	$ 5,000
Accounts receivable—net	30,000	$ 5,000	35,000
Inventory	40,000	10,000	50,000
Other current assets	10,000	—	10,000
Plant assets—net	60,000	20,000	80,000
Goodwill	—	65,000	65,000
	$145,000	$100,000	$245,000
Liabilities	$ 25,000	—	$ 25,000
Capital stock	100,000	—	100,000
Retained earnings	20,000	$(20,000)	—
Push-down capital	—	120,000	120,000
	$145,000	$100,000	$245,000

The entry to record the 100% push-down adjustment on Sandy's separate books is:

Accounts receivable	$ 5,000	
Inventory	10,000	
Plant assets	20,000	
Goodwill	65,000	
Retained earnings	20,000	
Push-down capital		$120,000

Observe that the balance of Sandy's retained earnings account is transferred to push-down capital, regardless of whether the push down is for 90% or 100% of the fair value/book value differential. This treatment is basic to push-down accounting, which requires a new accounting and reporting basis for the acquired entity. Push-down capital is an additional paid-in capital account. It includes the revaluation of subsidiary identifiable net assets and goodwill, based upon the price paid to acquire the subsidiary, and the subsidiary's retained earnings account balance, which is eliminated under the new entity concept of push-down accounting.

Consolidated balance sheet working papers to illustrate the effect of the push-down adjustments are presented in Exhibit 11–7. The balance sheet worksheet at the top of the exhibit reflects the 90% push-down adjustment that is compatible with parent company theory, and the worksheet at the bottom reflects the 100% push-down adjustment that is compatible with entity theory. Because the push-down adjustments are included in Sandy's separate balance sheets in Exhibit 11–7, the consolidation procedures are greatly simplified in relation to those illustrated in Exhibit 11–2. The simplification results from not having to allocate unamortized cost/book value differentials in the working papers under push-down accounting. The consolidated balance sheet amounts, however, are identical in Exhibit 11–7 under push-down accounting and in Exhibit 11–2, where the subsidiary balance sheets are maintained on an original cost basis.

Push-Down Procedures in Year After Acquisition

Consolidated financial statement working papers for Pedrich and Sandy corporations under push-down accounting procedures are illustrated for the year ended December 31, 20X2 in Exhibits 11–8 and 11–9. Exhibit 11–8 reflects the 90% push-down adjustment of parent company theory, and Exhibit 11–9 reflects the 100% push-down adjustment under entity theory. In both exhibits, the consolidation procedures are greatly simplified in relation to the comparable working papers for Pedrich and Sandy shown in Exhibits 11–3 and 11–4. As in the case of consolidated balance sheets, however, the amounts shown in the consolidated financial statements are identical.

In the consolidation working paper of Exhibit 11–9 (entity theory), the minority interest income of $1,250 is equal to 10% of Sandy's $12,500 net income as mea-

PEDRICH CORPORATION AND SUBSIDIARY
CONSOLIDATED BALANCE SHEET WORKING PAPERS AT JANUARY 1, 20X2

	Pedrich	90% Sandy	Adjustments and Eliminations	Consolidated
Parent Company Theory				
Assets				
Cash	$ 22,000	$ 5,000		$ 27,000
Accounts receivable—net	80,000	34,500		114,500
Inventories	90,000	49,000		139,000
Other current assets	20,000	10,000		30,000
Plant assets—net	220,000	78,000		298,000
Investment in Sandy	198,000		a 198,000	
Goodwill		58,500		58,500
Total assets	$630,000	$235,000		$667,000
Liabilities and Equity				
Liabilities	$ 80,000	$ 25,000		$105,000
Capital stock	400,000	100,000	a 100,000	400,000
Retained earnings	150,000	0		150,000
Push-down capital—Sandy		110,000	a 110,000	
Minority interest			a 12,000	12,000
Total equities	$630,000	$235,000		$667,000
Entity Theory				
Assets				
Cash	$ 22,000	$ 5,000		$ 27,000
Accounts receivable—net	80,000	35,000		115,000
Inventories	90,000	50,000		140,000
Other current assets	20,000	10,000		30,000
Plant assets—net	220,000	80,000		300,000
Investment in Sandy	198,000		a 198,000	
Goodwill		65,000		65,000
Total assets	$630,000	$245,000		$677,000
Liabilities and Equity				
Liabilities	$ 80,000	$ 25,000		$105,000
Capital stock	400,000	100,000	a 100,000	400,000
Retained earnings	150,000	0		150,000
Push-down capital—Sandy		120,000	a 120,000	
Minority interest			a 22,000	22,000
Total equities	$630,000	$245,000		$677,000

Exhibit 11–7   *Push-Down Accounting: Parent Company Versus Entity Approach*

PEDRICH CORPORATION AND SUBSIDIARY
CONSOLIDATION WORKING PAPERS—YEAR ENDED DECEMBER 31, 20X2

	Pedrich	90% Sandy	Adjustments and Eliminations	Minority Interest	Consolidated Statements
Income Statement					
Sales	$600,000	$200,000			$800,000
Income from Sandy	11,250		a 11,250		
Cost of sales	(300,000)	(129,000)			(429,000)
Operating expenses	(211,250)	(56,250)			(267,500)
Minority income				$ 3,500	(3,500)
Net income	$100,000	$ 14,750			$100,000
Retained Earnings					
Retained earnings	$150,000	$ 0			$150,000
Net income	100,000√	14,750√			100,000
Dividends	(80,000)	(10,000)	a 9,000	(1,000)	(80,000)
Retained earnings December 31, 20X2	$170,000	$ 4,750			$170,000
Balance Sheet					
Cash	$29,750	$ 13,000			$ 42,750
Accounts receivable—net	90,000	32,000			122,000
Inventories	100,000	48,000			148,000
Other current assets	30,000	17,000			47,000
Plant assets—net	200,000	74,100			274,100
Investment in Sandy	200,250		a 2,250 b 198,000		
Goodwill		52,650			52,650
	$650,000	$236,750			$686,500
Liabilities	$ 80,000	$ 22,000			$102,000
Capital stock	400,000	100,000	b 100,000		400,000
Retained earnings	170,000√	4,750√			170,000
Push-down capital—Sandy		110,000	b 110,000		
	$650,000	$236,750			
Minority interest January 1, 20X2			b 12,000	12,000	
Minority interest December 31, 20X2				$14,500	14,500
					$686,500

Exhibit 11–8   Push-Down Accounting—Parent Company Theory

PEDRICH CORPORATION AND SUBSIDIARY
CONSOLIDATION WORKING PAPERS—YEAR ENDED DECEMBER 31, 20X2

	Pedrich	90% Sandy	Adjustments and Eliminations	Minority Interest	Consolidated Statements
Income Statement Sales	$600,000	$200,000			$800,000
Income from Sandy	11,250		a 11,250		
Cost of sales	(300,000)	(130,000)			(430,000)
Operating expenses	(211,250)	(57,500)			(268,750)
Minority income				$ 1,250	(1,250)
Net income	$100,000	$ 12,500			$100,000
Retained Earnings Retained earnings	$150,000	$ 0			$150,000
Net income	100,000√	12,500√			100,000
Dividends	(80,000)	(10,000)	a 9,000	(1,000)	(80,000)
Retained earnings December 31, 20X2	$170,000	$ 2,500			$170,000
Balance Sheet Cash	$ 29,750	$ 13,000			$ 42,750
Accounts receivable—net	90,000	32,000			122,000
Inventories	100,000	48,000			148,000
Other current assets	30,000	17,000			47,000
Plant assets—net	200,000	76,000			276,000
Investment in Sandy	200,250		a 2,250 b 198,000		
Goodwill		58,500			58,500
	$650,000	$244,500			$694,250
Liabilities	$ 80,000	$ 22,000			$102,000
Capital stock	400,000	100,000	b 100,000		400,000
Retained earnings	170,000√	2,500√			170,000
Push-down capital—Sandy		120,000	b 120,000		
	$650,000	$244,500			
Minority interest January 1, 20X2			b 22,000	22,000	
Minority interest December 31, 20X2				$22,250	22,250
					$694,250

Exhibit 11–9 Push-Down Accounting—Entity Theory

sured under push-down accounting procedures. Similarly, the $22,250 minority interest at December 31, 20X2 is equal to 10% of Sandy's $222,500 stockholders' equity on that date. These minority interest items are determined under standard consolidation procedures. By contrast, in Exhibit 11–8 (parent company theory), the $3,500 minority interest income for 20X2 and the $14,500 minority interest at December 31, 20X2 do not have a direct reference to the $14,750 net income of Sandy or the $214,750 stockholders' equity of Sandy, as shown in Sandy's separate income statement and balance sheet under 90% push-down accounting. This is a problem that arises in the use of push-down accounting for a less-than-100%-owned subsidiary, where only the parent's percentage interest is pushed down on the subsidiary's books. In this case, separate cost-based records must be maintained by the subsidiary. The minority interest amount in Exhibit 11–8 can be determined directly from Sandy's separate cost-based statements as shown in Exhibit 11–3 (page 420). Minority shareholders are not expected to get meaningful information from consolidated financial statements, therefore, the 100% push-down approach under entity theory may be preferable, especially when the affiliated group has multiple partially owned subsidiaries.

Leveraged Buyouts

In a **leveraged buyout** (LBO), an investor group (often including company management, an investment banker, and financial institutions) acquires a company (Company A) from the public shareholders in a transaction financed with very little equity and very large amounts of debt. Usually, the investor group raises the money for the buyout by investing perhaps 10% of their own money and borrowing the rest. A holding company may be formed to acquire the shares of Company A. Usually debt raised by the investor group to finance the LBO is partially secured by Company A's own assets and is serviced with funds generated by Company A's operations and/or the sale of its assets. Because the loans are secured by Company A's assets, banks loaning money to the investor group often require that the debt appear on Company A's financial statements. If the previous owners were paid a high premium for their stock, which is often the case, and book values, rather than fair values, of the assets and liabilities are carried forward to the balance sheet of the new company (the acquired Company A), the debt incurred in the LBO may cause the new company's financial condition to look worse than it is. The popularity of LBOs is one reason many accountants support a change to push-down accounting for acquisitions, including LBOs, that would allow the assets of the acquired firm to be written up on its financial statements to reflect the purchase price.

For several years, the SEC and the FASB's Emerging Issues Task Force (EITF) wrestled with the question of whether fair values or book values (predecessor basis) should be carried forward in LBOs. Answers were finally provided in May 1989 in the EITF *Issue No. 88-16*, "Basis in Leveraged Buyout Transactions." The structure of a buyout influences the accounting basis. For example, a holding company may be used to acquire the net assets of Company A, a holding company may be used to acquire the equity of Company A, or an investor group may acquire Company A without using a holding company. The EITF consensus applied to LBOs in which a holding company is used to acquire all the equity of an operating company in a highly leveraged acquisition. The EITF sets forth tests for determining whether the LBO results in a change of the controlling interest. If there has been a change in control, a change in accounting basis is generally appropriate. The consensus provides complex rules based on the residual interest of each continuing shareholder for determining the accounting basis for the assets and liabilities carried forward to the books of the new entity. The final valuation on the subsidiary's books may be pre-LBO book values, fair values, or something in between, for example, 95% fair value and 5% book (predecessor) value.

Criticism of the consensus generally centers on its complexity, but it has also been challenged on conceptual grounds. In particular, critics do not like the resulting accounting basis if it reflects part fair value and part book value. The EITF argues that the method puts substance ahead of form—the new entity has new controlling shareholders and is similar to a purchase business combination.

Another Accounting Basis Solution

Corporations have tried to structure business combinations in ways to avoid goodwill. A corporation acquires a controlling interest in another company (Target), and, in the same transaction, Target issues additional shares to the parent in exchange for the parent's interest in a subsidiary. In substance, the parent company is selling its subsidiary to Target as part of the price of acquiring Target. The argument is that this is a combination of enterprises under common control. Therefore, the combination would not be a purchase and the transaction would be accounted for using historical costs.[7] The FASB's EITF addressed these combinations in *EITF Issue No. 90-13*, "Accounting for Simultaneous Common Control Mergers," and concluded that:

- The parent should account for the transfer of the subsidiary to Target as a purchase of Target under *APB Opinion No. 16*. Obtaining control of Target and the transfer of the subsidiary to Target cannot be separated and should be treated as one transaction.
- The parent should account for the transaction as a partial sale of the subsidiary (to the minority shareholders of Target) and a partial acquisition of Target. The parent should recognize gain or loss on the portion of the subsidiary sold.
- The parent should step up Target's assets and liabilities to the extent acquired by the parent and the subsidiary's assets and liabilities to the extent the ownership interest in the subsidiary was sold.

This structure for business combinations did not avoid purchase accounting and the resulting goodwill. The pressure to search for ways to avoid recording goodwill diminished in 1993 because goodwill became tax deductible. However, it is likely that corporations will continue to search for a structure that will avoid goodwill because of its financial reporting effects.

JOINT VENTURES

A **joint venture** is a form of partnership that originated with the maritime trading expeditions of the Greeks and Romans. The objective was to combine management participants and capital contributors in undertakings limited to the completion of specific trading projects. In recent times the joint venture has taken many different forms, such as partnership and corporate, domestic and foreign, and temporary as well as relatively permanent.

A common type of joint venture of the temporary type is the formation of syndicates of investment bankers to purchase securities from an issuing corporation and market them to the public. The joint venture enables several participants to share in the risks and rewards of undertakings that would be too large or too risky for a single venturer. It also enables them to combine technology, markets, and human resources to enhance the profit potential of all participants. Other areas in which joint ventures are common are land sales, oil exploration and drilling, and major construction projects.

New areas and uses for the joint venture form of business organization continue to emerge. For example, by mid-1994 in the telecommunications area nearly all major companies were seeking joint venture partners to gain size and capital. The purposes of the proposed joint ventures were to amass capital in order to bid in the multibillion-dollar auction for personal communications services (PCS) licenses and to build nationwide wireless telephone networks. One perceived advantage of these joint venture alliances is avoidance of expensive acquisition prices.[8]

Nature of Joint Ventures

A **joint venture** is a business entity that is owned, operated, and jointly controlled by a small group of investors (**venturers**) for the conduct of a specific business undertaking that provides mutual benefit for each of the venturers. It is common for each venturer to be active in the management of the venture and to participate in important decisions that typically require the consent of each venturer irrespective of ownership in-

---

[7]Under this assumption, the transaction would be accounted for under *Interpretation No. 39 of APB Opinion No. 16*, "Transfers and Exchanges Between Companies under Common Control."

[8]*Mergers & Acquisitions* (September/October 1994), p. 7

terest. Ownership percentages vary widely, and unequal ownership interests in a specific venture are commonplace.

Organizational Structures of Joint Ventures

Joint ventures may be organized as corporations, partnerships, or undivided interests. These forms are defined in the AICPA's Statement of Position "Accounting for Investment in Real Estate Ventures" (SOP 78–9) as follows:

> **Corporate Joint Venture**—A corporation owned and operated by a small group of venturers to accomplish a mutually beneficial venture or project.
> **General Partnership**—An association in which each partner has unlimited liability.
> **Limited Partnership**—An association in which one or more general partners have unlimited liability and one or more partners have limited liability. A limited partnership is usually managed by the general partner or partners, subject to limitations, if any, imposed by the partnership agreement.
> **Undivided Interest**—An ownership arrangement in which two or more parties jointly own property and title is held individually to the extent of each party's interest.

Financial reporting requirements for the investors in ventures differ according to the organizational structures.

Accounting for Corporate Joint Ventures

Investors who can participate in the overall management of a *corporate joint venture* should report their investments as equity investments (one-line consolidations) under the provisions of *APB Opinion No. 18*. The approach for establishing significant influence in corporate joint ventures is quite different from that for most common stock investments because *each venturer* usually has to consent to *each significant venture decision*, thus establishing an ability to exercise significant influence regardless of ownership interest. Even so, when a venturer cannot exercise significant influence over its joint venture for whatever reason, its investment in the venture is accounted for by the *cost method*.

An investment in the common stock of a corporate joint venture that exceeds 50% of the venture's outstanding shares is a *subsidiary investment*, for which parent-subsidiary accounting and reporting requirements are applicable. A corporate joint venture that is more than 50%-owned by another entity is not considered a joint venture for purposes of applying the provisions of *APB Opinion No. 18*, even though it continues to be described as a joint venture in financial releases.

Corporate joint ventures are described in *Opinion No. 18*, paragraph 2d, as follows:

> "Corporate joint venture" refers to a corporation owned and operated by a small group of businesses (the "joint venturers") as a separate and specific business or project for the mutual benefit of the members of the group. A government may also be a member of the group. The purpose of a corporate joint venture frequently is to share risks and rewards in developing a new market, product or technology; to combine complementary technological knowledge; or to pool resources in developing production or other facilities. A corporate joint venture also usually provides an arrangement under which each joint venturer may participate, directly or indirectly, in the overall management of the joint venture. Joint venturers thus have an interest or relationship other than as passive investors. An entity which is a subsidiary of one of the "joint venturers" is not a corporate joint venture. The ownership of a corporate joint venture seldom changes, and its stock is usually not traded publicly. A minority public ownership, however, does not preclude a corporation from being a corporate joint venture.

Note that a subsidiary (more than 50%-owned) of a joint venturer is *not* a corporate joint venture under *APB Opinion No. 18*. Instead, it would have to be consolidated under the provisions of *FASB No. 94*, "Consolidation of All Majority-Owned Subsidiaries."

Opinion No. 18 concludes that investors in the common stock of corporate joint ventures should account for their investments by the equity method in consolidated financial statements. The equity method best enables the investors to reflect the underlying nature of the venture.[9]

---

[9]*APB Opinion No. 18*, "The Equity Method of Accounting for Investments in Common Stock," paragraph 16.

Investments in the common stock of joint ventures, or other investments accounted for by the equity method, may be material in relation to the financial position or results of operations of the joint venture investor. If so, it may be necessary for the investor to provide summarized information about the assets, liabilities, and results of operations of its investees in its own financial statements. The required disclosures should be presented *individually* for investments in joint ventures that are material in relation to the financial position or results of operations of the investor. Alternatively, the required disclosures can be *grouped* for investments that are material as a group, but are not material individually.

Accounting for Unincorporated Joint Ventures

Accounting Interpretation No. 2 of APB Opinion No. 18 addresses the applicability of *Opinion No. 18* to investments in partnerships and undivided interests in joint ventures. Although the provisions of *Opinion No. 18* apply only to investments in common stock, and, therefore, do not cover unincorporated ventures, *Interpretation No. 2* explains that many of the provisions of *Opinion No. 18* are appropriate in accounting for investments in unincorporated entities. For example, partnership profits and losses accrued by investor-partners are generally reflected in the partners' financial statements. Elimination of intercompany profit in accounting for a partnership interest also seems appropriate, as does providing for deferred income tax liabilities on profits accrued by partner-investors. An example of this type of joint venture is the creation of a defense business partnership between Harsco Corporation and FMC Corporation in 1994. The new partnership was named United Defense, L.P., and was formed by combining Harsco's BMY-Combat Systems Division with FMC's Defense Systems Group. The following partial financial statement note described the joint venture as follows:

> The consolidated financial statements include the accounts of Harsco Corporation and its majority-owned subsidiaries ("Company"). Investments in United Defense, L.P., a 40% owned partnership and other unconsolidated entities are accounted for on the equity method. The income of unconsolidated entities is on a pre-tax basis for United Defense, L.P. as it is a partnership, and net of taxes for all other unconsolidated entities.[10]

In the Harsco example, Harsco's ownership interest in the partnership was only 40%, and Harsco accounted for its interest under the equity method. In contrast, Southdown owned a 75% partnership interest in Kosmos Cement Company; the other 25% interest was owned by Lone Star Cement. Southdown included the following partial financial statement note in its annual report:

> Kosmos Cement Company (Kosmos Cement) is a partnership which includes a cement plant located in Kosmosdale, Kentucky and a cement plant located near Pittsburgh, Pennsylvania along with related terminals and facilities. The partnership is 25% owned by Lone Star Industries, Inc. (Lone Star) and operated and 75% owned by the Company [Southdown]. The Company's Consolidated Balance Sheet includes 100% of the assets and liabilities of Kosmos Cement. Lone Star's 25% interest in Kosmos Cement and earnings therefrom have been reflected as "Minority interest in consolidated joint venture" and "Minority interest in earnings of consolidated joint venture" on the Company's Consolidated Balance Sheet and Statement of Consolidated Earnings, respectively.[11]

The previous discussion of the applicability of *Opinion No. 18* to partnerships also applies to undivided interests in joint ventures, where the investor-venturer owns an undivided interest in each asset and is proportionately liable for its share of each liability. However, the provisions of *Opinion No. 18* do not apply in some industries that have specialized industry practices. For example, the established industry practice in oil and gas ventures is for the investor-venturer to account for its pro rata share of the assets, liabilities, revenues, and expenses of a joint venture in its own financial statements. This reporting procedure is referred to as **pro rata** or **proportionate consolidation**. USX Corporation includes a note in its Summary of Principal Accounting Policies that "Investments in unincorporated oil and gas joint ventures, undivided

---

[10] *Harsco Corporation 1997 10-K*, page 34.
[11] *Southdown, Inc., 1996 Annual Report*, p. 47.

interest pipelines and jointly-owned gas processing plants are accounted for on a pro rata basis."[12]

Alternatively, *SOP 78-9* recommends against proportionate consolidation for undivided interests in real estate ventures subject to joint control by the investors. A venture is subject to joint control if decisions regarding the financing, development, or sale of property require the approval of two or more owner-venturers. Subsequently, a 1979 AICPA Issues Paper entitled "Joint Venture Accounting" recommended that a joint venture that is not subject to joint control, because its liabilities are several rather than joint, should be required to use the proportionate consolidation method.

One-Line Consolidation and Proportionate Consolidation

To illustrate the reporting alternatives for unincorporated joint ventures, assume that Price Corporation has a 50% undivided interest in Shield Company, a merchandising joint venture. Comparative financial statements under the two assumptions (accounting under the equity method and proportionate consolidation) appear in Exhibit 11–10. Column 1 presents a summary of Price's income statement and balance sheet, assuming that it uses the equity method of accounting for its investment in Shield, an unconsolidated joint venture company. Shield's income statement and balance sheet are summarized in column 2. In column 3, Price has consolidated its share (50%) of Shield's assets, liabilities, revenues, and expenses (from column 2)—in other words, a proportionate consolidation.

Note that Shield's $1,000,000 venture capital is eliminated in its entirety against the $500,000 investment in Shield balance, and against half of Shield's asset, liability, revenue, and expense account balances in the proportionate consolidation.

The Accounting Standards Executive Committee of the AICPA is reviewing certain inconsistencies in reporting unincorporated joint ventures that have arisen from the lack of authoritative guidance. Likewise, the Emerging Issues Task Force of the FASB is currently reviewing joint venture accounting.

	Equity Method—Price Corporation	Shield Unincorporated	Proportionate Consolidation—Price and Shield
Income Statement			
Revenues			
Sales	$2,000,000	$ 500,000	$2,250,000
Income from Shield	100,000	—	—
Total revenue	2,100,000	500,000	2,250,000
Expenses			
Cost of sales	1,200,000	200,000	1,300,000
Other expenses	400,000	100,000	450,000
Total expenses	1,600,000	300,000	1,750,000
Net income	$ 500,000	$ 200,000	$ 500,000
Balance Sheet			
Cash	$ 200,000	$ 50,000	$ 225,000
Accounts receivable	300,000	150,000	375,000
Inventory	400,000	300,000	550,000
Plant assets	800,000	800,000	1,200,000
Investment in Shield	500,000		
Total assets	$2,200,000	$1,300,000	$2,350,000
Accounts payable	$ 400,000	$ 200,000	$ 500,000
Other liabilities	500,000	100,000	550,000
Capital stock	1,000,000	—	1,000,000
Retained earnings	300,000	—	300,000
Venture capital	—	1,000,000	—
Total equities	$2,200,000	$1,300,000	$2,350,000

Exhibit 11–10 *The Equity Method and Proportionate Consolidation Compared*

---

[12]*USX Corporation Form 10-K* for the fiscal year ended December 31, 1997, p. U–7.

SUMMARY

This chapter covers several different theories related to consolidating the financial statements of a parent company and its subsidiaries. It also examines "new basis accounting" for assets and liabilities in a subsidiary's separate financial statements under push-down accounting, and illustrates accounting for corporate joint ventures.

The concepts and procedures underlying current consolidation practices are identified as the contemporary theory of consolidation to distinguish current practices from accounting practices under parent company and entity theories. The basic differences among the three theories are compared in a matrix in Exhibit 11–1. Nearly all of the differences disappear when subsidiaries are wholly owned.

Under push-down accounting, the cost/book value differentials determined in a purchase business combination are recorded in the separate books of the subsidiary. Push-down accounting is ordinarily required by the SEC for purchase business combinations in which all or substantially all of the ownership interests in the acquired company change hands. Some acquisitions can be structured to avoid push-down accounting.

A joint venture is a business entity that is owned, operated, and jointly controlled by a small group of investors for their mutual benefit. The joint venture investors are usually active in the management of the venture, and each venturer usually has the ability to exercise significant influence over the joint venture investee. Investors account for their investments in corporate joint ventures as one-line consolidations under the equity method. Similarly, investors account for investments in unincorporated joint ventures (partnerships and undivided interests) as one-line consolidations or proportionate consolidations, depending on the special accounting practices of the industries in which they operate.

APPENDIX: CONSOLIDATION UNDER A CURRENT COST SYSTEM

Many of the differences between the parent company, entity, and contemporary theories of consolidation arise because value changes are not recorded in the accounts of affiliated companies as they occur. Although entity theory is intended to provide a consistent valuation approach for majority and minority interests, it does not accomplish its objective because the net assets of the parent company are not revalued at the time of acquisition and because no revaluations occur after the date of a business combination.

This section of the chapter provides a brief digression from generally accepted accounting principles in order to consider how the consolidation process might be altered if a current cost approach were adopted. Conceivably, the adoption of a current cost system would eliminate many of the inconsistencies and complexities that arise in the preparation of consolidated financial statements.

Current Cost Accounting

U.S. companies may supplement their financial statements with current cost information as specified in *FASB Statement No. 89*.[13] This supplementary information includes current cost of inventories, property, plant, and equipment, and the effect on income from continuing operations of measuring cost of sales and depreciation on a current cost basis. Authoritative accounting bodies do not require business enterprises to issue current cost financial statements, so this section is limited to examining possible changes that a current cost system would have on the preparation of consolidated financial statements. The discussion assumes that implementation of a current cost system would involve the revaluation of all identifiable assets and liabilities on a current cost basis at each statement date, and that unidentifiable assets (that is, goodwill) would

---

[13] *FASB Statement No. 33*, which required certain large companies to disclose current cost information, was superseded by *FASB Statement No. 89* in December 1986. *Statement No. 89* encourages, but does not require, disclosure of supplementary current cost information.

continue to be recorded and amortized on a cost basis.[14] All changes in current costs of identifiable assets and liabilities are assumed to be included in the measurement of net income in the period of change. Also, goodwill or negative goodwill is assumed to be measured by the difference between the purchase price and the current cost of net assets acquired and amortized over a maximum period of 40 years. Under these assumptions, many of the problem areas of consolidations could conceivably be avoided.

Few consolidation adjustments are needed to consolidate the accounts of a parent company and its subsidiaries if all affiliates value their identifiable assets and liabilities on a current cost basis. Reciprocal accounts must still be eliminated, but the elimination process is greatly simplified. Reciprocal receivable and payable balances, including accounts for intercompany bond investments and bond liabilities,[15] should be precisely reciprocal under a current cost system, such that no income or equity accounts would be involved in the elimination process. Further, there are no constructive gains or losses on intercompany bond purchases because the purchase price of intercompany bonds is equivalent to the current cost of the liability at the time of its constructive retirement.

Under the historical cost system of accounting, the basis of income recognition is the sale of goods and services to other entities. In such a system, all gains and losses on intercompany transfers are deferred (unrealized) until subsequent sale outside the consolidated entity. Because changes in current cost form the basis for income recognition under a current cost accounting system, there is no need for deferring recognition of gains and losses on intercompany transfers. The assets are stated at their current costs, not their transfer prices, in both separate company and consolidated financial statements. Thus, under the current cost system assumed in this section, there are no unrealized gains or losses on intercompany purchase and sale transactions. This is because the basis for income recognition becomes changes in current cost, and any differences between intercompany transfer prices and current costs are recognized on the books of the purchasing affiliate during the period of the intercompany transactions.

Investment in subsidiary and underlying subsidiary equity amounts under a current cost system should be reciprocal except for any unamortized excess of purchase price over the current cost of net assets acquired. In other words, the initial difference between investment cost and current value of net assets acquired would lie solely in the goodwill or negative goodwill associated with a purchase business combination. In years subsequent to acquisition, this difference would be reduced through goodwill amortization and no additional differences would arise because there would be no unrealized or constructive gains or losses.

Identifiable assets and liabilities would be the same for a business combination accounted for under the pooling of interests method as under the purchase method, because all assets and liabilities would be recorded at their current costs. Thus, the only difference in the net assets under the two methods lies in the valuation of unidentifiable assets.

Minority interest computations under a current cost system would also be simplified. Income of minority stockholders under parent company or contemporary theory would be equal to the minority interest in subsidiary net income, and total minority interests at any date would be equal to the minority interest's share of the current cost of subsidiary net assets.

Consolidation Procedures Under Current Cost Accounting

Assume that Podunk Corporation acquires 80% of the outstanding stock of Sickle Corporation on January 2, 20X1 in a purchase business combination. Balance sheets of the two companies on a current cost basis just before the combination are as follows:

---

[14]Most current cost systems are not designed for the valuation of a business as a whole, but rather for the valuation of identifiable assets and liabilities. Unidentifiable assets are recorded only where necessary to reflect the acquisitions of groups of assets or entire business enterprises. Once recorded, the accounts for unidentifiable assets are not adjusted for changes in current costs.

[15]Current costs of bond liabilities and investments can be determined by references to market prices if current quotations are available. Otherwise, they would be determined by imputing current interest rates and using present value computations.

	Podunk	Sickle
Assets		
Cash	$ 50,000	$ 20,000
Accounts receivable	100,000	50,000
Inventories	250,000	80,000
Plant assets—net	500,000	300,000
Total	$900,000	$450,000
Liabilities and Equity		
Accounts payable	$ 60,000	$ 30,000
9% bonds payable	—	100,000
Capital stock, $10 par	500,000	300,000
Retained earnings	340,000	20,000
Total	$900,000	$450,000

The identifiable net assets of both Podunk and Sickle are fairly valued at their current costs and require no adjustment for purposes of the business combination. If Podunk issues 20,000 shares of stock with a market value of $400,000 for 80% of Sickle's outstanding shares, the investment is recorded as follows:

Investment in Sickle	$400,000	
Capital stock, $10 par		$200,000
Additional paid-in capital		200,000

To record acquisition of an 80% interest in Sickle.

A consolidated balance sheet for Podunk and Sickle immediately after acquisition shows goodwill of $144,000, equal to the excess of investment cost over current cost of net assets acquired [$400,000 − ($320,000 × 80%)]. A consolidation working paper entry to consolidate the balance sheets of the two companies is:

Capital stock—Sickle	$300,000	
Retained earnings—Sickle	20,000	
Goodwill	144,000	
Investment in Sickle		$400,000
Minority interest		64,000

The consolidated balance sheet prepared on a current cost basis immediately after the business combination appears as follows:

PODUNK CORPORATION AND SUBSIDIARY CONSOLIDATED BALANCE SHEET AT JANUARY 2, 20X1

Assets		
Current Assets		
Cash	$ 70,000	
Accounts receivable	150,000	
Inventories	330,000	
Total current assets		$ 550,000
Plant assets—net		800,000
Goodwill		144,000
Total assets		$1,494,000
Liabilities and Equity		
Liabilities:		
Accounts payable	$ 90,000	
9% bonds payable (at par value)	100,000	
Total liabilities		$ 190,000
Stockholders' equity		
Capital stock, $10 par	$ 700,000	
Additional paid-in capital	200,000	
Retained earnings	340,000	
Majority interest	1,240,000	
Minority interest	64,000	
Total stockholders' equity		1,304,000
Total liabilities and stockholders' equity		$1,494,000

Because the identifiable assets and liabilities of both parent and subsidiary are consolidated at their current costs, all assets and liabilities are valued consistently except for goodwill, which relates only to the majority interest. Assuming that the goodwill is amortized over a five-year period, the inconsistency will disappear at the end of five years. [Under entity theory, goodwill would be $180,000 ($144,000 ÷ 80%), and minority interest would be $100,000 (20% of $500,000 implied total valuation), and even this inconsistency would be eliminated.]

Intercompany Sales of Inventory Items in a Current Cost System

Assume that Podunk sells merchandise to Sickle for $20,000, that the merchandise was produced by Podunk during 20X2 at a cost of $12,000, and that it had a current cost of $15,000 at the time of sale. Podunk's profit of $8,000 on the sale is realized during 20X2, regardless of whether Sickle resells the merchandise or inventories it at year-end. However, if the goods have a current cost of $15,000 and remain unsold at year-end, Sickle will decrease its income for 20X2 in the amount of $5,000 by writing down the merchandise to its $15,000 year-end current cost. The entry on Sickle's books to record the write-down is:

Cost of sales	$5,000	
Inventory		$5,000
To reduce inventory to its current replacement cost at year-end.		

Although a separate account to record the $5,000 loss on the write-down to current cost could have been used, the adjustment to cost of sales is made in order to keep the illustration basic.

The net result of the intercompany sales transactions during 20X2 is to increase the combined income of Podunk and Sickle by $3,000—an $8,000 increase by Podunk and a $5,000 decrease by Sickle. Consolidated net income for 20X2 also increases $3,000 during 20X2, not as a result of the intercompany sale, but because the consolidated entity held merchandise during 20X2 while its current cost increased from $12,000 to $15,000.

A consolidation working paper entry to consolidate the accounts of Podunk and Sickle for the year is necessary to eliminate intercompany purchases and sales as follows:

Sales	$20,000	
Cost of sales		$20,000
To eliminate intercompany sales.		

This working paper elimination entry is needed in order to show the correct operating results of the consolidated entity, but it has no effect on consolidated net income. Notice that no working paper entry is needed to adjust the inventory. This is because the inventory is recorded on a current cost basis in the separate accounts of Sickle.

A brief analysis of the separate company and consolidated income statement effect of the $20,000 intercompany sale may be helpful. Consider the following partial consolidated income statement working papers in terms of increases (1) and decreases (2):

	Podunk	Sickle	Adjustments and Eliminations	Consolidated Income Statement
Sales	$+20,000	$ —	$−20,000	$ —
Cost of sales	+12,000	+5,000	−20,000	−3,000
Gross profit	$+ 8,000	$−5,000		$+3,000

Separate company cost of sales consist of the $12,000 historical cost on Podunk's books and $5,000 on Sickle's books from adjusting the inventory from $20,000 to its $15,000 current cost. When the intercompany sales and purchases are eliminated through the working paper entry, the final effects are to decrease consolidated cost of sales by $3,000 and increase consolidated net income by $3,000. This $3,000 is simply the increase in the current cost of the goods produced by Podunk and held within the consolidated entity at December 31, 20X2. Although some theorists would classify the $3,000 increase as a separate consolidated income statement item rather than as a reduction of consolidated cost of sales, this type of refinement does not seem necessary in view of the broad and general treatment accorded in this section. The previous discussion of the $20,000 downstream sale from Podunk to Sickle is equally applicable to an upstream sale by subsidiary to parent company.

Intercompany Sales of Plant Assets in a Current Cost System

Assume that Sickle owns land with a current cost of $8,000 on January 2, 20X2, that it sells the land to Podunk for $10,000 during 20X2, and that the land has a current cost of $8,500 at December 31, 20X2. Under these assumptions, Sickle will record a $2,000 gain at the time of sale and Podunk will record a $1,500 loss at year-end when it adjusts its land account to a current cost basis. Podunk will record the write-down to current cost as follows:

Loss on adjustment of land to current cost	$ 1,500	
Land		$ 1,500
To adjust the land account to its current cost at year-end.		

The combined effect of the intercompany land sale is to increase income for 20X2 by $500—a $2,000 gain to Sickle and a $1,500 loss to Podunk. These amounts are realized by Sickle and Podunk, respectively. For consolidated statement purposes, however, only the $500 net increase is included in consolidated net income. This $500 consists of the increase in the current cost of the land while it is being held within the consolidated entity (from $8,000 at the beginning of the year to $8,500 at year-end).

The land is adjusted on Podunk's books to its current cost at year-end, so the only working paper entry needed is as follows:

Gain on land	$ 1,500	
Loss on adjustment of land to current cost		$ 1,500
To offset gain and loss accounts from intercompany sale of land.		

The $500 gain not eliminated is included in the consolidated income statement as the only income statement effect of the intercompany sale of land. By this time, you should have discovered that the effect of intercompany transactions on consolidated net income is determined by changes in the current cost of assets held within the consolidated entity, and not by transfer prices.[16] A $500 increase in consolidated income would have resulted if the intercompany sale had occurred at $7,000, $9,000, or some other amount. As in the case of inventory items, the gain could be reflected in the consolidated income statement in various ways.

Constructive Retirement of Intercompany Bonds in a Current Cost System

If Podunk acquires 50% of Sickle's outstanding bonds (see page 438) for $48,000 on December 31, 20X2, there is no constructive gain on the bonds. This is because Sickle's bond liability on this date is $96,000—its current cost at December 31, 20X2 as established by Podunk's purchase of 50% of the bonds for $48,000. On its separate books, Sickle Corporation will recognize a $4,000 gain for 20X2 on the revaluation of its bond liability to a current cost basis. However, this gain is considered an adjustment of Sickle's bond interest expense for the year rather than a separate income statement item. The $4,000 decrease in Sickle's interest expense is reflected in Sickle's separate income statement and in the consolidated income statement for 20X2. The only working paper entry necessary for the intercompany bond holdings is:

9% bonds payable	$48,000	
Investment in Sickle bonds		$48,000
To eliminate reciprocal bond amounts.		

---

[16]No gains or losses are deferred under the current cost system visualized in this chapter, so it makes no difference if the sales are upstream or downstream.

Now assume that the bonds of Sickle are purchased on July 1, rather than on December 31, 20X2, and that Podunk pays $47,000 for 50% of Sickle's bonds. Also assume that all adjustments to current cost are made at year-end, at which time the current cost of the bonds is $96,000 ($48,000 for 50% of the bonds). Under these assumptions, Podunk and Sickle will make the following entries on their separate books during 20X2:

PODUNK'S BOOKS

July 1, 20X2

Investment in Sickle bonds	$47,000	
Cash		$47,000

    To record bond investment.

December 31, 20X2

Cash (or accrued interest receivable)	$ 2,250	
Investment in Sickle bonds	1,000	
Interest income		$ 3,250

    To record nominal interest on Sickle bonds and to adjust interest income
    for a $1,000 increase in the current cost of the bonds.

SICKLE'S BOOKS

December 31, 20X2

Interest expense	$ 5,000	
9% bonds payable	4,000	
Cash (or accrued interest payable)		$ 9,000

    To record nominal interest for the year and to adjust interest expense
    for the $4,000 decrease in the current cost of the bond liability.

After these entries are recorded, the separate books of Podunk show investment in Sickle bonds and interest income of $48,000 and $3,250, respectively. The separate books of Sickle show 9% bonds payable and interest expense of $96,000 and $5,000, respectively. The working paper entry to eliminate reciprocal bond investment and bond liability amounts will be for $48,000, just as in the previous example. However, an additional working paper entry is necessary to eliminate reciprocal interest income and interest expense as follows:

Interest income	$3,250	
Interest expense		$3,250
To eliminate reciprocal interest income and interest expense.		

This entry, which reduces the interest expense for the full amount of the intercompany interest income, results in interest expense of $1,750 ($5,000 − $3,250) in the consolidated income statement for the year. The $1,750 consists of the nominal interest of $6,750 on bonds outstanding during the year [($100,000 × 9% × $\frac{1}{2}$ year) + ($50,000 × 9% × $\frac{1}{2}$ year)] less the $5,000 decline in the current cost of bonds payable. (Others may prefer to show interest expense at $6,750 and to treat the $5,000 adjustment as a separate income item.) The $5,000 decrease in the current cost consists of a $3,000 decrease in the current cost of bonds constructively retired ($50,000 − $47,000) plus a $2,000 net decrease in the current cost of the bonds held outside of the consolidated entity at December 31, 20X2 ($50,000 − $48,000).

This type of analysis would not be necessary for practical accounting applications because the $1,750 net amount of interest expense results automatically from offsetting intercompany interest income against interest expense. It makes no difference whether it is the parent company's or subsidiary's bonds that are constructively retired because the analysis and computations under the current cost system described are exactly the same in either case.

SELECTED READINGS

Accounting Interpretation No. 2 of APB Opinion No. 18. "Investments in Partnerships and Ventures." New York: American Institute of Certified Public Accountants, November 1971.
Accounting Standards Executive Committee of the American Institute of Certified Public Accountants. Issues Paper. *Joint Venture Accounting.* New York: American Institute of Certified Public Accountants, 1979.

American Accounting Association's Financial Accounting Standards Committee. "Comment Letter to the FASB Discussion Memorandum 'New Basis of Accounting.'" *Accounting Horizons* (March 1994), pp. 119–121.

American Accounting Association's Financial Accounting Standards Committee. "Response to the FASB Discussion Memorandum 'Consolidation Policy and Procedures.'" *Accounting Horizons* (June 1994), pp. 120–125.

BIERMAN, HAROLD, JR. "Proportionate Consolidation and Financial Analysis." *Accounting Horizons* (December 1992), pp. 5–17.

Committee on Accounting Procedure. *Accounting Research Bulletin No. 51.* "Consolidated Financial Statements." New York: American Institute of Certified Public Accountants, 1959.

COLLEY, J. RON, and ARA G. VOLKAN. "Accounting for Goodwill." *Accounting Horizons* (March 1988), pp. 35–41.

COLLEY, J. RON, and ARA G. VOLKAN. "Business Combinations: Goodwill and Push-Down Accounting." *The CPA Journal* (August 1988), pp. 74–76.

CUNNINGHAM, MICHAEL E. "Push-Down Accounting: Pros and Cons." *Journal of Accountancy* (June 1984), pp. 72–77.

Emerging Issues Task Force. *EITF Issue No. 88-16.* "Basis in Leveraged Buyout Transactions." Stamford, CT: Financial Accounting Standards Board, 1989.

Financial Accounting Standards Board. Financial Accounting Series, No. 107-A. Discussion Memorandum. *An Analysis of Issues Related to Consolidation Policy and Procedures.* Norwalk, CT: Financial Accounting Standards Board, 1991.

Financial Accounting Standards Board. *EITF Issue No. 90-13.* Norwalk, CT: Financial Accounting Standards Board, 1990.

HENDRIKSEN, ELDON S. *Accounting Theory,* 4th Ed. Homewood, Ill.: Irwin, 1982.

HOLLEY, CHARLES L., EDWARD C. SPEDE, and MICHAEL C. CHESTER, JR. "The Push-Down Accounting Controversy," *Management Accounting* (January 1987), pp. 39–42.

International Accounting Standards Committee. *International Accounting Standards No. 31.* "Financial Reporting of Interests in Joint Ventures." London: IASC, reformatted 1994.

MOONITZ, MAURICE. *The Entity Theory of Consolidated Statements.* American Accounting Association Monograph No. 4. Sarasota, FL: American Accounting Association, 1944.

MORTENSEN, ROGER. "Accounting for Business Combinations in the Global Economy: Purchase, Pooling, or ____?" *Journal of Accounting Education,* Vol. 12, No. 1 (1994), pp. 81–87.

NURNBERG, HUGO, and JAN SWEENEY. "The Effect of Fair Values and Historical Costs on Accounting for Business Combinations." *Issues in Accounting Education* (Fall 1989), pp. 375–395.

PACTER, PAUL. "Revising GAAP for Consolidations: Join the Debate." *The CPA Journal* (July 1992), pp. 38–47.

Statement of Financial Accounting Standards No. 33. "Financial Reporting and Changing Prices." Stamford, CT: Financial Accounting Standards Board, 1979.

Statement of Position 78-9. "Accounting for Investment in Real Estate Ventures." New York: American Institute of Certified Public Accountants, Accounting Standards Division, 1978.

THOMAS, PAULA B., and J. LARRY HAGLER. "Push Down Accounting: A Descriptive Assessment." *Accounting Horizons* (September 1988), pp. 26–31.

WYATT, ARTHUR R. "A Critical Study of Accounting for Business Combinations." *Accounting Research Study No. 5.* New York: American Institute of Certified Public Accountants, 1963 (especially see pp. 81–86 on the fair value pooling concept).

ASSIGNMENT MATERIAL

QUESTIONS

1 Compare the contemporary, parent company, and entity theories of consolidated financial statements.

2 Which, if any, of the consolidation theories would be changed by FASB pronouncements? (For example, assume that a new FASB statement requires minority interest income to be computed as the minority interest share of subsidiary dividends declared.)

3 Under the entity theory of consolidation, a total valuation of the subsidiary is imputed on the basis of the price paid by the parent company for its controlling interest. Do you see any practical or conceptual problems with this approach to valuation?

4 Assume that Pabst Corporation acquires 60% of the voting common stock of Seller Corporation for $6,000,000 and that a consolidated balance sheet is prepared immediately after the business combination. Would total consolidated assets be equal to their fair values if the parent company theory were applied? If the entity theory were applied?

5 Why might the current practice of valuing the equity of minority shareholders at book value overstate the value of the minority interest?

6 Cite the conditions under which consolidated net income under parent company theory would equal income to majority stockholders under entity theory.

7 If investment income from a subsidiary is measured under the equity method and the statements are consolidated under the entity theory, will consolidated net income be equal to parent company net income?

8 Why are the income statement amounts under entity theory and contemporary theory the same if the subsidiary investment is made at book value? (Do not consider the different income statement presentations of majority and minority interests in responding to this question.)

9 Does contemporary practice correspond to parent company or entity theory in matters related to unrealized and constructive gains and losses on intercompany transactions?

10 To what extent does push-down accounting facilitate the consolidation process?

11 What is a joint venture and how are joint ventures organized?

12 What accounting and reporting methods are used by investor-venturers in accounting for their joint venture investments?

13 *Appendix* How are unrealized gains and losses eliminated in consolidating the financial statements of affiliated companies when current cost accounting is applied?

14 *Appendix* Describe the computation of the equity of minority shareholders when a current cost system of accounting is used (assume the contemporary theory of accounting except for the application of the current cost system).

15 *Appendix* How would the current cost of goodwill be determined under a current cost system of accounting?

16 *Appendix* How would different transfer prices for intercompany transactions affect consolidated assets and consolidated net income under a current cost system of accounting?

17 *Appendix* If a current cost system of accounting were used, would it still be necessary to eliminate intercompany sales and purchases? Intercompany receivables and payables? Discuss.

EXERCISES

E 11-1

1 The classification of minority interest income as an expense and minority interest as a liability is preferred under:
   a Parent company theory
   b Entity theory
   c Contemporary theory
   d None of the above

2 Contemporary theory is most similar to parent company theory in matters relating to:
   a Goodwill computations
   b Minority interest computations
   c Intercompany profit eliminations
   d Consolidated financial statement presentations

3 Contemporary theory is most similar to entity theory in matters relating to:
   a Goodwill computations
   b Minority interest computations
   c Intercompany profit eliminations
   d Consolidated financial statement presentations

4 When "consolidated income allocated to majority stockholders" under entity theory is compared to "consolidated net income" under contemporary theory, one would expect consolidated net income under contemporary theory to be:
   a Equal to consolidated income allocated to majority stockholders under entity theory
   b Greater than consolidated income allocated to majority stockholders under entity theory
   c Less than consolidated income allocated to majority stockholders under entity theory
   d Greater or less depending on the relationship of investment cost to book value acquired

5 Consolidated financial statement amounts and classifications should be identical under the contemporary, entity, and parent company theories of consolidation if:
   a All subsidiaries are acquired at book value
   b Only 100%-owned subsidiaries are consolidated
   c There are no intercompany transactions
   d All subsidiaries are acquired at book value and there are no intercompany transactions

6 When the fair values of an acquired subsidiary's assets and liabilities are recorded in the subsidiary's accounts (push-down accounting), the subsidiary's retained earnings will be:
   a Adjusted for the difference between the push-down capital and goodwill from the acquisition
   b Credited for the amount of the push-down capital
   c Transferred in its entirety to push-down capital
   d Credited for the difference between the total imputed value of the entity and the purchase price of the interest acquired

7 The most consistent statement of assets in consolidated financial statements would result from applying:
a Contemporary theory
b Parent company theory
c Entity theory
d A current cost system of accounting

E 11-2 **[Joint Ventures]**

1 A joint venture would not be organized as a(an):
a Corporation   **c** Partnership
b Proprietorship   **d** Undivided interest

2 Corporate joint ventures should be accounted for by the equity method, provided that the joint venturer:
a Cannot exercise significant influence over the joint venture
b Can participate in the overall management of the venture
c Owns more than 50% of the joint venture
d All of the above

3 An investor in a corporate joint venture would be least likely to:
a Be active in the management of the venture
b Have an ability to exercise significant influence
c Consent to each significant venture decision
d Hold title to a pro rata share of joint venture assets

4 Investors account for their investments in corporate joint ventures under the equity method if their individual ownership percentages are at least:
a 10%   **c** 50%
b 20%   **d** None of the above

5 Farver, Greta, and Higgs corporations own 60%, 25%, and 15%, respectively, of the common stock of Produce Corporation, a corporate joint venture that they organized for wholesaling fruits and vegetables. Which of the corporations should report their joint venture interests under the equity method?
a Farver, Greta, and Higgs
b Farver and Greta
c Greta and Higgs
d Farver and Higgs

E 11-3 **1** Peterson Company pays $720,000 for an 80% interest in Smith Corporation on December 31, 20X1, when Smith's net assets at book value and fair value are $800,000. Under entity theory, the minority interest at acquisition is:
a $144,000   **c** $180,000
b $160,000   **d** $200,000

2 Seattle Corporation sold inventory items to its parent company, Portland Corporation, during 20X2, and at December 31, 20X2 Portland's inventory included items acquired from Seattle at a gross profit of $50,000. If Seattle is an 80%-owned subsidiary of Portland, the amount of unrealized inventory profits to be eliminated in preparing the consolidated income statements of Portland and Subsidiary for 20X2 is $40,000 under:
a Parent company theory
b Contemporary theory
c Entity theory
d The equity method of accounting

3 A parent company that applies the entity theory of consolidation in preparing its consolidated financial statements computed income from its 90%-owned subsidiary under the equity method of accounting as follows:

Equity in subsidiary income ($200,000 × 90%)	$180,000
Goodwill amortization ($70,000 ÷ 10 years × 90%)	(6,300)
Income from subsidiary	$173,700

Given the foregoing information, minority interest income is:
a $20,000   **c** $18,000
b $19,300   **d** $17,300

Use the following information in answering questions 4 and 5:

Piedmont Corporation acquired an 80% interest in Swan Corporation on January 1, 20X1, when Swan's total stockholders' equity was $840,000. The book values and fair values of Swan's assets and liabilities were equal on this date. At December 31, 20X1, the consolidated balance sheet of Piedmont and Subsidiary shows unamortized goodwill from consolidation of $54,000, with a note that goodwill is being amortized over a 10-year period.

4 If the entity theory of consolidation was used, the purchase price of the 80% interest in Swan must have been:

      a $720,000   **c** $747,000
      b $732,000   **d** $900,000

  5 If the contemporary theory of consolidation was used, the purchase price of the 80% interest in Swan must have been:
      a $720,000   **c** $747,000
      b $732,000   **d** $900,000

E 11-4 Balance sheet information of Pond and Staff corporations at December 31, 20X1 is summarized as follows:

	Pond Book Value	Staff Book Value	Staff Fair Value
Current assets	$ 520,000	$ 50,000	$ 90,000
Plant assets—net	480,000	250,000	360,000
	$1,000,000	$300,000	$450,000
Current liabilities	$ 80,000	$ 40,000	$ 50,000
Capital stock	800,000	200,000	
Retained earnings	120,000	60,000	
	$1,000,000	$300,000	

On January 2, 20X2, Pond purchases 80% of Staff's outstanding shares for $500,000 cash.

Required
    1 Determine goodwill from the business combination under (a) parent company theory and (b) entity theory.
    2 Determine minority interest at January 2, 20X2 under (a) parent company theory and (b) entity theory.
    3 Determine the amount of total assets that would appear on a consolidated balance sheet prepared at January 2, 20X2 under (a) parent company theory and (b) entity theory.

E 11-5 On January 1, 20X5, Perry Corporation pays $300,000 for an 80% interest in Shelly Company, when Shelly's net assets have a book value of $275,000 and a fair value of $350,000. The $75,000 excess fair value is due to undervalued equipment with a five-year remaining useful life. Any goodwill is to be written off over a 10-year period.
    Separate incomes of Perry and Shelly for 20X5 are $500,000 and $50,000, respectively.

Required
    1 Calculate consolidated net income and minority interest income under (a) parent company theory and (b) entity theory.
    2 Determine unamortized goodwill at December 31, 20X5 under (a) parent company theory and (b) entity theory.

E 11-6 Stahl Corporation's recorded assets and liabilities are equal to their fair values on July 1, 20X1, when Polak Corporation purchases 72,000 shares of Stahl common stock for $1,800,000. Identifiable net assets of Stahl on this date are $1,710,000, and Stahl's stockholders' equity consists of $800,000 of $10 par common stock and $910,000 retained earnings. Any goodwill is to be amortized over 10 years.
    Stahl has net income for 20X1 of $80,000 earned evenly throughout the year and declares no dividends.

Required
    1 Determine the total value of Stahl's net assets at July 1, 20X1 under entity theory.
    2 Determine goodwill that would appear in a consolidated balance sheet of Polak Corporation and Subsidiary at July 1, 20X1 under (a) entity theory, (b) parent company theory, and (c) contemporary theory.
    3 Determine Polak's investment income from Stahl on an equity basis for 20X1.
    4 Determine minority interest in Stahl that will be reported in the consolidated balance sheet at December 31, 20X1 under entity theory.

E 11-7 Palumbo Company acquired an 80% interest in Seal Corporation at book value equal to fair value on January 1, 20X1. During the year, Seal sold $100,000 inventory items to Palumbo, and at December 31, 20X1, unrealized profits amounted to $30,000. Separate incomes of Palumbo and Seal for 20X1 were $500,000 and $300,000, respectively.

Required
    1 Determine consolidated net income for Palumbo Company and Subsidiary under the parent company theory of consolidation.
    2 Determine total consolidated income for Palumbo Company and Subsidiary, income to majority stockholders, and income to minority stockholders under the entity theory of consolidation.

E 11-8 Palid Corporation acquired an 80% interest in Stark Corporation at book value a number of years ago.

Separate incomes of Palid and Stark for 20X1 were $120,000 and $60,000, respectively. The only transactions between Palid and Stark during 20X1 were as follows:

1 Palid sold inventory items to Stark for $60,000. These items cost Palid $30,000, and half the items were inventoried at $30,000 by Stark at December 31, 20X1.
2 Stark sold land that cost $70,000 to Palid for $96,000 during 20X1. The land was held by Palid at December 31, 20X1.
3 Stark paid $24,000 dividends to Palid during 20X1.

Required: Compute consolidated net income for Palid Corporation and Subsidiary for 20X1 under:
1 Contemporary theory
2 Parent company theory
3 Entity theory

E 11-9 On January 1, 20X2, Pioneer Corporation acquired a 90% interest in Security Corporation for $2,520,000. The book values and fair values of Security's assets and equities on this date are as follows:

	Book Value	Fair Value
Cash	$ 200,000	$ 200,000
Accounts receivable—net	300,000	300,000
Inventories	500,000	600,000
Land	300,000	800,000
Buildings—net	700,000	1,000,000
Equipment—net	800,000	600,000
	$2,800,000	$3,500,000
Accounts payable	$ 550,000	$ 550,000
Other liabilities	450,000	550,000
Capital stock	1,000,000	
Retained earnings	800,000	
	$2,800,000	

Required

1 Prepare the journal entries on Security Corporation's books to push down the values reflected in the purchase price under *parent company theory*.
2 Prepare the journal entries on Security Corporation's books to push down the values reflected in the purchase price under *entity theory*.

E 11-10 Sun-Belt Land Development Corporation is a corporate joint venture that is jointly controlled and operated by five investor-venturers, four with 15% interests each and one with a 40% interest. Each of the five venturers is active in venture management. Land sales and other important venture decisions require the consent of each venturer. All venturers paid $15 per share for their investments on January 1, 20X1, and no changes in ownership interests have occurred since that time. During 20X2, Sun-Belt reported net income of $500,000 and paid dividends of $100,000. The stockholders' equity of Sun-Belt at December 31, 20X2 is as follows:

SUN-BELT LAND DEVELOPMENT CORPORATION
STOCKHOLDERS' EQUITY AT DECEMBER 31, 20X2

Common stock $10 par, 500,000 shares authorized, issued, and outstanding	$5,000,000
Additional paid-in capital	2,500,000
Total paid-in capital	7,500,000
Retained earnings	1,000,000
Total stockholders' equity	$8,500,000

Required: Determine the investment income for 20X2 and the investment account balance at December 31, 20X2, for the 40% venturer and for one of the 15% venturers.

E 11-11 **[Appendix]**

Assume that Seaside Company is a 90%-owned subsidiary of Prescott and that a current cost system of accounting is applicable to the separate company and consolidated financial statements of these affiliated companies. During 20X1, the following intercompany transactions took place between Prescott and Seaside:

1 Prescott sold merchandise that cost $18,000 and had a $20,000 current cost at the time of sale to Seaside for $25,000. At December 31, 20X1, 25% of this merchandise with a current cost of $5,500 remained unsold by Seaside.

2 Prescott acquired 10% of Seaside Company's outstanding bonds at December 31, 20X1 for $99,000. The book value of Seaside's bond liability before year-end adjustments on this date was $1,000,000.

3 On July 1, 20X1, Seaside sold land with a book value (current cost at January 1, 20X1) of $40,000 to Prescott for $50,000. This land had a current cost of $45,000 both at the time of sale and at December 31, 20X1.

Required

1 Prepare journal entries to record:

    a The foregoing transactions for 20X1 on the separate books of Prescott and Seaside. (Current cost adjustments are only made at year-end.)

    b Year-end adjustments on the separate books of Prescott and Seaside at December 31, 20X1.

2 Prepare the working paper entries related to the foregoing transactions that would be necessary to consolidate the financial statements of Prescott and Seaside at December 31, 20X1.

PROBLEMS

P 11-1 The adjusted trial balances of Picody Corporation and its 80%-owned subsidiary, Scone Corporation, at December 31, 20X5 are as follows:

	Picody	Scone
Cash	$ 32,000	$ 20,000
Receivables—net	120,000	180,000
Inventories	300,000	150,000
Plant assets—net	1,200,000	750,000
Investment in Scone	752,000	
Cost of sales	1,300,000	600,000
Depreciation	225,000	75,000
Other expenses	271,000	175,000
Dividends	200,000	50,000
	$4,400,000	$2,000,000
Accounts payable	$ 204,000	$ 100,000
Other liabilities	300,000	200,000
Capital stock	1,000,000	500,000
Retained earnings	800,000	200,000
Sales	2,000,000	1,000,000
Income from Scone	96,000	
	$4,400,000	$2,000,000

Picody acquired its interest in Scone for $640,000 on January 1, 20X4, when Scone's stockholders' equity consisted of $500,000 capital stock and $100,000 retained earnings. The excess cost was due to a $100,000 undervaluation of plant assets with a five-year remaining useful life and to goodwill with a 10-year amortization period. Picody uses a one-line consolidation in accounting for its investment in Scone.

Required: Prepare comparative consolidated balance sheets at December 31, 20X5 for Picody Corporation and Subsidiary under (a) parent company theory and (b) entity theory.

P 11-2 Pisces Corporation acquires an 80% interest in Scorpio Company on January 3, 20X1 for $160,000. On this date Scorpio's stockholders' equity consists of $100,000 capital stock and $70,000 retained earnings. The cost/book value differential is assigned to goodwill with a six-year amortization period. Immediately after acquisition, Scorpio sells equipment with a 10-year remaining useful life to Pisces at a gain of $5,000.

Adjusted trial balances of Pisces and Scorpio at December 31, 20X1 are as follows:

	Pisces	Scorpio
Current assets	$ 151,600	$ 90,000
Plant and equipment	400,000	200,000
Investment in Scorpio	168,400	—
Cost of sales	250,000	130,000
Depreciation	50,000	25,000
Other expenses	60,000	20,000
Dividends	50,000	10,000
	$1,130,000	$475,000

(Continued)

	Pisces	Scorpio
Accumulated depreciation	$ 150,000	$ 50,000
Liabilities	100,000	50,000
Capital stock	300,000	100,000
Retained earnings	163,600	70,000
Sales	400,000	200,000
Gain on plant assets	—	5,000
Income from Scorpio	16,400	—
	$1,130,000	$475,000

Required
1 Prepare a consolidated income statement for 20X1 using entity theory.
2 Prepare a consolidated balance sheet at December 31, 20X1 using entity theory.

P 11-3 Palace Corporation paid $595,000 cash for 70% of the outstanding voting stock of Sign Corporation on January 2, 20X2, when Sign's stockholders' equity consisted of $500,000 of $10 par common stock and $250,000 retained earnings. The book values of Sign's assets and liabilities were equal to their fair values on this date.

During 20X2, Palace Corporation had separate income of $300,000 and paid dividends of $150,000. Sign's net income for 20X2 was $90,000 and its dividends were $50,000. At December 31, 20X2, the stockholders' equities of Palace and Sign were as follows:

	Palace	Sign
Common stock ($10 par)	$1,400,000	$500,000
Retained earnings	450,000	290,000
Total stockholders' equity	$1,850,000	$790,000

There were no intercompany transactions between Palace Corporation and Sign Corporation during 20X2. Palace uses the equity method of accounting for its investment in Sign and amortizes goodwill over a 10-year period.

Required
1 Assume that Palace Corporation uses parent company theory for preparing consolidated financial statements for 20X2. Determine the following amounts:
  a Palace Corporation's income from Sign for 20X2
  b Goodwill that will appear in the consolidated balance sheet at December 31, 20X2
  c Consolidated net income for 20X2
  d Minority interest income for 20X2
  e Minority interest at December 31, 20X2
2 Assume that Palace Corporation uses entity theory for preparing consolidated financial statements for 20X2. Determine the following amounts:
  a Palace Corporation's income from Sign for 20X2
  b Goodwill that will appear in the consolidated balance sheet at December 31, 20X2
  c Total consolidated income for 20X2
  d Minority interest income for 20X2
  e Minority interest at December 31, 20X2

P 11-4 At December 31, 20X1, when the fair values of Smedley Corporation's net assets were equal to their book values of $240,000, Pierre Corporation acquired an 80% interest in Smedley Corporation for $224,000. One year later at December 31, 20X2, the comparative adjusted trial balances of the two corporations appear as follows:

	Pierre Corporation	Smedley Corporation
Cash	$ 40,800	$ 70,000
Accounts receivable	90,000	30,000
Inventory	160,000	40,000
Land	200,000	80,000
Buildings	900,000	200,000
Investment in Smedley	239,200	—
Cost of sales	375,000	200,000
Expenses	150,000	50,000
Dividends	120,000	30,000
Total debits	$2,275,000	$700,000

(Continued)

	Pierre Corporation	Smedley Corporation
Accumulated depreciation	$ 200,000	$ 60,000
Accounts payable	175,800	100,000
Capital stock	800,000	200,000
Retained earnings	360,000	40,000
Sales	700,000	300,000
Income from Smedley	39,200	—
Total credits	$2,275,000	$700,000

Additional Information
1 During 20X2, Smedley Corporation sold inventory items costing $15,000 to Pierre for $23,000. Half of these inventory items remain unsold at December 31, 20X2.
2 Goodwill is amortized over a 40-year period.

Required: Prepare comparative consolidated financial statements for Pierre Corporation and Subsidiary at and for the year ended December 31, 20X2 under
1 Contemporary theory
2 Parent company theory
3 Entity theory

P 11-5 Balance sheets for Packard Corporation and its 80%-owned subsidiary, Studs Building Supply Company, at December 31, 20X4 are summarized as follows.

	Packard	Studs
Assets		
Cash	$ 50,000	$ 20,000
Receivables—net	75,000	35,000
Inventories	110,000	30,000
Plant assets—net	215,000	85,000
Investment in Studs Building Supply	136,000	—
Total assets	$586,000	$170,000
Liabilities and Stockholders' Equity		
Accounts payable	$ 80,000	$ 15,000
Other liabilities	20,000	5,000
Total liabilities	100,000	20,000
Capital stock	300,000	100,000
Retained earnings	186,000	50,000
Stockholders' equity	486,000	150,000
Total equities	$586,000	$170,000

Additional Information
1 Packard Corporation paid $128,000 for its 80% interest in Studs on January 1, 20X3, when Studs had capital stock of $100,000 and retained earnings of $10,000.
2 Goodwill is amortized over a 10-year period.
3 At December 31, 20X4, Packard's inventory included items on which Studs had recorded gross profit of $20,000.

Required: Prepare comparative consolidated balance sheets for Packard Corporation and Subsidiary at December 31, 20X4 under the contemporary and entity theories of consolidation.

P 11-6 [AICPA adapted]
The individual and consolidated balance sheets and income statements of X and Y companies for the current year are presented on the next page.

Additional Information
1 X Company purchased its interest in Y Company several years ago.
2 X Company sells products to Y Company for further processing and also sells to firms outside the affiliated entity. The inventories of Y Company include an intercompany profit at both the beginning and the end of the year.
3 At the beginning of the current year, Y Company purchased bonds of X company having a maturity value of $100,000. These bonds are being held as available for sale securities and are, correspondingly, carried at fair value. No change in fair value has occurred over the course of the year. Y Company has agreed to offer X Company the option of reacquiring the bonds at Y's cost before deciding to dispose of them on the open market.

X AND Y COMPANIES' INDIVIDUAL AND CONSOLIDATED
BALANCE SHEETS AS OF THE END OF THE CURRENT YEAR

	X Company	Y Company	Consolidated
Assets			
Cash and receivables	$ 35,000	$108,000	$ 97,400
Inventories	40,000	90,000	122,000
Plant (net)	460,000	140,000	600,000
Goodwill from consolidation	—	—	30,000
Investment in Y	245,000	—	—
X bonds owned	—	103,000	—
Total assets	$780,000	$441,000	$849,400
Liabilities and Equity			
Current payables	$ 70,000	$ 23,000	$ 53,000
Dividends payable	10,000	8,000	12,400
Mortgage bonds (5%)	200,000	50,000	150,000
Capital stock	300,000	200,000	300,000
Retained earnings	200,000	160,000	217,000
Minority interest	—	—	117,000
Total liabilities and equity	$780,000	$441,000	$849,400

INDIVIDUAL AND CONSOLIDATED INCOME STATEMENTS
FOR THE CURRENT YEAR

	X Company	Y Company	Consolidated
Sales	$600,000	$400,000	$760,000
Cost of sales	(360,000)	(280,000)	(403,000)
Gross profit	240,000	120,000	357,000
Operating expenses	(130,000)	(54,000)	(189,000)
Operating profit	110,000	66,000	168,000
Interest revenue	1,800	5,000	1,800
Dividend revenue	11,200	—	—
	123,000	71,000	169,800
Interest expense	(10,000)	(3,000)	(8,000)
Provision for income tax	(56,000)	(34,000)	(90,000)
Nonrecurring loss	—	—	(3,000)
Minority share	—	—	(8,700)
Net income	$ 57,000	$ 34,000	$ 60,100
Dividends	(20,000)	(16,000)	(24,800)
Transfer to retained earnings	$ 37,000	$ 18,000	$ 35,300

Required: Answer the following questions on the basis of the preceding information.

1 Does X Company carry its investment in Y Company on the cost or equity basis? Explain the basis of your answer.

2 If Y Company's common stock has a stated value of $100 per share, how many shares does X Company own? How did you determine this?

3 When X acquired its interest in Y Company, the assets and liabilities of Y Company were recorded at their fair values. The $30,000 goodwill from consolidation represents un-amortized goodwill at the end of the current year. The original goodwill was $50,000 under entity theory, and the amortization is over a 10-year period. What was the amount of Y's retained earnings at the date that X Company acquired its interest in Y Company?

4 What is the nature of the nonrecurring loss appearing on the consolidated income statement? Reproduce the consolidating entry from which this figure originated and explain.

5 What is the amount of intercompany sales during the current year by X Company to Y Company?

6 Are there any intercompany debts other than the intercompany bondholdings? Identify any such debts, and state which company is the debtor and which is the creditor in each case. Explain your reasoning.

7 What is the explanation for the difference between the consolidated cost of goods sold and the combined cost of goods sold of the two affiliated companies? Prepare a schedule reconciling combined and consolidated cost of goods sold, showing the amount of inter-company profit in the beginning and ending inventories of Y Company and demonstrating how you determined the amount of intercompany profit. (*Hint:* A well-organized and labeled T-account for cost of goods sold will be an acceptable approach.)

8 Show how the $8,700 minority interest in total consolidated net income was determined.

9 Show how the total minority interest on the balance sheet ($117,000) was determined.

10 Beginning with the $200,000 balance in X Company's retained earnings at the end of the current year, prepare a schedule in which you derive the $217,000 balance of consolidated retained earnings at the end of the current year.

P 11-7 **[Push-down accounting]**

Played Corporation paid $480,000 cash for a 100% interest in Splash Corporation on January 1, 20X8, when Splash's stockholders' equity consisted of $200,000 capital stock and $80,000 retained earnings. Splash's balance sheet on December 31, 20X7 is summarized as follows:

	Book Value	Fair Value
Cash	$ 30,000	$ 30,000
Accounts receivable—net	70,000	70,000
Inventories	60,000	80,000
Land	50,000	75,000
Buildings—net	100,000	190,000
Equipment—net	90,000	75,000
Total assets	$400,000	$520,000
Accounts payable	$ 40,000	$ 40,000
Other liabilities	70,000	60,000
Capital stock	200,000	
Retained earnings	90,000	
Total equities	$400,000	

Played uses the equity method to account for its interest in Splash. The amortization periods for the fair value/book value differentials at the time of acquisition were as follows:

$20,000	Undervalued inventories (sold in 20X8)
25,000	Undervalued land
50,000	Undervalued buildings (10-year useful life remaining)
(15,000)	Overvalued equipment (five-year useful life remaining)
10,000	Other liabilities (two years before maturity)
20,000	Goodwill (10-year amortization period)

Required

1 Prepare a journal entry on Splash's books to push down the values reflected in the purchase price.

2 Prepare a balance sheet for Splash Corporation on January 1, 20X8.

3 Splash's net income for 20X8 under the new push-down accounting system is $90,000. What is Played's income from Splash for 20X8?

P 11-8 **[Push-down accounting]**

Parker Corporation paid $3,000,000 for an 80% interest in Sanue Corporation on January 1, 20X9, when the book values and fair values of Sanue's assets and liabilities were as follows:

	Book Value	Fair Value
Cash	$ 300,000	$ 300,000
Accounts receivable—net	600,000	600,000
Inventories	800,000	2,400,000
Land	200,000	200,000
Buildings—net	600,000	600,000
Equipment—net	1,000,000	500,000
	$3,500,000	$4,600,000
Accounts payable	$ 500,000	$ 500,000
Long-term debt	1,000,000	1,000,000
Capital stock, $1 par	800,000	
Retained earnings	1,200,000	
	$3,500,000	

Required

1 Prepare a journal entry on Sanue's books to push down 80% of the values reflected in the purchase price (the parent company theory approach).

2 Prepare a journal entry on Sanue's books to push down 100% of the values reflected in the purchase price (the entity theory approach).

3 Calculate the minority interest in Sanue on January 1, 20X9 under parent company theory.

4 Calculate the minority interest in Sanue on January 1, 20X9 under entity theory.

P 11-9   **[Push-down accounting]**

Power Corporation paid $180,000 cash for a 90% interest in Swing Corporation on January 1, 20X8, when Swing's stockholders' equity consisted of $100,000 capital stock and $20,000 retained earnings. Swing Corporation's balance sheets at book value and fair value on December 31, 20X7 are as follows:

	Book Value	Fair Value
Cash	$ 20,000	$ 20,000
Accounts receivable—net	50,000	50,000
Inventories	40,000	30,000
Land	15,000	15,000
Buildings—net	30,000	50,000
Equipment—net	70,000	100,000
Total assets	$225,000	$265,000
Accounts payable	$ 45,000	$ 45,000
Other liabilities	60,000	60,000
Capital stock	100,000	
Retained earnings	20,000	
Total equities	$225,000	

Additional Information

1   The amortization periods for the fair value/book value differentials at the time of acquisition are as follows:

Overvalued inventories (sold in 20X8)	$10,000
Undervalued buildings (10-year useful lives)	20,000
Undervalued equipment (five-year useful lives)	30,000
Goodwill (10-year amortization period)	Remainder

2   Power uses the equity method to account for its interest in Swing.

Required

1   Prepare a journal entry on Swing Corporation's books to push down the values reflected in the purchase price under parent company theory.
2   Prepare a journal entry on Swing Corporation's books to push down the values reflected in the purchase price under entity theory.
3   Prepare comparative balance sheets for Swing Corporation on January 1, 20X8 under the approaches of (1) and (2).

P 11-10   **[Push-down accounting]**

Use the information and assumptions from Problem P 11–9 for this problem. The accompanying financial statements are for Power and Swing corporations, one year after the business combination. Note that Swing's statements are presented first under contemporary theory with no push-down accounting, then under 90% push-down accounting, and finally, under 100% push-down accounting.

Swing mailed a check to Power on December 31, 20X8 to settle an account payable of $8,000. Power received the check in 20X9. The $8,000 amount is included in Power's December 31, 20X8 accounts receivable.

POWER CORPORATION AND SWING CORPORATION
COMPARATIVE FINANCIAL STATEMENTS
WITH AND WITHOUT PUSH-DOWN ACCOUNTING
AT AND FOR THE YEAR ENDED DECEMBER 31, 20X8

	Basic Accounting Power	Basic Accounting Swing	Push Down 90% Swing	Push Down 100% Swing
Income Statement				
Sales	$310,800	$110,000	$110,000	$110,000
Income from Swing	34,200			
Cost of sales	(140,000)	(42,000)	(33,000)	(32,000)
Depreciation expense	(29,000)	(17,000)	(24,200)	(25,000)
Other operating expenses	(45,000)	(11,000)	(14,600)	(15,000)
Net income	$131,000	$ 40,000	$ 38,200	$ 38,000

(Continued)

POWER CORPORATION AND SWING CORPORATION
COMPARATIVE FINANCIAL STATEMENTS
WITH AND WITHOUT PUSH-DOWN ACCOUNTING
AT AND FOR THE YEAR ENDED DECEMBER 31, 20X8

	Basic Accounting Power	Basic Accounting Swing	Push Down 90% Swing	Push Down 100% Swing
Retained Earnings				
Retained earnings—beginning	$147,000	$ 20,000	$ 0	$ 0
Add: Net income	131,000	40,000	38,200	38,000
Deduct: Dividends	(60,000)	(10,000)	(10,000)	(10,000)
Retained earnings—ending	$218,000	$ 50,000	$ 28,200	$ 28,000
Balance Sheet				
Cash	$ 63,800	$ 27,000	$ 27,000	$ 27,000
Accounts receivable	90,000	40,000	40,000	40,000
Dividends receivable	9,000			
Inventories	20,000	35,000	35,000	35,000
Land	40,000	15,000	15,000	15,000
Buildings—net	140,000	27,000	43,200	45,000
Equipment—net	165,000	56,000	77,600	80,000
Investment in Swing	205,200			
Goodwill			32,400	36,000
Total assets	$733,000	$200,000	$270,200	$278,000
Accounts payable	$125,000	$ 20,000	$ 20,000	$ 20,000
Dividends payable	15,000	10,000	10,000	10,000
Other liabilities	75,000	20,000	20,000	20,000
Capital stock	300,000	100,000	100,000	100,000
Push-down capital			92,000	100,000
Retained earnings	218,000	50,000	28,200	28,000
Total equities	$733,000	$200,000	$270,200	$278,000

Required: Prepare consolidation working papers for Power Corporation and Subsidiary for the year ended December 31, 20X8 under (a) 90% push-down accounting and (b) 100% push-down accounting.

P 11-11 **[Joint ventures]**
Pepper Corporation owns a 40% interest in Jerry Company, a joint venture that is organized as an undivided interest. In its separate financial statements, Pepper accounts for Jerry under the equity method, but for reporting purposes, the proportionate consolidation method is used.

Separate financial statements of Pepper and Jerry at and for the year ended December 31, 20X2 are summarized as follows:

	Pepper Corporation	Jerry Company
Combined Income and Retained Earnings Statements for the Year Ended December 31, 20X2		
Sales	$ 800,000	$300,000
Income from Jerry	20,000	—
Cost of sales	(400,000)	(150,000)
Depreciation expense	(100,000)	(40,000)
Other expenses	(120,000)	(60,000)
Net income	200,000	50,000
Beginning retained earnings	300,000	—
Beginning venture equity	—	250,000
Dividends	(100,000)	—
Retained earnings/venture equity	$ 400,000	$300,000
Balance Sheets at December 31, 20X2		
Cash	$ 100,000	$ 50,000
Receivables—net	130,000	30,000
Inventories	110,000	40,000
Land	140,000	60,000
Buildings—net	200,000	100,000
Equipment—net	300,000	180,000
Investment in Jerry	120,000	—
Total assets	$1,100,000	$460,000

(Continued)

	Pepper Corporation	Jerry Company
Accounts payable	$ 120,000	$100,000
Other liabilities	80,000	60,000
Common stock, $10 par	500,000	—
Retained earnings	400,000	—
Venture equity	—	300,000
Total equities	$1,100,000	$460,000

Required: Prepare working papers for a proportionate consolidation of the financial statements of Pepper Corporation and Jerry Company at and for the year ended December 31, 20X2.

P 11-12 **[Appendix]**

Separate financial statements on a current cost basis for Pringle and Slate at and for the year ended December 31, 20X2 are as follows:

	Pringle	Slate
Combined Income and Retained Earnings Statement for the Year Ended December 31, 20X2		
Sales	$800,000	$290,000
Income from Slate	13,000	—
Cost of sales	(695,000)	(200,000)
Expenses	(53,000)	(70,000)
Net income	65,000	20,000
Add: Beginning retained earnings	215,000	60,000
Deduct: Dividends	(30,000)	(10,000)
Retained earnings December 31, 20X2	$250,000	$ 70,000
Balance Sheet at December 31, 20X2		
Cash	$ 82,000	$ 40,000
Other current assets	180,000	70,000
Plant assets—net	490,000	190,000
Investment in Slate	198,000	—
Total assets	$950,000	$300,000
Liabilities	$100,000	$ 30,000
Capital stock	600,000	200,000
Retained earnings	250,000	70,000
Total equities	$950,000	$300,000

Additional Information
   1 Pringle acquired its 70% interest in Slate for $192,000 on December 31, 20X1.
   2 Goodwill is being amortized over a 10-year period.
   3 During 20X2, Pringle sold inventory items that cost $20,000 to Slate for $30,000. Half of these goods are inventoried by Slate at a current cost of $14,000 and are included in Slate's "other current assets" at December 31, 20X2.

Required: Prepare consolidation working papers for Pringle Corporation and Subsidiary at and for the year ended December 31, 20X2.

12

Accounting for Branch Operations

Previous chapters of this book have considered accounting and reporting procedures for consolidating the separate operations of parent companies and their subsidiaries. The objective of consolidation is to report the financial position and results of operations of separate legal entities as if there were only one economic entity. By contrast, branches are identifiable locations within a business entity for which separate accounting records are maintained. Branches are separate accounting entities, but they are not separate legal entities, and their financial statements are used only for internal reporting purposes. Financial statements for the business entity are prepared by combining the financial statements of the branches with those of the central reporting unit of the business.

This chapter distinguishes between sales agency and branch operations, describes accounting procedures for branch operations, and illustrates procedures for combining home office and branch financial statements in the preparation of financial statements for the business entity as a whole.

SALES AGENCIES AND BRANCHES

A technical distinction is commonly made between *sales agencies* and *branches*. **Sales agencies** are established to display merchandise and to take customers' orders, but they do not stock merchandise to fill customers' orders or pass on customer credit. The sales agency is not a separate accounting or business entity. Ordinarily, the only accounting records required for sales agencies are for cash receipts and disbursements, which are handled in essentially the same manner as petty cash systems. The central accounting system of the business maintains records of sales made through agency operations and related cost of sales and other expenses.

By contrast, a **branch operation** stocks merchandise, makes sales to customers, passes on customer credit, collects receivables, incurs expenses, and performs other functions normally associated with the operations of a separate business enterprise. Such activities are accounted for through separate branch accounting systems that parallel the systems of independent businesses except in the manner of accounting for ownership equities and in recording transactions between branches and the main office of the enterprise.

Many of the larger branch operations are the result of business combinations in which the surviving corporations establish branch entities to account for the operations of the combining corporations that are dissolved. In such cases, the existing information systems of the combining companies can be converted into home office and branch accounting systems with only minor adjustments. This method of combining accounting systems is often economical in that it avoids major changes in existing information systems and minimizes disruptions in normal business operations. This method also makes it easy to dispose of the new branch if operations prove unprofitable.

Although the technical distinctions for classifying sales agencies and branches may be important for marketing, advertising, and other business purposes, they are not particularly helpful for accounting purposes. Some sales agencies do carry stock in trade, and some branch operations have limited responsibility for maintaining customer records and approving credit. Many firms with branch operations have centralized customer credit and billing services on a regional or even a companywide basis. The accounting system for a remote business location, whether a branch or an agency, should be designed to accumulate information needed as economically as possible.

SALES AGENCY ACCOUNTS

Sales agencies do not require complete accounting systems to account for their limited activities. Ordinarily, cash receipts and disbursements records are sufficient for accounting at agency locations. Records for sales agency operations must be maintained in the central accounting system of the enterprise. The amount of data accumulated by the enterprise for agency operations may be limited to records of cash and display merchandise at agency offices, on the one hand, or comprise relatively complete asset and income data, on the other.

If detailed information for a sales agency is not deemed necessary, the following entries may suffice to account for agency operations.

1 Creation of an agency working capital fund:

Agency working capital	$5,000	
Cash		$5,000
To record transfer of cash to sales agency.		

2 Transfer of sample inventory to sales agency:

Sample inventory—agency	$9,000	
Merchandise inventory (or purchases)		$9,000
To transfer display merchandise to sales agency.		

3 Replenishment of agency working capital at month or year-end:

Salaries expense	$2,200	
Utilities expense	700	
Advertising expense	1,200	
Miscellaneous expense	300	
Cash		$4,400
To record expenses incurred by sales agency and replenishment of agency working capital.		

4 Adjustment of agency sample inventory at month or year-end:

Advertising expense	$3,000	
Sample inventory—agency		$3,000
To adjust agency sample inventory to net realizable value and to charge the write-down to advertising expense.		

These entries serve to account for agency expense transactions and cash and merchandise in possession of agency personnel. However, the system illustrated is not adequate for effective control over agency expenses or for measuring the contribution of agency operations to enterprise income, nor does it provide a basis for determining if agency operations are being performed efficiently.

An expansion of the system to accumulate agency sales and expense information provides a basis for comparing agency expenses over time and with expenses of similar sales agencies. It also enables profit evaluation of agency operations. The extent of detail accumulated for each sales agency depends upon the information needs of management.

Journal entries for an expanded agency recordkeeping system follow. The entries identify plant assets of the Newport sales agency separately. They also show sales, cost of sales, and expense information on an agency basis.

1 Purchase of Newport sales agency land and buildings:

Land—Newport sales agency	$ 2,000	
Buildings—Newport sales agency	18,000	
Cash		$20,000
Purchase of facilities for sales agency.		

2 Creation of a sales agency working capital fund:

Newport sales agency working capital	$ 4,000	
Cash		$ 4,000
To record transfer of cash to Newport sales agency.		

3 Transfer of display merchandise to sales agency:

Newport sales agency sample inventory	$ 8,000	
Merchandise inventory		$ 8,000
To record transfer of sample merchandise to sales agency.		

4 Payment of salaries to employees of sales agency:

Salaries expense—Newport sales agency	$ 3,000	
Cash		$ 3,000
To record payment of salaries to sales agency employees.		

5 Sales orders from sales agency are filled and customers are billed:

Accounts receivable	$12,000	
Sales—Newport sales agency		$12,000
To record credit sales made through Newport sales agency.		
Cost of sales—Newport sales agency	$ 6,000	
Merchandise inventory		$ 6,000
Cost of merchandise delivered to customers of sales agency.		

6 Replenishment of agency's working capital fund at year end:

Advertising expense—Newport sales agency	$ 1,800	
Utilities expense—Newport sales agency	400	
Other expenses—Newport sales agency	300	
Cash		$ 2,500
To record replenishment of sales agency working capital.		

7 Depreciation recorded on sales agency buildings:

Depreciation expense—Newport sales agency	$ 900	
Accumulated depreciation—Newport sales agency		$ 900
To record depreciation on sales agency buildings.		

8 Sample merchandise at sales agency adjusted to reflect shopwear:

Advertising expense—Newport sales Agency	$ 1,000	
Newport sales agency sample inventory		$ 1,000
To record adjustment of sample inventory to realizable value.		

The entries illustrated are examples of how an accounting system can be expanded to provide separate information for agency operations. Accumulation of such information is both practical and inexpensive even when an enterprise has a large number of sales agency operations.

BRANCH ACCOUNTING SYSTEMS

Branch accounting involves segmenting the accounting system of an enterprise into separate accounting systems for home office and branch operations. The home office records constitute the central accounting unit for the enterprise, and branch records constitute adjunct accounting systems for each branch operation. Separate home office and branch systems are used for accounting and internal reporting purposes, but the separate financial statements of the home office and branches have to be combined into a single set of financial statements for the enterprise in order to meet external reporting requirements.

The process of combining home office and branch financial statements is similar to the process of consolidating parent and subsidiary statements. Reciprocity is established between home office and branch records, reciprocal accounts are eliminated, and nonreciprocal accounts are combined. Unrealized profits from internal transfers between the home office and the branches must, of course, be eliminated in preparing combined financial statements for the enterprise.

Transactions Between the Home Office and the Branch

Transactions of the home office with external entities are recorded in the home office accounting records in the usual fashion. Similarly, transactions between a branch and unrelated entities are recorded on the branch books in accordance with established accounting procedures. Thus, the unique feature of home office and branch accounting lies in the manner of recording transactions between the home office and its branches.

The creation of a new branch requires entries on the books of both the home office and the branch. Assume that Expando Corporation creates a branch in Splinter, Montana, by transferring cash of $5,000 and equipment with a cost of $10,000 to the branch manager. Entries on the books of the home office and the branch are:

Home Office Books

Splinter branch	$15,000	
Cash		$ 5,000
Equipment		10,000

    To record transfer of cash and equipment
       to Splinter branch.

Branch Books

Cash	$ 5,000	
Equipment	10,000	
Home office		$15,000

    To record receipt of cash and equipment
       from home office.

The branch account on the home office books is an asset account representing the investment of the home office in branch net assets. The home office account on the branch books is an equity account that represents the equity of the home office in branch net assets. Thus, the branch and home office accounts are reciprocal, each representing the net assets of the branch. This reciprocal relationship between home office and branch accounts is a continuous relationship. Whenever the home office increases (debits) its branch account, the branch should increase (credit) its home office account. Similarly, any decrease (debit) in the home office account on the branch book should be accompanied by a decrease (credit) in the branch account on the home office books. The only reasons that differences between home office and branch accounts occur are time lags in recording information on the two sets of books and errors.

A second type of transaction between home office and branches is for merchandise transfers. Typically, branches are established to sell merchandise that is manufactured or purchased through home office operations. A branch manager may or may not have authority to purchase from outside suppliers. If Expando Corporation ships merchandise to the Splinter branch at its $8,000 home office cost, the following journal entries are required:

Home Office Books

Splinter branch	$8,000	
Shipments to Splinter branch		$8,000

    To record shipments at cost to Splinter branch.

Branch Books

Shipments from home office	$8,000	
Home office		$8,000

    To record shipments received from home office.

Two additional reciprocal accounts result from recording the merchandise transfer from home office to branch. The home office's shipments to branch account is a "contra purchases" account on the home office books, and the shipments from home office account on the branch books is essentially a "branch purchases" account. These accounts are used to determine the separate cost of sales for home office and branch operations, but, because they are reciprocal, they are eliminated in preparing combined financial statements for the enterprise.

Illustration of Home Office and Branch Accounting

Assume that Jiffy-Stop Corporation created a new branch outlet in Bee, Nebraska, at the beginning of 20X1 and that the transactions of the Bee branch during 20X1 are as follows:

1. Received cash of $20,000 from the home office.
2. Purchased equipment with a five-year life for $10,000 cash.
3. Received merchandise shipments from home office at the $16,000 home office cost.
4. Purchased merchandise from outside suppliers for $4,000 cash.
5. Sold merchandise for $30,000 cash.
6. Returned $1,000 of the merchandise acquired from the home office.
7. Paid expenses as follows:

Salaries	$6,000
Utilities	1,000
Rent expense	3,000
Other expenses	2,000

8. Remitted $15,000 to the home office.
9. Salaries payable at year-end were $1,000 and depreciation for the year was $2,000.
10. Branch inventory at year-end consisted of $1,000 merchandise acquired from outside suppliers and $5,000 acquired from home office.

Journal Entries Journal entries to record these transactions and related year-end events on the books of Bee branch are illustrated in Exhibit 12–1. The exhibit also shows journal entries on the home office books to reflect reciprocal home office items.

The closing entry of Bee branch contains a $2,000 credit to the home office account. This $2,000 is equal to branch income for the period and reflects the net asset increase from branch operations. A related adjusting entry on the home office books debits the Bee branch account for $2,000 and credits Bee branch profit for the period. This home office adjusting entry is roughly equivalent to a parent company entry to record its share of subsidiary income for a period under the equity method of accounting.

Cost of Sales Computations The journal entries illustrated in Exhibit 12–1 are based on periodic inventory procedures that provide detailed information about merchandise transfers between home office and branch locations. Although this detailed information can be used in the working papers to combine the home office and branch accounts for external reporting, it is convenient to group the separate inventory, purchases, and the shipment data into individual cost of sales categories for

Transaction	Home Office Books			Bee Branch Books		
1 Bee branch	$20,000		Cash	$20,000	
Cash		$20,000	Home office		$20,000
To transfer cash to Bee branch.			Receipt of cash from home office.		
2			Equipment	$10,000	
			Cash		$10,000
			To record purchase of equipment.		
3 Bee branch	$16,000		Shipments from home office	$16,000	
Shipments to Bee branch		$16,000	Home office		$16,000
To transfer merchandise to Bee branch at cost.			Receipt of merchandise from home office.		
4			Purchases	$ 4,000	
			Cash		$ 4,000
			To record cash purchases.		
5			Cash	$30,000	
			Sales		$30,000
			To record cash sales.		
6 Shipments to Bee branch	$ 1,000		Home office	$ 1,000	
Bee branch		$ 1,000	Shipments from home office		$ 1,000
Merchandise returned from Bee branch.			Merchandise returned to home office.		
7			Salaries expense	$ 6,000	
			Utilities expense	1,000	
			Rent expense	3,000	
			Other expenses	2,000	
			Cash		$12,000
			To record payment of expenses.		
8 Cash	$15,000		Home office	$15,000	
Bee branch		$15,000	Cash		$15,000
Cash received from Bee branch.			To record cash remittance to home office.		
9			*Adjusting Entries*		
			Salaries expense	$ 1,000	
			Salaries payable		$ 1,000
			Accrued salaries.		
			Depreciation expense—equipment	$ 2,000	
			Accumulated depreciation—equipment		$ 2,000
			Depreciation expense $10,000 ÷ 5 years.		
10 *Adjusting Entry*			*Closing Entry*		
Bee branch	$ 2,000		Sales	$30,000	
Bee branch profit		$ 2,000	Inventory	6,000	
To record Bee branch profit for the period.			Shipments from home office		$15,000
			Purchases		4,000
			Salaries expense		7,000
			Depreciation expense		2,000
			Utilities expense		1,000
			Rent expense		3,000
			Other expenses		2,000
			Home office		2,000
			To close income accounts to home office.		

Exhibit 12–1 Jiffy-Stop Corporation: Home Office and Branch Journal Entries

efficient preparation of working papers. Separate cost of sales computations for the home office and branch of Jiffy-Stop are as follows:

	Home Office	Bee Branch
Inventory January 1, 20X1	$ 85,000	$ —
Purchases	150,000	4,000
Shipments to branch	(15,000)	—
Shipments from home office	—	15,000
Goods available for sale	220,000	19,000
Inventory December 31, 20X1	(80,000)	(6,000)
Cost of sales	$140,000	$13,000

Data for home office purchases and inventories are included in the cost of sales computations without prior explanation.

Working Papers   Home office and branch accounting records may be combined, using either the trial balance or the financial statement working paper format. These approaches are illustrated in Exhibits 12–2 and 12–3 for the Jiffy-Stop Corporation. Data for the home office not previously introduced are included in the working papers to complete the illustrations.

Adjusted trial balances for Jiffy-Stop's home office and its Bee branch are shown in the first two columns of the trial balance working papers in Exhibit 12–2. The working paper procedures are comparable to those for the trial balance working papers used in preparing consolidated financial statements. Only two working paper entries are needed: one to establish reciprocity between the branch and home office accounts by eliminating the Bee branch profit and reducing the branch account to its preadjusted balance, and a second entry to eliminate reciprocal home office and branch account balances. These entries are similar to the consolidation working paper entries to eliminate income from subsidiaries against the parent company's investment in subsidiary account and, subsequently, to eliminate reciprocal investment and equity balances.

The same working paper entries are used in combining the home office and branch accounts in Exhibit 12–3 when the financial statement format is used. Under the financial statement format, however, the absence of a retained earnings account in the ledger of the branch necessitates a change in the retained earnings section of the working papers. The equity account of a branch is its home office account, so the branch column of the working papers shows changes in the home office account from current operations. Observe that working paper entry a of Exhibit 12–3 returns the Bee branch account on the home office books to its $20,000 preadjusted balance to establish reciprocity with the $20,000 preclosing balance of the home office account. Subsequently, entry b eliminates these reciprocal balances. Other aspects of the home office-branch working papers are the same as those for working papers of parent and subsidiary operations. Normally, only the combined financial statements that reflect the financial position and results of operations for the entity as a whole are used for external reporting purposes.

MERCHANDISE SHIPMENTS IN EXCESS OF COST

The procedures illustrated for Jiffy-Stop are based on merchandise shipments between the home office and Bee branch at home office cost. Many corporations, however, use transfer prices in excess of cost for internal shipments to their branches. Some corporations set transfer prices at normal sales prices, whereas others use standard markups. Still other corporations develop complex formulas for determining transfer prices. Reasons commonly cited for internal transfers of merchandise above cost include equitable allocation of income between the various units of the enterprise, efficiency in pricing inventories, and concealment of the true profit margins from branch personnel.

Shipments to Branch Recorded at Cost

When a home office ships merchandise to its branches at transfer prices in excess of cost, the accounting records of the home office are adjusted to permit measurement of actual cost of merchandise transferred. This is usually done through an inventory

JIFFY-STOP CORPORATION
HOME OFFICE AND BRANCH WORKING PAPERS
FOR THE YEAR ENDED DECEMBER 31, 20X1

	Home Office	Bee Branch	Adjustments and Eliminations	Income Statement	Retained Earnings	Balance Sheet
Debits						
Cash	$ 41,000	$ 9,000				$ 50,000
Accounts receivable	60,000					60,000
Inventories—ending	80,000	6,000				86,000
Land	20,000					20,000
Buildings—net	100,000					100,000
Equipment—net	52,000	8,000				60,000
Bee branch	22,000		a 2,000 b 20,000			
Cost of sales	140,000	13,000		$(153,000)		
Salaries expense	43,000	7,000		(50,000)		
Depreciation expense— buildings	5,000			(5,000)		
Depreciation expense— equipment	8,000	2,000		(10,000)		
Utilities expense	6,000	1,000		(7,000)		
Rent expense		3,000		(3,000)		
Other expenses	8,000	2,000		(10,000)		
Dividends	10,000				$(10,000)	
	$595,000	$51,000				$376,000
Credits						
Accounts payable	$ 50,000					$ 50,000
Salaries payable	4,000	$ 1,000				5,000
Capital stock	200,000					200,000
Retained earnings	110,000				110,000	
Home office		20,000	b 20,000			
Sales	229,000	30,000		259,000		
Bee branch profit	2,000		a 2,000			
	$595,000	$51,000				
Net income				$ 21,000	21,000	
Retained earnings December 31, 20X1					$121,000	121,000
						$376,000

Exhibit 12–2 *Combining Working Papers—Trial Balance Approach*

JIFFY-STOP CORPORATION
HOME OFFICE AND BRANCH WORKING PAPERS
FOR THE YEAR ENDED DECEMBER 31, 20X1

	Home Office	Bee Branch	Adjustments and Eliminations	Combined Statement
Income Statement				
Sales	$229,000	$30,000		$259,000
Bee branch profit	2,000		a 2,000	
Cost of sales	(140,000)	(13,000)		(153,000)
Salaries expense	(43,000)	(7,000)		(50,000)
Depreciation expense—buildings	(5,000)			(5,000)
Depreciation expense—equipment	(8,000)	(2,000)		(10,000)
Utilities expense	(6,000)	(1,000)		(7,000)
Rent expense		(3,000)		(3,000)
Other expenses	(8,000)	(2,000)		(10,000)
Net income	$ 21,000	$ 2,000		$ 21,000
Retained Earnings/Home Office				
Retained earnings January 1	$110,000			$110,000
Home office (preclosing)		$20,000	b 20,000	
Net income	21,000	2,000		21,000
Dividends	(10,000)			(10,000)
Retained earnings/home office	$121,000	$22,000		$121,000
Balance Sheet				
Cash	$ 41,000	$ 9,000		$ 50,000
Accounts receivable—net	60,000			60,000
Inventory	80,000	6,000		86,000
Land	20,000			20,000
Buildings—net	100,000			100,000
Equipment—net	52,000	8,000		60,000
Bee branch	22,000		a 2,000 b 20,000	
	$375,000	$23,000		$376,000
Accounts payable	$ 50,000			$ 50,000
Salaries payable	4,000	$ 1,000		5,000
Capital stock	200,000			200,000
Retained earnings	121,000			121,000
Home office		22,000		
	$375,000	$23,000		$376,000

Exhibit 12–3 *Combining Working Papers—Financial Statement Approach*

"loading" or unrealized profit account. For example, if Southern Fashion Mart's home office ships merchandise that costs $100,000 to its Tampa branch at a 20% markup based on cost, the home office and branch entries are:

Home Office Books

Tampa branch	$120,000	
Shipments to Tampa branch		$100,000
Loading in Tampa branch inventory		20,000

To record shipments to Tampa branch at 120% of cost.

Tampa Branch Books

Shipments from home office	$120,000	
Home office		$120,000

To record receipt of merchandise from home office.

Entries to record transfers of merchandise at prices in excess of cost do not change the reciprocal relationship between the home office and branch accounts, but they do affect the relationship between home office and branch shipment accounts, because the "shipments to branch" account is credited at cost and the "shipments from home office" account is debited at the transfer price. The difference between the shipment accounts lies in the markup that is reflected in the loading in branch inventories account. This loading account is frequently designated "unrealized profit in branch inventories."

When a branch receives merchandise at transfer prices that include a loading factor and sells that merchandise, its cost of goods sold is overstated and its income is understated. The home office increases its branch account and records branch profit or loss on the basis of income reported by the branch, so any branch profit recorded by the home office is similarly understated. This understatement of branch profit on home office books is corrected by a year-end adjusting entry that reduces the loading account to reflect amounts realized during the period through branch sales to outside entities.

Assume that the following account balances appear on the books of Southern Fashion Mart's home office and branch at December 31, 20X1 before adjusting entries are recorded:

Home Office Books

Tampa branch	$200,000 debit
Shipments to Tampa branch	100,000 credit
Loading in Tampa branch inventory	20,000 credit

Tampa Branch Books

Sales	$160,000 credit
Shipments from home office	120,000 debit
Expenses	30,000 debit
Home office	200,000 credit

If the Tampa branch has $12,000 inventory at transfer prices on December 31, 20X1, it reports income for the period of $22,000 (sales of $160,000, less cost of sales of $108,000 and other expenses of $30,000). The branch closing entry for the period is:

Sales	$160,000	
Inventory December 31, 20X1	12,000	
Shipments from home office		$120,000
Expenses		30,000
Home office		22,000

To close nominal accounts and transfer the balance
to the home office account.

This information is used by the home office to record branch profit for the period:

Tampa branch	$ 22,000	
Tampa branch profit		$ 22,000

To take up branch profit and to update the branch account.

The home office also adjusts its loading account to reflect the $2,000 unrealized profit in branch ending inventory [$12,000 − ($12,000 ÷ 120%)]:

Loading in Tampa branch inventory	$ 18,000	
Tampa branch profit		$ 18,000
To adjust branch loading account ($20,000 − $2,000)		
and branch profit for the period.		

After this entry is posted, the loading account will have a $2,000 balance equal to the $2,000 unrealized profit in the Tampa branch ending inventory, and the Tampa branch profit account will show a balance of $40,000. This $40,000 is the income of the branch on a cost basis, an amount that is subject to independent confirmation as follows:

Sales		$160,000
Shipments to branch (at cost)	$100,000	
Less: Inventory (at cost)	10,000	90,000
Gross profit		70,000
Other expenses		30,000
Branch income		$ 40,000

When the $40,000 branch profit is added to separate home office income for the period, the total equals combined net income for the enterprise. Although year-end entries for subsequent years are substantially the same as those illustrated, there will be a difference because the branch will have a beginning inventory stated at transfer prices, and the home office will have a beginning balance in its loading account equal to the unrealized profit in the branch beginning inventory. An example of branch accounting for Dasher Corporation at the end of this chapter illustrates accounting procedures for unrealized profits in both beginning and ending branch inventories.

Shipments to Branch Recorded at Billing Prices

Some firms enter merchandise shipments to their branches at billing prices and adjust the loading account at the end of the accounting period. When this approach is used, the balance of the loading account during an accounting period will reflect unrealized profit in branch beginning inventories, and the shipments to branch account will include the loading factor on shipments for the current period. The shipments to branch account (home office books) and the shipments from home office account (branch books) are reciprocals under this method.

To illustrate, Southern Fashion Mart's shipments to the Tampa branch could have been recorded at billing prices as follows:

Home Office Books		
Tampa branch	$120,000	
Shipments to Tampa branch		$120,000

With this entry, the home office and branch shipment accounts have equal balances, but two year-end adjusting entries are needed:

Home Office Books		
Shipments to Tampa branch	$ 20,000	
Loading in Tampa branch inventory		$ 20,000
To adjust shipments to a cost basis.		
Loading in Tampa branch inventory	$ 18,000	
Tampa branch profit		$ 18,000
To adjust branch profit for realization of markup		
on branch shipments.		

The first entry adjusts the shipments to branch and loading in branch inventory accounts to create balances of $100,000 and $20,000, respectively. The second entry to adjust branch profit for the loading factor is the same as the one shown earlier.

FREIGHT COSTS ON SHIPMENTS

The cost of transporting merchandise to its final sale location can be an important element of the cost of merchandise inventoried and sold. Accordingly, freight costs on merchandise shipped between home office and branch locations should be included in branch inventory and cost of goods sold measurements. Assume that merchandise is shipped from a home office to its branch at 125% of the $10,000 home office cost and that the home office pays $500 freight costs. The following home office and branch journal entries are required:

Home Office Books

Branch	$13,000	
Shipments to branch		$10,000
Loading in branch inventory		2,500
Cash		500

To record shipments to branch.

Branch Books

Shipments from home office	$12,500	
Freight-in on home office shipments	500	
Home office		$13,000

To record receipt of merchandise from home office.

If half the merchandise remains unsold at year-end, cost of branch sales is reported at $6,500, and the branch inventory is priced at its $6,250 home office cost, plus $250 freight-in. Branch inventory and cost of goods sold are reported in the same amount if the branch pays the transportation costs, but the freight transaction is not recorded on the home office books.

Merchandise cost should not include excessive freight charges from the transfer of merchandise between a home office and its branches or between branch locations. If the branch returns half the merchandise received from the home office because it is defective, or because of a shortage of inventory at the home office location, the home office cost of the merchandise should not include the freight charges to or from the branch. Assuming that the branch pays $250 to return half the merchandise to the home office, the branch and home office entries are:

Branch Books

Home office	$6,750	
Shipments from home office		$ 6,250
Freight-in on home office shipments		250
Cash		250

To record return of merchandise to the home office.

Home Office Books

Shipments to branch	$5,000	
Loading in branch inventory	1,250	
Loss on excessive freight charges	500	
Branch		$ 6,750

To record merchandise returned from branch location.

Total freight charges on the merchandise are charged to a home office "loss on excessive freight charges" account because the freight charges represent management mistakes or inefficiencies. Therefore, they are not considered normal operating or freight expenses.

A second example of excessive freight charges involves shipments between branches. Assume that the home office of Maxwell Industries ships merchandise at its $50,000 cost from Chicago to its St. Louis branch, and that it pays $2,000 freight charges on the merchandise. A few days later, the Omaha branch experiences a merchandise shortage and the merchandise is transferred from St. Louis to Omaha at a $1,200 cost paid by the St. Louis branch. The cost of shipping the merchandise from Chicago to Omaha would have been $1,800. Entries to record the initial shipment to the St. Louis branch and the subsequent transfer to the Omaha branch are shown in Exhibit 12–4.

In addition to adjusting shipment accounts and home office and branch accounts, the freight accounts must be adjusted. Total freight charges incurred were

ENTRIES TO RECORD SHIPMENT TO ST. LOUIS BRANCH

Home Office Books

St. Louis branch	$52,000	
Shipments to St. Louis branch		$50,000
Cash		2,000
To record shipment to St. Louis branch.		

St. Louis Branch Books

Shipments from home office	$50,000	
Freight-in on home office shipments	2,000	
Home office		$52,000
To record merchandise received from home office.		

ENTRIES TO RECORD TRANSFER FROM ST. LOUIS TO OMAHA

Home Office Books

Omaha branch	$51,800	
Loss on excessive freight charges	1,400	
Shipments to St. Louis branch	50,000	
St. Louis branch		$53,200
Shipments to Omaha branch		50,000
To record transfer of merchandise from St. Louis branch		
to Omaha branch.		

St. Louis Branch Books

Home office	$53,200	
Shipments from home office		$50,000
Freight-in on home office shipments		2,000
Cash		1,200
To record transfer of merchandise to Omaha branch.		

Omaha Branch Books

Shipments from home office	$50,000	
Freight-in on home office shipments	1,800	
Home office		$51,800
To record receipt of merchandise from home office via		
the St. Louis branch.		

Exhibit 12–4   *Maxwell Industries Excessive Freight Charges*

$3,200 ($2,000 + $1,200), but the cost of shipping merchandise from the home office directly to the Omaha branch would have been $1,800. Only $1,800 is recorded as an inventoriable cost on the books of the Omaha branch. The duplicate shipments are assumed to have resulted from home office management errors, so the $1,400 excessive freight is recorded as a home office loss. This accounting treatment is consistent with the accounting principle that inventory costs include only those costs necessary to get merchandise ready for final sale to customers.

HOME OFFICE—BRANCH EXPENSE ALLOCATION

The allocation of expenses among home office and branch operations is frequently necessary to provide an accurate measurement of income for the separate units of the enterprise. Advertising expense, for example, may relate to sales efforts of the home office and one or more branches. If such advertising is paid by the home office, that part related to branch sales should be allocated to the branches. Pension costs paid by the home office and home office general and administrative expenses may also be allocated to branch operations in order to provide complete profit information for each business unit. Another situation that requires expense allocation for complete profit information arises when plant asset records are centralized in the home office accounting system.

Some examples of accounting for these expense allocations follow. If a branch pays $5,000 for advertising that relates equally to branch and home office sales efforts, the $5,000 could be allocated as follows:

Branch Books

Advertising expense	$ 2,500	
Home office	2,500	
Cash		$ 5,000

To allocate advertising expense 50% to home office.

Home Office Books

Advertising expense	$ 2,500	
Branch		$ 2,500

To record advertising expense paid by branch.

Pension and general home office expenses of $50,000 and $120,000, respectively, that are incurred by the home office and allocated 25% each to the Denver and Cheyenne branches, would be recorded:

Home Office Books

Denver branch	$42,500	
Cheyenne branch	42,500	
Pension expense		$25,000
General expenses		60,000

To allocate pension and general expenses to branch operations.

Denver Branch Books

Pension expense	$12,500	
General expenses	30,000	
Home office		$42,500

To record expense allocations from home office.

Cheyenne Branch Books

Pension expense	$12,500	
General expenses	30,000	
Home office		$42,500

To record expense allocations from home office.

These examples illustrate the basic approach to expense allocations among home office and branch operations. Other expense items are allocated in similar fashion.

RECONCILIATION OF HOME OFFICE AND BRANCH ACCOUNTS

Reciprocity between home office and branch accounts will not exist at year-end if errors have been made in recording reciprocal transactions either on the home office or the branch books, or if transactions have been recorded on one set of books but not on the other. The approach for reconciling home office and branch accounts at year-end is similar to the approach used for bank reconciliations. A home office-branch reconciliation is illustrated in Exhibit 12–5 for Empire Corporation's home office and its Rochester branch at December 20X1 according to the following assumptions:

1 Balances on December 31, 20X1: Home office account (branch books), $452,300; Rochester branch account (home office books), $492,000.
2 The Rochester branch sent a check for $12,000 cash to the home office on December 31, 20X1. The home office did not receive the check until January 4, 20X2.
3 The home office shipped merchandise costing $20,000 to its Rochester branch on December 28, 20X1 at a transfer price of $25,000. The merchandise was not received by the Rochester branch until January 8, 20X2.
4 Advertising expenses of $8,500 were allocated by the home office to the Rochester branch. The expenses were recorded at $5,800 by the branch.

The following entry is made on the home office books to reflect cash in transit at December 31, 20X1:

Cash in transit	$12,000	
Rochester branch		$12,000

To record cash in transit on December 31, 20X1.

```
EMPIRE CORPORATION
HOME OFFICE—ROCHESTER BRANCH RECONCILIATION
AT DECEMBER 31, 20X1
```

	Home Office Account (Branch Books)	Rochester Branch Account (Home Office Books)
Balance per books, December 31, 20X1	$452,300	$492,000
Cash in transit—Rochester branch to home office	—	(12,000)
Shipments in transit to Rochester branch	25,000	—
Error correction: Advertising expenses of $8,500 were recorded as $5,800	2,700	—
Adjusted balances, December 31, 20X1	$480,000	$480,000

Exhibit 12–5   *Reconciliation of Home Office and Branch Accounts*

Although it is convenient to use the title "cash in transit" to ensure proper recording of the actual cash receipt, the cash is not in transit from the viewpoint of the combined entity, and it must be reported as cash and not cash in transit in the combined financial statements of the enterprise.

Correcting entries on the books of the Rochester branch to reflect the items in the reconciliation are as follows:

Shipments from home office—in transit	$25,000	
Home office		$25,000
To record merchandise in transit from the home office.		
Advertising expense	$ 2,700	
Home office		$ 2,700
To correct an error in recording an advertising expense allocation from home office as $5,800 rather than $8,500.		

When the accounts are updated to reflect these correcting entries, the home office and branch accounts have reciprocal balances.

ILLUSTRATION OF HOME OFFICE AND BRANCH ACCOUNTING

Dasher Corporation of Philadelphia has operated a sales branch in Dot, Rhode Island, for a number of years. All merchandise shipped to the Dot branch is transferred at normal sales prices, which are 125% of home office cost. The Dot branch also purchases merchandise from outside suppliers. This merchandise is sold by Dot at a 25% markup based on invoice cost. Balance sheets for Dasher Corporation's home office and its Dot branch at December 31, 20X1 are as follows:

```
DASHER CORPORATION HOME OFFICE AND BRANCH
BALANCE SHEETS AT DECEMBER 31, 20X1
```

	Home Office	Dot Branch
Assets		
Cash	$ 25,000	$11,000
Accounts receivable—net	42,000	23,000
Inventory	20,000	16,000
Plant assets—net	70,000	—
Dot branch	43,000	—
Total assets	$200,000	$50,000

(Continued)

DASHER CORPORATION HOME OFFICE AND BRANCH
BALANCE SHEETS AT DECEMBER 31, 20X1

	Home Office	Dot Branch
Liabilities and Equity		
Accounts payable	$ 14,000	$ 5,000
Other liabilities	10,000	2,000
Loading—branch inventory	1,600	—
Home office	—	43,000
Capital stock	150,000	—
Retained earnings	24,400	—
Total liabilities and equity	$200,000	$50,000

All plant asset records for Dasher's home office and Dot branch are maintained on the home office books. Half of the $16,000 branch inventory at December 31, 20X1 was received from local suppliers, and the remaining $8,000 was received from the home office at established transfer prices. A summary of the transactions of Dasher's home office and Dot branch for 20X2 follows, and journal entries to record the transactions are presented in Exhibit 12–6.

1 Dasher's sales for 20X2 were $281,750, of which $200,000 were home office sales and $81,750 were sales made by the Dot branch. All sales were on account.
2 Home office and branch purchases on account for 20X2 were $205,000 and $20,000, respectively. The home office shipped $40,000 of merchandise to Dot branch at a transfer price of $50,000.
3 The home office collected $195,000 on account during 20X2, and Dot branch collected $79,750.
4 The Dot branch transferred $55,000 cash to the home office during 20X2.
5 Payments on account were home office, $210,000; Dot branch, $21,000.
6 During 20X2, the home office paid operating expenses of $20,000, and Dot branch paid operating expenses of $2,000. Of the operating expenses paid by the home office, $1,000 was allocated to Dot branch.
7 Total depreciation for the year was $8,000, of which $1,500 was allocated to branch operations.

Year-end inventories are $25,000 for the home office and $10,000 for Dot branch, with half of the branch inventory consisting of merchandise acquired from the home office. Thus, total inventories for Dasher Corporation on a cost basis are $34,000, computed as follows:

Home office inventory	$25,000
Branch inventory acquired through purchases	5,000
Branch inventory transferred from home office: $5,000 ÷ 1.25	4,000
Total inventories	$34,000

Separate cost of sales calculations for inclusion in the combined working papers for the home office and the Dot branch are as follows:

	Home Office	Dot Branch
Inventory January 1, 20X2	$ 20,000	$16,000
Purchases	205,000	20,000
Shipments to branch	(40,000)	—
Shipments from home office	—	50,000
Goods available for sale	185,000	86,000
Inventory December 31, 20X2	(25,000)	(10,000)
Cost of sales	$160,000	$76,000

Trial balances prepared at December 31, 20X2, after the transactions summarized in Exhibit 12–6 were recorded, and inventory items grouped into cost of sales categories are shown in the first two columns of Exhibit 12–7. These trial balances

DASHER CORPORATION
HOME OFFICE AND DOT BRANCH JOURNAL ENTRIES
FOR THE YEAR 20X2

Item Number	Home Office Books			Dot Branch Books		
1	Accounts receivable	$200,000		Accounts receivable	$81,750	
	Sales		$200,000	Sales		$81,750
	To record sales on account.			To record sales on account.		
2	Purchases	$205,000		Purchases	$20,000	
	Accounts payable		$205,000	Accounts payable		$20,000
	To record purchases on account.			To record purchases on account.		
	Dot branch	$ 50,000		Shipments from home office	$50,000	
	Shipments to Dot branch		$ 40,000	Home office		$50,000
	Loading-branch inventory		10,000	To record receipt of merchandise from home office.		
	To transfer merchandise to Dot branch at 125% of cost.					
3	Cash	$195,000		Cash	$79,750	
	Accounts receivable		$195,000	Accounts receivable		$79,750
	To record collections on accounts receivable.			To record collections on accounts receivable.		
4	Cash	$ 55,000		Home office	$55,000	
	Dot branch		$ 55,000	Cash		$55,000
	To record receipt of cash from Dot branch.			To record cash remittance to home office.		
5	Accounts payable	$210,000		Accounts payable	$21,000	
	Cash		$210,000	Cash		$21,000
	To record payments on account.			To record payments on account.		
6	Operating expenses	$ 20,000		Operating expenses	$ 2,000	
	Cash		$ 20,000	Cash		$ 2,000
	To record payment of expenses.			To record payment of expenses.		
	Dot branch	$ 1,000		Operating expenses	$ 1,000	
	Operating expenses		$ 1,000	Home office		$ 1,000
	To record allocation of expenses to Dot branch.			To record expenses allocated from home office.		
7	Dot branch	$ 1,500		Operating expenses	$ 1,500	
	Operating expenses	6,500		Home office		$ 1,500
	Accumulated depreciation		$ 8,000	To record allocation of depreciation from home office.		
	To record depreciation allocated to Dot branch.					

Exhibit 12–6   Comparative Journal Entries for Home Office and Branch

were taken before the home office recorded income from Dot branch for the year, so the home office and branch accounts have reciprocal balances.

The working paper entries needed to combine the accounts of the home office and branch are reproduced in general journal form as follows:

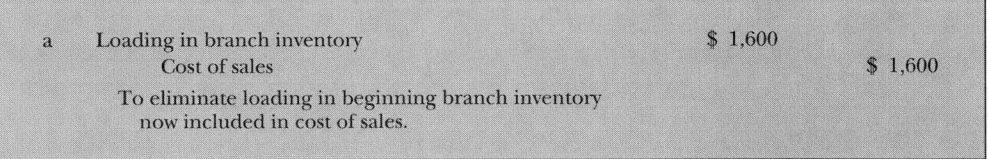

a	Loading in branch inventory	$ 1,600	
	Cost of sales		$ 1,600
	To eliminate loading in beginning branch inventory now included in cost of sales.		

DASHER CORPORATION
HOME OFFICE AND BRANCH WORKING PAPERS
FOR THE YEAR ENDED DECEMBER 31, 20X2

	Home Office	Dot Branch	Adjustments and Eliminations		Income Statement	Balance Sheet
Debits						
Cash	$ 45,000	$ 12,750				$ 57,750
Accounts receivable—net	47,000	25,000				72,000
Inventories	25,000	10,000		c 1,000		34,000
Plant assets—net	62,000					62,000
Dot branch	40,500			d 40,500		
Cost of sales	160,000	76,000	c 1,000	a 1,600 b 10,000	$(225,400)	
Operating expenses	25,500	4,500			(30,000)	
	$405,000	$128,250				$225,750
Credits						
Accounts payable	$ 9,000	$ 4,000				$ 13,000
Other liabilities	10,000	2,000				12,000
Loading in branch inventory	11,600		a 1,600 b 10,000			
Home office		40,500	d 40,500			
Capital stock	150,000					150,000
Retained earnings January 1, 20X2	24,400					24,400
Sales	200,000	81,750			281,750	
	$405,000	$128,250				
Net income					$ 26,350	26,350
						$225,750

Exhibit 12–7 *Combining Working Papers*

The home office and branch working papers in Exhibit 12–7 do not contain a retained earnings column. Dasher's net income for the period is the only item affecting the ending retained earnings balance, so it is convenient to omit the separate retained earnings column and to carry net income for the period directly to the balance sheet column.

Adjusting and closing entries for the Dot branch and home office are:

Dot Branch Closing Entry

Sales	$ 81,750	
Inventory December 31, 20X2	10,000	
Inventory January 1, 20X2		$ 16,000
Purchases		20,000
Shipments from home office		50,000
Operating expenses		4,500
Home office		1,250

Home Office Adjusting and Closing Entries

Dot branch	$ 1,250	
Dot branch profit		$ 1,250
Loading in branch inventory	$ 10,600	
Dot branch profit		$ 10,600

Unrealized profit per books of $11,600, less $1,000 unrealized profit in branch ending inventory = $10,600 adjustment.

Sales	$200,000	
Inventory December 31, 20X2	25,000	
Shipments to Dot branch	40,000	
Dot branch profit	11,850	
Inventory January 1, 20X2		$ 20,000
Purchases		205,000
Operating expenses		25,500
Retained earnings		26,350

The $1,250 income reported by the branch does not include any margin on goods received from the home office. This element of branch profit is recorded by the home office when it adjusts its loading account at year-end. Branch income for the year on a cost basis to the business entity is $11,850, an amount that appears in the separate home office income statement for 20X2.

Comparative balance sheets and income statements for Dasher Corporation's home office, its Dot branch, and its home office and branch combined appear in Exhibit 12–8 on page 474. These statements are presented to highlight differences between separate home office and branch statements and combined statements for the enterprise. Note that the cost of sales on the home office books is equal to 80% of home office sales ($160,000 ÷ $200,000), and that combined cost of sales is equal to 80% of combined sales ($225,400 ÷ $281,750), reflecting the companywide policy of setting sales prices at 25% above cost. This relationship does not exist between branch cost of sales and sales because branch shipments from the home office are recorded on the branch books at selling prices. All the items in the comparative statements have been covered individually, so additional discussion is not provided.

SUMMARY

Enterprises frequently conduct activities at diverse business locations by means of branches and sales agencies. Separate accounting systems are not required for sales agency operations, but the accounting system of the business entity may be expanded in order to provide information about agency operations for purposes of planning, control, and evaluation. By contrast, home office and branch operations are accounted for through separate home office and branch accounting systems. The home office accounts for its investment in the net assets of its branches by means of "branch" accounts that are reciprocal to "home office" accounts on the books of the branches. Reciprocal home office and branch accounts are eliminated when home office and branch financial statements are combined into financial statements for the enterprise.

Transactions between a home office and its branches require journal entries that are unique to home office and branch accounting systems. Entries to account for other transactions are recorded in the usual manner. Merchandise shipments to

```
DASHER CORPORATION
COMPARATIVE FINANCIAL STATEMENTS
AT AND FOR THE YEAR ENDED DECEMBER 31, 20X2
```

	Home Office	Dot Branch	Combined
Balance Sheets—December 31, 20X2			
Assets			
Cash	$ 45,000	$12,750	$ 57,750
Accounts receivable—net	47,000	25,000	72,000
Inventories December 31, 20X2	25,000	10,000	34,000
Dot branch	41,750	—	—
Plant assets—net	62,000	—	62,000
Total assets	$220,750	$47,750	$225,750
Liabilities and Equity			
Accounts payable	$ 9,000	$ 4,000	$ 13,000
Other liabilities	10,000	2,000	12,000
Loading—branch inventory	1,000	—	—
Home office	—	41,750	—
Capital stock	150,000	—	150,000
Retained earnings	50,750	—	50,750
Total liabilities and equity	$220,750	$47,750	$225,750
Income Statements—for 20X2			
Sales	$200,000	$81,750	$281,750
Dot branch income	11,850	—	—
	211,850	81,750	281,750
Cost of sales	(160,000)	(76,000)	(225,400)
Operating expenses	(25,500)	(4,500)	(30,000)
Net income	$ 26,350	$ 1,250	$ 26,350

Exhibit 12–8 *Separate Home Office and Branch and Combined Financial Statements*

branches and related transfer pricing strategies require special attention in order to avoid recognition of unrealized profits. Other areas of concern in home office-branch accounting include expense allocation, account reconciliation, and year-end accounting procedures. Separate home office and branch financial statements are used only for internal purposes. Financial statements for the enterprise as a whole are developed by combining the separate statements of the home office and its branches.

ASSIGNMENT MATERIAL

QUESTIONS

1 How does branch accounting differ from accounting for sales agencies?

2 Should a company maintain separate accounts for subsidiary records in order to identify the revenues and expenses associated with operations of each of its sale agencies? Discuss.

3 When are expenses paid by a sales agency recorded on the books of the central accounting unit of the enterprise?

4 Alternative account titles for the branch account on the books of the home office include "Tampa branch," "investment in Tampa branch," and "Tampa branch—current." Describe the nature and function of this account.

5 Explain the nature of the "shipments to branch" account on the home office books and the "shipments from home office" account on the branch books.

6 The accounts "shipments to branch" and "shipments from home office" may or may not have reciprocal balances. When should the account balances be reciprocal and when would they be different?

7 What advantages can you see for a firm to set transfer prices to its branches at normal sales prices?

8 Telestar Company ships merchandise to its Denver branch at 30% above cost. If the Denver branch has a beginning inventory of $39,000 and records shipments from home office of $780,000, what should be the year-end balance of the "loading" account on the books of the home office before adjusting entries? After adjusting entries, assuming that the ending inventory of the Denver branch is $58,500?

9 Topper Corporation's home office shipped merchandise to its Pine branch at a cost of $20,000 and also paid $1,000 shipping costs. Pine branch shipped this merchandise to Spruce branch a few days later and paid $500 shipping costs. If Topper's home office had shipped the merchandise directly to Spruce branch, the shipping cost would have been $900. Prepare journal entries on the books of the home office to record these transactions.

10 Does the allocation of home office expenses to branch operations affect the income of an enterprise? If not, what is the advantage of such allocation? Discuss.

11 Does the income of a home office plus the income of its branches equal the combined net income of the enterprise? Explain.

12 In preparing working papers to combine the adjusted trial balances of a home office and its branches, what is the advantage of combining the home office adjusted trial balance before recording the entry for branch profit or loss for the period?

EXERCISES

E 12-1 Arnimal Corporation is located in Dallas, Texas, and its branch is located in Forth Worth, Texas. Transactions and events affecting the Fort Worth branch during 20X9 are summarized as follows:

   1 Received shipments from the home office, billed at $10,000 home office cost.
   2 Purchased merchandise from Alta Wholesalers, $4,000.
   3 Sold merchandise to customers on account in the amount of $20,000.
   4 Paid operating expenses, $3,000.
   5 Returned 20% of the merchandise received in item 1 to the home office.
   6 Paid $2,000 for advertising, 50% of which is a home office expense.
   7 Received a debit memo from the home office for the following expenses allocated by the home office to the branch: depreciation expense, $500; other operating expenses, $200.
   8 Remitted $5,000 to the home office.
   9 Collected $14,000 on accounts receivable.
   10 Collected a note for the home office in the amount of $3,000 plus $150 interest.
   11 Received notice that the home office had collected $1,000 from a branch customer (assume that it was a customer included in item 3).
   12 Closed the nominal accounts to the revenue and expense summary account. Branch beginning and ending inventories were $1,900 and $2,000, respectively.
   13 Closed the balance of the revenue and expense summary account.

Required: Prepare journal entries to reflect the transactions and events in the accounts of the branch and the home office.

E 12-2 Yak Corporation's home office ships merchandise to its Vinton branch at a billing price of 120% of cost. During 20X4, the home office makes the following entry:

Vinton branch	$60,000	
Shipments to Vinton branch		$60,000

At year-end 20X4, $12,000 of this merchandise remains in the Vinton branch inventory.

Required: Prepare the entry or entries necessary on Yak's home office books at year-end 20X4 to adjust the branch inventory and branch profit to a cost basis.

E 12-3 Medina Corporation has operations in two locations—a main plant and a branch plant. The branch receives most of its inventory from the main plant, but it also purchases some items from local suppliers. The main plant transfers merchandise to the branch at 120% of cost, and this merchandise is inventoried by the branch at billed prices. The following data for the year 20X2 are available:

	Main Plant Books	Branch Plant Books
Inventory January 1	$ 126,000	$ 24,000
Purchases	1,400,000	48,000
Shipments to Branch	300,000	
Shipments from Home Office		360,000
Inventory/December 31	120,000	26,000

One-fourth of the beginning branch inventory was acquired from outside suppliers. The branch ending inventory includes $5,000 from outside suppliers.

Required: Determine the cost of goods sold amount to be included in the published income statement of Medina Corporation for the year 20X2.

E 12-4   Liberty Company operates two stores—the home office store and the Maywood branch. On December 31, 20X1, the Maywood branch account on the home office books has a balance of $340,000. On this same date, the Maywood branch books show a home office account balance of $319,000.

Both stores use a standard 120% markup on cost. However, Liberty's home office ships merchandise to the Maywood branch at cost. Maywood's ending inventory includes $20,000 of merchandise received from the home office.

Maywood remitted $15,000 to the home office on December 30, 20X1. However, the check was not delivered until January 5, 20X2. The home office allocated $5,000 general expenses to the Maywood branch, but this expense allocation had not been recorded by the Maywood branch at year-end.

Maywood paid $2,000 for advertising "after Christmas" sales that were to be allocated equally between the two stores. The home office has not recorded its share of this expense.

Required: Prepare a reconciliation of the home office and branch accounts.

E 12-5   Diazo Corporation operates a main store at its home office and a branch store in another state. The branch purchases most of its merchandise from the home office at 10% above home office cost. All merchandise acquired from other suppliers is accounted for by the branch at original cost. At September 30, 20X7, the records of the branch indicated the following:

September sales	$70,000	
Inventory September 1	17,600*	(50% from outside suppliers)
Shipments from home office	27,500	(at billed prices)
Purchases from outsiders	12,000	
Expenses	20,000	
Inventory September 30	15,000*	($4,000 from outside suppliers)

*Merchandise acquired from the home office is inventoried at billed prices.

Required

1 Prepare all necessary adjusting and closing entries on the branch books at September 30, 20X7.

2 Prepare all necessary adjusting entries on the home office books at September 30, 20X7 to adjust the home office records for the branch operations for September.

E 12-6   Eastland Corporation has two branches to which merchandise is transferred at cost plus 20%, plus freight charges. On November 30, 20X6, Eastland shipped merchandise that cost $5,500 to its Charlotte branch, and the $200 shipping charges were paid by Eastland. On December 15, 20X6, the Raleigh branch encountered an inventory shortage, and the Charlotte branch shipped the merchandise to the Raleigh branch at a freight cost of $160 paid by the Charlotte branch. Shipping charges from the home office to the Raleigh branch would have been $175.

1 Eastland will record the $5,500 shipment to the Charlotte branch, together with the $200 shipping charge, in a journal entry that includes the following:
   a Shipments from home office, $6,600
   b Shipments to Charlotte branch, $5,700
   c Unrealized profit—branch inventory, $1,100
   d Investment in Charlotte branch, $5,700

2 Charlotte branch should record the transfer of merchandise to the Raleigh branch by either a debit or a credit entry that includes the following:
   a Shipments from home office, $5,500
   b Raleigh branch, $6,975
   c Home office, $6,960
   d Inventory, $5,660

3 If the merchandise is unsold at year-end, the Raleigh branch will inventory the merchandise at:
   a $6,000   c $6,760
   b $6,975   d $6,775

4 If the merchandise is unsold at year-end, Eastland Corporation will include it as an asset in its *Annual Report to Stockholders* in the amount of:
   a $5,500   c $5,675
   b $5,660   d $5,875

E 12-7   On December 3, 20X3, the home office of Bristol Office Supply Company recorded a shipment of merchandise to its South Fork branch as follows:

South Fork branch	$30,000	
Shipments to South Fork branch		$25,000
Unrealized profit in South Fork branch inventory		4,000
Cash [for freight charges]		1,000

The South Fork branch sells 40% of the merchandise to outside entities during the rest of December 20X3. The books of the home office and Bristol branches are closed on December 31 of each year.

On January 5, 20X4, the South Fork branch transfers half of the original shipment to the Sandy branch, and the South Fork branch pays $500 freight on the shipment.

Required

1 Prepare the journal entry on the books of the South Fork branch to record receipt of the shipment from the home office on December 3, 20X3.
2 At what amounts should the 60% of the merchandise remaining unsold at December 31, 20X3 be included in (a) the inventory of the South Fork branch at December 31, 20X3 and (b) the published balance sheet of Bristol Office Supply Company at December 31, 20X3.
3 Prepare journal entries on the books of (a) the home office, (b) the South Fork branch, and (c) the Sandy branch for the January 5, 20X4 transfer, assuming that the freight cost of the merchandise from the home office to the Sandy branch would have been $600.

E 12-8 Summarized data taken from the trial balances of Manning Corporation's home office and branch at December 31, 20X5 are as follows:

	Home Office	Branch
Other assets	$340,000	$ 61,200
Branch	50,000	—
Inventory, January 1	10,000	4,800
Purchases	80,000	—
Shipments from home office	—	24,000
Expenses	20,000	10,000
	$500,000	$100,000
Liabilities	$ 25,200	$ 10,000
Loading in beginning branch inventory	800	—
Home office	—	50,000
Capital stock	200,000	—
Retained earnings, January 1	130,000	—
Sales	120,000	40,000
Shipments to branch	24,000	—
	$500,000	$100,000

The home office ships merchandise to its branch at 120% of home office cost. At December 31, 20X5, the home office inventory at cost was $15,000 and the branch inventory at transfer prices was $6,000.

Required

1 Prepare a schedule of cost of sales.
2 Prepare comparative home office, branch, and combined income statements for Manning Corporation for the year ended December 31, 20X5.

E 12-9 Naylor Corporation sells merchandise to independent retailers as well as to its own branch retail outlet for resale to customers. Sales to the branch outlet are made at 130% of Naylor's cost. Selected items from the trial balances of Naylor's home office and the branch outlet are as follows:

	Home Office Books	Branch Books
Debits:		
Inventory January 1	$120,000	$ 97,500
Purchases	630,000	—
Shipments from Naylor	—	312,000
Expenses	200,000	120,000
Credits:		
Shipments to branch	240,000	—
Sales	830,000	540,000
Unrealized profit in branch inventory	94,500	—

The December 31, 20X1 home office inventory is $90,000. Branch ending inventory at the transfer price is $39,000.

Required

  1 Prepare a closing entry for the branch and adjusting and closing entries for the home office.
  2 Prepare a combined income statement for Naylor Corporation using a cost of goods sold summary caption.

E 12-10 Home office and branch accounts for Michael Company showing activities for the month of July 20X7 follow:

HOME OFFICE ACCOUNT (BRANCH BOOKS)

Cash remitted to home office	$42,000	June 30, 20X7 balance	$15,000
Merchandise returned		Shipment from home	
to home office	3,000	office (cost)	32,000
Machine charged to home		Expenses allocated	
office	5,000	from home office	14,500
		Home office note collected	
		with $100 interest	2,100

INVESTMENT IN BRANCH ACCOUNT (HOME OFFICE BOOKS)

June 30, 20X7 balance	$15,000	Cash received from branch	$36,000
Shipments to branch (cost)	37,000	Machine purchased by branch	5,000
Expenses allocated to branch	15,400		
Note collected by branch	2,000		

Except for a branch error in recording expense allocations and a home office error in not recording interest, all differences in the accounts are due to timing differences in recording reciprocal information.

Required

  1 Prepare a reconciliation of the home office account (branch books) and the investment in branch account (home office books) as of July 31, 20X7.
  2 Prepare a single correcting journal entry to bring the home office account on the branch books up to date on July 31, 20X7.
  3 Prepare a single correcting journal entry to bring the investment in branch account on the home office books up to date on July 31, 20X7.

E 12-11 Summary adjusted trial balances for the home office and branch of Tanker Corporation at December 31, 20X3 are as follows:

	Home Office	Branch
Debits		
Other assets	$ 530,000	$165,000
Inventories January 1, 20X3	50,000	45,000
Branch	200,000	—
Purchases	500,000	—
Shipments from home office	—	240,000
Expenses	120,000	50,000
Dividends	100,000	—
Total debits	$1,500,000	$500,000
Credits		
Other liabilities	$ 90,000	$ 25,000
Capital stock	500,000	—
Retained earnings	100,000	—
Home office	—	175,000
Unrealized profit in branch inventory	10,000	—
Sales	537,500	300,000
Shipments to branch	200,000	—
Branch profit	62,500	—
Total credits	$1,500,000	$500,000

Additional Information

  1 The home office ships merchandise to its branch at 120% of home office cost.
  2 Inventories at December 31, 20X3 are $70,000 for the home office and $60,000 for the branch. The branch inventory is at transfer prices.

Required

1 Journalize the closing entries for the branch at December 31, 20X3.
2 Journalize the closing entries for the home office at December 31, 20X3.
3 Prepare a combined balance sheet for Tanker Corporation at December 31, 20X3.
4 Prepare a combined income statement for Tanker Corporation for the year ended December 31, 20X3.

E 12-12 Comparative data for Dalton Corporation's home office and its branches are summarized as follows:

	Home Office	Salina Branch	Wichita Branch
Cash	$ 67,000	$ 43,000	$ 46,000
Inventory January 1	83,000	22,000	33,000
Other current assets	50,000	20,000	25,000
Salina branch	90,000	—	—
Wichita branch	60,000	—	—
Shipments from home office	—	55,000	66,000
Purchases	150,000	—	—
Expenses	100,000	40,000	30,000
	$600,000	$180,000	$200,000
Current liabilities	$ 34,000	$ 10,000	$ 20,000
Capital stock	200,000	—	—
Retained earnings	40,000	—	—
Home Office	—	90,000	60,000
Loading—Salina branch	7,000	—	—
Loading—Wichita branch	9,000	—	—
Sales	200,000	80,000	120,000
Shipments to Salina branch	50,000	—	—
Shipments to Wichita branch	60,000	—	—
	$600,000	$180,000	$200,000

Ending inventories are $40,000 for the home office, $27,500 for the Salina branch, and $28,600 for the Wichita branch.

Required: Prepare an income statement for the home office of Dalton Corporation for the year (*not* a combined income statement).

PROBLEMS

P 12-1 Isaac Corporation retails merchandise through its home office store and through a branch store in a distant city. Separate ledgers are maintained by the home office and the branch. The branch store purchases merchandise from the home office (at 120% of home office cost), as well as from outside suppliers. Selected information from the December 31, 20X7 trial balances of the home office and branch is as follows:

	Home Office	Branch
Sales	$120,000	$60,000
Shipments to branch	16,000	—
Purchases	70,000	11,000
Inventory, January 1, 20X7	40,000	30,000
Shipments from home office	—	19,200
Expenses	28,000	12,000
Unrealized profit in branch inventory	7,200	—

Additional Information

1 The entire difference between the shipment accounts is due to the practice of billing the branch at cost plus 20%.
2 December 31, 20X7 inventories are $40,000 and $20,000 for the home office and the branch, respectively. (*Note:* The branch purchased 16% of its ending inventory from outside suppliers.)
3 Branch beginning and ending inventories include merchandise acquired from the home office as well as from outside suppliers. Merchandise acquired from the home office is inventoried at 120% of home office cost.

Required

1 Prepare a single closing journal entry for the branch books at December 31, 20X7.
2 Prepare journal entries to adjust the home office books for branch activities for 20X7. (*Hint:* Two entries are required.)
3 Prepare a single closing journal entry for the home office books at December 31, 20X7.
4 Prepare a combined income statement for Isaac Corporation for the year ended December 31, 20X7.

P 12-2 Fast-Stop has three all-night grocery stores located in western Virginia. Each store has a branch manager with authority to accept inventory items at home office cost plus 10% or to purchase from outside wholesalers, at his or her discretion.

Inventories at December 31, 20X1 were as follows:

Home office	$110,900 cost
Dublin branch	26,400 transfer price
Radford branch	29,700 transfer price
Blacksburg branch	46,200 transfer price

Summary information for Fast-Stop and its branches at December 31, 20X1 includes the following accounts and amounts.

	Home Office	Dublin Branch	Radford Branch	Blacksburg Branch
Cash	$ 42,000	$ 6,000	$ 44,000	$ 8,000
Inventories	60,900	37,400	33,000	18,700
Other current assets	45,100	26,600	40,000	53,300
Plant assets—net	200,000	—	—	—
Dublin branch	40,000	—	—	—
Radford branch	92,000	—	—	—
Blacksburg branch	50,000	—	—	—
Purchases	1,000,000	—	—	—
Shipments from home office	—	330,000	275,000	440,000
Expenses	20,000	50,000	48,000	80,000
	$1,550,000	$450,000	$440,000	$600,000
Liabilities	$ 46,900	$ —	$ —	$ —
Capital stock	400,000	—	—	—
Retained earnings	50,000	—	—	—
Home office	—	40,000	92,000	50,000
Unrealized profit in branch inventories	103,100	—	—	—
Shipments to Dublin branch	300,000	—	—	—
Shipments to Radford branch	250,000	—	—	—
Shipments to Blacksburg branch	400,000	—	—	—
Sales	—	410,000	348,000	550,000
	$1,550,000	$450,000	$440,000	$600,000

Required

1 Prepare adjusting and closing entries for the home office of Fast-Stop.
2 Prepare a combined income statement for Fast-Stop for 20X1.
3 Prepare a combined balance sheet for Fast-Stop at December 31, 20X1.

P 12-3 Separate financial statements of Tiller Company's home office and branch for 20X3 are summarized as follows:

	Home Office	Branch
Income Statements for the Year Ended December 31, 20X3		
Sales	$1,650,000	$800,000
Income from branch	218,000	—
Total revenue	1,868,000	800,000
Less: Cost of goods sold		
Beginning inventory	$ 250,000	$104,000*
Purchases	800,000	120,000
Shipments to branch	(200,000)	—
Shipments from home office	—	240,000

(Continued)

	Home Office	Branch
Goods available for sale	850,000	464,000
Inventory, December 31	(200,000)	(114,000)†
Cost of goods sold	650,000	350,000
Gross profit	1,218,000	450,000
Expenses	(700,000)	(270,000)
Net income	$ 518,000	$180,000

Retained Earnings Statement
for the Year Ended December 31, 20X3

Retained earnings—beginning	$ 132,000	—
Home office—preclosing balance	—	$250,000
Add: Net income	518,000	180,000
Less: Dividends	(400,000)	—
Retained earnings/home office balance—ending	$ 250,000	$430,000

Balance Sheet at December 31, 20X3

Cash	$ 64,000	$ 56,000
Accounts receivable—net	320,000	180,000
Inventories	200,000	114,000
Unrealized profit in branch inventory	(14,000)	—
Plant assets—net	800,000	200,000
Branch	430,000	—
Total assets	$1,800,000	$550,000
Accounts payable	$ 400,000	$ 80,000
Other liabilities	150,000	40,000
Capital stock	1,000,000	—
Retained earnings	250,000	—
Home office	—	430,000
Total equities	$1,800,000	$550,000

*Includes $72,000 acquired from home office at 120% of home office cost plus $32,000 acquired
through purchases.
†Includes $84,000 acquired from home office at 120% of home office cost plus $30,000 acquired
through purchases.

Required: Prepare working papers to combine the operations of Tiller's home office and branch
using the cost of goods sold summary approach with supporting schedules.

P 12-4 The after-closing balances of Carler Corporation's home office and its branch at January 1,
20X1 were as follows:

	Home Office	Branch
Cash	$ 7,000	$ 2,000
Accounts receivable—net	10,000	3,500
Inventory	15,000	5,500
Plant assets—net	45,000	20,000
Branch	28,000	—
Total assets	$105,000	$31,000
Accounts payable	$ 4,500	$ 2,500
Other liabilities	3,000	500
Unrealized profit—branch inventory	500	—
Home office	—	28,000
Capital stock	80,000	—
Retained earnings	17,000	—
Total equities	$105,000	$31,000

A summary of the operations of the home office and branch for 20X1 follows:

1 Home office sales: $100,000, including $33,000 to the branch. A standard 10% markup
on cost applies to all sales to the branch. Branch sales to its customers totaled $50,000.
2 Purchases from outside entities: home office, $50,000; branch, $7,000.
3 Collections from sales: home office, $98,000 (including $30,000 from branch); branch
collections, $51,000.
4 Payments on account: home office, $51,500; branch, $4,000.
5 Operating expenses paid: home office, $20,000; branch, $6,000.

6 Depreciation on plant assets: home office, $4,000; branch, $1,000.

7 Home office operating expenses allocated to the branch, $2,000.

8 At December 31, 20X1, the home office inventory is $11,000 and the branch inventory is $6,000, of which $1,050 was acquired from outside suppliers.

Required

1 Prepare journal entries to reflect the foregoing information in the accounts of the home office and the branch.

2 Post the journal entries to ledger accounts.

3 Prepare trial balances for the home office and branch.

4 Construct working papers to combine the activities of the home office and branch into financial statements.

5 Prepare closing entries for the branch and adjusting and closing entries for the home office.

P 12-5 Anselmo Company operates retail hobby shops from the main store and a branch store. Merchandise is shipped from the main store to the branch and billed to the branch at an arbitrary 10% markup. Trial balances of the main store and branch as of December 31, 20X6 are as follows:

	Main Store	Branch
Debits		
Cash	$ 1,500	$ 1,000
Accounts receivable—net	200	—
Inventory December 31, 20X5	3,500	2,500
Building—net	60,000	18,000
Equipment—net	30,000	12,000
Branch store	32,300	—
Purchases	240,000	11,000
Shipments from home office	—	99,000
Other expenses	15,000	7,000
	$382,500	$150,500
Credits		
Accounts payable	$ 15,000	$ 500
Unrealized inventory profit	9,200	—
Main store	—	30,000
Capital stock	50,000	—
Retained earnings	16,000	—
Sales	200,000	120,000
Shipments to branch	90,000	—
Profit from branch	2,300	—
	$382,500	$150,500

Inventories on hand at December 31, 20X6 at the main store and branch are $3,000 and $1,800, respectively. The December 31, 20X5 branch inventory includes merchandise purchased from outsiders of $300, and the December 31, 20X6 branch inventory includes $150 of merchandise purchased from outsiders.

Required

1 Prepare a schedule of cost of goods sold.

2 Prepare working papers to combine the main store and the branch accounts for the year 20X6.

P 12-6 Trial balances for Bear Corporation and its two branches at December 31, 20X6 are as follows:

	Home Office	Branch A	Branch B
Debits			
Cash	$ 15,000	$ 1,300	$ 6,400
Inventory January 1, 20X6	34,000	5,500	8,800
Other assets	300,000	150,000	125,000
Branch A	100,000	—	—
Branch B	81,000	—	—
Purchases	350,000	—	—
Shipments from home office	—	68,200	41,800
Other expenses	120,000	35,000	38,000
	$1,000,000	$260,000	$220,000

(Continued)

	Home Office	Branch A	Branch B
Credits			
Liabilities	$ 60,000	$ 16,000	$ 25,000
Home office	—	94,000	75,000
Sales	500,000	150,000	120,000
Shipments to Branch A	73,700	—	—
Shipments to Branch B	46,200	—	—
Loading in December 31,			
20X5 inventories	1,300	—	—
Capital stock	300,000	—	—
Retained earnings	18,800	—	—
	$1,000,000	$260,000	$220,000

Additional Information

1 Inventories on hand excluding all goods in transit on December 31, 20X6 are:

Home Office (cost)	$31,000
Branch A (billing prices)	7,260
Branch B (billing prices)	8,250

2 All differences between home office and branch accounts are due to cash in transit and merchandise in transit. (All cash in transit is from branch to home office.)

3 Bear consistently uses a standard markup on all goods shipped to its branches.

Required: Prepare working papers to combine the operations of Bear Corporation's home office and its branches at and for the year ended December 31, 20X6.

P 12-7 Selected information from the trial balances for the home office and the branch of Certy Company at December 31, 20X8 is provided. These trial balances cover the period from December 1 to December 31, 20X8. The branch acquires some of its merchandise from the home office (the branch is billed at 20% above the cost to the home office) and some of it from outsiders. Differences in the shipments accounts result entirely from the home office policy of billing the branch at 20% above cost.

	Home Office	Branch
Sales	$60,000	$30,000
Shipments to branch	8,000	—
Shipments to branch—loading	3,600	—
Purchases (outsiders)	35,000	5,500
Shipments from home office	—	9,600
Merchandise inventory December 1, 20X8	20,000	15,000
Expenses	14,000	6,000

Additional Information

Merchandise inventory, December 31, 20X8—home office, $20,000; branch, $10,000.

Required

1 How much of the December 1 inventory of the branch represents purchases from outsiders and how much represents goods acquired from the home office?

2 The ending inventory of the branch consists of merchandise purchased from the home office of $8,400; and from outsiders of $1,600. What entry is necessary on the home office books to adjust the "shipments to branch—loading" account at December 31, 20X8?

3 Prepare the income statement to be submitted by the branch to the home office for the month of December 20X8.

4 Prepare the income statement for the home office for December 20X8, showing separately the results of home office and branch operations (*not* a combined or consolidated statement).

P 12-8 Eastman Corporation has three distribution centers—the main office, Buffalo branch, and Carson branch. All merchandise is purchased through the main office and billed to the branches at 20% above cost. Trial balances for the three locations at December 31, 20X5 are as follows:

	Main Office	Buffalo Branch	Carson Branch
Cash	$ 26,000	$ 14,500	$ 25,000
Inventory December 31, 20X4	82,000	12,000	15,600
Shipments from main office	—	48,000	55,200
Buffalo branch	62,000	—	—
Carson branch	72,000	—	—
Other assets	300,000	50,000	60,000
Purchases	220,000	—	—
Expenses	38,000	9,500	10,200
	$800,000	$134,000	$166,000
Liabilities	$ 95,400	$ 20,000	$ 27,800
Shipments to Buffalo branch	54,000	—	—
Shipments to Carson branch	66,000	—	—
Sales	160,000	60,000	80,000
Unrealized profit in beginning branch inventories	4,600	—	—
Capital stock	350,000	—	—
Retained earnings	70,000	—	—
Main office	—	54,000	58,200
	$800,000	$134,000	$166,000

Additional Information

1 At December 31, 20X5, the Buffalo branch deposited $2,000 to the account of the main office.
2 On December 30, 20X5, the main office sent a $3,000 check to the Carson branch to replenish Carson's working capital.
3 Inventories at December 31, 20X5 are as follows:

Home office (cost)	$86,000
Buffalo branch (billed prices)	8,400
Carson branch (billed prices)	7,200

These inventories do not include goods in transit.

Required

1 Prepare a reconciliation of the main office and branch accounts on December 31, 20X5 before closing entries are made.
2 Calculate the separate and the combined inventories of the main office and the two branches on a cost basis at December 31, 20X5.
3 Compute the combined income of Eastman Corporation for the year ended December 31, 20X5.
4 Prepare a combined balance sheet for Eastman Corporation at December 31, 20X5.

P 12-9 Control Products Corporation has two branches, A and B, to which merchandise is billed at 20% above cost. Unadjusted trial balances of the three entities at December 31, 20X7 are summarized as follows:

	Home Office	Branch A	Branch B
Cash	$ 33,000	$ 22,000	$ 13,000
Inventory	80,000	18,000	24,000
Other current assets	50,000	25,000	23,000
Branch A	45,000	—	—
Branch B	42,000	—	—
Shipments from home office	—	60,000	36,000
Purchases	160,000	—	—
Expenses	90,000	25,000	20,000
	$500,000	$150,000	$116,000
Current liabilities	$ 40,000	$ 15,000	$ 11,000
Capital stock	100,000	—	—
Retained earnings	50,000	—	—
Home office	—	45,000	30,000

(Continued)

	Home Office	Branch A	Branch B
Loading—Branch A	13,000	—	—
Loading—Branch B	12,000	—	—
Sales	195,000	90,000	75,000
Shipments to Branch A	50,000	—	—
Shipments to Branch B	40,000	—	—
	$500,000	$150,000	$116,000

Additional Information

1. Merchandise that cost $10,000 was in transit from the home office to Branch B at December 31, 20X7.
2. Physical inventories at December 31, 20X7 were as follows:

Home office	$70,000 at cost
Branch A	21,000 at billed prices
Branch B	15,000 at billed prices (does not include merchandise in transit)

Required

1. Prepare working papers to combine home office and branch accounts for the year ended December 31, 20X7.
2. Prepare a reconciliation of the branch and home office accounts, starting with the balances given in the unadjusted trial balances and reconciling to the correct balances at December 31, 20X7, after all adjusting and closing entries have been made.

P 12-10 Trial balances for Homer Corporation and its two branches at December 31, 20X4 are as follows:

	Homer Home Office	Hampton Branch	Norfolk Branch
Debits			
Cash	$ 18,000	$ 5,000	$ 15,000
Receivables	30,000	12,000	26,000
Inventories January 1, 20X4	36,000	7,200	5,400
Other assets	200,000	42,800	47,600
Hampton branch	50,000	—	—
Norfolk branch	68,000	—	—
Shipments from home office	—	30,000	27,000
Purchases	120,000	—	—
Expenses	78,000	35,000	40,000
	$600,000	$132,000	$161,000
Credits			
Accounts payable	$ 40,000	$ 10,000	$ 30,000
Capital stock	200,000	—	—
Retained earnings	41,900	—	—
Home Office	—	42,000	61,000
Sales	250,000	80,000	70,000
Shipments to Hampton branch	36,000	—	—
Shipments to Norfolk branch	30,000	—	—
Loading—branch inventories	2,100	—	—
	$600,000	$132,000	$161,000

Additional Information

1. All shipments are billed at 120% of cost.
2. Ending inventories are $32,000, $8,400, and $4,800 for the home office, the Hampton branch, and the Norfolk branch, respectively. Ending inventories of the branches include the standard 20% loading factor but exclude goods in transit.
3. Goods in transit at billing prices on December 31, 20X4 are $6,000 to the Hampton branch and $3,000 to the Norfolk branch. Cash in transit from home office to the Hampton branch for operating expenses at December 31, 20X4 is $2,000. Cash in transit from the Norfolk branch to home office amounts to $4,000.
4. "Loading—branch inventories" represents unrealized profit in beginning inventories of the Hampton and Norfolk branches.

1 Prepare all journal entries necessary to adjust and close the books of the Hampton branch.
2 Prepare all journal entries necessary to adjust and close the books of the Norfolk branch.
3 Prepare all journal entries necessary to adjust and close the books of the home office.
4 Prepare an income statement for 20X4 and a balance sheet on December 31, 20X4 for Homer Corporation in a form that *reports revenue and expense details*, rather than branch profit and loss.

P 12-11 Comparative trial balances of the home office and the two branches of Toller Corporation at December 31, 20X2 were as follows:

	Home Office	Roca Branch	Lane Branch
Debits			
Cash	$ 5,000	$ 15,000	$ 22,000
Accounts receivable—net	80,000	30,000	40,000
Inventories	150,000	60,000	48,000
Roca branch	170,000	—	—
Lane branch	165,000	—	—
Plant assets (net)	730,000	250,000	200,000
Purchases	900,000	—	—
Shipments from home office	—	300,000	240,000
Expenses	300,000	75,000	50,000
Total debits	$2,500,000	$730,000	$600,000
Credits			
Accounts payable	$ 100,000	$ 45,000	$ 30,000
Other liabilities	80,000	15,000	5,000
Loading in branch inventories	108,000	—	—
Capital stock, $10 par	500,000	—	—
Retained earnings	262,000	—	—
Home office	—	170,000	165,000
Sales	1,000,000	500,000	400,000
Shipments to branches	450,000	—	—
Total credits	$2,500,000	$730,000	$600,000

Additional Information
Home office and branch inventories at December 31, 20X2 were:

Home office at cost	$120,000
Roca branch at billing prices	72,000
Lane branch at billing prices	96,000

All branch shipments are billed at 120% of home office cost.

Required

1 Compute the beginning inventory of Toller Corporation dated December 31, 20X1.
2 Compute the ending inventory of Toller Corporation at December 31, 20X2.
3 Prepare journal entries to close the books of the Roca branch and the Lane branch at December 31, 20X2.
4 Prepare journal entries to adjust and close the books of the home office at December 31, 20X2.
5 Prepare an income statement for the home office of Toller Corporation for the year ended December 31, 20X2 (*not* a combined income statement).
6 Prepare a combined balance sheet for Toller Corporation at December 31, 20X2.

13

Foreign Currency Concepts and Transactions

Foreign business activity by U.S. corporations has expanded rapidly over the years. In 1996, exports of U.S. goods rose to $611.7 billion, an increase of more than 6% from the previous year. Imports of foreign goods totaled $799.3 billion in 1996 (a 6.7% increase over 1995). In addition to import and export activities, U.S. corporations are heavily involved in foreign business operations through investments in foreign branches and foreign subsidiaries. For example, *The Coca-Cola Company 1997 Annual Report* reported that 66% of its net operating revenue and 76% of its operating income came from soft drink operations outside of North America. Only 29% of Coca Cola's volume comes from the United States. Coca Cola products are sold in nearly 200 countries worldwide. International operations, in total, represent a sizable part of American business activity and a significant area of accounting for U.S. corporations.

This chapter and Chapter 14 provide an introduction to accounting for international operations and an exposure to generally accepted accounting principles for translating foreign currency transactions and financial statements. Chapter 13 covers foreign currency concepts and definitions and accounting for foreign currency transactions. Chapter 14 covers translation and remeasurement of foreign currency financial statements into U.S. dollars, consolidating the financial statements of foreign subsidiaries with their U.S. parents,[1] and combining the operations of foreign branches with those of their U.S. home offices. An appendix to Chapter 14 covers the statement of cash flows for a parent company with a foreign subsidiary. A primary reference for these chapters is *FASB Statement No. 52,* "Foreign Currency Translation."

BRIEF BACKGROUND ON AUTHORITATIVE ACCOUNTING PRONOUNCEMENTS

Accounting standards for foreign operations and foreign exchange transactions began in 1939 with the issuance of *Accounting Research Bulletin (ARB) No. 4.* This pronouncement, which was reissued in 1953 as Chapter 12 of *ARB No. 43,* called for current accounts of foreign operations to be translated into U.S. dollars at current exchange rates, and noncurrent accounts to be translated at historical rates (the

---

[1]With the issuance of *FASB Statement No. 94,* "Consolidation of All Majority-Owned Subsidiaries," majority-owned foreign subsidiaries are consolidated unless parent control of the subsidiary is in doubt or the parent's control is temporary.

current-noncurrent method of translation). The basic procedures of accounting for foreign operations remained unchanged until the Financial Accounting Standards Board was formed in 1973.

The FASB placed a project on "Accounting for Foreign Currency Translation" on its original agenda, and in December 1973 it issued *Statement No. 1*, "Disclosure of Foreign Currency Translation Information." *Statement No. 1* did not change the accounting method used by firms to account for their foreign operations and transactions. However, it did require identification of the policies that were used and financial disclosure of foreign exchange adjustments reflected in income or deferred at year-end.

Both *FASB Statement No. 1* and Chapter 12 of *ARB No. 43* (except for a section on consolidation policies for foreign subsidiaries) were superseded by the issuance of *FASB Statement No. 8* in 1975. In developing *Statement No. 8*, the FASB considered a number of approaches to translating foreign currency financial statements into U.S. dollars, including:

1 The **current-noncurrent method**, specified in the 1939 pronouncement, which translates current accounts at current exchange rates and noncurrent accounts at historical rates.
2 The **monetary-nonmonetary method**, which translates monetary items at current exchange rates and nonmonetary items at historical exchange rates.
3 The **temporal method**, which translates items carried at past, current, and future prices in a manner that retains the accounting principles used to measure them. For example, cash, receivables and payables, and assets and liabilities carried at present or future prices are translated at the current exchange rate, and assets and liabilities carried at past prices are translated at applicable historical exchange rates.
4 The **current rate method**, which translates all assets and liabilities at the current exchange rate.

Although the FASB expressed a preference for the temporal method in *Statement No. 8*, it did not completely accept any of the methods considered. The method that the FASB adopted in *Statement No. 8* required translation of foreign statements in a manner that retained the measurement bases, which was essentially the temporal method.

From the time of its issuance in 1975, *Statement No. 8* had many critics. Much of the disagreement surrounding foreign currency translation related to the temporal method of translating foreign currency financial statements and the recognition of translation adjustments and gains and losses from foreign currency transactions in the income statement. Criticism of *Statement No. 8* often arose because foreign operations of different U.S. companies vary dramatically. Foreign operations of some companies have the objective of producing dollar profits for ultimate remittance to the United States. For these operations, the *Statement No. 8* requirement to recognize translation gains and losses as they arose was appropriate. Other companies finance their foreign operations locally (that is, within the foreign country) and evaluate them in terms of the local currency. *Statement No. 8* requirements to translate local borrowings at current rates and the assets purchased at historical rates were said to distort economic reality for these companies because the debt was repaid from local operations and the translation gains and losses were never realized. Still other companies finance foreign operations in the United States, transfer U.S. equipment and personnel to the foreign localities, sell the output in the world markets, and account for the operations in U.S. dollars. The translation gains and losses arising under *Statement No. 8* for such companies were labeled "fictitious" because the functional currency was the U.S. dollar and translation only distorted the nature of the operations.

In response to these arguments and in recognition of the differing nature of foreign operations among U.S. companies, the FASB issued *Statement No. 52*, "Foreign Currency Translation," in 1981.

OBJECTIVES OF TRANSLATION AND THE FUNCTIONAL CURRENCY CONCEPT

The objectives of translation under *FASB Statement No. 52* are set forth in paragraph 4 as (a) providing "information that is generally compatible with the expected economic effects of a rate change on an enterprise's cash flows and equity" and (b) reflecting "in consolidated statements the financial results and relationships of the individual consolidated entities as measured in their *functional currencies* in conformity with U.S. generally accepted accounting principles."

Functional Currency Concept

The FASB seeks to meet the objectives of *Statement No. 52* through application of the functional currency concept. An entity's *functional currency* is the currency of the primary environment in which it operates. Normally, a foreign entity's functional currency is the currency in which it generates and expends cash. When the functional currency is not obvious from cash flows, other factors may be considered. Economic indicators in addition to cash flows that are used in the determination of the functional currency include the following:

1 If *sales prices* of the foreign entity's products are determined by local competition or local government regulation, rather than by short-run exchange rate changes or worldwide markets, then the foreign entity's local currency may be the functional currency.

2 A *sales market* that is primarily in the parent company's country, or sales contracts that are normally denominated in the parent's currency, may indicate that the parent's currency is the functional currency.

3 *Expenses* such as labor and materials that are primarily local costs provide some evidence that the foreign entity's local currency is the functional currency.

4 If *financing* is denominated primarily in the foreign entity's local currency, and funds generated by its operations are sufficient to service existing and expected debt, then the foreign entity's local currency is likely to be the functional currency.

5 A high volume of *intercompany transactions and arrangements* indicates that the parent's currency may be the functional currency.

The FASB concluded that company management was in the best position to determine the functional currency of its foreign operations, and in the final analysis, the functional currency is based on management's judgment.

Statement No. 52 changed some traditional definitions by redefining foreign currency. Before the statement was issued, foreign currency meant a currency other than the currency of the country being referred to, or a currency other than the reporting currency of the enterprise being referred to. Local currency was the currency of a particular country being referred to or the reporting currency of a domestic or foreign operation being referred to. Under *Statement No. 52, foreign currency is a currency other than an entity's functional currency.* The statement provides no counterpart to local currency.

Assume, for example, that a U.S. company has a subsidiary in Germany, and the subsidiary's books of record are maintained in German marks. If the subsidiary's functional currency is the German mark, the U.S. dollar is a foreign currency from the viewpoint of the subsidiary. However, if the U.S. dollar is determined to be the subsidiary's functional currency, the mark would be a foreign currency from the subsidiary's viewpoint, even though it is the local currency and the currency of its accounting records.

Statement No. 52 permits two different methods for converting the financial statements of foreign subsidiaries into U.S. dollars, based on the foreign entity's functional currency. If the functional currency is the U.S. dollar, the foreign financial statements are remeasured into U.S. dollars using procedures similar to the temporal method. If the functional currency is the local currency of the foreign entity, the foreign financial statements are translated into U.S. dollars using the current rate method. A company should select the method that best reflects the nature of its foreign operations. Remeasurement and translation of foreign financial statements into U.S. dollars are covered in Chapter 14.

FOREIGN EXCHANGE CONCEPTS AND DEFINITIONS

The objective of a currency is to provide a standard of value, a medium of exchange, and a unit of measure. Currencies of different countries perform the first two functions with varying degrees of efficiency, but essentially all currencies provide a unit of measure for the economic activities and resources of their respective countries. That is, the financial activities and resources of a country are measured in the currency of that country. A transaction is *measured* in a particular currency if its magnitude is expressed in that currency.

Assets and liabilities are *denominated* in a currency if their amounts are fixed in terms of that currency. Transactions within a country (local transactions) are ordinarily both measured and denominated in that country's currency, and in the United States, one seldom investigates the possibility that a purchase or sale could be denominated (fixed) in a currency other than the U.S. dollar. In the case of transactions between business entities of different countries, however, the amounts receivable and payable are ordinarily denominated in the local currency of either the buying entity or the selling entity.[2] For example, if a U.S. firm sells merchandise to a British firm, the transaction amount will be denominated (fixed) in either U.S. dollars or British pounds, even though the U.S. firm will measure and record its account receivable and sales in U.S. dollars and the British firm will measure and record its purchase and account payable in British pounds. If the transaction is denominated in British pounds, the U.S. firm has to determine how many U.S. dollars the transaction represents in order to record it. If the transaction is denominated in U.S. dollars, the British firm has to determine how many British pounds the transaction represents. To measure the transaction in their own currencies, businesses around the world rely on exchange rates negotiated on a continuous basis in world currency markets.

Direct and Indirect Quotation of Exchange Rates

An **exchange rate** is the ratio between a unit of one currency and the amount of another currency for which that unit can be exchanged (converted) at a particular time. The exchange rate can be computed directly or indirectly. Assume that $1.60 can be exchanged for one British pound:

direct quotation (U.S. dollar equivalent):

$$\frac{\$1.60}{1} = \$1.60$$

indirect quotation (foreign currency per U.S. dollar):

$$\frac{1}{\$1.60} = .625 \text{ British pounds}$$

The first approach is referred to as a *direct quotation* (from a U.S. viewpoint) because the rate is expressed in U.S. dollars. It means that $1.60 is equivalent to one British pound (one unit of the foreign currency). The second approach is referred to as an *indirect quotation* (from a U.S. viewpoint) because the rate is expressed in British pounds (the foreign currency). It means that .625 British pounds is equivalent to one U.S. dollar. The Foreign Exchange section of *The Wall Street Journal* shows both direct (U.S. dollar equivalent) and indirect (currency per U.S. dollar) exchange rates on a daily basis.

Floating, Fixed, and Multiple Exchange Rates

Exchange rates may be fixed by a governmental unit or they may be allowed to fluctuate (float) with changes in the currency markets. **Official**, or **fixed**, **exchange rates** are set by a government and do not change as a result of changes in world currency markets. **Free**, or **floating**, **exchange rates** are those that reflect fluctuating market prices for a currency based on supply and demand and other factors in the world currency markets.

Floating Exchange Rates   Theoretically, a currency's value should reflect its buying power in world markets. For example, an increase in a country's inflation rate indicates that its currency's purchasing power is decreasing. The currency's value should

---

[2]Sometimes the amounts are denominated in the currency of a third country whose currency is relatively more stable than the currency of either the buyer or the seller.

fall in relation to other currencies. A large trade surplus indicates an increased demand for a country's currency and should result in that currency strengthening against other currencies. Conversely, a large trade deficit should lead to a decrease in the currency's value. Although inflation and trade are basic to floating exchange rates, other factors have sometimes been more influential. Investors buy securities in the world market, and interest rates rather than trade deficits may determine supply and demand for a country's currency. Speculative trading in currency movements also affects exchange rates.

To reduce its trade deficit, the U.S. government has occasionally asked other countries (Taiwan and Korea, for example) to let their currencies appreciate against the U.S. dollar. A decline in value of the dollar in relation to other major currencies should increase the price of foreign products in the United States and lead to a reduction of imports to this country. Similarly, U.S. goods can be sold in international markets for fewer foreign currency units. Even so, a weakening U.S. dollar has often done little to abate the U.S. consumers' demand for imported products, and changes in the exchange rates may have little effect on the trade deficit. Other factors that may affect a country's trade balance include interest rates[3] and tax rates.

Floating exchange rates are not always in the best interests of the world economy, so seven countries (United States, Japan, Germany, Britain, France, Italy, and Canada) joined together to keep the U.S. dollar, the German mark, and the Japanese yen within a secret range of exchange rates. The countries, called the Group of Seven (or G-7), try to "manage" the exchange rate through market intervention.

Fixed and Multiple Exchange Rates   When exchange rates are fixed, the issuing government is able to set (fix) different rates for different kinds of transactions. For example, it may set a preferential rate for imports or certain kinds of imports, and penalty rates for exports or certain kinds of exports, in order to promote the economic objectives of the country. Such rates are referred to as **multiple exchange rates**. For example, *The Wall Street Journal* on April 3, 1997 includes a quote for financial transactions in Uruguay ($.1003) but none for their "New Peso" used in other transactions.

The Euro   Beginning in January 1999, the euro will become the common currency for most of the countries (Austria, Belgium, Finland, France, Germany, Ireland, Italy, Luxembourg, the Netherlands, Portugal, and Spain) in the European Monetary Union. The conversion process is expected to take less than four years. In the first phase of conversion to a single European currency, national currencies of the participating countries will be fixed to the euro and noncash transactions may be denominated in either the euro or the old national currencies. The national currencies of EMU countries will no longer fluctuate in the market. Therefore, companies seeking to convert U.S. dollars to a European national currency, such as the Italian lira, will have to do so through the euro. After January 1, 2002, all noncash transactions must be denominated in the euro. The conversion schedule calls for the issuance of paper currency on January 1, 2002. By June 30, 2002, the conversion to the euro for all business and consumer transactions is scheduled to be complete and the old national currencies of the participating countries will no longer be used.

U.S. Change from Fixed to Floating Rates   Foreign currency translation was a pressing issue when the FASB was formed in 1973, largely because the United States changed from fixed to floating exchange rates in 1971, and major devaluations of the dollar occurred in 1971 and 1973. The change to floating exchange rates had a major impact on U.S. business firms with significant international operations and, quite naturally, led to a reexamination of accounting and reporting principles for foreign currency translation.

---

[3]Domestic savings in the United States has not been sufficient to finance the country's deficit, and the United States has had to bid up interest rates in the world capital markets.

Spot, Current, and Historical Exchange Rates

The exchange rates that are used in accounting for foreign operations and transactions (other than forward contracts[4]) are spot rates, current exchange rates, and historical exchange rates. Spot rate is a market term; current and historical rates are accounting terms. These are defined as follows:

> **Spot rate**—the exchange rate for immediate delivery of currencies exchanged
> **Current rate**—the rate at which one unit of currency can be exchanged for another currency at the balance sheet date or the transaction date
> **Historical rate**—the rate in effect at the date a specific transaction or event occurred

Spot, current, and historical rates may be either fixed or floating rates, depending upon the particular currency involved. Spot rates for foreign transactions between the United States and a country with fixed exchange rates will normally change in that foreign country only as a result of governmental action (except for transactions in the black market in the foreign country's currency). For example, the Argentine government can control the exchange rate in Buenos Aires, but not in New York. Spot rates for foreign transactions with a country that has floating exchange rates may change daily, or several times in a single day, depending on factors that influence the currency markets. However, note that there is only one spot rate for a given transaction.

The current rate for foreign currency transactions is the spot rate in effect for immediate settlement of the amounts denominated in foreign currency at the transaction date or at the balance sheet date. The current rate for translating foreign statements is the same as for foreign currency transactions, except where multiple exchange rates exist, in which case the rate to be used should be the rate applicable to dividend remittances (*FASB Statement No. 52*, paragraph 27).

Historical rates are the spot rates that were in effect on the date that a particular event or transaction occurred.

Foreign Exchange Quotations

Major U.S. banks facilitate international trade by maintaining departments that provide bank transfer services between American and foreign companies, as well as currency exchange services. Selling prices at 3:00 P.M. on April 7, 1998 for bank transfers of $1,000,000 or more in the United States for payment abroad for selected currencies were as follows:

	U.S. $ Equivalent	Currency per U.S. $
Britain (pound)	$1.6677	0.5996 pounds
Canada (dollar)	$0.7029	1.4226 $ Canadian
Japan (yen)	$0.007492	133.48 yen
Mexico (peso)	$0.1173	8.5250 pesos
Germany (mark)	$0.5444	1.8370 marks

These rates indicate the prices for immediate delivery of the selected currencies. For example, a payment of $1,667,700 to a U.S. banker at 3:00 P.M. on April 7, 1998 would have entitled a U.S. corporation to purchase British goods selling for 1,000,000 British pounds or to settle an account payable denominated at 1,000,000 British pounds. Similarly, a U.S. company could have purchased merchandise selling for 10,000,000 Canadian dollars for $7,029,000 at that time.

The U.S. bankers that provide foreign exchange services are, of course, remunerated for their services. The remuneration is the difference between the amount that they receive from U.S. corporations and the amount they pay out for the foreign currencies, or vice versa. For example, a bank that trades in foreign currency may offer to

---

[4]A *forward exchange contract* is an agreement to exchange different currencies at a specified future date and at a specified rate.

sell British pounds for $1.68 or buy them for $1.66 when the quoted rate for British bank notes is $1.67. Thus, a firm can buy 1,000,000 pounds for $1,680,000 or sell 1,000,000 pounds for $1,660,000 and the bank realizes a $10,000 gain in either case.

FOREIGN CURRENCY TRANSACTIONS OTHER THAN FORWARD CONTRACTS

Transactions within a country that are measured and recorded in the currency of that country are **local transactions**. The transactions of a British subsidiary would be recorded in British pounds, and its financial statements would be stated in British pounds. However, its financial statements must be converted into U.S. dollars before consolidation with a U.S. parent company. Translation of foreign currency financial statements is covered in Chapter 14.

This discussion of foreign currency transactions assumes the point of view of a U.S. firm whose functional currency is the U.S. dollar (which is also its local currency). **Foreign transactions** are transactions between countries or between enterprises in different countries. **Foreign currency transactions** are transactions whose terms are stated (denominated) in a currency other than an entity's functional currency (with this view, the US$). Thus, a foreign transaction may or may not be a foreign currency transaction. The most common types of foreign transactions are imports and exports of goods and services. Import and export transactions are foreign transactions, but they are not foreign currency transactions unless their terms are denominated in a foreign currency—that is, a currency other than the entity's functional currency. An export sale by a U.S. company to a Canadian company is a foreign currency transaction from the viewpoint of the U.S. company only if the invoice is denominated (fixed) in Canadian dollars. Translation is required if the transaction is denominated in a foreign currency, but not if it is denominated in the entity's functional currency.

FASB Requirements

The provisions of *FASB Statement No. 52* apply only to foreign currency transactions and to foreign currency financial statements. *Statement No. 52* (paragraph 16) requirements for foreign currency transactions other than forward exchange contracts are:

1 At the date the transaction is recognized, each asset, liability, revenue, expense, gain, or loss arising from the transaction shall be measured and recorded in the functional currency of the recording entity by use of the exchange rate in effect at that date.

2 At each balance sheet date, recorded balances that are denominated in a currency other than the functional currency of the recording entity shall be adjusted to reflect the current exchange rate.

Translation at the Spot Rate   The first requirement for foreign currency transactions is that they be translated into U.S. dollars at the spot rate in effect at the transaction date. Each asset, liability, revenue, and expense account arising from the transaction is translated into dollars. The unit of measurement is changed from the foreign currency to the U.S. dollar functional currency.

Assume that an American corporation imports inventory items from a Canadian firm when the spot rate for Canadian dollars is $.70. The invoice calls for payment of 10,000 Canadian dollars in 30 days. (*Note:* The $ sign used for the spot rate indicates direct quotation, or in other words, the U.S. dollar equivalent of one unit of foreign currency.)

The American importer records the transaction as follows:

Inventory	$7,000	
Accounts payable (fc)		$7,000
(Translation 10,000 Canadian dollars × $.70 spot rate.)		

Except for the foreign currency (fc) notation, the entry is recorded in the usual manner. The notation is used to indicate that the account payable is denominated in foreign currency. The inventory is both measured and denominated in U.S. dollars, so no subsequent adjustment is made to the inventory account.

If the account payable is settled when the spot rate is $.69, payment of the account is recorded:

Accounts payable (fc)	$7,000	
Exchange gain		$ 100
Cash		6,900

(Cash required equals 10,000 Canadian
dollars × the $.69 spot rate.)

The $100 exchange gain results because a liability measured at $7,000 is settled for $6,900. This gain reflects a change in the exchange rate between the transaction date and the date of settlement. If the exchange rate had changed to $.72, a $200 exchange loss would have resulted. Under the provisions of *Statement No. 52*, translation gains and losses are reflected in income in the period in which the exchange rate changes.

Exhibit 13–1 compares the accounting differences that arise when foreign transactions are denominated in an entity's functional currency (U.S. dollars) as opposed to foreign currency. In examining the exhibit, keep in mind that a transaction must be denominated in foreign currency to be a foreign currency transaction. When billing for a U.S. company is denominated in U.S. dollars, no translation is required and the provisions of *Statement No. 52* are not applicable.

Note that the exchange losses occurred only when the billing was in foreign currency, and that the losses were on settlement, not on initial recording.

Adjustment to Current Exchange Rate   The second requirement of *Statement No. 52* for foreign currency transactions is that cash and amounts owed by or to the enterprise that are denominated in foreign currency be adjusted to reflect the current exchange rate at the balance sheet date. This provision means that gains and losses on foreign currency transactions cannot be deferred until foreign currency is converted into U.S. dollars or until related receivables are collected or payables are settled. Instead, these amounts must be adjusted to reflect current exchange rates at the balance sheet date, and any exchange gains or losses that result from the adjustments must be reflected in current income.

Purchases Denominated in Foreign Currency

American Trading Company, a U.S. corporation, purchased merchandise from Kimetz Company of Switzerland on December 1, 20X8 for 10,000 Swiss francs, when the spot rate for Swiss francs was $.6600. American Trading closed its books at December 31, 20X8, when the spot rate for Swiss francs was $.6550, and settled the account on January 30, 20X9, when the spot rate was $.6650. These transactions and events are recorded by American Trading as follows:

December 1, 20X8		
Inventory	$6,600	
Accounts payable (fc)		$6,600
To record purchase of merchandise from Kimetz Company (10,000 Swiss francs × $.6600 rate).		
December 31, 20X8		
Accounts payable (fc)	$ 50	
Exchange gain		$ 50
To adjust accounts payable to exchange rate at year-end [10,000 Swiss francs × ($.6600 − $.6550)].		
January 30, 20X9		
Accounts payable (fc)	$6,550	
Exchange loss	100	
Cash		$6,650
To record payment in full to Kimetz Company (10,000 Swiss francs × $.6650 spot rate).		

SALES TRANSACTION

Assumption: U.S. Foods sells merchandise to London Industries Ltd. for $16,500, or 10,000 pounds when the exchange rate is $1.65, and receives payment when the exchange rate is $1.64.

IF BILLING IS IN U.S. DOLLARS

(Date of sale)

Accounts receivable	$16,500	
Sales		$16,500
To record sale to London Industries; invoice is $16,500		

(Date of receipt)

Cash	$16,500	
Accounts receivable		$16,500
To record collection in full from London Industries.		

IF BILLING IS IN BRITISH POUNDS

Accounts receivable (fc)	$16,500	
Sales		$16,500
To record sale to London Industries; billing is for 10,000 British pounds. (10,000 pounds × $1.65 = $16,500)		

Cash (fc)	$16,400	
Exchange loss	100	
Accounts receivable (fc)		$16,500
To record collection in full from London Industries. (10,000 pounds × $1.64 = $16,400)		

PURCHASE TRANSACTION

Assumption: U.S. Foods purchases merchandise from London Industries Ltd. for $8,250, or 5,000 pounds when the exchange rate is $1.65, and pays the account when the exchange rate is $1.67.

IF BILLING IS IN U.S. DOLLARS

(Date of purchase)

Inventory	$ 8,250	
Accounts payable		$ 8,250
To record purchase from London Industries; billing is $8,250.		

(Date of payment)

Accounts payable	$ 8,250	
Cash		$ 8,250
To record payment in full to London Industries.		

IF BILLING IS IN BRITISH POUNDS

Inventory	$ 8,250	
Accounts payable (fc)		$ 8,250
To record purchase from London Industries, billing is for 5,000 British pounds. (5,000 pounds × $1.65 = $8,250)		

Accounts payable (fc)	$ 8,250	
Exchange loss	100	
Cash		$ 8,350
To record payment in full to London Industries (5,000 pounds × $1.67 = $8,350).		

Exhibit 13–1   *Comparison of Purchase and Sale Transactions Denominated in U.S. Dollars Versus British Pounds*

The example shows that on December 1, 20X8, American Trading Company incurred a liability of $6,600 denominated in Swiss francs. On December 31, 20X8, the liability was adjusted to reflect the current exchange rate, and a $50 exchange gain was included in American Trading Company's 20X8 income statement. The exchange gain is the product of multiplying 10,000 Swiss francs by the change in the spot rate for Swiss francs between December 1 and December 31, 20X8. By January 30, 20X9, when the liability was settled, the spot rate for Swiss francs had increased to $.6650, and American Trading recorded a $100 exchange loss. The actual exchange loss is only $50 [10,000 francs × ($.6650 − $.6600)], but under *Statement No. 52* requirements, this loss is reported as a $50 exchange gain in 20X8 and a $100 exchange loss in 20X9.

Sales Denominated in Foreign Currency

On December 16, 20X8, American Trading Company sold merchandise to Kimetz Company for 20,000 Swiss francs, when the spot rate for Swiss francs was $.6600. American Trading closed its books on December 31, when the spot rate was $.6650, collected the account on January 15, 20X9, when the spot rate was $.6700, and held the cash until January 20, when it converted the Swiss francs into U.S. dollars at the $.6725 spot rate in effect on that date. American Trading records the transactions as follows:

December 15, 20X8

Accounts receivable (fc)	$13,200	
Sales		$13,200
To record sales to Kimetz		
(20,000 Swiss francs × $.6600 spot rate).		

December 31, 20X8

Accounts receivable (fc)	$ 100	
Exchange gain		$ 100
To adjust accounts receivable at year-end		
[20,000 Swiss francs × ($.6650 − $.6600)].		

January 15, 20X9

Cash (fc)	$13,400	
Accounts receivable (fc)		$13,300
Exchange gain		100
To record collection in full from Kimetz (20,000		
Swiss francs × $.6700) and recognize exchange gain		
for 20X9 [20,000 Swiss francs × ($.6700 − $.6650)].		

January 20, 20X9

Cash	$13,450	
Exchange gain		$ 50
Cash (fc)		13,400
To convert 20,000 Swiss francs into U.S. dollars		
(20,000 Swiss francs × $.6725).		

To summarize, American Trading recorded a $13,200 receivable denominated at 20,000 Swiss francs on December 15, 20X8. It then recognized an exchange gain of $100 from holding the receivable as the exchange rate increased to $.6650 at year-end, and another $100 exchange gain as the rate increased from $.6650 at December 31, 20X8 to $.6700 at the January 15, 20X9 settlement date. Because American Trading did not convert the Swiss francs into U.S. dollars on January 15, it speculated in exchange rate changes until January 20, when the 20,000 Swiss francs were converted into U.S. dollars. This speculation resulted in an additional $50 exchange gain for American Trading. A company that holds foreign currency units is a speculator in that currency, and under *Statement No. 52*, it recognizes gains and losses from changes in exchange rates as they occur.

FOREIGN CURRENCY DERIVATIVES AND HEDGING ACTIVITIES

Firms can often avoid gains and losses on foreign exchange transactions by immediate settlement of accounts denominated in a foreign currency or by hedging operations. A **hedging operation** is the purchase or sale of foreign currency contracts to offset the risks of holding receivables and payables denominated in a foreign currency. The usual strategy for avoiding the risks of exchange rate fluctuations is through forward contracts. A forward contract is an agreement to exchange different currencies at a specified future date and at a specified rate (the forward rate). Under *FASB Statement No. 133*, "Accounting for Derivative Instruments and Hedging Activities," such contracts are considered **derivative**[5] instruments. Based on *Statement 133*, derivative instruments represent rights or obligations and should be reported on the financial statements. Fair value is considered the only relevant measure for derivative instruments. Currency swaps and other agreements that are essentially the same as forward contracts are considered derivative instruments and subject to *Statement 133*. Although forward contracts are foreign currency transactions, they are treated differently depending on their nature and purpose in accordance with *Statement 52* and *Statement 133*. The FASB identifies three situations in which forward exchange contracts (or forward contracts, or futures) are used:

1 To speculate in foreign currency exchange price movements
2 A fair value hedge:
   a To hedge an exposed foreign currency asset or liability
   b To hedge a firm commitment
   c To hedge a net investment in a foreign entity
3 A cash flow hedge: To hedge a foreign currency forecasted transaction

Speculation

Exchange gains or losses on derivative instruments that speculate in foreign currency price movements are included in income in the periods in which the forward exchange rates change. Forward or future exchange rates for 30-, 90-, and 180-day delivery are quoted on a daily basis for the leading world currencies. A foreign currency derivative that is a speculation is valued at forward rates throughout the life of the contract (which is the fair value of the contract at that point in time). The basic accounting is illustrated in the following example.

On November 2, 20X7, U.S. International enters into a 90-day forward contract (future) to purchase 10,000 German marks when the current quotation for 90-day futures in German marks is $.5400. The spot rate for German marks on November 2 is $.5440. Exchange rates at December 31, 20X7 and January 30, 20X8 are as follows:

	December 31, 20X7	January 30, 20X8
30-day futures	$.5450	$.5480
Spot rate	.5500	.5530

Journal entries on the books of U.S. International to account for the speculation are as follows:

November 2, 20X7

Contract receivable (fc)	$5,400	
Contract payable		$5,400

To record contract for 10,000 marks × $.5400 exchange rate for 90-day futures.

December 31, 20X7

Contract receivable (fc)	$ 50	
Exchange gain		$ 50

To adjust receivable from exchange broker and recognize exchange gain (10,000 marks × $.5450 forward exchange rate for 30-day futures − $5400 per books).

---

[5]A foreign currency derivative instrument is a contract with a specified foreign exchange rate (the underlying) and specified number of currency units (the notional amount). The contract requires no initial investment (or a small initial investment) and permits net settlement. (See *Statement 133*, paragraphs 6 through 9 for a complete definition of derivative instruments.)

January 30, 20X8

Cash (fc)	$5,530	
Exchange gain		$ 80
Contract receivable (fc)		5,450

To record receipt of 10,000 marks. The current spot
rate for German marks is $.5530.

Contract payable	$5,400	
Cash		$5,400

To record payment of the liability to the exchange
broker denominated in dollars.

The entry on November 2 records U.S. International's right to receive 10,000 German marks from the exchange broker in 90 days. It also records U.S. International's liability to pay $5,400 to the exchange broker in 90 days. Both the receivable and the liability are recorded at $5,400 (10,000 marks × $.5400 forward rate), but only the receivable is denominated in German marks and is subject to exchange rate fluctuations.

At December 31, 20X7, the forward contract has 30 days until maturity. Under the provisions of *Statement No. 133*, the receivable denominated in German marks is adjusted to reflect the exchange rate of $.5450 for 30-day futures on December 31, 20X7. This is the fair value of the contract. The amount of the adjustment is included in U.S. International's income for 20X7.

On January 30, 20X8, U.S. International receives 10,000 German marks with a current value of $5,530 (10,000 marks × $.5530 spot rate). The translated value of the foreign currency received is $80 more than the recorded amount of the receivable, so an additional exchange gain results. U.S. International also settles its liability with the exchange broker on January 30.

A speculation involving the sale of foreign currency for future delivery is accounted for in a similar fashion, except that the receivable is fixed in U.S. dollars and the liability is denominated in foreign currency.

Fair Value Hedge of an Exposed Net Asset or Net Liability Position

A **foreign currency exposed net asset position** (exposed net asset position) is an excess of assets denominated in foreign currency over liabilities denominated in that foreign currency and translated at the current rate. A **foreign currency exposed net liability position** (exposed net liability position) is an excess of liabilities denominated in a foreign currency over assets denominated in that foreign currency and translated at the current rate. A forward contract to hedge an exposed net asset or exposed net liability position (a fair value hedge) may be used by importers to hedge accounts payable, and by exporters to hedge accounts receivable, denominated in foreign currency.

Forward Contract to Sell Foreign Currency   To hedge an exposed net asset position, a firm enters into a forward contract to sell foreign currency for future delivery. For example, a U.S. exporter sells merchandise to a Canadian company and records an account receivable denominated in Canadian dollars. To avoid exposure to exchange rate changes between the date of the sale and the date payment is due, the U.S. firm enters a contract with an exchange broker to sell the anticipated number of Canadian dollars at a specified forward rate at a future date. The U.S. firm receives the Canadian dollars as payment of the account receivable, delivers the Canadian dollars to the exchange broker, and receives U.S. dollars in exchange. Any exchange gain or loss on the account receivable is offset by an exchange loss (or gain) on the forward contract denominated in the same currency.

Forward Contract to Purchase Foreign Currency   To hedge an exposed net liability position, a firm enters into a forward contract to purchase foreign currency for future receipt. For example, a U.S. firm buys merchandise from a British firm. The invoice is denominated in British pounds and due in 30 days. To avoid exposure to exchange rate changes between the date of the purchase and the date payment is due in British pounds, the U.S. firm buys British pounds at a specified forward rate for receipt in 30 days. In this way any gain (or loss) on the account payable denominated in British pounds is offset by a loss (or gain) on the contract receivable denominated in the same foreign currency.

Exchange Gains and Losses   If the forward contracts are for the same number of foreign currency units and for the same time periods as the exposed net asset or net liability positions, the exchange gains or losses on the forward contracts will offset the exchange gains or losses on the exposed net asset or net liability positions in each period for which financial statements are prepared. In other words, no net exchange gains or losses result when an exposed net asset or liability position is completely hedged. Under *Statement 133*, both the gain and the offsetting loss must be reported in current earnings.

Cost of a Forward Contract   Generally, there is a cost of avoiding the risk of exchange rate changes, and that cost is the income effect of the hedging operation. The exchange broker ordinarily sets the forward rate at an amount different from the spot rate on the contract date to cover his or her own risk. Any difference between these rates is the cost of avoiding the risk of exchange rate fluctuations.

Hedging After-Tax Amounts   *Statement No. 133* continues *Statement No. 52's* policy of allowing the hedging of after-tax risks. If the forward contract is intended to provide a hedge on an after-tax basis, however, additional gains or losses may be deferred and treated as an offset to income taxes related to the transaction. Any gains or losses on the portion of a forward contract in excess of amounts intended to provide a hedge on an after-tax basis are recognized in income currently as exchange gains or losses.

Illustration: Hedge Against Exposed Net Asset Positions   U.S. Oil Company sells oil to Monato Company of Japan for 15,000,000 yen on December 1, 20X7. The billing date for the sale is December 1, 20X7, and payment is due in 60 days on January 30, 20X8. Concurrent with the sale, U.S. Oil enters into a forward contract to deliver 15,000,000 yen to its exchange broker in 60 days. Exchange rates for Japanese yen are as follows:

	December 1, 20X7	December 31, 20X7	January 30, 20X8
Spot rate	$.007500	$.007498	$.007497
30-day futures rate	$.007490	$.007498	$.007488
60-day futures rate	$.007490	$.007488	$.007486

The underscored rates are the relevant rates for accounting purposes. Journal entries to record the sale, the forward contract, year-end adjustments, and final settlement of accounts on the books of U.S. Oil follow. The forward contract, a derivative instrument, is carried at market value, which is the forward rate. The liability to the exchange broker is denominated in foreign currency.

December 1, 20X7

Accounts receivable (fc)	$112,500	
Sales		$112,500

    To record sales to Monato Company (15,000,000 yen × $.007500 spot rate).

Contract receivable	$112,350	
Contract payable (fc)		$112,350

    To record forward contract to deliver 15,000,000 yen in 60 days. Receivable: 15,000,000 yen × $.007490 forward rate.

At December 31, 20X7, the accounts receivable from the sale is adjusted to reflect the current exchange rate, and a $30 exchange loss is recorded. Calculating the exchange gain on the forward contract is a bit more complex. On the surface, the gain would appear to be the initial forward rate of .007490 × 15,000,000 less the current forward rate of .007489 × 15,000,000 ($112,350 − $112,335) which is $15. However, FASB had elected to discount this amount from the contract termination date to the financial statement date. If we assume that 6% is a reasonable discount rate this would be a discount of $.075 ($15 × .06 × 1/12). Further discussion of these derivatives will ignore this discounting feature as being not material. However, one should be aware that it is a required feature in calculating the gain or loss on forward contracts and may, for some firms, be material.

December 31, 20X7

Exchange loss	$ 30	
Accounts receivable (fc)		$ 30

    To adjust accounts receivable for current exchange rate
    [15,000,000 yen × ($.007500 − $.007498) = $30].

Contract payable (fc)	$ 15	
Exchange gain		$ 15

    To adjust contract payable to exchange broker to
    the current forward exchange rate. Payable:
    15,000,000 yen × ($.007490 − $.007489).

The exchange gain or loss on the underlying asset hedged will not be the same as the exchange gain or loss on the forward contract. This is due to the fact that the underlying asset is carried at the spot rate and the forward contract is carried at the forward rate. Over the contract period, the forward rate will approach the spot rate, exactly equaling it on the settlement date (and so must change at a different amount than the spot rate). This change in the relative value of the spot and forward rates determines the impact on net income. The impact of the basic change in exchange rate has been hedged and the change in the forward contract and the underlying hedge will offset each other. In this example, the net change in the relative value was $15 ($30 loss − $15 gain) for 20X7 and $135 ($15 loss + $120 loss) for 20X8.

January 30, 20X8

Cash (fc)	$112,455	
Exchange loss	15	
Accounts receivable (fc)		$112,470

    To record collection of receivable from
    Monato Company. Cash: 15,000,000 yen × $.007497.

Contract payable (fc)	$112,335	
Exchange loss	120	
Cash (fc)		$112,455

    To record delivery of 15,000,000 yen from Monato to
    foreign exchange broker in settlement of liability.

Cash	$112,350	
Contract receivable		$112,350

    To record receipt of cash from exchange broker.

In the final analysis, U.S. Oil Company makes a sale in the amount of $112,500. It takes a $150 charge on the transaction in order to avoid the risks of foreign currency price fluctuations, and it collects $112,350 in final settlement of the sale transaction. The $150 is charged to income over the term of the forward contract.

Hedge Against Exposed Net Liability Position   Accounting procedures for hedging an exposed net liability position are comparable to those illustrated for U.S. Oil Company except that the objective is to hedge a liability denominated in foreign currency, rather than a receivable. Normally, the forward rate for buying foreign currency for future receipt is ordinarily greater than the spot rate. For example, a forward contract to acquire 10,000 British pounds for receipt in 60 days might have a forward rate of $1.675 when the spot rate is $1.66. The forward contract is recorded:

Contract receivable (fc)	$16,750	
Contract payable		$16,750

The contract hedges any effect of changes in the exchange rate so that the net cost over the life of the contract will be the $150 differential between the spot and forward rates.

Result of Hedging The point is that forward rates are ordinarily set so that there is a cost to the firm for its hedging operations. Occasionally, the rates for futures are such that the hedging operations create credit balances, in which case hedging would increase income.

In summary, a forward contract is recorded at the forward rate while the underlying asset or liability is recorded at the spot rate (and adjusted to these respective rates and values at the financial statement date). Over the life of the contract, the initial difference between the spot and the forward rate is the cost of hedging the exchange rate risk. Since the gains and losses on both the hedge and the underlying are recorded in current earnings, the net cost that hits the income statement is the change in the relative value of the spot and forward rate.

If a firm enters a forward contract for foreign currency units in excess of the foreign currency units reflected in its exposed net asset or net liability position (a speculation in the currency), the difference ends up a gain or loss. This is due to the difference in the change in the value of the derivative and the change in the value of the underlying item hedged both hitting the income statement.

Fair Value Hedge of an Identifiable Foreign Currency Commitment

A **foreign currency commitment** is a contract or agreement denominated in foreign currency that will result in a foreign currency transaction at a later date. For example, a U.S. firm may contract to buy equipment from a Canadian firm at a future date with the invoice price denominated in Canadian dollars. The U.S. firm has an exposure to exchange rate changes because the future price in U.S. dollars may increase or decrease before the transaction is consummated. An identifiable foreign currency commitment differs from an exposed asset or liability position because the commitment does not meet the accounting tests for recording the related asset or liability in the accounts. The risk of the exposure still may be avoided by hedging. This situation is special because the underlying transaction being hedged is not recorded as an asset or liability. Therefore, some method must be established to record the change in the value of the underlying unrecorded commitment in order to record the derivative instrument as a hedge of the commitment. Once this mechanism has been created, both the change in the derivative instrument and the underlying commitment are recorded, in effect, offsetting each other, as with the case of a hedge of an asset or liability. A forward contract that is a hedge of a firm commitment is based on the forward rate, not the spot rate. Any gain or loss on the derivative and underlying contract is therefore based on the forward rate.

There is no requirement that the life of the forward contract has to begin at the foreign currency commitment date; however, the required accounting for the forward contract must begin at the designation date (in other words, when the forward contract is designated as a hedge of a foreign currency commitment).

Illustration: Hedge of an Identifiable Foreign Currency Purchase Commitment
On October 2, 20X7, American Stores Corporation contracts with Canadian Distillers for delivery of 1,000 cases of bourbon at a price of 60,000 Canadian dollars, when the spot rate for Canadian dollars is $.70. The bourbon is to be delivered in March and payment made in Canadian dollars on March 31, 20X8. In order to hedge this future commitment, American Stores purchases 60,000 Canadian dollars for delivery in 180 days at a forward exchange rate of $.725. Applicable forward rates on December 31, 20X7 and March 31, 20X8 (because the maturity is March 31, this rate is also the spot rate) are $.71 and $.68, respectively.

Assume that the derivative instrument (the forward contract) is designated as a hedge of this identifiable foreign currency commitment. The purchase of the forward contract on October 2, 20X7 is recorded as follows:

October 2, 20X7

Contract receivable (fc)	$43,500	
Contract payable		$43,500

    To record purchase of 60,000 Canadian dollars for
        delivery in 180 days at a forward rate of $.725.

By December 31, 20X7, the forward exchange rate for Canadian dollars decreases to $.71, and American Stores adjusts its receivable to reflect the 60,000 Canadian dollars at the 90-day forward exchange rate. This adjustment creates a $900 exchange loss on the futures contract as follows:

December 31, 20X7

Exchange loss	$ 900	
Contract receivable (fc)		$ 900

    To record exchange loss: 60,000
        Canadian dollars × ($.725 − $.71).

However, this loss is offset by the increase in the value of the underlying firm commitment shown below:

December 31, 20X7

Change in value of firm commitment in		
Canadian dollars (fc)	$ 900	
Exchange gain		$ 900

    To record exchange gain: 60,000 Canadian
        dollars × ($.725 − $.71). (Payment in Canadian
        dollars will cost fewer US$).

Journal entries on March 31, 20X8 to account for the foreign currency transaction and related forward contract are as follows:

March 31, 20X8

1. Contract payable	$43,500	
Cash		$43,500

    To record settlement of forward contract with the
        exchange broker (denominated in U.S. dollars).

2. Cash (fc)	$40,800	
Exchange loss	1,800	
Contract receivable (fc)		$42,600

    To record receipt of 60,000 Canadian dollars from the
        exchange broker when the exchange rate is $.68.

3. Change in value of firm commitment in Canadian dollars	$ 1,800	
Exchange gain		$ 1,800

    To record the change in the value of the underlying firm
        commitment.

4. Purchases	$43,500	
Change in value of firm commitment in Canadian		
dollars		$ 2,700
Accounts payable (fc)		40,800

    To record receipt of 1,000 cases of bourbon at a cost of
        60,000 Canadian dollars × forward exchange rate of
        $.725.

5. Accounts payable (fc)	$40,800	
Cash (fc)		$40,800

    To record payment of 60,000 Canadian dollars to
        Canadian Distillers.

Entry 1 records payment to the exchange broker for the 60,000 Canadian dollars at the contracted forward rate of $.725. The second entry reflects collection of the 60,000 Canadian dollars from the broker and records an additional exchange loss on the further decline of the exchange rate from the forward rate of $.71 at December 31, 20X7 to the $.68 spot rate (this is also the forward rate for the date of settlement) at March 31, 20X8. The third entry records the gain on the change in the dollar cost of the firm commitment to buy the bourbon since December 31, 20X7. The fourth entry on March 31 records receipt of the 1,000 cases of bourbon from Canadian Distillers and records the liability payable in Canadian dollars. It also incorporates the change in the firm commitment in the inventory value. In entry 5, Canadian Distillers is paid the 60,000 Canadian dollars in final settlement of the account payable.

Hedge of an Identifiable Foreign Currency Sales Commitment   Accounting procedures for hedging an identifiable foreign currency sales commitment are comparable to those illustrated for hedging a purchase commitment, except that the sales, rather than the purchases, account is adjusted for any deferred exchange gains or losses.

Cash Flow Hedge of an Anticipated Foreign Currency Transaction

A *committed* transaction qualifies as a foreign currency fair value hedge, whereas an *anticipated* foreign currency transaction is considered a **foreign currency cash flow hedge**. A cash flow hedge "applies to a derivative designated as a hedge of the foreign currency exposure of a foreign-currency-denominated forecasted transaction" (*Statement No. 133*, page 2). With an anticipated foreign currency transaction, there is no basis for adjusting the "value" of the underlying transaction as was done with the committed transaction. Therefore, the offset to the change in the value of the derivative contract (which still must be carried at fair value per *Statement No. 133*) is to other comprehensive income. Any "inefficiency" in the derivative contract will show up in the current income, as with any other derivative contract. An inefficiency occurs when the terms of the derivative do not exactly match the anticipated exposure.

Using the example above for American Stores but assuming an anticipated, rather than committed, transaction requires the following journal entries:

October 2, 20X7

Contract receivable (fc)	$43,500	
Contract payable		$43,500

To record purchase of 60,000 Canadian dollars for
delivery in 180 days at a forward rate of $.725.

By December 31, 20X7, the exchange rate for Canadian dollars decreases to $.71, and American Stores adjusts its receivable to reflect the 60,000 Canadian dollars at the current exchange rate. This adjustment creates a $900 exchange loss on the futures contract as follows:

December 31, 20X7

Other comprehensive income	$ 900	
Contract receivable (fc)		$ 900

To record exchange loss: 60,000 Canadian
dollars × ($.725 − $.71).

Journal entries on March 31, 20X8 to account for the foreign currency transaction and related forward contract are as follows:

March 31, 20X8

1. Contract payable	$43,500	
Cash		$43,500

To record settlement of forward contract with the
exchange broker (denominated in U.S. dollars).

2. Cash (fc)	$40,800	
Other comprehensive income	1,800	
Contract receivable (fc)		$42,600

To record receipt of 60,000 Canadian dollars from
the exchange broker when the exchange rate is $.68.

4. Purchases	$43,500	
Other comprehensive income		$ 2,700
Accounts payable (fc)		40,800

To record receipt of 1,000 cases of bourbon at a cost of 60,000 Canadian dollars × forward exchange rate of $.725.

With this entry, the gain or loss would effectively become part of regular income when the underlying purchases are sold or used.

5. Accounts payable (fc)	$40,800	
Cash (fc)		$40,800

To record payment of 60,000 Canadian dollars to Canadian Distillers.

Hedging a Net Investment in a Foreign Entity

U.S. firms with foreign investees may enter into forward exchange contracts or other foreign currency transactions to offset the effects of foreign currency fluctuations on their net investments. Gains and losses that arise from foreign currency transactions designated as, and effective as, economic hedges of a net investment in a foreign entity are recorded as translation adjustments of stockholders' equity. Classification as a **translation adjustment** means that these transaction gains and losses are included in comprehensive income (*FASB Statement No. 130*) but excluded from the determination of net income. This treatment is necessary because translation of the financial statements of a foreign subsidiary *with a functional currency other than the U.S. dollar* also produces translation adjustments, which are included in comprehensive income, rather than charges or credits to net income. Thus, the adjustment from hedging a net investment in a foreign entity offsets the adjustment from translating the foreign investees' financial statements into U.S. dollars.

Procedures to hedge a net investment in a foreign entity are not applicable to investees with a U.S. dollar functional currency. Hedges of these investments are accounted for as speculations. Gains and losses from remeasuring foreign-investee financial statements into U.S. dollars are included in net income for the period if the U.S. dollar is the investee's functional currency. Therefore, the gains and losses resulting from the hedge of the net investment must also be included in net income for the period. This means that the gain or loss on the hedge will offset the recognized gain or loss from the remeasurement. Translation and remeasurement of foreign currency financial statements are covered in the next chapter.

Illustration: Hedge of a Net Investment in a Foreign Entity   To illustrate the hedge of a net investment of a foreign entity, assume that Pinehurst Corporation, a U.S. Company, has a 40% equity investment in a British company, Bennett Ltd., acquired at book value equal to fair value. Bennett's functional currency is the British pound. An investee's assets and liabilities hedge each other, so only the net assets are exposed to the risk of exchange rate fluctuations. To hedge the foreign currency exposure, the translation adjustment from the hedging transaction must move in a direction opposite to the translation adjustment from the net assets of the investee. Thus, Pinehurst borrows British pounds to hedge the equity investment. Any translation losses on the equity investment will be fully or partially offset by the translation gains on the loan and vice versa.

The balance in Pinehurst's investment in Bennett account at December 31, 20X2 is $1,280,000, equal to 40% of Bennett's net assets of 2,000,000 pounds times a $1.60 year-end current exchange rate. On this date, Pinehurst has no translation adjustment balance relative to its investment in Bennett. In order to hedge its net investment in Bennett, Pinehurst borrows 800,000 pounds for one year at 12% interest on January 1, 20X3 at a spot rate of $1.60. The loan is denominated in pounds, with principal and interest payable on January 1, 20X4. Pinehurst records its loan as follows:

January 1, 20X3

Cash	$1,280,000	
Loan payable (fc)		$1,280,000

To record loan denominated in British pounds (800,000 pounds × $1.60 spot rate).

On November 1, 20X3, Bennett declares and pays a 100,000-pound dividend. Pinehurst records receipt of the dividend at the $1.75 spot rate on this date.

November 1, 20X3

Cash	$70,000	
Investment in Bennett		$ 70,000
To record receipt of dividends from Bennett (100,000 pounds × 40% × $1.75 spot rate).		

For 20X3, Bennett reports net income of 400,000 pounds. The weighted average exchange rate for translation of Bennett's revenue and expense items for the year is $1.70, and the current exchange rate at December 31, 20X3 is $1.80. These changes in Bennett's net assets are included in the following summary:

	British Pounds		U.S. Dollars
Net assets on January 1, 20X3	2,000,000	× $1.60	$3,200,000
Add: Net income for 20X3	400,000	× $1.70	680,000
Less: Dividends	(100,000)	× $1.75	(175,000)
Equity adjustment—change	—		435,000
Net assets on December 31, 20X3	2,300,000	× $1.80	$4,140,000

Pinehurst makes the following entry at December 31, 20X3 to take up its share of Bennett's income:

December 31, 20X3

Investment in Bennett	$446,000	
Income from Bennett		$ 272,000
Other comprehensive income		174,000
To record 40% share of Bennett's income (400,000 pounds × $1.70 weighted average exchange rate × 40% interest) and to record 40% share of translation adjustment ($435,000 × 40%).		

Also, Pinehurst adjusts the loan payable and the equity investment to the current rate at December 31, 20X3 and accrues interest on the loan:

Other comprehensive income	$160,000	
Loan payable (fc)		$ 160,000
To adjust loan payable denominated in British pounds to the current rate at year-end [800,000 pounds × ($1.80 − $1.60)].		

Interest expense	$163,200	
Exchange loss	9,600	
Interest payable		$ 172,800
To record interest expense (at weighted-average exchange rates) and accrue interest payable denominated in pounds at the year-end current rate as follows:		
Interest payable (800,000 pounds × 12% interest × 1 year × $1.80 current exchange rate)		$ 172,800
Less: Interest expense (800,000 pounds × 12% interest × 1 year × 1.70 weighted average exchange rate)		163,200
Exchange loss		$ 9,600

On January 1, 20X4, Pinehurst pays the loan and interest at the $1.80 spot rate as follows:

January 1, 20X4

Interest payable (fc)	$ 172,800	
Loan payable (fc)	1,440,000	
Cash		$1,612,800
To record payment of loan and interest denominated in British pounds when the spot rate is $1.80.		

As a result of the hedging operation, the changes in Pinehurst's investment in Bennett that were due to changing exchange rates were partially offset by its loan in British pounds. The equity adjustment from translation balance that appears in the stockholders' equity section of Pinehurst's December 31, 20X3 balance sheet is a $14,000 credit ($174,000 credit from the equity investment from translation, less $160,000 debit from adjustment of the loan denominated in British pounds).

Limit on Gain or Loss from Translation Adjustment   The gain or loss on an after-tax basis from the hedging operations that can be considered a translation adjustment is limited in amount to the *current* translation adjustment from the equity investment (see paragraph 129 of *Statement No. 52*).

Forward Contracts Summarized

The accounting required for a forward contract depends primarily on management's intent when entering into the transaction. In other words, the purpose of the transaction governs the accounting. Exhibit 13–2 summarizes the four types of forward contracts and the purpose, required accounting, and effect on income of each.

Additional Disclosures

The Financial Accounting Standards Board added a project on financial instruments and off-balance-sheet financing to its technical agenda in 1986. The goal was to develop broad standards for the accounting and reporting of financial instruments. As a result of this project, *FASB Statement No. 105*, "Disclosure of Information About Financial Instruments with Off-Balance-Sheet Risk and Financial Instruments with Concentrations of Credit Risk," was issued in 1990; *FASB Statement No. 107*, "Disclosures about Fair Value of Financial Instruments," was issued in 1991; and *FASB Statement No. 119*, "Disclosure about Derivative Financial Instruments and Fair Value of Financial Instruments," was issued in 1994. Some firms with substantial forward exchange contracts may have additional disclosure requirements under each of these statements.

The 1996 annual report of Harsco Corporation contains disclosures on their hedging activities in the "summary of significant accounting policies" as follows:

> The company's hedging strategy for the foreign currency exchange risk associated with its investment in Europe is based on projected foreign currency cash flows over periods up to 10 years. The company uses interest rate and cross currency interest rate swaps to effectively convert a portion of the company's U.S. dollar denominated debt into various European currencies. The company's investment in Europe and the foreign currency portion of these cross currency interest rate swaps are revalued in dollar terms each period to reflect current foreign currency exchange rates, with gains and losses recorded in the equity section of the balance sheet. To the extent that the notional amounts of these contracts exceed the company's investment in Europe, the related mark-to-market gains and losses are reflected currently in earnings. The net translation loss recognized in other income, including the gains and losses from those contracts not qualifying as hedges, was $14 million, $16 million and $3 million in 1996, 1995 and 1994. . . .
>
> The company also uses foreign currency forward contracts to hedge payments due on cross currency interest rate swaps and inter-company loans and, along with foreign currency options, to hedge material purchases, intercompany shipments and other commitments. . . . These contracts are not carried at fair value in the financial statements as the related gains and losses are recognized in the same period and classified in the same manner as the underlying transactions.[6]

SUMMARY

International accounting is concerned with accounting for foreign currency transactions and operations. The current accounting standard for foreign exchange transactions and financial statements is *FASB Statement No. 52*, "Foreign Currency Translation." *Statement No. 52* provides a functional currency concept: an entity's functional currency is the currency of the primary environment in which the entity operates.

---

[6] *Harsco Corporation 1996 Annual Report*, pages 39–40.

Classification	Purpose	Recognition	Expected Effect of Hedge and Related Foreign Currency Item
Speculation	To speculate in exchange rate changes.	Exchange gains and losses recognized currently, based on forward exchange rate changes.	Income effect equal to exchange gains and losses recognized.
Hedge of a net asset or liability position	To offset exposure to existing net asset or liability position.	Exchange gains and losses are recognized currently, but they are offset by related gains or losses on net asset or liability position.	Income effect equal to amortization of premium or discount. (Gains and losses offset.)
Hedge of an identifiable commitment	To offset exposure to a future purchase or sale and thereby lock in the price of an existing contract in U.S. dollars. commitment.	Exchange gains and losses are recognized currently, but they are offset by related gains or losses in the firm commitment.	Income effect equal to difference in the change in value of the hedge instrument versus the firm
Hedge of an anticipated transaction	To offset exposure of possible future purchase or sale.	Exchange gains or losses on the hedge counted in other comprehensive income until the underlying transaction is complete.	No immediate income effect. Adjusts underlying transaction.
Hedge of a net investment in a foreign entity	To offset exposure to an existing net investment in a foreign entity.	Exchange gains and losses are recognized as other comprehensive income and will offset translation adjustments recorded on the net investment.	Income effect equals the change in the future value of the hedge versus the value of the net investment.

Exhibit 13–2   Summary of Forward Contracts

Foreign currency transactions are transactions whose terms are denominated in a currency other than an entity's functional currency. Foreign currency transactions (other than forward contracts) are measured and recorded in U.S. dollars at the spot rate in effect at the transaction date. A change in the exchange rate between the date of the transaction and the settlement date results in an exchange gain or loss that is reflected in income for the period. At the balance sheet date, any remaining balances that are denominated in a currency other than the functional currency are adjusted to reflect the current exchange rate, and the gain or loss is charged to income.

Corporations use forward exchange contracts to avoid the risks of exchange rate changes and to speculate on foreign currency exchange price movements. *Statement No. 133* prescribes different provisions for forward contracts (and other derivatives), depending on their nature and purposes.

SELECTED READINGS

ESTRADA, ANETTE W., SUSAN W. MARTIN, and SANDER S. WECHSLER. "All Aboard for the Euro." *Management Accounting* (August 1998), pp. 37–41.

JOHNSON, L. TODD, HALSEY G. BULLEN, and VICTORIA W. KERN. "Hedge Accounting: Is Defferral the Only Option?" *Journal of Accountancy* (January 1994), pp. 53–58.

SOO, BILLY S., and LISA GILBERT SOO. "Accounting for the Multinational Firm: Is the Translation Process Valued by the Stock Market?" *The Accounting Review* (October 1944), pp. 617–637.

Statement of Financial Accounting Standards No. 52. "Foreign Currency Translation." Stamford, CT: Financial Accounting Standards Board, 1981.

Statement of Financial Accounting Standards No. 133. "Accounting for Derivative Instruments and Hedging Activities." Norwalk, CT: Financial Accounting Standards Board, 1998.

STEWARD, JOHN E. "The Challenges of Hedge Accounting." *Journal of Accountancy* (November 1989), pp. 48–56.

WILLIAMS, KATHY. "Are You Prepared for the Euro?" *Management Accounting* (May 1998), pp. 58–62.

ASSIGNMENT MATERIAL

QUESTIONS

1 Outline the evolution of accounting for foreign currency transactions and financial statements in terms of Professional Accounting Standards.

2 Distinguish between *measurement* and *denomination* in a particular currency.

3 Is the Canadian dollar a foreign currency? Explain.

4 Assume that one Canadian dollar can be exchanged for 0.72 U.S. dollars. What is the exchange rate if the exchange rate is quoted directly? Indirectly?

5 What is the difference between official and floating foreign exchange rates? Does the United States have floating exchange rates?

6 What is a spot rate with respect to foreign currency transactions? Could a spot rate ever be a historical rate? Could a spot rate ever be a fixed exchange rate? Discuss.

7 Describe the objectives of translation for purposes of preparing the financial statements of an enterprise.

8 Assume that a U.S. corporation imports electronic equipment from Japan in a transaction denominated in U.S. dollars. Is this transaction a foreign currency transaction? A foreign transaction? Explain.

9 How are assets and liabilities denominated in foreign currency measured and recorded at the transaction date? At the balance sheet date?

10 Criticize the following statement: "Exchange losses arise from foreign import activities, and exchange gains arise from foreign export activities."

11 When are exchange gains and losses reflected in the financial statements of a business enterprise?

12 A U.S. corporation imported merchandise from a British company for 1,000 British pounds when the spot rate was $1.45. It issued financial statements when the current rate was $1.47, and it paid for the merchandise when the spot rate was $1.46. What amount of exchange gain or loss will be included in the U.S. corporation's income statements in the period of purchase and in the period of settlement?

13 For what purpose or purposes might an enterprise enter into a "futures" derivative contract? In answering this question, you are to begin by defining the term forward exchange contract.

14 Do net exchange gains and losses arise from forward contracts (derivatives) that are designed to hedge a liability denominated in foreign currency?

15 Describe how to account for a forward contract that is intended as a hedge of an identifiable foreign currency commitment.

EXERCISES

E 13-1
1 If $1.5625 can be exchanged for 1 British pound, the direct and indirect exchange rate quotations are:
 a $1.5625 and 1 British pound, respectively
 b $1.5625 and 0.64 British pounds, respectively
 c $1.00 and 1.5625 British pounds, respectively
 d $1.00 and 0.64 British pounds, respectively

2 A U.S. firm purchases merchandise from a Canadian firm with payment due in 60 days and denominated in Canadian dollars. The U.S. firm will report an exchange gain or loss on settlement if the transaction is:

a Recorded in U.S. dollars
b Measured in U.S. dollars
c Not hedged through a forward contract
d Settled after an exchange rate change has occurred

3 Exchange gains and losses on accounts receivable and payable that are denominated in a foreign currency are:
a Accumulated and reported upon settlement
b Deferred and treated as transaction price adjustments
c Reported as equity adjustments from translation
d Recognized in the periods in which exchange rates change

4 Exchange gains and losses would be carried directly to stockholders' equity in a forward contract classified as a:
a Hedge of a net asset or liability position
b Hedge of a net investment in a foreign entity
c Hedge of a foreign currency commitment
d Speculation

5 An indication that a foreign subsidiary's functional currency is the currency of the parent company is provided by:
a Local financing of subsidiary operations
b A high volume of intercompany transactions
c Expenses that are primarily local costs
d Sales prices set by local competition in the subsidiary's country

6 A U.S. parent company has a subsidiary in Germany whose functional currency is the German mark. The U.S. dollar from the subsidiary's viewpoint is:
a A local currency
b A recording currency
c A foreign currency
d A common currency

E 13-2 Zimmer Corporation, a U.S. firm, purchased merchandise from Taisho Company of Japan on November 1, 20X2 for 10,000,000 yen, payable on December 1, 20X2. The spot rate for yen on November 1 was $.0075, and on December 1, the spot rate was $.0076.

Required
1 Did the dollar weaken or strengthen against the yen between November 1 and December 1, 20X2?
2 On November 1, 20X2, Zimmer recorded the account payable to Taisho in what amount?
3 On December 1, 20X2, Zimmer paid the 10,000,000 yen to Taisho. Prepare the journal entry to record settlement of the account on Zimmer's books.
4 If Zimmer had chosen to hedge its exposed net liability position on November 1, would it have entered a forward contract to purchase yen for future receipt or to sell yen for future delivery?

E 13-3 On December 16, 20X2, Rubbick Corporation, a U.S. firm, purchased merchandise from Hughes Company of Switzerland for 30,000 Swiss francs to be paid on January 15, 20X3. Relevant exchange rates for Swiss francs are:

December 16, 20X2	$.63
December 31, 20X2	$.66
January 15, 20X3	$.64

Required: Prepare all journal entries on Rubbick Corporation's books to account for the purchase on December 16, adjustment of the books on December 31, and payment of the account payable on January 15.

E 13-4 On November 16, 20X5, Littel Corporation of the United States sold inventory items to Candle Ltd. of Canada for 40,000 Canadian dollars (C$), to be paid on February 14, 20X6. Exchange rates for Canadian dollars on selected dates are as follows:

November 16, 20X5	$.70
December 31, 20X5	$.72
February 14, 20X6	$.71

Required: Determine the exchange gain or loss on the sale to Candle Ltd. to be included in Littel's income statements for the years 20X5 and 20X6.

E 13-5 Alliance Corporation, a U.S. company, sold inventory items to Royal Cabinets Ltd. of Great Britain for 120,000 British pounds on May 1, 20X2, when the spot rate was .6000 pounds. The invoice was paid by Royal on May 30, 20X2, when the spot rate was .6050 pounds.

Required: Prepare journal entries for the sale to Royal on May 1 and receipt of the 120,000 pounds on May 30.

E 13-6 **[AICPA adapted]**
1 On September 1, 20X7, Bain Corporation received an order for equipment from a foreign customer for 300,000 local currency units (LCU), when the U.S. dollar equivalent was $96,000. Bain shipped the equipment on October 15, 20X7 and billed the customer for 300,000 LCU when the U.S. dollar equivalent was $100,000. Bain received the customer's remittance in full on November 16, 20X7 and sold the 300,000 LCU for $105,000. In its income statement for the year ended December 31, 20X7, Bain should report a foreign exchange gain of:
   a $0   c $5,000
   b $4,000   d $9,000
2 On September 22, 20X4, Yumi Corporation purchased merchandise from an unaffiliated foreign company for 10,000 units of the foreign company's local currency. On that date, the spot rate was $.55. Yumi paid the bill in full on March 20, 20X5, when the spot rate was $.65. The spot rate was $.70 on December 31, 20X4. What amount should Yumi report as a foreign currency transaction loss in its income statement for the year ended December 31, 20X4?
   a $0   c $1,000
   b $500   d $1,500
3 On July 1, 20X4, Clark Company borrowed 1,680,000 local currency units from a foreign lender, evidenced by an interest-bearing note due on July 1, 20X5, which is denominated in the currency of the lender. The U.S. dollar equivalent of the note principal was as follows:

July 1, 20X4 (date borrowed)	$210,000
December 31, 20X4 (Clark's year-end)	240,000
July 1, 20X5 (date paid)	280,000

In its income statement for 20X5, what amount should Clark include as a foreign exchange gain or loss?
   a $70,000 gain   c $40,000 gain
   b $70,000 loss   d $40,000 loss
4 On July 1, 20X1, Stone Company lent $120,000 to a foreign supplier, evidenced by an interest-bearing note due on July 1, 20X2. The note is denominated in the currency of the borrower and was equivalent to 840,000 local currency units on the loan date. The note principal was appropriately included at $140,000 in the receivables section of Stone's December 31, 20X1 balance sheet. The note principal was repaid to Stone on the July 1, 20X2 due date, when the exchange rate was 8 LCU to $1. In its income statement for the year ended December 31, 20X2, what amount should Stone include as a foreign currency transaction gain or loss?
   a $0   c $15,000 gain
   b $15,000 loss   d $35,000 loss

E 13-7 Monroe Corporation imports merchandise from some Canadian companies and exports its own products to other Canadian companies. The *unadjusted* accounts denominated in Canadian dollars at December 31, 20X3 are as follows:

Account receivable from the sale of merchandise on December 16 to Carver Corporation. Billing is for 150,000 Canadian dollars and due January 15, 20X4	$103,500
Account payable to Forest Corporation for merchandise received December 2 and payable on January 30, 20X4. Billing is for 275,000 Canadian dollars	$195,250

Exchange rates on selected dates are as follows:

December 31, 20X3	$0.68
January 16, 20X4	$0.675
January 30, 20X4	$0.685

Required
   1 Determine the net exchange gain or loss from the two transactions that will be included in Monroe's income statement for 20X3.
   2 Determine the exchange gain or loss from settlement of the two transactions that will be included in Monroe's 20X4 income statement.

E 13-8 American TV Corporation had two foreign currency transactions during December 20X1 as follows:

December 12 Purchased electronic parts from Toko Company of Japan at an invoice price of 50,000,000 yen when the spot rate for yen was $.00750. Payment is due on January 11, 20X2.

December 15 Sold television sets to British Products Ltd. for 40,000 pounds when the spot rate for British pounds was $1.65. The invoice is denominated in pounds and is due on January 14, 20X2.

Required
1 Prepare journal entries to record the foregoing transactions.
2 Prepare journal entries to adjust the accounts of American TV Corporation at December 31, 20X1 if the current exchange rates are $.00760 and $1.60 for Japanese yen and British pounds, respectively.
3 Prepare journal entries to record payment to Toko Company on January 11, 20X2, when the spot rate for Japanese yen is $.00765, and to record receipt from British Products Ltd. on January 14, 20X2, when the spot rate for British pounds is $1.63.

E 13-9 Hayes Corporation, a U.S. importer, purchased merchandise from Cavilier Company of France for 100,000 francs on March 1, 20X8, when the spot rate for French francs was $.1630. The account payable denominated in francs was not due until May 30, 20X8, so Hayes immediately entered into a 90-day forward contract to hedge the transaction against exchange rate changes. The contract was made at a forward exchange rate of $.1650. Hayes settled the forward contract and the account payable on May 30, when the spot rate for francs was $.1600.

Required: Prepare the journal entries needed for Hayes to account for the purchase and forward contract on March 1, 20X8 and the subsequent settlements on May 30, 20X8.

E 13-10 Trendy Corporation purchases merchandise from Benetton S.p.A. of Italy for 10,000,000 lira. The merchandise is received on December 1, 20X8, with payment due in 60 days on January 30, 20X9. Also on December 1, 20X8, Trendy enters into a 60-day forward contract with the exchange broker to purchase the necessary 10,000,000 lira for delivery on January 30, 20X9 to hedge the Benetton transaction. Exchange rates for lira on selected dates are as follows:

	12/1/X8	12/31/X8	1/30/X9
Spot rate	$.00055	$.00056	$.00055
30-day futures	.00056	.00057	.00057
60-day futures	.00057	.00058	.00058

1 What is the net exchange gain or loss from this transaction and hedge that will be reported on Trendy's 20X8 income statement?
2 What effect will the transaction and hedge have on Trendy's income for 20X9?

E 13-11 **[AICPA adapted]**
On December 12, 20X1, Imp Company entered into three forward exchange contracts, each to purchase 100,000 local currency units in 90 days. Discounting is considered immaterial. The relevant exchange rates are as follows:

	Spot Rate	Forward Rate (for March 12, 20X2)
December 12, 20X1	$.88	$.90
December 31, 20X1	.98	.93

1 Imp entered into the first forward contract to hedge a purchase of inventory in November 20X1, payable in March 20X2. At December 31, 20X1, what amount of foreign currency transaction gain should Imp include in income from this forward contract?
  a $0   **c** $5,000
  b $3,000   **d** $7,000
2 Imp entered into the second forward contract to hedge a commitment to purchase equipment being manufactured to Imp's specifications. At December 31, 20X1, what amount of net gain or loss on foreign currency transactions should Imp include in income from this forward contract?
  a $0   **c** $5,000
  b $3,000   **d** $10,000
3 Imp entered into a third forward contract for speculation. At December 31, 20X1, what amount of foreign currency transaction gain should Imp include in income from this forward contract?
  a $0   **c** $5,000
  b $3,000   **d** $7,000

E 13-12   The accounts receivable of Bradley Corporation, a U.S. export company, include the following items denominated in foreign currency at December 31, 20X2, *before* adjusting entries are made as follows:

	Foreign Currency Units	Exchange Rate on Transaction Date	Balance per Books in U.S. Dollars
British pounds	50,000	$1.70	$ 85,000
German marks	200,000	.55	110,000
Swiss francs	100,000	.66	66,000
Japanese yen	10,000,000	.0076	76,000

On December 31, 20X2, the current exchange rates for British pounds, German marks, Swiss francs, and Japanese yen were $1.67, $.60, $.64, and $.0080, respectively.

Required
1 Determine the amount at which the foregoing receivables should be included in Bradley Corporation's December 31, 20X2 balance sheet.
2 Calculate the exchange gain or loss that should be included in Bradley's 20X2 income statement.

E 13-13   Kelly Corporation, a U.S. firm, had several foreign exchange transactions during 20X8. Prepare journal entries to record these transactions and year-end adjustments as described.

June 8   Purchased merchandise denominated at 10,000 British pounds when the spot rate was $1.60.

July 7   Paid the invoice of June 8 when the spot rate for British pounds was $1.61.

October 1   Sold merchandise to a Swiss firm for 30,000 Swiss francs when the spot rate for francs was $.670.

October 19 Settled the invoice of October 1 when the spot rate for francs was $.665.

November 16 Sold merchandise for 500,000 Swedish krona, payment to be received in krona in 60 days on January 16, 20X9. Spot rate for krona on this date was $.134.

November 16 Entered into a forward contract to deliver 500,000 krona to the exchange broker to hedge the sale of November 16 when the forward rate for 60-day futures in krona was $.1338 and the spot rate for krona was $.134.

December 31 Adjusted the accounts for the transactions of November 16 when the current exchange rate for krona was $.1343. The 15-day futures rate was $.1341 at December 31.

E 13-14   On April 1, 20X9, Windsor Ltd. of Canada ordered customized fittings from Ace Foundry, a U.S. firm, to be delivered on May 31, 20X9 at a price of 50,000 Canadian dollars. The spot rate for Canadian dollars on April 1, 20X9 was $.71. Also on April 1, in order to fix the sale price of the fittings at $35,250, Ace entered into a 60-day forward contract with the exchange broker to hedge the Windsor contract. This derivative met the conditions set forth in *FASB Statement No. 133* for a hedge of a foreign currency commitment. Exchange rates for Canadian dollars are as follows:

	April 1	May 31
Spot rate	$.710	$.725
60-day forward	.705	.715

Required: Prepare all journal entries on Ace Foundry's books to account for the commitment and related events on April 1 and May 31, 20X9.

E 13-15   On November 2, 20X1, Import Bazaar, a U.S. retailer, ordered merchandise from Matsushita Company of Japan. The merchandise is to be delivered to Import Bazaar on January 30, 20X2 at a price of 1,000,000 yen. Also on November 2, Import Bazaar hedged the foreign currency commitment with Matsushita by contracting with its exchange broker to buy 1,000,000 yen for delivery on January 30, 20X2. Exchange rates for yen are:

	11/2/X1	12/31/X1	1/30/X2
Spot rate	$.0075	$.0076	$.0078
30-day forward rate	.0076	.0078	.0079
90-day forward rate	.0078	.0079	.0080

Required

    1 Prepare the entry (or entries) on Import Bazaar's books on November 2, 20X1.

    2 Prepare the adjusting entry on December 31, 20X1.

E 13-16 Martin Corporation, a U.S. import-export firm, enters into a forward contract on October 2, 20X3 to speculate in German marks. The contract requires Martin to deliver 1,000,000 German marks to the exchange broker on March 31, 20X4.

    Quoted exchange rates for German marks are as follows:

	10/2/X3	12/31/X3	3/31/X4
Spot rate	$.6590	$.6500	$.6550
30-day forward	.6580	.6450	.6500
90-day forward	.6560	.6410	.6460
180-day forward	.6530	.6360	.6400

Required: Prepare the journal entries on Martin's books to account for the speculation throughout the life of the contract.

PROBLEMS

P 13-1 The accounts of Lincoln International, a U.S. corporation, show $81,300 accounts receivable and $38,900 accounts payable at December 31, 20X1, before adjusting entries are made. An analysis of the balances reveals the following:

Accounts receivable	
Receivable denominated in U.S. dollars	$28,500
Receivable denominated in 20,000 German marks	11,800
Receivable denominated in 25,000 British pounds	41,000
Total	$81,300

Accounts payable	
Payable denominated in U.S. dollars	$ 6,850
Payable denominated in 10,000 Canadian dollars	7,600
Payable denominated in 15,000 British pounds	24,450
Total	$38,900

    Current exchange rates for German marks, British pounds, and Canadian dollars at December 31, 20X1 are $.66, $1.65, and $.70, respectively.

Required

    1 Determine the net exchange gain or loss that should be reflected in Lincoln's income statement for 20X1 from year-end exchange adjustments.

    2 Determine the amounts at which the accounts receivable and accounts payable should be included in Lincoln's December 31, 20X1 balance sheet.

    3 Prepare journal entries to record collection of the receivables in 20X2 when the spot rates for German marks and British pounds are $.67 and $1.63, respectively.

    4 Prepare journal entries to record settlement of accounts payable in 20X2 when the spot rates for Canadian dollars and British pounds are $.71 and $1.62, respectively.

P 13-2 On April 1, 20X2, Baylor Corporation delivers merchandise to Rameau Corporation of France for 200,000 French francs when the spot rate for francs is 6.0496 francs. The receivable from Rameau is due May 30. Also on April 1, Baylor hedges its foreign currency asset and enters into a 60-day forward contract to sell 200,000 francs at a forward rate of 6.019 francs. The spot rate on May 30 was 5.992 francs.

Required

    1 Prepare journal entries to record the receivable from the sales transaction and the forward contract on April 1.

    2 Prepare journal entries to record collection of the receivable and settlement of the forward contract on May 30.

P 13-3 Shelton Corporation of New York is an international dealer in jewelry and engages in numerous import and export activities. Shelton's receivables and payables in foreign currency units before year-end adjustments on December 31, 20X7 are summarized as follows:

Foreign Currency	Currency Units	Rate on Date of Transaction	Per Books in U.S. Dollars	Current Rate on 12/31/X7
Accounts Receivable Denominated in Foreign Currency				
British pounds	100,000	$1.6500	$165,000	$1.6600
German marks	250,000	0.6600	165,000	0.6700
Swiss francs	160,000	0.6600	105,600	0.6400
French francs	500,000	0.1650	82,500	0.1700
Japanese yen	2,000,000	0.0075	15,000	0.0076
			$533,100	
Accounts Payable Denominated in Foreign Currency				
Canadian dollars	150,000	$0.7000	$105,000	$0.6900
German marks	50,000	0.6500	32,500	0.6700
Swedish krona	220,000	0.1300	28,600	0.1350
Japanese yen	4,500,000	0.0074	33,300	0.0076
			$199,400	

Required

1 Determine the amount at which the receivables and payables should be reported in Shelton's December 31, 20X7 balance sheet.

2 Calculate individual gains and losses on each of the receivables and payables and the net exchange gain that should appear in Shelton's 20X7 income statement.

3 Assume that Shelton wants to hedge its exposure to amounts denominated in German marks. Should it buy or sell marks for future delivery, in what amount or amounts?

P 13-4 Worldwide Corporation is an international firm that manufactures to the specifications of the purchaser and sells on a contract basis. The firm is headquartered in New York and its contracts are primarily with European firms.

The following transactions and events relate to one of its transactions and related hedging activities. Prepare all journal entries on Worldwide's books to account for the transactions and events.

November 16, 20X6   Contracted to deliver equipment to a British firm on February 14, 20X7. The contract is denominated in pounds, 400,000 pounds are due upon delivery, and the spot rate for pounds is $1.640 on November 16.

November 16, 20X6   Acquired a forward contract to sell 200,000 pounds for delivery on February 14, 20X7 at a forward rate of $1.630 in order to hedge 50% of the exposure.

December 31, 20X6   Current exchange rate for pounds on this date is $1.650 and the rate of a 45-day forward contract is $1.635.

February 14, 20X7   Worldwide delivers the equipment, collects the 400,000 pounds, delivers 200,000 pounds to the exchange broker, collects the amount due from the broker, and adjusts the sales account as appropriate. The spot rate for pounds on this date is $1.665.

P 13-5 The following items were included in the calculation of amounts appearing in the balance sheet of Mercer Corporation on December 31, 20X5:

Debit Balances

Account receivable from Freeport Ltd. of Great Britain
   (billing was for 100,000 British pounds (£)) $167,000
Contract receivable from exchange broker in U.S. dollars to hedge
   the receivable from Freeport for 30 days from December 16, 20X5   164,000
Contract receivable from exchange broker in Japanese yen to
   hedge payable to Matsushita for 90 days from December 2, 20X5   75,800

Credit Balances

Contract payable to exchange broker in pounds (for Freeport hedge) $165,500
Account payable to Matsushita Co. of Japan (billing was for
   10,000,000 yen)   75,500
Contract payable to exchange broker in U.S. dollars
   (for Matsushita hedge)   76,000

Selected exchange rates for British pounds and Japanese yen are as follows:

British pounds	12/16/X5	12/31/X5	1/15/X6
Spot rate	$1.650	$1.670	$1.680
Forward rate to sell £:			
on 1/15/X6	1.640	1.655	1.680

Japanese yen	12/02/X5	12/31/X5	3/01/X6
Spot rate	$.00754	$.00755	$.00750
Forward rate to buy yen:			
60-day forward	.00755	.00758	.00755
90-day forward	.00760	.00762	.00761

Required
1 Prepare journal entries on January 15, 20X6 to record collection of receivable from Freeport Ltd. and to settle the contract with the foreign exchange broker.
2 Prepare journal entries on March 1, 20X6 to record payment of the account to Matsushita and to settle the contract with the foreign exchange broker.

P 13-6   On October 2, 20X1, Flex-American Corporation, a U.S. company, entered into a forward contract to purchase 50,000 German marks for delivery in 180 days at a forward rate of $.6350. The forward contract is a derivative instrument hedging an identifiable foreign currency commitment as defined in *FASB Statement No. 133*. The spot rate for marks on this date was $.6250. Spot rates and forward rates for marks on December 31, 20X1 and March 31, 20X2 are:

	December 31, 20X1	March 31, 20X2
Spot rate	$.6390	$.6560
Forward rates		
30-day futures	.6410	.6575
90-day futures	.6420	.6615
180-day futures	.6450	.6680

Required: Prepare journal entries to:
1 Record the forward contract on October 2, 20X1
2 Adjust the accounts at December 31, 20X1
3 Account for settlement of the forward contract and record and adjust the related cash purchase on March 31, 20X2.

P 13-7   Bateman Industries, a U.S. corporation, anticipates a contract based on December 2, 20X1 discussions to sell heavy equipment to Ramsay Ltd. of Scotland for 500,000 British pounds. The equipment will likely be delivered and the amount collected on March 1, 20X2.

In order to hedge its anticipated commitment, Bateman entered into a forward contract on December 2 to sell 500,000 British pounds for delivery on March 1. The forward contract meets all the conditions of *FASB Statement No. 133* for a cash flow hedge of an anticipated foreign currency commitment.

Exchange rates for British pounds on selected dates are as follows:

British pounds	12/2/X1	12/31/X1	3/1/X2
Spot rate	$1.7000	$1.7100	$1.7200
90-day futures	1.6800	1.6900	1.7000

Required: Prepare the necessary journal entries on Bateman's books to account for:
1 The forward contract on December 2, 20X1.
2 Year-end adjustments relating to the forward contract on December 31, 20X1.
3 The delivery of the equipment and settlement of all accounts with Ramsay Ltd. and the exchange broker on March 1, 20X2.

P 13-8   Marlington Corporation, a U.S. firm, purchased equipment for 400,000 British pounds from Thacker Company Ltd. on December 16, 20X4. The terms were n/30, payable in British pounds.

On December 16, 20X4, Marlington also entered into a 30-day forward contract to hedge the account payable to Thacker. Exchange rates for British pounds on selected dates are as follows:

	12/16/X4	12/31/X4	1/15/X5
Spot rate	$1.67	$1.65	$1.64
Forward rate for 1/15/X5	1.68	1.66	1.64

Required

1 Prepare journal entries on December 16, 20X4 to record Marlington's purchase and the forward contract.
2 Prepare year-end journal entries for Marlington as needed on December 31, 20X4.
3 Prepare journal entries for Marlington's settlement of its accounts payable and the forward contract on January 15, 20X5.

P 13-9 Richmond-Davis Company, a U.S. firm, sold hospital equipment to Salem, Ltd. of Britain on November 2, 20X7 for 100,000 British pounds, payable in 90 days, on January 30, 20X8. Also, on November 2, Richmond-Davis entered into a 90-day forward contract to hedge its exposed net asset position. Exchange rates for pounds are as follows:

	November 2 20X7	December 31 20X7	January 30 20X8
Spot rate	$1.650	$1.660	$1.665
30-day forward	1.642	1.655	1.661
90-day forward	1.638	1.642	1.656
180-day forward	1.630	1.632	1.647

Required

1 Prepare journal entries to record the sale of merchandise to Salem, Ltd. and the related contract with the exchange broker.
2 Prepare adjusting entries for the sale and related hedge on December 31, 20X7.
3 Salem, Ltd. settles its account on January 30, 20X8. Prepare the journal entries necessary to settle the accounts with Salem, Ltd. and the exchange broker.

P 13-10 The unadjusted accounts of Stuart-American Corporation at December 31, 20X1 that relate to its forward exchange contracts are summarized as follows:

	In U.S. Dollars
Debit Balances	
Contract receivable from exchange broker in U.S. dollars (to hedge foreign currency commitment to Bennett, Ltd. of London due in 90 days from December 2.)	$168,000
Contract receivable from exchange broker in German marks (for speculation to purchase 200,000 marks in 90 days from December 2, 20X1)	130,000
Contract receivable from exchange broker in yen (to hedge payable to Toyaki for 120 days from November 1, 20X1)	76,000
Credit Balances	
Accounts payable to Toyaki Company of Japan (billing was for 10,000,000 Japanese yen)	$ 75,000
Contract payable to exchange broker in British pounds (to hedge a 100,000 pound sales commitment with Bennett, Ltd. of London)	168,000
Contract payable to exchange broker in U.S. dollars (for Toyaki hedge)	76,000
Contract payable to exchange broker in U.S. dollars (for speculation in German marks)	130,000

Exchange rates at December 31, 20X1 were as follows:

	Marks	Yen	Pounds
Current rate	$.640	$.0075	$1.715
Forward rates to purchase marks and yen and to sell pounds:			
30-day futures	$.660	$.0076	$1.700
60-day futures	.670	.0077	1.690
90-day futures	.680	.0078	1.680

Required

    1 Prepare a schedule to show the amounts at which the above accounts will appear in Stuart-American's December 31, 20X1 balance sheet.

    2 Compute the amount of exchange gain or loss that will appear in Stuart-American's 20X1 income statement.

P 13-11 The unadjusted accounts of Grandview International at December 31, 20X8 that related to its forward exchange contracts are summarized as follows:

	In U.S. Dollars
Debit Balances	
Accounts receivable from Nokia Company of Finland (billing was for 100,000 markka)	$22,000
Contract receivable from exchange broker in U.S. dollars (to hedge the receivable from Nokia for 60 days from December 1, 20X8)	21,000
Contract receivable from exchange broker in won (to hedge the payable to Cheil Textile Company for 120 days from November 1, 20X8)	13,000
Contract receivable from exchange broker in Canadian dollars (to hedge a 10,000 Canadian dollar purchase commitment from Sterling Corporation of Toronto for 60 days from December 1, 20X8)	8,400
Credit Balances	
Accounts payable to Cheil Textile Company of South Korea (billing was for 10,000,000 South Korean won)	12,000
Contract payable to exchange broker in markka (for Nokia hedge)	21,000
Contract payable to exchange broker in U.S. dollars (for Cheil hedge)	13,000
Contract payable to exchange broker in U.S. dollars (for Sterling hedge)	8,400

Exchange rates at December 31, 20X8 were as follows:

	Finnish Markka	South Korean Won	Canadian Dollars
Current rate	$.23	$.0014	$.81
Forward rates to sell markka and purchase won and Canadian dollars			
30-day futures	.22	.0015	.82
60-day futures	.21	.0016	.83

Required

    1 At what amount will the contract receivable from the exchange broker to hedge the account receivable from Nokia Company of Finland be included on Grandview's December 31, 20X8 balance sheet?

    2 At what amounts will the account payable from Cheil Textile Company and the related contract receivable from the exchange broker be included on Grandview's December 31, 20X8 balance sheet?

    3 Determine the exchange gain or loss for 20X8 on the forward contract to hedge the purchase commitment from Sterling.

P 13-12 Phillip Corporation of Atlanta paid $1,920,000 for a 40% interest in Slusser Company Ltd. of London on January 1, 20X1, when Slusser's net assets totaled 3,000,000 British pounds and the exchange rate for pounds was $1.60. A summary of changes in Slusser's net assets during 20X1 is as follows:

	British Pounds	Exchange Rates	U.S. Dollars
Net assets January 1	3,000,000	$1.60	$4,800,000
Add: Net income 20X1	600,000	1.55	930,000
Less: Dividends 20X1	(200,000)	1.54	(308,000)
Less: Equity adjustment from translation			(322,000)
Net assets December 31, 20X1	3,400,000	1.50	$5,100,000

Phillip Corporation anticipated a strengthening of the U.S. dollar against the British pound during the last half of 20X1, and it borrowed 1,200,000 pounds from a London bank for one year at 10% interest on July 1, 20X1 to hedge its net investment in Slusser. The loan was made when the exchange rate for British pounds was $1.55. The loan was denominated in British pounds and the current exchange rate at December 31, 20X1 was $1.50.

Required
  1 Prepare journal entries to account for Phillip's investment in Slusser during 20X1.
  2 Prepare journal entries for Phillip to:
    a Record the loan on July 1, 20X1.
    b Adjust the loan payable at December 31, 20X1.
    c Accrue interest on the loan at December 31, 20X1. (The interest, not a part of the hedge of the net investment, was incurred at a $1.525 average exchange rate.)

P 13-13 Pepperell Corporation, a U.S. firm, has a 25% interest in Spinoza Corporation, a foreign company based in the Netherlands whose functional currency is the guilder. The investment in Spinoza balance at December 31, 20X4 was $845,000, equal to 25% of the investee's net assets of 5,200,000 guilders × the $.65 current exchange rate on that date.

Because of anticipated strengthening of the U.S. dollar against the guilder, Pepperell negotiated a one-year, 15% loan of 1,300,000 guilders on January 1, 20X5 to hedge its net investment in Spinoza. It immediately invested the money in 9% U.S. government securities. These transactions were conducted while the spot rate for guilders was $.65.

During 20X5, the U.S. dollar strengthened against the guilder and the current exchange rate and spot rate for guilders at December 31, 20X5 stood at $.62. The average exchange rate for 20X5 was $.625. A summary of the equity changes of the foreign investee during 20X5 is as follows:

	Guilders	Exchange Rates	U.S. Dollars
Net assets January 1	5,200,000	× $.65	$3,380,000
Net income 20X5	832,000	× $.625	520,000
Equity adjustment—change			(160,160)
Net assets December 31	6,032,000	× $.62	$3,739,840

Required: Prepare journal entries on Pepperell's books to:
  1 Record the loan of 1,300,000 guilders
  2 Invest the $845,000 from the loan in U.S. securities
  3 Liquidate the U.S. securities at December 31, 20X5
  4 Settle the loan and interest with the Netherland lender at December 31, 20X5
  5 Account for the foreign investee during 20X5

14

Foreign Currency Financial Statements

U.S. multinational corporations apply the provisions of *FASB Statement No. 52* in converting the financial statements of their foreign subsidiaries and branches into U.S. dollars. *Statement No. 52* requires application of the functional currency concept under which *a foreign entity's functional currency is the currency of the primary economic environment in which it operates*. The foreign entity's functional currency affects (1) the procedures used to measure its financial position and results of operations and (2) whether exchange gains and losses will be included in consolidated net income or will be reported in other comprehensive income.

A U.S. company may have operations located outside the United States in which the books of record are maintained in the U.S. dollar and, therefore, the financial statements are prepared in U.S. dollars. Because these statements are not foreign currency financial statements, they are combined or consolidated according to the procedures described in Chapters 3 through 12, and they are not addressed in this chapter.

Several definitions from *Statement No. 52* are important to the functional currency concept. A **foreign currency** is a currency other than the entity's functional currency. If the functional currency of a German subsidiary is the German mark, the U.S. dollar is a foreign currency of the German subsidiary. If the functional currency of the German subsidiary is the U.S. dollar, the German mark is a foreign currency to the German subsidiary. The **local currency** is the currency of the country to which reference is made. Thus, the Canadian dollar is the local currency of a Canadian subsidiary of a U.S. firm. Note that the books of record and the subsidiary's financial statements will be prepared in the local currency in nearly all cases involving foreign currency financial statements, regardless of the determination of the functional currency. The **reporting currency** is the currency in which the consolidated financial statements are prepared—in other words, the currency of the parent company. The reporting currency for the consolidated statements of a U.S. firm with foreign subsidiaries is the U.S. dollar. **Foreign currency statements** are statements prepared in a currency that is *not* the reporting currency (the U.S. dollar) of the U.S. parent-investor.

APPLICATION OF THE FUNCTIONAL CURRENCY CONCEPT

Before the foreign currency statements of a foreign entity can be translated into U.S. dollars, they must be in conformity with the U.S. generally accepted accounting principles, and all account balances on the balance sheet date that are denominated in a foreign currency (from the foreign entity's point of view) must be adjusted to reflect current exchange rates. (This is similar to the year-end adjustments illustrated in Chapter 13 for U.S. firms with account balances denominated in a foreign currency.)

Under the objectives of the functional currency concept, a foreign entity's assets, liabilities and operations must be measured in its functional currency. Subsequently, the foreign entity's statement of financial position and results of operations have to be consolidated (subsidiary) or combined (branch) with those of the parent company in the currency of the reporting enterprise. The accounting procedures required to convert a foreign entity's financial statements into the currency of the U.S. parent depend on the functional currency of the foreign subsidiary or branch. Because the foreign entity's books are maintained in its local currency, which may be its functional currency or a foreign currency, the combining or consolidating may require translation, remeasurement, or both.

Translation   When the foreign entity's books are maintained in its functional currency (in other words, the local currency of the foreign entity is its functional currency), the statements are *translated* into the currency of the reporting entity. **Translation** involves expressing functional currency measurements in the reporting currency. A basic provision of *Statement No. 52* is that all elements of financial statements (assets, liabilities, revenues, and expenses) shall be translated using a current exchange rate. This is referred to as the **current rate method**. The functional currency is not the U.S. dollar, therefore, no direct impact on the reporting entity's cash flows is expected, and the effects of exchange rate changes are reported as stockholders' equity adjustments in other comprehensive income. The equity adjustments from translation are accumulated until sale or liquidation of the foreign entity investment, at which time they are reported as adjustments of the gain or loss on sale.

Remeasurement   When the foreign entity's books are not maintained in its functional currency, the foreign currency financial statements must be measured into the functional currency. Remeasurement obviates translation if the entity's functional currency is also the reporting currency. In other words, if the foreign currency financial statements are remeasured into a U.S. dollar functional currency, no translation is necessary because the reporting currency of the parent-investor is the U.S. dollar. The objective of remeasurement is to produce the same results as if the books were maintained in the functional currency. To accomplish this objective, both historical and current exchange rates are used in the remeasurement process. Under this method (the **temporal method**), monetary assets and liabilities are remeasured at current exchange rates, and other assets and equities are remeasured at historical rates. **Monetary assets and liabilities** are those in which the amounts are fixed in currency units. **Nonmonetary items** are those in which the amounts change with changes in market prices. The remeasurement produces exchange rate adjustments that are included in income because a direct impact on the enterprise's cash flows is expected.

Translation and Remeasurement of Foreign Currency Financial Statements

Patriot Corporation, a U.S. company, has a wholly owned subsidiary, Romel Corporation, that operates in Germany. The translation-remeasurement possibilities for the accounts of Romel are as follows:

	Functional Currency	Currency of Accounting Records	Required Procedures for Consolidating or Combining
Case 1	German mark	German mark	Translation
Case 2	U.S. dollar	German mark	Remeasurement
Case 3	Swiss franc	German mark	Remeasurement and translation

Under Case 1, Romel Corporation keeps its books in the local currency, marks, which is also the functional currency, and no remeasurement is needed, provided that the books reflect U.S. generally accepted accounting principles. The accounts do require translation to U.S. dollar amounts (the currency of the reporting enterprise), and

FASB Statement No. 52 requires translation under the *current rate method.* The current exchange rate at the balance sheet date is used to translate all assets and liabilities. Theoretically, the exchange rates in effect at transaction dates should be used to translate all revenues, expenses, and gains and losses. As a practical matter, it is expected that revenues and expenses will be translated at appropriate weighted average exchange rates for the period. The adjustments from translation are reported in other comprehensive income, as required by *FASB Statement No. 130,* "Reporting Comprehensive Income."

In Case 2, Romel's books are maintained in marks, but the functional currency is the U.S. dollar. Under *Statement No. 52,* the accounts of Romel are remeasured into the functional currency, which is also the currency of the reporting entity. In this case, remeasurement into the reporting currency obviates translation. The objective of remeasurement is to obtain the results that would have been produced if Romel's books of record had been maintained in the functional currency. Thus, remeasurement requires the use of historical exchange rates for some items and current rates for others and recognition of exchange gains and losses from measurement of all monetary assets and liabilities not denominated in the functional currency (the U.S. dollar in this case).

In Case 3, Romel's books are maintained in marks although the functional currency is Swiss francs. (This situation could arise if the subsidiary is a holding company for operations in Switzerland.) The consolidation requires a *remeasurement* of all assets, liabilities, revenues, expenses, and gains and losses into Swiss francs (the functional currency) and recognition of exchange gains and losses from remeasurement of the monetary assets and liabilities not denominated in Swiss francs. After the remeasurement is completed and Romel's financial statements are stated in Swiss francs, the statements are *translated* into U.S. dollars using the current rate method. This translation from the functional currency to the currency of the reporting entity will create translation adjustments, but such adjustments are not recognized in current income. Rather, they are reported in other comprehensive income.

A summary of exchange rates to be used for remeasurement and translation is provided in Exhibit 14–1. Once the functional currency has been determined, it should be "used consistently unless significant changes in economic facts and circumstances" indicate that the functional currency has changed. A change in functional currency is not considered a change in an accounting principle (*FASB Statement No. 52,* paragraph 45).

Intercompany Foreign Currency Transactions

Intercompany transactions between affiliated companies are foreign currency transactions if they produce receivable or payable balances denominated in a currency other than the entity's (parent's or subsidiary's) functional currency. Such intercompany foreign currency transactions result in exchange gains and losses that are included in income except when they produce intercompany balances of a long-term investment nature (that is, settlement is not expected in the foreseeable future), in which case the translation adjustments are reported in other comprehensive income as an equity adjustment from translation.

An intercompany transaction requires analysis to see if it is a foreign currency transaction for one, both, or neither of the affiliates. To illustrate the variables involved, assume that a U.S. parent company borrows $1,600,000 (1,000,000 pounds) from its British subsidiary. The following analysis shows that either the parent or the subsidiary will have a foreign currency transaction if the subsidiary's local currency is its functional currency.

	Currency in Which Loan is Denominated	Functional Currency of Subsidiary	Foreign Currency Transaction of	
			Subsidiary?	Parent?
Case 1	British pound	British pound	No	Yes
Case 2	British pound	U.S. dollar	Yes	Yes
Case 3	U.S. dollar	British pound	Yes	No
Case 4	U.S. dollar	U.S. dollar	No	No

When the U.S. dollar is the functional currency of the subsidiary, either both affiliates have a foreign currency transaction with offsetting effects (Case 2), or the in-

	Remeasurement to Functional Currency	Translation to Currency of Reporting Entity
Assets		
Cash, demand deposits, and time deposits	Current	Current
Marketable securities carried at cost:		
Equity securities	Historical	Current
Debt securities	Historical	Current
Accounts and notes receivable and related unearned		
discounts	Current	Current
Allowance for uncollectible accounts and notes	Current	Current
Inventories:		
Carried at cost	Historical	Current
Carried at lower of cost or market	*	Current
Prepaid insurance, advertising, and rent	Historical	Current
Refundable deposits	Current	Current
Property, plant, and equipment	Historical	Current
Accumulated depreciation on property, plant,		
and equipment	Historical	Current
Cash surrender value of life insurance	Current	Current
Deferred income tax assets	Current	Current
Patents, trademarks, licenses, and formulas	Historical	Current
Goodwill	Historical	Current
Other intangible assets	Historical	Current
Liabilities		
Accounts and notes payable and overdrafts	Current	Current
Accrued expenses	Current	Current
Deferred income tax liabilities	Current	Current
Deferred income	Historical	Current
Other deferred credits	Historical	Current
Bonds payable and other long-term debt	Current	Current
Stockholders' Equity		
Common stock	Historical	Historical[†]
Preferred stock carried at issuance price	Historical	Historical[†]
Other paid-in capital	Historical	Historical[†]
Retained earnings	Not remeasured	Not translated
Income Statement Items Related to Nonmonetary Items[‡]		
Cost of goods sold	Historical	Current
Depreciation on property, plant, and equipment	Historical	Current
Amortization of intangible items (patents,		
goodwill, etc.)	Historical	Current
Amortization of deferred income taxes	Current	Current
Amortization of deferred charges and credits	Historical	Current

*When the books are not maintained in the functional currency and the lower-of-cost-or-market rule is applied to inventories, inventories at cost are remeasured using historical rates. Then the historical cost in the functional currency is compared to market in the functional currency.

[†]Translation at historical rates is necessary for elimination of reciprocal parent investment and subsidiary equity accounts. It should be noted that conversion of all asset, liability, and equity accounts at current exchange rates would obviate the "equity adjustment from translation" component.

[‡]Income statement items related to monetary items are translated or remeasured at weighted average exchange rates to approximate the exchange rates in existence at the time of the related transactions. Intercompany dividends are converted at the rate in effect at the time of payment under both the remeasurement and translation approaches. Translation of income statement items at current rates is implemented by using weighted average exchange rates.

Exhibit 14–1 *Summary of Exchange Rates Used for Remeasurement and Translation*

tercompany transaction is not a foreign currency transaction (Case 4). Thus, only the cases in which the functional currency is the local currency of the subsidiary (Cases 1 and 3) have the potential to affect consolidated income. In these cases, translation adjustments will be reported as equity adjustments from translation if the loan is of a long-term investment nature; otherwise, they will be reported as exchange gains and losses.

Foreign Entities Operating in Highly Inflationary Economies

In a highly inflationary economy, the local currency rapidly loses value against goods and services. Generally, it is weakening against other currencies as well. The lack of a stable measuring unit presents special problems for converting foreign currency statements into U.S. dollars. For example, assume that at the end of year 1, $1 can be exchanged for 50 local currency units (LCU), a $.02 exchange rate, but at the end of year 2, $1 can be exchanged for 200 LCU, a $.005 exchange rate. An equity investment of 9,000,000 LCU at the end of year 1 is translated at $180,000 using the current exchange rate, but one year later the same investment of 9,000,000 LCU is translated at $45,000 using the current exchange rate. Under the current rate method, translation gains and losses are accumulated and reported in other comprehensive income. They are not recognized in income until the investment is sold.

The FASB recognized that the current rate method of translation would pose a problem for foreign entities operating in countries with high rates of inflation. Price level-adjusted financial statements are not basic financial statements under GAAP, so the FASB prescribed a practical alternative. The reporting currency (the U.S. dollar) has to be used to remeasure the financial statements of foreign entities in highly inflationary economies because the inflationary currency is not a functional measuring unit. Exchange gains and losses from remeasuring the financial statements of the foreign entity are recognized in the income for the period.

Statement No. 52 defines a "highly inflationary economy" as one with a cumulative three-year inflation rate of approximately 100% or more. Consider a foreign country with inflation data for a three-year period as follows:

	Index	Change in Index	Annual Rate of Inflation
January 1, 1999	120		
January 1, 2000	150	30	30 ÷ 120 (or 25%)
January 1, 2001	210	60	60 ÷ 150 (or 40%)
January 1, 2002	250	40	40 ÷ 210 (or 19%)

The three-year inflation rate is 108.3% [(250 − 120) ÷ 120], *not* 84% (25 + 40 + 19). Management applies judgment in the final determination to avoid frequent changes in the functional currency due to minor changes in the three-year inflation rate. The three-year inflation rate in this example exceeds 100%, so the usual criteria for identifying the functional currency are ignored and the U.S. dollar (the functional currency of the reporting entity) is the functional currency for purposes of preparing consolidated financial statements.

The 1993 annual report of Kimberly-Clark Corporation included the following financial statement note:

> Effective December 31, 1992, the Mexican economy was determined to no longer be hyperinflationary. As a result, the Mexican peso is considered to be the functional currency of the Corporation's operations in Mexico. In conjunction with this change, $25.3 million of deferred income taxes was charged to unrealized currency translation adjustments in 1992.[1]

Due to the increase in inflation in Mexico in recent years, the 1997 annual report of Kimberly-Clark Corporation included the following financial-statement note fragments indicating the change in the functional currency of the Mexican subsidiary (KCM) to the U.S. dollar.

> Prior to 1997 Mexico's economy was deemed to be non-hyperinflationary and because KCM has financed a portion of its operations in U.S. dollar obligations, KCM experienced foreign currency losses on these obligations as the value of the peso declined. Beginning in 1997, the Mexican economy was determined to be hyperinflationary because the country's cumulative inflation rate for the last three years had exceeded 100 percent. For accounting purposes, the functional currency of KCM became the U.S. dollar rather than the Mexican peso. Accordingly, changes in the value of the peso no longer result in foreign currency gains or losses attributable to the U.S. dollar obligations. However, changes in the value of the peso have resulted in gains or losses attributable to peso-denominated monetary assets held by KCM.

---

[1] *Kimberly-Clark Annual Report 1993*, p. 36.

The income statement and balance sheets of operations in hyperinflationary economies, i.e. Brazil, Mexico (effective January 1, 1997) and Venezuela, are translated into U.S. dollars using both current and historical rates of exchange. For balance sheet accounts translated at current exchange rates, such as cash and accounts receivable, the differences from historical exchange rates are reflected in income.[2]

Business Combinations

The assets and liabilities of a foreign entity are translated into U.S. dollars using the current exchange rate in effect on the date of the business combination. For a *pooling of interests business combination*, this involves translating the recorded assets and liabilities into U.S. dollars at book values.

In the case of a business combination accounted for as a *purchase*, the identifiable assets and liabilities of the foreign operations are adjusted to their fair values in local currency and translated at the exchange rate in effect on the date of the purchase business combination. Any difference between investment cost and translated net assets acquired is accounted for as goodwill or as an excess of net assets acquired over cost, as required by *APB Opinion No. 16*.

Cost/Book Value Differential   When the foreign entity's books are maintained in the functional currency, the excess of cost over book value acquired is assigned to assets, liabilities, and goodwill in local currency units and subsequently *translated* at current exchange rates under the current rate method. For example, assume that the excess is allocated 10,000 British pounds to equipment with a five-year life on January 1, 20X2, when the exchange rate is $1.50. If the average exchange rate for 20X2 is $1.45 and the year-end exchange rate is $1.40, depreciation on the excess for 20X2 will be $2,900 (2,000 pounds × $1.45); the undepreciated balance at December 31 will be $11,200 (8,000 pounds × $1.40); and the unrealized translation loss of $900 [$15,000 − ($2,900 + $11,200)] will be recorded in comprehensive income as an equity adjustment from translation.

When the foreign entity's books are not maintained in the functional currency, *remeasurement* is required and the excess allocated to equipment is amortized at the historical exchange rates in effect at the time of the business combination. Thus, the depreciation expense would be $3,000 (2,000 pounds × $1.50), and the undepreciated balance would be $12,000 (8,000 pounds × $1.50).

Minority Interest   The computation of the amount of a minority interest in a foreign subsidiary must be based on the translated or remeasured financial statements of the subsidiary. Similarly, the financial statements of a foreign investee must be translated or remeasured before the equity method of accounting is applied.

ILLUSTRATION—TRANSLATION UNDER STATEMENT NO. 52

The following illustration demonstrates the translation requirements of *Statement No. 52* in action.

Background Information

Pat Corporation, a U.S. firm, paid $525,000 cash to acquire all the stock of the British firm, Star Company Ltd., when the book value of Star's net assets was equal to fair value. This purchase business combination was consummated on December 31, 20X1, at which time the exchange rate for British pounds was $1.50. Star's assets and equities at acquisition on December 31, 20X1 were as follows:

	British Pounds	Exchange Rate	U.S. Dollars
Assets			
Cash	140,000	$1.50	210,000
Accounts receivable	40,000	1.50	60,000
Inventories (cost)	120,000	1.50	180,000
Plant assets	100,000	1.50	150,000
			(Continued)

---

[2]*Kimberly-Clark Annual Report 1997*, pp. 51–52.

	British Pounds	Exchange Rate	U.S. Dollars
Less: Accumulated depreciation	(20,000)	1.50	(30,000)
Total assets	380,000		570,000
Equities			
Accounts payable	30,000	1.50	45,000
Bonds payable	100,000	1.50	150,000
Capital stock	200,000	1.50	300,000
Retained earnings	50,000	1.50	75,000
Total equities	380,000		570,000

During 20X2, the British pound weakened against the U.S. dollar (in other words, a given number of U.S. dollars could be exchanged for more British pounds), and at year-end the current exchange rate was $1.40. Average exchange rates for 20X2 were $1.45. Star paid £30,000 dividends on December 1, 20X2, when the exchange rate was $1.42 (U.S.) per British pound.

Intercompany Transaction

The only intercompany transaction between the firms was an $84,000 (£56,000) non-interest-bearing advance by Star to Pat that was made on January 4, 20X2, when the exchange rate was still $1.50. The advance is denominated in U.S. dollars. Under the assumption that Pat determines Star's functional currency to be the British pound, the advance to Pat is a foreign currency transaction to Star, but not to Pat. Therefore, Star adjusts its advance to Pat account at year-end 20X2 to reflect the $1.40 current exchange rate. Star records an exchange gain because there is no evidence that the advance is of a long-term investment nature. The entry on Star's books is:

Advance to Pat	£4,000	
Exchange gain		£4,000

To adjust receivable denominated in dollars
[($84,000 ÷ $1.40) − £56,000 per books].

Star's adjusted trial balance at December 31, 20X2 reflects the advance to Pat in the amount of £60,000, and the exchange gain at £4,000.

Translating the Foreign Subsidiary's Adjusted Trial Balance

Pat has to translate Star's adjusted trial balance at December 31, 20X2 into U.S. dollars before it can either account for its investment under the equity method or consolidate its financial statements with those of Star. The translation of Star's accounts into U.S. dollars is shown in Exhibit 14-2, which illustrates translation working paper procedures. Under the *current rate method* required for foreign subsidiaries whose functional currency is not the U.S. dollar, all assets and liabilities are translated at the current exchange rate at the balance sheet date and all income statement items are translated at average exchange rates during the accounting period. Average rates are applied to approximate the current exchange rates in effect when the revenue and expense transactions were consummated during the period. The exchange rates in effect when dividends are paid are used in translating the dividends of a foreign subsidiary.

The stockholders' equity accounts of a subsidiary are not translated at current exchange rates. Capital stock and other paid-in capital accounts are translated at the exchange rate in effect when the subsidiary (or investee) was acquired. Retained earnings are not translated after acquisition, instead, *the retained earnings dollar amount consists of retained earnings at acquisition, plus income, less dividends after acquisition, all in translated dollar amounts.* In years subsequent to the year of acquisition, beginning retained earnings of one period is simply the prior year's ending retained earnings from the translated financial statements.

After all financial statement items have been translated into dollars, the trial balance debits and credits are totaled and *the amount needed to balance debits and credits is*

STAR COMPANY LTD.
TRANSLATION WORKSHEET FOR 20X2
(BRITISH POUNDS FUNCTIONAL CURRENCY)

	Trial Balance (in British Pounds)	Translation Rate	Trial Balance (in U.S. Dollars)
Debits			
Cash	110,000	$1.40	154,000
Accounts receivable	80,000	1.40	112,000
Inventories (FIFO)	120,000	1.40	168,000
Plant assets	100,000	1.40	140,000
Advance to Pat	60,000	1.40	84,000
Cost of sales	270,000	1.45	391,500
Depreciation	10,000	1.45	14,500
Wages and salaries	120,000	1.45	174,000
Other expenses	60,000	1.45	87,000
Dividends	30,000	1.42	42,600
Accumulated other comprehensive income			28,600
	960,000		1,396,200
Credits			
Accumulated depreciation	30,000	1.40	42,000
Accounts payable	36,000	1.40	50,400
Bonds payable	100,000	1.40	140,000
Capital stock	200,000	1.50	300,000
Retained earnings	50,000	computed	75,000
Sales	540,000	1.45	783,000
Exchange gain (advance)	4,000	1.45	5,800
	960,000		1,396,200

Exhibit 14–2   *Translation of Foreign Subsidiary Accounts into U.S. Dollars*

entered as an equity adjustment from translation and included in other comprehensive income. For example, the $28,600 equity adjustment on translation in Exhibit 14–2 is measured by subtracting the $1,367,600 debits from the $1,396,200 credits in the U.S. dollar column. Financial statements in dollars for the foreign entity are prepared directly from the translated trial balance. These are illustrated in Exhibit 14–3 for Star Company at and for the year ended December 31, 20X2.

Equity Method of Accounting

Pat records the investment in Star at its $525,000 cost on December 31, 20X1, and subsequently uses one-line consolidation procedures to account for its foreign subsidiary. Star's translated financial statements are used in applying the equity method. The entry to record receipt of the £30,000, or $42,600, dividend from Star on December 1, 20X2 is:

Cash	$42,600	
Investment in Star		$ 42,600

Pat received this dividend when the exchange rate was $1.42, so the dividends paid by Star also have to be translated into dollars at the current exchange rate in effect when the dividends were paid, $1.42 (see Exhibit 14–2).

Pat recognizes its equity in Star's income from 20X2 in an entry that also recognizes Star's unrecognized loss on translation. The entry for 20X2 is as follows:

Investment in Star	$93,200	
Other comprehensive income: equity adjustment on translation	28,600	
Income from Star		$121,800

```
STAR COMPANY LTD.
INCOME AND RETAINED EARNINGS STATEMENTS
FOR THE YEAR ENDED DECEMBER 31, 20X2
(IN U.S. DOLLARS)
```

Sales		$783,000
Less costs and expenses:		
Cost of sales	$391,500	
Depreciation	14,500	
Wages and salaries	174,000	
Other expenses	87,000	
Total costs and expenses		667,000
Operating income		116,000
Exchange gain		5,800
Net income		121,800
Retained earnings January 1		75,000
		196,800
Less: Dividends		42,600
Retained earnings December 31, 20X2		$154,200

```
STAR COMPANY LTD. BALANCE SHEET
AT DECEMBER 31, 20X2
(IN U.S. DOLLARS)
```

Assets	
Cash	$154,000
Accounts receivable	112,000
Inventories	168,000
Plant assets	140,000
Less: Accumulated depreciation	(42,000)
Advance to Pat	84,000
	$616,000
Equities	
Accounts payable	$ 50,400
Bonds payable	140,000
Capital stock	300,000
Retained earnings	154,200
Accumulated other comprehensive income	(28,600)
	$616,000

Exhibit 14–3   *Translated Financial Statements—British Pounds Functional Currency*

This entry recognizes 100% of Star's net income for 20X2, in dollars, as investment income, and it also enters the $28,600 unrecognized loss from translation on Pat's books. The recognized income of $121,800 less the $28,600 unrecognized loss on translation is the $93,200 investment increase from Star's operations in 20X2.

Goodwill Amortization   Pat's goodwill from its investment in Star is $150,000, equal to $525,000 investment cost less $375,000 book value and fair value of net assets acquired. Under the current rate method, the goodwill calculations are based on local currency units (British pounds), rather than U.S. dollar amounts. Thus, a first step in calculating goodwill amortization for Pat's investment in Star is to convert the $150,000 goodwill at acquisition into £100,000 goodwill by dividing $150,000 by the $1.50 exchange rate at acquisition on December 31, 20X1.

Current amortization on Pat's books is £100,000 ÷ 10 years × $1.45 average exchange rate for 20X2, or $14,500. Goodwill amortization for 20X2 is recorded on Pat's books as follows:

Income from Star	$14,500	
Other comprehensive income: equity adjustment		
from translation	9,500	
Investment in Star		$24,000

The equity adjustment on translation of goodwill that appears in the entry is the result of changes in exchange rates during 20X2, and the $24,000 credit to the investment in Star reflects the decrease in unamortized goodwill during the year, $150,000 − (£90,000 × $1.40). These relationships are summarized as follows:

	In Pounds	Exchange Rate	In Dollars
Beginning goodwill	100,000	$1.50	$150,000
Less: Amortization	10,000	1.45	14,500
	90,000		134,500
Equity adjustment	—		9,500
Ending goodwill	90,000	1.40	$126,000

Alternatively, the $9,500 equity adjustment can be computed as follows:

£10,000 amortization × ($1.50 − $1.45) exchange rate decline to midyear	$ 500
£90,000 unamortized goodwill × ($1.50 − $1.40) exchange rate decline for the year	9,000
Equity adjustment	$9,500

Similar adjustments are required when an excess of cost over book value is allocated to identifiable assets and liabilities and the current rate method is used.

Investment in Foreign Subsidiary   At this point, it may be helpful to summarize the changes in Pat's investment in Star account during 20X2:

Investment cost December 31, 20X1	$525,000
Less: Dividends received 20X2	(42,600)
Add: Equity in Star's net income	121,800
Less: Unrealized loss on translation	(28,600)
Less: Goodwill amortization	(14,500)
Less: Unrealized translation loss on goodwill	(9,500)
Investment balance December 31, 20X2	$551,600

The translated amount of Star's net assets at December 31, 20X2 is $425,600, as shown in Exhibit 14–3. Pat's $551,600 investment in Star balance on this date consists of the $425,600 equity in Star's net assets plus $126,000 unamortized goodwill. Pat also has unrealized losses from translation of $38,100 at December 31, 20X2, consisting of $28,600 translation losses on Star's net assets plus a $9,500 translation loss on goodwill. These unrealized losses are reflected in Pat's equity adjustment from translation account, which is reported in other comprehensive income. The equity adjustment is increased or decreased to reflect translation gains or losses during each period that the investment is held, and the final balance is treated as an adjustment of any gain or loss on sale or other disposal of the investment. *FASB Statement No. 52* requires disclosure of beginning and ending balances and changes to the translation adjustment account.

The functional currency concept provides a way to recognize exchange rate changes without affecting the income statement. When the local currency of a foreign entity is its functional currency, net assets can change without impacting income, the FASB reasoned. This may be because "a change in the exchange rate between the dollar and the other currency produces a change in the dollar equivalent of the net investment, but there is no change in the net assets of the other entity measured in its functional currency."[3] Or it might be argued that "the translation adjustment is

---

[3]Wig DeMoville and Roben Hatami, "Nonowner Equity Transactions—A Review," *The CPA Journal* (June 1990), p. 50.

merely a mechanical by-product of the translation process and thus represents a re-statement of previously reported equity."[4]

Consolidation

Working papers to consolidate the financial statements of Pat Corporation and Star Company Ltd. for the year ended December 31, 20X2 are illustrated in Exhibit 14–4. Although the account balances for Pat Corporation are introduced for the first time in the working papers, the amounts that appear are compatible with earlier assumptions. For example, the $107,300 income from Star ($121,800 equity in income less $14,500 goodwill amortization), the $551,600 investment in Star, and the $38,100 equity adjustment on translation appear in Pat's separate financial statements. The financial statements of Star that appear in the consolidation working papers of Exhibit 14–4 are based on those presented in Exhibit 14–3.

The procedures to consolidate a foreign subsidiary are basically the same as the procedures needed to consolidate a domestic subsidiary, and the sequence of working paper entries is the same. When the current rate method is used, however, the appearance of the equity adjustment from translation account does require special interpretation. For example, working paper entry a in Exhibit 14–4 is as follows:

a	Income from Star	$107,300	
	Dividends		$42,600
	Investment in Star		64,700

Although the objective of this working paper entry is the same as for similar entries encountered in earlier chapters, the $64,700 credit to the investment in Star account reduces the investment to $486,900, rather than to the $525,000 beginning-of-the-period balance. Actually, the $486,900 is the beginning-of-the-period balance less the $38,100 translation adjustments reflected in Pat's accumulated other comprehensive income: equity adjustment from translation account.

Working paper entry b is reproduced in journal form as follows:

b	Retained earnings—Star	$ 75,000	
	Goodwill	140,500	
	Capital stock—Star	300,000	
	Investment in Star		$486,900
	Other comprehensive income: equity adjustment—Star		28,600

The objective of this entry is to eliminate reciprocal equity in Star and investment in Star balances and enter unamortized goodwill as of the beginning of the accounting period. Because of unrealized translation losses under the current rate method, the objective is modified to include "less unrecognized translation losses." Thus, Star's $346,400 beginning-of-the-period equity less unrecognized translation losses ($75,000 retained earnings and $300,000 capital stock less $28,600) is eliminated against the $486,900 beginning-of-the-period investment balance. The $140,500 unamortized goodwill less unrecognized translation losses ($150,000 goodwill less $9,500 translation loss) is entered as the difference. Although less convenient, entry b may be divided into two working paper entries. The first entry eliminates reciprocal equity and investment balances at beginning-of-the-period amounts and enters beginning-of-the-period goodwill. A second entry adjusts the investment in Star account for unrealized translation losses, eliminates the unrealized translation loss for goodwill, and eliminates Star's remaining stockholders' equity account—the

[4]Ibid.

PAT CORPORATION AND SUBSIDIARY CONSOLIDATION WORKING PAPERS
TRANSLATION—FUNCTIONAL CURRENCY BRITISH POUND
FOR THE YEAR ENDED DECEMBER 31, 20X2

	Pat	Star	Adjustments and Eliminations	Consolidated Statements
Income Statement				
Sales	$1,218,300	$ 783,000		$2,001,300
Income from Star	107,300		a 107,300	
Cost of sales	(600,000)	(391,500)		(991,500)
Depreciation	(40,000)	(14,500)		(54,500)
Wages and salaries	(300,000)	(174,000)		(474,000)
Other expenses	(150,000)	(87,000)	c 14,500	(251,500)
Exchange gain		5,800		5,800
Net income	$ 235,600	$121,800		$ 235,600
Retained Earnings				
Retained earnings—Pat	$ 245,500			$ 245,500
Retained earnings—Star		$ 75,000	b 75,000	
Net income	235,600√	121,800√		235,600
Dividends	(100,000)	(42,600)	a 42,600	(100,000)
Retained earnings December 31, 20X2	$ 381,100	$154,200		$ 381,100
Balance Sheet				
Cash	$ 317,600	$ 154,000		$ 471,600
Accounts receivable	150,000	112,000		262,000
Inventories	300,000	168,000		468,000
Plant assets	400,000	140,000		540,000
Accumulated depreciation	(100,000)	(42,000)		(142,000)
Advance to Pat		84,000	d 84,000	
Investment in Star	551,600		a 64,700 b 486,900	
Goodwill			b 140,500 c 14,500	126,000
	$1,619,200	$616,000		$1,725,600
Accounts payable	$ 142,200	$ 50,400		$ 192,600
Advance from Star	84,000		d 84,000	
Bonds payable	250,000	140,000		390,000
Capital stock	800,000	300,000	b 300,000	800,000
Retained earnings	381,100√	154,200√		381,100
Accumulated other comprehensive income	(38,100)	(28,600)	b 28,600	(38,100)
	$1,619,200	$616,000		$1,725,600

Exhibit 14–4   *Working Papers Under the British Pound Functional Currency Assumption*

equity adjustment from translation account. These two entries would be journalized as follows:

Retained earnings—Star	$ 75,000	
Capital stock—Star	300,000	
Goodwill	150,000	
Investment in Star		$525,000
Investment in Star	$ 38,100	
Goodwill		$ 9,500
Other comprehensive income: equity adjustment		
from translation—Star		28,600

Working paper entry c enters current goodwill amortization as an expense (£10,000 × $1.45 average exchange rate) and reduces goodwill to its $126,000 unamortized amount at year-end (£90,000 × $1.40 exchange rate).

The final working paper entry eliminates the reciprocal advance to Pat and advance from Star balances. It should be noted that Pat's stockholders' equity balances, including its equity adjustment from translation, are equal to consolidated stockholders' equity balances because the equity method of accounting is used.

ILLUSTRATION—REMEASUREMENT UNDER STATEMENT NO. 52

When the functional currency of a foreign entity is the U.S. dollar, the foreign entity's accounts are *remeasured* into its U.S. dollar functional currency, and the net exchange gains or losses that result from the remeasurement are recognized in current income. To enable you to compare remeasurement and translation procedures, remeasurement procedures are applied to the Pat-Star example, assuming that Star's functional currency is the U.S. dollar and its books of record are maintained in British pounds. The objective of remeasurement is to produce the same results as if the books had been maintained in the U.S. dollar (see *FASB Statement No. 52*, paragraph 47).

Star's assets, liabilities, and stockholders' equity at acquisition on December 31, 20X1 are all remeasured using the $1.50 exchange rate in effect on that date. In other words, the remeasurement at acquisition is exactly the same as translation at acquisition. The $525,000 investment cost to Pat over the $375,000 net assets acquired in Star results in $150,000 goodwill. Under remeasurement procedures, however, goodwill is not adjusted for subsequent changes in exchange rates, and annual amortization over the 10-year period is $15,000 each year.

The £56,000($84,000) advance to Pat is not a foreign currency transaction of either Pat or Star because the advance is denominated in dollars and the functional currency of both Pat and Star is the U.S. dollar. As a result, Star does not adjust its advance to Pat to reflect the 60,000 British pound equivalent; instead, the £56,000 advance to Pat is remeasured at its $84,000 reciprocal amount on Pat's books. A remeasurement worksheet for Star Company Ltd. for 20X2 is illustrated in Exhibit 14–5. Except for the advance to Pat and the resulting $5,800 exchange gain under translation, Star's December 31, 20X2 trial balance in British pounds is the same as the one shown under the British pound functional currency assumption in Exhibit 14–2.

Star's monetary items other than the intercompany advance are remeasured at current exchange rates. These monetary items include cash, accounts receivable, accounts payable, and bonds payable, and the remeasurement produces the same amounts as translation under the current rate method. The advance to Pat and the dividends paid are translated at the reciprocal amounts in dollars that Pat recorded on its own books.

The cost of sales and inventory remeasurements shown in the worksheet assume first-in, first-out procedures and acquisition of the ending inventory items on Decem-

STAR COMPANY LTD.
REMEASUREMENT WORKSHEET FOR 20X2
(U.S. DOLLAR FUNCTIONAL CURRENCY)

	Trial Balance in British Pounds	Exchange Rate		Trial Balance in U.S. Dollars
Debits				
Cash	110,000	C	$1.40	154,000
Accounts receivable	80,000	C	1.40	112,000
Inventories (FIFO)	120,000	H	1.42	170,400
Plant assets	100,000	H	1.50	150,000
Advance to Pat	56,000**	R		84,000
Cost of sales	270,000	H		401,100
Depreciation	10,000	H	1.50	15,000
Wages and salaries	120,000	A*	1.45	174,000
Other expenses	60,000	A*	1.45	87,000
Dividends	30,000	R		42,600
Exchange loss				3,300
	956,000			1,393,400
Credits				
Accumulated depreciation	30,000	H	1.50	45,000
Accounts payable	36,000	C	1.40	50,400
Bonds payable	100,000	C	1.40	140,000
Capital stock	200,000	H	1.50	300,000
Retained earnings	50,000	Computed		75,000
Sales	540,000	A	1.45	783,000
	956,000			1,393,400

A Average exchange rate.

C Current exchange rate.

H Historical exchange rate.

R Reciprocal of U.S. dollar amounts.

*Assumed to be paid in cash during 20X2.

**A translation gain might need to be reported under British GAAP to the British Government. However, no gain or loss is reported under US GAAP, and the reciprocal rate is used.

Exhibit 14–5 *Remeasurement of Foreign Subsidiary Accounts into U.S. Dollars*

ber 1, 20X2, when the exchange rate was $1.42. Historical exchange rates are used in the computations as follows:

	Pounds	Exchange Rate	Dollars
Inventory December 31, 20X1	120,000	$1.50 H	$180,000
Purchases 20X2	270,000	1.45 A	391,500
	390,000		571,500
Inventory December 31, 20X2	120,000	1.42 H	170,400
Cost of sales	270,000		$401,100

Special procedures are required when inventories are priced under the lower-of-cost-or-market rule. These procedures are explained later in this chapter.

All of Star's plant assets were owned by Star when it became a subsidiary of Pat. Therefore, the plant assets, as well as the related depreciation expense and accumulated depreciation, are remeasured at the $1.50 exchange rate in effect at December 31, 20X1. If Star had acquired additional plant assets during 20X2, the additions and related depreciation would be remeasured at the exchange rates in effect when the additional assets were acquired.

Under *Statement No. 52*, expenses are remeasured at average rates during the period if they relate to monetary items (cash, receivables, and payables), and at historical exchange rates if they relate to nonmonetary items (such as plant assets, deferred charges, or intangibles). The wages and salaries and other expense items in Exhibit 14–5 are remeasured at average exchange rates, assuming they are related to monetary items. When a single expense account includes amounts related to both monetary and nonmonetary items, the remeasurement involves computations rather than application of a single average rate. The same reasoning applies to the remeasurement of sales, even though it would be rather unusual for sales to relate to nonmonetary items.

Capital stock and other paid-in capital items are remeasured at historical exchange rates, and there is no difference between the amounts that result from remeasurement and translation for these items. As explained earlier, the retained earnings balance is computed but not remeasured or translated. (Ending retained earnings is equal to beginning retained earnings plus remeasured income less remeasured dividends.)

After all items in the remeasurement worksheet, other than the exchange loss, are remeasured into the U.S. dollar functional currency, the trial balance debits and credits are totaled and the difference between debits and credits is determined. If the credits are greater, the difference is entered in the remeasurement working papers as the exchange loss for the period. Thus, the $3,300 exchange loss in Exhibit 14–5 is computed by subtracting $1,390,100 debits, excluding the exchange loss, from $1,393,400 total credits. Exchange gains and losses on remeasurement are recognized in income currently under the provisions of *Statement No. 52*. Exchange gains and losses on remeasurement and those arising from foreign currency transactions are combined for external reporting purposes. Separate disclosure of transaction and remeasurement gains and losses is provided in financial statement notes.

The Equity Method and Consolidation

All remeasurement gains and losses are recognized in current income, so the one-line consolidation entries under the U.S. dollar functional currency assumption are the same as those for a domestic subsidiary. The entries on Pat's books to account for its investment in Star are as follows:

Investment in Star	$525,000	
Cash		$525,000
To record acquisition on December 31, 20X1.		
Cash	$ 42,600	
Investment in Star		$ 42,600
To record dividends received on December 1, 20X2.		
Investment in Star	$ 87,600	
Income from Star		$ 87,600
To record investment income for 20X2 equal to Star's		
$102,600 net income less $15,000 goodwill amortization.		

The U.S. dollar amounts determined in the remeasurement worksheet of Exhibit 14–5 are used to prepare Star's financial statements in U.S. dollars. These financial statements are included in the consolidation working papers of Exhibit 14–6.

Pat's investment in Star account at December 31, 20X2 has a balance of $570,000 and is equal to Star's $435,000 net assets on that date plus $135,000 unamortized goodwill. These amounts are shown in the consolidation working papers of Exhibit 14–6.

Consolidation of a foreign subsidiary with a U.S. dollar functional currency is essentially the same as for a domestic subsidiary, once the foreign entity's financial statements have been remeasured in U.S. dollars. Although the remeasurement process is more complex than translation, the consolidation process is less complex because remeasurement does not produce unrealized translation gains and losses or equity adjustments from translation. The content of Exhibit 14–6 is not discussed in detail because the procedures applied are the same as those encountered in earlier chapters.

PAT CORPORATION AND SUBSIDIARY CONSOLIDATION WORKING PAPERS
REMEASUREMENT—FUNCTIONAL CURRENCY U.S. DOLLAR
FOR THE YEAR ENDED DECEMBER 31, 20X2

	Pat	Star	Adjustments and Eliminations		Consolidated Statements
Income Statement					
Sales	$1,218,300	$783,000			$2,001,300
Income from Star	87,600		a 87,600		
Cost of sales	(600,000)	(401,100)			(1,001,100)
Depreciation	(40,000)	(15,000)			(55,000)
Wages and salaries	(300,000)	(174,000)			(474,000)
Other expenses	(150,000)	(87,000)	c 15,000		(252,000)
Exchange loss		(3,300)			(3,300)
Net income	$ 215,900	$102,600			$ 215,900
Retained Earnings					
Retained earnings—Pat	$ 245,500				$ 245,500
Retained earnings—Star		$ 75,000	b 75,000		
Net income	215,900√	102,600√			215,900
Dividends	(100,000)	(42,600)		a 42,600	(100,000)
Retained earnings December 31, 20X2	$ 361,400	$135,000			$ 361,400
Balance Sheet					
Cash	$ 317,600	$154,000			$ 471,600
Accounts receivable	150,000	112,000			262,000
Inventories	300,000	170,400			470,400
Plant assets	400,000	150,000			550,000
Accumulated depreciation	(100,000)	(45,000)			(145,000)
Advance to Pat		84,000		d 84,000	
Investment in Star	570,000			a 45,000 b 525,000	
Goodwill			b 150,000 c 15,000		135,000
	$1,637,600	$625,400			$1,744,000
Accounts payable	$ 142,200	$ 50,400			$ 192,600
Advance from Star	84,000		d 84,000		
Bonds payable	250,000	140,000			390,000
Capital stock	800,000	300,000	b 300,000		800,000
Retained earnings	361,400√	135,000√			361,400
	$1,637,600	$625,400			$1,744,000

Exhibit 14–6 *Working Papers Under the U.S. Dollar Functional Currency Assumption*

Translation and Remeasurement Differences in Consolidated Statements

The differences between the consolidated financial statements of Pat Corporation and Subsidiary under the translation and remeasurement procedures are easily discernible when they are presented in comparative form. Such a format is provided in Exhibit 14–7, which shows more income under translation ($235,600 compared with $215,900) and greater net assets under remeasurement ($1,161,400 compared with $1,143,000). A substantial part of these differences lies in the $38,100 unrecognized translation losses that are excluded from net income when the statements are translated and subsequently deducted in other comprehensive income by means of the equity adjustment on translation account. In future years, however, unrecognized translation gains may result from the translation process and offset the unrecognized

---

PAT CORPORATION AND BRITISH SUBSIDIARY
CONSOLIDATED INCOME AND RETAINED EARNINGS STATEMENTS
FOR THE YEAR ENDED DECEMBER 31, 20X2

	Translation	Remeasurement
Sales	$2,001,300	$2,001,300
Less: Costs and expenses		
Cost of sales	991,500	1,001,100
Wages and salaries	474,000	474,000
Other expenses	237,000	237,000
Depreciation	54,500	55,000
Goodwill amortization	14,500	15,000
Total costs and expenses	1,771,500	1,782,100
Operating income	229,800	219,200
Exchange gain (loss)	5,800	(3,300)
Net income	235,600	215,900
Retained earnings January 1, 20X2	245,500	245,500
	481,100	461,400
Less: Dividends	100,000	100,000
Retained earnings December 31, 20X2	$ 381,100	$ 361,400

PAT CORPORATION AND BRITISH SUBSIDIARY
CONSOLIDATED BALANCE SHEETS AT DECEMBER 31, 20X2

	Translation	Remeasurement
Assets		
Cash	$ 471,600	$ 471,600
Accounts receivable	262,000	262,000
Inventories	468,000	470,400
Plant assets	540,000	550,000
Less: Accumulated depreciation	(142,000)	(145,000)
Goodwill	126,000	135,000
Total assets	$1,725,600	$1,744,000
Liabilities		
Accounts payable	$ 192,600	$ 192,600
Bonds payable	390,000	390,000
Total liabilities	582,600	582,600
Stockholder's Equity		
Capital stock	800,000	800,000
Retained earnings	381,100	361,400
Other comprehensive income: equity adjustment on translation	(38,100)	
Total stockholders' equity	1,143,000	1,161,400
Total liabilities and stockholders' equity	$1,725,600	$1,744,000

Exhibit 14–7 *Comparative Consolidated Financial Statements*

translation losses of 20X2, or even produce credit balances in the equity adjustment from translation account.

Disclosure for Changes in Translation Adjustments The Pat-Star illustration involves consolidation in the year of acquisition, so the impact of translation and remeasurement differences is relatively small. For many firms it can be substantial, however. Kimberly-Clark's translation adjustment—a loss—increased from $656.8 million in 1996 to $953.2 million in 1997. IBM's translation adjustment—also a loss—increased from $113 million to $888 million in the same time period.

Lower-of-Cost-or-Market Rule to Remeasure Inventories

Nonmonetary assets carried at cost are remeasured at historical rates and those carried at market are remeasured at current rates when the foreign entity's books of record are not maintained in the functional currency. Special care must be exercised in applying the lower-of-cost-or-market rule to inventories in remeasured statements because remeasured amounts are affected both by changes in exchange rates and by changes in replacement costs. Write-downs to market may be appropriate for both foreign currency statements and remeasured statements, for foreign currency statements but not remeasured statements, or for remeasured statements but not foreign currency statements. These three possibilities are illustrated as follows:

	Foreign Currency Units	Exchange Rate	U.S. Dollars
Case A: Inventory carried at market in both foreign currency statements and remeasured statements:			
Cost	1,000	$1.80 H	1,800
Replacement cost	950	1.85 C	1,758
Case B: Inventory carried at market in foreign currency statements, but cost in remeasured statements:			
Cost	1,000	$1.80 H	1,800
Replacement cost	950	1.92 C	1,824
Case C: Inventory carried at cost in foreign currency statements, but market in remeasured statements:			
Cost	950	$1.92 H	1,824
Replacement cost	1,000	1.80 C	1,800

As noted earlier, the H and C designations represent historical rates and current rates, respectively. In each of the three cases, it is assumed that replacement cost falls between the ceiling and the floor as required by *ARB No. 43*, Chapter 4. The write-downs to market in cases A and C are the result of applying the lower-of-cost-or-market rule in remeasurement statements and are reflected in cost of sales.

ILLUSTRATION—TRANSLATION WITH MINORITY INTEREST

The Pat and Star illustration provided an introduction to translation and consolidation procedures for foreign subsidiaries, but it omitted some important aspects of accounting for foreign subsidiaries. For example, intercompany profits, minority interests, long-term intercompany advances, and funds flow were not covered in that illustration. The following illustration provides an extended translation and consolidation example that includes minority interests, intercompany profits, and long-term intercompany advances. The statement of cash flows is illustrated in an appendix to this chapter.

Background Information

Pacific Corporation acquired a 90% interest in Sea Corporation, a French company, for $232,500 on January 1, 20X5. The exchange rate for French francs (Frs) on that date was $0.15, and Sea's stockholders' equity consisted of Fr 1,000,000 capital stock and Fr 500,000 retained earnings. Pacific designated Sea's functional currency to be the French franc.

Cost/Book Value Differential   The excess cost over book value from Pacific's investment in Sea Corporation is goodwill with a 10-year amortization period. Computations are as follows:

Investment in Sea	$232,500
Book value acquired	
(Fr 1,500,000 × $.15 exchange rate × 90%)	202,500
Goodwill in dollars	$ 30,000
Goodwill in francs ($30,000 ÷ $.15) = Fr 200,000	

Exchange Rates   Relevant exchange rates for 20X5 are as follows:

Current exchange rate January 1, 20X5	$.150
Average exchange rate for 20X5	.160
Exchange rate for dividends	.160
Current exchange rate December 31, 20X5	.170

Translation and Consolidation in the Year of Acquisition

A translation worksheet based on Sea Corporation's adjusted trial balance in francs at December 31, 20X5 is presented in Exhibit 14–8. The translation is based on the background information provided, and the procedures are comparable to those illustrated earlier in the chapter.

SEA CORPORATION TRANSLATION WORKSHEET
AT AND FOR THE YEAR ENDED DECEMBER 31, 20X5

	French Francs	Exchange Rate	U.S. Dollars
Cash	10,000	$.170	1,700
Accounts receivable	40,000	.170	6,800
Inventories	150,000	.170	25,500
Land	250,000	.170	42,500
Buildings	700,000	.170	119,000
Equipment	1,000,000	.170	170,000
Cost of sales	700,000	.160	112,000
Depreciation expense	200,000	.160	32,000
Operating expenses	150,000	.160	24,000
Dividends	100,000	.160	16,000
	3,300,000		549,500
Accumulated depreciation—buildings	100,000	.170	17,000
Accumulated depreciation—equipment	300,000	.170	51,000
Accounts payable	200,000	.170	34,000
Capital stock	1,000,000	.150	150,000
Retained earnings	500,000	.150	75,000
Sales	1,200,000	.160	192,000
Equity adjustment on translation			30,500
	3,300,000		549,500

Exhibit 14–8   Translation Worksheet—20X5

In interpreting Sea's U.S. dollar financial statements, one must consider the existence of the 10% minority interest. For example, compare Sea's stockholders' equity at the beginning and end of 20X5:

	January 1	December 31
Capital stock	$150,000	$150,000
Retained earnings	75,000	83,000
Equity adjustment	—	30,500
Stockholders' equity	$225,000	$263,500

The $8,000 increase in Sea's retained earnings comes from Sea's $24,000 net income less $16,000 dividends for 20X5. Sea's stockholders' equity increased by the $30,500 equity adjustment, for a total stockholders' equity increase of $38,500. Sea's stockholders' equity at December 31, 20X5 can be allocated between majority and minority interests as follows:

	90% to Pacific	10% to Minority Interests	Total
Stockholders' equity January 1	$202,500	$22,500	$225,000
Net income	21,600	2,400	24,000
Dividends	(14,400)	(1,600)	(16,000)
Equity adjustment	27,450	3,050	30,500
Stockholders' equity December 31	$237,150	$26,350	$263,500

Pacific's underlying equity in Sea Corporation is $237,150 at December 31, 20X5, and its investment in Sea equals underlying equity plus $30,600 unamortized goodwill (Fr 200,000 × 90% unamortized × $0.170 exchange rate).

One-Line Consolidation in Year of Acquisition   Pacific Corporation makes the following one-line consolidation entries in accounting for its investment in Sea for 20X5:

Cash	$14,400	
Investment in Sea		$14,400
To record dividends ($16,000 × 90%).		

Investment in Sea	$49,650	
Other comprehensive income: translation adjustment		$31,250
Income from Sea		18,400

To record income from Sea ($24,000 × 90% − $3,200 goodwill amortization) and equity adjustment computed as follows:

Equity adjustment from translation ($30,500 × 90%)	$27,450
Add: Equity adjustment from goodwill [$30,000 beginning balance − $3,200 amortization − (Fr 180,000 ending balance × $.17 current rate)]	3,800
Other comprehensive income: equity adjustment	$31,250

The investment in Sea account at December 31, 20X5 has a balance of $267,750. This balance consists of the $232,500 cost on January 1 plus $49,650 equity adjustment plus income for 20X5, less $14,400 dividends received. Alternatively, the balance of the investment account can be checked by adding $30,600 unamortized goodwill at December 31, 20X5 (Fr 180,000 goodwill × $.17 current exchange rate) to 90% of Sea's $263,500 stockholders' equity on that date. Remember that the equity adjustment from translation account in the subsidiary's U.S. dollar financial statements is a stockholders' equity account. This account may have a positive (credit) balance or negative (debit) balance, depending upon the direction of exchange rate movements.

Consolidation in Year of Acquisition   Working papers to consolidate the financial statements of Pacific Corporation and its French subsidiary at and for the year ended December 31, 20X5, are presented in Exhibit 14–9.

PACIFIC CORPORATION AND SUBSIDIARY
CONSOLIDATION WORKSHEET FOR THE YEAR ENDED DECEMBER 31, 20X5

	Pacific	Sea 90%	Adjustments and Eliminations		Minority Interest	Consolidated Statements
Income Statement Sales	$ 600,000	$ 192,000				$ 792,000
Income from Sea	18,400		a 18,400			
Cost of sales	(300,000)	(112,000)				(412,000)
Depreciation	(120,000)	(32,000)				(152,000)
Operating expense	(68,400)	(24,000)	c 3,200			(95,600)
Minority income					$ 2,400	(2,400)
Net income	$ 130,000	$ 24,000				$ 130,000
Retained Earnings Retained earnings	$ 120,000	$ 75,000	b 75,000			$ 120,000
Net income	130,000√	24,000√				130,000
Dividends	(50,000)	(16,000)		a 14,400	(1,600)	(50,000)
Retained earnings December 31, 20X5	$ 200,000	$ 83,000				$ 200,000
Balance Sheet Cash	$ 12,250	$ 1,700				$ 13,950
Accounts receivable	40,000	6,800				46,800
Inventories	80,000	25,500				105,500
Land	50,000	42,500				92,500
Buildings—net	150,000	102,000				252,000
Equipment—net	400,000	119,000				519,000
Investment in Sea	267,750			a 4,000 b 263,750		
Goodwill			b 33,800	c 3,200		30,600
	$1,000,000	$297,500				$1,060,350
Accounts payable	$ 68,750	$ 34,000				$ 102,750
Capital stock	700,000	150,000	b 150,000			700,000
Retained earnings	200,000√	83,000√				200,000
Accumulated other comprehensive income: equity adjustment*	31,250	30,500	b 30,500			31,250
	$1,000,000	$297,500				
Minority interest January 1, 20X5[†]				b 25,550	25,550	
Minority interest December 31, 20X5					$26,350	26,350
						$1,060,350

*Pacific's equity adjustment (90% × $30,500 equity adjustment) + $3,800 goodwill adjustment.
[†]Minority interest 10% × $255,500.

Exhibit 14–9   *Consolidation Working Papers—20X5*

In examining the consolidation worksheet, observe that the consolidated equity adjustment from translation is equal to Pacific Corporation's equity adjustment. That equity adjustment consists of 90% of Sea's $30,500 equity adjustment plus the $3,800 equity adjustment from goodwill. Under a one-line consolidation, the parent company equity adjustment balance is equal to the consolidated equity adjustment balance.

Entry a eliminates income and dividends from Sea and returns the investment account to its beginning balance plus the $31,250 equity adjustment.

a	Income from Sea	$ 18,400	
	Dividends		$ 14,400
	Investment in Sea		4,000

Although working paper entry a is relatively unaffected by the existence of the minority interest, entry b is subject to some complications that require explanation. Entry b is reproduced in general journal form for convenient reference.

b	Capital stock—Sea	$150,000	
	Retained earnings—Sea (beginning)	75,000	
	Equity adjustment—Sea	30,500	
	Goodwill	33,800	
	Investment in Sea		$263,750
	Minority interest (beginning)		25,550

The $33,800 goodwill amount in entry b is equal to beginning-of-the-period goodwill of $30,000 plus the $3,800 equity adjustment from goodwill for 20X5. The $263,750 investment in Sea amount in entry b is equal to the $232,500 beginning-of-the-period amount (cost) plus Pacific's $31,250 equity adjustment from translation. Finally, the $25,550 beginning minority interest amount is equal to Sea Corporation's $225,000 stockholders' equity at the beginning of the period plus Sea's $30,500 equity adjustment from translation times 10%.

To generalize, in the working paper entry to eliminate reciprocal investment and stockholders' equity balances and enter beginning-of-the-period unamortized cost/book value differentials and minority interest, the amounts entered are the usual beginning-of-the-period amounts adjusted for end-of-the-period equity adjustments from translation. Translation adjustments under the current rate method do not enter into the computations of minority interest income and consolidated net income, so the complications are limited to balance sheet items.

Entry c provides for the current year's goodwill amortization at the average exchange rate [(Fr 200,000 × $.160) ÷ 10 years]:

c	Operating expenses	$ 3,200	
	Goodwill		$ 3,200

Translation and Consolidation in Year After Acquisition

Pacific Corporation held its 90% interest in Sea Corporation throughout 20X6, and the only stockholders' equity changes of the two affiliated entities resulted from income, dividends, and equity adjustments from translation. A translation worksheet based on Sea's adjusted trial balance in francs at December 31, 20X6 is presented in Exhibit 14–10. Other information related to the year 20X6 is summarized in the paragraphs that follow.

TRANSLATION WORKSHEETS FOR SEA CORPORATION

	December 31, 20X5			December 31, 20X6		
	French Francs	Exchange Rate	U.S. Dollars	French Francs	Exchange Rate	U.S. Dollars
Cash	10,000	$.170	1,700	15,000	$.190	2,850
Accounts receivable	40,000	.170	6,800	25,000	.190	4,750
Inventories	150,000	.170	25,500	80,000	.190	15,200
Inventories				120,000	.175	21,000
Advance to Pacific				300,000	.190	57,000
Land	250,000	.170	42,500	250,000	.190	47,500
Buildings	700,000	.170	119,000	700,000	.190	133,000
Equipment	1,000,000	.170	170,000	1,000,000	.190	190,000
Equipment (new)				200,000	.190	38,000
Cost of sales	700,000	.160	112,000	480,000	.180	86,400
Cost of sales				360,000	.175	63,000
Depreciation expense	200,000	.160	32,000	200,000	.180	36,000
Operating expenses	150,000	.160	24,000	170,000	.180	30,600
Dividends	100,000	.160	16,000	100,000	.180	18,000
	3,300,000		549,500	4,000,000		743,300
Accumulated depreciation—buildings	100,000	.170	17,000	150,000	.190	28,500
Accumulated depreciation—equipment	300,000	.170	51,000	450,000	.190	85,500
Accounts payable	200,000	.170	34,000	250,000	.190	47,500
Notes payable				200,000	.190	38,000
Capital stock	1,000,000	.150	150,000	1,000,000	.150	150,000
Retained earnings	500,000	.150	75,000	550,000		83,000
Sales	1,200,000	.160	192,000	1,385,000	.180	249,300
Interest income				15,000	.180	2,700
Equity adjustment			30,500			58,800
	3,300,000		549,500	4,000,000		743,300

Exhibit 14–10 *Translation Worksheets—20X6*

Exchange Rates   Relevant exchange rates for 20X6 (and those from 20X5 for convenient reference) are as follows:

	20X5	20X6
Current exchange rate January 1	$.150	$.170
Exchange rate for intercompany sales	—	.175
Average exchange rate	.160	.180
Exchange rate for advance	—	.180
Exchange rate for dividends	.160	.180
Current exchange rate December 31	.170	.190

Advance from Subsidiary   Sea Corporation made a Fr 300,000 advance to Pacific on July 1, 20X6. This advance is long-term, denominated in francs, and bears interest at 10% per year. Pacific Corporation recorded the advance at $54,000 on July 1 but adjusted the advance to $57,000 to reflect current exchange rates at December 31, 20X6. The related debit of $3,000 was to Pacific's comprehensive income: equity adjustment account, as required by *FASB Statement No. 52* for translation adjustments from long-term intercompany balances and *Statement No. 130* dealing with comprehensive income.

Plant Asset Acquisitions   Neither Pacific Corporation nor Sea Corporation had plant disposals during 20X5 or 20X6, but both companies had acquisitions during 20X6. Pacific purchased buildings for $80,000 and equipment for $150,000. Sea purchased equipment for Fr 200,000 at December 31, 20X6, issuing a note payable for the purchase price, which is denominated in francs. A summary of plant asset changes for Pacific Corporation and Sea Corporation for 20X6 is as follows:

20X6	Land		Buildings—Net		Equipment—Net	
	Pacific	Sea	Pacific	Sea	Pacific	Sea
Balance January 1	$50,000	$42,500	$150,000	$102,000	$400,000	$119,000
Acquisitions	0	0	80,000	0	150,000	38,000
Depreciation	0	0	(50,000)	(9,000)	(100,000)	(27,000)
Exchange adjustment	0	5,000	0	11,500	0	12,500
Balance December 31	$50,000	$47,500	$180,000	$104,500	$450,000	$142,500

Intercompany Sales   Pacific Corporation sold inventory items that cost $70,000 to Sea Corporation for $84,000, denominated in dollars, during 20X6, when the exchange rate for francs was $.175. Sea measured its purchases and accounts payable at Fr 480,000 ($84,000 ÷ $.175), sold Fr 360,000 of the merchandise during 20X6, and included Fr 120,000 in its inventory at December 31, 20X6.

Translation   The translation worksheet presented in Exhibit 14–10 repeats the 20X5 translation data and shows the translation for 20X6. The difference between the $58,800 translation adjustment at year-end 20X6 and the $30,500 translation adjustment at year-end 20X5 is $28,300, the increase in the equity adjustment from translation for 20X6. This increase is allocated 90% to Pacific and 10% to minority interest.

One-Line Consolidation in Year After Acquisition   Pacific Corporation makes the following one-line consolidation entries in accounting for its investment in Sea for 20X6:

Cash	$16,200	
Investment in Sea		$16,200
To record dividends received ($18,000 × 90%).		

Investment in Sea	$54,170	
Comprehensive income: equity adjustment from		
translation		$28,870
Income from Sea		25,300

To record income from Sea ($36,000 × 90% − $3,600 goodwill amortization − $3,500 unrealized inventory profit) and equity adjustment ($28,300 × 90% + $3,400 from goodwill).

In addition, Pacific makes the following entry to adjust its advance from Sea account at year-end:

Comprehensive income: equity adjustment	$ 3,000	
Advance from Sea		$ 3,000

To adjust the advance from $54,000 to $57,000 to recognize a $0.01 exchange rate change on the 300,000 franc liability to Sea.

The balance of Pacific Corporation's investment in Sea account at December 31, 20X6 is $305,720, equal to 90% of Sea Corporation's $309,800 stockholders' equity on that date, plus $30,400 unamortized goodwill, less $3,500 unrealized inventory profit. Alternatively, the $305,720 investment in Sea account balance is equal to its $267,750 beginning balance, less $16,200 dividends received, plus $25,300 income from Sea, plus $28,870 equity adjustment from translation.

Consolidation in Year After Acquisition

Consolidation working papers for Pacific Corporation and Subsidiary are presented in Exhibit 14–11. These working papers are complicated by the existence of intercompany transactions and reciprocal items, but no new consolidation procedures are introduced.

PACIFIC CORPORATION AND SUBSIDIARY
CONSOLIDATION WORKSHEET FOR THE YEAR ENDED DECEMBER 31, 20X6

	Pacific	Sea 90%	Adjustments and Eliminations		Minority Interest	Consolidated Statements
Income Statement						
Sales	$ 700,000	$249,300	a 84,000			$ 865,300
Income from Sea	25,300		c 25,300			
Interest income		2,700	f 2,700			
Cost of sales	(400,000)	(149,400)	b 3,500	a 84,000		(468,900)
Depreciation	(150,000)	(36,000)				(186,000)
Operating expense	(72,600)	(30,600)	e 3,600			(106,800)
Interest expense	(2,700)			f 2,700		
Minority income					$ 3,600	(3,600)
Net income	$ 100,000	$ 36,000				$ 100,000
Retained Earnings						
Retained earnings	$ 200,000	$ 83,000	d 83,000			$ 200,000
Net income	100,000√	36,000√				100,000
Dividends	(50,000)	(18,000)		c 16,200	(1,800)	(50,000)
Retained earnings December 31, 20X6	$ 250,000	$101,000				$ 250,000
Balance Sheet						
Cash	$ 4,280	$ 2,850				$ 7,130
Accounts receivable	30,000	4,750		h 9,500		25,250
Inventories	100,000	36,200		b 3,500		132,700
Advance to Pacific		57,000		g 57,000		
Land	50,000	47,500				97,500
Buildings—net	180,000	104,500				284,500
Equipment—net	450,000	142,500				592,500
Investment in Sea	305,720			c 9,100 d 296,620		
Goodwill			d 34,000	e 3,600		30,400
	$1,120,000	$395,300				$1,169,980
Accounts payable	$ 55,880	$ 47,500	h 9,500			$ 93,880
Advance from Sea	57,000		g 57,000			
Note payable		38,000				38,000
Capital stock	700,000	150,000	d 150,000			700,000
Retained earnings	250,000√	101,000√				250,000
Accumulated other comprehensive income*	57,120	58,800	d 58,800			57,120
	$1,120,000	$395,300				
Minority interest January 1, 20X6†				d 29,180	29,180	
Minority interest December 31, 20X6					$30,980	30,980
						$1,169,980

*Pacific's equity adjustment (90% × $58,800 equity adjustment) + $7,200 goodwill adjustment − $3,000 advance adjustment.
†Minority interest 10% × $291,800.

Exhibit 14–11 *Consolidation Working Papers—20X6*

Working paper entries a and b of Exhibit 14–11 eliminate intercompany profits from Pacific Corporation's sales to Sea Corporation.

a	Sales	$84,000	
	Cost of sales		$84,000
b	Cost of sales	$ 3,500	
	Inventories		$ 3,500

Entry a eliminates the $84,000 transfer price from sales and cost of sales, and entry b defers recognition of the $3,500 unrealized profit in Sea's ending inventory. The intercompany sales in dollars are analyzed as follows:

	Transfer Price		Cost 5/6	Intercompany Profit 1/6
	In Francs	In Dollars		
Sold by Sea 75%	360,000	$63,000	$52,500	$10,500
Inventoried by Sea 25%	120,000	21,000	17,500	3,500
Total	480,000	$84,000	$70,000	$14,000

The translation worksheet in Exhibit 14–10 shows translation of the Fr 120,000 inventory and Fr 360,000 cost of sales at the $0.175 historical exchange rate at the time of transfer. These items are separated from other inventory and cost of sales items, which are translated at current and average exchange rates, respectively. Paragraph 25 of *FASB Statement No. 52* provides that:

> the elimination of intercompany profits that are attributable to sales or other transfers between entities that are consolidated, combined, or accounted for by the equity method in the enterprise's financial statements shall be based on the exchange rates at the dates of the sales or transfers. The use of reasonable approximations or averages is permitted.

When the inventory and cost of sales accounts are translated at historical exchange rates, the inventory profit elimination for a foreign subsidiary is the same as for a domestic subsidiary and no complications arise in the working papers.

Entry c eliminates income and dividends and returns the investment account to its beginning-of-the-period balance of $267,750 plus the $28,870 equity adjustment for 20X6.

c	Income from Sea	$ 25,300	
	Dividends		$ 16,200
	Investment in Sea		9,100

Working paper entry d from Exhibit 14–11 is relatively complex and is reproduced in general journal form for convenient reference and analysis as follows:

d	Capital stock—Sea	$150,000	
	Retained earnings—Sea (beginning)	83,000	
	Equity adjustment—Sea	58,800	
	Goodwill	34,000	
	Investment in Sea		$296,620
	Minority interest (beginning)		29,180

The $34,000 debit to goodwill is equal to the $30,600 beginning-of-the-period unamortized goodwill plus $3,400 equity adjustment to goodwill for the period. For convenience, the $34,000 goodwill amount may be calculated as goodwill amortization for the period (Fr 20,000 × $.18) plus unamortized goodwill at year-end (Fr 160,000 × $.19).

The $29,180 minority interest at January 1, 20X6 is 10% of Sea Corporation's capital stock and retained earnings at January 1, 20X6, plus $58,800 equity adjustment at December 31, 20X6—in other words, 10% × ($150,000 + $83,000 + $58,800). The change in Sea's equity adjustment for the period is reflected in the beginning minority interest amount because neither minority interest income nor dividends reflect translation adjustments. The $30,980 minority interest at December 31, 20X6 can be confirmed by comparing it with 10% of Sea's $309,800 stockholders' equity at year-end 20X6.

Entry e enters the current year's amortization (Fr 200,000 × $.18 average exchange rate), and entry f eliminates interest on the intercompany advance.

e	Operating expenses	$3,600	
	Goodwill		$3,600
f	Interest income	$2,700	
	Interest expense		$2,700

Working paper entry g debits advance from Sea for $57,000 and credits advance to Pacific for $57,000. The elimination of these reciprocal items requires no change in working paper procedures even though both amounts reflect a $3,000 increase because the Fr 300,000 ($54,000) advance was made on July 1, 20X6. The $3,000 increase in Sea's advance to Pacific is reflected in the $58,800 equity adjustment in Sea Corporation's U.S. dollar financial statements, and the $3,000 increase in Pacific's advance from Sea is recorded by Pacific as a direct debit to its equity adjustment account.

Pacific Corporation's $57,120 equity adjustment from translation at December 31, 20X6 is equal to the consolidated equity adjustment from translation on that date. The amount is calculated as follows:

Sea's $58,800 equity adjustment at	
December 31, 20X6 × 90%	$52,920
Equity adjustment from goodwill—20X5	3,800
Equity adjustment from goodwill—20X6	3,400
Equity adjustment from advance—20X6	(3,000)
Pacific's equity adjustment December 31, 20X6	$57,120

Comparative consolidated financial statements for Pacific Corporation and Subsidiary for 20X6 and 20X5 are presented in Exhibit 14–12. This information provides a convenient summary and comparison of the consolidated financial statement amounts.

ACCOUNTING FOR A FOREIGN BRANCH

This section of the chapter illustrates the remeasurement and translation of foreign branch operations into U.S. dollars.[5] The conversion of the accounts of a foreign branch into the currency of the home office is similar to the conversion process for foreign subsidiaries. If the functional currency of the branch is the currency of the home office, the accounts are remeasured into the home office's reporting currency, and gains or losses on remeasurement are recognized currently in income. If the local currency of the branch is its functional currency, the branch accounts are translated into the reporting currency of the home office, using the current rate method, and gains and losses on translation are deferred through an equity adjustment from translation account. In accounting for the foreign branches, the accounts that are unique to home office-branch accounting (reciprocal accounts) are converted into the currency of the reporting entity by reference to the reciprocal amounts that are recorded on the home office books.

---

[5]The use of foreign branches, rather than subsidiaries, may be on the rise, particularly by multinational companies with operations in Europe. A company may be able to save taxes and administrative and operating costs by creating a single European company with branches in separate countries. [Price Waterhouse, *International Tax Review* (November/December 1993).]

PACIFIC CORPORATION AND SUBSIDIARY
COMPARATIVE CONSOLIDATED FINANCIAL STATEMENTS
FOR THE YEARS ENDED DECEMBER 31, 20X6 AND 20X5

	20X6	20X5
Income Statement		
Sales	$ 865,300	$ 792,000
Cost of sales	(468,900)	(412,000)
Depreciation expense	(186,000)	(152,000)
Operating expense	(106,800)	(95,600)
Minority income	(3,600)	(2,400)
Net income	100,000	130,000
Other comprehensive income:		
Foreign currency translation adjustment	25,870	31,250
Comprehensive income	$ 125,870	$ 161,250
Retained Earnings		
Retained earnings January 1	$ 200,000	$ 120,000
Net income	100,000	130,000
Dividends	(50,000)	(50,000)
Retained earnings December 31	$ 250,000	$ 200,000
Balance Sheet		
Cash	$ 7,130	$ 13,950
Accounts receivable	34,750	46,800
Inventories	132,700	105,500
Land	97,500	92,500
Buildings—net	284,500	252,000
Equipment—net	592,500	519,000
Goodwill	30,400	30,600
Total assets	$1,179,480	$1,060,350
Accounts payable	$ 103,380	$ 102,750
Note payable	38,000	0
Capital stock	700,000	700,000
Retained earnings	250,000	200,000
Accumulated other comprehensive income: (Equity adjustment)	57,120	31,250
Minority interest	30,980	26,350
Total equities	$1,179,480	$1,060,350

Exhibit 14–12 *Comparative Financial Statements*

Illustration of Accounting for a Foreign Branch

Sun-Bud Corporation is a U.S. corporation with its home office in Detroit, Michigan. In addition to the Detroit operation, Sun-Bud has a branch in Toronto, Canada. All branch sales relate to merchandise acquired at cost from the home office. The current exchange rate was $.90 in December 20X1 when the Canadian branch was established, and $.92 in January 20X2, when the plant assets of the Canadian branch were acquired. During 20X2, the Canadian dollar weakened against the U.S. dollar. Relevant exchange rates for 20X2 were:

Current exchange rate December 31, 20X2	$.80
Average exchange rate for 20X2	$.85

Working papers to illustrate the translation of the Canadian branch accounts into U.S. dollars as of December 31, 20X2 are shown in Exhibit 14–13 under alternative U.S. dollar and Canadian dollar functional currency assumptions. The working papers also include the accounts of Sun-Bud's home office for reference purposes.

The beginning branch inventory of 40,000 Canadian dollars was acquired when the exchange rate was $.90, and the year-end inventories were $100,000 for the home

SUN-BUD CORPORATION
TRIAL BALANCE WORKING PAPERS
FOR THE YEAR ENDED DECEMBER 31, 20X2

	Home Office U.S. Dollars	Branch Canadian Dollars	Functional Currency U.S. Dollar		Functional Currency Canadian Dollar	
			Exchange Rate	U.S. Dollars	Exchange Rate	U.S. Dollars
Debits						
Cash	$ 480,000	30,000	$.80 C	$ 24,000	$.80 C	$ 24,000
Accounts receivable	91,000	25,000	.80 C	20,000	.80 C	20,000
Inventory—ending	100,000	42,500	.82 H	34,850	.80 C	34,000
Land	100,000	22,000	.92 H	20,240	.80 C	17,600
Equipment	500,000	375,000	.92 H	345,000	.80 C	300,000
Canadian branch	394,600					
Cost of goods sold	255,000	333,000	Computed	286,150	.85 A	283,050
Depreciation expense	80,000	27,500	.92 H	25,300	.85 A	23,375
Bad debts expense	4,550	1,300	.85 A	1,105	.85 A	1,105
Other operating expenses	340,000	17,400	.85 A	14,790	.85 A	14,790
Exchange loss				19,965		
Other comprehensive income: equity adjustment from translation						66,880
	$2,345,150	873,700		$791,400		$784,800
Credits						
Allowance for bad debts	$ 5,550	1,500	$.80 C	$ 1,200	$.80 C	$ 1,200
Accumulated depreciation	230,000	55,000	.92 H	50,600	.80 C	44,000
Accounts payable	65,000	2,000	.80 C	1,600	.80 C	1,600
Home office		411,200	R	394,600	R	394,600
Capital stock	700,000					
Retained earnings	344,600					
Sales	1,000,000	404,000	.85 A	343,400	.85 A	343,400
	$2,345,150	873,700		$791,400		$784,800

A   Average exchange rate.
C   Current exchange rate.
H   Historical exchange rate.
R   Reciprocal.

Exhibit 14–13   *Working Papers to Convert Branch Accounts into U.S. Dollars*

office and 42,500 Canadian dollars for the branch. The ending branch inventory was acquired when an $.82 exchange rate was in effect. Branch shipments in 20X2 were 335,500 Canadian dollars, or U.S. $285,000.

The information from Exhibit 14–13 is used to prepare combined financial statements for Sun-Bud and its Canadian branch. These combined statements are presented in Exhibit 14–14. The cost of goods sold computations are not apparent from an inspection of the working papers, so the following additional explanation is provided.

	Home Office U.S. Dollars	Branch Canadian Dollars		Branch Remeasured in U.S. Dollars
Inventory January 1	$170,000	40,000	× $.90 H	$ 36,000
Purchases	470,000			
Shipments (to branch) from home office	(285,000)	335,500	R	285,000
Goods available	355,000	375,500		321,000
Inventory December 31	100,000	42,500	× $.82 H	34,850
Cost of goods sold	$255,000	333,000		$286,150

SUN-BUD CORPORATION
COMPARATIVE INCOME AND RETAINED EARNINGS STATEMENTS
FOR THE YEAR ENDED DECEMBER 31, 20X2

	Remeasurement	Translation
Sales	$1,343,400	$1,343,400
Cost of goods sold	541,150	538,050
Gross profit	802,250	805,350
Depreciation expense	105,300	103,375
Bad debt expense	5,655	5,655
Other operating expenses	354,790	354,790
Exchange loss	19,965	
Total expenses	485,710	463,820
Net income	316,540	341,530
Retained earnings January 1, 20X2	344,600	344,600
Retained earnings December 31, 20X2	$ 661,140	$ 686,130

SUN-BUD CORPORATION
COMPARATIVE BALANCE SHEETS
AT DECEMBER 31, 20X2

	Remeasurement	Translation
Assets		
Cash	$ 504,000	$ 504,000
Accounts receivable—net	104,250	104,250
Inventories	134,850	134,000
Land	120,240	117,600
Equipment—net	564,400	526,000
Total assets	$1,427,740	$1,385,850
Equities		
Accounts payable	$ 66,600	$ 66,600
Capital stock	700,000	700,000
Retained earnings	661,140	686,130
Other comprehensive income:		
equity adjustment from translation		(66,880)
Total equities	$1,427,740	$1,385,850

Exhibit 14–14 *Comparative Financial Statements*

Under the U.S. dollar functional currency assumption, the combined cost of goods sold is $541,150 ($255,000 + $286,150), and under the Canadian dollar functional currency assumption, it is $538,050 [$255,000 + (333,000 Canadian dollars × $.85 average exchange rate)]. The elimination of reciprocal home office and shipment accounts has no effect on the combined financial statements.

SUMMARY

Before the results of foreign operations can be included in the financial statements of U.S. corporations, they have to be converted into U.S. dollars using procedures specified in *FASB Statement No. 52* that are based on the foreign entity's functional currency. If the U.S. dollar is determined to be the functional currency, the foreign entity's financial statements are remeasured into U.S. dollar financial statements using the temporal method, and the resulting exchange gain or loss is included in consolidated net income for the period. If the functional currency is determined to be the local currency of the foreign entity, the financial statements of that entity must be translated into U.S. dollars using the current rate method. The effects of the exchange rate changes from translation are accumulated in an equity adjustment from translation account and reported in other comprehensive income.

Foreign currency financial statements of subsidiaries operating in highly inflationary economies are remeasured as if the functional currency were the U.S. dollar.

Intercompany transactions between affiliated companies will result in a foreign currency transaction for either the parent or the subsidiary if the subsidiary's local currency is its functional currency. Alternatively, if the subsidiary's functional currency is the U.S. dollar, the intercompany transaction will be a foreign currency transaction to both affiliates or to neither affiliate.

On the date of a business combination, assets and liabilities are translated into U.S. dollars using current exchange rates.

APPENDIX: STATEMENT OF CASH FLOWS

The consolidated statement of cash flows (SCF) for a U.S. parent company and a foreign subsidiary is complicated by the existence of translation adjustments. Individual translation adjustments for the assets and liabilities have to be determined so that their effects can be eliminated in determining the cash flows for a period.

Illustration of a Consolidated Statement of Cash Flows for a Foreign Subsidiary and a U.S. Parent Company

Pac Corporation is a U.S. Company that purchased all the outstanding shares of Soy Corporation for $40,500 on January 1, 20X6. Soy is a foreign corporation and its functional currency is its local currency, the LCU. The stockholders' equity of Soy on January 1, 20X6 consisted of 2,000,000 LCUs capital stock and 200,000 LCUs retained earnings. The exchange rate for LCUs on January 1, 20X6 was $.018.

Cost/Book Value Differential The excess cost over the book value of Pac's investment in Soy is goodwill with a five-year amortization period. Goodwill from Pac's investment in Soy is computed as follows:

Investment in Soy	$40,500
Book value and fair value acquired (LCU 2,200,000 stockholders' equity × $.018 exchange rate)	39,600
Goodwill in U.S. dollars	$ 900
Goodwill in LCUs $900 ÷ $.018	50,000 LCU

Exchange Rates for 20X6 and 20X7 Exchange rates for the two years are as follows:

	20X6	20X7
Current exchange rate January 1	$.018	$.020
Average exchange rate for year	.019	.021
Exchange rate for dividends	.020	.022
Current exchange rate December 31	.020	.022

Goodwill Computations for 20X6 Goodwill amortization is computed as the goodwill in LCUs divided by the amortization period times the average exchange rate for the period:

$$50,000 \text{ LCU} \div 5 \text{ years} \times \$.019 \text{ average exchange rate} = \underline{\$190}$$

Unamortized goodwill under the current rate method is computed as the end-of-the-period balance of goodwill in LCUs times the December 31, 20X6 exchange rate:

$$(50,000 \text{ LCU} - 10,000 \text{ LCU amortization}) \times \$.020 = \underline{\$800}$$

The equity adjustment from translation of goodwill for 20X6 is computed as follows:

Beginning goodwill balance	$900
Less: Goodwill amortization for 20X6	(190)
Less: Ending unamortized goodwill	(800)
Equity adjustment from goodwill	$(90)

Goodwill Computations for 20X7   Goodwill amortization is computed as follows:

$$50,000 \text{ LCU} \div 5 \text{ years} \times \$.021 \text{ average exchange rate} = \underline{\underline{\$210}}$$

Unamortized goodwill at December 31, 20X7 is:

$$30,000 \text{ LCU} \times \$.022 \text{ current rate} = \underline{\underline{\$660}}$$

The equity adjustment for the translation of goodwill for 20X7 is computed as follows:

Beginning goodwill balance	$800
Less: Goodwill amortization for 20X7	(210)
Less: Unamortized goodwill at December 31, 20X7	(660)
Equity adjustment from goodwill	$(70)

Translation Worksheets   Translation worksheets of Soy Corporation for 20X6 and 20X7 are presented in Exhibit 14–15.

Investment in Soy Account Balance   Soy reports income of $5,700 in 20X6 [$17,100 sales − $5,700 cost of sales − $1,900 depreciation expense − $3,800 operating expenses] and income of $6,300 in 20X7 [$21,000 sales − $7,350 cost of sales − $2,100 depreciation expense − $5,250 operating expenses]. The investment in Soy account for 20X6 and 20X7 is analyzed as follows:

Investment cost January 1, 20X6		$40,500
Add: Income from Soy for 20X6:		
Equity in reported income	$5,700	
Less: Goodwill amortization	190	5,510
Less: 20X6 dividends		(4,000)
		42,010
Equity adjustment from translation		
and from goodwill ($4,700 + $90)		4,790
Investment in Soy balance December 31, 20X6		46,800
Add: Income from Soy for 20X7:		
Equity in reported income	$6,300	
Less: Goodwill amortization	210	6,090
Less: 20X7 dividends		(4,400)
		48,490
Equity adjustment from translation		
and from goodwill ($4,900 + $70)		4,970
Investment in Soy balance December 31, 20X7		$53,460

Consolidation Working Papers   Consolidation working papers for Pac Company and Subsidiary for 20X6 and 20X7 are presented in Exhibits 14–16 and 14–17, respectively. Pac's separate financial statements are introduced in the first column of the working papers, and Soy's financial statements are prepared from the worksheets in Exhibit 14–15.

Exhibit 14–18 is developed from the consolidated financial statements column of the working papers. It shows the year's changes from 20X6 to 20X7. This information is used in preparing the consolidated statement of cash flows.

As a first step in preparing the SCF, a reconciliation of the individual asset and liability translation adjustments for the year is needed, along with the change in the parent company (and consolidated) translation adjustment.

Translation Adjustments   Individual translation adjustments for cash and other balance sheet items are not needed in preparing the consolidation working papers, but they are needed in preparing the consolidated SCF. Because income statement items are translated at average exchange rates under the current rate method, and assets and liabilities at current exchange rates at the balance sheet date, each individual translation adjustment is ordinarily equal to the beginning balance of the account times the exchange rate change from beginning to midpoint in the year, plus the ending balance of the account times the exchange rate change from midpoint in the

TRANSLATION WORKSHEETS FOR SOY COMPANY

	For the Year 20X6			For the Year 20X7		
	LCUs	Exchange Rate	U.S. Dollars	LCUs	Exchange Rate	U.S. Dollars
Cash	590,000	$.020	$11,800	800,000	$.022	$17,600
Accounts receivable—net	310,000	.020	6,200	350,000	.022	7,700
Inventories	600,000	.020	12,000	650,000	.022	14,300
Plant assets—net	900,000	.020	18,000	800,000	.022	17,600
Cost of sales	300,000	.019	5,700	350,000	.021	7,350
Depreciation expense	100,000	.019	1,900	100,000	.021	2,100
Operating expenses	200,000	.019	3,800	250,000	.021	5,250
Dividends	200,000	.020	4,000	200,000	.022	4,400
Equity adjustment			0			0
	3,200,000		$63,400	3,500,000		$76,300
Accounts payable	100,000	.020	2,000	200,000	.022	$ 4,400
Capital stock	2,000,000	.018	36,000	2,000,000	.018	36,000
Retained earnings	200,000	.018	3,600	300,000	*	5,300
Sales	900,000	.019	17,100	1,000,000	.021	21,000
Equity adjustment year-end 20X6			4,700			4,700
Equity adjustment increase 20X7						4,900
	3,200,000		$63,400	3,500,000		$76,300

*Measured.

Exhibit 14–15   *Translation Worksheets for 20X6 and 20X7*

year to year-end. For example, the dollar translation adjustment of accounts receivable for 20X6 is determined as follows:

	Account Balance	×	Exchange Rate Change	=	Translation Adjustment
January 1, 20X7	310,000 LCU		($.021 avg. − $.020 beg.)		$310
December 31, 20X7	350,000 LCU		($.022 end. − $.021 avg.)		350
Translation adjustment of accounts receivable					$660

The translation adjustments for most other asset and liability items can be determined by using the procedure illustrated in Exhibit 14–19. In this example, the exchange rate change for the first half of 20X7 is $.001 ($.021 average exchange rate less $.020 beginning-of-the-period exchange rate), and the exchange rate change for the second half of 20X7 is also $.001 ($.022 end-of-the-period exchange rate less $.021 average exchange rate).

An exception to the usual procedure for determining the translation adjustments for balance sheet items occurs when actual cash flows differ from cash flows expected under the assumption that all cash receipts and cash disbursements are made at average exchange rates for the year. For example, when historical exchange rates are used for intercompany purchase transactions, those rates must be used in determining the translation adjustments, rather than average rates. A translation adjustment of cash is also needed for dividends, except when they are translated at average exchange rates. The calculation of individual translation adjustments for plant asset items requires special analysis for all acquisitions and disposals during a period.

The translation effect on consolidated net assets for a period is necessarily equal to the effect on consolidated stockholders' equity for that period.

Consolidated SCF Worksheet   A worksheet for the consolidated SCF using the indirect format is presented in Exhibit 14–20. The year's change column in that exhibit reflects consolidated balance sheet changes for Pac Corporation and Subsidiary between

PAC CORPORATION AND SUBSIDIARY
CONSOLIDATION WORKING PAPERS
FOR THE YEAR ENDED DECEMBER 31, 20X6

	Pac	Soy	Adjustments and Eliminations		Consolidated Statements
Income Statement Sales	$ 57,000	$17,100			$ 74,100
Income from Soy	5,510		a 5,510		
Cost of sales	(18,000)	(5,700)			(23,700)
Depreciation expense	(12,000)	(1,900)			(13,900)
Other operating expenses	(10,000)	(3,800)			(13,800)
Goodwill amortization			c 190		(190)
Net income	$ 22,510	$ 5,700			$ 22,510
Retained Earnings Retained earnings—Pac	$ 85,000				$ 85,000
Retained earnings—Soy		$ 3,600	b 3,600		
Net income	22,510	5,700			22,510
Dividends	(20,000)	(4,000)		a 4,000	(20,000)
Retained earnings December 31, 20X6	$ 87,510	$ 5,300			$ 87,510
Balance Sheet Cash	$ 49,000	$11,800			$ 60,800
Accounts receivable	55,100	6,200			61,300
Inventories	67,800	12,000			79,800
Plant assets—net	100,000	18,000			118,000
Investment in Soy	46,800			a 1,510 b 45,290	
Goodwill			b 990	c 190	800
Total assets	$318,700	$48,000			$320,700
Accounts payable	$ 26,400	$ 2,000			$ 28,400
Capital stock	200,000	36,000	b 36,000		200,000
Retained earnings	87,510	5,300			87,510
Accumulated other comprehensive income: equity adjustment from translation	4,790	4,700	b 4,700		4,790
Total equities	$318,700	$48,000			$320,700

Exhibit 14–16   *Consolidation Working Papers—20X6*

PAC CORPORATION AND SUBSIDIARY
CONSOLIDATION WORKING PAPERS
FOR THE YEAR ENDED DECEMBER 31, 20X7

	Pac	Soy	Adjustments and Eliminations		Consolidated Statements
Income Statement					
Sales	$ 57,000	$21,000			$ 78,000
Income from Soy	6,090		a 6,090		
Cost of sales	(18,000)	(7,350)			(25,350)
Depreciation expense	(12,000)	(2,100)			(14,100)
Other operating expenses	(10,000)	(5,250)			(15,250)
Goodwill amortization			c 210		(210)
Net income	$ 23,090	$ 6,300			$ 23,090
Retained Earnings					
Retained earnings—Pac	$ 87,510				$ 87,510
Retained earnings—Soy		$ 5,300	b 5,300		
Net income	23,090	6,300			23,090
Dividends	(20,000)	(4,400)		a 4,400	(20,000)
Retained earnings December 31, 20X7	$ 90,600	$ 7,200			$ 90,600
Balance Sheet					
Cash	$ 60,000	$17,600			$ 77,600
Accounts receivable	55,100	7,700			62,800
Inventories	49,800	14,300			64,100
Plant assets—net	108,000	17,600			125,600
Investment in Soy	53,460			a 1,690 b 51,770	
Goodwill			b 870	c 210	660
Total assets	$326,360	$57,200			$330,760
Accounts payable	$ 26,000	$ 4,400			$ 30,400
Capital stock	200,000	36,000	b 36,000		200,000
Retained earnings	90,600	7,200			90,600
Accumulated other comprehensive income: equity adjustment from translation	9,760	9,600	b 9,600		9,760
Total equities	$326,360	$57,200			$330,760

Exhibit 14–17   Consolidation Working Papers—20X7

PAC CORPORATION AND SUBSIDIARY
COMPARATIVE CONSOLIDATED FINANCIAL STATEMENTS
FOR THE YEARS ENDED DECEMBER 31, 20X7 AND 20X6

	20X7	20X6	Year's Change 20X7–20X6
Income Statement			
Sales	$ 78,000	$ 74,100	$ 3,900
Cost of sales	(25,350)	(23,700)	(1,650)
Depreciation expense	(14,100)	(13,900)	(200)
Other expenses	(15,250)	(13,800)	(1,450)
Goodwill amortization	(210)	(190)	(20)
Net income	$ 23,090	$ 22,510	$ 580
Retained Earnings			
Retained earnings January 1	$ 87,510	$ 85,000	$ 2,510
Net income	23,090	22,510	580
Dividends	(20,000)	(20,000)	
Retained earnings December 31	$ 90,600	$ 87,510	$ 3,090
Balance Sheet			
Cash	$ 77,600	$ 60,800	$16,800
Accounts receivable—net	62,800	61,300	1,500
Inventories	64,100	79,800	(15,700)
Plant assets—net	125,600	118,000	7,600
Goodwill	660	800	(140)
Total assets	$330,760	$320,700	$10,060
Accounts payable	$ 30,400	$ 28,400	$ 2,000
Capital stock	200,000	200,000	
Retained earnings	90,600	87,510	3,090
Other comprehensive income:			
equity adjustment	9,760	4,790	4,970
Total equities	$330,760	$320,700	$10,060

Exhibit 14–18   *Comparative Financial Statements and Year's Change*

PAC CORPORATION AND SUBSIDIARY
INDIVIDUAL ASSET AND LIABILITY TRANSLATION ADJUSTMENTS AND RECONCILIATION
AT AND FOR THE YEAR ENDED DECEMBER 31, 20X7

	1/1/X7 Balance In LCUs A	Rate Change 1st Half B	$ Change 1st Half of 20X7 C	12/31/X7 Balance In LCUs D	Rate Change 2nd Half E	$ Change 2nd Half of 20X7 F	Consolidated Translation Changes C + F
Cash	590,000	$.001	$ 590	800,000	$.001	$ 800	$1,390
Cash from dividends				200,000	.001	200	200
Accounts receivable	310,000	.001	310	350,000	.001	350	660
Inventories	600,000	.001	600	650,000	.001	650	1,250
Plant assets—net	900,000	.001	900	800,000	.001	800	1,700
Goodwill	40,000	.001	40	30,000	.001	30	70
			2,440			2,830	5,270
Accounts payable	100,000	.001	100	200,000	.001	200	(300)
			$2,340			$2,630	
Effect of translation changes on consolidated net assets							$4,970

Note: An adjustment of cash is needed for 20X7 dividends because the dividend rate of $.022 is not equal to the average exchange rate for the year.

Exhibit 14–19   *Individual Translation Adjustments*

PAC CORPORATION AND SUBSIDIARY
CONSOLIDATED STATEMENT OF CASH FLOWS WORKSHEET
FOR THE YEAR ENDED DECEMBER 31, 20X7

	Year's Change 20X7–20X6	Translation Adjustments	Year's Change Less Translation Adjustments	Cash Flows from Operating Activities	Cash Flows from Investing Activities	Cash Flows from Financing Activities
Balance Sheet						
Cash	$ 16,800	$ 1,590*	$ 15,210			
Accounts receivable	1,500	660	840	$ (840)		
Inventories	(15,700)	1,250	(16,950)	16,950		
Plant assets—net	7,600	1,700	5,900	14,100	$(20,000)	
Goodwill	(140)	70	(210)	210		
Total assets	$ 10,060	$ 5,270	$ 4,790			
Accounts payable	$ 2,000	$ 300	$ 1,700	1,700		
Capital stock	0	0	0			
Retained earnings	3,090	0	3,090	23,090		$(20,000)
Equity adjustment	4,970	4,970				
Total equities	$ 10,060	$ 5,270	$ 4,790			
				$ 55,210	$(20,000)	$(20,000)

*Presented in the SCF immediately below cash flows from financing activities.

Exhibit 14–20   *Worksheet for Consolidated Statement of Cash Flows*

December 31, 20X6 and 20X7. This information was presented earlier in Exhibit 14–18. A second column in the SCF worksheet shows the translation adjustments to individual balance sheet items as illustrated in Exhibit 14–19 and discussed in the preceding paragraph. The third column subtracts column 2 from column 1 to obtain the year's changes without translation adjustments. This information is pivotal in preparing a SCF

PAC CORPORATION AND SUBSIDIARY
CONSOLIDATED STATEMENT OF CASH FLOWS
FOR THE YEAR ENDED DECEMBER 31, 20X7

Cash Flows from Operating Activities		
Consolidated net income		$23,090
Noncash expenses, revenues, losses, and gains included in income:		
Depreciation	$ 14,100	
Goodwill amortization	210	
Increase in accounts receivable	(840)	
Increase in accounts payable	1,700	
Decrease in inventories	16,950	32,120
Net cash flows from operating activities		55,210
Cash Flows from Investing Activities		
Purchase of equipment	$(20,000)	
Net cash used in investing activities		(20,000)
Cash Flows from Financing Activities		
Dividends to Pac's stockholders	$(20,000)	
Net cash used in financing activities		(20,000)
Effect of exchange rate changes on cash		1,590
Net increase in cash		16,800
Cash and cash equivalents at beginning of year		60,800
Cash and cash equivalents at end of year		$77,600

Exhibit 14–21   *Consolidated Statement of Cash Flows*

for a consolidated entity with foreign subsidiaries. Once the translation effects are eliminated from the year's change information, preparation of the consolidated SCF is essentially the same as for a consolidated entity with only domestic subsidiaries.

Items in the "year's change less translation adjustments" column of Exhibit 14–20 are analyzed and carried to the "cash flows from operating activities," "cash flows from investing activities," or "cash flows from financing activities" columns, as appropriate. Information for consolidated net income, minority interest income, dividends, and depreciation is obtained from the consolidated income and retained earnings statements. Other information relating to plant asset purchases, goodwill amortization, and minority interest dividends is found in the consolidated working papers for 20X6 and in the background information for the illustration.

The consolidated SCF of Pac Corporation and Subsidiary for 20X7 is presented in Exhibit 14–21 on page 555. This statement is developed directly from the completed worksheet in Exhibit 14–20. The $1,590 translation adjustment of cash is shown as a separate line item immediately below the "cash flows from financing activities" section of the SCF.

SUMMARY

Before a consolidated statement of cash flows for a parent company and its foreign subsidiary can be prepared, the effects of individual translation adjustments for assets and liabilities must be identified. These adjustments are combined and reported as a separate line item under the heading "effect of exchange rate changes on cash."

SELECTED READINGS

DeMoville, Wig and Roben Hatami. "Nonowner Equity Transactions—A Review," *The CPA Journal* (June 1990), p. 50.
Huefner, Ronald J., J. Edward Ketz, and James A. Largay III. "Foreign Currency Translation and the Cash Flow Statement." *Accounting Horizons*, Vol. 3, no. 2. (June 1989), pp. 66–76.
Statement of Financial Accounting Standards No. 52. "Foreign Currency Translation." Stamford, CT: Financial Accounting Standards Board, 1981.

ASSIGNMENT MATERIAL

QUESTIONS

1 Do you agree that all financial statement items of a foreign entity are *translated* at current exchange rates under *FASB Statement No. 52*?

2 In the process of restructuring its manufacturing and distribution lines, a parent company changes its foreign subsidiary's functional currency. Does this accounting change require restatement of previously issued financial statements?

3 How does *Statement No. 52* define a highly inflationary economy?

4 What procedures may be required in accounting for a 60% interest in a foreign investee located in a highly inflationary economy?

5 Does the functional currency of a foreign subsidiary affect the initial recording of the business combination?

6 Explain how a pooling of interests business combination with a foreign subsidiary is recorded. What changes in recording the initial investment would be necessary if the business combination is accounted for under the purchase method?

7 Discuss the possible accounting problems that can arise in remeasuring inventory items that are accounted for under the lower-of-cost-or-market pricing procedure in the foreign entity's financial statements.

8 At what exchange rate would the retained earnings account of a foreign subsidiary be translated? Explain.

9 In consolidating the financial statements of a Canadian subsidiary that has a Canadian dollar functional currency with those of its U.S. parent, how are goodwill and goodwill amortization computed? Would the computation be different if the subsidiary had a U.S. dollar functional currency? Explain.

10 Is the "equity adjustment from translation" account ever eliminated? Explain.

11 How are expenses that relate to monetary items of a foreign subsidiary remeasured under *Statement No. 52*?

12 **Appendix** How is the effect of exchange rate changes in cash reported in a consolidated statement of cash flows?

EXERCISES

E 14-1

1 Under *FASB Statement No. 52*, a foreign entity's financial statements should be converted into U.S. dollars under the following methods for *translation* and *remeasurement*, respectively:
  a Current rate method and the monetary-nonmonetary method
  b Current rate method and the temporal method
  c Temporal method and the current-noncurrent method
  d Temporal method and the monetary-nonmonetary method

2 The exchange rate for converting a foreign entity's retained earnings into U.S. dollars for consolidation purposes is:
  a The historical rate **c** The current rate
  b The spot rate **d** None of the above

3 A German subsidiary of a U.S. firm has the French franc as its functional currency. Under the provisions of *FASB Statement No. 52*, the U.S. dollar from the subsidiary's viewpoint would be:
  a Its local currency **c** A foreign currency
  b Its recording currency **d** None of the above

4 Which one of the following foreign subsidiary accounts will be converted into the same number of U.S. dollars, regardless of whether *translation* or *remeasurement* is used?
  a Accounts receivable **c** Machinery
  b Inventories **d** Prepaid insurance

5 Which one of the following foreign subsidiary accounts will *not* be converted into the same number of U.S. dollars under *translation* as under *remeasurement*?
  a Cash **c** Capital stock
  b Inventories **d** Retained earnings

6 Which one of the following items from the financial statements of a foreign subsidiary would be translated into dollars using the historical exchange rate?
  a Accounts payable
  b Amortization of bond premium
  c Common stock
  d Inventories priced at the lower of cost or market

7 Average exchange rates are used to translate certain items from foreign income statements into U.S. dollars. Such averages are used to:
  a Approximate the effects of using the current exchange rates in effect on the transaction dates
  b Avoid using different exchange rates for some revenue and expense accounts
  c Eliminate large and temporary fluctuations in exchange rates that may reverse in the near future
  d Smooth out large exchange gains and losses

8 Palace Corporation made a long-term, dollar-denominated loan of $600,000 to its British subsidiary on January 1, 20X1, when the exchange rate for British pounds was $1.73. If the subsidiary's functional currency is its local currency, this transaction is a foreign currency transaction of:
  a The parent company but *not* the subsidiary
  b The subsidiary company but *not* the parent
  c Both the subsidiary and the parent
  d Neither the subsidiary nor the parent

9 Sumtora Corporation is a 100%-owned subsidiary of a U.S. corporation. The country in which Sumtora is located has been determined to have a "highly inflationary economy." Given this information, the functional currency of Sumtora is:
  a Its local currency
  b The U.S. dollar
  c Its recording currency
  d None of the above

10 An exchange gain on a long-term loan of a U.S. parent company to its British subsidiary whose functional currency is the British pound is:
  a Recognized in consolidated income currently
  b Deferred until the loan is settled
  c Treated as an equity adjustment from translation
  d Treated as an equity adjustment from remeasurement

11 A U.S. firm has a $10,000,000 investment in a foreign subsidiary, and the U.S. dollar is weakening against the currency of the country in which the foreign entity is located. On the basis of this information, one would expect the consolidated financial statements to show:
  a Translation gains
  b Translation losses
  c Stockholders' equity increase from equity adjustments
  d Stockholders' equity decrease from equity adjustments

12 Which one of the following would *not* give rise to changes in a parent company's equity adjustment from translation account?
  a Remeasurement of a foreign subsidiary's statements
  b Hedge of a net investment in a foreign subsidiary
  c Long-term intercompany loans to its foreign subsidiary
  d Translation of a foreign subsidiary's statements

E 14-2 **[AICPA adapted]**
  1 When preparing consolidated financial statements for a U.S. parent and its foreign subsidiary, the account balances expressed in foreign currency must be converted into the currency of the reporting entity. One objective of the translation process is to provide information that:
  a Reflects current exchange rates
  b Reflects current monetary equivalents
  c Is compatible with the economic effects of rate changes on the firm's cash flows
  d Reflects each translated account at its unexpired historical cost
  2 A company is translating account balances from another currency into dollars for its December 31, 20X5 statement of financial position and its calendar year 20X5 earnings statement and statement of cash flows. The average exchange rate for the year 20X5 should be used to translate:
  a Cash at December 31, 20X5
  b Land purchased at 20X3
  c Retained earnings at January 1, 20X5
  d Sales for 20X5
  3 If a parent company bills all sales to a foreign subsidiary in terms of dollars and is to be repaid in the same number of dollars, the purchases account on the subsidiary's trial balance will be converted to U.S. dollars by using:
  a The average exchange rate for the period
  b The exchange rate at the beginning of the period
  c The exchange rate at the end of the period
  d The amount showing in the parent's accounts for sales to the subsidiary
  4 A subsidiary's functional currency is the local currency, which has not experienced significant inflation. The appropriate exchange rate for translating the depreciation on plant assets in the income statement of the foreign subsidiary is the:
  a Exit rate
  b Historical exchange rate
  c Weighted average exchange rate over the economic life of each plant asset
  d Weighted average exchange rate for the current year
  5 The year-end balance of accounts receivable on the books of a foreign subsidiary should be translated by the parent company for consolidation purposes at the:
  a Historical rate   **c** Negotiated rate
  b Current rate   **d** Spot rate
  6 When remeasuring foreign currency financial statements into the functional currency, which of the following items would be remeasured using historical exchange rates?
  a Inventories carried at cost
  b Marketable equity securities reported at market values
  c Bonds payable
  d Accrued liabilities
  7 Park Company's wholly-owned subsidiary, Schnell Corporation, maintains its accounting records in German marks. Because all of Schnell's branch offices are in Switzerland, its functional currency is the Swiss franc. Remeasurement of Schnell's 20X4 financial statements resulted in a $7,600 gain, and translation of its financial statements resulted in an $8,100 gain. What amount should Park report as a foreign exchange gain in its income statement for the year ended December 31, 20X4?
  a $0   **c** $8,100
  b $7,600   **d** $15,700

E 14-3 On January 1, 20X8, Paily Company, a U.S. firm, purchases all the outstanding capital stock of Standt Ltd., a British firm, for $990,000, when the exchange rate for British pounds is $1.65. The book values of Standt's assets and liabilities are equal to fair values on this date, except for land that has a fair value of £200,000 and equipment with a fair value of £100,000.

  Summarized balance sheet information for Paily in U.S. dollars and for Standt in pounds just before the business combination is as follows:

	Paily	Standt
Current assets	$3,000,000	£100,000
Land	800,000	100,000
Buildings—net	1,200,000	250,000
		(Continued)

	Paily	Standt
Equipment—net	1,000,000	50,000
	$6,000,000	£500,000
Current liabilities	$ 600,000	£ 50,000
Notes payable	1,000,000	150,000
Capital stock	3,000,000	200,000
Retained earnings	1,400,000	100,000
	$6,000,000	£500,000

Required: Prepare a consolidated balance sheet for Paily Company and Subsidiary at January 1, 20X8, immediately after the business combination.

E 14-4 Stadt Corporation of the Netherlands is an 80%-owned subsidiary of Port Corporation, a US. firm, and its functional currency is the U.S. dollar. Stadt's books of record are maintained in guilders and its inventory is carried at the lower of cost or market.

> The current exchange rate for guilders at December 31, 20X8 is $.60.
>
> The historical cost of the inventory is 10,000 guilders.
>
> The replacement cost of the inventory is 9,000 guilders.
>
> The historical exchange rate is $.53.

Required: Determine the amount at which the inventory will be carried on (a) the foreign currency statements and (b) the remeasured statements.

E 14-5 On January 1, 20X5, Panama Corporation acquired all the stock of Simenon Company of Belgium for $1,200,000, when Simenon had 20,000,000 Belgium francs (BFr) capital stock and BFr 15,000,000 retained earnings. Simenon's net assets were fairly valued on this date and any cost/book value differential is goodwill with a 10-year amortization period. Simenon's functional currency is the Belgium franc. The exchange rates for Belgium francs for 20X5 were as follows:

January 1, 20X5	$.030
Average for 20X5	.032
December 31, 20X5	.034

Required

1 Calculate goodwill from the business combination on January 1, 20X5.

2 Determine goodwill amortization in U.S. dollars for 20X5.

3 Prepare a journal entry on Panama's books to record the goodwill amortization for 20X5.

E 14-6 Psalter Company acquired all the stock of Stanford Ltd. of Britain on January 1, 20X6 for $163,800, when Stanford had capital stock of £60,000 and retained earnings of £30,000. Stanford's assets and liabilities were fairly valued except for equipment with a three-year life that was undervalued by £6,000. Any remaining excess is goodwill with a useful life of 10 years.

Stanford's functional currency is the pound. Exchange rates for British pounds are as follows:

January 1, 20X6	$1.66
Average for the year 20X6	1.65
December 31, 20X6	1.64

Required:

1 Determine the unrealized translation gain or loss at December 31, 20X6 related to the cost/book value differential assigned to equipment.

2 Determine the unrealized translation gain or loss at December 31, 20X6 related to goodwill.

E 14-7 Packer Corporation of the United States purchased all the outstanding stock of Swiss Products Company of Switzerland for $1,350,000 cash on January 1, 20X9. The book values of Swiss's assets and liabilities were equal to fair values on this date except for land, which was valued at 1,000,000 Swiss francs. Summarized balance sheet information in Swiss francs (SFr) at January 1, 20X9 is as follows:

Current assets	SFr 800,000	Current liabilities	SFr 400,000
Land	600,000	Bonds payable	500,000
Buildings—net	400,000	Capital stock	1,000,000
Equipment—net	500,000	Retained earnings	400,000
	SFr 2,300,000		SFr 2,300,000

The functional currency of Swiss Products Company is the Swiss franc. Exchange rates for Swiss francs for 20X9 are:

Spot rate January 1, 20X9	$.75
Average rate 20X9	.76
Current rate December 31, 20X9	.77

Required: Determine the unrealized translation gain or loss at December 31, 20X9 relating to the excess allocated to the undervalued land.

E 14-8   [AICPA adapted]

1 Fay Corporation had a realized foreign exchange loss of $15,000 for the year ended December 31, 20X8 and must also determine whether the following items will require year-end adjustment.

> Fay had an $8,000 equity adjustment resulting from the translation of the accounts of its wholly owned foreign subsidiary for the year ended December 31, 20X8.

> Fay had an account payable to an unrelated foreign supplier payable in the supplier's local currency. The U.S. dollar equivalent of the payable was $64,000 on the October 31, 20X8 invoice date, and it was $60,000 on December 31, 20X8. The invoice is payable on January 30, 20X9.

> In Fay's 20X8 consolidated income statement, what amount should be included as foreign exchange loss?
> a $11,000   c $19,000
> b $15,000   d $23,000

2 On January 1, 20X8, the Ben Company formed a foreign subsidiary. On February 15, 20X8, Ben's subsidiary purchased 100,000 local currency units of inventory; 25,000 LCU of the original inventory purchased on February 15, 20X8 made up the entire inventory on December 31, 20X8. The subsidiary's functional currency is the U.S. dollar. The exchange rates were 2.2 LCU to $1 from January 1, 20X8 to June 30, 20X8 and 2 LCU to $1 from July 1, 20X8 to December 31, 20X8. The December 31, 20X8 inventory balance for Ben's foreign subsidiary should be remeasured into U.S. dollars in the amount of:
a $10,500   c $11,905
b $11,364   d $12,500

3 The Dease Company owns a foreign subsidiary with 3,600,000 local currency units of property, plant, and equipment before accumulated depreciation at December 31, 20X5. Of this amount, 2,400,000 LCU were acquired in 20X3, when the rate of exchange was 1.6 LCU to $1, and 1,200,000 LCU were acquired in 20X4, when the rate of exchange was 1.8 LCU to $1.

> The rate of exchange in effect at December 31, 20X5 was 2 LCU to $1. The weighted average of exchange rates in effect during 20X5 was 1.92 LCU to $1. The subsidiary's functional currency is the U.S. dollar.

> Assuming that the property, plant, and equipment are depreciated using the straight-line method over a 10-year period with no salvage value, how much depreciation expense relating to the foreign subsidiary's property, plant, and equipment should be charged in Dease's income statement for 20X5?
> a $180,000   c $200,000
> b $187,500   d $216,667

4 The Clark Company owns a foreign subsidiary that had net income for the year ended December 31, 20X5 of 4,800,000 local currency units, which was appropriately translated into $800,000.

> On October 15, 20X5, when the rate of exchange was 5.7 LCU to $1, the foreign subsidiary paid a dividend to Clark of 2,400,000 LCU. The dividend represented the net income of the foreign subsidiary for the six months ended June 30, 20X5, during which time the weighted average exchange rate was 5.8 LCU to $1.

> The rate of exchange in effect at December 31, 20X5 was 5.9 LCU to $1. What rate of exchange should be used to translate the dividend for the December 31, 20X5 financial statements?
> a 5.7 LCU to $1   c 5.9 LCU to $1
> b 5.8 LCU to $1   d 6.0 LCU to $1

5 The Jem Company used the current rate method when translating foreign currency amounts at December 31, 20X5. At that time, Jem had foreign subsidiaries with 1,500,000 local currency units in long-term receivables and 2,400,000 LCU in long-term debt. The rate of exchange in effect when the specific transactions occurred involving those foreign currency amounts was 2 LCU to $1. The rate of exchange in effect at December 31, 20X5 was 1.5 LCU to $1. The translation of the above foreign currency

amounts into U.S. dollars would result in long-term receivables and long-term debt, respectively, of:

a $750,000 and $1,200,000
b $750,000 and $1,600,000
c $1,000,000 and $1,200,000
d $1,000,000 and $1,600,000

6 Certain balance sheet accounts of a foreign subsidiary of Rowan at December 31, 20X9 have been translated into U.S. dollars as follows:

	Translated at Current Rates	Historical Rates
Note receivable, long term	$240,000	$200,000
Prepaid rent	85,000	80,000
Patent	150,000	170,000
	$475,000	$450,000

The subsidiary's functional currency is the currency of the country in which it is located. What total amount should be included in Rowan's December 31, 20X9 consolidated balance sheet for the three accounts?

a $450,000   c $475,000
b $455,000   d $495,000

7 On January 1, 20X2, Kiner Company formed a foreign branch. The branch purchased merchandise at a cost of 720,000 local currency units on February 15, 20X2. The purchase price was equivalent to $180,000 on this date. The branch's inventory at December 31, 20X2 consisted solely of merchandise purchased on February 15, 20X2 and amounted to 240,000 LCU. The exchange rate was 6 LCU to $1 on December 31, 20X2, and the average rate of exchange was 5 LCU to $1 for 20X2. Assume that the LCU is the functional currency of the branch. In Kiner's December 31, 20X2 balance sheet, the branch inventory balance of 240,000 LCU should be translated into U.S. dollars at:

a $40,000   c $60,000
b $48,000   d $84,000

E 14-9 Use the following information in answering questions 1 and 2.

Bradstreet Corporation has a 70% interest in Kasan Corporation of Switzerland, acquired in 20X5 at a price equal to book value and fair value of Kasan's net assets. Kasan's functional currency is the Swiss franc, and changes in Kasan's U.S. dollar, translated stockholders' equity for 20X8 are summarized as follows:

	Balance 1/1/X8	Change 20X8	Balance 12/31/X8
Capital stock	$10,000,000	none	$10,000,000
Other paid-in capital	8,000,000	none	8,000,000
Retained earnings	4,000,000	$1,500,000	5,500,000
Equity adjustment from translation	(2,000,000)	500,000	(1,500,000)
Total	$20,000,000	$2,000,000	$22,000,000

1 Kasan's U.S. dollar net income for 20X8 is $1,500,000, and Bradstreet accounts for its investment in Kasan as a one-line consolidation. Bradstreet's income from Kasan for 20X8 is:

a $2,000,000   c $1,400,000
b $1,500,000   d $1,050,000

2 The change in Bradstreet's investment in Kasan account for 20X8 is:

a $2,000,000   c $1,400,000
b $1,500,000   d $1,050,000

Use the following information in answering questions 3 and 4.

Martin Corporation loaned its 90% Colombian subsidiary 10,000,000 pesos denominated as $19,000 on July 1, 20X9, when the exchange rate for Colombian pesos was $.0019. The subsidiary's functional currency is its local currency, and the 20X9 average and year-end exchange rates are $.0018 and $.0016, respectively.

3 If the loan is short-term, the subsidiary's separate financial statements denominated in pesos at and for the year ended December 31, 20X9 should reflect:

a An exchange gain of 555,556 pesos
b An exchange loss of 1,875,000 pesos
c An equity adjustment of 1,875,000 pesos
d None of the above

4 If the loan is long-term, the consolidated financial statements of Martin Corporation and Subsidiary at and for the year ended December 31, 20X9 should reflect:
  a An exchange gain of $889
  b An exchange loss of $3,000
  c An equity adjustment of $2,700
  d None of the above

5 Inflation data of a foreign country for three years are as follows:

	Index	Change in Index	Annual Rate of Inflation
January 1, 20X6	150		
January 1, 20X7	200	50	50 ÷ 150 = 33%
January 1, 20X8	250	50	50 ÷ 200 = 25%
January 1, 20X9	330	80	80 ÷ 250 = 32%

The cumulative three-year inflation rate is:
  a 45%   **c** 120%
  b 90%   **d** 180%

E 14-10 Pender Corporation owns an 80% interest in Shinhan Ltd. of South Korea, purchased several years ago at book value equal to fair value. The functional currency of Shinhan is the U.S. dollar.
  Shinhan uses the FIFO inventory method. Data in won relating to Shinhan's cost of sales and inventory are as follows:

Inventory January 1, 20X7	9,000,000 won
Inventory December 31, 20X7	5,000,000 won
Purchases 20X7	86,000,000 won

The rate of exchange for the won on November 30, 20X7, when the ending inventory items were acquired, was $.00135. Other exchange rates for 20X7 are:

Exchange rate January 1, 20X7	$.0012
Exchange rate December 31, 20X7	.0014
Average exchange rate for 20X7	.0013

Required: Determine cost of sales and ending inventory amounts in U.S. dollars that will appear in Shinhan's remeasured financial statements.

E 14-11 **[AICPA adapted]**
Jay Company's 20X5 consolidated financial statements include two wholly owned subsidiaries, Jay Company of Australia (Jay A) and Jay Company of France (Jay F). Functional currencies are the U.S. dollar for Jay A and the franc for Jay F.

Required
  1 What are the objectives of translating a foreign subsidiary's financial statements?
  2 How are gains and losses arising from translating or remeasuring of each subsidiary's financial statements measured and reported in Jay's consolidated financial statements?
  3 *FASB Statement No. 52* identifies several economic indicators that are to be considered both individually and collectively in determining the functional currency for a consolidated subsidiary. List three of those indicators.
  4 What exchange rate is used to incorporate each subsidiary's equipment cost, accumulated depreciation, and depreciation expense in Jay's consolidated financial statements?

PROBLEMS

P 14-1 Parkway Corporation purchased a 40% interest in Scorpio Company of Germany for $1,080,000 on January 1, 20X6. The excess cost over book value is goodwill with a 10-year amortization period. A summary of Scorpio's net assets at December 31, 20X5 and at December 31, 20X6, after translation into U.S. dollars, is as follows:

	Capital Stock	Retained Earnings	Equity Adjustment	Net Assets
December 31, 20X5	$2,000,000	$400,000		$2,400,000
Net income		310,000		310,000
Dividends		(192,000)		(192,000)
Translation adjustment			$212,000	212,000
December 31, 20X6	$2,000,000	$518,000	$212,000	$2,730,000

Exchange rates for German marks were $.60 on January 1, 20X6, $.62 average for 20X6, $.64 when dividends were declared, and $.65 at December 31, 20X6. Scorpio had net assets of 4,000,000 marks at January 1, 20X6, 500,000 marks net income for 20X6, dividends of 300,000 marks, and ended the year with net assets of 4,200,000 marks.

Required
1 Calculate Parkway's income from Scorpio for 20X6.
2 Determine the balance of Parkway's investment in Scorpio account at December 31, 20X6.
3 Develop a proof of your calculation of the investment in Scorpio account balance at December 31, 20X6.

P 14-2 Placid Corporation purchased a 40% interest in Sorrier Company of France on January 1, 20X1 for $342,000, when Sorrier's stockholders' equity consisted of Fr 3,000,000 capital stock and Fr 1,000,000 retained earnings. Sorrier's functional currency is the French franc. The exchange rate at this time was $0.15 for French francs. Any goodwill is to be amortized over 10 years.

A summary of changes in the stockholders' equity of Sorrier during 20X1 (including relevant exchange rates) is as follows:

	French Francs	Exchange Rate	U.S. Dollars
Stockholders' equity January 1, 20X1	4,000,000	$.15 C	$600,000
Net income	800,000	.14 A	112,000
Dividends	(400,000)	.14 C	(56,000)
Equity adjustment			(84,000)
Stockholders' equity December 31, 20X1	4,400,000	.13 C	$572,000

Required: Determine the following
1 Goodwill from Placid's investment in Sorrier on January 1, 20X1
2 Goodwill amortization for 20X1
3 Unamortized goodwill at December 31, 20X1
4 Equity adjustment from goodwill for 20X1
5 Income from Sorrier for 20X1
6 Investment in Sorrier balance at December 31, 20X1

P 14-3 Pylon Corporation acquired all the outstanding capital stock of Sooth Company, Ltd. of London on January 1, 20X5 for $800,000, when the exchange rate for British pounds was $1.60 and Sooth's stockholders' equity consisted of £400,000 capital stock and £100,000 retained earnings. Sooth's functional currency is the British pound. Balance sheet accounts for Sooth at January 1, 20X5 in British pounds and U.S. dollars are summarized as follows:

	British Pounds	Exchange Rate	U.S. Dollars
Cash	50,000	$1.60	80,000
Accounts receivable—net	60,000	1.60	96,000
Inventories	40,000	1.60	64,000
Equipment	750,000	1.60	1,200,000
	900,000		1,440,000
Accumulated depreciation	250,000	1.60	400,000
Accounts payable	150,000	1.60	240,000
Capital stock	400,000	1.60	640,000
Retained earnings	100,000	1.60	160,000
	900,000		1,440,000

Exchange rates for 20X5 are as follows:

Current exchange rate January 1, 20X5	$1.60
Average exchange rate for 20X5	1.63
Rate for cash dividends	1.62
Current exchange rate December 31, 20X5	1.65

Sooth's adjusted trial balance in British pounds at December 31, 20X5 is as follows:

Debits

Cash	£	20,000
Accounts receivable—net		70,000
Inventories		50,000
Equipment		800,000
Cost of sales		350,000
Depreciation expense		80,000
Operating expenses		100,000
Dividends		30,000
		£1,500,000

Credits

Accumulated depreciation	£	330,000
Accounts payable		70,000
Capital stock		400,000
Retained earnings		100,000
Sales		600,000
		£1,500,000

Required

1 Prepare a translation worksheet to convert Sooth's December 31, 20X5 adjusted trial balance into U.S. dollars.

2 Prepare journal entries on Pylon's books to account for the investment in Sooth for 20X5.

P 14-4 Peter Corporation acquired 80% of the common stock of Schultz Corporation, a German company, for $3,200,000 on January 2, 20X6, when the stockholders' equity of Schultz consisted of 5,000,000 German marks capital stock and 2,000,000 marks retained earnings. The spot rate for marks on this date was $.50. Any cost/book value difference is goodwill to be amortized over a 10-year period, and Schultz's functional currency is the mark (DM).

Accounts from Schultz's adjusted trial balance in marks at December 31, 20X6 are as follows:

Debits

Cash	DM	1,000,000
Accounts receivable		2,000,000
Inventories		4,000,000
Equipment		8,000,000
Cost of sales		4,000,000
Depreciation expense		800,000
Operating expenses		2,700,000
Dividends		500,000
	DM	23,000,000

Credits

Accumulated depreciation—equipment	DM	2,400,000
Accounts payable		3,600,000
Capital stock		5,000,000
Retained earnings January 1		2,000,000
Sales		10,000,000
	DM	23,000,000

Relevant exchange rates in U.S. dollars for German marks are as follows:

Current exchange rate December 31, 20X6	$.60
Average exchange rate 20X6	.55
Exchange rate applicable to dividends	.54

Required

1 Prepare a translation worksheet for Schultz at December 31, 20X6.

2 Calculate Peter's income from Schultz for 20X6 on the basis of a one-line consolidation.

3 Determine the correct balance of Peter's investment in Schultz at December 31, 20X6.

P 14-5 Pardi Corporation of Chicago acquired all the outstanding capital stock of Sari Company of London on January 1, 20X6 for $1,200,000, when the exchange rate for British pounds was

$1.60 and Sari's stockholders' equity was £800,000, consisting of £500,000 capital stock and £300,000 retained earnings. The functional currency of Sari is the U.S. dollar.

Exchange rates for British pounds for 20X6 are:

Current rate December 31, 20X5	$1.60
Current rate December 31, 20X6	1.70
Average exchange rate for 20X6	1.65
Exchange rate for dividends	1.64

Sari's cost of goods sold consists of £200,000 inventory on hand at January 1, 20X6 and purchases of £600,000, less £150,000 inventory on hand at December 31, 20X6 that was acquired at an exchange rate of $1.68.

All of Sari's plant assets were on hand when Pardi acquired Sari, and Sari's other expenses were paid in cash or relate to accounts payable.

Sari's adjusted trial balance at December 31, 20X6 in British pounds is as follows:

Debits

Cash	£ 50,000
Accounts receivable	200,000
Short-term note receivable	50,000
Inventories	150,000
Land	300,000
Buildings—net	400,000
Equipment—net	500,000
Cost of sales	650,000
Depreciation expense	200,000
Other expenses	400,000
Dividends	100,000
	£3,000,000

Credits

Accounts payable	£ 180,000
Bonds payable—10%	500,000
Bond interest payable	20,000
Capital stock	500,000
Retained earnings	300,000
Sales	1,500,000
	£3,000,000

Required: Prepare a remeasurement worksheet to restate Sari's adjusted trial balance at December 31, 20X6 into U.S. dollars.

P 14-6 Pence Corporation, based in San Francisco, purchased 90% of Sevin Company's outstanding capital stock on January 1, 20X7 for $768,000. Sevin is a British company and the exchange rate for British pounds was $1.60 when Pence acquired its interest. Sevin's stockholders' equity on January 1, 20X7 consisted of £400,000 capital stock and £100,000 retained earnings. Sevin's functional currency is the British pound, and its comparative adjusted trial balances in pounds at December 31, 20X7 and 20X8 are as follows:

SEVIN COMPANY
ADJUSTED TRIAL BALANCES
IN BRITISH POUNDS AT DECEMBER 31,

	20X7	20X8
Debits		
Cash	30,000	50,000
Accounts receivable	60,000	90,000
Inventories	80,000	150,000
Equipment	900,000	1,000,000
Cost of sales	300,000	360,000
Depreciation expense	100,000	110,000
Operating expenses	80,000	90,000
Dividends	50,000	50,000
	1,600,000	1,900,000

(Continued)

SEVIN COMPANY
ADJUSTED TRIAL BALANCES
IN BRITISH POUNDS AT DECEMBER 31,

	20X7	20X8
Credits		
Accumulated depreciation—equipment	200,000	310,000
Accounts payable	200,000	220,000
Advance from Pence	20,000	20,000
Capital stock	400,000	400,000
Retained earnings	100,000	250,000
Sales	680,000	700,000
	1,600,000	1,900,000

Cost/Book Value Differential: The cost/book value differential from the investment in Sevin is goodwill with a 10-year amortization period. The original goodwill is $48,000 [$768,000 − (£500,000 × $1.60 exchange rate × 90%)].

Advance to Pence: On January 2, 20X7, Pence made a $30,000 (£20,000) short-term advance to Sevin. The advance is noninterest bearing and is denominated in pounds.

Summary of Exchange Rates

	20X7	20X8
Current exchange rate January 1	$1.60	$1.70
Average exchange rate	1.65	1.75
Exchange rate on the date of the advance	1.60	
Exchange rate for dividends	1.68	1.78
Current exchange rate December 31	1.70	1.80

Required

1 Prepare translation worksheets for Sevin Company for the years ended December 31, 20X7 and 20X8.
2 Calculate Pence's income from Sevin for 20X7 and 20X8.
3 Determine the investment in Sevin balance at year-end 20X7 and 20X8.

P 14-7 Philip Corporation, a U.S. firm, acquired 100% of Stuart Corporation's outstanding stock at book value on January 1, 20X8 for $112,000. Stuart is a New Zealand company and its functional currency is the U.S. dollar. The exchange rate for New Zealand dollars (NZ$) was $.70 when Philip acquired its interest. Stuart's stockholders' equity on January 1, 20X8 consisted of NZ$150,000 capital stock and NZ$10,000 retained earnings. The adjusted trial balance for Stuart at December 31, 20X8 is as follows:

Debits	
Cash	NZ$ 15,000
Accounts receivable—net	60,000
Inventories	30,000
Prepaid expenses	10,000
Land	45,000
Equipment	60,000
Cost of sales	120,000
Depreciation expense	12,000
Other operating expenses	28,000
Dividends	20,000
	NZ$400,000
Credits	
Accumulated depreciation	NZ$ 22,000
Accounts payable	18,000
Capital stock	150,000
Retained earnings	10,000
Sales	200,000
	NZ$400,000

Additional Information

1 Prepaid expenses (supplies) of NZ$18,000 were on hand when Philip acquired Stuart. Other operating expenses include NZ$8,000 of these supplies that were used in 20X8, and the remaining NZ$10,000 are on hand at year-end.

2 The NZ$120,000 cost of sales consists of NZ$50,000 inventory on hand at January 1, 20X8 and NZ$100,000 purchases during the year, less NZ$30,000 ending inventory that was acquired when the exchange rate was $.66.

3 The NZ$60,000 of equipment consists of NZ$50,000 included in the business combination and NZ$10,000 purchased during 20X8, at which time the exchange rate was $.68. A depreciation rate of 20% is applicable to all equipment for 20X8.

4 Exchange rates for 20X8 are summarized as follows:

Current exchange rate January 1, 20X8	$.70
Exchange rate when new equipment was acquired	.68
Average exchange rate for 20X8	.67
Exchange rate for December 31, 20X8 inventory	.66
Exchange rate for dividends	.66
Current exchange rate December 31, 20X8	.65

Required: Prepare a worksheet to remeasure the adjusted trial balance of Stuart Corporation into U.S. dollars at December 31, 20X8.

P 14-8 Paragon Corporation, a U.S. company, acquired a 90% interest in Freeman Corporation, an Australian company, on July 1, 20X4, when the exchange rate for Australian dollars (A$) was $.70. Paragon acquired its interest in Freeman at book value equal to fair value. Freeman's functional currency is the U.S. dollar. Relevant exchange rates for Australian dollars are:

Current rate December 31, 20X8	$.80
Current rate December 31, 20X7	.75
Average rate 20X8	.78

Freeman's adjusted trial balance in Australian dollars at December 31, 20X8 included the following accounts and amounts.

Debits		
Cash	A$	50,000
Accounts receivable		85,000
Inventories (at FIFO cost)		170,000
Land		200,000
Buildings		700,000
Equipment		230,000
Cost of sales		800,000
Depreciation expense—building		50,000
Depreciation expense—equipment		30,000
Other operating expenses		320,000
Dividends		200,000
Total debits		A$2,835,000

Credits		
Allowance for bad debts	A$	5,000
Accumulated depreciation—buildings		200,000
Accumulated depreciation—equipment		80,000
Accounts payable		150,000
Advance from Paragon		300,000
Capital stock		400,000
Retained earnings		200,000
Sales		1,500,000
Total credits		A$2,835,000

Information Relevant to Selected Balance Sheet Items

1 Freeman's inventories at December 31, 20X8 are A$170,000, acquired during the last quarter of 20X8 when the exchange rate was $.79. Inventories at December 31, 20X7 were A$250,000, acquired during the last quarter of 20X7 when the exchange rate was $.74.

2 The land (A$200,000) and buildings (A$700,000) have been held since the subsidiary was acquired on July 1, 20X4.

3 The equipment on hand since July 1, 20X4 is A$170,000, less accumulated depreciation of A$70,000, for a net amount of A$100,000. The rest of the equipment was acquired on December 31, 20X7 for A$60,000 and has accumulated depreciation of A$10,000, for a book value of A$50,000.

4 There have been no changes in Freeman's capital stock since Paragon purchased its 90% interest on July 1, 20X4. Freeman's December 31, 20X7 retained earnings in the remeasured balance sheet was $144,000.

5 Other operating expenses (other than A$2,000 bad debt expense) were incurred proportionately throughout 20X8.

6 Reciprocal amounts include the following:

Dividends. Paragon credited its investment in Freeman account for $135,000 for dividends received from Freeman.

Advance. The advance is denominated in Australian dollars. It is reported by Paragon at December 31, 20X8 as an "advance to Freeman" $240,000, and it is not of a long-term nature.

Required

1 Remeasure Freeman's trial balance into U.S. dollars.

2 Prepare income and retained earnings statements and a balance sheet for Freeman in U.S. dollars

P14-9   Pilot Corporation, a U.S. firm, purchased 80% of the outstanding stock of Saussure Corporation of Switzerland on January 1, 20X1 for $2,255,000, when the exchange rate for Swiss francs was $.55. Fair values were equal to book values of Saussure's assets and liabilities on this date, and its stockholders' equity consisted of Fr 3,000,000 capital stock and Fr 2,000,000 retained earnings. Any goodwill from the purchase is to be amortized over a 10-year period.

The current exchange rate for francs at December 31, 20X1 is $.65 and the average for the year is $.60. The exchange rate on November 1, 20X1, when dividends were declared, was $.63. Saussure's functional currency is its local currency. A translation worksheet for 20X1 is as follows:

	Francs	Exchange Rate	U.S. Dollars
Cash	1,000,000	$.65	$ 650,000
Accounts receivable	1,500,000	.65	975,000
Inventories (FIFO)	1,800,000	.65	1,170,000
Land	1,000,000	.65	650,000
Building	1,800,000	.65	1,170,000
Equipment	2,000,000	.65	1,300,000
Cost of sales	3,000,000	.60	1,800,000
Depreciation—building	200,000	.60	120,000
Depreciation—equipment	200,000	.60	120,000
Expenses	1,000,000	.60	600,000
Dividends	400,000	.63	252,000
	13,900,000		$8,807,000
Accumulated depreciation—building	900,000	$.65	$ 585,000
Accumulated depreciation—equipment	1,100,000	.65	715,000
Accounts payable	900,000	.65	585,000
Bonds payable	1,000,000	.65	650,000
Capital stock	3,000,000	.55	1,650,000
Retained earnings	2,000,000		1,100,000
Sales	5,000,000	.60	3,000,000
Equity adjustment from translation			522,000
	13,900,000		$8,807,000

Required

1 Determine the balance of Pilot's investment in Saussure account at December 31, 20X1.

2 Compute the goodwill and equity adjustment from translation that will appear in the consolidated balance sheet of Pilot Corporation and Subsidiary at December 31, 20X1.

P 14-10   Pic Corporation of the United States purchased 80% of the outstanding capital stock of Sol Company, a foreign company, for $75,000 on January 1, 20X1. At that time, Sol's stockholders' equity consisted of capital stock of LCU 500,000 and retained earnings of LCU 100,000. The exchange rate for LCU on January 1, 20X1 is $.15. Any cost-book value differential from the investment in Sol is goodwill with a 10-year amortization period. Pic's management determines that Sol's functional currency is the LCU.

Relevant exchange rates for the LCU are summarized as follows:

	20X1	20X2
Current exchange rate January 1	$.15	$.16
Average exchange for the year	.155	.165
Exchange rate for dividends	.158	.168
Current exchange rate December 31	.16	.17

Sol's translated adjusted trial balances for 20X1 and 20X2 are as follows:

	LCU	Rate	US$	LCU	Rate	US$
Debits:						
Cash	40,000	$.16	$ 6,400	60,000	$.17	$ 10,200
Accounts receivable	70,000	.16	11,200	100,000	.17	17,000
Inventories	60,000	.16	9,600	130,000	.17	22,100
Equipment	300,000	.16	48,000	400,000	.17	68,000
Building	600,000	.16	96,000	600,000	.17	102,000
Cost of sales	250,000	.155	38,750	310,000	.165	51,150
Depreciation expenses	100,000	.155	15,500	110,000	.165	18,150
Operating expenses	130,000	.155	20,150	140,000	.165	23,100
Dividends	50,000	.158	7,900	50,000	.168	8,400
	1,600,000		$253,500	1,900,000		$320,100
Credits:						
Accumulated depreciation— equipment	150,000	.16	$ 24,000	230,000	$.17	$ 39,100
Accumulated depreciation— building	50,000	.16	8,000	80,000	.17	13,600
Accounts payable	120,000	.16	19,200	140,000	.17	23,800
Capital stock	500,000	.15	75,000	500,000	.15	75,000
Retained earnings	100,000	.15	15,000	250,000		38,100
Sales	680,000	.155	105,400	700,000	.165	115,500
Equity adjustment			6,900			15,000
	1,600,000		$253,500	1,900,000		$320,100

Required: Determine the following:

1 Goodwill from the investment in Sol that will appear on the December 31, 20X1 and 20X2 consolidated balance sheets for Pic Corporation and Subsidiary.

2 The equity adjustment from translation that will appear on the December 31, 20X1 and 20X2 consolidated balance sheets for Pic Corporation and Subsidiary.

3 Minority interest that will appear on the December 31, 20X1 and 20X2 consolidated balance sheets for Pic Corporation and Subsidiary.

P 14-11   Pella Corporation, a U.S. firm, paid $308,000 for all the common stock of Sapir Company of Israel on January 1, 20X5, when the exchange rate for shekels was $.35. Sapir's equity on this date consisted of 500,000 shekels common stock and 300,000 shekels retained earnings. The $28,000 (80,000 shekels) excess is goodwill with a 10-year amortization period. Sapir's functional currency is the shekel.

Sapir's adjusted trial balance at December 31, 20X5 in shekels is as follows:

	Shekels		Shekels
Debits		*Credits*	
Cash	40,000	Accounts payable	120,000
Receivables—net	50,000	Other liabilities	60,000
Inventories	150,000	Advance from Pella	140,000
Land	160,000	Common stock	500,000
Equipment—net	300,000	Retained earnings 1/1	300,000
Buildings—net	500,000	Sales	600,000
Expenses	400,000		
Exchange loss (advance)	20,000		
Dividends	100,000		
	1,720,000		1,720,000

On January 2, 20X5, Pella advanced $42,000 (120,000 shekels) to Sapir. This advance was short-term, denominated in U.S. dollars, and made when the exchange rate for shekels was $.35. In June 20X5, Sapir paid a 100,000 shekel dividend when the exchange rate was $.33. The average and year-end exchange rates for shekels are $.32 and $.30, respectively.

Required

1 Prepare a worksheet to translate Sapir's adjusted trial balance at December 31, 20X5 into U.S. dollars.
2 Prepare the necessary journal entries for Pella to account for its investment in Sapir Company for 20X5.

P 14-12 PWA Corporation paid $1,710,000 for 100% of the stock of SAA Corporation, a French firm, on January 1, 20X5, when the stockholders' equity of SAA consisted of FFr 5,000,000 capital stock and FFr 3,000,000 retained earnings. SAA's functional currency is the French franc, and any cost/book value differential is goodwill with a 10-year amortization period.

On July 1, 20X5, PWA advanced $333,000 (FFr 1,800,000) to SAA when the exchange rate was $0.185. The advance is short-term and denominated in U.S. dollars.

Relevant exchange rates for francs for 20X5 are:

Rate at acquisition on January 1	$.190
Rate applicable to the advance on July 1	.185
Rate applicable to dividends on September 1	.185
Average rate for the year	.185
Current rate at December 31	.180

A translation worksheet for SAA's adjusted trial balance at December 31, 20X5 is as follows:

	French Francs	Exchange Rate	U.S. Dollars
Debits			
Cash	550,000	$.180 C	$ 99,000
Accounts receivable—net	500,000	.180 C	90,000
Inventories	1,500,000	.180 C	270,000
Land	1,600,000	.180 C	288,000
Equipment—net	3,000,000	.180 C	540,000
Buildings—net	5,000,000	.180 C	900,000
Expenses	4,000,000	.185 A	740,000
Exchange loss (advance)	50,000	.185 A	9,250
Dividends	1,000,000	.185 R	185,000
Equity adjustment from translation			84,750
	17,200,000		$3,206,000
Credits			
Accounts payable	750,000	.180 C	$ 135,000
Other liabilities	600,000	.180 C	108,000
Advance from PWA (short-term)	1,850,000	.180 C	333,000
Capital stock	5,000,000	.190 H	950,000
Retained earnings January 1	3,000,000	.190 H	570,000
Sales	6,000,000	.185 A	1,110,000
	17,200,000		$3,206,000

Financial statements for PWA and SAA at and for the year ended December 31, 20X5 are summarized as follows:

	PWA	SAA
Combined Income and Retained Earnings Statement for the Year Ended December 31, 20X5		
Sales	$ 569,500	$1,110,000
Income from SAA	342,250	—
Expenses	(400,000)	(740,000)
Exchange loss	—	(9,250)
Net income	511,750	360,750
		(Continued)

	PWA	SAA
Add: Beginning retained earnings	856,500	570,000
Less: Dividends	(300,000)	(185,000)
Retained earnings December 31	$1,068,250	$ 745,750

Balance Sheet at December 31, 20X5

	PWA	SAA
Cash	$ 90,720	$ 99,000
Accounts receivable—net	128,500	90,000
Advance to SAA	333,000	—
Inventories	120,000	270,000
Land	100,000	288,000
Equipment—net	600,000	540,000
Buildings—net	300,000	900,000
Investment in SAA	1,773,000	—
	$3,445,220	$2,187,000
Accounts payable	$ 162,720	$ 135,000
Advance from PWA	—	333,000
Other liabilities	308,500	108,000
Common stock	2,000,000	950,000
Retained earnings	1,068,250	745,750
Equity adjustment from translation	(94,250)	(84,750)
	$3,445,220	$2,187,000

Required

1 Prepare journal entries on PWA's books to account for its investment in SAA for 20X5.
2 Prepare consolidation working papers for PWA Corporation and Subsidiary for the year ended December 31, 20X5.

P 14-13 San Corporation is a 90%-owned foreign subsidiary of Par Corporation, acquired by Par on January 1, 20X8 at book value equal to fair value, when the exchange rates for LCUs of San's home country was $.24. San's functional currency is the LCU. Par made a LCU 200,000 loan to San on May 1, 20X8, when the exchange rate for LCU was $.23. The loan is short-term and denominated at $46,000. Adjusted trial balances of the affiliated companies at year-end 20X8 are as follows:

	Par in U.S. Dollars	San in LCU
Debits		
Cash	$ 47,000	150,000
Accounts receivable	90,000	180,000
Short-term loan to San	46,000	—
Inventories	110,000	230,000
Land	150,000	250,000
Buildings	300,000	600,000
Equipment	220,000	800,000
Investment in San (90%)	207,000	—
Cost of sales	400,000	200,000
Depreciation expense	81,000	100,000
Other expenses	200,000	120,000
Exchange loss	—	30,000
Dividends	100,000	100,000
Equity adjustment	39,600	—
	$1,990,600	2,760,000
Credits		
Accumulated depreciation—buildings	$ 120,000	300,000
Accumulated depreciation—equipment	60,000	400,000
Accounts payable	241,100	130,000
Short-term loan from Par	—	230,000
Capital stock	500,000	800,000
Retained earnings January 1	220,000	200,000
Sales	800,000	700,000
Income from San	49,500	—
	$1,990,600	2,760,000

San paid dividends in September when the exchange rate was $.21. The exchange rate for LCU was $.20 at December 31, 20X8, and the average exchange rate for 20X8 was $.22.

Required

1 Prepare a worksheet to translate San's adjusted trial balance into U.S. dollars at December 31, 20X8.
2 Prepare the necessary journal entries for Par to account for its investment in San for 20X8 under the equity method.
3 Prepare consolidation working papers for Par Corporation and Subsidiary for the year ended December 31, 20X8.

P 14-14   McAfee Corporation, a U.S. firm, operates a branch in a foreign country. The trial balance of the branch in the local currency units (LCU) of the country in which it is located is as follows:

BRANCH FACTORY
TRIAL BALANCE—DECEMBER 31, 20X6

	LCUs
Debits	
Cash	50,000
Accounts receivable	500,000
Operating supplies	800,000
Equipment	6,000,000
Operating expenses	5,000,000
Depreciation expense	600,000
	12,950,000
Credits	
Accumulated depreciation	1,100,000
Accounts payable	50,000
Home office	3,800,000
Sales revenue	8,000,000
	12,950,000

Additional Information

1 The branch purchased equipment for 5,000,000 LCU when it was formed on January 1, 20X5, and additional equipment on January 1, 20X6 for 1,000,000 LCU. Equipment is depreciated on a straight-line basis over 10 years with no salvage value.
2 Operating supplies are purchased proportionately throughout the year.
3 Sales and operating expenses are incurred evenly throughout the year.
4 Exchange rates in U.S. dollars on selected dates are as follows:

January 1, 20X5	$.105
Average 20X5	$.100
January 1, 20X6	$.095
Average 20X6	$.087
December 31, 20X6	$.085

5 The branch account on the home office books is correctly recorded at $375,000 U.S. on December 31, 20X6.

Required

1 Prepare working papers to remeasure the trial balance of MacAfee's foreign branch into U.S. dollars assuming a U.S. dollar functional currency.
2 Prepare working papers to translate the trial balance of MacAfee's foreign branch into U.S. dollars assuming the LCU is its functional currency.

P 14-15   **Appendix**

Perry Corporation, based in New York, acquired 75% of the outstanding shares of Smithe Corporation, a foreign company, on January 1, 20X7 for $1,421,000, when the exchange rate for local currency units of Smithe's home country was $1.40. At that date, Smithe's stockholders' equity was 1,300,000 LCU, consisting of 1,000,000 LCU capital stock and 300,000 LCU retained earnings. Any cost/book value differential from the investment in Smithe is assigned to goodwill with a 10-year amortization period. The functional currency of Smithe is its local currency unit. On January 2, 20X7, Smithe made a 40,000 LCU long-term noninterest-bearing advance to Perry, when the exchange rate was still $1.40. The advance is denominated in LCU. The adjusted trial balances of Smithe in LCU at December 31, 20X7 and 20X8 are as follows:

SMITHE COMPANY ADJUSTED TRIAL BALANCES AT DECEMBER 31

	20X7 in LCU	Exchange Rate	20X7 in Dollars	20X8 in LCU	Exchange Rate	20X8 in Dollars
Debits						
Cash	70,000	$1.45	101,500	80,000	$1.50	120,000
Accounts receivable	60,000	1.45	87,000	180,000	1.50	270,000
Inventories	150,000	1.45	217,500	200,000	1.50	300,000
Advance to Perry	40,000	1.45	58,000	40,000	1.50	60,000
Equipment	1,500,000	1.45	2,175,000	1,500,000	1.50	2,250,000
Cost of sales	600,000	1.43	858,000	700,000	1.48	1,036,000
Depreciation expense	150,000	1.43	214,500	150,000	1.48	222,000
Operating expenses	180,000	1.43	257,400	200,000	1.48	296,000
Dividends	50,000	1.42	71,000	50,000	1.47	73,500
	2,800,000		4,039,900	3,100,000		4,627,500
Credits						
Accumulated depreciation	300,000	1.45	435,000	450,000	1.50	675,000
Accounts payable	200,000	1.45	290,000	130,000	1.50	195,000
Capital stock	1,000,000	1.40	1,400,000	1,000,000	1.40	1,400,000
Retained earnings	300,000	1.40	420,000	320,000		449,100
Sales	1,000,000	1.43	1,430,000	1,200,000	1.48	1,776,000
Equity adjustment	—		64,900	—		132,400
	2,800,000		4,039,900	3,100,000		4,627,500

Relevant exchange rates for local currency units for 20X7 and 20X8 are summarized as follows:

	20X7	20X8
Current exchange rate January 1	$1.40	$1.45
Average exchange rate for year	1.43	1.48
Spot rate for dividends	1.42	1.47
Current exchange rate December 31	1.45	1.50

Financial statements for Perry Corporation for the two years ended December 31, 20X7 and 20X8 are summarized as follows:

PERRY CORPORATION

	20X7	20X8
Combined Income and Retained Earnings Statement for the Year Ended December 31		
Sales	$2,000,000	$2,100,000
Income from Smithe	69,355	160,580
Cost of sales	(900,000)	(900,000)
Depreciation expense	(200,000)	(250,000)
Operating expenses	(669,355)	(710,580)
Net income	300,000	400,000
Add: Retained earnings January 1	450,000	500,000
Deduct: Dividends	(250,000)	(250,000)
Retained earnings December 31	$ 500,000	$ 650,000
Balance Sheet at December 31		
Cash	$ 112,300	$ 59,500
Accounts receivable	150,000	195,000
Inventories	250,000	200,000
Equipment—net	2,000,000	2,100,000
Investment in Smithe	1,487,700	1,645,500
	$4,000,000	$4,200,000
Accounts payable	$ 393,405	$ 391,060
Advance from Smithe	58,000	60,000
Capital stock	3,000,000	3,000,000
Retained earnings	500,000	650,000
Equity adjustment	48,595	98,940
	$4,000,000	$4,200,000

Required

    1 Prepare consolidation working papers for Perry Corporation and Subsidiary for the years ended December 31, 20X7 and December 31, 20X8.

    2 Prepare a consolidated statement of cash flows for the year ended December 31, 20X8.

P 14-16 **[Appendix]**

Progress Corporation, a U.S. company based in New York, acquired 90% of the outstanding voting shares of Scheele Corporation, a foreign company, on January 1, 20X7 for $2,070,000. The functional currency of Scheele is its local currency unit. The exchange rate for LCUs at the time of the business combination was $.45. Also on January 1, 20X7, Progress made a $450,000 (1,000,000 LCU) short-term advance to Scheele. Adjusted trial balances of Progress and Scheele corporations at December 31, 20X7 and 20X8 are as follows:

ADJUSTED TRIAL BALANCES AT DECEMBER 31

	Progress Corporation		Scheele Corporation	
	20X7 in $	20X8 in $	20X7 in LCU	20X8 in LCU
Cash	406,200	183,800	100,000	600,000
Accounts receivable	1,200,000	1,400,000	400,000	1,000,000
Advance to Scheele	450,000	450,000		
Inventories	1,100,000	1,950,000	500,000	1,500,000
Investment in Scheele	2,196,000	2,426,250		
Equipment	2,500,000	3,000,000	9,000,000	9,000,000
Equity adjustment	247,800	389,950		
Cost of sales	4,300,000	4,800,000	3,000,000	3,600,000
Depreciation expense	600,000	700,000	900,000	900,000
Operating expenses	2,000,000	2,200,000	975,000	1,325,000
Exchange loss			125,000	75,000
	15,000,000	17,500,000	15,000,000	18,000,000
Accumulated depreciation	1,200,000	1,900,000	1,800,000	2,700,000
Accounts payable	1,700,000	1,500,000	1,075,000	1,100,000
Advance from Progress			1,125,000	1,200,000
Capital stock	3,000,000	3,000,000	4,000,000	4,000,000
Retained earnings	1,200,000	2,200,000	1,000,000	2,000,000
Income from Scheele	373,800	372,400		
Sales	7,526,200	8,527,600	6,000,000	7,000,000
	15,000,000	17,500,000	15,000,000	18,000,000

Additional Information

    1 The cost-book value difference is goodwill with 10-year amortization.

    2 The advance to Scheele is a noninterest-bearing loan denominated in U.S. dollars and adjusted on Scheele's books for exchange losses.

    3 Current exchange rates are $.40 at December 31, 20X7 and $.375 at December 31, 20X8. Average exchange rates are $.42 for 20X7 and $.38 for 20X8.

Required: Develop comparative consolidated financial statements for Progress Corporation and Subsidiary at and for the years ended December 31, 20X7 and 20X8. An income statement, a retained earnings statement, and a balance sheet are required for 20X7 and 20X8; and a statement of cash flows is required for 20X8.

15

Segment and Interim Financial Reporting

The purpose of this chapter is to discuss two forms of disaggregation of the information in financial reports. In the first part of the chapter, the consolidated financial data of an enterprise are disaggregated by operating segments under the provisions of *FASB Statement No. 131*, "Disclosures about Segments of an Enterprise and Related Information." The second part of the chapter covers financial reporting for a firm's operations in periods of less than one year. Guidelines for the preparation of partial-year reports are found in *APB Opinion No. 28*, "Interim Financial Reports."

Historically, the emphasis in financial reporting was on disclosure for the enterprise as a whole, with little concern for disaggregation of information reported for the business entity. With such an emphasis, it was not unusual for a small local business to disclose as much information about its operations and financial position as the largest national and multinational corporations disclosed about their financial affairs. This situation changed in the 1970s. Companies with significant operations in different industries and foreign countries now have to disclose information about those operations.

About the same time that investors and others were asking for financial information broken down by lines of business or products, they were also asking for more timely financial information. Balance sheets are prepared annually at a specific date, but income is earned throughout the reporting period. Investors want earnings data accumulated for shorter periods, such as by quarter, to show the progress of the enterprise. Some firms issued interim financial reports to shareholders, but the information provided was not consistent. The guidelines established by *APB Opinion No. 28* are applicable when publicly traded companies issue interim financial information to their security holders.

EVOLUTION OF SEGMENT REPORTING REQUIREMENTS

Segment reporting requirements can be traced to the 1964 hearings on economic concentration in American industry by the Subcommittee on Antitrust and Monopoly of the Senate Committee on the Judiciary.[1] These hearings were particularly con-

---

[1] K. Fred Skousen, "Chronicle of Events Surrounding the Segment Reporting Issue," *Journal of Accounting Research*, Vol. 8 (Autumn 1970), p. 294.

cerned with diversified companies or conglomerates. Testimony from the hearings included a recommendation that the SEC "require corporations to disclose revenues and profits for each of the operations engaged in."[2] In 1967, the Accounting Principles Board issued *Statement No. 2,* "Disclosure of Supplemental Financial Information by Diversified Companies," which encouraged, but did not require, diversified companies to disclose supplemental financial information about their industry segments.

The first financial reporting requirement for diversified companies became effective in 1969, when the SEC adopted "line-of-business" reporting requirements for its registrants. The basic SEC requirement consisted of disclosure of total sales revenue and income (or loss) before income taxes and extraordinary items for the most recent five-year period for *each line of business* with 10% or more of the enterprise's revenue or income before income taxes and extraordinary items. Applicability of the SEC rules was, of course, limited to SEC registrants and did not apply to all companies issuing financial statements under GAAP.

Reporting by diversified companies was one of the topics that appeared on the original agenda of the FASB in 1973. The FASB issued a discussion memorandum on the topic in 1974, and the SEC agreed to reconsider its line-of-business disclosure requirements when the FASB adopted a statement on segment reporting. The FASB issued *FASB Statement No. 14* in 1976. The following year, the SEC issued *Accounting Series Release (ASR) 236,* which adopted industry-segment rather than line-of-business requirements and brought the SEC requirements closer to those of *Statement No. 14.*

Statement No. 14 required business enterprises to report financial information disaggregated by industry segment and geographic area. It also required disclosures about export sales and major customers. The statement defined an industry segment as "a component of an enterprise engaged in providing a product or service or a group of related products or services primarily to unaffiliated customers . . . for profit (paragraph 10a)." Industry segments did not necessarily coincide with the division of operations within an enterprise and generating the required data was sometimes expensive and time consuming. Users of segment information complained about the lack of consistency between the segment data and the rest of the annual report.

Financial analysts found the segment information generated by *Statement 14* to be useful, but inadequate. Generally, they wanted more disaggregation of data, more information about each segment, and segment information in interim financial reports. A Research Report commissioned by the FASB and published in 1993 summarized the information needs of various users of segment data. For example, the report describes the particular segment information needs of lenders and creditors:

> Lenders and creditors seek information to help them assess the risks and prospective cash flows for an individual borrowing unit—the entity from whose cash flows the loan is expected to be repaid and by whose assets the loan may be secured. Often, the borrowing unit is an individual legal entity within a consolidated group of entities. Risks and prospects often differ from entity to entity within the group. Therefore, lenders and credit officers take the position that multicolumn *consolidating* financial statements are even more important to them than *consolidated* statements, because they are, in effect, disaggregation by borrowing unit.[3]

The FASB addressed these concerns in its reconsideration of segment disclosures, and in 1997, *Statement No. 131* superseded *Statement No. 14.* Generally, *Statement No. 131* aligns segment information reported in the financial statements with the disaggregated financial information that the enterprise generates internally for making operating decisions and evaluating segment performance.

SEGMENT REPORTING UNDER FASB STATEMENT NO. 131

FASB Statement No. 131 applies to public business enterprises, which are defined as enterprises that have issued debt or equity securities that are graded in a public market, that are required to file financial statements with the SEC, or that provide

---

[2]Ibid.

[3]Paul Pacter, *Reporting Disaggregated Information,* FASB Research Report, 1993, p. vii.

financial statements for the purpose of issuing securities in a public market. The standard requires an enterprise to report segment information on a single basis of segmentation, and that basis is determined by the way that management has organized the enterprise into units for internal decision making and performance evaluation. The standard refers to this approach as the *management approach* to segmentation. Under the management approach, segments used for external reporting are determined by the internal structure of the business. If internal reporting divisions are geographically based, segment reporting should be geographically based; if internal reporting is product-line or industry based, segment reporting should be similarly based. Only one set of segment reports is created. *Statement No. 131* (paragraph 4) concludes: "consequently, the segments are evident from the structure of the enterprise's internal organization, and financial statement preparers should be able to provide the required information in a cost-effective and timely manner."

Identification of Segment Reporting Responsibilities

All public enterprises are subject to the segment reporting provisions of *Statement No. 131*. However, the reporting responsibilities for an individual enterprise are determined by its operations in different industries and geographic areas and by its sales to major customers, in other words, by the extent of its diversification. *Statement No. 131* requires information be provided based on a single segmentation mechanism.

Segments determined by the management approach are called **operating segments**. *Statement 131* (paragraph 10) characterizes an operating segment as a component of an enterprise (1) that engages in business activities from which it may earn revenues and incur expenses, including intersegment revenues and expenses; (2) whose operating results are regularly reviewed by the enterprise's chief operating decision maker; and (3) for which discrete financial information is available. Some parts of an enterprise are not included in operating segments. Pension and other postretirement benefit plans are not operating segments. Likewise, corporate headquarters or functional departments that do not earn revenues are not operating segments.

Aggregation Criteria Similar operating segments may be combined if aggregation is consistent with the objectives of *Statement No. 131*, and the segments have similar economic characteristics. The segments also must be similar in each of the following areas: (a) the nature of the products and services, (b) the nature of the production processes, (c) the type or class of customer for their products and services, (d) the distribution method for products and services, and (e) if applicable, the nature of the regulatory environment (public utilities, for example).

Quantitative Thresholds Operating segments are reportable if they meet materiality thresholds. A segment is considered material, and therefore separately reportable, if one of the following three criteria is met.

1 Its reported revenue, including intersegment revenues, is 10% or more of the combined revenue of all operating segments.
2 The absolute value of its reported profit or loss is 10% or more of the greater of (a) the combined reported profit of all operating segments that reported a profit or (b) the absolute value of the combined reported loss of all operating segments that reported a loss.
3 Its assets are 10% or more of the combined assets of all operating segments.

Once reportable segments are identified, all other operating segments are combined with other business activities in an "all other" category for reporting purposes.

Reconsideration of Reportable Segments Reported segments must include 75% of all external revenue. If reportable segments do not meet this criteria, additional segments must be identified as reportable, even if they do not meet the quantitative thresholds. Two or more of the smaller segments that were not reportable on their own may be aggregated to form a reportable operating segment *only if* they meet a majority of the aggregation criteria.

Statement No. 131 does not specify the number of segments to be reported. However, too many segments would be considered overly detailed and, therefore, counter-productive. Although no firm limit was established, the FASB encourages enterprises who identify more than 10 reportable segments to consider additional aggregation.

Illustration of the 10 Percent Tests for Reportable Operating Segments

Phil-Brown Corporation has four operating segments determined on an industry basis. Phil-Brown selects which of its operating segments are reportable segments by applying the three materiality tests.

Revenue Test   The 10% revenue test is applied by computing the amount of each operating segment's revenue (revenue to external customers plus intersegment revenue) and by comparing that amount with 10% of the combined revenue (both internal and external) of all operating segments. This test is illustrated for the Phil-Brown Corporation as follows:

	Operating Segments Revenue	Intersegment Revenue		Test Value (10% × $670,000)	Reportable Segment Under Revenue Test?
Food	$150,000	$ 0	≥	$67,000	Yes
Paper	170,000	200,000	≥	67,000	Yes
Copper	40,000	0	<	67,000	No
Finance	60,000	50,000	≥	67,000	Yes
Total	$420,000	$250,000			

Total revenue for all segments equals $670,000, therefore, the test value for reportable segments is $67,000. Total revenue (external plus intersegment) of each of the operating segments is compared with the test value. The Food ($150,000), Paper ($370,000), and Finance ($110,000) segments are reportable segments under the revenue test. The Copper Segment is not a reportable segment.

Asset Test   The 10% asset test involves comparing the total amount of each operating segment's assets with 10% of the combined assets of all operating segments. The assets of a segment are those assets included in the measure of the segment's assets that are reviewed by the chief operating decision maker. Thus, general corporate assets may be included or excluded in the asset measurement, depending on the way management has organized the segments for making operating decisions.

Assume that all assets of Phil-Brown Corporation are assigned to operating segments other than those maintained for general corporate purposes.

	Operating Segments Identifiable Assets		Test Value (10% × $1,010,000)	Reportable Segment Under Asset Test?
Food	$200,000	≥	$101,000	Yes
Paper	250,000	≥	101,000	Yes
Copper	60,000	<	101,000	No
Finance	500,000	≥	101,000	Yes
Total	$1,010,000			

Food, Paper, and Finance segments all meet the 10% asset test for reportable operating segments.

Operating Profit Test   A segment's amount of operating profit or loss depends on the items of revenue and expense that management includes in the measurement reviewed by the chief operating decision maker. In applying the operating profit test to the identification of reportable segments, the absolute amount of each segment's operating profit or loss is compared with 10% of the greater of the combined operating profits of all profitable operating segments or the combined operating losses of all unprofitable operating segments. The test is illustrated as follows:

	Operating Segments Operating Profit	Operating Segments Operating Loss		Test Value (10% × $130,000)	Reportable Segment Under Operating Profit Test?
Food	$ 25,000		≥	$13,000	Yes
Paper	55,000		≥	13,000	Yes
Copper		$(10,000)	<	13,000	No
Finance	50,000		≥	13,000	Yes
Total	$130,000	$(10,000)			

After the $13,000 test value is determined, the test is applied to the absolute amounts of operating profit or loss for each segment. The Food, Paper, and Finance segments of Phil-Brown are reportable segments under the 10% operating profit test.

Reevaluation of Reportable The Copper Segment failed to meet any of the 10% tests for a reportable segment, so the reportable segments are Food, Paper and Finance. *Statement 131* further requires that total external revenue from the reportable operating segments constitute at least 75% of total consolidated revenue. In the Phil-Brown example, the test value is $315,000 ($420,000 × 75%). The external revenue of the Food, Paper, and Finance operating segments of $380,000 is greater than 75% of consolidated revenue, and no additional reportable segments need to be identified.

If the Copper Segment had been a reportable segment in the previous period and Phil-Brown's management considered it still to be significant, the Copper Segment would be reported separately as a reportable operating segment, even though it failed all of the 10% tests for this period.

Segment Disclosures

The disclosures required for operating segments are based on the identification of reportable segments. The basis of organization that is used to determine the operating segments (for example, products and services, geographic areas, regulatory environments, or some combination of these factors) must be disclosed, as well as any aggregation of operating segments used in arriving at these reportable segments. Each reportable segment must disclose the types of products and services from which it derives its income. Required disclosures must be made for each year for which financial statements are presented.

Profit/Loss and Asset Information A measure of *profit or loss* and *total assets* must be reported for each reportable operating segment. In addition, *Statement No. 131* (paragraph 27) requires the following information for each reportable segment "if the specified amounts are included in the measure of segment profit or loss reviewed by the chief operating decision maker":

1 Amount of revenue from external customers
2 Amount of revenue from other operating segments of the same enterprise
3 Interest revenue
4 Interest expense (If a segment's revenues are primarily interest and the chief operating decision maker relies on net interest revenue to evaluate performance, the segment may report interest revenue net of interest expense.)
5 Depreciation, depletion, and amortization expense
6 Unusual items (as described in *APB Opinion No. 31* paragraph 26)
7 Equity in the net income of investees accounted for by the equity method
8 Income tax expense or benefit
9 Extraordinary items
10 Significant noncash items other than depreciation, depletion, and amortization expense

Other disclosures about assets are required if the specified amounts are included for review by the chief operating decision maker. These include the amount of investment in equity investees, the total expenditures for additions to long-lived assets other than financial instruments and certain other items, and deferred tax assets.

Measurement   The amounts reported in segment information in the general-purpose financial statements depend on the amounts reported to the chief operating decision maker. If allocations of revenues, expenses, gains or losses are made to operating segments in determining the profit or loss measures for use by the chief operating decision maker, the allocations are also a part of the reported segment data. If assets are allocated to segments in internal reports, assets are allocated to segments for external reporting.

The enterprise must report the accounting basis of intersegment transactions (cost or market, for example). Also, any differences between the measurement of segment profit or loss and assets with the consolidated amounts that are not apparent from the required reconciliation described below must be disclosed. Changes in measurement methods from prior periods should be disclosed.

Reconciliation Requirements   In addition to the details provided on each segment, a reconciliation between the segment data and consolidated information must be provided for:

1 The total of the reportable segments' revenues and the reported consolidated revenues
2 The total reportable segments' profit or loss and consolidated income before taxes (However, if items like taxes and extraordinary items are included in segment profit or loss, segment profit or loss can be reconciled to consolidated income after these items are included.)
3 The total reportable segments' assets to consolidated assets
4 The total reportable segments' amounts for every other significant item of information disclosed, with their corresponding consolidated amount

Enterprisewide Disclosures

Enterprises must report limited information about products and services, geographic areas of operation, and major customers, regardless of the operating segmentation used. This additional information is only required if it is not provided as part of the reportable operating segment information.

Products and Services   Revenues from each product or service or group of similar products or services should be disclosed, or the fact that it is impractical to provide this information should be disclosed.

Geographic Information   Geographic information, if practicable, should include revenues from external customers attributed to the enterprise's home country and revenues attributed to all foreign countries in total. If revenue from one country is material (generally considered 10%), it should be disclosed separately. Similarly, long-lived assets must be disclosed by country of domicile and all other foreign countries in total, plus a separate reporting of any individual country where the assets are material.

Major Customers   Disclosure of the existence of major customers is also required. The fact that a single customer accounts for 10% or more of the enterprise's revenue must be disclosed, as well as the amount of revenue from each such customer and the segments reporting the revenue. Disclosure of the identity of the customer is not required. In calculating the 10% rule, a group of entities under common control count as a single customer. However, federal, state, and local governments count as different entities.

Exhibit 15–1 illustrates segment disclosures for Arc Corporation for one year. The disclosures are required for each year for which a complete set of financial statements is presented.

Segment Disclosures for Interim Reports

Statement No. 131 requires limited segment information to be included in interim reports. These requirements are covered in the next section of this chapter.

ARC CORPORATION SEGMENT DATA

	Fertilizer	Chemical	Finance	All Other*	Totals
Revenue from external customers	$130,000	$150,000	$ 9,000	$20,000*	$309,000
Intersegment revenue**	—	120,000	10,000	—	130,000
Interest revenue	1,000	8,200	—	300	9,500
Interest expense	900	6,800	—	800	8,500
Net interest revenue	—	—	1,200	—	1,200
Depreciation and amortization	15,000	18,000	9,000	3,000	45,000
Segment profit or (loss)	(9,000)	15,000	1,000	600	7,600
Income from equity investees	—	2,000	—	—	2,000
Segments assets	60,000	80,000	120,000	20,000	280,000
Expenditures for segment assets	7,000	6,000	2,500	1,000	16,500

*The "All Other" category includes the aerospace unit, whose principle product is propulsion engines, and an engineered-materials unit, whose principal product is fibers.

**All intersegment sales are made at market.

Reconciling Disclosures:

Revenue from reportable segments	$419,000
Other revenues	20,000
Less: Intersegment revenue	(130,000)
Consolidated revenue	$309,000
Total profit or loss from reportable segments	$ 7,000
Other profit or loss	600
	7,600
Less: Intersegment profits	(3,000)
Less: Unallocated amounts for corporate expenses	(1,200)
Income before income taxes and extraordinary items	$ 3,400
Total assets for reportable segments	$260,000
Other assets	20,000
Goodwill not allocated to segments	13,000
Other unallocated amounts	2,900
Consolidated assets	$295,900

Geographic Information:

	Revenues	Long-lived Assets
United States	$240,000	$85,000
Canada	60,000	9,000
Other foreign countries	9,000	—
	$309,000	$94,000

***Exhibit 15–1** Segment Disclosures*

INTERIM FINANCIAL REPORTING

Interim financial reports provide information about a firm's operations for less than a full year. They are commonly issued on a quarterly basis and typically include cumulative, year-to-date information, as well as comparative information for corresponding periods of the prior year. Before 1973, there was little uniformity in the content of interim financial reports issued to shareholders. This situation and the increasing importance of quarterly reports to investors subsequently led to the issuance of *APB Opinion No. 28*, "Interim Financial Reporting," in May 1973.

The guidelines for interim reporting are particularly applicable to publicly traded companies that are required to prepare quarterly reports pursuant to SEC and New York Stock Exchange requirements. Even so, the guidelines of *Opinion No. 28* are applicable whenever publicly traded companies issue interim financial information to their security holders (*APB Opinion No. 28*, paragraph 7).

Nature of Interim Reports

Conceptually, **interim financial reports** provide more timely, but less complete, information than annual financial reports. Interim reports reflect a trade-off between timeliness and reliability because estimates must replace many of the extensive reviews of receivables, payables, inventory, and the related income effects that support the measurements presented in annual financial reports, which have to meet audit requirements. The minimum-disclosure requirements of *Opinion No. 28* do not constitute fair presentations of financial position and results of operations in conformity with GAAP. Therefore, interim financial statements are usually labeled *unaudited*.

Under *APB Opinion No. 28*, each interim period is considered an integral part of each annual period, rather than a basic accounting period unto itself. Generally, interim-period results should be based on the accounting principles and practices used in the latest annual financial statements. Some modifications may be needed, however, to relate the interim-period to annual-period results in a meaningful manner. For example, interim statements may modify the procedures used in annual statements for product costs and other expenses.

Product Costs

Gross Profit Method   Firms using the gross profit method for pricing interim inventories must disclose the method and a reconciliation with the annual inventory amounts.

LIFO Inventories   If LIFO inventories are liquidated at an interim date but are expected to be replaced by year-end, cost of sales should include the cost of replacing the LIFO base, instead of giving effect to the interim liquidation. For example, a firm that experiences a liquidation of 100 units of a LIFO inventory during the first quarter of a year would charge cost of sales for the current cost of the 100 units, rather than the historical LIFO cost, if the 100 units are expected to be replaced by year-end. The amount of current cost in excess of the historical cost may be shown as a current liability on an interim balance sheet.

In case of a change to the LIFO inventory method, the cumulative effect of the change at the beginning of the period cannot be computed. If the change is made in the first period, that fact, but not the pro forma amounts, is disclosed. If the change is made in other than the first interim period, the change will be disclosed together with the financial information of prechange interim periods.[4]

Inventory Market Declines   Inventory market declines are not deferred beyond the interim period unless they are considered temporary such that no loss is expected for the fiscal year as a whole.

Standard Cost System   Planned variances under a standard cost system that are expected to be absorbed by year-end should usually be deferred at the interim date.

Expenses Other Than Product Costs

Annual Expenses in Interim Reports   Amounts charged to expense for annual purposes should be allocated to the interim periods that are expected to be benefited. The allocation procedures should be consistent with those used for annual reports. Major annual repairs are an example of this kind of allocation. Expenses arising in an interim period are not deferred unless they would be deferred at year-end. For exam-

---

[4]*FASB Statement No. 3*, "Reporting Accounting Changes in Interim Financial Statements," paragraphs 9–13.

ple, property taxes accrued or deferred for annual purposes are also accrued or deferred for interim periods.

Advertising Costs   Advertising costs are not deferred beyond an interim period unless the benefits clearly apply to subsequent interim periods.

Income Taxes   Income taxes for interim reporting are divided into (1) those applicable to income from continuing operations before income taxes, excluding unusual or infrequently occurring items, and (2) those applicable to significant, unusual, or infrequently occurring items, discontinued items, and extraordinary items.[5]

Income tax expense for an interim period is based on an estimated effective annual tax rate that is applied to taxable income from continuing operations, excluding unusual and infrequently occurring items. The year-to-date tax expense, less the tax expense recognized in earlier interim periods, is the tax expense for the current interim period. The tax effects of unusual and infrequently occurring items are calculated separately and added to the tax expense of the interim period in which these items are reported. Gains and losses on discontinued operations and extraordinary items are reported on a net-of-tax basis as in annual reports.

Computation of the Estimated Annual Effective Tax Rate

The following illustration shows how Small Corporation, a fictitious company, estimates its annual effective tax rate for the purpose of preparing quarterly financial reports. Small Corporation bases its estimate on the following assumed tax-rate schedule for corporations for the current year:

If Taxable Income Is:		The Tax Is:			
Over	But Not Over	Pay	+	Excess	Of the Amount Over
0	$ 50,000			15%	0
$ 50,000	75,000	$ 7,500	+	25	$ 50,000
75,000	100,000	13,750	+	34	75,000
100,000	335,000	22,250	+	39*	100,000
335,000	—			34	0

*A 5% additional tax rate applies to phase out the benefits of the graduated rates between $100,000 and $335,000 of taxable income.

Small Corporation estimates quarterly income for the calendar year 20X2 as follows:

Quarter	Estimated Income		Rate	Estimated Tax
1st	$ 20,000	×	15%	$ 3,000
2nd	30,000	×	15	4,500
3rd	25,000	×	25	6,250
4th	25,000	×	34	8,500
Totals	$100,000			$22,250

The estimated quarterly income and income tax estimates assume that Small anticipates no accounting changes, discontinued operations, or extraordinary items for the year. Thus, the estimated annual effective tax rate is 22.25%, equal to the estimated tax divided by the estimated income ($22,250 ÷ $100,000 = 22.25%). Income tax for the first quarter is $20,000 × 22.25%, or $4,450. This computation reflects the *integral theory such that each interim period is an essential part of an annual period, and not the discrete theory that each interim period is a basic, independent accounting period.* The integral theory is required by *APB Opinion No. 28.* If no

---

[5]See *FASB Interpretation No. 18,* "An Interpretation of *APB Opinion No. 28*," 1977.

changes in the estimates occur during the year, the income by quarter would be calculated as follows:

	First Quarter	Second Quarter	Third Quarter	Fourth Quarter	Fiscal
Income year-to-date	$20,000	$50,000	$75,000	$100,000	$100,000
Quarterly period income	$20,000	$30,000	$25,000	$ 25,000	$100,000
Tax expense (22.25%)	(4,450)	(6,675)	(5,563)	(5,563)	(22,250)
Net income	$15,550	$23,325	$19,438	$ 19,438	$ 77,750

Note that the estimated annual effective tax rate is applied to the year-to-date income, and prior-quarter income taxes are deducted to get the current quarterly income tax expense. For example, the third quarter tax expense is calculated as follows: $75,000 \times 22.25\% - (\$4,450 + \$6,675) = \$5,563$. This procedure provides for revision of the estimated annual effective tax rate to reflect changes in estimated income levels during the year. For example, if the $100,000 estimated income for the year had included $5,000 dividend income subject to an 80% dividend-received deduction, the annual effective tax rate would have been 20.89%. The calculation entails a $1,360 deduction for the tax savings on the dividends-received deduction: ($5,000 \times 80\% \times 34\%$ tax rate) = $1,360. The estimated annual effective tax rate would have been calculated: ($22,250 - $1,360) ÷ $100,000 = 20.89%.

GUIDELINES FOR PREPARING INTERIM STATEMENTS

The APB summarized the financial information to be disclosed in interim reports in *APB Opinion No. 28* guidelines. At a minimum, publicly traded companies should report:

1. **a** Sales or gross revenues
   b Provision for income taxes
   c Extraordinary items net of income taxes
   d Cumulative effect-type changes in accounting principles
   e Net income
2. Basic and diluted earnings per share
3. Seasonal revenue, costs, or expenses
4. Significant changes in estimates of income tax expense
5. Disposal of a segment of a business, extraordinary items, and unusual or infrequently occurring items
6. Contingent items
7. Changes in accounting principles and estimates
8. Significant changes in financial position

In addition, when interim data are reported on a regular basis, information should also be reported for the current year-to-date, or the last 12 months to date, with comparable information for the preceding year (*APB Opinion No. 18*, paragraph 30). If fourth-quarter reports are not issued, material disposals of business segments, extraordinary items, unusual and infrequently occurring items, and accounting changes for the quarter should be disclosed in notes to the annual report.[6]

Exhibit 15–2 shows a quarterly report for Sample Corporation and Subsidiaries for the three months ended September 30, 20X5. In addition to the 20X5 quarterly data, the Sample report gives the quarterly data for the previous year and year-to-date information for 20X4 and 20X5.

Segment Disclosures in Interim Reports *Statement No. 131* (paragraph 33) provides specific guidelines on what segment disclosures are to be included in interim reports. The interim reports must include the following information about each reportable segment: (1) revenue from external customers, (2) intersegment revenues, (3) a measure of segment profit or loss, (4) total assets for which there has been a material

---

[6]*FASB Statement No. 3*, paragraph 14.

SAMPLE CORPORATION AND SUBSIDIARIES
CONDENSED CONSOLIDATED STATEMENTS
OF INCOME (UNAUDITED)
DATA IN THOUSANDS EXCEPT PER SHARE AMOUNTS

	Three Months Ended September 30,		Nine Months Ended September 30,	
	20X5	20X4	20X5	20X4
Revenues	$2,469	$2,165	$6,725	$6,025
Cost and Expenses				
Cost of sales	1,624	1,409	4,412	3,936
Other operating expenses	691	613	1,969	1,763
Interest expense	26	29	76	77
	2,341	2,051	6,457	5,776
Income from continuing operations before income taxes	128	114	268	249
Income taxes	48	44	100	95
Income from continuing operations	80	70	168	154
Loss on discontinued operations*				34
Net income	$ 80	$ 70	$ 168	$ 120
Earnings per Common Share				
Continuing operations	$ 1.24	$ 1.08	$ 2.60	$ 2.38
Discontinued operations				(0.53)
Net earnings per common share	$ 1.24	$ 1.08	$ 2.60	$ 1.85
Cash Dividends per Common Share	$ 0.52	$ 0.50	$ 1.56	$ 1.50

*Earnings were negatively affected in the first six months of 20X4 by discontinued furniture operations.

Exhibit 15–2 *Quarterly Report*

change since the amount disclosed in the last annual report, (5) a description of any differences in the basis of segmentation or measurement of segment profit or loss since the last annual report, and (6) a reconciliation between segment and total profits, just as in the annual report.

In addition to a brief description of the products produced by each segment, Kimberly-Clark reported the following disclosure in its March 1998 quarterly financial statement footnote 7:

The following schedule presents information concerning consolidated operations by business segment for the three months ended March 31:

(Millions of Dollars)	1998[a]	1997
Net Sales:		
Personal Care Products	$1,331.4	$1,262.7
Tissue-Based Products	1,565.5	1,765.0
Newsprint, Paper and Other	165.1	224.5
Intersegment sales	(13.4)	(14.6)
Consolidated	$3,048.6	$3,237.6
Operating Profit:		
Personal Care Products	$ 212.9	$ 250.8
Tissue-Based Products	205.0	253.8
Newsprint, Paper and Other	37.1	40.8
Unallocated items—net	(10.7)	(1.1)
Consolidated	$ 444.3	$ 544.3

[a]Operating profit for the quarter for Personal Care Products and Tissue-Based Products includes $4.9 million and $9.3 million, respectively, of the charge related to the Announced Plan described in Note 2.

SEC Interim Financial Disclosures

The SEC requires that quarterly reports be prepared for the company's stockholders and for filing with the SEC. These reports are to be prepared in accordance with GAAP and are filed on Form 10-Q within 45 days from the end of a quarter. Fourth-quarter reports are not required, but SEC Rule 14a-3 requires inclusion of selected quarterly data in the annual report to shareholders. The quarterly reports are not audited, so the CPA's report states that a *review*, rather than an audit, has been made.

A company's Form 10-Q report to the SEC includes information in excess of the minimum reporting requirements under *APB Opinion No. 28*, as amended by *FASB Statement No. 3, FASB Statement No. 131*, and *FASB Interpretation No. 18*. In fact, financial information requirements for quarterly reporting are similar to the disclosures required in annual reports to the SEC. For example, Part I of Form 10-Q contains the following summary of contents:

> Part 1—Financial Information
>   Item 1—Consolidated Balance Sheet
>   Consolidated Statement of Income
>   Consolidated Statement of Cash Flows
>   Notes to Consolidated Financial Statements
>   Item 2—Management's Discussion of Financial Condition and Results of Operations

Comparative consolidated balance sheets are presented as of the end of the current quarter and at the prior year-end. The comparative consolidated income statements are presented for the current quarter and the same quarter of the prior year, as well as the current year-to-date and the prior year-to-date. Comparative consolidated statements of cash flows are presented for the current year-to-date and the prior year-to-date.

The information required in Form 10-Q in excess of that required by *APB Opinion No. 28* is available from the company to its shareholders upon request. Many companies, however, include essentially all the information from Form 10-Q in their regular quarterly reports. Exhibit 15–3 illustrates this extended disclosure

---

H. J. HEINZ COMPANY AND SUBSIDIARIES
CONSOLIDATED STATEMENTS OF INCOME
(DOLLARS IN THOUSANDS EXCEPT PER SHARE AMOUNTS—UNAUDITED)

	Three Months Ended		Six Months Ended	
	January 28, 1998 FY1998	January 29, 1997 FY1997	January 28, 1998 FY1998	January 29, 1997 FY1997
Sales	$2,236,034	$2,307,538	$6,733,386	$6,910,356
Cost of products sold	1,379,218	1,459,249	4,196,835	4,418,924
Gross profit	856,816	848,289	2,536,551	2,491,432
Selling, general and administrative expenses	512,776	502,998	1,369,517	1,445,107
Operating income	344,040	345,291	1,167,034	1,046,325
Interest income	7,462	8,324	23,004	28,701
Interest expense	64,848	70,496	190,956	204,481
Other expense, net	18,041	6,436	31,829	27,117
Income before income taxes	268,613	276,683	967,253	843,428
Provision for income taxes	80,457	102,296	346,930	311,991
Net income	$ 188,156	$ 174,387	$ 620,323	$ 531,437
Net income per share—diluted	$ .50	$ .47	$ 1.66	$ 1.42
Cash dividends per share	$ .315	$ .29	$ .92	$ .845

Exhibit 15–3   *H. J. Heinz Company Quarterly Report*

H. J. HEINZ COMPANY AND SUBSIDIARIES
CONSOLIDATED BALANCE SHEETS
(DOLLARS IN THOUSANDS—UNAUDITED)

	January 28, 1998 FY1998	April 30, 1997* FY1997
Assets		
Current Assets:		
Cash and cash equivalents	$ 195,979	$ 156,986
Short-term investments, at cost which approximates market	12,435	31,451
Receivables, net	1,037,415	1,118,874
Inventories	1,446,611	1,432,511
Prepaid expenses and other current assets	207,606	273,284
Total current assets	2,900,046	3,013,106
Property, plant and equipment	4,060,852	4,380,598
Less accumulated depreciation	1,728,564	1,901,378
Total property, plant and equipment, net	2,332,288	2,479,220
Goodwill, net	1,764,200	1,803,552
Other intangibles, net	617,068	627,096
Other non-current assets	514,188	514,813
Total other noncurrent assets	2,895,456	2,945,461
Total assets	$8,127,790	$8,437,787
Liabilities and Shareholders' Equity		
Current Liabilities:		
Short-term debt	$ 402,361	$ 589,893
Portion of long-term debt due within one year	13,382	573,549
Accounts payable	791,274	865,154
Salaries and wages	74,007	64,836
Accrued marketing	185,721	164,354
Accrued restructuring costs	127,259	210,804
Other accrued liabilities	302,566	315,662
Income taxes	153,861	96,163
Total current liabilities	2,050,431	2,880,415
Long-term debt	2,925,537	2,283,993
Deferred income taxes	247,462	265,409
Non-pension postretirement benefits	208,005	211,500
Other	364,342	356,049
Total long-term debt and other liabilities	3,745,346	3,116,951
Stockholders' Equity:		
Capital stock	107,988	108,015
Additional capital	245,917	175,811
Retained earnings	4,323,938	4,041,285
Cumulative translation adjustments	(364,110)	(210,864)
	4,313,733	4,114,247
Less:		
Treasury shares, at cost	1,940,798	1,629,501
Unfunded pension obligation	25,376	26,962
Unearned compensation relating to the ESOP	15,546	17,363
Total shareholders' equity	2,332,013	2,440,421
Total liabilities and shareholders' equity	$8,127,790	$8,437,787

*Summarized from audited fiscal year 1997 balance sheet

Exhibit 15–3 H. J. Heinz Company Quarterly Report (continued)

for the H. J. Heinz Company. In addition to the statements in the quarterly report that are reprinted in the exhibit, the company's 16-page report includes notes to the consolidated financial statements, a review of the financial information, a letter to shareholders from the company's chairman, and additional corporate information.

H. J. HEINZ COMPANY AND SUBSIDIARIES
CONSOLIDATED STATEMENTS OF CASH FLOWS
(DOLLARS IN THOUSANDS—UNAUDITED)

	Six Months Ended	
	January 28, 1998 FY1998	January 29, 1997 FY1997
Cash Provided by Operating Activities	$554,715	$434,858
Cash Flows from Investing Activities:		
Capital expenditures	(258,421)	(277,681)
Acquisitions, net of cash acquired	(136,351)	(179,627)
Proceeds from sale of Ore-Ida frozen food service foods business	490,739	
Purchases of short-term investments	(857,067)	(951,912)
Sales and maturities of short-term investments	880,710	962,226
Other items, net	28,864	25,741
Cash (used for) provided by investing activities	148,474	(421,253)
Cash Flows from Financing Activities:		
Proceeds from long-term debt,	3,934	45,185
Payments on long-term debt	(563,065)	(100,049)
Proceeds from commercial paper and short-term borrowings—net	481,438	468,693
Dividends	(337,670)	(310,239)
Purchase of treasury stock	(480,306)	(208,281)
Exercise of stock options	170,598	105,589
Other items, net	77,549	27,384
Cash provided by (used for) financing activities	(647,522)	28,282
Effect of exchange rate changes on cash and cash equivalents	(16,674)	(7,068)
Net increase in cash and cash equivalents	38,993	34,819
Cash and cash equivalents at beginning of year	156,986	90,064
Cash and cash equivalents at end of period	$195,979	$124,883

Exhibit 15–3   *H. J. Heinz Company Quarterly Report (continued)*

SUMMARY

Concern about segment disclosures increased throughout the 1960s—approximately the same period as the merger-and-acquisition boom years in which huge conglomerates were formed. In 1967, the APB recommended voluntary disclosures for diversified enterprises, and in 1969, the SEC adopted line-of-business disclosure requirements. It was not until 1977, however, that public firms issuing complete sets of financial statements in accordance with GAAP became subject to segment reporting requirements. That was the year in which *FASB Statement No. 14* became effective.

Under *Statement No. 14,* business enterprises disclosed information on their operations in different industries and geographic areas. In some circumstances, disclosures were also required for export sales and major customers. These reporting requirements were independent of each other, so a firm could be required to report information in one or more areas. Many firms had reporting responsibilities in all four areas.

Statement No. 131 eased the reporting requirements of *Statement No. 14,* and in the process, made the information more usable. Whereas *Statement No. 14* required disclosures about both industry segments and geographic segments, *Statement No. 131* requires disclosures about operating segments only. The operating segments of a public business enterprise are determined by the structure of the enterprise's internal organization. This method of identifying segments is called the management approach. The determination of which operating segments are reportable is based on aggregation criteria and materiality tests.

Disclosures required for each reportable operating segment include a description of the types of products and services from which it derives revenue and a measure of profit or loss and total assets. Other disclosures on revenues, expenses, gains, losses, and assets are required if the specified amounts are included in the measure of profit or loss and segment assets that are reviewed by the chief operating decision maker. Reportable segment data must be reconciled with the enterprise's consolidated amounts. Limited segment information is disclosed in quarterly reports.

Statement No. 131 requires other disclosures on an enterprisewide basis. Information about the enterprise's products and services, geographic areas, and major customers must be disclosed, unless the information is included as part of the segment disclosures.

Security analysts and other users of segment disclosures believe that segment information is important for effective analysis of financial statements because the operations in different industries and geographic areas vary with respect to risk, profitability, opportunities for expansion, and capital requirements.

Disclosure requirements for interim financial reports are found in *APB Opinion No. 28*, as amended by *FASB Statements No. 3* and *131*, and *FASB Interpretation No. 18*. Interim financial reports provide timely information. However, much of the information is based on estimates, and the reports are unaudited.

Each interim period is considered an integral part of the annual period. Interim-period information should be based on the accounting principles used in the last annual report, however, some modifications at the interim reporting date may be necessary so the interim-period results complement the annual results of operations.

The Securities and Exchange Commission requires additional disclosures in interim reports filed on Form 10-Q. Information above the minimum requirements of *APB Opinion No. 28* that is issued to shareholders in quarterly reports varies from company to company.

SELECTED READINGS

Accounting Principles Board Opinion No. 28. "Interim Financial Reporting." New York: American Institute of Certified Public Accountants, 1973.

BACKER, MORTON, and WALTER MCFARLAND. *External Reporting for Segments of a Business*. New York: National Association of Accountants, 1968.

DEPPE, LARRY A. "Disaggregated Information: Time to Reconsider." *Journal of Accountancy* (December 1994), pp. 65–70.

FASB Interpretation No. 18. "An Interpretation of *APB Opinion No. 28*." Stamford, CT: Financial Accounting Standards Board, 1977.

Financial Accounting Series. "Invitation to Comment." *Reporting Disaggregated Information by Business Enterprises*. Norwalk, CT: Financial Accounting Standards Board, 1993.

MAUTZ, ROBERT K. *Financial Reporting by Diversified Companies*. New York: Financial Executives Research Foundation, 1968.

PACTER, PAUL. *Reporting Disaggregated Information*. Financial Accounting Series. Norwalk, CT: Financial Accounting Standards Board, 1993.

SALTER, STEPHEN B., et al. "Reporting Financial Information by Segment: A Comment of the American Accounting Association on the IASC Draft Statement of Principles." *Accounting Horizons* (March 1996), pp. 118–123.

Statement of Financial Accounting Standards No. 3. "Reporting Accounting Changes in Interim Financial Statements." Stamford, CT: Financial Accounting Standards Board, 1974.

Statement of Financial Accounting Standards No. 131. "Disclosures about Segments of an Enterprise and Related Information." Stamford, CT: Financial Accounting Standards Board, 1997.

ASSIGNMENT MATERIAL

QUESTIONS

1 What is an operating segment?

2 What is a reportable segment according to *FASB Statement No. 131*? What criteria are used in determining what operating segments are also reportable segments?

3 How are the segments that are not reportable segments handled in the required disclosures of *FASB Statement No. 131*?

4 Revenue information for Mahoney Corporation is as follows:

Consolidated revenue (from the income statement)	$400,000
Intersegment sales and transfers	80,000
Combined revenues of all industry segments	$480,000

Does the 10% revenue test for a reportable segment apply to 10% of the $400,000 or 10% of the $480,000?

5 Describe the 10% operating profit test for determining reportable segments.

6 Describe the 10% asset test for determining reportable segments.

7 Describe the 10% revenue test for determining reportable segments.

8 Assume an enterprise has 10 operating segments. Five operating segments qualify as reportable segments by passing one of the 10% tests. However, their combined revenues from sales to unaffiliated customers total only 70% of the combined unaffiliated revenues from all operating segments. Should the remaining five operating segments be aggregated and shown as an "other segments" category? Explain.

9 What disclosures are required for the reportable segments and all remaining segments in the aggregate?

10 When is an enterprise required to include information in its financial statements about its foreign and domestic operations?

11 Must a major customer be identified by name?

12 Do the requirements of *FASB Statement No. 131* apply to financial statements for interim periods? If so, how?

13 Explain how a company estimates its annual effective tax rate for interim reporting purposes.

14 What is the difference between the integral theory and the discrete theory with respect to interim financial reporting?

15 Describe the minimum financial information to be disclosed in interim reports under the provisions of *APB Opinion No. 28.*

EXERCISES

E 15-1

1 The disclosure requirements for an operating segment do *not* include:
   a Unusual items
   b Income tax expense or benefit
   c Extraordinary items
   d Cost of goods or services sold

2 A reconciliation between the numbers disclosed in operating segments and consolidated numbers need *not* be provided for:
   a Cost of goods sold
   b Profit or loss
   c Net assets
   d Revenues

3 Each reportable segment is required to disclose the following information except for:
   a Extraordinary items
   b Depreciation, depletion, and amortization
   c Capital expenditures
   d Gross profit or loss

4 An enterprise is required to disclose information about its major customers if 10% or more of its revenue is derived from any single customer. This disclosure must include:
   a The products or services generating the revenue from such sales
   b The operating segment or segments making such sales and the total revenue from the customer
   c The name of the customer to whom the sales were made
   d The dollar amounts of revenue and any profit or loss on the sales

5 Which of the following is not a criteria for aggregating two or more operating segments?
   a The segments should have similar products or services
   b The segments should have similar production processes
   c The distribution of products should be similar
   d The segments should have similar amounts of revenue

6 Required segment disclosures in interim-period statements do not include:
   a A measure of segment profit or loss
   b Net interest revenue
   c A description of a change in segmentation from the last annual report
   d Intersegment revenue

E 15-2

Visclosky Corporation operates entirely in the United States but in different industries. It segments the business based on industry. Total sales of the segments, including intersegment sales, are as follows:

Concrete and stone products	$200,000
Construction	500,000
Lumber and wood products	900,000
Building materials	500,000
Other	50,000

Further analysis reveals sales from one segment to another as follows:

Lumber and wood products	$400,000
Building materials	200,000

Required

1 Determine which segments are reportable segments under both the 10% and the 75% revenue tests.
2 Prepare a schedule suitable for disclosing revenue by industry segment for external reporting.
3 Prepare a reconciliation of segment revenue to corporate revenue.

E 15-3   Superior Corporation's internal divisions are based on industry. The revenues, operating profits, and assets of the operating segments of Superior are presented in thousands of dollars as follows:

	Sales to Nonaffiliates	Inter-segment Sales	Total Sales	Operating Profit (Loss)	Assets
Food service industry	$300,000	$40,000	$340,000	$ 40,000	$200,000
Copper mine	80,000	—	80,000	(10,000)	60,000
Information systems	20,000	15,000	35,000	5,000	40,000
Chemical industry	130,000	20,000	150,000	30,500	217,000
Agricultural products	48,000	—	48,000	(15,500)	50,000
Pharmaceutical products	20,000	—	20,000	8,000	18,000
Foreign operations	15,000	—	15,000	5,000	20,000
Corporate Assets*					33,000
	$613,000	$ 75,000	$688,000	$ 63,000	$638,000

*Corporate assets include equity investees of $10,000 and general assets of $23,000.

Required: Determine the reportable segments of Superior Corporation.

E 15-4   The sales in thousands of dollars of the segments of Worldwide Corporation (Worldwide is organized on a geographic basis) for 20X6 are as follows:

	Unaffiliated Sales	Intersegment Sales	Total
United States	$50,000	$15,000	$ 65,000
Canada	18,000	8,000	26,000
Europe	10,000	1,000	11,000
Latin America	7,000	3,000	10,000
Japan	3,000	—	3,000
Korea	1,000	—	1,000
	$89,000	$27,000	$116,000

The $89,000 sales to unaffiliated customers is the amount of revenue reported in Worldwide's consolidated income statement.

Required: Illustrate the disclosure of Worldwide's domestic and foreign revenue in a form acceptable for external reporting, including reconciliation with consolidated revenue.

E 15-5   **[AICPA adapted]**
1 Correy Corporation and its divisions are engaged solely in manufacturing operations. The following data (consistent with prior years' data) pertain to the industries in which operations were conducted for the year ended December 31, 20X7:

Industry	Total Revenue	Operating Profit	Assets at December 31, 20X7
A	$10,000,000	$1,750,000	$20,000,000
B	8,000,000	1,400,000	17,500,000
C	6,000,000	1,200,000	12,500,000
D	3,000,000	550,000	7,500,000
E	4,250,000	675,000	7,000,000
F	1,500,000	225,000	3,000,000
	$32,750,000	$5,800,000	$67,500,000

In its segment information for 20X7, how many reportable segments does Correy have?
a Three   b Four   c Five   d Six

2 Kaycee Corporation's revenues for the year ended December 31, 20X1 were as follows:

Consolidated revenue per income statement	$1,200,000
Intersegment sales	180,000
Intersegment transfers	60,000
Combined revenues of all segments	$1,440,000

Kaycee has a reportable segment if that segment's revenues exceed:
a $6,000   **c** $120,000
b $24,000   **d** $144,000

3 The following information pertains to Aria Corporation and its divisions for the year ended December 31, 20X8:

Sales to unaffiliated customers	$2,000,000
Intersegment sales of products similar to those sold to unaffiliated customers	600,000
Interest earned on loans to other industry segments	40,000

The intersegment interest is not reported by the divisions on internal reports reviewed by the chief operating officer. Aria and all of its divisions are engaged solely in manufacturing operations. Aria has a reportable segment if that segment's revenue exceeds:
a $264,000   **c** $204,000
b $260,000   **d** $200,000

4 The following information pertains to revenue earned by Timm Company's operating segments for the year ended December 31, 20X2:

Segment	Sales to Unaffiliated Customers	Intersegment Sales	Total Revenues
Alo	$ 5,000	$ 3,000	$ 8,000
Bix	8,000	4,000	12,000
Cee	4,000	—	4,000
Dil	43,000	16,000	59,000
Combined	60,000	23,000	83,000
Elimination	—	(23,000)	(23,000)
Consolidated	$60,000	—	$60,000

In conformity with the revenue test, Timm's reportable segments were:
a Only Dil
b Only Bix and Dil
c Only Alo, Bix, and Dil
d Alo, Bix, Cee, and Dil

Use the following information in answering questions 5 and 6: Grum Corporation, a publicly owned corporation, is subject to the requirements for segment reporting. In its income statement for the year ended December 31, 20X8, Grum reported revenues of $50,000,000, operating expenses of $47,000,000, and net payroll costs of $15,000,000. Grum's combined identifiable assets of all industry segments at December 31, 20X8 were $40,000,000.

5 In its 20X8 financial statements, Grum should disclose major customer data if sales to any single customer amount to at least:
a $300,000   **c** $4,000,000
b $1,500,000   **d** $5,000,000

6 In its 20X8 financial statements, if Grum is organized on an industry basis, it should disclose foreign operations data on a specific country if revenues from that country's operations are at least:
a $5,000,000   **c** $4,000,000
b $4,700,000   **d** $1,500,000

7 Selected data for a segment of a business enterprise are to be separately reported in accordance with *FASB Statement No. 131* when the revenues of the segment exceed 10% of the:
a Combined net income of all segments reporting profits
b Total revenues obtained in transactions with outsiders
c Total revenues of all the enterprise's operating segments
d Total combined revenues for all segments reporting profits

8 In financial reporting of segment data, which of the following items is used in determining a segment's operating income?

a Income tax expense

b Sales to other segments

c General corporate expense

d Gain or loss on discontinued operations

E 15-6 A summary of the segment operations of the Johnson-Miller Corporation for the year ended December 31, 20X2 follows:

	United States	Canada	Germany	Japan	Mexico	Other Foreign	Consolidated
Sales to unaffiliated customers	$ 70,000	$12,000	$ 6,000	$ 7,000	$3,000	$2,000	$100,000
Interarea transfers	20,000			$ 6,000			
Total revenue	$ 90,000	$12,000	$ 6,000	$13,000	$3,000	$2,000	$100,000
Operating profit	$ 16,000	$ 2,000	$ 3,000	$ 2,000	$1,000	$1,000	$ 25,000
Segment assets	$100,000	$15,000	$17,000	$18,000	$4,000	$3,000	$200,000

1 For which of the following geographic areas would separate disclosures be required if only the 10% revenue test is considered?

a United States, Canada, and Japan

b United States and Canada

c United States and Japan

d United States, Canada, Germany, and Japan

2 For which of the following geographic areas would separate disclosures be required if only the 10% asset test is considered?

a United States

b United States and Canada

c United States, Japan, and Germany

d United States, Canada, Germany, and Japan

3 For which of the following geographic areas would separate disclosures be required if *all* relevant tests are considered?

a United States, Canada, Germany, and Japan

b United States, Japan, and Germany

c United States, Canada, and Japan

d United States and Canada

E 15-7 **1** Interim reporting under *APB Opinion No. 28* guidelines refers to financial reporting:

a On a monthly basis

b On a quarterly basis

c On a regular basis

d For periods less than a year

2 A liquidation of LIFO inventories for interim reporting purposes may create a problem in measuring cost of sales. Accordingly, cost of sales in interim periods should:

a Be determined using the gross profit method

b Include the income effect of the LIFO liquidation

c Include the expected cost of replacing the liquidated LIFO base

d None of the above

3 Baker Company's effective annual income tax rates for the first two quarters of 20X2 are 34% and 30% for the first and second quarter, respectively. Assume that Baker's pretax income is $120,000 for the first quarter and $90,000 for the second quarter. Income tax expense for the second quarter is computed:

a $90,000 × 30%

b ($120,000 + $90,000) × 30%

c ($120,000 × 34%) + ($90,000 × 30%)

d ($210,000 × 30%) − ($120,000 × 34%)

4 Assume corporate tax rates of 15% on the first $50,000 of taxable income, 25% on taxable income between $50,000 and $75,000, 34% on taxable income between $75,000 and $100,000, and 39% on taxable income between $100,000 and $335,000. If a corporation estimates its pretax income at $20,000 for the first quarter, $25,000 for the second quarter, $30,000 for the third quarter, and $35,000 for the fourth quarter, its estimated annual effective tax rate is:

a 23.77%   **c** 24.67%

b 25%   **d** 34%

E 15-8 The estimated and actual pretax incomes of Endicott Corporation by quarter for 20X3 were as follows:

	1st Quarter	2nd Quarter	3rd Quarter	4th Quarter
Estimated pretax income	$30,000	$30,000	$40,000	$50,000
Actual pretax income	30,000	40,000	40,000	40,000

Endicott calculated its estimated annual effective income tax rate to be 27.8333%, based on estimated pretax income and existing income tax rates.

Required: Prepare a schedule to calculate Endicott Corporation's net income by quarter.

E 15-9 **[AICPA adapted]**
1 An inventory loss from a market price decline occurred in the first quarter, and the decline was not expected to reverse during the fiscal year. However, in the third quarter, the inventory's market price recovery exceeded the market decline that occurred in the first quarter. For interim financial reporting, the dollar amount of net inventory should:
   a Decrease in the first quarter by the amount of the market price decline and increase in the third quarter by the amount of the decrease in the first quarter
   b Decrease in the first quarter by the amount of the market price decline and increase in the third quarter by the amount of the market price recovery
   c Decrease in the first quarter by the amount of the market price decline and *not* be affected in the third quarter
   d Not be affected in either the first quarter or the third quarter
2 Farr Corporation had the following transactions during the quarter ended March 31, 20X2:

Loss on early extinguishment of debt	$ 70,000
Payment of fire insurance premium for calendar year 20X2	100,000

What amount should be included in Farr's income statement for the quarter ended March 31, 20X2?

	Extraordinary Loss	Insurance Expense
a	$70,000	$100,000
b	$70,000	$ 25,000
c	$17,500	$ 25,000
d	0	$100,000

3 An inventory loss from a permanent market decline of $360,000 occurred in May 20X1. Cox Company appropriately recorded this loss in May 20X1, after its March 31, 20X1 quarterly report was issued. What amount of inventory loss should be reported in Cox's quarterly income statement for the three months ended June 30, 20X1?
   a $0   c $180,000
   b $90,000   d $360,000
4 On July 1, 20X5, Dolan Corporation incurred an extraordinary loss of $300,000, net of income tax saving. Dolan's operating income for the full year ending December 31, 20X5 is expected to be $500,000. In Dolan's income statement for the quarter ended September 30, 20X5, how much of this extraordinary loss should be disclosed?
   a $300,000   c $75,000
   b $150,000   d $0
5 In January 20X3, Pine Company paid property taxes of $80,000 covering the calendar year 20X3. Also in January 20X3, Pine estimated that its year-end bonuses to executives would amount to $320,000 for 20X3. What is the total amount of expense relating to these two items that should be reflected in Pine's quarterly income statement for the three months ended June 30, 20X3?
   a $100,000   c $20,000
   b $80,000   d $0

E 15-10 Trapper Manufacturing Company records sales of $1,000,000 and cost of sales of $550,000 during the first quarter of 20X1. Trapper uses the LIFO inventory method, and its inventories are computed as follows:

Beginning LIFO inventory at January 1	10,000 units at $5	$50,000
Ending LIFO inventory at March 31	6,000 units at $5	$30,000

Before year-end, Trapper expects to replace the 4,000 units liquidated in the first quarter. The current cost of the inventory units is $8 each.

Required: At what amount will Trapper report cost of sales in its first-quarter interim report?

PROBLEMS

P 15-1 The following information has been accumulated for use in preparing segment disclosures for Ledbetter Corporation:

	Sales to Unaffiliated Customers	Sales to Affiliated Customers	Total Sales
Apparel	$164,000	—	$ 164,000
Construction	112,000	—	112,000
Furniture	208,000	$ 6,000	214,000
Lumber and wood products	175,000	90,000	265,000
Paper	90,000	—	90,000
Textiles	50,000	170,000	220,000
Tobacco	93,000	—	93,000
Total	$892,000	$266,000	$1,158,000

Required
1 Determine Ledbetter's reportable segments under the 10% revenue test.
2 Are additional reportable segments required under the 75% revenue test?
3 Prepare a schedule to disclose revenue by operating segment for external reporting. Assume that the paper and tobacco segments, both sold in grocery stores, share similar operating characteristics on four of the five aggregation criteria.

P 15-2 The following data for 20X8 relate to Hawkeye Industries, a worldwide conglomerate:

Segments	Sales to Unaffiliated Customers	Intersegment Sales	Operating Profit (Loss)	Assets
Food	$300,000	$ 50,000	$45,000	$310,000
Chemical	110,000	40,000	23,000	150,000
Textiles	65,000	5,000	(8,000)	60,000
Furniture	48,000	—	9,000	40,000
Beverage	62,000	10,000	18,000	60,000
Oil	15,000	—	(2,000)	25,000
Segment	600,000	105,000	85,000	645,000
Corporate	—	—	(7,000)	15,000
Consolidated	$600,000	0	$78,000	$660,000

Required: Answer the following questions relating to Hawkeye's required segment disclosures and show computations.
1 Which segments are reportable segments under (a) the revenue test, (b) the operating profit test, and (c) the asset test?
2 Do additional reportable segments have to be identified?

P 15-3 Daton-Paulo Corporation's home country is the United States, but it also has operations in Canada, Mexico, Brazil, and South Africa and reports internally on a geographic basis. Information relevant to Daton-Paulo's operating segment disclosure requirement for the year ended December 31, 20X2 is presented in summary form as follows:

	United States	Canada	Mexico	Brazil	South Africa	Consolidated
Sales to unaffiliated customers	$120,000	$13,000	$20,000	$22,000	$15,000	$190,000
Intersegment transfers	29,000	11,000			10,000	
Total revenue	$149,000	$24,000	$20,000	$22,000	$25,000	$190,000
Operating profit	$ 24,000	$ 6,000	$ 8,000	$ 5,000	$ 7,000	$ 50,000
Identifiable assets	$150,000	$30,000	$19,000	$20,000	$31,000	$305,000

Required
1 Prepare schedules to show which of Daton-Paulo's operating segments require separate disclosure under (a) the 10% revenue test, (b) the 10% asset test, and (c) the 10% profit test.
2 Which of Daton-Paulo's operating segments meet at least one of the tests for segment reporting?
3 Prepare a schedule to disclose Daton-Paulo's segment operations from the information given.

P 15-4 Mid-America Corporation has five major operating segments and operates in both domestic and foreign markets. Mid-America is organized internally on an industry basis. Information about its revenue from operating segments and foreign operations for 20X1 is as follows:

SALES TO UNAFFILIATED CUSTOMERS

	Domestic	Foreign	Total
Foods	$ 150,000	$ 30,000	$ 180,000
Soft drinks	650,000	250,000	900,000
Distilled spirits	500,000	50,000	550,000
Cosmetics	200,000	—	200,000
Packaging	110,000	—	110,000
Other (four minor segments)	240,000	—	240,000
	$1,850,000	$330,000	$2,180,000

SALES TO AFFILIATED CUSTOMERS

	Domestic	Foreign	Total
Foods	$ 30,000	$ —	$ 30,000
Soft drinks	160,000	—	160,000
Distilled spirits	—	20,000	20,000
Cosmetics	—	—	—
Packaging	10,000	—	10,000
Other (four minor segments)	—	—	—
	$200,000	$20,000	$220,000

A Japanese subsidiary of Mid-America operates exclusively in the soft-drink market. All other foreign operations are carried out through Canadian subsidiaries, none of which are included in the soft-drink business.

Only the soft-drink and distilled-spirits segments are reportable segments under the asset and operating profit tests for segments.

Required

1 Determine which industry segments are reportable segments under the revenue test for segment reporting. Assume no further aggregation is possible. Would the possible aggregation of smaller segments change your response?
2 Prepare a schedule suitable for disclosing Mid-America's revenue by segment for 20X1, assuming no further aggregation is possible.
3 Prepare a schedule suitable for disclosing Mid-America's revenue by geographic area for 20X1.

P 15-5 Selected information, which is reported to the chief operating officer, for the five segments of Random Choice Company for the year ended December 31, 20X1 is as follows:

	Food	Tobacco	Lumber	Textiles	Furniture	General Corporate	Consolidated
Revenue Data							
Sales to unaffiliated customers	$12,000	$10,000	$7,000	$18,000	$7,000		$54,000
Sales to affiliated customers	5,000	7,000		8,000			
Income from equity investees				3,000		$6,000	9,000
Total revenue	$17,000	$17,000	$7,000	$29,000	$7,000	$6,000	$63,000
Expense Data							
Cost of sales	$10,000	$ 9,000	$4,000	$16,000	$4,000		$23,000
Depreciation expense	1,000	2,000	2,500	3,000	500		9,000
Other operating expenses	2,000	2,000	1,000	2,000	1,000		8,000
Interest expense	2,000			2,000		$3,000	7,000
Income taxes	1,000	2,000	(250)	3,000	750	1,500	8,000
Net income	$ 1,000	$ 2,000	$ (250)	$ 3,000	$ 750	$1,500	$ 8,000

(Continued)

	Food	Tobacco	Lumber	Textiles	Furniture	General Corporate	Consolidated
Asset Data							
Segment assets	$18,000	$19,000	$6,000	$22,000	$7,000		$ 72,000
Investment in affiliates				20,000		$40,000	60,000
General corporate assets						4,000	4,000
Intersegment advances	1,000	2,000					
Total assets	$19,000	$21,000	$6,000	$42,000	$7,000	$44,000	$136,000

The lumber segment has not been a reportable segment in prior years and is not expected to be a reportable segment in future years.

Required

1 Prepare schedules to show which of the segments are reportable segments under:
  a The 10% revenue test
  b The 10% operating profit test
  c The 10% asset test
2 Which of the segments meet at least one of the tests for reportable segments?
3 Must additional reportable segments be identified?
4 Prepare a schedule for appropriate disclosure of the above segmented data in the financial report of Random Choice Company for the year ended December 31, 20X1.

P 15-6 The consolidated income statement of Truetest Company for 20X2 appears as follows:

TRUETEST CONSOLIDATED INCOME STATEMENT FOR THE YEAR ENDED DECEMBER 31, 20X2

Sales	$360,000
Interest income	10,000
Income from equity investee	30,000
Total revenue	400,000
Cost of sales	$180,000
General expenses	40,000
Selling expenses	50,000
Interest expense	10,000
Minority interest income	15,000
Income taxes	45,000
Total expenses	340,000
Income before extraordinary loss	$ 60,000
Extraordinary loss (net of income taxes)	10,000
Consolidated net income	$ 50,000

Truetest's operations are conducted through three domestic operating segments with sales, expenses, and assets as follows:

	Chemical	Food	Drug	Corporate
Sales (including intersegment sales)	$160,000	$140,000	$120,000	
Cost of sales (including intersegment cost of sales)	80,000	70,000	60,000	
General expenses	15,000	10,000	10,000	$ 5,000
Selling expenses	20,000	15,000	15,000	
Interest expense (unaffiliated)	5,000		5,000	
Identifiable assets	200,000	180,000	150,000	200,000
Investment in equity investee				300,000

The $10,000 interest income is not related to any industry segment. Consolidated total assets are $1,000,000. The chemical and food segments had intersegment sales of $35,000 and $25,000, respectively.

Required: Prepare a schedule of required disclosures for Truetest's industry segments in a form acceptable for reporting purposes.

P 15-7 The information that follows is for Colby Company at and for the year ended December 31, 20X9. Colby's operating segments are cost centers currently used for internal planning and control purposes. Amounts shown in the "Total Consolidated" column are amounts prepared under GAAP for external reporting. (*Data are in thousands of dollars.*)

	Food Industry	Packing Industry	Textile Industry	Foreign Operations	All Other Industries	Corporate	Total Consolidated
Income Statement							
Sales to unaffiliated customers	$950	$500	$300	$250	$400		$2,400
Income from equity investees							100
Cost of sales to unaffiliated customers	(600)	(350)	(175)	(125)	(250)		(1,500)
Operating expense	(200)	(75)	(150)	(75)	(75)	$ (25)	(600)
Interest expense							(20)
Income taxes							(150)
Minority interest income							(30)
Income (loss)	$150	$ 75	$(25)	$ 50	$ 75	$ (25)	$ 200
Assets							
Current assets	$300	$100	$ 75	$100	$225	$ 25	$ 825
Plant assets—net	400	400	250	100	175	25	1,350
Advances	50		25			50	
Equity investments						1,000	1,000
Total assets	$750	$500	$350	$200	$400	$1,100	$3,175
Intersegment Transfers							
Sales†	$ 60	$ 60	$ 30	$ 50			
Purchases†	$100	$ 25		$ 75			

†Amounts have been eliminated from the income data given.

Required
1 Prepare a schedule to determine which of Colby's operating segments are reportable segments under (a) the 10% revenue test, (b) the 10% operating profit test, and (c) the 10% asset test.
2 Prepare a schedule to show how Colby's segment information would be disclosed under the provisions of *FASB Statement No. 131.*

P 15-8 Trotter Corporation is subject to income tax rates of 20% of its first $50,000 pretax income and 34% on amounts in excess of $50,000. Quarterly pretax accounting income for the calendar year is estimated by Trotter to be:

Quarter	Estimated Pretax Income
1st	$ 20,000
2nd	30,000
3rd	60,000
4th	50,000
Total	$160,000

No changes in accounting principles, discontinued items, unusual or infrequently occurring items, or extraordinary items are anticipated for the year. The fourth quarter's pretax income is, however, expected to include $20,000 dividends from domestic corporations, for which an 80% dividend-received deduction is available.

Required
1 Calculate the estimated annual effective tax rate for Trotter Corporation for 20X2.
2 Prepare a schedule showing Trotter's estimated net income for each quarter and the calendar year 20X2.

16

Partnerships— Formation, Operations, and Changes in Ownership Interests

In this and the succeeding chapter, the focus is on accounting for partnership entities. This chapter describes general matters relating to the partnership form of business organization, including partnership formation, accounting for partnership operations, and accounting for changes in ownership interests. A special kind of partnership, the limited partnership, which is frequently used in professional partnerships like CPA firms, is described at the end of this chapter. Chapter 17 covers matters relating to the dissolution and liquidation of partnerships. Although accounting for partnership equities differs from that of other types of business organizations; asset, liability, and income accounting usually follow GAAP comparable to other entities. In other words, the analysis and recording of transactions not affecting ownership interests are ordinarily the same for partnerships as for proprietorships and corporations.

NATURE OF PARTNERSHIPS

The advantages of the partnership over the proprietorship form of business organization include sharing the investment needed, the talents required, and the risks involved in a particular business venture. The partnership form of organization is found in many areas of business, including service industries, retail trade, wholesale and manufacturing operations, and the professions, particularly the legal, medical, and public accounting professions. Partnerships are governed by state statutes. The National Conference of Commissioners on Uniform State Laws in 1914 developed the Uniform Partnership Act that was eventually adopted, with some variations, by all 50 states except Louisiana. The Revised Uniform Partnership Act (RUPA) was promulgated by the National Conference in 1992 and it has been adopted, with revision, by several states. California, for example, adopted RUPA to govern all partnerships formed after December 31, 1996. The Uniform Partnership Act still provides legal guidance for general partnerships in most states, and its provisions generally apply to the formation, operation, and dissolution of partnerships in the United States. References made to the Act in Chapters 16 and 17 refer to the Uniform Partnership Act, which appears as an appendix to this chapter. It is important to remember, however, that each state has its own variation of partnership law.

Partnership Characteristics

Partnership is defined in Section 6 of the Uniform Partnership Act as "an association of two or more persons to carry on as co-owners a business for profit." One legal feature of a partnership is its **limited life**. Under the Act, the legal life of a partnership terminates with the admission of a new partner, the withdrawal or death of an old partner, voluntary dissolution by the partners, or involuntary dissolution such as through bankruptcy proceedings. However, the termination of a partnership association does not necessarily terminate the partnership as a separate business and accounting entity. Partnership business operations frequently continue without substantial interference in spite of the admission and withdrawal of partners.

Another legal feature of a partnership is **mutual agency**. Each partner is assumed to be an agent for all partnership activities with the power to bind all other partners by his or her actions on behalf of the partnership. The implications of mutual agency are particularly significant when considered in conjunction with the **unlimited liability** feature of partnerships. Each partner is liable for all partnership debts and, in case of insolvency, may be required to use personal assets to pay partnership debts authorized by any partner.

Articles of Partnership

A partnership may be formed by a simple oral agreement among two or more people to operate a business for profit. The *ease of formation* feature of partnerships should not, however, encourage unsound business practices. Even though oral agreements may be legal and binding, **partnership agreements** should be in writing and at a minimum should specify:

1 The nature of the business
2 The rights and duties of each of the partners
3 The initial investment of each of the partners, including the amounts at which noncash assets are to be recorded
4 Provisions for additional investments and withdrawals
5 The manner in which profits and losses are to be shared
6 Procedures for dissolving the partnership

In the absence of a specific agreement for dividing profits and losses, all partners share equally, irrespective of investments made or time devoted to the business (Section 18 of the Act).

Partnership Financial Reporting

The accounting reports of partnerships are designed to meet the needs of three user groups—the partners, the partnership creditors, and the Internal Revenue Service (IRS). Partners need accounting information for planning and controlling partnership assets and activities and for making personal investment decisions with respect to their partnership investments. In the absence of an agreement to the contrary, every partner has access to the partnership books at all times (Section 19 of the Act). Credit grantors such as banks and other financial institutions frequently require financial reports in support of loan applications and other credit matters relating to partnerships.

Although partnerships do not pay federal income taxes, they are required to submit financial information returns to the IRS. This allows the IRS to verify that each partner pays income taxes on his or her share of partnership income. Outside of these three specific user groups, there is no widespread or public interest in the financial reports of partnerships, therefore, partnerships are not expected to prepare annual reports for public circulation.

INITIAL INVESTMENTS IN A PARTNERSHIP

All property brought into the partnership or acquired by the partnership is partnership property (Section 8[1] of the Act). Initial investments in a partnership are recorded in capital accounts maintained for each partner. If Ashley and Becker each invest $20,000 cash in a new partnership, the investments are recorded:

Cash	$20,000	
Ashley capital		$20,000
To record Ashley's original investment of cash.		
Cash	$20,000	
Becker capital		$20,000
To record Becker's original investment of cash.		

Noncash Investments

When property other than cash is invested in a partnership, the cost of the noncash property is measured and recorded at the fair value of the property at the time of the investment. Conceptually, the fair value should be determined by independent valuations, but as a practical matter, the fair value of noncash property is determined by agreement of all partners, because agreement is essential to partnership formation. The amounts involved should be specified in the written partnership agreement. Assume, for example, that C. Cola and R. Crown enter into a partnership with the following investments:

	C. Cola (Fair Value)	R. Crown (Fair Value)
Cash	—	$ 7,000
Land (cost to C. Cola, $5,000)	$10,000	—
Building (cost to C. Cola, $30,000)	40,000	—
Inventory items (cost to R. Crown, $28,000)	—	35,000
Total	$50,000	$42,000

The valuations to be recorded must be agreed upon by both Cola and Crown and are recorded as follows:

Land	$10,000	
Building	40,000	
C. Cola capital		$50,000
To record C. Cola's original investment of land and building at fair value.		
Cash	$ 7,000	
Inventory	35,000	
R. Crown capital		$42,000
To record R. Crown's original investment of cash and inventory items at fair value.		

Partnership investments are recorded at fair value because all property brought into the partnership becomes partnership property, and any gains or losses from use or disposal of such property will be divided in the profit and loss sharing ratios of the partners. Thus, equitable treatment of the partners requires that noncash property be recorded at its fair value. Assume that the investments of C. Cola and R. Crown are recorded at original cost to the individual partners, that the noncash assets are immediately sold at their fair values, and that the partnership is liquidated. C. Cola invests assets with a fair value of $50,000 but receives only $46,000 (half of the $92,000 fair value) in liquidation. Crown invests assets with a fair value of $42,000 and receives $46,000 in liquidation. Entries on the partnership books to reflect the accounting under these assumptions are shown in Exhibit 16–1.

Although immediate sale and liquidation of partnership investments is unusual, the computation of the $4,000 inequity is equally applicable when unrecorded gains (and losses) on property contributed by individual partners are realized through use in partnership operations. Recording partners' noncash investments at their fair value ensures that any gains and losses on subsequent disposition of the property through use or through sale will be equitable. Such gains or losses are correctly divided in the profit and loss sharing ratios provided in the partnership agreement.

	Investment at Original Cost		Investment at Fair Value	
1. To record C. Cola's investment:				
Land	$ 5,000		$10,000	
Building	30,000		40,000	
C. Cola capital		$35,000		$50,000
2. To record R. Crown's investment:				
Cash	$ 7,000		$ 7,000	
Inventory	28,000		35,000	
R. Crown capital		$35,000		$42,000
3. To record sale of assets at fair value:				
Cash	$85,000		$85,000	
Land		$ 5,000		$10,000
Building		30,000		40,000
Inventory		28,000		35,000
Gain on sale		22,000		none
4. To distribute the gain on sale equally:				
Gain on sale	$22,000		none	
C. Cola capital		$11,000		none
R. Crown capital		11,000		none
5. To distribute cash in final liquidation of the partnership:				
C. Cola capital	$46,000		$50,000	
R. Crown capital	46,000		42,000	
Cash		$92,000		$92,000

Exhibit 16–1   *Comparison of Initial Investment Involving Noncash Assets*

Bonus or Goodwill on Initial Investments

A different problem of valuation arises when partners agree on relative capital interests that are not aligned with their investments of identifiable assets. For example, C. Cola and R. Crown could agree to divide initial partnership capital equally, even though C. Cola contributed $50,000 in identifiable assets and R. Crown contributed $42,000. Such an agreement implies that R. Crown is contributing an unidentifiable asset such as individual talent, established clientele, or banking connections to the partnership. The alternative interpretation that C. Cola is making a gift to R. Crown is unacceptable because it implies irrational conduct, and it conflicts with the accountant's assumption of rational and honest conduct of business affairs.

The partnership agreement specifies equal capital interests, so the capital account balances of C. Cola ($50,000) and R. Crown ($42,000) have to be adjusted to meet the conditions of the agreement. Either of two approaches may be used to adjust the capital accounts—the bonus approach or the goodwill approach. Under the **bonus approach**, the unidentifiable asset is not recorded on the partnership books and the only journal entry necessary is as follows:

C. Cola capital	$4,000	
R. Crown capital		$4,000

To establish equal capital interests of $46,000 by recording
a $4,000 bonus from C. Cola to R. Crown.

When the goodwill approach is used, the unidentifiable asset contributed by Crown is measured on the basis of C. Cola's $50,000 investment for a 50% interest. C. Cola's investment implies total partnership capital of $100,000 ($50,000 ÷ 50%) and goodwill of $8,000 ($100,000 total capital − $92,000 identifiable assets). The unidentifiable asset is recorded:

Goodwill	$8,000	
R. Crown capital		$8,000

To establish equal capital interests of $50,000 by recognizing
R. Crown's investment of an $8,000 unidentifiable asset.

Both approaches are equally effective in aligning the capital accounts with the agreement and are equitable in assigning capital interests to individual partners. A decision to use one approach over the other will depend on partner attitudes toward recording the $8,000 unidentifiable asset under the goodwill method and to C. Cola's reaction to receiving a $46,000 capital credit for a $50,000 investment under the bonus approach.

ADDITIONAL INVESTMENTS AND WITHDRAWALS

The partnership agreement should establish guidelines for additional investments and withdrawals made after partnership operations have begun. Additional investments are credited to the investing partner's capital account at fair value at the time of the investment. Withdrawals of large and irregular amounts are ordinarily charged directly to the withdrawing partner's capital account. The entry for such a withdrawal might be:

Smith capital	$20,000	
Cash		$20,000
To record the withdrawal of cash.		

Drawings

The business rewards of partners are in the form of partnership profits, so partners do not have take-home pay as do the employees of the partnership business. Instead, active partners commonly withdraw regular amounts of money on a weekly or monthly basis in anticipation of their share of partnership profits. Such withdrawals are called **drawings**, **drawing allowances**, or sometimes **salary allowances**, and they are usually charged to the partners' drawing accounts rather than directly to the capital accounts. For example, if Townsend and Lee withdraw $1,000 from the partnership each month, the monthly withdrawals would be recorded:

Townsend drawing	$ 1,000	
Cash		$ 1,000
To record Townsend's drawing allowance for January.		

Lee drawing	$ 1,000	
Cash		$ 1,000
To record Lee's drawing allowance for January.		

The drawing accounts should be closed to the capital accounts at the end of each accounting period. Thus, the final effect is the same as if direct charges had been made to the capital accounts. The use of drawing accounts does, however, provide a record of each partner's drawings during an accounting period. This record may be compared with drawings allowed in the partnership agreement in order to establish an accounting control over excessive drawings. (Drawings balances are also a factor in many profit and loss sharing agreements, and will be discussed in conjunction with such agreements.) If Townsend draws $1,000 each month during the year, his drawing account balance at year-end will be $12,000, and his drawing account will be closed by the following entry:

Townsend capital	$12,000	
Townsend drawing		$12,000
To close Townsend's drawing account.		

Regardless of the name given to regular withdrawals by partners, such withdrawals are disinvestments of essentially the same nature as large and irregular withdrawals, and the effect on the capital accounts after closing entries will be the same for each dollar withdrawn. Drawing accounts should be closed to capital accounts before a partnership balance sheet is prepared.

Loans and Advances

A partner may make a personal loan to the partnership. This situation is provided for in Section 18(c) of the Act, which specifies that "a partner, who in the aid of the partnership makes any payment or advance beyond the amount of capital which he agreed to contribute, shall be paid interest from the date of the payment or advance." Such loans or advances and accrued interest thereon are correctly regarded as liabilities of the partnership. Similarly, partnership loans and advances to an individual partner are considered partnership assets. Matters concerning loans and advances to or from partners should be covered in the partnership agreement.

PARTNERSHIP OPERATIONS

The operations of a partnership are similar in most respects to those of other forms of organizations operating in the same line of business. In measuring partnership income for a period, however, the expenses should be scrutinized to make sure that personal expenses of the partners are not included among the business expenses of the partnership. If personal expenses of a partner are paid with partnership assets, the payment is charged to the drawing or capital account of the partner whose personal obligations have been settled. Drawings and salary allowances should be closed to the capital accounts of the partners, rather than to an income summary account. Salary allowances, whether debited to partner salary or drawing accounts, are part of the net income allocated to the partners.

General-purpose financial statements of a partnership include an income statement, a balance sheet, a statement of partnership capital, and a statement of cash flows. The statement of partnership capital is the only one of these statements that is unique to the partnership form of organization, so it is the only statement that will be illustrated at this time.

Assume that Ratcliffe and Yancey are partners sharing profits in a 60:40 ratio, respectively. Data relevant to the partnership's equities for the year 20X2 are as follows:

Partnership net income 20X2	$34,500
Ratcliffe capital January 1, 20X2	40,000
Ratcliffe additional investment 20X2	5,000
Ratcliffe drawing 20X2	6,000
Yancey capital January 1, 20X2	35,000
Yancey drawing 20X2	9,000
Yancey withdrawal 20X2	3,000

This information is reflected in the statement of partners' capital that appears in Exhibit 16–2. Although other forms of presentation are acceptable, the format illustrated in Exhibit 16–2 is used because it provides a comparison of capital changes before and after the division of partnership net income. An ability to compare beginning capital balances and net contributed capital is helpful to the partners in setting investment and withdrawal policies and in controlling abuses of the established policies. In the case of incomplete partnership records, the format illustrated

---

RATCLIFFE AND YANCEY
STATEMENT OF PARTNERS' CAPITAL
FOR THE YEAR ENDED DECEMBER 31, 20X2

	60% Ratcliffe	40% Yancey	Total
Capital balances January 1, 20X2	$40,000	$35,000	$75,000
Add: Additional investments	5,000	—	5,000
Deduct: Withdrawals	—	(3,000)	(3,000)
Deduct: Drawings	(6,000)	(9,000)	(15,000)
Net contributed capital	39,000	23,000	62,000
Add: Net income for 20X2	20,700	13,800	34,500
Capital balances December 31, 20X2	$59,700	$36,800	$96,500

Exhibit 16–2   *Format for a Statement of Partners' Capital*

also provides a convenient means of computing net income—which is simply the difference between net contributed capital and ending capital as shown in the total column. (Note that the preclosing capital account balances are $45,000 [$40,000 + $5,000] for Ratcliffe and $32,000 [$35,000 − $3,000] for Yancey.)

Closing entries for the Ratcliffe and Yancey partnership at December 31, 20X2 are as follows:

December 31, 20X2		
Revenue and expense summary	$34,500	
Ratcliffe capital		$20,700
Yancey capital		13,800

To divide net income for the year 60% to Ratcliffe and 40% to Yancey.

December 31, 20X2		
Ratcliffe capital	$ 6,000	
Yancey capital	9,000	
Ratcliffe drawing		$ 6,000
Yancey drawing		9,000

To close partner drawing accounts to capital accounts.

PROFIT AND LOSS SHARING AGREEMENTS

Partnership income may be divided equally among the partners, and equal division is required in the absence of a profit and loss sharing agreement. However, partners may agree to share profits in a specified ratio, such as the 60:40 division illustrated for the Ratcliffe and Yancey partnership. The division of partnership income according to specified ratios is easy to comprehend and requires no further explanation, other than to note that profit sharing agreements also apply to the division of losses unless the agreement specifies otherwise.

Although agreements to share profits and losses equally or in specified ratios are common, other more-complex profit sharing agreements are also encountered in practice. An equitable division of profits (and losses) frequently requires that consideration be given to the time that partners devote to the partnership business and the capital invested in the business by individual partners. If one partner manages the partnership, the partnership agreement may allow the managing partner a salary allowance equal to the amount he or she could earn in an alternative employment opportunity before remaining profits are allocated. *Such salary allowances are, of course, only provisions of the profit sharing agreement and are not expenses of the partnership.* Similarly, if one partner invests significantly more than another in a partnership venture, the agreement may provide an interest allowance on capital investments before remaining profits are divided. As in the case of salary allowances, *interest allowances are merely provisions of the partnership agreement and have no effect on the measurement of partnership income.*

Service Considerations in Profit and Loss Sharing Agreements

As mentioned previously, the equitable distribution of partnership income may require a salary allowance to a partner who devotes time to the partnership business while other partners work elsewhere. Salary allowances may also be used to provide a differential between the fair value of the talents of different partners, all of whom devote their time to the partnership. Another possibility for differentiation in the profit and loss sharing agreement is to provide salary allowances to active partners plus a bonus to the managing partner in order to encourage profit maximization. These alternatives are illustrated for the partnership of Bob, Gary, and Pete. Bob is the managing partner, Gary is the sales manager, and Pete works outside the partnership.

Salary Allowances in Profit Sharing Agreements Assume that the partnership agreement provides that Bob and Gary receive salary allowances of $12,000 each, after which remaining income is allocated equally among the three partners. If partnership net income is $60,000 for 20X1 and $12,000 for 20X2, the income allocations would be as shown in Exhibit 16–3. The 20X1 allocation is $24,000 each to Bob and Gary

INCOME ALLOCATION SCHEDULE—20X1

		Bob	Gary	Pete	Total
Net income	$60,000				
Salary allowances to					
Bob and Gary	(24,000)	$12,000	$12,000		$24,000
Remainder to divide	36,000				
Divided equally	(36,000)	12,000	12,000	$12,000	36,000
Remainder to divide	0				
Net income allocation		$24,000	$24,000	$12,000	$60,000

INCOME ALLOCATION SCHEDULE—20X2

		Bob	Gary	Pete	Total
Net income	$12,000				
Salary allowances to					
Bob and Gary	(24,000)	$12,000	$12,000		$24,000
Remainder to divide	(12,000)				
Divided equally	12,000	(4,000)	(4,000)	$(4,000)	(12,000)
Remainder to divide	0				
Net income allocation		$ 8,000	$ 8,000	$(4,000)	$12,000

Exhibit 16–3   *Salary Allowances in Profit Sharing Agreements*

and $12,000 to Pete. The 20X2 allocation is $8,000 income to Bob and Gary and a $4,000 loss to Pete. Note that the partnership agreement has been followed in 20X2, even though the salary allowances of $24,000 exceeded partnership net income of $12,000. The income allocation schedule follows the order of the profit sharing agreement even when the partnership has a loss. Salary allowances, in that case, simply increase the loss to be divided equally.

Journal entries to distribute partnership income to individual capital accounts for 20X1 and 20X2 follow.

December 31, 20X1		
Revenue and expense summary	$60,000	
Bob capital		$24,000
Gary capital		24,000
Pete capital		12,000
Partnership income allocation for 20X1.		

December 31, 20X2		
Revenue and expense summary	$12,000	
Pete capital	4,000	
Bob capital		$ 8,000
Gary capital		8,000
Partnership income allocation for 20X2.		

Income allocation schedules such as those shown in Exhibit 16–3 can be used as explanations of the closing entries to distribute partnership income to individual capital accounts.

In partnership accounting, partner salary allowances are not expenses in the determination of partnership net income; instead, they are a means of achieving an equitable division of income among the partners based on time and talents devoted to partnership business. This point has already been established. However, there are situations in which calculations of income after salary allowances may be useful. These situations include performance comparisons and measurements of business success.

Calculating partnership income after salary allowances is appropriate in comparing the performance of a partnership business with similar businesses operated under the corporation form of organization. Stockholders who devote their time to corporate affairs are employees, and their salaries are deducted in measuring corporate net income. Failure to adjust partnership income for salary allowances may, therefore, result in invalid comparisons. Other adjustments, such as for corporate income taxes, also have to be made for valid comparisons.

Calculation of partnership income after salary allowances is also appropriate in assessing the success of a business. The financial success of a partnership business lies in its earning a fair return for the services performed by partners, for capital invested in the business, and for the risks taken. If partnership income is not greater than the combined amounts that active partners could earn by working outside of the partnership, then the business is not a financial success. Income after salary allowances (or imputed salaries) should be sufficient to compensate for capital invested and risks undertaken.

Bonus and Salary Allowances   The partnership agreement of Bob, Gary, and Pete provides that Bob receive a bonus of 10% of partnership net income for managing the business; that Bob and Gary receive salary allowances of $10,000 and $8,000, respectively, for services rendered; and that the remaining partnership income be divided equally among the three partners. If partnership net income is $60,000 in 20X1 and $12,000 in 20X2, the partnership income is allocated as shown in Exhibit 16–4.

The allocation schedules illustrated follow the order of the profit sharing agreement in allocating the bonus, the salary allowances, and the remainder to individual partners. The bonus is computed on the basis of partnership net income as the concept of "partnership net income" is generally understood in accounting practice. Partners may, however, intend for salary allowances to be deducted in determining the base for computing the bonus. If this had been the intent, the bonus illustrated for 20X1 would have been $4,200 [($60,000 − $18,000) × 10%] rather than 6,000, and the final net income allocation would have been $26,800, $20,600, and $12,600 for Bob, Gary, and Pete, respectively. Sometimes the partners may intend for the bonus, as well as salary allowances, to be deducted in determining the base for the bonus

INCOME ALLOCATION SCHEDULE—20X1					
		Bob	Gary	Pete	Total
Net income	$60,000				
Bonus to Bob	(6,000)	$ 6,000			$ 6,000
Remainder to divide	54,000				
Salary allowances to					
Bob and Gary	(18,000)	10,000	$ 8,000		18,000
Remainder to divide	36,000				
Divided equally	(36,000)	12,000	12,000	$12,000	36,000
Remainder to divide	0				
Net income allocation		$28,000	$20,000	$12,000	$60,000

INCOME ALLOCATION SCHEDULE—20X2					
		Bob	Gary	Pete	Total
Net income	$12,000				
Bonus to Bob	(1,200)	$ 1,200			$ 1,200
Remainder to divide	10,800				
Salary allowances to					
Bob and Gary	(18,000)	10,000	$ 8,000		18,000
Remainder to divide	(7,200)				
Divided equally	7,200	(2,400)	(2,400)	$ (2,400)	(7,200)
Remainder to divide	0				
Net income allocation		$ 8,800	$ 5,600	$ (2,400)	$12,000

Exhibit 16–4   *Bonus and Salary Allowances in Profit Sharing Agreements*

computation. Had this been the intent in the Bob, Gary, and Pete partnership agreement, the bonus would have been $3,818, computed as follows:

$$\text{Let B} = \text{bonus}$$
$$B = 10\% \ (\$60,000 - \$18,000 - B)$$
$$B = \$6,000 - \$1,800 - .1B$$
$$1.1B = \$4,200$$
$$\underline{\underline{B = \$3,818}} \text{ (rounded)}$$
$$\textit{Check: } \$60,000 - \$18,000 - 3,818 = \$38,182 \text{ bonus base}$$
$$\$38,182 \times 10\% = \$3,818 \text{ bonus}$$

The intent of the partners may not be apparent when technical accounting terms are used, so the partnership agreement should be precise in specifying measurement procedures to be used in determining the amount of a bonus.

Capital as a Factor in Profit Sharing Agreements

Capital is an important factor in the earning process of many businesses, and the capital contributions of partners are frequently considered in profit and loss sharing agreements. Total partnership income may be allocated on the basis of relative capital balances of the partners, or interest may be allowed on relative capital balances as one of several factors to be considered in achieving an equitable allocation of partnership net income.

If capital is to be considered in the division of partnership income, the profit sharing agreement should be specific with respect to the concept of capital to be applied. For example, capital may refer to beginning capital balances, ending capital balances, or average capital balances. In addition, several interpretations of average capital balances are possible, and capital balances may be determined before or after drawing accounts are closed to the partner's capital accounts. Thus, the precise concept of capital to be used should be designated in the partnership agreement.

When beginning capital balances are used in allocating partnership income, additional investments during the accounting period are discouraged because the partners making such investments are not compensated in the division of income until a later period. A similar problem arises when ending capital balances are used. Year-end investments are encouraged, but there is no incentive for a partner to make any investments before year-end. Also, there is no penalty for withdrawals if the amounts withdrawn are reinvested before the period's end. These considerations suggest that weighted average capital balances provide the most equitable basis for allocating partnership income, and a weighted average interpretation of capital should be assumed in the absence of evidence to the contrary. Average capital balances means weighted average unless another interpretation of average capital is specified in the agreement.

Usually the drawing allowances specified in a partnership agreement may be withdrawn without affecting the capital balances to be used in dividing partnership income. That is, drawing account balances up to the amounts specified in the agreement would not be deducted in determining average or year-end capital balances of the partners. Drawings in excess of allowable amounts would be charged against the partners' capital accounts in computing average or ending capital balances for purposes of dividing partnership income. Excess drawing should be charged directly to the partner's capital account on a timely basis. Drawing account balances may be excessive and, if so, they should be adjusted before average or ending capital is computed.

Income Allocated in Relation to Partnership Capital   The partnership of Ace and Butch was formed on January 1, 20X1, with each partner investing $20,000 cash. Changes in the capital accounts during 20X1 are summarized as follows:

	Ace	Butch
Capital balances January 1, 20X1	$20,000	$20,000
Investment April 1	2,000	—

(Continued)

	Ace	Butch
Withdrawal July 1	—	(5,000)
Investment September 1	3,000	—
Withdrawal October 1	—	(4,000)
Investment December 28	—	8,000
Capital balances December 31, 20X1	$25,000	$19,000

The beginning, ending, and average capital amounts for Ace and Butch for 20X1 are as follows:

COMPARISON OF CAPITAL BASES

	Beginning Capital Investment	Ending Capital Investment	Weighted Average Capital Investment
Ace	$20,000	$25,000	$22,500
Butch	20,000	19,000	16,500

Computations for the weighted average capital investments of Ace and Butch are shown in Exhibit 16–5. Actual investments are multiplied by the number of months outstanding to get dollar-month investment computations. Total dollar-month investments are divided by 12 to get weighted average annual capital balances. Ordinarily, computations to the nearest half-month are considered adequate, although the weighted average balances could easily be made on a weekly, or even daily, basis.

The Ace and Butch example can now be extended under the further assumption that partnership net income is to be divided on the basis of capital balances, and that net income for 20X1 is $100,000. Allocation of partnership income to Ace and Butch under each of the three capital bases would be:

Beginning Capital Balances

Ace $100,000 × 20/40	$ 50,000
Butch $100,000 × 20/40	50,000
Total income	$100,000

Ending Capital Balances

Ace $100,000 × 25/44	$ 56,818.18
Butch $100,000 × 19/44	43,181.82
Total income	$100,000.00

Average Capital Balances

Ace $100,000 × 225/390	$ 57,692.31
Butch $100,000 × 165/390	42,307.69
Total income	$100,000.00

If the partnership agreement of Ace and Butch specifies that income will be divided based on capital balances, but it fails to specify how capital balances are to be computed, the weighted average computation is used. The $100,000 partnership income for 20X1 is allocated $57,692.31 to Ace and $42,307.69 to Butch.

Interest Allowances on Partnership Capital Although capital investments may be used as the sole basis for income allocation, they may also be used as one of several income allocation provisions in a partnership agreement. For example, an agreement may provide for interest allowances on partnership capital in order to encourage capital investments, as well as salary allowances to recognize time devoted to the business. Remaining profits may then be divided equally or in any other ratio specified in the profit sharing agreement.

	Dollar-Month Investment	
Average Capital Investment of Ace		
$20,000 × 3 months (January 1 to April 1)	$ 60,000	
22,000 × 5 months (April 1 to September 1)	110,000	
25,000 × 4 months (September 1 to December 31)	100,000	
12 months	$270,000	
Ace's average capital investment ($270,000 ÷ 12 months)		$22,500
Average Capital Investment of Butch		
$20,000 × 6 months (January 1 to July 1)	$120,000	
15,000 × 3 months (July 1 to October 1)	45,000	
11,000 × 3 months (October 1 to December 28)	33,000	
12 months	$198,000	
Butch's average capital investment ($198,000 ÷ 12 months)		$16,500

Exhibit 16–5   *Computation of Weighted Average Capital Investment*

Consider the following information relating to the capital and drawing accounts of the Russo and Stokes partnership for the calendar year 20X1:

	Russo	Stokes
Capital Accounts		
Capital balances January 1, 20X1	$186,000	$114,000
Additional investments June 1, 20X1	24,000	36,000
Withdrawal July 1, 20X1	—	−10,000
Capital balances December 31, 20X1 (before drawings)	$210,000	$140,000
Drawing Accounts		
Drawing account balances* December 31, 20X1	$ 10,000	$ 12,000

*Account titles may be labeled partner salaries rather than partner drawings. In either case, the balances should be closed to partner capital accounts and not to the income summary.

The partnership agreement provides that the partnership income is to be divided equally after salary allowances of $12,000 per year for each partner, and after interest allowances at a 10% annual rate on average capital balances. Schedules showing the income allocations for 20X1 under this agreement are illustrated in Exhibit 16–6. The first schedule (Part A) assumes that partnership net income for 20X1 is $91,000, and the second schedule (Part B) assumes a partnership loss for 20X1 of $3,000.

The average capital balances for Russo and Stokes, as used in the exhibit, are computed as follows:

	Dollar-Month Investment	
Average Capital Investment of Russo		
$186,000 × 5 months	$ 930,000	
$210,000 × 7 months	1,470,000	
12 months	$2,400,000	
Average capital ($2,400,000 ÷ 12 months)		$200,000
Average Capital Investment of Stokes		
$114,000 × 5 months	$ 570,000	
$150,000 × 1 month	150,000	
$140,000 × 6 months	840,000	
12 months	$1,560,000	
Average capital ($1,560,000 ÷ 12 months)		$130,000

```
┌─────────────────────────────────────────────────────────────────────────┐
│ PART A—PARTNERSHIP INCOME ASSUMED TO BE $91,000                           │
│ INCOME ALLOCATION SCHEDULE                                                │
│                                                                           │
│                                          Russo       Stokes      Total    │
│                                                                           │
│ Net income                 $91,000                                        │
│ Salary allowances          (24,000)     $12,000     $12,000     $24,000   │
│ Remainder to divide         67,000                                        │
│ Interest allowances:                                                      │
│   $200,000 × 10%           (20,000)      20,000                   20,000   │
│   $130,000 × 10%           (13,000)                  13,000       13,000   │
│ Remainder to divide         34,000                                        │
│ Divided equally            (34,000)      17,000      17,000       34,000   │
│ Remainder to divide              0                                        │
│    Net income allocation                $49,000     $42,000     $91,000   │
│                                                                           │
│ PART B—PARTNERSHIP LOSS ASSUMED TO BE $3,000                              │
│ INCOME ALLOCATION SCHEDULE                                                │
│                                                                           │
│                                          Russo       Stokes      Total    │
│                                                                           │
│ Net loss                  $(3,000)                                        │
│ Salary allowances          (24,000)     $12,000     $12,000     $24,000   │
│ Remainder to divide        (27,000)                                       │
│ Interest allowances:                                                      │
│   $200,000 × 10%           (20,000)      20,000                   20,000   │
│   $130,000 × 10%           (13,000)                  13,000       13,000   │
│ Remainder to divide        (60,000)                                       │
│ Divided equally             60,000      (30,000)    (30,000)    (60,000)  │
│ Remainder to divide              0                                        │
│    Net income (loss) allocation         $ 2,000     $ (5,000)   $ (3,000) │
└─────────────────────────────────────────────────────────────────────────┘
```

Exhibit 16–6   *Interest and Salary Allowances in Profit Sharing Agreements*

Exhibit 16–6 shows that all provisions of the profit sharing agreement are used in allocating partnership income, regardless of whether the partnership has net income or net loss. The full amount of salary allowances as provided in the agreement is included in the income division, even though Russo only withdrew $10,000 of the $12,000 allowable amount.

In Part A of Exhibit 16–6, partnership income of $91,000 was divided $49,000 to Russo and $42,000 to Stokes. The division of the $3,000 net loss in Part B was allocated as $2,000 income to Russo and a $5,000 loss to Stokes. In both cases, the partnership agreement provided for a $7,000 income allocation differential between the two partners. The amount of this differential was the same for the income and loss situations because the residual income amount was divided equally. A 60:40 division of income after salary and interest allowances, for example, would have resulted in a larger differential in Part A (that is, greater than $7,000) and a smaller differential in Part B (less than $7,000). One must be careful in making generalizations about the effect of various profit sharing provisions on final income allocations.

CHANGES IN PARTNERSHIP INTERESTS

The admission of a new partner or the withdrawal or death of an existing partner dissolves the existing legal partnership entity. However, dissolution does not necessarily result in the termination of the partnership operations or of the partnership as a separate business and accounting entity. **Partnership dissolution** under the Act is simply "the change in the relation of the partners caused by any partner ceasing to be associated in the carrying on as distinguished from the winding up of the business" (Section 29 of the Act).

When a partnership is legally dissolved by the admittance of a new partner or by the retirement or death of an existing partner, a new partnership agreement is necessary for the continuing operations of the partnership business. A question arises as to whether the assets of the continuing partnership business should be revalued. Some argue that because legal dissolution terminates the old partnership, all assets transferred to the new partnership should be revalued in the same manner as if the assets had been sold to a corporate entity. Others argue that changes in partnership interests are not unlike changes in the stockholders of a corporation, and that private sales of ownership interests provide no basis for revaluation of the business entity. These alternative views reflect the concepts of the legal and business entities, respectively. Both views have merit, and this text does not emphasize either view. Instead, both views are discussed and illustrated in the following sections on changes in partnership interests. The revaluation approach is generally referred to as the **goodwill procedure**, and the absence of revaluation is referred to as the **bonus procedure**.

Assignment of an Interest to a Third Party

A partnership is not dissolved when a partner assigns his or her interest in the partnership to a third party because such an assignment does not in itself change the relations among partners. Such assignment only entitles the assignee to receive the assigning partner's interest in future partnership profits and in partnership assets in the event of liquidation. The assignee does not become a partner, however, and does not obtain the right to share in management of the partnership (Section 27 of the Act). If the assignee does not become a partner, the only change required on the partnership books is for transfer of the capital interest of the assignor partner to the assignee.

The assignment by Mark to Conn of his 25% interest in the Pilar-Mark partnership is recorded:

Mark capital	XXX	
Conn capital		XXX

The amount of the capital transfer is equal to the recorded amount of Mark's capital at the time of the assignment, and it is independent of the consideration received by Mark for his 25% interest. If the recorded amount of Mark's capital is $50,000, then the amount of the transfer entry is $50,000, regardless of whether Conn pays Mark $50,000 or some other amount.

Admission of a New Partner

A new partner can be admitted with the consent of all continuing partners in the business. However, the old partnership is dissolved and a new agreement is necessary for the continuing operations of the partnership business. In the absence of a new agreement, all profits and losses in the new partnership are divided equally under the provisions of the Act.

A person may become a partner in an existing partnership *by purchasing an interest from one or more of the existing partners* with the consent of all continuing partners in the new partnership entity or *by investing money or other resources in the partnership*. In either case, the partnership books should be closed to update the capital accounts in anticipation of a new partnership agreement. These situations are similar in the sense that the old partnership is legally dissolved, and capital and income interests will be based on a new partnership agreement. The situations are dissimilar in the sense that the partnership entity receives no new resources when a third party purchases an interest directly from existing partners, but it does receive new resources when a third party becomes a partner by direct investment in the partnership. The partners in the new agreement can agree upon any capital and profit sharing interests they choose, so the role of the accountant is largely one of advising the partners on matters concerning the equitable allocation of capital and income interests in the new agreement.

PURCHASE OF AN INTEREST FROM EXISTING PARTNERS

With the consent of all continuing partners, a new partner may be admitted into an existing partnership by purchasing an interest directly from the existing partners. The old partnership is dissolved, its books are closed, and a new partnership agreement governs the continuing business operations. If the capital accounts are aligned with the profit and loss sharing ratios before and after the admission of a new partner, the net assets of the old partnership are probably valued correctly.

For example, Alfano and Bailey are partners with capital balances of $50,000 each, and they share profits and losses equally. Cobb purchases one-half of Alfano's interest from Alfano for $25,000, and a new partnership of Alfano, Bailey, and Cobb is formed such that Alfano and Cobb each have a 25% interest in the capital and profits of the new partnership. The only entry required to record Alfano's transfer to Cobb is:

Alfano capital	$25,000	
Cobb capital		$25,000

To record Cobb's admission into the partnership with the purchase of one-half of Alfano's interest.

In this case, the capital and income interests are aligned before and after the admission of Cobb, and the evidence indicates that the net assets of the old partnership were correctly valued. That is, Cobb's payment of $25,000 for a 25% interest in the capital and future income of the partnership implies a total valuation for the partnership of $100,000 ($25,000 ÷ 0.25). The net assets of the old partnership were recorded at $100,000, so no basis for revaluation arises.

Now assume that Alfano and Bailey have capital balances of $50,000 and $40,000, respectively, that they share profits equally, and that they agree to take Cobb into the partnership with a payment of $25,000 directly to Alfano. The partners may agree that half of Alfano's capital balance is to be transferred to Cobb (as in the previous example), that the net assets are not to be revalued, and that future profits will be shared 25%, 50%, and 25% to Alfano, Bailey, and Cobb, respectively. Although it seems equitable, there is no compelling reason for such an agreement, because the capital and income interests were not aligned either before or after the admission of Cobb.

	Old Partnership			New Partnership		
	Capital Investment		Income Interest	Capital Investment		Income Interest
Alfano	$50,000	$\frac{5}{9}$	50%	$25,000	$\frac{5}{18}$	25%
Bailey	40,000	$\frac{4}{9}$	50%	40,000	$\frac{8}{18}$	50%
Cobb				25,000	$\frac{5}{18}$	25%
	$90,000			$90,000		

Also note that the $25,000 payment of Cobb to Alfano does not provide evidence as to the correct valuation of partnership net assets, because the payment was for five-eighteenths of the partnership net assets but 25% of future partnership profits. If revaluation is desirable, the asset value should be based on appraisals or evidence other than the amount of Cobb's payment to Alfano.

Revaluation/Goodwill Procedure

A third possibility is that Alfano and Bailey have capital balances of $50,000 and $40,000, respectively, that they share profits equally, and that Cobb is admitted to the partnership with a total payment of $50,000 directly to the partners. Cobb is to have a 50% interest in the capital and income of the new partnership. Alfano and Bailey will each have a 25% interest in future income of the partnership. Several additional questions of equity arise concerning the valuation of total partnership assets, the capital transfers to Cobb, and the division of the $50,000 payment between Alfano and Bailey. Cobb's $50,000 payment for a 50% interest in both capital and future income implies a $100,000 valuation for total partnership assets. If assets are to be revalued, the revaluation should be recorded prior to Cobb's admission to the partnership. The revaluation could be recorded:

Goodwill (or identifiable net assets)	$10,000	
Alfano capital		$ 5,000
Bailey capital		5,000

When assets are revalued and goodwill is recorded, goodwill should be amortized over a maximum of 40 years in accordance with *APB Opinion No. 17*. If the assets are revalued and identifiable asset accounts are adjusted, the amount of the adjustments will be amortized or depreciated over the remaining asset lives. Although the revaluation procedure is commonly referred to as the goodwill procedure, goodwill should not be recorded until all identifiable assets have been adjusted to their fair values. Thus, the approach is comparable to the approach used to record business combinations under the purchase method or the acquisition of operating divisions or groups of assets.

The previous entry recording goodwill of $10,000 gives Alfano and Bailey capital balances of $55,000 and $45,000, respectively. If equal amounts of capital are to be transferred to Cobb, the entry to record Cobb's admission to the partnership is:

Alfano capital	$25,000	
Bailey capital	25,000	
Cobb capital		$50,000

Equal amounts of capital are transferred by Alfano and Bailey, so it would seem equitable for Alfano and Bailey to share equally the $50,000 received from Cobb. The capital balances are summarized as follows:

CAPITAL BALANCES

	Before Revaluation	Revaluation	After Revaluation	Capital Transferred	Capital After Transfer	
Alfano	$50,000	$ 5,000	$ 55,000	$–25,000	$ 30,000	(30%)
Bailey	40,000	5,000	45,000	–25,000	20,000	(20%)
Cobb				50,000	50,000	(50%)
	$90,000	$10,000	$100,000	$ 0	$100,000	

Alternatively, it may be desirable to realign the capital balances of Alfano and Bailey in the new partnership such that each will have a 25% interest in the capital and income of the new partnership. In this case, the admission of Cobb would be recorded:

Alfano capital	$30,000	
Bailey capital	20,000	
Cobb capital		$50,000

A division of the cash received from Cobb equal to the capital transfers ($30,000 and $20,000) would then seem equitable. In this case, the capital changes are as follows:

CAPITAL BALANCES

	Before Revaluation	Revaluation	After Revaluation	Capital Transferred	Capital After Transfer	
Alfano	$50,000	$ 5,000	$ 55,000	$–30,000	$ 25,000	(25%)
Bailey	40,000	5,000	45,000	–20,000	25,000	(25%)
Cobb				50,000	50,000	(50%)
	$90,000	$10,000	$100,000	$ 0	$100,000	

Nonrevaluation/Bonus Procedure

If the assets of the new partnership are not to be revalued, but equal amounts of capital are to be transferred to Cobb, a single entry is adequate to record the transfer:

Alfano capital	$22,500	
Bailey capital	22,500	
Cobb capital		$45,000

Equal amounts of capital and equal rights to future income are transferred by Alfano and Bailey to Cobb, so an equal division of the $50,000 received from Cobb seems equitable. In this case, each of the old partners receives $2,500 in excess of the amount of capital transferred ($25,000 received less $22,500 capital transferred). This $2,500 excess for Alfano and Bailey represents half of the $10,000 unrecorded asset values that will accrue to the benefit of Cobb in future income allocations. The capital accounts before and after the admission of Cobb are as follows:

CAPITAL BALANCES

	Per Books	Capital Transferred	Capital After Transfer	
Alfano	$50,000	$−22,500	$27,500	(30.6%)
Bailey	40,000	−22,500	17,500	(19.4%)
Cobb		45,000	45,000	(50.0%)
	$90,000	$ 0	$90,000	

Should Alfano and Bailey desire to equate their capital and income interests in the new partnership, Alfano would receive $30,000 of the amount paid by Cobb, and Bailey would receive $20,000. The entry to record the capital transfer in this case would be:

Alfano capital	$27,500	
Bailey capital	17,500	
Cobb capital		$45,000

The capital transfers of Alfano and Bailey are computed by deducting $22,500, the desired capital balances (25% of $90,000 total capital), from their existing capital balances of $50,000 and $40,000, respectively. As in the previous illustration where assets were not revalued, Alfano and Bailey each receive $2,500 more than the amount of capital transferred, again equal to their respective shares of unrecorded asset values that will accrue to the benefit of Cobb. A summary of the capital balances follows:

CAPITAL BALANCES

	Per Books	Capital Transferred	Capital After Transfer	
Alfano	$50,000	$−27,500	$22,500	(25%)
Bailey	40,000	−17,500	22,500	(25%)
Cobb		45,000	45,000	(50%)
	$90,000	$ 0	$90,000	

The decision to revalue or not to revalue partnership assets when a new partner is admitted through payments to existing partners is less important than equity considerations surrounding capital transfers and cash distributions. Comparable treatment of all partners is the objective, regardless of asset revaluation. Although the evidence supporting revaluation is not always convincing, a revaluation based on the price paid by an incoming partner does have the advantage of establishing a capital balance for that partner equal to the amount of his or her investment. For example, Cobb's capital credit was equal to his $50,000 payment to Alfano and Bailey when the assets were revalued. It was only $45,000 when the assets were not revalued. Also, the amounts of capital transfer and cash allocations are easier to determine when assets are revalued because gains and losses relating to the old partnership are formally recorded in the accounts.

INVESTING IN AN EXISTING PARTNERSHIP

A new partner may be admitted into an existing partnership by investing cash or other assets in the business, or by bringing clients or individual talents into the business that will contribute to future profitability. In this case, the old partnership is legally dissolved and the investment of the new partner is recorded under the provisions of the new partnership agreement. As in the case of a purchase of an interest, the net assets of the old partnership may or may not be revalued. However, because new assets are being invested in the business, the basis for revaluation is not necessarily determined by the investment of the new partner. If the amount invested by the new partner implies that the old partnership has unrecorded asset values, a total valuation of the new business based on the investment of the new partner seems appropriate. On the other hand, if the capital interest granted to the new partner is greater than the amount of his or her investment, and the identifiable assets of the old partnership are recorded at their fair values, there is an implication that the new partner is bringing goodwill into the business. In this case, the total valuation of the new business is determined by reference to the capital of the old partnership.

The evidence provided by the amount of an investment only relates to the total value of the business. Values for identifiable assets have to be determined on an individual basis by appraisal or other valuation technique, so it is assumed that the identifiable assets of the old partnership are recorded at their fair values, in the absence of evidence to the contrary. If identifiable assets of a partnership are to be revalued, the revaluation must be based on appraisals or other evidence relating to specific assets.

Partnership Investment at Book Value

Andrew and Boyles have capital balances of $40,000 each and share profits equally. They agree to admit Criner to a one-third interest in capital and profits of a new Andrew, Boyles, and Criner partnership for a $40,000 cash investment. Criner's $40,000 investment is equal to the capital interest that she receives [($80,000 + $40,000) ÷ 3], so the issue of revaluation does not arise. Criner's investment is recorded on the partnership books:

Cash	$40,000	
Criner capital		$40,000
To record Criner's $40,000 cash investment for a one-third interest in partnership capital and income.		

Partnership Assets Revalued (Goodwill to Old Partners)

Now assume that Andrew and Boyles, who have capital balances of $40,000 each and share profits equally, agree to admit Criner to a one-third interest in the capital and profits of a new partnership for a cash investment of $50,000. Because Criner is willing to invest $50,000 for a one-third interest in the $80,000 recorded assets plus her $50,000 investment ($130,000 assets), there is an implication that the old partnership has unrecorded asset values. The amount of unrecorded assets is determined by reference to Criner's investment. By implication, total assets of the new partnership will be $150,000 ($50,000 ÷ $\frac{1}{3}$). The value of unrecorded assets must be $20,000, the excess of the $150,000 total value, less the $80,000 recorded assets plus the $50,000 new investment. If the assets are revalued, the following entries are made:

Goodwill	$20,000	
Andrew capital		$10,000
Boyles capital		10,000
To revalue the assets of the old partnership based on the amount of Criner's investment.		
Cash	$50,000	
Criner capital		$50,000
To record Criner's investment in the partnership for a one-third interest in capital and income.		

The $20,000 recorded as goodwill in the first entry is credited to the old partners in their old profit and loss sharing ratios. Conceptually, the revaluation constitutes a final act of the old partnership, and all further entries are those of the new partnership. The second entry merely records Criner's $50,000 cash investment and capital credit in equal amounts. A summary of the capital balances before and after the $20,000 revaluation and the investment of Criner is as follows:

CAPITAL BALANCES

	Before Revaluation	Revaluation	After Revaluation	New Investment	Capital After Investment	
Andrew	$40,000	$10,000	$ 50,000		$ 50,000	$\frac{1}{3}$
Boyles	40,000	10,000	50,000		50,000	$\frac{1}{3}$
Criner				$50,000	50,000	$\frac{1}{3}$
	$80,000	$20,000	$100,000	$50,000	$150,000	

Partnership Assets Not Revalued (Bonus to Old Partners)

If the partners decide against revaluation, the only entry required to record Criner's admittance into the partnership is as follows:

Cash	$50,000	
Andrew capital		$ 3,333
Boyles capital		3,333
Criner capital		43,334

To record Criner's investment in the partnership and to allow Andrew and Boyles a bonus due to unrecorded asset values.

In this case, partnership net assets are increased only by the amount of the new investment. The new partner's capital account is credited for her one-third interest in the $130,000 capital of the new partnership, and the difference between the investment and capital credit of the new partner is allocated to the capital accounts of the old partners in relation to the old profit sharing agreement. This situation is referred to as a *bonus to old partners* because the old partners receive capital credits for a part of the new partner's investment. The goodwill and bonus procedures are comparable in the sense that each partner would receive $50,000 if the business were immediately sold for $150,000. The capital balances before and after the admission of Criner are as follows:

CAPITAL BALANCES

	Per Books	Investment	Capital After Investment	
Andrew	$40,000	$ 3,333	$ 43,333	$\frac{1}{3}$
Boyles	40,000	3,333	43,333	$\frac{1}{3}$
Criner		43,334	43,334	$\frac{1}{3}$
	$80,000	$50,000	$130,000	

Partnership Assets Revalued (Goodwill to New Partner)

Suppose that Andrew and Boyles agreed to admit Criner into the partnership *for a 40% interest* in the capital and profit with an investment of $50,000. In this case, there is an implication that Criner is bringing goodwill into the partnership. That is, Andrew and Boyles must be willing to admit Criner to a 40% interest in the $80,000 recorded assets plus her $50,000 investment (40% × $130,000 = $52,000) because they expect Criner's total contribution to exceed her cash investment. Accordingly, the total value of the partnership is determined by reference to the 60% interest retained in the new partnership capital and profits by Andrew and Boyles. Total capital of the new partnership is $133,333 ($80,000 old capital assumed to be fairly valued ÷ 60%), and the admission of Criner is recorded:

Cash	$50,000	
Goodwill	3,333	
Criner capital		$53,333

To admit Criner to a 40% interest in capital and profits.

Total capital of the new partnership is $133,333 ($80,000 old capital + $50,000 new investment + $3,333 goodwill), and Criner has a 40% interest in that new capital. A summary of the capital balances before and after the admittance of Criner is as follows:

CAPITAL BALANCES

	Per Books	Investment Plus Goodwill	Capital After Investment	
Andrew	$40,000		$ 40,000	30%
Boyles	40,000		40,000	30%
Criner		$53,333	53,333	40%
	$80,000	$53,333	$133,333	

Partnership Assets Not Revalued (Bonus to New Partner)

Instead of allowing goodwill to the incoming partner, the bonus procedure can be used. Under this procedure the assets are not revalued, but the capital balances of Andrew and Boyles must be reduced to meet the 40% condition of the agreement. Total assets of the new partnership are $130,000, and Criner's 40% interest is $52,000. The $2,000 difference between Criner's capital credit of $52,000 and her $50,000 investment is considered a bonus to Criner. Partnership assets are not revalued, so the excess $2,000 credited to Criner's account must be charged against the capital accounts of Andrew and Boyles in relation to their old profit and loss sharing ratios. Criner's admittance to the partnership under the bonus procedure is recorded:

Cash	$50,000	
Andrew capital	1,000	
Boyles capital	1,000	
Criner capital		$52,000

To record Criner's investment of $50,000 for a 40% interest in the partnership and allow her a $2,000 bonus.

The capital accounts of the partnership before and after the admittance of Criner are as follows:

CAPITAL BALANCES

	Per Books	Investment	Capital After Investment	
Andrew	$40,000	$(1,000)	$ 39,000	30%
Boyles	40,000	(1,000)	39,000	30%
Criner		52,000	52,000	40%
	$80,000	$50,000	$130,000	

Basis for Revaluation

The revaluation/goodwill and nonrevaluation/bonus procedures are alternative approaches for recording changes in partnership interests through direct investments in an existing partnership. In deciding whether the goodwill or bonus relates to the old partners or the new partner, the investment of the new partner is analyzed in terms of the nonrevaluation/bonus procedure. Under the nonrevaluation assumption, the capital credit of the new partner is determined by multiplying the new partner's capital interest by the net assets of the old partnership plus the investment. The analysis is as follows:

If investment of new partner	=	capital credit of new partner	⇒	no bonus (or goodwill)
If investment of new partner	>	capital credit of new partner	⇒	bonus to old partners (or goodwill to old partners if assets are revalued)
If investment of new partner	<	capital credit of new partner	⇒	bonus to new partner (or goodwill to new partner if assets are revalued)

The amount of the old partnership capital provides no basis for revaluation of the old partners' capital, so any revaluation relating to the old partners' capital should be based on the investment of the new partner. Similarly, the amount of the new partner's investment provides no basis for revaluation of the new partner's capital, therefore, any revaluation of the new partner's capital should be related to the old partnership capital retained. Application of this scenario prevents the downward adjustment of identifiable net assets of the old partnership, which are assumed to be recorded at amounts equal to their fair values. If the evidence indicates an undervaluation or overvaluation of recorded net assets, adjustments should be made before comparing the new partner's investment and capital credit to identify bonus or goodwill.

A summary of the procedures used in the previous examples to compute the amounts of goodwill and bonus for Criner's investments is as follows:

	$50,000 Investment for a 1/3 Interest	$50,000 Investment for a 40% Interest
Nonrevaluation—Bonus		
Criner's investment	$ 50,000	$ 50,000
Criner's capital credit:		
$130,000 × $\frac{1}{3}$	43,334	
$130,000 × 40%		52,000
Bonus to old partners ($50,000 > $43,334)	$ 6,666	
Bonus to Criner ($50,000 < $52,000)		$ 2,000
Revaluation—Goodwill		
Total capital:		
$50,000 ÷ $\frac{1}{3}$ (based on Criner's investment)	$150,000	
$80,000 ÷ 60% (based on old partnership capital)		$133,333
Book value of old partnership assets + Criner's investment	130,000	130,000
Goodwill (other identifiable assets) to old partners	$ 20,000	
Goodwill to Criner		$ 3,333

DISSOLUTION OF A CONTINUING PARTNERSHIP THROUGH DEATH OR RETIREMENT

The retirement or death of a partner from a continuing partnership business dissolves the old partnership and requires a settlement with the retiring partner or with the estate of the deceased partner. In the absence of a partnership agreement to the contrary, the settlement is in accordance with Section 42 of the Act. This section provides that the retiring partner or the estate of a deceased partner "may have the value of his interest at the date of dissolution ascertained, and shall receive as an ordinary creditor an amount equal to the value of his interest in the dissolved partnership with interest." The valuation is at the date of dissolution, so it follows that partnership books should be closed as of the date of death or retirement. When there is a time lag between death or retirement and final settlement, the capital balance of the deceased or retiring partner should be reclassified as a liability. Any interest (or other return) accruing on the liability up to the date of final settlement is considered an expense of the continuing partnership entity.

In recording the settlement, the accounting depends upon whether the retiring partner (or the estate of the deceased partner) receives an amount equal to the final balance of his or her capital account or something more or less than his or her final capital. If the retiring partner (or the estate of a deceased partner) is paid an amount equal to the final balance of his or her capital account, the only entry necessary is a charge to his or her capital account and a credit to cash for the amount paid. When the settlement with a retiring partner is more or less than the final capital account balance, the revaluation/goodwill and nonrevaluation/bonus procedures provide alternate methods of accounting for the settlement.

To illustrate the goodwill and bonus procedures, assume that Bonnie, Clyde, and Dillinger are partners with profit sharing percentages of 40%, 20%, and 40%, respectively, and that Dillinger decides to retire. The capital and income interests of the three partners on the date of Dillinger's retirement are as follows:

	Capital Balances	Percentage of Capital	Profit and Loss Percentage
Bonnie	$ 70,000	35%	40%
Clyde	50,000	25	20
Dillinger	80,000	40	40
Total capital	$200,000	100%	100%

Excess Payment to Retiring Partner

The partners agree that the business is undervalued on the partnership books and that Dillinger will be paid $92,000 in final settlement of his partnership interest. The excess payment to Dillinger can be recorded by three methods: (1) Dillinger may be granted a bonus, (2) partnership capital may be revalued to the extent of the excess payment to Dillinger, or (3) partnership capital may be revalued based on the amount implied by the excess payment.

Bonus to Retiring Partner   Dillinger's withdrawal from the partnership under the bonus procedure is recorded as follows:

Dillinger capital	$80,000	
Bonnie capital	8,000	
Clyde capital	4,000	
Cash		$92,000

This entry reflects the fact that Bonnie and Clyde granted a $12,000 bonus to Dillinger that was charged to their capital accounts in their 40:20 relative profit sharing ratios.

Goodwill Equal to Excess Payment Is Recorded   A second method of recording Dillinger's withdrawal is to record the $12,000 excess of cash paid to Dillinger over his capital account balance as goodwill:

Dillinger capital	$80,000	
Goodwill	12,000	
Cash		$92,000

Under this approach, goodwill is recorded only to the extent paid for by the continuing partnership. The problem with this approach is that it provides a revaluation of Dillinger's share of partnership assets, but it does not provide a revaluation of Bonnie and Clyde's capital interests. Thus, it is argued that this approach is inconsistent and logically unsound.

Revaluation of Total Partnership Capital Based on Excess Payment   A third approach for recording Dillinger's retirement is to revalue total partnership capital on the basis of the $12,000 excess payment. Under this method, total partnership capital is revalued as follows:

Goodwill (other assets)	$30,000	
Bonnie capital		$12,000
Clyde capital		6,000
Dillinger capital		12,000

The total undervaluation of the partnership is measured by the amount implied by the excess payment. In this case, the $30,000 is computed by dividing the $12,000 excess payment by Dillinger's 40% profit sharing percentage. Dillinger's retirement is then recorded:

Dillinger capital	$92,000	
Cash		$92,000

Total partnership capital implied by Dillinger's retirement settlement could have been computed by capitalizing the $92,000 payment to Dillinger to obtain a total partnership valuation of $230,000 ($92,000 ÷ 40%). This approach is acceptable when the capital and income interests of the retiring (or deceased) partner are aligned. In the absence of such alignment, this alternate approach produces erroneous results. For example, assume the same facts as before except that Bonnie, Clyde, and Dillinger have capital balances of $70,000, $60,000, and $70,000, respectively. Capitalizing the $92,000 payment to Dillinger by 40% produces a total partnership valuation of $230,000 and the same $30,000 goodwill computation as before. However, the results are erroneous because Dillinger's capital balance is only $82,000 after the goodwill is recorded [$70,000 + ($30,000 × 40%)]. The actual goodwill implied by the $92,000 payment to Dillinger is $55,000 [($92,000 − $70,000) ÷ 40%], and Dillinger's share is $22,000. Dillinger's capital account is increased to $92,000, the amount of the cash payment, when the implied goodwill is recorded.

Payment to Retiring Partner Less than Capital Balance

Suppose that Dillinger is paid $72,000 in final settlement of his capital interest. In this case, the three partners may have agreed that the business is worth less than its book value.

Overvalued Assets Written Down A retirement payment to Dillinger of $8,000 less than his final capital balance implies that existing partnership capital is overvalued by $20,000 [($80,000 − $72,000) ÷ 40%]. If the evidence available supports this implication, the overvalued assets should be identified and reduced to their fair values. The revaluation and payment to Dillinger are recorded:

Bonnie capital	$ 8,000	
Clyde capital	4,000	
Dillinger capital	8,000	
Net assets		$20,000
Dillinger capital	$72,000	
Cash		72,000

This method of recording Dillinger's withdrawal is appropriate if the $72,000 paid to Dillinger is the result of a valuation provided for under the Act. However, it would not be appropriate if the $72,000 were determined by prior agreement of the partners without regard to total partnership capital at the time of withdrawal.

Bonus to Continuing Partners If evidence indicates that partnership capital is fairly valued, the retirement of Dillinger would be recorded under the bonus procedure as follows:

Dillinger capital	$80,000	
Bonnie capital		$ 5,333
Clyde capital		2,667
Cash		72,000

This method of recording provides a bonus to Bonnie and Clyde. The bonus is measured by the excess of Dillinger's capital balance over the cash paid by the partnership for his 40% interest.

LIMITED PARTNERSHIPS

Under some circumstances, the unlimited liability characteristic of general partnerships may be circumvented by creating a special kind of partnership called a limited partnership. The Uniform Limited Partnership Act provides legal guidance for limited partnerships. The limited partnership consists of at least one general partner and one or more limited partners. The general partner is like any partner in a general partnership, and he or she has unlimited liability for partnership debt. The limited partner is basically an investor whose risk is limited to his or her equity investment in the partnership. The limited partner is *excluded* from the management of the business. If he or she takes part in management, he or she loses the limited partner status and becomes a general partner with unlimited liability.

A limited partnership is more difficult to form than a general partnership. The limited partnership agreement *must be written*, signed by the partners, and filed with the appropriate public official in the state where the partnership is created. If the statute is not carefully followed, the courts may find the partnership to be a general partnership, rather than a limited partnership.

Joint Ventures

Joint ventures have the characteristics of partnerships, except that the joint venture is usually set up for a specific limited purpose. When the activity is complete, the venture is terminated. For this reason, the agency power of joint ventures is limited. Joint ventures are covered in Chapter 11 of this book.

SUMMARY

Partnership accounting procedures are similar to those for other forms of business organization, except for procedures relating to the measurement of partnership capital interests. Accounting measurements relating to the capital and income interests of partners are based on the partnership agreement, or in the absence of an agreement, on the Uniform Partnership Act, except for partnerships in states that have not adopted the Act. The partnership agreement should be in writing and should cover matters relating to the amount and valuation of capital contributions, additional investments and withdrawals, loans to partners, profit sharing arrangements, changes in partnership interests, and various other matters. These areas are discussed in the chapter, and related accounting concepts and procedures are illustrated.

SELECTED READINGS

Special Report. "Limited Liability CPA Firms: An Attractive Choice." *Journal of Accountancy* (July 1995), pp. 20–21.

WOEHLKE, JAMES A., WILLIAM B. KELLIHER, BRIAN L. SCHORR, and WALTER M. PRIMOFF. "LLCs: The Business Planner's Dream Entity." *The CPA Journal* (June 1995), pp. 16–22.

ASSIGNMENT MATERIAL

QUESTIONS

1 Explain why the noncash investments of partners should be recorded at their fair values.
2 Is there a conceptual difference between partner drawings and withdrawals? A practical difference?
3 In the absence of an agreement for the division of profits, how are they divided under the Uniform Partnership Act? Does your answer also apply to losses? Does it apply if one partner invests three times as much as the other partners?
4 Why do some profit sharing agreements provide for salary and interest allowances?
5 Are partner salary allowances expenses of the partnership?
6 When a profit sharing agreement specifies that profits be divided in the ratio of capital balances, how should capital balances be computed?
7 Explain how a partner could have a loss from partnership operations for a period even though the partnership had net income.
8 The concept of partnership dissolution has a technical meaning under the provisions of the Uniform Partnership Act. Explain the concept.
9 If a partner sells his or her partnership interest directly to a third party, the partnership may or may not be dissolved. Under what conditions is the partnership dissolved?
10 If a partnership is dissolved with the death or retirement of a partner, how do you explain the fact that some partnerships have been in existence for 50 years or more?
11 How does the purchase of an interest from existing partners differ from acquiring an interest by investment in a partnership?
12 What alternative approaches can be used in recording the admission of a new partner?
13 Why is the goodwill procedure best described as a revaluation procedure?
14 Explain the bonus procedure for recording an investment in a partnership. When is the bonus applicable to old partners, and when is it applicable to new partners?

15 The goodwill procedure was used to record the investment of a new partner in the XYZ Partnership, but immediately thereafter, the entire business was sold for an amount equal to the recorded capital of the partnership. Under what conditions would the amounts received in final liquidation of the partnership have been the same as if the bonus procedure had been used?

16 Bob invests $10,000 cash for a 25% interest in the capital and earnings of the BOP Partnership. Explain how this investment could give rise to (a) recording goodwill, (b) the write-down of the partnership assets, (c) a bonus to old partners, and (d) a bonus to Bob.

EXERCISES

E 16-1 Carson and Lamb establish a partnership to operate a used-furniture business under the name of C&L Furniture. Carson contributes furniture that cost $60,000 and has a fair value of $90,000. Lamb contributes $30,000 cash and delivery equipment that cost $40,000 and has a fair value of $30,000. The partners agree to share profits and losses 60% to Carson and 40% to Lamb.

Required: Calculate the dollar amount of inequity that will result if the initial noncash contributions of the partners are recorded at cost rather than fair market value.

E 16-2 Arnold, Beverly, and Carolyn are partners who share profits and losses 40:40:20, respectively, after Beverly, who manages the partnership, receives a bonus of 10% of income after deducting the bonus. Partnership income for the year is $506,000.

Required: Prepare a schedule to allocate partnership income to Arnold, Beverly, and Carolyn.

E 16-3 The partnership agreement of Vannah, Wanine, and Ully provides that profits are to be divided as follows:

- Ully receives a salary of $12,000 and Wanine receives a salary of $9,000 for time spent in the business.
- All partners receive 10% interest on average capital balances.
- Remaining profits and losses are divided equally among the three partners.

On January 1, 20X2 the capital balances were Vannah, $100,000; Wanine, $80,000; and Ully, $75,000. Vannah invested an additional $20,000 on July 1 and withdrew $20,000 on October 1. Ully and Wanine had drawings of $9,000 each during the year.

Required: Prepare a schedule to allocate partnership net income of $14,000 for 20X2.

E 16-4 Melanie and David created a partnership to own and operate a health-food store. The partnership agreement provided that Melanie receive a salary of $10,000 and David a salary of $5,000 to recognize their relative time spent in operating the store. Remaining profits and losses were divided 60:40 to Melanie and David, respectively. Income for 20X3, the first year of operations, of $13,000 was allocated $8,800 to Melanie and $4,200 to David.

On January 1, 20X4 the partnership agreement was changed to reflect the fact that David could no longer devote any time to the store's operations. The new agreement allows Melanie a salary of $18,000, and the remaining profits and losses are divided equally. In 20X4 an error was discovered such that the 20X3 reported income was understated by $4,000. The partnership income of $25,000 for 20X4 included this $4,000 related to 20X3.

Required: Prepare a schedule to allocate the $25,000 reported 20X4 partnership income to Melanie and David.

E 16-5 On December 31, 20X2 the total partnership capital (assets less liabilities) for the Bird, Cage, and Dean partnership is $372,000. Selected information related to the preclosing capital balances is as follows:

	Bird Capital	Cage Capital	Dean Capital	Total Capital
Balance January 1	$120,000	$ 90,000	$140,000	$350,000
Investments 20X2		20,000	20,000	40,000
Withdrawals 20X2	(30,000)		(30,000)	(60,000)
Drawings 20X2	(10,000)	(10,000)	(10,000)	(30,000)
	$ 80,000	$100,000	$120,000	$300,000

Required: Prepare a statement of partnership capital for the Bird, Cage, and Dean partnership at year-end 20X2.

E 16-6 Capital balances and profit and loss sharing ratios of the partners in the BIG Entertainment Galley are as follows:

Batty capital (50%)	$140,000
Iggy capital (30%)	160,000
Grabby capital (20%)	100,000
Total	$400,000

Batty needs money and agrees to assign half of his interest in the partnership to Yessir for $90,000 cash. Yessir pays $90,000 directly to Batty. Yessir does not become a partner.

Required

1 Prepare a journal entry to record the assignment of half of Batty's interest in the partnership to Yessir.
2 What is the total capital of the BIG partnership immediately after the assignment of the interest to Yessir?

E 16-7 The capital accounts of the Klaxon and Bell partnership on September 30, 20X1 were:

Klaxon capital (75% profit percentage)	$140,000
Bell capital (25% profit percentage)	60,000
Total capital	$200,000

On October 1, Ring was admitted to a 40% interest in the partnership when he purchased 40% of each existing partner's capital for $120,000, paid directly to Klaxon and Bell.

Required: Determine the capital balances of Klaxon, Bell, and Ring after Ring's admission to the partnership if goodwill is *not* recorded.

E 16-8 Bowen and Monita are partners in a retail business and divide profits 60% to Bowen and 40% to Monita. Their capital balances at December 31, 20X5 are as follows:

Bowen capital	$180,000
Monita capital	180,000
Total capital	$360,000

Partnership assets and liabilities have book values equal to fair values. The partners agree to admit Johnson into the partnership. Johnson purchases a one-third interest in partnership capital and profits directly from Bowen and Monita (one-third of each of their capital accounts) for $150,000.

Required: Prepare journal entries for the admission of Johnson into the partnership, assuming that partnership assets are revalued.

E 16-9 The capital balances and profit and loss sharing percentages for the Sprint, Telico, and Univar partnership at December 31, 20X1 are as follows:

Sprint capital (30%)	$80,000
Telico capital (50%)	$90,000
Univar capital (20%)	$70,000

The partners agree to admit Vernon into the partnership on January 1, 20X2 for a 20% interest in the capital and income of the business.

Required

1 Prepare the journal entry(s) to record Vernon's admission to the partnership assuming that he invests $50,000 in the partnership for the 20% interest and that partnership capital is *revalued*.
2 Prepare the journal entry(s) to record Vernon's admission to the partnership assuming that he invests $70,000 in the partnership for the 20% interest and that partnership capital is *revalued*.

E 16-10 Capital balances and profit sharing percentages for the partnership of Manda, Nimball, and Ojas on January 1, 20X6 are as follows:

Manda (36%)	$140,000
Nimball (24%)	100,000
Ojas (40%)	160,000
	$400,000

On January 3, 20X6 the partners agree to admit Roscoe into the partnership for a 25% interest in capital and earnings for his investment in the partnership of $120,000. Partnership assets are not to be revalued.

Required
1 Determine the capital balances of the four partners immediately after the admission of Roscoe.
2 What is the profit and loss sharing ratio for Manda, Nimball, Ojas, and Roscoe?

E 16-11 Capital balances and profit and loss sharing ratios for the Nixon, Mann, and Peter partnership on December 31, 20X1, just before the retirement of Nixon, are as follows:

Nixon capital (30%)	$64,000
Mann capital (30%)	$70,000
Peter capital (40%)	$80,000

On January 2, 20X2, Nixon is paid $85,000 cash upon his retirement.

Required: Prepare the journal entry(s) to record Nixon's retirement assuming that goodwill, as implied by the payment to Nixon, is recorded on the partnership books.

E 16-12 A balance sheet at December 31, 20X5 for the Beck, Dee, and Lynn partnership is summarized as follows:

Assets	$80,000	Liabilities	$20,000
Loan to Dee	10,000	Beck capital (50%)	30,000
	$90,000	Dee capital (40%)	30,000
		Lynn capital (10%)	10,000
			$90,000

Dee is retiring from the partnership. The partners agree that partnership assets, excluding Dee's loan, should be adjusted to their fair value of $100,000 and that Dee should receive $31,000 for her capital balance net of the $10,000 loan. No goodwill is to be recorded.

Required: Determine the capital balances of Beck and Lynn immediately after Dee's retirement.

E 16-13 Kathy and Eddie formed the K & E partnership several years ago. Capital account balances on January 1, 20X5 were:

Kathy	$496,750
Eddie	$268,250

The partnership agreement provides Kathy with an annual salary of $10,000 plus a bonus of 5% of partnership net income for managing the business. Eddie is provided an annual salary of $15,000 with no bonus. The remainder is shared evenly. Partnership net income for 20X5 was $30,000. Eddie and Kathy each invested an additional $5,000 during the year to finance a special purchase. Year-end drawing account balances were $15,000 for Kathy and $10,000 for Eddie.

Required:
1 Prepare an income allocation schedule.
2 Create the journal entries to update the equity accounts at the end of the year.
3 Determine the capital balances as of December 31, 20X5.

E 16-14 The capital account balances and profit and loss sharing ratios of the Byder, Cegal, Danner, and Evita Partnership on December 31, 20X5 after closing entries are as follows:

Byder (30%)	$ 60,000
Cegal (20%)	50,000
Danner (40%)	50,000
Evita (10%)	40,000
Total capital	$200,000

Cegal is retiring from the partnership and the partners agree that he will receive a cash payment of $70,000 in final settlement of his interest. The book values of partnership assets and liabilities are equal to fair values except for a building with a book value of $30,000 and a fair value of $50,000.

Required
1 Prepare the journal entry (entries) to record Cegal's retirement assuming that assets are revalued to the basis implied by the excess payment to Cegal.

2 Prepare the journal entry (entries) to record Cegal's retirement assuming that assets and liabilities are revalued only to the extent of the excess payment to Cegal.

3 Prepare the journal entry (entries) to record Cegal's retirement assuming the bonus approach is used.

E 16-15   **1** Bill and Ken enter into a partnership agreement in which Bill is to have a 60% interest in capital and profits and Ken is to have a 40% interest in capital and profits. Bill contributes the following:

	Cost	Fair Value
Land	$ 10,000	$20,000
Building	100,000	60,000
Equipment	20,000	15,000

There is a $30,000 mortgage on the building that the partnership agrees to assume. Ken contributes $50,000 cash to the partnership. Bill and Ken agree that Ken's capital account should equal Ken's $50,000 cash contribution and that goodwill should be recorded. Goodwill should be recorded in the amount of:

a $10,000   c $16,667
b $15,000   d $20,000

2 Thomas and Mark are partners having capital balances of $50,000 and $60,000, respectively. They admit Jay to a one-third interest in partnership capital and profits for an investment of $65,000. If the goodwill procedure is used in recording Jay's admission to the partnership:

a Jay's capital will be $58,333
b Total capital will be $175,000
c Mark's capital will be $70,000
d Goodwill will be recorded at $15,000

3 On December 31, 20X6, Tina and Webb, who share profits and losses equally, have capital balances of $170,000 and $200,000, respectively. They agree to admit Zen for a one-third interest in capital and profits for his investment of $200,000. Partnership net assets are not to be revalued. Capital accounts of Tina, Webb, and Zen, respectively, immediately after Zen's admission to the partnership are:

a $170,000, $200,000, and $200,000
b $165,000, $195,000, and $200,000
c $175,000, $205,000, and $190,000
d $185,000, $215,000, and $200,000

4 Finney and Rhoads have capital balances of $100,000 and $80,000, respectively, and they share profits equally. The partners agree to accept Chesterfield for a 25% interest in capital and profits for her investment of $90,000. If goodwill is recorded, the capital account balances of Finney and Rhoads immediately after Chesterfield's admittance to the partnership will be:

a Finney, $100,000 and Rhoads, $120,000
b Finney, $111,250 and Rhoads, $91,250
c Finney, $145,000 and Rhoads, $125,000
d Finney, $120,000 and Rhoads, $120,000

5 The balance sheet of the Fred, Gini, and Peggy partnership on December 31, 20X6, together with profit sharing ratios, revealed the following:

Cash	$240,000	Fred capital (30%)	$200,000
Other assets	360,000	Gini capital (30%)	170,000
		Peggy capital (40%)	230,000
	$600,000		$600,000

Gini is retiring from the partnership and the partners agreed that she should receive $200,000 cash as payment in full for her share of partnership assets. If the goodwill implied by the settlement with Gini is recorded on the partnership books, total partnership assets after Gini's withdrawal should be:

a $566,667   c $430,000
b $500,000   d $400,000

E 16-16   **1** Shirley purchased an interest in the Tony and Olga partnership by paying Tony $40,000 for half of his capital and half of his 50% profit sharing interest. At the time, Tony's capital balance was $30,000 and Olga's capital balance was $70,000. Shirley should receive a credit to her capital account of:

a $15,000   c $25,000
b $20,000   d $33,333

2 Linkous and Quesenberry are partners with capital balances of $50,000 and $70,000, respectively, and they share profits and losses equally. The partners agree to take Duncan into the partnership for a 40% interest in capital and profits, while Linkous and Quesenberry each retain a 30% interest. Duncan pays $60,000 cash directly to Linkous and Quesenberry for his 40% interest, and goodwill implied by Duncan's payment is recognized on the partnership books. If Linkous and Quesenberry transfer equal amounts of capital to Duncan, the capital balances after Duncan's admittance will be:

  a Linkous, $35,000; Quesenberry, $55,000; Duncan, $60,000

  b Linkous, $45,000; Quesenberry, $45,000; Duncan, $60,000

  c Linkous, $36,000; Quesenberry, $36,000; Duncan, $48,000

  d Linkous, $26,000; Quesenberry, $46,000; Duncan, $48,000

  Use the following information in answering questions 3 and 4:

     Dr. McCall and Dr. Newby are partners with capital balances of $70,000 and $50,000, respectively, and they share profit and losses equally. Dr. Oakes is admitted to the partnership with a contribution of $50,000 cash for a one-third interest in the partnership capital and in future profits and losses.

3 If the goodwill is recognized in accounting for the admission of Dr. Oakes, what amount of goodwill will be recorded?

  a $60,000   **c** $10,000

  b $20,000   **d** $6,667

4 If no goodwill is recognized, the capital balances of Drs. McCall and Newby immediately after the admission of Dr. Oakes will be:

  a McCall, $65,000 and Newby, $45,000

  b McCall, $66,667 and Newby, $46,666

  c McCall, $67,500 and Newby, $47,500

  d McCall, $70,000 and Newby, $50,000

5 The December 31, 20X8 balance sheet of the Bennett, Carter, and Davis partnership is summarized as follows:

Cash	$100,000	Carter loan	$100,000
Other assets, at cost	500,000	Bennett capital	100,000
		Carter capital	200,000
		Davis capital	200,000
	$600,000		$600,000

The partners share profits and losses as follows: Bennett, 20%; Carter 30%; and Davis, 50%. Carter is retiring from the partnership and the partners have agreed that "other assets" should be adjusted to their fair value of $600,000 at December 31, 20X8. They further agree that Carter will receive $244,000 cash for his partnership interest exclusive of his loan, which is to be paid in full, and that no goodwill implied by Carter's payment will be recorded.

     After Carter's retirement, the capital balances of Bennett and Davis, respectively, will be:

  a $116,000 and $240,000

  b $101,714 and $254,286

  c $100,000 and $200,000

  d $73,143 and $182,857

E 16-17 **[AICPA adapted]**

1 Cobb, Inc., a partner in TLC Partnership, assigns its partnership interest to Bean, who is not made a partner. After the assignment, Bean asserts the rights to:

  I Participate in the management of TLC

  II Cobb's share of TLC's partnership profits

  Bean is correct as to which of these rights?

  a I only   **c** I and II

  b II only   **d** Neither I nor II

2 When property other than cash is invested in a partnership, at what amount should the noncash property be credited to the contributing partner's capital account?

  a Fair value at the date of contribution

  b Contributing partner's original cost

  c Assessed valuation for property tax purposes

  d Contributing partner's tax basis

3 Arthur Plack, a partner in the Brite Partnership, has a 30% participation in partnership profits and losses. Plack's capital account had a net decrease of $60,000 during the calendar year 20X4. During 20X4, Plack withdrew $130,000 (charged against his capital account) and contributed property valued at $25,000 to the partnership. What was the net income of the Brite Partnership for 20X4?

  a $150,000   **c** $350,000

  b $233,333   **d** $550,000

4 Fox, Greg, and Howe are partners with average capital balances during 20X6 of $120,000, $60,000, and $40,000, respectively. Partners receive 10% interest on their average capital balances. After deducting salaries of $30,000 to Fox and $20,000 to Howe, the residual profit or loss is divided equally. In 20X6 the partnership sustained a $33,000 loss before interest and salaries to partners. By what amount should Fox's capital account change?

a $7,000 increase
b $11,000 decrease
c $35,000 decrease
d $42,000 increase

5 Beck, an active partner in the Beck and Cris partnership, receives an annual bonus of 25% of partnership net income after deducting the bonus. For the year ended December 31, 20X8, partnership net income before the bonus amounted to $300,000. Beck's 20X8 bonus should be:

a $56,250   c $62,500
b $60,000   d $75,000

E 16-18   [AICPA adapted]

1 Partners Allen, Baker, and Coe share profits and losses 50:30:20, respectively. The balance sheet at April 30, 20X5 follows:

Assets		Equities	
Cash	$ 40,000	Accounts payable	$100,000
Other assets	360,000	Allen capital	74,000
		Baker capital	130,000
		Coe capital	96,000
	$400,000		$400,000

The assets and liabilities are recorded and presented at their respective fair values. Jones is to be admitted as a new partner with a 20% capital interest and a 20% share of profits and losses in exchange for a cash contribution. No goodwill or bonus is to be recorded. How much cash should Jones contribute?

a $60,000   c $75,000
b $72,000   d $80,000

2 Elton and Don are partners who share profits and losses in the ratio of 7:3, respectively. On November 5, 20X8 their respective capital accounts were as follows:

Elton	$ 70,000
Don	60,000
	$130,000

On that date they agreed to admit Kravitz as a partner with a one-third interest in the capital and profits and losses upon his investment of $50,000. The new partnership will begin with a total capital of $180,000. Immediately after Kravitz's admission, what are the capital balances of Elton, Don, and Kravitz, respectively?

a $60,000, $60,000, $60,000
b $63,000, $57,000, $60,000
c $63,333, $56,667, $60,000
d $70,000, $60,000, $50,000

3 William desires to purchase a one-fourth capital and profit and loss interest in the partnership of Eli, George, and Dick. The three partners agree to sell William one-fourth of their respective capital and profit and loss interests in exchange for a total payment of $40,000. The capital accounts and the respective percentage interests in profits and losses immediately before the sale to William are:

Eli capital (60%)	$ 80,000
George capital (30%)	40,000
Dick capital (10%)	20,000
	$140,000

All other assets and liabilities are fairly valued, and implied goodwill is to be recorded prior to the acquisition by William. Immediately after William's acquisition, what should be the capital balances of Eli, George, and Dick, respectively?

a $60,000, $30,000, $15,000
b $69,000, $34,500, $16,500
c $77,000, $38,500, $19,500
d $92,000, $46,000, $22,000

4 The capital accounts of the partnership of Newton, Sharman, and Jackson on June 1, 20X7 are presented, along with their respective profit and loss ratios:

Newton	$139,200	$\frac{1}{2}$
Sharman	208,800	$\frac{1}{3}$
Jackson	96,000	$\frac{1}{6}$
	$444,000	

On June 1, 20X7, Sidney was admitted to the partnership when he purchased, for $132,000, a proportionate interest from Newton and Sharman in the net assets and profits of the partnership. As a result of this transaction, Sidney acquired a one-fifth interest in the net assets and profits of the firm. Assuming that implied goodwill is *not* to be recorded, what is the combined gain realized by Newton and Sharman upon the sale of a portion of their interests in the partnership to Sidney?

a $0   c $62,400
b $43,200   d $82,000

5 Kern and Pate are partners with capital balances of $60,000 and $20,000, respectively. Profits and losses are divided in the ratio of 60:40. Kern and Pate decided to form a new partnership with Grant, who invested land valued at $15,000 for a 20% capital interest in the new partnership. Grant's capital account should be credited for:

a $12,000   c $16,000
b $15,000   d $19,000

6 James Dixon, a partner in an accounting firm, decided to withdraw from the partnership. Dixon's share of the partnership profits and losses was 20%. Upon withdrawing from the partnership, he was paid $74,000 in final settlement for his partnership interest. The total of the partners capital accounts *before* recognition of partnership goodwill prior to Dixon's withdrawal was $210,000. After his withdrawal, the remaining partners' capital accounts, excluding their share of goodwill, totaled $160,000. The total agreed-upon goodwill of the firm was:

a $120,000   c $160,000
b $140,000   d $250,000

7 On June 30, 20X8 the balance sheet for the partnership of Williams, Brown, and Lowe, together with their respective profit and loss ratios, is summarized as follows:

Assets, at cost	$300,000	Williams loan	$ 15,000
		Williams capital (20%)	70,000
		Brown capital (20%)	65,000
		Lowe capital (60%)	150,000
			$300,000

Williams has decided to retire from the partnership, and by mutual agreement the assets are to be adjusted to their fair value of $360,000 at June 30, 20X8. It is agreed that the partnership will pay Williams $102,000 cash for his partnership interest exclusive of his loan, which is to be repaid in full. Goodwill is to be recorded in this transaction, as implied by the excess payment to Williams. After Williams's retirement, what are the capital account balances of Brown and Lowe, respectively?

a $65,000 and $150,000
b $97,000 and $246,000
c $73,000 and $174,000
d $77,000 and $186,000

E 16-19 The partnership agreement of Kray, Lamb, and Mann provides for the division of net income as follows:

1 Lamb, who manages the partnership, is to receive a salary of $11,000 per year.
2 Each partner is to be allowed interest at 10% on beginning capital.
3 Remaining profits are to be divided equally.

During 20X1, Kray invested an additional $4,000 in the partnership. Lamb withdrew $5,000, and Mann withdrew $4,000. No other investments or withdrawals were made during 20X1. On January 1, 20X1 the capital balances were Kray, $65,000; Lamb, $75,000; and Mann, $70,000. Total capital at year-end was $252,000.

Required: Prepare a statement of partners' capital for the year ended December 31, 20X1.

E 16-20 After operating as partners for several years, Grosby and Hambone decided to sell one-half of each of their partnership interests to Iota for a total of $70,000, paid directly to Grosby and Hambone.

At the time of Iota's admittance to the partnership, Grosby and Hambone had capital balances of $45,000 and $65,000, respectively, and shared profits 45% to Grosby and 55% to Hambone.

Required

    1 Calculate the capital balances of each of the partners immediately after Iota is admitted as a partner.

    2 In designing a new partnership agreement, how should profits and losses be divided?

    3 If a new partnership agreement is not established, how will profits and losses be divided?

E 16-21 The Case, Donley, and Early partnership balance sheet and profit and loss percentages at June 30, 20X6 are summarized as follows:

Assets	$500,000	Case capital (30%)	$140,000
		Donley capital (30%)	175,000
		Early capital (40%)	185,000
	$500,000		$500,000

On July 1, 20X6 the partners agree that Ms. Case is to retire immediately and receive $161,000 for her partnership interest.

Required: Prepare journal entries to illustrate *three* possible methods of accounting for the retirement of Ms. Case.

PROBLEMS

P 16-1 Ellen, Fargo, and Gary are partners who share profits and losses 20%, 20%, and 60%, respectively, after Ellen and Fargo each receive a $12,000 salary allowance. Capital balances on January 1, 20X6 are as follows:

Ellen (20%)	$ 69,000
Fargo (20%)	85,500
Gary (60%)	245,500

During 20X6, Gary invested an additional $20,000 in the partnership, and Ellen and Fargo each withdrew $12,000, equal to their salary allowances as provided by the profit and loss sharing agreement. The partnership net assets at December 31, 20X6 were $481,000.

Required: Prepare a statement of partnership capital for the year ended December 31, 20X6.

P 16-2 The partnership of Mortin and Oscar is being dissolved, and the assets and equities at book value and fair value and profit and loss sharing ratios at January 1, 20X1 are as follows:

	Book Value	Fair Value
Cash	$ 20,000	$ 20,000
Accounts receivable—net	100,000	100,000
Inventories	50,000	200,000
Plant assets—net	100,000	120,000
	$270,000	$440,000
Accounts payable	$ 50,000	$ 50,000
Mortin capital (50%)	120,000	
Oscar capital (50%)	100,000	
	$270,000	

Mortin and Oscar agree to admit Trent into the partnership for a one-third interest. Trent invests $95,000 cash and a building to be used in the business with a book value to Trent of $100,000 and a fair value of $120,000.

Required:

    1 Prepare a balance sheet for the Mortin, Oscar, and Trent partnership on January 2, 20X1, just after the admission of Trent, assuming that the assets are revalued and goodwill is recognized.

    2 Prepare a balance sheet for Mortin, Oscar and Trent partnership on January 2, 20X1, after the admission of Trent, assuming that the assets are not revalued.

P 16-3 Ashe and Barbour are partners with capital balances on January 1, 20X6 of $40,000 and $50,000, respectively. The partnership agreement provides that each partner be allowed 10% interest on beginning capital balances; that Ashe receive a salary allowance of $12,000 per year and a 20% bonus of partnership income after interest, salary allowance, and bonus; and that remaining income be divided equally.

Required: Prepare an income distribution schedule to show how the $105,000 partnership net income for 20X6 should be divided.

P 16-4 The partnership agreement of Alex, Carl, and Erika provides that profits are to be divided as follows:

1 Alex is to receive a salary allowance of $10,000 for managing the partnership business.
2 Partners are to receive 10% interest on average capital balances.
3 Remaining profits are to be divided 30%, 30%, and 40% to Alex, Carl, and Erika, respectively.

Alex had a capital balance of $60,000 at January 1, 20X1 and had drawings of $8,000 during the year ended December 31, 20X1. Carl's capital balance on January 1, 20X1 was $90,000, and he invested an additional $30,000 on September 1, 20X1. Erika's beginning capital balance was $110,000, and she withdrew $10,000 on July 1 but invested an additional $20,000 on October 1, 20X1.

The partnership has a net loss of $12,000 during 20X1, and the accountant in charge allocated the net loss as follows: $200 profit to Alex, $4,800 loss to Carl, and $7,400 loss to Erika.

Required

1 A schedule to show the correct allocation of the partnership net loss for 20X1
2 A statement of partnership capital for the year ended December 31, 20X1
3 Journal entries to correct the books of the partnership at December 31, 20X1, assuming that all closing entries for the year have been recorded

P 16-5 A summary of changes in the capital accounts of the Katie, Lynda, and Molly partnership for 20X2, before closing partnership net income to the capital accounts, is as follows:

	Katie Capital	Lynda Capital	Molly Capital	Total Capital
Balance January 1, 20X2	$80,000	$80,000	$90,000	$250,000
Investment April 1	20,000			20,000
Withdrawal May 1		(15,000)		(15,000)
Withdrawal July 1	(10,000)			(10,000)
Withdrawal September 1			(30,000)	(30,000)
	$90,000	$65,000	$60,000	$215,000

Determine the allocation of the 20X2 net income to the partners under each of the following sets of independent assumptions:

1 Partnership net income is $60,000, and profit is divided on the basis of average capital balances during the year.
2 Partnership net income is $50,000, Katie gets a bonus of 10% of income for managing the business, and the remaining profits are divided on the basis of beginning capital balances.
3 Partnership net loss is $35,000, Molly receives a $12,000 salary, each partner is allowed 10% interest on beginning capital balances, and the remaining profits are divided equally.

P 16-6 The partnership of Jones, Keller, and Glade was created on January 2, 20X6, with each of the partners contributing cash of $30,000. Reported profits, withdrawals, and additional investments were as follows:

	Reported Net Income	Withdrawals	Additional Investments
20X6	$19,000	$4,000 Keller 5,000 Jones	$5,000 Glade
20X7	$22,000	$8,000 Glade 3,000 Keller	$5,000 Jones
20X8	$29,000	$2,000 Glade 4,000 Keller	$6,000 Glade

The partnership agreement provides that partners are to be allowed 10% interest on the beginning-of-the-year capital balances, that Jones is to receive a $7,000 salary allowance, and that remaining profits are to be divided equally.

After the books were closed on December 31, 20X8, it was discovered that depreciation had been understated by $2,000 each year and that the inventory taken at December 31, 20X6 was understated by $8,000.

Required

    1 Calculate the balances in the three capital accounts on January 1, 20X9.

    2 Calculate the balances that should be in the three capital accounts on January 1, 20X9.

    3 Give the journal entry (one entry) to correct the books on January 1, 20X9.

P 16-7   The partnership of Addie and Bailey is being dissolved, and its assets and equities at book value and fair value just prior to dissolution on January 1, 20X8 are as follows:

	Book Value	Fair Value
Assets		
Cash	$ 15,000	$ 15,000
Accounts receivable—net	45,000	40,000
Inventories	50,000	60,000
Plant assets—net	90,000	105,000
	$200,000	$220,000
Equities		
Accounts payable	$ 30,000	$ 30,000
15% note payable	50,000	40,000
Addie capital (60%)	64,000	
Bailey capital (40%)	56,000	
	$200,000	

On January 2, 20X8, Addie and Bailey take Cathy into the new partnership of Addie, Bailey, and Cathy for a 40% interest in capital and profits.

Required

    1 Prepare journal entries for the admission of Cathy into the partnership for an investment of $150,000, assuming that assets (including any goodwill) are revalued.

    2 Prepare a balance sheet for the Addie, Bailey, and Cathy partnership on January 2, 20X8, just after the admission of Cathy.

P 16-8   The capital accounts of the Abed, Batak, and Cabel partnership at December 31, 20X6, together with profit and loss sharing ratios, are as follows:

Abed (25%)	$ 75,000
Batak (25%)	100,000
Cabel (50%)	125,000

The partners agree to admit Darling into the partnership.

Required: Prepare the journal entry or entries to admit Darling into the partnership and calculate the partners' capital balances immediately after his admission under each of the following independent assumptions.

    1 Cabel sells half of her interest to Darling for $90,000, and the partners agree to admit Darling into the partnership.

    2 Darling invests $75,000 cash in the partnership for a 25% interest in the partnership capital and profits, and partnership assets are revalued.

    3 Darling invests $80,000 cash in the partnership for a 20% interest in the capital and profits, and partnership assets are revalued.

    4 Darling invests $90,000 cash in the partnership for a 30% interest in the capital and profits, and partnership assets are *not* revalued.

P 16-9   Three partners, Pat, Mike, and Hay, have capital balances and profit sharing ratios at December 31, 20X3 as follows:

Pat	$144,000	profit ratio $\frac{2}{5}$
Mike	216,000	profit ratio $\frac{1}{2}$
Hay	90,000	profit ratio $\frac{1}{10}$

On January 1, 20X4, Con invests $85,080 in the business for a one-sixth interest in capital and income.

Required

    1 Prepare journal entries giving *two* alternative solutions for recording Con's admission to the partnership.

    2 Prepare journal entries giving *two* alternative solutions for recording Con's admission to the partnership if she purchased a one-sixth interest from each of the partners, rather than paying the $85,080 into the business.

P 16-10 The AT Partnership was organized several years ago, and on January 1, 20X2 the partners agree to admit Carmen for a 40% interest in capital and earnings. Capital account balances and profit and loss sharing ratios at January 1, 20X2 before the admission of Carmen are as follows:

Aida (50%)	$500,000
Thais (50%)	280,000

Required: Prepare journal entries to record the admission of Carmen for a 40% interest in the capital and rights to future profits under the following independent assumptions.
1. Carmen pays $450,000 directly to Aida and Thais for 40% of each of their interests, and the *bonus* procedure is used.
2. Carmen pays $600,000 directly to Aida and Thais for 40% of each of their interests, and *goodwill* is recorded.
3. Carmen invests $450,000 in the partnership for her 40% interest, and *goodwill* is recorded.
4. Carmen invests $600,000 in the partnership for her 40% interest, and *goodwill* is recorded.

P 16-11 Harry, Iona, and Jerry formed a partnership on January 1, 20X4, with each partner contributing $20,000 cash. Although the partnership agreement provided that Jerry receive a salary of $1,000 per month for managing the partnership business, Jerry has never withdrawn any money from the partnership. Harry withdrew $4,000 in each of the years 20X4 and 20X5, and Iona invested an additional $8,000 in 20X4 and withdrew $8,000 during 20X5. Due to an oversight, the partnership has not maintained formal accounting records, but the following information as of December 31, 20X5 is available:

Cash on hand	$ 28,500
Due from customers	20,000
Merchandise on hand (at cost)	40,000
Delivery equipment—net of depreciation	37,000
Prepaid expenses	4,000
Assets	$129,500
Due to suppliers	$ 14,600
Wages payable	4,400
Note payable	10,000
Interest payable	500
Liabilities	$ 29,500

Additional Information
1. The partners agree that income for 20X4 was about half of the total income for the first two years of operations.
2. Although profits were not divided in 20X4, the partnership agreement provides that profits, after allowance for Jerry's salary, are to be divided each year on the basis of beginning-of-the-year capital balances.

Required: Prepare statements of partnership capital for the years ended December 31, 20X4 and December 31, 20X5.

P 16-12 The partnership of Drinkard and Boone was formed and commenced operations on March 1, 20X8, with Drinkard contributing $30,000 cash and Boone investing cash of $10,000 and equipment with an agreed-upon valuation of $20,000. On July 1, 20X8, Boone invested an additional $10,000 in the partnership. Drinkard made a capital withdrawal of $4,000 on May 2, 20X8 but reinvested the $4,000 on October 1, 20X8. During 20X8, Drinkard withdrew $800 per month and Boone, the managing partner, withdrew $1,000 per month. These drawings were charged to salary expense. A preclosing trial balance taken at December 31, 20X8 is as follows:

	Debit	Credit
Cash	$ 9,000	
Receivables—net	15,000	
Equipment—net	50,000	
Other assets	19,000	
Liabilities		$ 17,000
Drinkard capital		30,000
Boone capital		40,000
Service revenue		50,000
Supplies expense	17,000	
Utilities expense	4,000	
Salaries to partners	18,000	
Other miscellaneous expenses	5,000	
Total	$137,000	$137,000

1 Journalize the entries necessary to close the partnership books assuming that there is no agreement regarding profit distribution.
2 Prepare a statement of partnership capital assuming that the partnership agreement provides for monthly salary allowances of $800 and $1,000 for Drinkard and Boone, respectively, and for the division of remaining profits in relation to average capital balances.
3 Prepare a profit distribution schedule for the Drinkard and Boone partnership assuming monthly salary allowances of $800 and $1,000 for Drinkard and Boone, respectively; interest allowances at a 12% annual rate on average capital balances; and remaining profits divided equally.

P 16-13 A condensed balance sheet for the Peter, Quarry, and Sherel partnership at December 31, 20X7 and their profit and loss sharing percentages on that date are as follows:

CONDENSED BALANCE SHEET AT DECEMBER 31, 20X7

Cash	$ 15,000	Liabilities	$ 50,000
Other assets	185,000	Peter capital (50%)	75,000
Total assets	$200,000	Quarry capital (30%)	50,000
		Sherel capital (20%)	25,000
		Total liabilities and capital	$200,000

On January 1, 20X8 the partners decided to bring Tom into the partnership for a one-fourth interest in the capital and profits of the partnership. The following proposals for Tom's admittance into the partnership were considered:

1 Tom would purchase one-half of Peter's capital and right to future profits directly from Peter for $60,000.
2 Tom would purchase one-fourth of each partner's capital and rights to future profits by paying a total of $45,000 directly to the partners.
3 Tom would invest $55,000 cash in the partnership for a 25% interest in capital. Future profits would be divided $37\frac{1}{2}$%, $22\frac{1}{2}$%, 15% and 25% for Peter, Quarry, Sherel, and Tom, respectively.

Required: Prepare journal entries with supporting computations to show Tom's admittance into the partnership under each of the above proposals assuming that:

a Partnership net assets are not to be revalued
b Partnership net assets are to be revalued

P 16-14 Killer and Lassie have been operating an accounting firm as partners for a number of years, and at the beginning of 20X8, their capital balances were $60,000 and $75,000, respectively. During 20X8, Killer invested an additional $10,000 on April 1 and withdrew $6,000 on August 30. Lassie withdrew $12,000 on May 1 and withdrew another $6,000 on November 1. In addition, Killer and Lassie withdrew their salary allowances of $18,000 and $24,000, respectively. At year-end 20X8, total capital of the Killer and Lassie partnership was $182,000. Killer and Lassie share income after salary allowances in a 60:40 ratio.

Required
1 Determine average capital balances for Killer and Lassie for 20X8.
2 Allocate 20X8 partnership income to Killer and Lassie.

APPENDIX
UNIFORM PARTNERSHIP ACT (1914)

Part I

Preliminary Provisions

§ 1. Name of Act

This act may be cited as Uniform Partnership Act.

§ 2. Definition of Terms

In this act, "Court" includes every court and judge having jurisdiction in the case.

"Business" includes every trade, occupation, or profession.
"Person" includes individuals, partnership, corporations, and other associations.

"Bankrupt" includes bankrupt under the Federal Bankruptcy Act or insolvent under any state insolvent act.

"Conveyance" includes every assignment, lease, mortgage, or encumbrance.

"Real Property" includes land and any interest or estate in land.

§ 3. Interpretation of Knowledge and Notice

(1) A person has "knowledge" of a fact within the meaning of this act not only when he has actual knowledge thereof, but also when he has knowledge of such other facts as in the circumstances shows bad faith.

(2) A person has "notice" of a fact within the meaning of this act when the person who claims the benefit of the notice:
   (a) States the fact to such person, or
   (b) Delivers through the mail, or by other means of communication, a written statement of the fact to such person or to a proper person at his place of business or residence.

§ 4. Rules of Construction

(1) The rule that statutes in derogation of the common law are to be strictly construed shall have no application to this act.

(2) The law of estoppel shall apply under this act.

(3) The law of agency shall apply under this act.

(4) This act shall be so interpreted and construed as to effect its general purpose to make uniform the law of those states which enact it.

(5) This act shall not be construed so as to impair the obligations of any contract existing when the act goes into effect, nor to affect any action or proceedings begun or right accrued before this act takes effect.

§ 5. Rules for Cases Not Provided for in This Act

In any case not provided for in this act the rules of law and equity, including the law merchant, shall govern.

Part II

Nature of a Partnership

§ 6. Partnership Defined

(1) A partnership is an association of two or more persons to carry on as co-owners a business for profit.

(2) But any association formed under any other statute of this state, or any statute adopted by authority, other than the authority of this state, is not a partnership under this act, unless such association would have been a partnership in this state prior to the adoption of this act; but this act shall apply to limited partnerships except in so far as the statutes relating to such partnerships are inconsistent herewith.

§ 7. Rules for Determining the Existence of a Partnership

In determining whether a partnership exists, these rules shall apply:

(1) Except as provided by section 16 persons who are not partners as to each other are not partners as to third persons.

(2) Joint tenancy, tenancy in common, tenancy by the entireties, joint property, common property or part ownership does not itself establish a partnership, whether such co-owners do or do not share any profits made by the use of the property.

(3) The sharing of gross returns does not of itself establish a partnership, whether or not the persons sharing them have a joint or common right or interest in any property from which the returns are derived.

(4) The receipt by a person of a share of the profits of a business is prima facie evidence that he is a partner in the business, but no such inference shall be drawn if such profits were received in payment:
   (a) As a debt by installments or otherwise,
   (b) As wages of an employee or rent to a landlord,
   (c) As an annuity to a widow or representative of a deceased partner,
   (d) As interest on a loan, though the amount of payment varies with the profits of the business,
   (e) As the consideration for the sale of a good-will of a business or other property by installments or otherwise.

§ 8. Partnership Property

(1) All property originally brought into the partnership stock or subsequently acquired by purchase or otherwise, on account of the partnership, is partnership property.

(2) Unless the contrary intention appears, property acquired with partnership funds is partnership property.

(3) Any estate in real property may be acquired in the partnership name. Title so acquired can be conveyed only in the partnership name.

(4) A conveyance to a partnership in the partnership name, though without words of inheritance, passes the entire estate of the grantor unless a contrary intent appears.

Part III

Relations of Partners to Persons Dealing with the Partnership

§ 9. Partner Agent of Partnership as to Partnership Business

(1) Every partner is an agent of the partnership for the purpose of its business, and the act of every partner, including the execution in the partnership name of any instrument, for apparently carrying on in the usual way the business of the partnership of which he is a member binds the partnership, unless the partner so acting has in fact no authority to act for the partnership in the particular matter, and the person with whom he is dealing has knowledge of the fact that he has no such authority.

(2) An act of a partner which is not apparently for the carrying on of the business of the partnership in the usual way does not bind the partnership unless authorized by the other partners.

(3) Unless authorized by the other partners or unless they have abandoned the business, one or more but less than all the partners have no authority to:
  (a) Assign the partnership property in trust for creditors or on the assignee's promise to pay the debts of the partnership,
  (b) Dispose of the good-will of the business,
  (c) Do any other act which would make it impossible to carry on the ordinary business of a partnership,
  (d) Confess a judgment,
  (e) Submit a partnership claim or liability to arbitration or reference.

(4) No act of a partner in contravention of a restriction on authority shall bind the partnership to persons having knowledge of the restriction.

§ 10. Conveyance of Real Property of the Partnership

(1) Where title to real property is in the partnership name, any partner may convey title to such property by a conveyance executed in the partnership name; but the partnership may recover such property unless the partner's act binds the partnership under the provisions of paragraph (1) of section 9, or unless such property has been conveyed by the grantee or a person claiming through such grantee to a holder for value without knowledge that the partner, in making the conveyance, has exceeded his authority.

(2) Where title to real property is in the name of the partnership, a conveyance executed by a partner, in his own name, passes the equitable interest of the partnership, provided the act is one within the authority of the partner under the provisions of paragraph (1) of section 9.

(3) Where title to real property is in the name of one or more but not all the partners, and the record does not disclose the right of the partnership, the partners in whose name the title stands may convey title to such property, but the partnership may recover such property if the partners' act does not bind the partnership under the provisions of paragraph (1) of section 9, unless the purchaser or his assignee, is a holder for value, without knowledge.

(4) Where the title to real property is in the name of one or more or all the partners, or in a third person in trust for the partnership, a conveyance executed by a partner in the partnership name, or in his own name, passes the equitable interest of the partnership, provided the act is one within the authority of the partner under the provisions of paragraph (1) of section 9.

(5) Where the title to real property is in the names of all the partners a conveyance executed by all the partners passes all their rights in such property.

§ 11. Partnership Bound by Admission of Partner

An admission or representation made by any partner concerning partnership affairs within the scope of his authority as conferred by this act is evidence against the partnership.

§ 12. Partnership Charged with Knowledge of or Notice to Partner

Notice to any partner of any matter relating to partnership affairs, and the knowledge of the partner acting in the particular matter, acquired while a partner or then present to his mind, and the knowledge of any other partner who reasonably could and should have communicated it to the acting partner, operate as notice to or knowledge of the partnership, except in the case of a fraud on the partnership committed by or with the consent of that partner.

§ 13. Partnership Bound by Partner's Wrongful Act

Where, by any wrongful act or omission of any partner acting in the ordinary course of the business of the partnership or with the authority of his co-partners, loss or injury is caused to any person, not being a partner in the partnership, or any penalty is incurred, the partnership is liable therefore to the same extent as the partner so acting or omitting to act.

§ 14. Partnership Bound by Partner's Breach of Trust

The partnership is bound to make good the loss:
- (a) Where one partner acting within the scope of his apparent authority receives money or property of a third person and misapplies it; and
- (b) Where the partnership in the course of its business receives money or property of a third person and the money or property so received is misapplied by any partner while it is in the custody of the partnership.

§ 15. Nature of Partner's Liability

All partners are liable
- (a) Jointly and severally for everything chargeable to the partnership under sections 13 and 14.
- (b) Jointly for all other debts and obligations of the partnership; but any partner may enter into a separate obligation to perform a partnership contract.

§ 16. Partner by Estoppel

- (1) When a person, by words spoken or written or by conduct, represents himself, or consents to another representing him to any one, as a partner in an existing partnership or with one or more persons not actual partners, he is liable to any such person to whom such representation has been made, who has, on the faith of such representation, given credit to the actual or apparent partnership, and if he has made such representation or consented to its being made in a public manner he is liable to such person, whether the representation has or has not been made or communicated to such person so giving credit by or with the knowledge of the apparent partner making the representation or consenting to its being made.
  - (a) When a partnership liability results, he is liable as though he were an actual member of the partnership.
  - (b) When no partnership liability results, he is liable jointly with the other persons, if any, so consenting to the contract or representation as to incur liability, otherwise separately.
- (2) When a person has been thus represented to be a partner in an existing partnership, or with one or more persons not actual partners, he is an agent of the persons consenting to such representation to bind them to the same extent and in the same manner as though he were a partner in fact, with respect to persons who rely upon the representation. Where all the members of the existing partnership consent to the representation, a partnership act or obligation results; but in all other cases it is the joint act or obligation of the person acting and the persons consenting to the representation.

§ 17. Liability of Incoming Partner

A person admitted as a partner into an existing partnership is liable for all the obligations of the partnership arising before his admission as though he had been a partner when such obligations were incurred, except that his liability shall be satisfied only out of partnership property.

Part IV

Relations of Partners to One Another

§ 18. Rules Determining Rights and Duties of Partners

The rights and duties of the partners in relation to the partnership shall be determined, subject to any agreement between them, by the following rules:
- (a) Each partner shall be repaid his contributions, whether by way of capital or advances to the partnership property and share equally in the profits and surplus remaining after all liabilities, including those to partners, are satisfied; and must contribute towards the losses, whether of capital or otherwise, sustained by the partnership according to his share in the profits.
- (b) The partnership must indemnify every partner in respect of payments made and personal liabilities reasonably incurred by him in the ordinary and proper conduct of its business, or for the preservation of its business or property.
- (c) A partner, who in aid of the partnership makes any payment or advance beyond the amount of capital which he agreed to contribute, shall be paid interest from the date of the payment or advance.

(d) A partner shall receive interest on the capital contributed by him only from the date when repayments should be made.

(e) All partners have equal rights in the management and conduct of the partnership business.

(f) No partner is entitled to remuneration for acting in the partnership business, except that a surviving partner is entitled to reasonable compensation for his services in winding up the partnership affairs.

(g) No person can become a member of a partnership without the consent of all the partners.

(h) Any difference arising as to ordinary matters connected with the partnership business may be decided by a majority of the partners; but no act in contravention of any agreement between the partners may be done rightfully without the consent of all the partners.

§ 19. Partnership Books

The partnership books shall be kept, subject to any agreement between the partners, at the principal place of business of the partnership, and every partner shall at all times have access to and may inspect and copy any of them.

§ 20. Duty of Partners to Render Information

Partners shall render on demand true and full information of all things affecting the partnership to any partner or the legal representative of any deceased partner or partner under legal disability.

§ 21. Partner Accountable as a Fiduciary

(1) Every partner must account to the partnership for any benefit, and hold as trustee for it any profits derived by him without the consent of the other partners from any transaction connected with the formation, conduct, or liquidation of the partnership or from any use by him of its property.

(2) This section applies also to the representatives of a deceased partner engaged in the liquidation of the affairs of the partnership as the personal representatives of the last surviving partner.

§ 22. Right to an Account

Any partner shall have the right to a formal account as to partnership affairs:

(a) If he is wrongfully excluded from the partnership business or possession of its property by his co-partners,

(b) If the right exists under the terms of any agreement

(c) As provided by section 21,

(d) Whenever other circumstances render it just and reasonable.

§ 23. Continuation of Partnership Beyond Fixed Term

(1) When a partnership for a fixed term or particular undertaking is continued after the termination of such term or particular undertaking without any express agreement, the rights and duties of the partners remain the same as they were at such termination, so far as is consistent with a partnership at will.

(2) A continuation of the business by the partners or such of them as habitually acted therein during the term, without any settlement or liquidation of the partnership affairs, is prima facie evidence of a continuation of the partnership.

Part V

Property Rights of a Partner

§ 24. Extent of Property Rights of a Partner

The property rights of a partner are (1) his rights in specific partnership property, (2) his interest in the partnership, and (3) his right to participate in the management.

§ 25. Nature of a Partner's Right in Specific Partnership Property

(1) A partner is co-owner with his partners of specific partnership property holding as a tenant in partnership.

(2) The incidents of this tenancy are such that:

(a) A partner, subject to the provisions of this act and to any agreement between the partners, has an equal right with his partners to possess specific partnership property for partnership purposes; but he has no right to possess such property for any other purpose without the consent of his partners.

(b) A partner's right in specific partnership property is not assignable except in connection with the assignment of rights of all the partners in the same property.

(c) A partner's right in specific partnership property is not subject to attachment or execution, except on a claim against the partnership. When partnership property is attached for a partnership debt the partners, or any of them, or the representatives of a deceased partner, cannot claim any right under the homestead or exemption laws.

(d) On the death of a partner his right in specific partnership property vests in the surviving partner or partners, except where the deceased was the last surviving partner, when his right in such property vests in his legal representative. Such surviving partner or partners, or the legal representative of the last surviving partner, has no right to possess the partnership property for any but a partnership purpose.

(e) A partner's right in specific partnership property is not subject to dower, curtesy, or allowances to widows, heirs, or next of kin.

§ 26. Nature of Partner's Interest in the Partnership

A partner's interest in the partnership is his share of the profits and surplus, and the same in personal property.

§ 27. Assignment of Partner's Interest

(1) A conveyance by a partner of his interest in the partnership does not of itself dissolve the partnership, nor, as against the other partners in the absence of agreement, entitle the assignee, during the continuance of the partnership, to interfere in the management or administration of the partnership business or affairs, or to require any information or account of partnership transactions, or to inspect the partnership books; but it merely entitles the assignee to receive in accordance with his contract the profits to which the assigning partner would otherwise be entitled.

(2) In case of a dissolution of the partnership, the assignee is entitled to receive his assignor's interest and may require an account from the date only of the last account agreed to by all the partners.

§ 28. Partner's Interest Subject to Charging Order

(1) On due application to a competent court by any judgment creditor of a partner, the court which entered the judgment, order, or decree, or any other court, may charge the interest of the debtor partner with payment of the unsatisfied amount of such judgment debt with interest thereon; and may then or later appoint a receiver of his share of the profits, and of any other money due or to fall due to him in respect of the partnership, and make all other orders, directions, accounts and inquiries which the debtor partner might have made, or which the circumstances of the case may require.

(2) The interest charged may be redeemed at any time before foreclosure, or in case of a sale being directed by the court may be purchased without thereby causing a dissolution:

(a) With separate property, by any one or more of the partners, or

(b) With partnership property, by any one or more of the partners with the consent of all the partners whose interests are not so charged or sold.

(3) Nothing in this act shall be held to deprive a partner of his right, if any, under the exemption laws, as regards his interest in the partnership.

Part VI

Dissolution and Winding up

§ 29. Dissolution Defined

The dissolution of a partnership is the change in the relation of the partners caused by any partner ceasing to be associated in the carrying on as distinguished from the winding up of the business.

§ 30. Partnership not Terminated by Dissolution

On dissolution the partnership is not terminated, but continues until the winding up of partnership affairs is completed.

§ 31. Causes of Dissolution

Dissolution is caused:

(1) Without violation of the agreement between the partners,

(a) By the termination of the definite term or particular undertaking specified in the agreement;

(b) By the express will of any partner when no definite term or particular undertaking is specified;

(c) By the express will of all the partners who have not assigned their interests or suffered them to be charged for their separate debts, either before or after the termination of any specified term or particular undertaking;

(d) By the expulsion of any partner from the business bona fide in accordance with such a power conferred by the agreement between the partners;

(2) In contravention of the agreement between the partners, where the circumstances do not permit a dissolution under any other provision of this section, by the express will of any partner at any time;

(3) By any event which makes it unlawful for the business of the partnership to be carried on or for the members to carry it on in partnership;

(4) By the death of any partner;

(5) By the bankruptcy of any partner or the partnership;

(6) By decree of court under section 32.

§ 32. Dissolution by Decree of Court

(1) On application by or for a partner the court shall decree a dissolution whenever:

(a) A partner has been declared a lunatic in any judicial proceeding or is shown to be of unsound mind,

(b) A partner becomes in any other way incapable of performing his part of the partnership contract,

(c) A partner has been guilty of such conduct as tends to affect prejudicially the carrying on of the business,

(d) A partner willfully or persistently commits a breach of the partnership agreement, or otherwise so conducts himself in matters relating to the partnership business that it is not reasonably practicable to carry on the business in partnership with him,

(e) The business of the partnership can only be carried on at a loss,

(f) Other circumstances render a dissolution equitable.

(2) On the application of the purchaser of a partner's interest under sections 28 or 29 [should read 27 or 28];

(a) After the termination of the specified term or particular undertaking,

(b) At any time if the partnership was a partnership at will when the interest was assigned or when the charging order was issued.

§ 33. General Effect of Dissolution on Authority of Partner

Except so far as may be necessary to wind up partnership affairs or to complete transactions begun but not then finished, dissolution terminates all authority of any partner to act for the partnership,

(1) With respect to the partners,

(a) When the dissolution is not by the act, bankruptcy or death of a partner; or

(b) When the dissolution is by such act, bankruptcy or death of a partner, in cases where section 34 so requires.

(2) With respect to persons not partners, as declared in section 35.

§ 34. Rights of Partner to Contribution from Co-partners after Dissolution

Where the dissolution is caused by the act, death or bankruptcy of a partner, each partner is liable to his co-partners for his share of any liability created by any partner acting for the partnership as if the partnership had not been dissolved unless

(a) The dissolution being by act of any partner, the partner acting for the partnership had knowledge of the dissolution, or

(b) The dissolution being by the death or bankruptcy of a partner, the partner acting for the partnership had knowledge or notice of the death or bankruptcy.

§ 35. Power of Partner to Bind Partnership to Third Persons after Dissolution

(1) After dissolution a partner can bind the partnership except as provided in Paragraph (3).

(a) By any act appropriate for winding up partnership affairs or completing transactions unfinished at dissolution;

(b) By any transaction which would bind the partnership if dissolution had not taken place, provided the other party to the transaction

(I) Had extended credit to the partnership prior to dissolution and had no knowledge or notice of the dissolution; or

(II) Though he had not so extended credit, had nevertheless known of the partnership prior to dissolution, and having no knowledge or notice of dissolution, the fact of dissolution had not been advertised in a newspaper of general circulation in the place (or in each place if more than one) at which the partnership business was regularly carried on.

(2) The liability of a partner under Paragraph (1b) shall be satisfied out of partnership assets alone when such partner had been prior to dissolution

    (a) Unknown as a partner to the person with whom the contract is made; and

    (b) So far unknown and inactive in partnership affairs that the business reputation of the partnership could not be said to have been in any degree due to his connection with it.

(3) The partnership is in no case bound by any act of a partner after dissolution

    (a) Where the partnership is dissolved because it is unlawful to carry on the business, unless the act is appropriate for winding up partnership affairs; or

    (b) Where the partner has become bankrupt; or

    (c) Where the partner has no authority to wind up partnership affairs; except by a transaction with one who

        (I) Had extended credit to the partnership prior to dissolution and had no knowledge or notice of his want of authority; or

        (II) Had not extended credit to the partnership prior to dissolution and, having no knowledge or notice of his want of authority, the fact of his want of authority had not been advertised in the manner provided for advertising the fact of dissolution in Paragraph (1b II).

(4) Nothing in this section shall affect the liability under Section 16 of any person who after dissolution represents himself or consents to another representing him as a partner in a partnership engaged in carrying on business.

§ 36. Effect of Dissolution on Partner's Existing Liability

(1) The dissolution of the partnership does not of itself discharge the existing liability of any partner.

(2) A partner is discharged from any existing liability upon dissolution of the partnership by an agreement to that effect between himself, the partnership creditor and the person or partnership continuing the business; and such agreement may be inferred from the course of dealing between the creditor having knowledge of the dissolution and the person or partnership continuing the business.

(3) Where a person agrees to assume the existing obligations of a dissolved partnership, the partners whose obligations have been assumed shall be discharged from any liability to any creditor of the partnership who, knowing of the agreement, consents to a material alteration in the nature or time of payment of such obligations.

(4) The individual property of a deceased partner shall be liable for all obligations of the partnership incurred while he was a partner but subject to the prior payment of his separate debts.

§ 37. Right to Wind Up

Unless otherwise agreed the partners who have not wrongfully dissolved the partnership or the legal representative of the last surviving partner, not bankrupt, has the right to wind up the partnership affairs; provided, however, that any partner, his legal representative or his assignee, upon cause shown, may obtain winding up by the court.

§ 38. Rights of Partners to Application of Partnership Property

(1) When dissolution is caused in any way, except in contravention of the partnership agreement, each partner, as against his co-partners and all persons claiming through them in respect of their interests in the partnership, unless otherwise agreed, may have the partnership property applied to discharge its liabilities, and the surplus applied to pay in cash the net amount owing to the respective partners. But if dissolution is caused by expulsion of a partner, bona fide under the partnership agreement and if the expelled partner is discharged from all partnership liabilities, either by payment or agreement under section 36(2), he shall receive in cash only the net amount due him from the partnership.

(2) When dissolution is caused in contravention of the partnership agreement the rights of the partners shall be as follows

    (a) Each partner who has not caused dissolution wrongfully shall have,

        (I) All the rights specified in paragraph (1) of this section, and

        (II) The right, as against each partner who has caused the dissolution wrongfully, to damages for breach of the agreement.

    (b) The partners who have not caused the dissolution wrongfully, if they all desire to continue the business in the same name, either by themselves or jointly with others, may do so, during the agreed term for the partnership and for that purpose may possess the partnership property, provided they secure the payment by bond approved by the court, or pay to any partner who has caused the dissolution wrongfully, the value of his interest in the partnership at the dissolution, less any

damages recoverable under clause (2a II) of this section, and in like manner indemnify him against all present or future partnership liabilities.
(c) A partner who has caused the dissolution wrongfully shall have:
   (I) If the business is not continued under the provisions of paragraph (2b) all the rights of a partner under paragraph (1), subject to clause (2a II), of this section,
   (II) If the business is continued under paragraph (2b) of this section the right as against his co-partners and all claiming through them in respect of their interests in the partnership, to have the value of his interest in the partnership, less any damages caused to his co-partners by the dissolution, ascertained and paid to him in cash, or the payment secured by bond approved by the court, and to be released from all existing liabilities of the partnership; but in ascertaining the value of the partner's interest the value of the good-will of the business shall not be considered.

§ 39. Rights Where Partnership Is Dissolved for Fraud or Misrepresentation

Where a partnership contract is rescinded on the ground of the fraud or misrepresentation of one of the parties thereto, the party entitled to rescind is, without prejudice to any other right, entitled:
(a) To a lien on, or a right of retention of, the surplus of the partnership property after satisfying the partnership liabilities to third persons for any sum of money paid by him for the purchase of an interest in the partnership and for any capital or advances contributed by him, and
(b) To stand, after all liabilities to third persons have been satisfied, in the place of the creditors of the partnership for any payments made by him in respect to the partnership liabilities; and
(c) To be indemnified by the person guilty of the fraud or making the representation against all debts and liabilities of the partnership.

§ 40. Rules for Distribution

In settling accounts between the partners after dissolution, the following rules shall be observed, subject to any agreement to the contrary:
(a) The assets of the partnership are:
   (I) The partnership property,
   (II) The contributions of the partners necessary for the payment of all the liabilities specified in clause (b) of this paragraph.
(b) The liabilities of the partnership shall rank in order of payment as follows:
   (I) Those owing creditors other than partners,
   (II) Those owing to partners other than for capital and profits,
   (III) Those owing to partners in respect of capital,
   (IV) Those owing to partners in respect of profits.
(c) The assets shall be applied in the order of their declaration in clause (a) of this paragraph to the satisfaction of the liabilities.
(d) The partners shall contribute, as provided by section 18 (a) the amount necessary to satisfy the liabilities; but if any, but not all, of the partners are insolvent, or, not being subject to process, refuse to contribute, the other partners shall contribute their share of the liabilities, and, in the relative proportions in which they share the profits, the additional amount necessary to pay the liabilities.
(e) An assignee for the benefit of creditors or any person appointed by the court shall have the right to enforce the contributions specified in clause (d) of this paragraph.
(f) Any partner or his legal representative shall have the right to enforce the contributions specified in clause (d) of this paragraph, to the extent of the amount which he has paid in excess of his share of the liability.
(g) The individual property of a deceased partner shall be liable for the contributions specified in clause (d) of this paragraph.
(h) When partnership property and the individual properties of the partners are in possession of a court for distribution, partnership creditors shall have priority on partnership property and separate creditors on individual property, saving the rights of lien or secured creditors as heretofore.
(i) Where a partner has become bankrupt or his estate is insolvent the claims against his separate property shall rank in the following order:
   (I) Those owing to separate creditors,
   (II) Those owing to partnership creditors,
   (III) Those owing to partners by way of contribution.

§ 41. Liability of Persons Continuing the Business in Certain Cases

(1) When any new partner is admitted into an existing partnership, or when any partner retires and assigns (or the representative of the deceased partner assigns) his rights in partnership property to two or more of the partners, or to one or more of the partners and one or more third persons, if the business is continued without liquidation of the partnership affairs, creditors of the first or dissolved partnership are also creditors of the partnership so continuing the business.

(2) When all but one partner retire and assign (or the representative of a deceased partner assigns) their rights in partnership property to the remaining partner, who continues the business without liquidation of partnership affairs, either alone or with others, creditors of the dissolved partnership are also creditors of the person or partnership so continuing the business.

(3) When any partner retires or dies and the business of the dissolved partnership is continued as set forth in paragraphs (1) and (2) of this section, with the consent of the retired partners or the representative of the deceased partner, but without any assignment of his right in partnership property, rights of creditors of the dissolved partnership and of the creditors of the person or partnership continuing the business shall be as if such assignment had been made.

(4) When all the partners or their representatives assign their rights in partnership property to one or more third persons who promise to pay the debts and who continue the business of the dissolved partnership, creditors of the dissolved partnership are also creditors of the person or partnership continuing the business.

(5) When any partner wrongfully causes a dissolution and the remaining partners continue the business under the provisions of section 38(2b), either alone or with others, and without liquidation of the partnership affairs, creditors of the dissolved partnership are also creditors of the person or partnership continuing the business.

(6) When a partner is expelled and the remaining partners continue the business either alone or with others, without liquidation of the partnership affairs, creditors of the dissolved partnership are also creditors of the person or partnership continuing the business.

(7) The liability of a third person becoming a partner in the partnership continuing the business, under this section, to the creditors of the dissolved partnership shall be satisfied out of partnership property only.

(8) When the business of a partnership after dissolution is continued under any conditions set forth in this section the creditors of the dissolved partnership, as against the separate creditors of the retiring or deceased partner or the representative of the deceased partner, have a prior right to any claim of the retired partner or the representative of the deceased partner against the person or partnership continuing the business, on account of the retired or deceased partner's interest in the dissolved partnership or on account of any consideration promised for such interest or for his right in partnership property.

(9) Nothing in this section shall be held to modify any right of creditors to set aside any assignment on the ground of fraud.

(10) The use by the person or partnership continuing the business of the partnership name, or the name of a deceased partner as part thereof, shall not of itself make the individual property of the deceased partner liable for any debts contracted by such person or partnership.

§ 42. Rights of Retiring or Estate of Deceased Partner When the Business Is Continued

When any partner retires or dies, and the business is continued under any of the conditions set forth in section 41(1, 2, 3, 5, 6), or section 38(2b) without any settlement of accounts as between him or his estate and the person or partnership continuing the business, unless otherwise agreed, he or his legal representative as against such persons or partnership may have the value of his interest at the date of dissolution ascertained, and shall receive as an ordinary creditor an amount equal to the value of his interest in the dissolved partnership with interest, or, at his option or at the option of his legal representative, in lieu of interest, the profits attributable to the use of his right in the property of the dissolved partnership; provided that the creditors of the dissolved partnership as against the separate creditors, or the representative of the retired or deceased partner, shall have priority on any claim arising under this section, as provided by section 41(8) of this act.

§ 43. Accrual of Actions

The right to an account of his interest shall accrue to any partner, or his legal representative, as against the winding up partners or the surviving partners or the person or partnership continuing the business, at the date of dissolution, in the absence of any agreement to the contrary.

Part VII

Miscellaneous Provisions

§ 44. When Act Takes Effect

This act shall take effect on the ___ day of ___ one thousand nine hundred and ___.

§ 45. Legislation Repealed

All acts or parts of acts inconsistent with this act are hereby repealed.

17

Dissolution
and Liquidation
of a Partnership

The dissolution of a partnership is simply the change in the relationship of the partners that terminates the partnership as a legal entity. Upon dissolution, the partnership entity may continue under a new agreement, as discussed in Chapter 16, or the partnership may be terminated both as a legal and as a business entity. The termination of a partnership as a business entity involves winding up the affairs of the partnership business and is referred to as **partnership liquidation**. In this chapter, the focus will be on partnership dissolution that involves liquidation of the partnership business.

THE LIQUIDATION PROCESS

In general, the liquidation of a partnership involves:

Converting noncash assets into cash

Recognizing gains and losses and liquidating expenses incurred during the liquidation period

Settling all liabilities

Distributing cash to the partners according to the final balances in their capital accounts

This general description of the liquidation process assumes that the partnership is solvent in the sense that partnership assets exceed partnership liabilities. It also assumes that all partners have equity in partnership net assets, that there are no partner loan balances, and that all assets are converted into cash before any cash is distributed to the partners. As these assumptions are relaxed, the liquidation process becomes more complex. Accordingly, this chapter begins with simple liquidations for solvent partnerships and proceeds to installment liquidations and liquidations of insolvent partnerships.

The rules for distributing assets in the liquidation of a partnership are covered in Section 40 of the Uniform Partnership Act. Section 40b gives the rank order of payment as follows:

Amounts owed to creditors other than partners

Amounts owed to partners other than for capital and profits[1]

---

[1]There is a presumption that money advanced to a partnership by a partner is a capital contribution. The partner will need evidence, such as a promissory note, that the money was a loan.

Amounts due to partners with respect to their capital interests

Amounts due to partners in respect of profits

Although the Act lists profits as a fourth level of priority, all profits and losses and drawing balances should be closed to the capital accounts before any distributions are made. Capital accounts are assumed to be updated before each distribution, so the fourth level is not relevant to the discussion in this chapter. Additional comment on level II priority is also necessary because partnership property should never be distributed to a partner with a negative capital balance. Thus, partners' loan balances should be offset against capital balances in determining the amount of distributions to partners. Once the amount to be distributed to a particular partner is determined, that partner's loan balance should be charged before his or her capital account is reduced. This strategy is discussed further under the heading "Debit Capital Balances in a Solvent Partnership" and in conjunction with installment liquidations.

Simple Partnership Liquidation

A simple liquidation of a partnership refers to the conversion of all partnership assets into cash and a single distribution of cash to partners in final settlement of the affairs of the partnership. To illustrate a simple liquidation, assume that the balance sheet of Holmes and Kaiser at December 31, 20X1 is as follows:

HOLMES AND KAISER
BALANCE SHEET
AT DECEMBER 31, 20X1

Assets		Liabilities and Equity	
Cash	$ 10,000	Accounts payable	$ 40,000
Accounts receivable—net	30,000	Loan from Holmes	10,000
Inventory	30,000	Holmes capital	25,000
Plant assets—net	40,000	Kaiser capital	35,000
	$110,000		$110,000

Holmes and Kaiser share profits and losses 70% and 30%, respectively, and agree to liquidate their partnership as soon as possible after January 1, 20X2. The inventory items are sold for $25,000, plant assets are sold for $30,000, and $22,000 is collected in final settlement of the accounts receivable. As the final step in the partnership liquidation, the $87,000 available cash is distributed to the creditors and the partners.

Order of Payment	
I To creditors for accounts payable	$40,000
II To Holmes for his loan balance	10,000
III To Holmes for his capital balance	8,900
To Kaiser for his capital balance	28,100
Total distribution	$87,000

The amounts of cash distributed to the partners are equal to the partners' capital account balances after all losses on liquidation are recognized. Journal entries for the partnership during the liquidation period are shown in Exhibit 17–1. Losses during the liquidation period are charged directly to the capital accounts in the 70% and 30% profit sharing ratios. The established profit and loss sharing ratios are used during the liquidation period unless the partnership agreement specifies a different division of profits and losses during liquidation. In the case of agreements providing for salary and interest allowances, however, only the residual profit and loss sharing ratios would be applied during the liquidation period. This is because the gains and losses on liquidation are essentially adjustments of prior profits that would have been shared in the residual profit sharing ratios if they had been recognized prior to dissolution.

A liquidating partnership should maintain a summary of transactions and balances during the liquidation stage. This summary of transactions and balances is provided for in the Holmes and Kaiser partnership by the partnership liquidation state-

Journal Entries to Record the Liquidation

Cash	$25,000	
Holmes capital	3,500	
Kaiser capital	1,500	
Inventory		$30,000

    To record sale of inventory items and allocation of the $5,000
loss to the partners' capital accounts in their residual profit
and loss sharing ratios.

Cash	$30,000	
Holmes capital	7,000	
Kaiser capital	3,000	
Plant assets—net		$40,000

    To record sale of plant assets and allocation of the $10,000 loss to
the partners' capital accounts in their residual profit and loss
sharing ratios.

Cash	$22,000	
Holmes capital	5,600	
Kaiser capital	2,400	
Accounts receivable—net		$30,000

    To record collection of $22,000 of accounts receivable and to
write off the remaining $8,000 receivables as a loss charged to
the partners' capital accounts in their residual profit and loss
sharing ratios.

Accounts payable	$40,000	
Cash		$40,000

    To record payment of nonpartner liabilities.

Loan from Holmes	$10,000	
Cash		$10,000

    To pay loan from Holmes.

Holmes capital	$ 8,900	
Kaiser capital	28,100	
Cash		$37,000

    To distribute cash to partners in final liquidation of the
partnership.

Exhibit 17–1   *Simple Liquidation—Holmes and Kaiser Partnership*

ment shown in Exhibit 17–2. Liquidation statements are convenient references for use during the liquidation process, but, of course, they do not take the place of formal journalizing and posting during the phase-out period. In examining the liquidation statement for Holmes and Kaiser, note that assets are dichotomized into cash and noncash categories and that liabilities consist of priority (rank I or nonpartner) liabilities and partner (rank II) liabilities. Also note that all losses (and gains) are distributed to the partners' capital accounts as soon as they are recognized. With the capital accounts updated, the final distribution of cash to the partners is equal to the predistribution balances in the partners' capital accounts.

Debit Capital Balances in a Solvent Partnership

In liquidations of partnerships that are solvent, there will be sufficient resources to pay creditors and distribute some cash to partners. However, the process of liquidation may result in losses that force the capital accounts of some partners into debit balances. When this happens, those partners with debit balances have an obligation to partners with credit balances, and they can be required to use their personal assets to settle their partnership obligations. If the partners with debit balances are without personal resources, the partners with equity will have to assume losses equal to the debit balances. Such losses would be shared in the relative profit and loss sharing ratios of the partners with capital.

HOLMES AND KAISER PARTNERSHIP
STATEMENT OF PARTNERSHIP LIQUIDATION
FOR THE PERIOD JANUARY 1, 20X2 TO JANUARY 31, 20X2

	Cash	Noncash Assets	Priority Liabilities	Holmes Loan	(70%) Holmes Capital	(30%) Kaiser Capital
Balances January 1, 20X2	$10,000	$100,000	$40,000	$10,000	$25,000	$35,000
Sale of inventory	25,000	(30,000)			(3,500)	(1,500)
	35,000	70,000	40,000	10,000	21,500	33,500
Sale of plant assets	30,000	(40,000)			(7,000)	(3,000)
	65,000	30,000	40,000	10,000	14,500	30,500
Collection of receivables	22,000	(30,000)			(5,600)	(2,400)
	87,000	—	40,000	10,000	8,900	28,100
Payment of liabilities	(40,000)		(40,000)			
	47,000		—	10,000	8,900	28,100
Payment of Holmes loan	(10,000)			(10,000)		
	37,000			—	8,900	28,100
Final distribution to partners	(37,000)				(8,900)	(28,100)
	—				—	—

Exhibit 17–2   *Statement of Partnership Liquidation*

Assume that the partnership of Jay, Jim, and Joe is in the process of liquidation and the partnership accounts have the following balances after all assets have been converted into cash and all liabilities have been paid:

	Debit	Credit
Cash	$25,000	
Jay capital (40%)	3,000	
Jim capital (40%)		$16,000
Joe capital (20%)		12,000
Total	$28,000	$28,000

If Jay is personally solvent, he should pay $3,000 into the partnership to eliminate his debit capital account balance. His payment of $3,000 will bring the partnership cash up to $28,000, which can then be distributed to Jim and Joe in final liquidation of the partnership. If Jay is unable to make his debit balance good, his debit balance represents a $3,000 loss to be charged to Jim and Joe according to their relative profit and loss sharing ratios. Jim's share of the loss is $2,000 ($3,000 × .4/.6), and Joe's share is $1,000 ($3,000 × .2/.6). In this case, the $25,000 is distributed $14,000 to Jim and $11,000 to Joe, and the partnership business is terminated.

When a partner with a debit capital balance has a loan receivable from the partnership, the rule of offset suggests that the loan be used to offset the debit capital balance up to the amount of the debit balance. For example, assume that the partnership of Jay, Jim, and Joe had account balances as follows:

	Debit	Credit
Cash	$25,000	
Loan from Jay		$ 5,000
Jay capital (40%)	8,000	
Jim capital (40%)		16,000
Joe capital (20%)		12,000
Total	$33,000	$33,000

Under the rule of offset, the loan from Jay would not be paid even though it has a higher priority ranking in liquidation than the capital interests of Jim and Joe. Instead it would be offset against Jay's debit capital balance, leaving Jay with a $3,000 obligation to Jim and Joe. If Jay is personally solvent, application of the rule of offset poses no problem. Jay simply pays $3,000 to the partnership so that Jim and Joe can receive the balances in their capital accounts in final liquidation. In this case, the rule of offset produces the same result as payment of the $5,000 loan balance to Jay, followed by the collection of $8,000 from Jay's personal assets.

If Jay is personally insolvent, however, the situation is changed considerably. In this case, Jay's personal creditors would have a prior claim on any money paid to Jay because personal creditors have a prior claim on personal assets. Under the rule of offset, $25,000 cash would be paid: $14,000 to Jim and $11,000 to Joe. Alternatively, if the $5,000 loan balance is paid directly to Jay, his personal creditors would be paid the amount of their claims up to $5,000, leaving less than $25,000 for distribution to Jim and Joe. Because of insufficient evidence that the rule of offset is generally accepted by the courts, it has been recommended that the rule not be applied without agreement from the partners, when a partner-creditor is personally insolvent.[2] Upon dissolution and subject to the rights of creditors, partners can agree to different property distributions than provided for under the Act.[3]

SAFE PAYMENTS TO PARTNERS

Ordinarily, the process of liquidating a business takes considerable time, and some cash may become available for distribution to partners after all liabilities are paid, but before all noncash assets are converted into cash. If the partners decide to distribute available cash before all noncash assets are sold (and before all gains or losses are recognized), the question arises as to how much cash can be safely distributed to the individual partners. **Safe payments** are distributions that can be made to partners with assurance that the amounts distributed are not excessive, in other words, that the resources distributed will not have to be returned to the partnership.

The measurement of safe payments to partners is based on the following assumptions: (1) all partners are personally insolvent (that is, partners could not make any payments into the partnership), and (2) all noncash assets represent possible losses (that is, noncash assets should be considered losses for purposes of determining safe payments). In addition, when calculating safe payments, the partnership may withhold specific amounts of cash on hand to cover liquidation expenses, unrecorded liabilities, and general contingencies. The amounts of cash withheld are contingent losses to the partners and are considered losses for purposes of determining safe payments.

Application of Safe Payments Schedule

Assume that the partnership of Buzz, Maxine, and Nancy is in the process of liquidation and that its account balances are as follows:

Debits		Credits	
Cash	$ 80,000	Loan payable to Nancy	$ 20,000
Loan due from Maxine	10,000	Buzz capital (50%)	50,000
Land	20,000	Maxine capital (30%)	70,000
Buildings—net	140,000	Nancy capital (20%)	110,000
	$250,000		$250,000

All liabilities other than to partners have been paid, and the partners expect the sale of the land and buildings to take several months. Therefore, they agree that all cash on hand other than $10,000 to cover expenses and contingencies should be distributed immediately. Given this information, a schedule of safe payments is prepared to determine the amount of cash that can be safely distributed to each partner. A safe payments schedule for the Buzz, Maxine, and Nancy partnership is illustrated in Exhibit 17–3.

---

[2]Stephen A. Zeff, "Right of Offset vs. Partnership Act in Winding-up Process," *Accounting Review* (January 1957), pp. 68–70.

[3]*Anderson v. Anderson*, 1958, 138 A.2d 880, 215 Md.-483.

BUZZ, MAXINE, AND NANCY PARTNERSHIP
SCHEDULE OF SAFE PAYMENTS

	Possible Losses	Buzz Equity (50%)	Maxine Equity (30%)	Nancy Equity (20%)
Partners' equities (capital ± loan balances)		$50,000	$60,000	$130,000
Possible loss on noncash assets				
Book value of land and buildings	$160,000	(80,000)	(48,000)	(32,000)
		(30,000)	12,000	98,000
Possible loss on contingencies				
Cash withheld for contingencies	10,000	(5,000)	(3,000)	(2,000)
		(35,000)	9,000	96,000
Possible loss from Buzz				
Buzz's debit balance allocated 60:40 to Maxine and Nancy		35,000	(21,000)	(14,000)
		0	(12,000)	82,000
Possible loss from Maxine				
Maxine's debit balance assigned to Nancy			12,000	(12,000)
			0	$ 70,000

Exhibit 17–3   *Safe Payments Schedule*

The safe payments schedule begins with the equity of each partner shown on the top line. Partner equity is determined by combining the capital and loan balances for each of the partners. Possible losses are allocated to the partners in their profit and loss sharing ratios and are deducted from partner equity balances in the safe payments schedule in the same manner that actual losses would be deducted. The possible losses shown in Exhibit 17–3 include the $160,000 book value of the land and buildings, the only noncash assets, and the $10,000 cash withheld from distribution. After possible losses are deducted from the equity of each partner for purposes of safe payment calculations, some partners may show negative equity. If so, the negative amounts must be allocated to the partners with equity in their relative profit and loss sharing ratios. Allocations in the schedule are continued until none of the partners shows negative equity. At that point, the amount shown for partners with equity balances will be equal to the cash available for distribution. In the example shown in Exhibit 17–3, the allocations are continued until Nancy's equity shows a $70,000 balance and the equity of Buzz and Maxine is at zero. Thus, the $70,000 can be safely distributed to Nancy, but nothing can be safely distributed to either Buzz or Maxine.

Note that the safe payments schedule is used *only* to determine the amount of advance distribution. That is, the safe payments schedule does not affect account balances or the statement of partnership liquidation. Actual cash distributed to Nancy is recorded in the usual fashion, with Nancy's loan balance being reduced to zero before her capital account is charged. The journal entry is:

Loan payable to Nancy	$20,000	
Nancy capital	50,000	
Cash		$70,000

After this entry is recorded, the account balances of the Buzz, Maxine, and Nancy partnership are as follows:

Debits		Credits	
Cash	$ 10,000	Buzz capital (50%)	$ 50,000
Loan due from Maxine	10,000	Maxine capital (30%)	70,000
Land	20,000	Nancy capital (20%)	60,000
Buildings—net	140,000		
	$180,000		$180,000

The partnership loan to Maxine can be charged to the capital balance of Maxine at any time, subject to the approval of the partners. Observe that the $10,000 loan to Maxine does not affect the determination of safe payments because the computations are based on the equity rather than the capital balances of the partners. Ordinarily, partnership loans to partners should be charged against partner capital balances at the beginning of the liquidation process.

Advance Distribution Requires Partner Approval

Any distribution to partners before all gains and losses have been realized and recognized requires approval of all partners. Assume that Xavier, Young, and Zebula are partners sharing profits and losses equally, and that the partnership is in the process of liquidation with the following account balances after all nonpartner liabilities have been paid:

Debits		Credits	
Cash	$30,000	Xavier loan	$15,000
Equipment	45,000	Young capital	30,000
Xavier capital	10,000	Zebula capital	40,000
	$85,000		$85,000

If available cash is to be distributed, it should be paid $10,000 to Young and $20,000 to Zebula according to the following safe payment computations:

	Possible Losses	Xavier Equity	Young Equity	Zebula Equity
Partners' equities		$ 5,000	$30,000	$40,000
Possible loss on noncash asset:				
Equipment	$45,000	(15,000)	(15,000)	(15,000)
		(10,000)	15,000	25,000
Possible loss on Xavier's debit				
balance shared 50:50		10,000	(5,000)	(5,000)
Safe payments		—	$10,000	$20,000

Xavier may object to the immediate distribution of the $30,000 cash to Young and Zebula because his $15,000 loan to the partnership has a higher priority in liquidation than the capital balances of Young and Zebula. The objection simply means that the partners do not agree to the advance distribution of cash, and accordingly, all distributions to partners are delayed until all assets are converted into cash and a final settlement can be made.

INSTALLMENT LIQUIDATIONS

An **installment liquidation** involves the distribution of cash to partners as it becomes available during the liquidation period and before all liquidation gains and losses have been realized. The alternative is a simple liquidation, in which no cash is distributed to partners until all gains and losses on liquidation are realized and reflected in the partners' capital account balances.

General Principles of Installment Liquidation

An orderly liquidation of a solvent partnership may be carried out with distributions of available cash on a regular basis until all noncash assets are converted into cash. Liabilities other than those to partners must, of course, be paid before any distributions are made to partners. Once cash is available for distribution to partners, the amounts to be distributed to individual partners can be determined by the preparation of a schedule of safe payments for each installment distribution. A safe payments schedule will not be necessary, however, when the capital accounts at the start of the liquidation process are in the relative profit and loss sharing ratios of the partners, and there are no loan or advance balances with the partners. In this case, all distributions to partners will be made in the relative profit and loss sharing ratios.

When installment payments to partners are determined by reference to safe payments schedules, the order of distributions will be such that the remaining capital balances (equity balances if there are loans with partners) after each distribution will be ever closer to alignment with the profit and loss sharing ratios of the partners. Once all partners are included in an installment distribution, the remaining capital balances (equities) will be aligned, and further installment payments will be in the profit sharing ratios. Thus, even though the capital accounts (equities) are not aligned at the start of the liquidation process, if all partners are included in the first installment, future installment payments to partners will be in the profit sharing ratios, and additional safe payment schedules are not necessary.

Installment Liquidation Illustration

The partnership of Duro, Kemp, and Roth is to be liquidated as soon as possible after December 31, 20X1, and all cash on hand except for a $20,000 contingency balance is to be distributed at the end of each month until the liquidation is completed. Profits and losses are shared 50%, 30%, and 20% to Duro, Kemp, and Roth, respectively. A balance sheet of the partnership at December 31, 20X1 contains the following accounts and balances:

DURO, KEMP, AND ROTH
BALANCE SHEET
AT DECEMBER 31, 20X1

Assets		Liabilities and Capital	
Cash	$ 240,000	Accounts payable	$ 300,000
Accounts receivable—net	280,000	Note payable	200,000
Loan to Roth	40,000	Loan from Kemp	20,000
Inventories	400,000	Duro capital (50%)	340,000
Land	100,000	Kemp capital (30%)	340,000
Equipment—net	300,000	Roth capital (20%)	200,000
Goodwill	40,000		
	$1,400,000		$1,400,000

A summary of liquidation events is as follows:

January 20X2—The loan to Roth is offset against his capital balance, the goodwill is written off, $200,000 is collected on account, inventory items that cost $160,000 are sold for $200,000, and cash is distributed.

February 20X2—Equipment with a book value of $80,000 is sold for $60,000, the remaining inventory items are sold for $180,000, liquidation expenses of $4,000 are paid, a liability of $8,000 is discovered, and cash is distributed.

March 20X2—The land is sold for $150,000, liquidation expenses of $5,000 are paid, and cash is distributed.

April 20X2—Additional equipment is sold for $150,000, the remaining equipment and receivables are written off, and all cash on hand is distributed in final liquidation of the partnership.

January Liquidation Events   The events of the Duro, Kemp, and Roth partnership during the month of January 20X2 are recorded as follows:

Roth capital	$ 40,000	
Loan to Roth		$ 40,000
To offset loan against capital.		
Duro capital	$ 20,000	
Kemp capital	12,000	
Roth capital	8,000	
Goodwill		$ 40,000
To write off goodwill.		

	Cash		$200,000	
	Accounts receivable			$200,000

To record collection of receivables.

	Cash		$200,000	
	Inventories			$160,000
	Duro capital			20,000
	Kemp capital			12,000
	Roth capital			8,000

To record sale of inventory items at a gain.

	Accounts payable		$300,000	
	Note payable		200,000	
	Cash			$500,000

To record payment of nonpartner liabilities.

	Loan from Kemp		$ 20,000	
	Kemp capital		100,000	
	Cash			$120,000

To record distribution of cash to Kemp.

In addition to being recorded in the accounts, each of the foregoing entries should be reflected in a statement of partnership liquidation, such as the one shown in Exhibit 17–4. A liquidation statement is a continuous record that summarizes all transactions and events during the liquidation period, and it will not be complete until the liquidation is finalized. Thus, the statement shown in Exhibit 17–4 for January events is really an interim statement. However, interim liquidation statements are probably more important than the final liquidation statement, because interim statements show the progress that has been made toward liquidation to date and can provide a basis for current decisions as well as future planning. The completed liquidation statement can do little more than provide interested parties with an ability to check on what has been done. The partnership liquidation statement may be an acceptable legal document for partnerships that are liquidated through a bankruptcy court.[4]

DURO, KEMP, AND ROTH
STATEMENT OF PARTNERSHIP LIQUIDATION
FOR THE PERIOD JANUARY 1, 20X2 TO FEBRUARY 1, 20X2

	Cash	Noncash Assets	Priority Liabilities	50% Duro Capital	Kemp Loan	30% Kemp Capital	20% Roth Capital
Balances January 1	$240,000	$1,160,000	$500,000	$340,000	$20,000	$340,000	$200,000
Offset Roth loan		(40,000)					(40,000)
Write-off of goodwill		(40,000)		(20,000)		(12,000)	(8,000)
Collection of receivables	200,000	(200,000)					
Sale of inventory items	200,000	(160,000)		20,000		12,000	8,000
Predistribution balances January 31	640,000	720,000	500,000	340,000	20,000	340,000	160,000
January distribution (see Exhibit 17–5)							
Creditors	(500,000)		(500,000)				
Kemp	(120,000)				(20,000)	(100,000)	
Balances February 1	20,000	720,000	0	340,000	0	240,000	160,000

Exhibit 17–4 Interim Statement of Partnership Liquidation

[4]When a partnership is liquidated under Chapter 7 of the Bankruptcy Act, court approval is required for all distributions.

DURO, KEMP, AND ROTH
SCHEDULE OF SAFE PAYMENTS
JANUARY 31, 20X2

	Possible Losses	50% Duro Capital	30% Kemp Capital and Loan	20% Roth Capital
Partners' equities January 31, 20X2 (see Statement of Liquidation)		$340,000	$360,000	$160,000
Possible loss on noncash assets (see Statement of Liquidation)	$720,000	(360,000)	(216,000)	(144,000)
		(20,000)	144,000	16,000
Possible loss on contingencies: cash withheld	20,000	(10,000)	(6,000)	(4,000)
		(30,000)	138,000	12,000
Possible loss from Duro: debit balance allocated 60:40		30,000	(18,000)	(12,000)
		—	$120,000	—

Exhibit 17–5   *First Installment—Safe Payments Schedule*

In the cash distribution that is made on January 31, 20X2 (see Exhibit 17–4), the partnership has $140,000 remaining after all nonpartner debts have been paid. Of this amount, $20,000 is retained by the partnership for contingencies, and $120,000 is available for distribution to the partners. The safe payments schedule that appears in Exhibit 17–5 shows that the full $120,000 should be distributed to Kemp. The partnership has a $20,000 loan payable to Kemp, so the first $20,000 distributed to Kemp is applied to the loan, and the remaining $100,000 is charged to Kemp's capital account.

February Liquidation Events   Journal entries to record the February 20X2 events of the Duro, Kemp, and Roth liquidation are:

Cash	$ 60,000	
Duro capital	10,000	
Kemp capital	6,000	
Roth capital	4,000	
Equipment—net		$ 80,000

To record sale of equipment at a $20,000 loss.

Cash	$180,000	
Duro capital	30,000	
Kemp capital	18,000	
Roth capital	12,000	
Inventories		$240,000

To record sale of remaining inventory items at a $60,000 loss.

Duro capital	$ 2,000	
Kemp capital	1,200	
Roth capital	800	
Cash		$ 4,000

To record payment of liquidation expenses.

Duro capital	$ 4,000	
Kemp capital	2,400	
Roth capital	1,600	
Accounts payable		$ 8,000

To record identification of an unrecorded liability.

Accounts payable		$ 8,000		
Cash			$ 8,000	

To record payment of accounts payable.

Duro capital		$ 84,000		
Kemp capital		86,400		
Roth capital		57,600		
Cash			$228,000	

To record distribution of cash to partners.

These entries are reflected in the liquidation statement that appears in Exhibit 17–6. The liquidation statement is for the period January 1, 20X2 to March 1, 20X2. Computations for the amount of cash distributed to partners on February 28, 20X2 are shown in Exhibit 17–7. All the partners are included in the February 28 distribution, so all future distributions will be in the profit and loss sharing ratios, provided that the liquidation proceeds as planned.

Note that the plan of distribution can be upset by events such as the distribution of noncash assets to specific partners. In the liquidation of a medical practice partnership, for example, it might be expected that the doctors would withdraw equipment early in the liquidation process in order to continue their own practices. When noncash assets are distributed to partners, the fair value of such assets should be determined, and any difference between fair value and book value should be recognized as a partnership gain or loss. The distribution of noncash assets to specific partners and the valuation of the property distributed must be approved by all partners.

DURO, KEMP, AND ROTH
STATEMENT OF PARTNERSHIP LIQUIDATION
FOR THE PERIOD JANUARY 1, 20X2 TO MARCH 1, 20X2

	Cash	Noncash Assets	Priority Liabilities	50% Duro Capital	Kemp Loan	30% Kemp Capital	20% Roth Capital
Balances January 1	$240,000	$1,160,000	$500,000	$340,000	$20,000	$340,000	$200,000
Offset Roth loan		(40,000)					(40,000)
Write-off of goodwill		(40,000)		(20,000)		(12,000)	(8,000)
Collection of receivables	200,000	(200,000)					
Sale of inventory items	200,000	(160,000)		20,000		12,000	8,000
Predistribution balances January 31	640,000	720,000	500,000	340,000	20,000	340,000	160,000
January distribution (see Exhibit 17–5)							
Creditors	(500,000)		(500,000)				
Kemp	(120,000)				(20,000)	(100,000)	
Balances February 1	20,000	720,000	0	340,000	0	240,000	160,000
Equipment sale	60,000	(80,000)		(10,000)		(6,000)	(4,000)
Sale of inventory items	180,000	(240,000)		(30,000)		(18,000)	(12,000)
Liquidation expenses	(4,000)			(2,000)		(1,200)	(800)
Liability discovered			8,000	(4,000)		(2,400)	(1,600)
Predistribution balances February 28	256,000	400,000	8,000	294,000		212,400	141,600
February distribution (see Exhibit 17–7)							
Creditors	(8,000)		(8,000)				
Partners	(228,000)			(84,000)		(86,400)	(57,600)
Balances March 1	20,000	400,000	0	210,000		126,000	84,000

Exhibit 17–6 *Interim Statement of Partnership Liquidation*

```
DURO, KEMP, AND ROTH
SCHEDULE OF SAFE PAYMENTS
FEBRUARY 28, 20X2
```

	Possible Losses	50% Duro Capital	30% Kemp Capital	20% Roth Capital
Partners' equities February 28, 20X2 (see Statement of Liquidation)		$294,000	$212,400	$141,600
Possible loss on noncash assets (see Statement of Liquidation)	$400,000	(200,000)	(120,000)	(80,000)
		94,000	92,400	61,600
Possible loss on contingencies: cash withheld	20,000	(10,000)	(6,000)	(4,000)
		$ 84,000	$ 86,400	$ 57,600

Exhibit 17–7   *Second Installment—Safe Payments Schedule*

March and April Liquidation Events   By March 20X2 the liquidation of the Duro, Kemp, and Roth partnership has progressed to a point where partner capital balances are in their relative profit and loss sharing ratios. Journal entries for the events of March and April are as follows.

Entries for March

Cash	$150,000	
Duro capital		$ 25,000
Kemp capital		15,000
Roth capital		10,000
Land		100,000

To record sale of land at a $50,000 gain.

Duro capital	$ 2,500	
Kemp capital	1,500	
Roth capital	1,000	
Cash		5,000

To record payment of liquidation expenses.

Duro capital	$ 72,500	
Kemp capital	43,500	
Roth capital	29,000	
Cash		$145,000

To record the March distribution of cash to partners.

Entries for April

Cash	$150,000	
Duro capital	35,000	
Kemp capital	21,000	
Roth capital	14,000	
Equipment—net		$220,000

To record sale of the remaining equipment at a
$70,000 loss.

Duro capital	$ 40,000	
Kemp capital	24,000	
Roth capital	16,000	
Accounts receivable		$ 80,000

To record write-off of remaining receivables.

Duro capital	$ 85,000	
Kemp capital	51,000	
Roth capital	34,000	
Cash		$170,000

To record distribution of cash to partners in final liquidation.

These entries are reflected in a complete liquidation statement for the partnership in Exhibit 17–8. The complete liquidation statement covers the period January 1 to April 30, 20X2. The March and April cash distributions to partners are in the relative profit and loss sharing ratios, so safe payment computations are not necessary. The $145,000 distributed to partners on March 31 is determined by subtracting the $20,000 cash reserve from the $165,000 cash balance immediately before the distribution. All remaining cash is remitted to the partners in the final installment distribution on April 30, 20X2.

CASH DISTRIBUTION PLANS

Safe payment schedules are an effective method of computing the amount of safe payments to partners and preventing excessive payments to any partner. However, the approach is inefficient if numerous installment distributions are made to partners, because a safe payment schedule must be prepared for each distribution until the

DURO, KEMP, AND ROTH
STATEMENT OF PARTNERSHIP LIQUIDATION
FOR THE PERIOD JANUARY 1, 20X2 TO APRIL 30, 20X2

	Cash	Noncash Assets	Priority Liabilities	50% Duro Capital	Kemp Loan	30% Kemp Capital	20% Roth Capital
Balances January 1	$240,000	$1,160,000	$500,000	$340,000	$20,000	$340,000	$200,000
Offset Roth loan		(40,000)					(40,000)
Write-off of goodwill		(40,000)		(20,000)		(12,000)	(8,000)
Collection of receivables	200,000	(200,000)					
Sale of inventory items	200,000	(160,000)		20,000		12,000	8,000
Predistribution balances January 31	640,000	720,000	500,000	340,000	20,000	340,000	160,000
January distribution (see Exhibit 17–5)							
Creditors	(500,000)		(500,000)				
Kemp	(120,000)				(20,000)	(100,000)	
Balances February 1	20,000	720,000	0	340,000	0	240,000	160,000
Equipment sale	60,000	(80,000)		(10,000)		(6,000)	(4,000)
Sale of inventory items	180,000	(240,000)		(30,000)		(18,000)	(12,000)
Liquidation expenses	(4,000)			(2,000)		(1,200)	(800)
Liability discovered			8,000	(4,000)		(2,400)	(1,600)
Predistribution balances February 28	256,000	400,000	8,000	294,000		212,400	141,600
February distribution (see Exhibit 17–7)							
Creditors	(8,000)		(8,000)				
Partners	(228,000)			(84,000)		(86,400)	(57,600)
Balances March 1	20,000	400,000	0	210,000		126,000	84,000
Sale of land	150,000	(100,000)		25,000		15,000	10,000
Liquidation expenses	(5,000)			(2,500)		(1,500)	(1,000)
Predistribution balances March 31	165,000	300,000		232,500		139,500	93,000
March distribution (50:30:20)	(145,000)			(72,500)		(43,500)	(29,000)
Balances April 1	20,000	300,000		160,000		96,000	64,000
Sale of equipment	150,000	(220,000)		(35,000)		(21,000)	(14,000)
Write-off of receivables		(80,000)		(40,000)		(24,000)	(16,000)
Predistribution balances April 30	170,000	0		85,000		51,000	34,000
April distribution (50:30:20)	(170,000)			(85,000)		(51,000)	(34,000)
Liquidation completed April 30	0			0		0	0

Exhibit 17–8   *Final Statement of Partnership Liquidation*

capital balances are aligned with the profit and loss sharing ratios. The safe payment schedule approach is also deficient as a planning device because it does not provide information that will help the partners project when they can expect to be included in cash distributions. These deficiencies of the safe payment approach can be overcome by preparing a cash distribution plan at the start of the liquidation process.

The development of a **cash distribution plan** (also referred to as a cash predistribution plan) for the liquidation of a partnership involves a ranking of the partners in terms of their vulnerability to possible losses, the use of the vulnerability ranking to prepare a schedule of assumed loss absorption, and the development of a cash distribution plan from the assumed-loss-absorption schedule. In illustrating the preparation of a cash distribution plan, the Duro, Kemp, and Roth example is used again.

Vulnerability Ranks

At the inception of the liquidation process, Duro, Kemp, and Roth had capital balances of $340,000, $340,000, and $200,000, respectively, but their equities (capital ± loan balances) were $340,000, $360,000, and $160,000, respectively. In determining their vulnerability to possible losses, the equity of each partner is divided by his or her profit sharing ratio to identify the maximum loss that the partner could absorb without reducing his or her equity below zero. **Vulnerability rankings** for Duro, Kemp, and Roth are determined as follows:

DURO, KEMP, AND ROTH VULNERABILITY RANKING

	Partner's Equity		Profit Sharing Ratio		Loss Absorption Potential	Vulnerability Ranking (1 most vulnerable)
Duro	$340,000	÷	.5	=	$ 680,000	1
Kemp	360,000	÷	.3	=	1,200,000	3
Roth	160,000	÷	.2	=	800,000	2

The vulnerability ranks indicate that Duro is most vulnerable to losses because his equity would be reduced to zero with a total partnership loss on liquidation of $680,000. Kemp, on the other hand, is least vulnerable because his equity is sufficient to absorb his share of liquidation losses up to $1,200,000. This interpretation helps explain why Kemp received all the cash distributed to partners in the first installment distribution in the previous illustration.

Assumed Loss Absorption

A **schedule of assumed loss absorption** is prepared as a second step in developing the cash distribution plan. This schedule starts with the preliquidation equities and charges each partner's equity with its share of the loss that would exactly eliminate the equity of the most vulnerable partner. The next step is to charge each remaining partner's equity with its share of the loss that would exactly eliminate the equity of the next most vulnerable partner. This process is continued until the equities of all but the least vulnerable partner have been reduced to zero. A schedule of assumed loss absorption for the Duro, Kemp, and Roth partnership is as follows:

DURO, KEMP, AND ROTH SCHEDULE OF ASSUMED LOSS ABSORPTION

	(50%) Duro	(30%) Kemp	(20%) Roth	Total
Preliquidation equities	$340,000	$360,000	$160,000	$860,000
Assumed loss to absorb Duro's equity (allocated 50:30:20)	(340,000)	(204,000)	(136,000)	(680,000)
Balances	—	156,000	24,000	180,000
Assumed loss to absorb Roth's equity (allocated 60:40)		(36,000)	(24,000)	(60,000)
Balances		$120,000	—	$120,000

The partnership loss that exactly eliminates Duro's equity is $680,000, an amount computed in preparing the vulnerability ranks. After Duro's equity is reduced to zero in the first step, losses are divided 60% to Kemp and 40% to Roth until Roth's equity is reduced to zero. The additional partnership loss that reduces Roth's equity to zero is $60,000—Roth's $24,000 equity divided by his 40% profit sharing ratio after Duro is eliminated from consideration (in other words, it is assumed that Duro is personally insolvent). After Roth's equity has been reduced to zero, the equity of Kemp, the least vulnerable partner, stands at $120,000.

Cash Distribution Plan

Kemp should receive the first $120,000 distributed to the partners. A cash distribution plan for the Duro, Kemp, and Roth partnership is prepared from the schedule of assumed loss absorption as follows:

DURO, KEMP, AND ROTH CASH DISTRIBUTION PLAN

	Priority Liabilities	Kemp Loan	Duro	Kemp	Roth
First $500,000	100%				
Next $20,000		100%			
Next $100,000				100%	
Next $60,000				60	40%
Remainder			50%	30	20

In developing the cash distribution plan, the first cash available for distribution goes to nonpartner creditors. These consist of the $300,000 accounts payable and the $200,000 note payable of the Duro, Kemp, and Roth partnership at December 31, 20X1. The next $20,000 goes to Kemp to settle his loan to the partnership, because partner loans have a higher priority than partner capital balances. The next $100,000 available is distributed to Kemp in consideration of his capital balance. This distribution aligns the capital and profit sharing ratios of Kemp and Roth. The next $60,000 is shared 60% and 40% between Kemp and Roth. This distribution completes the alignment of all capital balances and profit sharing ratios, and the remaining distributions are in accordance with the profit sharing ratios.

Kemp can analyze the cash distribution plan on January 1, 20X2 and determine that he will begin to receive cash after $500,000 has been paid to priority creditors. Similarly, Roth and Duro can use the plan to determine their chances of recovering some or all of their partnership equities. For example, if Duro expects $800,000 to be realized from all partnership assets, he can easily compute the amount he would receive [($800,000 − $680,000) × 50% = $60,000].

Cash Distribution Schedule

Further application of the cash distribution plan can be illustrated by assuming that the Duro, Kemp, and Roth partnership is liquidated in two installments, with $550,000 cash being distributed in the first installment and $250,000 in the second and final installment. Under these assumptions, the cash distribution plan would be used in preparing a **cash distribution schedule** such as the following one.

DURO, KEMP, AND ROTH CASH DISTRIBUTION SCHEDULE

	Cash Distributed	Priority Liabilities	Kemp Loan	Duro Capital	Kemp Capital	Roth Capital
First Installment						
Priority creditors	$500,000	$500,000				
Kemp loan	20,000		$20,000			
Kemp capital (remainder)	30,000				$ 30,000	
	$550,000	$500,000	$20,000		$ 30,000	
Second Installment						
Kemp capital	$ 70,000				$ 70,000	
Kemp and Roth (60:40)	60,000				36,000	$24,000
Remainder (50:30:20)	120,000			$60,000	36,000	24,000
	$250,000			$60,000	$142,000	$48,000

The $550,000 cash distributed in the first installment is allocated $500,000 to nonpartner liabilities and $20,000 to repay the loan from Kemp. The remaining $30,000 is paid to Kemp to reduce the balance of his capital account. In the second installment distribution, as shown in the cash distribution schedule, Kemp receives the first $70,000 in order to align his capital balance with that of Roth. The next $60,000 is allocated to Kemp and Roth in accordance with their 60:40 relative profit and loss sharing ratios, and the final $120,000 is allocated to Duro, Kemp, and Roth in their 50 : 30 : 20 relative profit and loss sharing ratios. The information from the cash distribution schedule is used in the same manner as information from safe payment schedules. That is, the cash payments indicated by the cash distribution schedules are entered in the statement of partnership liquidation and in the partnership records as cash distributions are actually made.

The preparation of a cash distribution plan is more time-consuming than the preparation of a single safe payments schedule. However, as shown here, the cash distribution plan provides a flexible and efficient means of determining safe payments to partners. In addition, the cash distribution plan serves a planning, as well as a computational, function.

INSOLVENT PARTNERS AND PARTNERSHIPS

The order for distributing assets in the liquidation of a partnership was listed early in this chapter as:

    I Amounts owed to creditors other than partners
    II Amounts owed to partners other than for capital and profits
    III Amounts due to partners with respect to their capital interests
    IV Amounts due to partners in respect of profits

This order of distribution is specified in Section 40b of the Act. With respect to an insolvent partner, Section 40i of the Act gives the following rank order for claims against the separate property of a bankrupt partner:

    I Those owing to separate creditors
    II Those owing to partnership creditors
    III Those owing to partners by way of contribution

These priority rankings have important implications for the liquidation of partnerships that are insolvent (partnership assets < partnership liabilities) and for the liquidation of partnerships that are solvent (partnership assets ≥ partnership liabilities), but one or more of the individual partners is insolvent (personal assets < personal liabilities). Partnership creditors must first seek recovery of their claims from partnership property, and the creditors of individual partners must first seek recovery of their claims from individual property. Thus, individual and partnership properties are marshaled separately in establishing the priority of claims.

Partnership Solvent—One or More Partners Personally Insolvent

In the liquidation of a solvent partnership, partnership creditors recover the full amount of their claims from partnership property. The partnership must be careful not to distribute partnership property to an insolvent partner. This distribution makes the assets personal assets, and his or her personal creditors have a priority claim on the assets. Otherwise, personal creditors only have a claim to the extent of the insolvent partner's equity in such partnership assets. Also, if an insolvent partner has a credit capital balance and a solvent partner has an equal debit balance (that is, partnership assets = partnership liabilities = 0), the personal creditors of the insolvent partner have a claim against the personal assets of the solvent partner to the extent of the debit capital balance.

Even though the partnership is solvent, individual partners may have debit balances in their capital accounts at the time of dissolution, or they may end up with debit capital balances as a result of losses and expenses incurred during the liquidation process. Such partners are obligated to the partners with equity in the partnership for the amount of such debit balances. However, if a partner with a debit capital balance is personally insolvent (personal assets < personal liabilities), the full amount of that partner's personal assets will go to his or her personal creditors (rank I) under the Act, and amounts owing to partners by way of contribution (rank III) will not share in distribution of that partner's personal assets. In some states, however, it is possible under *common law or bankruptcy law* for the partners to share in the personal assets of an insolvent partner with a debit capital balance.[5]

To illustrate, West, York, and Zeff are partners sharing profits 30%, 30%, and 40%, respectively. West is personally insolvent with personal assets of $50,000 and personal liabilities of $100,000. The partnership account balances after all partnership liabilities have been paid are as follows:

	Case A	Case B	Case C
Cash	$60,000 dr	—	—
West capital (30%)	18,000 cr	$18,000 cr	$21,000 dr
York capital (30%)	18,000 cr	27,000 dr	9,000 cr
Zeff capital (40%)	24,000 cr	9,000 cr	12,000 cr

In Case A, the $18,000 partnership equity of West should not be paid directly to West because her personal creditors have a prior claim against her $18,000 equity in partnership assets.

In Case B, the personal creditors of West have a claim against the personal assets of York to the extent of the $18,000 that York owes West. Zeff also has a claim against York for $9,000.

In Case C, West has a debit balance in her capital account and is insolvent. Under the provisions of the Act, York and Zeff are not allowed to share in the personal assets of West. Thus, they must share the $21,000 loss from West in their relative profit sharing ratios of 3:7 and 4:7.

Insolvent Partnership

When a partnership is insolvent, the cash available after all noncash assets have been converted into cash will not be sufficient to pay partnership creditors.[6] Partnership creditors will obtain partial recovery from partnership assets (rank I) and will call upon individual partners to use their personal resources to satisfy remaining claims (rank II). Although personal creditors have a prior claim (rank I) on personal assets, partnership creditors can seek recovery of their claims from the personal assets of any partner who is personally solvent. Under the Act, partners are required to contribute the amounts necessary to satisfy partnership liabilities. The Act is specific in stating that a partner must contribute his or her share of the payment to satisfy the liabilities, as well as his or her relative share of the liabilities of any partners who are insolvent or who cannot or will not contribute their share of the liabilities (see Section 40b of the Act). A partner who pays more than his or her share of partnership liabilities does, of course, have a claim against partners with debit capital balances.

Rose, Faye, and Kate are partners sharing profits equally, and their partnership is in the process of liquidation. After all assets have been converted into cash and all available cash applied to payment of partnership liabilities, the following account balances remain on the partnership books:

Liabilities	$90,000 cr
Rose capital ($\frac{1}{3}$)	30,000 dr
Faye capital ($\frac{1}{3}$)	30,000 dr
Kate capital ($\frac{1}{3}$)	30,000 dr

---

[5]A trustee in a partnership case under the Bankruptcy Act of 1978 has a claim against the estate of each general partner that is also a debtor in a bankruptcy case (11 U.S.C. paragraph 723[c]).

[6]As used in this chapter, an insolvent partnership means that partnership liabilities exceed the fair value of partnership assets. Under the Bankruptcy Act of 1978, a partnership is insolvent if partnership liabilities exceed the fair value of partnership assets plus the excess of each general partner's personal assets over personal debts (11 U.S.C. paragraph 101[26]B).

Provided that all partners have personal resources of at least $30,000, each partner should pay $30,000 into the partnership in full satisfaction of partnership liabilities. However, the creditors may collect the full $90,000 deficiency from any one of the partners. For example, creditors may collect the $90,000 from Rose, in which case the remaining partnership balances would be:

Rose capital	$60,000 cr
Faye capital	30,000 dr
Kate capital	30,000 dr

If Faye and Kate can each pay $30,000 into the partnership, the fact that the creditors proceeded against Rose is of no great concern. However, if the creditors proceeded against Rose because Kate is personally insolvent, and Faye's net personal assets are only $35,000, the situation is changed considerably. In this case, Rose and Faye share equally the $30,000 loss on Kate's insolvency, after which Rose will have a $45,000 credit capital balance and Faye, a $45,000 debit capital balance. Faye's personal assets are only $35,000, so Rose proceeds to collect the $35,000 from Faye, and the remaining $10,000 debit balance in Faye's capital account is written off as a loss to Rose.

The examples in this section illustrate some of the more general problems that arise in liquidations of partnerships that are insolvent or in which there are insolvent partners. Many legal complications can arise in partnership liquidations, so the accountant should not hesitate to seek legal counsel as the need arises.

SUMMARY

The liquidation of a partnership involves the conversion of noncash assets into cash, the recognition of gains and losses during the liquidation period, the payment of liabilities, and the distribution of cash to partners in final termination of the business entity. A simple liquidation refers to the conversion of all assets into cash before any distributions are made to partners.

A primary financial statement of a liquidating partnership is the statement of partnership liquidation, which summarizes all financial transactions and events during the liquidation period. This statement may also be used as a legal document for liquidations carried out under the jurisdiction of a court. When partnerships are liquidated by means of installment distributions to partners, cash is distributed to partners after liabilities have been paid but before all gains and losses on liquidation are recognized in the accounts. To prevent excessive payments to any partner, the amount of cash to be distributed is computed on the basis of two assumptions—that all partners are personally insolvent and that all noncash assets are actual losses. Under these assumptions, there are two primary approaches for computing the amounts that can be safely paid to partners in each installment distribution. The first approach is to prepare a safe payments schedule for each installment distribution, and the second approach is to prepare a cash distribution plan that can be used throughout the liquidation process.

The Act specifies priorities for the distribution of partnership assets in liquidations and for the distribution of the personal assets of insolvent partners. Partnership creditors rank first in recovering their claims from partnership property, and personal creditors rank first in recovering their claims from personal property. Priorities for other claims depend upon whether the partnership or the individual partners are insolvent, and each case requires separate analysis. The determination of property rights and creditor claims involves complex legal interpretations, so competent legal advice is frequently needed.

ASSIGNMENT MATERIAL

QUESTIONS

1 How does liquidation of a partnership differ from dissolution of a partnership?
2 What is a simple partnership liquidation and how are distributions to partners determined?
3 The Uniform Partnership Act specifies a priority ranking for distribution of partnership assets in liquidation. What is the ranking?

4 Under what conditions would partnership assets be distributed for partner capital interests before partner's loans to the partnership are paid?

5 What assumptions are made in determining the amount of distributions to individual partners prior to the recognition of all gains and losses on liquidation?

6 Why are partner equities rather than partner capital balances used in the preparation of safe payment schedules?

7 How do safe payment computations affect partnership ledger account balances?

8 What is a statement of partnership liquidation and how is the statement helpful to partners and other parties involved in partnership liquidation?

9 If a partnership in liquidation has satisfied all of its nonpartner liabilities and has cash available for distribution to partners, under what circumstances would it be permissible to divide available cash in the profit and loss sharing ratios of the partners?

10 What are vulnerability ranks and how are they used in the preparation of cash distribution plans for partnership liquidations?

11 If a partnership is insolvent, how does one determine the amount of cash to distribute to individual partners?

12 When all partnership assets have been distributed in the liquidation of a partnership, some partners may have debit capital balances whereas others have credit capital balances. How are such balances disposed of if the partners with debit balances are personally solvent? If they are personally insolvent?

EXERCISES

E 17-1 The partnership of Folly and Frill is in the process of liquidation. On January 1, 20X5 the ledger shows account balances as follows:

Cash	$10,000	Accounts payable	$15,000
Accounts receivable	25,000	Folly capital	40,000
Lumber inventory	40,000	Frill capital	20,000

On January 10, 20X5 the lumber inventory is sold for $25,000, and during January, accounts receivable of $21,000 are collected. No further collections on the receivables are expected. Profits are shared 60% to Folly and 40% to Frill.

Required: Prepare a schedule showing how the cash available on February 1, 20X5 should be distributed.

E 17-2 After closing entries were made on December 31, 20X6, the ledger of Mike, Nancy, and Okey contained the following balances:

Cash	$39,000	Accounts payable	$ 5,000
Inventory	16,000	Mike capital (40%)	15,000
		Nancy capital (30%)	8,000
		Okey capital (30%)	27,000

Due to unsuccessful operations, the partners decide to liquidate the business. During January some of the inventory is sold for $10,000, and on January 31, 20X7 all available cash is distributed. It is not known if the remaining inventory items can be sold.

Required: Prepare all journal entries necessary to account for the transactions of the partnership during January 20X7.

E 17-3 Terry, Vivian, and Walter have decided to liquidate their partnership. Account balances on January 1, 20X6 are as follows:

Cash	$120,000	Accounts payable	$ 40,000
Other assets	120,000	Terry capital (30%)	85,000
	$240,000	Vivian capital (30%)	25,000
		Walter capital (40%)	90,000
			$240,000

The partners agree to keep a $10,000 contingency fund and to distribute available cash immediately.

Required: Determine the amount of cash that should be paid to each partner.

E 17-4 Jan, Kim, and Lee announce plans to liquidate their partnership immediately. The assets, equities and profit and loss sharing ratios are summarized as follows.

Loan to Kim	$ 20,000	Accounts payable	$ 60,000
Other assets	180,000	Jan capital (50%)	59,000
	$200,000	Kim capital (30%)	29,000
		Lee capital (20%)	52,000
			$200,000

The other assets are sold for $120,000, and an overlooked bill for landscaping services of $5,000 is discovered. Kim cannot pay her partnership debt at the present time, but she expects to have the money in a month or two.

Required: Determine how cash should be distributed to creditors and partners.

E 17-5 The profit and loss sharing agreement of the partnership of Anita, Bernice, and Colleen provides that the partners are allowed 10% interest on their average capital balances for the year; Anita is allowed a $15,000 salary, and the remainder is divided 50% to Anita, 30% to Bernice, and 20% to Colleen. The December 31, 20X8 after-closing balances are as follows:

Net assets	$100,000	Anita capital	$ 40,000
		Bernice capital	35,000
		Colleen capital	25,000
			$100,000

In January 20X9 the partnership is preparing to liquidate the business and discovers that the year-end inventory was overvalued by $10,000, resulting in an error in calculating the 20X8 net income.

Required: Determine the correct capital balances of Anita, Bernice, and Colleen.

E 17-6 The profit and loss sharing agreement of the partnership of Ali, Bart, and Carrie provides a salary allowance for Ali and Carrie of $10,000 each. Partners receive a 10% interest allowance on their average capital balances for the year. The remainder is divided 40% to Ali, 20% to Bart, and 40% to Carrie. The December 31, 20X8 after-closing balances are as follows:

Net assets	$150,000	Ali capital	$ 60,000
		Bart capital	25,000
		Carrie capital	65,000
			$150,000

In January 20X9 the partnership is preparing to liquidate the business and discovers that the year-end inventory was erroneously undervalued by $15,000, resulting in an error in calculating the 20X8 net income.

Required: Determine the correct capital balances of Ali, Bart, and Carrie.

E 17-7 A condensed balance sheet with profit sharing percentages for the Evers, Freda, and Grace partnership on January 1, 20X1 shows the following:

Cash	$100,000	Liabilities	$ 80,000
Other assets	500,000	Evers capital (40%)	100,000
		Freda capital (40%)	250,000
		Grace capital (20%)	170,000
	$600,000		$600,000

On January 2, 20X1 the partners decide to liquidate the business, and during January they sell assets with a book value of $300,000 for $170,000.

Required: Prepare a safe payment schedule to show the amount of cash to be distributed to each partner if all available cash, except for a $10,000 contingency fund, is distributed immediately after the sale.

E 17-8 The partnership of Jerry, Joan, and Jill is in the process of liquidation. Its account balances on November 30, 20X8 are:

Cash	$ 8,000	Accounts payable	$ 4,000
Inventory	16,000	Due to Joan	4,000
Goodwill	8,000	Jerry capital	10,800
Receivable from Jerry	3,000	Joan capital	13,200
		Jill capital	3,000

Profits and losses are shared 40:50:10 to Jerry, Joan, and Jill, respectively.

Required: Prepare a statement of liquidation and a safe payments schedule for immediate distribution of all cash on hand.

E 17-9 The Larry, Moe, and Curly Partnership became insolvent on January 1, 20X1, and the partnership is being liquidated as soon as practicable. In this respect the following information for the partners has been marshaled:

	Capital Balances	Personal Assets	Personal Liabilities
Larry	$ 70,000	$80,000	$40,000
Moe	(60,000)	30,000	50,000
Curly	(30,000)	70,000	30,000
Total	$(20,000)		

Assume that residual profits and losses are shared equally among the three partners. Based on this information, calculate the *maximum* amount that Larry can expect to receive from the partnership liquidation.

E 17-10 The partnership of Alice, Betty, and Carle became insolvent during 20X1, and the partnership ledger shows the following balances after all partnership assets have been converted into cash and all available cash distributed:

	Debit	Credit
Accounts payable		$ 30,000
Alice capital		20,000
Betty capital	$120,000	
Carle capital		70,000
	$120,000	$120,000

Profit and loss sharing percentages for the three partners are Alice, 30%; Betty, 40%; and Carle, 30%. The personal assets and liabilities of the partners are as follows:

	Alice	Betty	Carle
Personal assets	$60,000	$110,000	$60,000
Personal liabilities	50,000	60,000	40,000

Required: Prepare a schedule to show the phaseout of the partnership and final closing of the books if the partnership creditors recover $30,000 from Betty.

E 17-11 After all partnership assets were converted into cash and all available cash distributed to creditors, the ledger of the Daniel, Eric, and Fred partnership showed the following balances:

	Debit	Credit
Accounts payable		$20,000
Daniel capital (40%)		10,000
Eric capital (30%)		60,000
Fred capital (30%)	$90,000	
	$90,000	$90,000

The percentages indicated are residual profit and loss sharing ratios. Personal assets and liabilities of the partners are as follows:

	Daniel	Eric	Fred
Personal assets	$50,000	$50,000	$100,000
Personal liabilities	45,000	40,000	40,000

The partnership creditors proceed against Fred for recovery of their claims, and the partners settle their claims against each other in accordance with the Act.

Required: Prepare a schedule to show the phaseout of the partnership and final closing of the books.

E 17-12 The partnership of Ace, Ben, Cid, and Don was dissolved on January 5, 20X1, and the account balances at June 30, 20X1, after all noncash assets are converted into cash, are as follows:

	Debits	Credits
Cash	$200,000	
Cid capital (20%)	170,000	
Don capital (10%)	80,000	
Accounts payable		$400,000
Ace capital (50%)		40,000
Ben capital (20%)		10,000
	$450,000	$450,000

Additional Information

1 The percentages indicated represent the relevant profit and loss sharing ratios.
2 Personal assets and liabilities of the partners at June 30, 20X1 are as follows:

	Personal Assets	Personal Liabilities
Ace	$600,000	$300,000
Ben	100,000	150,000
Cid	400,000	300,000
Don	100,000	20,000

3 Ace pays $200,000 into the partnership, and partnership liabilities are paid on July 1, 20X1.
4 On July 15, 20X1, Cid pays $100,000 into the partnership and Don pays $80,000. No further contributions from either Cid or Don are possible.
5 Losses from the bankruptcy of Cid are divided among the solvent partners on July 15, 20X1.
6 Available cash is distributed and the partnership books are closed on July 31, 20X1.

Required: Prepare a liquidation statement for the Ace, Ben, Cid, and Don partnership for the period June 30, 20X1 to July 31, 20X1.

E 17-13 The partnership of Denver, Elsie, Fannie, and George is being liquidated over the first few months of 20X2. The trial balance at January 1, 20X2 is as follows:

	Debits	Credits
Cash	$ 200,000	
Accounts receivable	56,000	
Inventory	142,000	
Equipment (net)	300,000	
Land	150,000	
Loan to Denver	20,000	
Accounts payable		$400,000
Denver capital (20%)		170,000
Elsie capital (10%)		80,000
Fannie capital (50%)		140,000
Geroge capital (20%)		78,000
	$868,000	$868,000

Additional Information

1 The partners agree to retain $20,000 cash on hand for contingencies and distribute the rest of the available cash at the end of each month.

2 In January half of the receivables were collected. Inventory that cost $75,000 was liquidated for $45,000. The land was sold for $250,000.

Required: Prepare a schedule of safe payments for the Denver, Elsie, Fannie, and George partnership for January 31, 20X2.

E 17-14 The assets and equities of the Quen, Reed, and Stac partnership at the end of its fiscal year on October 31, 20X2 are as follows:

Assets		Equities	
Cash	$ 15,000	Liabilities	$ 50,000
Receivables—net	20,000	Loan from Stac	10,000
Inventory	40,000	Quen capital (30%)	45,000
Plant assets—net	70,000	Reed capital (50%)	30,000
Loan to Reed	5,000	Stac capital (20%)	15,000
	$150,000		$150,000

The partners decide to liquidate the partnership. They estimate that the noncash assets, other than the loan to Reed, can be converted into $100,000 cash over the two-month period ending December 31, 20X2. Cash is to be distributed to the appropriate parties as it becomes available during the liquidation process.

1 The partner most vulnerable to partnership losses on liquidation is:

a Quen   c Reed and Quen equally

b Reed   d Stac

2 If $65,000 is available for the first distribution, it should be paid to:

	Priority Creditors	Quen	Reed	Stac
a	$60,000	$ 5,000	$ 0	$ 0
b	60,000	1,500	2,500	1,000
c	50,000	5,000	0	10,000
d	50,000	12,000	0	3,000

3 If a total amount of $7,500 is available for distribution to partners after all non-partner liabilities are paid, it should be paid as follows:

	Quen	Reed	Stac
a	$7,500	$ 0	$ 0
b	0	3,750	3,750
c	2,250	3,750	1,500
d	2,500	2,500	2,500

E 17-15 1 In a partnership liquidation, the final cash distribution to the partners should be made in accordance with the:

a Partner profit and loss sharing ratios

b Balances of partner capital accounts

c Ratio of the capital contributions by partners

d Safe payments computations

2 In accounting for the liquidation of a partnership, cash payments to partners after all non-partner creditors' claims have been satisfied, but before final cash distribution, should be according to:

a Relative profit and loss sharing ratios

b The final balances in partner capital accounts

c The relative share of gain or loss on liquidation

d Safe payments computations

3 After all noncash assets have been converted into cash in the liquidation of the Maris and DeMarco partnership, the ledger contains the following account balances:

	Debit	Credit
Cash	$34,000	—
Accounts payable	—	$25,000
Loan payable to Maris	—	9,000
Maris capital	8,000	—
DeMarco capital	—	8,000

Available cash should be distributed: $25,000 to accounts payable and:
- **a** $9,000 for loan payable to Maris
- **b** $4,500 each to Maris and DeMarco
- **c** $1,000 to Maris and $8,000 to DeMarco
- **d** $8,000 to Maris and $1,000 to DeMarco

4 The partnership of Gwen, Bill, and Sissy is liquidating and the ledger shows the following:

Cash	$ 80,000
Inventories	100,000
Accounts payable	60,000
Gwen capital (50%)	40,000
Bill capital (25%)	45,000
Sissy capital (25%)	35,000

If all available cash is distributed immediately:
- **a** Gwen, Bill, and Sissy should get $26,667 each
- **b** Gwen, Bill, and Sissy should get $6,667 each
- **c** Gwen should get $10,000, and Bill and Sissy should get $5,000 each
- **d** Bill should get $15,000 and Sissy, $5,000

5 The following balance sheet summary, together with residual profit sharing ratios, was developed on April 1, 20X6, when the Dick, Frank, and Helen partnership began its liquidation:

Cash	$140,000	Liabilities	$ 60,000
Accounts receivable	60,000	Loan from Frank	20,000
Inventories	85,000	Dick capital (20%)	75,000
Plant assets—net	200,000	Frank capital (40%)	200,000
Loan to Dick	25,000	Helen capital (40%)	155,000
	$510,000		$510,000

If available cash except for a $5,000 contingency fund is distributed immediately, Dick, Frank, and Helen, respectively, should receive:
- **a** $0, $80,000, and $15,000
- **b** $16,000, $32,000, and $32,000
- **c** $0, $70,000, and $5,000
- **d** $0, $72,500, and $7,500

6 The partnership of Unsel, Vance, and Wayne was dissolved on June 30, 20X6, and account balances after noncash assets were converted into cash on September 1, 20X6 are:

Cash	$50,000	Accounts payable	$120,000
		Unsel capital (30%)	90,000
		Vance capital (30%)	(60,000)
		Wayne capital (40%)	(100,000)

Personal assets and liabilities of the partners at September 1, 20X6 are:

	Personal Assets	Personal Liabilities
Unsel	$ 80,000	$90,000
Vance	100,000	61,000
Wayne	190,000	80,000

If Wayne contributes $70,000 to the partnership to provide cash to pay the creditors, what amount of Unsel's $90,000 partnership equity would appear to be recoverable?
- **a** $90,000
- **b** $81,000
- **c** $79,000
- **d** None of the above

E 17-16 [AICPA adapted]
Use the following information in answering questions 1, 2, and 3. Q, R, S, and T are partners sharing profits and losses equally. The partnership is insolvent and is to be liquidated. The status of the partnership and each partner is as follows:

	Partnership Capital Balance	Personal Assets (Exclusive of Partnership Interest)	Personal Liabilities (Exclusive of Partnership Interest)
Q	$ 15,000	$100,000	$40,000
R	10,000	30,000	60,000
S	(20,000)	80,000	5,000
T	(30,000)	1,000	28,000
Total	$(25,000)		

Assume that the Uniform Partnership Act applies to these questions:

1 The partnership creditors:
   a Must first seek recovery against S because he is personally solvent and he has a negative capital balance
   b Will *not* be paid in full regardless of how they proceed legally because the partnership assets are less than partnership liabilities
   c Will have to share R's interest in the partnership on a pro rata basis with R's personal creditors
   d Have first claim to partnership assets before any partner's personal creditors have rights to the partnership assets

2 The partnership creditors may obtain recovery of their claims:
   a In the amount of $6,250 from each partner
   b From the personal assets of either Q or R
   c From the personal assets of either S or T
   d From the personal assets of either Q or S for some or all of their claims

3 If Q pays the full amount owed to partnership creditors from his personal assets, then:
   a Q's partnership loss will be increased by $25,000
   b Q's partnership loss will be increased by $12,500
   c Q will have a $40,000 total partnership loss
   d Q's partnership loss will be the same as if S had paid partnership creditors from his personal assets

4 X, Y, and Z have capital balances of $30,000, $15,000, and $5,000, respectively, in the XYZ partnership. The general partnership agreement is silent as to the manner in which partnership losses are to be allocated but does provide that partnership profits are to be allocated as follows: 40% to X, 25% to Y, and 35% to Z. The partners have decided to dissolve and liquidate the partnership. After paying all creditors, the amount available for distribution will be $20,000. X, Y, and Z are individually solvent. Under the circumstances, Z will:
   a Receive $7,000
   b Receive $12,000
   c Personally have to contribute an additional $5,500
   d Personally have to contribute an additional $5,000

5 The following condensed balance sheet is presented for the partnership of Smith and Jones, who share profits and losses in the ratio of 60 : 40, respectively:

Other assets	$450,000	Accounts payable	$120,000
Smith, loan	20,000	Smith, capital	195,000
	$470,000	Jones, capital	155,000
			$470,000

The partners have decided to liquidate the partnership. If the other assets are sold for $385,000, what amount of the available cash should be distributed to Smith?
   a $136,000   c $159,000
   b $156,000   d $195,000

PROBLEMS

P 17-1 Barney, Betty, and Rubble are partners in a business that is in the process of liquidation. On January 1, 20X2, the ledger accounts show the balances indicated:

Cash	$25,000	Barnes capital	$72,000
Inventory	72,000	Betty capital	28,000
Supplies	18,000	Rubble capital	15,000

The cash is distributed to partners on January 1, 20X2. Inventory and supplies are sold for a lump-sum price of $81,000 on February 9, 20X2, and on February 10, 20X2, cash on hand is distributed to the partners in final liquidation of the business.

Required

1 Prepare the journal entry to distribute available cash on January 1, 20X2. Include a safe payment schedule as proper explanation of who should receive cash.

2 Prepare journal entries necessary on February 9, 20X2 to record the sale of assets and distribution of the gain or loss to the partners' capital accounts.

3 Prepare the journal entry to distribute cash on February 10, 20X2 in final liquidation of the business.

P 17-2 The December 31, 20X4 balance sheet of the Chan, Dickerson, and Grunther partnership, along with the partners' residual profit and loss sharing ratios, is summarized as follows:

Assets		Equities	
Cash	$ 60,000	Accounts payable	$ 90,000
Receivables	120,000	Loan from Dickerson	50,000
Inventories	150,000	Chan capital (20%)	95,000
Due from Chan	15,000	Dickerson capital (30%)	160,000
Other assets	255,000	Grunther capital (50%)	205,000
	$600,000		$600,000

The partners agree to liquidate their partnership as soon as possible after January 1, 20X5 and to distribute all cash as it becomes available.

Required: Prepare a cash distribution plan to show how cash will be distributed as it becomes available.

P 17-3 Fred, Flint, and Wilma announced the liquidation of their partnership beginning on January 1, 20X8. Profits and losses are divided 30% to Fred, 20% to Flint, and 50% to Wilma. Balance sheet items are summarized as follows:

Cash	$ 45,000	Accounts payable	$ 20,000
Accounts receivable—net	25,000	Fred capital (30%)	75,000
Inventories	25,000	Flint capital (20%)	30,000
Plant assets—net	80,000	Wilma capital (50%)	60,000
Flint loan	10,000		
	$185,000		$185,000

Required: Prepare a cash distribution plan as of January 1, 20X8 for the Fred, Flint, and Wilma partnership.

P 17-4 The partnership of Gary, Henry, Illa, and Joseph is preparing to liquidate. Profit and loss sharing ratios are shown in the summarized balance sheet at December 31, 20X8 as follows:

Cash	$200,000	Other liabilities	$100,000
Inventories	200,000	Gary loan	100,000
Loan to Henry	20,000	Gary capital (40%)	200,000
Other assets	510,000	Henry capital (30%)	320,000
		Illa capital (20%)	100,000
		Joseph capital (10%)	110,000
	$930,000		$930,000

Required

1 The partners anticipate an installment liquidation. Prepare a cash distribution plan as of January 1, 20X9 that includes a $50,000 contingency fund to help the partners predict when they will be included in cash distributions.

2 During January 20X9, the inventories are sold for $100,000, the other liabilities are paid, and $50,000 is set aside for contingencies. The partners agree that loan balances should be closed to capital accounts and remaining cash (less the contingency fund) should be distributed to partners. How much cash should each partner receive?

P 17-5 Eli, Joe, and Ned agree to liquidate their consulting practice as soon as possible after the close of business on July 31, 20X6. The trial balance on that date shows the following account balances.

	Debits	Credits
Cash	$13,000	
Accounts receivable	12,000	

(Continued)

	Debits	Credits
Furniture and fixtures	35,000	
Accounts payable		$ 6,000
Loan from Eli		4,000
Eli capital		20,000
Joe capital		15,000
Ned capital		15,000
	$60,000	$60,000

The partners share profits and losses 20%, 30%, and 50% to Eli, Joe, and Ned, respectively, after Ned is allowed a monthly salary of $4,000.

August transactions and events are as follows:

1 The accounts payable are paid.
2 Accounts receivable of $8,000 are collected in full. Ned accepts accounts receivable with a face value and fair value of $3,000 in partial satisfaction of his capital balance. The remaining accounts receivable are written off as uncollectible.
3 Furniture with a book value of $25,000 is sold for $15,000.
4 Furniture with a book value of $4,000 and an agreed upon fair value of $1,000 is taken by Joe in partial settlement of his capital balance. The remaining furniture and fixtures are donated to Goodwill Industries.
5 Liquidation expenses of $3,000 are paid.
6 Available cash is distributed to partners on August 31.

Required: Prepare a statement of partnership liquidation for the Eli, Joe, and Ned partnership for the month of August.

P 17-6 Jones, Smith, and Tandy are partners in a furniture store that began liquidation on January 1, 20X1, at which time the ledger contained the following account balances:

	Debit	Credit
Cash	$ 15,000	
Accounts receivable	20,000	
Inventories	65,000	
Land	50,000	
Buildings	100,000	
Accumulated depreciation—buildings		$ 40,000
Furniture and fixtures	50,000	
Accumulated depreciation—furniture and fixtures		30,000
Accounts payable		80,000
Jones capital (20%)		40,000
Smith capital (30%)		60,000
Tandy capital (50%)		50,000
	$300,000	$300,000

The following transactions and events occurred during the liquidation process:

January   Inventories were sold for $20,000 cash, collections on account totaled $14,000, and half of the amount due to creditors was paid.

February   Land costing $40,000 was sold for $60,000, the remaining land and buildings were sold for $40,000, half of the remaining receivables were collected, and the remainder were uncollectible.

March   The remaining liabilities were paid and available cash was distributed to the partners in final liquidation.

Required: Prepare a statement of liquidation for the Jones, Smith, and Tandy partnership.

P 17-7 The after-closing trial balance of the Link, Mack, and Nell partnership at December 31, 20X8 was as follows:

	Debit	Credit
Cash	$ 47,000	
Receivables—net	25,000	
Loan to Mack	8,000	
Inventories	20,000	
Plant assets—net	50,000	

(Continued)

	Debit	Credit
Accounts payable		$ 55,000
Loan from Link		15,000
Link capital (50%)		40,000
Mack capital (30%)		20,000
Nell capital (20%)		20,000
Total	$150,000	$150,000

Additional Information

1 The partnership is to be liquidated as soon as the assets can be converted into cash. Cash realized on conversion of assets is to be distributed as it becomes available, except that $10,000 is to be held to provide for contingencies during the liquidation period.

2 Profits and losses on liquidation are to be divided in the percentages indicated in the trial balance.

Required

1 Prepare a cash distribution plan for the Link, Mack, and Nell partnership.

2 If $25,000 cash is realized from the receivables and inventories during January 20X9, how should the cash be distributed at the end of January? (Assume that this is the first distribution of cash during the liquidation period.)

P 17-8 The partnership of Jason, Kelly, and Becky, who share partnership profits 50%, 30%, and 20%, respectively, decide to liquidate their partnership. They need the cash from the partnership as soon as possible but do not want to sell the assets at firesale prices, so they agree to an installment liquidation. A summary balance sheet on January 1, 20X2, is as follows:

Cash	$ 16,500	Accounts payable	$ 21,000
Accounts receivable	28,000	Loan from Becky	9,500
Inventory	20,500	Jason capital	69,000
Equipment—net	101,000	Kelly capital	47,000
Loan to Jason	14,000	Becky capital	33,500
	$180,000		$180,000

Cash is distributed to the partners at the end of each month, with $5,000 retained for possible contingencies in the liquidation process.

During January 20X2, Jason agreed to offset his capital balance with his loan from the partnership, $25,000 was collected on the accounts receivable, and the balance is determined to be uncollectible. Liquidation expenses of $2,000 were paid.

During February 20X2, $18,000 was collected from the sale of inventories and $90,000 collected from the sale of equipment. Additional liabilities of $3,000 were discovered, and $2,000 of liquidation expenses were paid. All cash was then distributed in a final liquidation.

Required: Prepare a statement of partnership liquidation with supporting safe payment schedules for each cash distribution.

P 17-9 The balance sheet of Roger, Susan, and Tom, who share partnership profits 30%, 30%, and 40%, respectively, included the following balances on January 1, 20X2, the date of dissolution:

Cash	$ 20,000	Liabilities	$ 40,100
Other assets	130,000	Roger loan	5,000
Loan to Susan	10,000	Roger capital	9,900
		Susan capital	45,000
		Tom capital	60,000
	$160,000		$160,000

During January 20X2 part of the firm's assets are sold for $40,000. In February the remaining assets are sold for $21,000. Assume that available cash is distributed to the proper parties at the end of January and at the end of February.

Required: Prepare a statement of partnership liquidation with supporting safe payment schedules for each cash distribution. (It will not be possible to determine the actual gains and losses in January.)

Account balances for the Ral, Tom, and Vic partnership on October 1, 20X5 are as follows:

Cash	$ 21,000	Accounts payable	$ 80,000
Accounts receivable	63,000	Note payable	50,000
Inventory	120,000	Ral capital (30%)	43,600
Equipment	150,000	Tom capital (50%)	150,000
Ral loan	15,000	Vic capital (20%)	45,400
	$369,000		$369,000

The partners have decided to liquidate the business. Activities for October and November are as follows:

October

1. Ral is short of funds and the partners agree to charge her loan to her capital account.
2. $40,000 is collected on the accounts receivable; $4,000 is written off as uncollectible.
3. Half the inventory is sold for $50,000.
4. Equipment with a book value of $55,000 is sold for $60,000.
5. The $50,000 bank note plus $600 accrued interest is paid in full.
6. The accounts payable are paid.
7. Liquidation expenses of $2,000 are paid.
8. Except for a $5,000 contingency fund, all available cash is distributed to partners at the end of October.

November

9. The remaining equipment is sold for $38,000.
10. Vic accepts inventory with a book value of $20,000 and a fair value of $10,000 as payment for part of her capital balance. The rest of the inventory is written off.
11. Accounts receivable of $10,000 are collected. The remaining receivables are written off.
12. Liquidation expenses of $800 are paid.
13. Remaining cash, including the contingency fund, is distributed to the partners.

Required: Prepare a statement of partnership liquidation for the period October 1 through November 30.

P 17-11 The balance sheet of the Tucker, Gilliam, and Simpson partnership at December 31, 20X1 follows:

TUCKER, GILLIAM, AND SIMPSON PARTNERSHIP BALANCE SHEET
AT DECEMBER 31, 20X1

Assets		*Liabilities*	
Cash	$120,000	Accounts payable	$ 65,000
Receivables—net	80,000	Due to Simpson	35,000
Due from Gilliam	10,000	Total liabilities	100,000
Inventories	90,000		
Land	50,000	*Capital*	
Buildings—net	120,000	Tucker capital (20%)	$130,000
Machinery—net	30,000	Gilliam capital (30%)	110,000
		Simpson capital (50%)	160,000
		Total capital	400,000
Total assets	$500,000	Total liabilities and capital	$500,000

On January 1, 20X2, the partners agree to dissolve the partnership, distribute available cash immediately except for $10,000 to be held to cover contingencies, and liquidate the other assets as soon as possible. Profit sharing percentages are indicated in the balance sheet.

Required

1. Prepare a schedule showing the cash distribution on January 1, 20X2.
2. Prepare a cash distribution plan to show how all cash could be safely distributed to partners as it becomes available (assume no cash has been distributed).

P 17-12 The adjusted trial balance of the Jee, Moore, and Olsen partnership at December 31, 20X6 was as follows:

Cash	$ 50,000
Accounts receivable—net	100,000
Nonmonetary assets	800,000
Loan to Jee	50,000
Expenses	400,000
Total debits	$1,400,000

Accounts payable	$ 80,000
Loan from Olsen	20,000
Jee capital	300,000
Moore capital	450,000
Olsen capital	350,000
Revenue	200,000
Total credits	$1,400,000

Additional Information

1 Partnership profits are divided 20%, 40%, and 40% to Jee, Moore, and Olsen, respectively, after salary allowances of $25,000 each to Jee and Moore for time devoted to the business.
2 Due to the disastrous results of 20X6, the partners agreed to liquidate the business as soon as possible after January 1, 20X7, and to distribute available cash on a weekly basis.
3 During the first week in January, $85,500 was collected on the accounts receivable and cash was distributed on January 8, 20X7.

Required

1 Prepare the journal entries to close the partnership books at December 31, 20X6.
2 Develop a cash distribution plan for the partnership as of January 1, 20X7.
3 Prepare a cash distribution schedule for the January 8, 20X7 distribution of available cash.

P 17-13 The after-closing trial balances of the Beams, Plank, and Timbers partnership at December 31, 20X1 included the following accounts and balances:

Cash	$120,000
Accounts receivable—net	140,000
Loan to Timbers	20,000
Inventory	200,000
Plant assets—net	200,000
Trademarks	20,000
Total debits	$700,000
Accounts payable	$150,000
Notes payable	100,000
Loan from Plank	10,000
Beams capital (profit sharing ratio, 50%)	170,000
Plank capital (profit sharing ratio, 30%)	170,000
Timbers capital (profit sharing ratio, 20%)	100,000
Total credits	$700,000

The partnership is to be liquidated as soon as possible, and all available cash except for a $10,000 contingency balance is to be distributed at the end of each month prior to the time that all assets are converted into cash.

During January 20X2, $100,000 was collected from accounts receivable, inventory items with a book value of $80,000 were sold for $100,000, and available cash was distributed.

During February 20X2, Beams received plant assets with a book value of $60,000 and a fair value of $50,000 in partial settlement of her equity in the partnership. Also during February, the remaining inventory items were sold for $60,000, liquidation expenses of $2,000 were paid, and a liability of $8,000 was discovered. Cash was distributed on February 28.

During March 20X2 the plant assets were sold for $110,000, the remaining noncash assets were written off, final liquidation expenses of $5,000 were paid, and cash was distributed. The dissolution of the partnership was completed on March 31, 20X2.

Required: Prepare a statement of partnership liquidation for the Beams, Plank, and Timbers partnership for the period January 1, 20X2 to March 31, 20X2.

18

Corporate Liquidations, Reorganizations, and Debt Restructurings for Financially Distressed Corporations

This chapter examines accounting and legal matters relating to financially distressed corporations.[1] Some corporations are able to recover from financial adversity through internal operating and policy changes, whereas others with more serious financial problems are forced to seek additional remedies. In general, these remedies are classified as direct agreements with creditors, reorganizations, and liquidations.

A debtor corporation is considered insolvent when it is unable to pay its debts as they come due, or when its total debts exceed the fair value of its assets. The inability to make payment in due course is referred to as **equity insolvency**. Having total debts that exceed the fair value of total assets is referred to as **bankruptcy insolvency**. Debtor corporations that are insolvent in the equity sense may be able to avoid bankruptcy proceedings by negotiating an agreement directly with creditors. Debtor corporations that are insolvent in the bankruptcy sense will ordinarily be reorganized or liquidated under the supervision of a bankruptcy court.

A petition for relief can be filed with a bankruptcy court by either the debtor or the creditors. Therefore, a direct agreement between the parties can be reached only when both agree that resolving the matter out of court is in their own best interests.

BANKRUPTCY REFORM ACT OF 1978

The federal government has preempted legislation of state governments that deals with bankruptcies since 1898. The 1898 Bankruptcy Act and its numerous amendments were repealed when Congress enacted Title 11 of the United States Code (U.S.C.), the Bankruptcy Act, which reflects the entire bankruptcy law and became effective October 1, 1979. The 1978 act, frequently referred to as the Bankruptcy Reform Act, provided a comprehensive law of bankruptcy as well as new bankruptcy judges and new bankruptcy courts (as separate but adjunct to each U.S. district court). The part of the 1978 act dealing with judges and courts stated that bankruptcy judges were to be appointed by the president for a period of 14 years. This provision dealing with bankruptcy court judges was ruled unconstitutional in 1982 in the *North-*

---

[1]Municipalities, railroads, stockbrokers, and commodity brokers are excluded from the discussion in this chapter. Bankruptcies of these entities are covered by special provisions of Title 11 of the United States Code.

ern Pipeline case, because bankruptcy judges were given the powers, but not the protection, of district court judges, who were appointed for life. In response to this and other controversies, a series of amendments to the 1978 law were passed, and bankruptcy judges are now appointed by federal appeals-court judges.

Since its inception, the 1978 bankruptcy law has been used to protect firms from a variety of obligations. In 1983 several companies filed for bankruptcy in an attempt to have their collective bargaining contracts set aside (Wilson Foods and Continental Airlines, for example). Other companies threatened bankruptcy unless their employees agreed to substantial pay cuts or other concessions. Under pressure from organized labor, Congress passed a law in 1984 to clarify the Bankruptcy Code in relation to wage contracts. The law provides that a bankruptcy court can grant wage reductions only if they are "necessary." The 1984 law has been interpreted in several court rulings, appeals, and reversals.

Not all bankruptcy filings occur because the debtor corporation is insolvent. Solvent corporations have filed for bankruptcy protection in an attempt to break leases and renegotiate purchase contracts. Some companies seek bankruptcy protection when they are faced with product-liability lawsuits. For example, A. H. Robins filed for bankruptcy protection when thousands of Dalkon Shield users filed claims against the company. Similarly, Dow Corning Corporation filed for bankruptcy when it faced 19,000 lawsuits stemming from silicone breast implants. Texaco filed for bankruptcy protection to prevent seizure of its assets in settlement of a $10.3 billion judgment awarded to Pennzoil by the Texas state courts. Companies in bankruptcy have generally been protected from environmental cleanup obligations incurred prior to the bankruptcy filing. In the LTV Corporation bankruptcy case a U.S. district judge ruled that a company in bankruptcy proceedings cannot be required to pay cleanup costs incurred *after* the bankruptcy petition is filed if the costs relate to pollution that occurred *before* the filing, regardless of when the contamination was discovered.

The jurisdiction of the bankruptcy court covers all cases under Title 11 of the U.S.C. A case begins with the filing of a petition under which a debtor is initially brought into bankruptcy court. In general, the petition is filed in the district where the debtor's principal place of business or principal assets have been located for at least 180 days. Either the debtor corporation or its creditors may file the petition. If the debtor corporation files the petition, the proceedings are termed a **voluntary bankruptcy proceeding**; if creditors file, it is an **involuntary bankruptcy proceeding**. Most bankruptcy filings are voluntary.

A petition commencing a case by or against a corporate debtor may be filed under either Chapter 7 or Chapter 11 of the Bankruptcy Act. **Chapter 7 of the Bankruptcy Act** *covers straight bankruptcy under which liquidation of the debtor corporation is expected,*[2] and **Chapter 11 of the Bankruptcy Act** *covers rehabilitation of the debtor and anticipates reorganization of the debtor corporation.* The bankruptcy court has the power (subject to various requests and conditions) to dismiss a case, to enter the order for relief (in other words, accept the petition), or to convert a Chapter 11 reorganization case into a Chapter 7 liquidation case or vice versa.

Chapter 13 of the Bankruptcy Act provides an alternative to liquidation for financially troubled individuals and small sole proprietorships (those with unsecured debts of less than $250,000 and secured debts of less than $750,000) that have regular income. Larger sole proprietorships file under Chapter 11. The purpose of Chapter 13 filings is to work out a plan whereby creditors are fully or partially paid over an extended period of time without liquidating the debtor's estate. The debtor may convert a Chapter 13 filing to a Chapter 11 or a Chapter 7 case. Alternatively, creditors can petition the court to transfer the Chapter 13 case to Chapter 11 or 7. Chapter 12

---

[2]Not all liquidations result from financial adversity. Voluntary liquidations are often based on the belief that the market value of the company's stock is less than the amount that could be realized by selling the company's assets. This type of liquidation does not involve restructurings or judicial remedies, and established accounting principles are applicable to winding up the company's affairs through liquidating dividends. For a discussion of voluntary liquidations, see Ronald J. Kudle, *Voluntary Corporate Liquidations* (Westport, CT: Quorum Books, Greenwood Press, 1988), or George E. Nogler and Kenneth B. Schwartz, "Financial Reporting and Auditors' Opinions on Voluntary Liquidations," *Accounting Horizons* (September 1989), pp. 12–20.

of the Bankruptcy Act is similar to Chapter 13 except that it applies to family farmers with regular income. Chapter 12 and Chapter 13 cases will not be discussed further.

The Office of U.S. Trustee

The Bankruptcy Reform Act created the Office of U.S. Trustee to be responsible for the administrative duties of bankruptcy cases. U.S. trustees are appointed by the U.S. Attorney General for seven-year terms. The duties of the U.S. trustee are to maintain and supervise a panel of private trustees eligible to serve in Chapter 7 cases, to serve as trustee or interim trustee in some bankruptcy cases (such as in a Chapter 7 case where a qualified private trustee is not available), to supervise the administration of bankruptcy cases, and to monitor appointed creditors' committees and preside over creditor meetings.

A 1994 amendment to the Bankruptcy Act charged the U.S. trustee with reviewing professional fees charged in a bankruptcy case for reasonableness.

Duties of the Debtor Corporation

In addition to specific obligations related to Chapter 7 liquidation cases and Chapter 11 reorganization cases, the debtor corporation is required to perform the following duties:

- File a list of creditors, a schedule of assets and liabilities, and a statement of debtor's financial affairs
- Cooperate with the trustee as necessary to enable the trustee to perform his duties
- Surrender all property to the trustee, including books, documents, records, and papers relating to the estate in cases involving a trustee
- Appear at hearings of the court as required

Identifying creditors and filing documents may take several months. It is an important task because creditors who have been notified of the bankruptcy proceedings may receive a percentage of their claims. Those creditors not notified are entitled to the full amount.

Duties of the Bankruptcy Judge

The role of the bankruptcy judge is judicial. The judge settles disputes that occur during the case and approves all payments of debts incurred before the bankruptcy filing, as well as other payments that are considered extraordinary. In U.S. trustee districts, the judge remains outside the administration of the case.

A 1994 amendment to the Bankruptcy Act established the authority of bankruptcy judges to hear jury trials involving allegedly improper transfers of the debtor's assets (such as fraudulent conveyance of assets[3] or preferential treatment of creditors). The bankruptcy judge may conduct jury trials in civil proceedings if designated by the district court to do so and with the consent of all parties.

The 1994 amendment to the Bankruptcy Act allows the court to establish a time schedule for the various steps in the bankruptcy proceedings.

LIQUIDATION

The Federal Office of Court Administration reported that of the 53,993 business bankruptcy filings for the twelve months ended June 30, 1997, 31,444 were filed under Chapter 7 of the Bankruptcy Act. Chapter 7 liquidations are cheaper and faster than Chapter 11 reorganizations. A Chapter 7 liquidation case is commenced *voluntarily* when a debtor corporation files a petition with the bankruptcy court or *involun-*

---

[3]Fraudulent transfer is "a transfer of an interest or an obligation incurred by the debtor, within one year prior to the date the petition was filed, with the intent to hinder, delay, or defraud creditors or whereby the debtor received less than fair equivalent value and the debtor (1) was insolvent before or became insolvent as the result of such transfer, (2) was left with unreasonably small business capital, or (3) intended to incur debts beyond the ability to pay such debts as they matured. Fraudulent transfers may be voided." Grant W. Newton, *Bankruptcy and Insolvency Accounting*, 2nd ed. (New York: John Wiley & Sons, 1981), p. 636.

tarily through filing by three or more entities[4] holding noncontingent, unsecured claims aggregating at least $10,000. A single creditor with an unsecured claim of $10,000 or more may also file a petition, provided that there are fewer than 12 unsecured creditors. The court will grant the order for relief (accept the petition) under Chapter 7 if the creditors prove their claims, or if the debtor fails to contest the petition on a timely basis. The order for relief prevents creditors from seeking payment of their claims directly from the debtor. If the creditors fail to prove their alleged claims, the court will dismiss the case. The debtor may respond to the petition by filing for protection from creditors under Chapter 11.

If an order for relief under Chapter 7 is granted, the U.S. trustee (or the court) will appoint an interim trustee to take possession of the debtor corporation's estate until a trustee is elected. (An interim trustee may be appointed at any time after commencement of a case if the court considers it necessary to preserve the property of the estate or prevent losses). The election for trustee takes place at a meeting of creditors, and only unsecured creditors with undisputed claims are eligible to vote. A trustee will be elected if creditors holding a minimum of 20% in amount of claims vote for a candidate and one candidate obtains the votes of creditors holding a majority in amount of claims actually voting. If a trustee is not elected, the interim trustee serves as trustee. The unsecured creditors eligible to vote may also elect a creditors' committee of three to 11 members to consult with the trustee and to submit questions regarding the debtor's estate to the court.

Duties of the Trustee in Liquidation Cases

The filing of a case creates an estate. *The trustee takes possession of the estate, converts the estate assets into cash, and distributes the proceeds according to priority of claims, as directed by the bankruptcy court.* Other duties of the trustee in a liquidation case are:

- To investigate the financial affairs of the debtor
- To provide information about the debtor's estate and its administration to parties in interest
- To examine creditor claims and object to claims that appear improper
- If authorized to operate the debtor's business, to provide periodic reports and summaries of operations, a statement of receipts and disbursements, and other information as the court specifies
- To file final reports on trusteeship as required by the court

The trustee has the power to void (invalidate) certain transfers of property of the debtor or certain obligations incurred by the debtor. These items are referred to as *preferences*, and those that a trustee can void are *voidable preferences*. A transfer is voidable only if the debtor was insolvent in the bankruptcy sense at the time of the transfer. When a transfer is voided, the trustee recovers the property or its value for the benefit of the debtor's estate.

Transfers made within 90 days of filing can be voided by the trustee. The time is extended to a year if the transfer is to an insider. A corporation's insiders are its officers and directors and their relatives, the corporation's affiliates, the officers and directors of the affiliates, and their relatives. A transfer in payment of a debt incurred in the ordinary course of business, made under ordinary terms, and paid within 45 days of its incurrence is not voidable (utility bills, personal services, cash sales). However, any transfer made within one year of filing can be voided if it is made with an intent to hinder, delay, or defraud any entity, or if the debtor is insolvent or becomes insolvent as a result of the transaction, and the debtor received less than equivalent value in the transaction.

Payment of Claims

Claims in a Chapter 7 liquidation case are paid in the order shown in Exhibit 18–1. Claims secured by valid liens are paid to the extent of the proceeds from property pledged as security. If the proceeds are insufficient to satisfy the claims of secured creditors, the amounts not satisfied are unsecured, nonpriority claims (or general un-

---

[4]An entity under Title 11 means person, estate, trustee, or governmental unit. *Person* means individual, partnership, or corporation, but not a governmental unit.

```
┌──────────────────────────────────────────────────────────────────────────────┐
│  I. Secured Claims                                                             │
│     Claims secured by valid liens.                                             │
│ II. Unsecured Priority Claims                                                  │
│     1 Administrative expenses incurred in preserving and liquidating the estate│
│       including trustee's fees and legal and accounting fees.                  │
│     2 Claims incurred between the date of filing an involuntary petition and   │
│       the date an interim trustee is appointed.                                │
│     3 Claims for wages, salaries, and commissions earned within 90 days of     │
│       filing the petition and not exceeding $4,000 per individual.             │
│     4 Claims for contributions to employee benefit plans arising from services │
│       rendered within 180 days of filing the petition and limited to $4,000    │
│       per employee.                                                            │
│     5 Claims of individuals not to exceed $1,800 arising from the purchase,    │
│       lease, or rental of property that was not delivered or the purchase of   │
│       services that were not provided by the debtor.                           │
│     6 Claims of governmental units for income or gross receipts taxes, property│
│       taxes, employment taxes, excise taxes, and customs duties that originated│
│       within one to four years before filing (periods vary for different       │
│       claims). Taxes collected or withheld for which the debtor is liable and  │
│       penalties related to the foregoing are also included.                    │
│ III. Unsecured Nonpriority Claims                                              │
│     1 Allowed claims that were timely filed.                                   │
│     2 Allowed claims where proof of claims was filed late.                     │
│     3 Allowed claims (secured and unsecured) for any fine, penalty, or         │
│       forfeiture, or for multiple, exemplary, or punitive charges arising prior│
│       to the order for relief or appointment of trustee.                       │
│     4 Claims for interest on the unsecured priority claims or the unsecured    │
│       nonpriority claims.                                                      │
│ IV. Stockholders' Claims                                                       │
│     Remaining assets are returned to the debtor corporation or its             │
│     stockholders.                                                              │
└──────────────────────────────────────────────────────────────────────────────┘
```

Exhibit 18–1   *Ranking of Claims in Chapter 7 Liquidation Cases*

secured claims). Unsecured claims are divided into priority and nonpriority classes for Chapter 7 liquidation cases (see Exhibit 18–1). Unsecured, priority claims are paid in full before any distributions are made to unsecured, nonpriority claims. Further, claims within the unsecured-priority-claims class are ranked 1 through 6, such that claims in the first rank (administrative expenses) are paid in full before any distribution is made for claims in the second rank, and so forth. Within each of the six priority ranks, however, distributions are made on a pro rata basis when available cash is insufficient to pay all claims of that rank. Equivalent procedures apply to cash distributions in the four ranks included within the unsecured, nonpriority class. Stockholders under a Chapter 7 liquidation case are included in distributions only when all valid creditor claims have been fully satisfied.

ILLUSTRATION OF A LIQUIDATION CASE

Stilldown Corporation experienced a large operating loss in 20X1 and the first half of 20X2. By July 20X2 its accounts payable were overdue, and its accounts receivable had been pledged to support a bank loan that was in default. Stilldown's creditors were unwilling to extend additional credit or amend the terms of any of their loans, and on August 1, 20X2, Stilldown filed a voluntary petition for relief under Chapter 7 of the Bankruptcy Act.

A balance sheet prepared as of the date of filing is presented in Exhibit 18–2. Although the balance sheet shows stockholders' equity of $13,000 on a going-concern basis, historical cost valuations are not good indicators of financial condition for a liquidating company.[5] An accounting statement that does provide relevant information for a liquidating company is the *statement of affairs.*

---

[5]Generally accepted accounting principles are based on the assumption that a firm will continue to operate in the foreseeable future. However, this "going concern" assumption is inappropriate for firms in serious financial difficulty. When available evidence contradicts the "going concern" assumption, independent auditors issue "going concern" qualifications (or disclaimers) in their audit reports.

```
STILLDOWN CORPORATION
BALANCE SHEET
AUGUST 1, 20X2
```

Assets

Current Assets		
Cash	$ 3,000	
Marketable securities (at market)	7,000	
Accounts receivable (net of estimated uncollectible accounts)	25,000	
Inventories	50,000	
Prepaid expenses	4,000	$ 89,000
Long-Term Assets		
Land	$ 15,000	
Building—net	40,000	
Equipment—net	30,000	
Intangible assets	6,000	91,000
Total assets		$180,000

Liabilities and Stockholders' Equity

Current Liabilities		
Accounts payable	$ 65,000	
Wages payable	13,000	
Property taxes payable	2,000	
Note payable—bank	25,000	
Notes payable—suppliers	5,000	
Interest payable	7,000	$117,000
Long-Term Liabilities		
Mortgage payable		50,000
Total liabilities		167,000
Stockholders' Equity		
Capital stock	$200,000	
Retained earnings	(187,000)	
Total stockholders' equity		13,000
Total liabilities and stockholders' equity		$180,000

Exhibit 18–2   *Debtor Corporation's Balance Sheet at the Time of Filing a Petition with the Bankruptcy Court*

Statement of Affairs

A trustee's duties may include filing a statement of financial affairs with the bankruptcy court. This statement is a legal document prepared for the bankruptcy court. The accountant's **statement of affairs** is a financial statement that emphasizes liquidation values and provides relevant information for the trustee in liquidating the debtor corporation. It also provides information that may be useful to creditors and to the bankruptcy court.

A statement of affairs is prepared as of a specific date, and it shows balance sheet information with assets measured at expected net realizable values and classified on the basis of availability for fully secured, partially secured, priority, and unsecured creditors. Liabilities are classified in the statement of affairs as priority, fully secured, partially secured, and unsecured. Historical cost valuations are included in the statement for reference purposes.

An illustrative statement of affairs for Stilldown Corporation is presented in Exhibit 18–3. Information for the statement is derived from the balance sheet (see Exhibit 18–2) as of the filing date and other sources, such as appraisals for the expected liquidation values of assets and contractual agreements with creditors concerning the security of their claims. The mortgage payable, together with $5,000 interest payable, is secured by the land and building. All accounts receivable are pledged as security for the bank loan, plus $2,000 unpaid interest that is included in interest payable.

STILLDOWN CORPORATION
STATEMENT OF AFFAIRS—ON AUGUST 1, 20X2

Assets

Book Value		Realizable Values—Liability Offsets for Secured Creditors		Realizable Value Available for Unsecured Creditors
	Pledged for Fully Secured Creditors			
$ 55,000	Land and building—net		$60,000	
	Less: Mortgage payable	$50,000		
	Interest payable	5,000	55,000	$ 5,000
	Pledged for Partially Secured Creditors			
25,000	Accounts receivable		$22,000	
	Less: Note payable to bank	$25,000		
	Interest payable	2,000	27,000	0
	Available for Priority and Unsecured Creditors			
3,000	Cash			3,000
7,000	Marketable securities			7,000
50,000	Inventories			55,000
4,000	Prepaid expenses			0
30,000	Equipment—net			12,000
6,000	Intangible assets			0
	Total available for priority and unsecured creditors			82,000
	Less: Priority liabilities			15,000
	Total available for unsecured creditors			67,000
	Estimated deficiency			8,000
$180,000				$75,000

Liabilities and Stockholders' Equity

Book Value		Secured and Priority Claims	Unsecured Nonpriority Claims
	Priority Liabilities		
$ 13,000	Wages payable	$13,000	
	Property taxes payable	2,000	
		15,000	
	Fully Secured Creditors		
50,000	Mortgage payable	50,000	
5,000	Interest payable	5,000	
		55,000	
	Partially Secured Creditors		
25,000	Note payable—bank	25,000	
2,000	Interest payable	2,000	
		27,000	
	Less: Accounts receivable pledged	22,000	$ 5,000
	Unsecured Creditors		
65,000	Accounts payable		65,000
5,000	Notes payable to suppliers		5,000
	Stockholders' Equity		
200,000	Capital stock		
(187,000)	Retained earnings		
$180,000			$75,000

Exhibit 18–3   *Statement of Affairs*

It is expected that Stilldown's assets can be converted into cash within three months and that the realizable values will be as follows:

Cash	$ 3,000
Marketable securities	7,000
Accounts receivable	22,000
Inventories (net of selling expenses)	55,000
Prepaid expenses	none
Land and building	60,000
Equipment	12,000
Intangible assets	none
	$159,000

Assets pledged as security for creditor claims are offset against the claims of secured creditors in the asset section of the statement of affairs. Any excess of the realizable value of assets pledged over related claims is carried to the right-hand column of the statement to indicate the amount available for unsecured creditors. An excess of secured creditor claims over the realization value of assets pledged as security indicates that the claims are only partially secured. The unsecured portion is shown in the liability section of the statement as an unsecured, nonpriority claim. (Note that the offset for partially secured creditors is shown in both the asset and the liability sections of the statement.)

The $8,000 estimated deficiency shown in the statement of affairs is a balancing figure that represents the excess of general unsecured claims over the total amount expected to be available to holders of such claims. Alternatively, the $8,000 estimated deficiency can be computed by subtracting the expected realizable value of assets from total liabilities ($167,000 − $159,000) or by deducting the $21,000 expected losses on assets ($180,000 book value − $159,000 realizable value) from the $13,000 stockholders' equity as shown in the historical balance sheet.

Trustee Accounting

A trustee in a Chapter 7 bankruptcy case takes over the assets of the debtor corporation. The trustee is accountable for those assets until being released by the bankruptcy court. The Bankruptcy Act does not cover procedural accounting details such as whether the trustee should create a new set of accounting records to establish accountability for the estate and show the eventual discharge of responsibility, or whether the corporation's existing accounting records should be continued under the direction of the trustee.

The trustee for Stilldown Corporation in this illustration creates a new set of accounting records. The assets are recorded on the trustee's books at recorded book values, rather than at expected realizable values, because of the subjectivity involved in estimating realizable amounts at the time of filing. Contra asset accounts are omitted from the trustee's books because they are not meaningful in a liquidation case and because it is desirable to keep the trustee accounts as simple as possible. The following entry could be prepared to open the trustee's books for Stilldown:

Cash	$ 3,000	
Marketable securities	7,000	
Accounts receivable	25,000	
Inventories	50,000	
Prepaid expenses	4,000	
Land	15,000	
Building	40,000	
Equipment	30,000	
Intangible assets	6,000	
Accounts payable		$65,000
Wages payable		13,000
Property taxes payable		2,000
Note payable—bank		25,000
Notes payable—suppliers		5,000
Interest payable		7,000
Mortgage payable		50,000
Estate equity		13,000
To record custody of Stilldown Corporation in liquidation.		

Subsequent to assuming custody of the estate, the trustee records gains, losses, and liquidation expenses directly in the estate equity account. Any unrecorded assets or liabilities that are discovered by the trustee are also entered in the estate equity account. To distinguish assets and liabilities included in the initial estate and those acquired or incurred by the trustee, the assets and liabilities recorded after the trustee takes charge of the estate are identified as "new."

Transactions and events during the first month of Stilldown's trusteeship are described and journal entries to record them in the trustee's books are illustrated as follows:

1 A previously unrecorded utility bill for $500 is received.

Estate equity	$ 500	
Utilities payable—new		$ 500

2 Intangible assets are deemed worthless and are written off.

Estate equity	$ 6,000	
Intangible assets		$ 6,000

3 All inventory items are sold for $48,000, of which $18,000 is on account and $30,000 is in cash.

Cash	$30,000	
Accounts receivable—new	18,000	
Estate equity	2,000	
Inventories		$50,000

4 The equipment is sold for $14,200 cash.

Cash	$14,200	
Estate equity	15,800	
Equipment		$30,000

5 Wages and property taxes owed on August 1 (priority liabilities) are paid.

Wages payable	$13,000	
Property taxes payable	2,000	
Cash		$15,000

6 Land and building are sold for $64,000 cash, and the mortgage payable and related interest are paid.

Cash	$64,000	
Land		$15,000
Building		40,000
Estate equity		9,000
Mortgage payable	$50,000	
Interest payable	5,000	
Cash		$55,000

7 Insurance policies (included in prepaid expenses) are canceled, and a $1,000 cash refund is received.

Cash	$ 1,000	
Prepaid expenses		$ 1,000

8 Accounts receivable of $21,000 are collected from the amounts owed to Stilldown at August 1. The remaining $4,000 is uncollectible.

Cash	$21,000	
Estate equity	4,000	
Accounts receivable		$25,000

9 The $21,000 received on account is applied to the bank note payable and related interest.

Interest payable	$ 2,000	
Note payable—bank	19,000	
Cash		$21,000

10 Estate administration expenses of $3,000 are paid.

Estate equity	$ 3,000	
Cash		$ 3,000

11 Trustee fees of $2,000 are accrued.

Estate equity	$ 2,000	
Trustee's fee payable—new		$ 2,000

After the transactions and events through August 31 are entered on the trustee's books, financial statements can be prepared as needed to show progress toward liquidation and financial position as of August 31, 20X2.

Statement of Cash Receipts and Disbursements   The statement of cash receipts and disbursements is prepared directly from entries in the cash account, which appears in summary form as follows:

CASH

Balance, August 1, 20X2	$ 3,000	Wages and property taxes	$ 15,000
Inventory items sold	30,000	Mortgage and interest	
Equipment sold	14,200	payment	55,000
Land and building sold	64,000	Bank notes and interest	21,000
Insurance refund	1,000	Administrative expenses	3,000
Accounts receivable	21,000	Balance forward	39,200√
	133,200		133,200
Balance, August 31, 20X2	$ 39,200		

Exhibit 18–4 illustrates the trustee's interim statement of cash receipts and cash disbursements for the period August 1 to August 31, 20X2. All disbursements require approval of the court, so the statement should be a useful financial summary.

Statement of Changes in Estate Equity   Data contained in the estate equity account provide the basis for preparation of the statement of changes in estate equity (or deficit). That account appears in summary form as follows:

ESTATE EQUITY (DEFICIT)

Utility bill discovered	$ 500	August 1, 20X1 balance	$13,000
Intangibles written off	6,000	Land and building gain	9,000
Inventory loss	2,000		
Equipment loss	15,800		
Accounts receivable written off	4,000		
Administrative expenses	3,000		
Trustee's fee	2,000	Balance forward (deficit)	11,300√
	33,300		33,300
August 31, 20X2	$11,300		

Exhibit 18–5 illustrates the statement of changes in estate equity for Stilldown Corporation from August 1 to August 31, 20X2. Observe that the statement separates gains and losses on asset realization from expenses involved in liquidating the corporation.

STILLDOWN CORPORATION IN TRUSTEESHIP
STATEMENT OF CASH RECEIPTS AND DISBURSEMENTS
FROM AUGUST 1 TO AUGUST 31, 20X2

Cash balance, August 1, 20X2		$ 3,000
Add: Cash receipts		
Sale of inventory items	$30,000	
Sale of equipment	14,200	
Sale of land and building	64,000	
Refund from insurance policy	1,000	
Collection of receivables	21,000	
Total cash receipts		130,200
		133,200
Deduct: Cash disbursements		
Wages payable (priority claim)	$13,000	
Property taxes payable (priority claim)	2,000	
Mortgage payable and interest (fully secured)	55,000	
Bank note payable and interest (for secured portion)	21,000	
Administrative expenses (priority item)	3,000	
Total cash disbursements		94,000
Cash balance, August 31, 20X2		$ 39,200

Exhibit 18–4   *Trustee's Interim Statement of Cash Receipts and Cash Disbursements*

STILLDOWN CORPORATION IN TRUSTEESHIP
STATEMENT OF CHANGES IN ESTATE EQUITY
FROM AUGUST 1 TO AUGUST 31, 20X2

Estate equity August 1, 20X2		$ 13,000
Less: Net loss on asset liquidation		
(see schedule below)	$18,800	
Liability for utilities discovered	500	
Administrative expenses	3,000	
Trustee's fee	2,000	
Net decrease for the period		(24,300)
Estate deficit August 31, 20X2		$ 11,300

SCHEDULE OF NET LOSSES ON ASSET LIQUIDATION

	Book Value August 1 −	Proceeds on Realization =	Gain or (Loss)
Accounts receivable	$25,000	$21,000	$ (4,000)
Inventories	50,000	48,000	(2,000)
Land and building	55,000	64,000	9,000
Equipment	30,000	14,200	(15,800)
Intangible assets	6,000	0	(6,000)
Net loss on liquidation of assets			$(18,800)

Exhibit 18–5 *Trustee's Statement of Changes in Estate Equity and Schedule of Net Losses on Asset Liquidation*

Balance Sheet   A balance sheet is prepared directly from the ledger account balances of the trustee and is presented in Exhibit 18–6. Two key amounts that appear in the balance sheet—cash and estate deficit—are supported by amounts from the statements of cash receipts and disbursements (Exhibit 18–4) and changes in estate equity (Exhibit 18–5). The statements presented in Exhibits 18–4, 18–5, and 18–6 are in a format familiar to accountants, but you will want to compare these financial statements with the traditional statement of realization and liquidation that is presented in Exhibit 18–7.

STILLDOWN CORPORATION IN TRUSTEESHIP
BALANCE SHEET
ON AUGUST 31, 20X2

Assets	
Cash	$39,200
Marketable securities	7,000
Accounts receivable—new	18,000
Prepaid expenses	3,000
Total assets	$67,200
Liabilities and Deficit	
Accounts payable	$65,000
Utilities payable—discovered	500
Trustee's fee payable—new	2,000
Note payable—bank (unsecured portion)	6,000
Notes payable—suppliers	5,000
Total liabilities	78,500
Less: Estate deficit	11,300
Total liabilities less deficit	$67,200

Exhibit 18–6 *Trustee's Interim Balance Sheet During the Liquidation Phase*

STILLDOWN CORPORATION IN TRUSTEESHIP
STATEMENT OF REALIZATION AND LIQUIDATION
AUGUST 1, 20X2 TO AUGUST 31, 20X2

Assets

Assets to Be Realized [Noncash assets at August 1]			Assets Realized: [Proceeds from sale, disposal, or write-off]		
Marketable securities	$ 7,000		Accounts receivable	$21,000	
Accounts receivable	25,000		Inventories	48,000	
Inventories	50,000		Prepaid expenses	1,000	
Prepaid expenses	4,000		Land and building	64,000	
Land	15,000		Equipment	14,200	
Building	40,000		Intangible assets	none	$148,200
Equipment	30,000				
Intangible assets	6,000	$177,000			
Assets Acquired: [New noncash assets received]			Assets Not Realized: [Noncash assets at August 31]		
Accounts receivable—new		18,000	Marketable securities	$ 7,000	
			Prepaid expenses	3,000	
			Accounts receivable—new	18,000	28,000

Liabilities

Liabilities to Be Liquidated: [Liabilities at August 1]			Liabilities Liquidated: [Amounts paid on liabilities]		
Accounts payable	$65,000		Wages payable	$13,000	
Wages payable	13,000		Property taxes payable	2,000	
Property taxes payable	2,000		Note payable—bank	19,000	
Note payable—bank	25,000		Interest payable	7,000	
Notes payable—suppliers	5,000		Mortgage payable	50,000	91,000
Interest payable	7,000				
Mortgage payable	50,000	167,000	Liabilities Not Liquidated: [Liabilities at August 31]		
Liabilities Incurred or Discovered: [Amounts incurred or discovered but unpaid at August 31]			Accounts payable	$65,000	
Liability discovered for utilities	$ 500		Notes payable—suppliers	5,000	
			Liability discovered for utilities	500	
Trustee's fee payable—new	2,000	2,500	Trustee's fee payable—new	2,000	78,500

Income or Loss and Supplemental Items

Supplementary Expenses: [Expenses excluding asset losses and write-offs]			Supplementary Revenues: [Revenues excluding gains on assets or liability settlements]		
Liability discovered for utilities	$ 500		None		
Trustee's fee	2,000		Net Loss		24,300
Administrative expenses —new	3,000	5,500			
		$370,000			$370,000

Exhibit 18–7 *Statement of Realization and Liquidation*

Statement of Realization and Liquidation The purpose of introducing the statement of realization and liquidation in this chapter is to make readers aware of the statement and its intended uses and limitations. The Bankruptcy Act does not require such a statement, instead it allows the judge in a bankruptcy case to prescribe the form in which information is presented to the court.

A **statement of realization and liquidation** is an activity statement that is intended to show progress toward the liquidation of a debtor's estate. Its original purpose was to inform the bankruptcy court and interested creditors of the accomplishments of the trustee. A statement of realization and liquidation for Stilldown Corporation is presented in Exhibit 18–7. The statement is presented in its traditional format except for bracketed explanations of the various categories.

An examination of Stilldown's statement of realization and liquidation shows that the statement is complex and that its format is unusual. In addition, the logic of the statement's construction is not immediately apparent. These considerations, together with the fact that the statement does a poor job of showing progress toward liquidation, have resulted in the statement's decline. Although a number of alternative formats for the statement have been proposed, many accountants feel that basic financial statements with supporting schedules provide more relevant information about liquidation activity.

Winding Up the Case

During September 20X2 the trustee for Stilldown Corporation collected the $18,000 accounts receivable, sold the marketable securities for $7,300, sold supplies (included in prepaid expenses) for $995, wrote off the remaining prepaid expenses, and distributed cash in final liquidation of the estate. Journal entries on the trustee's books to record these transactions and events follow:

Cash	$18,000	
Accounts receivable—new		$18,000
Collection of receivable in full.		
Cash	$ 7,300	
Marketable securities		$ 7,000
Estate equity		300
Sale of marketable securities for cash.		
Cash	$ 995	
Estate equity	2,005	
Prepaid expenses		$ 3,000
Sale of supplies and write-off of prepaid expenses.		

After these entries are entered in the trustee's records, the account balances are as follows:

	Debit	Credit
Cash	$65,495	
Accounts payable		$65,000
Utilities payable		500
Trustee's fee payable—new		2,000
Note payable—bank (unsecured portion)		6,000
Notes payable—suppliers		5,000
Estate equity	13,005	
	$78,500	$78,500

The trustee's fee is a priority claim, so it is paid in full, and the remaining claims of $76,500 (all first-rank unsecured creditors) receive 83¢ on the dollar ($63,495 ÷ $76,500) in final settlement of their claims. Entries to record the cash distributions are:

Trustee's fee payable—new	$ 2,000	
Cash		$ 2,000
To record payment of trustee's fee.		
Accounts payable	$53,950	
Utilities payable	415	
Note payable—bank	4,980	
Notes payable—suppliers	4,150	
Cash		$63,495
To record payment of 83¢ on the dollar to the general		
unsecured creditors.		

When the debtor is an individual, the court will grant a discharge voiding most existing liabilities or claims unless the debtor has (1) transferred, removed, destroyed, mutilated, or concealed property of the estate with intent to hinder, delay, or defraud; (2) made fraudulent statements under oath; (3) presented a false claim; (4) withheld information; or (5) failed to meet certain other conditions. However, corporations are not eligible for discharge because their liabilities are limited to corporate assets. A case involving a corporation is closed when the estate is fully administered and the trustee is dismissed. The trustee makes the following entry in closing out the Stilldown Corporation case:

Accounts payable	$11,050	
Utilities payable	85	
Note payable—bank	1,020	
Notes payable—suppliers	850	
Estate equity		$13,005

To close the trustee's records.

REORGANIZATION

Less than 20% of business bankruptcy cases filed each year are filed under Chapter 11. Even so, the Chapter 11 reorganization cases usually involve the largest amounts of money.

A Chapter 11 reorganization case is initiated voluntarily when a debtor corporation files a petition with the bankruptcy court, or involuntarily when creditors file a petition in accordance with the same $10,000 claim limitations applicable to Chapter 7 filings. The act of filing commences the case and initiates a hearing before the bankruptcy court. As mentioned earlier, the court may enter an order for relief under Chapter 11 (in other words, grant the petition for protection from creditors), convert the case to a Chapter 7 liquidation, or dismiss the case (for example, the case will be dismissed if the bankruptcy court believes that the filing was an act of bad faith). A U.S. trustee is appointed by the bankruptcy judge to be responsible for the administration of the Chapter 11 case.

Trustee or Debtor in Possession

In a Chapter 11 case, a private trustee may be appointed for cause, but otherwise the debtor corporation is continued in possession of the estate. A trustee may be appointed in cases involving fraud, dishonesty, or gross mismanagement, or if the court rules that appointment of a trustee is in the best interest of creditors, equity holders, and other parties with an interest in the estate. For the most part, bankruptcy judges have been reluctant to appoint private trustees to operate businesses in reorganization cases because it is assumed that company management is more qualified to operate and reorganize insolvent companies.[6] If the court orders the appointment of a private trustee, one is appointed by the U.S. trustee or by the bankruptcy court in non-U.S. trustee districts. Within 30 days of the order to appoint a private trustee, any party in interest in the case may request the election of a disinterested person to serve as trustee, and the U.S. trustee will call a meeting of creditors for that purpose. The option to elect a trustee is an important change provided by 1994 Bankruptcy Reform Act.

The duties of a trustee include:

- Being accountable for the property received from the debtor, including operations of the debtor's business
- Filing a list of creditors, schedules of assets and liabilities, and a statement of financial affairs (if not filed by the debtor)
- Furnishing information to the court about the debtor's estate and its administration

---

[6]One notable exception was the Eastern Airlines bankruptcy case. Eastern is often cited as an example of how badly a reorganization case can turn out for creditors. The bankruptcy judge appointed a private trustee to operate Eastern after company management lost $1.2 billion during the year the company operated under the protection of the bankruptcy court. The bankruptcy judge further noted that Eastern's management had been unable to make reliable forecasts even in the short run. [*The Wall Street Journal*, April 20, 1990, p. A3, and June 17, 1993.]

- Examining creditor claims and objecting to claims that appear to be improper (normally, only the trustee can object)
- Filing a reorganization plan or reporting why a plan will not be filed
- Filing final reports on the trusteeship as required by the court

A **debtor in possession** performs the duties of a trustee. It negotiates with the creditors, stockholders, and others in creating a plan of reorganization that will be confirmed by the bankruptcy court.

When a trustee is not appointed in a Chapter 11 case, an examiner will be appointed if loans to outsiders other than for goods and services exceed $5,000,000, or if the court concludes that such appointment is in the interests of the creditors, equity holders, or other parties with an interest in the estate. A primary function of the examiner is to value the debtor's assets and report such valuations to the court.

Committee Representation

Creditors' committees are responsible for protecting the interests of the creditors they represent and making sure that the assets of the debtor are preserved. The committees may review the debtor's transactions and object in bankruptcy court to those that they believe are not in the best interests of the creditors they represent. All negotiations between prepetition creditors and the debtor in possession must take place through the creditors' committees.

Unlike Chapter 7 cases, creditors' committees are not elected in Chapter 11 cases. A creditors' committee is *appointed by the U.S. trustee* as soon as practicable after the bankruptcy court grants an order for relief under Chapter 11. The creditors' committee (usually seven members) is selected from the largest unsecured creditors. Subsequently, the composition of that committee may be changed and other committees of creditors or equity holders may be appointed. The selection of creditors' committees can be extremely important to the final disposition of a reorganization case. If creditor committees begin fighting against each other, a simple and timely reorganization is nearly impossible.

Governmental units are generally not eligible to serve on creditor committees. Prior to 1994, the Pension Benefit Guaranty Corporation (PBGC) sat on creditor committees, but only as a nonvoting member. The 1994 Bankruptcy Reform Act gave the PBGC voting rights on creditor committees.

Operating Under Chapter 11

Reorganization may take from six months to several years. In the meantime, subject to restrictions of the Bankruptcy Code and the bankruptcy court, the debtor in possession continues operating the business while working out a reorganization plan that is acceptable to all parties concerned. On the day of the bankruptcy filing, the company's existing bank accounts and books are closed and new accounts and books reopened.

Usually, the company will arrange a new line of credit with its banks to enable it to continue to operate. This is often referred to as debtor-in-possession financing. New financing agreements must be approved by the bankruptcy court.

Possible Benefits of Chapter 11 Protection to the Debtor in Possession   With the bankruptcy court's approval, the company may be able to reduce its labor costs through layoffs or wage reductions, or by terminating its pension plans. As mentioned earlier, the 1984 law made it more difficult to use bankruptcy to break labor contracts. Also, with the bankruptcy court's approval, the company can reject certain executory contracts and unexpired leases. (**Executory contracts** are those that have not been completely performed by both parties, such as purchase commitments.) Any claims for damages resulting from the cancellation of unfavorable contracts are treated as unsecured debt. Interest on unsecured debt stops at the time of filing. This can be a big factor for some companies. Interest of nearly $3 million a day was accruing on Pennzoil's $10.3 billion award from Texaco until the date of Texaco's Chapter 11 filing.

Creditors subject to the jurisdiction of the bankruptcy court may not commence or continue a lawsuit to take possession of the debtor's property without permission of the bankruptcy court; however, secured creditors may receive payments to protect their interest in collateral that the debtor continues to use in its operations. This is particularly applicable when the debtor continues to use collateralized property subject to depreciation, depletion, or amortization. Payments to the secured creditor may reduce the loan balance as the value of the collateral declines.

Financially distressed companies that find it necessary to restructure or swap debt may have difficulty gaining the necessary support from bondholders without filing for bankruptcy. A debt restructuring plan typically requires approval of 95% of each class of bondholders and a majority of stockholders. However, a debt restructuring under the bankruptcy court requires only two-thirds approval of each class of bondholders.

Disadvantages of a Chapter 11 Filing   A Chapter 11 filing creates the obvious disadvantage for the debtor corporation of losing the confidence of its lenders, suppliers, customers, and employees. Beyond this stigma of bankruptcy, there is the additional disadvantage of operating a business in competitive markets when capital expenditures, acquisitions, disposals of assets, borrowing money, and so on, require prior approval of the court. Depending on the circumstances of a particular case, the bankruptcy court may impose so many restrictions on company management that even day-to-day operations of the business become difficult. The company may have to sell off its profitable units to meet creditor demands for emerging from Chapter 11. The biggest disadvantage to the debtor is the cost of the bankruptcy proceedings.[7] Lawyers and other advisers are hired by the creditors' committees and the stockholders' committees, as well as by the debtor, but they are all paid from the debtor's assets. Expenses of the creditors' committees may also be reimbursed. Soaring fees in bankruptcy cases prompted some judges to cut fees that they considered unreasonable. The 1994 amendments to the Bankruptcy Act specifically granted the court the authority to award compensation less than the compensation requested when the fees seem unreasonable. The motion for reduced compensation can come from the court, the U.S. trustee, the trustee for the estate, or any other party in interest. In determining the reasonableness of billed fees, the court will consider the time spent on the services, the rates charged, the benefit to the debtor's estate of the services, and the necessity of the service to the administration of the estate. Several provisions of the 1994 Bankruptcy Reform Act that were identified earlier should lower administrative and legal costs.

The Plan of Reorganization

The intent of debtor relief under Chapter 11 is reorganization, and the final objective of the court proceedings is confirmation of a **reorganization plan** that is "fair and equitable" to all interests concerned. Only the debtor corporation may file a plan during the first 120 days after the order for relief is granted. Subsequently, the debtor, the trustee, the creditors' committees, an equity security holders' committee, or other parties in interest may file plans.

To reduce bankruptcy expenses and reduce the time a debtor must operate under bankruptcy court restrictions, some firms file preapproved reorganization plans with the court at the same time they file under Chapter 11 (often called a prepackaged bankruptcy). In other words, the terms of the debt restructuring have been worked out with creditors, and some or all creditors have agreed to the plan before the bankruptcy filing.

Chapter 11 provisions stipulate that the plan of reorganization must:

- Identify classes of claims (except for the administrative expenses, claims arising after an involuntary filing but before the order for relief or appointment of a trustee, and certain tax claims that are given priority)
- Specify any class of claims that is not impaired (a class of claims is *impaired* unless the plan leaves unaltered the legal rights of each claim in the class)
- Specify any class of claims that is impaired

---

[7]Finley Kumble is a good example of how costly and drawn-out bankruptcy cases can be. The company filed for bankruptcy in 1988. During the next six years while in Chapter 11, the trustee collected $60 million in cash for creditors. However, 80% of the money went for operating and administering the bankruptcy case, including $37 million for lawyers, trustees, and accountants. [*The Wall Street Journal*, April 8, 1994, pp. B1 and B5.]

- Treat all claims within a particular class alike
- Provide adequate means for the plan's execution (such as retention of property by the debtor, merger, modification of a lien, and extension of maturity dates)
- Prohibit the issuance of nonvoting equity securities
- Contain provision for selection of officers and directors that is consistent with the interests of creditors, equity holders, and public policy

A reorganization plan may provide for sale of the debtor's property and distribution of the proceeds. A debtor corporation may prefer to liquidate under Chapter 11 instead of Chapter 7 because it expects that an orderly sale by company management will raise more money than a liquidating sale by a trustee.

A reorganization plan may be confirmed by the court if it is accepted by each class of creditors and stockholders whose claims or interests will be impaired. Alternatively, the plan may be confirmed even if it is rejected by some impaired classes, a "cramdown," if the bankruptcy judge determines the plan is fair and equitable.

Acceptance of a plan by a class of claims requires approval by at least two-thirds in amount and more than half in number of claims. Classes of claims that are unimpaired are assumed to have accepted the plan, and classes that receive nothing are assumed to have rejected it without the necessity of a vote. In order for the bankruptcy court to confirm a plan, each class of claims must have accepted the plan or not be impaired under it. Within each class, each holder of a claim must either have accepted the plan or receive (or retain an interest) not less than that holder would receive if the debtor corporation were liquidated.

After the necessary approval has been obtained, the court holds a confirmation hearing to entertain objections to confirmation and to confirm that the plan is "fair and equitable." Confirmation by the court constitutes discharge of the debtor except for claims provided for in the reorganization plan.

The ranking of unsecured creditors in a large reorganization case is seldom simple and is often the result of negotiation rather than rule. Many reorganizations are complicated by professional investors who buy debt claims from the original holders at deep discounts and then push for settlements to turn a quick profit from their investment.

Two years after R. H. Macy & Company filed for Chapter 11, Federated Department Stores purchased half of Macy's billion-dollar secured creditor claims held by Prudential Insurance Company of America for $449.3 million and took an option to buy the rest. This gave Federated the ability to block any takeover attempt by another retailer while it negotiated its own Macy takeover with the eight major creditor committees.

Shareholders have also become more aggressive in bankruptcies. One reason for the increased shareholder activism is the increase in investors that speculate in the stock of companies in Chapter 11. Another reason is the rise of lawyers and financial advisers who specialize in leading equity committees against creditors and management. When solvent companies seek bankruptcy reorganization (A. H. Robins and Texaco, for example), shareholders have equity to protect.

The value of claims in a bankruptcy case can also be controversial. When a company is financially distressed, bondholders may give concessions to the debtor by swapping their bonds for new bonds issued at a discount. In the LTV Corporation case, the bankruptcy judge ruled that bondholders filing claims must value their bonds at the "fair market value of property given in the exchange transaction." Bondholders who paid par for their bonds and did not participate in LTV's swap could claim par plus accrued interest.[8]

FINANCIAL REPORTING DURING REORGANIZATION

In 1990 the Accounting Standards Executive Committee (AcSEC) of the AICPA issued Statement of Position (SOP) 90–7, "Financial Reporting by Entities in Reorganization under the Bankruptcy Code," to provide guidance for financial reporting by

---

[8] *The Wall Street Journal,* January 31, 1990, p. A3.

firms during Chapter 11 reorganization and when they emerge from Chapter 11. Before issuance of the SOP, there was no prescribed accounting for a reorganization under Chapter 11, and practices were diverse. For example, prepetition liabilities (those existing at the time of filing) are stayed, so some firms classified them as long-term and other firms classified them as current.

Under the SOP, the objective of financial statements prepared for a company operating under Chapter 11 is to reflect the financial evolution during the bankruptcy proceedings. Therefore, the financial statements should distinguish the transactions and events directly related to the reorganization from the ongoing operations of the business.

Effects of Chapter 11 Proceedings on the Balance Sheet

The balance sheet should present prepetition liabilities that are subject to compromise separately from those that are not subject to compromise. **Prepetition liabilities subject to compromise** are the unsecured and undersecured liabilities incurred before the company entered Chapter 11 proceedings. A secured claim is undersecured if the collateral is worth less than the amount of the claim. The entire amount of an undersecured claim is included in prepetition liabilities subject to compromise. **Liabilities not subject to compromise** include fully secured liabilities incurred before the Chapter 11 filing and all postpetition claims. These claims should be classified as current or noncurrent in a classified balance sheet. **Postpetition liabilities** are those that are incurred after the filing of the Chapter 11 petition, and that are not associated with prebankruptcy events.

Prepetition claims discovered after the Chapter 11 filing are included in the balance sheet at the allowed amount of the claims, rather than the amount at which they may be settled. Claims that cannot be reasonably estimated should be disclosed in notes to the financial statements under the provisions of *FASB Statement No. 5*, "Accounting for Contingencies."

Effects of Chapter 11 Proceedings on the Income Statement and the Statement of Cash Flows

Professional fees and similar expenses related directly to the Chapter 11 proceedings are expensed as incurred. "Income, expenses, realized gains and losses, and provisions for losses that result from the restructuring of the business should be reported separately in the income statement as *reorganization items*, except for those required to be reported as discontinued operations" (SOP 90–7, paragraph 27).

Interest expense to be reported is the amount that will be paid during the proceedings, or the probable amount to be allowed as a priority, secured, or unsecured claim. Amounts by which reported interest expense differs from contractual interest should be disclosed. Interest income earned as a result of bankruptcy proceedings is reported separately as a reorganization item. Generally, this includes all interest income.

Earnings per share for Chapter 11 companies should be reported as usual. If the issuance of common stock or common stock equivalents under a reorganization plan is probable, that fact should be disclosed.

Cash flow items relating to reorganization should be disclosed separately from cash flow items relating to the ongoing operations of the business in the statement of cash flows. The SOP recommends the direct method of presenting cash flows.

Supplementary Combined Financial Statements

The AcSEC concluded that consolidated financial statements that include one or more companies operating under Chapter 11 do not provide adequate information about the bankruptcy proceedings. Therefore, the SOP requires that *condensed combined financial statements* for all entities in reorganization proceedings be presented as supplementary information. Intercompany receivables and payables should be disclosed, with receivables written down if necessary. Consolidation may be inappropriate for some subsidiaries in bankruptcy, particularly if a trustee is appointed to operate the company in bankruptcy.

FINANCIAL REPORTING FOR THE EMERGING COMPANY

Ordinarily, a corporate reorganization involves a restructuring of liabilities and capital accounts and a revaluation of the firm's assets. Participation of stockholders in the reorganized company depends upon whether they are deemed to have an equitable interest by the bankruptcy court. Many companies cannot emerge from bankruptcy as independent companies, and their reorganization plans include sale of the company. In providing for the plan's execution, the debtor corporation typically amends its charter to provide for the issuance of new securities for cash or in exchange for creditor claims (that is, some creditors may become stockholders).

The financial condition of companies filing for bankruptcy court protection varies drastically. Occasionally, profitable corporations file for protection under Chapter 11. Settlements under a reorganization plan are influenced by the ability of the interested parties to negotiate and manipulate their relative positions through creditors' and equity holders' committees. Bankruptcy judges also have broad discretionary powers in bankruptcy settlements. A provision of the Bankruptcy Code known as the doctrine of equitable subordination allows judges to move unsecured creditors ahead of secured creditors in certain situations in the interest of "fairness."

Reorganization Value

Determining the reorganization value of the entity emerging from bankruptcy is an important part of the reorganization plan. The emerging entity's **reorganization value** approximates fair value of the entity without considering liabilities. In other words, it approximates the amount a willing buyer would pay for the assets of the entity at the time of the restructuring. Generally, the reorganization value is determined by discounting future cash flows for the reconstituted business, plus the expected proceeds from assets not required in the new business. The discount rates should reflect the business and financial risks involved. (SOP 90–7, paragraph 9.)

The reorganization value determines how much creditors will recover and how much stock of the reorganized company each class of creditors will receive when the company emerges from bankruptcy. For example, in the Macy bankruptcy case, senior creditors were owed $3.1 billion and public bondholders, $1.2 billion. Macy's board of directors debated a $3.5 billion reorganization value under one plan and a $3.8 billion value under another. Senior creditors would receive a smaller stake in the reorganized company under the higher reorganization value, and bondholders would receive almost nothing under the lower value. The unsecured bondholders' committee pushed for a reorganization value of $4 billion, and another plan put forth by Federated Department Stores, a major creditor, was based on a $3.35 billion reorganization value. After months of negotiation, Federated and Macy filed a joint plan that called for the merger of the two companies and a reorganization value of $4.1 billion.

Financial reporting by a company whose reorganization plan has been confirmed by the court is determined by whether the reorganized entity is essentially a new company that qualifies for fresh start reporting. The SOP provides two conditions that must be met for **fresh start reporting**:

1 The reorganization value of the emerging entity's assets immediately before the date of confirmation of the reorganization plan is less than the total of all postpetition liabilities and allowed claims.
2 Holders of existing voting shares immediately before confirmation of the reorganization plan receive less than 50% of the emerging entity. This loss of control must be substantive and not temporary.

When both of these conditions are met, the emerging entity is in effect a new company and it should adopt fresh start reporting.

Fresh Start Reporting

Fresh start reporting results in a new reporting entity with no retained earnings or deficit balance.

Allocating the Reorganization Value to Identifiable Assets   The reorganization value of the company should be allocated to tangible and identifiable intangible assets according to the purchase method of accounting for transactions as set forth in *APB Opinion No. 16*, "Business Combinations."[9] Any amount of reorganization value not attributed to the tangible and identifiable intangible assets is reported as an unidentifiable intangible asset, "reorganization value in excess of amounts allocable to identifiable assets." The assumptions used in determining the excess during the allocation period should be consistent with the assumptions used in determining the reorganization value. (The maximum allocation period is 40 years, but a much shorter period is presumed.)

Reporting Liabilities   Liabilities, other than deferred income taxes, should be reported at their current value at the confirmation date of the reorganization plan. Deferred taxes are reported as required in *FASB Statement No. 109*, "Accounting for Income Taxes." Benefits realized from prior net operating loss carryforwards are applied, first, to reduction of the reorganization value in excess of amounts allocable to identifiable assets and to other intangibles until exhausted and, finally, as a reduction of income tax expense.

Final Statements of Old Entity   The final statements of the old entity as of and for the period ending on the date of confirmation of the plan should disclose the effects of the adjustments on the individual asset and liability accounts resulting from adopting fresh start reporting. The statements should also show the effect of debt forgiveness. It is expected that the ending balance sheet of the old entity will be the same as the opening balance sheet of the new entity, including a zero retained earnings balance.

Disclosures in Initial Financial Statements of New Entity   Paragraph 39 of the SOP lists the following disclosures that should be included in notes to the initial financial statements of the new entity:

- Adjustments to the historical amounts of individual assets and liabilities
- The amount of debt forgiveness
- The amount of prior retained earnings or deficit eliminated
- Significant factors relating to the determination of reorganization value

Comparative Financial Statements   Fresh start financial statements of the new entity are not comparable with those prepared by the predecessor company before confirmation of the reorganization plan. If predecessor statements are required by the SEC or another regulatory agency, a clear distinction should be made between the fresh start statements of the new entity and the statements of the predecessor company.

Reporting by Entities That Do Not Qualify for Fresh Start

Companies emerging from reorganization that do not meet the criteria for fresh start reporting should report liabilities compromised at their present values as determined at appropriate interest rates under *APB Opinion No. 21*, "Interest on Receivables and Payables." Forgiveness of debt should be reported as an extraordinary item. Quasi-reorganization accounting should *not* be used for any entities emerging from bankruptcy court protection.

---

[9]See Chapter 1, "Business Combinations," for a discussion on assigning fair values to specific categories of assets, and then allocating the total purchase price, or in this case, the reorganization value, to those assets on the basis of the assigned fair values.

ILLUSTRATION OF A REORGANIZATION CASE

Baker Corporation files for protection from creditors under Chapter 11 of the bankruptcy act on January 5, 20X2. Baker is a debtor in possession, and at the time of filing, its balance sheet includes the following items:

Current assets		
Cash	$ 50,000	
Accounts receivable—net	500,000	
Inventory	300,000	
Other current assets	50,000	$ 900,000
Plant assets		
Land	$200,000	
Building—net	500,000	
Equipment—net	300,000	
Goodwill	200,000	1,200,000
		$2,100,000
Current liabilities		
Accounts payable	$600,000	
Taxes payable	150,000	
Accrued interest on 15% bonds	90,000	
Note payable to bank	260,000	$1,100,000
15% bonds payable (partially secured with land and building)		1,200,000
Stockholders' deficit		
Capital stock	$500,000	
Deficit	(700,000)	(200,000)
		$2,100,000

On the filing date, Baker's bank accounts and books are closed, and a new set of books is opened. The company is able to arrange short-term financing with the bank (with the bankruptcy court's approval) in order to continue operations while working out a reorganization plan.

During 20X2, no prepetition liabilities are paid and no interest is accrued on the bank note or the bonds payable. The bankruptcy court allows Baker Corporation to invest $100,000 in new equipment in August 20X2. This new equipment has a useful life of five years, and Baker uses straight-line depreciation calculated to the nearest half-year. The building is being depreciated at a rate of $50,000 per year and the old equipment at a rate of $60,000 per year. Goodwill amortization is $50,000 per year.

Costs related to the bankruptcy, including all expenses of the creditor committees and the equity holder committee, are expensed as incurred and paid in cash.

Reclassification of Liabilities Subject to Compromise

At the beginning of 20X2, Baker reclassifies the liabilities subject to compromise into a separate account by that name. The entry to record the reclassification is as follows:

Accounts payable	$ 600,000	
Taxes payable	150,000	
Accrued interest on 15% bonds	90,000	
Note payable to bank	260,000	
15% bonds payable (partially secured)	1,200,000	
Liabilities subject to compromise		$2,300,000

To reclassify liabilities subject to compromise.

The $2,300,000 prepetition claims are included in the December 31, 20X2 balance sheet as a separate category, with a supplemental schedule to show details of the amount.

Disclosing Reclassified Liabilities in the Financial Statements The balance sheet disclosures to report the reclassification in accordance with the provisions of the AICPA's SOP 90–7 on financial reporting for entities in reorganization are included in Exhibit 18–8. The exhibit presents a combined income and retained earnings statement for 20X2, as well as a balance sheet at December 31, 20X2.

Although the reclassification of liabilities subject to compromise poses no difficulties in preparing balance sheets and income statements, it does complicate the preparation of the cash flow statement. In particular, the year's changes in the account balances that are reclassified must be separated from changes that affect operations and cash flows for the period. Exhibit 18–9 presents a cash flow working paper for Baker Corporation's 20X2 statement of cash flows, and Exhibit 18–10 presents the cash flows statement. Only the direct method of presenting the cash flow statement is illustrated because that is the format recommended in the SOP.

BAKER CORPORATION
INCOME AND RETAINED EARNINGS STATEMENT
FOR THE YEAR 20X2

Sales	$ 1,000,000
Cost of sales	(430,000)
Wages and salaries	(250,000)
Depreciation and amortization	(170,000)
Other expenses	(50,000)
Earnings before reorganization items	100,000
Professional fees related to bankruptcy proceedings	(450,000)
Net loss	(350,000)
Beginning deficit	(700,000)
Deficit December 31, 20X2	$(1,050,000)

BALANCE SHEET AT DECEMBER 31, 20X2

Current assets		
Cash	$ 150,000	
Accounts receivable—net	350,000	
Inventory	370,000	
Other current assets	50,000	$ 920,000
Plant assets		
Land	$ 200,000	
Building—net	450,000	
Equipment—net	330,000	
Goodwill	150,000	1,130,000
		$2,050,000
Current liabilities		
Short-term borrowings	$ 150,000	
Accounts payable	100,000	
Wages and salaries payable	50,000	$ 300,000
Liabilities subject to compromise*		2,300,000
Stockholders' deficit		
Capital stock	$ 500,000	
Deficit	(1,050,000)	(550,000)
		$2,050,000

*Liabilities subject to compromise:	
Partially secured 15% bonds payable plus $90,000 interest,	
secured by first mortgage on land and building	$1,290,000
Priority tax claim	150,000
Accounts payable and unsecured note to bank	860,000
	$2,300,000

Exhibit 18–8   *Balance Sheet and Income Statement During Chapter 11 Reorganization*

The cash flow working papers in Exhibit 18–9 show an initial reconciling entry to eliminate the effect of the entry that reclassified liabilities subject to compromise. This is necessary because a reclassification entry has no cash flow effects.

One other item in Exhibit 18–9 that is unique to firms in reorganization is professional fees relating to bankruptcy proceedings. Cash paid for these items is classified as cash flows from operating activities, but separate disclosure of operating cash flows *before* and *after* the operating cash flows from the professional fees of bankruptcy proceedings is recommended. This disclosure is illustrated in Exhibit 18–10, which presents the statement of cash flows for Baker Corporation for the year 20X2.

BAKER CORPORATION AND SUBSIDIARY
WORKING PAPERS FOR THE STATEMENT OF CASH FLOWS (DIRECT METHOD)
FOR THE YEAR ENDED DECEMBER 31, 20X2

	Year's Change	Reconciling Items Debit	Reconciling Items Credit	Cash Flow from Operations	Cash Flow— Investing Activities	Cash Flow— Financing Activities
Asset Changes						
Cash	100,000					
Accounts receivable—net	(150,000)	b 150,000				
Inventories	70,000		c 70,000			
Other current assets	0					
Land	0					
Buildings—net	50,000	e 50,000				
Equipment—net	30,000	e 70,000	g 100,000			
Goodwill	(50,000)	e 50,000				
Total asset changes	50,000					
Changes in Equities						
Accounts payable	(500,000)	c 100,000	a 600,000			
Taxes payable	(150,000)		a 150,000			
Accrued interest—15% bonds	(90,000)		a 90,000			
Short-term borrowings	150,000	f 150,000				
Note payable to bank	(260,000)		a 260,000			
Wages and salaries payable	50,000		d 50,000			
15% bonds payable	(1,200,000)		a 1,200,000			
Liabilities subject to compromise	2,300,000	a 2,300,000				
Common stock	0					
Deficit*	(350,000)					
Total equity changes	(50,000)					
Changes in the Deficit*						
Sales	1,000,000		b 150,000	1,150,000		
Cost of goods sold	(430,000)		c 30,000	(400,000)		
Wages and salaries	(250,000)	d 50,000		(200,000)		
Depreciation and amortization	(170,000)		e 170,000			
Other expenses	(50,000)			(50,000)		
Professional fees paid for reorganization*	(450,000)			(450,000)		
Change in deficit†	(350,000)					
Proceeds from short-term borrowing			f 150,000			150,000
Purchase of equipment		g 100,000			100,000	
		3,020,000	3,020,000	50,000	100,000	150,000

* Requires separate disclosure in the "cash flow from operating activities" section.

† Deficit changes replace amounts in the deficit account for reconciling purposes.

Exhibit 18–9   *Working Papers for the Statement of Cash Flows*

BAKER CORPORATION
STATEMENT OF CASH FLOWS
FOR THE YEAR ENDED DECEMBER 31, 20X2

Cash flows from operating activities

Cash received from customers (sales $1,000,000 + decrease in accounts receivable $150,000)	$1,150,000
Cash paid to suppliers (cost of sales $430,000 + increase in inventory $70,000 − increase in accounts payable $100,000)	(400,000)
Cash paid to employees (wages and salaries $250,000 − increase in wages payable $50,000)	(200,000)
Cash paid for other expenses	(50,000)
Net cash flows provided by operating activities before reorganization items	500,000

Operating cash flows from reorganization

Professional fees paid for services relating to bankruptcy proceedings	(450,000)
Net cash provided by operating activities	50,000

Cash flows from investing activities

Capital expenditures	$(100,000)	
Net cash used in investing activities		(100,000)

Cash flows from financing activities

Net short-term borrowings	$ 150,000	
Net cash provided by financing activities		150,000
Net increase in cash		$ 100,000

Reconciliation of net income to net cash provided by operating activities

Net loss	$ (350,000)
Adjustments to reconcile net loss to net cash provided by operations:	
Depreciation and amortization	170,000
Increase in postpetition payables (operating activities)	150,000
Decrease in accounts receivable	150,000
Increase in inventory	(70,000)
Cash provided by operating activities	$ 50,000

Exhibit 18–10   *Statement of Cash Flows During Chapter 11 Reorganization*

Operations Under Chapter 11

During the next six months, Baker continues to operate under Chapter 11 of the Bankruptcy Code while it works out a reorganization plan, and by June 30, 20X3, Baker has a plan. Balance sheet and income statement amounts reflecting operations for the first six months of 20X3 are summarized as follows:

COMPARATIVE BALANCE SHEETS 20X3

	January 1	June 30	Change
Cash	$ 150,000	$ 300,000	$150,000
Accounts receivable	350,000	335,000	(15,000)
Inventory	370,000	350,000	(20,000)
Other current assets	50,000	30,000	(20,000)
Land	200,000	200,000	—
Building—net	450,000	425,000	(25,000)
Equipment—net	330,000	290,000	(40,000)
Goodwill	150,000	125,000	(25,000)
Assets	$2,050,000	$2,055,000	$ 5,000

(Continued)

COMPARATIVE BALANCE SHEETS 20X3

	January 1	June 30	Change
Liabilities subject to compromise	$2,300,000	$2,300,000	$ —
Short-term loan	150,000	75,000	(75,000)
Accounts payable	100,000	125,000	25,000
Wages and salaries	50,000	55,000	5,000
Liabilities	2,600,000	2,555,000	(45,000)
Common stock	500,000	500,000	—
Deficit	(1,050,000)	(1,000,000)	50,000
Equities	$2,050,000	$2,055,000	$ 5,000

INCOME STATEMENT FOR SIX MONTHS ENDING JUNE 30, 20X3

Sales		$ 600,000
Cost of sales		(200,000)
Wages and salaries expense		(100,000)
Depreciation and amortization		
Building	$25,000	
Old equipment	30,000	
New equipment	10,000	
Goodwill	25,000	(90,000)
Other expenses		(30,000)
Earnings before reorganization items		180,000
Professional fees related to bankruptcy proceedings		(130,000)
Net income		50,000
Beginning deficit		(1,050,000)
Ending deficit		$(1,000,000)

The Reorganization Plan

After extensive negotiations among the parties of interest, a reorganization value of $2,200,000 is agreed upon, and a plan of reorganization is filed with the court. The terms of Baker's proposed reorganization plan include the following:

1 Baker's 15% bonds payable were secured with the land and building. The bondholders agree to accept $500,000 new common stock, $500,000 senior debt of 12% bonds, and $100,000 cash payable December 31, 20X3.
2 The priority tax claims of $150,000 will be paid in cash as soon as the reorganization plan is confirmed by the bankruptcy court.
3 The remaining unsecured, nonpriority, prepetition claims of $950,000 will be settled as follows:
   a Creditors represented by the accounts payable will receive $275,000 subordinated debt and $140,000 common stock.
   b The $90,000 accrued interest on the 15% bonds will be forgiven.
   c The $260,000 note payable to the bank will be exchanged for $120,000 subordinated debt and $60,000 common stock.
4 Equity holders will exchange their stock for $100,000 common stock of the emerging company.

Fresh Start Reporting

The reorganization value is compared with the total postpetition liabilities and allowed claims at June 30 to determine if fresh start reporting is appropriate:

Postpetition liabilities	$ 255,000
Allowed claims subject to compromise	2,300,000
Total liabilities on June 30, 20X3	2,555,000
Less: Reorganization value	(2,200,000)
Excess liabilities over reorganization value	$ 355,000

The excess liabilities over reorganization value indicates that the first condition for fresh start reporting is met. The reorganization plan calls for the old equity holders to retain less than a 50% interest in the emerging company, so the second condition also is met, and fresh start reporting is appropriate. A summary of the proposed reorganized capital structure is as follows:

Postpetition liabilities	$ 255,000
Taxes payable	150,000
Current portion of senior debt, due December 31, 20X3	100,000
Senior debt, 12% bonds	500,000
Subordinated debt	395,000
Common stock	800,000
	$2,200,000

The plan is approved by each class of claims and confirmed by the bankruptcy court on June 30, 20X3. Baker Corporation records the provisions of the reorganization plan and the adoption of fresh start reporting in the books of the old entity as follows:

Accounts payable (prepetition)	$ 600,000	
Interest (prepetition)	90,000	
Bank note (prepetition)	260,000	
15% bonds payable (prepetition)	1,200,000	
12% senior debt		$500,000
12% senior debt—current		100,000
Subordinated debt		395,000
Common stock (new)		700,000
Gain on debt discharge		455,000

To record settlement of the prepetition claims. (The summary account "prepetition claims subject to compromise" could have been used.)

Common stock (old)	$ 500,000	
Common stock (new)		$100,000
Additional paid-in capital		400,000

To record exchange of stock by equity holders.

Baker's assets that have fair values different from their recorded book values on June 30, 20X3 are summarized as follows:

	Fair Value	Book Value	Difference
Inventory	$ 375,000	$ 350,000	$ 25,000
Land	300,000	200,000	100,000
Buildings—net	350,000	425,000	(75,000)
Equipment—net	260,000	290,000	(30,000)
Goodwill	0	125,000	(125,000)
	$1,285,000	$1,390,000	$(105,000)

The entries to adjust Baker's assets for the fair value/book value differences and record the fresh start are:

Inventory	$ 25,000	
Land	100,000	
Loss on asset revaluation	105,000	
Building—net		$ 75,000
Equipment—net		30,000
Goodwill		125,000

To adjust Baker's assets to their fair values.

Reorganization value in excess of identifiable assets	$250,000	
Gain on debt discharge	455,000	
Additional paid-in capital	400,000	
Loss on asset revaluation		$ 105,000
Deficit		1,000,000

To eliminate the deficit and additional paid-in capital and to record the excess reorganization value and the fresh start.

Working papers to show the effect of the reorganization plan on Baker's balance sheet are presented in Exhibit 18–11.

BAKER CORPORATION
COMPARATIVE BALANCE SHEETS AT JUNE 30, 20X3

	Preconfirmation Balance Sheet	Adjustments to Record Confirmation of Plan		Reorganized Balance Sheet
		Debits	Credits	
Assets				
Cash	$ 300,000			$ 300,000
Accounts receivable	335,000			335,000
Inventory	350,000	a 25,000		375,000
Other current assets	30,000			30,000
Land	200,000	b 100,000		300,000
Building	425,000		c 75,000	350,000
Equipment	290,000		d 30,000	260,000
Goodwill	125,000		e 125,000	—
Reorganization excess	—	f 250,000		250,000
	$2,055,000			$2,200,000
Equities (postpetition claims)				
Short-term bank loan	$ 75,000			$ 75,000
Accounts payable	125,000			125,000
Wages payable	55,000			55,000
(prepetition claims) Accounts payable—old	600,000	h 600,000		—
Taxes payable	150,000			150,000
Interest	90,000	i 90,000		—
Bank note	260,000	j 260,000		—
15% bonds payable	1,200,000	g 1,200,000		—
(stockholders' equity) Capital stock—old	500,000	k 500,000		—
Deficit	(1,000,000)	c 75,000 d 30,000 e 125,000	a 25,000 b 100,000 f 250,000 g 100,000 h 185,000 i 90,000 j 80,000 k 400,000	—
(new equities) Current portion—bonds	—		g 100,000	100,000
12% senior debt	—		g 500,000	500,000
Subordinated debt	—		h 275,000 j 120,000	395,000
Common stock—new	—		g 500,000 h 140,000 j 60,000 k 100,000	800,000
Retained earnings—new	—			0
	$2,055,000			$2,200,000

Exhibit 18–11 *Working Papers to Show Confirmation of Reorganization Plan with Fresh Start Reporting*

The first column of the working papers reflects the balance sheet at June 30, 20X3, immediately before recognizing the terms of the reorganization plan and establishing fresh start reporting. Entries a through f in the adjustment columns adjust the identifiable assets to their reorganization value, which approximates fair value. Baker's goodwill is eliminated, and the excess reorganization value over the fair value of identifiable assets is entered. Working paper entries g through k impose the terms of the reorganization plan.

Note that the last column, "reorganized balance sheet," is both the final balance sheet of the old entity and the opening balance sheet of the new emerging entity. Although the opening balance sheet of the new entity reflects the reorganization values of the assets, SOP 90–7 provides that the adjustments to historical cost should be disclosed in notes to the initial financial statements. The new Baker Corporation should also disclose the amount of debt forgiveness, the deficit eliminated, and key factors used in the determination of the reorganization value.

TROUBLED DEBT RESTRUCTURINGS

Accounting requirements for troubled debt restructuring fall under the jurisdiction of two different FASB statements. The creditors utilize *FASB Statement No. 114* "Accounting by Creditors for Impairment of a Loan." However, the debtor still uses the older *FASB Statement No. 15* "Accounting by Debtors and Creditors for Troubled Debt Restructuring." These are primarily applicable to troubled debt restructurings arranged through direct negotiations between a debtor company and its creditors, and they do not apply to a general restatement of a debtor's liabilities under the bankruptcy act or in a quasi-reorganization. Settlements of specific liabilities adjudicated through federal bankruptcy or other courts are covered by *Statement No. 15*, provided that the settlements are not a part of a general liability restatement.

Concept of a Troubled Debt Restructuring

A **troubled debt restructuring** occurs when a *creditor* "for economic or legal reasons related to the debtor's financial difficulties grants a concession to the debtor that it would not otherwise consider." Satisfaction of a debt by foreclosure, repossession, transfer of assets, or granting an equity interest in the debtor corporation is included in the term "troubled debt restructuring." It makes no difference whether the concession is negotiated between a debtor and a creditor or is imposed by law or a court.

Troubled debt restructurings are classified for accounting purposes as:

1 Transfer of assets in full settlement
2 The grant of an equity interest in full settlement
3 A modification of terms (for example, reduction of interest rates, extension of maturities, reduction in amounts of principal or interest)
4 Some combination of the above types

A debt restructuring is *not* a troubled debt restructuring if the fair value of assets received or equity interest transferred at least equals the carrying value of the creditor's receivable (creditor's viewpoint) or the debtor's payable (debtor's viewpoint). The carrying amounts of the debt (payable and receivable) may be different, so a restructuring can be a troubled debt restructuring for the debtor but not for the creditor. Differences can stem from the write-down of a receivable to its expected net realizable value (either directly or through an allowance account) or from the sale of a receivable to a third party at an amount that reflects the debtor's financial difficulties.

In addition, a debt restructuring is *not* a troubled debt restructuring if an interest rate reduction reflects decreased market interest rates, if new debt securities are issued to the creditor that reflect current market rates of interest, or if the restructuring involves changes in lease agreements.

Debtor Accounting

A debtor that transfers third-party receivables, real estate, or other assets to a creditor in full settlement of a payable recognizes a gain on restructuring for the excess of the carrying value of the payable over the fair value of the assets transferred. The debtor also recognizes a gain or loss on the difference between the book value and fair value of assets transferred to the creditor (this is not a restructuring gain or loss). Foreclosures and repossessions are accounted for in the same manner as asset transfers.

When a debtor issues or grants an equity interest to a creditor in full settlement of a payable, the excess of the carrying value of the payable over the fair value of the equity interest is recognized as a gain on restructuring. The debtor accounts for the equity interest issued at its fair value, but legal fees or other direct costs of granting an equity interest reduce the carrying amount of the equity interest granted.

Modification of the terms of a debt includes adjustments such as reducing the stated interest rate, extending the maturity date, reducing the face amount or accrued interest on the debt, or some combination of these adjustments. The debtor in a troubled debt restructuring accounts for a modification of terms prospectively. The carrying amount of the payable does not change unless it exceeds total future cash payments under the new terms. In this case the payable is reduced to an amount equal to future cash payments (principal and interest), and a gain on restructuring is recognized. Subsequently, all cash payments are accounted for as reductions in the payable.

When total future cash payments under a modification of terms exceed the carrying value of the payable, the debtor does not reduce the payable or recognize a gain. Instead, the debtor calculates an effective interest rate that equates future cash payments and the carrying amounts of the payable, and applies that rate in determining interest expense and principal components of future payments.

If a troubled debt restructuring involves a combination of asset transfers, granting an equity interest, and modification, the procedures are applied as described, but restructuring gains on asset transfers and equity interests granted are measured and recorded before the modifications are considered.

A debtor's individual gains on troubled debt restructurings are aggregated and reported as an extraordinary item on a net-of-tax basis if the effect is material. Direct costs incurred in a restructuring, other than those associated with granting an equity interest, are deducted in measuring gains on the restructurings of payables. Disclosures are required for aggregate gains on restructurings and related per share amounts, aggregate gains or losses on asset transfers, and principal changes and terms involved in each restructuring.

Creditor Accounting

Receivables of third parties, real estate, other assets, or equity securities received from a debtor in a troubled debt restructuring are recorded by the creditor at their fair values at the time of restructuring. The excess of the recorded amount of the receivable satisfied over the fair value of assets received is recorded as a loss. Creditor repossessions or foreclosures are accounted for in the same manner as other assets received from the debtor.

When the terms of a receivable are modified in a troubled debt restructuring, the creditor measures the loan in accordance with the provisions of *FASB Statement No. 114*, "Accounting by Creditors for Impairment of a Loan." The loan is impaired when it is probable (likely) that the creditor will not be able to collect all amounts due according to the contractual terms of the loan agreement including both principal and interest. The creditor measures the loan impairment based on the present value of the expected future cash flows discounted at the loan's effective interest rate. The effective interest rate is the original contractual rate (not the rate in the restructuring agreement), adjusted for any deferred loan fees, premium, or discount. When the loan is acquired at a discount that relates to the loan's credit quality, the effective interest rate is the discount rate that equates the present value of the investor's estimate of the loan's future cash flows with the purchase price of the loan.

As a practical expedient, the impairment may be measured based on the loan's observable market price, if available, or the fair value of collateral if the loan is collateral-dependent. Collateral-dependent means that the loan is expected to be repaid solely from the underlying collateral.

If the measure of the impaired loan is less than the recorded investment in the loan[10] (including accrued interest, net deferred loan fees or costs, and unamortized premium or discount), a valuation allowance is credited with a corresponding debit to bad debt expense. If there is a significant change in the market price or underlying collateral for the loan, the creditor adjusts the valuation account. However, the net carrying amount of the loan cannot exceed the recorded investment in the loan.

For troubled debt restructurings that involve a combination of asset transfers, equity interests, and modifications of terms, asset transfers and equity interests received by the creditor are measured and recorded before the modifications are considered. Otherwise, the procedures described are applicable.

A creditor's losses on restructuring are included in income in the period of restructuring to the extent that they are not offset against allowances for uncollectible amounts. Legal fees and direct costs incurred by a creditor are treated as expenses when incurred. A creditor is required to disclose:

1 The recorded investment in impaired loans, including (a) the amount for which there is a related allowance for credit losses and the amount of the allowance and (b) the amount of that recorded investment for which there is no related allowance for credit losses.
2 The creditor's policy for recognizing interest income on impaired loans.
3 The average recorded investment in impaired loans for each period and the time the loans were impaired within the period.

ILLUSTRATION OF A TROUBLED DEBT RESTRUCTURING

Slump Corporation is a financially distressed corporation with assets and liabilities as of January 1, 20X2 as follows:

		Book Value
Assets		
Cash		$ 5,000
Accounts receivable	$28,000	
Less: Uncollectible receivables	3,000	25,000
Inventory		60,000
Plant and equipment—net		360,000
Total assets		$450,000
Liabilities and Stockholders' Equity		
Accounts payable		$ 72,500
15% note payable—due December 1, 20X1		50,000
Interest on note payable		7,500
10% note payable—due January 1, 20X3		100,000
Interest payable on note		5,000
Capital stock, $100 par		200,000
Retained earnings		15,000
Total liabilities and stockholders' equity		$450,000

Transfer of Assets

Slump Corporation enters into an agreement with one of its suppliers, Kile Corporation, to transfer its accounts receivable (fair value $23,000) as payment in full for a $30,000 account payable owed to Kile. The concession was granted by Kile in order to

---

[10]The *net carrying amount of a loan* is net of a valuation allowance; the *recorded investment in the loan* does not consider a valuation allowance, but does reflect any direct write-down of the loan [*FASB Statement No. 114*, footnote 2].

make the best of a difficult situation. Slump and Kile record the troubled debt restructuring as follows:

SLUMP'S BOOKS

Loss on transfer of accounts receivable	$ 2,000	
Estimated uncollectible receivables	3,000	
Accounts receivable		$ 5,000
To restate receivables at fair value.		
Accounts payable—Kile	$30,000	
Accounts receivable		$23,000
Gain on restructuring of debt		7,000
To transfer receivables to Kile in full settlement of an account payable.		

KILE'S BOOKS

Investment in accounts receivable	$23,000	
Loss on settlement of receivables	5,500	
Estimated uncollectible receivables	1,500	
Accounts receivable—Slump		$30,000
To record acceptance of receivables of Slump in full settlement of account.		

The entries on Slump's books reflect a loss on transfer because the fair value of the receivables was less than book value at the time of restructuring. Slump also records a gain from cancellation of a $30,000 liability to Kile by transferring accounts receivable with a fair value of $23,000. This $7,000 gain is a gain from a troubled debt restructuring and is reported on Slump's income statement for 20X2 as an extraordinary item, if material when considered with other gains on restructuring.

Kile's entry to record the restructuring assumes that a $1,500 provision for uncollectible accounts receivable has been provided. Thus, Kile's loss is only $5,500, the $28,500 book value of the receivable from Slump less the $23,000 fair value of receivables accepted in full settlement. Kile's loss is included in its income for the period in accordance with *APB Opinion No. 30* tests for unusual nature and infrequency of occurrence.

Grant of an Equity Interest

Slump Corporation issues 500 shares of its stock to Equity Finance Company in full settlement of the 15% note payable and accrued interest. The shares have a fair value of $50,000, and the debt is carried at its $40,000 cost by Equity Finance, which purchased the note from the original payee. This restructuring is a troubled debt restructuring for Slump Corporation because it satisfies a $57,500 liability for an equity interest worth $50,000. Slump records the restructuring:

SLUMP'S BOOKS

15% note payable	$50,000	
Interest on note payable	7,500	
Capital stock, $100 par		$50,000
Gain on restructuring of debt		7,500
To record grant of equity interest in full settlement of note.		

The restructuring is not a troubled debt restructuring from the creditor's viewpoint because there is no loss to Equity Finance. The transaction is a reciprocal exchange that involves a monetary liability, so Equity Finance should record a $10,000 gain and enter the equity investment at its fair value when received.

Modification of Terms

Bussy Bank, holder of Slump's 10% note, agrees to a modification of terms such that the bank will accept $55,000 on December 31, 20X2 and December 31, 20X3 in full settlement of the debt, including interest. The carrying value of the debt on both

Slump's books and Bussy Bank's books is $105,000, indicating that Bussy Bank has not provided for the previous impairment of the note receivable.

Total payments in the new agreement exceed $105,000, so Slump records no gain or loss when the agreement is consummated. In accounting for the debt in subsequent periods, however, an effective interest rate has to be computed to equate the two future payments of $55,000 with the $105,000 carrying value of the debt. *Calculation* (P = present value of an annuity):

$$\$55,000 \times P_{2\,years\,?\,interest} = \$105,000$$
$$\$105,000 \div \$55,000 = 1.909091 \text{ present value factor}$$
$$1.909091 = \text{annuity factor for two periods at } 3.158\% \text{ effective interest}$$

Payments of $55,000 at December 31, 20X2 and 20X3, are recorded by Slump as follows:

December 31, 20X2

Note payable	$46,684	
Interest payable (January 1, 20X2)	5,000	
Interest expense	3,316	
Cash		$55,000

To record payment to Bussy Bank. Interest for 20X2 is computed as $105,000 × 3.158% effective interest rate = $3,316.

December 31, 20X3

Note payable	$53,316	
Interest expense	1,684	
Cash		$55,000

To record payment to Bussy Bank Interest for 20X3 is computed as $1,684 ($105,000 − $55,000 + $3,316) × 3.158% effective interest rate = $1,684

Bussy accounts for the modification of terms under the provisions of *FASB Statement 114*. Bussy determines that the loan is impaired because it will not collect the 10% contractual rate of interest for the two years. Bussy measures the impaired loan based on the present value of future cash flows of two receipts of $55,000 each at the end of 20X2 and 20X3. These cash payments are discounted by the effective interest rate (in this case, the 10% contractual rate).

At the time of the restructuring, Bussy Bank computes the present value of its restructured note receivable from Slump as follows:

Present value of $55,000 in one year at 10% interest:

$$\text{Present value factor} = (1 + i)^{-N} = (1 + 10\%)^{-1} = .909091$$
$$\$55,000 \times .909091 = \$50,000$$

Present value of $55,000 in two years at 10% interest:

$$\text{Present value factor} = (1 + i)^{-N} = (1 + 10\%)^{-2} = .826446$$
$$\$55,000 \times .826446 = \$45,455$$

The Bussy Bank makes the following entry on January 1, 20X2 to recognize the restructuring of its loan to Slump:

Note from Slump	$95,455	
Loss on restructured note	9,545	
10% note from Slump		$100,000
Interest receivable		5,000

To record loss from restructuring Slump's loan.

Bussy Bank would record receipt of the $55,000 in the following manner:

BUSSY BOOKS

	20X2	20X3
Cash	$55,000	$55,000
Mortgage receivable	$45,455	$50,000
Interest revenue	9,545	5,000

SUMMARY

A debtor corporation that cannot solve its financial problems internally may be able to obtain relief by direct negotiation with creditors. Failing this, the debtor may seek protection from creditors by filing a petition for bankruptcy under Title 11 of the U.S.C. Either the debtor or the creditors can file a petition. A petition filed under Chapter 11 of the Bankruptcy Act covers reorganization of the debtor; a Chapter 7 filing covers liquidation of the debtor.

In a Chapter 7 liquidation case, a trustee and creditors' committee are elected by the unsecured creditors. The trustee takes possession of the debtor's estate, converts the assets into cash, and distributes the proceeds according to the priority of claims, as directed by the bankruptcy court.

In a Chapter 11 reorganization case, the U.S. trustee appoints a creditors' committee as soon as practicable after the filing. A trustee may be appointed for cause, but generally the debtor continues in possession. The debtor corporation continues operations while it works out a reorganization plan that is fair and equitable.

The AICPA's Statement of Position, "Financial Reporting by Entities in Reorganization Under the Bankruptcy Code," prescribes financial reporting for companies operating under Chapter 11. Some companies emerging from Chapter 11 are essentially new companies and qualify for fresh start reporting. Emerging companies that do not meet the criteria for fresh start reporting account for their liabilities in accordance with *APB Opinion No. 21*, "Interest on Receivables and Payables."

In a troubled debt restructuring, a creditor grants a concession to the debtor because of the debtor's financial troubles. For example, the creditor may accept assets or an equity interest from the debtor in full settlement of a debt, or the creditor may modify the terms of a debt by lowering interest rates, extending maturities, and so on. The concession may be negotiated directly between the debtor and creditor, or it may be imposed by a court. *FASB Statement Nos. 15 and 114* prescribe accounting procedures for troubled debt restructurings.

SELECTED READINGS

ALTMAN, EDWARD I. *Corporation Financial Distress*. New York: John Wiley, 1983. "Bankruptcy," Title 11 United States Code, 1978.

ARUTT, DIANE, et al. "Implementation of SFAS No. 114, *Accounting by Creditors for Impairment of a Loan*." *The CPA Journal* (January 1995), pp. 36–41.

American Accounting Association's Financial Accounting Standards Committee. "Response to the FASB Exposure Draft 'Accounting by Creditors for Impairment of a Loan.'" *Accounting Horizons* (September 1993), pp. 114–117.

BRADLEY, MICHAEL and MICHAEL ROSENZWEIG. "The Untenable Case for Chapter 11." *The Yale Law Journal*, Vol. 101 (1992), pp. 1043–1095.

FRETT, JEROME. "Bankruptcy: When Is It Good News?" *Journal of Accountancy* (November 1991), pp. 135–138.

HERZ, ROBERT, H. and EDWARD J. ABAHOONIE, "Restructuring Business in the 1990s." *Journal of Accountancy* (April 1992), pp. 28–33.

KUDLA, RONALD J. *Voluntary Corporate Liquidations*. Westport, CT: Quorum Books, Greenwood Press, 1988.

NEWTON, GRANT W. *Bankruptcy and Insolvency Accounting: Practice and Procedure*, 2nd ed. New York: John Wiley, 1981.

PARISER, DAVID B. "Financial Reporting Implications of Troubled Debt." *The CPA Journal* (February 1989), pp. 32–40.

ROBBINS, JOHN, AL GOLL, and PAUL ROSENFELD. "Accounting for Companies in Chapter 11 Reorganization." *Journal of Accountancy* (January 1991), pp. 74–80.

Statement of Financial Accounting Standards No. 15. "Accounting by Debtors and Creditors for Troubled Debt Restructurings." Stamford, CT: Financial Accounting Standards Board, 1977.

Statement of Financial Accounting Standards No. 114. "Accounting by Creditors for Impairment of a Loan." Norwalk, CT: Financial Accounting Standards Board, 1993.

Statement of Financial Accounting Standards No. 118. "Accounting by Creditors for Impairment of a Loan—Income Recognition and Disclosures." Norwalk, CT: Financial Accounting Standards Board, 1994.

Statement of Position 90–7. "Financial Reporting by Entities in Reorganization under the Bankruptcy Code." Executive Committee of the Accounting Standards Division of the American Institute of Certified Public Accountants, 1990.

ASSIGNMENT MATERIAL

QUESTIONS

1 What is the distinction between *equity insolvency* and *bankruptcy insolvency*?

2 Is a Title 11 case under the Bankruptcy Act of 1978 the same as a Chapter 11 case? Discuss.

3 Bankruptcy proceedings may be designated as *voluntary* or *involuntary*. Distinguish between the two types, including the requirements for the filing of an involuntary petition.

4 Consider the following statement: "A bankrupt company is liquidated under Chapter 7 of the Bankruptcy Act, but a company that is not bankrupt will be rehabilitated under Chapter 11." Do you agree? Discuss.

5 What are the duties of the U.S. trustee under the Bankruptcy Act of 1978? Do U.S. trustees supervise the administration of all bankruptcy cases?

6 What obligations does a debtor corporation have in a bankruptcy case?

7 Is a trustee appointed in Title 11 cases? In all Chapter 7 cases? Discuss.

8 Do you agree with the following statement? "Trustees and creditor committees are appointed in Chapter 11 cases and elected in Chapter 7 cases."

9 Describe the duties of a trustee in a liquidation case under the Bankruptcy Act of 1978.

10 Which unsecured claims have priority in a Chapter 7 liquidation case? Discuss in terms of priority ranks.

11 Does the Bankruptcy Act of 1978 establish priorities for holders of unsecured, nonpriority claims (that is, general unsecured claims)?

12 What is the purpose of a statement of affairs and how are assets valued in this statement?

13 Does the Bankruptcy Act require a trustee to prepare a statement of realization and liquidation for the bankruptcy court?

14 Does filing a case under Chapter 11 of the Bankruptcy Act mean that the company will not be liquidated? Discuss.

15 What is a "debtor in possession" reorganization case?

16 When can a creditor committee file a plan of reorganization under a Chapter 11 case?

17 Discuss the requirements for approval of a plan of reorganization.

18 Does acceptance of a plan by two-thirds in amount and more than half in number of claims constitute confirmation of a reorganization plan? Discuss.

19 Describe *prepetition liabilities subject to compromise* on the balance sheet of a company operating under Chapter 11 of the Bankruptcy Act.

20 The *reorganization value* of a firm emerging from Chapter 11 bankruptcy is used to determine the accounting of the reorganized company. Explain reorganization value as used in the AICPA's SOP 90–7, "Financial Reporting by Entities in Reorganization Under the Bankruptcy Code."

21 The SOP provides two conditions that must be met for an emerging firm to use fresh start reporting. What are these two conditions?

22 A firm emerging from Chapter 11 bankruptcy that does not qualify for fresh start reporting must still report the effect of the reorganization plan on its financial position and results of operations. How is debt forgiveness reported in the reorganized company's financial statements?

23 What is a troubled debt restructuring? Is it possible for an extinguishment of debt to be a troubled debt restructuring for the debtor corporation but not for the creditor?

24 When does the debtor corporation recognize a loss on the restructuring of debt?

25 If the terms of a debt are modified such that future payments of the debtor are greater than the carrying value of the debt, how does the debtor company account for the modification?

EXERCISES

E 18-1

1 Insolvency in the bankruptcy sense means:

a Book value of assets is greater than liabilities

b Fair value of assets is less than liabilities

c Inability to meet financial obligations as they come due

d Liabilities are greater than book value of assets

2 Discharge of a debtor corporation's liabilities other than those provided for in the reorganization plan results when:
  a The plan is accepted by a majority of unsecured creditors
  b Each class of claims has accepted the plan or is not impaired under it
  c Each holder of a claim has accepted the plan or will receive at least as much as if the company were liquidated
  d The court confirms that the plan is fair and equitable

3 Election of a trustee in a Chapter 7 case requires:
  a Approval by a majority of creditors
  b Approval by a majority of claims represented
  c Approval by a majority in amount and at least 20% of claims eligible to vote
  d Approval of two-thirds in amount and a majority of holders of all claims

4 The order of payments for unsecured priority claims in a Chapter 7 bankruptcy case is such that:
  a Tax claims of governmental units are paid before claims for administrative expenses incurred by the trustee
  b Tax claims of governmental units are paid before claims of employees for wages
  c Claims of employees for wages are paid before administrative expenses incurred by the trustee
  d Claims incurred between the filing of an involuntary petition and appointment of a trustee are paid before claims for contributions to employee benefit plans

5 A judge in a corporate bankruptcy case may *not*:
  a Dismiss a case
  b Transfer a Chapter 11 case to Chapter 7
  c Transfer a Chapter 7 case to Chapter 11
  d Transfer a Chapter 7 case to Chapter 5

6 A debtor's duties under a Chapter 7 bankruptcy case do *not* include:
  a Filing a schedule of assets and liabilities with the court
  b Surrendering the firm's property to the trustee
  c Relinquishing stockholders' claims in the estate
  d Cooperating with the trustee

7 A specific duty of a U.S. trustee in a bankruptcy case is to:
  a Preside over the meetings of creditors' committees
  b Convert the estate assets into cash
  c Investigate the financial affairs of the debtor
  d Operate the debtor's business

8 A corporation may *not* be a debtor in possession if:
  a The case is initiated in a voluntary filing
  b The case is initiated in an involuntary filing
  c Loans other than for goods and services exceed $5,000,000
  d The court concludes that appointment of a trustee is in the best interests of creditors

9 Among other provisions, a Chapter 11 plan for reorganization must:
  a Rank claims according to their liquidation priorities
  b Not impair the claims of secured creditors
  c Provide adequate means for the plan's execution
  d Treat all claims alike

10 Which of the following claims *would not* be entitled to a priority in a Chapter 7 bankruptcy proceeding?
  a Administrative expenses incurred by the trustee
  b Salaries payable of $1,500
  c Claims of governmental units for taxes
  d Claims of creditors for $2,000 interest

11 Under Chapter 11 of the Bankruptcy Act:
  a Only involuntary filings are accepted by the court
  b The court is required to appoint a trustee
  c A solvent corporation may file a petition for relief from creditors
  d Only the debtor corporation can file a reorganization plan

12 A "debtor in possession" case is:
  a A voluntary case
  b An involuntary case
  c A Chapter 7 case
  d A Chapter 11 case

13 The term *insider* is frequently used in relation to preferential transfers under the Bankruptcy Act. Which of the following is *not* an insider?
  a An officer of the corporation
  b An officer of an affiliated corporation
  c The family members of a client corporation's president
  d A family member of the corporation's controller

E 18-2 **1** A troubled debt restructuring does *not* require:
  a A concession imposed by law or a court
  b A debtor company with financial difficulties
  c A creditor to grant a concession to the debtor
  d A creditor concession related to the debtor's financial difficulties

  2 Which of the following debt restructurings could be a troubled debt restructuring?
  a Interest rate reductions that reflect decreased market interest rates
  b Restructuring as part of a general restatement of liabilities under the Bankruptcy Act
  c Book value of assets transferred exceeds the carrying value of the debt
  d New debt securities issued to the creditor reflect current interest rates

  3 Modification of terms of a debt in a troubled debt restructuring does not result in a gain for the debtor at the time of restructuring unless the:
  a Principal amount of the debt is reduced
  b Present value of future cash payments is less than the carrying value of the debt
  c Absolute amount of future cash payments (principal and interest) is less than the carrying value of the debt
  d Modification is required by law or action of a bankruptcy court

  4 In accounting for troubled debt restructurings that involve a combination of asset transfers, granting of equity interests, and modifications of terms:
  a Asset transfers and equity interests granted are measured and recorded before modifications
  b Modifications are recorded before asset transfers
  c Equity interests granted are recorded before asset transfers
  d Modifications are recorded first, equity interests next, and then asset transfers

  5 Which statement with respect to gains and losses on troubled debt restructurings is correct?
  a Debtor gains on restructuring and gains or losses on asset transfers are combined and the net amount is reported as an extraordinary item.
  b Creditor losses on restructurings are extraordinary only if they meet the requirements of *APB Opinion No. 30* for extraordinary items.
  c Debtor gains and creditor losses on restructurings are extraordinary items, if material.
  d Debtor gains on restructurings are treated as extraordinary, and losses on restructurings are included in income in the period of restructuring.

E 18-3 Use the following information in answering questions 1 and 2:
  Craftmaker Company filed for protection from creditors under Chapter 11 of the Bankruptcy Act on July 1, 20X4. Craftmaker had the following liabilities at the time of filing:

10% mortgage bonds payable, secured by a building with a book value and fair value of $100,000	$200,000
Accrued interest on mortgage (January 1–July 1)	10,000
Accounts payable	80,000
Priority tax claims	50,000
	$340,000

  1 The December 31, 20X4 balance sheet will show prepetition liabilities of:
  a $340,000 (the claims at filing)
  b $240,000 (the original claims less the secured portion of the mortgage bonds)
  c $350,000 (the original claims plus six months' interest on the bonds)
  d $290,000 (the original claims less the priority tax claims)

  2 Two and a half years after filing the petition for bankruptcy, Craftmaker's management, its creditors, the equity holders, and other parties in interest, agree on a reorganization value of $500,000. Which of the following statements is most likely?
  a The reorganization value approximates the appraised value of the firm as a going concern less the prepetition liabilities.
  b The reorganization value approximates the fair value of the assets less the fair value of the prepetition and postpetition liabilities.
  c The reorganization value approximates the fair value of the assets less the book value of the postpetition liabilities and the estimated settlement value of the prepetition liabilities.
  d The reorganization value approximates the fair value of the entity without considering the liabilities.

  3 Universal Industries, a parent company with five wholly owned operating subsidiaries, is in the process of preparing consolidated financial statements for the year. Two of Universal's subsidiaries are operating as debtors in possession under Chapter 11 of the Bankruptcy Act. Which of the following statements is correct?

a *FASB Statement No. 94*, "Consolidation of All Majority-owned Subsidiaries," prohibits Universal Industries from consolidating the financial statements of the two subsidiaries in bankruptcy with those of the other affiliated companies.

b *FASB Statement No 94*, "Consolidation of All Majority-owned Subsidiaries," requires that the financial statements of all five of the subsidiaries be consolidated with those of the parent company.

c If Universal's consolidated financial statements include the operations of the two subsidiaries in bankruptcy, *Statement of Position 90–7* requires that condensed combined financial statements for all entities in reorganization be presented as supplementary financial statements.

d If Universal's consolidated financial statements do **not** include the operations of the two subsidiaries in bankruptcy, those subsidiaries must be accounted for under the cost method.

4 When fresh start reporting is used, the initial financial statement disclosures should not include:

a Adjustments made in the amounts of individual assets and liabilities

b The amount of debt forgiven

c The amount of prior retained earnings or deficit eliminated

d Current and prior-year EPS amounts

E 18-4 Freidrich Corporation holds a $100,000 note receivable from Moody Supply Company. It has been learned that Moody Supply filed for Chapter 7 bankruptcy and that the expected recovery of nonsecured claims is 35¢ on the dollar. Moody's note payable to Freidrich is secured by inventory items with an estimated recoverable value of $30,000.

Required: Determine Freidrich's expected recovery on the note.

E 18-5 Deadtrack Corporation is being liquidated under Chapter 7 of the Bankruptcy Act. After all noncash assets have been liquidated, $40,000 cash remains to pay the following approved claims:

Administrative expenses including trustee fees	$ 10,000
Salaries (includes CEO's salary of $8,000)	20,000
Property taxes	16,000
Claims between filing of the involuntary petition and appointment of the trustee	5,000
Accounts payable, unsecured	15,000
Notes payable, unsecured	30,000
Interest on unsecured notes payable	4,000
Total unpaid claims	$100,000

Required: Determine the amount to be paid to unsecured priority creditors in settlement of their claims.

E 18-6 Handyman Hardware has been operating under Chapter 11 of the Bankruptcy Code for the past 15 months. On March 31, 20X5, just before confirmation of its reorganization plan, Handyman's reorganization value is estimated at $2,000,000. A balance sheet for Handyman prepared on the same date is summarized as follows:

Current assets	$ 500,000
Plant assets	2,000,000
	$2,500,000
Postpetition liabilities	$ 800,000
Prepetition liabilities subject to compromise*	1,000,000
Fully secured debt	600,000
Capital stock	600,000
Deficit	(500,000)
	$2,500,000

*Represents allowed claims. The reorganization plan calls for payment of $100,000 and issuance of $200,000 notes and $250,000 common stock in settlement of the prepetition liabilities.

Required: 1 On the basis of the reorganization value, does Handyman Hardware qualify for fresh start reporting? 2 What other conditions must be met for fresh start reporting? Show calculations.

E 18-7 Holiday Corporation is in bankruptcy and is being liquidated by a court-appointed trustee. The financial report that follows was prepared by the trustee just before the final cash distribution:

Assets	
Cash	$100,000

Approved claims	
Mortgage payable (secured by property that was sold for $50,000)	$ 80,000
Accounts payable, unsecured	50,000
Administrative expenses payable, unsecured	8,000
Salaries payable, unsecured	2,000
Interest payable, unsecured	10,000
Total approved claims	$150,000

The administrative expenses are for trustee fees and other costs of administering the debtor corporation's estate.

Required: Show how the $100,000 cash will be distributed to holders of each of the approved claims.

E 18-8 Kassum Company experienced cash flow problems during 20X2, and on June 30, 20X2 was unable to pay principal and interest on a $50,000 debt to its principal supplier, Genair Corporation. In view of Kassum Company's distressed financial condition, Genair agreed to accept machinery with a book value of $52,000 and a fair value of $45,000 in full satisfaction of the $50,000 debt and $7,500 accrued interest.

Required: Prepare journal entries on the books of Kassum Company and Genair Corporation to record the troubled debt restructuring that was consummated on July 30, 20X2.

E 18-9 On January 1, 20X3, Second National Bank sold its $25,000, 15% note receivable from Milan Company to Stable Finance Company for $20,000, in anticipation of Milan's default on the loan. Stable did not accrue interest on the note during the first half of 20X3 because of the uncertain financial condition of Milan and the speculative nature of the investment. Milan Company was unable to pay the note and $1,875 accrued interest on its June 30, 20X3 due date.

During August 20X3, Stable Finance and Milan negotiated an agreement under which Milan was to issue 1,000 shares of its $10 par common stock to Stable Finance in full satisfaction of the debt. The restructuring was consummated on August 31, at which time the stock had a fair value of $23,000, and accrued interest on the debt was $2,500 ($25,000 $\times$ 15% $\times \frac{2}{3}$ year).

Required

1 Is this a troubled debt restructuring? Discuss.

2 Prepare journal entries on the books of Milan Company to record the restructuring, assuming that it is a troubled debt restructuring.

E 18-10 Crash Corporation was unable to pay its $100,000, 12% note and $6,000 interest to Crimp Bank on December 31, 20X7. Due to the financially distressed condition of Crash, Crimp Bank agreed to extend the due date on the note for two years, and to reduce the interest rate from 12% to 3% simple interest payable when the loan is due, provided that the $6,000 accrued interest was paid immediately. This agreement was consummated on December 31, 20X7, on which date Crash paid the $6,000 interest due. The present value of $1 due in two periods at 12% interest is .7972 and at 3% interest is .9426.

Required

1 Is this a troubled debt restructuring for Crash? For Crimp Bank?

2 Calculate the gain or loss on restructuring to be recorded on December 31, 20X7 by Crash and by Crimp Bank.

E 18-11 [AICPA adapted]

1 On December 31, 20X3, Marsh Company entered into a debt restructuring agreement with Saxe Company, which was experiencing financial difficulties. Marsh restructured a $100,000 note receivable as follows:

Reduced the principal obligation to $70,000.

Forgave $12,000 of accrued interest.

Extended the maturity date from December 31, 20X3 to December 31, 20X5.

Reduced the interest rate from 12% to 8%. Interest will be payable annually on December 31, 20X4 and 20X5.

The present value of $1 due in two periods at 8% interest is .8573 and at 12% interest is .7972. The present value of an ordinary annuity of $1 for two periods at 8% interest is 1.7833 and at 12% interest is 1.6901.

At December 31, 20X3, Marsh computes a loss on the receivable from Saxe Company of (rounded):

a $65,269   c $42,002
b $46,731   d $34,731

2 During 20X2, Peterson Company experienced financial difficulties and is likely to default on a $500,000, 15%, three-year note dated January 1, 20X1, payable to Forest National Bank. On December 31, 20X2 the bank agreed to settle the note and unpaid interest of $75,000 for 20X2 for $50,000 cash and marketable securities having a current market value of $375,000. Peterson's acquisition cost of the securities is $385,000. Ignoring income taxes, what amount should Peterson report as a gain from the debt restructuring in its 20X2 income statement?

a $65,000   c $140,000
b $75,000   d $150,000

3 Carr Company is indebted to Apex Company under a $700,000, 12%, four-year note dated December 31, 20X1. Annual interest of $84,000 was paid on December 31, 20X2 and 20X3. During 20X4, Carr experienced financial difficulties and is likely to default on the note and interest unless concessions are made. On December 31, 20X4, Apex agreed to restructure the debt as follows.

Interest for 20X4 was reduced from $84,000 to $40,000, payable on January 31, 20X5.

Interest for 20X5 was waived.

The $700,000 principal amount was reduced to $600,000.

Ignoring income taxes, how much should Carr report as extraordinary gain on debt restructuring in its income statement for the year ended December 31, 20X4?

a $0   c $100,000
b $60,000   d $144,000

4 Hull Company is indebted to Apex under a $500,000, 12%, three-year note dated December 31, 20X4. Because of Hull's financial difficulties developing in 20X6, Hull owed accrued interest of $60,000 on the note at December 31, 20X6. Under a troubled debt restructuring on December 31, 20X6, Apex agreed to settle the note and accrued interest for a tract of land having a fair value of $450,000. Hull's acquisition cost of the land is $360,000. Ignoring income taxes, on its 20X6 income statement Hull should report its troubled debt restructuring as:

	Other Income	Extraordinary Gain
a	$200,000	0
b	$140,000	0
c	$ 90,000	$ 50,000
d	$ 90,000	$110,000

E 18-12 The creditors of Downy Corporation agreed to the following financial concessions in recognition of Downy's deteriorating financial condition:

1 Freshline Company, one of Downy's suppliers, agrees to accept merchandise at its normal selling price of $30,000 in full satisfaction of its $32,400 overdue account receivable from Downy. The cost of the merchandise to Downy was $24,000. Freshline's account receivable from Downy included a $3,000 allowance for doubtful accounts.

2 Downy Corporation's bank, Glidden Fidelity, agrees to accept 2,000 shares of Downy's $10 par common stock with a current market price of $20 per share in full satisfaction of a $45,000 note and $4,000 accrued interest due from Downy. Glidden Fidelity Bank has provided a $10,000 bad debt allowance for this note.

Required

1 Prepare journal entries on Downy's books to account for the restructuring transaction.
2 Prepare journal entries on the books of Freshline Company and Glidden Fidelity Bank to account for the restructuring transactions.

PROBLEMS

P 18-1 The balance sheet of Slim-Line Corporation appeared as follows on March 1, 20X2, when an interim trustee was appointed by the U.S. trustee to assume control of Slim-Line's estate in a Chapter 7 case.

Assets		Liabilities and Stockholders' Equity	
Cash	$ 2,000	Accounts payable	$25,000
Accounts receivable—net	4,000	Note payable—unsecured	20,000
Inventories	18,000	Revenue received in advance	500
Land	10,000	Wages payable	1,500
Buildings—net	50,000	Mortgage payable	40,000
Intangible assets	13,000	Capital stock	20,000
		Retained earnings deficit	(10,000)
Assets	$97,000	Liabilities and equity	$97,000

Additional Information

1 Creditors failed to elect a trustee and, accordingly, the interim trustee became trustee for the case.
2 The land and buildings are pledged as security for the mortgage payable.
3 In January 20X2, Slim-Line received $500 from a customer as a payment in advance for merchandise that is no longer marketed.
4 Activities of the trustee during March are summarized as follows:
   a $3,800 is collected on the receivables.
   b Inventories are sold for $9,700.
   c Land and buildings bring a total of $45,000.
   d Nothing is realized from the intangible assets.
   e Administrative expenses of $4,100 are incurred by the trustee.

Required

1 Prepare a separate set of books for the trustee to assume possession of the estate and convert its assets into cash.
2 Prepare financial statements on March 31 for Slim-Line in Trusteeship (balance sheet, cash receipts and disbursements, and changes in estate equity).
3 Prepare journal entries on the trustee's books to distribute available cash to creditors and close the case.

P 18-2 Daniel Corporation filed a petition under Chapter 7 of the Bankruptcy Act in January 20X6. On March 15, 20X6 the trustee provided the following information about the corporation's financial affairs.

	Book Values	Estimated Realizable Values
Assets		
Cash	$ 20,000	$ 20,000
Accounts receivable—net	100,000	75,000
Inventories	150,000	70,000
Plant assets—net	250,000	280,000
Total assets	$520,000	
Liabilities		
Liability for priority claims	$ 80,000	
Accounts payable—unsecured	150,000	
Note payable, secured by accounts receivable	100,000	
Mortgage payable, secured by all plant assets	220,000	
Total liabilities	$550,000	

Required

1 Determine the amount expected to be available for unsecured claims.
2 Determine the expected recovery per dollar of unsecured claims.
3 Estimate the amount of recovery for each class of creditors.

P 18-3 Marble Corporation is a financially distressed corporation with assets and liabilities at book value on June 30, 20X6 as follows:

Assets		Liabilities	
Cash	$ 70,000	Accounts payable	$ 50,000
Accounts receivable less $5,000		15% note payable	100,000
uncollectible receivables	45,000	Interest on note payable	15,000
Inventory	80,000	15% mortgage payable	300,000
Plant and equipment—net	405,000	Interest on mortgage payable	30,000
Total assets	$600,000	Total liabilities	$495,000

Additional Information

1 On July 1, 20X6, Nappy Supply Corporation, Marble's sole supplier, accepted all of Marble's accounts receivable with a fair value of $38,000 in full settlement of the accounts payable liability.
2 On July 5, 20X6, Onze Finance Corporation accepted 1,000 shares of Marble Corporation's $10 par common stock with a fair value of $80 per share in full settlement of the note payable and interest.
3 Also on July 5, 20X6, Lateral Bank agreed to accept $45,000 per year for eight years in full settlement of the mortgage payable and interest. The current interest rate on July 5 was 12% and the present value of the eight future payments on that date was $223,544.

Required:

1 Calculate Marble Corporation's gain or loss on restructuring its debt in accordance with the provisions of *FASB Statement No. 15*.
2 How much gain or loss should Nappy, Onze and Lateral Bank recognize on the troubled debt restructuring?

P 18-4 Fabulous Fakes Corporation is being liquidated under Chapter 7 of the Bankruptcy Act. All assets have been converted into cash and $374,500 cash is available to pay the following claims:

1	Administrative expenses of preserving and liquidating the debtor corporation's estate	$ 12,500
2	Merchandise creditors	99,000
3	Local government for property taxes	4,000
4	Local bank for unsecured loan (principal is $30,000 and interest is $4,500)	34,500
5	State government for gross receipts taxes	3,000
6	Employees for unpaid wages during the month before filing (includes $5,000 for the company president and less than $4,000 for each of the other employees)	48,000
7	Customers for prepaid merchandise that was not delivered	1,500
8	Holders of the first mortgage on the company's real estate that was sold for $240,000 (includes $220,000 principal and $8,500 interest)	228,500

Assume that all the claims are allowed and that they were timely filed.

Required

1 Rank the claims according to priority under the Bankruptcy Act.
2 Show how the available cash will be distributed in final liquidation of the corporation.

P 18-5 Galax Corporation experienced financial difficulties during the current year and was able to obtain concessions from several of its creditors to enable continued operations. Information relating to each of the concessions is as follows:

1 Galax transfers inventory items with a normal selling price of $21,000 (cost $15,000) to Renner Corporation in full satisfaction of a $20,000 note and $3,000 accrued interest. The book value of the note and interest on Renner's book was $22,000 ($23,000 less $1,000 allowance for uncollectible notes).
2 First Piedmont Finance Company accepts 3,000 shares of Galax Corporation's $10 par common stock in full satisfaction of a $50,000 note and $2,500 accrued interest. The stock has a book value of $60,000 and a fair value of $40,000. First Piedmont acquired the note and accrued interest for $35,000 just before the restructuring.
3 The First National Bank of Danville extends the $100,000 mortgage on Galax's plant for two years and reduces the interest rate from 15% to 6% in order to make the best of a difficult situation. In return, Galax pays the $3,750 accrued interest immediately. The PV of $1 due in two periods at 15% interest is .7561 and at 6% is .8900. The PV of an annuity of $1 for two periods at 15% is 1.6257 and at 6% is 1.8334.

Required: Prepare journal entries on the books of Galax Corporation and each of its creditors to account for the restructurings described.

P 18-6 Daryl Corporation filed a petition under Chapter 7 of the U.S. Bankruptcy Act on June 30, 20X2. Data relevant to its financial position as of this date are:

	Book Value	Estimated Net Realizable Values
Cash	$ 2,200	$ 2,200
Accounts receivable—net	15,000	13,500
Inventories	20,000	22,500
Equipment—net	55,000	28,000
Total assets	$92,200	$66,200
Accounts payable	$26,400	
Rent payable	7,600	
Wages payable	12,000	
Note payable plus accrued interest	31,000	
Capital stock	55,000	
Retained earnings (deficit)	(39,800)	
Total liabilities and equity	$92,200	

Required
1 Prepare a statement of affairs assuming that the note payable and interest are secured by a mortgage on the equipment and that wages are less than $4,000 per employee.
2 Estimate the amount that will be paid to each class of claims if priority liquidation expenses including trustee fees are $4,000 and estimated net realizable values are actually realized.

P 18-7 The unsecured creditors of Dawn Corporation filed a petition under Chapter 7 of the Bankruptcy Act on July 1, 20X6 to force Dawn into bankruptcy. The court order for relief was granted on July 10 at which time an interim trustee was appointed to supervise liquidation of the estate. A listing of assets and liabilities of Dawn Corporation as of July 10, 20X6, along with estimated realizable values, is as follows:

	Book Values	Estimated Realizable Values
Assets		
Cash	$ 80,000	$ 80,000
Accounts receivable—net	210,000	160,000
Inventories	200,000	210,000
Equipment—net	150,000	60,000
Land and buildings–net	250,000	140,000
Intangible assets	10,000	—
	$900,000	$650,000
Accounts payable	$400,000	
Note payable	100,000	
Wages payable (from June and July)	24,000	
Taxes payable	76,000	
Mortgage payable $200,000, plus $5,000 unpaid interest to July 10	205,000	
Capital stock	300,000	
Retained earnings deficit	(205,000)	
	$900,000	

Additional Information
1 Accounts receivable are pledged as security for the note payable.
2 No more than $1,000 is owed to any employee.
3 Taxes payable are a priority item.
4 Inventory items include $50,000 acquired on July 5, 20X6 and the unpaid invoice is included in accounts payable.
5 The mortgage payable and interest are secured by the land and buildings.
6 Trustee fees and other costs of liquidating the estate are expected to be $11,000.

Required
1 Prepare a statement of affairs for Dawn Corporation on July 10, 20X6.
2 Develop a schedule showing how available cash will be distributed to each class of claims assuming (a) the estimated realizable values are actually received and (b) the trustee and other fees of liquidating the estate are $11,000.

P 18-8   The balance sheet of Everlast Window Corporation at June 30, 20X1 contains the following items:

Assets

Cash	$ 40,000
Accounts receivable—net	70,000
Inventories	50,000
Land	30,000
Building–net	200,000
Machinery—net	60,000
Goodwill	50,000
	$500,000

Equities

Accounts payable	$110,000
Wages payable	60,000
Property taxes payable	10,000
Mortgage payable	150,000
Interest on mortgage payable	15,000
Note payable—unsecured	50,000
Interest payable—unsecured	5,000
Capital stock	200,000
Retained earnings deficit	(100,000)
	$500,000

The company is in financial difficulty and its stockholders and creditors have requested a statement of affairs for planning purposes. The following information is available:

1 The company estimates that $63,000 is the maximum amount collectible for the accounts receivable.
2 Except for 20% of the inventory items that are damaged and worth only $2,000, the cost of the other items is expected to be recovered in full.
3 The land and building have a combined appraisal value of $170,000 and are subject to the $150,000 mortgage and related accrued interest.
4 The appraised value of the machinery is $20,000.
5 Wages payable and property taxes payable are unsecured priority items that do not exceed any limitations of the Bankruptcy Act.

Required

1 Prepare a statement of affairs for Everlast Window Corporation as of June 30, 20X1.
2 Compute the estimated settlement per dollar of unsecured liabilities.

P 18-9   Lowstep Corporation filed for relief under Chapter 11 of the Bankruptcy Act on January 2, 20X2. A summary of Lowstep's assets and equities on this date, and at June 30, 20X2, is shown below. Estimated fair values of Lowstep's assets at June 30 are also shown.

	January 2, 20X2	June 30, 20X2 Per Books	June 30, 20X2 Estimated Fair Value
Assets			
Cash	$ 200	$ 6,700	$ 6,700
Trade receivables—net	800	1,000	1,000
Inventories	2,000	1,600	2,000
Prepaid items	500	—	—
Land	1,000	1,000	2,000
Buildings—net	3,000	2,900	1,500
Equipment—net	2,000	1,800	1,800
Goodwill	4,500	4,000	0
	$14,000	$19,000	$15,000
Equities			
Accounts payable	$ 1,000	$ 3,000	
Wages payable	500	1,000	
Bank note payable (includes $500 interest)	5,000		
Long-term note payable (secured with equipment)	6,000		
Prepetition liabilities allowed		12,500	
Common stock	7,000	7,000	
Deficit	(5,500)	(4,500)	
	$14,000	$19,000	

The parties-in-interest agree to a reorganization plan on July 1, 20X2, and a hearing to confirm that the plan is fair and equitable is scheduled for July 8. Under the reorganization plan, the reorganization value is set at $16,000, and the debt and equity holders will receive value as follows:

	To Receive Cash Consideration	To Receive Noncash Consideration
Postpetition claims		
Accounts payable (in full)	$3,000	
Wages payable (in full)	1,000	
Prepetition claims		
Accounts payable (80%)	800	
Wages payable (80%)	400	
Bank note payable and interest (80%)		$ 2,000 note payable
		2,000 common stock
Long-term note payable (80%)		1,800 note payable
		3,000 common stock
Common stockholders*		2,000 common stock
	$5,200	$10,800

*Reorganization value over consideration allocated to creditors.

The reorganization plan is confirmed on July 8, 20X2 under the new name of Highstep Corporation. There are no asset or liability changes between July 1 and July 8.

Required
1 Is the reorganization of Lowstep eligible for fresh start accounting? Show calculations.
2 Prepare journal entries to adjust Lowstep's accounts for the reorganization plan.
3 Prepare a fresh start balance sheet as of July 8, 20X2.

19

An Introduction to Accounting for State and Local Governmental Units—Part I

Accounting and financial reporting practices of businesses and other nongovernment entities differ significantly from those of state and local government entities. The accounting profession recognizes these differences as important enough to warrant having different standards-setting bodies for these two broad categories of organizations. Generally accepted accounting principles of state and local governments (hereafter referred to as SLGs) are established by the **Governmental Accounting Standards Board (GASB)** under the auspices of the Financial Accounting Foundation. GAAP for businesses and other nongovernment (essentially, private not-for-profit) organizations are established by the GASB's "sister" organization, the Financial Accounting Standards Board. Indeed, GAAP for government entities and for businesses never have been established by the same standards-setting bodies. Just as there were predecessor bodies for the FASB, there were predecessor bodies for the GASB.

The primary source of GAAP for states, cities, counties, towns, school districts, special districts and authorities, and other local government entities is the statements and interpretations of the GASB. This guidance is codified by the GASB (and annually updated) in *Codification of Governmental Accounting and Financial Reporting Principles*. The primary FASB standards covering accounting and financial reporting for nongovernment, not-for-profit organizations are *FASB Statement No. 116*, "Accounting for Contributions Received and Contributions Made;" *FASB Statement No. 117*, "Financial Statements of Not-for-Profit Organizations;" and *FASB Statement No. 124*, "Accounting for Certain Investments Held by Not-for-Profit Organizations." The organizations covered by these standards include not-for-profit colleges and universities, health care entities, voluntary health and welfare organizations, and other not-for-profit organizations that are not governments.

Government colleges and universities typically apply the guidance in the AICPA's audit guide, *Audits of Colleges and Universities*, as modified by GASB standards. Nongovernment colleges and universities must apply FASB standards. Implementation of FASB standards for nongovernment colleges and universities is addressed in the AICPA audit guide, "Audits of Not-for-Profit Organizations." The National Association of College and University Business Officials publishes a useful, up-to-date practice manual covering college and university accounting and reporting for both government and nongovernment institutions. It is called the *Financial Accounting and Reporting Manual* (FARM). Government health care entities must comply with GASB standards; nongovernment health care providers must comply with FASB standards. The AICPA's accounting and audit guide, *Audits of Health Care Organizations*, discusses and illustrates the financial reporting requirements for both government and nongovernment health care organizations. Similarly, voluntary health and welfare organizations and other not-for-profit organizations that are governments must follow GASB standards, which permit them to apply the guidance in AICPA pronouncements that were developed for those entities. Nongovernment voluntary health and welfare organizations and other not-for-profit organizations must apply the FASB guidance. Implementation of the FASB guidance is addressed in *Audits of Not-for-Profit Organizations*—the AICPA audit guide. Clearly, it is important to properly distinguish between government and nongovernment entities. Therefore, the audit guides contain a definition of a government that must be applied to each college or university, health care entity, voluntary health and welfare organization, or other not-for-profit organization to determine which guidance applies.

This chapter and Chapter 20 summarize accounting and reporting principles for state and local governmental units and illustrate fund accounting practices using a municipal accounting system as a model. Except for the federal government, state and local governmental units constitute the largest single category of nonprofit organizations in terms of the dollar volume of annual expenditures.

HISTORICAL DEVELOPMENT OF ACCOUNTING PRINCIPLES FOR STATE AND LOCAL GOVERNMENTAL UNITS

The most important continuous source of accounting principles for state and local governmental units has been the Government Finance Officers Association[1] and its committees on governmental accounting. *Municipal Accounting and Auditing*, in 1951, and *Governmental Accounting, Auditing, and Financial Reporting (GAAFR)*,[2] in 1968, comprised more or less complete frameworks of accounting principles peculiar to governmental units. They also provided standards for evaluating the financial reports of governmental units, including audited financial statements that were issued in accordance with GAAP. In 1974 the AICPA issued its Industry Audit Guide, *Audits of State and Local Governmental Units*, in which it noted that *GAAFR's* accounting and reporting principles constituted GAAP except where they were modified by the audit guide.

The AICPA's audit guide prompted the 1979 revision of *GAAFR* to update and clarify governmental accounting and financial reporting principles, and to incorporate pertinent aspects of the audit guide. The Government Finance Officers Association established a new committee, the National Council on Governmental Accounting (NCGA) to develop the 1979 *GAAFR* Restatement. As part of this project, the NCGA issued *Governmental Accounting and Financial Reporting Principles, Statement No. 1 (NCGA1)* in 1979. The following year, a new nonauthoritative *GAAFR* was issued as a comprehensive volume to explain and illustrate the principles of *NCGA1*. Also in 1980, the AICPA issued *Statement of Position 80–2*, which amended *Audits of State and Local Governmental Units* to recognize the principles of *NCGA1* as generally accepted accounting principles.

The Governmental Accounting Standards Board

In 1984 the Financial Accounting Foundation (which oversees the FASB) formed the Governmental Accounting Standards Board to establish and improve standards for governmental accounting and financial reporting. The AICPA Council declared that Rule 203 of its Rules of Conduct applies to GASB's pronouncements. Therefore, those pronouncements constitute GAAP for governments.

In July 1984, GASB issued *GASB Statement No. 1, Authoritative Status of NCGA Pronouncements and AICPA Industry Audit Guide*, in which it affirmed that:

> All NCGA Statements and Interpretations heretofore issued and currently in effect are considered as being encompassed within the conventions, rules, and procedures referred to as "generally accepted accounting principles," and are continued in force until altered, amended, supplemented, revoked, or superseded.

---

[1]The Government Finance Officers Association was the Municipal Finance Officers Association before changing its name in 1985.

[2]Both publications were issued by the National Committee on Governmental Accounting, one of the governmental accounting committees of the Municipal Finance Officers Association.

The GASB in 1985 integrated all effective accounting and reporting standards from these various sources into one publication called *Codification of Governmental Accounting and Financial Reporting Standards*. The *Codification* is revised annually. At this writing, the GASB has issued 32 statements of standards and five interpretations setting forth government accounting and reporting requirements. The GASB issues concepts statements, technical bulletins, and implementation guides as well.

GAAP Hierarchy for State and Local Government Entities

During the first five years of GASB's existence, a discussion arose about the jurisdiction of GASB and FASB over government-owned "special entities" such as hospitals, colleges and universities, and public utilities. In 1990 the Financial Accounting Foundation approved distribution of an agreement for a GAAP hierarchy for state and local governmental units, including special entities. That agreement, modified slightly in 1991 by *Statement on Auditing Standards No. 69*, lists the following categories, in descending order, as GAAP guidelines for state and local governments:[3]

1 *GASB Statements and GASB Interpretations.* This category also includes FASB pronouncements made applicable to state and local governments by a GASB Statement or Interpretation.
2 *GASB Technical Bulletins.* This category also includes AICPA Industry Audit and Accounting Guides and Statements of Position if specifically made applicable to state and local governments by the AICPA and cleared by the GASB.
3 *Consensus positions* of GASB Emerging Issues Task Force and AICPA Practice Bulletins if specifically made applicable to state and local governments by the AICPA and cleared by the GASB. [No GASB EITF exists currently.]
4 *Implementation Guides* published by the GASB staff and *industry practices* that are widely recognized and prevalent in state and local government.
5 *Other accounting literature* [including FASB standards not made applicable to governments by a GASB standard].

The Environment of Governmental Accounting

General government activities involve providing goods and services to citizens on the basis of need, without regard to their ability to pay. The goods and services to be provided, and the level to be provided, are determined by the citizens through their elected officials or by mandate or persuasion from a higher level of government. General government activities are usually financed by taxes and by intergovernmental grants and subsidies, and there may be no relationship between the people receiving the services and those paying for them. Resource allocation involves establishing fixed dollar budgets and restricting the use of resources to various general governmental projects and programs. For example, taxes may be levied to finance a specific program, the state government may provide monies to finance a specific service at the local level, or borrowed resources may be restricted to a specific project. The existence of restrictions on resources is the primary reason for fund accounting, which is a major feature of governmental accounting. **Fund accounting** is the use of multiple accounting entities (funds or account groups) to account for resources segregated according to purpose.

Most general purpose units of government engage in business-type activities in addition to general government activities. In these activities the government typically provides services to users for a fee that is intended to recover all, or at least the primary portion, of the costs of providing the service. Some of these activities involve providing services to the constituency—e.g., water and sewer services, electric service, golf courses, public docks and wharves, and transit systems. Others involve providing services to departments or agencies within the government—e.g., central motor pools, self-insurance activities, and central printing and data processing services. Because of these two different models of financing and providing services, governments are said to have a "dual nature."

---

[3]Statement on Auditing Standards No. 69, "The Meaning of *Present Fairly in Conformity with Generally Accepted Accounting Principles* in the Independent Auditor's Report," Auditing Standards Board.

OVERVIEW OF BASIC GOVERNMENTAL ACCOUNTING MODELS AND PRINCIPLES

Because of the pervasive practice of controlling government operations in part by restricting use of financial resources to specific purposes and because of the differing bases for allocating financial resources to specific uses in general government activities and business-type activities, governments are accounted for under a system that requires multiple accounting entities for a single government. These accounting entities are referred to as funds. Each fund is used to account for and report on a certain business-type activity of a government or a certain subset of its general government financial resources that are to be used for a certain purpose or purposes. Indeed, not only are funds separate accounting entities, but there is a different accounting model used for business-type activity funds than that needed for general government activity funds. Thus, just as governments have a dual nature, they have "dual accounting models."

Fund Definition and Categories

GASB defines a fund as:

> . . . a fiscal and accounting entity with a self-balancing set of accounts recording cash and other financial resources [and, if proprietary or trust funds, non-financial resources], together with all related liabilities and residual equities or balances, and changes therein, which are segregated for the purpose of carrying on specific activities or attaining certain objectives in accordance with special regulations, restrictions, or limitations.[4]

Note that because a fund is an accounting entity, each fund has:

- Its own accounting equation
- Its own journals, ledgers, and other accounting records needed to account for the effects of transactions on the net assets/activities accounted for in the fund
- Financial statements that report on the fund itself.

Business-type activities are accounted for in a category of funds called **proprietary funds**. **General government activities** are accounted for in **governmental funds**. There are two types of proprietary funds and four types of governmental funds. However, just as a person who knows how to account for and report one type of business can account for and report other types of businesses—with the exception of transactions or events unique to the other businesses—one who knows how to account for one type of proprietary fund knows most of what is needed to account for all other proprietary funds. Likewise, one who can account for one type of governmental fund knows most of what is needed to account for all governmental funds.

A third category of funds is the fiduciary or trust and agency funds. Most funds in this category are accounted for either like proprietary funds or like governmental funds. Hence, learning how to account for the other two fund categories enables one to account for most fiduciary funds as well. Therefore, we will focus on accounting for governmental funds and proprietary funds as we begin to discuss the models.

The Proprietary Fund Accounting Model

The most effective way to understand the nature and working of funds is to understand the basic accounting model—including the accounting equation and financial statements. Proprietary funds are explained first because accounting for a proprietary fund is very similar to accounting for a business. Indeed, the GASB requires governments to apply a substantial portion of the FASB's standards to proprietary funds.

The accounting equation for a proprietary fund is the same as that for a business:

$$\begin{array}{c}\text{Current}\\\text{Assets}\end{array} + \begin{array}{c}\text{Noncurrent}\\\text{Assets}\end{array} - \begin{array}{c}\text{Current}\\\text{Liabilities}\end{array} - \begin{array}{c}\text{Long-Term}\\\text{Liabilities}\end{array} = \begin{array}{c}\text{Contributed}\\\text{Capital}\end{array} + \begin{array}{c}\text{Retained}\\\text{Earnings}\end{array}$$

---

[4]*GASB Cod. Sec. 1100.102.*

Because the same accounting equation is used, most transactions and events also are accounted for and reported in identical or similar ways. The following are among the transactions typically accounted for the same by proprietary activities of a government and similar businesses:

- Sales and service revenues
- Purchase and use of inventory
- Uncollectible accounts and bad debts expense
- Purchases of fixed assets, supplies, or materials
- Depreciation of fixed assets
- Supplies, utilities, and salary expenses
- Capital leases
- Debt issuance, interest, and debt retirement

Proprietary funds report revenues and expenses using the accrual basis of accounting. The required proprietary fund financial statements are:

- Balance sheet
- Statement of revenues, expenses, and changes in retained earnings (or fund equity)
- Statement of cash flows

The first two statements are essentially the same as their business financial statement counterparts—except for (a) some different measurement rules for specific assets, liabilities, revenues, and expenses such as pensions, and (b) the effects of certain types of government transactions that businesses typically do not have. The statement of cash flows is not unlike the business cash flow statement, but the GASB does define cash somewhat differently than the FASB and requires a different classification of cash flows.

The essence of the discussion about proprietary funds is that one's business accounting background is directly applicable to proprietary fund accounting for most transactions and purposes. The transactions and events that are unique to governments or that are accounted for differently than for a business enterprise will be the focus of much of our discussion of proprietary funds.

The General Government Accounting Model

Accounting for general government activities (e.g., public safety, general administration, and the judicial system) requires two types of accounting entities. These accounting entities are the governmental funds and the account groups. Governments use four types of governmental funds (these four types are discussed later) and two account groups.

Governmental Funds Governmental funds, in their purest and simplest form, are essentially *working capital* entities. The accounting equation for a governmental fund is:

$$\frac{\text{Current}}{\text{Assets}} - \frac{\text{Current}}{\text{Liabilities}} = \frac{\text{Fund}}{\text{Balance}}$$

Although this equation becomes complicated by practical considerations, it is important to continue to think of governmental funds as working capital entities even as you address more advanced issues.

The required financial statements for a governmental fund are:

- Balance sheet
- Statement of revenues, expenditures, and changes in fund balance (GAAP basis of accounting)
- Statement of revenues, expenditures, and changes in fund balance—budget and actual (budgetary basis of accounting)

The simplest way to understand the fundamental nature and content of the first two statements is to relate them to the accounting equation. A balance sheet is in essence a detailed presentation of the accounting equation. Thus, a governmental-fund balance sheet lists accounts and amounts for cash, receivables, inventories, investments, accounts payable, salaries payable, short-term notes payable, etc., rather than just current assets and current liabilities.

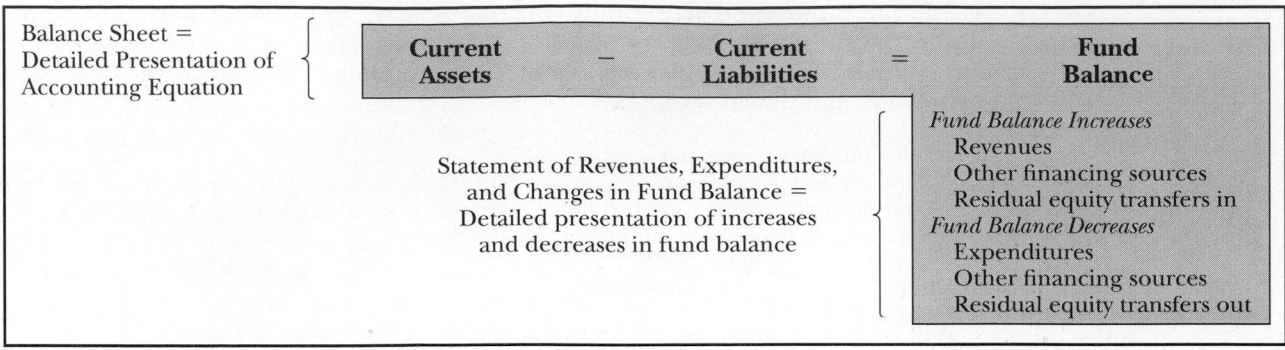

Exhibit 19–1   Governmental Fund Financial Statements

Likewise, the fundamental nature of the statement of revenues, expenditures, and changes in fund balance can be understood in relation to the accounting equation as illustrated in Exhibit 19–1. Do not make the mistake of viewing this statement as a variation of an income statement or statement of revenues, expenses, and changes in retained earnings. The statement of revenues, expenditures, and changes in fund balance simply reports increases and decreases in fund balance (which essentially means increases and decreases in working capital). This makes the statement more similar to a statement of cash flows than to an income statement. No equivalent of an income statement is presented for governmental funds.

The increases in fund balance in a statement of revenues, expenditures, and changes in fund balance are classified into three categories and the decreases are classified into three categories. These categories will be discussed more thoroughly later, but as the exhibit indicates, increases are reported as either revenues, other financing sources, or residual equity transfers in. Decreases are classified as expenditures, other financing uses, or residual equity transfers out.

Account Groups   Obviously, the governmental funds are not adequate to account for all the assets and liabilities of general government activities. Fixed assets and long-term liabilities are excluded from the governmental fund equation. General government activities, however, require significant investments in fixed assets, and governments commonly incur large debt obligations associated with general government operations. General government fixed assets (i.e., all fixed assets except those of specific proprietary or similar fiduciary funds) are referred to as "general fixed assets." These fixed assets are accounted for in a separate accounting entity called the General Fixed Assets Account Group (GFAAG). The GFAAG serves as an accountability listing of the fixed assets used in general government activities. Its accounting equation is:

$$\text{Fixed Assets} = \text{Investment in General Fixed Assets}$$

Note that just as fixed assets do not "fit" into the governmental fund accounting equation, depreciation of those fixed assets is not a change in working capital of any governmental fund and is not accounted for in them. Although governments are permitted to record accumulated depreciation in the GFAAG, few do so. Hence, the GFAAG typically is affected only when a government acquires a general fixed asset or disposes of an existing general fixed asset.

General government long-term liabilities (i.e., all government long-term liabilities except those of specific proprietary or similar fiduciary funds) are referred to as "general long-term debt." These long-term liabilities include bonds, notes, warrants, claims and judgments liabilities, unfunded pension obligations, et cetera. They are accounted for in a separate accounting entity called the General Long-Term Debt Account Group (GLTDAG). The GLTDAG serves as an accountability listing of the long-term liabilities incurred in general government activities. Its accounting equation is:

$$\begin{array}{c} \text{Amount to Be Provided} \\ \text{in Future Years to Retire} \\ \text{General Long-Term} \\ \text{Debt Principal} \end{array} + \begin{array}{c} \text{Amount Available in} \\ \text{Debt Service Funds to} \\ \text{Retire General Long-} \\ \text{Term Debt Principal} \end{array} = \text{Long-Term Liabilities}$$

Applying the Models—Transaction Analysis

To solidify your understanding of the proprietary (or business-type activity) accounting model and the general government accounting model, consider the effects of several transactions on each of those models. Note that all the activities, assets, liabilities, equity, revenues, expenses, and other changes of a particular business-type activity are accounted for in a single accounting entity—the appropriate proprietary fund. A general government activity may require several types of governmental funds as well as the two account groups in order to account for all the associated assets, liabilities, fund balance and changes therein. The various types of governmental funds are discussed later. In this section we do not identify the particular fund affected. The purpose is to explain and illustrate the governmental fund model. The accounting and reporting for the same transaction is the same in every governmental fund, regardless of the specific type of governmental fund.

Some proprietary activity transactions have essentially the same impact on a proprietary fund that the same transaction of a general government activity has on a governmental fund. This is true for most transactions that affect only working capital accounts. Consider the analysis of the following four transactions as reflected in Exhibit 19–2.

Transactions:

1 Incurred salary cost of $1,000.
2 Charges for services rendered, $500, were billed and collected immediately.
3 Borrowed $3,000 on a 1-year, 6% note six months before year-end.
4 Year-end accrual of interest on the note.

Note that the analysis is identical except that increases and decreases in proprietary fund net assets affect retained earnings and increases and decreases in governmental fund net assets affect fund balance. Likewise, the amounts reported in the operating statements of the funds—the statement of revenues, expenses, and changes in retained earnings for the proprietary fund and the statement of revenues, expenditures, and changes in fund balance for the governmental fund—are similar. Transaction 1 would be reported as expenses of $1,000 in a proprietary fund and as expenditures of $1,000 in a governmental fund. Transaction 2 should be reported as revenues of $500 in each case. Transaction 3 does not affect the operating statement of either a proprietary fund or a governmental fund. Transaction 4 should be reported as interest expense of $90 in a proprietary fund and as $90 of interest expenditures in a governmental fund.

In many other cases, identical transactions have different impacts on a proprietary fund accounting entity than on the general government accounting entities—i.e., the governmental funds and account groups. This is particularly true for transactions that relate to long-term liabilities or fixed assets. The full effect of such

Business-Type Activity					General Government Activity				
Proprietary Fund	*No. 1*	*No. 2*	*No. 3*	*No. 4*	*Governmental Fund*	*No. 1*	*No. 2*	*No. 3*	*No. 4*
Current Assets		+500	+3,000		Current Assets			+500	+3,000
Noncurrent Assets					Current Liabilities	+1,000		+3,000	+90
Current Liabilities	+1,000		+3,000	+90	Fund Balance	−1,000	+500		−90
Long-Term Liabilities					General Long-Term Debt Account Group is not affected by any of these transactions.				
Contributed Capital					General Fixed Assets Account Group is not affected by any of these transactions.				
Retained Earnings	−1,000	+500		−90					

Exhibit 19–2 *Transaction Analysis—Only Working Capital Accounts Affected*

transactions of business-type activities are accounted for completely within a proprietary fund. The same transaction of a general government activity typically requires entries in both the governmental funds and in one of the account groups. Consider the analysis of the following four transactions in Exhibit 19–3.

5 Borrowed $5,000 by issuing a three-year note.
6 Purchased computer equipment costing $800 for cash.
7 Sold a truck for $1,000. It was originally purchased three years ago for $9,000, had an estimated residual value of $1,200, and is fully depreciated.
8 Computed depreciation on the computer equipment for the year, $250.

Notice the dramatic difference in the accounting and reporting of these transactions under the two models. Transactions 5 and 6 do not affect a proprietary fund's net assets or equity and are not reported in the statement of revenues, expenses, and changes in retained earnings. However, both of these transactions do affect working capital. Therefore, the fund balance of a governmental fund is affected by both transactions, and both transactions are reflected in the statement of revenues, expenditures, and changes in fund balance for a governmental fund. Transaction 5 increases fund balance. Fund balance increases resulting from issuance of general long-term debt are reported as other financing sources in governmental funds. This transaction would be reported as "long-term note proceeds, $5,000" in the statement of revenues, expenditures, and changes in fund balance. Transaction 6 is reported as expenditures for capital outlay, $800, in a governmental fund statement of revenues, expenditures, and changes in fund balance.

Transaction 7 affects the proprietary fund retained earnings and the governmental fund fund balance, but in very different ways. A proprietary fund would report a $200

Proprietary Activity					General Government Activity				
Proprietary Fund	*No. 5*	*No. 6*	*No. 7*	*No. 8*	*Governmental Fund*	*No. 5*	*No. 6*	*No. 7*	*No. 8*
Current Assets	+5,000	−800	+1,000		Current Assets	+5,000	−800	+1,000	
Noncurrent Assets		+800	−1,200 (Book value)	−250	Current Liabilities				
Current Liabilities					Fund Balance	+5,000	−800	+1,000	
Long-Term Liabilities	+5,000				*General Fixed Assets Account Group*				
Contributed Capital									
Retained Earnings			−200	−250	Fixed Assets		+800	−9,000	
					Investment in GFA		+800	−9,000	
					General Long-Term Debt Account Group				
					Amount to Be Provided in Future Years	+5,000			
					Amount Available in Debt Service Funds				
					Long-Term Liabilities	+5,000			

Exhibit 19–3   *Transaction Analysis—Non-Working-Capital Accounts Affected*

loss on disposal of fixed assets for transaction 7 whereas a governmental fund would report the $1,000 of "proceeds from the sale of fixed assets" as an other financing source.

Transaction 8 requires $250 of depreciation expense to be reported in the proprietary fund operating statement. However, if the computers are general fixed assets, no depreciation expense is reported in the governmental fund because depreciation is not a use of working capital and the fixed asset is not an asset of the fund. Likewise, governments typically choose not to reflect accumulated depreciation in the GFAAG.

After mastering the transaction analysis for a generic proprietary fund and that for a generic governmental fund and the account groups, three primary elements remain to establish a good understanding of the basic governmental accounting model. The first is to know and distinguish the specific types of funds. The second is to be able to identify and classify interfund transactions, which are simply transactions between two funds. The third is to understand the basis of accounting used for each type of fund.

Proprietary Fund Types

Governments account for their business-type activities in one of two types of proprietary funds—enterprise funds and internal service funds. Some governments do not have enterprise or internal service funds; other governments have several of each type. The primary distinction between the two types of proprietary funds is that *internal service funds* are used to account for activities operated and financed on a business-type basis that provide goods or services either solely or almost solely to *internal customers*—i.e., other departments or agencies of the government. *Enterprise funds* are used to account for business-type activities through which a government serves primarily *outside customers*, typically the public. Enterprise fund activities often provide services to internal customers as well, but those customers are not the predominant customers.

Common examples of activities accounted for in internal service funds include centralized data processing services, central motor pools and garages, centralized risk financing activities, and central stores. Activities commonly accounted for in enterprise funds include public (government-owned) gas and electric utilities, water and sewer departments, government trash and garbage services, parking garages, civic centers, toll roads, mass transit services, and golf courses.

The formal definitions of the specific fund types are included in Exhibit 19–4. Note that part a of the *enterprise fund* definition requires an activity to be accounted for in an enterprise fund if all of the following are true:

- Provides goods or services
- To the public
- For a fee, and
- Fee revenue is intended to cover (primarily) the full cost (expenses, including depreciation) of providing the goods or services

Activities that do not meet the mandatory criterion may still be accounted for in enterprise funds under part b of the definition. Part b provides that any activity for which the governing body deems capital maintenance or net income information useful may be accounted for using an enterprise fund. Many civic centers and transit authorities are classified as enterprise funds under this option criterion.

Notice that the internal service fund definition requires that departments or agencies that provide goods or services to other departments or agencies on a cost-reimbursement basis are accounted for in these funds. Providing goods or services on a cost-reimbursement basis means for a fee intended to cover the costs (expenses) of providing the good or service. Hence, as noted earlier, the key distinction between the two types of proprietary funds is whether they primarily serve the public and/or external entities or they predominantly serve internal departments and agencies.

Governmental Fund Types

Four types of governmental funds, in addition to the account groups, are used to account for general government activities. Each governmental fund is a working capital entity. Each is used to account for only a portion of the general government working capital. *The difference between these funds, then, is the purpose or purposes for which the work-*

Governmental Fund Types

 1 The *general fund*—to account for all financial resources except those required to be accounted for in another fund.

 2 *Special revenue funds*—to account for the proceeds of specific revenue sources (other than expendable trusts or for major capital projects) that are legally restricted to expenditure for specified purposes.

 3 *Capital projects funds*—to account for financial resources to be used for the acquisition or construction of major capital facilities (other than those financed by proprietary funds and trust funds).

 4 *Debt service funds*—to account for the accumulation of resources for, and the payment of, general long-term debt principal and interest.

Proprietary Fund Types

 5 *Enterprise funds*—to account for operations (a) that are financed and operated in a manner similar to private business enterprises—where the intent of the governing body is that the costs (expenses, including depreciation) of providing goods or services to the general public on a continuing basis be financed or recovered primarily through user charges; or (b) where the governing body has decided that periodic determination of revenues earned, expenses incurred, and/or net income is appropriate for capital maintenance, public policy, management control, accountability, or other purposes.

 6 *Internal service funds*—to account for the financing of goods or services provided by one department or agency to other departments or agencies of the governmental unit, or to other governmental units, on a cost-reimbursement basis.

Fiduciary Fund Types

 7 *Trust and agency funds*—to account for assets held by a governmental unit in a trustee capacity or as an agent for individuals, private organizations, other governmental units, and/or other funds. These include (a) expendable trust funds, (b) nonexpendable trust funds, (c) pension trust funds, and (d) agency funds.

Exhibit 19–4   Fund Type Definitions

ing capital accounted for in each of them may or must be used. A *capital projects fund* is used to account for resources to be used to construct or acquire a major general government fixed asset and the related current liabilities. A *debt service fund* is used to account for resources to be used to pay principal, interest, and related charges on general long-term debt. *Special revenue funds* are used to account for general government financial resources restricted for other specific purposes. And, the *general fund* is used to account for working capital available for general use. A government has only one general fund. It may have any number of each of the other fund types. Recall that each of these governmental funds has the same accounting equation, financial statements, et cetera, discussed and illustrated above for a generic governmental fund. The only added complexity is that one must understand which governmental fund is affected in order to account for general government activities properly.

Fiduciary (Trust and Agency) Fund Types

As indicated in Exhibit 19–4, trust and agency funds include three types of trust funds as well as agency funds. Pension trust funds are used to account for government pension plans. Many local governments participate in state pension plans, which are reported by the state, and do not have pension trust funds. States and some local governments will have pension trust funds. The basic difference between expendable and nonexpendable trusts is that the corpus or principal of an expendable trust can be expended for some purpose(s). The corpus or principal of a nonexpendable trust cannot be expended.

Expendable trusts are accounted for in **expendable trust funds**. The primary accountability objective for an expendable trust fund is similar to that of governmental funds—to assure that the resources are expended only for the permitted purposes. Thus, Expendable Trust Funds are accounted for in a manner similar to governmental funds. Expendable trust funds have the same accounting equation and same types of financial statements as governmental funds.

Nonexpendable trust funds are accounted for like proprietary funds because of the need to demonstrate whether or not the principal of the fund has been maintained. They require use of the same accounting equation and presentation of the same basic financial statements as proprietary funds.

The accounting equation for *pension trust funds* is somewhat unique. Also, the financial statements presented for pension trust funds are different from those presented for other funds.

Agency funds are essentially "receive-hold-remit" or "bill-collect-hold-remit" accountability devices, though they are also used for other purposes. The accounting equation for an agency fund is:

$$\text{Assets} = \text{Liabilities}$$

Every asset received by an agency fund results in a corresponding increase in liabilities or decrease in another asset. Agency funds have no equity or fund balance and, therefore, have no operations to report. A Combining Statement of Agency Fund Assets and Liabilities is the basic agency fund financial statement. This statement simply presents the beginning and ending balances of each agency fund asset and liability account along with the gross increases and decreases in each of these accounts. No revenues, expenditures or expenses, or transfers are reported in an agency fund.

Applying the Model Using Specific Funds

A useful way to solidify your understanding of the funds and the model at this point is to test your understanding using transactions. The following general government transactions are analyzed in Exhibit 19–5.

1 Issued general obligation bonds, par value of $3,000, at 101 to finance construction of a government office building.
2 Transferred the premium on the bonds to the fund used to account for payment of principal and interest on the bonds.
3 Incurred and paid construction costs of $1,300 on the building.
4 Levied and collected sales taxes restricted to use for economic development, $600.
5 Paid general government employees salaries, $450. Another $35 of salaries accrued but have not been paid.
6 Borrowed $500 on a six-month note to finance general operating costs of the government.

Note that the transaction analysis is the same as for general government activities in the previous section on applying the model. All that is added is that we have named the specific governmental fund affected by each transaction.

		Governmental Fund			General Fixed Assets Account Group		General Long-Term Debt Account Group		
No.	Fund	Accounting Equation			Accounting Equation		Accounting Equation		
		CA	CL	FB	FA	Investment in GFA	Amount to Be Provided	Amount Available	Long-Term Liabilities
1	CPF	+3,030		+3,030			+3,000		+3,000
2a	CPF	−30		−30					
2b	DSF	+30		+30			−30	+30	
3	CPF	−1,300		−1,300	+1,300	+1,300			
4	SRF	+600		+600					
5	GF	−450	+35	−485					
6	GF	+500		+500					

Legend:
CA—Current assets; CL—Current liabilities; CPF—Capital projects fund; DSF—Debt service fund; FA—Fixed assets; FB—Fund balance; GF—General fund; SRF—Special revenue fund

Exhibit 19–5 *General Government Transaction Analysis Using Specific Funds*

Bases of Accounting

Another key aspect of the proprietary fund and governmental fund models is the basis of accounting used for each. Consistent with having fundamentally different accounting equations and models, governmental and proprietary funds use different bases of accounting. The GASB specifies the basis of accounting to be used for each type of fund:

> . . . The modified accrual or accrual basis of accounting, as appropriate, should be used in measuring financial position and operating results.
>
> *Governmental fund* revenues and expenditures should be recognized on the modified accrual basis. Revenues should be recognized in the accounting period in which they become available and measurable. Expenditures should be recognized in the accounting period in which the fund liability is incurred, if measurable, except for unmatured interest on general long-term debt which should be recognized when due.
>
> *Proprietary fund* revenues and expenses should be recognized on the accrual basis. Revenues should be recognized in the accounting period in which they are earned and become measurable; expenses should be recognized in the period incurred, if measurable.
>
> *Fiduciary fund* revenues and expenses or expenditures (as appropriate) should be recognized on the basis consistent with the fund's accounting measurement objective. Nonexpendable trust and pension trust funds should be accounted for on the accrual basis; expendable trust funds should be accounted for on the modified accrual basis. Agency fund assets and liabilities should be accounted for on the modified accrual basis.
>
> *Transfers* should be recognized in the accounting period in which the interfund receivable and payable arise. (GASB Cod. Sec. 1100.108)

In essence, the "accrual" basis refers to recognition of revenues and expenses of proprietary funds and similar (proprietary-type) trust funds as in business accounting. The "modified accrual" basis refers to recognition of revenues and expenditures using the "flows of financial resources" measurement focus of governmental funds and similar (governmental-type) trust funds.

Because proprietary and similar trust funds recognize revenues and expenses on much the same basis as businesses, the modified accrual basis of accounting used by governmental and expendable trust funds is emphasized in this discussion.

Governmental and Expendable Trust Funds—Revenues   The modified accrual basis of accounting is used for governmental and expendable trust funds. The modified accrual basis requires that revenues be measurable and "available" in order to be recognized. To be available, the revenues must be both

1 *collected* within the period or soon enough thereafter to pay liabilities incurred for expenditures of the period, *and*
2 *legally available* for expenditure in the period

Recognition of revenues that do not meet these "available" criteria must be *deferred* (recorded as "deferred revenues," a liability) initially. Then revenues are recognized when "available." (Thus, revenues may be recognized later in governmental funds than in proprietary funds.)

Revenues are legally available if the government's legal claim to the resources has been established by the end of the period and the resources were raised for the purpose of financing the budget of the current period or prior periods. A government's legal claim to revenues is established in different ways depending upon the nature of the revenues.

- For taxes assessed by a government, the tax levy establishes the government's claim to the resources. Taxes levied to finance a period's budget become legally available in that period.
- A government's claim to charges for services of general government departments is established by performing the service.
- Its claim to sales taxes is established by a business making a taxable sale.
- Its claim to income taxes results from taxpayers earning taxable income.

The "collected soon enough after year-end to pay liabilities for current expenditures" criteria is not defined in the GASB Codification. However, with respect to property tax revenue recognition the Codification limits this period to not more than 60 days after the end of the fiscal year. Most government accountants extend this "not more than 60 days" limitation to all other governmental fund revenues as well.

Recognize that modified accrual revenue recognition is not "cash-basis" revenue recognition. Governments often recognize revenue in one fiscal year that is collected during (not more than) the first 60 days of the subsequent fiscal year. Likewise, governments that collect revenues in one fiscal year that are not legally available for use until the next fiscal year cannot recognize those revenues in the year they are collected because the "legal availability" criterion is not met.

An exception to the 60-day rule was established by the GASB in GASB Statement No. 31, "Accounting and Financial Reporting for Certain Investments and for External Investment Pools." This statement requires most investments to be reported at their fair value. Investment income of each fund of a government, therefore, is increased or decreased by the net change in the fair value of investments. Investments are not classified into categories as required for businesses; the change in fair value of investments required to be accounted for at fair value always affects investment income. Investment income can be reported as a single line item in the financial statements, with the effect of the change in fair value disclosed in the notes, or the detail may be presented in the financial statements as follows, for example:

Interest income	XXX
Net increase (decrease) in fair value of investments	YYY
Total investment income	ZZZ

Note that the change in fair value of investments that must be accounted for under that approach is recognized in investment income without regard to the 60-day rule.

A final point is that governmental fund revenues are recognized on the *net revenue* approach. Revenues are recognized *net* of allowances for uncollectible accounts rather than for the gross amounts earned or levied. Therefore, whereas a proprietary fund that levied charges on customers of $1,000 but expected $10 to prove uncollectible would report revenues of $1,000 and expenses of $10, a governmental fund in a similar scenario would report only the net realizable value, or $990, as revenues.

Governmental and Expendable Trust Funds—Expenditures   As noted above, governmental funds report expenditures, not expenses. With limited exceptions, governmental fund *expenditures are recognized in the period that the fund liability is incurred.* Expenses essentially reflect the cost of assets or services used by an entity. Expenditures, as used in government accounting, typically reflect the use of governmental fund working capital. Thus, expenditures normally reflect the cost of goods or services acquired during a period, whether or not consumed, and the maturing of general long-term debt principal.

Many operating expenses and expenditures occur simultaneously. For instance, the use of electricity results in an expense and an expenditure in the same amounts at the same point in time. The same is true for salaries and wages of government employees. In governmental funds, it is the expenditure, not the expense that is reported.

For other items, the timing of recognition of expense and expenditure differs dramatically. Purchase of a fixed asset that is to be used over a 10-year period results in a capital outlay expenditure in the year of acquisition and no additional expenditures in the next nine years. The cost of this fixed asset would be assigned to expense over the 10-year period of its use, however. Finally, retirement of general long-term debt principal is reported as expenditures. Debt principal retirement is not recognized as expenses at any point in time.

It is significant that expenditures are recognized in the period that a governmental fund liability is incurred, not in the period that the government as a whole incurs a liability. As a result, expenditures are recognized when the fire department buys water from the Water Enterprise Fund. A general fund liability is incurred (to the enterprise fund) as a result of this transaction; the government as a whole has not incurred a liability.

Likewise, the government as a whole sometimes incurs liabilities that do not result in fund liabilities being incurred at the same point in time. This may be true with general government claims and judgments, compensated absences, or pension contributions, for instance. In these cases, long-term liabilities that are reported in the GLTDAG have been incurred. Because these long-term liabilities are not fund liabilities, expenditures are not recorded until they become current liabilities and/or are paid.

The primary exception to recognizing expenditures when a governmental fund incurs a liability is that *interest and principal expenditures* on *general* long-term debt *usually* are *recorded "when due."* Indeed, these expenditures are never required to be reported before the legal due date, *but are permitted to be accrued if* (a) they are due *early* in the next year *and* (b) the financial *resources* for their payment have been *provided* in the current year.

Classification of Revenues, Expenses, and Expenditures   The GASB also discusses the classification of revenues, expenditures, and expenses, stating:

> Governmental fund revenues should be classified by fund and source. Expenditures should be classified by fund, function (or program), organization unit, activity, character, and principal classes of objects.
>
>   Proprietary fund revenues and expenses should be classified in essentially the same manner as those of similar business organizations, functions, or activities. (GASB Cod. Sec. 1100.110)

Revenues and expenses of proprietary funds are classified in the same manner as for similar business organizations, but the GASB describes rather precise classification requirements for the revenues and expenditures of governmental funds. **Governmental fund revenues** are increases in fund financial resources other than from interfund transfers and debt issue proceeds.

Sources of governmental fund revenues are taxes, licenses and permits, intergovernmental revenues, charges for services, fines and forfeits, and miscellaneous other sources. All the sources are reasonably self-explanatory except for intergovernmental revenue sources. **Intergovernmental revenues** include the following four sources of governmental financing:

> **Grants**—[contributions or gifts from other governmental units (for example, state grants for highways) to be used for specified purposes.] *Capital grants* are contributions or gifts restricted by the grantor for the acquisition or construction of fixed (capital) assets. *Operating grants* are contributions or gifts that are intended to finance operations or that may be used for either operations or capital outlays at the discretion of the grantee. (GASB Cod. Sec. G60.501, 509)
>
> **Shared revenue**—a revenue levied by one government but shared on a predetermined basis, often in proportion to the amount collected at the local level, with another government or class of government. (GASB Cod. Sec. G60.514.)
>
> **Entitlements**—the amount of payment to which a state or local government is entitled as determined by the federal or other government . . . pursuant to an allocation formula contained in applicable statutes. (GASB Cod. Sec. G60.504.)
>
> **Payments in lieu of taxes**—amounts paid by one governmental unit to another for revenues lost because governmental units cannot tax each other (for example, payments by a state university to a town in which it is located).

Accounting and Reporting for Certain Grants and Other Financial Assistance[5]
Pass-through grants are amounts received by a governmental unit (the recipient government) to transfer to or spend on behalf of a secondary recipient. Pass-through grants are recognized as revenues and expenses or expenditures in a governmental, proprietary, or trust fund. If the recipient government has *no* administrative or financial involvement in the program, the pass-through grant may be accounted for in an agency fund.

   On-behalf payments for fringe benefits and salaries are direct payments made by one entity (the paying entity) to a third-party recipient for the employees of another, legally separate entity (the employer entity). The employer entity should recognize revenue equal to the amount received (and receivable at year-end) by the third-party entity. Expenses or expenditures are recognized equal to revenues *unless* the employer is legally responsible for the payment, in which case the employer follows accounting standards for that type of transaction. For example, a state government (the paying entity) may make contributions to a pension plan (third-party recipient) for employees

---

[5] *GASB Statement No. 24.*

of public school districts (the employer entity) within the state. The public school district should recognize revenue equal to the amount received by the pension plan for the year. The school district will also recognize expenditures equal to the revenue for the period unless it is legally responsible for the payments. If it is legally responsible, the school district will recognize expenditures using pension accounting standards.

State governments account for distributions of food stamp benefits in the general fund or a special revenue fund. Revenues and expenditures are recognized at the same time—when the benefits are distributed.

Governmental fund expenditures are decreases in fund financial resources other than from interfund transfers (or from long-term debt retirements using refunding bond proceeds). The typical expenditure classifications for governmental funds that are required are summarized in Exhibit 19–6. At least the fund and function or program classifications are required for external financial reporting.

Interfund Transfers and General Long-Term Debt Proceeds

Other features of the government accounting models that must be understood are the treatment of the proceeds from issuing general long-term debt and accounting for and reporting interfund transactions. Because a government uses several funds to account for its activities, it is common for there to be transactions between funds. Such funds are called interfund transactions. Examples include sales of services from an enterprise or internal service fund department to other departments, shifts of general fund resources to capital projects funds to cover part of the cost of a capital project, and interfund loans. Interfund transactions are classified into several types. Each type of interfund transaction is reported differently in the financial statements, as discussed below.

Interfund Loans and Advances   **Interfund loans** are loans that are made by one fund to another and must be repaid. The receivable and payable resulting from an interfund loan appear in different funds, and they must be disclosed in a combined balance sheet. The interfund receivable and payable are not eliminated as such bal-

By Fund	**By Activity (Line of Work to Perform a Function)**[*]
Governmental Funds	Police Administration
General Fund (GF)	Traffic Control
Special Revenue Fund (SRF)	Street Cleaning
Capital Projects Fund (CPF)	
Debt Service Fund (DSF)	**By Organization Unit**[*]
Proprietary Funds	City Council
Enterprise Fund (EF)	Police Department
Internal Service Fund (ISF)	Fire Department
Fiduciary Funds	Planning Department
Trust Fund (TF)	Nondepartmental
Agency Fund (AF)	
	By Object of Expenditure
By Function (Broad Purposes)[*]	*Current Expenditures*
General Government	Personal Services
Public Safety	Supplies
Highways and Streets	Other Services and Charges
Sanitation	*Capital Outlays*
Health and Welfare	Land
Culture and Recreation	Buildings
Education	Improvements Other Than Buildings
	Machinery and Equipment
By Character Classification	Construction Work in Process
Current Expenditures	*Debt Service*
Capital Outlays	Principal
Debt Service	Interest
Intergovernmental	

[*]Indicates that examples rather than complete classifications are provided.

Exhibit 19–6   *Summary of Expenditure Classifications*

ances would be in the consolidated financial statements of a parent company and subsidiary.

Quasi-External Transactions   **Quasi-external transactions** are those that would be treated as revenues, expenditures, or expenses if they involved organizations external to the governmental unit. Payments in lieu of taxes from a proprietary fund to the general fund, or internal service fund billings to departments are examples of quasi-external transactions. These transactions *are accounted for as revenues, expenditures, or expenses of the funds involved* even though they are not revenues, expenditures, or expenses of the governmental unit.[6] Any receivable and payable balances will appear on the balance sheets of the respective funds and should be disclosed in a combined balance sheet.

Reimbursements   A reimbursement is necessary when an expenditure applicable to one fund is made by a different fund. The **reimbursement** interfund transaction is recorded as *an expenditure or expense (as appropriate) in the reimbursing fund and as a reduction of the expenditure or expense in the fund that is reimbursed.* This accounting assures that the revenue, expenditure, or expense appears only in the proper fund.

Interfund Transfers   Interfund transfers are classified as residual equity transfers and operating transfers. **Residual equity transfers** are nonrecurring and nonroutine transfers of equity between funds, such as an initial capital contribution from the general fund for organizing a proprietary fund or the transfer of a residual balance of a discontinued fund to the general fund or a debt service fund. All other interfund transfers are operating transfers. **Operating transfers** typically are legally authorized, recurring shifts of resources from one fund to another that do not represent revenues and expenditures or expenses to the funds involved. For example, resources accumulated by the general fund are transferred to the debt service fund, through which the money will be expended to service the debt.

Proceeds of General Long-Term Debt Issues   Proceeds of general long-term debt issues increase fund balance (and working capital) of a governmental fund. The cash received increases current assets of the governmental fund, but the liability is recorded in the general long-term debt account group, not in the fund. The fund balance increase should be reported as *bond issue proceeds*, or a similar title, and shown as *other financing sources* in the statement of revenues, expenditures, and changes in fund balance of the recipient fund.

THE ROLE OF THE BUDGET, BUDGETARY ACCOUNTING, AND BUDGETARY REPORTING

In addition to GAAP reporting models that differ from business accounting and financial reporting, the role and impact of the budget is dramatically more significant in governments. The supply and demand mechanism does not serve as an automatic allocation mechanism for general government resources as it does for business. The mechanism does not function effectively because there is not a direct, proportionate relationship between the resources provided to a government by an individual and the quantity, quality, and type of services received by that particular individual. In the absence of the supply and demand resource-allocation mechanism, governments use fixed dollar budgets as one key mechanism to allocate general government resources to various activities and purposes. Indeed, resource use typically must be authorized by laws or ordinances called appropriations.

The GASB recognizes the importance of the budget in one of the basic principles it sets forth, stating:

> An annual budget should be adopted by every governmental unit. The accounting system should provide the basis for appropriate budgetary control.
>
> Budgetary comparisons should be included in the appropriate financial statements and schedules for governmental funds for which an annual budget has been adopted. (GASB Cod. Sec. 1100.109)

---

[6]GASB Cod. Sec. 1800.103 and 1800.104.

Budgeting is considered especially important in general government accounting, and the budget document is often considered more significant than the financial reports. In addition, the accounting system is required to provide appropriate budgetary control either formally through the use of budgetary accounts (typical in the general fund, special revenue funds, and other governmental funds) or informally through the maintenance of separate budgetary records and comparisons. A comparison of actual and budgetary amounts is required to be included in the annual operating statements of all governmental funds for which an annual budget has been adopted.

Interim and Annual Financial Reports

The GASB's discussion of financial reporting covers the need for interim reports, the content of a comprehensive annual financial report, and the numerous requirements for external general purpose financial statements when they are issued separately from the corresponding annual report. The GASB's basic principle on financial reporting states, in part:

> Appropriate interim financial statements and reports of financial position, operating results, and other pertinent information should be prepared to facilitate management control of financial operations, legislative oversight, and, where necessary or desired, for external reporting purposes.
>
> A comprehensive annual financial report should be prepared and published, covering all funds and account groups of the primary government (including its blended component units) and providing an overview of all discretely presented component units of the reporting entity—including introductory section; appropriate combined, combining, and individual fund statements; notes to the financial statements; required supplementary information; schedules; narrative explanations; and statistical tables. . . .
>
> General purpose financial statements of the reporting entity may be issued separately from the comprehensive annual financial report. Such statements should include the basic financial statements and notes to the financial statements that are essential to the fair presentation of financial position and results of operations (and cash flows of those fund types and discretely presented component units that use proprietary fund accounting). (GASB Cod. Sec. 1100.112. a–c.)

GASB Statement No. 14, "The Financial Reporting Entity," explains that the financial reporting entity is made up of the primary government, organizations for which the primary government is financially accountable, and other organizations whose exclusion would cause the reporting entity's financial statements to be misleading or incomplete. Component units are legally separate organizations for which the elected officials of the primary government are financially accountable. Some component units are so closely related to the primary government that their financial data should be blended with that of the primary government. Most component units, however, are to be discretely presented in the financial statements. The general purpose financial statements are emphasized in Chapter 20.

BUDGETING

A **budget** is a plan of financial operation consisting of an estimate of proposed expenditures for a given period and the proposed means of financing them. Ordinarily, the preparation of a budget is the responsibility of the executive branch of government—the mayor, city manager, governor, and so on. Approval of a budget, however, is a legislative responsibility. A legislative body may approve a proposed budget as submitted by the chief executive, or it may amend the executive budget prior to approval. *When approved by the legislative body, the budget for expenditures becomes a spending ordinance that has the force of law. An approved revenue plan also has the force of law* because it provides the governmental unit with the power to levy taxes, to sell licenses, to charge for services, and so on, in the amount or at the rate approved.

Appropriations *are approved or authorized expenditures*, and they provide legislative control over the expenditure budget prepared by the executive branch. Such control may be in detail, as when the legislative body makes appropriations for each item included in the budget. The legislative body may, however, approve expenditures (make appropriations) by category (by department, for example), or in total. Line-item approval provides maximum control over the executive by the legislative branch because *any* change in the budget must be approved by the legislative body. If appropriations are made by department, however, the executive could allocate more resources to some items within a department (supplies, for example) and less to others (salaries, for example) without legislative approval of the change.

Appropriations may be restricted by allotments. **Allotments** are divisions of the appropriation authority by time period. In other words, the yearly appropriations may be allotted to months or quarters to prevent expenditure of the appropriation too early in the year. Further, allotments may be necessary for coordinating revenues collected with payments for expenditures (i.e., managing cash flows.)

A current budget is normally for a one-year period, and it includes the operating budget as well as the capital budget for the current period. A capital budget should not be confused with a capital program. A **capital budget** simply represents the current portion of a capital program, whereas a **capital program** represents a plan of capital expenditures to be incurred each year over a fixed period of years.

Budgetary Approaches

Traditionally, the budgets of local governmental units have been prepared on a line-item basis in order to provide maximum control over expenditures. Although this approach does achieve its control objective in the sense of helping to avoid overspending of amounts appropriated, many believe it is not a good approach for planning and evaluation. The fact that actual expenditures are in legal compliance with amounts appropriated does not provide assurance that expenditures are effective in meeting the needs of citizens or that resources are used efficiently in obtaining goods and services needed to carry out governmental programs.

Program and performance budgeting are alternative budgeting approaches that have been developed to improve the planning and evaluation functions of governmental budgets. A **program budget** organizes the proposed expenditure budget in terms of total cost of programs to be carried out or functions to be performed. Under this approach, the budget is organized into programs for public safety, health and welfare, recreation, ecology, public works, and so on (and the total cost of each program); rather than in terms of an object of expenditure classification including salaries, utilities, supplies, fringe benefits, insurance, automobiles, gasoline, repairs, and so on. The program approach permits the ranking of programs and the scaling of costs so that available resources are directed toward essential and high-priority programs before funds are appropriated for other programs. Proponents consider program budgeting a superior planning approach that can improve the *effectiveness* with which limited resources are allocated to fulfill the needs of citizens.

A **performance budget** is one that emphasizes measurable performance of work programs and activities so that input costs can be compared with output benefits. Performance budgeting is primarily an evaluation approach, and it frequently involves cost accounting calculations such as the cost per mile of streets resurfaced, per ton mile of garbage hauled, per credit hour of instruction, and so on. Such information can be helpful in determining how *efficiently* resources are being used in providing public goods and services to citizens.

Another budgeting approach is **zero-base budgeting**. Under this approach, all appropriations are to be made without direct reference to prior years' programs or expenditures (that is, from zero base). The intent is to prevent appropriations for ineffective programs that might otherwise be approved year after year. Like the program approach, zero-base budgeting is primarily a tool for planning rather than for control or evaluation.

THE GENERAL FUND AND SPECIAL REVENUE FUNDS

The *general fund (GF)* is the entity used to account for all unrestricted resources except those required to be accounted for in another fund. In more descriptive terms, the GF is the entity that is used to account for the general operations of government, including the revenue received and the expenditures made in providing public goods and services to citizens. If a general purpose government has only one fund accounting entity, that fund is a general fund.

A *special revenue fund (SRF)* is the entity used to account for the proceeds of specific revenue sources (other than expendable trusts or for major capital projects or debt service on general long-term debt) that are restricted by law or administrative action to expenditures for specified purposes. A government has only one general fund. It can have many special revenue funds, or none at all. If specific revenue sources are earmarked for education, a special revenue education fund should be utilized to account for the earmarked resources. Similarly, if a city receives state or federal funds specifically designated to be used for highway construction or maintenance, a SRF should be created to account for such fund resources.

Earmarked revenues are accounted for in separate special revenue funds to show compliance with legal or administrative requirements. Outside of this need to separate earmarked revenue sources, there is no essential difference between a SRF and a GF. Indeed, if a special revenue fund is not legally or contractually required, governments have the option of accounting for a special revenue source in the general fund. Both types of funds are governmental funds, use the modified accrual basis, and typically integrate their budgets into their accounting systems. Because the accounting requirements for special revenue funds are the same as for a general fund, only general fund accounting procedures are illustrated.

ACCOUNTING FOR THE GENERAL FUND

The after-closing trial balance of the Town of Blair General Fund at June 30, 20X1 shows the following ledger account balances:

Debits	
Cash	$31,000
Taxes receivable—delinquent	15,000
Accounts receivable	3,000
Supplies inventory	6,000
Total debits	$55,000

Credits	
Allowances for uncollectible taxes—delinquent	$ 1,000
Vouchers payable	14,000
Note payable (short-term)	15,000
Reserve for encumbrances	9,000
Unreserved fund balance	16,000
Total credits	$55,000

Events for the year July 1, 20X1 to June 30, 20X2 of the Town of Blair include recording an approved budget, accounting for revenues from various sources, accounting for expenditures with encumbrance controls, preparing year-end adjusting and closing entries, and finally, preparing the general fund financial statements.

Revenues

Under the modified accrual basis of accounting, *revenues are recognized in the period in which they become susceptible to accrual.* Susceptible to accrual means the taxes must be measurable and available to finance expenditures of the period. Ordinarily, this means that revenues from property taxes are recognized when taxpayers are billed for the amount of taxes levied. If taxes are not collected by year-end or within 60 days thereafter, revenues are not recognized. A liability, deferred tax revenues, is recorded. Likewise, if taxes are collected in a period before they become legally available to finance expenditures, the amount received is recorded as deferred taxes (called taxes collected in advance in this case), and revenue is not recognized until the next period when it becomes available to cover expenditures.

Unlike levied taxes, where the governmental entity establishes the tax base, taxpayer-assessed taxes, such as sales and income taxes, require the taxpayer to determine the tax base. Taxpayer-assessed tax revenues, net of estimated refunds, are recognized when they become measurable and available.

Assuming they are to be collected within not more than 60 days after year-end, revenues from garbage collection and other city services are recognized when bills are rendered for services performed. But revenues from licenses, permits, fines, and the like cannot be measured objectively until cash is actually received. Therefore, revenues from these sources are usually recognized when cash is collected.

Collected sales taxes held by merchants at the end of the fiscal year should be accrued by the taxing authority if they will be remitted in time to pay liabilities of the current period. The same is true for taxes collected and held by one government agency at year-end for another.

Expenditures

Expenditures are decreases in the net financial resources of a governmental fund, as noted earlier. Under modified accrual accounting, *expenditures are normally recorded when the related fund liability is incurred.* This concept should not be confused with the expense concept, in which expenses are recognized when the related goods or services are used. Under modified accrual accounting, salaries, supplies, utilities, and fixed assets alike are recorded as expenditures when the related liabilities are incurred. In each of these cases, the net financial resources (assets minus liabilities) are reduced when the liabilities are incurred because the related resources are not recognized as assets of the general fund.

Encumbrances

Because expenditures, as measured on a government's budgetary basis, in a period are limited by law to those for which appropriations have been made, it is extremely important to keep expenditures within authorized levels. Approving expenditures without considering outstanding purchase orders or unperformed contracts could result in overspending appropriations. For example, assume that total appropriations for the year exceed actual expenditures to date by $4,000 and that an additional equipment purchase for $3,000 is approved. If $2,000 of supplies are on order, and expenditures are made for both the equipment and the supplies, actual expenditures for the period will exceed appropriations by $1,000. Encumbrance accounting helps prevent this type of situation. *Encumbrance* means *commitment*, and **encumbrance accounting** records commitments made for goods on order and for unperformed contracts. Encumbrance accounting provides additional control over expenditures. Encumbrances are not reported in the GAAP-basis operating statement.

If the full amount of an appropriation is not expended during the period covered by an appropriation, a question arises as to whether the unexpended portion can be carried over as authorization for expenditures in the succeeding year. Although laws of the governmental unit will cover this matter, a common position is that all appropriations lapse at the end of the year for which they are made, except that committed appropriations (that is, encumbrances outstanding) can continue to serve as authorizations for the items on order or under contract. Note that the after-closing trial balance for the Town of Blair includes a credit account "Reserve for Encumbrances" of $9,000. This fund balance account communicates the amount of committed appropriations that is carried over to serve as authorization for the actual expenditures as they occur in the succeeding year. One of the first entries to be made in the year beginning July 1, 20X1 is to reclassify this account to identify it as a carry-over from the prior year:

GF		
Reserve for encumbrances	$9,000	
Reserve for encumbrances—prior year		$9,000

Alternatively, the town could have re-established the encumbrances account and recorded appropriations of $9,000.

The Budget

The Town of Blair approved the following GF budget for the fiscal year July 1, 20X1 to June 30, 20X2.

TOWN OF BLAIR
GENERAL FUND BUDGET SUMMARY
FOR THE YEAR JULY 1, 20X1 TO JUNE 30, 20X2

Revenue Sources	
Taxes	$250,000
Licenses and permits	20,000
Intergovernmental revenue	40,000
Charges for services	60,000
Fines and forfeits	15,000
Rents and royalties	10,000
Miscellaneous revenues	5,000
Total budgeted revenues	400,000
Expenditures	
Current services	
General government	45,000
Public safety	140,000
Highways and streets	90,000
Sanitation	55,000
Health and welfare	20,000
Recreation	30,000
Capital outlays	15,000
Total appropriations	395,000
Budgeted increase in fund balance	$ 5,000

The revenue categories used in the budget are the revenue sources illustrated in the GASB Codification. Budgeted expenditures as itemized in the general fund budget summary are organized by character class (current services, capital outlays, and debt service) and by function within the current services category. Expenditures for each of the functions (for example, public safety) could be further divided into those applicable to specific departments or other organization units (such as police department and fire department). Expenditures in each of the organization units could also be presented in terms of the object of expenditure classification (personal services, supplies, and other services and charges). Exhibit 19–6 illustrated just some of the possibilities of expenditure classification.

Recording the Budget   On July 1, 20X1, the approved budget of Blair is recorded. The following general journal entry is made to record the budget in the accounts of the GF.

GF		
Estimated revenues	$400,000	
Appropriations		$395,000
Unreserved fund balance		5,000

To record the budget for the year July 1, 20X1 to June 30, 20X2.

The entry records total estimated revenues and total appropriations in the general ledger and credits the budgeted excess to the fund balance account. However, *detailed subsidiary revenue and expenditure ledgers* are used to record line-item revenue and expenditure amounts, even if the budget is approved in terms of the broad categories reflected in the budget summary. In the case of legislative approval by category, however, the city manager (or chief executive) would have authority to authorize shifts from one line-item expenditure to another within the broad categories approved. The broad categories are used for budgeting and reporting purposes but not for accounting purposes. In other words, there is no account called taxes or general government, but the accounting system is organized to permit aggregation of the detailed items into these categories.

Subsidiary Ledgers   Details of the planned revenues (such as property taxes, sales taxes, and license revenue) are recorded in a *subsidiary revenue ledger*, and appropriation details (such as police supplies, mayor's office expenses, and maintenance of city hall) are recorded in a *subsidiary expenditure ledger*. By recording estimated revenues for individual items as debits in the subsidiary revenue ledger and actual revenue items as credits, the subsidiary account balances during the year will reveal differences between actual and budgeted revenue for each item to date, as well as the final excess or deficiency at year-end. Similarly, by recording encumbrances and actual expenditures as debits and appropriations as credits, the account balances shown in the individual accounts of the subsidiary expenditure ledger represent unencumbered, unexpended appropriations for each expenditure item. These subsidiary ledger techniques provide the means of achieving *formal budgetary control* over the items included in the approved budget.

Reporting the Budget in Financial Statements   Compliance with the approved budget is required for the general fund and for special revenue funds. To demonstrate compliance with the budget, a *statement of revenues, expenditures, and changes in fund balance—budget and actual* must be prepared as one of the required financial statements of governmental funds. As its title implies, the statement compares budgeted and actual operating results and is presented using the budgetary basis of accounting, which often differs from GAAP. (Some governments adopt cash basis budgets, for instance.) This statement is illustrated for the Town of Blair at the end of this section of the chapter.

Transactions for the Year

Accounting for Property Taxes   When the treasurer of Blair sends out property tax bills of $200,000, revenue is recognized as follows:

GF

Taxes receivable—current	$200,000	
Allowance for uncollectible taxes—current		$ 2,000
Revenue		198,000
To record the property tax levy.		

This entry assumes that 1% of property tax levies will not be collectible and that the rest of the taxes will be collected either during the current year or within not more than 60 days thereafter. Therefore, revenue is recognized for 99% of the amount billed. Uncollectible taxes are not expenditures in governmental accounting; instead they are revenue adjustments as illustrated. Like accounts receivable, taxes receivable is a control account for individual amounts owed. The *current* designation for taxes receivable is used to distinguish current taxes receivable from taxes that are past due. Any balances remaining in the "taxes receivable—current" and "allowance for uncollectible taxes—current" accounts after the due date for payment are reclassified as "taxes receivable—delinquent" and "allowance for uncollectible taxes receivable—delinquent." Note that the after-closing trial balance for the Town of Blair's general fund at June 30, 20X1, includes a debit account, "taxes receivable—delinquent" of $15,000, and a credit account, "allowance for uncollectible taxes—delinquent," of $1,000.

Collections of current property taxes of $176,000 and past due taxes of $14,000 are recorded in the usual manner for receivables as follows:

GF

Cash	$190,000	
Taxes receivable—current		$176,000
Taxes receivable—delinquent		14,000
To record collection of property taxes.		

When a specific property tax bill ($1,000) is determined to be uncollectible, it is written off with the following entry:

GF

Allowance for uncollectible taxes—delinquent	$ 1,000	
Taxes receivable—delinquent		$ 1,000
To record write-off of uncollectible account.		

Charges for Service Revenue is recognized when bills for garbage collection ($60,200) are sent out. Assuming $200 is estimated to be uncollectible and the remainder is expected to be collected by year-end (or within 60 days thereafter), the entry is recorded:

GF		
Accounts receivable	$ 60,200	
Allowance for uncollectible accounts		$ 200
Revenue		60,000
To record charges for garbage collection.		

When customers pay their garbage bills ($58,000), the payment is entered as follows:

GF		
Cash	$ 58,000	
Accounts receivable		$ 58,000
To record collection of receivables for garbage collection service.		

Revenue from Other Sources Except for taxpayer-assessed tax revenues, revenue from most other sources is recognized as cash is received. Thus, the collection of fees ($20,000) from business licenses is recorded:

GF		
Cash	$ 20,000	
Revenue		$ 20,000
To record collection of business license fees.		

Other revenues for the 20X1–20X2 fiscal year are recognized as cash is received. The amount in the following entry includes all revenue items not listed individually:

GF		
Cash	$124,000	
Revenue		$124,000
To summarize other revenue items for the year.		

Although the general ledger ordinarily includes only one revenue account, it is important to remember that the detailed revenue sources have to be recorded individually in a *subsidiary revenue ledger*.

Recording Expenditures When the payroll for salaries ($20,000) is vouchered for payment, a GF entry is made as follows:

GF		
Expenditures	$ 20,000	
Vouchers payable		$ 20,000
To record accrual of salaries.		

Accounting for Encumbrances During the year, snow removal equipment expected to cost $15,000 is ordered. The following encumbrance entry is made at the time the purchase order is placed to recognize a commitment to pay for the equipment when it is received:

GF		
Encumbrances	$ 15,000	
Reserve for encumbrances		$ 15,000
To record a purchase order for $15,000 of snow-removal equipment.		

This information helps prevent overspending because encumbrances can be deducted from unexpended appropriations to determine unencumbered appropriations (that is, maximum additional authorizations):

Appropriations (authorized expenditures)	$ X
Less: Expenditures to date	Y
Unexpended appropriations	X−Y
Less: Encumbrances	Z
Unencumbered appropriations	$X−Y−Z

The remaining expenditure authority is reflected by the amount of unencumbered appropriations. When the snow removal equipment is received, the entry recording the encumbrance is reversed:

GF

Reserve for encumbrances	$15,000	
Encumbrances		$ 15,000

    To reverse the encumbrance entry for snow-removal
      equipment.

The entry to record the receipt of the equipment is unaffected by the encumbrance entries and is recorded for the actual amount of the invoice. Assuming that the actual cost of the equipment purchased is $14,000, the expenditure is recorded:

GF

Expenditures	$14,000	
Vouchers payable		$ 14,000

    To record the purchase of snow-removal equipment.

Note that the amount of the encumbrance was an estimate of the actual cost, which was $1,000 less than the estimate. Like formal budgetary accounting, encumbrance accounting does not affect the recording of actual transactions and events.

As noted in the transaction analysis illustrating application of the general government accounting model earlier in the chapter, the acquisition of fixed assets (such as the snow-removal equipment) decreases net assets (working capital) of the fund because fixed assets are not recorded as assets in the GF. Instead, they are recorded in the general fixed assets account group as explained further in Chapter 20.

In July 20X1, Blair received the equipment that had been ordered in the previous fiscal year, and for which an encumbrance of $9,000 had been recorded. Recall that one of the first entries of the current year was to reclassify the reserve for encumbrances as reserve for encumbrances—prior year to show the authorization for items related to and chargeable against the prior year's appropriations. If the actual invoice is $8,500, the entry to record receipt of the equipment is:

GF

Expenditures—prior year	$ 8,500	
Vouchers payable		$ 8,500

    To record receipt of equipment ordered during the
      prior year and chargeable against the prior year's
      reserve for encumbrances.

If the actual invoice had been more than the encumbered amount carried over from the prior year, the difference would have been charged to the current year's expenditures.

Supplies Supply acquisitions accounted for under a periodic inventory system are recorded as expenditures when the related liability is incurred. The expenditure is adjusted at year-end for the change in inventory during the year. Thus, expenditures are reported for the cost of supplies or materials used or consumed during the year. (This consumption method approach is optional now, but the GASB has indicated that it will be required in the future.) Under this method, the sequence of acquiring supplies is recorded:

GF

Encumbrances	$ 6,000	
Reserve for encumbrances		$ 6,000

    To record the purchase order for operating supplies.

GF

Reserve for encumbrances	$ 6,000	
Encumbrances		$ 6,000

    To reverse the encumbrance entry upon receipt of the
      supplies.

GF

Expenditures	$ 6,000	
Vouchers payable		$ 6,000

    To record receipt of operating supplies.

Under the purchase method, this entry decreases the net assets of the general fund because supply purchases are recorded as expenditures rather than assets. (Accounting for supplies on hand requires a year-end adjusting entry that is explained shortly.)

When an additional $5,000 of supplies is ordered, the entry is:

GF		
Encumbrances	$ 5,000	
Reserve for encumbrances		$ 5,000
To record encumbrances for a purchase order for supplies.		

These supplies have not been received at year-end, June 30, 20X2.

Other Transactions for the Year   The note payable that was outstanding at June 30, 20X1 becomes due and is paid:

GF		
Note payable	$ 15,000	
Cash		$ 15,000

A summary entry for the remainder of the various expenditures throughout the year is as follows:

GF		
Expenditures	$348,040	
Vouchers payable		$348,040
Summary entry for accrual of salaries, purchase of supplies and fixed assets, and so on.		

GF		
Vouchers payable	$388,000	
Cash		$388,000
To record payment of all vouchers for the year in summary form.		

Year-end Procedures

Adjusting Entries   Recall that the entry to purchase supplies was recorded as expenditures rather than assets. If supplies that cost $9,000 are on hand at the balance sheet date and the consumption method is used, however, the $6,000 beginning-of-the-period supplies on hand account would be adjusted by $3,000 at year-end; in other words, to a final balance of $9,000, and expenditures would be reduced. (The reserve for inventory, not expenditures, is adjusted under the purchases method.)

GF		
Supplies inventory	$ 3,000	
Expenditures		$ 3,000
To adjust the supplies inventory and supplies expenditures accounts.		

Assume that uncollected taxes on June 30, 20X2 are past due. Accordingly, the $24,000 taxes receivable—current and $2,000 allowance for uncollectible taxes—current are reclassified as delinquent. The entry for this reclassification is:

GF		
Taxes receivable—delinquent	$ 24,000	
Allowance for uncollectible taxes—current	2,000	
Taxes receivable—current		$ 24,000
Allowance for uncollectible taxes—delinquent		2,000
To reclassify past-due taxes receivable as delinquent.		

Blair's adjusted general fund trial balance at June 30, 20X2 includes the following accounts and balances:

Debits

Cash	$ 20,000
Taxes receivable—delinquent	24,000
Accounts receivable	5,200
Supplies inventory	9,000
Estimated revenues	400,000
Expenditures	378,500
Expenditures—prior year	8,500
Encumbrances	5,000
Total debits	$850,200

Credits

Allowance for uncollectible taxes—delinquent	$ 2,000
Allowance for uncollectible accounts	200
Vouchers payable	16,000
Reserve for encumbrances—prior year	9,000
Reserve for encumbrances	5,000
Unreserved fund balance	21,000
Appropriations	395,000
Revenues	402,000
Total credits	$850,200

Closing Entries   By year-end, the budgetary accounts will have served their purpose and must be closed. The most direct method of closing budgetary accounts is to reverse the original entry to record the budget. At June 30, 20X2 the accounts for Blair could be closed as follows:

GF

Appropriations	$395,000	
Unreserved fund balance	5,000	
Estimated revenues		$400,000
To close the budgetary accounts.		

This closing approach emphasizes the fact that formal budgetary accounting does not affect actual revenues, expenditures, or any balance sheet account. When this entry is made to close the appropriations and estimated revenue accounts, the unreserved fund balance account is returned to its $16,000 beginning-of-the-year balance.

Actual revenues and expenditures are closed directly to the unreserved fund balance account. Under the assumption that committed appropriations can be carried over to the succeeding fiscal period to serve as authorization for items on order, any outstanding encumbrances at year-end would also be closed to the unreserved fund balance account. The adjusted trial balance shows that Blair had revenue of $402,000, expenditures of $378,500 for the current year, and encumbrances outstanding at June 30, 20X2 of $5,000. The entry to close these accounts is:

GF

Revenues	$402,000	
Expenditures		$378,500
Encumbrances		5,000
Unreserved fund balance		18,500
To close revenue, expenditures, and encumbrances accounts.		

This entry relates to current-year budgeted revenues and appropriations. Actual revenues exceeded expenditures against current year appropriations by $23,500, of which $5,000 is committed for supplies ordered but not yet received. The $5,000 reserve for encumbrances account (that is, the credit related to the $5,000 closed out) is not closed at year-end, but rather is reflected in the fund balance section of the balance sheet. The uncommitted and unappropriated amount is credited to unreserved fund balance. The $8,500 expenditure from the prior year's appropriations is charged against the prior year's reserve for encumbrances account.

GF		
Reserve for encumbrances—prior year	$ 9,000	
Expenditures—prior year		$ 8,500
Unreserved fund balance		500

To close prior-year reserve for encumbrances and related expenditures and credit the fund balance for the excess.

Financial Statements

As noted in discussing the general government accounting model, the required general fund financial statements are a balance sheet, statement of revenues, expenditures, and changes in fund balance prepared on the modified accrual (GAAP) basis of accounting, and statement of revenues, expenditures, and changes in fund balance—budget and actual (prepared on the budgetary basis of accounting, which often differs from GAAP). The statements for the Town of Blair General Fund in our example are presented in Exhibits 19–7 to 19–9.

Note that the statement of revenues, expenditures, and changes in fund balance in Exhibit 19–8 is a very simple one. Each change in fund balance (working capital) for the general fund in this example was classified as revenues or expenditures. Exhibit 19–1 indicated that three categories of increases and three categories of decreases may be found in a statement of revenues, expenditures, and changes in fund balance. For simplicity, such items were not included in this example. The other categories are shown in Exhibit 19–8 (without amounts) to better illustrate the statement. The examples in the next chapter incorporate these other types of fund balance changes.

Note that the balance sheet in Exhibit 19–7 does not include fixed assets or long-term debt. This is consistent with the accounting model and makes governmental fund balance sheets relatively straightforward. Note that the total fund balance reported articulates with the ending fund balance reported in the statement of revenues, expenditures, and changes in fund balance, which explains changes in total fund balance.

Finally, the statement of revenues, expenditures, and changes in fund balance—budget and actual is presented in Exhibit 19–9. This statement typically includes the same classifications as the GAAP operating statement. Often, however, the amounts reported for revenues, expenditures, fund balance, et cetera differ between the two statements. These differences exist when a government uses a non-GAAP basis of accounting for budgeting purposes, as the Town of Blair does. The budget and actual comparison statement must be presented on the budgetary basis of accounting even if it differs from GAAP. The differences between the two statements must be reconciled on the face of the statements, as done here, or in the notes to the financial statements. The reconciliation can explain differences between GAAP-basis and budgetary-basis fund balance amounts or differences between the excess of revenues and other financing sources over expenditures and other financing uses reported in the two statements.

SUMMARY

Accounting principles for state and local governmental units have been developed through the efforts of the Government Finance Officers Association and its committees and, more recently, the Governmental Accounting Standards Board. The *GASB Codification of Governmental Accounting and Financial Reporting* provides GAAP for the financial statements of state and local governmental units. Twelve basic accounting principles from *NCGA1* and included in the *GASB Codification* establish the objectives and underlying support for accounting and reporting practices of state and local governments.

Accounting requirements for the general fund are the same as for special revenue funds, and the discussion of accounting procedures for the general fund applies equally to special revenue funds. The essential difference between a general fund and a special revenue fund lies in the fact that general fund revenues are available to fi-

TOWN OF BLAIR GENERAL FUND
BALANCE SHEET
AT JUNE 30, 20X2

Assets

Cash	$20,000	
Taxes receivable—delinquent (net of $2,000 estimated uncollectible taxes)	22,000	
Accounts receivable (net of $200 estimated uncollectible accounts)	5,000	
Supplies inventory	9,000	
Total assets		$56,000

Liabilities and Fund Balance

Vouchers payable		$16,000
Fund equity		
Reserve for encumbrances	$ 5,000	
Unreserved fund balance	35,000	
Total fund balance		40,000
Total liabilities and fund balance		$56,000

Exhibit 19–7   *General Fund Balance Sheet*

TOWN OF BLAIR GENERAL FUND
STATEMENT OF REVENUES, EXPENDITURES, AND
CHANGES IN FUND BALANCE
FOR THE FISCAL YEAR ENDED JUNE 30, 20X2

Revenues

Taxes	$255,000
Licenses and permits	18,000
Intergovernmental revenues	40,000
Charges for services	62,000
Fines and forfeits	12,000
Rents and royalties	11,000
Miscellaneous revenue	4,000
Total revenues	402,000

Expenditures

Current services	
General government	$ 41,500
Public safety	133,000
Highway and streets	86,300
Sanitation	54,700
Health and welfare	19,500
Recreation	29,500
Capital outlays	22,500
Total expenditures	387,000
Excess of revenues over expenditures	15,000

Other Financing Sources (Uses)

General long-term debt proceeds	—
Operating transfers in	—
Operating transfers out	—
Excess of revenues and other financing sources over expenditures and other financing uses	15,000
Fund balance at July 1, 20X1	25,000
Residual equity transfers in	—
Residual equity transfers out	—
Fund balance at June 30, 20X2	$ 40,000

Exhibit 19–8   *General Fund GAAP Basis Statement of Operations*

TOWN OF BLAIR GENERAL FUND
STATEMENT OF REVENUES, EXPENDITURES,
AND CHANGES IN FUND BALANCE
BUDGET AND ACTUAL (BUDGETARY BASIS)
FOR THE YEAR ENDED JUNE 30, 20X2

	Budget	Actual (Budgetary Basis)	Variance Favorable (Unfavorable)
Revenues			
Taxes	$250,000	$255,000	$ 5,000
Licenses and permits	20,000	18,000	(2,000)
Intergovernmental revenue	40,000	40,000	—
Charges for services	60,000	62,000	2,000
Fines and forfeits	15,000	12,000	(3,000)
Rents and royalties	10,000	11,000	1,000
Miscellaneous revenue	5,000	4,000	(1,000)
Total revenues	400,000	402,000	2,000
Expenditures and Encumbrances			
Current services			
General government	$ 45,000	$ 44,500	$ 500
Public safety	140,000	135,000	5,000
Highways and streets	90,000	86,300	3,700
Sanitation	55,000	54,700	300
Health and welfare	20,000	19,500	500
Recreation	30,000	29,500	500
Capital outlays	15,000	14,000	1,000
Total expenditures	395,000	383,500*	11,500
Excess of revenue over expenditures	5,000	18,500	13,500
Budgetary fund balance June 30, 20X1	16,000	16,000	—
Add: Excess prior year's encumbrance over actual expenditure	—	500	500
Budgetary fund balance at June 30, 20X2	$ 21,000	$ 35,000	$14,000
Encumbrances outstanding fund balance of June 30, 20X2		5,000	
GAAP fund balance at June 30, 20X2		$ 40,000	

*Actual expenditures on a budgetary basis includes the $5,000 supplies purchase commitment chargeable against the 20X2 appropriations, but excludes the $8,500 expenditure chargeable against the prior year's carryover appropriation.

Exhibit 19–9   *General Fund Budgetary Comparison Statement*

nance the general needs of government, whereas the revenues of special revenue funds are restricted to specific uses. General and special revenue activities normally are controlled with formal budgetary procedures and accounting practices. Compliance with the budget is demonstrated by presenting statements comparing actual and budgeted revenues and expenditures. The basic accounting cycle for a general fund from recording the budget at the beginning of the year to preparation of financial statements at year-end is illustrated.

SELECTED READINGS

Audits of State and Local Governmental Units, Audit and Accounting Guide. New York: American Institute of Certified Public Accountants, 1998.

BERRY, LEONARD EUGENE, and GORDON B. WARWOOD. *Governmental and Nonprofit Accounting: A Book of Readings.* Homewood, IL: Richard D. Irwin, 1984.

Governmental Accounting Standards Board. *Codification of Governmental Accounting and Financial Reporting Standards.* Norwalk, CT: Governmental Accounting Standards Board, 1998.

Governmental Accounting Standards Board. *Statement No. 31,* "Accounting and Financial Reporting for Certain Investments and for External Investment Pools." Norwalk, CT: Governmental Accounting Standards Board, 1997.

Governmental Accounting Standards Board. *Concepts Statement No. 2,* Service Efforts and Accomplishments Reporting." Norwalk, CT: Governmental Accounting Standards Board, 1994.

Government Finance Officers Association of the United States and Canada. *Governmental Accounting, Auditing, and Financial Reporting.* Chicago: Municipal Finance Officers Association of the United States and Canada, 1994.

National Council on Government Accounting. *Governmental Accounting and Financial Reporting Principles, Statement 1.* Chicago: Municipal Finance Officers Association of the United States and Canada, 1979.

ASSIGNMENT MATERIAL

QUESTIONS

1 What organization provides GAAP for state and local governmental units? Explain.

2 Describe the concept of a fund as used in connection with governmental accounting. How many funds might be used by a single governmental unit? How many fund types?

3 Distinguish between governmental funds, proprietary funds, and fiduciary funds. Which funds are classified as governmental funds?

4 List the four types of governmental funds. What is the primary distinction among them?

5 What is the accounting equation for a governmental fund? What are the required financial statements?

6 List the two types of proprietary funds. What distinguishes them from each other?

7 What is the accounting equation for a proprietary fund? What are the required financial statements?

8 Why aren't fixed assets recorded in the accounts of a general fund? Explain.

9 What is the modified accrual basis and to which fund types is it applicable?

10 Are interfund transfers expenditures? Expenses? Explain.

11 What is an appropriation? How can budgetary approval be arranged to give the legislative body maximum control over the budget? How can it be arranged to give the executive maximum flexibility?

12 Distinguish between the line-item, program, performance, and zero-base approaches to budgeting.

13 What is included in the revenue source designated "intergovernmental revenues"?

14 If revenue needed from property taxes to balance the budget is $200,000 and a 3 percent loss on uncollectible taxes is expected, at what amount should taxpayers be billed?

15 Assume that supplies on hand at the beginning of the year amount to $60,000, that supply purchases, which were recorded in expenditures during the year are $400,000, that supplies on hand at year-end are $40,000, and that the consumption basis of accounting for supplies is used. What adjusting entry for supplies should be made at year-end?

16 What are encumbrances and how do encumbrance accounting practices help control expenditures?

17 If a government has cash interest on general fund investments during the year of $65,000 and the fair value of its investments decreases by $1,000 during the year, what amount should it report as investment income in its general fund?

EXERCISES

E 19-1   1 A common objective of a governmental fund is:
  a The maintenance of capital of the fund
  b Profitable operations
  c The receipt of resources from designated sources and the use of resources for authorized purposes
  d The financing of police departments, fire departments, and road construction

2 The term *appropriation*, as used in governmental accounting, is:
  a A budget request   c An authorization to spend
  b A commitment   d An allotment

3 An example of a governmental expenditure that would not be an expense of a profit-oriented organization is:
  a Supplies used   c Interest
  b Accrued wages and salaries d Capital outlays

4 Which one of the following general ledger accounts of a city's general fund would normally have a credit balance?
  a Estimated revenues   c Appropriations
  b Encumbrances   d Expenditures

5 Which one of the following categories of interfund transactions is reported in the revenue and expenditure or expense classifications of a governmental unit?

   a Quasi-external transactions   **c** Operating transfers

   b Reimbursements   **d** Residual equity transfers

E 19-2   **1** Depreciation expense accounts would likely be found in the:

   a General fund   **c** Debt service fund

   b Capital projects fund   **d** Enterprise fund

2 A personal property tax levy is ordinarily:

   a Greater than budgeted revenue from property taxes

   b Equal to expected property tax receipts

   c Greater than personal property assessments

   d Equal to valuations of taxable personal property

3 When the *purchases basis* of accounting for supplies is used, the financial statements of the related fund entity:

   a Need not show material amounts of supplies on hand as an asset

   b Must disclose the cost of supplies used during the period

   c Should reflect the actual cost of supplies purchased as expenditures for the period

   d Need not disclose a fund balance reserve for material amounts of supplies on hand

4 When the *consumption basis* of accounting for supplies is used, the financial statements of the related fund entity:

   a Must show supply purchases as expenditures of the period

   b Must show a fund balance restriction for material amounts of supplies on hand

   c Must reflect the fact that perpetual inventory procedures have been used in accounting for supplies

   d Must show supplies on hand as an asset

5 If a general fund budget includes an appropriation for supplies used, there is an implication that:

   a *Supplies on hand* is not a fund resource

   b The consumption basis is being used for supplies

   c Budgetary accounts are not integrated into the fund accounting system

   d A perpetual supplies inventory is maintained

E 19-3   **[AICPA adapted]**

1 The primary emphasis in accounting and reporting for governmental funds is on:

   a Flow of current financial resources

   b Income determination

   c Capital transfers

   d Transfers relating to proprietary activities

2 The general purpose financial statements of a state government:

   a May *not* be issued separately from the comprehensive annual financial report

   b Are comprised of the combined financial statements and related notes

   c Are synonymous with the comprehensive annual financial report

   d Contain more detailed information regarding the state government's finances than is contained in the comprehensive annual financial report

3 Under the modified accrual basis of accounting for a governmental unit, revenues should be recognized in the accounting period in which they:

   a Are earned and become measurable

   b Are collected

   c Become available and measurable

   d Become available and earned

4 Authority granted by a legislative body to make expenditures and to incur obligations during a fiscal year is the definition of an:

   a Appropriation

   b Allocation

   c Encumbrance

   d Expenditure

5 For state and local governmental units, generally accepted accounting principles often require that encumbrances outstanding at year-end be reported as:

   a Expenditures   **c** Deferred liabilities

   b Reservations of fund balance **d** Current liabilities

      6 The estimated revenues control account balance of a governmental fund type is eliminated when:

   a The budget is recorded

   b The budgetary accounts are closed

   c Appropriations are closed

   d Property taxes are recorded

E 19-4

1 The accounts *estimated revenues* and *appropriations* appear in the trial balance of the general fund. These accounts indicate:

   a The use of cash basis accounting

   b The use of accrual basis accounting

   c The formal use of budgetary accounts

   d The informal use of budgetary accounts

2 When a complete system of encumbrance accounting is used (in other words, all commitments are encumbered), the authorizations remaining available for expenditures at any interim date will be equal to:

   a Appropriations less encumbrances

   b Appropriations less expenditures

   c Appropriations plus encumbrances less expenditures

   d Appropriations less expenditures and encumbrances

3 Encumbrance accounting is designed to:

   a Prevent overspending of amounts appropriated

   b Replace expenditure accounting for governmental organizations

   c Prevent excessive appropriations

   d Prevent or reduce waste in governmental spending

4 Reserve accounts for supplies and other items are frequently found in the fund balance section of balance sheets of governmental funds. Such accounts are used to show:

   a That a commitment has been made but a liability does not yet exist

   b That resources equal to the amount of the reserve are on hand but are not available for appropriation

   c Negative assets or resources

   d The amount of appropriation that is being carried over to the next fiscal period

5 Reserve for encumbrance accounts in general fund balance sheets at year-end indicate:

   a The amount of net assets required to complete the transaction(s) in the succeeding period

   b Noncompliance with GAAP

   c Cash on hand

   d Valuation reserves

E 19-5 **[AICPA adapted]**

1 Of the items listed, those most likely to have parallel accounting procedures, account titles, and financial statements are:

   a Special revenue funds and trust funds

   b Internal service funds and debt service funds

   c The general fixed assets account group and the general long-term debt account group

   d The general fund and special revenue funds

2 A budgetary fund balance reserved for encumbrances in excess of a balance of encumbrances indicates:

   a An excess of vouchers payable over encumbrances

   b An excess of purchase orders over invoices received

   c An excess of appropriations over encumbrances

   d A recording error

3 The encumbrance account of a governmental unit is debited when:

   a The budget is recorded

   b A purchase order is approved

   c Goods are received

   d A voucher payable is recorded

4 The *reserve for encumbrances—past year* account typically represents amounts recorded by a governmental unit for:

   a Anticipated expenditures in the next year

   b Expenditures for which purchase orders were made in the prior year but expenditure and disbursement will be in the current year

   c Excess expenditures in the prior year that will be offset against the current-year budgeted amounts

   d Unanticipated expenditures of the prior year that become evident in the current year

5 Encumbrances outstanding at year-end in a state's general fund should be reported as a:

   a Liability in the general fund

   b Fund balance reserve in the general fund

   c Liability in the general long-term debt account group

   d Fund balance designation in the general fund

6 When equipment was purchased with general fund resources, an appropriate entry was made in the general fixed assets account group. Which of the following accounts would have been increased in the general fund?

   a Due from general fixed assets account group

   b Expenditures

c Appropriations

d No entry should be made in the general fund

E 19-6   **[AICPA adapted]**

1 For the budgetary year ending December 31, 20X3, Maple City's general fund expects the following inflows of resources:

Property taxes, licenses, and fees	$9,000,000
Proceeds of debt issue	5,000,000
Interfund transfers for debt service	1,000,000

In the budgetary entry, what amount should Maple record for estimated revenues?

a $9,000,000   **c** $14,000,000

b $10,000,000   **d** $15,000,000

2 During its fiscal year ended June 30, 20X3, Cliff City issued purchase orders totaling $5,000,000, which were properly charged to encumbrances at that time. Cliff received goods and related invoices at the encumbered amounts totaling $4,500,000 before year-end. The remaining goods of $500,000 were not received until after year-end. Cliff paid $4,200,000 of the invoices received during the year. What amount of Cliff's encumbrances were outstanding at June 30, 20X3?

a $0   **c** $500,000

b $300,000   **d** $800,000

3 The following information pertains to property taxes levied by Oak City for the calendar year 20X2:

Collections during 20X2	$500,000
Expected collections during the first 60 days of 20X3	100,000
Expected collections during the balance of 20X3	60,000
Expected collections during January 20X4	30,000
Estimated to be uncollectible	10,000
Total levy	$700,000

What amount should Oak report for 20X2 net property tax revenues?

a $700,000   **c** $600,000

b $690,000   **d** $500,000

4 The following information pertains to Pine City's general fund for 20X9:

Appropriations	$6,500,000
Expenditures	5,000,000
Other financing sources	1,500,000
Other financing uses	2,000,000
Revenues	8,000,000

In 20X9, Pine's total fund balance increased by:

a $3,000,000   **c** $1,500,000

b $2,500,000   **d** $1,000,000

5 The following information pertains to Park Township's general fund at December 31, 20X2:

Total assets, including $200,000 of cash	$1,000,000
Total liabilities	600,000
Reserved for encumbrances	100,000

Appropriations do not lapse at year end. At December 31, 20X2, what amount should Park report as unreserved fund balance in its general fund balance sheet?

a $200,000   **c** $400,000

b $300,000   **d** $500,000

6 The following information pertains to Cobb City:

20X3 governmental fund revenues that became measurable and available in time to be used for payment of 20X3 liabilities	$16,000,000
Revenues earned in 20X1 and 20X2 and included in the $16,000,000 indicated	2,000,000
Sales taxes collected by merchants in 20X3 but not required to be remitted to Cobb until January 20X4	3,000,000

For the year ended December 31, 20X3, Cobb should recognize revenues of:

a $14,000,000   **c** $17,000,000
b $16,000,000   **d** $19,000,000

1 Revenue received by one governmental unit from a specific revenue source of another governmental unit is:

  a Classified as miscellaneous revenue
  b An example of a grant
  c An example of shared revenue
  d An example of internal service revenue

2 Intergovernmental revenue is an important source of revenue to state and local governmental units. Which of the following revenue sources is *not* an example of intergovernmental revenue?

  a Payments in lieu of taxes (except from a governments own funds)
  b Grants
  c Charges for services
  d Entitlements

3 A city receives pass-through grants from the state. The city has responsibility for reviewing applications and determining eligibility of potential recipients as well as for funding the administration of the program at the local level. These pass-through grants should not be accounted for in:

  a An agency fund
  b A governmental fund
  c A proprietary fund
  d A trust fund

4 The general fund unreserved fund balance account balance is best described as a measurement of:

  a Assets less liabilities of the fund
  b The balancing figure in a fund balance sheet
  c The amount of fund assets available for appropriation for general uses
  d Revenue less expenditures during the lifetime of the fund

5 Estimated uncollectible taxes are:

  a Reported in the *reserve* section of a general fund balance sheet
  b Credited when expenditures are debited for uncollectible taxes
  c Recorded when property tax revenue is accrued
  d Direct charges against the fund balance account

6 During the year ended June 30, 20X4, $80,000 cash was transferred from the general fund to other funds of the city of Huntsville. The $80,000 consists of:

  • $18,000 to the Electric Utility Fund of which $16,000 was for current year services and $2,000 was for services received in the year ended June 30, 20X3
  • $50,000 to the Central Purchasing Fund to provide initial capital for the fund
  • $12,000 to the City Hall Capital Projects Fund to repay a temporary loan

In the statement of revenues, expenditures, and changes in fund balance of the general fund for the year ended June 30, 20X4, residual equity transfers to other funds should be shown in the amount of:

  a $50,000   **c** $68,000
  b $62,000   **d** $78,000

The adopted budget of a city includes anticipated revenues of $1,000,000 and appropriations of $980,000. Revenue from sources other than property taxes are estimated as follows:

Licenses and permits	$ 12,000
Intergovernmental revenue	200,000
Charges for services	10,000
Fines and forfeits	4,000
Rents and royalties	3,000
Miscellaneous	1,500
	$230,500

The total assessed valuation of taxable property in the city is $20,000,000 and a 5 percent loss on uncollectible taxes is expected.

Required

  1 What amount of estimated revenue from property taxes should be included in the budget?
  2 Determine the property tax rate.

E 19-9 Purchase orders totaling $6,000 for supplies are outstanding at June 30, 20X7, the close of the fiscal year. The supplies are received on July 18, 20X7 at a cost of $5,800.

Prepare the journal entries needed in the 20X7–20X8 fiscal year assuming that committed appropriations can be carried over to the next period.

E 19-10 The following events and transactions relate to the levy and collection of property taxes for Medville Township.

March 21, 20X3—Property tax bills for $1,600,000 are sent to property owners. An estimated 2 percent of the property tax levies are uncollectible. The taxes are due on May 1.

May 4, 20X3—$1,300,000 in taxes have been collected. The remaining receivables are reclassified as delinquent.

May 5–December 31, 20X3—An additional $150,000 of taxes are collected.

November 1, 20X3—A $5,000 tax receivable account is determined to be uncollectible and is written off.

January 1, 20X4–February 28, 20X4—An additional $87,750 of 20X3 taxes are collected.

Required
1 Prepare summary journal entries for the events and transactions described above for the Medville general fund.
2 How will property taxes be presented in the December 31, 20X3 balance sheet?
3 What amount of property tax revenues should be reported for 20X3?

E 19-11 A general ledger trial balance for Galax City contained the following balances at June 30, 20X7, just before closing entries were made:

Due from other funds	$ 600
Unreserved fund balance	3,000
Estimated revenues	18,000
Revenues	17,380
Appropriations	17,500
Expenditures—current year	16,450
Expenditures—prior year	1,900
Encumbrances	1,000
Operating transfers in	3,200
Reserve for encumbrances	1,000
Reserve for encumbrances—prior year	2,000

Required: Prepare the necessary closing entries.

E 19-12 A general ledger trial balance at June 30, 20X3 for Fortune City is as follows:

	Debits	Credits
Cash	$ 12,000	$ —
Taxes receivable	30,000	—
Allowance for uncollectible taxes	—	2,000
Due from other funds	3,000	—
Supplies inventory, June 30, 20X3	4,000	—
Estimated revenues	300,000	—
Expenditures	290,000	—
Expenditures—prior year	5,000	—
Encumbrances	6,000	—
Vouchers payable	—	15,000
Due to other funds	—	5,000
Reserve for encumbrances	—	6,000
Reserve for encumbrances—prior year	—	5,000
Reserve for inventory	—	2,000
Unreserved fund balance	—	10,000
Appropriations	—	300,000
Revenues	—	305,000
	$650,000	$650,000

Fortune City uses a purchase basis in accounting for supplies.

Required: Prepare a general fund balance sheet as of June 30, 20X3.

E 19-13 The trial balance of the general fund of Idaho City before closing at December 31, 20X2 contained the following accounts and balances:

Unreserved fund balance	$ 25,000
Estimated revenues	100,000
Appropriations	95,000
Encumbrances	4,000
Reserve for encumbrances	4,000
Reserve for encumbrances—prior year	5,000
Revenues	101,000
Expenditures	94,000
Expenditures—prior year	4,800
Operating transfers out	18,000
Operating transfers in	27,000
Residual equity transfers in	12,000

Required

Prepare a statement of revenues, expenditures, and changes in (total) fund balance for Idaho City's general fund in 20X2. (Details of revenue and expenditure accounts are omitted to simplify the requirement.)

E 19-14 Use transaction analysis to determine the effects of each of the following transactions. Assume that a general government activity is involved.

1 Salaries paid totaled $30,000. Additional salaries incurred, but not paid, totaled $2,500.
2 Levied property taxes of $100,000. $98,000 was collected during the year. The balance is expected to be uncollectible.
3 Borrowed $60,000 by issuing a nine-month note bearing interest at 7%.
4 Repaid the note plus interest when due.
5 Borrowed $600,000 by issuing bonds at par. The bonds mature in 10 years.
6 Purchased equipment costing $25,000, by making a down payment of $10,000 and signing a one-year, 5% note for the balance of the cost. The purchase occurred at mid-year.
7 Sold equipment at the end of its expected useful life. The equipment had no expected residual value when acquired (at a cost of $13,000), but sold for $1,200.
8 Determined that it is probable that a lawsuit involving a claim against a department will result in a settlement of at least $50,000. However, it is not expected that any payments will be required for two years or more.

E 19-15 Repeat Exercise 19-14 under the assumption that the transactions involve a proprietary activity instead of a general government activity.

PROBLEMS

P 19-1   **A** Patton County entered into the following transactions. The county's fiscal year-end is December 31. Analyze the effects of each transaction on the accounting equations of each fund or account group affected by the transaction. (Reflect any interest accruals that Patton County would be required to make at year-end.)

B Indicate how each transaction would be reported in the operating statement of each fund affected by the transaction.

1 Patton County issued $10 million of general obligation, 8%, 10-year bonds at 101 on October 1, 20X8. Bond interest is payable semiannually on March 31 and September 30. The bonds were issued to finance construction of a new county office building.
2 The county board of supervisors voted to use the premium on the bonds to pay principal and interest charges on the debt when they mature. Resources were transferred to the appropriate fund.
3 The county paid $2 million to High Rise Construction Company during 20X8 for work completed during the year. The company billed the county another $500,000 for work performed during 20X8, but for which the county has not yet paid.
4 Reflect any interest accrual required or permitted at year-end. (*Hint:* Unmatured interest and principal on general long-term debt are not accrued.)
5 The county purchased a truck for a general government department. The cost of the truck, $22,000, was paid in cash.
6 The county-owned-and-operated electric utility billed residents and businesses $500,000 for electricity sales. Ninety percent of the amount billed was collected; $10,000 is expected to be uncollectible. In addition, the county expects to collect $30,000 of the outstanding receivables during the first two months of the next fiscal year and the remaining $10,000 at some point later in that year.

7 The county-owned-and-operated electric utility billed other departments and agencies of the county $50,000 for electricity sales. Ninety percent of the amount billed was collected during the year.

8 In 20X9 the county paid $1,800,000 from its general fund to the fund from which the bonds are to be repaid. The purpose of shifting the resources was to provide for the principal and interest payments to be made during the fiscal year.

9 The county paid the first interest payment on the bonds when due, March 31, 20X9.

10 The county paid the second interest payment on the bonds when due, September 30, 20X9, and also repaid $1 million of bond principal on that date.

P 19-2 **A** The City of Nancy entered into the following transactions. The city's fiscal year end is December 31. Analyze the effects of each transaction on the accounting equations of each fund or account group affected by the transaction. (Reflect any interest accruals that the City of Nancy would be required to make at year-end.)

B Indicate how each transaction would be reported in the operating statement of each fund affected by the transaction.

1 Nancy paid salaries to general government employees, $95,000.

2 Nancy purchased an automobile by issuing a $25,000, 8% note to the vendor. The purchase occurred at mid-year and the note is a one-year note.

3 Nancy transferred general fund resources to a fund to be used to account for a new central data processing department that will provide data processing services to all departments on a cost-reimbursement basis.

4 The city sold general fixed assets with an original cost of $300,000 for $30,000 at the end of their useful life. The use of the resources received is not restricted.

5 In the second fiscal year, the city repaid the principal and interest on the note issued in no. 2 at the due date of the note.

6 Vacation and sick leave of $40,000 were paid to general government employees during the year. The liability for accumulated, unused vacation and sick leave for general government employees increased by $135,000 during the year. All of the liability increase is long-term.

7 $500,000 of "profits" from the airport enterprise fund were transferred to the general fund of the city to subsidize general fund operations.

8 Interest income collected on Nancy's general fund investments totaled $70,000 for the year. The fair value of the general fund's equity in the state investment pool, which is the city's primary investment medium, increased $1,300 during the year.

P 19-3 The *unadjusted* trial balance for the general fund of the City of Three Rivers at December 31, 20X8 is as follows:

	Debit	Credit
Accounts receivable	$ 25,000	—
Allowance for bad debts	—	$ 2,000
Allowance for uncollectible taxes	—	30,000
Appropriations	—	900,000
Cash	40,000	—
Due from agency fund	10,000	—
Due to utility fund	—	20,000
Encumbrances	50,000	—
Estimated revenues	910,000	—
Expenditures	858,000	—
Fund balance	—	26,000
Reserve for encumbrances	—	50,000
Revenues	—	910,000
Taxes receivable—delinquent	210,000	—
Taxes received in advance	—	10,000
Vouchers payable	—	155,000
	$2,103,000	$2,103,000

Supplies on hand at December 31, 20X8 are $3,000. The $50,000 encumbrance relates to equipment ordered November 28 for the Department of Public Works, but not received by year-end.

Required: Prepare a balance sheet for the general fund of the City of Three Rivers at December 31, 20X8.

P 19-4 The preclosing account balances of the general fund of the City of Chico on June 30, 20X3 were as follows:

Debits

Cash	$ 80,000
Taxes receivable—delinquent	160,000
Supplies inventory	18,000
Estimated revenues	1,000,000
Expenditures	940,000
Operating transfers out	10,000
Encumbrances	20,000
	$2,228,000

Credits

Allowance for uncollectible taxes— delinquent	$ 30,000
Vouchers payable	40,000
Notes payable	60,000
Reserve for encumbrances	20,000
Reserve for supplies	18,000
Unreserved fund balance	120,000
Revenues	980,000
Appropriations	960,000
	$2,228,000

The unreserved fund balance at the beginning of the year was $80,000, and there were no carryover encumbrances at the beginning of the fiscal year.

Required
1 Prepare a statement of revenues, expenditures, and changes in total fund balance for the year ended June 30, 20X3.
2 Prepare a general fund balance sheet at June 30, 20X3.

P 19-5 Prepare entries in the general fund to record the following transactions and events:
1 Estimated revenues for the fiscal year were $250,000 and appropriations were $248,000.
2 The tax levy for the fiscal year, of which 99% is believed to be collectible, was $200,000.
3 Taxes collected were $150,000.
4 A short-term loan of $15,000 was made to the special revenue fund.
5 Orders for supplies were placed in the amount of $18,000.
6 The items ordered in 5 were received. Actual cost was $18,150 and vouchers for that amount were prepared.
7 Materials were acquired from the stores fund (an internal service fund) in the amount of $800 (without encumbrance).
8 A $5,000 payment (transfer) was made to the debt service fund.
9 A cash payment of $15,000 was made for the purchase of equipment.
10 Licenses were collected in the amount of $3,000.
11 The balance of taxes receivable became delinquent.
12 Delinquent taxes of $30,000 were collected before year-end. The remaining net realizable value of delinquent taxes is expected to be collected uniformly over the first four months of the next fiscal year.

P 19-6 Prepare the journal entries required to record the following transactions in the general fund of Barek Township. Indicate other funds or account groups that would be affected by the transaction.
1 Borrowed $75,000 by issuing six-month tax anticipation notes.
2 Ordered equipment with an estimated cost of $33,000.
3 Received the equipment along with an invoice for its actual cost, $33,250.
4 Transferred $200,000 of general fund resources to a debt service fund.
5 On January 1, the township levied property taxes of $1,000,000. The township expects to collect all except $100,000 by the end of the fiscal year or within not more than 60 days thereafter. Of the remaining $100,000, half is expected to prove uncollectible.
6 The township received a $100,000 restricted grant for certain library programs from another unit of government. The grant will be accounted for in the general fund.
7 The township incurred $75,000 of expenditures for the programs covered by the library grant.

P 19-7 **[AICPA adapted]**
The comptroller of the City of Helmaville recently resigned. In his absence, the deputy comptroller attempted to calculate the amount of money required to be raised from prop-

erty taxes for the general fund for the fiscal year ending June 30, 20X7. The calculation is to be made as of January 1, 20X6, to serve as a basis for setting the property tax rate for the following fiscal year. The mayor has requested you to review the deputy comptroller's calculations and obtain other necessary information to prepare a formal statement for the general fund that will disclose the amount of money required to be raised from property taxes for the fiscal year ending June 30, 20X7. Following are the calculations prepared by the deputy comptroller:

City resources other than proposed tax levy:	
Estimated general fund working balance, January 1, 20X6	$ 352,000
Estimated receipts from property taxes (January 1, 20X6–June 30, 20X6)	2,222,000
Estimated revenue from investments (January 1, 20X6–June 30, 20X7)	442,000
Estimated proceeds from sale of general obligation bonds in August 20X6	3,000,000
	$6,016,000
General fund requirements:	
Estimated expenditures (January 1, 20X6–June 30, 20X6)	$1,900,000
Proposed appropriations (July 1, 20X6–June 30, 20X7)	4,300,000
	$6,200,000

Additional Information

1 The general fund working balance required by the city council for July 1, 20X7 is $175,000.
2 Property tax collections are due in March and September of each year. Your review indicates that during the month of February 20X6 estimated expenditures will exceed available funds by $200,000. Pending collection of property taxes in March 20X6, this deficiency will have to be met by the issuance of 30-day tax anticipation notes of $200,000 at an estimated interest rate of 9% per annum.
3 The proposed general obligation bonds will be issued by the city water fund and will be used for the construction of a new water pumping station.

Required: Prepare a statement as of January 1, 20X6, calculating the property tax levy required for the City of Helmaville general fund for the fiscal year ending June 30, 20X7.

P 19-8 **[AICPA adapted]**
The following summary of transactions was taken from the accounts of the Annaville School District general fund *before* the books had been closed for the fiscal year ended June 30, 20X5:

	Postclosing Balances June 30, 20X4	Preclosing Balances June 30, 20X5
Cash	$400,000	$ 700,000
Taxes receivable	150,000	170,000
Estimated uncollectible taxes	(40,000)	(70,000)
Estimated revenues	—	3,000,000
Expenditures	—	2,842,000
Expenditures—prior years	—	—
Encumbrances	—	91,000
	$510,000	$6,733,000
Vouchers payable	$ 80,000	$ 408,000
Due to other funds	210,000	142,000
Reserve for encumbrances	60,000	91,000
Unreserved fund balance	160,000	182,000
Revenues from taxes	—	2,800,000
Miscellaneous revenues	—	130,000
Appropriations	—	2,980,000
	$510,000	$6,733,000

Additional Information

1 The estimated taxes receivable for the year ended June 30, 20X5 were $2,870,000, and taxes collected during the year totaled $2,810,000.

2 An analysis of the transactions in the vouchers payable for the year ended June 30, 20X5 follows:

	Debit (Credit)
Current expenditures	$(2,700,000)
Expenditures for prior years	(58,000)
Vouchers for payment to other funds	(210,000)
Cash payments during the year	2,640,000
Net change	$ (328,000)

During the year the general fund was billed $142,000 for services performed on its behalf by other city funds.

On May 2, 20X5 commitment documents were issued for the purchase of new textbooks at a cost of $91,000.

Required: Based upon the data presented, reconstruct the *original detailed journal entries* that were required to record all transactions for the fiscal year ended June 30, 20X5, including the recording of the current year's budget. Do *not* prepare closing entries at June 30, 20X5.

P 19-9 **[AICPA adapted]**

The following information was abstracted from the accounts of the general fund of the City of Rom after the books had been closed for the fiscal year ended June 30, 20X8:

	Trial Balance June 30, 20X7	Transactions July 1, 20X7 to June 30, 20X8 Debit	Transactions July 1, 20X7 to June 30, 20X8 Credit	Postclosing Trial Balance June 30, 20X8
Cash	$700,000	$1,820,000	$1,852,000	$668,000
Taxes receivable	40,000	1,870,000	1,828,000	82,000
	$740,000			$750,000
Allowances for uncollectible taxes	$ 8,000	8,000	10,000	$ 10,000
Vouchers payable	132,000	1,852,000	1,840,000	120,000
Fund balance:				
Reserve for encumbrances	—	1,000,000	1,070,000	70,000
Unreserved	600,000	140,000	60,000	
			30,000	550,000
	$740,000			$750,000

Additional Information: The budget for the fiscal year ended June 30, 20X8 provided for estimated revenues of $2,000,000 and appropriations of $1,940,000.

Required: Prepare journal entries to record the budgeted and actual transactions for the fiscal year ended June 30, 20X8.

P 19-10 The following information regarding the fiscal year ended December 31, 20X0 was drawn from the accounts and records of the Velander County general fund.

Revenues and other asset inflows:	
Taxes	$10,000,000
Licenses and permits	2,000,000
Intergovernmental grants	300,000
Proceeds of short-term note issuances	1,000,000
Collection of interfund advance to other fund	450,000
Receipt of net assets of terminated fund	2,000,000
Expenditures and other asset outflows:	
General government expenditures	8,000,000
Public safety expenditures	1,500,000
Judicial system expenditures	1,000,000
Health and welfare expenditures	1,200,000
Equipment purchases	600,000
Payment to debt service fund to cover future debt service on general government bonds	320,000
Unreserved fund balance, January 1, 20X0	$ 2,200,000

Prepare a statement of revenues, expenditures, and changes in fund balance for the Velander County general fund for the year ended December 31, 20X0.

20

An Introduction to Accounting for State and Local Governmental Units—Part II

The preceding chapter reviewed accounting standards for state and local governmental units and explained procedures relevant to accounting for the general fund and special revenue funds. These two governmental funds almost always must use formal budgetary accounting practices. Other governmental funds also may integrate their budgets into their accounting systems when an annual budget is legally adopted or when it is considered necessary for control purposes.

This chapter assumes that the funds in the illustrations do not use formal budgetary accounting. The chapter includes those governmental funds not covered in the preceding chapter (capital projects funds and debt service funds), accounting procedures for the general fixed assets and the general long-term debt account groups, and accounting procedures applicable to proprietary funds (internal service funds and enterprise funds) and fiduciary funds (trust funds and agency funds).

Individual fund and account group financial statements are illustrated in the sections that cover different funds and account groups. *General purpose financial statements* are combined statements presented in a columnar format with separate columns for the individual fund types and account groups of the primary government (including its blended component units) and one or more columns for the discretely presented component units. Thus, a final section of the chapter explains the process of combining the financial statements of individual funds of a particular fund type into combining financial statements for the fund type, and the development of combined financial statements for all fund types and account groups for external reporting purposes.

CAPITAL PROJECTS FUNDS

The acquisition of minor general fixed assets from expenditures of annual appropriations are accounted for in the general fund or special revenue funds. But major general fixed assets are not financed through appropriations of these funds. The purpose of **capital projects funds (CPF)** is to account for resources segregated for the acquisition of major capital facilities other than those financed by trust and proprietary funds. Typical sources of financing include the proceeds of bond issues, grants and shared revenues, transfers from other funds, and contributions from property owners. *GASB Statement No. 6* explains that when capital improvements are financed by special assessment debt for which the government is not obligated in any manner, the proceeds from the special assessment debt should be described as contributions from property owners rather than bond proceeds.[1]

Capital projects funds are governmental funds. Like general and special revenue funds, capital projects funds are essentially working capital entities. They are used to account for working capital to be used for major general government capital projects. *Capital projects funds use modified accrual accounting and revenue and expenditure accounts.* Ordinarily, a separate CPF is created to account for each major capital project. A CPF is created when it is legally authorized, and it exists for the life of the project. Formal budgetary accounting often is not used unless numerous capital projects are financed through the same fund or facilities are being constructed with the governmental unit as the primary contractor.

CPFs most often acquire fixed assets by purchase or construction. Encumbrance accounting procedures are used to account for commitments made to contractors and for material and supply orders.

The next section illustrates the accounting and reporting for a CPF during a two-year construction project.

Accounting for a Capital Projects Fund

The City of Budding authorizes the construction of a new city hall on January 1, 20X1 in the amount of $1,000,000. Financing for the project consists of $500,000 from a $6\frac{1}{2}\%$ serial bond issue, $400,000 from a federal grant, and $100,000 from the general fund. Transactions and events during the life of the project are as follows:

20X1

1 The city transfers $100,000 from the GF to the city hall capital projects fund (a CPF created to account for the city hall construction).
2 Planning and architect's fees are paid in the amount of $40,000.
3 The contract is awarded to the lowest bidder for $950,000.
4 The bonds are sold for $502,000 (at a premium of $2,000).
5 The amount of the premium is transferred to the debt service fund.
6 The construction is certified to be 50% complete and a bill for $475,000 is received from the contractor.
7 Contracts payable, less a 10% retained percentage, is paid.
8 The books are closed and financial statements are prepared.

20X2

9 The amount due from the federal grant is received.
10 Construction is completed and the contractor is paid.
11 Closing entries are recorded.
12 Remaining cash is transferred to the GF.

Creation of the CPF When the city hall CPF is created, a memorandum entry is made in the CPF noting the $1,000,000 authorization.

> *CPF*
> Memorandum—city hall project authorization $1,000,000

Interfund Transfer (1) Transaction 1 increases CPF current assets and fund balance. As discussed in Chapter 19, nonreciprocal interfund transactions like this one are called transfers. This transfer does not involve termination of a fund or provision of permanent initial or expansion capital to a proprietary fund. Thus, it is an *operating transfer*, not a residual equity transfer. Fund balance increases from operating transfers are reported as other financing sources, not as revenues.

This transaction also decreases GF current assets and fund balance. The decrease in GF fund balance is another financing use, not an expenditure. The $100,000 transfer requires an entry in both funds. The GF entry to record the transfer is:

> *GF*
> Other financing uses—operating transfer to city hall CPF $ 100,000
>   Cash $100,000
>   To record transfer to city hall CPF.

---

[1]GASB, Cod. Sec. S40.119.

The corresponding entry in the CPF to receive the $100,000 is:

CPF
Cash	$100,000	
Other financing sources—operating transfer		
from general fund		$100,000
To record receipt of funds from the GF.		

Recording Expenditures (2) Payments for planning and architect's fees are recorded:

CPF
Expenditures	$ 40,000	
Cash		$ 40,000
To record payments for planning and architect's fees.		

Recording Encumbrances (3) When the contract is awarded to a contractor, an encumbrance entry is made for the full amount of the contract:

CPF
Encumbrances	$950,000	
Reserve for encumbrances		$950,000
To record encumbrances for the amount of the contract.		

Accounting for the Bond Proceeds (4 and 5) Proceeds of bond issues are recognized in the CPF at the time the bonds are sold. The sale of the bonds increases CPF current assets (cash). The bond liability is long-term so it is accounted for in the general long-term debt account group, not in the CPF. Thus, the CPF fund balance increases by the amount of the bond proceeds ($502,000). This fund balance increase is classified as an other financing source (bond issue proceeds), not as revenues.

The bonds were sold at a premium. Although the full amount of the proceeds is recorded in the CPF, the premium is not available to finance the project. Premiums often are set aside to service the debt. Thus, the premium is transferred to the debt service fund through which the bond liability will be serviced. (The corresponding entry for the debt service fund is illustrated in the next section of this chapter.) Journal entries for the sale of bonds and transfer of the premium are:

CPF
Cash	$502,000	
Other financing sources—proceeds from		
bond issue		$502,000
To record sale of bonds.		
Other financing uses—operating transfer to debt		
service fund	$ 2,000	
Cash		$ 2,000
To transfer the premium to the city hall debt service fund.		

If the bonds had been sold at a discount, the amount received would have been recorded as bond proceeds. The sale of bonds at a discount requires reducing the project authorization or transferring additional resources to the CPF.

Progress Payments and Retained Percentages (6 and 7) A construction contract often provides that a portion of the contractor's remuneration be withheld until completion of the construction project and final inspection. Note that the fixed asset (construction in progress) is not recorded in the CPF. (It should be recorded in the general fixed assets account group.) The fixed asset does not represent CPF working capital. Instead, the incurrence of the contract payable liability increases CPF liabilities and decreases CPF fund balance. This fund balance decrease is reported as an expenditure. Accounting entries for the amount owed on partial completion of the contract and the first progress payment on the contract are recorded:

```
CPF
Reserve for encumbrances                        $475,000
    Encumbrances                                             $475,000
    To reverse half of the amount encumbered.


Expenditures                                    $475,000
    Contracts payable                                        $427,500
    Contracts payable—retained percentage                     47,500
    To record expenditures and a 10% retained percentage
      on the city hall construction.


Contracts payable                               $427,500
    Cash                                                     $427,500
    To record partial payment to the contractor.
```

Adjusting and Closing Entries (8)

At the end of the fiscal year, the CPF books are closed and financial statements are prepared. The city hall construction project has not been completed and the statements for the CPF are interim statements from the standpoint of the project.

Intergovernmental Revenue   The grant from the federal government is intergovernmental revenue. Under modified accrual accounting, revenue is recognized on restricted grants when qualifying costs have been incurred (and other significant conditions, if any, have been met), assuming either (1) cash was received in advance of the expenditures or (2) cash will be received within not more than 60 days into the next fiscal year.[2]

Because the amount of the federal grant to the city hall project is not received at the time the books are closed, it should be accrued, provided that the commitment is firm. Revenue is recognized if the receivable will be collected in not more than 60 days into the next fiscal year. Otherwise, deferred revenue is credited. Failure to recognize revenue from the grant could make the CPF appear to be in financial difficulty for interim reporting purposes when, in fact, it has progressed as planned.

```
CPF (Adjusting Entry)
Due from federal government                     $400,000
    Revenue                                                  $400,000
    To accrue revenue from the federal grant.
```

This entry assumes that the federal government has agreed to contribute $400,000 to the project regardless of the total cost. Therefore, because more than $400,000 of costs were incurred in 20X1, the full $400,000 is recorded as revenue. If the grant had specified that the federal government would pay 40% of the cost of the project up to $400,000, the entry would be for $206,000 ($515,000 × 0.4).

```
CPF (Adjusting Entry)
Due from federal government                     $206,000
    Revenue                                                  $206,000
```

Likewise, if the grant proceeds had been received in advance of expenditure, and the grant were for 40% of the cost, the following grant entries would have been required for 20X1:

```
CPF
Cash                                            $400,000
    Deferred revenue                                         $400,000
    To record receipt of grant.


CPF (Adjusting Entry)
Deferred revenue                                $206,000
    Revenue                                                  $206,000
    To record grant revenue.
```

---

[2]Some experts contend that the collection criterion does not apply to intergovernmental grants.

Closing Entry—20X1   A closing entry for the CPF is recorded as follows:

CPF (Closing Entry)

Revenue	$400,000	
Other financing sources—Operating transfer from general fund	100,000	
Other financing sources—proceeds from bond issue	502,000	
Expenditures		$515,000
Other financing uses—operating transfer to debt service fund		2,000
Encumbrances		475,000
Unreserved fund balance		10,000

To close the books at the end of 20X1.

Unissued Bonds at an Interim Statement Date

The bonds to finance the city hall capital project have been issued by December 31, 20X1, but in some cases there will be authorized but unissued bonds at an interim reporting date. The existence of the unissued bonds would be disclosed only in a statement note. The authorization of the bonds does not represent a CPF asset. Assets are received only upon bond issuance.

Required Financial Statements for the CPF

Required financial statements for capital projects funds are the same as for all other governmental funds—a balance sheet, a statement of revenues, expenditures, and changes in fund balance (GAAP basis), and a budgetary comparison statement on the

---

CITY OF BUDDING
CITY HALL CAPITAL PROJECTS FUND
BALANCE SHEET
AT DECEMBER 31, 20X1

Assets		
Cash		$132,500
Due from federal government		400,000
Total assets		$532,500
Liabilities		
Contracts payable—retained percentage		$ 47,500
Fund Balance		
Reserve for encumbrances	$475,000	
Unreserved fund balance	10,000	
Total fund balance		485,000
Total liabilities and fund balance		$532,500

CITY OF BUDDING
CITY HALL CAPITAL PROJECTS FUND
STATEMENT OF REVENUES, EXPENDITURES,
AND CHANGES IN FUND BALANCE
FOR THE YEAR ENDED DECEMBER 31, 20X1

Revenues		
Revenue from federal grant		$400,000
Expenditures		
Architect fees	$ 40,000	
Construction costs	475,000	515,000
Excess of expenditures over revenue		(115,000)
Other Financing Sources (Uses)		
Bond proceeds	$502,000	
Operating transfer from general fund	100,000	
Operating transfer to debt service fund	(2,000)	600,000
Excess of revenues and other financing sources over expenditures and other uses		485,000
Fund balance, January 1, 20X1		—
Fund balance December 31, 20X1		$485,000

Exhibit 20–1   *Capital Projects Fund Financial Statements*

budgetary basis of accounting. (The budgetary comparison statement is called the statement of revenues, expenditures, and changes in fund balance—budget and actual. It is only required for governmental funds with legally adopted annual budgets.) As required by GAAP, the capital projects fund revenue from the federal grant is reported separate from transfers. In the statement of revenues, expenditures, and changes in fund balances, operating transfers into a fund and proceeds from bond issues are reported as *other financing sources*. Similarly, operating transfers out of a fund are reported as *other financing uses* and distinguished from expenditures.

The illustrations provided by the *GASB Codification* show other financing sources (uses) below the excess of revenues over expenditures (as shown in Exhibit 20–1 on page 763). Some municipal reports combine revenues and other financing sources to show the line-item *total sources of financial resources*. Similarly, expenditures and other financing uses are combined to show *total uses of financial resources*.

Entries for 20X2

Reinstatement of Encumbrances   At the start of year 20X2, the $475,000 encumbrance that was closed to unreserved fund balance at the end of the year 20X1 is reinstated in the accounts as follows:

CPF

Encumbrances	$475,000	
Unreserved fund balance		$475,000

To reinstate the encumbrances.

Receipt of Grant (9)   When the federal grant is received, it is recorded:

CPF

Cash	$400,000	
Due from federal grant		$400,000

To record receipt of the federal grant.

Completion of the Project (10)   The journal entries to record completion of construction and payment to the contractor are as follows:

CPF

Reserve for encumbrances	$475,000	
Encumbrances		$475,000

To remove encumbrances when construction is complete.

Expenditures	$475,000	
Contracts payable		$475,000

To record expenditures on city hall construction.

Contracts payable	$475,000	
Contracts payable—retained percentage	47,500	
Cash		$522,500

To record final payment to contractor.

Closing Entries (11)   An entry is made to close expenditures:

CPF

Unreserved fund balance	$475,000	
Expenditures		$475,000

To close the expenditures to fund balance.

Residual Equity Transfer (12)   The transfer of the remaining fund balance to the general fund in final termination of the city hall CPF is recorded as follows:

CPF

Residual equity transfer to GF	$ 10,000	
Cash		$ 10,000

To record transfer of cash to the general fund.

Unreserved fund balance	$ 10,000	
Residual equity transfer to GF		$ 10,000

To close city hall CPF ledger.

A corresponding entry is required in the general fund to receive the cash transferred. That entry is:

GF

| Cash | $ 10,000 | |
| Residual equity transfer from CPF | | $ 10,000 |

To record receipt of cash from City Hall CPF.

The $10,000 transfer to the general fund is a residual equity transfer because the fund is being terminated. Residual equity transfers are presented separately as increases or decreases in fund balance in the statement of revenues and expenditures and changes in fund balance.

Required Financial Statement (20X2)   Because the city hall CPF was terminated in 20X2, it has no balance sheet items to report at the end of 20X2. The only statement required is a statement of revenues, expenditures, and changes in fund balance as follows:

CITY OF BUDDING
CITY HALL CAPITAL PROJECTS FUND
STATEMENT OF REVENUES, EXPENDITURES, AND CHANGES
IN FUND BALANCE
FOR THE YEAR ENDED DECEMBER 31, 20X2

Revenues	$ —
Expenditures	
Construction costs	475,000
Total expenditures over revenues	(475,000)
Fund balance, December 31, 20X1	485,000
Residual equity transfer to GF	(10,000)
Fund balance, December 31, 20X2	$ —

For *internal reporting purposes*, a statement of revenues, expenditures, and changes in fund balance should be prepared covering the entire term of the project from January 1, 20X1 through December 31, 20X2.

DEBT SERVICE FUNDS

Debt service funds (DSF) are governmental funds that are used to account for the receipt of resources from designated sources (such as taxes or transfers from the general fund) and to account for the use of these resources to make principal and interest payments on general long-term debt obligations. Ordinarily, a separate DSF is created to account for servicing each general long-term debt issue. Although debt service funds make interest and principal payments on general long-term debt, the liability for general long-term debt is recorded in the **general long-term debt (GLTD)** account group and *not* in the DSF. Thus, the records of debt service funds and general long-term debt account groups have to be coordinated. When long-term debt matures, expenditures are recorded in the DSF and the liability for the debt is reduced in the GLTD account group.

Revenues and expenditures of debt service funds are accounted for on the modified accrual basis. Under modified accrual accounting, expenditures are ordinarily recognized in the accounting period in which related fund liabilities are incurred. However, interest expenditures and principal retirement expenditures on general long-term debt are recognized when due (in other words, typically in the year of payment). The unmatured amounts are not accrued at year-end. This exception is made to avoid showing an expenditure and a liability for debt service in one period and the transfer of resources from the general fund or other sources to pay the liability in the following period.[3]

---

[3]Accrual is permitted, but not required, if two conditions are met. First, the resources to be used for payment must be available in the DSF by year end. Second, the payment must be due early (first few days) in the next year.

The operations of debt service funds for serial bond issues are much different than for term bond issues. In the case of a serial bond issue, where bonds are retired at regular intervals, resources typically are received as needed to service the debt and no significant balances are carried over from one period to the next. However, the operations of debt service funds for term bond issues have the objectives of accumulating resources to retire all of the debt at maturity, as well as making periodic interest payments. Debt service funds for term bond issues involve both sinking fund operations and operations for current debt service. Thus, they are much more complex than for serial bond issues. Formal budgetary accounting is ordinarily needed for term bond issues but not for serial bond issues. Only serial bond debt service fund operations are illustrated in this chapter.

Accounting for the Debt Service Fund

Assume the $500,000, $6\frac{1}{2}\%$ serial bond issue of the City of Budding that was issued for $502,000 on July 1, 20X1 has interest payment dates of January 1 and July 1 of each year. Principal amounts of $50,000 are due each year starting on July 1, 20X2, and cash for all debt service is to be provided by transfers from the general fund. Amounts needed for debt service payments are transferred from the general fund during the month before the due date. Under these assumptions, the required journal entries for the city hall debt service fund for 20X1 and 20X2 are as follows:

DSF July 1, 20X1

Cash	$ 2,000	
Other financing sources—operating transfer		
from city hall CPF		$ 2,000
To record receipt of issue premium from city hall CPF.		

DSF December 20X1

Cash	$14,250	
Other financing sources—operating transfer		
from general fund		$14,250
To record receipt of resources for the January 1, 20X2 interest payment from the general fund, less the $2,000 already accumulated.		
($500,000 × .065 × .5 year) − $2,000 = $14,250.		

DSF Closing Entries—20X1

Other financing sources—operating transfer from		
city hall CPF	$ 2,000	
Other financing sources—operating transfer from		
general fund	14,250	
Unreserved fund balance		$16,250
To close the accounts.		

DSF January 1, 20X2

Expenditures	$16,250	
Cash		$16,250
To record payment of interest due on $6\frac{1}{2}\%$ serial bond issue.		

DSF June 20X2

Cash	$66,250	
Other financing sources—operating transfer from		
general fund		$66,250
To record receipt of $16,250 for interest payment plus $50,000 for the first serial payment due July 1, 20X2.		

DSF July 1, 20X2

Expenditures	$66,250	
Cash		$66,250
To record payment of principal and interest on the serial bond issue.		

DSF December 20X2

Cash	$14,625	
Other financing sources—operating transfer from general fund		$14,625

To record receipt of cash from GF for the January 1, 20X3
interest payment ($450,000 × 6½% × ½ year).

DSF Closing Entries—20X2

Other financing sources—operating transfer from general fund	$80,875	
Unreserved fund balance	1,625	
Expenditures		$82,500

To close the accounts.

Financial Statements for DSF

The financial reporting requirements for a debt service fund include the same statements as those required for other governmental funds. Comparative statements for the debt service fund of the City of Budding are shown in Exhibit 20–2. The illustration assumes that an annual budget is not adopted. Thus, a budgetary comparison statement is not required.

Operating Transfers The entries in December 20X1, June 20X2, and December 20X2 to record receipt of cash from the general fund are considered operating transfers that are made in connection with the normal operations of government. Operating transfers are not revenues or expenditures of either fund involved in the transaction. Instead, operating transfers are reported as "other financing sources (uses)." In

---

CITY OF BUDDING
CITY HALL DEBT SERVICE FUND
BALANCE SHEET
AT DECEMBER 31, 20X2 AND 20X1

	20X2	20X1
Assets		
Cash	$14,625	$16,250
Total assets	$14,625	$16,250
Liabilities and Fund Balance		
Fund balance	$14,625	$16,250
Total liabilities and fund balance	$14,625	$16,250

CITY OF BUDDING
CITY HALL DEBT SERVICE FUND
STATEMENT OF REVENUES, EXPENDITURES,
AND CHANGES IN FUND BALANCE
FOR THE YEARS ENDED DECEMBER 31, 20X2 AND 20X1

	20X2	20X1
Revenues	—	—
Expenditures		
Interest	$32,500	—
Principal retirement	50,000	
Total expenditures	82,500	
Excess of revenues over expenditures	(82,500)	—
Other financing sources (uses)		
Operating transfers in	80,875	$16,250
Excess of revenues and other financing sources over (under) other financing uses	(1,625)	16,250
Fund balance, January 1	16,250	—
Fund balance, December 31	$14,625	$16,250

Exhibit 20–2   *Debt Service Fund Statements*

this case, the $2,000 transfer of the bond premium on July 1, 20X1, the $14,250 December 20X1 operating transfer for the payment of interest, the $66,250 operating transfer in June 20X2 for interest and the first principal payment, and the $14,625 operating transfer in December 20X2 for interest are reported as other financing sources in the DSF and as other financing uses in the GF or in the CPF.

Note that interest payable is not accrued on December 31, 20X1 and 20X2 for interest payments due on January 1, 20X2 and 20X3. The interest could be recorded because the amounts payable are due on January 1, and resources are available in the DSF at year-end to cover the interest payments due early in the next fiscal year. Interest could not be accrued at December 31 if the general fund operating transfers were made on January 1 to pay interest on January 1.

SPECIAL ASSESSMENT ACTIVITIES

Public improvements that benefit a limited group of property owners are sometimes financed through special taxes levied against the property owners deemed to benefit from the improvements. These special tax levies are known as special assessment levies, or just **special assessments**. The more common types of special assessment projects include street paving, the construction of sidewalks, and the installation of sewer lines. Ordinarily, a special assessment project originates when property owners in an area petition the government to construct the improvements desired. If the project is authorized, the government obtains the financing, makes the improvement, and levies special assessments on the property owners for some or all of the cost incurred. The special assessments levied may be paid immediately, in which case the governmental unit is repaid for the resources it uses in constructing the improvement, and the special assessment project is terminated. In many cases, however, special assessment bonds are issued to pay the construction costs, and the special assessments are collected in installments over the term of the special assessment bond issue. Interest charged on the unpaid balances of special assessment receivables is used to cover the interest on the special assessment bonds. No serious problem of financing the special assessment project arises if special assessments are not paid as they come due. This is because the governmental unit has power to enforce collection through seizure of the real property against which special assessments are levied.

The primary unique feature of general government special assessment capital projects is that a long-term special assessment receivable is created by special assessment levies collected in installments over future years. The GASB requires fairly straightforward application of the governmental accounting model to these transactions. Capital improvements related to special assessment projects are accounted for in capital project funds. The special assessment receivables and debt service on special assessment debt for which the government is obligated in some manner are accounted for in a debt service fund, and the related special assessment obligation is accounted for in the general long-term debt account group. Alternatively, the debt service on special assessment debt for which the governmental unit is not obligated in any manner is accounted for in an agency fund, and the related special assessment obligation is only disclosed in notes to the financial statements.[4]

ACCOUNT GROUPS

An account group is a self-balancing set of accounts with equal debits and credits, but account groups are not funds because they are not fiscal entities. Fixed assets that are assets of the general government and unmatured long-term liabilities that are liabilities of the general government are accounted for in account groups. Thus, a governmental unit needs two account groups—the general fixed assets account group and the general long-term debt account group.

Recall that the accounting equation for the general fixed assets account group is:

$$\text{Fixed assets} = \text{Investment in general fixed assets}$$

---

[4]GASB, Cod. Sec. S40.

The accounting equation for the general long-term debt account group is:

Amount to be provided in future years to retire general long-term debt + Amount available in DSFs to retire general long-term debt = General long-term debt payable

GENERAL FIXED ASSETS ACCOUNT GROUP

General fixed assets of a governmental unit include all fixed assets other than those accounted for in proprietary funds (enterprise or internal service funds) or trust funds. Thus, they include fixed assets purchased by or through a general fund, special revenue fund, or capital projects fund, as well as many of those acquired through donation, capital leases, and foreclosures. When fixed assets are acquired through a governmental fund, the purchase transactions are recorded as expenditures in the governmental funds, but the property acquired is recorded in the **general fixed assets** (GFA) account group, except for the purchase of *public domain* or *infrastructure general fixed assets.* Public domain or infrastructure fixed assets consist of roads, bridges, curbs and gutters, streets and sidewalks, and similar assets of general government activities. The capitalization and reporting of infrastructure fixed assets in the GFA account group is optional [GASB Cod. Sec. 1400.109].

General Fixed Asset Acquisitions

Fixed assets acquired by purchase are recorded at their cost. Those acquired by gift are recorded at their fair values at the time of receipt. (Fixed assets acquired by lease agreements are covered later in this chapter.) Depreciation on general fixed assets is not recorded in the accounts of governmental funds because it is not a change in financial resources or working capital. Accumulated depreciation may be recorded (optional) in the GFA account group, but typically is not. Fixed asset classifications include the following:

> Land
> Buildings
> Improvements other than buildings
> Machinery and equipment
> Construction in progress

Entries in the GFA accounts are signaled by transactions in the governmental funds. Thus, expenditure transactions for capital outlays in governmental funds must be coordinated with general fixed asset records. If an entry is made in the general fund to record a $15,000 expenditure for a police car, the following entry is made in the GFA account group:

GFA Account Group		
Machinery and equipment	$ 15,000	
Investment in general fixed assets—general revenue		$ 15,000
To record acquisition of police car through general revenue sources.		

Similarly, if the capital projects fund records a $100,000 expenditure for a building acquired through a federal grant, the following entry in the GFA account group is made:

GFA Account Group		
Buildings	$100,000	
Investment in general fixed assets—federal grant		$100,000
To record acquisition of a building through federal grant.		

The credit entry for recording fixed assets in the GFA account group is to the account "investment in general fixed assets" with the source of financing being specified.

Expenditures on incomplete construction projects of capital projects funds are recorded in the GFA account group as incurred, rather than when construction is complete. Thus, costs incurred on a building contract are recorded as expenditures in the CPF and as construction in progress in the GFA account group. Upon completion of the building, the amounts recorded as construction in progress in the GFA account group are reclassified as buildings (or another appropriate classification).

Recording Accumulated Depreciation

Although the recording of accumulated depreciation in the GFA account group is optional, if it is recognized, the entry is recorded in the following format:

GFA Account Group
Investment in general fixed assets (grants, donations, etc.)   XXX
      Accumulated depreciation (buildings, equipment, etc.)   XXX

In this manner, accumulated depreciation is reflected in the accounts, but depreciation expense is never recorded.

Asset Dispositions

When general fixed assets are sold, retired, or abandoned, an entry is made debiting the investment in general fixed assets account and crediting the land, building, or other fixed assets account for its recorded amount (book value if accumulated depreciation is recorded). The entry in the GFA account group, therefore, is typically a reversal of the initial acquisition entry and is independent of the amount received, if any, for the asset retired. Proceeds from the sale of general fixed assets are usually recorded as other financing sources in the general fund.

Financial Statements for the GFA Account Group

The financial statements prepared for the GFA account group are a statement of changes in general fixed assets and a statement of general fixed assets (balance sheet). These are illustrated in Exhibit 20–3. The statement of changes in general fixed assets could be expanded to include accumulated depreciation and the book value of general fixed assets where the optional accumulated depreciation is recorded. A statement of general fixed assets is required when governments need to present more detail than is included in the combined balance sheet. Changes in general fixed assets are required to be reported in the general purpose financial statements, but they can be reported in statement form or in a financial statement note.

GENERAL LONG-TERM DEBT ACCOUNT GROUP

General long-term debt is the *unmatured principal* of bonds, warrants, notes, special assessment debt for which the government is obligated in some manner, or other forms of noncurrent or long-term indebtedness that is not a specific liability of any proprietary fund or trust fund. Governmental funds do not record the obligations for general long-term debt in their accounts. These obligations are recorded in the **general long-term debt** account group, where the debt is classified as term bonds, serial bonds, and other general long-term liabilities. *The amounts recorded for general long-term debt obligations (credit) are balanced by accounts that show the amounts available in DSFs to be used to pay general long-term debt and amounts to be provided for (raised) in the future for payment of the obligations (debits).*

Recording General Long-Term Debt Obligations

When a general obligation serial bond issue is sold, the proceeds received are recorded in a governmental fund. Most commonly, general government bonds are issued to finance construction or acquisition of general government fixed assets. In this situation, a capital projects fund is used to account for the bond proceeds. At the same time, an entry for the bond liability is recorded in the GLTD account group. For example, the issuance of the serial bond issue for construction of the Budding City Hall (page 761) would be recorded in the GLTD account group as follows:

GLTD Account Group
Amount to be provided for payment of serial bonds $ 500,000
      Serial bonds payable $ 500,000

Note that the bonds are recorded at their face value, not their present value.

CITY OF GOWER
STATEMENT OF CHANGES IN GENERAL FIXED ASSETS*
FOR THE FISCAL YEAR ENDED JUNE 30, 20X2

	Balance July 1, 20X1	Additions	Deductions	Balance June 30, 20X2
Land	$ 109,000	$ 10,500	$ 10,000	$ 109,500
Buildings	1,000,000	300,000	75,000	1,225,000
Improvements other than buildings	410,000	81,000	—	491,000
Equipment	230,000	70,000	30,000	270,000
Construction in progress	251,000	251,000	—	502,000
Total assets	$2,000,000	$712,500	$115,000	$2,597,500

* Footnote disclosure is acceptable.

CITY OF GOWER
STATEMENT OF GENERAL FIXED ASSETS*
ON JUNE 30, 20X2

Assets	
Land	$ 109,500
Buildings	1,225,000
Improvements other than buildings	491,000
Equipment	270,000
Construction in progress	502,000
	$2,597,500
Investment in General Fixed Assets	
General revenues	$ 392,500
General obligation bonds	1,000,000
State shared revenues	250,000
Federal grants	500,000
State grants	300,000
Donations	155,000
	$2,597,500

*Optional

Exhibit 20–3   *Financial Statements for General Fixed Assets Account Group*

As serial bonds are retired through the debt service fund, entries are made in the GLTD account group to reduce the recorded obligation. The July 1, 20X2 entry in the DSF for retirement expenditures of $50,000 par of the city hall bonds (page 766) requires the following entry in the GLTD account group:

GLTD Account Group

Serial bonds payable	$ 50,000	
Amount to be provided for payment of serial bonds		$ 50,000

In the case of term bonds, in which resources are accumulated in the DSF to retire the full amount of the obligation at maturity, the sequence of recording in the GLTD account group is as follows:

1 Assume that $1,000,000 term bonds are issued with the proceeds being recorded in the CPF. The corresponding entry in the GLTD account group is:

GLTD Account Group

Amount to be provided for payment of term bonds	$1,000,000	
Term bonds payable		$1,000,000

2 If $50,000 is accumulated in the DSF for future retirement of these term bonds, the corresponding entry in the GLTD account group is:

GLTD Account Group

Amount available for payment of term bonds	$ 50,000	
Amount to be provided for payment of term bonds		$ 50,000

3 When bonds are retired through the DSF, the entry in the GLTD account group is:

GLTD Account Group

Term bonds payable	$1,000,000	
Amount available for payment of term bonds		$1,000,000

Financial Statements for GLTD Account Group

The financial statements that are usually prepared for general long-term debt are a statement of changes in general long-term debt and a statement of general long-term debt (balance sheet). These statements are illustrated in Exhibit 20–4. The statement of general long-term debt is required if there is not sufficient detail for fair presentation in the combined balance sheet. Changes in general long-term debt must be re-

---

CITY OF RUTHERFORD
STATEMENT OF CHANGES IN GENERAL LONG-TERM DEBT*
FOR THE FISCAL YEAR ENDED JUNE 30, 20X2

	Balance July 1, 20X1	Additions	Deductions	Balance June 30, 20X2
Serial bonds payable	$ 500,000	$1,000,000	$200,000	$1,300,000
Term bonds payable	2,000,000	—	—	2,000,000
Capital lease liabilities	400,000	500,000	47,250	852,750
Claims and judgments payable	—	1,200,000	—	1,200,000
Vacation pay payable	700,000	80,000	—	780,000
Total liabilities	$3,600,000	$2,780,000	$247,250	$6,132,750

* Footnote disclosure is acceptable.

CITY OF RUTHERFORD
STATEMENT OF GENERAL LONG-TERM DEBT*
AT JUNE 30, 20X2

Amount available to retire term bonds	$ 770,000
Amount available to retire serial bonds	150,000
Total amount available to retire general long-term debt	920,000
Amount to be provided to retire:	
Term bonds	1,230,000
Serial bonds	1,150,000
Capital lease liabilities	852,750
Claims and judgments payable	1,200,000
Vacation pay payable	780,000
Total amount to be provided in future years to retire debt	5,212,750
Total available and to be provided	$6,132,750

General Long-Term Debt

Term bonds	
6% general obligation bonds due July 1, 20X9	$2,000,000
Serial bonds	
$5\frac{1}{2}$% general obligation bonds due $100,000 annually	1,000,000
6% special assessment debt with government commitment due $60,000 annually	300,000
Capital lease liabilities	852,750
Claims and judgments payable	1,200,000
Vacation pay payable	780,000
Total general obligation debt	$6,132,750

*Optional

Exhibit 20–4   *Statements for General Long-Term Debt Account Group*

ported in the general purpose financial statements—either in a statement as illustrated or in a note to the financial statements.

Defeasance of Debt

Debt refundings occur when new debt is issued and the proceeds are used to repay an old debt issue. A current refunding occurs when the old debt is repaid immediately. An advance refunding occurs when the proceeds of the new debt issue are placed with an escrow agent and invested until they are used to repay principal and interest of the old debt. Advance refundings usually result in the defeasance of debt in a legal sense or in substance. Legal defeasance occurs when the debt is legally satisfied even though the debt is not actually paid. In substance defeasance occurs when the debt is considered defeased for accounting and financial reporting purposes even though legal defeasance has not occurred. For accounting and financial reporting purposes, debt is defeased in substance if the debtor irrevocably places cash or certain other assets with an escrow agent in a trust to be used solely for satisfying payments of both interest and principal on the defeased debt, the assets of the trust are only cash and risk-free securities, and the investment maturities are matched with the debt service payment schedule.

Governmental Funds   *GASB Statement No. 7*, "Advance Refundings Resulting in Defeasance of Debt," provides guidance for accounting and reporting for advance refundings of debt reported in the general long-term debt account group.[5] The proceeds from advance refundings that result in defeasance of debt are reported in the fund receiving the proceeds as an "other financing source—proceeds of refunding bonds." Use of the proceeds to pay the escrow agent (or to repay the bondholders) is reported as an "other financing use—payments to refunded bond escrow agent" (or "other financing use—principal retirement" if bondholders are paid). Any payments to the escrow agent (or to bondholders) from sources other than the bond proceeds are reported as "debt service expenditures." Finally, the GLTD account group is adjusted for increases or decreases in the long-term debt.

Proprietary Activities   *GASB Statement No. 23*, "Accounting and Financial Reporting for Refundings of Debt Reported by Proprietary Activities," establishes accounting standards for current refundings and advance refundings resulting in defeasance of debt reported by proprietary funds (and other governmental entities using proprietary fund accounting).[6] In accounting for refundings, the difference between the reacquisition price (the amount required to repay the old debt in a refunding transaction) and the net carrying amount of the old debt (amount due at maturity adjusted for unamortized premium or discount and issuance costs of the old debt) should be deferred and amortized as a component of interest expense over the remaining life of the old debt or the life of the new debt, whichever is shorter. The deferred amount is reported as an addition to or deduction from the new debt in the balance sheet. In essence, the deferred amount is deferring the gain or loss that would have been recognized if borrowed resources had not been used. The subsequent accounting and reporting for the deferred amount is similar to that for premiums and discounts.

ACCOUNTING FOR LEASES IN GOVERNMENTAL FUNDS

Lease agreements of state and local governments are accounted for under the provisions of *FASB Statement No. 13*, "Accounting for Leases," as amended and interpreted by *NCGA Statement No. 5*, "Accounting and Financial Reporting Principles for Lease Agreements by State and Local Governments" and by *GASB Statement No. 13*, "Accounting and Reporting for Leases with Scheduled Rent Increases." A lease agreement that is financed from general government resources must be accounted for under governmental fund accounting principles. [See GASB Cod. Sec. L20.]

Operating lease payments are typically recorded as rental expenditures. Operating leases with scheduled rent increases that are reported in governmental funds should recognize rental revenue or expenditures each period using the modified accrual basis of accounting.[7]

---

[5]GASB, Cod. Sec. D20.106-108.
[6]GASB, Cod. Sec. D20.109-110.
[7]Measurement criteria are provided in GASB, Cod. Sec. L20.109 and .110.

When *capital leases* are used to acquire general fixed assets by purchase or construction, the asset is capitalized in the general fixed assets account group at the inception of the lease at the present value of the minimum lease payments determined by *FASB Statement No. 13* criteria. For example, if a government enters into a general government capital lease with an initial down payment of $50,000 and a present value of minimum lease payments of $500,000, the following entries are required:

GFA Account Group

Machinery and equipment	$500,000	
Investment in general fixed assets—capital lease		$500,000

At the same time, a liability in the same amount is recorded in the general long-term debt account group.

GLTD Account Group

Amount to be provided for payment of capital lease	$450,000	
Capital lease payable		$450,000

The governmental fund acquiring the general fixed asset through a capital lease records an expenditure and other financing source [GASB Cod. Sec. L20.115]. For example:

GF

Expenditures	$500,000	
Cash		$ 50,000
Other financing sources—capital lease		450,000

PROPRIETARY FUNDS

Proprietary funds of governmental units are used to account for business-type activities that provide goods and services to users and finance those services largely from user charges. The objective of proprietary funds is to maintain capital and/or produce income, and full accrual accounting procedures apply. Thus, proprietary funds have revenue and expense, *not expenditure*, accounts. Revenues are recognized in the accounting period in which they *are earned and become measurable*, and expenses are recognized in the period *incurred*, if measurable. The availability criterion for governmental fund revenue recognition does not apply to proprietary fund and similar trust fund revenue recognition.

Recall that the accounting equation for proprietary funds is

$$\begin{array}{c} \text{Current} \\ \text{assets} \end{array} + \begin{array}{c} \text{Noncurrent} \\ \text{assets} \end{array} - \begin{array}{c} \text{Current} \\ \text{liabilities} \end{array} - \begin{array}{c} \text{Long-term} \\ \text{liabilities} \end{array} = \begin{array}{c} \text{Contributed} \\ \text{capital} \end{array} + \begin{array}{c} \text{Retained} \\ \text{earnings} \end{array}$$

The fixed assets of proprietary funds are **fund fixed assets** and not general fixed assets. Long-term liabilities incurred by a proprietary fund and to be serviced from its revenues are **fund liabilities,** not general long-term debt. Lease agreements of proprietary funds are accounted for entirely within the fund under the provisions of *FASB Statement No. 13*, "Accounting for Leases," except for operating leases with scheduled rent increases. Operating leases with scheduled rent increases (in other words, the increases are fixed by contract) that are reported in proprietary funds and similar trust funds should recognize rental revenue as it accrues over the lease term.

As noted in the last chapter, proprietary funds are required to present three financial statements. The required statements are a balance sheet, statement of revenues, expenses, and changes in retained earnings (or changes in fund equity), and statement of cash flows.

The Governmental Accounting Standards Board addressed the issue of which accounting and reporting standards apply to proprietary activities in *GASB Statement No. 20*, "Accounting and Financial Reporting for Proprietary Activities." Governmental proprietary activities *must apply*:

- All applicable GASB statements and
- All FASB and predecessor standards issued before November 30, 1989[8] that do not conflict with GASB standards.

---

[8]November 30, 1989 is the date that the Financial Accounting Foundation reaffirmed that the GASB was responsible for setting the standards for state and local governments.

Governmental proprietary activities *may either apply*:

- All FASB standards issued after November 30, 1989, as long as they do not conflict with GASB standards, *or*
- No FASB standards issued after November 30, 1989, even if they modify or rescind earlier issued FASB statements (This election does not completely prohibit applying a FASB standard. In essence, they are in the lowest level of the GAAP hierarchy.)

The two types of funds within the proprietary fund classification are internal service funds and enterprise funds.

INTERNAL SERVICE FUNDS

Internal service funds (ISF) are proprietary funds that are used to account for the financing of goods and services provided by one department or agency to other departments or agencies of the governmental unit, or to other governmental units, on a cost-reimbursement basis. Account classifications used by an ISF are those that would be used in accounting for similar operations of a private business enterprise.

The key difference between an ISF and an enterprise fund lies in the user group for which the goods and services are intended. Enterprise funds provide goods and services primarily to the general public, whereas internal service funds provide their goods and services primarily to other departments or agencies within the same governmental unit (or, on a limited basis, to other governmental units). Even though the user groups for enterprise and internal service funds are different, the accounting is identical. Also, the financial statement requirements are the same.

Centralized purchasing, motor pools, printing shops, and self-insurance are examples of internal service fund operations. Each activity offers potential efficiencies through economies of scale, improved services, and better control.

In many cases, the initial financing of an ISF is provided by a contribution of cash and/or operating facilities from the governmental unit, after which the ISF is expected to be self-sustaining. Alternatively, the governmental unit may provide a long-term advance to the ISF to be repaid out of future operating flows of the fund. A contribution is classified as part of the fund equity of the ISF, whereas an advance is recorded as a liability of the ISF. Interfund advances are long-term liabilities and receivables. Short-term interfund loans are recorded as *due to Fund A, due from Fund B,* and so on.

Accounting for an Internal Service Fund

The City of Carlton creates a central motor pool fund with a cash contribution of $200,000 from the general fund and a contribution of existing motor vehicles with a fair value of $120,000. The cash contribution is recorded as a $200,000 residual equity transfer in the GF and is reported as a direct charge to the beginning fund balance of the GF [GASB Cod. Sec. 1800.107]. The equipment transferred is removed from the records of the general fixed assets account group at its original cost, or book value if accumulated depreciation has been recorded. In the records of the central motor pool fund, the capital contribution is recorded:

ISF		
Cash	$200,000	
Motor vehicles	120,000	
Residual equity transfer from GF		$200,000
Contributed capital from municipality		120,000

To record establishment of the fund. (The residual equity transfer is closed to the contributed capital account.)

A building is constructed on land owned by the city at a cost of $100,000, equipment is purchased for $50,000, and operating supplies are acquired for $20,000. These cash expenditures, in summary form, are recorded as follows:

ISF		
Building	$100,000	
Equipment	50,000	
Supplies on hand	20,000	
Cash		$170,000

To record purchase of building, equipment, and supplies.

During the first year of operation, the central motor pool fund supplies motor pool vehicles to municipal departments and bills these departments at a predetermined rate based on miles driven. The rate is set to cover all costs of operating the motor pool and servicing the vehicles, including the cost of replacing worn-out vehicles. Journal entries to record revenue and expense transactions and year-end entries are shown below in summary form. Note the similarity to business accounting entries.

Due from general fund	$ 60,000	
Due from special revenue fund	30,000	
Due from enterprise fund	40,000	
Service revenue		$130,000
To charge user funds for vehicle services.		
Cash	$100,000	
Due from general fund		$ 60,000
Due from enterprise fund		40,000
To record collections from user funds.		
Salaries expense	$ 40,000	
Utilities expense	8,000	
Supplies expense	30,000	
Cash		$ 78,000
To record payments for expense items.		

Adjusting Entries

Supplies expense	$ 5,000	
Supplies on hand		$ 5,000
To adjust supplies expense and supplies on hand accounts at year-end.		
Salaries expense	$ 4,000	
Accrued salaries payable		$ 4,000
To accrue salaries.		
Depreciation expense—building	$ 5,000	
Accumulated depreciation—building		$ 5,000
To record depreciation on building ($100,000 ÷ 20 years).		
Depreciation expense—vehicles	$ 20,000	
Accumulated depreciation—vehicles		$ 20,000
To record depreciation on vehicles (200,000 miles driven × 10 cents per mile).		
Depreciation expense—equipment	$ 10,000	
Accumulated depreciation—equipment		$ 10,000
To record depreciation on equipment ($50,000 ÷ 5 years).		

Closing Entries

Residual equity transfer from GF	$200,000	
Contributed capital from municipality		$200,000
Service revenue	$130,000	
Supplies expense		$ 35,000
Salaries expense		44,000
Utilities expense		8,000
Depreciation expense—building		5,000
Depreciation expense—vehicles		20,000
Depreciation expense—equipment		10,000
Retained earnings		8,000
To close revenue and expense accounts to retained earnings.		

```
CITY OF CARLTON
CENTRAL MOTOR POOL FUND
BALANCE SHEET
AT DECEMBER 31, 20X1

Current Assets
Cash                                         $ 52,000
Due from special revenue fund                  30,000
Supplies on hand                               15,000
    Total current assets                                   $ 97,000

Plant Assets
Building (net of accumulated depreciation)     95,000
Vehicles (net of accumulated depreciation)    100,000
Equipment (net of accumulated depreciation)    40,000
    Total plant assets                                       235,000
        Total assets                                        $332,000

Liabilities and Fund Equity
Accrued salaries payable                                   $   4,000
Fund equity
    Contributed capital from municipality     320,000
    Retained earnings                           8,000
        Total fund equity                                    328,000
        Total liabilities and fund equity                   $332,000
```

Exhibit 20–5   ISF Balance Sheet

Financial Statements of the ISF

The required financial statements of an internal service fund include a balance sheet, a statement of revenues, expenses, and changes in retained earnings (or fund equity), and a statement of cash flows. Financial statements for the central motor pool fund are shown in Exhibits 20–5, 20–6, and 20–7. For illustrative purposes, the operating statement in Exhibit 20–6 includes certain items such as nonoperating revenues and expenses and operating transfers that did not affect the central motor pool ISF.

```
CITY OF CARLTON
CENTRAL MOTOR POOL FUND
STATEMENT OF REVENUES, EXPENSES,
AND CHANGES IN RETAINED EARNINGS
FOR THE YEAR ENDED DECEMBER 31, 20X1

Operating Revenues
Service revenues                                          $130,000

Operating Expenses
Supplies expense                             $35,000
Salaries expense                              44,000
Utilities expense                              8,000
Depreciation expense                          35,000
    Total operating expenses                                122,000
        Operating income                                      8,000

Nonoperating revenues (expenses)
Investment income                                —
Interest expense                                 —
Gain on sale of fixed assets                     —              —
        Income before operating transfers                     8,000
Operating transfers in                                         —
Operating transfers out                                        —
        Net income                                            8,000
Retained earnings, January 1, 20X1                             —
Retained earnings, December 31, 20X1                      $   8,000
```

Exhibit 20–6   ISF Statement of Revenues, Expenses, and Changes in Retained Earnings

```
CITY OF CARLTON
CENTRAL MOTOR POOL FUND
STATEMENT OF CASH FLOWS
FOR THE YEAR ENDED DECEMBER 31, 20X1
```

Direct Method

Cash Flows from Operating Activities

Cash received from customers		$100,000
Less: Cash paid to suppliers	$ (50,000)	
Cash paid for salaries	(40,000)	
Cash paid for utilities	(8,000)	(98,000)
Cash flows from operating activities		2,000

Cash Flows from Noncapital Financing Activities

Cash received from residual equity transfer from general fund	200,000	
Cash from noncapital financing activities		200,000

Cash Flows from Capital and Related Financing Activities

Purchase of building	(100,000)	
Purchase of equipment	(50,000)	
Net cash used in capital and related financing activities		(150,000)
Increase in cash for 20X1		52,000
Cash, January 1, 20X1		—
Cash, December 31, 20X1		$ 52,000

Indirect Method

Cash Flows from Operating Activities

Operating income		$ 8,000
Noncash expenses, revenues, losses and gains included in income		
Depreciation	$ 35,000	
Due from special revenue fund	(30,000)	
Supplies on hand	(15,000)	
Accrued salaries payable	4,000	6,000
Cash flows from operating activities		2,000

Cash Flows from Noncapital Financing Activities

Cash received from residual equity transfer from general fund	200,000	
Cash from noncapital financing activities		200,000

Cash Flows from Capital and Related Financing Activities

Purchase of building	(100,000)	
Purchase of equipment	(50,000)	
Net cash used in capital and related financing activities		(150,000)
Increase in cash for 20X1		52,000
Cash, January 1, 20X1		—
Cash, December 31, 20X1		$ 52,000

Exhibit 20–7 *ISF Cash Flow Statement (Includes Alternative Methods)*

Statement of Cash Flows for Proprietary and Nonexpendable Trust Funds

GASB Statement No. 9, "Reporting Cash Flows of Proprietary and Nonexpendable Trust Funds and Government Entities That Use Proprietary Fund Accounting," establishes standards for cash flow reporting for proprietary and nonexpendable trust funds and other governmental entities that use proprietary fund accounting. Public employee retirement systems and pension trust funds are exempt from the requirement.

FASB No. 95, "Statement of Cash Flows," specifies a three-section format for cash flow statements of business enterprises: operating activities, investing activities, and financing activities. *GASB Statement No. 9* requires a cash flow statement with four separate sections for governments: cash flows from operating activities, cash flows from noncapital financing activities, cash flows from capital and related financing activities, and cash flows from investing activities. The content and application of the four separate sections of the statement of cash flows for proprietary funds and government entities that use proprietary fund accounting are reviewed here:

Cash Flows from Operating Activities   Cash *inflows* of the operating activities section include:

> Receipts from sales of goods or services
> Receipts from quasi-external operating transactions
> Receipts from other funds for reimbursements of operating transactions
> All other receipts not included in one of the other three sections

Cash *outflows* of the operating activities section include:

> Payments for materials used in providing services or manufacturing goods for resale
> Principal payments to suppliers of those materials or goods on account or under short-term or long-term notes payable
> Payments to suppliers for other goods and services
> Payments to employees for salaries
> Payments to other governments as grants for operating activities
> Payments for taxes and in lieu of taxes
> All other cash payments not included in one of the other three sections

Cash Flows from Noncapital Financing Activities   Items to be considered cash *inflows* for the noncapital financing activities section include:

> Proceeds from bonds and notes not clearly issued specifically for the acquisition, construction or improvement of capital assets
> Receipts from grants and subsidies and receipts from other funds (except those restricted for capital purposes or operating activities)
> Receipts from property taxes and other taxes collected for the governmental enterprise and not restricted for capital purposes

Cash *outflows* for this section include:

> Repayments of amounts borrowed (including interest payments) other than those related to acquiring or constructing capital assets
> Amounts paid for grants and subsidies (except those for specific operating activities of the grantor government)
> Cash paid to other funds except for quasi-external transactions

Cash Flows from Capital ("Fixed Asset") and Related Financing Activities   Capital and related activities include acquiring and disposing of capital assets used in providing goods and services, including borrowing money to finance fixed asset construction or acquisition and repaying it with interest. Cash *inflows* include amounts from capital grants (i.e., grants for the sole purpose of acquiring, constructing, or improving a fixed asset), contributions, special assessments, insurance proceeds, and so on, as long as they are received specifically to defray the cost of acquiring, constructing, or improving capital assets. Cash received from sale or disposal of fixed assets is included in this section also.

Cash *outflows* include amounts to acquire, construct, or improve capital assets, and to repay amounts borrowed (including interest), as long as the purpose of the borrowing was directly related to acquiring, constructing or improving capital assets.

Cash Flows from Investing Activities   Investing activities include making and collecting loans and acquiring and disposing of investments in debt or equity instruments. Cash *inflows* include collections of loans and sales of investment securities (other than from cash equivalents) and the receipt of interest and dividends. Cash *outflows* include making loans and payments to acquire investment securities (other than for cash equivalents). Cash equivalents are defined as short-term, highly liquid investments that are both readily convertible into known amounts of cash and so near their maturity that they present insignificant risk of changes in value because of changes in interest rates. Ordinarily, these include investments with remaining maturities when purchased of three months or less.

Direct or Indirect Method of Preparing Cash Flows Statement   The statement of cash flows can be prepared using either the direct or indirect method of presenting cash flows from operating activities. Both methods are illustrated in Exhibit 20–7 for the internal service fund. GASB encourages use of the direct method. Only one method, direct or indirect, should be used in a combined or combining statement of cash flows.

ENTERPRISE FUNDS

Enterprise funds (EF) are used to account for activities that are financed and operated similarly to those of private business enterprises. Typically, the goods and services of enterprise funds are provided *to the general public on a continuing basis* with the costs being financed primarily through user charges. Activities that do not fully meet this norm may also be accounted for in an enterprise fund, if desired by the governing body for certain reasons. Mass transit authorities sometimes are treated as enterprise funds under this option criterion. Because the objective of an enterprise fund is to maintain capital and/or generate net income, full accrual accounting procedures are applicable. Like internal service funds, enterprise funds are proprietary funds that use revenue and expense accounts and accrual accounting practices similar to those of private business enterprises.

The fixed assets acquired and the long-term liabilities incurred by an EF are *fund fixed assets* and *long-term fund liabilities*. Therefore, they are recorded in the enterprise fund and not in the general fixed assets and general long-term debt account groups. Often, the long-term debt obligations are in the form of revenue bonds secured only by enterprise fund operations. If such bonds are also secured by the "full faith and credit" of the governmental unit, the liability is still recorded in the fund, but a contingent liability also must be disclosed in the notes related to general long-term debt.

The GASB Codification permits the use of enterprise fund accounting for any service for which there is a significant potential for financing through user charges. The types of operations accounted for through enterprise funds are about as diverse as those found in private enterprise. They range from the operation of electric and water utilities that are intended to produce income, to swimming pool and golf course operations where costs are intended to be recovered primarily from user charges to activities such as mass transit authorities and civic centers that are often heavily subsidized from general government revenues.

Initial financing of many enterprise funds is typically the same as for an ISF. The governmental unit makes a capital contribution (a residual equity transfer in the general fund) or provides a long-term advance to the enterprise fund, and future operations are expected to cover all costs, including depreciation on fund fixed assets, so that operations can continue indefinitely without further capital contributions.

The income or loss of an enterprise fund is closed to retained earnings, as in private business enterprises. Thus, a closing entry for an enterprise fund might appear as follows:

EF		
Service revenue	$100,000	
Interest income	2,000	
Cost of supplies used		$ 40,000
Utility expense		16,000
Depreciation expense		20,000
Interest expense		6,000
Retained earnings		20,000

Customer Deposits   Utility-type enterprise funds often require customer deposits to assure timely payment for services. Deposits are normally required before service starts and are refunded when service is terminated. Land developers may also be required to make good faith deposits to finance the cost of extending utilities service lines. Such assets should be segregated and reported as restricted assets in the enterprise fund balance sheet. Customer deposits remain in current liabilities until applied against unpaid billings or refunded to customers.

Grants Intergovernmental operating grants (which can be used either only for operations or for operations and capital assets acquisition) should be recognized in the period qualifying expenditures are incurred (assuming any other significant conditions have been met also). Operating grants are reported as nonoperating revenues in proprietary funds. Intergovernmental capital grants are recognized as contributed capital, not as revenues, in the period qualifying expenditures are incurred (assuming any other significant conditions have been met).

Required Financial Statements

Required financial statements for an enterprise fund consist of a balance sheet, an operating statement (statement of revenues, expenses, and changes in retained earnings), and a statement of cash flows. The financial statements of an enterprise fund are similar to those of a business enterprise. Enterprise funds do not pay property taxes or income taxes, and these items are noticeably absent from the operating statement. In addition, an enterprise fund does not have capital stock and paid-in capital, and in place of stockholders' equity, its balance sheet shows a fund equity section, such as the following:

Fund Equity	
Contributed capital from municipality	$800,000
Retained earnings	150,000
Total fund equity	$950,000

One other difference from the statements of private businesses that may be found in the financial statements of an enterprise fund lies in such interfund account titles as due from general fund (for utility charges), due to internal service fund (for supply acquisitions), advance from general fund (for long-term financing), and operating transfers and residual equity transfers. Such items constitute only minor differences from private enterprise accounting.

COMBINING FINANCIAL STATEMENTS

A governmental unit may have a number of enterprise funds, as well as numerous funds for each of the other fund types except the general fund. The GASB Codification requires that combining financial statements be included in a comprehensive annual financial report. Combining financial statements are used to aggregate individual fund account balances to produce relevant totals by fund type. The total data for each fund type are presented in a column in the corresponding combined financial statement.

The concept of combining financial statements is illustrated in Exhibit 20–8 for the balance sheets of the Town of Blacksburg, Virginia's four enterprise funds—waste management, water and sewer, golf course, and transit system. Financial statement items for these individual enterprise funds are combined in the statement illustrated, and only the totals are used in the combined balance sheet column for enterprise funds. Similar combining statements for other fund types are needed to meet the requirements for a comprehensive annual financial report.

FIDUCIARY FUNDS

Fiduciary fund types are used to account for assets held by a governmental unit as trustee or agent for individuals, private organizations, and other governmental units. The fiduciary grouping includes trust funds and agency funds, which are similar in the sense that the governmental unit acts in a fiduciary capacity for both types of funds. The accounting emphasis for trust and agency funds lies in showing how the government's fiduciary responsibilities have been met. A separate agency or trust fund may be used for each agreement under which the governmental unit acts as agent or trustee.

TOWN OF BLACKSBURG, VIRGINIA
ENTERPRISE FUNDS
COMBINING BALANCE SHEET
JUNE 30, 1997

	Water and Sewer	Waste Management	Golf Course	Transit System	Total
Assets					
Current assets:					
Cash and temporary investments	$ 1,742,992	$ 51,950	$ 82,025	$ 623,957	$ 2,500,924
Cash with fiscal agent	10,000	—	—	—	10,000
Utilities receivable, net of allowance for uncollectibles	721,033	126,645	—	—	847,678
Accounts receivable, net	260,342	3,443	—	34,538	298,323
Accrued interest	20,428	—	—	8,387	28,815
Receivable from other governments	—	—	—	324,582	324,582
Prepaid expenses	631	—	—	—	631
Inventories	—	—	7,041	12,744	19,785
Total current assets	2,755,426	182,038	89,066	1,004,208	4,030,738
Property, plant and equipment:					
Land	56,314	—	376,947	157,000	590,261
Buildings	—	—	214,525	3,321,928	3,536,453
Water system—Plant	5,949,709	—	—	—	5,949,709
Sewer system—Plant	4,368,032	—	—	—	4,368,032
Equipment	2,363,095	15,124	128,425	4,410,754	6,917,398
Construction in progress	171,094	—	—	—	171,094
Total property, plant and equipment	12,908,244	15,124	719,897	7,889,682	21,532,947
Less accumulated depreciation	5,509,700	5,658	140,061	4,460,240	10,115,659
Net property, plant & equipment	7,398,544	9,466	579,836	3,429,442	11,417,288
Total assets	$10,153,970	$191,504	$668,902	$4,433,650	$15,448,026
Liabilities and Fund Equity					
Liabilities:					
Current liabilities:					
Accounts payable	$ 742,387	$ 71,906	$ 10,096	$ 49,056	$ 873,445
Accrued expenses	137,745	1,284	11,364	57,944	208,337
Current maturities of long-term debt	182,000	—	5,000	—	187,000
Current maturities of capital lease obligations	145,285	—	—	—	145,285
Customer deposits	103,125	—	—	—	103,125
Deferred revenue	175,469	—	—	—	175,469
Total current liabilities	1,486,011	73,190	26,460	107,000	1,692,661
Long-term debt (net of discount)	2,436,535	—	134,320	—	2,570,855
Long-term capital lease obligation	1,537,449	—	—	—	1,537,449
Total liabilities	5,459,995	73,190	160,780	107,000	5,800,965
Fund equity:					
Contributed capital	1,191,677	—	381,370	3,288,961	4,862,008
Retained earnings	3,502,298	118,314	126,752	1,037,689	4,785,053
Total fund equity	4,693,975	118,314	508,122	4,326,650	9,647,061
Total liabilities and fund equity	$10,153,970	$191,504	$668,902	$4,433,650	$15,448,026

Source: Adapted from Town of Blacksburg, Virginia, Comprehensive Annual Financial Report, June 30, 1997.

Exhibit 20–8 *Combining Balance Sheet*

The basis of accounting for fiduciary funds follows the nature and measurement objective of the fund. Agency funds do not have revenues, expenditures, or expenses because their operations are of a custodial nature. Expendable trust funds are accounted for on a modified accrual basis in the same manner as governmental funds because they have the same "source and use" measurement objective. Nonexpendable trust funds have a capital maintenance or income objective and are accounted for in the same manner as proprietary funds. Somewhat unique guidance applies to pension trust funds.

Agency funds are used to account for resources that governments hold in a custodial or agency capacity. Governments account for some assets held in an agency capacity in other funds as well. The accounting equation for an agency fund is simply

$$\text{Assets} = \text{Liabilities}$$

There is no fund balance or equity. The primary financial statement for agency funds is a statement of changes in assets and liabilities. This statement usually consists of four columns. The first and last columns are essentially beginning and ending balance sheets. The middle columns are for disclosing additions and deductions for each asset and liability account. The statement is essentially an accountability-type reconciliation of beginning and ending balances.

A local government acts as an agent for the federal government when it withholds income and social security taxes from employee payrolls. It acts as an agent for the state government when it collects sales taxes on goods and services sold to the public. But separate **agency funds (AF)** need not be used for such agency relationships because normal liability accounting procedures are adequate to show how the governmental unit's fiduciary responsibilities have been met.

The debt service transactions of a special assessment bond issue for which the government is *not obligated in any manner* are reported in an agency fund to reflect the fact that the government's duties are limited to acting as an agent for the assessed property owners and bondholders. Thus, the government acts as agent for the property owners in collecting special assessments and remitting the amounts collected to bondholders.

Agency funds are needed when the government's agency responsibilities involve numerous transactions, include several different governmental units, and/or do not arise from normal and recurring operations of any other fund. For example, if a county unit of government serves as a tax collection agency for all towns and cities located within the county, an agency fund is created to show the county's acceptance of responsibility for collecting taxes for other governmental units and the fulfillment of that responsibility.

Accounting for an Agency Fund

Assume that Wise County collects property taxes for its own purposes as well as for the cities of Ansley, Broken Bow, and Custer, and that total property tax levies for 20X1 are as follows:

Wise County	$100,000	50%
Ansley	50,000	25
Broken Bow	20,000	10
Custer	30,000	15
Total	$200,000	100%

When the tax levies are certified to the county for collection, a tax agency fund is used to record the county's custodial responsibility for collecting the taxes:

AF		
Taxes receivable for local governmental units	$200,000	
Liability to Wise County		$100,000
Liability to Ansley		50,000
Liability to Broken Bow		20,000
Liability to Custer		30,000

If $180,000 of the levy is collected and $160,000 is remitted to the respective units of government during 20X1, the collection and remittance are recorded as follows:

AF		
Cash	$180,000	
Taxes receivable for local governmental units		$180,000
To record collection of taxes receivable.		

If Wise County charges Ansley, Broken Bow, and Custer a fee of 1% of taxes collected, the total charges would be $900 ($90,000 collected for these three cities times 1%), and the collection fees would be recorded:

AF		
Liability to Ansley	$ 450	
Liability to Broken Bow	180	
Liability to Custer	270	
Due to general fund (of Wise County)		$ 900
To charge cities a 1% fee for taxes collected for them.		

AF		
Due to general fund	$ 800	
Liability to Wise County	80,000	
Liability to Ansley	39,600	
Liability to Broken Bow	15,840	
Liability to Custer	23,760	
Cash		$160,000
To record remittance of taxes collected.		

Financial Statements for AF

Financial statements for the tax collection agency fund of Wise County are shown in Exhibit 20–9. Because agency funds do not have revenues and expenditures, the only statement in the exhibit is a statement of changes in assets and liabilities.

TRUST FUNDS [TF]

Expendable trust funds are those in which trust fund assets can be expended as needed to meet the objectives of the trust. The accounting emphasis in such trust funds is on showing the source of resources received and the use of those resources in meeting the governmental unit's fiduciary responsibilities as trustee. Expendable trust funds are accounted for in the same manner as governmental funds. Thus, their revenues and expenditures are accounted for on a modified accrual basis, and the required financial statements are a balance sheet, a statement of revenues, expendi-

---

WISE COUNTY
TAX COLLECTION AGENCY FUND
STATEMENT OF CHANGES IN ASSETS AND LIABILITIES
FOR THE YEAR ENDED DECEMBER 31, 20X1

	Balance January 1, 20X1	Additions	Deductions	Balance December 31, 20X1
Assets				
Cash	—	$180,000	$160,000	$20,000
Taxes receivable	—	200,000	180,000	20,000
Total assets	—	$380,000	$340,000	$40,000
Liabilities				
Due to General Fund	—	$ 900	$ 800	$ 100
Liability to Wise County	—	100,000	80,000	20,000
Liability to Ansley	—	50,000	40,050	9,950
Liability to Broken Bow	—	20,000	16,020	3,980
Liability to Custer	—	30,000	24,030	5,970
Total liabilities	—	$200,900	$160,900	$40,000

Exhibit 20–9   *Agency Fund Statement of Changes in Assets and Liabilities*

tures, and changes in fund balance, and, for those with legally adopted annual budgets, a budgetary comparison statement. A recent GASB standard, *GASB Statement No. 32*, "Accounting and Financial Reporting for Internal Revenue Code Section 457 Deferred Compensation Plans" only requires governments to report such deferred compensation plans in their financial statements if the government has fiduciary responsibility for the plan. If the government has fiduciary responsibility, it will account for the plan as an expendable trust fund.

Nonexpendable trust funds are those for which the principal must be maintained. The income may or may not be expendable. A trust fund in which the principal is nonexpendable but the income may be expended for purposes provided in the trust document is known as an **endowment trust fund**. An example of the endowment type of nonexpendable trust fund is a cemetery trust where some of the proceeds from sales of cemetery lots are placed in trust to provide perpetual care of the cemetery. The trust principal is required to be maintained intact, but the income can be expended for maintenance of the cemetery. Alternatively, many loan funds are nonexpendable both as to income and as to principal. In such trust funds, all amounts loaned are required to be repaid with interest and no part of the trust fund assets can be expended. Losses from bad debts can, of course, reduce trust fund assets.

Nonexpendable trust funds are accounted for in the same manner as proprietary fund types. That is, they record their revenues and expenses on an accrual accounting basis, including depreciation on their fund fixed assets and interest expense on their fund long-term liabilities. Required financial statements for nonexpendable trust funds are a balance sheet, a statement of revenues, expenses, and changes in fund equity, and a statement of cash flows.

Accounting for a Nonexpendable Trust Fund

On January 2, 20X1, the City of Plenty was named trustee for an apartment building that was placed in trust at the death of A. C. Olds. The trust document stipulated that the $250,000 trust fund principal be maintained intact and that income be transferred to the general fund to pay for recreational equipment and supplies for the city's parks, playgrounds, and recreation center. Transactions and events for the Olds Trust Fund for 20X1 are described, together with summary journal entries to record the items.

1 The trust fund principal consists of the apartment building with a fair value of $280,000, and land with a fair value of $70,000, less a $100,000, 7% mortgage payable to be serviced and retired from trust assets:

TF
Land	$ 70,000	
Apartment building	280,000	
Mortgage payable		$100,000
Trust fund principal		250,000

2 Rentals from the apartment building for 20X1 consist of $45,000 cash received and $5,000 rentals due on December 31, 20X1:

TF
Cash	$ 45,000	
Rent receivable	5,000	
Rental revenues		$ 50,000

3 Building maintenance costs for the year are $16,000, of which $2,000 remains unpaid at year-end:

TF
Maintenance expense	$ 16,000	
Accounts payable		$ 2,000
Cash		14,000

4 During 20X1, $3,500 mortgage interest is paid and $3,500 is accrued at year-end. In addition, a $10,000 principal payment on the mortgage is due January 1, 20X2:

TF

Interest expense	$ 7,000	
Interest payable		$ 3,500
Cash		3,500

5 Depreciation expense on the apartment building for 20X1 is $17,500 ($280,000 ÷ 16 years):

TF

Depreciation expense	$17,500	
Accumulated depreciation—building		$17,500

6 The $9,500 of income of the trust for the year is transferred to the general fund to finance purchases of recreational equipment:

TF

Other financing uses—operating transfer to general fund	$ 9,500	
Cash		$ 9,500

7 Closing entries for the year are recorded:

TF

Rental revenues	$50,000	
Maintenance expense		$16,000
Depreciation expense		17,500
Interest expense		7,000
Other financing uses—operating transfer to general fund		9,500

Financial Statements for a Nonexpendable Trust Fund

Financial statements for the Olds Trust Fund for the year ended December 31, 20X1, are shown in Exhibits 20–10, 20–11, and 20–12. Because the trust fund is classified as nonexpendable, a balance sheet, a statement of revenues, expenses, and changes in fund equity, and a statement of cash flows are required.

PENSION TRUST FUNDS

Accounting and reporting for public employee retirement systems (PERS) is done through a pension trust fund. PERS are not subject to the regulations of ERISA (the federal government's Employee Retirement Income Security Act), and consequently, some governmental pension plans are fully funded, others are partially funded, and still others make *all* pension payments from current revenue. Pension trust fund accounting and financial reporting requirements are set forth primarily in *GASB Statement No. 25*, "Financial Reporting for Defined Benefit Pension Plans and Note Disclosures for Defined Contribution Plans." *GASB Statement No. 27*, "Accounting for Pensions by State and Local Governmental Employers," provides guidance for financial accounting and reporting for state and local governmental employers' pension expenses, expenditures, assets, and liabilities. FASB pension accounting guidance is never to be applied by governments.

GASB Statement No. 25 This statement covers information that should be reported about the pension plan, whether the plan issues a separate report or is included in the financial reports of the plan sponsor or participating employer. Two financial statements are required for defined benefit pension plans:

> *Statement of plan net assets*—reports the fair value and composition of plan assets, liabilities, and net assets held in trust for pension benefits.
>
> *Statement of changes in plan assets*—reports the principal year-to-year changes resulting from contributions, net investment income, benefit payments, and so on.

```
CITY OF PLENTY
OLDS TRUST FUND
BALANCE SHEET
AT DECEMBER 31, 20X1
```

Assets
Current assets
  Cash $ 18,000

Assets		
Current assets		
Cash	$ 18,000	
Rent receivable	5,000	
Total current assets		$ 23,000
Plant assets		
Land	70,000	
Apartment building (net of $17,500 depreciation)	262,500	
Total plant assets		332,500
Total assets		$355,500
Liabilities and Fund Equity		
Current liabilities		
Accounts payable	2,000	
Interest payable	3,500	
Mortgage payable—current portion	10,000	
Total current liabilities	15,500	
Long-term liabilities		
Mortgage payable—less current portion	90,000	
Total liabilities		$105,500
Fund equity		
Fund balance—principal		250,000
Total liabilities and fund equity		$355,500

Exhibit 20–10   *Balance Sheet for Nonexpendable Trust Fund*

These statements do not indicate the financial soundness of a pension plan. Rather, the statements essentially reflect the current balance of financial resources available to pay pension benefits and the changes in that balance during the year without any indication of its adequacy. The adequacy or inadequacy of the plan net assets is indicated in one of two schedules that must be presented as required supplementary information immediately *after* the financial statement notes. The schedules

```
CITY OF PLENTY
OLDS TRUST FUND
STATEMENT OF REVENUES, EXPENSES,
AND CHANGES IN FUND EQUITY
FOR THE YEAR ENDED DECEMBER 31, 20X1
```

Operating revenues		
Rental Revenue		$ 50,000
Operating expenses		
Maintenance expense	$16,000	
Depreciation expense	17,500	
Total operating expenses		33,500
Operating income		16,500
Nonoperating income (expense)		
Interest expense		7,000
Income before operating transfers		9,500
Operating transfer to general fund		9,500
Net income		—
Fund equity, January 1, 20X1		—
Contributions		250,000
Fund equity, December 31, 20X1		$250,000

Exhibit 20–11   *Statement of Revenues, Expenses, and Changes in Fund Equity*

```
┌─────────────────────────────────────────────────────────────────────┐
│ CITY OF PLENTY                                                        │
│ OLDS TRUST FUND                                                       │
│ STATEMENT OF CASH FLOWS                                               │
│ FOR THE YEAR ENDED DECEMBER 31, 20X1                                  │
│ ─────────────────────────────────────────────────────────────────── │
│ Direct Method                                                         │
│ ─────────────────────────────────────────────────────────────────── │
│ Cash Flows from Operating Activities                                  │
│ Cash received from tenants                                 $45,000    │
│ Cash paid for maintenance                                  (14,000)   │
│   Cash flows from operating activities                      31,000    │
│                                                                       │
│ Cash Flows from Noncapital Financing Activities                       │
│ Cash paid for operating transfers                           (9,500)   │
│                                                                       │
│ Cash Flows from Capital and Related Financing Activities              │
│ Cash paid for interest                                      (3,500)   │
│                                                                       │
│ Cash Flows from Investing Activities                                  │
│ None                                                            —     │
│ Net increase in cash                                        18,000    │
│ Cash, January 1, 20X1                                           —     │
│ Cash, December 31, 20X1                                    $18,000    │
└─────────────────────────────────────────────────────────────────────┘
```

Exhibit 20–12   *Statement of Cash Flows for Nonexpendable Trust Fund*

provide information on the funded status of the plan and the extent to which required employer contributions are being fully funded. The schedules include information for six plan years. The required schedules are:

> *Schedule of funding progress*—reports actuarial value of assets, actuarial accrued liability, and the relationship between the two over time. *GASB Statement No. 25* establishes parameters for measuring the actuarially determined information.
>
> *Schedule of employer contributions*—reports annual required employer contributions and the percentage of which is recognized by the plan as contributed.

Disclosures accompanying the schedules should include actuarial methods and significant assumptions used for financial reporting as well as any major factors that affect the user's ability to interpret trends.

GASB Statement No. 25 also provides disclosure requirements for defined contribution plans, including a brief plan description, summary of significant accounting policies, fair value of plan assets (unless reported at fair value), and information about contributions and investment concentrations.

GASB Statement No. 27   This statement "establishes standards for the measurement, recognition, and display of pension expenditures/expenses and related liabilities, assets, note disclosures, and, if applicable, required supplementary information in the financial reports of state and local governmental employers."[9] Employers in single-employer and agent multiple-employer defined benefit pension plans should measure and disclose their *annual pension cost* on the accrual basis of accounting, regardless of the amount recognized as pension expenditures/expenses on the modified accrual or accrual basis. The annual pension cost will equal the employer's annual required contributions unless the employer has a net pension obligation for past under- or over-contributions. *GASB Statement No. 27* defines *net pension obligation* as "the cumulative difference between annual pension cost and the employers' contributions to the plan, including the pension liability or asset at transition, if any." When an employer has a net pension obligation at the beginning of a year, annual

---

[9] *GASB Statement No. 27*, Summary.

pension cost is equal to the annual required contributions plus one year's interest on the net pension obligation plus or minus an adjustment to the annual required contribution to offset the effect of actuarial amortization of past under- or over-contributions.

Governmental and expendable trust funds should recognize pension expenditures on the modified accrual basis, meaning expenditures will equal actual contributions plus/minus any change in the current portion of the net pension obligation. A long-term liability balance in the net pension obligation is reported in the general long-term debt account group. An asset balance (cumulative net contributions greater than cumulative pension cost) is *not* recognized in the financial statements, but should be disclosed.

Proprietary and similar trust funds and other entities that use proprietary fund accounting should recognize pension expense on the accrual basis. Net pension obligations or assets should be recognized as fund liabilities or assets.

Statement No. 27 requires disclosure of the plan and funding policy, annual pension cost for *three* years, and if applicable, (also for three years) components of annual pension cost, change for the year in the net pension obligation, and the year-end balance of the net pension obligation. Disclosure about the plan's funding progress is also required in notes or supplements.

Employers that participate in a cost-sharing multiple-employer defined benefit pension plan typically pay the required contribution each year. In this case, the pension expenditure or expense equals the employer's contractually required contributions. Likewise, employers participating in defined contribution plans typically pay the required contribution and should recognize pension expenditures or expenses equal to the employer's required contributions to the plan. In both cases a liability is recognized for unpaid contributions. If this liability is noncurrent, expenditures of governmental funds are reduced by the increase in the long-term liability for unpaid contributions.

COMBINED FINANCIAL STATEMENTS

GASB Statement No. 14 explains that the financial reporting entity is made up of the primary government and its component units. Each state government and each general purpose local government is a primary government according to *GASB 14.* A special purpose government is a primary government if it has a separately elected governing body, is legally separate, and is fiscally independent of other state or local governments. Component units are legally separate organizations for which the primary government is financially accountable. They can also be other organizations for which the nature and significance of their relationship with the primary government are such that exclusion would result in the reporting entity's statements being misleading or incomplete. Some component units are so closely related to the primary government that they should be blended with the primary government. For component units that provide services primarily to the public or to other entities, blending is to be used only if a voting majority of the primary government governing body serves on the component unit governing board and also constitutes a voting majority of that board (i.e., the component unit has substantively the same governing body as the primary government). Therefore, most component units are discretely presented in the reporting entity's financial statements.

Discrete presentation means that the component unit's financial data are presented in a column(s) separate from the primary government's financial data. Supporting information for the individual component units should be provided in the statement notes of the reporting entity or in combining statements in the general purpose financial statements.

The financial statements illustrated up to this point have been for individual funds or fund types. Except for the general fund, a governmental unit may have several individual funds within each type of fund.

When a governmental unit has more than one fund of a given type, the individual statements for that type of fund are usually combined for external reporting pur-

CITY OF ROANOKE, VIRGINIA
COMBINED BALANCE SHEET
ALL FUND TYPES, ACCOUNT GROUPS AND DISCRETELY PRESENTED COMPONENT UNITS
JUNE 30, 1997 (WITH COMPARATIVE TOTALS FOR JUNE 30, 1996)

	Govermental Fund Types				Proprietary Fund Types	
	General	Special Revenue	Debt Service	Capital Projects	Enterprise	Internal Service
Assets and Other Debits						
Cash and Cash Equivalents	$ 1,354,870	$ 463,258	$9,107,653	$33,304,919	$ 31,074,108	$15,139,198
Investments	4,922,128	—	—	—	—	301,054
Interest and Dividends Receivable	196,474	807,706	—	—	—	—
Due from Other Governmental Units	5,383,345	—	—	1,651,425	1,043,712	17,116
Due from Other Funds	316,806	—	40,678	27,198	284,688	757,174
Due from Primary Government	—	—	—	—	—	—
Due from Component Units	866	131,866	—	—	—	—
Taxes Receivable	6,265,855	—	—	—	—	—
Accounts Receivable	869,340	786,052	—	15,779	687,802	12,137
Allowance for Uncollectible Receivables	(2,236,679)	—	—	—	—	—
Notes Receivable	—	6,000,000	—	—	—	—
Inventory	—	—	—	—	1,004,918	927,432
Other Assets	—	—	—	—	139,715	—
Land	—	—	—	—	6,457,833	68,152
Buildings and Structures	—	—	—	—	167,107,051	160,279
Equipment and Other Fixed Assets	—	—	—	—	9,950,837	25,610,074
Accumulated Depreciation	—	—	—	—	(58,858,351)	(16,021,543)
Construction in Progress	—	—	—	—	9,220,721	434,020
Amount Available in Debt Service Fund	—	—	—	—	—	—
Amount to be Provided for Retirement of General Long-term Debt	—	—	—	—	—	—
Total Assets and Other Debits	$17,073,005	$8,188,882	$9,148,331	$34,999,321	$168,113,034	$27,405,093

Source: City of Roanoke, Virginia, Comprehensive Annual Financial Report, 1997.

Exhibit 20–13   *Combined Balance Sheet—All Fund and Account Groups*

poses. Thus, individual debt service fund balances are combined into a single set of financial statements for all debt service funds. Similarly, all individual capital project funds are combined into a single set of financial statements for all capital project funds. Expendable and nonexpendable trust funds are combined separately. This combining process continues until there is only one set of financial statements for each type of fund. These statements are called combining statements. (See Exhibit 20–8 for an example.)

The total columns from the combining statements for each type of fund are presented in combined financial statements for external reporting, with separate columns for each type of fund. Combined statements may or may not contain total columns. In this manner, the number of financial statements required for external financial reporting in accordance with GAAP and that make up the general purpose financial statements within the comprehensive annual financial report is reduced to the following for most governments:

1 A combined balance sheet for all fund types and account groups and discretely presented component units.

Fiduciary Fund Type	Account Groups		Totals Memorandum Only	Component Units		Memorandum Only Totals Reporting Entity	
Trust and Agency	General Fixed Assets	General Long-Term Debt	Primary Government	School Board	Housing Authority	June 30, 1997	June 30, 1996
$ 900,615	$ —	$ —	$ 91,344,621	$ 8,025,555	$ 555,356	$ 99,925,532	$ 95,770,583
208,790,254	—	—	214,013,436	273,091	5,885,083	220,171,610	181,509,601
1,202,117	—	—	2,206,297	—	—	2,206,297	2,184,373
7,026	—	—	8,102,624	2,045,091	720,230	10,867,945	12,727,433
201,066	—	—	1,627,610	1,109,177	250,211	2,986,998	4,126,654
—	—	—	—	14,163	3,951,305	3,965,468	4,447,062
14,531	—	—	147,263	—	—	147,263	215,346
—	—	—	6,265,855	—	—	6,265,855	5,711,228
—	—	—	2,371,110	—	2,862,743	5,233,853	5,342,041
—	—	—	(2,236,679)	—	—	(2,236,679)	(1,528,191)
—	—	—	6,000,000	—	—	6,000,000	6,000,000
—	—	—	1,932,350	—	—	1,932,350	1,832,513
18,000	—	—	157,715	—	203,494	361,209	267,399
—	17,219,564	—	23,745,549	1,612,521	9,013,329	34,371,399	33,120,669
—	62,869,372	—	230,136,702	63,987,685	41,582,410	335,706,797	302,593,480
—	6,125,954	—	41,686,865	26,835,551	2,881,655	71,404,071	62,641,426
—	—	—	(74,879,894)	—	—	(74,879,894)	(71,316,030)
—	5,108,245	—	14,762,986	14,534,723	—	29,297,709	48,805,121
—	—	9,148,331	9,148,331	—	—	9,148,331	8,797,456
—	—	68,914,608	68,914,608	33,874,851	11,237,435	114,026,894	116,228,330
$211,133,609	$91,323,135	$78,062,939	$645,447,349	$152,312,408	$79,143,251	$876,903,008	$819,476,494

2 A combined statement of revenues, expenditures, and changes in fund balances for all governmental fund types and discretely presented component units.

3 A combined statement of revenues, expenditures, and changes in fund balances—budget and actual—for general and special revenue fund types (and similar governmental fund types of the primary government for which annual budgets have been legally adopted),

4 A combined statement of revenues, expenses, and changes in retained earnings (or equity) for all proprietary fund types and discretely presented component units, and

5 A combined statement of cash flows for all proprietary fund types and discretely presented component units.

The general purpose financial statements also include notes to the financial statements and required supplementary information. Expendable trust funds may be incorporated in the combined governmental fund-type statements; nonexpendable trust funds may be incorporated in the proprietary fund-type statements. Governments with pension trust funds or external investment pools also must include a statement of changes in net assets in their general purpose financial statements.

Examples of the required statements are presented in Exhibits 20–13 through 20–17 to illustrate the basic financial reports for governmental units. The basic

CITY OF ROANOKE, VIRGINIA
COMBINED BALANCE SHEET
ALL FUND TYPES, ACCOUNT GROUPS AND DISCRETELY PRESENTED COMPONENT UNITS
JUNE 30, 1997 (WITH COMPARATIVE TOTALS FOR JUNE 30, 1996)

	Govermental Fund Types				Proprietary Fund Types	
	General	Special Revenue	Debt Service	Capital Projects	Enterprise	Internal Service
Liabilities, Fund Equity, and Other Credits						
Liabilities:						
Accounts Payable and Accrued Expenses/Expenditures	$ 3,062,480	$ 271	$ —	$ 85,827	$ 2,686,885	$ 190,217
Claims Payable	—	—	—	—	—	7,490,066
Due to Other Governmental Units	50,375	411,906	—	—	—	—
Due to Other Funds	640,559	36,459	—	—	915,207	33,776
Due to Primary Government	—	—	—	—	—	—
Due to Component Units	14,163	—	—	—	—	—
Deferred Revenue	3,366,162	7,740,246	—	—	—	—
Revenue Bonds Payable	—	—	—	—	—	—
General Obligation Bonds Payable	—	—	—	—	46,725,000	—
Notes Payable	—	—	—	—	—	—
Capital Lease Payable Component Unit	—	—	—	—	3,829,924	—
Section 108 Loans Payable	—	—	—	—	—	—
Literary Fund Loans	—	—	—	—	—	—
VPSA School Bonds	—	—	—	—	—	—
Compensated Absences Payable	—	—	—	—	284,735	327,558
Other Liabilities	—	—	—	—	174,648	—
Total Liabilities	7,133,739	8,188,882	—	85,827	54,616,399	8,041,617
Fund Equity and Other Credits:						
Investment in General Fixed Assets	—	—	—	—	—	—
Contributed Capital	—	—	—	—	54,083,418	6,887,173
Retained Earnings						
Designated for Uninsured Claims	—	—	—	—	—	2,662,464
Undesignated	—	—	—	—	59,413,217	9,813,839
Fund Equity:						
Reserved for Encumbrances	3,199,750	—	—	2,714,074	—	—
Reserved for Employee Retirement Benefits	—	—	—	—	—	—
Reserved for Health Insurance	—	—	—	—	—	—
Reserved for Operations	—	—	—	—	—	—
Unreserved:						
Designated for Workers' Compensation*	—	—	—	—	—	—
Designated for Debt Service	—	—	9,148,331	—	—	—
Designated for Capital Equipment	6,489,516	—	—	—	—	—
Designated for Uninsured Claims	250,000	—	—	—	—	—
Designated for Future Years' Expenditures	—	—	—	32,199,420	—	—
Total Fund Equity and Other Credits	9,939,266	—	9,148,331	34,913,494	113,496,635	19,363,476
Total Liabilities, Fund Equity and Other Credits	$17,073,005	$8,188,882	$9,148,331	$34,999,321	$168,113,034	$27,405,093

*Designations of unreserved fund balance reflect management intent and are optional.

Exhibit 20–13   Continued

Fiduciary Fund type	Account Groups		Totals Memorandum Only	Component Units		Memorandum Only Totals Reporting Entity	
Trust and Agency	General Fixed Assets	General Long-Term Debt	Primary Government	School Board	Housing Authority	June 30, 1997	June 30, 1996
$ 207,146	$ —	$ —	$ 6,232,826	$ 1,111,507	$ 1,239,257	$ 8,583,590	$ 9,387,414
—	—	—	7,490,066	5,005,313	—	12,495,379	11,684,385
420,997	—	—	883,278	—	176,600	1,059,878	779,395
1,609	—	—	1,627,610	1,109,177	250,211	2,986,998	4,126,654
—	—	—	—	14,531	—	14,531	32,268
—	—	—	14,163	—	—	14,163	364,809
—	—	—	11,106,408	—	—	11,106,408	11,086,810
—	—	—	—	—	3,907,405	3,907,405	3,968,358
—	—	68,385,215	115,110,215	13,465,109	5,790,000	134,365,324	141,620,646
—	—	—	—	—	5,392,536	5,392,536	5,855,596
—	—	—	3,829,924	—	—	3,829,924	3,909,226
—	—	5,475,000	5,475,000	—	—	5,475,000	5,660,000
—	—	—	—	3,576,000	—	3,576,000	3,812,000
—	—	—	—	13,498,015	—	13,498,015	9,468,742
—	—	4,202,724	4,815,017	3,335,727	142,720	8,293,464	8,063,456
—	—	—	174,648	—	481,395	656,043	789,275
629,752	—	78,062,939	156,759,155	41,115,379	17,380,124	215,254,658	220,609,034
—	91,323,135	—	91,323,135	106,970,480	52,908,633	251,202,248	233,656,732
—	—	—	60,970,591	—	1,014,290	61,984,881	61,099,774
—	—	—	2,662,464	—	—	2,662,464	—
—	—	—	69,227,056	—	935,776	70,162,832	61,825,437
—	—	—	5,913,824	7,690,207	—	13,604,031	16,385,149
210,503,857	—	—	210,503,857	—	—	210,503,857	173,212,961
—	—	—	—	136,545	—	136,545	—
—	—	—	—	—	3,365,633	3,365,633	3,034,226
—	—	—	—	15,227	—	15,227	37,790
—	—	—	9,148,331	—	—	9,148,331	8,797,456
—	—	—	6,489,516	976,819	—	7,466,335	7,382,668
—	—	—	250,000	300,000	—	550,000	2,650,373
—	—	—	32,199,420	(4,892,249)	3,538,795	30,845,966	30,785,894
210,503,857	91,323,135	—	488,688,194	111,197,029	61,763,127	661,648,350	598,867,460
$211,133,609	$91,323,135	$78,062,939	$645,447,349	$152,312,408	$79,143,251	$876,903,008	$819,476,494

CITY OF ROANOKE
COMBINED STATEMENT OF REVENUES, EXPENDITURES, AND CHANGES IN FUND BALANCES
ALL GOVERNMENTAL FUND TYPES AND DISCRETELY PRESENTED COMPONENT UNITS
YEAR ENDED JUNE 30, 1997 (WITH COMPARATIVE TOTALS FOR JUNE 30, 1996)

	Governmental Fund Types			
	General	Special Revenue	Debt Service	Capital Projects
Sources of Financial Resources				
Revenues:				
Local Taxes	$113,654,246	$ —	$ —	$ —
Permits, Fees, and Licenses	680,100	—	—	—
Fines and Forfeitures	990,906	—	—	—
Rents and Interest	1,037,250	—	443,374	1,572,128
Intergovernmental	36,626,633	4,604,893	—	706,043
Charges for Services	5,008,863	—	—	—
Miscellaneous	487,418	—	—	411,045
Total Revenues	158,485,416	4,604,893	443,374	2,689,216
Other Sources:				
General Obligation Bond Proceeds	—	—	—	—
VPSA School Bond Proceeds	—	—	—	—
Literary Fund Loan Proceeds	—	—	—	—
Transfers from Other Funds	—	674,316	7,787,654	2,504,062
Transfers from Primary Government	—	—	—	—
Total Sources of Financial Resources	158,485,416	5,279,209	8,231,028	5,193,278
Uses of Financial Resources				
Expenditures:				
Current:				
General Government	10,011,252	—	—	—
Judicial Administration	3,895,334	270,247	—	—
Public Safety	35,907,383	408,740	—	—
Public Works	22,428,196	—	—	—
Health and Welfare	20,975,329	892,761	—	—
Education	—	—	—	—
Parks, Recreation, and Cultural	3,914,258	11,359	—	—
Community Development and Housing Activities	2,730,491	1,867,235	—	—
Nondepartmental	35,537	—	—	—
Debt Service:				
Principal Retirement	—	—	3,662,433	—
Interest and Paying Agent Charges	—	—	4,217,720	—
Major Capital Outlay	—	—	—	5,665,585
Total Expenditures	99,897,780	3,450,342	7,880,153	5,665,585
Other Uses:				
Transfers to Governmental Fund Types	10,409,911	556,121	—	—
Transfers to Proprietary Fund Types	4,292,422	—	—	—
Transfers to Primary Government	—	—	—	—
Transfers to Component Units	41,919,407	1,272,746	—	—
Total Uses of Financial Resources	156,519,520	5,279,209	7,880,153	5,665,585
Excess of Revenues and Other Sources Over (Under) Expenditures and Other Uses	1,965,896	—	350,875	(472,307)
Net Income from Component Unit Proprietary Activities	—	—	—	—
Fund Balances—July 1	10,382,064	—	8,797,456	35,385,801
Residual Equity Transfer	(2,408,694)	—	—	—
Fund Balances—June 30	$ 9,939,266	$ —	$9,148,331	$34,913,494

Source: City of Roanoke, Virginia, Comprehensive Annual Financial Report, 1997.

Exhibit 20–14   *Combined Statement of Revenues, Expenditures, and Changes in Fund Balances*

Totals Memorandum Only	Component Units		Memorandum Only Totals Reporting Entity	
Primary Government	School Board	Housing Authority	Year Ended June 30, 1997	Year Ended June 30, 1996
$113,654,246	$ —	$ —	$113,654,246	$109,327,584
680,100	—	—	680,100	649,546
990,906	—	—	990,906	903,916
3,052,752	252,755	2,826,299	6,131,806	5,839,030
41,937,569	49,159,602	10,675,639	101,772,810	103,101,277
5,008,863	3,345,608	6,648,255	15,002,726	13,430,967
898,463	664,909	242,181	1,805,553	920,059
166,222,899	53,422,874	20,392,374	240,038,147	234,172,379
—	—	—	—	31,300,000
—	4,600,325	—	4,600,325	4,006,579
—	—	—	—	2,200,000
10,966,032	3,372,466	—	14,338,498	12,761,542
—	41,919,407	868,521	42,787,928	40,744,190
177,188,931	103,315,072	21,260,895	301,764,898	325,184,690
10,011,252	—	—	10,011,252	10,095,409
4,165,581	—	—	4,165,581	3,912,837
36,316,123	—	—	36,316,123	35,257,162
22,428,196	—	—	22,428,196	22,434,846
21,868,090	—	—	21,868,090	19,659,114
—	89,286,785	—	89,286,785	84,249,226
3,925,617	—	—	3,925,617	4,271,845
4,597,726	—	19,203,203	23,800,929	27,680,314
35,537	—	39,544	75,081	255,411
3,662,433	2,246,833	705,811	6,615,077	6,484,527
4,217,720	1,557,984	675,397	6,451,101	4,983,783
5,665,585	10,482,584	331,618	16,479,787	21,371,580
116,893,860	103,574,186	20,955,573	241,423,619	240,656,054
10,966,032	3,372,466	—	14,338,498	12,761,542
4,292,422	—	—	4,292,422	3,834,477
	50,000	—	50,000	20,000
43,192,153	—	—	43,192,153	41,051,604
175,344,467	106,996,652	20,955,573	303,296,692	298,323,677
1,844,464	(3,681,580)	305,322	(1,531,794)	26,861,013
—	—	155,417	155,417	65,386
54,565,321	7,908,129	7,379,465	69,852,915	42,926,516
(2,408,694)	—	—	(2,408,694)	—
$ 54,001,091	$ 4,226,549	$ 7,840,204	$ 66,067,844	$ 69,852,915

CITY OF ROANOKE, VIRGINIA
STATEMENT OF REVENUES, EXPENDITURES, AND CHANGES IN UNRESERVED FUND
BALANCE—BUDGET (NON-GAAP BUDGETARY BASIS) AND ACTUAL
GENERAL FUND
YEAR ENDED JUNE 30, 1997

	Revised Budget	Actual	Variance—Favorable (Unfavorable)
Sources of Financial Resources			
Fund Balance July 1, 1996	$ 10,382,064	$ 10,382,064	$ —
Revenues:			
Local Taxes	111,168,908	113,654,246	2,485,338
Permits, Fees, and Licenses	562,200	680,100	117,900
Fines and Forfeitures	875,500	990,906	115,406
Rents and Interest	1,138,326	1,037,250	(101,076)
Intergovernmental	35,945,352	36,626,633	681,281
Charges for Services	5,273,148	5,008,863	(264,285)
Miscellaneous	560,451	487,418	(73,033)
Total Revenues	**155,523,885**	**158,485,416**	**2,961,531**
Total Sources of Financial Resources	**165,905,949**	**168,867,480**	**2,961,531**
Uses of Financial Resources			
Expenditures:			
General Government	10,347,213	10,213,312	133,901
Judicial Administration	4,113,018	4,013,524	99,494
Public Safety	37,419,626	36,660,452	759,174
Public Works	24,785,289	24,342,106	443,183
Health and Welfare	21,981,830	20,990,341	991,489
Parks, Recreation, and Cultural	4,057,971	4,045,477	12,494
Community Development	2,857,603	2,796,781	60,822
Nondepartmental	113,873	35,537	78,336
Total Expenditures	**105,676,423**	**103,097,530**	**2,578,893**
Other Uses:			
Transfers to Governmental Fund Types	10,409,911	10,409,911	—
Transfers to Proprietary Fund Types	4,292,422	4,292,422	—
Transfers to Component Units	41,919,407	41,919,407	—
Total Other Uses	**56,621,740**	**56,621,740**	**—**
Total Uses of Financial Resources	**162,298,163**	**159,719,270**	**2,578,893**
Residual Equity Transfer	(2,408,694)	(2,408,694)	—
Fund Balance June 30, 1997	**$ 1,199,092**	**$ 6,739,516**	**$5,540,424**

Source: City of Roanoke, Virginia, Comprehensive Annual Financial Report, 1997.

Exhibit 20-15   *Combined Budgetary Comparison Statement*

statements, except for notes to the financial statements that have been omitted from this reproduction, come from the 1997 *Comprehensive Annual Financial Report of the City of Roanoke, Virginia.* The comprehensive document exceeds 100 pages and includes an introduction, combining financial statements and individual fund financial statements and schedules, supplemental schedules, and other statistical information.

General purpose financial statements are used primarily for efficient presentation of data. The notes to the financial statements indicate that the City of Roanoke is the primary government of the reporting entity and that the Greater Roanoke Transit Company, a separate legal entity, is reported as a blended component unit under the provisions of *GASB Statement No. 14.* Roanoke has two discretely presented component units, the City of Roanoke School Board and the Redevelopment and Housing Authority. The statement notes also provide addresses where complete financial statements of the discretely presented components can be obtained, as required by *Statement No. 14.*

CITY OF ROANOKE, VIRGINIA
COMBINED STATEMENT OF REVENUES, EXPENSES AND
CHANGES IN RETAINED EARNINGS
PROPRIETARY FUND TYPES
YEAR ENDED JUNE 30, 1997 (WITH COMPARATIVE TOTALS FOR JUNE 30, 1996)

	Proprietary Fund Types		Memorandum Only Totals	
	Enterprise	Internal Service	Year Ended June 30, 1997	Year Ended June 30, 1996
Operating Revenues				
Charges for Services	$23,705,981	$21,456,884	$ 45,162,865	$ 31,782,024
Other	202,002	—	202,002	162,086
Total Operating Revenues	23,907,983	21,456,884	45,364,867	31,944,110
Operating Expenses				
Personal Services	8,136,176	5,188,415	13,324,591	12,738,348
Other Services and Charges	10,640,110	13,749,888	24,389,998	9,904,745
Materials and Supplies	1,423,013	1,091,369	2,514,382	2,420,575
Depreciation	3,597,422	1,239,298	4,836,720	5,841,919
Total Operating Expenses	23,796,721	21,268,970	45,065,691	30,905,587
Operating Income	111,262	187,914	299,176	1,038,523
Nonoperating Revenues (Expenses)				
Gain (Loss) on Disposition of Fixed Assets	403,410	(14,494)	388,916	500,000
Operating Grants	1,564,678	—	1,564,678	1,633,530
Interest Revenue	833,278	766,393	1,599,671	2,904,759
Interest Expense	(2,183,544)	—	(2,183,544)	(1,284,673)
Other	—	301,054	301,054	—
Net Nonoperating Revenues	617,822	1,052,953	1,670,775	3,753,616
Income Before Operating Transfers	729,084	1,240,867	1,969,951	4,792,139
Operating Transfers				
Transfers from Other Funds	3,347,581	1,718,469	5,066,050	5,206,570
Transfer from Component Units	—	50,000	50,000	20,000
Transfers to Other Funds	(773,628)	—	(773,628)	(1,372,093)
Net Income	3,303,037	3,009,336	6,312,373	8,646,616
Depreciation Charged to Contributed Capital	1,954,182	169,193	2,123,375	2,197,826
Increase in Retained Earnings/Fund Balance	5,257,219	3,178,529	8,435,748	10,844,442
Retained Earnings—July 1	54,155,998	6,889,080	61,045,078	50,200,636
Residual Equity Transfer	—	2,408,694	2,408,694	—
Retained Earnings—June 30	$59,413,217	$12,476,303	$ 71,889,520	$ 61,045,078

Source: City of Roanoke, Virginia, Comprehensive Annual Financial Report, 1997. (The pension trust fund column is omitted because it will not be presented in this statement in future years. Instead, the city will present a statement of changes in plan net assets for its pension trust fund.)

Exhibit 20–16   *Combined Statement of Revenues, Expenses and Changes in Retained Earnings*

PROPOSED REPORTING MODEL CHANGES

The GASB has issued an exposure draft proposing major changes in the basic financial statements required for governments. The GASB's new reporting model would continue to require presentation of certain fund-based financial statements—particularly for major funds. These funds would be reported similarly to the way that they are currently reported. However, in addition to the fund-based financial statements, the GASB's proposed model would require "entity-wide" financial statements presented on a revenue and expense basis.

To get an overview of these entity-wide financial statements—a statement of net assets and a statement of activities, examine Exhibits 20–18 and 20–19. Note in the

CITY OF ROANOKE, VIRGINIA
COMBINED STATEMENT OF CASH FLOWS
PROPRIETARY FUND TYPES
YEAR ENDED JUNE 30, 1997 (WITH COMPARATIVE TOTALS FOR JUNE 30, 1996)

	Proprietary Fund Types		Memorandum Only Totals	
	Enterprise	Internal Service	June 30, 1997	June 30, 1996
Cash Flows from Operating Activities:				
Cash Received from Customers	$24,131,940	$23,028,928	$47,160,868	$31,753,439
Cash Payments to Suppliers for Goods and Services	(7,388,091)	(3,630,895)	(11,018,986)	(9,035,386)
Cash Payments to Other Funds for Interfund Services	(5,332,867)	(386,552)	(5,719,419)	(3,898,418)
Cash Payments for Personal Services	(8,152,671)	(5,358,970)	(13,511,641)	(12,265,446)
Cash Payments for Claims	—	(4,900,896)	(4,900,896)	—
Other Operating Revenues	189,257	—	189,257	172,098
Net Cash Provided by Operating Activities	**3,447,568**	**8,751,615**	**12,199,183**	**6,726,287**
Cash Flows from Noncapital Financing Activities:				
Operating Grants Received	1,557,956	—	1,557,956	1,652,788
Operating Transfers from Other Funds	3,347,581	1,718,469	5,066,050	5,206,570
Operating Transfers from Component Units	—	50,000	50,000	20,000
Operating Transfers to Other Funds	(773,628)	—	(773,628)	(1,372,093)
Residual Equity Transfer Received	—	2,408,694	2,408,694	—
Interfund Loan Received	254,424	15,273	269,697	182,907
Interfund Loan Paid	—	(182,907)	(182,907)	—
Net Cash Provided by Noncapital Financing Activities	**4,386,333**	**4,009,529**	**8,395,862**	**5,690,172**
Cash Flows from Capital and Related Financing Activities:				
Acquisition and Construction of Fixed Assets	(3,526,391)	(2,790,120)	(6,316,511)	(7,218,215)
Proceeds from Sale of Fixed Assets	370,000	—	370,000	—
Principal Paid on Bond Maturities	(1,970,000)	—	(1,970,000)	(1,955,000)
Principal Paid on Capital Lease Obligation	(79,302)	—	(79,302)	(78,843)
Interest Paid on Bonds and Capital Lease	(3,101,689)	—	(3,101,689)	(3,152,893)
Contributed Capital Remitted	—	—	—	(32,568)
Contributed Capital Received	538,259	—	538,259	1,121,030
Net Cash Used for Capital and Related Financing Activities	**(7,769,123)**	**(2,790,120)**	**(10,559,243)**	**(11,316,489)**
Cash Flows from Investing Activities:				
Interest Revenue	1,533,196	741,162	2,274,358	1,575,527
Total Cash Provided by Investing Activities	**1,533,196**	**741,162**	**2,274,358**	**1,575,527**
Net Increase in Cash and Cash Equivalents	**1,597,974**	**10,712,186**	**12,310,160**	**2,675,497**
Cash and Cash Equivalents at July 1	29,476,134	4,427,012	33,903,146	31,227,649
Cash and Cash Equivalents at June 30	**$31,074,108**	**$15,139,198**	**$46,213,306**	**$33,903,146**
Reconciliation of Operating Income to Net Cash Provided by Operating Activities:				
Operating Income	$ 111,262	$ 187,914	$ 299,176	$ 40,720
Adjustments to Reconcile Operating Income to Net Cash Provided by Operating Activities:				
Depreciation	3,597,422	1,239,298	4,836,720	5,841,919
Changes in Assets and Liabilities:				
(Increase) Decrease Due from Other Governmental Units	170,762	13,591	184,353	(80,434)
Decrease Due from Other Funds	205,291	40,547	245,838	251,455
Decrease Due from Component Units	—	17,644	17,644	3,196
(Increase) Decrease Accounts Receivable	116,590	14,296	130,886	(143,828)
Increase Inventory	(71,939)	(27,898)	(99,837)	(109,199)
Decrease Other Assets	40,446	—	40,446	627
Increase (Decrease) Accounts Payable and Accrued Expenses	132,766	30,714	163,480	(7,348)
Increase Claims Payable	—	7,490,066	7,490,066	—
Increase (Decrease) Due to Other Funds	(789,116)	(259,372)	(1,048,488)	868,086
Increase (Decrease) Compensated Absences Payable	(27,106)	4,815	(22,291)	47,606
Increase (Decrease) Other Liabilities	(38,810)	—	(38,810)	13,487
Total Adjustments	**3,336,306**	**8,563,701**	**11,900,007**	**6,685,567**
Net Cash Provided by Operating Activities	**$ 3,447,568**	**$ 8,751,615**	**$12,199,183**	**$ 6,726,287**

Noncash Investing, Capital and Financing Activities:

The Civic Center, City Information Systems and Fleet Management Fund received fixed assets costing $142,809, $321,379 and $61,482, respectively, as contributed capital from other funds.

The Risk Management Fund received $301,054 of Trigon Common Stock during the year as part of Trigon's conversion to a public stock corporation. The stock is recorded as an investment as its fair market value on the date of demutualization.

See Notes to Financial Statements

Source: City of Roanoke, Virginia, Comprehensive Annual Financial Report, 1997. (The pension trust fund column is omitted because it will not be presented in this statement in future years. Instead, the city will present a statement of changes in plan net assets for its pension trust fund.)

Exhibit 20–17 *Combined Statement of Cash Flows*

statement of net assets that all general government assets and liabilities, including fixed assets and general long-term debt, are aggregated in one column. This column actually includes most internal service fund assets and liabilities because general government departments are typically the largest customers of internal service funds. The aggregated general government information on a capital-maintenance or flow-of-economic-resources basis actually is the most significant change in the new model. The information in the business activities column is basically the same as is currently provided by the enterprise funds columns in combined financial statements. This approach, if adopted, will be a radical step in government reporting standards and require considerable cost and effort for governments to implement. Among other tasks, all general fixed assets infrastructure will have to be inventoried, capitalized, and depreciated. Most governments do not capitalize general fixed assets infrastructure currently.

Many other changes are proposed in the GASB's exposure draft on the reporting model as well. These proposed changes range from redefining enterprise fund activities and fiduciary funds to requiring presentation of a management discussion and analysis section, to eliminating the distinction between contributed capital and retained earnings.

SAMPLE CITY
STATEMENT OF NET ASSETS
DECEMBER 31, 2002

| | Primary Government | | | |
	Governmental Activities	Business-type Activities	Total**	Component Units
Assets				
Cash and cash equivalents	$ 13,597,899	$ 10,279,143	$ 23,877,042	$ 303,935
Investments	27,365,221	—	27,365,221	7,428,952
Receivables (net)	12,833,132	3,609,615	16,442,747	4,042,290
Internal receivables	175,000	—	—	—
Inventories	322,149	126,674	448,823	83,697
Capital assets, net	170,022,760	151,388,751	321,411,511	37,744,786
Total assets	224,316,161	165,404,183	389,545,344	49,603,660
Liabilities				
Accounts payable	6,783,310	751,430	7,534,740	1,803,332
Internal payables	—	175,000	—	—
Deferred revenue	1,435,599	—	1,435,599	38,911
Long-term liabilities	92,538,378	78,908,559	171,446,937	28,532,790
Total liabilities	100,757,287	79,834,989	180,417,276	30,375,033
Net Assets				
Invested in capital assets, net of related debt	90,701,684	73,088,574	163,790,258	15,906,392
Restricted for:				
Capital projects	24,715,566	—	24,715,566	492,445
Debt service	3,020,708	1,451,996	4,472,704	—
Community development projects	4,811,043	—	4,811,043	—
Other purposes	3,214,302	—	3,214,302	—
Unrestricted (deficit)	(2,904,429)	11,028,624	8,124,195	2,829,790
Total net assets	$123,558,874	$ 85,569,194	$209,128,068	$19,228,627

**After elimination of internal balances.
Source: GASB Exposure Draft, "Basic Financial Statements—and Management's Discussion and Analysis—for State and Local Governments."

Exhibit 20–18   *Entity-wide Statement of Net Assets*

SAMPLE CITY
STATEMENT OF ACTIVITIES
FOR THE YEAR ENDED DECEMBER 31, 2002

| | | Primary Government | |
| | | Program Revenues | |
Functions/Programs	Expenses	Charges for Services	Grants and Contributions
Primary government			
General government	$ 9,571,410	$ 3,146,915	$ 843,617
Public safety	34,844,749	1,198,855	1,369,993
Public works	10,128,538	850,000	2,252,615
Engineering services	1,299,645	704,793	—
Health and sanitation	6,738,672	5,612,267	575,000
Cemetery	735,866	212,496	—
Culture and recreation	11,532,350	3,995,199	2,450,000
Community development	2,919,389	—	2,580,000
Interest on long-term debt	6,068,121	—	—
Water	3,595,733	4,159,350	1,159,909
Sewer	4,912,853	7,170,533	486,010
Parking facilities	2,796,283	1,344,087	—
Total primary government	$95,143,609	$28,394,495	$11,717,144
Component units:			
Landfill	$ 3,382,157	$ 3,857,858	$ 11,397
Public school system	31,186,498	705,765	3,937,083
Total component units	$34,568,655	$ 4,563,623	$ 3,948,480

General revenues:
  Taxes
    Real estate
    Other
  Grants and contributions not restricted to specific programs
  Interest and investment earnings
  Miscellaneous
    Total general revenues
      Excess (deficiency) of revenues over expenses before special item
  Special item:
    Gain on sale of park land
      Excess (deficiency) of revenues over expenses
  Transfers
      Change in net assets
  Net assets—beginning
  Net assets—ending

Source: GASB Exposure Draft, "Basic Financial Statements—and Management's Discussion and Analysis—for State and Local Governments."

Exhibit 20–19 *Entity-wide Statement of Activities*

At this writing, GASB is deliberating on responses to its exposure draft and the results of public hearings and forums held on this project. The final statement, even if adopted by early 1999, is not expected to go into effect until 2002 or 2003.

SUMMARY

Capital projects funds and debt service funds are governmental funds that use the modified accrual basis of accounting. Capital projects funds are used to account for the acquisition of major capital facilities, and debt service funds are used to account for the receipt and use of resources to service general long-term debt obligations. Neither capital projects funds nor debt service funds record fixed assets or depreciation

| | Net (Expense) Revenue | | |
Governmental Activities	Business-type Activities	Total	Component Units Net (Expense) Revenue
$ (5,580,878)	$ —	$ (5,580,878)	
(32,275,901)	—	(32,275,901)	
(7,025,923)	—	(7,025,923)	
(594,852)	—	(594,852)	
(551,405)	—	(551,405)	
(523,370)	—	(523,370)	
(5,087,151)	—	(5,087,151)	
(339,389)	—	(339,389)	
(6,068,121)	—	(6,068,121)	
—	1,723,526	1,723,526	
—	2,743,690	2,743,690	
—	(1,452,196)	(1,452,196)	
(58,046,990)	3,015,020	(55,031,970)	
			$ 487,098
			(26,543,650)
			(26,056,552)
34,168,449	—	34,168,449	21,893,273
13,308,487	—	13,308,487	—
1,457,820	—	1,457,820	6,461,708
1,958,144	601,349	2,559,493	881,763
884,907	104,925	989,832	22,464
51,777,807	706,274	52,484,081	29,259,208
(6,269,183)	3,721,294	(2,547,889)	3,202,656
2,653,488	—	2,653,488	—
(3,615,695)	3,721,294	105,599	3,202,656
501,409	(501,409)	—	
(3,114,286)	3,219,885	105,599	3,202,656
126,673,160	82,349,309	209,022,469	16,025,971
$123,558,874	$85,569,194	$209,128,068	$19,228,627

> The amounts reported in the net (expense) revenue columns are intended to give the reader an idea of the relative extent to which each function relies upon or contributes to the general revenues of the government.

in their accounts, nor are they used to account for general long-term debt. General fixed assets and general long-term debt are recorded in separate self-balancing account groups.

Internal service funds, enterprise funds, and nonexpendable trust funds have operations that are similar to those of private business enterprises, and accordingly, the accounting and reporting requirements are quite similar to those of private businesses with the same or similar types of activities. Expendable trust funds have measurement objectives that are comparable to those of governmental funds, and their accounting requirements are essentially the same. Because the operations of agency funds are primarily custodial, agency fund assets and liabilities are accounted for on a modified accrual basis, and revenue and expenditure accounting is not applicable.

ASSIGNMENT MATERIAL

QUESTIONS

1 What is the purpose of capital projects funds? Are all general fixed assets of a governmental unit acquired through capital projects funds? Explain.

2 How are capital projects funds financed and when would a capital projects fund be terminated?

3 If bonds issued to finance a capital project are sold at a premium, is the amount of project authorization increased by the premium? Discuss.

4 Are debt service funds used to account for debt service on all long-term obligations of a governmental unit? If not, which long-term debt obligations are excluded?

5 How are retirements of general long-term debt reported when they are financed with refunding bond proceeds?

6 Describe a transaction that would affect the general fund, the debt service fund, and the general long-term debt account group at the same time.

7 Is interest paid through the debt service fund recorded on an accrual basis? Explain.

8 How do special assessment levies differ from general tax levies?

9 Which funds and/or account groups may be used to account for the activities of a general government, special assessment construction project with long-term financing? Explain.

10 In which funds should the depreciation on general fixed assets be recognized?

11 Explain the account "investment in general fixed assets." When is the account balance increased and when is it decreased?

12 Is the account "amount provided for retirement of term bonds payable" an asset, a liability, or a fund equity account? Explain.

13 The first payment on a five-year capital lease for a street sweeper is recorded in the general fund on January 1, 20X1. What other funds and/or account groups might be affected? Discuss.

14 How are enterprise and internal service funds similar? How are they different?

15 Cite some governmental operations that might be accounted for through an internal service fund.

16 What financial statements are needed for an enterprise fund to meet the requirements for fair presentation in accordance with GAAP?

17 Are the accounts "capital contribution from municipality," "contributed capital from municipality," and "advance from municipality" synonomous? Discuss.

18 What fund types are included in the fiduciary fund category?

19 Compare the financial reporting requirements of expendable and nonexpendable trust funds.

20 Are all the agency responsibilities of a governmental unit accounted for through agency funds? Explain.

21 How many columns (not including total columns) are needed for a combined balance sheet of a governmental unit with a general fund, two special revenue funds, three internal service funds, four enterprise funds, a general fixed assets account group, and a general long-term debt account group? Explain.

22 Do pension trust fund financial statements indicate if the plan is fully funded? Explain.

23 A government retires enterprise fund debt with a carrying value of $8,300,000 with advance refunding proceeds of $7,700,000. Does the government report an extraordinary gain on the early retirement of debt? Explain.

EXERCISES

E 20-1
1 Loup City should use a capital projects fund to account for:
  a Proceeds of a capital grant to finance a new civic center that will not provide services primarily on a user-charge basis
  b Construction of sewer lines by the water and sewer utility to be financed by user costs
  c The accumulation of resources to retire bonds issued to construct the town hall
  d Construction of an addition to the airport terminal owned by the Loup City Municipal Airport, an enterprise fund

2 When a capital projects fund is dissolved by paying any remaining assets to another fund, the decrease in fund balance is a (an):
  a Expenditure
  b Operating transfer
  c Residual equity transfer
  d Reimbursement

3 Which of the following items would be least likely to appear in the balance sheet of a capital projects fund?

a Due from federal government (for grant)

b Due from general fund or from the debt service fund

c Proceeds from bond issue

d Construction in progress

4 Three financial statements may be required to present the results of operations and financial position of a capital projects fund. Which of the following is *not* one of these required statements?

a Statement of cash flows

b Statement of revenues, expenditures, and changes in fund balance

c Statement of revenues, expenditures, and changes in fund balance—budget and actual

d Balance sheet

5 Assets financed through a capital projects fund should be capitalized and reported in annual reports:

a Only when construction is completed

b On the basis of expenditures to date

c On the basis of expenditures and encumbrances to date

d On the basis of amounts paid to date

6 A capital projects fund received proceeds of a $5 million bond issue that was sold for $5,020,000 during December 20X1. The premium was required by law to be made available for interest payments on the issue. Which of the following funds or account groups would not be affected by the transaction?

a Internal service fund

b Capital projects fund

c Debt service fund

d General long-term debt account group

E 20-2

1 Montgomery County issues general obligation serial bonds to finance construction of a sheriff's office. Which of the following funds and/or account groups are affected by the transaction?

a Special revenue fund

b Capital projects fund and general fund

c Capital projects fund, general fund, and general long-term debt account group

d Capital projects fund and general long-term debt account group

2 On April 1, 20X1 the City of Greenspur sold an 8%, $100,000 serial bond issue with interest payment dates of April 1 and October 1. The related debt service fund received and paid out $4,000 during 20X1. If a balance sheet is prepared on December 31, 20X1:

a It will show a fund balance deficit of $2,000

b It should show interest payable of $2,000

c Interest should not be accrued

d Interest from October 1 to December 31 should be accrued according to the *GASB Codification*

3 When general obligation term bonds are retired, an entry debiting "bonds payable" and crediting "amounts provided for repayment of bonds" is recorded in the:

a Special revenue fund

b General long-term debt account group

c Debt service fund

d General fund

4 Assume that assets are accumulated in the debt service fund during the current year to retire general obligation term bonds in the future. This event:

a Requires an entry in the general long-term debt account group

b Is recognized in the debt service fund only

c Would be recognized in both the general fund and the debt service fund

d Would not affect the general long-term debt account group

5 The city's debt as reported in its general long-term debt account group is defeased using proceeds from an advance refunding under *GASB Statement 7* when:

a The debt matures

b The refunding debt issue is sold

c The proceeds of the refunding issue are deposited in an irrevocable trust with an escrow agent under certain specified guidelines

d The general long-term debt is actually paid

E 20-3

1 General fixed assets:

a Include all fixed assets of a government

b Include those fixed assets that are not accounted for in an enterprise, trust, or internal service fund

c Are usually acquired with the resources of nonexpendable funds

d Should be depreciated on a straight-line basis according to GAAP

2 The capital maintenance objective is characteristic of:
  a An internal service fund
  b A general fund
  c A debt service fund
  d An expendable trust fund

3 One would not expect to find fixed asset accounts in:
  a A capital projects fund
  b An internal service fund
  c A pension trust fund
  d An enterprise fund

4 Accounts for accumulated depreciation may appear in the ledger of a:
  a General fixed assets account group
  b General fund
  c Special revenue fund
  d Capital projects fund

5 The cash received from the sale of vehicles used by the sheriff's office would probably be recorded in:
  a The general fund
  b The general fixed assets account group
  c A capital projects fund
  d A debt service fund

6 A municipality's debt service fund regularly receives cash from the general fund to pay interest and serial payments on the city's outstanding serial bond issue. The transfer of cash from the general fund is:
  a Recorded as an expenditure of the general fund and revenue of the debt service fund
  b A quasi-external transaction that will appear in the operating statements of the respective funds, even though it is not an expenditure or revenue of the governmental unit
  c An operating transfer that will be included as "other financing sources and uses" in the respective funds
  d Paid immediately to outside interests and therefore has no effect on the financial statements of the debt service fund

E 20-4   **[AICPA adapted]**

1 It is inappropriate to record depreciation expense in a (an):
  a Enterprise fund
  b Internal service fund
  c Nonexpendable trust fund
  d Capital projects fund

2 The receipts from a special tax levy to retire and pay interest on general obligation bonds issued to finance the construction of a new City Hall should be recorded in a:
  a Debt service fund
  b Capital projects fund
  c Revolving interests fund
  d Special revenue fund

3 The *amount available in debt service funds* is an account of a governmental unit that would be included in the:
  a Liability section of the general long-term debt account group
  b Liability section of the debt service fund
  c "Other debits" section of the general long-term debt account group
  d Asset section of the debt service fund

4 *Proceeds of general obligation bonds* is an account of a governmental unit that typically would be included in the:
  a Enterprise fund
  b General fund
  c Capital projects fund
  d General long-term debt account group

5 Equipment in general governmental service that had been constructed 10 years before by a capital projects fund was sold. The receipts were accounted for as an other financing source. Entries are necessary in the:
  a General fund and capital projects fund
  b General fund and general fixed assets account group
  c General fund, capital projects fund, and enterprise fund
  d General fund, capital projects fund, and general fixed assets account group

6 Cash secured from property tax revenue was transferred for eventual payment of principal and interest on general obligation bonds. The bonds had been issued when land had been acquired several years ago for a city park. Upon the transfer, an entry would *not* be made in which the following:

a Debt service fund
b General fixed assets account group
c General long-term debt account group
d General fund

E 20-5 **[AICPA adapted]**

1 The billings for transportation services provided to other governmental units are recorded by the internal service fund as:
a Interfund exchanges
b Intergovernmental transfers
c Transportation appropriations
d Operating revenues

2 Flac City recorded a 20-year building rental agreement as a capital lease. The building lease asset was reported in the general fixed assets account group. Where should the lease liability be reported in Flac's combined balance sheet?
a General long-term debt account group
b Debt service fund
c General fund
d A lease liability should not be reported

3 Which of the following does not affect an internal service fund's net income?
a Depreciation expense on its fixed assets
b Operating transfers in
c Operating transfers out
d Residual equity transfers

4 Central County received taxes from various towns and cities for capital projects financed by Central's long-term debt. A special tax was assessed by each local government, and a portion of the tax was restricted to repay the long-term debt of Central's capital projects. Central should account for the restricted portion of the special tax in which of the following funds?
a Internal service fund
b Enterprise fund
c Capital projects fund
d Debt service fund

5 Lisa County issued $5,000,000 of general obligation bonds at 101 to finance a capital project. The $50,000 premium was to be used for payment of principal and interest. This transaction should be accounted for in the:
a Capital projects fund, debt service fund, and general long-term debt account group
b Capital projects fund and debt service fund only
c Debt service fund and the general long-term debt account group only
d Debt service fund only

6 In 20X8, Beech City issued $400,000 of bonds, the proceeds of which were restricted to the financing of a capital project. The bonds will be paid wholly from special assessments against benefited property owners. However, Beech is obligated to provide a secondary source of funds for repayment of the bonds in the event of default by the assessed property owners. In Beech's general purpose financial statements, this $400,000 special assessment debt should:
a Not be reported
b Be reported in the special assessment fund
c Be reported in the general long-term debt account group
d Be reported in an agency fund

E 20-6

1 Charges for services are a major source of revenue for:
a A debt service fund
b A trust fund
c An enterprise fund
d A capital projects fund

2 A city provides initial financing for its enterprise fund with the stipulation that the amount advanced be returned to the general fund within five years. In recording the payment to the enterprise fund, the general fund should:
a Debit the account *contribution to enterprise fund*
b Debit the *expenditures* account
c Credit a *due from enterprise fund* account
d Credit a *reserve for advance to enterprise fund* account

3 Jonesville acquires equipment for the magistrate's office through a capital lease that is financed from general government resources. In accounting for the acquisition:

a Lease payments are recorded as rental expenditures.

b The equipment is capitalized in the general fixed assets account group and a liability is recorded in the general long-term debt account group at the inception of the lease. Expenditures and other financing sources are recorded in the general fund.

c The acquisition is accounted for through a general fund but neither the general fixed assets nor general long-term debt account groups are affected.

d The acquisition must be accounted for through an internal service fund.

4 If enterprise fund assets are financed through general obligation bonds, rather than revenue bonds, the debt:

a Is not an enterprise fund liability

b Must be serviced through a debt service fund

c Is an enterprise fund liability if enterprise fund revenues are intended to service the debt

d Is reported both as a long-term fund liability and a general obligation liability

5 An internal service fund would most likely be created to provide:

a Debt service

b Perpetual care of cemeteries

c Centralized purchasing

d Tax collection and recording services

6 Enterprise funds should be used in accounting for government activities that involve:

a Providing goods and services to the public

b Providing goods and services subject to user charges

c Providing goods and services to the public if a substantial amount of revenue is derived from user charges

d Collection of money from the public

E 20-7 **1** Fiduciary funds include four different types of funds. Which of the following is *not* one of these types?

a Agency funds

b Tax collection funds

c Nonexpendable trust funds

d Pension trust funds

2 Agency funds maintain accounts for:

a Liabilities

b Revenues

c Fund balance

d Expenditures

3 The trust fund that is most likely to be nonexpendable is:

a A pension fund

b A loan fund

c A special deposit fund

d A revenue sharing fund

4 Agency responsibilities:

a Must be accounted for in agency funds according to GAAP

b May often be accounted for as liabilities of the general fund

c Are infrequently encountered in accounting for governments

d Arise whenever assets are placed in trust for particular purposes

5 If Craig County established a separate fund entity to account for state income taxes collected and remitted to the state, the fund would likely be:

a An agency fund

b An internal service fund

c An endowment fund

d A trust fund

6 Each year Harman County invests $100,000 from general revenue in marketable securities to provide for the eventual retirement of general obligation term bonds. The investment activity is accounted for in:

a A nonexpendable trust fund

b An expendable trust fund

c A debt service fund

d The general fund

E 20-8 **[AICPA adapted] 1** Maple Township issued these bonds during the year ended June 30, 20X8:

Bonds issued for the garbage collection enterprise fund that will service the debt	$500,000
Revenue bonds to be repaid with admission fees collected by the township zoo enterprise fund	350,000

What amount of these bonds should be accounted for in Maple's general long-term debt account group?

a $0   c $500,000

b $350,000   d $850,000

2 Lori Township received a gift of an ambulance having a market value of $80,000. What account in the general fixed assets account group should be debited for this $80,000 gift?

a None (memorandum entry only)

b Investment in general fixed assets from gifts

c Machinery and equipment

d General fund assets

3 Customers' security deposits that cannot be spent for normal operating purposes were collected by a governmental unit and accounted for in an enterprise fund. A portion of the amount collected was invested in marketable debt securities and a portion in marketable equity securities. How would each portion be classified in the balance sheet?

	Portion in Marketable Debt Securities	Portion in Marketable Equity Securities
a	Unrestricted asset	Restricted asset
b	Unrestricted asset	Unrestricted asset
c	Restricted asset	Unrestricted asset
d	Restricted asset	Restricted asset

4 Brockton City serves as a collecting agency for the local independent school district and for a local water district. For this purpose, Brockton has created a single agency fund and charges the other entities a fee of 1% of the gross amounts collected. (The service fee is treated as a general fund revenue.) During the latest fiscal year, a gross amount of $268,000 was collected for the independent school district and $80,000 for the water district. As a consequence of the foregoing, Brockton's general fund should:

a Recognize receipts of $348,000

b Recognize receipts of $344,520

c Record revenue of $3,480

d Record encumbrances of $344,520

5 Through an internal service fund, Wood County operates a centralized data processing center to provide services to Wood's other departments. In 20X9, this internal service fund billed Wood's parks and recreation fund $75,000 for data processing services. What account should Wood's internal service fund credit to record this $75,000 billing to the parks and recreation fund?

a Operating revenues control

b Interfund exchanges

c Intergovernmental transfers

d Data processing department expenses

E 20-9 **[AICPA adapted]**

Rock County has acquired equipment through a noncancelable lease-purchase agreement dated December 31, 20X1. This agreement requires no down payment and the following minimum lease payments:

December 31	Principal	Interest	Total
20X2	$50,000	$15,000	$65,000
20X3	50,000	10,000	60,000
20X4	50,000	5,000	55,000

1 What account should be debited for $150,000 in the general fund at inception of the lease if the equipment is a general fixed asset and Rock does *not* use a capital projects fund?

a Other financing uses control

b Equipment

c Expenditures control

d Memorandum entry only

2 What account should be credited for $150,000 in the general fixed assets account group at inception of the lease if the equipment is a general fixed asset?

a Fund balance from capital lease transactions

b Other financing sources control—capital leases

c Expenditures control—capital leases

d Investment in general fixed assets—capital leases

3 What journal entry is required for $150,000 in the general long-term debt account group at the inception of the lease if the lease payments are to be financed with general government resources?

  a Debit: Expenditures control   Credit: Other financing sources control
  b Debit: Other financing uses control   Credit: Expenditures control
  c Debit: Amount to be provided for lease payments   Credit: Capital lease payable
  d Debit: Capital lease payable   Credit: Amount to be provided for lease payments

4 If the lease payments are required to be made from the general fund, what account or accounts should be debited in the general fund for the December 31, 20X2 lease payment of $65,000?

  a Expenditures control, $65,000
  b Other financing sources control, $50,000; and expenditures control, $15,000
  c Amount to be provided for lease payments, $50,000; and expenditures control, $15,000
  d Expenditures control, $50,000; and amount to be provided for lease payments, $15,000

5 If the equipment is used in enterprise fund operations and the lease payments are to be financed with enterprise fund revenues, what account should be debited for $150,000 in the enterprise fund at inception of the lease?

  a Expenses control
  b Expenditures control
  c Other financing sources control
  d Equipment

6 If the equipment is used in internal service fund operations and the lease payments are financed with internal service fund revenues, what account or accounts should be debited in the internal service fund for the December 31, 20X2 lease payment of $65,000?

  a Expenditures control, $65,000
  b Expenses control, $65,000
  c Capital lease payable, $50,000; and expenses control, $15,000
  d Expenditures control, $50,000; and expenses control, $15,000

E 20-10   [AICPA adapted]

1 The following revenues were among those reported by Ariba Township in 20X9:

Net rental revenue (after depreciation) from a parking garage owned by Ariba	$ 40,000
Interest earned on investments held for employee's retirement benefits	100,000
Property taxes	6,000,000

What amount of the foregoing revenues should be accounted for in Ariba's governmental type funds?

  a $6,140,000   **c** $6,040,000
  b $6,100,000   **d** $6,000,000

2 Kew City issued the following long-term obligations:

Revenue bonds to be repaid from admission fees collected from users of the city swimming pool	$1,000,000
General obligation bonds issued for the city water and sewer fund which will service the debt	$1,800,000

Although these bonds are expected to be paid from enterprise funds, the full faith and credit of the city has been pledged as further assurance that the obligations will be paid. What amount of these bonds should be accounted for in the general long-term debt account group?

  a $0   **c** $1,800,000
  b $1,000,000   **d** $2,800,000

3 The following proceeds received by Grove City in 20X7 are legally restricted to expenditure for specified purposes:

Donation by a benefactor mandated to an expendable trust fund to provide meals for the needy	$ 300,000
Sales taxes to finance the maintenance of tourist facilities in the shopping district	900,000

What amount should be accounted for in Grove's special revenue funds?

  a $0   **c** $900,000
  b $300,000   **d** $1,200,000

4 In connection with Albury Township's long-term debt, the following cash accumulations are available to cover payment of principal and interest on:

Bonds for financing of water treatment plant
construction $1,000,000
General long-term obligations   400,000

The amount of these cash accumulations that should be accounted for in Albury's debt service funds is:

  a $0   **c** $1,000,000
  b $400,000   **d** $1,400,000

> Use the following information in answering questions 5 and 6:
> On December 31, 20X7, Vane City paid a contractor $3,000,000 for the total cost of a new municipal annex built in 20X7 on city-owned land. Financing was provided by a $2,000,000 general obligation bond issue sold at face amount on December 31, 20X7, with the remaining $1,000,000 transferred from the general fund.

5 What account and amount should be reported in Vane's 20X7 financial statements for the general fund?

  a Other financing uses control, $1,000,000
  b Other financing sources control, $2,000,000
  c Expenditures control, $3,000,000
  d Other financing sources control, $3,000,000

6 What accounts and amounts should be reported in Vane's 20X7 financial statements for the capital projects fund?

  a Other financing sources control, $2,000,000; general long-term debt, $2,000,000
  b Revenues control, $2,000,000; expenditures control, $2,000,000
  c Other financing sources control, $3,000,000; expenditures control, $3,000,000
  d Revenue control, $3,000,000; expenditures control, $3,000,000

E 20-11 For each of the following unrelated transactions that might appear in a capital projects fund, indicate the other funds or account groups in which journal entries would be made:

  1 Received a short-term loan from the general fund for temporary financing.
  2 Awarded a contract to the lowest bidder.
  3 Received proceeds from a term bond issue sold at a premium. The premium is transferred to the appropriate fund (to be used to service the bonds).
  4 Construction of a building is half-completed and the contractor submits a bill for half of the contract price.
  5 Paid the water and sewer utility for installing sewer lines.

E 20-12 The City of Radford is replacing the equipment in the treasurer's office. The old equipment was financed by a state grant and purchased in 20X1 at a cost of $30,000. At the time of the purchase, the equipment had an estimated useful life of 10 years and estimated salvage value of $2,000. The equipment is sold after eight years for $5,000.

Required: Prepare journal entries in the general fund and the general fixed assets account group to record the sale of the equipment. The city does not record accumulated depreciation in its account group.

E 20-13 Ravana Township is constructing a town hall, financed in part by a 6%, $400,000 serial bond issue. The bonds are sold at a discount of $4,000. The general fund will be able to transfer resources equal to the amount of the discount if needed to complete the project.

Required: Prepare journal entries in the capital projects fund and the general long-term debt account group to account for the sale of the bonds.

E 20-14 Prepare the journal entries that would be required in the general fixed assets account group to account for the following unrelated transactions and events.

  1 A fire truck was sold for $50,000 cash. Its original cost when purchased from general revenues was $175,000.
  2 Used police cars were sold for $4,500. These cars were purchased for $16,000 through state grant revenue.
  3 A flood destroyed street cleaning equipment and $5,000 was received from insurance on the equipment. The cost of the equipment was $8,000.
  4 Construction on the city hall was completed at a total cost of $680,000. The city hall project was financed by equal amounts of general obligation bond proceeds and federal revenue sharing funds. Expenditures on the project in prior years were $200,000.
  5 Land with a current value of $50,000 was donated to the city. The cost to the donor was $26,000.

E 20-15 The Police Complex Capital Projects Fund was established in 20X1 for construction in the authorized amount of $5,000,000. Financing was from a $4,000,000, 20-year, term bond issue that was sold at par and from general fund transfers in the amount of $1,000,000. Amounts for repayment of the term bonds were transferred from a special revenue fund to a sinking fund, starting in 20X1.

The project was completed in 20X3 and the remaining fund balance was transferred to the fund responsible for servicing the long-term debt. A summary of revenues, expenditures, and encumbrances related to the project (but not including transfers for debt service) is as follows:

	20X1	20X2	20X3
Bond proceeds and operating transfers	$5,000,000	none	none
Expenditures for the year	1,000,000	$2,500,000	$1,450,000
Encumbrances outstanding at December 31	4,000,000	1,500,000	none

Indicate which of the following funds or account groups are affected by activities related to the police complex in each of the three years, 20X1, 20X2, and 20X3.

1 General fund
2 Special revenue fund
3 Debt service fund
4 Capital projects fund
5 General fixed assets account group
6 General long-term debt account group

E 20-16 The City of Lite established a tax agency fund to collect property taxes for the City of Lite, Bloomer County, and Bloomer School District. Total tax levies of the three governmental units were $200,000 for 20X1, of which $60,000 was for the City of Lite, $40,000 for Bloomer County, and $100,000 for Bloomer School District.

The tax agency fund charges Bloomer County and Bloomer School District a 2% collection fee that it transfers to the general fund of the City of Lite in order to cover costs incurred for agency fund operations.

During 20X1 the tax agency fund collected $150,000 of the 20X1 levies and remitted $100,000 to the various governmental units. The $100,000 includes $1,400 collection fees that were remitted to Lite's general fund.

Required: Prepare a statement of changes in assets and liabilities for the City of Lite Tax Agency Fund at December 31, 20X1.

E 20-17 Prepare all journal entries, other than adjusting and closing entries, to account for the activities described below that relate to the construction and financing of a new recreation center for the City of Unitas for the calendar year 20X1. Prepare entries for all funds and account groups affected and identify the fund or account group to which each journal entry relates.

March 1, 20X1—Sold $1,000,000 general obligation, 6% serial bonds at a premium of 1% to finance construction of a new recreation center. An additional $200,000 was received (in cash) from a federal grant to bring the total financing up to the $1,200,000 authorized expenditures for the project.

March 8, 20X1—The premium was transferred to another fund for debt service.

October 1, 20X1—The general fund transferred $20,000 to provide for the bond debt service. This $20,000 together with the issue premium was used to pay the $30,000 interest that came due on the project during 20X1.

March 1 to December 31, 20X1—A contract for $1,150,000 was let for the recreation center. Contract expenditures of $500,000 were recorded and paid and engineering costs of $15,000, not under contract, were paid. Encumbrances of $650,000 relating to the construction contract were outstanding at December 31.

PROBLEMS

P 20-1 The Town of Simmonsville has $3,000,000 of 6% bonds outstanding. Interest on the general obligation, general government indebtedness is payable semiannually each March 31 and September 30. December 31 is the fiscal year-end. Record the following transactions in the town's debt service fund.

1 Received a transfer from the general fund to provide financing for the March 31, 20X0 interest payment.
2 Paid the interest due on March 31, 20X0.

3 Received a transfer from the general fund to provide financing for the September 30, 20X0 interest payment and retirement of $1,000,000 of the bonds.

4 Paid the interest on September 31, 20X0 and repaid $1,000,000 of the bonds.

5 December 31 is the fiscal year-end. Record any appropriate adjustments.

6 Received a transfer from the general fund to provide financing for the March 31, 20X1 interest payment.

7 Paid the interest due on March 31, 20X1.

P 20-2 Prepare all the entries required in all the funds and account groups of a city to record the following transactions.

1 The city leased vehicles with a capitalizable cost (i.e., present value of minimum lease payments) of $1,500,000, including a $300,000 downpayment at the inception of the lease. The lease is properly classified as a capital lease. The vehicles are for the use of general government departments. The interest rate implicit in the lease agreement is 10%.

2 The city paid the first annual lease payment at the end of the first year of the lease, $500,000.

3 Advance refunding bonds were issued at par, $4,000,000.

4 The proceeds of the advance refunding bonds were paid into an irrevocable trust. The trust meets the conditions necessary for an outstanding bond issue with a par value of $4,200,000 to be considered defeased in substance.

5 Repeat No. 4. Assume that the refunding bond proceeds plus $500,000 of previously accumulated cash were paid to the trust to defease the $4,200,000 of outstanding bonds.

6 The general fund paid claims and judgments during the year of $300,000. Additionally, the long-term liability for general government claims and judgments increased by $600,000 during the year.

P 20-3 The City of Highview authorized construction of a $600,000 addition to the municipal building in September 20X2. The addition will be financed by $200,000 from the general fund and a $400,000 serial bond issue to be sold in April 20X3.

Required: Prepare journal entries for the capital projects fund and any other fund or account group involved to the extent of requiring journal entries to record the transactions described.

1 On October 1, 20X2 the general fund transferred $200,000 to the capital projects fund.

2 On November 1, 20X2 a contract for the addition was awarded to Smiley Construction for $580,000.

3 On April 15, 20X3 the $400,000, 7% bonds were sold for $401,000 and the premium was transferred to the debt service fund.

4 On May 2, 20X3 construction was completed and Smiley Construction submitted a bill for $580,000.

5 On May 12, 20X3 the bill to Smiley Construction was paid in full. The CPF was closed, the remaining cash was transferred to the general fund.

P 20-4 On June 15, 20X1, Loup City authorizes the issuance of $500,000 par of 6% serial bonds to be issued on July 1, 20X1 and to mature in annual serials of $100,000 beginning on July 1, 20X5. The proceeds of the bond issue are to be used to finance a new city hall.

During the fiscal year ended June 30, 20X2, the following events and transactions occurred:

July 1, 20X1—A contract for construction of the city hall is awarded to Kircher Construction Company for $480,000.

July 1, 20X1—$250,000 par value of 6% serial bonds are sold at a premium of 2%.

December 20, 20X1—A bill is received from Kircher Construction Company for one-third of the contract price.

January 1, 20X2—Kircher Construction Company is paid for work completed to date, less a 10% retained percentage to ensure performance.

January 1, 20X2—Bond interest due is paid with funds transferred from the general fund and from the premium that was made available for interest payments.

June 30, 20X2—A bill is received from Kircher Construction Company for one-third of the contract price.

Required

1 Prepare journal entries to account for the transactions and events described in each of the funds and account groups affected. Identify the fund or account group for each journal entry.

2 Prepare a closing journal entry for the capital projects fund at June 30, 20X2.

P 20-5 Comparative adjusted trial balances for the Motor Pool of Douwe County at June 30, 20X1 and June 30, 20X2 are as follows:

	June 30, 20X2	June 30, 20X1
Cash	$ 37,000	$ 44,000
Due from general fund	—	8,000
Due from electric fund	4,000	3,000
Supplies on hand	14,000	12,000
Autos	99,000	80,000
Supplies used	68,000	60,000
Salaries expense	25,000	20,000
Utilities expense	9,000	8,000
Depreciation	16,000	15,000
Operating transfer to general fund	12,000	—
	$284,000	$250,000
Accumulated depreciation—autos	$ 56,000	$ 40,000
Accounts payable	11,000	10,000
Advance from general fund (current)	5,000	5,000
Contribution from general fund	50,000	50,000
Retained earnings	42,000	35,000
Revenue from billings	120,000	110,000
	$284,000	$250,000

Required: Prepare financial statements for the Motor Pool at and for the year ended June 30, 20X2. (The statement of cash flows is to be included.)

P 20-6 Selected activities relating to fixed assets of Progressive City for 20X3 are described in the following list. Prepare journal entries for additions to and deletions from the general fixed assets account group using the five major classifications of assets illustrated by the GASB.

General Fund

1 Office equipment is purchased for $6,000. $40,000 is paid and a three-month note is issued for the balance.
2 A new fire truck is purchased for $235,000.
3 Park equipment costing $8,000 is received and installed.
4 New radar equipment costing $8,000 is purchased and old radar equipment costing $4,000 is sold for $100. No depreciation had been recorded.
5 The roof on City Hall is replaced at a cost of $3,000.
6 $2,500 is received from the sale of buildings that cost $40,000 a number of years ago.

Motor Pool Fund

7 A new automobile is purchased for $15,000 and an old automobile costing $10,000 with $6,000 depreciation recorded is sold for $4,500.

Sewer Construction Fund

8 Initial expenditures on a new sewer system of $40,000 are vouchered during the year. The total cost of the system is estimated at $100,000 to be financed 50% by federal grants and 50% from a bond issue.

Street Paving Fund

9 Street paving costing $20,000 is completed for this special assessment project during the year. Expenditures of $6,000 had been recorded in the prior year.

Other

10 Land with a value of $20,000 is donated to the city during the year.

P 20-7 The accounts of the general fund, the debt service fund, the general fixed assets account group, and the general long-term debt account group of Ampora, Illinois, were merged on June 30, 20X8 by an inexperienced bookkeeper. The combined account balances are included in a trial balance as follows:

TRIAL BALANCE
AMPORA, ILLINOIS
ON JUNE 30, 20X8

Cash ($8,000 is for debt service)	$ 68,000
Current taxes receivable	32,000

(Continued)

Delinquent taxes receivable		8,000
Land		30,000
Buildings		90,000
Construction in progress		35,000
Investments (restricted for debt service)		45,000
Amount provided for payment of bonds		53,000
Amount to be provided for payment of bonds		47,000
Vouchers payable (GF)		$ 20,000
Due to internal service fund		4,000
Reserve for encumbrances		5,000
Bonds payable		100,000
Investment in general fixed assets—general revenue		55,000
Investment in general fixed assets—federal grant		100,000
Fund balance ($53,000 belongs to DSF)		124,000
	$408,000	$408,000

Required: Prepare balance sheets for each of the funds or account groups involved. All account balances that apply to more than one fund or account group have been identified in the combined trial balance.

P 20-8 On January 1, 20X2, J. G. Monee created a student aid trust fund to which he donated a building valued at $40,000 (his cost was $25,000), bonds having a market value of $50,000, and $10,000 cash. The trust agreement stipulated that principal was to be maintained intact and earnings were to be used to support needy students. Consider gains on investments and depreciation as adjustments of earnings rather than of trust fund principal.

Activities for 20X2

1 During the year, net rentals of $4,000 were collected for building rental (net rentals equal gross rentals less $12,000 out-of-pocket costs).
2 The bonds were sold for $55,000 on June 30, 20X2. Of the proceeds, $3,000 represented interest accrued from January 1 to June 30.
3 Stocks were purchased for $60,000 cash.
4 Depreciation on the building was calculated at $2,000 for the year.
5 Dividends receivable of $6,000 were recorded at December 31, 20X2.

Required: Prepare balance sheets for the student aid principal trust fund and the student aid earnings trust fund at December 31, 20X2.

P 20-9 **[AICPA adapted]**
In a special election held on May 1, 20X7, the voters of the City of Nicknar approved a $10,000,000 issue of 6% general obligation bonds maturing in 20 years. The proceeds of this sale will be used to help finance the construction of a new civic center. The total cost of the project was estimated at $15,000,000. The remaining $5,000,000 will be financed by a state grant for the project, which has been awarded. A capital projects fund was established to account for this project and was designated the civic center construction fund. The formal project authorization was appropriately recorded in a memorandum entry.

The following transactions occurred during the fiscal year beginning July 1, 20X7 and ending June 30, 20X8:

1 On July 1 the general fund loaned $500,000 to the civic center construction fund for defraying engineering and other expenses.
2 Preliminary engineering and planning costs of $320,000 were paid to Akron Engineering Company. There had been no encumbrance for this cost.
3 On December 1 the bonds were sold at 101. The premium on bonds was transferred to the debt service fund.
4 On March 15 a contract for $12,000,000 was entered into with Candu Construction Company for the major part of the project.
5 Orders were placed for materials estimated to cost $55,000.
6 On April 1 a partial payment of $2,500,000 was received from the state.
7 The materials that were previously ordered were received at a cost of $51,000 and paid.
8 On June 15 a progress billing of $2,000,000 was received from Candu Construction for work done on the project. As per the terms of the contract, the city will withhold 6% of any billing until the project is completed.
9 The general fund was repaid the $500,000 previously loaned.

Required

1 Prepare journal entries to record the transactions in the civic center construction fund for the period July 1, 20X7 through June 30, 20X8 and the appropriate closing entries at June 30, 20X8.
2 Prepare a balance sheet for the civic center construction fund on June 30, 20X8.

P 20-10   A government has $5,000,000 of general government, general obligation bonds outstanding. Prepare the journal entries required to record the following:

Situation A
The government issues $5,300,000 of bonds at par and pays the proceeds to the trust department of a bank to establish an irrevocable trust to provide for all future debt service requirements on the old debt issue. The defeasance in substance criteria are met.

Situation B
Same as Situation A, except the government has to pay a total of $5,500,000 into the trust to defease the debt. The additional $200,000 was accumulated previously in the debt service fund.

P 20-11   The City of Melborne authorized the construction of a new recreation center at a total cost of $1,000,000 on June 15, 20X7. On the same date, the city approved a $1,000,000, 8%, 10-year general obligation serial bond issue to finance the project. During the year July 1, 20X7 to June 30, 20X8, the following transactions and events occurred relative to the recreation center project.

1 On July 1, 20X7 the city sold $500,000 par of the authorized bonds, with interest payment dates on December 31 and June 30 and the first serial retirement to be made on June 30, 20X8. The bonds were sold at 102.

2 On July 5, 20X7 a construction contract for the recreation center was let in the amount of $960,000.

3 On December 15, 20X7 the contractor's bill for $320,000 was received based on certification that the work was one-third completed.

4 The contractor was paid for one-third of the contract less a 10% retained percentage to assure performance.

5 On December 30, 20X7 the GF transferred $30,000 to the fund responsible for servicing the serial bonds.

6 Interest on the serial bonds was paid on December 31, 20X7 with the money transferred from the GF and the CPF.

7 On June 15, 20X8 the contractor's bill for $320,000 was received based on certification that the work was two-thirds completed.

8 On June 28, 20X8 the GF transferred $90,000 to the fund responsible for servicing the serial bonds; $40,000 for interest and $50,000 for principal.

9 Interest and principal on the serial bonds were paid on June 30, 20X8.

10 On June 30, 20X8 the city sold the remaining $500,000 par of authorized bonds at par.

Required

1 Prepare all journal entries in all the funds and account groups necessary to account for the transactions and events given. (If amounts are not known, use XXX.)

2 Prepare financial statements for the CPF for the year ended June 30, 20X8.

P 20-12   **[AICPA adapted]**
The following transactions represent practical situations frequently encountered in accounting for municipal governments. Each transaction is independent of the others.

1 The city council of Bernardville adopted a budget for the general operations of the government during the new fiscal year. Revenues were estimated at $695,000. Legal authorizations for budgeted expenditures were $650,000.

2 Taxes of $160,000 were levied for the special revenue fund of Millstown. One percent was estimated to be uncollectible.

3 a On July 25, 20X3 office supplies estimated to cost $2,390 were ordered for the city manager's office of Bullersville. Bullersville, which operates on a calendar year, does not maintain an inventory of such supplies.

   b The supplies ordered July 25 were received on August 9, 20X3, accompanied by an invoice for $2,500.

4 On October 10, 20X3 the general fund of Washingtonville repaid to the utility fund a loan of $1,000 plus $40 interest. The loan had been made earlier in the fiscal year.

5 A prominent citizen died and left 10 acres of undeveloped land to Harper City for a future school site. The donor's cost of the land was $55,000. The fair value of the land was $85,000.

6 a On March 6, 20X3 Dahlstrom City issued 4% special assessment bonds payable, due March 6, 20X8 at face value of $90,000. Interest is payable annually. Dahlstrom City, which operates on a calendar year, will use the proceeds to finance a curbing project. The city is secondarily liable to bondholders of this issue.

   b On October 29, 20X3 the full $84,000 cost of the completed curbing project was accrued. Also, appropriate closing entries were made with regard to the project.

7 a Conrad Thamm, a citizen of Basking Knoll, donated common stock valued at $22,000 to the city under a trust agreement. Under the terms of the agreement, the principal amount is to be kept intact; use of revenue from the stock is restricted to financing academic college scholarships for needy students.

   b On December 14, 20X3 dividends of $1,100 were received on the stock donated by Mr. Thamm.

   c The fair value of the stock at the end of the fiscal year was $23,000.

8 a On February 23, 20X3 the Town of Lincoln, which operates on the calendar year, issued 4% general obligation bonds with a face value of $300,000 payable in 10 years, to finance the construction of an addition to the city hall. Total proceeds were $308,000.

b On December 31, 20X3 the addition to the city hall was officially approved, the full cost of $297,000 was paid to the contractor, and appropriate closing entries were made with regard to the project. (Assume that no entries have been made with regard to the project since February 23, 20X3.)

Required: For each transaction prepare the necessary journal entries for all funds and account groups involved.

P 20-13 **[AICPA adapted]**
The City of Happy Hollow has engaged you to examine its financial statements for the year ended December 31, 20X1. The city was incorporated as a municipality and began operations on January 1, 20X1. A budget was approved by the city council and was recorded, but all transactions have been recorded on the cash basis. The bookkeeper has provided an operating fund trial balance as follows:

Debits	
Cash	$238,900
Expenditures	72,500
Estimated revenues	114,100
	$425,500
Credits	
Appropriations	$102,000
Revenues	108,400
Bonds payable	200,000
Premium on bonds payable	3,000
Fund balance	12,100
	$425,500

Additional Information

1 Examination of the appropriation-expenditure ledger revealed the following information:

	Budgeted	Actual
Personal services	$ 45,000	$38,500
Supplies	19,000	11,000
Equipment	38,000	23,000
Total	$102,000	$72,500

2 Supplies and equipment in the amounts of $4,000 and $10,000, respectively, had been received, but the vouchers had not been paid at December 31.

3 At December 31 outstanding purchase orders for supplies and equipment not yet received were $1,200 and $3,800, respectively.

4 The inventory of supplies on December 31 was $1,700 by physical count. The decision was made to record the inventory of supplies. A city ordinance requires that expenditures be based on purchases, not on the basis of usage.

5 Examination of the revenue subsidiary ledger revealed the following:

	Budgeted	Actual
Property taxes	$102,600	$ 96,000
Licenses	7,400	7,900
Fines	4,100	4,500
Total	$114,100	$108,400

It was estimated that 5% of the property taxes would not be collected. Accordingly, property taxes were levied in an amount so that collections would yield the budgeted amount of $102,600.

6 On November 1, 20X1, Happy Hollow issued 8% general obligation term bonds with $200,000 face value for a premium of $3,000. Interest is payable each May 1 and November 1 until maturity 14 years from the date of issuance. The city council ordered that the cash from the bond premium be set aside and restricted for the eventual retirement of the debt principal. The bonds were issued to finance the construction of a city hall, but no contracts had been let as of December 31.

Required

1 Prepare a worksheet showing adjustments and distributions to the proper funds or groups of accounts in conformity with generally accepted accounting principles applicable to governmental entities. (Formal adjusting entries are not required.)

2 Identify the financial statements that should be prepared for the general fund. (You are not required to prepare these statements.)

3 Draft formal closing entries for the general fund.

P 20-14 **[AICPA adapted]**

The City of Merlot operates a central garage through an internal service fund to provide garage space and repairs for all city-owned and -operated vehicles. The central garage fund was established by a contribution of $200,000 from the general fund on July 1, 20X6, at which time the building was acquired. The after-closing trial balance at June 30, 20X8 was as follows:

	Debit	Credit
Cash	$150,000	
Due from general fund	20,000	
Inventory of materials and supplies	80,000	
Land	60,000	
Building	200,000	
Accumulated depreciation—building		$ 10,000
Machinery and equipment	56,000	
Accumulated depreciation—machinery and equipment		12,000
Vouchers payable		38,000
Contribution from general fund		200,000
Retained earnings		306,000
	$566,000	$566,000

The following information applies to the fiscal year ended June 30, 20X9:

1 Materials and supplies were purchased on account for $74,000.

2 The inventory of materials and supplies at June 30, 20X9 was $58,000, which agreed with the physical count taken.

3 Salaries and wages paid to employees totaled $230,000 including related costs.

4 A billing was received from the enterprise fund for utility charges totaling $30,000, and was paid.

5 Depreciation of the building was recorded in the amount of $5,000. Depreciation of the machinery and equipment amounted to $8,000.

6 Billings to other departments for services rendered to them were as follows:

General fund	$262,000
Water and sewer fund	84,000
Special revenue fund	32,000

7 Unpaid interfund receivable balances at June 30, 20X9 were as follows:

General fund	$ 6,000
Special revenue fund	16,000

8 Vouchers payable at June 30, 20X9 were $14,000.

Required

1 For the period July 1, 20X8 through June 30, 20X9, prepare journal entries to record all the transactions in the central garage fund accounts.

2 Prepare closing entries for the central garage fund at June 30, 20X9.

P 20-15 Prepare journal entries to record the following grant-related transactions of an enterprise fund activity. Explain how these transactions should be reported in the enterprise fund's financial statements, including the statement of cash flows.

1 Received an operating grant in cash from the state, $3,000,000.

2 Incurred qualifying expenses on the grant program, $1,200,000.

3 Received a federal grant to finance construction of a processing plant, $7,000,000. (The cash was received in advance.)

4 Incurred and paid construction costs on the processing plant, $4,000,000.

21

Voluntary Health and Welfare Organizations, Health Care Entities, and Colleges and Universities

This chapter provides an introduction to accounting principles and reporting practices of not-for-profit voluntary health and welfare organizations, other not-for-profit organizations (such as churches and museums), health care entities, and colleges and universities. Each of these organization types is important for the resources it controls and for its impact on society.

The four organization types are alike in the sense that they are not-for-profit organizations and have service objectives. However, their service objectives, sources of financing, and degree of autonomy vary significantly, and these differences are reflected in their financial reporting requirements. Further, some of these organizations are considered governments in the accounting literature and are required to follow the pronouncements of the GASB. Others are nongovernment not-for-profit organizations whose standards are established by the FASB.

SOURCES OF ACCOUNTING PRINCIPLES FOR NONGOVERNMENT, NOT-FOR-PROFIT ENTITIES

One of the first challenges that must be addressed in accounting and reporting for a not-for-profit organization is to determine whether it must follow GASB or FASB standards. Appropriate AICPA audit guides, such as *Audits of Not-for-Profit Organizations*, contain a "definition" of a government that must be applied to each organization to determine if it is a government that must follow GASB standards. If it is not a government, FASB standards must be applied. Applying this definition sometimes produces results that most would not have presumed. Even a "for-profit" entity can be a government. The Columbus Clippers, a AAA professional baseball team, is a government organization under the definition, which is reproduced in Exhibit 21–1, and must follow the government GAAP hierarchy. This hierarchy establishes the GASB as the standards-setting body. All nongovernment, not-for-profit organizations—whether voluntary health and welfare organizations, health care organizations, colleges and universities, or other—apply essentially the same guidance. The primary FASB standards that provide unique guidance for such entities are *FASB Statement No. 116*, "Accounting for Contributions Received and Contributions Made," which establishes accounting standards for contributions, and *Statement No. 117*, "Financial Statements of Not-for-Profit Organizations," which identifies the required statements to be presented by nongovernment, not-for-profit organizations.

Public corporations* (or bodies corporate and politic) are governmental organizations. Other organizations are governmental organizations if they have one or more of the following characteristics:

- Popular election of officers or appointment (or approval) of a controlling majority by officials of one or more state or local governments
- The potential for dissolution by a government, with the net assets reverting to a government, or
- The power to enact *and* enforce a tax levy

Furthermore, organizations are presumed to be governmental if they have the ability to issue directly (rather than through a state or municipal authority) debt that pays interest exempt from federal taxation. However, organizations possessing only that ability (to issue tax-exempt debt) and none of the other governmental characteristics may rebut the presumption that they are governmental if their determination is supported by compelling, relevant evidence.

Black's Law Dictionary defines a public corporation as: An artificial person (e.g., [a] municipality or a governmental corporation) created for the administration of public affairs. Unlike a private corporation it has no protection against legislative acts altering or even repealing its charter. Instrumentalities created by [the] state, formed and owned by it in [the] public interest, supported in whole or part by public funds, and governed by managers deriving their authority from [the] state. Sharon Realty Co. v. Westlake, Ohio Com.Pl., 188 N.E.2d 318, 323, 25 O.O.2d 322. A public corporation is an instrumentality of the state, founded and owned in the public interest supported by public funds and governed by those deriving their authority from the state. York County Fair Ass'n v. South Carolina Tax Commission, 249 S.C. 337, 154 S.E.2d 361, 362.
Source: AICPA, *Audits of Health Care Organizations,* para 1.02c.

Exhibit 21–1 *Definition of Governments*

Government health care organizations are to follow the guidance in the AICPA audit guide, "Audits of Health Care Organizations." *GASB Statement No. 15*, "Governmental College and University Accounting and Financial Reporting Models," permits government colleges and universities to use either the AICPA college guide model or the governmental model for accounting and financial reporting by governmental colleges and universities. The AICPA college guide model and the provisions of the health care audit guide are illustrated later in this chapter.

GASB Statement No. 29, "The Use of Not-for-Profit Accounting Principles by Governmental Entities," prohibits government organizations from applying FASB standards such as FASB Statements 116, 117, and 124 that relate solely or primarily to not-for-profit organizations. Government voluntary health and welfare organizations and other not-for-profit organizations have two options to choose. One is to apply the standard government accounting model described in Chapters 19 and 20. The other is to apply the AICPA model that the entity was using when the GASB adopted *Statement 29*. This second option is not available for entities that were not using the AICPA model when *Statement 29* became effective or that were formed subsequently. Voluntary health and welfare guidance under this option is derived from the AICPA audit guide, *Audits of Voluntary Health and Welfare Organizations*. Other not-for-profit organization guidance under this option is found primarily in AICPA *Statement of Position (SOP) 78–10*.

Thus, GAAP for government-supported colleges and universities are different from those for private colleges and universities. The same is true of hospitals, voluntary health and welfare organizations and other nonprofit organizations that are governments under the definition in Exhibit 21–1.

ACCOUNTING PRINCIPLES APPLICABLE TO MOST NONGOVERNMENT, NOT-FOR-PROFIT ENTITIES

Because the FASB issued *Statements No. 93, 116,* and *117* for the purpose of standardizing accounting and financial reporting in not-for-profit entities, this chapter will begin with a summary of accounting principles applicable to nongovernment, not-for-profit organizations in general. These general principles apply to nongovernmental voluntary health and welfare organizations, nongovernmental health care entities, and private colleges and universities for which the FASB provides GAAP. These common principles are then illustrated for a voluntary health and welfare organization. The next section of the chapter reviews some accounting and reporting practices of health care entities and compares those practices with practices of a governmental health care entity. A final section of the chapter illustrates financial accounting and reporting for governmental colleges and universities that are accounted for under GASB pronouncements.

Accrual Basis of Accounting

Not-for-profit organizations account for revenues and expenses using the accrual basis of accounting. *Statement No. 117* requires that not-for-profit organizations that issue GAAP basis financial statements recognize depreciation expense on long-lived assets. Depreciation should be recorded even if the assets are gifts. Certain works of art and certain historical treasures that meet the definition of "collections" need not be capitalized or depreciated.

The audit and accounting guide, *Audits of Not-for-Profit Organizations*, describes revenues of not-for-profit organizations as inflows of assets from major ongoing activities. Gains are increases in net assets from peripheral or incidental transactions. Expenses are outflows of assets or the incurrence of liabilities resulting from the organization's major ongoing activities, and losses are decreases in net assets from peripheral or incidental transactions or events outside the control of the not-for-profit entity. Revenues and expenses are reported at gross amounts. Most gains and losses are reported net, and investment income is reported net of related expenses.

Classification of Net Assets

The reporting requirements of *Statement No. 117* are based on a division of net assets into three classifications. These classes of net assets are totally dependent on the existence or absence of donor-imposed restrictions. The three classes of net assets are defined in *Statement No. 116*:

- **Permanently restricted net assets** are the portion of net assets whose use is limited by donor-imposed *stipulations that do not expire and cannot be removed* by action of the not-for-profit entity.
- **Temporarily restricted net assets** are the portion of net assets whose use is limited by donor-imposed *stipulations that either expire* (time restrictions) *or can be removed by the organization fulfilling the stipulations* (purpose restrictions).
- **Unrestricted net assets** are the portion of net assets that carry *no donor-imposed stipulations*.

The organization's net assets, revenues, expenses, gains, and losses are classified according to the three classes of net assets. This division of net assets into unrestricted, temporarily restricted, and permanently restricted classifications is the core of the financial statement presentations for not-for-profit entities. Revenues, gains, and losses can be reported in each net asset class, but expenses are reported only in the unrestricted net assets class.

Contributions

For some not-for-profit entities, contributions are a major source of revenue. *Statement No. 116* defines a **contribution** as "an unconditional transfer of cash or other assets to an entity or a settlement or cancellation of its liabilities in a voluntary, nonreciprocal transfer by another entity acting other than as an owner."[1] Note the characteristics of the transfer from the definition: (1) the transfer is unconditional; (2) the transfer is to or from an entity acting other than as an owner; (3) the transfer is voluntary; and (4) the transfer is nonreciprocal (in other words, the asset is received or the liability canceled without value given in exchange).

Note also that the transfer involves cash or "other assets." Examples of other assets include buildings, securities, use of facilities, services, and **unconditional promises to give**. *Statement No. 116* describes a promise to give as a written or oral

---

[1]*FASB Statement No. 116*, Appendix D.

agreement to contribute cash or other assets to another entity. The promise should be verifiable by evidence such as pledge cards or tape recordings of oral promises. A promise to give may be conditional or unconditional.

- A **conditional promise to give** depends on the occurrence of a specified future and uncertain event to bind the promisor. Conditional promises to give should be recognized as contribution revenue and receivables when the conditions are substantially met (in other words, when the conditional promise to give becomes unconditional).
- An **unconditional promise to give** depends only on the passage of time or demand by the promisee for performance. Promises to give are considered unconditional if the possibility that a condition will not be met is remote.[2] Unconditional promises to give are recognized as contribution revenue and receivables in the period in which the promise is received.

A conditional gift of cash or other asset that may have to be returned to the donor if the condition is not met should be accounted for as a refundable advance (liability).

Restricted and Unrestricted Support

Generally, restricted and unrestricted contributions are measured at fair value and recognized as revenues or gains in the period they are received, and as assets, decreases of liabilities, or expenses, depending on the form of the benefits received. (Contributed services and collections are discussed later.) Contributions are separated into the three classes of net assets: (1) those that increase unrestricted net assets, (2) those that increase temporarily restricted net assets, and (3) those that increase permanently restricted net assets.

- Unrestricted contributions are reported as unrestricted support that increases unrestricted net assets.
- Restricted contributions are reported as restricted support that increases either permanently restricted net assets or temporarily restricted net assets.[3]

Unconditional promises to give with payments due in future periods—next year or later—are reported as restricted support (in other words, as contribution revenues in temporarily restricted net assets, based on the time restriction) in the period the promises are received, even if the resources are not restricted for specific purposes.[4]

Contributions made are recognized as expenses in the period made and are measured at fair value.

Donor-Imposed Restriction Distinguished from Donor-Imposed Condition A donor-imposed condition provides that the donor's money is returned or the donor is released from the promise to give if the condition is not met. Donor-imposed restrictions simply limit the use of contributed assets. If it is unclear whether donor stipulations are conditions or restrictions, the promise is presumed to be conditional.

Gifts of Long-Lived Assets Gifts of long-lived assets may be restricted or unrestricted, depending on the organization's accounting policy or the donor's restriction. If the contributed long-lived assets are restricted by the donor for use for a certain period of time, the assets are reported as restricted support in temporarily restricted net assets. Depreciation is recorded as an expense in unrestricted net assets, and there is a reclassification for the amount of the depreciation from temporarily restricted to unrestricted net assets.

If the donor contributes the long-lived assets with no restrictions or if the assets are purchased with contributions restricted to the acquisition of long-lived assets, the

---

[2]When the contribution is recognized as revenue because not meeting the condition is remote, a contingent liability should be disclosed in notes to the financial statements.

[3]Donor-restricted contributions whose restrictions are met in the same reporting period may be reported as unrestricted support as long as the policy is followed consistently.

[4]An exception is provided when the donor explicitly stipulates that the contribution is intended to support current-period activities, in which case it is reported as unrestricted support.

organization can choose either of two accounting methods, which should be used consistently. The accounting policy must be disclosed in notes to the financial statements. The methods are as follows:

1 The organization may adopt an accounting policy that implies a time restriction that expires over the useful life of the donated asset. As in the case of contributed long-lived assets with an explicit donor-imposed time restriction, the gift is reported as restricted support in temporarily restricted net assets. Depreciation is recorded as an expense in unrestricted net assets, which results in a reclassification for the amount of the depreciation from temporarily restricted to unrestricted net assets. (This also applies to assets purchased with cash that was restricted to the purchase of long-lived assets.)

2 If no policy implying a time restriction exists and there are no donor-imposed restrictions, the gifts are unrestricted support.

Expiration of Donor-Imposed Restrictions   Expiration of a donor-imposed restriction is recognized in the period in which the restriction is satisfied (i.e., when a time restriction is met or a purpose restriction satisfied). If a given contribution is subject to more than one restriction, the effect of the expiration of the restrictions is recognized in the period in which the last restriction expires. When the temporary restriction is met (either by the passage of time or by the incurrence of expenses for the restricted purpose), resources in the temporarily restricted net assets are reclassified as unrestricted net assets and reported as net assets released from restrictions in the activities statement. The expense is reported on the financial statements as a decrease in unrestricted net assets. "Net assets released from restrictions" is reported in the statement of activity as an increase in unrestricted net assets and a corresponding decrease in temporarily restricted net assets.

When an expense is incurred for which there are both unrestricted and temporarily restricted net assets available, the donor-imposed restriction is fulfilled to the extent of the expense.

If donor-imposed restrictions are met in the same period that the contributions are received, the contributions may be reported as unrestricted if the following conditions are met. First, the policy must be disclosed in the notes and followed consistently, and second, the organization must have the same policy for temporarily restricted investment income whose restrictions are met in the same period as income is recognized.

Investments and Investment Income

Investments made by a not-for-profit organization are initially recorded at their cost, and investments received as contributions are recorded at fair value in the appropriate net asset classification. Investment income should be recognized as earned and reported as an increase in unrestricted, temporarily restricted, or permanently restricted net assets, depending on donor-imposed restrictions on the use of the investment income. Realized gains and losses are recognized when investments are sold and are reported as changes in unrestricted, temporarily restricted, or permanently restricted net assets.

FASB Statement No. 124, "Accounting for Certain Investments Held by Not-for-Profit Organizations," requires investments in debt securities to be reported at their fair values. Investments in equity securities that have readily determinable fair values also must be reported at fair values. Changes in fair values are to be reported in the statement of activities. The fair value accounting requirement does not apply to equity investments that are accounted for by the equity method or investments in consolidated subsidiaries.

Additionally, financial statements should disclose the investment objectives of the organization and should include other information as follows:

- The aggregate carrying value by major types of investments and the bases for the reported carrying values
- The methods and significant assumptions used to determine the carrying value of investments *other than* equity securities that do not have readily determinable fair values and debt securities
- Contractual maturities of debt securities

- The nature of and carrying value for any investment or group of investments that represents a significant concentration of risk
- The composition of the investment return included in the change in net assets for the period, including investment income, realized gains and losses on investments carried at other than fair value, and net holding gains and losses on investments carried at fair value
- A reconciliation of the investment return to the amounts presented in the statement of activities if there is a discrepancy

Transfers That Are Not Contributions

Contributions do not include transfers that are exchange transactions, transfers where the not-for-profit enterprise is acting as an agent, trustee, or intermediary for the donor, or tax exemptions, tax incentives, and tax abatements.

Exchange Transactions   Exchange transactions are reciprocal transfers where both parties give and receive approximately equal value. Sales of products and services are exchange transactions. Exchange transactions are sometimes difficult to distinguish from contributions. Assume that a not-for-profit organization sends calendars (premiums) to potential donors in a fund-raising appeal. The recipients keep the premium whether or not they make a donation. In this case the donations are contributions and the cost of premiums is a fund-raising expense. The same is true if the not-for-profit organization gives the premiums only to donors, but the premiums are nominal in relation to the donations. If donors receive gifts that approximate the value of their donations, however, the transaction is an exchange.

Dues charged to members of not-for-profit entities may have characteristics of both contributions and exchange transactions. The portion of the dues representing contributions will be recognized as revenue when received, but the portion representing an exchange transaction will be recognized as revenue as it is earned. Grants must also be analyzed to determine if they are exchange transactions. The grant is an exchange transaction if the potential public benefit is secondary to the grantor's potential direct benefit.

Resources received in exchange transactions are classified as unrestricted revenues and unrestricted net assets even if the resource provider limits use of the resources.

Agency Transactions   An agency transaction is one in which assets are transferred to the not-for-profit organization, but the not-for-profit organization has little or no discretion over the use of those assets, and the assets are passed on to a third party. The resource provider is using the not-for-profit entity as an agent or intermediary to transfer assets to a third-party donee. The receipt of assets in an agency transaction increases the assets and liabilities of the not-for-profit entity and disbursement of those assets decreases assets and liabilities. The cash received and paid is reported as cash flows from operating activities in the statement of cash flows.

Gifts in Kind   Gifts in kind are contributions if the not-for-profit entity has discretion over the disposition of the resources. If it has little or no discretion over the disposition, the gifts are accounted for as agency transactions. Gifts in kind that are contributions are measured at fair value, if practicable. When fair value cannot be reasonably determined, the gifts should not be recorded as contributions. Instead, the items are recorded as sales revenue when they are sold. Cost of sales is the cost of getting the inventory ready for sale.

Contributed Services

Contributed services are recognized only if the services received (1) create or enhance nonfinancial assets of the organization or (2) require specialized skills, are provided by individuals possessing those skills, and would typically need to be purchased if not provided by donation. Contributed services that do not meet the criteria should not be recognized. However, information about services contributed to the organization's programs and activities should be described.

Measurement Principles

Contributions received and contributions made are measured at fair value. *Statement No. 116* identifies quoted market prices as the best estimate of fair values for both monetary and nonmonetary assets. Other valuation methods that might be used include quoted market prices for similar assets or independent appraisals. If a reasonable estimate for fair value cannot be made, the contribution should not be recognized.

Unconditional Promises to Give   Contribution revenues and the related receivables are measured at the fair value of the assets received or the liabilities satisfied. When the contributed asset is received, contributions (pledges) receivable is decreased and the appropriate asset account is increased. A change in the fair value of the contributed asset between the date recorded as contribution revenue and the date it is received by the not-for-profit entity is accounted for as follows:

- No additional revenue is recognized if the fair value increases.
- If the fair value decreases, the difference is recognized in the period the decrease occurred and reported as a change in the net asset class in which the revenue was originally reported or in the class where the net assets are represented.

Unconditional promises to give that the not-for-profit entity expects to collect within one year of the financial statement date may be measured at their *net realizable value* (gross amount less an allowance for uncollectible accounts). However, unconditional promises to give that are *not* expected to be collected within the year are measured at the present value of the amounts expected to be collected (estimated future cash flows). The discount rate to be used in computing the present value should be a risk-free rate of return for a like time period.[5] The discount rate should be determined at the time the receivable is recognized and should not be revised for market rate changes. The discount is amortized using the interest rate method (see *APB Opinion No. 21*, paragraph 15). Amortization of the discount is included in contribution revenue and as an increase in the appropriate net asset class.

Conditional Promises to Give   Conditional promises to give are measured at the fair value of the asset at the time it is received. (The conditional promise to give is not recorded as an asset or as contribution revenue until it is received or becomes unconditional.)

Collections

Statement No. 116 encourages retroactive capitalization of collections of works of art, historical treasures, and similar items, but it does not require it. Collections may be capitalized retroactively using cost or fair value at acquisition, current cost, or current market value. The same method need not be used for all items. Collections that are not capitalized, or that are capitalized prospectively, should be described. Contributed collection items should be recognized as revenues or gains if the collection is capitalized and they should not be recognized unless the collection is capitalized.

When collection items are not recognized, the costs of collection items, proceeds from sales, and proceeds from insurance recoveries are shown as increases or decreases of the appropriate net asset class on the activities statement, separately from revenues, expenses, gains, and losses. An entity that capitalizes its collections prospectively should report proceeds from sales and insurance recoveries of items not previously capitalized separately from revenues, expenses, gains, and losses.

Financial Statements

FASB Statement No. 117 requires not-for-profit organizations to provide a set of financial statements that includes a statement of financial position, statement of activities, statement of cash flows, and accompanying notes. Voluntary health and welfare organizations also must provide a statement of functional expenses. The goal of the reporting requirement is to establish consistent standards for reporting basic information. The statements and notes should include:

- Information required by GAAP for which not-for-profit entities are not specifically exempt
- Information required by applicable specialized accounting and reporting principles and practices

---

[5]AICPA audit guide, *Not-for-Profit Organizations*, paragraph 5.52.

The organization's net assets, revenues, expenses, gains, and losses are classified according to the three classes of net assets—unrestricted, temporarily restricted, and permanently restricted. The classifications are based totally on the existence or absence of donor-imposed restrictions.

Statement of Financial Position   The balance sheet reports assets, liabilities, and net assets. Other balance sheet characteristics include:

- The statement's focus is on the organization as a whole. Thus, total assets, total liabilities, and total net assets are disclosed.
- Net assets are reported in total and by the three classes of net assets—unrestricted, temporarily restricted, and permanently restricted. Permanently and temporarily restricted amounts can be reported on the face of the balance sheet or in notes.
- Assets do not need to be disaggregated on the basis of donor restrictions, but assets received with donor-imposed restrictions that limit their use to long-term purposes should be separated from assets available for current use.
- Comparative statements from the prior period are not required.

Like assets and liabilities should be aggregated into homogeneous groups. Information on the organization's liquidity can be provided by sequencing assets and liabilities by nearness of conversion to cash and use of cash, classifying assets and liabilities as current and noncurrent, and/or providing disclosures about liquidity and restrictions in notes.

Permanent restrictions *may* have separate lines for (1) holdings (land, art, and so on, to be used for specific purposes, preserved and not sold) and (2) permanent endowment funds (assets donated that must be invested to provide a permanent source of income). Temporarily restricted net assets *may* use separate lines on the face of the balance sheet or in notes to distinguish between restrictions for:

1 Support of particular operating activities (*purpose restriction*)
2 Investment for specified term (*time restriction*)
3 Use in specified future period
4 Acquisition of long-lived assets

Statement No. 117 does not prohibit a display of funds in the balance sheet, but if funds are presented, they must be arranged and labeled so that interfund balances are eliminated from total amounts. The reporting of aggregated amounts is still required when fund information is presented.

Statement of Activities   The statement of activities provides information about the change in amount and nature of net assets and about how resources are used to provide various programs or services.

The focus of the activities statement is on the organization as a whole. The amount of *change in net assets* for the period must be reported. This amount should articulate to net assets in the balance sheet. Revenues, expenses, gains, and losses should be presented by net asset class. The statement should also report the amount of change in permanently restricted net assets, temporarily restricted net assets, and unrestricted net assets. An intermediate measure (such as operating revenues over expenses) *may* be included.

Revenues increase unrestricted net assets unless use of the assets received is limited by donor-imposed restrictions. *Expenses* always decrease unrestricted net assets. Expenses can not be reported in the temporarily restricted or permanently restricted net asset classes. Donor-restricted contributions are reported as restricted revenues or gains (restricted support) and increases in temporarily restricted or permanently restricted net assets. Donor-restricted contributions whose restrictions are met in the same reporting period may be reported as unrestricted *if* the organization follows a consistent policy and that policy is disclosed. Reclassifications are reported separately.

Gains and losses on investments are increases or decreases in unrestricted net assets unless their use is restricted by explicit donor stipulations or by law.

Further classifications of revenues, expenses, gains, and losses, such as operating or nonoperating, recurring or nonrecurring, and so on, are optional. In any case, the statement of activities must report the change in unrestricted net assets for the period.

Generally, gross revenues and expenses are reported.[6] Gains and losses from peripheral or incidental transactions or events beyond the control of the organization may be reported at net amounts.

Expenses should be reported by functional classification (i.e., major classes of program services and supporting services) in the statement or notes. *Program services* are the activities that distribute goods and services to beneficiaries, customers, or members that fulfill the purpose or mission of the organization. *Supporting services* are all activities other than program services. Supporting services include:

1 Management and general—oversight, business management, general recordkeeping, budgeting, financing, and related administrative activities
2 Fund-raising—publicizing and conducting fund-raising campaigns, maintaining donor mailing lists, conducting special fund-raising events, preparing and distributing fund-raising manuals, instructions and other materials, and other activities to solicit contributions
3 Membership-development activities—soliciting for prospective members and membership dues, membership relations, and so on.

Statement of Functional Expenses   Voluntary health and welfare organizations must report expenses classified by function and by natural classification (salaries, rent, etc.) in a matrix format as a separate statement. Other not-for-profit organizations are encouraged (but *not* required) to provide this additional expense information.

Statement of Cash Flows   *FASB Statement No. 95*, "Statement of Cash Flows," is amended by *Statement No. 117* to extend the provisions to not-for-profit organizations. Not-for-profit organizations use the same classifications and definitions as business enterprises, except that the description of financing activities is expanded to include resources that are donor-restricted for long-term purposes. Investing activities of permanent endowments are reported as cash flows of investing activities.

Recall that cash restricted for long-term purposes *cannot* be aggregated in the balance sheet with cash available for current uses. Similarly, cash and cash equivalents that are restricted for long-term purposes can be excluded from cash in the cash flows statement.

Not-for-profit organizations are encouraged to use the direct method for presenting cash flows, but the indirect method is permitted. A schedule should be provided to reconcile the change in net assets in the statement of activities to net cash flows from operating activities if the direct method is used.

Financial Statement Disclosures for Contributions

Not-for-profit entities should disclose unconditional promises to give as (1) amounts of promises receivable in less than one year, in one to five years, and in more than five years, and (2) the allowance for uncollectible promises receivable.

Disclosures in notes for conditional promises to give include the total amounts promised and a description and amount for each group of promises having similar characteristics.

VOLUNTARY HEALTH AND WELFARE ORGANIZATIONS

Voluntary health and welfare organizations encompass a diverse group of not-for-profit entities that are supported by and provide voluntary services to the public. They may expend their resources to solve basic social problems in the areas of health or welfare, or to alleviate such problems at the community level or on an individual basis. The 1995 audit and accounting guide, *Audits of Not-for-Profit Organizations*, provides guidance for accounting and reporting for all nongovernment voluntary health and welfare organizations.

---

[6]Investment revenues may be reported net of custodial and advisory fees as long as the expense is disclosed on the face of the statement or in notes.

Governmental voluntary health and welfare organizations follow the guidance in the 1974 AICPA industry audit guide, *Audits of Voluntary Health and Welfare Organizations*. Governmental voluntary health and welfare organizations are not illustrated.

Fund Accounting

Historically, many not-for-profit entities used fund accounting principles, both for internal accounting and for reporting information in their financial statements. Fund accounting is not required by any FASB statement or interpretation and it is not required by *Audits of Not-for-Profit Organizations. FASB Statement No. 117* does not require reporting by funds, but it does not prohibit reporting by funds as additional information as long as the information required by *Statement No. 117* is presented and all interfund balances are eliminated. The disclosure focus must be on the entity as a whole, not on the funds.

Not-for-profit entities receive resources from contributions, charges for services, grants, appropriations, and so on, and the use of some of these resources is restricted for specific activities or purposes. Fund accounting principles provide a convenient method for segregating the accounting records of resources restricted for specific purposes. Many not-for-profit organizations continue to use fund accounting for internal accounting, but it is not required by GAAP, and it is rarely presented in financial statements of nongovernment, voluntary health and welfare organizations. Therefore, fund accounting is not discussed or illustrated for nongovernment organizations.

Revenues and Expenses

The financial statements of voluntary health and welfare organizations are subject to generally accepted accounting principles that include APB Opinions, FASB statements, and other authoritative pronouncements, except when such pronouncements are inapplicable. Thus, as noted earlier, revenues and expenses are recorded as earned and incurred under the accrual basis of accounting.

Contributions are the major sources of support for voluntary health and welfare organizations. Revenues are reported in the net asset class to which they relate. Revenues with no donor-imposed restrictions increase unrestricted net assets; revenues with donor-imposed restrictions increase temporarily restricted or permanently restricted net assets. Expenses decrease unrestricted net assets. Expenses are classified as *program services* and *supporting services* and are reported on a functional basis under these classifications. Program services relate to the expenses incurred in providing the organization's social service activities. Supporting services consist of administrative expenses and fund-raising costs. In reporting expenses in the statement of activities, the functional classifications might appear as follows:

Expenses

Program Services
Research
Public education
Professional education
Community services

Supporting Services
Management and general
Fund-raising

The functional basis of reporting expenses results in an informative but highly aggregated form of statement presentation. To overcome the limitations of aggregation, voluntary health and welfare organizations prepare a separate statement of functional expenses. This statement reconciles the functional classifications with basic object-of-expenditure classifications such as salaries, supplies, postage, and awards and grants. The statement of functional expenses is a *required* statement for voluntary health and welfare organizations. The FASB encourages its presentation for other not-for-profit entities, but does not require it.

Financial Reporting

The basic financial statements of nongovernment, voluntary health and welfare organizations include the same statements required for other not-for-profit organizations (a statement of financial position, a statement of activities, and a statement of cash flows) plus one additional statement, the statement of functional expenses.

A national, voluntary health and welfare organization may have financially interrelated local affiliates. Unless the local organizations are independent of the national organization, with separate purposes and separate governing boards, the financial statements of the national and local organizations are combined for reporting in accordance with GAAP.

Sample financial statements for a fictitious voluntary health and welfare organization are presented in Exhibits 21–2, 21–3, 21–4, and 21–5.

Sample Journal Entries

The following *unrelated* journal entries provide examples of some typical accounting procedures for several fictitious, voluntary health and welfare organizations.

Contributions   A group of concerned citizens organized a voluntary health and welfare organization called the Neighborhood Assistance Fund (NAF) in 20X5. As part of its fund-raising effort in 20X5, NAF distributed decals to all residents in the community. The decals cost NAF $145. As a result of the campaign, the organization received $4,000 unrestricted cash contributions and unconditional promises to give to-

---

VOLUNTARY HEALTH AND WELFARE ORGANIZATION
STATEMENTS OF FINANCIAL POSITION
DECEMBER 31, 20X7 AND 20X6

	20X7	20X6
Assets		
Cash and cash equivalents	$ 4,000	$ 2,500
Accounts receivable	500	400
Inventories	2,500	1,600
Contributions receivable	15,000	12,000
Short-term investments	1,000	—
Assets restricted to investments in land, buildings, and equipment	1,500	800
Land, buildings, and equipment (less accumulated depreciation of $4,000 in 20X6 and $3,500 in 20X5)	6,000	7,000
Assets restricted for endowment	5,000	5,000
Total assets	$35,500	$29,300
Liabilities and Net Assets		
Liabilities		
Accounts payable	$ 2,300	$ 1,900
Grants payable	1,550	—
Mortgage payable	3,000	6,000
Interest payable	50	100
Total liabilities	6,900	8,000
Net assets		
Unrestricted	7,100	3,500
Temporarily restricted	16,500	12,800
Permanently restricted	5,000	5,000
Total net assets	28,600	21,300
Total liabilities and net assets	$35,500	$29,300

Exhibit 21–2   *Balance Sheet for Nongovernment Voluntary Health and Welfare Organization*

```
┌─────────────────────────────────────────────────────────────────────┐
│ VOLUNTARY HEALTH AND WELFARE ORGANIZATION                             │
│ STATEMENT OF ACTIVITIES                                               │
│ FOR THE YEAR ENDED DECEMBER 31, 20X7                                  │
└─────────────────────────────────────────────────────────────────────┘
```

Changes in unrestricted net assets
  Revenues and gains

Contributions		$29,500	
Membership revenues		8,200	
Fees		400	
Special event	$7,500		
Less: Direct costs	4,000	3,500	
Income from investments		50	
Total unrestricted revenues and gains			$41,650
Net assets released from restrictions			
Satisfaction of program restriction		$ 5,000	
Expiration of time restriction		10,000	
Total net assets released from restrictions			15,000
Total unrestricted revenues, gains, and			
other support			56,650
Expenses and losses			
Program services			
Public health and education		$26,000	
Research		10,000	36,000
Supporting services			
Fund raising		11,000	
Management and general		6,050	17,050
Total expenses and losses			53,050
Increase in unrestricted net assets			3,600

Changes in temporarily restricted net assets

Contributions	$18,550	
Income on investments	150	
Net assets released from restrictions	(15,000)	
Increase in temporarily restricted net assets		3,700

Changes in permanently restricted net assets

	—
Increase in net assets	7,300
Net assets at the beginning of the year	21,300
Net assets at the end of the year	$28,600

Exhibit 21–3   *Statement of Activities*

taling $6,000. Of this $6,000 contribution receivable, $2,000 is not collectible until 20X6. A presumption exists that the $2,000 due in 20X6 is restricted for use in 20X6. NAF estimates that 10% of the pledges will be uncollectible. The following entries are made in 20X5.

Fund raising expenses	$ 145	
Cash		$ 145
To record payment for decals used in fund raising.		
Cash	$4,000	
Unrestricted support—contributions		$4,000
To record cash contributions.		
Contributions receivable	$6,000	
Allowance for uncollectible contributions		$ 600
Unrestricted support—contributions		3,600
Temporarily restricted support—contributions		1,800

  To record unrestricted promises to give, promises restricted
    for use in 20X6, and estimated uncollectibles.

```
VOLUNTARY HEALTH AND WELFARE ORGANIZATION
STATEMENT OF CASH FLOWS—INDIRECT METHOD
YEAR ENDED DECEMBER 31, 20X7

Cash flows from operating activities
   Change in net assets                                                    $7,300
   Adjustments to reconcile change in net assets to
      cash used by operating activities
   Depreciation                                              $    500
   Increase in contributions receivable                        (3,000)
   Increase in accounts receivable                               (100)
   Increase in inventories                                       (900)
   Increase in accounts payable                                   400
   Increase in grants payable                                   1,550
   Decrease in interest payable                                   (50)
   Increase in amount restricted for plant                      (700)      (2,300)
      Net cash provided by operating activities                             5,000

Cash flows from investing activities
   Cash paid for short-term investments                        (1,000)
   Sale of equipment                                              500
      Net cash used for investing activities                                 (500)

Cash flows from financing activities
   Payment on mortgage liability                               (3,000)
      Net cash used in financing activities                                 (3,000)
Increase in cash and cash equivalents                                       1,500
Cash and cash equivalents at beginning of year                              2,500
   Cash and cash equivalents at end of year                                $4,000
```

Exhibit 21–4   *Statement of Cash Flows (Indirect Method)*

NAF collected $3,600 of the contributions receivable due in 20X5 and wrote off the remaining $400 as uncollectible.

```
Cash                                              $3,600
Allowance for uncollectible contributions            400
   Contributions receivable                                   $4,000
   To record collection of contributions receivable.
```

The full $2,000 due in 20X6 is collected in 20X6. When the receivables are collected, any difference between the estimated amount of uncollectibles and the actual amount is reported as a gain or loss in the appropriate net asset class. The implied

```
VOLUNTARY HEALTH AND WELFARE ORGANIZATION
STATEMENT OF FUNCTIONAL EXPENSES
FOR THE YEAR ENDED DECEMBER 31, 20X7
```

	Total	Public Health and Education	Research	Fund Raising	Management and General
Salaries	$12,370	$ 5,000	$ 3,050	$ 2,320	$ 2,000
Grants	10,000	5,000	5,000	—	—
Supplies	25,050	13,820	1,200	7,330	2,700
Professional fees	1,280	580	300	250	150
Office expense	3,850	1,400	350	1,000	1,100
Depreciation	500	200	100	100	100
	$53,050	$26,000	$10,000	$11,000	$ 6,050

Exhibit 21–5   *Statement of Functional Expenses*

time restriction is met, so $1,800 of temporarily restricted net assets are reclassified as unrestricted net assets.

Cash	$2,000	
Allowance for uncollectible contributions	200	
Contributions receivable		$2,000
Unrestricted support		200

To record collection of receivables and recognize support for the difference between the estimated and actual allowance for uncollectible amounts.

Temporarily restricted net assets—reclassifications out	$1,800	
Unrestricted net assets—reclassifications in		$1,800

To reclassify net assets for which the restriction has been met.

A donor gives NAF $1,000 that is restricted for a playground project. NAF purchases supplies for the playground project for $900. Expenses are reported as changes in unrestricted net assets. An entry is made to reclassify $900 of temporarily restricted net assets. The reclassification is entered even if unrestricted resources were used to pay for the playground supplies.

Cash	$1,000	
Restricted support—contributions		$1,000

To record gift restricted for special project.

Expenses—community service	$ 900	
Cash		$ 900

To record purchase of supplies to be used in playground project.

Temporarily restricted net assets—reclassifications out	$ 900	
Unrestricted net assets—reclassifications in		$ 900

To reclassify net assets restricted for the playground project for which the restriction has been met.

Donated Long-Lived Assets Action Against Poverty, a voluntary health and welfare organization, has a policy of implying a time restriction on donated fixed assets over the life of the asset. On January 1, 20X2, Martin Construction donated a used van to Action Against Poverty. The fair value of the van is $1,500 and it has a three-year remaining useful life. The van will be used in the organization's community service program.

The donated van is initially recorded as temporarily restricted support. Depreciation expense on the van is classified by functional expense. The amount of depreciation expense is reclassified from temporarily restricted net assets to unrestricted net assets.

Equipment	$1,500	
Restricted support—contribution		$1,500

To record receipt of donated van.

Depreciation expense—community service	$ 500	
Accumulated depreciation—equipment		$ 500

To record depreciation.

Temporarily restricted net assets—reclassifications out	$ 500	
Unrestricted net assets—reclassifications in		$ 500

To record reclassification of net assets for which the temporary restriction is satisfied.

Special Event Fund Raisers Gross revenues and expenses are generally reported for special events in which attendees receive a benefit and the special event is related to the major ongoing activities of the organization. However, if the special event is peripheral to the organization's ongoing activities, the receipts and related costs *may* be reported at a net amount of gain or loss. If a net gain or loss is reported, the direct costs are not included in the statement of functional expenses.

A fund-raising event for a voluntary health and welfare organization featured a dinner and dance. Ticket sales for the dinner totaled $950 and expenses of the fund raiser amounted to $650. If the special event is incidental to the activities of the organization, the proceeds of the special event may be reported as gains and net of direct costs.

Cash	$ 950	
Unrestricted gains—special event		$ 950
To record proceeds from a fund-raising event.		
Unrestricted support—special event	$ 650	
Cash (or vouchers payable)		$ 650
To charge costs of fund-raising event against support		
from the event.		

If not incidental, the gross proceeds should be reported as revenues and direct costs should be included in expenses.

Gifts in Kind   Throughout the summer a voluntary health and welfare organization receives donations of used housewares and furniture that are sold at a rummage sale held in August. Fair values for the donated items cannot be reasonably determined, but the cost of storing and moving the items to the rummage sale location is $550. Proceeds from the sale are $6,595. Because the fair value cannot be determined, the items are not recorded as contributions.

Cost of goods sold	$ 550	
Cash		$ 550
To pay costs of storing and moving rummage sale items.		
Cash	$6,595	
Unrestricted revenues—sales		$6,595
To record proceeds from rummage sale.		

Alternatively, if the fair value of donated items can be reasonably determined, the gifts in kind are recorded as contributions. Office-Mate Company donates office supplies with a fair value of $390 to a voluntary health and welfare organization. Office-Mate puts no restrictions on the use of the donated items. The organization records the gift as follows:

Inventory of office supplies	$ 390	
Unrestricted support—contributed supplies		$ 390
To record receipt of office supplies.		

Membership Fees   Memberships give members certain benefits, such as the right to receive the organization's newsletters, and so on. Dues from members may represent exchange transactions, contributions, or both, depending on the benefits provided to members. For example, a voluntary health and welfare organization charges dues of $30 a year, which entitles members to a quarterly magazine. The fair value of the four publications is approximately $30. If the organization receives $3,000 in memberships, it records the exchange transaction as an asset and liability as follows:

Cash	$3,000	
Unearned membership dues		$3,000
To record dues from members.		

When the first quarterly magazine is issued, one-fourth of the dues are earned and recognized as revenues. Revenues from exchange transactions are classified as unrestricted.

Unearned membership dues	$ 750	
Unrestricted revenues—membership dues		$ 750
To record revenues earned from publication.		

Alternatively, assume that a voluntary health and welfare organization charges dues of $30 a year, but the member benefits are negligible. The full amount of the dues are recognized as contributions when received with a credit to "unrestricted support—contributions."

In cases in which the fair value of member benefits is less than the amount of dues, the transfers should be divided between contributions and revenues. An organization may have levels of memberships, but the more expensive memberships do not entitle the members to additional benefits. The excess payments are classified as contributions. For example, the Kidney Foundation offers regular memberships for $10 and sustaining memberships for $50 and over. All members are entitled to the same educational materials that are distributed when the dues are received. The foundation received 4,000 regular memberships ($40,000) and 100 sustaining memberships ($15,000), which are recorded:

Cash	$55,000	
Unrestricted revenues—dues		$41,000
Unrestricted support—contributions		14,000
To record revenue and support from the sale of memberships.		

Donated Securities and Investment Income   Securities with a fair value of $5,000 are received with the stipulation that they permanently endow a special education project. Income earned on the securities is restricted to use for the special education project. Dividend income is $475.

Securities	$ 5,000	
Permanently restricted support—contribution		$ 5,000
To record receipt of securities permanently restricted for a special education project.		

Cash	$ 475	
Temporarily restricted revenue—investment income		$ 475
To record investment income restricted for special education project.		

Supplies   The Asthma Support Group had supplies on hand of $1,600 at January 1, 20X2. The organization purchased supplies for $1,500 during the year and received donations of supplies that had a fair value of $2,050. At the end of the 20X2 calendar year, the inventory on hand was $750. The supplies were allocated to public education programs, $2,000; community service programs, $1,400; fund-raising expenses, $600; and general administration, $400. Entries to summarize these events are:

Materials and supplies inventory	$ 3,550	
Unrestricted support—contributions		$ 2,050
Cash		1,500
To record donated materials and supplies and to record purchase of supplies.		

Expenses—management and general	$ 400	
Expenses—public education programs	2,000	
Expenses—community service	1,400	
Expenses—fund-raising	600	
Materials and supplies inventory		$ 4,400
To record allocation of supplies expense.		

Donated Services and Payment of Salaries   An accounting firm donated its services to audit the books of the Mental Health Association. The audit would have cost the Association $1,200 if the services had not been donated. The Mental Health Association paid salaries allocated to program services and administration as follows: public education programs, $6,000; community services, $4,000; and management and general, $2,000.

Expenses—management and general	$ 1,200	
Unrestricted support—donated services		$ 1,200
To record donated services allocated to management and general expenses.		

Expenses—public education programs	$ 6,000	
Expenses—community services	4,000	
Expenses—management and general	2,000	
Cash		$12,000
To record salaries allocated to program services and administration.		

Depreciation   Equipment owned by Mental Health Services is used in providing services to the organization's clients. There are no explicit or implicit donor-imposed restrictions on the fixed assets. The $8,000 depreciation expense on the equipment is allocated to the programs and general administration of the organization as follows:

Depreciation expense—research programs	$ 1,000	
Depreciation expense—public education programs	2,000	
Depreciation expense—community services	4,000	
Depreciation expense—management and general	1,000	
Accumulated depreciation		$ 8,000
To record depreciation allocated to programs and general administration.		

Fixed Asset Purchase with Restricted Resources   Equipment costing $40,000 was purchased by the Heart Research Institute. The equipment was financed by $30,000 from contributions with donor-imposed restrictions that were accumulated for purchase of the equipment and $10,000 from general resources.

Equipment	$40,000	
Cash		$40,000
To record payment for the purchase of equipment.		
Temporarily restricted net assets—reclassifications out	$30,000	
Unrestricted net assets—reclassifications in		$30,000
To record reclassification of temporarily restricted net assets.		

HOSPITALS AND OTHER HEALTH CARE ORGANIZATIONS

Hospitals and other health care providers constitute a significant area of accounting, both in terms of entities represented and in terms of cost of services provided. Health care providers include clinics, ambulatory care organizations, continuing-care retirement communities, health maintenance organizations, home health agencies, hospitals, government-owned health care entities, and nursing homes that provide health care. Health care entities may be organized as not-for-profit entities, government entities, or private business enterprises owned by investors (stockholders, partners, or sole proprietors). Accounting and reporting standards for health care organizations are generally covered in the audit and accounting guide, *Audits of Health Care Organizations.* The audit guide provides guidance on accounting and reporting for both government and nongovernment health care organizations even though there are significant differences in the two. The discussion in this chapter generally refers to hospitals as a matter of convenience, but the principles apply to other health care organizations as well.

Accounting and reporting for a nongovernment, not-for-profit hospital is based upon the same standards and principles as for any other nongovernment, not-for-profit organization. However, there are several uniquenesses that warrant specific discussion. First, there are unique revenue sources such as patient service revenues and premium fees. Also, the expense classifications used are relatively unique to hospitals. Finally, the audit guide requires health care organizations to present a statement of operations reporting a performance measurement and the change in unrestricted net assets along with a statement of changes in net assets, instead of a statement of activities. This financial statement approach is permitted by *Statement No. 117.* Each of these uniquenesses is discussed in the following sections.

Revenues and Gains

Revenue is reported in the period in which services are rendered. Operating revenues consist of patient service revenues, premium fee revenues, and other operating revenues. Some examples of patient service revenues and other operating revenues are given in Exhibit 21–6.

Patient Service Revenue   Patient service revenues include room and board, nursing services, and other professional services. Patient service revenues typically are recorded at established (gross) rates as the services are provided but are *reported* net of amounts that are considered deductions from revenues. The objective is to report the amount

```
┌─────────────────────────────────────────────────────────────────────────┐
│  Patient Service Revenues          Other Operating Revenues               │
│  Routine care                      Tuition from educational programs      │
│  Nursing                           Research and specific purpose grants   │
│  Delivery and labor rooms          Miscellaneous                          │
│  Emergency room                       Rental revenue for hospital space, clinics, etc. │
│  Recovery rooms                        Gift shop, television rental, telephone, cafeteria │
│  Medical and surgical supplies         Medical record transcripts         │
│  Laboratory—clinical and pathology     Donated medicine, linen, and office supplies │
│  EKG-EEG                                                                  │
│  Radiation therapy                                                        │
│  Pharmacy                                                                 │
│  Anesthesiology                                                           │
│  Physical therapy                                                         │
│  Respiratory therapy                                                      │
│  Hemodialysis                                                             │
│  Speech therapy                                                           │
│  Ambulance                                                                │
└─────────────────────────────────────────────────────────────────────────┘
```

Exhibit 21–6   *Examples of Hospital Revenue Classifications*

that the hospital is entitled to collect and intends to collect as patient service revenues. Charity care—services provided free of charge to patients who qualify under a hospital's charity care policy—are excluded from both gross and net patient service revenues. Allowance accounts are used to reduce receivables for estimated deductions from revenues, as well as for estimated bad debt expenses. Deductions from revenues include:

> *Courtesy allowances*—discounts for doctors and employees
>
> *Contractual adjustments*—discounts arranged with third-party payors (Medicare and Blue Cross, for example) that frequently have agreements to reimburse at less-than-established rates

Premium Fees   Premium fees, also known as subscriber fees or capitation fees, are revenues from agreements under which a hospital provides any necessary patient services (perhaps from a contractually established list of services) for a specific fee. The fee is usually a specific fee per member per month. The fees are earned whether the standard charges for services actually rendered are more or less than the amount of the fee—i.e., without regard to services actually provided in the period. Therefore, they are reported separately from patient service revenues. This is a growing portion of hospital revenues in many hospitals.

Other Operating Revenues   The "other operating revenue" classification includes revenue from services to patients other than for health care and revenues from sales and services provided to nonpatients. This classification might include tuition from schools operated by the hospital, rentals of hospital space, charges for preparing and reproducing medical records, room charges for telephone calls and television, proceeds from cafeterias, gift shops, snack bars, and so on.

Classification of Operating Expenses

Operating expenses of hospitals are reported on an accrual basis and normally include functional categories for nursing services (medical and surgical, intensive care, nurseries, operating rooms), other professional services (laboratories, radiology, anesthesiology, pharmacy), general services (housekeeping, maintenance, laundry), fiscal services (accounting, cashier, credits and collections, data processing), administrative services (personnel, purchasing, insurance, governing board), interest, and depreciation provisions.

Although accounts are maintained for employee and contractual allowances, these items are not expenses. As discussed earlier, they are revenue deductions that are subtracted from gross patient service revenues to arrive at the net patient service revenue reported in the statement of operations.

Provision for Bad Debts   The provision for bad debts is an expense. The difference between charity care and bad debts expense is that charity care results from the hospital's policy of providing health care to individuals who meet certain financial criteria, whereas bad debt expense results from extending credit.[7] Health care services provided as charity care were never intended to provide cash flows.

Statement of Operations and Other Hospital Financial Statements

Basic statements for nongovernment, not-for-profit health care entities consist of a balance sheet, a statement of operations, a statement of changes in net assets, and a statement of cash flows. Exhibits 21–7, 21–8, 21–9, and 21–10 illustrate these basic statements for a nongovernment hospital.

CARE HOSPITAL
STATEMENT OF FINANCIAL POSITION
AT DECEMBER 31, 20X2

Current Assets		
Cash and cash equivalents		$ 60,000
Investments		540,000
Accounts receivable—patients, less $120,000		
estimated uncollectible receivables		1,080,000
Accounts receivable—Medicare		400,000
Receivable from limited use assets		100,000
Inventories and prepaid items		170,000
Total current assets		2,350,000
Assets Limited as to Use		
by Board for capital improvements		230,000
Property, Plant, and Equipment		
Land		650,000
Buildings	$5,000,000	
Fixed equipment	2,000,000	
Movable equipment	1,500,000	
	8,500,000	
Less: Accumulated depreciation	2,800,000	5,700,000
Total property, plant, and equipment		6,350,000
Assets restricted for plant purposes		300,000
Assets restricted for endowment		1,420,000
Total assets		$10,650,000
Current Liabilities		
Accounts payable		$ 300,000
Accrued interest		150,000
Accrued salaries		210,000
Payroll taxes payable		140,000
Accrued pension expense		50,000
Current portion of long-term debt		100,000
Total current liabilities		950,000
Long-Term Debt		
Notes payable		500,000
Bonds payable (net of current portion)		900,000
Mortgage payable		3,000,000
Total long-term liabilities		4,400,000
Total liabilities		5,350,000
Net assets		
Unrestricted		$ 3,220,000
Temporarily restricted		660,000
Permanently restricted		1,420,000
Total net assets		5,300,000
Total liabilities and net assets		$10,650,000

Exhibit 21–7   *Nongovernment, Not-for-Profit Hospital Statement of Financial Position*

---

[7]AICPA, *Audits of Health Care Organizations*, Glossary.

```
CARE HOSPITAL
STATEMENT OF OPERATIONS
FOR THE YEAR ENDED DECEMBER 31, 20X2
```

Unrestricted revenues, gains, and other support		
Net patient service revenues	$7,740,000	
Other operating revenues	950,000	
Unrestricted donations	150,000	
Unrestricted income from endowments	120,000	
Income from board-designated funds	20,000	
Net assets released from restrictions upon satisfaction of program restrictions	50,000	
Total unrestricted revenues, gains and other support		$9,030,000
Expenses and losses		
Nursing services	$2,700,000	
Other professional services	1,800,000	
General services	1,500,000	
Fiscal services	500,000	
Administrative services	300,000	
Medical malpractice costs	180,000	
Provision for uncollectible accounts	600,000	
Provision for depreciation	400,000	
Total expenses and losses		7,980,000
Excess (Deficiency) of revenues, gains, and other support over expenses and losses		1,050,000
Net assets released from restrictions for plant assets purposes		20,000
Increase in unrestricted net assets		$1,070,000

Exhibit 21–8   *Nongovernment, Not-for-Profit Hospital Statement of Operations*

Note that the statement of operations and the statement of changes in net assets taken together present essentially the same information as a statement of activities. The statement of cash flows illustrated in Exhibit 21–10 is prepared using the indirect method. Although comparative current- and prior-year statements are not shown, most hospitals issue comparative statements.

Accounting and Reporting for Government Hospitals

Although government hospitals must apply government GAAP as established by the GASB, the differences in accounting and reporting for government and nongovernment hospitals are fairly limited. The key differences are: the financial statements distinguish between unrestricted and restricted funds instead of net asset classes; restricted contributions are recognized when the restrictions are met rather than when

```
CARE HOSPITAL
STATEMENT OF CHANGES IN NET ASSETS
FOR THE YEAR ENDED DECEMBER 31, 20X2
```

	Unrestricted	Temporarily Restricted	Permanently Restricted	Total
Balance, January 1, 20X2	$2,150,000	$450,000	$1,010,000	$3,610,000
Excess of revenues, gains, and other support over expenses and losses	1,050,000	—	—	1,050,000
Contributions	—	270,000	300,000	570,000
Restricted investment income	—	10,000	110,000	120,000
Net assets released from restrictions	20,000	(70,000)	—	(50,000)
Changes in net assets	1,070,000	210,000	410,000	1,690,000
Balance, December 31, 20X2	$3,220,000	$660,000	$1,420,000	$5,300,000

Exhibit 21–9   *Nongovernment, Not-for-Profit Hospital Statement of Changes in Net Assets*

CARE HOSPITAL
STATEMENT OF CASH FLOWS (*INDIRECT METHOD*)
FOR THE YEAR ENDED DECEMBER 31, 20X2

Cash Flows from Operating Activities and Gains and Losses

Change in net assets		$1,690,000
Adjustments to reconcile change in net assets to net cash used by operating activities		
Provision for depreciation	$ 400,000	
Provision for uncollectible accounts	600,000	
Decrease in Medicare accounts receivable	40,000	
Decrease in unearned interest (limited-use assets)	15,000	
Increase in accounts payable and accrued expenses	60,000	
Increase in patient accounts receivable	(195,000)	
Increase in inventories and supplies	(40,000)	880,000
Net cash provided by operating activities and gains and losses		2,570,000
Cash Flows from Investing Activities		
Purchase of property, plant, and equipment	(2,280,000)	
Purchase of investments	(300,000)	
Cash invested in limited use assets	(350,000)	
Net cash used by investing activities		(2,930,000)
Cash Flows from Financing Activities		
Proceeds from contributions restricted for investment in endowment	300,000	
Other financing activities		
Proceeds from long-term note payable	500,000	
Repayment of bonds payable	(100,000)	
Repayment of mortgage note payable	(800,000)	
Net cash used by financing activities		(100,000)
Net decrease in cash for 20X2		(460,000)
Cash and cash equivalents at beginning of year		520,000
Cash and cash equivalents at end of year		$ 60,000

Exhibit 21–10   *Nongovernment, Not-for-Profit Hospital Statement of Cash Flows*

unconditional pledges or gifts are received; a statement of changes in fund balances replaces the statement of changes in net assets; the government cash flow statement is used instead of the *FASB Statement No. 95* cash flow statement approach; and all investment income, including changes in the fair value of other than trading securities, is included in the performance measure presented in the statement of operations.

Unrestricted vs. Restricted Funds

Government hospital accounting systems that are maintained on a fund basis have major fund categories for donor-restricted and unrestricted resources. These categories, including the major restricted fund subgroups normally found in hospital accounting, are summarized in Exhibit 21–11 with notations of the general nature and scope of activities included in the subgroups.

Unrestricted Fund Category   The unrestricted fund category contains all resources that are not restricted by donors or grantors, including board-designated assets and other assets whose use is limited by a third party other than a donor. *Board-designated funds* are included within the unrestricted fund grouping because the governing board can rescind its own actions and direct the resources to general operating uses. The assets of the unrestricted fund include such items as cash, receivables, inventories, and prepaid expenses, as well as property, plant, and equipment used for general operations of the hospital or other health care provider. Any related long-term debt is also included in the unrestricted fund category. The primary difference between the assets that comprise the unrestricted fund and those that affect unrestricted net assets in a nongovernment hospital is pledges receivable with an implied time restriction.

Unrestricted Funds

Unrestricted Funds—to account for all unrestricted resources of the health care provider including assets limited as to use, agency funds, and property, plant, and equipment (and related long-term debt) used in the general operations of the entity. Assets limited as to use includes such items as resources that the governing board has set aside for specific purposes, proceeds from a debt issue that must be used in accordance with the indenture requirements, and assets that are restricted by agreements with outside entities other than a donor or grantor.

Restricted Funds

Specific Purpose Funds—to account for resources restricted by donors for specific operating purposes.
Plant Replacement and Expansion Funds—to account for resources restricted by donors for property, plant, and equipment.
Endowment or Pure Endowment Funds—to account for resources restricted indefinitely by endowment agreement (permanent restriction as to principal) or for a specified time period (term endowment).

Exhibit 21–11 *Fund Accounting Structure for Government Hospitals*

These pledges are temporarily restricted under *FASB Statement No. 117* because of the time restriction, but would be reported as part of the unrestricted fund in a government hospital (if reportable at all).

Hospitals receive and hold resources of patients, residents, physicians, and others under agency relationships. Such resources are reported as assets of the unrestricted fund in the financial statements and as liabilities until the resources are returned to the principal or disbursed to another party on behalf of the principal. Related cash receipts and disbursements are included as cash flows from operating activities in the statement of cash flows, but the statement of operations and statement of changes in fund balances are not affected.

Assets of the unrestricted fund also include the proceeds of debt issues and funds deposited with trustees that are limited to use according to the trust agreement. (If the donor deposits the funds with the trustee and controls disposition of the trust, the assets are not included in the hospital's unrestricted fund.)

Donor-Restricted Funds Category The donor-restricted funds category is used to account for resources restricted by donors or grantors and consists of three subgroups that correspond to the donor or grantor restrictions. Specific purpose funds are used to account for resources restricted by the donor for specific operating purposes. Plant replacement and expansion funds are used to account for resources that donors have restricted to acquisitions of property, plant, or equipment. The endowment funds consist of pure endowments (permanently restricted) and term endowments (temporarily restricted) and include resources restricted by endowment agreements. Hospital endowment funds do not include quasi- or board-designated endowments (in other words, resources set aside by the governing board).

Restricted Contributions

Government hospitals do not report donor-restricted contributions as revenues or support when received. Rather, they are reported as increases in the restricted funds column of the statement of changes in fund balances. When qualifying costs are incurred, an "amount released from restrictions is reported." Amounts released from restrictions of specific purpose funds or of endowment funds (for term endowments that become available for unrestricted use) are reported in "revenues, gains and other support." Therefore, they affect the performance measurement in the statement of operations. Amounts released from restrictions associated with property, plant, and equipment are reported after the performance measurement as direct additions to unrestricted fund balance. Amounts released from restrictions are also reported as decreases in restricted fund balances.

Government Hospital Financial Statements

The basic financial statements for government hospitals are a balance sheet, a statement of operations, a statement of changes in fund balances, and a statement of cash flows. The purpose of each statement is similar to its nongovernment counterpart. The most obvious differences arise from not using net asset classes, the differences in treatment of restricted gifts, and the use of different guidance for the cash flow statement compared to a nongovernment, not-for-profit hospital. The government hospital balance sheet differs from the balance sheet in Exhibit 21–7 primarily in the presentation of fund balance instead of net asset classes. The statement would be the same if Care Hospital were a government hospital except that the balance sheet would report unrestricted fund balance of $3,220,000 instead of unrestricted net assets. It would report restricted fund balance of $2,080,000 and total fund balance of $5,300,000. The government hospital statement of operations and statement of changes in fund balances are presented in Exhibits 21–12 and 21–13 so that you can observe the differences between those and the equivalent statements for nongovernment, not-for-profit hospitals. Observe that the key differences between the government and nongovernment hospital statements of operations for Care Hospital are:

- Amounts released from restrictions for operating purposes are recognized as revenues in the government hospital statement.
- Operating and nonoperating income are distinguished in the government hospital statement.

The government hospital cash flow statement is presented using the same guidance as for government proprietary funds so it is not illustrated here.

CARE (GOVERNMENT) HOSPITAL
STATEMENT OF OPERATIONS
FOR THE YEAR ENDED DECEMBER 31, 20X2

Net patient service revenues	$7,740,000
Other Revenues:	
Other operating revenues	950,000
Amounts released from restrictions for operating purposes	50,000
Total other operating revenues	1,000,000
Total operating revenues	8,740,000
Expenses:	
Nursing services	2,700,000
Other professional services	1,800,000
General services	1,500,000
Fiscal services	500,000
Administrative	300,000
Medical malpractice costs	180,000
Uncollectible accounts	600,000
Depreciation	400,000
Total expenses	7,980,000
Operating income	760,000
Nonoperating Gains and Losses:	
Unrestricted endowment income	120,000
Other unrestricted investment income	20,000
Unrestricted contributions	150,000
Total nonoperating gains	290,000
Excess of Revenues and Gains over Expenses and Losses	1,050,000
Amounts released from restrictions for acquisitions of fixed assets	20,000
Increase in unrestricted fund balance	$1,070,000

Exhibit 21–12 *Government Hospital Statement of Operations*

```
CARE (GOVERNMENT) HOSPITAL
STATEMENT OF CHANGES IN FUND BALANCES
FOR THE YEAR ENDED DECEMBER 31, 20X2
```

	Unrestricted	Restricted
Fund balance, January 1, 20X2	$2,150,000	$1,460,000
Excess of revenues and gains over expenses and losses	1,050,000	
Restricted grants and contributions		570,000
Restricted investment income		120,000
Amounts released from restrictions used for specific operating programs*		(50,000)
Amounts released from restrictions used for purchase of property and equipment	20,000	(20,000)
Fund balance, December 31, 20X2	$3,220,000	$2,080,000

*Note that this amount does not have to be added to the unrestricted fund here because it is already included in revenues (see Exhibit 21–12) and thus the "Excess of revenues and gains over expenses and losses."

Exhibit 21–13 *Government Hospital Statement of Changes in Fund Balances*

Sample Journal Entries

The following *unrelated* situations describe some typical activities of a government hospital. The journal entries are provided to demonstrate how the concepts are implemented in the accounting system. Only general ledger accounts are shown. For all but the last two items covered, the entries would be the same in a nongovernment, not-for-profit hospital except that the fund designation is not reported and therefore does not have to be maintained from a GAAP viewpoint.

Recording Patient Service Revenue   Gross charges at established rates for services rendered to patients of Nancy Memorial Hospital amounted to $1,300,000. The hospital had contractual adjustments with insurers and Medicare of $300,000. Hospital staff and their dependents received courtesy discounts of $9,000.

Unrestricted Fund		
Accounts receivable	$1,300,000	
Patient service charges		$1,300,000
To record patient service charges at established rates.		
Courtesy discounts	$ 9,000	
Contractual adjustments	300,000	
Accounts receivable		$ 309,000
To record courtesy discounts and contractual adjustments.		

Wages and Salaries   The hospital pays salaries and wages allocated to functional categories as follows: nursing services, $55,000; other professional services, $15,000; general services, $170,000; fiscal services, $12,000; and administrative services, $20,000.

Unrestricted Fund		
Nursing services expense	$ 55,000	
Other professional services	15,000	
General services	170,000	
Fiscal services	12,000	
Administrative services	20,000	
Wages and salaries payable		$ 272,000
To record accrual of payroll.		

Purchase and Use of Supplies   The Caleb County Clinic purchases materials and supplies for $130,000. The supplies usage by the major functional categories during the year is as follows: nursing services, $50,000; other professional services, $40,000; general services, $20,000; fiscal services, $5,000; and administrative services, $8,000.

Unrestricted Fund

Inventory of materials and supplies	$130,000	
Cash (accounts payable)		$130,000

    To record purchase of supplies.

Nursing services expense	$ 50,000	
Other professional services expense	40,000	
General services expense	20,000	
Fiscal services expense	5,000	
Administrative services expense	8,000	
Inventory of materials and supplies		$123,000

    To record usage of materials and supplies.

Other Operating Revenues   Joshua County Hospital charges patients rent for telephones and televisions in their rooms. Throughout the year, the hospital offers several health care courses, for which tuition is charged. Revenue for television and telephone rental was $72,000 for the year, and the tuition charges for courses were $24,000.

Unrestricted Fund

Cash (or accounts receivable)	$ 96,000	
Other operating revenue		$ 96,000

    To record revenue from television and telephone
    rentals and fees charged for health care courses.

Depreciation   Luke County Hospital recognizes depreciation on its equipment, $50,000; and building, $20,000. Luke's movable (or minor) equipment is depreciated on an inventory basis and is determined to be $5,500.

Unrestricted Fund

Depreciation expense	$ 75,500	
Accumulated depreciation—equipment		$ 50,000
Accumulated depreciation—building		20,000
Movable equipment		5,500

    To record depreciation on major equipment,
    building, and movable equipment.

Contributions   Matthew Community Hospital received unrestricted cash donations of $250,000.

Unrestricted Funds

Cash	$250,000	
Unrestricted support—nonoperating gains		$250,000

    To record receipt of unrestricted contributions.

Donated Assets   Municipal Hospital of Joniville received marketable equity securities valued at $500,000 that were donor restricted for the purchase of diagnostic equipment (income from the securities is also restricted.) The donation is recorded in a restricted fund until the funds are used to purchase the equipment.

Plant Replacement and Expansion Fund (Diagnostic Equipment)

Marketable equity securities	$500,000	
Fund balance		$500,000

    To record donation of securities.

    Because income is donor restricted, dividends from the securities are recorded in the plant replacement and expansion fund as earned. For example:

Plant Replacement and Expansion Fund (Diagnostic Equipment)

Cash	$ 12,500	
Fund balance—investment income		$ 12,500

    To record receipt of dividend income restricted to the
    acquisition of diagnostic equipment.

Assume these securities that now have a book value of $550,000 are sold for $600,000 and the proceeds used to purchase the diagnostic equipment, which costs $560,000. The following entries might be made:

Plant Replacement and Expansion Funds (Diagnostic Equipment)

Cash	$600,000	
Marketable equity securities		$550,000
Fund balance—investment income		50,000
To record sale of securities.		

Fund balance—amount released from restrictions	$560,000	
Cash		$560,000
To record satisfaction of restrictions by purchase of equipment costing $560,000.		

Unrestricted Fund

Equipment	$560,000	
Accounts payable (or cash)		$560,000
To record purchase of diagnostic equipment.		

Cash	$560,000	
Amounts released from restrictions for plant purposes		$560,000
To record reimbursement for equipment from plant replacement and expansion fund.		

COLLEGES AND UNIVERSITIES

The usual objective of a college or university is to provide educational services to its constituents. Colleges and universities frequently provide their services on the basis of social desirability and finance them, at least in part, without reference to those receiving the benefits. The objectives of college and university accounting are to show the sources from which resources have been received and how those resources were utilized in meeting educational objectives. Traditionally, fund accounting practices were generally used in achieving the accounting objectives.

The primary authority over accounting principles for private (nongovernment) colleges and universities is the Financial Accounting Standards Board. FASB standards have been incorporated into the AICPA audit guide, *Audits of Not-for-Profit Organizations,* which provides accounting and reporting guidance for private colleges and universities as well as voluntary health and welfare organizations and other not-for-profit organizations. Although private colleges and universities may use the same fund accounting practices internally has government colleges and universities, the private institutions' net assets and revenues, expenses, gains, and losses must be classified based on the existence or absence of donor-imposed restrictions, in accordance with FASB pronouncements. The required financial statements of private, not-for-profit colleges and universities are the same as those for voluntary health and welfare organizations except for the statement of functional expenses.

Primary authority over accounting principles for governmental colleges and universities is held by the GASB. *GASB Statement No. 15* identifies two models as acceptable for accounting and financial reporting by governmental colleges and universities—the AICPA College Guide Model and the Governmental Model.

The "AICPA College Guide Model" follows the guidance of the AICPA audit guide, *Audits of Colleges and Universities,* as amended by *SOP 74–8,* and modified by all applicable GASB pronouncements. Most government colleges and universities follow the AICPA College Guide Model. Note that even though a government college or university elects to follow the audit guide, it must also apply relevant GASB pronouncements.

The "Governmental Model" follows the standards established by National Council on Governmental Accounting *Statement 1,* "Governmental Accounting and Financial Reporting Principles," as amended by subsequent NCGA and GASB pronouncements. Colleges using the Governmental Model use governmental and proprietary funds to report their operations.

GASB pronouncements apply to all governmental entities, including colleges and universities that are governmental entities. *Audits of Colleges and Universities* constitutes GAAP for government colleges and universities that follow the AICPA College Guide Model, until the provisions are changed by GASB pronouncements. Thus, *Audits of Colleges and Universities* remains effective for government colleges and universities using the AICPA College Guide Model even though it has been superseded by *Audits of Not-for-Profit Organizations* for private colleges and universities. In addition to the audit guide, much college and university implementation guidance comes from the *Financial Accounting and Reporting Manual*, an accounting manual prepared by the National Association of College and University Business Officers (NACUBO). The illustrations in this chapter are for a *government* college or university that follows the AICPA College Guide Model.

Fund Groupings

The accounting and reporting systems of colleges and universities that use fund accounting are divided into six fund groups. These groups are further divided into subgroups as needed for planning, control, decision making, and reporting purposes. This fund accounting structure is summarized in Exhibit 21–14, which also sketches the nature and scope of activities included in each group.

General Accounting and Reporting Matters for Governmental Colleges and Universities

Colleges and universities are encouraged by the NACUBO to prepare operating and capital budgets, but they are not required to integrate budgetary accounting into their accounting systems. If formal budgetary accounting is used, it can be applied in a manner similar to that used for governmental entities.

Basic financial statements for government colleges and universities following the AICPA College Guide Model include a balance sheet for all fund groups, a statement of changes in fund balances for all fund groups, and a statement of revenues, expenditures, and other changes for the current funds grouping. Revenues are classified by source and expenditures by function.

Audits of Colleges and Universities specifies that the accounts and reports be maintained on an accrual basis. This is interpreted to mean that revenues are recognized when earned and that expenditures are recognized when the related materials or services are received. *Accrual accounting*, as the term is used here, differs from its usage with respect to business entities and private colleges, because public colleges and universities do not report expenses or net income. Deferred expenses (supplies, for example) and accrued liabilities (salaries, for example) are reflected in the current funds balance sheet. With respect to depreciation, government colleges and universities are guided by *GASB Statement No. 8*, "Applicability of *FASB Statement No. 93*, 'Recognition of Depreciation by Not-for-Profit Organizations,' to Certain State and Local Governmental Entities."[8] Therefore, governmental colleges and universities typically do not report depreciation. Expenditures for plant asset replacements and renewals are reported as current fund expenditures when acquired directly through current funds.

Current Funds of Colleges and Universities

Only resources that are expendable for operating purposes are included in the **current funds grouping**. The current funds grouping contains two subgroups—one for unrestricted current funds and the other for restricted current funds. When expendable resources are restricted by donors or outside entities to expenditures for specific operating purposes, they are classified as restricted current funds. *GASB Statement No. 19*, "Governmental College and University Omnibus Statement," provides that Pell

---

[8]Nongovernment colleges and universities report depreciation expense on capital assets under the provisions of *FASB Statement No. 93* and *FASB Statement No. 117*.

Unrestricted Current Funds—to account for financial resources expendable for operating purposes in carrying out the objectives of the college or university (encompasses instruction, research, extension, and public service). This category includes auxiliary enterprises (such as residence halls, food services, intercollegiate athletics, college stores, and student unions), and separate subfunds may be used for each enterprise.

Restricted Current Funds—to account for financial resources expendable for operating purposes but restricted by donors* or other outside agencies to a specific purpose.

Loan Funds

Individual Loan Funds—to account for resources available for student and faculty loans and related loan activity. Because resources may be restricted externally by donors or internally by the governing body, the accounting records must enable the sources and the restrictions to be identified.

Endowment and Similar Funds

Endowment Funds—to account for resources received from donors and outside agencies with the stipulation that principal be maintained in perpetuity and income be expended for general or specified purposes or added to principal.

Term Endowment Funds—to account for resources received from donors or outside agencies with the stipulation that principal may be expended after some time period or event has occurred.

Quasi-Endowment Funds—to account for resources designated by the governing board (internally designated) to be invested indefinitely with income being expended as directed.

Annuity and Life Income Funds

Annuity Funds—to account for resources acquired under the condition that the college or university make stipulated periodic payments to individuals as provided by agreement with the donor.

Life Income Funds—to account for funds contributed to the college or university under the requirement that the income be paid (usually until death) to a designated beneficiary.

Plant Funds

Unexpended Plant Funds—to account for unexpended resources to be used for acquisition of physical property.

Renewal and Replacement Fund—to account for resources to be used for renewal or replacement of existing property.

Retirement of Indebtedness Funds—to account for resources set aside for debt service and debt retirements relating to institutional properties.

Investment in Plant Funds—to account for plant investments including land, buildings, improvements other than buildings and equipment (including books), and liabilities relating to plant assets.

Agency Funds

Individual Funds—to account for resources held by a college or university as custodian or agent for student or faculty groups.

*Donors refers to both donors and grantors.

Exhibit 21–14   *Fund Accounting Structure for Colleges and Universities*

grants should be reported in the restricted current fund.[9] Otherwise, resources expendable for operating purposes are included in the **unrestricted current funds** subgroup. Because the current funds grouping encompasses resources received and expended for instruction, research, extension, and public service, as well as for the operation of **auxiliary enterprises** (student unions, dormitories, residence halls, intercollegiate athletics, and so on), it is an extremely important area of accounting for all educational institutions. By contrast, the scope and magnitude of activities accounted for through the other fund groupings vary widely from one institution to another.

Only current funds of colleges and universities report revenues and expenditures. Financial reporting of the other fund groupings is done through the balance sheet and the statement of changes in fund balances.

---

[9]*GASB Statement No. 19* also provides guidance on the classification of risk financing activities. If risk financing activities are accounted for through a single fund, it should be the unrestricted current fund.

Current Funds Revenues and Transfers

The term *revenue* is used in accounting only for current unrestricted funds and current restricted funds. Other fund groupings use the term *additions* to report activities that increase funds. The restricted current funds group has both revenue and additions. Current funds revenue-control accounts include:

Tuition and fees
Appropriations (federal, state, and local)
Government grants and contracts (federal, state, and local)
Private gifts, grants, and contracts
Endowment income
Sales and services of educational activities
Sales and services of auxiliary enterprises
Sales and services of hospitals
Other sources
Independent operations

Transfers of unrestricted resources from other funds to the current funds are classified as nonmandatory transfers in the statement of revenues, expenditures, and other changes. Required transfers from the current funds are reported as mandatory transfers. Discretionary transfers made by the university are nonmandatory transfers. Transfers are not included in revenue.

Revenue of Restricted Current Funds Group The restricted current funds group includes resources expendable for operating purposes that are *restricted by donors or other outside entities* for specific purposes. *Additions* to current restricted funds consist of restricted gifts, restricted endowment fund income, restricted contracts and grants from private organizations or governmental units, and restricted income from investments of current restricted fund resources. *Revenue* of current restricted funds is recognized to the extent that such funds are expended during the period for the specified purposes. The timing of revenue recognition coincides with the removal of donor restrictions. Thus, the revenue of current restricted funds for a period is equal to current restricted fund expenditures for that period.[10]

Revenue of Auxiliary Enterprises The revenue of auxiliary enterprises includes amounts earned in providing facilities and services to faculty, staff, and students. It includes amounts charged for residence halls, food services, intercollegiate athletics, and college unions, as well as sales and receipts from college stores, barber shops, movie houses, and so on. The revenue of auxiliary enterprises does *not* include interdepartmental transactions of service departments.

Service Department Activities In accounting for the activities of service departments, such as storerooms, motor pools, and print shops, the accounting records are normally maintained on a cost-reimbursement basis, and no revenues or expenditures are recorded. Instead, the cost is reflected in the expenditures of the departments or divisions receiving the goods and services.

Revenue of Unrestricted Current Funds Group Revenue of unrestricted current funds includes tuition and fees, unrestricted gifts, grants, and government appropriations, as well as unrestricted income earned from unrestricted resources. It also includes unrestricted income earned by endowment and similar funds, but it does *not* include net capital gains of endowment funds. Capital gains and losses from endowment fund investments typically are accounted for in those funds.

---

[10]This is a major difference between accounting for private and governmental colleges and universities. Under the provisions of *FASB Statement No. 116*, donor-restricted contributions are recognized as revenue using the same guidelines as used for unrestricted revenue—in other words, in the period unconditionally pledged or received.

Current Fund Expenditures and Transfers

Expenditures   The term *expenditures* is used only in accounting for the current funds. Current fund expenditures include all expenditures incurred in accordance with generally accepted accounting principles except expenditures for renewals and replacements of plant and equipment. For reporting purposes, current fund expenditures are classified broadly as *educational and general expenditures* and *expenditures of auxiliary enterprises*. Expenditures are classified on a functional basis in the statement of current funds revenues, expenditures, and other changes. Functional classifications include:

Instruction—expenditures for the instruction program

Research—expenditures to produce research outcome

Public service—expenditures for activities to provide noninstructional services to external groups

Academic support—expenditures to provide support for instruction, research, and publications

Student services—amounts expended for admissions and registrar, and amounts expended for students' emotional, social, and physical well-being

Institutional support—amounts expended for administration and the long-range planning of the university

Operation and maintenance of plant—expenditures of current operating funds for operating and maintaining the physical plant (net of amounts to auxiliary enterprises and university hospitals)

Scholarships and fellowships—expenditures from restricted or unrestricted funds in the form of grants to students

Transfers   Sometimes current fund resources are transferred to other fund groups as directed by the governing board of a college or university or as stipulated in a binding agreement with outside entities. For example, the governing board may authorize transfers to a quasi-endowment fund to provide income for designated future purposes (board-designated), a bond indenture may require amounts to be set aside for debt service or renewal or replacement of the educational plant (a binding agreement), or a gift agreement for a student loan fund may require matching transfers by the college or university (a binding agreement). Transfers of current funds resources to other funds under binding agreements are **mandatory transfers** and are so classified for reporting purposes. Discretionary or board-designated transfers are nonmandatory transfers.

Sample Journal Entries for the Unrestricted Current Fund

The journal entries presented here illustrate the recording of some typical events and transactions that would occur in the unrestricted current funds of colleges and universities. The examples are unrelated, and subsidiary account references are not included. The functional basis of classifying the expenditures and the revenue sources would be designated in the subsidiary accounts.

Tuition and Fees and Transfers   The full amount of tuition and fees (net of refunds) assessed against students for educational purposes is recognized as revenue. Tuition waivers for scholarships or staff benefits and estimated bad debts are recorded as expenditures.

When *some portion* of the tuition and fees is externally restricted for activities other than current operations, the full amount of the tuition and fees is recorded as revenue in the unrestricted current funds, then the restricted amount is recorded as a mandatory transfer to the appropriate fund. When specific fees are assessed solely for legally or contractually restricted purposes (in other words, the *total* amount of the fees assessed is externally restricted), the fees are recorded directly as additions to the fund balance of the appropriate fund.

Student tuition and fees for Harvey College total $300,000. Ten percent of this amount is legally restricted for debt service on the educational plant. Student tuition and fees also include $5,000 of tuition waivers provided under the fellowship program. Bad debts are estimated at 3% of gross revenue from student tuition and fees, or $9,000. The following entries are made in the *unrestricted current fund*:

Accounts receivable	$300,000	
Revenues—educational and general		$300,000

To record tuition and fees.

Expenditures—educational and general	$ 5,000	
Accounts receivable		$ 5,000

To record tuition waivers.

Expenditures—educational and general	$ 9,000	
Allowance for uncollectible accounts		$ 9,000

To record allowance for uncollectible accounts.

Mandatory transfer—principal and interest	$ 30,000	
Due to plant fund for retirement of indebtedness		$ 30,000

To record legally binding transfer to plant funds to
retire debt.

In this example, only a portion of the fees is restricted. Therefore, the full amount of the revenue is reported in the unrestricted current funds subgroup, with the restricted portion being treated as a mandatory transfer to the plant funds.

If the governing board of Harvey College had restricted a portion of the tuition and fees for nonoperating purposes, the full amount of tuition and fees would be recorded as revenue in the unrestricted current fund and the restricted (designated) portion would be treated as a nonmandatory transfer to the appropriate fund.

Appropriations from Federal, State, and Local Governments

Appropriations include unrestricted amounts for current operations that are received, or made available, from legislative acts or from a local taxing authority. Restricted appropriations are classified as unrestricted if the governing board can change a restriction without going through a legislative process. R. E. Robinson Junior College receives an appropriation from the state for current operations of $700,000.

Cash	$700,000	
Revenues—educational and general		$700,000

To record appropriations from the state government.

Sales and Services of Educational Activities

Unrestricted current fund revenue may be generated from sales of goods and services that are related incidentally to educational activities of the university. In other words, the goods and services sold are a by-product of training or instruction. An example of this category of revenue is the dairy creamery of a land grant university that has $550 revenue from sales of its products.

Cash	$ 550	
Revenue—educational and general		$ 550

To record sales related to educational activities.

Purchase of Supplies and Materials

Because colleges and universities use accrual accounting, an expenditure is recognized when the supplies and materials are used. The purchase of supplies and materials increases an inventory account when the liability is incurred. The supplies inventory, if significant, is included in the financial statements as an asset (deferred charge or prepaid expenditure). For example, McCoy Community College purchases supplies and materials for $350,000 to be used in educational instruction. The purchase is recorded:

Supplies and materials inventory	$350,000	
Accounts payable		$350,000

To record purchase of supplies and materials.

If McCoy uses $320,000 of the supplies during the period, an entry is made as follows:

Expenditures—educational and general	$320,000	
Supplies and materials inventory		$320,000

To record utilization of supplies related to
instructional purposes.

If, however, an expenditure is recorded when the inventory is received and the liability incurred, an adjustment is made at the end of the period to recognize any significant inventory on hand as an asset (deferred charge) and decrease the expenditures amount.

Payment of Salaries and Wages   When salaries of $200,000 are paid from unrestricted current funds, Hopper College records payment as follows:

Expenditures—educational and general	$200,000	
Cash (salaries payable)		$200,000
To record expenditures for salaries.		

Sales and Services of Auxiliary Enterprises   Auxiliary enterprises are entities that exist to provide goods or services to students, faculty, and staff for fees related to the cost of those goods and services. All revenue directly derived from the operations of auxiliary enterprises is classified as *auxiliary revenue* and is reported in the current funds subgroups. All expenditures are classified as *auxiliary enterprise expenditures* and reported in the current funds. Fixed assets and long-term debt of auxiliary enterprises are accounted for in the plant fund.

The dining hall at Morris Community College had sales of $60,800 and purchased $30,000 supplies during May. The supplies used by the auxiliary enterprise during the period amounted to $28,000. Salaries paid to auxiliary employees were $31,000. Summary entries are:

Cash	$ 60,800	
Revenues—auxiliary enterprises		$ 60,800
To record sales and services related to auxiliary enterprises.		
Supplies inventory	$ 30,000	
Cash (or accounts payable)		$ 30,000
To record purchase of supplies.		
Expenditures—auxiliary enterprises	$ 28,000	
Supplies inventory		$ 28,000
To record utilization of supplies related to auxiliary enterprises.		
Expenditures—auxiliary enterprises	$ 31,000	
Cash		$ 31,000
To record expenditures for salaries of auxiliary enterprises.		

Note that when a liability is incurred for the supplies, the inventory account is debited. The expenditure for supplies is not recognized until the supplies are used.

Mandatory Transfers for Loan Fund Matching Grants   Donors of gifts and grants for specific purposes may require that the college or university provide matching gifts under a binding agreement. For example, the federal government gives Hicks University a $100,000 grant for student loans if Hicks provides matching funds. Hicks will record its matching gift to the student loan funds as a *mandatory transfer*:

Mandatory transfer—loan fund matching grant	$100,000	
Due to loan funds (or cash)		$100,000
To record mandatory transfer to loan fund under binding agreement to provide matching funds.		

Nonmandatory Transfers   Funds transferred back to the unrestricted current funds from other funds are *nonmandatory transfers*, rather than revenue. Transfers made from unrestricted current funds to other funds at the discretion of the governing board of the college or university are also nonmandatory transfers. For example, the governing board of Bettinger College directs that $150,000 from unrestricted current funds be transferred to the student loan fund and that $200,000 be transferred to the renewal and replacement fund for the future renovation of the theater arts building:

Nonmandatory transfers to loan funds	$150,000	
Nonmandatory transfers to plant fund for renewal and replacement	200,000	
Cash		$350,000

To record transfers to loan funds and renewal and replacement fund.

Expenditure for Plant Assets   Current funds expenditures may include the cost of minor plant assets provided that current fund resources are budgeted for and used by operating departments for the assets required. For more significant asset purchases, financial resources are transferred from the current funds to the plant fund making the purchase.

Isler Institute purchases equipment directly through unrestricted current funds in the amount of $35,000. The entry made in the *unrestricted current funds* grouping is:

Expenditures—educational and general	$ 35,000	
Accounts payable		$ 35,000

To record purchase of equipment.

A separate entry is made in the *investment in plant accounts* to record the equipment:

Equipment	$ 35,000	
Net investment in plant		$ 35,000

To record purchase of equipment through current unrestricted funds.

Isler Institute purchases land as a building site for a new testing laboratory. The land costs $200,000, and financial resources are available in the unrestricted current funds. For this purchase, however, the $200,000 is transferred to the unexpended plant funds grouping for making the purchase. The entry in the unrestricted current funds is:

Nonmandatory transfer to unexpended plant funds	$200,000	
Cash		$200,000

To transfer money to plant funds for the purchase of land.

The entries in the plant funds are:

Unexpended Plant Fund

Cash	$200,000	
Fund balance—unrestricted		$200,000

To record transfer from unrestricted current fund.

Fund balance—unrestricted	$200,000	
Cash		$200,000

To record purchase of land for cash.

Investment in Plant

Land	$200,000	
Net investment in plant		$200,000

To record purchase of land.

Academic Year Different from Fiscal Year   Revenues and related expenditures of an academic year that falls within two different fiscal years should be recognized in the period in which classes are predominately conducted. Revenue received but not earned is reported in the balance sheet as *deferred credits*. Any prepaid expenditures are *deferred charges*. Adjusting entries might be as follows:

Revenues—educational and general	
Deferred credits (or deferred revenues)	

To defer revenue received but not earned.

Deferred charges	
Expenditures—educational and general	

To record prepaid expenses.

At the beginning of the next year, the entries are reversed to remove the liability, recognize revenue, and record utilization of prepaid items.

Closing Entries   At year-end, the revenues, expenditures, and mandatory and nonmandatory transfer accounts are closed to the fund balance account.

Sample Entries for Restricted Current Funds

Financial resources in the restricted current funds grouping are expendable for current operating purposes, but they are restricted by donors or other outside agencies to a specific purpose. When cash or other financial resources are received, they are recorded as increases in the fund balance. When the restrictions are met by incurring expenditures for the specified purpose, revenue is recognized. In other words, revenues and expenditures are equal.

An entry to record the receipt of cash that is restricted for specific purposes is as follows:

Cash	$500,000	
Fund balances—gift		$200,000
Fund balances—grants		250,000
Fund balances—endowment income		50,000
To record receipt of cash.		

Expenditures are made during the period for specific purposes stipulated by the donors and grantors:

Expenditures—educational and general	$400,000	
Expenditures—auxiliary enterprises	50,000	
Cash		$450,000
To record expenditures incurred.		

At the end of the period, revenue is recognized in the amount of the expenditures and the fund balances are adjusted:

Fund balances—gifts	$200,000	
Fund balances—grants	200,000	
Fund balances—endowment income	50,000	
Revenues—educational and general		$400,000
Revenues—auxiliary enterprises		50,000
To recognize revenue for the period.		

Statement of Current Funds Revenues, Expenditures, and Other Changes

A reporting format for current funds revenues, expenditures, and other changes of a state-supported university following the AICPA College Guide Model is illustrated in Exhibit 21–15. (The statement is illustrative only and has no relationship to the preceding unrelated sample entries.) Separate statement columns are used for unrestricted and restricted current funds subgroups. As expected, revenues and expenditures of restricted current funds are equal.

Although mandatory transfers are not expenditures, they are distinguished from nonmandatory transfers and are reported in a manner similar to that for expenditures. The mandatory transfer from current funds for principal and interest is included in the combined statement of changes in fund balances for all fund groupings as a mandatory transfer to the *retirement of indebtedness* subgroup of the plant funds group. Similarly, the mandatory transfer for matching loan funds would be an addition to the loan funds group. Although Exhibit 21–15 does not illustrate mandatory transfers for auxiliary enterprises, mandatory transfers relating to dormitory bond indenture agreements are frequently found in the auxiliary enterprise category.

The "other transfers and additions (deductions)" section of Exhibit 21–15 shows $30,000 restricted receipts over transfers to revenues. This is a type of reconciling item that represents additions to the restricted current fund subgroup over amounts recognized as revenue. As explained earlier, revenue recognition of restricted current

STATEMENT OF CURRENT FUNDS REVENUES, EXPENDITURES, AND OTHER CHANGES
FOR THE YEAR ENDED JUNE 30, 20X2

	Unrestricted	Restricted	Total
Revenues			
Tuition and fees	$1,000,000		$1,000,000
State appropriations	1,200,000		1,200,000
Federal grants and contracts	50,000	$100,000	150,000
Private grants and gifts	400,000	250,000	650,000
Endowment income	75,000	20,000	95,000
Sales and services of educational departments	60,000		60,000
Sales and services of auxiliary enterprises	800,000		800,000
Total current revenues	3,585,000	370,000	3,955,000
Expenditures and Mandatory Transfers			
Educational and General			
Instruction	1,500,000	40,000	1,540,000
Research	600,000	250,000	850,000
Public service and extension	100,000		100,000
Academic support	50,000		50,000
Student services	40,000		40,000
Libraries	70,000	20,000	90,000
Operation and maintenance of plant	80,000		80,000
Scholarships and grants		60,000	60,000
General administration	90,000		90,000
Educational and general expenditures	2,530,000	370,000	2,900,000
Mandatory Transfers			
Principal and interest	40,000		40,000
Renewals and replacements	60,000		60,000
Loan fund matching grants	5,000		5,000
Total educational and general	2,635,000	370,000	3,005,000
Auxiliary Enterprises			
Expenditures	760,000		760,000
Total expenditures and mandatory transfers	3,395,000	370,000	3,765,000
Other Transfers and Additions (Deductions)			
Restricted receipts over transfers to revenues		30,000	30,000
Quasi-endowment fund created	(40,000)		(40,000)
Restricted resources refunded to grantor		(20,000)	(20,000)
Net increases in fund balances	$ 150,000	$ 10,000	$ 160,000

Exhibit 21–15   *Government College and University Operating Statement for Current Funds (AICPA College Guide Model)*

funds requires removal of donor restrictions through expenditures for specific operating purposes.

A statement of current funds revenues, expenditures, and other changes is the only separate statement for a fund group that is required for college and university reporting. Other statements (balance sheet and statement of changes in fund balances) include all fund groups.

Loan Funds

Resources held by colleges and universities under agreements to provide loans to faculty, staff, and students are accounted for in the **loan funds** group. Fund assets consist of cash, loans, receivables, and temporary investments. Liabilities, if any, consist of amounts payable for operating expenses, loan refunds, and so on. Loan fund additions consist of gifts, bequests, gains on investments, interest on loans, and endowment fund income restricted to loans. Decreases result from loans written off, losses on investments, administrative expenses (if legally permitted), and refunds. Interest on student loans, if significant, must be accrued. Sources of loan funds available are disclosed, and restrictions are identified in presenting the loan fund balances in the combined balance sheet.

Endowment and Similar Funds

The **endowment fund** group consists of endowments, term endowments, and quasi-endowments. Annuity and life income funds, if insignificant, are also included in this group. The "similar funds" designation is used when annuity and life income funds are included.

A separate fund is used for each endowment. The usual assets are cash, certificates of deposit, and investments in securities, real estate, and so on. Liabilities typically consist of debts related to fund assets such as mortgage payable or taxes payable. Income measurement includes changes in fair value of investments per *GASB Statement 31* and depreciating fixed assets held to produce income. Endowment fund income is:

1 Credited to current restricted funds if restricted but expendable for current operating purposes, *or*
2 Credited to endowment, plant, or loan fund balances if so specified by the terms of the endowment agreement, *or*
3 Credited to revenue of unrestricted current funds if available for current expenditure without restrictions.

The assets and liabilities of endowment funds are combined for presentation in the balance sheet of the college or university, but separate fund balances typically are reported for endowments, term endowments, and quasi-endowments.

Annuity and Life Income Funds

The assets of annuity and life income funds consist of cash and various types of investments that are reported in a manner comparable to that used for endowment funds. Annuity fund liabilities consist of debts related to fund assets and the actuarial amount of annuities payable. Fund balances of annuity funds are increased by new gifts in excess of the present value of annuities payable (classified as additions) and decreased when remaining balances are transferred to other funds upon termination. Liabilities of life income funds consist of debts related to fund assets and life income payments currently due. Increases in the fund balances of life income funds consist of new gifts (additions) and investment gains less losses. (Income earned by a standard life income fund constitutes a payment currently due and does not increase the fund balance.) Decreases result from transfers to other funds when life income agreements are terminated.

Plant Funds

The **plant funds** group comprises four subgroups: unexpended plant funds, renewal and replacement funds, retirement of indebtedness funds, and investment in plant accounts. The first three funds are used to account for financial resources of the college or university. The last subgroup, the investment in plant accounts, is used to account for the physical plant and related long-term debt.

Unexpended Plant Funds and Renewal and Replacement Funds   **Unexpended plant funds** are used to account for resources held for additions and improvements to the physical plant, whereas **renewal and replacement funds** are used for resources held for renewal and replacements of the existing plant. Assets of unexpended plant funds and renewal and replacement funds include cash, receivables, and investments. Fund balance additions include gifts, donations, investment income, and transfers from other funds (including mandatory transfers for renewal and replacement funds). Deductions for unexpended plant funds include losses on investments and expenditures for new or improved facilities, and fund-raising costs. Renewal and replacement fund deductions consist of outlays for renovations, major repairs, and replacements. Separation of the fund balance into restricted and unrestricted (including board-designated) components is required for each subgroup.

Retirement of Indebtedness Fund   Assets of a **retirement of indebtedness fund** consist of liquid resources for current debt service and investments held for future debt retirement, including sinking fund investments. Fund balance additions include mandatory transfers, voluntary transfers, investment income and gains, gifts, and so on. Deductions consist of principal and interest payments, investment losses, and custodial expenses. The assets may consist of restricted and unrestricted resources, so a separation of the fund balance into restricted and unrestricted components is essential.

Investment in Plant Accounts   The assets of the **investment in plant accounts** consist of the physical plant (land, buildings, improvements other than buildings, and equipment, which includes library books). Assets acquired by purchase or construction are valued at cost, and those acquired by donation are valued at fair value. All liabilities relating to plant assets are also included in this category. The excess of assets over liabilities is designated as "net invested in plant" rather than fund balance. Additions arise from expenditures of unexpended plant funds, renewal and replacement funds, and current funds that require capitalization. Additions also result from gifts of books, equipment, and so on. Deductions in the net investment in plant arise from sales and other disposals. Accumulated depreciation may be recorded on depreciable plant assets, and, if so, the charge is reported as a deduction in the net investment in plant account.

Financial statements of the four plant fund groups are included in the balance sheet and the statement of changes in fund balances for the college or university. Separate columns may be used for each plant fund subgroup, or a single column may be used for all subgroups provided that restricted and unrestricted fund balances for the subgroups are disclosed.

Agency Funds of Colleges and Universities   **Agency funds** are used to account for assets held by the college or university for individual students and faculty members and for their organizations. Transactions of agency funds only affect asset and liability accounts and do not result in revenues and expenditures. Agency fund assets and liabilities are included in a column of the college or university combined balance sheet, and no other financial statement presentations are required for basic reporting purposes.

Other Financial Statements for the AICPA College Guide Model

In addition to the statement of current funds revenues, expenditures and other changes that was illustrated in Exhibit 21–15, the basic financial statements for government colleges and universities include a balance sheet (all funds) and a statement of changes in fund balances (all funds). The balance sheet in Exhibit 21–16 and the statement of changes in fund balances in Exhibit 21–17 are presented in a columnar format without separate columns for the four plant fund subgroupings. For alternative presentations that illustrate the details of the plant fund subgroups and a layered balance sheet format, the reader is referred to the *Financial Accounting and Reporting Manual* of the NACUBO or the industry audit guide *Audits of Colleges and Universities.*

Financial statements of government colleges and universities that are component units of a state or local governmental unit must be included within the financial report of the government. The relationship between the primary government and its component units is discussed in Chapter 20. The college or university's financial statements may be discretely presented in a separate column to the right of the fund types of the primary government. *GASB Statement No. 14* provides that the reporting entity's combined statements include one or more columns to display balances for discretely presented component units use.[11] The discretely presented component unit column should be to the right of the columns for the primary government and should be clearly labeled. (See Chapter 20, Exhibits 20–13, 20–14, 20–15, and 20–16 for examples of discretely presented component units.) A college or university will be discretely presented in the combined balance sheet in the typical fashion. However, the primary government will have to include a statement of changes in fund balances and a statement of current funds revenues, expenditures, and other changes for discretely presented component units that use the AICPA College Guide Model.

The college or university itself may have component units. In other words, the component unit may serve as a "primary government" when it issues its own separate financial statements. The provisions of *GASB Statement No. 14* are applied in layers from the bottom up. Therefore, the separate financial statements of the college or

---

[11] *GASB Statement No. 14*, "The Financial Reporting Entity," paragraph 45.

BALANCE SHEET
ON JUNE 30, 20X2

	Current Funds		Loan Funds	Endowment and Similar Funds	Annuity and Life Income Funds	Plant Funds
	Unrestricted	Restricted				
Assets						
Cash	$ 95,000	$ 25,000	$ 4,000	$ 60,000	$150,000	$ 55,000
Investments	500,000	140,000	40,000	1,515,000	650,000	500,000
Accounts receivable (less allowances)	70,000					
Loans to students			50,000			
Unbilled charges		20,000				
Due from unrestricted funds						45,000
Inventories	170,000					
Prepaid expenses	15,000					
Deposits with trustees						200,000
Land						700,000
Improvements other than buildings						1,500,000
Buildings						8,000,000
Equipment						600,000
Library books						1,100,000
	$850,000	$185,000	$94,000	$1,575,000	$800,000	$12,700,000
Liabilities						
Accounts payable	$ 90,000	$ 55,000				$ 37,000
Accrued liabilities	40,000					
Students' deposits	25,000					
Due to other funds	45,000					
Annuities payable					$400,000	
Life income payable					30,000	
Notes payable						350,000
Bonds payable						2,100,000
Mortgages payable						5,200,000
Fund Balances						
Current funds	650,000	130,000				
Loan funds—restricted			$80,000			
Loan funds—unrestricted			14,000			
Endowment and similar funds						
Endowment				$1,000,000		
Term endowment				100,000		
Quasi-endowment— unrestricted				475,000		
Annuity and life income funds						
Annuity					270,000	
Life income					100,000	
Plant funds						
Restricted						700,000
Unrestricted						63,000
Net investment in plant						4,250,000
	$850,000	$185,000	$94,000	$1,575,000	$800,000	$12,700,000

Exhibit 21–16   *Governmental College and University Combined Balance Sheet*

university should include its discretely presented component units in the same manner as described for the primary government. The separately issued financial statements of a college or university that is a component unit of another government should disclose that fact, and notes to the financial statements should identify the primary government and describe the relationship between the college or university and the primary government.

STATEMENT OF CHANGES IN FUND BALANCES
FOR THE YEAR ENDED JUNE 30, 20X2

	Current Funds		Loan Funds	Endowment and Similar Funds	Annuity and Life Income Funds	Plant Funds
	Unrestricted	Restricted				
Revenues and Other Additions						
Unrestricted current fund revenues	$3,585,000					
Expired term endowments—restricted						$ 10,000
State appropriations—restricted						20,000
Federal grants and contracts—restricted		$100,000				
Private gifts, grants, and contracts—restricted		250,000	$40,000	$ 500,000	$100,000	
Investment income—restricted		20,000	8,000			13,000
Realized gains on investments—restricted			1,000	15,000		
Interest on loans receivable			11,000			
Expended on plant facilities						300,000
Retirement of indebtedness						15,000
Matured annuity restricted to endowment				30,000		
Total revenues and other additions	3,585,000	370,000	60,000	545,000	100,000	358,000
Expenditures and Other Deductions						
Educational and general expenditures	2,530,000	370,000				
Auxiliary enterprises expenditures	760,000					
Refunded to grantors		20,000				
Loan cancellations and write-offs			8,000			
Administrative costs			3,000			
Expended for plant facilities						320,000
Retirement of indebtedness						15,000
Interest on indebtedness						5,000
Disposal of plant facilities						65,000
Expired term endowments restricted to plant				10,000		
Matured annuity restricted to endowment					30,000	
Total expenditures and other deductions	3,290,000	390,000	11,000	10,000	30,000	405,000
Transfers Among Funds—Additions (Deductions)						
Mandatory						
Principal and interest	(40,000)					40,000
Renewals and replacements	(60,000)					60,000
Loan fund matching grant	(5,000)		5,000			
Restricted receipts over transfers to revenue		30,000				
Quasi-endowment fund created						
Net change—increase	(40,000)			40,000		
(decrease)	150,000	10,000	54,000	575,000	70,000	53,000
Fund balance—beginning	500,000	120,000	40,000	1,000,000	300,000	4,960,000
Fund balance—end of year	$ 650,000	$130,000	$94,000	$1,575,000	$370,000	$5,013,000

Exhibit 21–17   *College and University Combined Statement of Changes in Fund Balances*

SUMMARY

The FASB has issued several statements aimed at improving comparability in the financial statements of all nongovernment, not-for-profit entities that issue statements in accordance with GAAP. Thus, nongovernment voluntary health and welfare organizations, health care entities, and colleges and universities prepare a set of financial statements that present unrestricted net assets, temporarily restricted net assets, permanently restricted net assets, and total net assets, as well as changes in each class of net assets and in total. In accomplishing this comparability, however, the comparability between a particular not-for-profit type and its government counterpart has been lost. The GASB intends to issue its own pronouncements on accounting and financial reporting in these areas in the near future, but at this time, improved comparability between government and nongovernment, not-for-profit entities does not appear to be a priority with either the FASB or the GASB.

Accounting and reporting guidance for nongovernment, voluntary health and welfare organizations and colleges and universities comes from the AICPA audit guide, *Audits of Not-for-Profit Organizations. Health Care Organizations* provides guidance for health care entities. Government colleges and universities that use the AICPA College Guide Model follow the AICPA industry audit guide, *Audits of Colleges and Universities.* Government voluntary health and welfare organizations follow *Audits of Voluntary Health and Welfare Organizations.* The chapter first summarizes the accounting principles common to all nongovernment, not-for-profit entities and then illustrates the applications of those principles to voluntary health and welfare organizations and health care entities. Nongovernment colleges and universities apply the same principles as voluntary health and welfare organizations. Accordingly, they are not illustrated separately. Accounting for government colleges and universities that follow the AICPA Audit Guide Model is illustrated in the last section of the chapter.

Nongovernment, not-for-profit organizations may use fund accounting practices, but fund accounting is not required by any FASB pronouncement or by the respective audit guides. Not-for-profit organizations use accrual accounting for revenues and expenses.

Financial statements of nongovernment, not-for-profit entities include the statement of financial position, statement of activity, and statement of cash flows. Voluntary health and welfare organizations also prepare a statement of functional expenses. The financial statements and notes should include all information required by GAAP and for which not-for-profit entities are not specifically exempt, as well as information required by applicable specialized accounting and reporting principles and practices. The focus of the financial statements is on the entity as a whole.

Government hospital and nongovernment not-for-profit hospital reporting are quite similar. The differences are highlighted in the chapter. Government colleges and universities use fund accounting practices and accrual accounting, but depreciation is not recorded. The operating statement of a government college or university (the statement of current funds revenues, expenditures, and other changes) is a revenues and expenditures statement for current funds only.

SELECTED READINGS

American Institute of Certified Public Accountants. *Audits of Colleges and Universities,* 2nd ed., Industry Audit Guide. New York: AICPA, 1975.

American Institute of Certified Public Accountants. *Health Care Organizations,* Audit and Accounting Guide. New York: AICPA, 1997.

American Institute of Certified Public Accountants. *Audits of Not-for-Profit Organizations,* Audit and Accounting Guide. New York: AICPA, 1996.

American Institute of Certified Public Accountants. *Audits of Voluntary Health and Welfare Organizations,* Industry Audit Guide, New York: AICPA, 1974.

ANTHONY, ROBERT N. "The Foolishness of FASB's Nonprofit Classes." *Management Accounting* (July 1993), pp. 53–57.

ANTHONY, ROBERT N. "The Nonprofit Accounting Mess." *Accounting Horizons* (June 1995), pp. 44–53.

BAILEY, LARRY P., and RAYMOND R. POTEAU. "Accounting Rule Making—A Two Headed Monster?" *The CPA Journal* (June 1994), pp. 28–31.

BENSON, MARTHA L., Alan S. GLAZER, and HENRY R. JAENICKE. "Coping with NPO Standards—It's Not Difficult." *Journal of Accountancy* (September 1998), pp. 67–74.

BROWN, KEN W. "How Colleges Can Profit Through Depreciation." *Management Accounting* (January 1998), pp. 18–22.

BROWN, VICTOR H. and SUSAN E. WEISS. "Toward Better Not-for-Profit Accounting and Reporting." *Management Accounting* (July 1993), pp. 48–52.

CAPIN, GREGORY B. and JOEL TANENBAUM. "How to Report a Joint Activity." *Journal of Accountancy* (October 1998), pp. 37–44.

CHASE, BRUCE W. "Get Ready, Here They Come." *Journal of Accountancy* (January 1995), pp. 79–82.

Financial Accounting and Reporting Manual for Higher Education. Washington, D.C.: National Association of College and University Business Officers, 1990.

MCELDOWNEY, JOHN E., THOMAS L. BARTON, and DAVID RAY. "Look Out for Cletus William." *The CPA Journal* (December 1993), pp. 44–47.

PELFREY, SANDRA, "SFAS No. 117 and Its Impact on Not-for-Profit Colleges and Universities." *The CPA Journal* (November 1993), pp. 54–56.

Statement of Financial Accounting Standards No. 93. "Recognition of Depreciation by Not-for-Profit Organizations." Stamford, CT: Financial Accounting Standards Board, 1987.

Statement of Financial Accounting Standards No. 116. "Accounting for Contributions Received and Contributions Made." Norwalk, CT: Financial Accounting Standards Board, 1993.

Statement of Financial Accounting Standards No. 117. "Financial Statements of Not-for-Profit Organizations." Norwalk, CT: Financial Accounting Standards Board, 1993.

Statement of Position 74–8. "Financial Accounting and Reporting by Colleges and Universities." New York: American Institute of Certified Public Accountants, 1974.

ASSIGNMENT MATERIAL

QUESTIONS

1 What statements are included in a set of financial statements for nongovernment, not-for-profit entities?

2 How does one determine whether a hospital, college, or voluntary health and welfare organization should be reported in accordance with FASB standards or GASB standards?

3 Explain the difference between a conditional promise to give and an unconditional promise to give. Explain the difference between donor-imposed conditions and donor-imposed restrictions.

4 Do all not-for-profit entities record depreciation on all of their property? Explain.

5 How are unconditional promises to give with collections due in the next period accounted for?

6 How is the expiration of a time restriction recognized?

7 Are gifts in kind always reported as unrestricted support that increase unrestricted net assets?

8 Expenses of voluntary health and welfare organizations include classifications for program services and supporting services. Explain these classifications.

9 If a nongovernment, not-for-profit hospital incurs expenses for which restricted donations are available, but uses unrestricted resources for those expenses, should it report net assets released from restrictions in its statement of operations. Explain?

10 Explain the key differences between a statement of operations of a government hospital and that of a nongovernment, not-for-profit hospital.

11 What is the purpose of the statement of functional expenses of voluntary health and welfare organizations?

12 Under what circumstances are contributed services reported in the statement of activities of a nongovernment, voluntary health and welfare organization?

13 Describe the resources that are accounted for in the unrestricted funds of a government hospital.

14 Are board-designated funds of hospitals included in the unrestricted funds or the restricted funds category? Explain.

15 In which fund grouping of a government hospital would medical equipment and related long-term liabilities be recorded?

16 What fund grouping of government hospitals corresponds to the restricted current funds grouping of colleges and universities?

17 Health care entities frequently provide charity care to qualified individuals. How is charity care reported in the financial statements of a hospital?

18 How are net patient service revenues of hospitals measured, and in which hospital financial statement are they reported?

19 What are the three major revenue groupings of hospitals? Give an example of a revenue item that would be included in each grouping.

20 Are provisions for bad debts and depreciation of hospitals reported as expenses or expenditures? Explain.

21 What is the operating statement of a government university? Describe the difference in a set of financial statements for a government university and a private university.

22 What subgroups are included in the current funds grouping of college and university accounting systems that follow the AICPA College Guide Model?

23 Identify three types of endowment funds that may be included in the endowment and similar funds grouping of a university, and explain the differences in the three types.

24 Explain the differences that one would expect to find in the composition of the assets and liabilities of annuity and life income funds.

25 In which fund group and subgroup of a government university would you expect to find an account or accounts for library books?

26 Kepper Junior College, a state-supported institution, received $40,000 from federal grants for accounting research during 20X2. The college expended $25,000 in 20X2 and $12,000 in 20X3, and refunded $3,000 to the U.S. government in 20X4. In what fund or funds should the grant resources be recorded, and how should the grant activity be accounted for in each of the three years?

27 Is it true that revenue and expenditures of a university's service departments (centralized purchasing, for example) are excluded from the university's revenues and expenditures? Explain.

28 What is a *mandatory transfer* as the term is used in college and university accounting?

29 Assume that a university receives $5,000 of unrestricted income from endowment fund investments. Is this transaction recorded in the endowment fund? Explain.

EXERCISES

E 21-1

1 Net assets that are restricted by the governing board of a nongovernment, not-for-profit organization are reported as a part of:

   a Permanently restricted net assets
   b Temporarily restricted net assets
   c Unrestricted net assets
   d Either permanently restricted or temporarily restricted net assets, depending on the term of the restriction

2 Unconditional promises to give are recognized as contribution revenue under *FASB Statement 116* when:

   a The promise is received
   b The related receivable is collected
   c The time or purpose restriction is satisfied
   d The future event that binds the promisor occurs

3 Which of the following it *not* a characteristic of a conditional promise to give:

   a Depends on the occurrence of a specified future and uncertain event to bind the promisor
   b Gift may have to be returned to donor if condition is not met
   c Recognized as contribution revenue when the conditions are substantially met
   d Depends on demand by the promisee for performance

4 Contributed long-lived assets that are donor restricted for a certain time period are reported by a nongovernment, not-for-profit entity as:

   a Unrestricted support in unrestricted net assets
   b Restricted support in permanently restricted net assets
   c Restricted support in temporarily restricted net assets
   d Unrestricted support in temporarily restricted net assets

5 Long-lived assets are purchased by a nongovernment, not-for-profit entity with cash that was restricted for that purpose. The assets are reported in temporarily restricted net assets. Depreciation expense is reported in unrestricted net assets.

   a The depreciation expense is incorrectly reported.
   b An amount equal to the depreciation is reclassified from temporarily restricted to unrestricted net assets.
   c An amount equal to the depreciation is reclassified from unrestricted to temporarily restricted net assets.
   d An amount equal to the depreciation is reported as revenues.

E 21-2

1 When a temporary restriction on resources of a nongovernment, not-for-profit entity is met by the incurrence of an expense for the restricted purpose:

   a The expense is reported in the statement of activity as an increase in unrestricted net assets
   b Amounts reported in the temporarily restricted net assets are reclassified as unrestricted net assets
   c The entry is a debit to expense and a credit to the program services
   d The expense is reported in restricted net assets

2 A nongovernment, not-for-profit entity gives donors a sweatshirt imprinted with its logo when they pay $15 dues. The value of the sweatshirt is approximately $15. This transaction is most likely reported as:

  a An exchange transaction
  b An agency transaction
  c A contribution
  d A gift in kind

3 How will a nongovernment, not-for-profit entity record an agency transaction in which it receives resources?

  a No entry is made in the accounts.
  b Debit the asset account and credit contribution revenue.
  c Debit the asset account and credit temporarily restricted net assets.
  d Debit the asset account and credit a liability account.

4 Unconditional promises to give that are collectible within one year of the financial statement date:

  a Should be reported at their gross amount
  b Should be reported at the gross amount less an allowance for uncollectible accounts
  c Should be reported at the present value of the amounts expected to be collected, using the donor's incremental borrowing rate
  d Should not be reported until collected

5 In preparing the statement of cash flows for a nongovernment, not-for-profit entity, cash contributions that are restricted for long-term purposes are classified as:

  a Operating activities
  b Investing activities
  c Financing activities
  d Capital and related financing activities

E 21-3   **1** Voluntary health and welfare organizations include voluntary:

  a Hospitals
  b Health, welfare, and community service organizations
  c Social clubs
  d Fine arts associations

2 Which of the following statements is not required for nongovernment, voluntary health and welfare organizations that issue financial statements in accordance with GAAP?

  a Balance sheet
  b Statement of support, revenues and expenses, and changes in retained earnings
  c Statement of functional expenses
  d Statement of cash flows

3 Voluntary health and welfare organizations:

  a Are required to use fund accounting principles to segregate unrestricted and restricted net assets
  b May report by funds if interfund balances are eliminated and the required disclosures of *FASB Statement No. 117* are presented
  c Must report by funds if fund accounting principles are used for internal accounting purposes
  d Are prohibited from reporting by funds, even if fund accounting is used for internal accounting purposes

4 Fund-raising costs of voluntary health and welfare organizations are classified as:

  a Functional expenditures
  b Program services
  c Supporting services
  d Management and general expenses

5 Volunteers collect money and nonperishable food for the Food Pantry, a nongovernment, voluntary health and welfare organization, by going house to house once each year for donations. The services of the volunteers should be accounted for as follows:

  a The fair value of the service is estimated and recorded as contributions that increase unrestricted net assets.
  b The fair value of the service is estimated and recorded as contributions that increase either unrestricted net assets or temporarily restricted net assets, depending on donor-imposed restrictions on the resources collected.
  c The per diem wage rates of the donors are recorded in unrestricted net assets.
  d None of the above.

6 Unconditional promises to give (pledges) of nongovernment, voluntary health and welfare organizations are recognized as revenue and support in the period in which:

  a The pledges are received
  b Cash is received from the pledges
  c All restrictions on pledged resources have been removed
  d Pledged resources are expended

E 21-4

1 A university that is a component unit of a state or local government:
  a Is not required to issue separate financial statements, but its financial data must be included in the primary government's financial report
  b Issues separate financial statements and is reported in the financial report of the primary government under the cost or equity method
  c Issues separate financial statements that are also discretely presented in component unit columns of the primary government's financial report
  d Issues separate financial statements, but is not included in the primary government's financial report

2 The operations of dormitories and dining halls for colleges and universities that use fund accounting are reported in the fund grouping:
  a Current funds—unrestricted
  b Current funds—restricted
  c Plant funds
  d Specific purpose funds

3 A university that follows the AICPA College Guide Model should follow the accounting guidance in *Audits of Colleges and Universities* and as modified by:
  a All GASB and FASB statements and interpretations
  b All GASB statements and interpretations but no FASB pronouncements
  c All GASB statements and interpretations and all applicable FASB pronouncements issued before November 30, 1989
  d All FASB pronouncements but no GASB statements and interpretations

4 Required financial statements for a private, not-for-profit college includes which of the following?
  a A statement of cash flows
  b A statement of functional expenses
  c A statement of changes in fund balances
  d A statement of revenues, expenditures, and other changes

5 A *quasi-endowment*, as the term is used in college and university accounting, is a fund for which:
  a The donor restricts both principal and income
  b The donor restricts principal but income can be used for any bona fide operating purpose
  c The governing board sets principal resources aside and specifies how the income is to be used
  d The governing board promises a life income to the donor

6 Which of the following statements best describes how depreciation is used by universities?
  a Depreciation is recorded only in auxiliary funds of both government and nongovernment universities.
  b Government universities record depreciation expense in the investment in plant funds subgroup; private universities do not record depreciation expense.
  c Replacement cost depreciation is a unique feature of university accounting.
  d Depreciation expense is recorded by private universities, but not by government universities.

E 21-5

1 A university that follows the AICPA College Guide Model issues revenue bonds for a new dormitory, and construction is completed during the current year. In its combined balance sheet at year end, the university should report the debt under the category:
  a Plant funds—unexpended
  b Plant funds—renewal and replacement
  c Plant funds—retirement of indebtedness
  d Plant funds—investment in plant

2 Auxiliary enterprises in government college and university accounting are reported under the major fund category:
  a Current funds
  b Endowment and similar funds
  c Plant funds
  d Enterprise funds

3 Which of the following subgroups of a government university's accounting system is most likely to have resources free of external restrictions?
  a Term endowments
  b Annuity funds
  c Restricted current funds
  d Unexpended plant funds

4 The current funds grouping of a state university accounting system includes:
  a Books
  b Unexpended research grants
  c Resources restricted by the governing body for student loans
  d Bonds payable

5 Unrestricted current funds resources transferred to a city university's renewal and replacement fund subgroup in accordance with the provisions of a bond indenture are classified as:
  a Mandatory transfers
  b Provisions for funded depreciation
  c Other transfers
  d Expenditures

6 A government university recognizes revenue from a grant to supplement faculty salaries when:
  a The grant is awarded
  b Grant resources are received
  c Expenditures are made for the salary supplements
  d The amount of the grant is both measurable and available

E 21-6 **1** A principal source of revenue for hospitals is from patient services. Patient services revenue for hospitals is *recorded* at:
  a Amounts actually billed to patients
  b The hospital's full established rates for services provided
  c Amounts actually received from patients
  d Amounts actually billed to patients less discounts granted

2 Donated services to a nongovernment, not-for-profit hospital meet the criteria in *FASB Statement No. 116* for recognition as donated services. The donated services:
  a Should be reported as an addition in the specific purpose funds grouping
  b Should be reported as unrestricted support and expense in the statement of operations
  c Should be reported as unrestricted support and expense in the statement of operations of unrestricted funds
  d Should be reported as an addition in the enterprise fund

3 The provision for bad debts of a not-for-profit hospital is:
  a Reported as an operating expense in the statement of operations
  b Reported as a deduction from gross patient service revenues in the statement of operations of unrestricted funds
  c Reported in the statement of functional expenses
  d Disclosed in notes to the financial statements, but not reported in the financial statements

4 Charity care provided by a not-for-profit hospital:
  a Is reported as an operating expense in the statement of operations of unrestricted funds
  b Is reported as a deduction from gross patient service revenues in the statement of operations of unrestricted funds
  c Is excluded from both gross patient service revenue and expense
  d Is reported in the statement of functional expenses

5 Discounts allowed to third-party payors in hospital accounting are recorded as
  a Charity care
  b Contractual allowances
  c Courtesy allowances
  d Mandatory discounts

6 Hospital room charges for telephone and television rentals should be classified as
  a Patient service revenues
  b Other operating revenues
  c Nonoperating gains
  d Premium fees

E 21-7 **1** Long-term debt of a government hospital is accounted for in the:
  a Unrestricted fund
  b Board-designated funds
  c Restricted funds
  d Plant replacement and expansion funds

2 A hospital bills patients at gross rates and provides for courtesy allowances for employees when they settle their accounts at less than gross rates. In accordance with this system, the journal entry to record courtesy allowances would appear
  a Debit—cash; debit—courtesy allowance; credit—accounts receivable
  b Debit—courtesy discount; credit—allowance for courtesy discounts
  c Debit—cash; debit—patient service revenue; credit—accounts receivable
  d Debit—accounts receivable; credit—courtesy allowances; credit—patient service revenue

3 Unrestricted income from a nongovernment health care entity's permanent endowment investments should be reported:
  a In the permanently restricted net assets as unrestricted support—nonoperating gains
  b In the statement of operations as unrestricted support—operating gains
  c In the statement of operations as unrestricted revenues—investment income
  d In the permanently restricted net assets as restricted revenues—investment income

4 A nongovernmental health care entity that issues financial statements as required by the *Health Care Organizations* Audit Guide should provide:

    a A statement of financial position, a statement of activities, and a statement of revenues and expenses of unrestricted funds

    b A statement of financial position, a statement of operations, a statement of changes in net assets, and a statement of cash flows

    c A statement of financial position, a statement of activities, and a statement of cash flows

    d A statement of financial position, a statement of revenues and expenses of unrestricted funds, and a statement of functional expenses

5 A nongovernment health care entity receives a gift of cash that is specified by the donor to be used for cancer research. The contribution will most likely be reported in:

    a Unrestricted net assets

    b Temporarily restricted net assets

    c Permanently restricted net assets

    d Either a or b, depending on the mission and activities of the health care entity

E 21-8

1 Depreciation and amortization of hospital property and equipment:

    a Is required for both government and nongovernment hospitals

    b Is not recorded in the statement of operations, but accumulated depreciation is disclosed in the statement of financial position

    c Is reported in the plant replacement and expansion fund of hospitals that use fund accounting

    d Is optional on donated property

2 Oliver Hardwick, a roofing contractor, repaired the roof on the Mosely Clinic, a nongovernment health care entity, at no charge to the clinic. The estimate for the job was $3,000.

    a The donated services meet the criteria in *FASB Statement No. 116* and should be reported in the statement of operations as unrestricted support-donated services.

    b The donated services should be described in notes to the financial statements, but not included in the statement of operations.

    c Only donated services that directly provide health care to patients can be recognized in the financial statements.

    d The donated services are a direct addition to the current fund.

3 The following items are classified as "assets limited as to use" in the general funds of a hospital:

Board designated funds for long-term investments	$50,000
Resources deposited with trustee under indenture agreement	30,000

How much of these amounts should be classified as temporarily restricted net assets?

    a $80,000   **c** $30,000

    b $50,000   **d** 0

4 Land is given to a not-for-profit hospital with the stipulation that upon its ultimate sale the proceeds will be permanently invested. The land donation should be reported in changes in:

    a Unrestricted net assets

    b Temporarily restricted net assets

    c Permanently restricted net assets

    d A specific purpose fund

6 The resources restricted for plant replacement and expansion for a not-for-profit hospital total $360,000. $250,000 of this balance represents amounts restricted by donors for the acquisition of fixed assets. The other $110,000 of the fund balance represents amounts restricted under agreements with third parties other than donors.

    a The resources are treated as temporarily restricted net assets of $360,000

    b The resources are treated as temporarily restricted net assets of $250,000 and permanently restricted net assets of $110,000

    c The resources are treated as temporarily restricted net assets of $250,000 and unrestricted net assets of $110,000

    d None of the above

E 21-9 A nongovernment voluntary health and welfare organization receives $20,000 of unconditional promises to give with no donor-imposed restrictions. Of this amount $14,000 is due during the current period and $6,000 is due in the next period. The organization estimates that 3% of the pledges will be uncollectible.

Required: Prepare a journal entry (or entries) to record the pledges and indicate the effect that the pledges will have on the net asset classifications.

E 21-10   A nongovernment voluntary health and welfare organization receives a $200 cash gift that is restricted for use in a project to provide immediate assistance to qualified people with temporary hardships. Money is given to a qualified individual during the same period.

Required: Prepare *all* journal entries to record the events described.

E 21-11   A voluntary health and welfare organization summarizes its expenses by functions, as follows:

Education	$20,400
Fund raising	11,400
Management and general	5,500
Public health	15,700
Research	12,000

Required: Determine the expenses for program services and for supporting services.

E 21-12   In January 20X6 the Grand Diner restaurant donated restaurant equipment to the Food Kitchen, a nongovernment, voluntary health and welfare organization. The equipment has a fair value of $6,000 and a remaining useful life of four years, with no scrap value. No restrictions are imposed on the use of the equipment, either by Grand Diner or the Food Kitchen.

     Also in 20X6 a church donated $8,000 to the Food Kitchen that is restricted to the purchase of a new truck. The money was invested in a CD that pays 5% interest. Accrued interest on the investment totaled $215 on December 31, 20X6. The income from the investment is also restricted for the purchase of a truck.

Required: Prepare journal entries to account for these transactions in 20X6. Discuss the effect on the net asset classifications and the financial statements.

E 21-13   The following list of definitions relate to the accounting of a state university that follows the AICPA College Guide Model. Identify the terms defined.
1 Entities that exist to provide goods and services to students, faculty, and staff for fees related to the cost of such services
2 Transfers of current fund resources to other funds at the governing board's discretion
3 Fund used to account for resources held by the university for other entities. Transactions of this fund affect only asset and liability accounts
4 Fund used to account for donor-restricted resources with the agreement that the principal may be expended after some time period or event
5 Transfers of current fund resources to other funds under binding agreements
6 Fund used to account for resources that are expendable for operating purposes, but are donor restricted to a specific purpose
7 Fund used to account for resources designated by the governing board to be invested indefinitely with income being expended as directed
8 Amounts for current operations that are received from legislative acts or from a local taxing authority
9 Funds used to account for resources set aside for debt service and debt retirements relating to institutional properties
10 Direct increases (credits) to the fund balance account for funds other than current funds

E 21-14   Classify the listed items of a government hospital according to the following categories:
   A   Patient service revenues
   B   Other operating revenues
   C   Nonoperating gains
   D   Excluded from revenues and gains

1 Sales from operations of a gift shop in the hospital
2 Charges for nursing care
3 Proceeds from the hospital cafeteria
4 Rent received from Radiology Associates for hospital space
5 Bandages and other supplies that are donated to the hospital by Med-Tech Corporation on a regular basis
6 Tuition for classes of the nursing school operated by the hospital
7 Donated services from a CPA firm that provides interim audits at no charge
8 Interest earned on unrestricted investments
9 Charges for emergency room services
10 Ambulance service

E 21-15 Bedford Community College assessed its students $750,000 tuition for the 20X7 fall term. The college estimates bad debts will be 1% of the gross assessed tuition. Bedford's scholarship program provides for tuition waivers totaling $65,000. Because of class cancellations, $15,000 is refunded to the students.

Required: Determine the amount of revenue to be reported in the unrestricted current fund of Bedford Community College.

E 21-16 Dalton State University received donations of $3 million in 20X6 that were restricted to certain research projects on the feasibility of growing tobacco for pharmaceutical uses. The university incurred $1.2 million of expenditures on this research in 20X6.

Required: Prepare journal entries in the appropriate fund to record the above information. Also, explain how this information should be reported in the university's statement of current funds revenues, expenditures, and other changes.

PROBLEMS

P 21-1 At the beginning of 20X3, the citizens of North Pike created Share Shop, a voluntary health and welfare organization. Share receives donations of money, nonperishable groceries, and household items from contributors. The food and household items are distributed free of charge to families on the basis of need. Share allocates expenses 80% to community services and 20% to management and general services, unless otherwise noted.

Share has one paid administrator with a yearly salary of $14,600. An accountant donates accounting services to Share that have a fair value of $900 and are allocated to management and general. Work is also done by regular volunteers whose services cannot be measured.

A local transit company has provided free warehouse space for the operations of Share Shop. Fair value of rent for the warehouse is $3,000 a year. Utilities of $1,800 are paid by Share for 20X3.

During the year, Share purchased supplies for $300. At December 31, 20X3, the supplies inventory was insignificant. Expenses incurred in determining which families were eligible for Share's services and other accounting and reporting expenses totaled $6,000.

Donated assets for 20X3 included nonperishable groceries with a fair value of $60,000 and household items with a fair value of $40,000. During the year, the Shop distributed three-fourths of the groceries and half of the household items. No portion of these distributions was allocated to management and general services.

In addition to the donated assets, Share received cash donations of $10,000 and pledges of $20,000. Share estimated that 10% of the pledges would be uncollectible. At year-end 20X3, $15,000 of the pledges had been collected. Share estimates that only $1,000 of the remaining pledges will be uncollectible.

Town Council of North Pike made a $25,000 grant to Share Shop that will be paid in January 20X4.

Required: Prepare summary entries for Share Shop for the year 20X3.

P 21-2 The following selected items were taken from the accounts of Mitch Deskins Memorial Hospital, a not-for-profit hospital at December 31, 20X6:

Debits	
Administrative services	$ 310,000
Contractual allowances	400,000
Depreciation	200,000
Employee discounts	100,000
General services	290,000
Loss on sale of assets	50,000
Nursing services	1,000,000
Other professional services	500,000
Provision for bad debts	150,000
Credits	
Donated medicine	$ 300,000
Income from investment in affiliate	80,000
Patient service revenues	2,500,000
Television rentals to patients	50,000
Unrestricted donations	200,000
Unrestricted income from investments of endowment funds	270,000
Restricted donations for fixed asset purchases	300,000
Restricted donations for specific operating purposes	100,000

Required: Use the information given to prepare a statement of operations for Mitch Deskins Memorial Hospital at December 31, 20X6. Assume that $80,000 of expenses were for purposes for which restricted donations were available and that fixed assets costing $97,000 were purchased from donations restricted for their purchase.

P 21-3 The following information relates to revenues, expenditures, and transfers of the current funds of a state-supported junior college:

Tuition and fees	
Total assessed	$2,000,000
Tuition waivers	120,000
Appropriations	
State	800,000
Local	300,000
Auxiliary enterprises	
Sales	500,000
Expenditures	480,000
Endowment income	
Restricted to research	70,000
Unrestricted	20,000
Private gifts and grants	
Restricted to student scholarships	300,000
Unrestricted	80,000
Expenditures	
Instruction	2,100,000
Research	100,000
Student services	120,000
Operation of plant	180,000
Scholarships (does not include tuition waivers)	200,000
Mandatory transfer to retirement of indebtedness plant fund for mortgage bond sinking fund requirement	100,000
Transfer from unrestricted current fund to endowment fund	50,000

Required: Prepare a statement of current fund revenues, expenditures, and other changes.

P 21-4 The following information was taken from the accounts and records of the Amoruso Society, a nongovernment, not-for-profit organization. The balances are as of December 31, 20X5 unless otherwise stated.

Unrestricted Support—Contributions	$3,000,000
Unrestricted Support—Membership Dues	400,000
Unrestricted Revenues—Investment Income	83,000
Temporarily Restricted Gain on Sale of Investments	5,000
Expenses—Education	300,000
Expenses—Research	2,300,000
Expenses—Fund Raising	223,000
Expenses—Management and General	117,000
Restricted Support—Contributions	438,000
Restricted Revenues—Investment Income	22,500
Permanently Restricted Support—Contributions	37,000
Unrestricted Net Assets, January 1, 20X5	435,000
Temporarily Restricted Net Assets, January 1, 20X5	5,000,000
Permanently Restricted Net Assets, January 1, 20X5	40,000

The unrestricted support from contributions was all received in cash during the year. Additionally, the Society received pledges totaling $425,000. The pledges should be collected during 20X6, except for the estimated uncollectible portion of $16,000. The Society spent $3,789,000 of restricted resources on construction of a major capital facility during 20X5, and $500,000 of research expenses were for research financed from restricted donations.

Required: Prepare the statement of activities for the Amoruso Society for 20X5.

P 21-5 Prepare journal entries to record the following transactions in the appropriate funds of a government university. (Indicate the fund for each entry.)
1 Tuition and fees assessed total $6,000,000. 80% is collected by year end, scholarships are granted for $200,000, and $100,000 is expected to be uncollectible.
2 Revenues collected from sales and services of the university bookstore, an auxiliary enterprise, were $800,000.

3 Salaries and wages were paid, $2,600,000. $170,000 of this was for employees of the university bookstore.

4 Unrestricted resources were paid to the fund to be used to service the long-term mortgage on the university's buildings, $1,000,000.

5 Mortgage payments totaled $960,000. $600,000 was for interest.

6 Restricted contributions for a specific academic program were received, $440,000.

7 Expenditures for the restricted program were incurred and paid, $237,000.

8 Equipment was purchased from resources previously set aside for that purpose, $44,000.

P 21-6 Three wealthy friends, Rick Richardson, C. D. Hypes, and Jack Petersen, each decided to donate $5,000,000 to the organization of their choice. Mr. Richardson chose to contribute to a local voluntary health and welfare organization, Mr. Hypes to the local state university, and Mr. Petersen to the county hospital. Each donation was made on May 21, 20X3. Prepare the entries required for each of the recipient organizations under the following scenarios.

    1 No restrictions are placed on the use of the donated resources

        a Prepare the May 21, 20X3 entry.

        b Prepare any entries necessary in 20X4 if $2,300,000 of the gift is used to finance operating expenses.

    2 The donation was restricted to research.

        a Prepare the May 21, 20X3 entry.

        b Prepare any entries necessary in 20X4 if $2,300,000 of the gift is used to finance research expenses.

    3 The donation was restricted for construction of a fixed asset.

        a Prepare the May 21, 20X3 entry.

       b Prepare any entries necessary in 20X4 if $2,300,000 of the gift is used to finance construction costs.

P 21-7 The Good Grubb Food for the Hungry Institute is a nongovernment, not-for-profit organization that provides free meals for the destitute in a large metropolitan area. Record the following transactions in the accounts of Good Grubb.

    1 Unrestricted cash gifts that were received last year, but designated for use in the current year, totaled $20,000.

    2 Unrestricted pledges of $65,000 were received. Five percent of pledges typically prove uncollectible. Additional cash contributions during the year totaled $35,000.

    3 Donations of food totaled $150,000. The inventory of food on hand decreased by $1,200 during the year.

    4 Expenses were incurred as follows: Salary of director, $10,000; facility rental, $8,000; purchases of food, $70,000; and supplies, $27,000. Supplies inventory increased by $5,000 during the year.

    5 Restricted pledges of $300,000 were received during the year. The pledges are restricted for use in constructing a new kitchen and dining hall.

P 21-8 In October 1997 Gravel Hill Christian Church, an historic country church that was established in 1835 in Simmonsville, Virginia, began a campaign to improve its worship facility. Beginning with a $30 contribution from an 11-year-old young lady, Michelle Harris, the church raised $7,200 in cash donations restricted for use in constructing the improvement. $4,000 was received in 1997 and $3,200 in 1998. All of these resources were expended in 1998 to complete the project.

    In addition, the following services were provided to the church free of charge in completing the improvement. Mr. Bob Ballagh, a local plumber, and Tom Lovejoy, a local electrician, provided plumbing and electrical services valued at $1,200. Carpenters Mike Linkous and Jim Harris contributed framing and finishing work valued at $3,000. Lonnie Oliver contributed the installation of a septic system. His services were valued at $2,500. All of these services were contributed in 1998.

    The church pianist, Margaret Estes, who retired from her CPA practice in 1992 before *SFAS Nos. 116 and 117* became effective, was asked by the building fund treasurer, Carolyn Harris, to explain how to account for and report these events. Mrs. Estes comes to you and asks you to explain how these events are to be reported under the requirements of the current standards.

Required: Prepare journal entries to record these events in accordance with the requirements of *SFAS Nos. 116 and 117*. Also, explain or illustrate how to report these events in the financial statements of Gravel Hill Christian Church.

APPENDIX A

SEC Influence on Accounting

The influence of the Securities and Exchange Commission on the development of accounting and reporting principles is well-recognized by accountants. Congress gave the SEC authority to establish accounting principles when it passed the Securities Exchange Act of 1934, under which the SEC was created. Initially, the administration of the Securities Act of 1933 was assigned to the Federal Trade Commission. But a year later, the 1934 act created the Securities and Exchange Commission and made it responsible for establishing regulations over accounting and auditing matters for firms under its jurisdiction. Thus, the SEC has the authority to prescribe accounting principles for entities that fall under its jurisdiction.[1]

A combination of inadequate regulation of securities at the federal and state levels, the stock market crash of 1929, and the Great Depression of the 1930s all contributed to the enactment of new securities legislation in the early 1930s.

THE 1933 SECURITIES ACT

A primary objective of the Securities Act of 1933 was "to provide full and fair disclosure of the character of securities sold in interstate and foreign commerce and the mails, and to prevent fraud in the sale thereof . . ." (Securities Act of 1933). Another objective of the 1933 act was to protect investors against fraud, deceit, and misrepresentation. There have been many amendments, but these objectives still constitute the primary thrust of the 1933 act.

The Securities Act of 1933 is often called the "truth in securities act." This is because *the SEC's objective is to prevent the issuers of securities from disclosing false, incomplete, or otherwise misleading information to prospective buyers of their securities.* The SEC emphasizes that its objective is not to pass judgment on the merits of any firm's securities. The SEC imposes severe penalties on firms and individuals that violate its disclosure requirements.

---

[1]For example, in 1993 the SEC issued *Staff Accounting Bulletin No. 93*, which requires discontinued operations that have not been divested within one year of their measurement dates to be accounted for prospectively as investments held for sale.

Issuance of Securities in Public Offerings

The Securities Act of 1933 is concerned with the issuance of specific securities to investors in public offerings. Such securities are required to be *registered with the SEC* and to be *advertised in a prospectus* before being offered for sale to the public.

Exempt Security Issues   Certain security issuances are exempt from the 1933 act. A partial list of exempt securities includes those issued by governmental units, not-for-profit organizations, firms in bankruptcy and subject to court order, firms in stock splits or in direct sales to existing shareholders (private placements), and firms issuing intrastate securities with sales limited to residents of that state.

Issues of $5,000,000 or Less   *Regulation A* provides less-restrictive registration procedures for security issuances not exceeding $5,000,000. Regulation A permits firms to use an *offering circular* rather than a prospectus as required for full registration.

The Prospectus   The **prospectus** is a part of the registration statement that provides detailed information about the background of the registrant firm, including its development, its business, and its financial statements. An **offering circular** is like a prospectus, but has fewer disclosure requirements. A copy of the prospectus is required to be presented to prospective buyers before the securities are offered for sale. A **preliminary prospectus** (also known as a *red herring prospectus*) is a communication that identifies the nature of the securities to be issued, states that they have not been approved or disapproved by the SEC, and explains how to obtain the prospectus when it becomes available.

THE SECURITIES EXCHANGE ACT OF 1934

The Securities Exchange Act of 1934 created the Securities and Exchange Commission and gave it authority to administer the 1933 act as well as regulate the trading of securities on national exchanges. Subsequently, the 1934 act was amended to include securities traded in over-the-counter markets, provided that the firms have total assets of more than $10 million and at least 500 stockholders. Firms that want their securities traded on the national exchanges, or in over-the-counter markets subject to the net-asset and stockholder limitations, must file **registration statements** with the SEC. Form 10 is the primary form that is used for registering securities on national stock exchanges or in over-the-counter markets. This registration for trading purposes is required in addition to the registration prepared for new security issuances under the 1933 act.

Additional Periodic Reporting Requirements   Companies covered by the 1934 act also have periodic reporting responsibilities. These include filing 10-K annual reports, 10-Q quarterly reports, and 8-K current "material event" reports with the SEC. The information in these reports is publicly available so that company officers, directors, and major stockholders (insiders) will not be able to use it to gain an unfair advantage over the investing public. In other words, the objective is to provide full disclosure of all material facts about the company and thereby contribute to a more-efficient and ethical securities market.

The SEC and National Exchanges   In addition to the registration and periodic reporting rules for companies whose stock is publicly traded, the Securities Exchange Act contains registration and reporting requirements for the national securities exchanges. The SEC has responsibility for monitoring the activities of the national exchanges and assuring their compliance with applicable legal provisions. The 1934 act also gave the SEC broad enforcement powers over stockbrokers and dealers and over accountants that are involved in SEC work.

Additional Responsibilities of the SEC

Subsequent to the Securities Exchange Act of 1934, the SEC acquired regulatory and administrative responsibilities under the Public Utilities Holding Company Act of 1935, the Trust Indenture Act of 1939, the Investment Company Act of 1940, the Investment Advisers Act of 1940, the Securities Investor Protection Act of 1970, and the Foreign Corrupt Practices Act of 1977. These acts are listed for identification purposes, but the SEC's responsibility under them is not discussed in this appendix.

THE REGISTRATION STATEMENT FOR SECURITY ISSUES

Firms issuing securities to the public under the Securities Act of 1933 are required to provide full and fair disclosure of all material facts about those securities. The disclosures are provided in a registration statement that is filed with the SEC at least 20 days before the securities are offered for sale to the public. The 20-day waiting period may be extended if the SEC finds deficient or misleading information in the registration statement. In addition, if an amendment to the registration statement is filed, the amended statement is treated as a new one for purposes of applying the 20-day rule.

Security Registration

The registration of securities with the SEC is ordinarily a major undertaking for the registrant company. It involves developing a registration team consisting of financial managers, legal counsel, security underwriters, public accountants, and other professionals as needed. The team plans the registration process in detail, assigns responsibility for each task, coordinates the efforts of all team members, and maintains a viable timetable throughout each phase of the project. Because of its complexity, the coordination of efforts is sometimes referred to as a balancing act.

Registering Securities Under the Integrated Disclosure System   In 1980 the process of registering securities was changed when the SEC adopted an **integrated disclosure system** for almost all reports required by the 1933 and 1934 securities acts. The integrated system revised the registration forms and streamlined the process for filing with the SEC. As a result, the registration statement is now completed in accordance with instructions for the particular registration form deemed appropriate for a specific registrant company.

For example, Form S-1 is a general form to be used by firms going public (issuing securities to the public for the first time) and by firms that have been SEC registrants for fewer than three years. It is also a residual form to be used unless another form is specified. Forms S-2 and S-3 are forms with fewer disclosure requirements than S-1. They are used primarily for registrations of established firms that have been SEC registrants for more than three years and that meet certain other criteria. Form S-4 is used for registering securities issued in a business combination. Firms issuing securities under *Regulation A* use Form 1-A. A number of other registration forms are applicable to selected types of security issues and firm situations.

THE INTEGRATED DISCLOSURE SYSTEM

The basic regulations of the Securities and Exchange Commission are found in *Regulation S-X*, which prescribes rules for the form and content of financial statements filed with the SEC, and *Regulation S-K*, which covers the nonfinancial statement disclosures of the registration statements and other periodic filings with the SEC. Before the 1980s, the two regulations sometimes had conflicting requirements, and firms often had difficulty in identifying the appropriate rules and procedures for reporting to the SEC.

From 1933 to 1980 the SEC issued numerous *Accounting Series Releases (ASRs)*—official supplements to AICPA and FASB pronouncements—and *Staff Accounting Bulletins (SABs)*—informal interpretations by the SEC staff on GAAP and S-X provisions. The issuance of these ASRs and SABs often increased the difficulty of complying with SEC regulations because their provisions were sometimes inconsistent with GAAP or other SEC regulations.

Codification of SABs and ASRs

In implementing the integrated disclosure system, the SEC issued *SAB No. 40* to codify *SABs 1* through *38*. This was done to revise the content of the SABs to conform to GAAP, to eliminate duplicate material contained in some SABs, and in some cases to recognize FASB pronouncements as meeting the SEC's requirements. The SEC also codified the relevant accounting-related ASRs into *Financial Reporting Release (FRR) No. 1*. Thus, the current series consists of FRRs rather than ASRs.

Objectives of Integrated Disclosure System

The objectives of the integrated disclosure system are to simplify the registration process, to reduce the cost of compliance with SEC regulations, and to improve the quality of information provided to investors and other parties. *Under the integrated system, the disclosures included in SEC filings and those distributed to investors via prospectuses, proxy statements, and annual reports are essentially the same.*

Standardization of Audited Financial Statements

The integrated disclosure system amended Regulation S-X in order to standardize the financial statement requirements in most SEC filings. For example, Regulation S-X, which prescribes the form and content of financial statements filed with the SEC, was amended in 1992 to conform certain of its accounting and disclosure requirements to those contained in FASB Statements, including *FASB Statement No. 109,* "Accounting for Income Taxes" (effective December 15, 1992), *FASB Statement No. 95,* "Statement of Cash Flows" (effective July 15, 1988), *FASB Statement No. 91,* "Accounting for Nonrefundable Fees and Costs Associated with Originating or Acquiring Loans and Initial Direct Costs of Leases" (effective December 15, 1987), and *FASB Statement No. 69,* "Disclosures about Oil and Gas Producing Activities" (effective December 15, 1982). This permits the financial statements included in annual reports to shareholders to be the same as those included in the prospectus, the 10-K, and other reports filed with the SEC. Note that the SEC's proxy rules govern the content of annual reports to shareholders. Under current rules, the content of the annual report to shareholders is the same as in 10-K filings. **Form 10-K** is the general form for the annual report that registrants file with the SEC. It is required to be filed within 90 days after the end of the registrant company's fiscal year. The 10-K report must be signed by the chief executive officer, the chief financial officer, the chief accounting officer, and a majority of the company's board of directors.

The 10-K disclosures required by the SEC for public companies are summarized in Exhibit A–1. As shown in the exhibit, the SEC divides the disclosures into four

---

SUMMARY OF REQUIRED DISCLOSURES UNDER SEC FORM 10-K

Part I
Item 1 Business (nature and history of the business, industry segments, etc.)
Item 2 Properties (location, description and use of property, etc.)
Item 3 Legal proceedings (details of pending legal proceedings)
Item 4 Voting by security holders (items submitted to shareholders for voting)

Part II
Item 5 Market for common equity (place traded, shares, dividends, etc.)
Item 6 Selected financial data (five-year trend data for net sales, income from continuing operations including EPS, total assets, long-term debt, cash dividends, etc.)
Item 7 Management's discussion and analysis (discussion of the firms' liquidity, capital resources, operations, financial condition, etc.)
Item 8 Financial statements and supplementary data (requirements include audited balance sheets for two years and audited income statements and statements of cash flows for three years. Also, three-year and five-year summaries are required for selected statement items.)
Item 9 Changes in accountants and disagreements on accounting matters (changes in accountants and accounting changes, disagreements, disclosures, etc.)

Part III
Item 10 Directors and executive officers (names, ages, positions, etc.)
Item 11 Executive compensation (names, positions, salaries, stock options, etc.)
Item 12 Security ownership of beneficial owners and management (listing of insider owners of securities.)
Item 13 Certain relationships (business relations and transactions with management, etc.)

Part IV
Item 14 Exhibits, financial statement schedules, and 8-K reports (supporting schedules of securities, borrowings, subsidiaries, ratios, etc.)

Exhibit A-1 *Summary of Required Disclosures Under Form 10-K*

groups. This is done in order to distinguish the information required to be disclosed in annual reports to shareholders from the complete 10-K information package required for filings with the SEC. For example, the information included in Part II of the exhibit is primarily accounting information that is required for annual reports filed with the SEC as well as the annual reports distributed to the company's shareholders. The disclosure requirements summarized in Parts I, III, and IV of the exhibit are only required for SEC filings, but they may be included in annual reports to shareholders.

In implementing its integrated disclosure system, the SEC eliminated a number of differences between reports filed with the SEC and those contained in annual reports to shareholders. This permitted public companies to meet many of the SEC filing requirements by reference to disclosures made in the annual reports to shareholders. That is, companies can include copies of their annual shareholder reports in their 10-K filings and satisfy many SEC disclosure requirements with one report. Information incorporated by reference to other reports is encouraged by the SEC and is not required to be duplicated. This "incorporation by reference" ruling has resulted in a substantial increase in the size of corporate annual reports and a corresponding decrease in the size of 10-K reports filed with the SEC.

Form 8-K Form 8-K is a report that requires registrants to inform the SEC about significant changes that take place regarding firm policies or financial condition. The report must be submitted within 15 days (five days in some cases) of the occurrence of the event. Items that might be disclosed in Form 8-K include changes in management, major acquisitions or disposals of assets, lawsuits, bankruptcy filings, and unexpected changes in directors.

Form 10-Q Form 10-Q contains quarterly data prepared in accordance with GAAP. The form is filed within 45 days of the end of each of the registrant's first three quarters. Chapter 15 of this text describes and illustrates the SEC requirements for quarterly reports.

SEC DEVELOPMENTS

Regulation S The SEC issued **Regulation S** in 1990 to clarify the applicability of U.S. securities laws across national boundaries. Generally, the regulation provides that sales of securities outside the United States are not subject to the 1933 Securities Act. The regulation also provides "safe harbor" rules to exempt any U.S. companies that sell securities offshore from SEC registration requirements.

The EDGAR System The Securities and Exchange Commission introduced a massive new computerized system to facilitate the process of filing, reviewing, and disseminating corporate information to the public in 1984. [URL: http://www.sec.gov/edaux/searches.htm] **EDGAR** is an abbreviation for the SEC's system entitled Electronic Data Gathering Analysis and Retrieval System. One of the SEC's goals under the integrated-disclosure system is to provide investors, analysts, and other interested parties with instant access to corporate information on file with the SEC.

Small Business Although most SEC registrants are large public companies, the capital needs of small-business issuers (under $25 million in both revenue and public float) have been addressed by the SEC, and new financial rules for small-business enterprises were adopted in 1992 and 1993. Those rules provide new opportunities for small firms to raise capital to start and/or expand their businesses. Rule 504 relating to certain tax-exempt private offerings was amended to allow issuers other than development-stage enterprises to raise up to $1,000,000 in any 12-month period without registering under the 1933 Securities Act. Also, safe-harbor rules for information or trends and future events that may affect future operating results have been revised.

Year 2000 In 1996, the SEC began reporting regularly to Congress on the readiness of the securities industry and public companies to meet the information processing challenges of the year 2000. The SEC takes the problem very seriously and explains that failure to assess the problem, fix noncompliant systems, and then test those systems "could endanger the nation's capital markets and place at risk the assets of millions of investors." The SEC's approach has been as follows:

1 Industry oversight—includes educating members of the securities industry on the Year 2000 problems, monitoring their progress in solving the problem, supporting the Securities Industry Associations' industry-wide testing program, and participating in industry-wide contingency planning groups to minimize the effects of unexpected problems that occur.
2 Issuer disclosure—Staff Legal Bulletin No. 5 provides specific guidance for disclosures about a company's Year 2000 issues.
3 Internal commission systems—the SEC believes that the EDGAR database is Year 2000 compliant, as well as most other SEC systems. However, testing continues. The SEC has contingency plans in place so that if any system does fail, it will have a minimum impact.
4 Investor education—the SEC provides information about the scope of the Year 2000 problem and maintains a Year 2000 page on its Web site.

SUMMARY

This appendix provides an overview of securities legislation related to financial accounting and reporting. It also explains the function of the Securities and Exchange Commission and its authority to prescribe accounting principles. SEC requirements that are relevant to particular topics are integrated into the chapters throughout this book. For example, in Chapters 3 and 12, the SEC's requirement to push down the purchase price of a subsidiary to the subsidiary's financial statements is discussed and illustrated; in Chapter 8, the SEC's position on recognizing gain on a subsidiary's stock sales is discussed; and in Chapter 15, the history of the SEC's efforts in requiring segment disclosures is traced and SEC requirements for interim reports are illustrated.

SELECTED READINGS

American Accounting Association's Securities and Exchange Commission Liaison Committee. "Mountaintop Issues: From the Perspective of the SEC." *Accounting Horizons* (March 1995), pp. 79–86.
IANNACONI, TERESA E. "The SEC's Expanded Role in Small Business Capital Formation." *Journal of Accountancy* (August 1993), pp. 47–48.
JAYSON, SUSAN. "EDGAR Update: No More Fear of Filing." *Management Accounting* (March 1994), pp. 24–26.
SKOUSEN, K. FRED. *An Introduction to the SEC*, 5th ed. Cincinnati: South-Western Publishing Co., 1991.

Estates and Trusts

Estate and trust accounting is frequently referred to as **fiduciary accounting** because estate and trust managers operate in a good-faith custodial or stewardship relationship with beneficiaries of the estate or trust property. A fiduciary is a person whom other people hold in particular confidence. Fiduciaries may be executors, trustees, administrators, and guardians, depending on the nature of their duties and the demands of custom.

In legal terms, **fiduciary** is an individual or an entity authorized to take possession of the property of others. Upon taking possession of estate or trust property, the fiduciary (administrator of an estate or trustee of a trust, for example) has an obligation to administer it in the best interest of all beneficiaries. Although similar practices are used in accounting for estates and trusts, there are a number of differences between the two types of entities. These include the manner in which the entities are created, the objectives of their activities, and the time spans of their existence. These differences are discussed and accounting practices for estates and trusts are reviewed and illustrated in this appendix.

CREATION OF AN ESTATE

An estate comes into existence at the death of an individual. If the deceased person (**decedent**) had a valid will in force at the time of death, he or she is said to have died **testate**.[1] In the absence of a valid will, the decedent is said to have died **intestate**. The estate consists of the property of the decedent at the time of death. Ordinarily, a **personal representative** of the decedent is appointed by a probate court to take control of the decedent's property, but some flexibility is provided if a valid will is in force at the time of death. In this case, the personal representative may leave real or tangible personal property under the control of the person presumably entitled to it under the terms of the will.

---

[1]People with sizable estates usually have lawyers draw up their wills. The lawyer can provide for the eventual validation of the will and also help with estate planning so that property is distributed according to the client's wishes and taxes are minimized.

PROBATE PROCEEDINGS

The personal representative of the deceased (or other interested party) files a petition with the appropriate probate court requesting that an existing will be **probated**, that is, for the will to be validated. The hearing of the probate court to establish validity is called a **testacy proceeding**, because its purpose is to determine whether the deceased died testate or intestate. Under the **Uniform Probate Code** [§ 1-201 (30)], the term *personal representative* includes both executor and administrator, as well as other designations for persons who perform the same functions.

Confirmation

A confirmation by a probate court that a will is valid means that the decedent died testate. Ordinarily, this leads to appointment of the personal representative named in the will as **executor** of the will. It also leads to the presumption that estate property will be distributed in accordance with the provisions of the will, in the absence of extenuating circumstances.

A person dies intestate when he or she dies without leaving a will. Failure of the probate court to validate a will submitted for probate also means that the decedent died intestate. In either case, the court appoints an **administrator** to take control of the estate and supervise the distribution of estate assets in accordance with applicable state laws.

Uniform Probate Code

The state laws governing probate and distributions of estate property vary considerably and do not provide a uniform basis for classifying the legal and accounting characteristics of estates. Therefore, the discussion and illustrations in this appendix are based on the 1974 edition of the Uniform Probate Code, which was approved by the National Conference of Commissioners on Uniform State Laws. The Uniform Probate Code has been approved by the American Bar Association, even though most states have not adopted it.

ADMINISTRATION OF THE ESTATE

The personal representative (executor or administrator) of the estate is a fiduciary who is expected to observe the standards of care applicable to trustees. Appointment by a probate court gives the executor authority to carry out the written instructions of the decedent, including the settlement and distribution of the estate. The executor is expected to perform this duty as expeditiously and efficiently as possible.

Within 30 days after appointment, the personal representative (executor or administrator) must inform the *heirs* and *devisees* of his or her appointment and provide selected information about certain other matters. **Heirs** are the persons entitled to the property of the decedent under the statutes of intestate succession. **Intestate succession** is the order in which estate property is distributed to the surviving spouse, parents, children, and so on, if any estate property is not effectively distributed by will. **Devisees** are those persons designated in a will to receive a *devise* (a testamentary disposition of real or personal property). Under the Uniform Probate Code, "to devise" means to dispose of real or personal property by will. A specific devise is the gift of an object, and a general devise is a gift of money.

Intestate Succession

Under the Uniform Probate Code, as amended, the entire estate of a person who dies intestate passes to the spouse if (1) the decedent has no living descendants or (2) all surviving descendants are also descendants of the surviving spouse. If there are descendants from a prior marriage or relationship, the surviving spouse receives the first $100,000 (the amount varies by state) and one-half of the remaining intestate estate. The remaining part of the estate not passing to the spouse (or the entire estate if there is no surviving spouse) passes to the descendants as directed in the state code.

Inventory of Estate Property

The executor or administrator of a will is required to prepare and file an inventory of property owned by the deceased within three months of appointment. This inventory must list the property in reasonable detail and show the fair market value on the date of death for each item of property. Any encumbrance on the property (such as a lien or other claim) must also be disclosed for each item. This inventory is filed with the probate court, and additional copies must be provided to interested persons on request. If appraisers are employed to assist in valuing the property, their names and addresses must accompany the property inventory. Subsequent discovery of property omitted from the inventory, or errors in valuing certain items, are corrected by preparing and filing a new or supplementary inventory of the estate property. Personal items of limited value are usually excluded from the inventory.

Exempt Property and Allowances

The Uniform Probate Code entitles the surviving spouse to a **homestead allowance** that is exempt from, and has priority over, all claims against the estate. The amount of the allowance varies but in some states it is $15,000. In the absence of a surviving spouse, the minor children would share the allowance equally. The surviving spouse also has an entitlement of up to $10,000 (varies by state) in household furniture, automobiles, and personal effects from the estate, depending on whether or not the property has been used to secure a loan. In the absence of a surviving spouse, the minor children share this property jointly.

The surviving spouse and minor children who were dependent on the deceased are also entitled to a *reasonable* family allowance to be paid out of the estate property during the period in which the estate is being administered. This family allowance is exempt from and has priority over all claims except the homestead allowance.

Claims Against the Estate

Under the Uniform Probate Code, the personal representative publishes a notice in a newspaper of general circulation in the county for three consecutive weeks. The purpose is to announce his or her appointment and to notify creditors to present their claims within four months of the date of first publication of the notice.

Claims against the estate *that arose before death* and were not presented within four months (three years, if the required notice to creditors was not published) are barred forever against the estate, the personal representative, the heirs, and the devisees [Uniform Probate Code, § 3-801-3].

All claims against the decedent's estate *that arose after death* are barred as claims against the estate, the personal representative, the heirs, and the devisees unless presented as:

1 A claim based on a contract with the personal representative within four months after performance is due and discharged, or
2 Any other claim within four months after it arises.

Classification of Claims   When estate assets are insufficient to pay all claims in full, payments are made as follows [Uniform Probate Code, § 3-805]:

1 Costs and expenses of administration of the estate
2 Reasonable funeral expenses and reasonable and necessary medical and hospital expenses of the last illness of the decedent
3 Debts and taxes with preference under federal or state law
4 All other claims

No preference is given for payment within a given class of claims.

Secured Claims   Payment of secured claims against the estate depends on the amount allowed if the creditor surrenders his security. However, if the assets of the estate are encumbered by mortgage, pledge, lien, or other security interest, the personal representative may pay the encumbrance if it appears to be in the best interests of the estate [Uniform Probate Code, § 3-814].

ACCOUNTING FOR THE ESTATE

The executor (personal representative) records the inventory of estate property in a self-balancing set of accounts that show:

1 The property for which responsibility has been assumed
2 The manner in which that responsibility is subsequently discharged

The executor does not accept responsibility for obligations of the decedent (testator), so the liabilities of the estate are not recorded until paid.

Estate Principal and Income

The focus of fiduciary accounting lies in distinguishing between principal and income. That focus applies to accounting for both estates and trusts. Estates frequently realize income from various investments between the time that the property inventory is filed by the executor and the time the estate is fully administered. A primary reason for dividing estate principal and income is that the beneficiaries are likely to be different. For example, some devises specified in the will are distributed to the devisees from estate principal, but the income may accrue to the residual beneficiaries of the estate. **Residual beneficiaries** are those entitled to the remainder of the estate after all other rightful claims on the estate have been satisfied.

The National Conference of Commissioners on Uniform State Laws approved a Revised Uniform Principal and Income Act in 1978 to provide guidance in distinguishing between estate principal and income. That act provides that expenses incurred in settling a decedent's estate be charged against the principal of the estate. These expenses include debts, funeral expenses, estate taxes, interest and penalties, family allowances, attorney's fees, personal representative's fees, and court costs [Uniform Probate Code, § 5].

Alternatively, income (less expenses) earned after death on assets included in the decedent's estate is distributed to the specific devisee to whom the property was devised. Any remaining income that accrues during the period of estate administration is distributed to the devisees in proportion to their interests in the undivided (residual) assets of the estate.

Estate Income, Gains, and Losses   In accounting for the decedent's estate, the receipts due but unpaid at the date of death are a part of the estate principal. These include items such as interest, dividends, rents, royalties, and annuities due at the time of death. After death, earnings from income-producing property are estate income, unless the will specifically provides otherwise. That is, amounts earned for the items listed would be classified as income, rather than principal, if they came due during the period of estate administration. In accounting for interest income on bond investments included in the estate inventory, no provision is made for amortization of bond issue premiums and discounts. This is because the bonds (and other securities) are included in the estate inventory at fair market value, and any gains or losses on disposal are adjustments of estate principal.

Depreciation is a related matter that requires interpretation under the Uniform Principal and Income Act [Uniform Probate Code, §§ 13a(2) and c(3)]. The act provides that a reasonable allowance for depreciation be made on depreciable property of the estate, except that no depreciation is to be made on real property used by a beneficiary as a residence or on personal property held by a trustee who is not then making a depreciation allowance.

ILLUSTRATION OF ESTATE ACCOUNTING

On April 1, 20X6, Harry Olds entered the hospital with a terminal illness. He died May 1, 20X6, at the age of 70. Laura Hunt, Harry's only daughter, was appointed executor of the estate by the probate court, which also confirmed that Harry had died testate. The will provided specific devises at estimated values to be awarded as follows:

Summer home to his daughter, Laura Hunt	$45,000
1973 Datsun 240Z to his grandson, Gary Hunt	8,000
200 shares of FFF stock to his friend, Michael Wallace	5,000
All other personal effects to Harry's widow, Gloria Olds	

The following general devises of cash were also provided:

Laura Hunt, in lieu of fees as executor	$19,000
Sara Tyson, Harry's housekeeper	6,000
First Methodist Church	5,000
Humane Society	10,000
Gloria Olds is to receive the income in excess of expenses during the administration of the estate.	
The residue of the estate is to be placed in trust, with the income used to support Harry's widow during her lifetime. Upon her mother's death, Laura gets the remainder of the estate.	

Laura informed the heirs and devisees of her appointment as executor of Harry's estate on May 19, 20X6, and at the same time, placed the required notice to creditors in the newspaper. On June 15, 20X6, she filed the estate inventory that appears in Exhibit B-1 with the probate court.

Laura subsequently prepared the following entries to record transactions and events during the period of estate administration:

May 19, 20X6

Memorandum: Placed a notice in the *Montgomery County News Messenger* that creditors of the estate of Harry Olds should present their claims against the estate within four months.

June 15, 20X6   Recorded the inventory of estate assets as of May 1, 20X6:

Cash—principal	$ 30,000
Savings account	93,000
Certificate of deposit, due 8/1/20X6	100,000
Certificate of deposit, due 7/1/20X6	100,000
Note receivable—George Stein	20,000
Rocky Mountain Power common stock	40,000
Southern Natural Gas common stock	30,000
FFF Company common stock	5,000
Danville municipal bonds	58,000

HARRY OLDS, TESTATOR
INVENTORY OF ESTATE ASSETS
AS OF THE DATE OF DEATH ON MAY 1, 20X6

Description of Property	Fair Value
Cash in Commercial National Bank	$ 30,000
Cash in savings account at First National Bank	93,000
Certificate of deposit, 8%, 18 months, due August 1 (includes $10,000 accrued interest)	110,000
Certificate of deposit, 9%, one-year, due July 1 (includes $7,500 interest)	107,500
Note receivable plus $1,500 accrued interest from George Stein, 10%, due June 1	21,500
Rocky Mountain Power common stock, 1,000 shares	40,000
Southern Natural Gas common stock, 2,000 shares	30,000
Danville City 9%, $50,000 par municipal bonds	58,000
Interest on Danville City bonds, due June 1	1,875
Dividends receivable—utility stocks	1,500
Summer home	45,000
FFF common stock, 200 shares	5,000
1973 Datsun 240Z	8,000
Personal effects*	—
	$551,375

*The probate court permitted Laura to exclude Harry's personal effects other than specific devises from the inventory.

Submitted by Laura Hunt, executor on June 15, 20X6.

Exhibit B–1   *Inventory of Estate Assets*

Summer home	45,000	
1973 Datsun 240Z	8,000	
Interest receivable on CDs	17,500	
Interest receivable—George Stein	1,500	
Interest receivable—municipal bonds	1,875	
Dividends receivable—common stock	1,500	
Estate principal		$551,375

June 16, 20X6 Cashed dividend checks received May 5 on utility stock:

| Cash—principal | $ 1,500 | |
| Dividends receivable—common stock | | $ 1,500 |

June 18, 20X6 Collected interest of $2,250 on Danville City bonds. Interest of $375 was earned after the date of death:

Cash—principal	$ 1,875	
Cash—income	375	
Interest receivable—municipal bonds		$ 1,875
Estate income		375

June 23, 20X6 Funeral expenses of $4,500 were paid:

| Funeral expenses | $ 4,500 | |
| Cash—principal | | $ 4,500 |

June 24, 20X6 Collected the $20,000 George Stein note and $1,650 interest. Interest of $150 was earned after the date of death:

Cash—principal	$ 21,500	
Cash—income	150	
Note receivable—George Stein		$ 20,000
Interest receivable—George Stein		1,500
Estate income		150

June 25, 20X6 Discovered and cashed a certificate of deposit that matured on April 15 and was excluded from the estate inventory. The proceeds were $10,800:

| Cash—principal | $ 10,800 | |
| Assets subsequently discovered | | $ 10,800 |

June 28, 20X6 Paid hospital and medical bills in excess of amounts paid by Medicare and private health insurance policies:

| Hospital and medical expenses | $ 19,000 | |
| Cash—principal | | $ 19,000 |

July 1, 20X6 Cashed the certificate of deposit that was due on July 1:

Cash—principal	$107,500	
Cash—income	1,500	
Certificate of deposit		$100,000
Interest receivable on CD		7,500
Estate income		1,500

July 12, 20X6 Paid cash to general devisees as provided in the will:

Devise—Laura Hunt	$ 19,000	
Devise—Sara Tyson	6,000	
Devise—First Methodist Church	5,000	
Devise—Humane Society	10,000	
Cash—principal		$ 40,000

August 1, 20X6 Recorded interest from savings account for the quarter ending July 31:

| Cash—income | $ 1,395 | |
| Estate income | | $ 1,395 |

August 1, 20X6 Cashed in the certificate of deposit due August 1:

Cash—principal	$110,000	
Cash—income	2,000	
Certificate of deposit		$ 100,000
Interest receivable on CD		10,000
Estate income		2,000

August 5, 20X6 Received dividend checks on utilities stock:

Cash—income	$ 1,500	
Estate income		$ 1,500

August 15, 20X6 Paid a $500 mechanics bill on the Datsun 240Z that was incurred on April 10, 20X6 and submitted for payment on August 10:

Debts of decedent paid	$,500	
Cash—principal		$ 500

August 15, 20X6 Delivered specific devises as provided in the will. Personal effects not included in the estate inventory were left with the widow, Gloria Olds:

Devise—summer home to Laura Hunt	$ 45,000	
Devise—1973 Datsun 240Z to Gary Hunt	8,000	
Devise—FFF stock to Michael Wallace	5,000	
Summer home		$ 45,000
1973 Datsun 240Z		8,000
FFF Company common stock		5,000

August 28, 20X6 Payment of attorney fees and court costs:

Attorney fees paid	$ 4,500	
Court costs paid	500	
Cash—principal		$ 5,000

August 31, 20X6 Distribution of estate income to Gloria Olds:

Distribution to Gloria Olds	$ 6,920	
Cash—income		$ 6,920

Closing Entries

Entries to close the nominal accounts to estate income and estate principal on August 31 are as follows:

Estate principal	$127,000	
Funeral expenses paid		$ 4,500
Hospital and medical expenses paid		19,000
Devise—Laura Hunt		64,000
Devise—Sara Tyson		6,000
Devise—First Methodist Church		5,000
Devise—Humane Society		10,000
Debts of decedent paid		500
Devise to Gary Hunt		8,000
Devise to Michael Wallace		5,000
Attorney fees paid		4,500
Court costs paid		500
Estate Income	$ 6,920	
Distribution to Gloria Olds		$ 6,920
Assets subsequently discovered	$ 10,800	
Estate principal		$ 10,800

After these closing entries are made, the remaining account balances are as follows:

Cash—principal	$214,175
Savings account	93,000
Rocky Mountain Power common stock	40,000
Southern Natural Gas common stock	30,000
Danville municipal bonds	58,000
Estate principal	$435,175

August 31, 20X6   Laura Hunt transfers estate property to Ed Jones, trustee for Gloria Olds, in accordance with the income trust established by Harry Olds' will:

Estate principal		$435,175
Cash—principal	$214,175	
Savings account	93,000	
Rocky Mountain Power common stock	40,000	
Southern Natural Gas common stock	30,000	
Danville municipal bonds	58,000	

Charge-Discharge Statement

The **charge-discharge statement** is a document prepared by the personal representative (executor or administrator) to show accountability for estate property received and maintained or disbursed in accordance with the will (or the probate court in intestate cases). A charge-discharge statement shows progress in the administration of the estate and termination of responsibility when the will has been fully administered. A final charge-discharge statement by Laura Hunt for her father's estate is shown in Exhibit B-2. The statement consists of two major parts: one for estate principal and

---

ESTATE OF HARRY OLDS
CHARGE-DISCHARGE STATEMENT
FOR THE PERIOD OF ESTATE ADMINISTRATION
MAY 1 TO AUGUST 31, 20X6

Estate Principal

I charge myself for:

Assets included in estate inventory	$551,375	
Assets discovered after inventory	10,800	
Total estate principal charge		$562,175

I credit myself for:

Funeral expenses paid	$ 4,500	
Hospital and medical expenses paid	19,000	
Mechanic's bill paid	500	
Attorney fees and court costs	5,000	$ 29,000
Devises paid in cash to:		
Laura Hunt	$ 19,000	
Sara Tyson	6,000	
First Methodist Church	5,000	
Humane Society	10,000	40,000
Devises distributed in kind to:		
Laura Hunt (summer home)	$ 45,000	
Gary Hunt (Datsun 240Z)	8,000	
Michael Wallace (FFF stock)	5,000	58,000
Transferred to Ed Jones, trustee for Gloria Olds:		
Cash—principal	$214,175	
Savings account	93,000	
Rocky Mountain Power Company stock	40,000	
Southern Natural Gas Company stock	30,000	
Danville municipal bonds	58,000	435,175
Total estate principal discharge		$562,175

Estate Income

I charge myself for:

Estate income received during estate administration	$ 6,920

I credit myself for:

Payment of estate income to Gloria Olds as directed by the will	$ 6,920

Respectfully submitted: Laura Hunt, Estate Executor, August 31, 20X6.

Exhibit B–2   *Charge-Discharge Statement*

one for estate income. The extent of detail is determined by the complexity of the estate, the number of devises, and instructions from the probate court.

Income Taxes on Estate Income

Income on resources held by the estate while it is being settled is taxable, even though the inheritance may not be taxable to the beneficiary. The tax may be paid by the estate or by the beneficiary if estate property has already been distributed to the beneficiary. Estates and trusts file federal income tax returns on Form 1041, *U.S. Fiduciary Income Tax Return.* The beneficiary's share of income is reported on Schedule K-1 of Form 1041.

For tax purposes, the beneficiary treats each item of income earned on estate property in the same way that it is treated by the estate. For example, if interest is earned on bonds held by the estate, the beneficiary classifies the income as interest. If the estate receives dividends from stock holdings, the beneficiary classifies the income as dividends. The fiduciary of the estate must provide this information to the beneficiary on Schedule K-1.

ACCOUNTING FOR TRUSTS

The will of Harry Olds resulted in the creation of an income trust for Gloria Olds. A trust created pursuant to a will is referred to as **testamentary trust**. The fiduciary that administers a trust is the **trustee**. A trustee may be a business entity or a natural person. As in the case of estates, guidance in accounting for trusts comes from state laws, the Uniform Trusts Act, the Uniform Probate Code, and the Revised Uniform Principal and Income Act.

The entry made by Ed Jones, the trustee, to open the books for the creation of the Gloria Olds Trust is as follows:

Cash	$214,175	
Savings account	93,000	
Rocky Mountain Power common stock	40,000	
Southern Natural Gas common stock	30,000	
Danville municipal bonds	58,000	
Trust fund principal		$435,175
To record receipt of property transferred from Laura Hunt, executor.		

A primary concern in accounting for trust entities is distinguishing between principal and income. This is especially true of income trusts such as the one created for Gloria Olds because the principal amount of the trust is to be maintained intact to provide income for Mrs. Olds's care until her death. Separate *trust fund principal* and *trust fund income* accounts are used to separate principal and income balances for accounting purposes. The use of separate principal and income cash accounts, however, is of limited value, and the practice is usually not necessary.

Chapter 20 of this book discusses trust funds of governmental units and illustrates accounting and reporting practices for them.

SUMMARY

When a person dies without a valid will, he or she dies intestate. The deceased person's estate is distributed under the statutes of intestate succession. When the decedent has a valid will in force, he or she dies testate. The probate court normally names the personal representative named in the will as executor of the estate. The executor is a fiduciary charged with carrying out the provisions of the will, including the settlement and distribution of the estate.

The executor records an inventory of the estate in a self-balancing set of accounts; however, obligations of the decedent are not recorded until paid. The executor must distinguish between estate principal and income in accounting for the estate. Guidance for distinguishing estate principal and estate income is found in the

Uniform Principal and Income Act. The executor prepares a charge-discharge statement to show accountability for estate property and progress in the administration of the estate. A final charge-discharge statement is prepared when the estate has been fully administered.

SELECTED READINGS

BERNSTEIN, PHYLLIS J., STEPHEN J. ROJAS, and MURRAY B. SCHWARTZBERG. "A Primer on Trusts." *Journal of Accountancy* (May 1993), pp. 57–61.

HIRA, LABH S. "Revocable Trusts: Appealing, But Beware." *Journal of Accountancy* (October 1991), pp. 91–96.

WILSON, DOUGLAS D., "Providing Guidance to Executors and Trustees," *Journal of Accountancy* V. 184, No. 4 (October 1997), pp. 37–43.

Glossary

Acquisition: a business combination in which one corporation acquires control over the operations of another entity.

Actual Retirement of Bonds: the repurchase and retirement of bonds by the issuing affiliate.

Additions (Governmental Colleges and Universities): increases to the fund balance of fund groupings other than current unrestricted funds and current restricted funds to the extent that expenditures have not been made.

Administrator: the court-appointed representative who takes control of the estate of a person who died intestate and supervises the estate's distribution.

Affiliate: a subsidiary in a technical sense, although the term is sometimes used to refer to 20% to 50%-owned equity investees.

Agency Funds (Governmental Accounting): used to account for resources held by the governmental unit as agent for other funds, other governmental units, or individuals.

Agency Theory: a theory of intercompany bondholdings that allocates constructive gains and losses to the issuing affiliate.

Allotments: divisions of the appropriation authority by time period.

Annuity Funds: a college and university fund type to account for resources acquired under the condition that stipulated periodic payments be made to individuals as directed by the donor of the resources.

Appropriations: budget authorizations of expenditures.

Auxiliary Enterprises: a college and university activity encompassing student unions, dormitories, resident halls, and intercollegiate athletics that are intended to be self-sustaining.

Bankruptcy Insolvency: a condition in which an entity has total debts in excess of the fair market value of its assets.

Bonus Procedure (Partnerships): the adjustment of partner capital balances as an alternative to revaluing partnership assets or recording goodwill.

Branch Operation: a company outlet that stocks goods, makes sales, maintains accounting records, and functions much like a separate business enterprise.

Budget: a plan of financial operations including proposed expenditures for a period and the means of financing them.

Business Combination: a uniting of previously separate business entities through acquisition by one entity of another entity's net assets or a majority of its outstanding voting common stock, or through an exchange of common stock.

Capital Budget (Governmental Accounting): the current portion of a capital program.

Capital Program (Governmental Accounting): a plan of capital expenditures by year over a fixed period of years.

Capital Projects Funds (Governmental Accounting): used to account for resources to be used for acquisition or construction of major general government capital facilities.

Cash Distribution Plan (Partnerships): a plan developed at the beginning of the liquidation period that shows how cash will be distributed throughout the phase-out period.

Cash Distribution Schedule (Partnerships): a schedule of cash distributions made to creditors and partners in a partnership liquidation.

Chapter 11 of the Bankruptcy Act: Chapter 11 covers rehabilitation of the debtor and anticipates a reorganization of the debtor corporation.

Chapter 7 of the Bankruptcy Act: Chapter 7 covers straight bankruptcy under which the debtor entity is expected to be liquidated.

Charge-Discharge Statement (Estates and Trusts): a document prepared by the executor or administrator of an estate to show accountability for property received and disbursed.

Charity Care: hospital terminology for services provided free of charge to qualifying patients.

Conditional Promise to Give (Not-for-Profit Accounting): a pledge that is dependent upon the occurrence or failure to occur of an uncertain future event.

Conglomeration: the combination of firms in unrelated and diverse product lines and/or service functions.

Connecting Affiliates Relationship: a type of affiliation structure involving indirect or mutual holdings between a parent company and its subsidiaries.

Consolidation: (1) a business combination in which a new corporation is formed to take over two or more business entities that then go out of existence; (2) in a generic sense, it means the same as acquisition or merger; (3) the process of combining parent company and subsidiary financial statements.

Constructive Retirement of Bonds: the repurchase of bonds of one affiliate by another so that the bonds are held within the parent-subsidiary affiliation and, in effect, retired.

Constructive Retirement of Preferred Stock: the purchase of a subsidiary's preferred stock by the parent company results in a retirement of the preferred stock from the viewpoint of the consolidated entity.

Contemporary Theory: the current theory underlying consolidated financial statements; it reflects certain aspects of both entity and parent company theory.

Contribution (Not-for-Profit Accounting): a transfer of cash or other assets to an entity or a settlement or cancellation of its liabilities from a voluntary nonreciprocal transfer.

Conventional Approach of Accounting for Mutually Held Common Stock: parent company stock held by a subsidiary is accounted for as being constructively retired for consolidation purposes.

Conversion to Equity Method Approach: an approach used in the preparation of consolidation working papers when the parent company has used an incomplete equity or cost method in accounting for its subsidiaries: the parent company's accounts are converted to the equity method as the first working paper entry.

Corporate Joint Venture: a joint venture organized under the corporate form of business organization.

Current Funds: a college and university fund grouping to account for resources expendable for operating purposes; includes unrestricted current funds and restricted current funds.

Current Rate: the exchange rate in effect at the balance sheet date or the transaction date.

Current Rate Method: translation of all assets, liabilities, revenues, and expenses at current exchange rates.

Debtor in Possession: a Chapter 11 case where the debtor corporation keeps control of the business and performs the duties of a trustee.

Debt Service Funds (Governmental Accounting): used to account for the accumulation of resources for payment of principal and interest on general long-term debt.

Decedent: a person that is deceased.

Defeasance of Debt: occurs when the debt is legally satisfied even though the debt is not actually paid (legal defeasance) or when the debtor irrevocably places cash or certain other assets with an escrow agent in a trust for the payment of the debt (in substance defeasance).

Denominated: to denominate in a currency is to fix the amount in units of that currency.

Devisees: those persons designated in a will to receive real or personal property.

Direct Holdings: direct investments in voting stock of one or more investee companies.

Direct Quotation: the expression of an exchange rate in U.S. dollars (U.S. dollar equivalent).

Donor-Imposed Conditions (Not-for-Profit Accounting): the occurrence or failure to occur of an uncertain future event that releases the donor from its obligation.

Donor-Imposed Restrictions (Not-for-Profit Accounting): specifications of how or when the assets promised or received must be used.

Downstream Sale: sales or other intercompany transactions from parent company to subsidiary.

Drawings (Partnerships): regular partner withdrawals as provided in the partnership agreement and closed to partner capital at year-end.

EDGAR System: the SEC's electronic data gathering, analysis, and retrieval system. Forms filed with the SEC can be downloaded from the EDGAR system at http://www.sec.gov/edaux/formlynx.htm by providing the form desired and company name.

Encumbrance Accounting: recording commitments made for goods on order and for unperformed contracts to prevent overspending of amounts appropriated.

Endowment Funds (Not-for-Profit Accounting): used to account for gifts and bequests received from donors under endowment agreements (hospitals); a fund type for colleges and universities to account for resources received from donors or outside agencies with the stipulation that the principal be maintained in perpetuity and income be used as directed.

Endowment Trust Funds (Governmental Accounting): a trust fund in which the principal must remain intact but the earnings may be expended for authorized purposes.

Enterprise Funds (Governmental Accounting): used to account for operations that are financed and operated in a manner similar to private enterprise.

Entitlements (Governmental Accounting): payments to which state and local governmental units are entitled based on an allocation formula.

Entity Theory: a theory under which consolidated financial statements are prepared from the view of the total business entity.

Equity Adjustment on Translation: an exchange gain or loss that is reported as a stockholders' equity adjustment (and in other comprehensive income).

Equity Insolvency: the inability of an entity to pay its debts as they come due.

Equity in Subsidiary Realized Income: the parent company's or minority interest's share of subsidiary income adjusted for intercompany gains and losses and amortization of cost/book value differentials.

Equity Method: accounting for a common stock investment on an accrual basis; earnings increase the investment and dividends decrease it.

Exchange Rate: the ratio between a unit of one currency and the amount of another currency for which it can be exchanged.

Executor: the court-appointed representative who takes control of the estate of a decedent who died testate and supervises its distribution.

Executory Contracts: contracts that have not been completely performed by the parties to the contract (purchase commitments and leases, for example).

Expendable Funds: those in which resources can be expended to meet the objective of the fund.

Expendable Trust Funds: a trust fund in which the assets can be expended as needed to meet the fund's objectives.

Expenditures: decreases in the net financial resources of a governmental type fund other than those caused by transfers or similar other financing uses.

Fair Value/Cost Method (for Equity Investments): if the stock is not marketable, a common stock investment is accounted for at its original cost. If the stock is marketable, the investment is carried at fair market value with an associated adjunct/contra equity account for the change in value from original cost (assuming an available-for-sales security). In both cases, dividends received are recorded as income from the investment.

Family Allowance: an allowance to a surviving spouse and minor children to be paid out of estate property during the period of estate administration.

Father-Son-Grandson Relationship: a type of affiliation structure involving indirect or mutual holdings between a parent company and its subsidiaries.

Fiduciary: an individual or entity authorized to take possession of the property of others.

Fiduciary Accounting: a term used to describe accounting for estates and trusts whose managers have a custodial or stewardship relationship with the trust or estate beneficiaries.

Fiduciary Funds: a category of funds to account for assets held by the government as trustee or agent; includes expendable, nonexpendable, and pension trust funds and agency funds.

Fixed Exchange Rates: exchange rates set by a government and subject to change only by that government. (Also *official exchange rates.*)

Floating Exchange Rates: exchange rates that are market driven and reflect supply and demand factors, inflation, and so on. (Also *free exchange rates.*)

Foreign Currency: a currency other than the entity's functional currency.

Foreign Currency Commitment: a contract or agreement that will result in a foreign currency transaction at a later date.

Foreign Currency Cash Flow Hedge: a derivative instrument that hedges against the effect of the change in the relative value of two currencies due to the inherent exposure in forecasted transactions denominated in the foreign currency.

Foreign Currency Fair Value Hedge: a derivative instrument that hedges against the effect of the change in the relative value of two currencies due to the inherent exposure of holding an asset, liability or firm commitment denominated in a foreign currency.

Foreign Currency Statements: the financial statements of a foreign subsidiary or other foreign entity and expressed in its local currency.

Foreign Currency Transactions: transactions whose terms are denominated in a currency other than the entity's functional currency.

Foreign Transactions: transactions between entities in different countries.

Form 8-K: form to disclose significant changes in firm policies, financial condition, etc., to the SEC.

Form 10-K: basic form for the annual report that firms file with the SEC.

Form 10-Q: form for quarterly reports that firms file with the SEC.

Fraudulent Transfer: a transfer of an interest or an obligation incurred by the debtor within one year prior to the date of filing a bankruptcy petition with the intent to defraud creditors.

Free Exchange Rates: exchange rates that are market driven and reflect supply and demand factors, inflation, and so on. (Also *floating exchange rates*.)

Fresh Start Reporting: accounting under a reorganization plan that meets prescribed conditions and enables the new entity to eliminate its prior deficit and report zero retained earnings.

Functional Currency: the currency of the primary environment in which an entity operates.

Fund: a fiscal and accounting entity with a self-balancing set of accounts that records cash and other assets together with related liabilities and residual balances.

Fund Accounting or Fund Basis: financial systems that are segmented into separate accounting and reporting entities (funds) on the basis of their objectives and restrictions on their operations and resources.

Fund Balance: assets less liabilities of a governmental fund; often is essentially the working capital of a governmental fund.

Fund Equity: an amount equal to assets less liabilities of a fund.

Fund Fixed Assets (Governmental Accounting): fixed assets related to specific proprietary or trust funds and accounted for in those funds.

Fund Long-Term Liabilities (Governmental Accounting): long-term liabilities of proprietary and trust funds are designated fund long-term liabilities and accounted for in those funds.

General Fixed Assets (Governmental Accounting): all fixed assets not classified as fund fixed assets; general fixed assets are accounted for in the general fixed assets account group.

General Fund (Governmental Accounting): used to account for all financial resources not accounted for in another fund.

General Government Activities: in a simple situation, they are essentially taxpayer finance activities made available to all members of a government's constituency without charges for use. These activities commonly include general administration, public safety, education, the judicial system, and so on.

General Long-Term Debt (Governmental Accounting): all unmatured long-term liabilities other than fund long-term liabilities; accounted for in the general long-term debt account group.

General Partnership: an association in which each partner has unlimited liability.

Goodwill Procedure (Partnerships): the adjustment of assets and liabilities to fair values and recording goodwill as an alternative to adjusting partner equity balances (also, a partnership revaluation approach).

Governmental Accounting Standards Board (GASB): the standards-setting body for governmental accounting and financial reporting.

Governmental Fund Expenditures: decreases in fund financial resources other than from interfund transfers and other financing uses.

Governmental Fund Revenues: increases in fund financial resources other than from transfers, debt issue proceeds, and interfund reimbursement transactions.

Governmental Funds: a category of funds used to account for most governmental functions that are basically different from private enterprise; they include the general fund, special revenue funds, capital projects funds, and debt service funds.

Grants: contributions from other governmental units to be used for specific purposes.

Hedging Operations: purchase or sale of a foreign currency contract to offset the risks of holding receivables or payables denominated in a foreign currency.

Heirs: the persons entitled to the property of the decedent under the statutes of intestate succession.

Historical Rate: the exchange rate in effect at the time a specific transaction or event occurred.

Homestead Allowance: an allowance to a surviving spouse that has priority over all other claims against the estate.

Horizontal Integration: the combination of firms in the same business lines or markets.

IASC: International Accounting Standards Committee.

Incomplete Application of the Equity Method: accounting for an equity investee without considering amortization of cost-book value differentials or intercompany profits (also called the simple equity method).

Indirect Holdings: investments that enable an investor company to control an investee that is not directly owned through an investee that is directly owned.

Indirect Quotation: the expression of an exchange rate in foreign currency units (foreign currency per U.S. dollar).

Installment Liquidation (Partnerships): distribution of cash as it becomes available during the liquidation period.

Interfund Loans: loans made by one fund to another and that must be repaid.

Intergovernmental Revenue: revenues received from other governmental units.

Interim Financial Reports: unaudited financial reports that are issued for periods of less than a full year and frequently are called quarterly reports.

Internal Service Funds (Governmental Accounting): used to account for financing goods and services provided by one department to other departments on a cost-reimbursement basis.

Intestate: having died without a valid will.

Intestate Succession: the order in which intestate estate property is distributed to the surviving spouse, descendants, parents, and so on.

Investment in Plant Accounts: used by colleges and universities to account for the physical plant, which includes land, buildings, improvements other than buildings, and equipment including library books, and for related debt.

Involuntary Bankruptcy Proceedings: the filing is involuntary if the creditors file the bankruptcy petition.

Joint Venture: a business entity that is owned, operated, and jointly controlled by a small group of investors (venturers) for a specific undertaking; it may be temporary or relatively permanent, and it may be corporate or partnership.

Leveraged Buyout: acquisition of a publicly-held company directly from its shareholders in a transaction financed primarily by debt.

Liabilities Not Subject to Compromise: the fully secured liabilities incurred before a Chapter 11 bankruptcy filing and all post-petition claims.

Life Income Funds: a college and university fund type to account for resources acquired under the condition that the income be paid to a designated individual until death.

Limited Life: the legal life of partnerships terminates with the admission of a new partner, death or retirement of an old partner, etc.

Limited Partnership: an association in which one or more partners have limited liability and at least one partner has unlimited liability.

Loan Funds: a college and university fund grouping to account for resources available for student and faculty loans.

Local Currency: the currency of the country being referred to.

Local Transactions: transactions within a country that are measured in the currency of that country.

Mandatory Transfers (Colleges and Universities): transfers of resources under binding agreements with outside agencies or donors; a matching gift to a student loan fund, for example.

Measurement Focus (Governmental Accounting): that which is expressed in reporting an entity's financial performance and position.

Merger: a business combination in which one corporation takes over the operations of another entity and that entity goes out of existence; also, a business combination or an acquisition in a generic sense.

Minority Interest: the stockholder interest in a subsidiary not owned by the parent company.

Monetary Assets and Liabilities: are assets and liabilities in which the amounts are fixed in currency units. If the value of the currency unit changes, it is still settled with the same number of units.

Monetary–Nonmonetary Method: translation of monetary items at current exchange rates and nonmonetary items at historical rates.

Multiple Exchange Rates: fixed exchange rates with preferential rates set for different kinds of transactions.

Mutual Agency (Partnerships): each partner has the power to bind all other partners, in the absence of notification to the contrary.

Mutual Holdings: two or more affiliated companies that hold stock in each other.

Negative Goodwill: the excess of the fair market value of assets acquired in a purchase business combination over the investment cost.

Nonexpendable Funds (Governmental Accounting): funds that have a profit or capital maintenance objective; includes enterprise and internal service funds as well as nonexpendable trust funds.

Nonexpendable Trust Funds: principal is maintained intact but income may or may not be expendable.

Nonmandatory Transfers (Colleges and Universities): funds transferred back to unrestricted current funds or transfers at the discretion of the governing board.

Nonmonetary Items: are items that would change with changes in market price or changes in the value of the currency.

Nonprofit or Not-for-Profit Entities: nonbusiness organizations that have neither individual ownership nor private-profit objectives.

Offering Circular: similar to a prospectus, but with fewer disclosure requirements.

Official Exchange Rates: exchange rates set by a government and subject to change only by that government. (Also *fixed exchange rates*.)

One-line Consolidation: another name for the equity method of accounting; under the equity method the investor's income and consolidated net income are equal.

Operating Profit Test: a test to determine if an operating segment is a reportable segment of the enterprise.

Operating Segment: a component of an enterprise engaged in providing goods and services to unaffiliated or affiliated customers for a profit.

Operating Transfers (Governmental Accounting): legally authorized shifts of resources from one fund to another that are not revenues, expenditures or expenses, or residual equity transfers.

Parent Company Theory: a theory under which consolidated financial statements are prepared from the view of parent company stockholders.

Parent-Subsidiary Relationship: a relationship that gives one corporation the power to control another corporation through its majority common stock ownership.

Partnership: an association of two or more persons to carry on as co-owners in a business for profit.

Partnership Agreement: a contract between partners covering duties of partners, investments, withdrawals, profit sharing, and so on. Without this agreement, these issues are settled by the Uniform Partnership Act.

Partnership Dissolution: the change in the relation of partners when any partner is no longer involved in carrying on the business. The business may continue as an operating business despite the dissolution of the partnership.

Partnership Liquidation: the process of converting assets into cash, settling all liabilities, and distributing any remaining cash to partners.

Par Value Theory: a theory of intercompany bond holdings that allocates constructive gains or losses between the purchasing and issuing affiliates on the basis of the par value of the bonds.

Patient Service Revenue (Hospitals): revenue from board and room, nursing services, and other professional services, and recorded on an accrual basis.

Payments in Lieu of Taxes: payments by one governmental unit to another for revenues lost because governments cannot tax each other. Also, similar payments from a government's enterprise fund to its other tax-supported funds.

Performance Budget: a budget that emphasizes measurable performance of work programs and activities.

Permanently Restricted Net Assets (Not-for-Profit Accounting): the portion of a not-for-profit entity's net assets whose use is limited by donor-imposed stipulations that do not expire and cannot be removed by action of the entity.

Personal Representative: a person named by the probate court to take control of a decedent's estate.

Piecemeal Acquisition: a corporation gains control of a subsidiary through a series of separate stock purchases.

Plant Funds: a college and university fund grouping to account for unexpended plant funds, renewal and replacement funds, retirement of indebtedness funds, and investment in plant funds.

Plant Replacement and Expansion Funds (Hospitals): a hospital fund group to account for donor-restricted resources for plant, property and equipment.

Pledge (Nonprofit Accounting): a written or oral promise to contribute cash or other assets to the organization.

Pooling of Interests Method: a business combination consummated through an exchange of common shares and accounted for on a book value basis.

Postpetition Liabilities: liabilities incurred after a Chapter 11 filing and not associated with pre-bankruptcy events.

Preacquisition Dividends: dividends paid on an equity investment prior to the date the investment was acquired during the year.

Preacquisition Earnings: income on an equity investment from beginning of the year up to the date the investment was acquired during the year.

Preferences: certain transfers of property of a debtor or certain obligations incurred by a debtor prior to filing a bankruptcy petition.

Preliminary Prospectus: a preliminary communication about securities to be issued that also explains how to get a copy of the prospectus filed with the SEC.

Prepetition Liabilities: liabilities of the debtor corporation at the time of a bankruptcy filing.

Prepetition Liabilities Subject to Compromise: unsecured and undersecured liabilities incurred before a Chapter 11 bankruptcy filing.

Probate: to probate a will is to validate a will.

Program Budget: an expenditure budget of the total cost of programs to be carried out or functions to be performed.

Proportionate or Pro Rata Consolidation: a practice in accounting for joint ventures in which each investor-venturer accounts for its share of assets, equities, revenues, and expenses.

Proprietary Funds (Governmental Accounting): a category of funds to account for operations that are similar to those of private business enterprises; including enterprise funds and internal service funds.

Prospectus: information about an SEC registrant firm that includes its type of business, company background, and financial statements; it is a part of the SEC registration statement.

Purchase Method: a method of accounting for a business combination in which one corporation acquires a controlling interest in another entity; the acquisition is accounted for on a fair value basis.

Pure Endowments: endowments for which the principal is permanently restricted. (*Quasi-endowments* can be changed by the governing board.)

Push-Down Accounting: establishment of a new basis of subsidiary accounting based on the price paid by the parent company.

Quasi-Endowment Funds: a college and university fund type to account for resources designated by the governing board to be invested indefinitely, with income being expended as directed.

Quasi-External Transactions: those that would be revenues and expenses or expenditures for organizations external to the governmental unit.

Registration Statements: statements required to be filed with the SEC for firms that issue securities to the public, and for firms whose shares are traded on national stock exchanges.

Regulation S: a 1990 regulation to clarify the applicability of security laws across national boundaries.

Reimbursements: transactions between two funds of a government that constitute reimbursements of a fund for expenditures or expenses initially made from it that are properly applicable to another fund. Reimbursements are recorded as expenditures or expenses in the reimbursing fund and as reductions of expenditures or expenses in the reimbursed fund.

Remeasurement: the conversion of a foreign entity's financial statements from another currency into its own functional currency.

Renewal and Replacement Funds (Colleges and Universities): used to account for the resources held by colleges and universities for renewal and replacement of the physical plant.

Reorganization Items: income, expenses, realized gains and losses, and provisions for losses that result from restructuring a business under Chapter 11 of the Bankruptcy Act.

Reorganization Plan: a plan for rehabilitation of the debtor corporation in a Chapter 11 case; to be confirmed, the plan must be fair and equitable to all interests concerned.

Reorganization Value: an approximation of the amount a willing buyer would pay for the assets of the corporation at the time of restructuring.

Reportable Operating Segment: an operating segment for which information is required to be reported.

Reporting Currency: the currency in which consolidated financial statements are prepared.

Residual Beneficiaries: those entitled to the remainder of an estate after all other rightful claims have been satisfied.

Residual Equity Transfer (Governmental Accounting): nonrecurring or nonroutine transfers of equity between funds.

Restricted Current Funds (Colleges and Universities): encompasses resources expendable currently but restricted to expenditures for specified operating purposes.

Restricted Funds (Hospitals): a hospital fund grouping that includes specific purpose funds, plant replacement and expansion funds, and endowment funds.

Retirement of Indebtedness Fund: used in college and university accounting for liquid resources held for current debt service, and investments held for future debt retirement.

Safe Payments (Partnerships): distributions that can be made to partners with assurance that the amounts are not excessive.

Salary Allowances (Partnerships): partner salary allowances are drawings authorized in lieu of salaries because partner rewards come from sharing in partnership earnings.

Sales Agency: a business office established to display merchandise and take customer orders, but not to fill orders or grant credit.

Schedule of Assumed Loss Absorption: used in developing the cash distribution plan in a partnership liquidation. Each partner's equity is charged with a loss amount to eliminate the equity of the most vulnerable partner, and so on.

Shared Revenues (Governmental Accounting): specific revenue sources shared with other governmental units; sales taxes and gasoline taxes are examples.

Special Assessments: special tax levies against benefited property owners for improvements that benefit the owner's property.

Special Revenue Funds (Governmental Accounting): used to account for proceeds from specific revenue sources that are legally restricted to specified purposes.

Specific Purpose Funds (Hospitals): a hospital fund group to account for resources restricted by donors for specific operating purposes.

Spot Rate: the exchange rate in effect for immediate delivery of the currencies exchanged.

Statement of Affairs: a financial statement that shows liquidation values of a bankrupt entity and provides estimates of possible recovery for unsecured creditors.

Statement of Functional Expenses (Voluntary Health and Welfare Organizations): a financial statement that shows the costs associated with the program services or other activities of the organization.

Statement of Realization and Liquidation: statement showing progress toward liquidation in a bankruptcy case.

Step-by-Step Acquisitions: acquiring an equity interest in a series of separate stock purchases.

Subsidiary: a corporation in which the controlling stockholders' interest lies with a parent company that controls its decisions and operations.

Substantially All Test: used in determining if 90% of the combining entity's voting common stock is exchanged, required in a pooling of interests.

Temporal Method: translation of items carried at past, current, and future prices in a manner that retains their measurement bases.

Temporarily Restricted Net Assets (Not-for-Profit Accounting): the portion of a not-for-profit entity's net assets whose use is limited by donor-imposed stipulations that either expire or can be removed by fulfilling the stipulations.

Temporary Differences: differences in taxable income and accounting income that originate in one accounting period and reverse in a later period.

Term Endowment Funds: a college and university fund type to account for resources received from donors or outside agencies with the stipulation that the principal may be expended after a period of time or the occurrence of some event.

Term Endowments: endowments for which the principal is temporarily restricted.

Testacy Proceeding: a hearing of a probate court to determine if the deceased died testate or intestate (that is, with or without a will).

Testate: having died with a valid will in force.

Testamentary Trust: a trust that is created pursuant to a will.

Translation: expressing functional currency measurements in the reporting currency.

Translation Adjustment (also *Equity Adjustment on Translation*): an exchange gain or loss that is reported as an equity adjustment in other comprehensive income.

Treasury Stock Approach: accounting for parent company stock held by a subsidiary as treasury stock in consolidated statements.

Troubled Debt Restructuring: occurs when a creditor grants a concession to a debtor because of the debtor's financial difficulties.

Trust and Agency Funds: used to account for assets held in a trustee capacity or as agent for individuals, private organizations, and other governmental units.

Trustee: a lawyer appointed by the U.S. trustee or by the bankruptcy court to assume control of the debtor's estate and coordinate its administration with the court.

Unconditional Promises to Give (Nonprofit Accounting): a pledge without conditions.

Undivided Interest (Joint Ventures): an ownership arrangement in which two or more parties own property and title is held individually to the extent of each party's interest.

Unexpended Plant Funds: used by colleges and universities to account for resources held for additions and improvements to the physical plant.

Uniform Probate Code: a document prepared by the National Conference of Commissioners on Uniform State Laws that provides guidelines for estate and trust administration.

Unlimited Liability: each partner is liable for all partnership debts. Limited partners in a limited partnership, which is allowed in some states, do not have unlimited liability.

Unrestricted Current Funds (Colleges and Universities): encompasses resources received and expended for instruction, research, extension, and public services, as well as auxiliary enterprises.

Unrestricted Funds (Hospitals): used to account for all resources of a hospital not restricted by donors or grantors.

Unrestricted Net Assets (Not-for-Profit Accounting): the portion of net assets of a not-for-profit entity that carries no donor-imposed restrictions.

Upstream Sale: sales or other intercompany transactions from subsidiary to parent company.

U.S. Trustee: an administrative officer of the bankruptcy court; appointed by the attorney general for five-year terms.

Venturers: the owner participants in a joint venture.

Vertical Integration: the combination of firms with operations in different but successive stages of production and/or distribution.

Voidable Preferences: preferences that can be voided by a trustee in a bankruptcy case.

Voluntary Bankruptcy Proceedings: the filing is voluntary if the debtor files the bankruptcy petition.

Voluntary Health and Welfare Organizations: a diverse group of nonprofit entities that is supported by donations and seeks to solve basic social problems of health and welfare.

Vulnerability Ranking (Partnerships): a ranking of partners on the basis of the amount of partnership losses they could absorb without reducing their capital accounts below zero.

Zero-Base Budgeting: making budgetary appropriations without direct reference to prior years' programs or expenditure budgets.

Index

Negative goodwill. *See also* Goodwill
  in business combinations, 17–18
  in equity method, 45, 46–47
Net revenue approach, 731
Nonexpendable trust funds, 728, 785–87
Nonmandatory transfers, 848–49
Nonmonetary items, 520. *See also* Foreign
  currency
North American Free Trade Agreement
  (NAFTA), 18
Not-for-profit entities. *See also* Colleges
  and universities; Health care
  entities; Voluntary health and
  welfare organizations
  accrual basis of accounting, 819, 843
  classification of net assets, 819
  collections, 823
  contributions (*see* Contributions)
  financial statements, 823–25
  investments and investment income,
    821–22
  source of accounting principles for,
    817–18
  transfers that are not contributions,
    822
Not-for-profit organization accounting,
  719–20. *See also* Governmental
  accounting; Not-for-profit
  entities
Nynex Corporation, 2

Offering circular, 868
Office Depot, 2
Official exchange rates, 490. *See also*
  Foreign currency
On-behalf payments for fringe benefits
  and salaries, 732–33
One-line consolidation. *See also* Equity
  method
  overview, 41
  and proportionate consolidation, 435
  and separate income tax returns,
    381–82
Operating profit test, 578–79. *See also*
  Segment reporting
Operating segments, 577. *See also*
  Segment reporting
Operating transfers, 734
Options, subsidiaries with, 375–77
Ownership interest
  acquisitions during accounting period
    consolidation procedures, 287–89
    preacquisition dividends, 286–87, 288
    preacquisition earnings, 285–86, 288
  piecemeal acquisitions, 291–93
  pooling of interests during accounting
    period, 289–91
  sale of
    during accounting period, 295,
      297–99
    at beginning of period, 294–95, 296
  subsidiary stock transactions
    dividends and splits, 304–6
    sale of additional shares, 300–303
    treasury stock, 303–4

Parent company theory
  consolidated balance sheet, 422,
    424–25
  consolidated income statement, 422,
    424
  consolidation after acquisition, 419,
    420, 423–25
  consolidation at acquisition, 417–19

versus entity and contemporary
  theories, 413–16
  on goodwill, 416–17
  overview, 412
Parent-subsidiary relationship, 68. *See also*
  Ownership interest
Partnership agreements, 600
Partnership dissolution, 611–12
Partnerships
  articles of, 600
  characteristics of, 600
  dissolution through death or
    retirement, 619–21
  drawings, loans, and advances, 603–4
  financial reporting, 600
  initial investment in, 600–603
  interest changes, 611–12
  investment in existing, 615–19
  legislation history, 599
  limited, 621–22
  liquidation of (*see under* Liquidation)
  operations, 604–5
  profit and loss sharing agreements
    capital as factor in, 608–11
    service considerations, 605–8
  purchase of interest from existing
    partner, 612–15
Par value theory, 246
Pass-through grants, 732
Patient service revenues, 833–34
Payments in lieu of taxes, 732
Pennzoil, 676
Pension trust funds, 729, 788–89
Percentage allocation method, 384. *See
  also* Income taxes
Performance budgets, 736
Permanently restricted net assets, 819
Personal representative, 873
Piecemeal acquisition, 291–93
Plant assets
  cost method intercompany sale,
    225–27, 228
  depreciable
    downstream sale of, 211–13, 214
    upstream sale of, 213, 215–19
  equity method intercompany sale,
    220–23
  incomplete equity method
    intercompany sale, 223–25
  intercompany sales of, in current cost
    system, 440
  inventory purchased for use as, 227, 229
  nondepreciable
    downstream sale of, 206–7
    subsequent year sale to outside
      entity, 208, 210
    upstream sale of, 208–10
  sold at other than fair value, 219–20
  unrealized profit summary illustration,
    230
Plant funds, 852–53
Plant replacement and expansion funds,
  838
Pledges, 819–20
Pooling of interests method
  accounting for subsidiary investments
    in, 87–88
  APB conditions for, 5–8
  combining stockholder's equities, 8–11
  disclosure requirements, 22
  expenses related to, 13
  midyear, 289–91
  with minority interest, 88–90
  overview, 5

versus purchase method, 19–22
  reporting combined operations in,
    11–13
  substantially all test, 7–8
Postpetition liabilities, 692
Preacquisition dividends, 286–87, 288
Preacquisition earnings, 285–86, 288
Preferences, 678
Preferred stock. *See also* Stock
  constructive retirement of, 369–70,
    372
  equity method accounting, 50–51
  subsidiary
    acquired by parent, 368–72
    convertible, 374–75
    not held by parent, 366–68
Preliminary prospectus, 868
Premium fees, 834
Prepetition liabilities subject to
  compromise, 692
Probate proceedings, 874
Program budgets, 736
Proportionate consolidation, 434–35
Proprietary funds. *See under*
  Governmental accounting
Pro rata consolidation, 434
Prospectus, 868
Provision for bad debts, 834–35
Prudential Insurance Company of
  America, 691
Public Utilities Holding Company Act
  (1935), 868
Purchased income. *See* Preacquisition
  earnings
Purchase method
  conditions for, 13–14
  cost allocation, 14–16
  disclosure requirements, 22
  illustration, 16–18
  overview, 5
  versus pooling of interests method,
    19–22
Pure endowment funds, 838
Push-down accounting
  overview, 84–85, 425–26
  year after acquisition, 427, 429–31
  year of acquisition, 426–27

Quasi-endowment funds, 844
Quasi-external transactions, 734

Red herring prospectus, 868
Registration statements, 868, 869
Regulation S, 871
Reimbursement interfund transactions,
  734
Remeasurement, 520–21. *See also* Foreign
  currency
Renewal and replacement funds, 844,
  852
Reorganization. *See also* Chapter 11 of
  the Bankruptcy Act;
  Liquidation
  committee representation, 689
  financial reporting during, 691–93
  fresh start reporting, 693–94, 699–702
  operating under Chapter 11, 689–90,
    698–99
  plan of, 690–91, 699
  reclassification of liabilities subject to
    compromise, 695–98
  trustee or debtor in possession, 688–89
  types of, 391, 393
  value of emerging company, 693